Scotland

THE ROUGH GUIDE

There are more than one hundred Rough Guide titles
covering destinations from Amsterdam to Zimbabwe

Forthcoming titles include
Bali • Mexico
Moscow • Thailand • Venice

Rough Guide Reference Series
Classical Music • European Football • The Internet • Jazz
Opera • Reggae • Rock Music • World Music

Rough Guide Phrasebooks
Czech • French • German • Greek • Hindi & Urdu • Indonesian • Italian
Mandarin Chinese • Mexican Spanish • Polish • Portuguese
Russian • Spanish • Thai • Turkish • Vietnamese

Rough Guides on the Internet
http://www.roughguides.com

ROUGH GUIDE CREDITS

Text editor: Amanda Tomlin
Series editor: Mark Ellingham
Editorial: Martin Dunford, Jonathan Buckley, Samantha Cook, Jo Mead, Kate Berens, Ann-Marie Shaw, Paul Gray, Sarah Dallas, Chris Schüler, Julia Kelly, Helena Smith, Caroline Osborne, Kieran Falconer, Judith Bamber, Olivia Eccleshall, Orla Duane (UK); Andrew Rosenberg (US)
Production: Susanne Hillen, Andy Hilliard, Judy Pang, Link Hall, Nicola Williamson, Helen Ostick

Picture research: Eleanor Hill
Cartography: Melissa Flack, Maxine Burke
Online editors: Alan Spicer (UK); Geronimo Madrid (US)
Finance: John Fisher, Celia Crowley, Catherine Gillespie, Neeta Mistry
Marketing & Publicity: Richard Trillo, Simon Carloss, Niki Smith (UK); Jean-Marie Kelly, SoRelle Braun (US)
Administration: Tania Hummel, Alexander Mark Rogers

ACKNOWLEDGEMENTS

The authors would like to thank Caledonian MacBrayne Ferries; Historic Scotland; National Trust for Scotland; the Scottish Tourist Board, and everyone at the regional tourist boards, in particular Toni MacPherson at the Dundee tourist office and Pam Wells at the Aberdeen tourist board; Alasdair Enticknap, Val and Gordon Humphries; Ian Dunn; Thom Dibdin and Gordon McCulloch; Emma Burtles; Stewart Appleby; Kirsty and Stewart Blackstock, Meg and Andy Rodger; Catriona McCartney; Dave Ashcroft; Tony Clift; Dorothy and Sandy Logie; Roly Duncan; Brian Smith; Nick Bell; Fiona Cook; Valerie and Ian Pragnell; and Stewart Cruickshank.

The editor thanks Nikky Twyman for proofreading; Maxine Burke for cartography; and Link Hall for production.

PUBLISHING INFORMATION

This third edition published February 1998 by Rough Guides Ltd, 62–70 Shorts Gardens, London WC2H 9AB. Reprinted in September 1998. Distributed by the Penguin Group:
Penguin Books Ltd, 27 Wrights Lane, London W8 5TZ
Penguin Books USA Inc., 375 Hudson Street, New York 10014, USA
Penguin Books Australia Ltd, 487 Maroondah Highway, PO Box 257, Ringwood, Victoria 3134, Australia
Penguin Books Canada Ltd, 10 Alcorn Avenue, Toronto, Ontario, Canada M4V 1E4
Penguin Books (NZ) Ltd, 182–190 Wairau Road, Auckland 10, New Zealand
Typeset in Linotron Univers and Century Old Style to an original design by Andrew Oliver.
Printed in England by Clays Ltd, St Ives PLC
Illustrations in Part One and Part Three by Edward Briant.

Illustrations on p.1 & p.545 by Henry Iles
© The Rough Guides Ltd 1998
No part of this book may be reproduced in any form without permission from the publisher except for the quotation of brief passages in reviews.
624pp - Includes index
A catalogue record for this book is available from the British Library
ISBN 1-85828-220-9

Scotland

THE ROUGH GUIDE

written and researched by

Alastair Hamilton, Rob Humphreys, Catherine Logie, Sophie Pragnell, Donald Reid and Julian Ward

with additional contributions by

Dave Abram, Wayne Alderson, Donald Greig, Colin Irwin, Phil Lee, Gordon McLachlan, Mike Parker, Helena Smith and Tania Smith

THE ROUGH GUIDES

We set out to do something different when the first Rough Guide was published in 1982. Mark Ellingham, just out of university, was travelling in Greece. He brought along the popular guides of the day, but found they were all lacking in some way. They were either strong on ruins and museums but went on for pages without mentioning a beach or taverna. Or they were so conscious of the need to save money that they lost sight of Greece's cultural and historical significance. Also, none of the books told him anything about Greece's contemporary life – its politics, its culture, its people, and how they lived.

So with no job in prospect, Mark decided to write his own guidebook, one which aimed to provide practical information that was second to none, detailing the best beaches and the hottest clubs and restaurants, while also giving hard-hitting accounts of every sight, both famous and obscure, and providing up-to-the-minute information on contemporary culture. It was a guide that encouraged independent travellers to find the best of Greece, and was a great success, getting shortlisted for the Thomas Cook travel guide award, and encouraging Mark, along with three friends, to expand the series.

The Rough Guide list grew rapidly and the letters flooded in, indicating a much broader readership than had been anticipated, but one which uniformly appreciated the Rough Guide mix of practical detail and humour, irreverence and enthusiasm. Things haven't changed. The same four friends who began the series are still the caretakers of the Rough Guide mission today: to provide the most reliable, up-to-date and entertaining information to independent-minded travellers of all ages, on all budgets.

We now publish 100 titles and have offices in London and New York. The travel guides are written and researched by a dedicated team of more than 100 authors, based in Britain, Europe, the USA and Australia. We have also created a unique series of phrasebooks to accompany the travel series, along with an acclaimed series of music guides, and a best-selling pocket guide to the Internet and World Wide Web. We also publish comprehensive travel information on our web site:

and http://www.roughguides.com

HELP US UPDATE

We've gone to a lot of effort to ensure that this new edition of The Rough Guide to Scotland is accurate and up-to-date. However, things change – places get "discovered", opening hours are notoriously fickle, restaurants and rooms raise prices or lower standards, extra buses are laid on or off. If you feel we've got it wrong or left something out, we'd like to know, and if you can remember the address, the price, the time, the phone number, so much the better.

We'll credit all contributions, and send a copy of the next edition (or any other Rough Guide if you prefer) for the best letters. Please mark letters: "Rough Guide Scotland Update" and send to:
Rough Guides, 62–70 Shorts Gardens, London WC2H 9AB, or Rough Guides, 375 Hudson St, 9th floor, New York NY 10014. Or send email to: mail@roughguides.co.uk
Online updates about this book can be found on Rough Guides' website at http://www.roughguides.com

READERS' LETTERS

We would also like to thank all the readers who have taken the time and trouble to write in with comments, suggestions and helpful advice: Judy Zavos; Mark Bennett and Ann Warren; Craig Sluite; Nikki Knox; John Stevens; Suzanne Burkenshaw; Marja Gastelaars; W Ayotte; Ian Duckett; M S McCleery; S. Medlik; Martin Staniforth; Jane Cooper; Tim Cook; Philip Denton; DW Emslie; Andrew and Sarah Kelly; Monica Staaf; Chikako Nakazawa; Jane Cooper; George Robertson; Damian O'Brien; Catherine Spencer; Adam Smith; Peter Humphris; Suzanne Veletta; David Goodway; Kevin Byrne; Dorothy Baker; John Campbell; S. Dawson; Patricia Eccles; Brenda Gamlin; Anthony Harris; Helene Hubers; Helen Kara; Alice McLure; Ralph Moore; Helen Mycroft; Sarah and Susan Schmidt; Jean Davidson Sinclair; Raymond Lyons, DW Moore; Ben de Bruijin; Michela Fraschi; Joan Lawler; Adele M Payne.

CONTENTS

Introduction xi

PART THREE CONTEXTS 545

LIST OF MAPS

MAP SYMBOLS

Symbol	Description		Symbol	Description
⚊⚊	Railway		▲	Campsite
▬▬	Motorway		◉	Hotel
══	Road		▣	Restaurant
-----	Path		✕	Airport
– – –	Ferry route		Ⓤ	Underground station
⚊⚊	Waterway		★	Bus stop
--⚊--	Chapter division boundary		Ⓟ	Parking
▬·▬·▬	International boundary		ⓘ	Tourist office
∴	Ruins		⊠	Post office
♯	Castle		Ⓒ	Telephone
⌂	Abbey		⚱	Whisky distillery
⏛	Stately home		■	Building
⚔	Battlefield		⊞	Church
◓	Cave		▨	Park
▲	Peak		▨	National park
⚲	Waterfall		▨	Beach

INTRODUCTION

With a population of just five million, most of whom are concentrated around the central belt, Scotland boasts vast tracts of glorious empty wilderness, whose unique beauty is hard to beat. Despite the best efforts of an unreliable and often inhospitable climate, it is, quite simply, a wonderfully rewarding and diverse country to visit, encompassing everything from the rolling countryside of the Borders to the wild and weather-beaten islands that arc around its west and north coasts. Many parts of the mainland are surprisingly accessible, with remote lochs, glens and Highland mountains lying less than two hours' travel from Edinburgh and Glasgow, two of Britain's most complex and intriguing cities.

For centuries Scotland was a divided nation, with Gaelic-speaking, cattle-raising clans concentrated to the north and west, and English-speaking Scots, distinguished by their Norman-style feudal loyalties and allegiances, dominant to the south and east. These two linguistically distinct Scotlands developed on separate lines, their mutually antagonistic populations creating the first of several overlapping sources of national tension. After the Reformation, religion became another flashpoint, not just between Catholic and Protestant, but also amongst a host of reformist sects. Later still, industrialization divided the rural from the urban, generating the class-conscious, socialist-minded cities of central and eastern Scotland. Such tensions are still apparent today in the complex relationships between incomers and natives, between the landed and the stranded, and between the progressive core of the cities and the drug-ridden poverty of their fringes.

In the background lurks Scotland's problematic relationship with England. In 1707, the Act of Union united the English and Scottish parliaments ending centuries of political strife, and shortly afterwards, in 1745, the failure of Bonnie Prince Charlie's Jacobite rebellion gave the English and their Scottish allies the chance to bring the Gaels to heel. However, the union only partly integrated the two nations with Scotland retaining separate legal and education systems, and, to this day, its relationship with its southern neighbour remains anomalous. During the Conservative governments of the 1980s and 1990s, the huge majority of Scots consistently favoured the opposition – Labour in the cities, the Liberal Democrats in the Highlands and a strong thread of Nationalist support throughout the northeast, in particular. This created further ill-will towards the union, and left many Scots feeling resentful and disenfranchised. However, the landslide victory of the Labour party in the 1997 general election, which left the Conservatives with no seats at all in Scotland, turned this around. In September 1997, a referendum was held in which Scots voted resoundingly in favour of their own parliament, with limited tax-levying powers. New legislation will give the Scots control over many of the issues which directly affect them, such as health, law and order, and the environment, though Westminster is to remain in charge of other areas such as defence, foreign affairs and major tax decisions. It remains to be seen whether this devolution of power will satisfy the Scots, or simply fuel their desire for complete independence from the United Kingdom, a question which will not begin to be properly addressed until the year 2000, when an elected assembly will sit in Edinburgh for the first time in three hundred years.

Where to go

If you're short of time, you can still sample a little of everything by starting at either – or both – of the country's great cities, Glasgow and Edinburgh, before moving on up

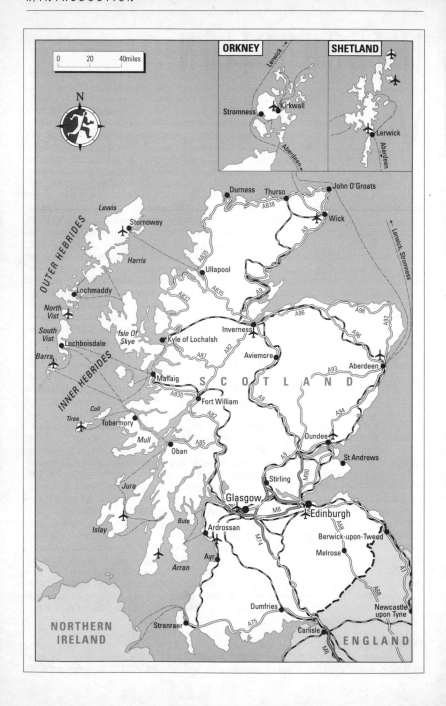

the west coast, where stunning land and seascapes are studded with reminders of Scotland's long and fractious history.

Travelling around mainland Scotland is comparatively easy: the road network reaches almost every corner of the country, trains serve the major towns and an extensive bus system links all but the most remote villages. Hikers are well served, too: all of the country's parks and most of the wilderness areas are crisscrossed by popular walking trails. Without your own transport, it's more difficult to move around the islands, where, especially on the Western Isles, bus services deteriorate and are often impossible to coordinate with ferry sailing times. Almost all of the ferries are operated by Caledonian MacBrayne, who provide a splendidly punctual and efficient service, along with various island-hopping discount tickets to reduce the substantial costs of ferry travel. Reasonably priced accommodation is available almost everywhere, at its least expensive (and sometimes grimmest) in the youth hostels, and more popularly in hundreds of family-run B&Bs.

The majority of visitors begin their tour of Scotland in the capital, **Edinburgh**, a handsome and ancient town famous for its magnificent castle and the Palace of Holyroodhouse, as well as for the excellence of its museums – not to mention the **Edinburgh International Festival**, a world-acclaimed arts shindig held for three weeks, in August and early September. From here it's just a short journey west to the capital's rival, lively **Glasgow**, a sprawling industrial metropolis that was once the second city of the British Empire. In recent years, though its industrial base remains in decline, Glasgow has done much to improve its image, aided in particular by the impressive architectural legacy of its late eighteenth- and nineteenth-century heyday.

Southern Scotland, often underrated, features some of the country's finest scenery, especially among the elevated river valleys surrounding **Moffat** and in the forests and flat-peaked hills of the **Galloway Forest Park**, close to the **Solway coast**. Away to the east lie the better-known ruins of the four medieval Border abbeys of Melrose, Dryburgh, Jedburgh and Kelso. **Jedburgh** is the pick of the bunch, but the trim town of **Melrose**, tucked into the one of the prettiest parts of the valley of the River Tweed, is the best peg on which to hang your visit, especially as it's close to **Abbotsford**, the intriguing, treasure-crammed mansion of Sir Walter Scott.

To the north of Edinburgh, across the Firth of Forth, **Central Scotland**'s varied landscape embraces deep and shadowy glens, jagged-edged mountains and the well-walked hills of the **Trossachs**. It's here you'll find the impressive remains of **Stirling** castle and, on the coast, prosperous **St Andrews**, home of golf. **Northeast Scotland** may seem at first to have less to offer, but you could consider following the **Speyside** malt whisky trail, taking a walk in the tranquil and majestic valleys of the **Angus glens**, or making a visit to oil-rich **Aberdeen**, the nation's third largest city, or **Deeside**, home to Queen Victoria's "dear paradise", Balmoral.

Most visitors move on from the central belt to **Argyll**, a sparsely populated territory of sea lochs and mountains. Mainland Argyll points out towards the southernmost reaches of the **Hebrides**, the long chain of rocky islands necklacing Scotland's Atlantic shoreline. **Bute** and **Arran**, with its striking granite peaks, are accessible by ferry from Ardrossan in Ayrshire. From Oban you can reach the gorgeous scenery of **Mull**, and the quieter islands of **Islay** and **Jura**, wonderful places for a walking holiday.

Up along the coast, reached by boat from Mallaig or Kyleakin, is **Skye**, the most visited of the Hebrides, made famous by the exploits of Flora MacDonald, who smuggled Bonnie Prince Charlie "over the sea to Skye" after his defeat at the Battle of Culloden. The harsh rocky promontories that make up the bulk of the island are serrated by scores of deep sea lochs, together creating some of the western coast's fiercest scenery. The island also boasts the snow-tipped **Cuillins**, whose clustered summits offer perhaps the most challenging climbing in the country, and the bizarre rock formations of the Quiraing ridge on the **Trotternish peninsula**. The only settlement of any size is **Portree**, draped around the cliffs of a narrow bay, but many visitors prefer to explore the isolated hotels, B&Bs and youth hostels scattered across the island.

From Uig, on the west coast of Skye, and from Oban and Ullapool, there are frequent boats across to the **Western Isles**, an elongated archipelago extending south from the single island of **Lewis and Harris**, to the uninhabited islets below **Barra**. The Isles are some of the last bastions of the Gaelic language, and you'll find many road signs in Gaelic only. Of the islands, Lewis is distinguished by the prehistoric standing stones of **Callanish**, one of the best-preserved monuments of its type in Europe, while North Harris possesses a remarkably hostile landscape of forbiddingly bare mountains giving way to the wide sandy beaches and lunar-like hills of South Harris.

Back on the mainland, the **Highlands**, whose multitude of mountains, sea cliffs, glens and lochs cover the northern two-thirds of the country, is probably the region most commonly associated with Scotland. Its great popularity belies its stark remoteness, despite a number of internationally known sights, not least **Loch Ness**, midway along the Great Glen and home to the eponymous monster. **Inverness**, near the site of the **Battle of Culloden**, is an obvious base for exploring the region, although **Fort William**, at the opposite end of the Great Glen close by **Ben Nevis**, Scotland's highest peak, is a possible alternative, especially if you're heading west.

In the far north, boats leave for the cluster of islands that make up the agricultural **Orkney Islands**, whose main town, **Kirkwall**, crowds round its magnificent medieval cathedral. Further north, 200 miles north of Aberdeen, are the much more rugged **Shetland Islands**, where the bustling and historic harbour at **Lerwick** shelters craft from every corner of the North Atlantic. Orkney and Shetland, both with a rich Norse heritage, differ not only from each other, but also quite distinctly, in dialect and culture,

SCOTLAND'S CLIMATE

Average daily maximum temperatures in °C and monthly rainfall in mm

	Jan	Feb	Mar	Apr	May	June	July	Aug	Sept	Oct	Nov	Dec
Dumfries												
°C	5.6	6.0	8.2	11.2	14.4	17.3	18.3	18.1	15.9	12.9	8.6	6.8
mm	103	72	66	55	71	63	77	93	104	106	109	104
Edinburgh												
°C	6.2	6.4	8.5	11.2	14.2	17.1	18.4	18.2	16.3	13.3	9	71
mm	47	39	39	38	49	45	69	73	57	56	58	56
Fort William												
°C	6.3	6.7	8.6	11.2	14.5	16.6	17.2	17.3	15.4	12.8	8.8	7.3
mm	200	132	152	111	103	124	137	150	199	215	220	238
Lerwick												
°C	5.1	4.9	6	7.8	10	12.5	13.7	14	12.5	10.3	7.4	6
mm	127	93	93	72	64	64	67	78	113	119	140	147
Perth												
°C	5.7	6	8.4	11.8	14.9	18	19.1	18.6	16.2	12.9	8.5	6.6
mm	70	52	47	43	57	51	67	72	63	65	69	82
Tiree												
°C	7.2	7	8.3	10.3	12.7	14.8	15.8	16.1	14.7	12.6	9.6	8.2
mm	120	71	77	60	56	66	79	83	123	125	123	123
Wick												
°C	5.6	5.7	7.3	9.3	11.3	14.2	15.4	15.4	14.1	11.8	8.2	6.5
mm	81	58	55	45	47	49	61	74	68	73	90	82

from mainland Scotland. These far-flung, sea- and wind-buffeted islands, offer some of the country's wildest scenery, finest bird-watching and stunning archeological remains.

When to go

The pressure systems rolling in off the Atlantic pretty much control Scotland's volatile **climate**, especially on the west coast, where a bright, sunny morning can soon turn into a wet and windy afternoon. The west coast is appreciably wetter than the rest of the country, but milder in winter, due to the moderating influence of the Gulf Stream. There's no way of predicting when the fine weather will arrive, though spring and early autumn have proved good bets in recent years: you just have to trust your luck and be well prepared, even in high summer. Always pack warm and waterproof clothing – and an umbrella.

PART ONE

THE

BASICS

GETTING THERE FROM ENGLAND, IRELAND AND EUROPE

Crossing the border from England into Scotland is straightforward, with train and bus services forming part of the British national network. Flights are another option, though fares can be high. If you're driving from the south the two main routes run up the east of England via the A1 and up the west side of the country using the M6 and the A74; only the latter offers at least dual-carriageway driving the whole way. It takes the best part of a day to get from London to Edinburgh or Glasgow by car; although it is possible, if you drive flat out and encounter no road-work delays, to get to either city in around eight hours. If you'd prefer a slower, more scenic route, take the A68 up through eastern England and over the border at Carter Bar (this route adds a couple of hours to the journey time).

FLIGHTS

You can fly direct to Scotland's **main airports** – Edinburgh, Glasgow and Aberdeen – in an hour or so from all five London airports (Heathrow, Gatwick, Stansted, Luton and City) as well as from various provincial airports, and from Ireland (for a full rundown of routes and carriers, see box below). There's usually a confusingly wide array of fares. The **best deals** are special-offer tickets,

AIRLINES

Aer Lingus
Eire ☎01/844 4777
UK ☎0645/737747
Air UK ☎0345/666777
British Airways ☎0345/222111
British Midland ☎0345/554554
Business Air ☎0500/340146

Easyjet ☎0990/292929
Gill Airways ☎0191/286 2222
Icelandair ☎0171/388 5599
Ryanair
Eire ☎01/677 4422
UK ☎0541/569569
Sabena ☎0345/125254

FLIGHT AGENTS IN BRITAIN

Campus Travel, 52 Grosvenor Gardens, London SW1 0AG; ☎0171/730 3402.
Also many branches around the country.

Council Travel, 28a Poland St, London W1 3DB; ☎0171/437 7767.
Flights and student discounts.

Destination Group, 41–45 Goswell Rd, London EC1; ☎0171/253 9000.
Good discount fares.

STA Travel, 86 Old Brompton Rd, London SW7; ☎0171/361 6161.
Offices nationwide.

Trailfinders, 42–50 Earls Court Rd, London W8 6FT; ☎0171/938 3366.
Many branches nationwide.

Travel Bug, 597 Cheetham Hill Rd, Manchester M8 5EJ; ☎0161/721 4000.
Large range of discounted tickets.

Union Travel, 93 Piccadilly, London W1; ☎0171/493 4343.
Competitive air fares.

FLIGHTS TO SCOTLAND

What follows is a summary of **direct flights** to Scotland from England, Wales, Ireland and Europe, with departure points and destinations listed in alphabetical order. For telephone numbers of the airline companies, see box on p.3. Additional flight information is available on BBC Ceefax (pp.455–454) and ITV Teletext (pp.298–299).

BA = British Airways; BD = British Midland; EI = Aer Lingus; FI = Icelandair; II = Business Air; LX = Crossair; RY = Ryanair; SN = Sabena; U2 = Easyjet; UK = Air UK; WF = Wilderoe's Flyveselskap; 9C = Gill Airways.

From	To	Frequency	Duration	Carrier
Amsterdam	Aberdeen	1–4 daily	35min	UK/BD
	Edinburgh	5–6 daily	30min	UK/BD
	Glasgow	1–5 daily	35min–2hr 25min	UK/BD/FI
	Inverness	1 daily	1hr 35min	UK
Belfast	Aberdeen	1–2 daily	1hr 5min	BA
	Edinburgh	1–3 daily	50min	BA
	Glasgow	2–6 daily	45min	BA
Bergen	Shetland	2 weekly	1hr 5min	WF
Birmingham	Aberdeen	Mon–Fri 1–3 daily	1hr 35min	BA
	Edinburgh	3–7 daily	1hr	BA
	Glasgow	3–12 daily	1hr 10min	BA
Bristol	Aberdeen	1–2 daily	2hr 25min	BA
	Edinburgh	2–8 daily	1hr 25min	BA
	Glasgow	4–8 daily	1hr 25min	BA
Brussels	Glasgow	1–2 daily	1hr 10min	SN
Cardiff	Aberdeen	1 daily	2hr 40min	BA
	Edinburgh	Mon–Fri 3 daily	2hr 5min	BA
Cork	Glasgow	1–2 daily (not Sun)	2hr 30min	EI
Donegal	Glasgow	5 weekly	1hr 5min	EI
Dublin	Aberdeen	1 daily	2hr 50min	EI
	Edinburgh	2–4 daily	1hr 10min	EI/RY
	Glasgow	3–6 daily	1hr	EI
East Midlands	Aberdeen	Mon–Fri 1–2 daily	1hr 25min	BD
	Edinburgh	1–4 daily	55min	BD
	Glasgow	1–4 daily	55min	BD
Jersey	Aberdeen	1 daily	3hr 40min	BA
	Edinburgh	2–3 daily	3hr	BA/BD
	Glasgow	Sat & Sun 3–6 daily	1hr 20min	BD
Leeds Bradford	Aberdeen	Mon–Fri 3 daily	1hr 20min	BA
	Edinburgh	6 daily	1hr	9C
	Glasgow	1–3 daily	1hr	BD
London City	Edinburgh	3 daily	1hr 15min	UK
	Glasgow	1–3 daily	1hr 25min	UK
London Gatwick	Aberdeen	3–4 daily	1hr 45min	BA
	Edinburgh	4–6 daily	1hr 25min	BA
	Glasgow	3–5 daily	1hr 25min	BA
London Heathrow	Aberdeen	4–7 daily	1hr 15min	BA
	Edinburgh	hourly	1hr 15min	BA/BD
	Glasgow	hourly	1hr 15min	BA/BD
	Inverness	3 daily	1hr 30min	BA

continued opposite . . .

From	To	Frequency	Duration	Carrier
London Luton	Aberdeen	2–3 daily	1hr 20min	BA
	Edinburgh	hourly	1hr 10min	U2
	Glasgow	3–5 daily	1hr 35min	U2
	Inverness	1 daily	1hr 30min	U2
London Stansted	Aberdeen	2–3 daily	1hr 25min	BA
	Edinburgh	3–5 daily	1hr 15min	BA
	Glasgow	5–10 daily	1hr 15min	BA/RY
	Inverness	1 daily	1hr 30min	UK
Manchester	Aberdeen	2–8 daily	1hr 20min	BA/II
	Edinburgh	2–8 daily	1hr 5min	BA/II
	Glasgow	2–8 daily	1hr 10min	BA/II
	Dundee	Mon–Fri 2 daily	1hr 45min	II
Southampton	Aberdeen	Mon–Fri 1 daily	2hr 40min	BA
	Edinburgh	1–3 daily	1hr 35min	BA
	Glasgow	1–3 daily	1hr 35min	BA

valid only on specific flights and sold a week or more in advance; these tend to leave from airports such as Luton and Stansted, and are often subject to rigid restrictions, but the savings can make the extra effort well worthwhile. The next cheapest seats are **Apex** (Advance Purchase Excursion) tickets, available on all flights, at about half the price of a full-price economy class scheduled ticket. The full Apex fare must be paid at least two weeks before departure, and only fifty percent will be returned if the booking is cancelled. Anyone under 26 should also check out specialist agencies such as Campus Travel or STA Travel, who offer **youth deals**, including Domestic Air Passes (also known as Hopper Passes; see p.29) on British Airways flights, which can get you to Inverness and the Hebrides for a fraction of the published fare. Addresses for discount agents are listed overleaf.

There are flights almost hourly to Edinburgh and Glasgow from **London**, and nearly as many to Aberdeen. As a broad guide to what you're likely to pay, reckon on around £30 (plus £10 airport tax) for a rock-bottom one-way ticket from Luton or Stansted to Edinburgh or Glasgow with Easyjet. Occasionally, you may find even cheaper offers, such as Ryanair's superb-value fares of £19 single from Stansted to Prestwick (Glasgow), which is bookable a minimum of seven days in advance. Full return fares on British Airways, British Midland or Air UK, the other three main carriers, start at around £100, rising to double that for the most flexible tickets; Apex rates and reductions for young persons and students apply in most cases. Note, too, that **airport tax**, currently £10, is levied on all domestic flights to Scotland.

Coming from **Ireland**, the best deals are also with Ryanair, who operate three flights a day from Dublin to Glasgow Prestwick. Their Apex fare is around IR£60 return (with an additional IR£15 airport tax), while the full published fare with Aer Lingus can cost three or four times that amount. From **Belfast**, your only option is British Airways, who have several daily flights to Edinburgh, Glasgow and Aberdeen; the Apex fare is around £70. Again, see below for full details on airlines and routes.

TRAINS

Glasgow and Edinburgh are both served by frequent direct **InterCity** services from **London**, and are easily reached from other main English towns and cities, though you may have to change trains en route. Since 1996, when the British rail network was privatized, two separate companies have operated services from Euston to Scotland: GNER trains run up the east coast to Edinburgh, while Virgin trains go to Glasgow via the west coast. Ordinary standard-class **fares** with both companies are high, with first class costing an extra 33 percent, but with some forward planning you can take advantage of five types of reduced-fare ticket (see p.6), all of which come with their own restrictions and conditions. On Sundays, on many long-distance services, you can convert your standard-class ticket to a first-class one by paying a £7 supplement – well worth it if you're facing a six-hour journey on a popular route.

RAIL ENQUIRIES

Timetable information ☎0345/484950
International rail enquiries ☎0990/848848
GNER ☎0345/484950
Virgin ☎0345/222333
Le Shuttle ☎0990/353535; Calais
☎03/21.00.60.00
Eurostar ☎0345/303030; Paris/Lille
☎01/45.82.50.50; Brussels ☎02/224 8856

Journey times from London can be as little as 4hr 30min to Edinburgh and 5hr to Glasgow; from Manchester, reckon on around 2hr 30min to Edinburgh and 3hr to Glasgow. From either of these two points allow another 2hr 30min to Aberdeen and 3hr 30min to Inverness. Other than Edinburgh, these cities, along with Fort William, are served by overnight **sleeper trains**, for which reservations cost an additional £27 and can be made at any mainline station.

Eurostar operates frequent train services through the **Channel Tunnel** to London, Waterloo from Lille (2hr), Paris (3hr) and Brussels (3hr 15min). You then have to change trains, and stations, to Euston for the onward journey. If you are driving from mainland Europe, you might want to take the frequent train service – Le Shuttle – that carries you and your car from Calais to Folkestone in 35 minutes; fares range from £89 off season to £149 in high summer.

TICKETS AND PASSES

In decreasing order of cost, **Savers** are return tickets that can be used on all trains on Saturdays, Sundays and public holidays, on most weekday trains outside rush hour for the outward journey and all trains for the return leg. If you buy a return ticket at any station outside the rush hour, you'll routinely be issued with a Saver. **SuperSavers**, cheaper still, cannot be used on Fridays nor on a dozen other specified days of the year, and are not valid for any peak-hour service to or from London. Saver and SuperSaver tickets are valid for a month (outward travel has to be on the date of issue), and can be used on the London Underground if your journey involves crossing from one London station to another. **Apex** tickets are issued in limited numbers on certain InterCity journeys of 150 miles or more, and have to be booked at least seven days before travelling; a

seat reservation is included with the ticket. The rock-bottom **SuperApex** tickets have to be booked at least fourteen days in advance, and are available in limited numbers on InterCity services from London to a range of destinations in Scotland. **Children** aged 5–15 pay half the adult fare on most journeys, but there are no discounts on Apex and SuperApex tickets. Under-5s travel free, but are not entitled to their own seat on crowded trains.

To take the London–Edinburgh service as an example, a standard single fare costs £70, which is more than the majority of the reduced return fares: a Saver return costs £73.50, a SuperSaver £64, an Apex costs £48, and a SuperApex just £34. For all these tickets you should book as far in advance as you possibly can – many Apex and SuperApex are sold out weeks before the travel date.

Three discount **passes**, all valid for a year, are available in Britain to nationals and foreign visitors alike. The **Young Person's Railcard** costs £18 and gives 34 percent reductions on all standard, Saver and SuperSaver fares to full-time students studying in Britain and anyone who is between 16 and 26 years of age. A **Senior Citizens' Railcard**, also £18 and offering 34 percent reductions, is available to all those aged 60 or over. For both passes you'll need to show proof of age (for foreign visitors your passport is preferred) and provide two passport-size photographs. Foreign students will need to show proof of full-time study in Britain. Another option is the **Family Railcard**, which costs £20 and gives a variety of discounts from 21 to 34 percent for up to four adults, travelling with children (visitors will need to show their passports). Even more enticingly, it allows up to four children aged 5–15 to travel anywhere in the country for a flat fare of £2 each (which includes a seat reservation). If all your children are under 5, you must buy at least one £2 fare to qualify for the discount.

For those under 26 (and resident in a European country for at least six months), **InterRail** passes may be a cost-effective way to travel if Scotland is part of a longer European trip. They offer discounts on UK train travel, on cross-Channel ferries and Eurostar (check with a travel agent or at a main train station for any discounts on other ferry routes). There are two types of pass: the **InterRail "All-zone"** (£279 for a month), and the **InterRail Zonal** (price varies according to the number of zones you want to travel in and the duration of your trip). For those over 26, the **InterRail 26 Plus** pass (£275 for a month or £215 for 15 days) covers all of Europe except France, Belgium, Switzerland, Spain, Italy, Portugal and Morocco. Remember that none of the InterRail passes are valid in the country of purchase.

BUSES

Inter-town **bus** services (known as **coaches** in Scotland and the rest of Britain) duplicate many train routes, often at half the price or less. The frequency of service is usually comparable to the train, and in some instances the difference in journey time isn't that great; buses are also reasonably comfortable, and on longer routes often have drinks and sandwiches available on board. Two of the main operators between England and Scotland are National Express (☎0990/808080) and its subsiduary company Scottish Citylink Coaches (☎0990/505050). They both offer the same reduced rates to children (thirty percent); if you're a student, under 25 or a senior citizen you have to buy a one-year pass for £8 to get this discount. See "Getting around" (p.24) for details of train passes.

Direct buses run from most provincial British cities to **Edinburgh**, **Glasgow**, **Aberdeen** and **Inverness**. Tickets are widely available from bus stations and hundreds of agents throughout England. Typical fares from London to Glasgow and Edinburgh (journeys of around 7hr 45min) are £30 return on National Express's Overnight Explorer service, which leaves every evening from Victoria coach station, and has the added advantage of saving you the cost of overnight accommodation. The journeys to Aberdeen and Inverness take around eleven and twelve hours respectively, with the ticket to both costing £49 return. There's a 25 percent **discount** on bookings made seven days in advance.

A fun alternative for travellers wishing to take in some of the highlights of England and Wales en route to Scotland is the popular Go Blue Banana London–Edinburgh **backpackers' minibus tour**. Beginning in London, the bus takes three days to reach Edinburgh, with overnight stops in Bath and Chester, and visits en route the Brecon Beacons in Wales, the Lake District, Hadrian's Wall, and a string of breweries and distilleries. Tickets for the three-day trip cost £85, including the bus back from Edinburgh to London after the tour, but not

including any food or accommodation. For more details, contact Go Blue Banana in Edinburgh (☎0131/556 2000).

FERRIES

The only way to get to the Scottish mainland direct by **ferry from Europe** is on the Smyril Line service which links Shetland with Norway, the Faroe Islands, Iceland and Denmark (June–Aug only). The most direct route is from **Bergen** in Norway **to Lerwick** in Shetland and then on **to Aberdeen** by P&O Scottish Ferries. The first leg of the journey to Lerwick (1 weekly) takes 12 hours and costs £55 single, with the crossing to Aberdeen (6 weekly) taking fourteen hours and costing £50. If you want to take a car, add another £50 or so for each sector. It's also possible to take the same ferry from **Hansthölm** in Denmark **to Shetland** (1 weekly) via Faroe.

There's a greater choice of ferry services from Europe to ports in England, the most convenient of which are those to Newcastle or Hull in the northeast, from where it's an easy two-hour drive across the border into Scotland. North Sea Ferries sail daily **to Hull from Rotterdam and Zeebrugge**: both crossings take about fourteen hours and cost from around £150 single for up to four people and a small car, while foot passengers pay around £60 one-way. From Scandinavia, Color Line sail **to Newcastle from Bergen** and/or **Stavanger** one to three times a week; the journey takes 24–26 hours depending on whether it's direct.

From June to August, Scandinavian Seaways runs one service a week from Gothenburg in **Sweden to Newcastle**, taking about 23 hours and costing £136 per person (with an extra £54 for a car). From April to October they also operate a **Hamburg to Newcastle** service, four times a week. It takes just under 24 hours and costs £74 per person (plus £54 for cars). The same company also runs the Ijmuiden (**Amsterdam**) **to Newcastle** route, which takes around seventeen hours and costs £46 per person £54 for car. Note that all these rates can increase considerably during peak periods.

A further alternative is to take one of the very frequent ferries to England from the **French ports**; there's more choice of sailings this way, though the drive up to Scotland from the south coast can easily take a full day. Hoverspeed, Stena Sealink and P&O offer regular sailings from Calais to Dover (the shortest route), for which the lowest fare for a foot passnger is £24 (or £50–120 for small car). For full details of ferry routes and prices call the ferry companies direct; telephone numbers are listed in the box below.

From Ireland, there two main ferry routes to Scotland – Larne to Cairnryan and Belfast to Stranraer. P&O European Ferries runs several crossings daily from **Larne to Cairnryan** (2hr 30min by ferry; 1hr by jetliner); fares for foot pasengers are £44–54, and for a car with five pas-

sengers £250–380. Stena Sealink operates five ferries daily on the **Belfast to Stranraer** route (1hr 40min–3hr), with a car and five passengers costing £99–380 and foot passengers £24–44. In addition, Hoverspeed runs daily Seacat catamarans on this route, taking just 1hr 30min, and costing between £180–280 return, depending on the season and sailing times. All ferry companies from Ireland also offer much cheaper five-day return fares, as well as rock-bottom day-return fares. For more details, call the companies.

FERRY COMPANIES

Color Line ☎0191/296 1313; Bergen ☎5554 8660; Oslo ☎22944400.

Hoverspeed/Seacat Belfast ☎0345/523523; Calais ☎03/21.46.14.14.

North Sea Ferries Rotterdam ☎01819/55500; Zeebrugge ☎050/54.22.22.

P&O European Ferries ☎01581/200276; Paris ☎01/44.51.00.51; Calais ☎03/21.46.04.40; Larne ☎0990/980777.

P&O North Sea Ferries ☎01482/377177.

P&O Scottish Ferries ☎01224/572615.

Scandinavian Seaways ☎0191/293 6262; Amsterdam ☎25/503 4546; Gothenburg ☎31/650650; Hamburg ☎40/389 0371.

Smyril Line ☎01224/572615; Torshavn, Faroe ☎01/5900.

Stena Sealink ☎01776/702262; Calais ☎03/21.96.70.70; Larne ☎01574/273616; Belfast ☎01232/884090.

GETTING THERE FROM THE USA AND CANADA

The majority of airlines fly from the USA and Canada to London with connections to any number of Scottish airports (see p.10). However, if you are planning on travelling throughout the British Isles you might want to fly into London and take a slower, more

scenic route up to Scotland, either by rail or road.

Only **Glasgow** is served by nonstop direct flights from North America. Flights to **Edinburgh** tend to route through London or Dublin; to get to **Aberdeen** or **Inverness** you can fly to London or Manchester and hop on a British Airways, British Midland, or Air UK shuttle. Aberdeen is also well served with flights from Paris, Amsterdam and Scandinavia. For the **Scottish Islands** there are many internal flights from Glasgow and Edinburgh, or you can take any of a number of ferries from the west coast or from Aberdeen. See p.3 for the full picture on flying to Scotland from other parts of Britain.

Figure on seven hours' flying time nonstop from New York to Glasgow, or seven hours to London with an extra hour and a quarter to Glasgow or Edinburgh (not including stopover time). Add an extra four or five hours to travel from the West Coast. Most eastbound flights cross the Atlantic overnight, reaching Britain the next morning, although a few flights from the East Coast leave early in the morning, landing late the same evening.

SHOPPING FOR TICKETS

Barring special offers, the absolute cheapest of the airlines' published fares is a winter **Super Apex** ticket, sometimes known as a "Eurosaver". However, these are only available at certain times of the year and on certain routes, and your stay is limited to between seven and 21 days. You're more likely, therefore, to get an **Apex** ticket, which also carries certain restrictions: you have to book – and pay – at least 21 days before departure, spend at least seven days abroad (maximum stay three months), and you tend to get penalized if you change your schedule. Some airlines also issue **Special Apex** tickets to people younger than 24, often extending the maximum stay to a year. In addition, many airlines offer youth or student fares to **under-26s**; a passport or driving licence are sufficient proof of age, though these tickets are subject to availability and can have eccentric booking conditions. It's worth remembering that most cheap return fares involve spending at least one Saturday night away and that many tickets will only permit you a percentage refund if you need to cancel or alter your journey, so make sure you check the restrictions carefully before buying a ticket.

You can normally cut costs further by going through a **specialist flight agent** – either a **consolidator**, who buys up blocks of tickets from the airlines and sells them at a discount, or a **discount agent**, who in addition to selling discounted flights may also offer special student and youth fares and a range of other travel-related services such as insurance, rail passes, car rentals, tours and the like. Bear in mind, though, that these companies make their money by dealing in bulk – don't expect them to answer lots of questions, and remember that the penalties for changing your plans can be stiff. Some agents specialize in **charter flights**, which may be cheaper than anything available on a scheduled flight, but again departure dates are fixed and withdrawal penalties are high (check the refund policy). If you travel a lot, **discount travel clubs** are another option – the annual membership fee may be worth it for benefits such as cut-price air tickets and car rental.

However, you shouldn't automatically assume that tickets purchased through a travel specialist will be cheapest – once you get a quote, check with the airlines and you may turn up an even better deal. **Students** might be able to find cheaper flights through the major student travel agencies, such as STA Travel, Nouvelles Frontières and, for Canadian students, Travel CUTS.

A further possibility is to see if you can arrange a **courier flight**, although the hit-or-miss nature of these makes them most suitable for the single traveller who travels light and has a very flexible schedule. In return for shepherding a parcel through customs and possibly giving up your baggage allowance, you can expect to get a heavily discounted ticket. For information about courier flights you could contact Halbart Express (☎718/656-5000), or Now Voyager (☎212/431-1616) in New York. For more options, consult *A Simple Guide to Courier Travel* (Pacific Data Sales Publishing).

If you are travelling to Scotland as part of a much longer journey, you might want to consider buying a **Round-the-World (RTW) ticket**. Some travel agents can sell you an "off-the-shelf" RTW ticket that will have you touching down in about half a dozen cities (London is easily arranged, but a Scottish connection will probably have to be added on separately); others will have to assemble one for you, which can be tailored to your needs but is likely to be more expensive.

The newest tool for finding low price air fares is the **World Wide Web**. There are a number of new sites, where you can look up fares and even book tickets. You can search in the travel sections of your Web browser, or try one of the following locations: Travelocity at *www.travelocity.com*; Travel Information Service at *www.ibm.tiss.com*; or FLIFO Cyber Travel Agent at *www.flifo.com*. In addition, you could link up with Discount Airfares Worldwide On-Line at *www.etn.nl/discount.htm*, which is a hub of consolidator and discount agent Web links, maintained by the non-profit European Travel Network.

Regardless of where you buy your ticket, **fares** will depend on the season. Fares to Scotland are highest from around early June to mid-September, when the weather is best; they drop during the "shoulder" seasons – mid-September to early November, and mid-April to early June – and you'll get the best prices during the low season, November through to April when only a few hardy souls feel like vacationing in Scotland (excluding Christmas and New Year when prices are hiked up and seats are at a premium). Note also that flying at the weekend ordinarily adds up to $50 to the round-trip fare; price ranges quoted below assume midweek travel.

FLIGHTS FROM THE USA

There are several daily **nonstop flights to Glasgow** from US cities: British Airways flies from New York, American from Chicago, and Northwest from Boston. You can also fly to London on any of those airlines, as well as on Virgin, TWA, Continental and Delta, and take a connecting flight to Scotland.

Low-season Apex fares to Glasgow from New York and other East Coast cities cost $400–500, and from the West Coast $500–600. During the shoulder season prices rise to $500–550 from New York, $700–800 from Los Angeles; and in the summer fares can reach $700–800 from New York and up to $1000 from Los Angeles.

Should you fly direct to London, British Airways, British Midland, Air UK, EasyJet and

AIRLINES IN THE USA AND CANADA

Aer Lingus ☎1-800/223-6537 or 212/557-1110; *www.aerlingus.ie.*
Flies to Dublin from Boston and New York, with one-hour connecting flights to Glasgow.

Air Canada in BC ☎1-800/663-3721; in Alberta Saskatchewan and Manitoba, ☎1-800/542-8940; in eastern Canada ☎1-800/268-7240; in US ☎1-800/776-3000; *www.aircanada.ca*
Nonstop flights from Toronto to Glasgow, also flies to London daily from Toronto, Montréal or Vancouver, or to Manchester from Toronto.

American Airlines ☎1-800/624-6262; *www.americanair.com*
Daily nonstop flights from Chicago to Glasgow, also has several daily nonstop flights to London from New York, Boston, Chicago, Miami, Dallas and Los Angeles. Also flies from New York and Chicago into Manchester.

British Airways in US ☎1-800/247-9297; in Canada ☎1-800/668-1059; *www.british-airways.com*
Daily (except Sun) nonstop flights from New York to Glasgow. Also flies daily to London Heathrow from twenty North American cities, and to Manchester and Birmingham with numerous connecting flights to Glasgow, Edinburgh, Aberdeen, Inverness, Orkney (Kirkwall), Shetland (Lerwick) and Stornoway.

British Midland ☎1-800/788-0555; *www.iflybritishmidland.com*
Offers hourly flights each day to Glasgow and Edinburgh from London.

Canadian Airlines in Canada ☎1-800/665-1177; in US ☎1-800/426-7000; *www.cdnair.ca*
Direct flights from Toronto to London, with connections throughout Canada.

Continental Airlines ☎1-800/231-0856; *www.flycontinental.com*
Nonstop flights from New York (Newark) and Houston to London, and from Newark to Manchester and Birmingham.

Delta Airlines ☎1-800/241-4141 or 404/765-5000; *www.delta-air.com*
Daily nonstop flights to London (Gatwick) from New York, Boston, Cincinnati, Atlanta, Miami, Orlando, Los Angeles and San Francisco. Also flies from Atlanta to Manchester.

Icelandair ☎1-800/223-5500; *www.icelandair.com*
Flights to Glasgow from New York (daily), Boston (five weekly), Baltimore (daily), as well as less regular services from Orlando, Fort Lauderdale and Halifax; all flights with a one- to two-hour stopover in Iceland. Worth checking for low rates.

Northwest Airlines ☎1-800/447-4747; *www.nwa.com*
Regular nonstop flights from Boston to Glasgow, which run more frequently in summer. Also daily nonstop flights from Boston, Detroit and Minneapolis to London.

TWA ☎1-800/892-4141; *www.twa.com*
Daily nonstop flights to London (Gatwick) from St Louis, Baltimore and Philadelphia.

United Airlines ☎1-800/538-2929; *www.ual.com*
Flies to London (Heathrow) from New York, Chicago, Washington DC, Los Angeles and San Francisco, with connecting flights on British Midland to Edinburgh and Glasgow.

Virgin Atlantic Airways ☎1-800/862-8621; *www.fly.virgin.com/atlantic*
Nonstop flights to London from New York, Boston, Miami, Orlando, Los Angeles and San Francisco with connecting flights on British Midland to Edinburgh and Glasgow.

DISCOUNT TRAVEL COMPANIES IN THE USA AND CANADA

Air Brokers International, 323 Geary St, Suite 411, San Francisco, CA 94102 (☎1-800/883-3273 or 415/397-1383; www.aimnet.com/~airbrokr). Consolidator and specialist in RTW tickets.

Air Courier Association, 191 University Blvd, Suite 300, Denver, CO 80206 (☎303/278-8810; www.aircourier.org). Courier flight broker, charging an annual fee of $28, plus $30 initiation.

Airhitch, 2641 Broadway, New York, NY 10025 (☎1-800/326-2009 or 212/864-2000; www.airhitch.org). Standby-seat broker. For a set price, they guarantee to get you on a flight as close to your preferred destination as possible, within a week.

Airtech, 588 Broadway, Suite 204, New York, NY 10012 (☎1-800/575-TECH or 212/219-7000). Standby-seat broker; also deals in consolidator fares and courier flights.

Cheap Tickets, Inc. Offices throughout the US. (☎1-800/377-1000 or 212/570-1179). Consolidator.

Council Travel, 205 E 42nd St, New York, NY 10017 (☎1-800/226-8624; www.ciee.org), and branches in many other US cities. Student/budget travel agency. A sister company, Council Charter (☎1-800/800-8222), specializes in charter flights.

Educational Travel Center, 438 N Frances St, Madison, WI 53703 (☎1-800/747-5551 or 608/256-5551; www.edtrav.com). Student/youth and consolidator fares.

High Adventure Travel, 353 Sacramento St, Suite 600, San Francisco, CA 94111 (☎1-800/350-0612 or 415/912-5600; www.highadv.com). Round-the-world tickets. The Web site features an interactive database that lets you build your own RTW itinerary.

International Association of Air Travel Couriers, 8 South J St, PO Box 1349, Lake Worth, FL 33460 (☎561/582-8320; www.courier.org). Courier-flight broker. Membership $45 per year.

New Frontiers/Nouvelles Frontières, 12 E 33rd St, New York, NY 10016 (☎1-800/366-6387 or ☎212/779-0600); 1001 Sherbrook E, Suite 720, Montréal, H2L 1L3 (☎514/526-8444); and other

branches in LA, San Francisco and Québec City. French discount travel firm.

Now Voyager, 74 Varick St, Suite 307, New York, NY 10013 (☎212/431-1616; www.nowvoyagertravel.com). Courier flight broker and consolidator.

Skylink, 265 Madison Ave, 5th Fl, New York, NY 10016 (☎1-800/AIR-ONLY or 212/573-8980) with branches in Chicago, Los Angeles, Montréal, Toronto and Washington DC. Consolidator.

STA Travel, 10 Downing St, New York, NY 10014 (☎1-800/781-4040 or 212/627-3111; www.sta-travel.com), and other branches in the Los Angeles, San Francisco and Boston areas. Worldwide discount travel firm specializing in student/youth fares; also student IDs, travel insurance, car rental, rail passes, etc.

Student Flights, 5010 E Shea Blvd, Suite 104A, Scottsdale, AZ 85254 (☎1-800/255-8000 or ☎602/951-1177; www.isecard.com). Student/youth fares, student IDs.

TFI Tours International, 34 W 32nd St, New York, NY 10001 (☎1-800/745-8000 or 212/736-1140), and other offices in Las Vegas and Miami. Consolidator.

Travac Tours, 989 6th Ave, New York, NY 10018 (☎1-800/872-8800 or 212/563-3303; www.travac.com). Consolidator and charter broker.

Travel Avenue, 10 S Riverside, Suite 1404, Chicago, IL 60606 (☎1-800/333-3335 or 312/876-6866; www.travelavenue.com). Full-service travel agent that offers discounts in the form of rebates.

Travel CUTS, 187 College St, Toronto, ON M5T 1P7 (☎1-800/667-2887 [Canada only] or 416/979-2406), and other branches all over Canada. Organization specializing in student fares, IDs and other travel services.

UniTravel, 1177 N Warson Rd, St Louis, MO 63132 (☎1-800/325-2222 or 314/569-2501). Consolidator.

Worldtek Travel, 111 Water St, New Haven, CT 06511 (☎1-800/243-1723 or 203/772-0470). Discount travel agency.

Ryanair offer the greatest selection of onward connections to Scotland (see p.3). Aer Lingus also serves Edinburgh, and United can ticket you straight through to several Scottish destinations on British Midland. Flying to Manchester in the north of England is another possibility, though this won't be any cheaper than the direct Apex fare to Glasgow.

FLIGHTS FROM CANADA

Air Canada flies daily nonstop to **Glasgow from Toronto** in summer (four times a week in winter). From other Canadian cities you can fly via London on Air Canada or British Airways (see p.3 for details of onward travel to Scotland), or alternatively fly to Chicago, New York or Boston and pick up a nonstop flight to Glasgow from there. In addition, Air Canada also has direct flights from Toronto to Manchester.

Low-season midweek Apex fares from Toronto and Montréal to Glasgow should set you back CAN$600–700; from Vancouver between CAN$800–900. During the shoulder seasons fares are around CAN$650–750 from Toronto, CAN$850–950 from Vancouver, and in high season expect to pay $750–950 from Toronto and $950–1150 from Vancouver.

PACKAGES AND INCLUSIVE TOURS

Although you may want to see Scotland at your own speed, you shouldn't dismiss out of hand the idea of a package deal. Many agents and airlines put together very flexible deals, sometimes amounting to no more than a flight plus car or train pass and accommodation, which can actually work out better value than the same arrangements made on arrival, especially in the case of fly-drive deals, as car rental is expensive in Britain.

There are also many tour operators that specialize in travel to Scotland. Most can do packages of the standard highlights, and many also organize **walking or cycling trips** through the countryside, with any number of theme tours based around Scotland's literary heritage, history, pubs, gardens, golf – you name it. A few possibilities are listed in the box below, and a good travel agent will be able to point out others. For further listings, contact the British Tourist Authority (☎1-800/462-2748) or check out the Scottish Tourist Board's website at *www.holiday.scotland.net*. Be sure to examine the fine print of any deal, and make sure the operator is a member of the United States Tour Operator Association (USTOA) or approved by the American Society of Travel Agents (ASTA).

NORTH AMERICAN TOUR OPERATORS TO SCOTLAND

Abercrombie & Kent ☎1-800/323-7308; *www.abercrombiekent.com*
Land and rail tours of Scotland.

Above the Clouds Trekking ☎1-800/233-4499; *www.gorp.com/abvclds.htm*
Week-long walking tours of the Highlands.

British Coastal Trails ☎1-800/473-1210; *www.bctwalk.com*
Walking trips in the Borders and Western Isles.

British Travel International ☎1-800/327-6097
Offers self-catering country cottages and B&B accommodation in Scotland and can arrange air tickets, rail and bus passes.

CIE Tours International ☎1-800/243-8687; *www.cietours.com*
Escorted bus tours and deluxe castle tours of Scotland.

English Lakeland Ramblers ☎1-800/724-8801; *www.ramblers.com*
Week-long walking tours in the Highlands and Islands.

Especially Britain ☎1-800/869-0538
Fly-drives and independent rail tours staying in B&Bs, country houses and castles.

Golf International Inc ☎800/833-1389
Scottish golf vacation specialist.

Himalayan Travel ☎1-800/225-2380; *www.gorp.com/himtravel.htm*
Hiking and walking tours of Scotland.

Home At First ☎1-800/523-5842
Rents out cottages and flats in Scotland.

Jerry Quinlan's Celtic Golf ☎1-800/535-6148 or 609/884-8090; *www.jqcelticgolf.com*
Customized golf tours of Scotland's best links.

Journeys Through Scotland ☎1-800/828-7583
Customized sightseeing and golf tours.

Lord Addison Travel ☎1-800/326-0170; *www.lordaddison.com*
Small escorted specialist tours, including garden tours and history tours, such as the "Bonnie Prince Charlie tour".

McFarland Ltd ☎1-800/437-2687; *www.reveretvl.com*
Scottish specialist who can book hotels and arrange BritRail passes.

Prestige Tours ☎1-800/890-7375
A variety of Scottish tours.

Sterling Tours ☎1-800/727-4359; *www.sterlingtours.com*
Scottish specialist offering a variety of independent itineraries, some packages.

GETTING THERE FROM AUSTRALIA AND NEW ZEALAND

There are no direct flights to Scotland from Australia or New Zealand, and mostly you will have to route through London then get an onward flight north. Travelling time is twenty hours plus, so you might be better off including a stopover – and a good night's sleep – in your itinerary. Fares obviously depend on the time of the year: low-season rates run from mid-January to the end of February and October to November; high season is mid-May to August, and December to mid-January; and shoulder season is the rest of the year. Unlike with some destinations, prices do not vary according to the time of the week. Tickets purchased direct from the airlines tend to be more expensive, while travel agents can offer better deals and have the latest information on special offers and stopovers – the best discounts are often available through Flight Centres and STA, who can also advise on visa regulations. Students and under-26s can usually get a further ten percent off published prices.

All the fares quoted below are from Australia's east coast, unless otherwise stated, to London. From Perth you'll pay $200–400 less on flights routed through Asia and Africa, and the same amount more for flights via the Americas. In addition, you'll need to add on an extra A$150–300, depending on the season, for the flight to Glasgow or Edinburgh; most travel agents will be able to book this leg for you in advance, though you may find it cheaper to wait and pick up a low-cost flight in London (see p.3 for details). Alternatively, you may prefer to travel overland

from London by bus or train. BritRail train passes can be good value if you intend to do a lot of travelling in the UK, but must be bought before you leave home (see p.25 for full details).

The cheapest scheduled flights to London are **via Asia** with Philippine Airlines, Garuda and Royal Brunei, all of which charge around A$1500 in low season, and A$1899 in high season, and involve a transfer in the carrier's hub city. Aeroflot's lowest fare starts at A$1750, though for A$1799 (low season) you can fly with Virgin Atlantic/Malaysia Airlines via Kuala Lumpur. In the mid-range, Thai Airways, Cathay Pacific and Singapore Airlines all fly direct to London for A$1999–2510, while British Airways and Qantas both quote published fares of A$2399 in low season up to A$3199 in high season. Many of the airlines also offer fly-drive packages and stopovers in their hub cities for no extra cost; JAL, for example, flies from Sydney, Cairns and Brisbane several times a week including a stopover in Tokyo or Osaka and fourteen-day car hire in London, with fares starting at A$1999.

Via Africa the lowest fares start at A$1899, with Qantas/Air France via Johannesburg and Paris on the way out and back via southeast Asia. Qantas/SAA flights via Johannesburg start at A$2200, while low-season British Airways flights via Johannesburg or Harare start from A$2400.

Flights are pricier **via North America**, with United Airlines offering the cheapest deal via Los Angeles and either New York, Washington or Chicago for A$2299–2899, while Air New Zealand via Auckland and Los Angeles, and Canadian Airlines via Toronto or Vancouver, both charge around A$2499–3099.

Currently the best fare of all on offer is the Britannia Airways **charter flight** which runs several times a month to Gatwick and Manchester via Singapore and Abu Dhabi. Fares start at A$1299 in low season and range up to A$1899 in high season, though the flight only runs between November and April.

From New Zealand, the cheapest scheduled flights to London Heathrow (with an extra NZ$150–300 for flights to Edinburgh and Glasgow) are with Thai Airways, Korean Air and JAL, all of whom fly via their respective home cities for around NZ$2199–2699. British Airways' daily flight from Auckland costs from NZ$2599, including a connecting flight to Edinburgh or

AIRLINES IN AUSTRALIA AND NEW ZEALAND

Aeroflot, Australia ☎02/9262 2233.
Daily flights from Sydney to London Heathrow via
Moscow and Bangkok.

Air New Zealand, Australia ☎132476; New
Zealand ☎09/357 3000.
Daily direct flights to London Heathrow from
major Australian cities via Asia and from major
New Zealand cities via Los Angeles.

Air France, Australia ☎02/9321 1000; New
Zealand ☎09/303 3521.
Several flights a week to London from major
Australian cities via Johannesburg and Paris, and
return via Paris and Singapore/Bangkok/Hong
Kong: code-shares with Qantas.

Britannia Airways, Australia ☎02/9251 1299.
Several flights a month from Sydney, Brisbane,
Cairns and Auckland to London Gatwick and once
a week to Manchester via Bangkok and Abu Dhabi:
flights only run between November and April.

British Airways, Australia ☎02/9258 3300;
New Zealand ☎09/356 8690.
Daily direct flights from Sydney to London
Heathrow via Singapore/Los Angeles, and twice-
weekly via Harare or Johannesburg; daily flights
from Auckland via Los Angeles, with onward connections to Scotland.

Canadian Airlines, Australia ☎02/9299 7843 or
1800/251 321; New Zealand ☎09/309 0735.
Several flights a week to London Heathrow via
Vancouver/Toronto from Sydney, Melbourne and
Auckland.

Cathay Pacific, Australia ☎131747; New
Zealand ☎09/379 0861.
Several flights a week to London and
Manchester from Brisbane, Sydney, Melbourne,
Perth, Cairns and Auckland, via Hong Kong.

Garuda, Australia ☎02/334 9944 or 1-800/800
873; New Zealand ☎09/366 1855.
Several flights weekly from major Australian and
New Zealand cities to London Gatwick via
Denpasar or Jakarta.

Japanese Airlines (JAL), Australia ☎02/9272
1111; New Zealand ☎09/379 9906.
Daily flights to London Heathrow via Tokyo or
Osaka from Brisbane and Sydney, and several
weekly flights from Cairns and Auckland: onward
connections to Edinburgh on British Midland.

KLM, Australia ☎02/9231 6333 or 1-800/505
747.
Twice-weekly flights from Sydney to London
Heathrow via Amsterdam and Singapore.

Korean Air, Australia ☎02/9262 6000; New
Zealand ☎09/307 3687.
Several flights a week to London from Sydney,
Auckland and once a week from Christchurch, via
Seoul.

Malaysia Airlines (MAS), Australia ☎13 2627;
New Zealand ☎09/373 2741.
Several flights a week to London Heathrow from
Sydney, Melbourne, Perth and Auckland via
Kuala Lumpur. With onward connections to Leeds
and Bradford.

Philippine Airlines, Australia ☎02/9251 2044.
Twice weekly flights to London Gatwick from
Sydney and Brisbane via Manila and Frankfurt.

Qantas, Australia ☎131211; New Zealand
☎09/357 8900 or 0800/808 767.
Daily flights from major Australasian cities to
London Heathrow via Singapore/Bangkok. Also
daily flights to Hong Kong and twice-weekly
flights to Beijing.

Royal Brunei Airlines, Australia ☎07/3221
7757.
Three flights weekly to London from Brisbane,
and two weekly from Darwin and Perth, via Abu
Dhabi and Brunei.

South African Airways (SAA), Australia
☎02/9223 4402.
Flights to London from major Australian cities via
Perth and Johannesburg/Harare: code-shares
with Qantas.

Singapore Airlines, Australia ☎131011; New
Zealand ☎09/379 3209.
Daily flights to London Heathrow and
Manchester from Brisbane, Sydney, Melbourne,
Perth and Auckland via Singapore.

Thai Airways, Australia ☎131960; New
Zealand ☎09/377 3886.
Several flights a week to London Heathrow via
Bangkok from Brisbane, Sydney, Melbourne,
Perth and Auckland.

United Airlines, Australia ☎131777; New
Zealand ☎09/377 3886.
Daily flights to London Heathrow and
Manchester via Los Angeles Chicago, New York
or Washington from Sydney, Melbourne and
Auckland.

Virgin Atlantic, Australia ☎02/9352 6199.
Daily flights to London Heathrow via Kuala
Lumpur from Sydney, Melbourne, and Adelaide:
code-shares with Malaysia Airlines.

Glasgow. The most direct route to London is via North America with United Airlines stopping in Los Angeles and Chicago for NZ$2599 (low season) and NZ$2999 (high season). As with Australia, the cheapest fare of all is on Britannia Airways' charter flight from Auckland to Gatwick and Manchester that runs several times a month from November to April. Fares from Auckland are NZ$1450 low season, NZ$1850 shoulder season and NZ$2150 high season.

DISCOUNT AGENTS IN AUSTRALIA AND NEW ZEALAND

Anywhere Travel, 345 Anzac Parade, Kingsford, Sydney (☎02/9663 0411).

Brisbane Discount Travel, 260 Queen St, Brisbane (☎07/3229 9211).

Budget Travel, 16 Fort St, Auckland, plus branches around the city (☎09/366 0061 and ☎0800/808 040).

Destinations Unlimited, 3 Milford Rd, Auckland (☎09/373 4033).

Flight Centres, 82 Elizabeth St, Sydney, plus branches nationwide (☎13 1600); 205 Queen St, Auckland (☎09/309 6171), plus branches nationwide.

Northern Gateway, 22 Cavenagh St, Darwin (☎08/8941 1394).

STA Travel, 702 Harris St, Ultimo, Sydney; 256 Flinders St, Melbourne, plus offices in state capitals and major universities (telesales ☎1300/360 960); 10 High St, Auckland, plus branches in Wellington, Christchurch, Dunedin, Palmerston North, Hamilton and at major universities (telesales ☎09/366 6673). Web site: *www.statravelaus.com.au.*

Thomas Cook, 175 Pitt St, Sydney; 257 Collins St, Melbourne, plus branches in other state capitals (telesales ☎1800/063 913); 96 Anzac Ave, Auckland (☎09/379 3920).

SPECIALIST AGENTS

Adventure Specialists, 69 Liverpool St, Sydney (☎02/9261 2927).
Offers a selection of walking and cycling holidays throughout Scotland.

Adventure World, 73 Walker St, North Sydney (☎02/9956 7766 and 1800/221 931), plus branches in Brisbane and Perth; 101 Great South Rd, Remuera, Auckland (☎09/524 5118).
Based in London, but with an extensive variety of tours throughout Scotland.

Best of Britain, 352a Military Rd, Cremorne, Sydney (☎02/9909 1055).
Can arrange flights, accommodation, car rental, tours, canal boats and B&Bs throughout Scotland.

British Travel, 1st Floor, 200 Adelaide Terrace, East Perth (☎08/9221 7999).
Specializes in all aspects of UK travel including charter flights from Australia.

Explore Holidays, corner of Marsden and Pennet Hills roads, Carlingford (☎02/9872 6222). Can organize guest-house, farm, country inn and hotel accommodation throughout Scotland, as well as special-interest and rambling trips.

Destinations Adventure, 2nd Floor, Premier Building, corner of Queen and Durham streets, East Auckland (☎09/309 0464).
New Zealand agents for Peregrine Adventures.

Peregrine Adventures, 258 Lonsdale St, Melbourne (☎03/9663 8611), plus offices in Brisbane, Sydney, Adelaide and Perth.
Adventure travel company specializing in small-group walking and cycling holidays in Scotland, with travel between main points by minibus.

Sundowners, 151 Dorcas St, South Melbourne (☎03/9600 1934).
Russian and Trans-Siberian Railway specialists; escorted group tours and independent travel by train to Scotland via Moscow.

Wiltrans/Maupintour, Level 10, 189 Kent St, Sydney (☎02/9225 0899).
Fully escorted tours around Scotland's historic homes and gardens, staying in upmarket accommodation.

YHA Travel Centre,
422 Kent St, Sydney (☎02/9261 1111); 205 King St, Melbourne (☎03/9670 9611); 38 Stuart St, Adelaide (☎08/8231 5583); 154 Roma St, Brisbane (☎07/3236 1680); 236 William St, Perth (☎08/9227 5122); 69a Mitchell St, Darwin (☎08/8981 2560); 28 Criterion St, Hobart (☎03/6234 9617); 36 Customs House, Auckland (☎09/379 4224).
Organizes budget accommodation throughout England, Wales and Scotland for YHA members.

If you're visiting Sotland as part of a longer trip, a **round-the-world (RTW) ticket** can work out very good value. Currently the best deals on offer are Cathay Pacific/United's "Globetrotter", Air New Zealand/KLM/Northwest's "World Navigator" and Qantas/BA's "Global Explorer" tickets. All allow six stopovers worldwide with limited backtracking, and start at A$2499/NZ$3089. For more flexibility, Singapore Airlines/TWA's "Easyworld" ticket (only available in Australia) allows unlimited stopovers worldwide (except in the US where the limit is eight) with limited backtracking for a flat rate of A$3109. Note that, while it's easy enough to include London on a round-the-world itinerary, a stop in Scotland may involve backtracking and can be harder to arrange; you may find it cheaper to buy the London to Scotland leg separately, or to travel overland (see p.5 for details).

VISAS, CUSTOMS REGULATIONS AND TAX

Citizens of all European countries – except Albania, Bulgaria, Romania and all states of the former Soviet Union (other than the Baltic states) – can enter Britain with just a passport, generally for up to three months. US, Canadian, Australian and New Zealand citizens can stay for up to six months. Citizens of all other nationalities require a visa, obtainable from the British Consular or Mission office in the country of application. All overseas consulates in Scotland are detailed in the listings sections for Edinburgh and Glasgow.

LONG STAYS AND WORK PERMITS

For stays of longer than six months, US, Canadian, Australian and New Zealand citizens can apply to the British Embassy (see box below) in person or by post for an **Entry Clearance Certificate**. Unless you're a resident of an EU country, you need a **permit** to work legally in the UK, although without the backing of an established employer or company this can be very difficult to obtain. Persons aged between 17 and 27 may, however, apply for a **Working Holiday-Maker Entry Certificate**, which entitles you to stay in the UK for up to two years and to do casual work. The

BRITISH EMBASSIES ABROAD

Australia (High Commission) Commonwealth Ave, Yarralumla, Canberra, ACT 2600 (☎06/6257 1982).

Canada (High Commission) 80 Elgin St, Ottawa, ON K1P 5K7 (☎613/237-1530).

Ireland 31–33 Merrion Rd, Dublin 4 (☎01/269 5211).

Netherlands Koningslaan 44, Amsterdam (☎676 43 43).

New Zealand (High Commission) 44 Hill St, Wellington (☎04/495 0889).

USA 3100 Massachusetts Ave NW, Washington, DC 20008 (☎202/462-1340).

Details of British immigration and visa requirements are listed on the Foreign and Commonwealth Office's **Web site** (*www.fco.gov.uk*), from which you can download the full range of application forms and information leaflets. In addition, an independent charity, the **Immigration Advisory Service** (IAS), County House, 190 Great Dover St, London SE1 4YB (☎0171/357 6917), offers free and confidential advice to anyone applying for Entry Clearance into the UK.

certificates are only available abroad, from British embassies and consulates, and when you apply you must have proof of a valid return or onward ticket, and the means to support yourself while you're in Britain. Note, too, that the certificates are valid from the date of entry into Britain – you won't be able to recoup time spent out of the country during the two-year period.

In North America, full-time, bona fide college students can get temporary work or study permits through the **Council of International Education Exchange** (CIEE), 205 E 42nd St, New York, NY 10017 (☎212/822 2600; *www.ciee.org*). In addition, Commonwealth citizens with a parent or grandparent born in the UK can apply for a **Certificate of Entitlement to the Right of Abode**, which permits them to work in Britain. If you're unsure about whether or not you may eligible for one of these, contact your nearest British Mission (embassy or consulate), or the Foreign and Commonwealth Office in London (☎0171/270 1500 or 238 4633).

CUSTOMS AND TAX

Travellers coming into Britain directly from another **EU** country do not have to make a declaration to customs at their place of entry and can effectively bring almost as much wine or beer across the Channel as they like. However, there are still strict restrictions – details of which are prominently displayed in all duty-free outlets – on tax- or duty-free goods, so you can't invest in a stockpile of cheap cigarettes, wherever you're coming from.

There are **import restrictions** on a variety of articles and substances, from firearms to furs derived from endangered species, none of which should bother the average tourist. However, if you need any clarification on British import regulations, contact HM Customs and Excise, Dorset House, Stamford Street, London SE1 9PJ (☎0171/928 3344). You cannot bring pets into Britain on holiday, as tight quarantine restrictions apply to animals brought from overseas (except Northern and Southern Ireland).

Many goods in Britain, with the chief exceptions of books and food, are subject to **Value Added Tax** (VAT), which currently increases the cost of an item by 17.5 percent. Visitors from non-EU countries can save a lot of money through the Retail Export Scheme, which allows a refund of VAT on goods to be taken out of the country – though savings will usually be minimal, if anything, for EU nationals, because of their own VAT rates. Note that not all shops participate in this scheme – those doing so display a sign to this effect – and that you cannot reclaim VAT charged on hotel bills or other services.

MONEY, BANKS AND COSTS

The basic unit of currency in Britain is the pound sterling (£), divided into 100 pence (p). Coins come in denominations of 1p, 2p,

5p, 10p, 20p, 50p and £1 – there's a rare £2 coin in circulation as well. Bank of England and Northern Ireland banknotes are legal tender in Scotland; in addition the Bank of Scotland, the Royal Bank of Scotland and the Clydesdale Bank issue their own banknotes in denominations of £1, £5, £10, £20, £50 and £100 – legal tender in the rest of Britain, no matter what shopkeepers south of the border might say. Shopkeepers will carefully scrutinize any £20 or £50 notes, as forgeries are widespread, and you'd be well advised to do the same. The quickest test is to hold the note up to the light to make sure there's a thin wire filament running from top to bottom; this is by no means foolproof, but it will catch most fakes.

CARRYING MONEY

There are no exchange controls in Britain, so you can bring in as much money as you like. The easiest and safest way to carry your money is in travellers' cheques, available for a small commission (usually one percent) from any major bank. The most commonly accepted travellers' cheques are American Express (Amex), followed by Visa and Thomas Cook – most cheques issued by banks will be one of these brands. You'll usually pay commission again when you cash each cheque, normally another one percent or so, or a flat rate, though no commission is payable on Amex cheques exchanged at Amex offices. Make sure you keep a record of the cheques as you cash them, so that you'll be able to get the value of all uncashed cheques refunded immediately if you lose them.

Most hotels, shops and restaurants in Scotland accept the major **credit cards** – Access/MasterCard, Visa, Amex and Diners Club – although they're less useful in rural areas; smaller establishments all over the country, such as B&Bs, will often accept cash only. You can get cash advances from selected banks and bureaus de change on credit cards, though there will invariably be a minimum amount you can draw.

If you have a PIN number, you can take money out with Visa and Access/MasterCard at Bank of Scotland, Clydesdale and Royal Bank of Scotland **cashpoint machines**, and you can use Visa cards in TSB Scotland machines. Bank of Scotland and Royal Bank of Scotland cashpoints take Lloyds and Barclays cash cards, while Clydesdale takes Midland and National Westminster cards. Bank of Scotland, Clydesdale and most building society cashpoints are in the Link network and accept all affiliated cards.

BANKING HOURS

In every sizeable town in Scotland and, surprisingly, in some small places, you'll find a branch of at least one of the big high-street banks: Bank of Scotland, Royal Bank of Scotland, Clydesdale and TSB Scotland. However, on some islands, and in remoter parts, you may find there is only a mobile bank that runs to a timetable, usually available from the local post office. General **opening hours** are Monday to Friday 9.15am until 4pm or 4.45pm, though all are open until 5.45pm on Thursdays. Almost everywhere, banks are the best places in which to **change money and cheques**; outside banking hours you'll have to use a **bureau de change**, widely found in most city centres, often at train stations or airports. Avoid changing money or cheques in hotels, where the rates are normally very poor.

EMERGENCIES

If, as a foreign visitor, you run out of money or there is some kind of emergency, the quickest way to get **money sent out** is to contact your bank at home and have them wire the cash to the nearest bank. You can do the same thing through Thomas Cook or American Express if there's a branch nearby. Americans and Canadians can also have cash sent out through Western Union (information in UK ☎0800/833833) to a nearby bank or post office. Make sure you know when it's likely to arrive, since you won't be notified by the receiving office. Remember, too, that you'll need some form of identification when you pick up the money.

COSTS

Scotland has become an expensive place to visit, although in general it is marginally less pricey than England. The minimum expenditure, if you're camping, hitching a lot of the time and preparing most of your own food, would be in the region of £25 a day, rising to around £35 a day using the hostelling network, some public transport and grabbing the odd meal. Couples staying at budget B&Bs, eating at unpretentious restaurants and visiting a fair number of tourist attractions, are looking at around £50 each per day; if you're renting a car, staying in comfortable B&Bs or hotels and eating well, you should reckon on at least £70–80 a day per person. Single travellers should budget on spending around sixty percent of what a couple would spend (single rooms cost more than half a double). If you're visiting **Edinburgh**, which can get pricey, allow at least an extra £10 or so a day to get full pleasure out of the place.

TIPPING

There are no fixed rules for **tipping** in Scotland. If you think you've received good service, particularly in restaurants or cafés, you may want to leave a tip of ten to fifteen percent, but check first that service has not already been included. It is not normal, however, to leave tips in pubs, although bar staff are sometimes offered drinks, which they may accept in the form of money (the assumption is they'll spend this on a drink after closing time). Taxi drivers, on the other hand, will expect tips on long journeys – ten percent is the norm. The other occasion when you'll be expected to tip is in upmarket hotels where, in common with most other countries, porters, bellboys and table waiters rely on being tipped to bump up their often dismal wages.

YOUTH AND STUDENT DISCOUNTS

Various offical youth/student ID cards are widely available and most will soon pay for themselves in savings.

Full-time students are eligible for the **International Student ID Card** (ISIC), which entitles the bearer to special fares on local transport, and discounts at museums, theatres and other attractions. For Americans, there's also a health benefit, providing up to US$3000 in emergency medical coverage and US$100 a day for sixty days in the hospital, plus a 24-hour hotline to call in the event of a medical, legal or financial emergency. The card, which costs US$20 for Americans, CAN$30 for Canadians, A$10 for Australians and NZ$15 in New Zealand, is available from branches of Council Travel, STA and Travel CUTS (see p.11 and p.15 for addresses).

You only have to be 25 or younger to qualify for the **Go-25 Card**, which costs the same as the ISIC and carries the same benefits. It can be purchased through Council Travel in the US and around the world, Hostelling International in Canada (see "Accommodation", p.30) and STA in Australia and New Zealand.

INSURANCE, HEALTH AND EMERGENCIES

Wherever you're travelling from, it's a good idea to have some kind of travel insurance, which covers you for loss of possessions and money, as well as the cost of all medical and dental treatment. If you're travelling to Scotland from elsewhere in Britain, you may well be covered by your domestic insurance policy.

The amount of cover you get varies according to the premium, but a standard policy should always cover the cost of cancellation and curtailment of flights, medical expenses, travel delay, accident, missed departures, lost baggage, lost passport, personal liability and legal expenses.

Policies can start from as low as £13 per month, and it's always worth shopping around to get a good price. Some insurance companies refuse to cover travellers over 65, or stop at 69 or 74 years of age, and most that do charge hefty premiums. The best policies for **older travellers**, with no upper age limit, are offered by Age Concern (☎01883/346964).

Whatever your policy, if you have anything stolen, get a copy of the police report of the incident, as this is essential to substantiate your claim.

INSURANCE COMPANIES IN THE UK

Campus Travel (see p.3 for address).

Columbus Travel Insurance, 17 Devonshire Square, London EC2M 4SQ (☎0171/375 0011).

Endsleigh Insurance, Cranfield House, 97–107 Southampton Row, London WC1B 4AG (☎0171/436 4451).

Marcus Hearne & Co Ltd, 65–66 Shoreditch High St, London E1 6JL (☎0171/739 3444).

STA (see p.3 for address).

Worldwide, The Business Centre, 1–7 Commercial Rd, Tonbridge, Kent TN12 6YT (☎01732/773366).

NORTH AMERICAN COVER

Before buying an insurance policy, check that you're not already covered. **Canadian provincial health plans** typically provide some overseas medical coverage, although they're unlikely to pick up the full tab in the event of a mishap. Holders of official **student/teacher/youth cards** (see p.19) are covered for accident coverage and hospital in-patient benefits, and the annual membership fee is far less than the cost of comparable insurance. **Students** may also find that their student health coverage extends during the vacations and for one term beyond the date of last enrolment. Bank and **credit cards** (particularly American Express) often provide certain levels of medical or other insurance, and travel insurance may also be included if you use a major credit or charge card to pay for your trip. In addition, **homeowners' or renters'** insurance often covers theft or loss of documents, money and valuables while overseas.

If you do need to purchase a separate travel insurance **policy**, be aware that they can vary hugely: some are comprehensive, while others cover only certain risks (accidents, illnesses, delayed or lost luggage, cancelled flights, etc). In particular, ask whether the policy pays medical costs up front or reimburses you later, and whether it provides for medical evacuation to your home country. For policies that include lost or stolen luggage, check exactly what is and isn't covered, and make sure the per-article limit will cover your most valuable possessions. A specialist travel insurance company (see box above) can give you advice about various policies and ensure that you get one suited to your needs.

The lowest **premiums** are usually available through student/youth travel agencies: for example, ISIS policies (for students of any age)

for eight to fifteen days cost $60 with medical coverage, and $45 without; for a month you'll pay $110 and $85 respectively; and for two months the charge is $165 with medical coverage, $135 without. Non-students will pay a bit more: Travel Assistance International, for example, offers a fifteen-day policy including medical cover for $75–95, and a thirty-day plan for $105–130. If you're planning to do any "dangerous sports" (skiing, mountaineering, etc), check whether these activities are covered: some companies levy a surcharge.

Most North American travel policies apply only to items lost, stolen or damaged while in the custody of an identifiable, responsible third party – hotel porter, airline, luggage consignment, etc. Even in these cases you will have to contact the local police within a certain time limit to have a complete report made out so that your insurer can process the claim.

AUSTRALASIAN COVER

Travel insurance policies in Australia and New Zealand tend to be put together by airlines and travel agent groups, and are all fairly similar in terms of coverage and price. A typical policy for the UK covering medical costs, lost baggage and personal liability will cost around A$100/NZ$110 for two weeks, A$170/NZ$190 for one month, and A$250/NZ$275 for two months.

The following companies offer some of the widest cover available and can be arranged direct or through most travel agents: Ready Plan, 141 Walker St, Dandenong, Melbourne (☎03/9791 5077 or 1800/337 462), and 10/63 Albert St, Auckland (☎09/379 3208); and Cover More, Level 9, 32 Walker St, North Sydney, (☎02/9202 8000), with branches also in Victoria and Queensland.

THE MIDGE

Despite being around a millimetre long, and enjoying a life span on the wing of just a few weeks, the **midge** (*culicoides*) – a tiny biting fly prevalent in the Highlands (mainly the west coast) and islands – is considered to be second only to the weather as the major deterrent to tourism in Scotland. More than thirty varieties of midge exist here, though only half of these actually bite humans. Ninety percent of all midge bites are down to the female *culicoides impunctatus* or Highland midge (the male does not bite). To some, these persistent creatures are merely a nuisance; others have a violent allergic reaction when bitten. The easiest way to avoid midges is to visit in the winter, since they only appear between April and October; less drastic deterrents include smoke and noise – wind, direct sunlight, heavy rain and drought also discourage them. Basically, midges love still, damp, overcast or shady conditions and are at their meanest around sunrise and sunset. You'll soon notice if they're near; cover up arms and legs and try to avoid wearing dark colours, which attract them. Various repellents are worth a try, among them Autan and Jungle Formula, widely available from pharmacists, and the herbal remedy citronella. An alternative to repellents for protecting your face, especially if you are walking or camping, is the midge net, which you secure by tucking under your hat. Although they appear ridiculous at first, midge nets are commonplace and extremely useful.

HEALTH

No vaccinations are required for entry into Britain. Citizens of all **EU** countries are entitled to free medical treatment at National Health Service hospitals on production of an **E111** form (available from post offices, DSS offices or travel agents); you can just show your passport, but will have to pay on the spot and claim the money back later. Citizens of other countries will be charged for all medical services except those administered by accident and emergency units at National Health Service hospitals. Thus a **US** citizen who has been hit by a car would not be charged if the injuries simply required stitching and setting in the emergency unit, but would if admission to a hospital ward were necessary. Health insurance is therefore extremely advisable for all non-EU nationals. In **Australia**, Medicare has a reciprocal health-care arrangement with Britain.

Pharmacists can dispense only a limited range of drugs without a doctor's prescription. Most are open standard shop hours, though in large towns some may close as late as 10pm – local newspapers carry lists of late-opening pharmacies. **Doctors' surgeries** tend to be open from about 9am to noon and then for a couple of hours in the evening; outside surgery hours, you can turn up at the casualty department of the local hospital for complaints that require immediate attention – unless it's an emergency, in which case ring for an ambulance ☎999.

THE POLICE

For the most part the Scottish **police** continue to be approachable and helpful to visitors. If you're lost in a major town, asking a police officer is generally the quickest way to get help – alternatively, you could ask a **traffic warden**, a much-maligned species of law enforcer responsible for parking restrictions and other vehicle-related matters. They're distinguishable by their flat caps with a yellow band, and by the fact that they are generally armed with a book of parking-fine tickets; police officers on street duty wear a peaked flat hat with a black and white chequered band, and are generally armed with a truncheon (baton).

As with any country, Scotland's major towns have their danger spots, but these tend to be inner-city housing estates where no tourist has any reason to be. The chief risk on the streets is pickpocketing, so carry only as much money as you need, and keep all bags and pockets fastened. Should you have anything stolen or be involved in some incident that requires reporting, go to the local police station (addresses in the major cities are listed in the Guide); the ☎999 number should only be used in emergencies.

EMERGENCIES

For Police, Fire Brigade, Ambulance and, in certain areas, Mountain Rescue or Coastguard, dial ☎999.

INFORMATION AND MAPS

SCOTTISH TOURIST BOARD OFFICES

Scotland: 23 Ravelston Terrace, Edinburgh EH4 3EU (☎0131/332 2433).

England: 19 Cockspur St, London SW1 5BL (☎0171/930 8661 or 8662 or 8663).

If you want to do a bit of research before arriving in Scotland, you should contact the British Tourist Authority (BTA) in your country or write direct to the main office of the Scottish Tourist Board (STB), marking your letter "Information Department" – the addresses are given below. The BTA and STB will send you a wealth of free literature, some of it just rose-tinted

BRITISH TOURIST AUTHORITY OFFICES

Australia 210 Clarence St, 4th Floor, Sydney, NSW 2000 (☎02/267 4555).

Canada 111 Avenue Rd, Suite 450, Toronto, ON M5R 3J8 (☎416/961-8124).

Ireland 18–19 College Green, Dublin 2 (☎1/670 8000).

New Zealand Suite 305, 3rd Floor, Dilworth Building, corner of Customs and Queen streets, Auckland (☎09/303 1805).

USA 551 5th Ave, Suite 701, New York, NY 10176 (☎1-800/Go Britain or 212/986-2200); 625 N Michigan Ave, Suite 1510, Chicago, IL (walk-in service only).

REGIONAL TOURIST BOARDS IN SCOTLAND

Aberdeen & Grampian Tourist Board, Migvie House, North Silver Street, Aberdeen AB10 1RJ (☎01224/632727).

Angus & City of Dundee Tourist Board, 4 City Square, Dundee DD1 3BA (☎01382/434664).

Argyll, The Isles, Loch Lomond, Stirling & Trossachs Tourist Board, Old Town Jail, St John's Street, Stirling (☎01786/471301).

Ayrshire & Arran Tourist Board, Burns House, Burns Statue Square, Ayr KA7 1UT (☎01292/288688).

Dumfries and Galloway Tourist Board, 64 Whitesands, Dumfries DG1 2RS (☎01387/253862).

Edinburgh and the Lothians Tourist Board, 4 Rothesay Terrace, Edinburgh EH3 7RY (☎0131/557 1700).

Glasgow and the Clyde Valley Tourist Board, 11 George Square, Glasgow G2 1DY (☎0141/204 4772).

Highlands of Scotland Tourist Board, Peffery House, Strathpeffer IV14 9HA (☎01463/421160).

Kingdom of Fife Tourist Board, 7 Hanover Court, North Street, Glenrothes KY7 5SB (☎01334/472021).

Orkney Tourist Board, 6 Broad St, Kirkwall, Orkney KW15 1DH (☎01856/872856).

Perthshire Tourist Board, Lower City Mills, West Mill Street, Perth PH1 5QP (☎01738/627958).

Scottish Borders Tourist Board, Shepherd Mills, Whinfield Road, Selkirk TD7 4DT (☎01750/20555).

Shetland Island Tourism, Market Cross, Lerwick, Shetland ZE1 0LU (☎01595/693434).

Western Isles Tourist Board, 26 Cromwell St, Stornoway, Isle of Lewis HS1 2DD (☎01851/703088).

MAP OUTLETS

IN THE UK

Blackwell's Map and Travel Shop, 53 Broad St, Oxford OX1 3BQ (☎01865/792792).

Call of the Wild, 21 Station St, Keswick, Cumbria CA12 5HH (☎01768/771014).

Daunt Books, 83 Marylebone High St, London W1M 3DE (☎0171/224 2295); 193 Haverstock Hill, London NW3 4QL (☎0171/794 4006).

Heffers Map Shop, 3rd Floor, in Heffers Stationery Department, 19 Sidney St, Cambridge, CB2 3HL (☎01223/568467). Mail order available from here; more maps and travel literature at their bookshop at 20 Trinity St.

HMSO Books, 71 Lothian Rd, Edinburgh EH3 9AZ (☎0131/228 4181).

James Thin Melven's Bookshop, 29 Union St, Inverness, IV1 1QA (☎01463/233500).

John Smith and Sons, 57–61 St Vincent St, Glasgow G2 5TB (☎0141/221 7472).

Latitude, 34 The Broadway, Darkes Lane, Potters Bar, Herts EN6 2HW (☎01707/663090). Mail-order catalogue available.

The Map Shop, 30a Belvoir St, Leicester, LE1 6QH (☎0116/2471400). Mail order available.

The Map Shop, 15 High St, Upton-upon-Severn, Worcestershire WR8 0HJ (☎01684/593146). Free catalogue and mail order available.

National Map Centre, 22–24 Caxton St, London SW1H 0QU (☎0171/222 2466).

Newcastle Map Centre, 55 Grey St, Newcastle upon Tyne, NE1 6EF (☎0191/261 5622).

Stanfords, 12–14 Long Acre, London WC2E 9LP (☎0171/836 1321); maps by mail or phone order are available on this number. Other branches are located within Campus Travel at 52 Grosvenor Gardens, London SW1W 0AG (☎0171/730 1314); within the British Airways offices at 156 Regent St, London W1R 5TA (☎0171/434 4744); and at 29 Corn St, Bristol BS1 1HT (☎0117/929 9966).

The Travel Bookshop, 13–15 Blenheim Crescent, London W11 2EE (☎0171/229 5260).

IN NORTH AMERICA

Adventurous Traveler Bookstore, PO Box 1468, Williston, VI 05495 (☎1-800/282-3963; *www.AdventurousTraveler.com*).

Book Passage, 51 Tamal Vista Blvd, Corte Madera, CA 94925 (☎415/927-0960).

The Complete Traveler Bookstore, 199 Madison Ave, New York, NY 10016 (☎212/685-9007).

Map Link, 30 S La Petera Lane, Unit #5, Santa Barbara, CA 93117 (☎805/692-6777).

The Map Store Inc, 1636 1st St, Washington DC, 20006 (☎202/628-2608).

Open Air Books and Maps, 25 Toronto St, Toronto, ON M5R 2C1 (☎416/363-0719).

Phileas Fogg's Books & Maps, #87 Stanford Shopping Center, Palo Alto, CA 94304 (☎1-800/533-FOGG).

Rand McNally, 444 N Michigan Ave, Chicago, IL 60611 (☎312/321-1751); 150 E 52nd St, New York, NY 10022 (☎212/758-7488); 595 Market St, San Francisco, CA 94105 (☎415/777-3131); call ☎1-800/333-0136 for other locations, or for maps by mail order.

Sierra Club Bookstore, 6014 College Ave, Oakland, CA 94618 (☎510/658-7470).

Travel Books & Language Center, 4931 Cordell Ave, Bethesda, MD 20814 (☎1-800/220-2665).

Traveler's Bookstore, 22 W 52nd St, New York, NY 10019 (☎212/664-0995).

Ulysses Travel Bookshop, 4176 St-Denis, Montréal (☎514/843-9447).

World Wide Books and Maps, 736 Granville St, Vancouver, BC V6Z 1E4 (☎604/687-3320).

IN AUSTRALIA AND NEW ZEALAND

Bowyangs, 372 Little Bourke St, Melbourne, VIC 3000 (☎03/9670 4383).

The Map Shop, 16a Peel St, Adelaide, SA 5000 (☎08/8231 2033).

Perth Map Centre, 891 Hay St, Perth, WA 6000 (☎08/9322 5733).

Speciality Maps, 58 Albert St, Auckland (☎09/307 2217).

Travel Bookshop, 20 Bridge St, Sydney, NSW 2000 (☎02/9241 3554).

Worldwide Maps and Guides, 187 George St, Brisbane, Queensland (☎07/3221 4330).

advertising copy, but much of it extremely useful – especially the maps, city guides and event calendars. If you want more hard facts on a particular area, approach the area tourist boards, which are listed on p.22. Some are extremely helpful, others give the impression of being harassed to breaking point by years of understaffing, but all of them will have a few leaflets worth scanning before you set out.

Tourist offices (sometimes called Tourist Information Centres) exist in virtually every Scottish town – you'll find their phone numbers and opening hours in the relevant sections of the Guide. The average opening hours are much the same as standard shop hours, with the difference that in summer they'll often be open on a Sunday and for a couple of hours after the shops have closed on weekdays; opening hours are generally shorter in winter, and in more remote areas the office may well be closed for the season. All centres offer information on accommodation (and can usually book rooms – see "Accommodation"), local public transport, attractions and restaurants as well as town and regional maps. In many cases their services are free, but a growing number of offices make a small charge for an accommodation list or a town guide with an accompanying street plan.

MAPS

Many bookshops will have a selection of maps of Scotland and Britain in general, but see the box on p.23 for a list of travel specialists. Virtually every service station in Scotland stocks one or more of the big **road atlases**. The best of these are the large-format ones produced by the AA, RAC, Collins and Ordnance Survey, which cover all of Britain at around 3miles:1in and include larger-scale plans of major towns. You could also invest in the excellent **fold-out maps** published by Michelin and Bartholomew; the latter includes clear town plans of the major cities. Another option is the official tourist map series published by Estate Publications, perfect if you're driving or cycling round one particular region since it marks all the major tourist sights as well as youth hostels and campsites.

If you're after more detail, the most comprehensive **maps** of Scotland are produced by the **Ordnance Survey** series – renowned for its accuracy and clarity. The 204 maps in their 1:50,000 (a little over 1mile:1in) *Landranger* series cover the whole of Britain and show enough detail to be useful for most walkers. Their more detailed 1:25,000 Pathfinder series, which also covers the whole of Britain, is invaluable for serious hiking. For many of the walks in this guide, the use of Ordnance Survey maps is strongly recommended (see p.43). The full Ordnance Survey range is only available at a few big-city stores, although in any walking district of Scotland you'll find the relevant maps in local shops or tourist offices.

GETTING AROUND

As you'd expect, the efficiency of Scotland's train and bus services is largely dictated by geography and population density. The majority of Scots live in the central belt, which spreads from Glasgow in the west to Edinburgh, virtually on the east coast. Public transport here is efficient and most places are easily accessible by train and bus. To the south and north it can be a different story: off the main routes, public transport services are few and far between, particularly in more remote regions such as the Highlands, although with careful planning practically everywhere is accessible and you'll have no trouble getting to the main

tourist destinations. In most parts of Scotland, especially if you take the scenic backroads, the low level of traffic makes driving wonderfully unstressful.

TRAINS AND RAIL PASSES

UK government policies over the past decade or so have led to a severe decline in **rail services** all over Britain, and Scotland is no exception. For the time being, **ScotRail** runs the majority of train services, reaching all the major towns, sometimes on lines rated as among the great scenic routes of the world. For a rundown of the different fares available, see "Getting there from England, Ireland and Europe".

You can buy tickets for ScotRail trains at stations or from major travel agents. For busy long-distance **InterCity** routes, it's advisable to **reserve** a seat. Seat reservations to Edinburgh, Glasgow, Aberdeen or Inverness are included in the price of the ticket if you book in advance. The ticket offices at many rural and commuter stations are closed at weekends; in these instances there's sometimes a vending machine on the platform. If the machines aren't working, you can buy your ticket on board, but if you've embarked at a station that does have a machine and you haven't bought a ticket there's a spot fine of £10.

In addition, ScotRail offers a number of **travel passes** and **special tickets**. The **Freedom of Scotland Travelpass** gives unlimited train travel and is valid on all CalMac west coast ferry links (see ferry information on p.28), as well as offering 33 percent reductions on many buses and on some P&O Orkney and Shetland ferries. It costs £99 for eight consecutive days, £139 for fifteen

---

> **TRAIN INFORMATION AND BOOKING IN SCOTLAND**
>
> Details of all ScotRail fares, train times, reservations and other information can be obtained by calling **National Rail Enquiries** ☎0345/484950. **ScotRail telesales** ☎0345/550033.

---

days (or £110 for eight out of fifteen days), and comes complete with timetables and a card allowing discounts at tourist attractions, shops and restaurants throughout Scotland. The **ScotRail Rover** is perhaps the most flexible option, allowing unlimited travel on ScotRail for varying periods; prices range from £62 for four out of eight consecutive days' travel, to £118 for twelve out of fifteen days. ScotRail also do three other regional Rover passes: the West Highland (covering the area from Glasgow to Fort William), which costs £40 for four out of eight days; the North Highland, which for the same price is valid on all lines from Thurso to Aberdeen; and the Festival Cities, which includes routes from Glasgow to Edinburgh and Stirling, and costs £25 for three out of seven days. The Freedom of Scotland and the ScotRail Rover passes are both available from ScotRail telesales (see above).

If you plan to do a lot of travelling around the UK, your best bet is to buy one of the range of BritRail passes, which allow unlimited travel in Scotland, England and Wales. These passes can not be bought in the UK and are only available for purchase before you leave your home country, through local travel agents or the specialist companies listed below. The **BritRail Classic Pass** allows unlimited standard-class travel for eight

---

consecutive days for US$260/A$280/NZ$330; fifteen days costs US$402/A$395/NZ$480; 22 days costs US$518/A$555/NZ$660; and one month for US$598/A$605/NZ$725. Under-26s pay US$210/A$225/NZ$265 for eight days; US$322/A$315/NZ$425 for fifteen days; US$417/A$445/NZ$530 for 22 days; or US$481/A$485/NZ$580 for one month. Seniors (aged 60+ and only available for first-class travel) pay US$320/A$355/NZ$425 for eight days, US$492/A$505/NZ$605 for fifteen days, US$642/A$705/NZ$840 for 22 days, or US$733/A$770/NZ$925 for one month.

Better value if you're not travelling every day is the **BritRail Flexipass**, which allows four days of travel within a one-month period for US$219/A$240/NZ$290; eight days out of a month for US$325/A$345/NZ$410; or fifteen days out of a month for US$485/A$550/NZ$660. Under-26s pay US$175/A$195/NZ$230 for four days out of a month, US$255/A$275/NZ$330 for eight days in one month, or US$389/A$440/NZ$530 for fifteen days out of two months. For Seniors (60+ and only available for first-class travel) the prices are US$275/A$310/NZ$370 for four days out of a month; US$395/A$440/NZ$530 for eight days in one month; and US$599/A$705/NZ$850 for fifteen days in a month.

A great bargain for **travellers with children** allows one free child pass for each paying adult, and if four adults are travelling together on a BritRail pass, two of the four can purchase the pass for half-price. BritRail Pass holders can also get special rates on the London to Paris Eurostar.

BUSES

Travelling around Scotland by **bus** may take a little longer than using the train, but works out considerably cheaper. There's a plethora of regional companies, but by far the biggest national operators are Scottish Citylink (☎0990/898989), a subsidiary company of National Express. With train travel being so expensive, bus services have become very popular, so for busy routes and at weekends and holidays it's a good idea to buy a "reserved-journey ticket", which guarantees you a seat.

If you plan to do a lot of travelling by bus, it may be worth buying a **Tourist Trail Pass**, which offers unlimited travel on the National Express and Scottish Citylink network: it costs £49 for three days; £79 for five days;on any eight days within sixteen it costs £95 for students and under-23s, £119 for others; for any fifteen days within

thirty, you'll pay £145 and £179 respectively. In England you can buy them both from major travel agents, at Gatwick and Heathrow airports and at the British Travel Centre, 12 Regent St, London W1 (walk-in service only). In Scotland, outlets include St Andrew Square Bus Station, Edinburgh, and Buchanan Bus Station, Glasgow, as well as other local bus stations. In **North America** these passes are available from British Travel International (☎1-800/327-6097) and US National Express (☎540/298-1395).

Local bus services are run by a bewildering array of companies, and it's increasingly the case that private companies duplicate the busiest routes in an attempt to undercut the commercial opposition, leaving the remoter spots neglected. As a general rule, the further away from urban areas you get, the less frequent and more expensive bus services become.

Those rural areas not covered by other forms of public transport are served by the **postbus** network, which operates 140 minibuses carrying mail and three to ten fare-paying passengers. They set off in the morning – usually around 8am from the main post office and collect mail (or deliver it) from/to the nether regions. It's an extremely cheap way to travel, costing about £2 or so for every 25 miles, and can be a convenient way of getting to hidden-away B&Bs, although often excruciatingly slow. You can get a booklet of routes and timetables from the Royal Mail Public Relations Unit, 102 West Port, Edinburgh EH3 9HS (☎0131/228 7407), and the Scottish Tourist Board in London (see p.22).

BUS TOURS

If you're backpacking, a cheap, flexible and fun way of travelling around Scotland is on one of the popular **"jump-on-jump-off" minibus** services that operate out of Edinburgh. Among the oldest of the established operators is the bizarrely named Go Blue Banana company, whose minibus calls at Pitlochry, Inverness, Loch Ness, Kyleakin and Isle of Skye, Fort William, Oban, Loch Lomond and Glasgow before returning to Edinburgh. It runs every day except Sunday, throughout the year, stopping at independent hostels along the route – which saves you the hassle of lugging of your bags around – and you can spend as long as you like at each place. A ticket for one circuit costs £85: for further details, contact Go Blue Banana at 16 High St, Edinburgh (☎0131/556 2000). Haggis Backpackers, at 11 Blackfriars St,

Edinburgh EH1 1NB (☎0131/557 9393) operates a similar service in large Mercedes buses, complete with punchy sound systems.

Both the companies mentioned above also run backpackers' **minibus tours** of Scotland. Prices start at about £75 for a three-day round-trip from Edinburgh, taking in Loch Ness, Skye, Glen Coe and other Highland highlights, while a six-day guided tour, combining most of Scotland's main tourist destinations, costs around £139; these fares do not include food and accommodation, but the tour companies can help with hostel booking. The same applies to the popular Rabbie's Trail Burners tours, which also start in Edinburgh (207 High St, Edinburgh; ☎0131/226 3133), offering a range of one-, two- or three-day tours in Mercedes sixteen-seater minibuses, with knowledgeable driver-guides. If you're pushed for time and want to do a whistlestop tour of England and Wales en route to Scotland, another option worth considering is the Go Blue Banana London to Edinburgh trip, outlined in "Getting there" on p.7.

DRIVING AND HITCHING

If you want to cover a lot of the country in a short time, or just want more flexibility, you'll need your own transport. In order to **drive** in Scotland you must have a current driving licence; foreign nationals will need to supplement this with an international driving permit, available from state and national motoring organizations for a small fee. If you're bringing your own car into the country you should also carry your vehicle registration or ownership document at all times. Furthermore, you must be adequately insured, so be sure to check your existing policy.

In Scotland, as in England, you drive on the left, which can lead to a few tense days of acclimatization for many overseas drivers. **Speed limits** are 30–40mph (50–65kmph) in built-up areas, 70mph (110kmph) on motorways and dual carriageways, and 60mph (100kmph) on most other roads. As a rule, assume that in any area with street lighting the speed limit is 30mph (50kmph) unless stated otherwise. Out in the remoter regions, many roads are still **single-track**, with passing places – these should also be used to enable cars to overtake you. In the Highlands, the roads are littered with sheep who are entirely oblivious to cars, so slow down and edge your way past – should you kill one, it is your duty to inform the local farmer.

The three major motoring organizations, the Automobile Association (AA), the Royal Automobile Club (RAC) and Green Flag Emergency Assistance, all operate 24-hour emergency **breakdown** services. The AA and RAC also provide many other motoring services, including a reciprocal arrangement for free assistance through many overseas motoring organizations – check the situation with yours before setting out. On motorways the AA and RAC can be called from roadside booths; elsewhere ring ☎0800/887766 for the AA; ☎0800/828282 for the RAC; and ☎0800/400600 for Green Flag. In remote areas, however, particularly in the Highlands, you may have a long wait for assistance. You can ring these emergency numbers even if you are not a member of the respective organization, although a substantial fee will be charged. In addition, it may be worth investing in a policy with home-relay, as spare parts can be hard to get hold of in the Highlands, and most standard policies will only get you to the nearest garage, where you can find yourself stranded for days until the part you need is sent from Inverness or Glasgow. If you're touring the remoter parts of Scotland, bear in mind, too, that some regions of the country, particularly the far north, have comparatively few garages and petrol stations.

Like the rest of Britain, it's inadvisable for anyone travelling alone to **hitch** in Scotland, even in the central region where there's a good motorway network and a lot of traffic. In remote areas, especially in the Highlands, there's a long tradition of giving lifts, but locals clearly have priority, and you may have to wait a long time before you're picked up.

CAR AND MOTORBIKE RENTAL

Car rental in Scotland is expensive, and, especially if you're travelling from North America, you'll probably find it cheaper to arrange things in advance through one of the multinational chains. If you do rent a car, the least you can expect to pay is around £135 a week – the rate for a small hatchback from Holiday Autos, one of the most competitive rental agencies; reckon on paying £40 per day direct from one of the multi-nationals, £5 or so less at a local firm. Most companies prefer you to pay with a credit card, otherwise you may have to leave a deposit of £100–150. There are very few automatics at the lower end of the price scale – if you want one, you should book well ahead. To rent a car you

MOTORING ORGANIZATIONS

American Automobile Association (AAA). Each state has its own club – check the phone book for local address and phone number. The AAA can refer members to overseas auto associations, and can provide international drivers' licences and *carnets de passage* (for those planning to transport cars across certain international boundaries).

Australian Automobile Association, 212 Northbourne Ave, Canberra ACT 2601 (☎61/6247 7311).

Automobile Association, Fanum House, Basingstoke, Hants RG21 4EA (☎0990/448866).

Canadian Automobile Association (CAA). Each region has its own club – check the phone book for local address and phone number. Benefits are comparable to the AAA's (see above), and membership rates vary.

New Zealand Automobile Association, PO Box 1794, Wellington (☎64/473 8738).

Royal Automobile Club, RAC House, PO Box 700, Bristol BS99 1RB (☎0800/550550).

CAR RENTAL FIRMS

IN BRITAIN
Avis ☎0990/900500.
Budget ☎0800/181181.
Eurodollar ☎01895/223300.
Europcar ☎0345/222525.
Hertz ☎0990/996699.
Holiday Autos ☎0990/300400.
Thrifty ☎0990/168238.

IN AUSTRALIA
Avis ☎1800/225 533.
Budget ☎132727.
Hertz ☎133039.

IN NEW ZEALAND
Avis ☎09/526 2847.
Budget ☎09/375 2222.
Hertz ☎09/309 0989.

IN NORTH AMERICA

Alamo ☎1-800/522-9696; *www.goalamo.com*
Auto Europe ☎1-800/223-5555; *www.wrld.com/ae*
Avis ☎1-800/331-1084; *www.avis.com*
Budget ☎1-800/527-0700; *www.budgetrentacar.com*
Dollar ☎1-800/421-6868; *www.dollarcar.com*
Enterprise Rent-a-Car ☎1-800/325-8007; *www.pickenterprise.com*
Europe by Car ☎1-800/223-1516; *www.europebycar.com*

Hertz ☎1-800/654-3001; in Canada ☎1-800/263-0600; *www.hertz.com*
Holiday Autos ☎1-800/422-7737; *www.holiday/colauto.com*
National ☎1-800/CAR-RENT; *www.nationalcar.com*
Thrifty ☎1-800/367-2277; *www.thrifty.com*
US Rent-a-Car ☎1-800/777-9377.
Value ☎1-800/468-2583.

need to show your driving licence; few companies will rent to drivers with less than a year's experience and most will only rent to people between 21 and 70 years of age.

Motorbike rental is ludicrously expensive, at around £50 a day/£220 a week for a 500cc machine, and around £90/£325 for a one-litre tourer, including everything from insurance, helmets and luggage.

FERRIES

Scotland has 130 inhabited islands, and ferries play an important part in travelling around the country. Most ferries carry cars and vans, for which advance reservations can be made – highly advisable, particularly during the busy summer season (April–Oct). Of the major operators, Caledonian MacBrayne (abbreviated by most people and throughout this book to CalMac) covers the majority of routes.

CalMac has a virtual monopoly on services on the River Clyde and those to the Inner and Outer Hebrides, sailing to 23 islands altogether. They aren't cheap, but they do have two types of **reduced-fare pass**, the Island Hopscotch and the Island Rover. The Hopscotch offers a range of

FERRY OFFICES AND INFORMATION IN SCOTLAND

Caledonian MacBrayne Ltd, The Ferry Terminal, Gourock, Renfrewshire PA19 1QP (☎01475/650100).

Orkney Islands Shipping Co Ltd, Head Office, 4 Ayre Rd, Kirkwall KW15 1QX (☎01856/872044).

P&O Scottish Ferries, PO Box 5, Jamieson's Quay, Aberdeen AB9 8DL (☎01224/572615).

Western Ferries (Clyde) Ltd, 16 Woodside Crescent, Glasgow G3 7UT (☎0141/332 9766).

economy fares for cars and passengers on 24 preset routes and is valid for one month from the date of the first journey. It's the best option for anyone planning to make several short ferry trips between islands, though you do have to follow a set itinerary. Marginally more flexible is the Island Rover pass, which entitles you to eight or fifteen consecutive days of unlimited ferry travel, though again you must inform CalMac of your exact itinerary in advance. The eight-day pass costs £37 for passengers and £190 for cars, while the fifteen-day pass costs £53 and £285 respectively. Schedules vary and are highly complicated, but you can get details from the address above.

P&O Scottish Ferries sail **to Orkney and Shetland** from Aberdeen and Scrabster (Thurso). To Shetland from Aberdeen takes 13hr and costs about £92 single for a foot passenger, plus £80 or so for a small car. The ferry from Aberdeen to Orkney takes 8hr and costs £40, plus £100 or so for a car, while Scrabster to Orkney takes 1hr 45min and costs £13.50, plus a further £45 for a car. On all routes you should book in advance if you are taking a vehicle. The various Orkney islands are linked to each other by services run by the Orkney Islands Shipping Co Ltd.

In addition, Western Ferries operate between Gourock and Dunoon on the mainland to the islands of Islay and Jura, and numerous small operators round the Scottish coast run day-excursion trips; their phone numbers are listed in the relevant chapters in the Guide.

It is possible to book ferry tickets in advance **in North America**, if you're organized enough to know exactly when you'll be making the crossing. For sailings to/from France, Belgium or the Netherlands, contact BritRail Travel International (☎1-888/274-8724) or Scots American (☎1-201/768-1187); to/from Scandinavia, contact Bergen Line (☎1-800/323-7436) or Scandinavian Seaways (☎1-800/533-3755). In **Australia** and **New Zealand**, you can book ferry tickets in advance at branches of Thomas Cook (see p.15).

INTERNAL FLIGHTS

Scotland has seventeen internal airports, many of them on the islands and useful if you are short on time. Most flights are operated by British Airways Express (☎0345/222111), who fly between Edinburgh, Glasgow, Aberdeen and Inverness and to some of the main islands. Airports are listed below; call them, or British Airways Express, for timetable information. They'll also be able to fill you in on any cost-cutting special tickets and fares, such as the **Hopper Pass** sold through youth agents such as STA Travel (see p.3, p.11 or p.15 for address), which entitles students and those under 26 to sizeable discounts – ideal if you're travelling to and from some of the larger islands; note, however, that Shetland is not included in the scheme.

To find out which airports serve which destinations, consult the "Travel details" section of the relevant chapter.

AIRPORTS IN SCOTLAND

Aberdeen ☎01224/722331.	**Fair Isle** ☎01595/760222.	**Sumburgh** ☎01950/460654.
Barra Northbay ☎01871/890283.	**Glasgow** ☎0141/887 1111.	**Tingwall** ☎01595/840306.
Benbecula ☎01870/602051.	**Inverness** ☎01463/232471.	**Tiree** ☎01879/220309.
Campbeltown ☎01586/552571.	**Islay** ☎01496/302361.	**Unst** ☎01957/711620.
Dundee ☎01382/643242.	**Kirkwall** ☎01856/872421.	**Wick** ☎01955/602215.
Edinburgh ☎0131/333 1000.	**Stornoway** ☎01851/702256.	

ACCOMMODATION

The prevalence of bed and breakfasts (B&B) and hostels in Scotland ensures that budget accommodation is easy to come by. There are also scores of upmarket hotels, ranging from bland business-oriented places in the centres of the big towns to plush converted country mansions and ancient castles. Most tourist offices will book all kinds of accommodation for you when you arrive, although usually there is a small fee for this service. In some areas you will pay a deposit that's deducted from your first night's bill (usually ten percent), in others the office will take a percentage or flat-rate commission – on average around £3 – and occasionally it's free. Another useful service operated by the majority of tourist offices is the "Book-a-Bed-Ahead" service, which locates accommodation in your next port of call, and costs from £2.50.

HOTELS AND B&BS

The STB operates a nationwide system for grading **hotels, guest houses and B&Bs**, which is updat-

ed annually – although by no means everyone participates, and you shouldn't assume that a particular B&B is no good if it's ungraded. There are so many of these establishments in Scotland that the grading inspectors can't possibly keep track of them all, and in the rural backwaters some of the most enjoyable accommodation is to be found in welcoming and beautifully located houses whose facilities may technically fall short of official standards. All accommodation in the scheme is graded into four categories: Approved, Commended, Highly Commended and Deluxe. Within these, one to five Crowns are awarded for "facilities" which theoretically cover the condition of buildings and grounds, the quality of the food and general comfort as well as the warmth of welcome and the efficiency and friendliness shown by the staff. It's probably also worth using the grades supplied by the AA and the RAC as they independently combine evaluation of facilities with a degree of subjective judgement. Though there's not a hard and fast correlation between standards and price, you'll probably be paying in the region of £40 per night for a double room at a one-star hotel (breakfast included), rising to around £70 in a three-star, and from around £120 for a five-star. In some larger towns and cities the big hotels often offer cut-price deals at the weekend to fill rooms vacated by the week's business trade, but these places tend to be soulless multinational chain operations. If you can afford it, stay in a refurbished old building – many towns have atmospheric coaching inns and such like, while out in the countryside you'll find converted mansions and castles, often with brilliant restaurants attached.

ACCOMMODATION PRICE CODES

Throughout this book, accommodation **prices** have been graded with the numbers below, according to the cost of the least expensive double room in high season. Although costs will rise slightly overall with the life of this edition, the relative comparisons should remain valid. The bulk of the recommendations will fall in categories ② to ⑤; those in the highest categories are limited to places that are especially attractive. Bear in mind that many of the swanky chain hotels slash their tariffs at the weekend, and that many of the cheaper places will also have more expensive rooms. Note that in our accommodation listings price codes are not given for youth hostels – all youth hostel accommodation costs under £10 per person per night, except in the odd rare case, where we have quoted the price in the review.

① under £20
② £20–30
③ £30–40

④ £40–50
⑤ £50–60
⑥ £60–70

⑦ £70–80
⑧ £80–100
⑨ over £100

At the lower end of the scale, hotels merge almost imperceptibly into **B&Bs** – often known as **guest houses** in resorts and other tourist towns. These range from ordinary private houses with a couple of bedrooms set aside for paying guests and a dining room for the consumption of a rudimentary breakfast, to rooms as well furnished as those in hotels costing twice as much, with delicious home-prepared breakfasts, and an informal hospitality that a larger place couldn't match. B&Bs are also graded by the STB, the AA and the RAC. As a guideline to costs, it's easy to find a grade 1 STB place for under £35 per night a double; grade 4 places go for around £80. As many B&Bs, even the pricier ones, have a very small number of rooms, you should certainly book as far in advance as possible.

Another important point to remember in rural Scotland is that many B&Bs, as well as hotels, are only open for the summer season, roughly from Easter to October. You'll always find somewhere to stay outside this period, but the choice may be pretty limited.

HOSTELS

The network of the **Scottish Youth Hostels Association (SYHA)** consists of some eighty properties, usually offering bunk-bed accommodation in single-sex dormitories or smaller rooms. A few of these places are spartan establishments of the sort traditionally associated with the wholesome, fresh-air ethic of the early hostels, but most have moved well away from this and are beginning to offer private facilities with no curfew.

All the hostels referred to as "youth hostels" in the Guide are official *SYHA* properties unless stated otherwise. For Scottish residents, membership – which includes membership of the hostelling associations in the sixty countries affiliated to the **International Youth Hostels Federation (IYHF)** – costs £2.50 per year for under-18s, £6 for others, and can be obtained either by writing to or visiting the *SYHA* offices listed overleaf, or in person at most *SYHA* hostels. Visitors from elsewhere in Britain and foreign nationals who wish to join the IYHF can do so at the *SYHA* offices or most Scottish youth hostels for a £9 fee. Youth hostel members are entitled to half-price entry to all National Trust for Scotland properties (see p.37).

The vast majority of hostels charge between £4 and £10 a night, with only a few top-grade establishments (normally those in large cities) charging more than this. The cost of hostel **meals**, where available, is low: breakfast is around £2.50, and evening meals start at around £4. Nearly all hostels have kitchen facilities, for those who prefer self-catering. If you need to check any tariffs in advance, phone the hostel, or consult the current *SYHA Handbook*, which comes free when you pay your membership subscription.

At any time of the year, particularly in the popular city hostels, it's best to **book** well in advance, and it's essential at Easter, Christmas and from May to August. You can book by post, telephone and, in many cases, by fax, and your bed will be held until 6pm on the day of arrival. Some hostels, particularly in the Highlands, are closed for the whole of the winter except for the Christmas and New Year period. Even if you haven't booked, always phone ahead – we've given phone numbers in the Guide. Most hostels are closed from 10am to 5pm with an 11.30pm curfew, but some stay open all day. Length of stay is normally unlimited. Once again, it's worth getting hold of a copy of the current *SYHA Handbook*, which clarifies the intricacies of the system.

Allied to the *SYHA*, the **Gatliff Hebridean Hostels Trust** is a charitable organization that rents out very simple croft accommodation in the Hebridean islands. Accommodation is very basic, almost primitive, and many of these hostels have no phone, but the settings are invariably spectacular. In Shetland, Camping Böds, operated by the **Shetland Amenity Trust,** offer similarly simple accommodation: you need all your usual camping equipment, except, of course, a tent.

In addition, the **Independent Backpackers Hostels Association,** is an association of 37 independent hostels, mainly situated in the Highlands and islands, though including three in Edinburgh. These are mostly family-run places with no membership and no curfew, and many stay open all year. Housed in buildings ranging from croft houses to converted churches, they all have dormitories, hot showers, common rooms and self-catering kitchens, while many organize a range of outdoor activities. Prices hover around £9 per person per night. A brochure listing all the properties is available from Peter Thomas, Croft Bunkhouse, 7 Portnalong, Isle of Skye IV47 8SL (☎01478/640254). Detailed reviews of most independent hostels in Scotland are featured in the relevant sections of this book, and in more detail in the excellent *Accommodation for Groups* by Sam Dalley (published by Backpacker

SYHA OFFICES

Aberdeen 11 Ashvale Place, AB1 6QD
(☎01224/588156).

Ayr Craigweil House, Craigweil Rd, KA7 BJ (no phone).

Dundee 86 Bell St, DD1 1JG (☎01382/322150).

Edinburgh 161 Warrender Park Rd, EH9 1EQ
(☎0131/229 8660).

Glasgow 12 Renfield St, G2 5AL (☎0141/226 3976).

Stirling *SYHA* National Office, 7 Glebe Crescent, FK8 2JA (☎01786/891400).

YOUTH HOSTEL ASSOCIATIONS

Australia Australian Youth Hostels Association, Level 3, 10 Mallett St, Camperdown, NSW (☎02/565 1325).

Canada Hostelling International Canada, Room 400, 205 Catherine St, Ottawa, ON K2P 1C3 (☎1-800/663-5777 or ☎613/237-7884). Annual membership adults $26.75, under-18s free when accompanied by parents; two-year memberships cost $35.

England and Wales Youth Hostel Association (*YHA*), Trevelyan House, 8 St Stephen's Hill, St Albans, Herts AL1 2DY (☎017278/45047). London information office: 14 Southampton St, London WC2E 7HY (☎0171/836 1036).

Ireland An Óige, 61 Mountjoy St, Dublin 7 (☎01/830 4555).

New Zealand Youth Hostels Association of New Zealand, PO Box 436, Christchurch 1 (☎03/799970).

Northern Ireland Youth Hostel Association of Northern Ireland, 22 Donegal Rd, Belfast, BT12 5JN (☎01232/324733).

Scotland Scottish Youth Hostel Association (*SYHA*), 7 Glebe Crescent, Stirling, FK8 2JA (☎01786/451181).

USA Hostelling International-American Youth Hostels (*HI-AYH*), 733 15th St NW, Suite 840, PO Box 37613, Washington, DC 20005 (☎202/783-6161; *www.hostel.com*). Annual membership adults $25, youths (under 18) $10, seniors (55 or over) $15, families $35.

Press and distributed by Cordee Books and Maps, 3a De Montfort St, Leicester LE1 7HD (☎0116/254 3579).

CAMPING, CARAVANNING AND SELF-CATERING

There are hundreds of **campsites** in Scotland, most of which are open from April to October. The most expensive sites, which charge about £9 to pitch a tent, are usually well equipped with shops, a restaurant, a bar and occasionally sports facilities. At the other end of the scale, farmers sometimes offer pitches on their land for as little as £2.50 per night. The AA lists and grades campsites in its publication *Camping and Caravanning in Britain and Ireland*, and the area tourist boards can all supply lists of their recommended sites. In the most popular parts of rural Scotland – especially in the Highlands and the islands – tents have to share space with **caravans**. The great majority are permanently moored at their sites, while the ranks of nose-to-tail trailers in the vicinity of some of Scotland's

finest scenery might make you think that half the population of Britain shacks up in a caravan for the midsummer break.

For **North Americans** planning to do a lot of camping, an international camping carnet is a sound investment, available from home motoring organizations, or from Family Campers and RVers (FCRV), 4804 Transit Rd, Building 2, Depew, NY 14043 (☎1-800/245-9755). The carnet is good for discounts at member sites and serves as useful identification. FCRV annual membership costs $25, and the carnet an additional $10.

You may prefer more robust **self-catering** accommodation, and there are thousands of STB-approved properties for rent by the week, ranging from city penthouses to secluded cottages. The least you can expect to pay for four-berth self-catering accommodation in summer would be around £150 per week, but for something special – such as a well-sited coastal cottage – you should budget for twice that amount. A good source of accommodation is the STB's *Scotland: Self-Catering* guide. Updated annually, this full-colour brochure lists over 1200 properties, ranging from cottages and chalets to luxurious apartments, with colour photographs of most places included. Copies can be bought or odered through any Scottish tourist office (see p.22).

Another cheap self-catering option, especially if you're staying a week or more, is **campus accommodation.** Many Scottish universities open their halls of residence to overseas visitors during the summer break, and rooms vary from tiny single rooms in long, lonely corridors, to relatively comfortable places in small shared apartments. The British Universities Accommodation Consortium (BUAC) has full details: contact them at Box 1547, University Park, Nottingham NG7 2RD (☎0115/950 4571) for a brochure.

FOOD AND DRINK

Though the Scots still tend to regard eating as a necessity rather than the focal point of the day, the quality of Scottish food has improved by leaps and bounds in recent years. Scottish produce – superb meat, fish and game, a wide range of dairy products, the best soft fruit in Europe and a bewildering variety of traditional baked goodies – is of outstanding quality and has to some extent been rediscovered of late. Bear in mind, too, that in the larger cities the presence of various immigrant communities has led to a fine array of ethnic restaurants.

In many hotels and B&Bs you'll be offered a **Scottish breakfast**; similar to its English counterpart of sausage, bacon and egg but with the addition of porridge – properly made with genuine oatmeal and traditionally eaten with salt rather than sugar, though the latter is always on offer. You may also be served kippers or Arbroath smokies (delicately smoked haddock with butter), or a large piece of haddock eaten with a poached egg on top. Oatcakes (plain, slightly salty biscuits) and a "buttery" – a butter-enriched bread related to the French croissant – will often feature. Scotland's staple drink, like England's, is **tea**, drunk strong and with milk, though **coffee** is just as readily available everywhere.

The quintessential Scots dish is **haggis**, a sheep's stomach bag stuffed with spiced liver, offal, oatmeal and onion and traditionally eaten with bashed neeps (mashed turnips) and chappit tatties (mashed potatoes). The humble haggis has become rather trendy in recent years, and you can even, in the big cities, get a vegetarian version. Other staples include steak and kidney pie and shepherd's pie (minced beef covered with mashed potato and baked), as well as **stovies**, a tasty mash of onion and fried potato heated up with minced beef. In this cold climate home-made soup is generally welcome; try **Scots broth**, made with combinations of lentil, split pea, mutton stock or vegetables and barley.

Scots **beef** is delicious, especially the Aberdeen Angus breed; menus will specify if your steak falls into that fine category. **Venison**, the meat of the red deer, also features large – low in cholesterol and very tasty, it's served roasted or in casseroles, often flavoured with juniper or with a whisky sauce. If you like **game** and can afford it, splash out on grouse, the most highly prized of all game birds, strong, dark and succulent, best eaten with bread sauce. Pheasant is also worth a try: less rich than other game, more like a tasty chicken – you can eat it stuffed with oatmeal or with a mealie pudding, a kind of vegetarian black pudding made from onion, oatmeal and spices.

Scotland has a huge variety of fresh **fish** to choose from. In the coastal towns, prawns, oysters, crab and scallops are always available, while inland salmon is a must, especially the more delicately flavoured wild salmon – though this will always cost more than the farmed variety. Both are served either hot with melted butter, small new potatoes and a creamy Hollandaise sauce, or cold in a salad. Trout is also farmed in Scotland, often fried in oatmeal and eaten with bacon. Look out especially for the wild brown trout, whose firm pink flesh is nearly as good as salmon.

Puddings, often smothered in butterscotch sauce or syrup, are taken very seriously in Scotland. One traditional favourite is Cranachan, made with toasted oatmeal steeped in whisky and folded into whipped cream flavoured with fresh raspberries; on the same lines, Atholl Brose, related to the English syllabub, is made with oatmeal, whisky and cream. For the ultimate dessert decadence, try the clootie dumpling, a sweet, stodgy fruit pudding soaked in a cloth for hours. If it all sounds a bit rich you might prefer the black bun, a peppery fruitcake encased in a thin pastry and traditionally eaten at New Year, or the many home-made shortbreads – far superior to the commercial varieties. One Scottish institution that satisfies the Scots' sweet tooth is the **high tea**, consisting of a cooked main course and a plethora of cakes, washed down with tea or coffee and eaten between about 5pm and 6.30pm.

As for **fast food**, fish and chips is as popular in Scotland as in England and "**chippies**" abound, serving battered fish (invariably known as a "fish supper" even if eaten at lunchtime), haggis, oatmeal-based numbers such as black and mealie puddings, and artery-clogging, battered, deep-fried Mars bars. For alternative fast food, in the major towns there are all the usual **pizza** and **burger** outlets, and the more recent **baked potato** shops.

WHERE TO EAT

For **budget food** in Scotland you'll find hordes of **cafés** – which range from the most basic "greasy

spoons" to vaguely French-style **brasseries**, where you can have anything from a glass of wine to a cup of coffee, as well as a simple meal. Many provincial towns have **tearooms** of sorts, where you can sample Scottish baking. Some of the cheapest places to eat in Scotland are the **pubs**, many of which serve food all day – indeed, in the smallest villages these might be your only option.

The ranks of Scottish **gastronomic restaurants** grow with each passing year, with cordon bleu chefs producing high-class dishes with a Scottish slant that certainly rival their English and European counterparts. Outside Edinburgh and Glasgow many of these are found in hotels but are happy to serve non-residents, though you could easily land up paying £25–50 a head.

In central Scotland, particularly in Edinburgh and Glasgow, the **Indian** and **Chinese** communities ensure there is a good choice of restaurants, offering quality meals at fair prices. Some of the **French** restaurants in Edinburgh are excellent, and Scotland's large **Italian** community means there are numerous good trattorias. On the whole, though, you won't find the range of choice that exists south of the border, and outside the big cities **vegetarians** are still looked on somewhat askance, though the situation is slowly improving.

The restaurant listings in the Guide include a mix of high-quality and budget establishments. As a general rule on **costs**, if we call a place inexpensive, you can expect to pay under £10 a head, without drinks; moderate means it will cost between £10 and £20; expensive from £20 to £30; and very expensive over £30.

DRINK

As in the rest of Britain, Scottish **pubs**, which originated as travellers' hostelries and coaching inns, are *the* great social institution, and the pub crawl, a drunken trawl through as many pubs as possible in one night, is a national pastime. The focal points of any community, the local British pub can vary from oak-beamed and ingle-nooked inns with heaps of atmosphere, open fires and polished brass fittings, to blaring, noisy theme pubs, lined wall-to-wall with jukeboxes and pinball machines. Most pubs are owned by large breweries who favour their own cask-conditioned real ales served from the distinctive Scottish tall font (for more on types of beer, see below). Many of them, especially outside the big cities, are no-nonsense spit-and-sawdust public bars with an almost exclusively male clientele, making some visitors, especially women, feel highly uncomfortable. However, there are plenty of places that can be as welcoming as the full name, "public house", suggests, along with – in Edinburgh and Glasgow at least – a rash of upbeat, trendy café-bars favoured by a young, pre-clubbing set.

Scotland was ahead of England in changing to all-day **opening hours**, and pubs are generally open from Monday to Saturday 11am to 11pm, with "last orders" called by the bar staff about fifteen minutes before closing time. On Sunday the hours are reduced; many pubs are closed in the afternoon and last orders are called at 10.30pm. In general, you have to be 16 to enter a pub unaccompanied, though some places have special family rooms for people with children, and beer gardens where younger kids can run free. The legal drinking age is 18.

BEER

Beer is the staple drink in Scotland's pubs, the indigenous variety a thick, dark **ale** with a full head served in pints or half-pints at room temperature, much like the English bitter (in Scotland known as **heavy**). Scottish beers are graded by the shilling: a system used since the 1870s and indicating the level of potency – the higher the shilling mark, the stronger or "heavier" the beer. A pint costs anything from £1.50 to £2.20, depending on the brew and the locale of the pub.

Scotland's biggest-name breweries are McEwan's and Younger's, part of the mighty Scottish and Newcastle group, and Tennents, owned by the English firm Bass. The beers produced by these companies tend to be heavier, smoother and stronger than their English equivalents, especially McEwan's Export, a mass-produced, highly potent brew, and Tennents' Fowler's Wee Heavy, a famously tasty smooth ale. Younger's Tartan, though less flavoursome, is Scotland's biggest seller.

However, if you really want to discover how good Scottish beer, once renowned throughout the world for its strength, can be, look out for the products of the small **local breweries** scattered throughout Scotland. Edinburgh's Caledonian Brewery makes nine good cask beers, and operates from Victorian premises using much of their original equipment, including the only direct-fired coppers left in Britain. Others to look out for are Bellhaven, brewed in Dunbar near Edinburgh, whose 80-shilling Export is a typical Scottish ale; Maclays, a hoppy, lightish ale brewed in Alloa; and Traquair, in the Borders, which does a wonderfully smooth House Ale. The dry, fruity Alice Ale, brewed in Inverness, and the Orkney Brewery's Raven Ale, could be life-savers in the north, where good beer is hard to come by.

Blond Pilsner beers, or **lagers**, are served all over Scotland, along with European and American bottled varieties, but the major Scottish brews have little to fear from these pale and often tasteless competitors. **Wines** sold in pubs are generally appalling – strange in view of the excellent selection sold in off-licences and supermarkets.

WHISKY

Scotland's national drink is **whisky** – *uisge beatha*, the "water of life" in Gaelic – traditionally drunk in pubs with a half-pint of beer on the side, a combination known as a "nip and a hauf".

Whisky has been produced in Scotland since the fifteenth century, and really took off in popularity after the 1780 tax on claret made wine too expensive for most people. The taxman soon caught up with illicit whisky distilling and drove the stills underground, and today many malt distilleries operate on the site of simple cottages that once distilled the stuff illegally. In 1823 Parliament revised its Excise Laws, in the process legalizing whisky production, and today the drink is Scotland's chief export. There are two types of whisky: single malt, made from malted barley, and grain whisky, which (relatively cheap to produce), is made from maize and a small amount of malted barley in a continuous still. **Blended**, which accounts for more than ninety percent of all sales, is as the name suggests, a blend of the two types.

Grain whisky forms about seventy percent of the average bottle of blended whisky, but the distinctive flavour of the different blends comes from the malt whisky which is added to the grain in different quantities. The more expensive the blend, the higher the proportion of skilfully chosen and aged malts that have gone into it. Among many brand names, Johnnie Walker, Bells, Teachers and The Famous Grouse are some of the most widely available. All have a similar flavour, and are often drunk with mixers such as lemonade or mineral water.

Despite the dominance of the blended whiskies, **single malt whiskies** are infinitely superior, and best drunk neat to appreciate their distinctive flavours. Malt whisky is made by soaking barley in water for two or three days until it swells, after which it is left to germinate for up to twelve days, allowing the starch in the barley seed to become soluble. The malted barley is dried and peated, mashed with hot water and fermented with yeast to convert the sugar into crude alcohol, which is then twice distilled and the vapours condensed as a spirit, aged for a minimum of three years in oak casks. Single malts vary enormously depending on the peat used for drying, the water used for mashing, and the type of oak cask used in the maturing process, but they fall into four distinct groups – Highland, Lowland, Campbeltown and Islay, with the majority falling

into the Highland category and being produced largely on Speyside. You can get the best-known blends – among them Glenlivet, Glenmorangie, MacAllan, Talisker, Laphroaig, Highland Park and Glenfiddich, the top seller – in most of the pubs.

Most distilleries have a highly developed nose for PR and offer free tours that range from slick and streamlined to small and friendly. All of them offer visitors a "wee dram" as a finale, and you can buy bottles of the stuff – though prices are no lower at source than in the shops.

POST AND PHONES

Virtually all post offices are open Monday to Friday 9am to 5.30pm and Saturday 9am to 12.30pm or 1pm; in small communities you'll find sub-post offices operating out of a shop, open the same hours, even if the shop itself is open for longer. Stamps can be bought at post-office counters, from vending machines outside, or from an increasing number of newsagents, usually in books of four or ten.

A first-class letter to anywhere in the British Isles currently costs 26p and should – in theory – arrive the next day; second-class letters cost 20p, and take from two to four days. Airmail letters of less than 20g (0.7oz) also cost 26p to EU countries, and 31p to non-EU European countries. Letters to other overseas destinations cost from 43p for 10g, and 63p for 20g. Pre-stamped aerogrammes conforming to overseas airmail weight limits of under 10g can be bought for 36p from post offices only. For more information about Royal Mail postal services, phone ☎0345/740740.

Most public **payphones** in Scotland are operated by British Telecom (BT) and, in towns, at least, are widespread. Many BT payphones take all coins from 10p upwards, although an increasing proportion only accept **phonecards**, available from post offices and newsagents which display the BT logo. These cards come in denominations of £2, £3, £5, £10 and £20; some BT phones accept credit cards too.

Inland calls are cheapest between 6pm and 8am. **Reduced-rate periods** for most **interna-**

tional calls are 6pm to 8am from Monday to Friday and all day on Saturday and Sunday. Any number that begins with ☎0800 is free.

Throughout the Guide, telephone numbers are prefixed by the area code, except in the case of the big cities, when the area code is indicated once only, in a shaded box.

OPERATOR SERVICES AND PHONE CODES

Operator ☎100.
Directory assistance ☎192.
Overseas directory assistance ☎153.
International operator ☎155.

OPENING HOURS AND HOLIDAYS

Traditionally shop hours in Scotland have been Monday to Saturday 9am to 5.30pm or 6pm, but now many places stay open on Sundays and late at night, with Thursday or Friday the favoured evenings. The big supermarkets also tend to stay open until 8pm or 9pm from Monday to Saturday, as do many of the stores in the shopping complexes that are springing up on the outskirts of many major towns. Many provincial towns still retain an "early closing day" when shops close at 1pm – Wednesday is the favourite.

Unlike in England, Scotland's **"bank holidays"** mean just that: they are literally days when the banks are closed rather than general public holidays, and they vary from year to year. They include January 2, the Friday before Easter, the first and last Monday in May, the last Monday in August, St Andrew's Day (November 30), Christmas Day (December 25) and Boxing Day (December 26).

New Year's Day, January 1, is the only fixed **public holiday**, but all Scottish towns and cities have a one-day holiday in both spring and autumn – dates vary from place to place but normally fall on a Monday. If you want to know the exact dates, you can get a booklet detailing them from the Glasgow Chamber of Commerce, 30 George Square, Glasgow G2 1EQ.

SIGHTS, MUSEUMS AND MONUMENTS

Apart from the really big museums, and a number of attractions high on the tourist trail, Scotland's tourist season runs from Easter to October, and outside this period many indoor attractions are shut – though ruins, parks and gardens are normally accessible year-round. We've given full details of opening hours and admission charges in the Guide.

Many of Scotland's most treasured sights – from castles and country houses to islands, gardens and tracts of protected landscape – come under the control of the privately run **National Trust for Scotland**, 5 Charlotte Square, Edinburgh EH2 4DU (☎0131/226 5922), or the state-run **Historic Scotland**, Longmore House, Salisbury Place, Edinburgh EH9 15H (☎0131/668 8600), shown respectively as the "NTS" or "HS" in the Guide. Both organizations charge an entry fee for most places, and these can be quite high, especially for the more grandiose NTS estates. If you think you'll be visiting more than half a dozen owned by the NTS, or more than a dozen owned by HS, it's worth taking **annual**

membership (NTS £25, family £42; HS £18, family £37), which allows free entry to their properties.

In addition, both the NTS and HS offer short-term passes that give discounts on admission prices. The **National Trust Touring Pass**, which costs £14 for an adult and £25 for a family, is valid for seven days and gives free admission to all NTS properties. The HS **Scottish Explorer** seven-day ticket allows free entry to seventy monuments, castles and other properties and costs £12 or £26 for a family; a two-week equivalent costs £17/£35. **Members of the IYHF** (see p.31) are automatically eligible for half-price entry into all NTS properties.

A lot of Scottish **stately homes** remain in the hands of the landed gentry, who tend to charge around £5 for admission to edited highlights of their domain. Many other old buildings, albeit rarely the most momentous structures, are owned by local authorities, and admission is often cheaper, sometimes free. Municipal art galleries and museums are usually free, as are most of the state-owned museums, although "voluntary" donations are normally solicited.

The majority of fee-charging attractions in Scotland give 25–50 percent **reductions** for senior citizens, the unemployed, full-time students and children under 16, with under-5s being admitted free almost everywhere. Proof of age will be required in most cases. The entry charges quoted in the Guide are the full adult charges.

North Americans can buy the Scottish Explorer and National Trust Touring passes at travel agents or directly from Especially Britain (see under "Getting there from the USA and Canada"). A further option, only open to overseas visitors, is the **Great British Heritage Pass**, which gives free admission to some 600 sites throughout Britain, including many which are not run by the NTS or HS. Costing $45 for seven days, around $70 for 15 days and $90 for a month, it can be purchased through most travel agents at home, on arrival at any large UK airport, from British Airways offices and the British Travel Centre, 22 Regent St, London W1 (walk-in service only).

THE MEDIA

The principal British daily newspapers are all available in Scotland, often in a specific Scottish edition. The tabloids are as popular as in England – among them Rupert Murdoch's sex-and-scandal *Sun*, the self-consciously ridiculous *Daily Sport*, and the vaguely left-wing *Mirror*, the only tabloid that manages anything approximating an antidote to the *Sun*'s reactionary politics. The "quality" end of the market is cornered by the Murdoch-owned *Times*, the staunchly Conservative *Daily Telegraph*, the *Independent*, which strives worthily to live up to its name, and the *Guardian*, which inhabits a niche marginally left of centre.

The **Scottish press**, in the main rather staid and parochial, produces two major serious daily newspapers: Edinburgh's liberal-left *Scotsman* and the Glasgow's centre-right *Herald*. Scotland's biggest-selling daily paper, though, is the downmarket *Daily Record*, from the same stable as the *Daily Mirror*. The provincial daily press is more widely read than its English counterpart, with the two biggest-selling regional titles being Aberdeen's famously parochial *Press and Journal*, widely read in the northeast, the Highlands and the islands, and the right-wing *Dundee Courier*, mostly sold in Perth, Angus and Fife. For an insight into life in the Highlands and islands, the weekly *Oban Times* is a must, as is the more radical, campaigning weekly, the *West Highland Free Press*, printed on Skye. All carry articles in Gaelic as well as English. Further north, the lively *Shetland Times* and the sedate *Orcadian* are essential reading.

Many national **Sunday newspapers** have a Scottish section north of the border, but Scotland's own Sunday "heavy" is the serious *Scotland on Sunday*, known for its excellent political reporting and arts reviews. Far more fun and widely read, is the anachronistic *Sunday Post*, published by Dundee's mighty Thomson and Legg publishing group and read by more than half the population. It's a wholesome paper, uniquely Scottish, and has changed little since the 1950s, since when its two long-running cartoon strips, *Oor Wullie* and *The Broons*, have acquired something of a cult status.

When it comes to **specialist periodicals**, the best-selling weekly news magazine is the dry, scholarly *Economist*. The earnest socialist alternative, the *New Statesman and New Society*, has so few readers that it's stuck with the nickname "The Staggers", while the satirical bi-weekly *Private Eye* is a much-loved institution that prides itself on printing the stories the rest of the press won't touch, and on surviving the consequent stream of libel suits. The lively, weekly *Big Issue*, produced by homeless people and sold by vendors on every city street, has a separate Scottish edition and often carries features by well-known writers. Scottish **monthlies** include the *Scottish Field*, a lowbrow version of England's *Tatler*, covering the interests and pursuits of the landed gentry, and the widely read *Scots Magazine*, an old-fashioned middle-of-the-road publication which promotes family values, a stiff upper lip and lots of good fresh air. *USA Today* is the most widely available **North American paper**, though only the larger newsagents will stock it; you can also find *Time* and *Newsweek* in quality bookstores and newsagents. For visitors to Glasgow and Edinburgh, the fortnightly **listings magazine** *The List* is a must, covering all events in both cities.

TELEVISION AND RADIO

In Scotland there are five main **television channels**, the state-owned BBC1 and BBC2, and the independent commercial channels, ITV, Channel Four and Channel 5. Though assailed by government critics of late, the **BBC** is just about maintaining its worldwide reputation for in-house quality productions, ranging from expensive costume dramas to intelligent documentaries – split between the avowedly mainstream BBC1 and the more rarefied fare of BBC2. Three companies, the populist STV, which serves most of southern Scotland and parts of the West Highlands, the Aberdeen-based Grampian, and Border Televsion which transmits from Carlisle, form the **ITV** network in Scotland. This is complemented by the more eclectic and less mainstream broadcasting of the partly subsidized **Channel Four**, and the downmarket **Channel 5**, which shows good movies, but can't yet be recieved in many parts of Scotland. A plethora of **satellite** and, in the cities, **cable stations** are also available, though the dominant force is still Rupert Murdoch's **BSkyB**, which offers unlimited news, sport, movies, soaps, home shopping and game shows. For the time being, however, the old terrestrial stations still attract the majority of viewers.

Market forces are also eating away at the **BBC radio** network, which broadcasts six main channels in Scotland, though most of them originate largely from London. Radio One plays almost exclusively mainstream pop music; Radio Two specializes in MOR music; Radio Three broadcasts predominantly classical music; Radio Four is a blend of current affairs, arts and drama; and Radio Five Live, the newest station, transmits a mix of sport and news. The award-winning BBC Radio Scotland offers a Scottish perspective on news, politics, arts, music, travel and sport, and provides a Gaelic network in the northwest with local programmes in Shetland, Orkney, the north and the borders.

A web of **local commercial radio** stations stretches from Shetland to the Borders, mostly mixing rock and pop music with news, but a few tiny community-based stations such as Lochbroom FM in Ullapool – famed for its daily midge count – transmit documentaries and discussions on local issues. The most populated areas of Scotland also receive UK commercial radio: Classic FM lures listeners from Radios 2 and 3, Virgin Radio competes head to head with Radio 1 and Talk Radio UK offers phone-ins and chat.

EVENTS AND ENTERTAINMENT

Scotland offers a huge range of annual events, reflecting contemporary culture and heritage as well as its world-renowned tartan image. Many tourists will want to home straight in on bagpipes, ceilidhs and Highland Games, but it's worth bearing in mind that there's more to Scotland than this: numerous regional celebrations perpetuate ancient customs and accentuate the differences between Scotland and England, while the Edinburgh Festival and Glasgow's Mayfest are arts festivals on an international scale. Scotland's sporting events range from Highland Games, International Rugby and golf championships to home-grown pastimes such as curling – an activity that can be loosely described as

EVENTS CALENDAR

December 31 and January 1: Hogmanay and Ne'er Day. More important to the Scots than Christmas. Festivities revolve around the "first-footing", when at midnight crowds of revellers troop into neighbours' houses bearing gifts. Traditionally the first foot should be a dark-haired stranger carrying coal and salt (so the house won't lack for warmth or food), and a bottle of whisky (for obvious reasons).

January 1: Stonehaven fireball ceremony. Locals swing fireballs on long sticks to welcome New Year and ward off evil spirits.

January 1: Kirkwall Boy's and Men's Ba' Games, Orkney. Mass, drunken football game through the streets of the town, with the castle and the harbour the respective goals – as a grand finale the players jump into the harbour.

January 11: Burning of the Clavie, Burghead, Moray. Burning tar barrel is carried through the town and then rolled down Doorie Hill. Charred fragments of the Clavie offer protection against the evil eye.

Last Tuesday in January: Up-Helly-Aa, Lerwick, Shetland. Norse fire festival culminating in the burning of a specially built Viking longship. Visitors will need an invite from one of the locals, or you can buy a ticket for the Town Hall celebrations; see p.522.

January 25: Burns Night. Burns suppers all over Scotland. Dinners held to commemorate Scotland's greatest poet, involving haggis, whisky and lots of poetry recital.

February: Scottish Curling Championship held in a different (indoor) venue each year.

February: Aberdeen Angus Bull Sales at Perth.

February–March: Five Nations Rugby Tournament.

March 1: Whuppity Scourie at Lanark. Local children race round the church beating each other with home-made paper weapons as they go: a representation (it's thought) of the chasing away of winter or the warding off of evil spirits.

March: Edinburgh Folk Festival.

April: Scottish Grand National at Ayr. Not quite as testing as the English equivalent steeplechase but an important event on the Scottish racing calendar.

April: Rugby Sevens (seven-a-side rugby tournament) in full swing all over the Borders.

April: Kate Kennedy procession at St Andrews. An exclusively male university tradition in honour of distinguished figures in the town and university's history. The role of Kate, niece of the founder of the university, and mythologized as a great beauty, is always played by a first-year student.

April: Shetland Folk Festival.

May 1: Beltane Fire Festival on Calton Hill in Edinburgh.

May: Mayfest. Glasgow's recent and very successful answer to the Edinburgh Festival.

bowls on ice, which originated in Scotland nearly five hundred years ago and is now played all over the world – and shinty, a simple form of hockey (see p.42). Soccer is the national game, and weekly league matches are held from August to May (see p.42).

It's important to bear in mind that a few of the smaller, more obscure events, particularly those with a pagan bent, are in no way created for tourists, and indeed do not always welcome the casual visitor. If in doubt, check at the local tourist office. The STB publishes a weighty and complete list of Scottish events annually in December: it's free and you can get it from area tourist offices or direct from their headquarters.

HIGHLAND GAMES

Despite their name, **Highland Games** are held all over Scotland, from May until mid-September:

they vary in size and differ in the range of events they offer. Although the most famous ones are at Oban, Cowal and especially Braemar, often the smaller ones are more fun. They probably originated in the fourteenth century as a means of recruiting the best fighting men for the clan chiefs, and were popularized by Queen Victoria to encourage the traditional dress, music, games and dance of the Highlands; various royals still attend the Games at Braemar. The most distinctive events are known as the "**heavies**" – tossing the caber, putting the stone, and tossing the weight over the bar – all of which require prodigious strength and skill. Tossing the caber is the most spectacular, when the athlete must run carrying an entire tree trunk and attempt to heave it end over end in a perfect, elegant throw. Just as important as the sporting events are the **piping competitions** – for individuals and bands – and **dancing com-**

May: Scottish FA Cup Final in Glasgow.

Late May: Atholl Highlanders Parade at Blair Castle, Perthshire. The annual parade and inspection of Britain's last private army by their colonel-in-chief, the Duke of Atholl.

Late May: Scottish Hebridean Islands Peak Race. The biggest combined sailing and fell-running competition in the world.

June–August: Riding of the Marches in the border towns of Hawick, Selkirk, Annan, Dumfries, Duns, Peebles, Jedburgh, Langholm and Lauder. The Rides originated to check the boundaries of common land owned by the town and also to commemorate warfare between the Scots and the English. Nowadays individual Ridings have their own special ceremonies, though they all start with a parade of pipes and brass bands.

June: Shinty Camanachd Cup Final, usually in Inverness. Finals of the intensely competitive games between the northern towns who play Scotland's own stick-and-ball game.

June: Royal Highland Agricultural Show, Ingliston, near Edinburgh. Scotland's biggest and best.

June: Highland Games at Campbeltown, Aberdeen and Grantown-on-Spey.

July: Scottish Open Golf Championship, held at a different venue each year.

July: Glasgow International Folk Festival.

July: Highland Games at Caithness, Elgin, Glengarry, North Uist, Inverness, Inveraray, Mull, Lewis, Durness, Lochaber, Dufftown, Halkirk.

August: Edinburgh International Festival and Fringe. One of the world's great arts jamborees, detailed in full on p.96.

August: Edinburgh Military Tattoo held on the Castle esplanade. Massed pipe bands and drums by floodlight.

August: World Pipe Band Championship at Glasgow.

August: International Horse Trials at Blair Atholl.

August: Horse festival on South Ronaldsay in Orkney. Small children dress as horses and drag decorative wooden ploughs along the beach in a competition to turn the straightest furrows.

August: Northern Meeting Piping Championships at Inverness.

August: Highland Games at Dunoon (Cowal), Mallaig, Skye, Dornoch, Aboyne, Strathpeffer, Assynt, Bute, Glenfinnan, Argyllshire, Glenurquhart and Invergordon.

September: Highland Games at Braemar.

September: Ben Nevis Race for amateurs to the top of the highest mountain in Scotland and back again.

October: The National Mod. Competitive festival of all aspects of Gaelic performing arts, held in varying venues.

October: Glenfiddich Piping Championships at Blair Atholl for the world's top ten solo pipers.

November: St Andrew's Day celebrations at St Andrews.

petitions, where you'll see girls as young as three years old tripping the quick, intricate steps of such traditional dances as the Highland Fling.

FOOTBALL

Soccer, or **football** as it's more commonly known in Britain, is far and away Scotland's most popular spectator sport, and one of the few areas of Scottish life that has remained truly independent from the English. A potent source of pride for Scots everywhere, the national team has consistently managed to hold its own in international competitions, qualifying for five World Cups in a row between 1974 and 1990, and putting in sterling performances at the last two European Championships.

Behind Scotland's soccer success is a thriving league, established in 1874, and dominated from the start by the two Glasgow teams, **Rangers** (aka the "Old Firm") and **Celtic** – the former representing the city's Protestant community, and the latter its Catholics. The sectarian, and occasionally violent, rivalry between these two is one of the least attractive aspects of the Scottish game, but Rangers' and Celtic's stranglehold over the Premier Division has arguably been just as damaging. Although the 1980s saw Dundee United and Aberdeen break the deadlock between the two teams, the old pattern has reasserted itself during the 1990s, with Rangers winning every league title since 1989, and Celtic being the only other side to come anywhere close. During the past few seasons, calls have been mounting for both clubs to join the English Premiership, which would give them the kind of tough opposition they need to achieve greater success at international level. However, the loss of the two flagship clubs would lead to the Scottish league no longer remaining a credible European contender, and serve an undeserved deathblow to the nation's rich footballing tradition.

With a couple of exceptions (notably Jock Stein's legendary Celtic sides of the 1970s), Scottish soccer has traditionally been renowned less for its great teams than for its outstanding individuals – **players** such as Denis Law of Manchester United, Kenny Dalglish of Celtic and Liverpool, Billy Bremner at Leeds and Graeme Souness in the famous Liverpool side of the early 1980s, as well as **managers** of near-mythical status like Jock Stein, Sir Matt Busby, Bill Shankly and, of course, Alex Ferguson, present manager of Manchester United. These days, **Paul Gascoigne**, of Glasgow Rangers, is the biggest star playing in Scotland, but with increasing numbers of talented local players remaining at home rather than drifting south across the border (a consequence of the relative ease with which English sides can now recruit players from the Continent), the grassroots standard of Scottish football is on the rise, and soccer enthusiasts should definitely take in a game or two while they're here.

The **season** begins in early August and ends in mid-May, with weekend fixtures kicking off at 3pm; you can also watch live matches on television on Monday and Friday evenings, and on Saturday afternoons. Match **tickets** are a little less expensive in Scotland than England, ranging from £10 to £20 for big games; the major clubs operate telephone credit-card booking services (see the relevant listings section for details). For a quick overview of the Scottish soccer scene, check out the *Daily Mail's* Soccernet **Web site**, at *www.soccernet.com/ scottish/index.html*, which features the homepages of each Premier Division club, with news and match-report archives.

SHINTY

Played throughout Scotland but with particular strongholds in the West Highlands and Speyside, the game of **shinty** arrived in the country from Ireland around 1500 years ago. Until the latter part of the nineteenth century, it was played on an informal basis and teams from neighbouring villages had to come to an agreement about rules before matches could begin. However, in 1893, the sport's governing body, the **Camanachd Association** – from the Gaelic for "shinty", *camanachd* – was set up to formalize the rules. The first **Camanachd Cup Final** was held in Inverness in 1896, with Glasgow Cowal going down 2:0 to Kingussie.

Today, shinty is still fairly close to its Irish roots in the game of hurling, with each team having twelve players including a goalkeeper, and each goal counting for a point. The game, sometimes described as "hockey with injuries", isn't for the faint-hearted; it's played at a furious pace, with sticks – called *camans* or *cammocks* – flying alarmingly in all directions. Support is enthusiastic and vocal, and if you're in the Highlands during the season – roughly parallel with the soccer season – it's well worth trying to catch a match: check with tourist offices or the local paper to see if there are any local fixtures.

SPORTS AND OUTDOOR PURSUITS

Like their English neighbours, the Scots are sports mad, especially when it comes to football, which is played with near religious zeal in the main towns and cities. The majority of visitors, however, spend little time in urban centres, preferring instead the open spaces of rural Scotland – a landscape that's perfect for outdoor pursuits. Within striking distance of Glasgow and Edinburgh, vast stretches of glens and moorland offer walking for even the toughest hiker, spectacular mountains on which some of the world's great mountaineers have cut their teeth, and which (in winter) provide great skiing. For more sedate walkers, numerous marked trails range from hour-long ambles to coast-to-coast treks. The shoreline, lochs and rivers give opportunities for fishing as well as sailing and numerous watersports, including surfing, and there are plenty of fine beaches for less structured fresh-air activities or just slobbing around. Scotland, of course, is also the "home of golf": it's relatively cheap here and there are proportionally more courses than anywhere else in the world.

WALKING AND CLIMBING

The whole of Scotland offers superb opportunities for hill **walking**, from the smooth, grassy hills and moors of the **Southern Uplands** to the wild and rugged country of the northwest. Scotland has several **Long Distance Footpaths** (LDPs) which will take days to walk, though you can, of course, just do a section of them. The major ones are the **Southern Upland Way**, which crosses the country from coast to coast in the south, and, at 212 miles, is the longest. The best known, however, is the **West Highland Way**, a 95-mile hike from Glasgow to Fort William via Loch Lomond and Glen Coe. The gentler **Speyside Way**, in Aberdeenshire, is a mere thirty miles. The green signposts of the Scottish Rights of Way Society point to these and many other cross-country routes; while in the wilder parts the accepted freedom to roam allows extensive mountain walking, rock climbing, orienteering and allied activities.

Scotland's main climbing areas are in the **Highlands**, which boast many challenging peaks as well as great hill walks. There are 279 mountains over 3000ft (914m) in Scotland, known as **Munros** after the man who first classified them: many walkers "collect" them, and it's possible to chalk up several in a day. Serious climbers will probably head for **Glen Coe** or **Torridon**, which offer difficult routes in spectacular surroundings. These and some of the other finest Highland areas (Lawers, Kintail, West Affric) are in the ownership of the National Trust for Scotland, while Blaven and Ladhar Bheinn (Knoydart) are John Muir Trust properties; both allow year-round access. Elsewhere there may be restricted access during lambing (dogs are particularly unwelcome in April and May) and deerstalking seasons (mid-August to the third week in October). The booklet *Heading for the Scottish Hills* (published by the Scottish Mountaineering Club or SMC) provides such information on all areas.

Numerous short walks (from accessible towns and villages) and several major walks are covered in the Guide. However, you should only use these notes as general outlines and always in conjunction with a good map. Where possible we have given details of the best maps to use – in most cases one of the Ordnance Survey (OS) series (see p.24). You should never attempt walks beyond your abilities and always follow the guidelines below. Other useful sources for information on walks are listed in the box on p.44. If you decide to follow one of the walks and haven't got a map with you, head for the nearest tourist office who will usually supply OS and other local maps, safety advice and guidebooks/leaflets, as will shops in most areas. Among the many **guidebooks** available for serious walking and climbing, the SMC's series of *District Guides* offer blow-by-blow accounts of climbs written by professional mountaineers – for other good walking guides see the "Books" section of Contexts (p.585).

SAFETY IN THE SCOTTISH HILLS

Scottish mountains are not high, but, due to rapid weather changes, they are potentially extremely dangerous and should be treated with respect. Every year, in every season, climbers and hill walkers die on Scottish mountains. If the weather looks as if it's closing in, *get down fast.*

It is essential that you are properly equipped – even for what appears to be an easy expedition in apparently settled weather – with proper warm, fluorescent and waterproof layered clothing, supportive footwear and adequate maps, a compass (which you should know how to use) and food. Always leave word of your route and what time you expect to return; and remember to contact the person again to let them know that you are back.

HORSE RIDING

Pony trekking as an organized leisure activity originated in Scotland, when the late Lieutenant Commander Jock Kerr Hunter set up the first rid-

---

USEFUL ADDRESSES FOR WALKERS

Cordee (Book Distributors), 3a de Montfort St, Leicester LE1 7HD (☎0116/254 3579). Produces extensive book lists and distributes all SMC publications.

John Muir Trust, Freepost, Musselburgh, Midlothian EH21 7BR (☎0131/665 0596). An organization that purchases land for conservation and public access and can give details of public rights of way.

Mountaineering Council of Scotland, 4a St Catherine's Rd, Perth, Perthshire PH1 5SE (☎01738/638227). The representative body for all mountain activities publishes details of estate

boundaries and contact phone numbers to help climbers and walkers check on estate activities before setting out.

National Trust for Scotland, 5 Charlotte Square, Edinburgh EH2 4DU (☎0131/226 5922).

Ramblers Association Scotland, 23 Crusader House, Haig Business Park, Markinch, Fife KY7 6AQ (☎01592/611177).

Scottish Rights of Way Society, John Cotton Business Centre, 10–12 Sunnyside, Edinburgh EH7 5RA (☎0131/652 2937) .

Scottish Youth Hostel Association, 7 Glebe Crescent, Stirling FK8 2JA (☎01786/451181).

WALKING HOLIDAY COMPANIES

Assynt Guided Holidays, Birchbank, Knockan,Elphin, Sutherland (☎01854/666215). Mountain walks, or glen and loch-side ambles, and fishing trips, with one of Scotland's most knowledgeable guides.

C-N-Do Scotland WS, Unit 77, Stirling Enterprise Park, Stirling FK7 7RP (☎01786/445703). Munro bagging for novices and experts, in small groups and with qualified leaders.

The Glencoe Specialists, 19b Carnoch, Glencoe, Argyll PA39 4HS (☎01855/811472; *www.ourworld.compuserve.com/ homepages/Hadrian-Mountaineering*). Year-round programme of gentle walks and scrambles on Skye, and around Glen Coe/Ben Nevis.

Highland Activity Holidays, 99 Norheim, Dufftown, Glenfiddich AB55 4AR

(☎01340/820892). Gentle guided walking holidays based in a guest house or two-star hotel.

North-West Frontiers, Ullapool, Ross-shire IV26 2SZ (☎01854/612628; *www.ourworld. compuserve.com/homepages/NWF*). Guided mountain trips with small groups in the north-west Highlands, starting in Inverness; May to October only.

Ossian Guides, Sanna, Newtonmore, Inverness-shire PH20 1DG (☎01540/673402). Walking, scrambling and photo-treks with qualified leaders throughout the Highlands.

Rua Reidh Lighthouse, Melvaig, Gairloch, Wester Ross (☎01445/771263). Accompanied and self-guided wilderness walks on the west coast; from three-night to one-week itineraries. Family multi-activity holidays also available.

ing school here fifty or so years ago, to encourage people to explore the country via its old drove roads. Since then, equestrian centres have mushroomed, and miles of the most beautiful lochsides, heather-clad moorland and long sandy beaches are now accessible on horseback, to novices as well as experienced riders.

The Scottish Tourist Board produces a glossy brochure listing around sixty **riding centres** across the country, all of them approved by either the Trekking and Riding Society of Scotland (TRSS) or the British Horse Society (BHS). Membership of these schemes ensures the centre is inspected each year, that the horses are well looked after, and that the staff are properly qualified. As a rule, any centre will offer the option of **pony trekking** (leisurely ambles on sure-footed Highland Ponies), **hacking** (for experienced riders who want to go for a short ride at a fastish pace), and **trail riding** (over longer distances, for riders who feel secure at a canter). In addition, a network of special **horse and rider B&Bs** in Scotland means you can ride independently on your own horse.

A four-day route was recently inaugurated in the Borders region, using private tracks, open country and quiet bridleways. For more information about the **Beccleuch Country Ride**, and the B&B network mentioned above, contact the Scottish Borders Tourist Board (☎01835/863435), or the BRS/TRSS, Boreland, Fearnan, Aberfeldy, Perthshire PH15 2PG (☎01877/830274).

CYCLING AND MOUNTAIN BIKING

Despite the recent boom in the sale of mountain bikes, **cyclists** are still treated with notorious neglect by many motorists and by the people who plan the country's traffic systems. Very few of Scotland's towns have proper cycle routes, but if you're hellbent on tackling the congestion, pollution and aggression of city traffic, get a **helmet** and a secure **lock** – cycle theft in Scotland is an organized and highly effective racket. The rural backroads are infinitely more enjoyable, particularly in the gentle landscape of the south of the country, whose generally amiable gradients and a decent density of pubs and B&Bs make it a perfect area for cycle touring. Your main problem out in the countryside will be finding spare parts – anything more complex than inner tubes or tyres can be very hard to come by.

Cycling is popular in the Highland walking areas, but cyclists should always keep to tracks

where a right to cycle exists, and to pass walkers at considerate speeds. Footpaths, unless otherwise marked, are for pedestrian use only. The Forestry Commission has recently established 1150 miles of excellent off-road routes all over the country, which are detailed in numerous *Cycling in the Forest* leaflets (available from Forest Enterprise offices listed below and from most tourist offices). Waymarked and graded, these are best attempted on **mountain bikes** with multi-gears, although many of the gentler routes may be tackled on hybrid and standard road cycles.

Transporting your bike by train is a good way of getting to the interesting parts of Scotland without a lot of hard pedalling. Bikes are not allowed on InterCity express trains, but on most other intertown routes are carried at £3.50 per journey; always check the route you wish to travel accepts bikes, and reserve as far in advance as possible. Bus and coach companies, including National Express and Scottish Citylink rarely accept cycles unless they are dismantled and boxed. One notable exception is the Bike Bus Company (☎0131/229 6274), which operates a minibus and trailer service out of Edinburgh for cyclists.

Bike rental is available at shops in most large towns and many tourist centres, although the specimens on offer are often pretty heavy and basic – all right for a brief spin, but not for any serious touring. Expect to pay in the region of £10–20 per day; most rental outlets also give good discounts for multi-day hire.

Another option is to shell out on a **cycling holiday package**. These can take all forms, but generally include transport of your luggage to each stop, prebooked accommodation, detailed route instructions, a packed lunch and backup support. Most holiday companies offer some budget packages, with hostel instead of hotel or B&B accommodation, and the cost-cutting option of using your own bike. For a list of recommended cycling holiday specialists, see the box on p.46.

Britain's biggest **cycling organization**, the Cycle Touring Club or CTC (see box on p.46), provides lists of tour operators and rental outlets in Scotland, and supplies members with touring and technical advice, as well as insurance. As a general introduction, the Scottish Tourist Board's *Cycling in Scotland* brochure is worth sending off for, with practical advice and suggestions for itineraries around the country. Recommended as a

USEFUL ADDRESSES FOR CYCLISTS

The Scottish Cyclists' Union, The Velodrome, Meadowbank Stadium, London Road, Edinburgh EH7 6AY (☎0131/652 0187). This organization produces an annual handbook and calendar of cycling events – mainly road, mountain-bike and track races.

Cyclists' Touring Club, 69 Meadrow, Godalming, Surrey GU7 3HS (☎01483/417217).

Britain's largest cycling organization, and a good source of general advice; they also have lists of cyclist-friendly B&Bs and cafés in Scotland.

Forest Enterprise, 21 Church St, Inverness, Invernesshire IV1 1EL (☎01463/232811). The best source of information of Scotlands extensive network of forest trails – ideal for mountain biking at all levels of ability.

CYCLING HOLIDAY OPERATORS

Bespoke Highland Tours, The Bothy, Camusdarach, Arisaig, Inverness-shire PH39 4NT (☎01687/450272).

Roundabout Scottish Cycling Holidays, 4 Observatory Lane, Glasgow G12 9AH (☎0141/337 3877).

Scottish Border Trails, Venlaw High Road, Peebles EH45 8RL (☎01721/722934).

Scottish Youth Hostel Association: Breakaway Holidays, 7 Glebe Crescent, Stirling FK8 2JA (☎01786/891400).

more detailed guide is *Cycling in Scotland & North East England* by Philip Routledge (available from Sigma Leisure, 1 South Oak Lane, Wilmslow, Cheshire SK9 6AR; £7.95 plus £2 p&p), which crams dozens of maps, routes and general information into 220 pages.

GOLF

There are over 400 **golf courses** in Scotland, where the game is less elitist, cheaper and more accessible than anywhere else in the world. Golf in its present form took shape in the sixteenth century on the dunes of Scotland's east coast, and today you'll find some of the oldest courses in the world on these early coastal sites, known as "links". If you want a round of golf, it's often possible just to turn up and play, though it's sensible to phone ahead and book, and essential for the championship courses (see below).

Public courses are owned by the local council, while **private** courses belong to a club. You can play on both – occasionally the private courses require that you be a member of another club, and the odd one asks for introductions from a member, but these rules are often waived for overseas visitors and all you need to do is pay a one-off fee. The cost of one round will set you back between around £5 for small, nine-hole courses, up to more than £20 for eighteen holes. Simply pay as you enter and play. In remote areas the courses are sometimes unmanned – just put the admission fee into the honour box. Most courses have **resi-**

dent professionals who give lessons, and some rent equipment at reasonable rates. Renting a caddy car will add an extra few pounds depending on the swankiness of the course.

Scotland's **championship** courses, which often host the British Open tournament, are renowned for their immaculately kept greens and challenging holes and, though they're favoured by serious players, anybody with a valid handicap certificate can enjoy them. **St Andrews** (☎01334/475757) is *the* destination for golfers: it's the home of the Royal and Ancient Golf Club, the worldwide controlling body that regulates the rules of the game. Of its five courses, the best known is the Old Course, a particularly intriguing ground with eleven enormous greens and the world-famous "Road Hole". If you want to play, there's no introduction needed, but you'll need to book months in advance and have a handicap certificate – handicap limits are 24 for men and 36 for women. You could also enter your name for the daily right-to-play lottery – contact the club before 2pm on the day you'd like to play. One of the easiest championship courses to get into is Carnoustie, in Angus (☎01241/853249), though you should still try to book as far ahead as possible. No handicap certificate is required for play here before 1.30pm on Saturday and 11am on Sunday. Other championship courses include Gleneagles in Perthshire (☎01764/663543), Royal Dornoch in Sutherland (☎01862/810219), and Turnberry in Ayrshire (☎01655/331000). A round of golf at any of these will set you back at least £20, double that if you rent a human caddie – and you'll be expected to tip over and above that. Near Edinburgh, Muirfield, considered by professional players to be one of the most testing grounds in the world, is also one of the most elitist – women can only play if accompanied by a man and aren't allowed into the clubhouse.

Worth shelling out for if you're coming to Scotland primarily to play golf, is the Great Scottish Golf Tour ticket, which entitles you to up to two rounds at a choice of fourteen courses, including Carnoustie and Montrose, over three or five days (£60/£95). The tickets are available from the *Alyth Hotel*, Aalyth, Perthshire PH11 8AF (☎01828/632447).

FISHING

Scotland's serrated coastline – with the deep sea lochs of the west, the Firths of the east and the myriad offshore islands– encompasses the full gamut of marine habitats, and ranks among the cleanest coasts in Europe. Combine this with an abundance of salmon, sea trout, brown trout and pike, acres of open space, and easy access, and you have an angler's paradise par excellence. Whether you're into game, coarse- or sea- fishing, you'll be spoilt for choice. The only element in short supply is company; Scotland may offer wonderful **fishing**, but its unpolluted, open waters don't attract anywhere near the numbers of anglers you'd expect.

Nor will you get bogged down in fishing beaurocracy. No licence is needed to fish in Scotland, although nearly all land is privately owned and its fishing therefore controlled by a landlord/lady or his/her agent. Permission, however, is usually easy to obtain: **permits** can be bought without hassle at local tackle shops, or through fishing clubs in the area – if in doubt, ask at the nearest tourist office. The other thing to bear in mind is that salmon and sea trout have strict **seasons**, which vary between districts but usually stretch from late August until late February. Once again, individual tourist offices will know the precise dates, or you can check in the Scottish Tourist Board's excellent *Fish Scotland* brochure (free from any tourist office or by post; see p.22). It provides a rough introduction to game-, coarse- and sea-angling, with tips on how to find the famous sea marks and salmon beats, and a rundown of less-well-known fishing spots. Other sources of useful information are the Scottish Federation of

Sea Anglers, Brian Burn, Flat 2, 16 Bellevue Rd, Ayr KA7 2SA (☎01292/264735), and the Scottish Anglers National Association, c/o David Wilkie, Administration Office, Caledonia House, South Gyle, Edinburgh EH12 9DQ (☎0131/339 8808).

BEACHES

Scotland is ringed by fine **beaches** and bays, most of them clean and many of them deserted even in high summer – perhaps hardly surprising, given the bracing winds and icy water. Few people come to Scotland for a beach holiday, but it's worth sampling one or two, even if you never shed as much as a sweater. A rash of slightly melancholy seaside towns lies within easy reach of Glasgow, while on the east coast the relatively low cliffs and miles of sandy beaches are ideal for walking. Bizarrely enough, given the low temperature of the water, the beaches in the northeast are beginning to figure on surfers' itineraries, attracting enthusiasts from all over Europe (see below). Perhaps the most beautiful beaches of all are to be found on Scotland's islands: endless, isolated stretches that on a sunny day can be the epitome of the Scottish Hebridean dream.

In order to comply with EU directives on bathing-water quality, Scotland's 23 dirtiest beaches have been monitored over the past decade for pollution, and measures implemented to ensure they clean up their act. Great strides have been made over the past few years, and currently only two of the bathing beaches identified – **Girvan** and **Tunberry** – remain on the blacklist.

SURFING

Unlikely though it may seem, Scotland is fast gaining a reputation as a **surfing** destination, with a good selection of excellent quality breaks. It may not have the sunshine of Hawaii, and the water is steely-grey rather than turquoise-blue, but there are world-class waves to be found. **Thurso** is the number-one spot on the **north coast**, and boasts one of the finest reef breaks in Europe. In addition, the rest of this coastline – Sango Bay, Torrisdale, Farr Bay and Armadale, in particular – offers waves comparable to those in Hawaii, Australia and Indonesia. However, Scotland's northern coastline lies on the same latitude as Alaska and Iceland, so the water temperature is very low: even in midsummer it rarely exceeds 15°C, and in winter can drop to as low as to 7°C. The one vital accessory, therefore, is a good wet suit (ideally a

TOP TEN SCOTTISH BREAKS

*1. **Thurso East**, just below the castle; see p.479. One of the best right-hand reef breaks in Europe.

*2. **Brimm's Ness**, five miles west of Thurso; see p.479. A selection of reef breaks that pick up the smallest of swells.

3. **Pease Bay**, near Dunbar, 26 miles east of Edinburgh; see p.120. A popular break suited to all abilities; can get very crowded.

4. **Fraserburgh**, 39 miles north of Aberdeen; see p.413. A number of beach and reef breaks – beginners should stick to the beach.

*5 **Skirza Harbour**, three miles south of John O'Groats; see p.480. An excellent left-hand reef break on the far northeast tip of Scotland.

6. **Sandside Bay**, on the north coast, ten miles west of Thurso; see p.479. Reef and beach breaks,

but dubious water quality due to the proximity of the Dounreay nuclear power station.

*7. **Torrisdale Bay**, Bettyhill, on the north coast of the Highlands; see p.478. An excellent right-hand river-mouth break.

8. **Sandwood Bay**, a day's hike south of Cape Wrath in Sutherland; see p.476. Beach breaks on one of the most scenic and remote shorelines in Britain, only accessible on foot.

9. **Machrihanish Bay**, Mull of Kintyre; see p.312. Four miles of beach breaks on one of Scotland's loneliest peninsulas.

*10. **Valtos**, on the Uig peninsula, Lewis; see p.351. A break on one of the Outer Hebrides' most exquisite shell-sand beaches.

*Experienced surfers only.

5/3mm steamer) wet-suit boots and, outside of summer, gloves and a hood, too.

In addition to Thurso, there are several other excellent breaks, many of which lie within easy reach of large cities, such as **Pease Bay**, near Edinburgh, and **Fraserburgh**, near Aberdeen. The beaches of the **Moray Firth** also offer a good North Sea swell. Of the islands, the west coasts of **Coll**, **Tiree** and **Islay** get great swell from the Atlantic and have good beaches, while the spectacular west coast offers numerous possibilities, in particular one of Britain's most isolated beaches, **Sandwood Bay**. In the Outer Hebrides, the best breaks are to be found along the northern coastline of **Lewis**, near Carloway and Bragar.

Many of these beaches are surrounded by stunning scenery, and you'd be unlucky to encounter another surfer for miles. However, this isolation – combined with the cold water and big, powerful waves – means that, in general, much of

Scottish surf is best left to **experienced surfers** (see box above). If you're a beginner, get local advice before you go in, and be aware of your limitations; remember, if you get caught in a current off the west coast the next stop might be Iceland.

The popularity of surfing in Scotland has led to a spate of **surf shops** opening up: Clan, 45 Hyndland St, Partick, Glasgow (☎0141/339 6523); Granite Reef, 45 Justice St, Aberdeen (☎01224/621193); ESP, 6 Greyfriars St, Elgin (☎01343/550129); and Mach, 1146 Argyle St, Glasgow (☎0141/334 5559), can all rent or sell equipment, and provide good information about the local breaks and events on the surfing scene. Two further sources of information are *Surf UK* by Wayne "Alf" Alderson (Fernhurst Books; £13.95), with details on over four hundred breaks around Britain, and the bimonthly *Surf* magazine (£3.00), which is good for grassroots info on the Scottish surfing scene.

TRAVELLERS WITH DISABILITIES

Scotland has numerous specialist tour operators catering for physically handicapped travellers, and the number of non-specialist operators who welcome clients with disabilities is increasing. For more information on these operators, you should get in touch with Disability Scotland, Princes House, 5 Shandwick Place, Edinburgh EH2 4RG (☎0131/229 8632). It has a comprehensive computer database covering all aspects of disabled holidays in Scotland, publishes a full directory, and is happy to deal with queries; also see the box below for other useful organizations in Britain.

Should you go it alone, you'll find that Scottish attitudes towards travellers with disabilities are often begrudging, and years behind advances towards independence made in North America and Australia. Access to theatres, cinemas and other public places has improved recently, but **public transport** companies rarely make any effort to help disabled people, though some ScotRail

---

ADDRESSES FOR TRAVELLERS WITH DISABILITIES

BRITAIN
Access Travel, 16 Haweswater Ave, Astley, Lancashire M29 7BL (☎01942/888844, fax 891811). Tour operator that can arrange flights, transfer and accommodation. This is a small business, personally checking out places before recommendation.

Holiday Care Service, 2nd Floor, Imperial Building, Victoria Rd, Horley, Surrey RH6 7PZ (☎01293/774535, fax 784647; Minicom ☎01293/776943). Provides free lists of accessible accommodation abroad – European, American and long-haul destinations – plus a list of accessible attractions in the UK. Information on financial help for holidays available.

Mobility International, 228 Borough High St, London SE1 1JX (☎0171/403 5688). Puts out a quarterly newsletter that keeps up-to-date with developments in disabled travel.

RADAR (Royal Association for Disability and Rehabilitation), 12 City Forum, 250 City Rd, London EC1V 8AF (☎0171/250 3222; Minicom ☎0171/250 4119). A good source of advice on holidays and travel. They produce an annual holiday guide for the UK (£7, includes p&p), which includes some information on Scotland.

Tripscope, The Courtyard, Evelyn Road, London W4 5JL (☎0181/994 9294, fax 994 3618). This registered charity provides a national telephone information service offering free advice on UK and international transport and travel for those with a mobility problem.

NORTH AMERICA
Directions Unlimited, 720 N Bedford Rd, Bedford Hills, NY 10507 (☎1-800/533-5343). Tour operator specializing in custom tours for people with disabilities.

Jewish Rehabilitation Hospital, Laval, Canada (☎514/688-9550; *axis@musica.mcgill.ca*). Friendly service providing general advice about travelling abroad with disabilities. Will reply to email queries.

Mobility International USA, PO Box 10767, Eugene, OR 97440 (voice and TDD: ☎503/343-1284). Information and referral services, access guides, tours and exchange programmes. Annual membership $25 (includes quarterly newsletter).

Society for the Advancement of Travel for the Handicapped (SATH), 347 5th Ave, Suite 610, New York, NY 10016 (☎212/447-7284). Non-profit travel-industry referral service that passes queries onto its members as appropriate, allow plenty of time for a response.

Travel Information Service, Moss Rehabilitation Hospital, 1200 W Tabor Rd, Philadelphia, PA 19141 (☎215/456-9600; TTY for the hearing impaired: ☎215/456-9602). Telephone information and referral service.

Twin Peaks Press, Box 129, Vancouver, WA 98666 (☎360/694-2462 or 1-800/637-2256). Publisher of the *Directory of Travel Agencies for the Disabled* ($19.95), listing more than 370 agencies worldwide; *Travel for the Disabled* ($19.95); the *Directory of Accessible Van Rentals* ($9.95); and *Wheelchair Vagabond* ($14.95), loaded with personal tips.

AUSTRALIA AND NEW ZEALAND
ACROD, PO Box 60, Curtin, ACT 2605 (☎06/6282 4333). Compiles lists of organizations, accommodation, travel agencies and tour operators.

Disabled Persons Assembly, PO Box 10, 138 The Terrace, Wellington (☎04/472 2626).

InterCity services now accommodate wheelchair users in comfort. Wheelchair users and blind or partially sighted people are automatically given 30–50 percent reductions on train fares, and people with other disabilities are eligible for the **Disabled Persons Railcard** (£15 per year), which gives a third off most tickets. There are no bus discounts for the disabled, and of the major **car-rental** firms only Hertz offers models with hand controls at the same rate as conventional vehicles, and even these are only available in the more expensive categories. **Accommodation** is the same story, with modified suites for people

with disabilities available only at higher-priced establishments and perhaps the odd B&B.

Useful **publications** include RADAR's annually updated *Holidays in the British Isles: A Guide for Disabled People*. Two other publications to look out for are *The World Wheelchair Traveller* by Susan Abbott and Mary Ann Tyrrell (AA Publications), which includes basic hints and advice, and our own *Nothing Ventured/Able to Travel: Disabled People Travel the World* by Alison Walsh (Rough Guides), which has practical advice and inspiring accounts of disabled travel worldwide.

DIRECTORY

Electricity In Britain the current is 240V AC. North American appliances need a transformer and adapter; Australasian appliances need only an adapter.

Gaelic In some areas of Scotland, particularly in the Highlands and islands, road signs are bilingual English/Gaelic. In the Guide, the Gaelic translation is given – in italics and parentheses – the first time any village or island is mentioned, after which the English name is used. The main exception to this rule is in the Western Isles, where signposting is exclusively in Gaelic – we've reflected this in the main text by giving the Gaelic first and putting the English in parentheses. Thereafter we've used the Gaelic, except for the islands and ferry ports which are more familiar in the English, as they appear on CalMac timetables.

Laundry Coin-operated laundries are found in nearly all Scottish cities and some towns, and are open about twelve hours a day from Monday to Friday, less on weekends. A wash followed by a spin or tumble dry costs about £2.30; a "service wash" (your laundry done for you in a few hours) costs about £1 extra.

Public toilets Found at all train and bus stations and signposted on town high streets: a fee of 10p or 20p is usually charged.

Smoking Although many Scots still smoke, the last decade has seen a dramatic change in attitudes towards smoking and a significant reduction in the consumption of cigarettes. Smoking is now outlawed from just about all public buildings and on public transport, and many restaurants and hotels have become totally non-smoking. Smokers are advised, when booking a table or a room, to check their vice is tolerated there.

Time Greenwich Mean Time (GMT) is in force from late October to late March, after which the clocks go forward an hour for British Summer Time (BST). GMT is five hours ahead of the US Eastern Standard Time and ten hours behind Australian Eastern Standard Time.

Videos Visitors from North America planning to use their video cameras in Britain should note that Betamax video cassettes are less easy to obtain in Scotland, where VHS is the commonly used format, so bring a supply with you.

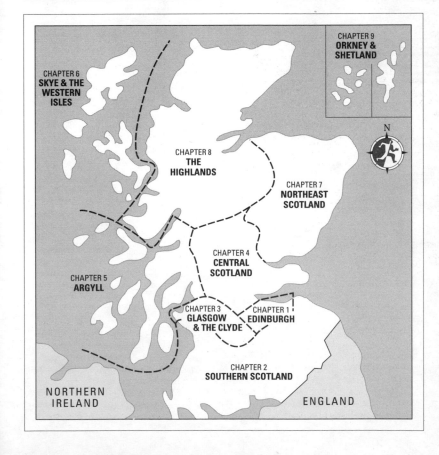

CHAPTER 9
**ORKNEY &
SHETLAND**

CHAPTER 6
**SKYE & THE
WESTERN
ISLES**

CHAPTER 8
**THE
HIGHLANDS**

CHAPTER 7
**NORTHEAST
SCOTLAND**

N

CHAPTER 4
**CENTRAL
SCOTLAND**

CHAPTER 5
ARGYLL

CHAPTER 3
**GLASGOW
& THE CLYDE**

CHAPTER 1
EDINBURGH

CHAPTER 2
SOUTHERN SCOTLAND

NORTHERN
IRELAND

ENGLAND

CHAPTER ONE

EDINBURGH

Well-heeled **EDINBURGH**, the showcase capital of Scotland, is a cosmopolitan and cultured city. Its setting is undeniably striking; perched on a series of extinct volcanoes and rocky crags which intrude on the generally flat landscape of the Lothians, with the sheltered shoreline of the Firth of Forth to the north. "My own Romantic town", Sir Walter Scott called it, although it was another native author, Robert Louis Stevenson, who perhaps best captured the feel of his "precipitous city", declaring that "No situation could be more commanding for the head of a kingdom; none better chosen for noble prospects."

The centre has two distinct parts. North of the **Castle Rock**, the dignified, Grecian-style **New Town** was immaculately laid out during the Age of Reason, after the announcement of a plan to improve conditions in the city. The **Old Town**, on the other hand, with its tortuous alleys and tightly packed closes, is unrelentingly medieval, associated in popular imagination with its underworld lore of the schizophrenic Deacon Brodie, inspiration for Stevenson's *Dr Jekyll and Mr Hyde*, and the body snatchers Burke and Hare. Edinburgh earned its nickname of "Auld Reekie" for the smog and smell generated by the Old Town, which for centuries swam in sewage tipped out of the windows of cramped tenements.

Set on the crag which sweeps down from the towering fairytale **Castle** to the royal **Palace of Holyroodhouse**, the Old Town preserves all the key reminders of its role as a capital, while, in contrast, a tantalizing glimpse of the wild beauty of Scotland's scenery can be had immediately beyond the palace in **Holyrood Park**, an extensive area of open countryside dominated by **Arthur's Seat**, the largest and most impressive of the volcanoes.

In August and early September, around a million visitors flock to the city for the **Edinburgh International Festival**, in fact a series of separate festivals that make up the largest arts extravaganza in the world. Among the city's many museums, the **National Gallery of Scotland** boasts as choice an array of Old Masters as can be found anywhere; its offshoot, the **Scottish National Gallery of Modern Art**, has Britain's oldest specialist collection of twentieth-century painting and sculpture.

On a less elevated theme, the city's distinctive howffs (pubs), allied to its brewing and distilling traditions, make it a great **drinking** city. The presence of three **universities**, plus several colleges, means that there is a youthful presence for most of the year – a welcome corrective to the stuffiness which is often regarded as Edinburgh's Achilles heel.

Some history

It was during the **Dark Ages** that the name of Edinburgh – at least in its early forms of Dunedin or Din Eidyn ("fort of Eidyn") – first appeared. Castle Rock, a strategic fort atop one of the volcanoes, served as the nation's **southernmost border post** until 1018, when King Malcolm I established the River Tweed as the permanent frontier. In the reign of Malcolm Canmore the castle became one of the main seats of the court, and the town, which was given privileged status as a **royal burgh**, began to grow. In 1128 King David established Holyrood Abbey at the foot of the slope, later allowing its monks to found a separate burgh, known as **Canongate**.

Robert the Bruce granted Edinburgh a **new charter** in 1329, giving it jurisdiction over the nearby port of **Leith**, and during the following century the prosperity brought by foreign trade enabled the newly fortified city to establish itself as the permanent **capital of Scotland**. Under King James IV, the city enjoyed a short but brilliant **Renaissance era**, which saw not only the construction of a new palace alongside Holyrood Abbey, but also the granting of a royal charter to the College of Surgeons, the earliest in the city's long line of academic and professional bodies.

This period came to an abrupt end in 1513 with the calamitous defeat by the English at the Battle of Flodden, which led to several decades of political instability. In the 1540s, King Henry VIII's attempt to force a royal union with Scotland led to the sack of Edinburgh, prompting the Scots to turn to France: French troops arrived to defend the city, while the young queen Mary was dispatched to Paris as the promised bride of the

Dauphin. While the French occupiers succeeded in removing the English threat, they themselves antagonized the locals, who had become increasingly sympathetic to the ideals of the **Reformation**. When the radical preacher John Knox returned from exile in 1555, he quickly won over the city to his Calvinist message.

James VI's rule saw the foundation of the University of Edinburgh in 1582, but following the **Union of the Crowns** in 1603 the city was totally upstaged by London: although James promised to visit every three years, it was not until 1617 that he made his only return trip. In 1633 Charles I visited Edinburgh for his coronation, but soon afterwards precipitated a crisis by introducing episcopacy to the Church of Scotland, in the process making Edinburgh a bishopric for the first time. Fifty years of religious turmoil followed, culminating in the triumph of **presbyterianism**. Despite these vicissitudes, Edinburgh expanded throughout the seventeenth century and, constrained by its walls, was forced to build both upwards and inwards.

The **Union of the Parliaments** of 1707 dealt a further blow to Edinburgh's political prestige, though the guaranteed preservation of the national church and the legal and educational systems ensured that it was never relegated to a purely provincial role. On the contrary, it was in the second half of the eighteenth century that Edinburgh achieved the height of its intellectual influence, led by an outstanding group, including David Hume and Adam Smith. Around the same time, the city began to expand beyond its medieval boundaries, laying out a **New Town**, a masterpiece of the Neoclassical style.

Industrialization affected Edinburgh less than any other major city in the nation, and it never lost its white-collar character. Nevertheless, the city underwent an enormous **urban expansion** in the course of the century, annexing, among many other small burghs, the large port of Leith.

In 1947 Edinburgh was chosen to host the great **International Festival** which served as a symbol of the new peaceful European order; despite some hiccups, it has flourished ever since, in the process helping to make tourism a mainstay of the local economy. In 1975 the city carried out another territorial expansion, moving its boundaries westwards as far as the old burgh of South Queensferry and the Forth Bridges. Four years later, an inconclusive referendum on Scottish devolution delayed Edinburgh's revival of its role as a governmental capital, and Glasgow, previously the poor relation, began to challenge the city's status as a cultural centre. The keen rivalry between the two cities was most recently manifested in a hard-fought campaign, won by Glasgow, for the title of City of Architecture 1999.

In the general election of May 1997, Edinburgh astonished all pundits by voting out its last two Conservative Members of Parliament. Britain's new Labour government immediately implemented its promise of a referendum on the subject of devolution, to which Scotland voted resoundingly in favour of its own parliament with tax-levying powers. The site of the new parliament is a subject of much debate in Edinburgh, with the **Old Royal High School** being the strongest contender. Whichever location is finally chosen, Scotland's capital will in the near future be an important political centre once more.

The telephone code for Edinburgh is ☎0131.

Arrival, information and transport

Although Edinburgh occupies a large area relative to its population – less than half a million people – most places worth visiting lie within the compact city centre, which is easily explored on foot. This is divided clearly and unequivocally between the maze-like **Old Town**, which lies on and around the crag linking the Castle and the Palace, and the **New Town**, laid out in a symmetrical pattern on the undulating ground to the north.

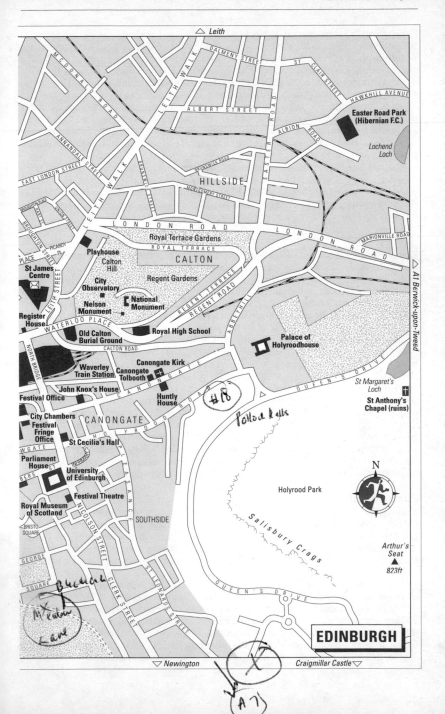

Edinburgh International Airport (☎333 1000) is at Turnhouse, seven miles west of the city centre, close to the start of the M8 motorway to Glasgow. Regular shuttle buses (£3.20) connect to Waverley Station in the town centre; taxis charge around £11 for the same journey. Conveniently situated at the eastern end of Princes Street in the New Town, **Waverley Station** (☎556 2451) is the terminus for all mainline trains. The central exit takes you out onto Waverley Bridge, with Princes Street to the north and the Old Town to the south. The northern exit leads straight up the stairway to Princes Street itself, while the southern exit leads to Market Street, the outer fringe of the Old Town.

There's a second mainline train stop, Haymarket Station, just under two miles west on the lines from Waverley to Glasgow, Fife and the Highlands, although this is only really of use if you're staying nearby.

The bus terminal for local and intercity services is on St Andrew Square, two minutes' walk from Waverley Station, on the opposite side of Princes Street. One of the major bus companies, SMT (Scottish Midland Transport), has a shop (☎558 1616) at the southeastern corner of the bus station, where timetables are kept and tickets sold for several of the confusing array of private bus operators.

Information

Edinburgh's main **tourist office** is at 3 Princes St beside the northern entrance to the station (April & Oct Mon–Sat 9am–6pm, Sun 10am–6pm; May, June & Sept Mon–Sat 9am–7pm, Sun 10am–7pm; July & Aug Mon–Sat 9am–8pm, Sun 10am–8pm; Nov–March Mon–Sat 9am–6pm, Sun 10am–8pm; ☎557 1700). Although inevitably flustered at the height of the season, it's efficiently run, with scores of free leaflets; when the office is closed, there's a 24-hour computerized information service at the door. The much smaller **airport branch** is in the main concourse, directly opposite Gate 5 (April–Oct Mon–Sat 8.30am–9.30pm, Sun 9.30am–9.30pm; Nov–March Mon–Fri 9am–6pm, Sat 9am–5pm, Sun 9.30am–5pm; ☎333 2167). For up-to-date maps of the city head for one of the major book stores – Waterstones, 13–14 Princes St, is the nearest to Waverley Station.

Of the guided tours available, the best are the Guide Friday open-topped buses, which depart from Waverley Station and cruise through the city streets, allowing you to get on and off at leisure. Lothian Region Transport (LRT) has various coach tours leaving from Waverley Bridge, while several companies along the Royal Mile offer walking tours of the street, including Edinburgh Walking Tours (☎557 4700), Mercat Tours (☎661 4541) and Robin's Tours (☎661 0125). Forth Helicopter Services, Edinburgh Airport (☎339 8877), offer spectacular aerial sightseeing trips of the city for £29 per person (10min), or £50 including the Forth Bridges (15min).

City transport

Most of Edinburgh's **public transport** services terminate on or near Princes Street, the city's main thoroughfare, which lies at the extreme southern end of the New Town. Edinburgh is well-served by **buses**, although even locals are confused by the consequences of deregulation, with several companies offering competing services along similar routes. Each bus stop usually lists the different companies together with the route numbers that stop there.

Most useful are the maroon buses operated by Lothian Regional Transport (LRT); all buses referred to in the text are run by them unless otherwise stated. Timetables and passes are available from the ticket centres at 31 Waverley Bridge (☎225 8616) or 27 Hanover St (☎554 4494). A good investment, especially if you're staying far out or want to explore the suburbs, is the £10 pass allowing a week's unlimited travel on LRT buses; passport photo needed. You can also buy an LRT day pass for £2.20, or, of course, tickets from the driver, for which you'll need exact change.

The green buses run by Eastern Scottish, and the green and yellow buses of Lowland Scottish link the capital with outlying towns and villages. Most services depart from and terminate at the St Andrew Square bus station.

The city is well endowed with taxi ranks, especially around Waverley Bridge. Costs start at £1.20 for the first 340yd and 20p for each additional 240yd. The phone numbers of the main local cab companies are: Capital Castle Cabs (☎228 2555), Central Radio Taxis (☎229 2468) and City Cabs (☎228 1211).

It is emphatically *not* a good idea to take a **car** into central Edinburgh: despite the presence of several expensive multistorey car parks, looking for somewhere to park involves long, fruitless searches. Traffic calming has been introduced in several key areas – Princes Street is now one-way for cars and has a speed limit of 20mph and Charlotte Square has adopted a complicated traffic-flow system – and there is talk of imposing road-pricing in the future. Bus lanes must be left clear during rush hours, and cars parked on yellow lines are regularly clamped or towed away, with a retrieval fee of £120. Most ticket and parking-meter regulations cease at 5.30pm Monday to Friday, and at 1.30pm on Saturday.

Edinburgh is a reasonably cycle-friendly city – although hilly – with several **cycle paths**. The local cycling action group, Spokes (☎313 2114), publishes an excellent cycle map of the city. For rental, try Central Cycles, 13 Lochrin Place (☎228 6333), Edinburgh Cycle Hire, 29 Blackfriars St (☎556 5560), or Sandy Gilchrist Cycles, 1 Cadzow Place (☎652 1760).

Accommodation

As befits its status as a top tourist city, Edinburgh has a larger and wider choice of **accommodation** than any other place in Britain outside London. The greatest number of places to stay can be found in the streets immediately north of Haymarket Station, Royal Terrace and the lower reaches of the New Town, and to the south, the inner suburbs of Bruntsfield and Newington, where numerous hotels and guest houses line the major roads into the city from England.

In addition to Edinburgh's **hotels**, hundreds of **private houses** offer B&B deals at low rates, but in order to protect the guest-house trade from excessive competition, they are only open between Easter and October. There is also a decent choice of both official and private **hostels**, and three **campsites** attached to caravan parks. Surprisingly, the wide range of **campus accommodation** is neither as cheap nor as convenient as might be expected. **Self-catering** is an alternative, extremely cost-effective for groups intending to stay a week or more, with some enticing addresses available for let.

Advance reservations are very strongly recommended during the Festival: turning up on spec entails accepting whatever is left (which is unlikely to be good value) or else

---

ACCOMMODATION PRICE CODES

Throughout this book, accommodation **prices** have been graded with the codes below, according to the cost of the least expensive double room in high season. Price codes are not given for campsites, most of which charge under £10 per person. Almost all hostels charge less than £10 a night for a bed – the few exceptions to this rule have the prices quoted in the text. For a full account of the accommodation price codes, see p.30.

① under £20	④ £40–50	⑦ £70–80
② £20–30	⑤ £50–60	⑧ £80–100
③ £30–40	⑥ £60–70	⑨ over £100

commuting from the suburbs. The **tourist office** (see p.58) sends out accommodation lists for free, and can reserve any type of accommodation in advance for a non-refundable £3 fee: call in personally when you arrive or write in advance to Edinburgh Marketing Central Reservations Department, 3 Princes St, Edinburgh EH2 2QP (☎557 9677), stating requirements. In Waverley Station, Thomas Cook runs a hotel reservation service (daily 7am–10.30pm; ☎556 0030) which makes a £5 non-refundable charge for bookings.

Hotels

Although considerably more expensive than the guest houses, Edinburgh's **hotels** are generally of a high standard and cover a wide range of tastes, from the hub of New Town elegance to quieter retreats out of the centre.

Old Town

Apex International Hotel, 31–35 Grassmarket (☎300 3456). Large, new, reasonably priced hotel with upper rooms enjoying views across to the castle. ⑥.

Point Hotel, 34–59 Bread St (☎221 9919). Minimalist conversion of a former Co-op supermarket, handily placed in the heart of the Old Town. ⑧.

New Town

Albany Hotel, 39–43 Albany St (☎556 0397). Georgian listed building with many period features and comfortable rooms in a quiet street a couple of minutes' walk south of the bus station. ⑧.

Argus Hotel, 14 Coates Gardens (☎337 6159). Smallish rooms in a low-key hotel close to Haymarket Station. ⑤.

Claymore Hotel, 6 Royal Terrace (☎556 2693). Small, family-run hotel on one of the city's most desirable streets. ⑤.

Clifton Private Hotel, 1 Clifton Terrace (☎337 1002). Another family-run hotel, in roomy Victorian town house directly opposite Haymarket Station. ⑤.

Halcyon Hotel, 8 Royal Terrace (☎556 1032). A very reasonably priced unpretentious hotel, considering the location. ⑥.

Howard Hotel, 32–36 Great King St (☎557 3500). Top-of-the-range (£180 a night) elegant townhouse hotel. Lavishly decorated and serving excellent food. ⑨.

Old Waverley Hotel, 43 Princes St (☎556 4648). Large, recently refurbished, grand hotel in ideal location, right across from Waverley Station and with sweeping city views. Good restaurant, *Cranston's*, serving mainly Scottish dishes, with several vegetarian options. ⑨.

Parliament House Hotel, 15 Calton Hill (☎478 4000). Smart new hotel in great central location, halfway up Calton Hill; includes three rooms for disabled visitors. ⑧.

Ritz Hotel, 14–18 Grosvenor St (☎337 4315). Posh five-storey hotel close to Haymarket Station. Some rooms feature antique four-poster beds. ⑦.

Rothesay Hotel, 8 Rothesay Place (☎225 4125). Quiet West End hotel in a Georgian terrace close to St Mary's Cathedral; bright high-ceilinged rooms. ⑦.

Roxburghe Hotel, 38 Charlotte Square (☎225 3921). Characterful traditional hotel, right on the corner of Edinburgh's most beautiful square. ⑨.

Royal British Hotel, 20 Princes St (☎556 4901). Swanky hotel with a prime location on Edinburgh's main street, offering stunning views. ⑨.

Leith

Camore Hotel, 7 Links Gardens (☎554 7897). Georgian house with many attractive original features including marble fireplaces. Also has great views over Leith Links, Calton Hill and Arthur's Seat. ⑤.

Malmaison, 1 Tower Place (☎555 6868). Popular harbourside Leith hotel: each room has its own highly distinctive decoration. ⑧.

South of the centre

Allison House Hotel, 15–17 Mayfield Gardens (☎667 8049). Popular, well-run and recently expanded hotel with "honesty" bar – guests serve themselves and pay on departure. ⑤.

Arthur's View Hotel, 10 Mayfield Gardens (☎667 3468). Pleasant, friendly hotel in convenient Southside location. ⑦.

Braid Hills Hotel, 134 Braid Rd (☎447 8888). Old-fashioned, baronial-style hotel in a residential area up in the hilly southern outskirts, with fine views (10min drive from the city). ⑧.

Bruntsfield Hotel, 69–74 Bruntsfield Place (☎229 1393). Large, comfortable and peaceful hotel overlooking Bruntsfield Park, a mile south of Princes Street. ⑨.

Donmaree Hotel, 21 Mayfield Gardens (☎667 3641). Victorian mansion on the south side of the city, with a pleasant first-floor lounge and luxurious conservatory. ⑨.

Prestonfield House Hotel, Priestfield Road (☎668 3346). Luxury hotel in a seventeenth-century mansion set in its own park below Arthur's Seat. A new wing has just been added, raising the number of rooms from a tiny five to a still trim 31. Peacocks strut around on the lawns and Highland cattle low in the adjacent fields. ⑨.

Teviotdale House Hotel, 53 Grange Loan (☎667 4376). Peaceful non-smoking hotel, offering luxurious standards at reasonable prices. Particularly renowned for the huge home-cooked Scottish breakfasts. ⑦.

Thrums Private Hotel, 14–15 Minto St (☎667 5545). Excellent hotel in large Georgian house with equally classy restaurant. ⑥.

West of the centre

Jarvis Ellersly Country House Hotel, 4 Ellersly Rd (☎337 6888). Edwardian country mansion set in walled garden in quiet suburban Corstorphine, between the city centre and the airport. Predominantly business clientele. ⑨.

Norton House Hotel, Ingliston (☎333 1275). Country house with spacious rooms and a conservatory restaurant, set in extensive parkland a mile from the airport; owned by the Virgin group. ⑨.

Guest houses

Edinburgh's innumerable **guest houses** are excellent value for money and far more personal places to stay than the larger city hotels.

New Town

Ardenlee Guest House, 9 Eyre Place (☎556 2838). Welcoming, non-smoking guest house, with exceptionally comfortable and spacious rooms. Breakfast includes some vegetarian options, and private parking is available. ⑤.

Dickie Guest House, 22 E Claremont St (☎556 4032). Friendly B&B in a Victorian town house on the eastern edge of the New Town. ⑤.

Drummond House, 17 Drummond Place (☎557 9189). There are just four rooms in this luxurious and expensive guest house in the heart of the New Town, which is an attractive alternative to the large hotels. ⑧.

Galloway Guest House, 22 Dean Park Crescent (☎332 3672). Friendly, family-run place in elegant Stockbridge, within walking distance of the centre. ④.

Marrakech Guest House, 30 London St (☎556 4444). In a residential street just a few minutes' walk south of the bus station; has small rooms and a superb Moroccan restaurant in the basement. ⑤.

St Bernard's Guest House, 22 St Bernard's Crescent (☎332 2339). Well located in Georgian Stockbridge, with tasteful pink rooms. ⑤.

Sibbet House, 26 Northumberland St (☎556 1078). Small, sumptuous family guest house, where British sang-froid is challenged by a communal breakfast table, an occasion regularly enlivened by the host's bagpipe-playing. ⑦.

Six Mary's Place, Raeburn Place (☎332 8965). Collectively run, "alternative" guest house; has a no-smoking policy, and offers excellent home-cooked vegetarian meals. ⑥.

Stuart House, 12 E Claremont St (☎557 9030). Homely, bright refurbished Georgian house in eastern New Town, a few minutes' walk from the bus station; no smoking. ⑦.

South of the centre

Hopetoun Guest House, 37 Mayfield Rd (☎667 7691). Bright, friendly non-smoking guest house with just three rooms. Great views of Arthur's Seat and Blackford Hill. ⑤.

International Guest House, 37 Mayfield Gardens (☎667 2511). One of the best of the Mayfield guest houses, with comfortable, well-equipped rooms. ⑤.

Kenvie Guest House, 16 Kilmaurs Rd (☎668 1964). Comfortable, homely guest house in a quiet street, close to the Royal Commonwealth Pool. Rooms are non-smoking. ④.

Ravensneuk Guest House, 11 Blacket Ave (☎667 5347). Good-value rooms set in a quiet conservation area, close to the Royal Commonwealth Pool and Holyrood Park. ⑤.

Town House, 65 Gilmore Place (☎229 1985). Small but friendly Victorian guest house close to the King's Theatre; no-smoking. ⑤.

Leith and Inverleith

A-Haven Guest House, 180 Ferry Rd (☎554 6559). Exceptionally friendly place; among the best of a number of guest houses on one of Edinburgh's main east–west arteries. ⑤.

Ashlyn Guest House, 42 Inverleith Row (☎552 2954). Right by the Botanic Garden, and within walking distance of the centre. Non-smoking. ⑤.

Bonnington Guest House, 202 Ferry Rd (☎554 7610). Comfortable, friendly guest house pleasantly sited just by the park. ⑤.

Ravensdown Guest House, 248 Ferry Rd (☎552 5438). Another place on Ferry Road, with a fine panoramic view across Inverleith playing fields to the city centre. ④.

Sheridan Guest House, 1 Bonnington Terrace (☎554 4107). Comfortable guest house in elegant Victorian terrace. ④.

East of the centre

Daisy Park Guest House, 41 Abercorn Terrace (☎669 2503). Relaxed atmosphere and close to the sea. ④.

Devon House Guest House, 2 Pittville St (☎669 6067). Pleasant rooms, only 2min from the shore. ③.

Joppa Turrets Guest House, 1 Lower Joppa (☎669 5806). The place to come if you want an Edinburgh holiday by the sea: a quiet establishment right by the beach in Joppa, five miles east of the city centre. ③.

Stra'ven Guest House, 3 Brunstane Rd North (☎669 5580) Splendid lounge and friendly service in an elegant well-kept guest house; non-smoking. ④.

Self-catering apartments

Canon Court Apartments, 20 Canonmills (☎474 7000). All mod cons available in these smart, comfortable apartments on the northern edge of the New Town, near the Water of Leith. Prices start at £39 a night for one person and rise to £624 for six people for a week.

Crosswoodhill Farm, West Calder, West Lothian (☎01501/785205). Eighteen miles and 35min by car from the centre of Edinburgh, this rural farm has two self-catering properties, sleeping five and six and surrounded by attractive countryside and farm animals. Prices start from £220 a week in low season, up to £440 in high season.

National Trust for Scotland, 5 Charlotte Square (☎243 9331). Has a two-room apartment in Gladstone's Land (the finest house on the Royal Mile) available for rent. Minimum period one week; open March–Oct only. Sleeps two and costs from £210 per week.

No. 5 Self Catering Apartments, 5 Abercorn Terrace (☎669 1044). These Georgian houses in Portobello have apartments for three people for £120–320 per week; for two, £90–225; single units, £60–95; reduced rates for longer stays.

Rosslyn Castle, Roslin, Midlothian (☎01628/825925). For a very special holiday, hire this fifteenth-century castle dramatically sited on a rock high above the River Esk and just 5min walk from Rosslyn Chapel (seven miles from city centre). Sleeps up to seven people and costs £606–1308 a week.

Royal Mile Enterprises, c/o Vivien Andersen, 3 Doune Terrace (☎225 7189). Two apartments for rent in a historical tenement on the Royal Mile; minimum stay three nights. Sleeps two to four and costs £470 per week.

West End Apartments, c/o Brian Matheson, 2 Learmonth Terrace (☎332 0717 or 226 6513). Five apartments in a West End town house; minimum let two nights. Sleeps up to five and costs £180–600 per week.

Campus accommodation

Heriot-Watt University Riccarton Campus, Currie (☎451 3115). Rather inconveniently sited at the extreme western fringe of the city, but open all year. ⑤.

Jewel and Esk Valley College, 24 Milton Rd E (☎657 7523). Again the location, about 5 miles east of the centre, is not ideal, but it's served directly by bus #44 and lies just beyond the terminus of bus #5. Open all year, except Dec. ④.

Napier University, 219 Colinton Rd (☎455 4921). Reasonable location in the southern inner suburbs, but open July to mid-Sept only. Minimum stay 2 nights. Buses #23 and #27 will take you to Princes Street. ⑥.

University of Edinburgh Pollock Halls of Residence, 18 Holyrood Park Rd (☎667 1971). Unquestionably the best setting of any of the campuses, right beside the Royal Commonwealth Pool and Holyrood Park. Open Easter and late June to mid-Sept only. ⑤.

Hostels

Belford Hostel, 6–8 Douglas Gardens (☎225 6209). Housed in a converted Arts and Crafts church, just west of the centre, close to the Dean Village. Has dorm beds and doubles and no curfew.

Bruntsfield Hostel, 7 Bruntsfield Crescent (☎447 2994). Strictly run *SYHA* youth hostel, overlooking Bruntsfield Links a mile south of Princes Street; take bus #11, #15 or #16. 2am curfew; closed Jan.

Cowgate Tourist Hostel, 112 Cowgate (☎226 2153). Basic, excellent-value accommodation in small apartments with kitchens, in the heart of the Old Town. Laundry facilities. Open July–Sept only; no curfew.

Edinburgh Backpackers Hostel, 65 Cockburn St (☎539 8695). Busy well-run hostel just off the Royal Mile.

Edinburgh Central Youth Hostel, Robertson Close, Cowgate. Lively SYHA hostel open June–Aug only; beds cost £10.15 in July and Aug, £9.15 in June. Advance bookings through Edinburgh District Office, 161 Warrender Park Rd, Edinburgh EH9 1EQ (☎229 8660).

Eglinton Hostel, 18 Eglinton Crescent (☎337 1120). The most expensive of the SYHA hostels, with beds costing £11.95 in high season and £10.95 in low season including continental breakfast, but it's well-sited west of the centre, near Haymarket Station. It's easier-going than its Bruntsfield counterpart, but still with a 2am curfew; closed Dec.

High Street Hostel, 8 Blackfriars St (☎557 3984). Privately run venture with room for 130 people, just off the Royal Mile. Slightly cramped, but its lively atmosphere makes up for it. Open 24hr, all year.

Royal Mile Backpackers, 105 High St (☎557 6120) Reasonably priced dormitories, clean and friendly and in a great location.

Campsites

Mortonhall Caravan Park, 38 Mortonhall Gate, Frogston Rd E (☎664 1533). A good site, five miles out, near the Braid Hills; take bus #11 from Princes Street. Open March–Oct.

Silverknowes Caravan Site, Marine Drive, Silverknowes (☎312 6874). Pleasant campsite, popular with backpackers, close to the shore in the western suburbs, a 30min ride from the centre by bus #14. Open April–Sept.

Slatebairns Caravan Club Site, Roslin, Midlothian (☎440 2192). Caravans and tents are welcome at this attractive countryside site with good facilities, situated seven miles from the city centre (bus #87A). Open Easter–Sept.

The Old Town

The **OLD TOWN**, although only about a mile long and 300yd wide, represents the total extent of the twin burghs of Edinburgh and Canongate for the first 650 years of their existence, and its general appearance and character remain indubitably medieval. Containing as it does the majority of the city's most famous tourist sights, it makes by far the best starting point for your explorations.

In addition to the obvious goals of the **Castle**, the **Palace of Holyroodhouse** and **Holyrood Abbey**, there are scores of historic monuments along the length of the **Royal Mile** linking the two. Inevitably, much of the Old Town is sacrificed to hard-sell tourism, and can be uncomfortably crowded throughout the summer, especially during the Festival. A welcome antidote, and a reminder that the Old Town is by no means fossilized for the benefit of tourists, is provided by the area to the south, notably Chambers Street, location of the **Royal Museum of Scotland** and the **University of Edinburgh**.

While it's possible to cover the highlights of the Old Town in the course of a single day, a detailed visit requires several times as long. No matter how pressed you are, make sure you spare time for the wonderfully varied scenery and breathtaking vantage points of **Holyrood Park**, an extensive tract of open countryside on its eastern edge.

The Castle

The history of Edinburgh, and indeed of Scotland, is indissolubly bound up with its **Castle** (daily: April–Sept 9.30am–6pm; Oct–March 9.30am–5pm; £5.50), which dominates the city from its lofty seat atop an extinct volcanic rock. It requires no great imaginative feat to comprehend the strategic importance that underpinned the Castle's, and hence Edinburgh's, pre-eminence within Scotland: in the dramatic view from Princes Street (perhaps most impressive under the clear, bright skies of spring), the north side rears high above an almost sheer rockface; the southern side is equally formidable, the western, where the rock rises in terraces, only marginally less so. Would-be attackers, like modern tourists, were forced to approach the Castle from the crag to the east on which the Royal Mile runs down to Holyrood.

The Castle's disparate styles reflect its many changes in usage, as well as advances in military architecture: the oldest surviving part, **St Margaret's Chapel**, is from the twelfth century, while the most recent additions date back to the 1920s. Nothing remains from its period as a seat of the Scottish court in the reign of Malcolm Canmore; indeed, having been lost to (and subsequently recaptured from) the English on several occasions, the defences were dismantled by the Scots themselves in 1313, and only rebuilt in 1356 when the return of King David II from captivity introduced a modicum of political stability. Thereafter, it gradually developed into Scotland's premier castle, with the dual function of fortress and royal palace. It last saw action in 1745, when the Young Pretender's forces, fresh from their victory at Prestonpans, made a half-hearted attempt to storm it. Subsequently, advances in weapon technology diminished its importance, but under the influence of the Romantic movement it came to be seen as a great national monument. A grandiose "improvement" scheme, which would have transformed it into a bloated nineteenth-century vision of the Middle Ages, was considered, but, perhaps fortunately, only a few elements of it were actually built.

Though you can easily take in the views and wander round the Castle yourself, you might like to join one of the somewhat overheated **guided tours** offered by kilted locals, furiously hamming up a thick Scottish brogue as they talk of war, boiling oil and the roar of the cannon.

The Esplanade

The Castle is entered via the **Esplanade**, a parade ground laid out in the eighteenth century and enclosed a hundred years later by ornamental walls, the southern one of which commands fine views towards the Pentland Hills. Each evening during the Festival (see p.96), the Esplanade is the setting for the city's most shameless and spectacular demonstration of tourist kitsch, the Edinburgh Military Tattoo. Despite opposition from traditionalists, plans have been mooted to move the Tattoo to a permanent auditorium in Princes Street Gardens, which will reduce the cost of erecting and dismantling the spectators' grandstands each year.

Dotted around are several military monuments, including an equestrian **statue of Field Marshal Earl Haig**, the controversial Edinburgh-born commander of the British forces in World War I, whose trench warfare strategy of sending men "over the top" led to previously unimaginable casualties.

The lower defences

The **Gatehouse** to the Castle is a Romantic-style addition of the 1880s, complete with the last drawbridge ever built in Scotland. It was later adorned with appropriately heroic-looking statues of Sir William Wallace and Robert the Bruce.

Rearing up behind is the most distinctive and impressive feature of the Castle's silhouette, the sixteenth-century **Half Moon Battery**, which marks the outer limit of the actual defences. Continuing uphill, you pass through the **Portcullis Gate**, a handsome Renaissance gateway of the same period, marred by the addition of a nineteenth-century upper storey equipped with anachronistic arrow slits rather than gunholes.

Beyond is the six-gun **Argyle Battery**, built in the eighteenth century by Major-General Wade, whose network of military roads and bridges still forms an essential part of the transport infrastructure of the Highlands. Further west on **Mill's Mount Battery**, a well-known Edinburgh ritual takes place – the daily firing of the one o'clock gun. Originally designed for the benefit of ships in the Firth of Forth, it's now used as a time signal by city-centre office workers. Both batteries offer wonderful panoramic views over Princes Street and the New Town to the coastal towns and hills of Fife across the Forth.

Up the tortuously sloping road, the **Governor's House** is a 1740s mansion whose harled masonry and crow-stepped gables are archetypal features of vernacular Scottish architecture. It now serves as the officers' mess for members of the garrison, while the governor himself lives in the northern side wing. Behind stands the largest single construction in the Castle complex, the **New Barracks**, built in the 1790s in an austere Neoclassical style. The road then snakes round towards the enclosed citadel at the uppermost point of Castle Rock, entered via **Foog's Gate**.

St Margaret's Chapel

At the eastern end of the citadel, **St Margaret's Chapel** is the oldest surviving building in the Castle, and probably also in Edinburgh itself. Used as a powder magazine for 300 years, this tiny Norman church was rediscovered in 1845 and was eventually rededicated in 1934, after sympathetic restoration. Externally, it is plain and severe, but the interior preserves an elaborate zigzag archway dividing the nave from the sanctuary. Although once believed to have been built by the saint herself, and mooted as the site of her death in 1093, its architectural style suggests that it actually dates from about thirty years later, and was thus probably built by King David I as a memorial to his mother.

The battlements in front of the chapel offer the best of all the Castle's panoramic views. They are interrupted by the **Lang Stairs**, which provide an alternative means of access from the Argyle Battery via the side of the Portcullis Gate. Just below the battlements there's a small **cemetery**, the last resting place of the **soldiers' pets**: it is kept in immaculate condition, particularly when contrasted with the dilapidated state of some of the city's public cemeteries. Continuing eastwards, you skirt the top of the Forewall and Half Moon Batteries, passing the 110ft-deep **Castle Well** en route to **Crown Square**, the highest, most secure and most important section of the entire complex.

The Palace

The eastern side of Crown Square is occupied by the **Palace**, a surprisingly unassuming edifice built round an octagonal stair turret heightened last century to bear the Castle's main flagpole. Begun in the 1430s, the Palace's present Renaissance appearance is thanks to King James IV, though it was remodelled for Mary, Queen of Scots and her consort Henry, Lord Darnley, whose entwined initials (MAH), together with the date 1566, can be seen above one of the doorways. This gives access to a few historic rooms, the most interesting of which is the tiny panelled bedchamber at the extreme southeastern corner, where Mary gave birth to James VI. Along with the rest of the Palace, the room was remodelled for James's triumphant homecoming in 1617 though this was to be the last time it served as a royal residence.

Another section of the Palace has recently been refurbished with a detailed audio visual presentation on the **Honours of Scotland**, the originals of which are housed in the Crown Room at the very end of the display. These magnificent crown jewels – the only pre-Restoration set in the United Kingdom – serve as one of the most potent images of Scotland's nationhood. They were last used for the Scottish-only coronation of Charles II in 1651, an event which provoked the wrath of Oliver Cromwell, who made exhaustive attempts to have the jewels melted down. Having narrowly escaped his clutches by being smuggled out of the Castle and hidden in a rural church, the jewels later served as symbols of the absent monarch at sittings of the Scottish Parliament before being locked away in a chest following the Union of 1707. For over a century

---

THE STONE OF DESTINY

Legend has it that the Stone of Destiny (also called the Stone of Scone) was "Jacob's Pillow", on which he dreamed of the ladder of angels from earth to heaven. Its real history is obscure, but it is known that it it was moved from Ireland to Dunadd by missionaries, and thence to Dunstaffnage, from where Kenneth MacAlpine, king of the Dalriada Scots, brought it to the abbey at Scone in 838. There it remained for almost five hundred years, used as a coronation throne on which all kings of Scotland were crowned.

In 1296, an over-eager Edward I stole what he believed to be the Stone and installed it at Westminster Abbey, where, apart from a brief interlude in 1950 when it was removed by Scottish nationalists and hidden in Arbroath for several months, it remained for seven hundred years. All this changed in December 1996 when, after an elaborate ceremony-laden journey from London, the Stone returned to Scotland, one of many doomed attempts by the Conservative government to convince the Scottish people that the Union was a good thing. Much to the annoyance of the people of Perth and the curators of Scone Palace, and to the general indifference of the Scottish public, the Stone was placed in Edinburgh Castle.

However, speculation surrounds the authenticity of the Stone, for the original is said to have been intricately carved, while the one seen today is a plain block of sandstone. Many believe that the canny monks at Scone palmed this off onto the English king and that the real Stone of Destiny lies hidden in an underground chamber, its whereabouts a mystery to all but a chosen few.

they were out of sight and eventually presumed lost, before being rediscovered in 1818 as a result of a search initiated by Sir Walter Scott.

Of the three pieces comprising the Honours, the oldest is the **sceptre**, which bears statuettes of the Virgin and Child, St James and St Andrew, rounded off by a polished globe of rock crystal: it was given to James IV in 1494 by Pope Alexander VI, and refashioned by Scottish craftsmen for James V. Even finer is the **sword**, a swaggering Italian High Renaissance masterpiece by the silversmith Domenico da Sutri, presented to James IV by the great artistic patron Pope Julius II. Both the hilt and the scabbard are engraved with Julius's personal emblem, showing the oak tree and its acorns, the symbols of the Risen Christ, together with dolphins, symbols of the Church. The jewel-encrusted **crown**, made for James V by the Scottish goldsmith James Mosman, incorporates the gold circlet worn by Robert the Bruce and is surmounted by an enamelled orb and cross.

The glass case containing the Honours has recently been rearranged to create space for its newest addition, the **Stone of Destiny**. This remarkably plain object now lies incongruously next to the opulent Crown Jewels.

Around Crown Square

The south side of **Crown Square** is occupied by the **Great Hall**, built under James IV as a venue for banquets and other ceremonial occasions. Until 1639 the meeting place of the Scottish Parliament, it later underwent the indignity of conversion and subdivision, firstly into a barracks, then a hospital. During this time, its hammerbeam roof – the earliest of three in the Old Town – was hidden from view. It was restored towards the end of the last century, when the hall was decked out in the full-blown Romantic manner.

On the west side of the square, the eighteenth-century **Queen Anne Barracks** house part of the **Scottish United Services Museum**, with displays on each of the different Scottish military regiments, plus the navy and air force. Note the model of the ship *The Great George*, made by French prisoners incarcerated in the Castle during the eighteenth and early nineteenth centuries.

In 1755, the castle church of St Mary on the north side of the square was replaced by a barracks, which in turn was skilfully converted into the quietly reverential **Scottish National War Memorial** in honour of the 150,000 Scots who fell in World War I.

The rest of the complex

From Crown Square, you can descend to the **Vaults**, a series of cavernous chambers erected by order of James IV to provide an even surface for the showpiece buildings above. They were later used as a prison for captured foreign nationals, who have bequeathed a rich legacy of graffiti. One of the rooms houses the famous fifteenth-century siege gun, **Mons Meg**, which could fire a 500-pound stone nearly two miles. A seventeenth-century visitor, the London poet, John Taylor, commented: "It is so great within, that it was told me that a child was once gotten there." In 1754, Mons Meg was taken to the Tower of London, where it stayed till Sir Walter Scott persuaded George IV, on the occasion of his 1822 state visit to Scotland, to return it.

Directly opposite the entrance to the Vaults is the **Military Prison**, built in 1842, when the design and function of jails was a major topic of public debate. The cells, though designed for solitary confinement, are less forbidding than might be expected. Finally, beyond the Governor's House, and overlooking the two-tier western defences, the late nineteenth-century **Hospital** is a continuation of the Scottish United Services Museum.

The Royal Mile

The **Royal Mile**, the name given to the ridge linking the Castle with Holyrood, was described by Daniel Defoe, in 1724, as "the largest, longest and finest street for Buildings and Number of Inhabitants, not in Bretain only, but in the World". Almost

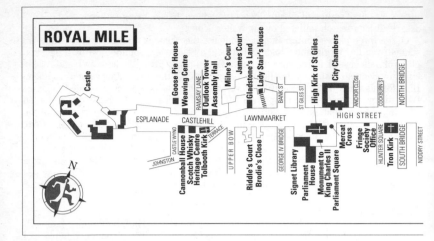

exactly a mile in length, it is divided into four separate streets – Castlehill, Lawnmarket, High Street and Canongate. From these, branching out in a herringbone pattern, a series of tightly packed closes and steep lanes are entered via archways known as pends. After the construction of the New Town, the Royal Mile degenerated into a notorious slum, but has since shaken off that reputation, becoming once again a highly desirable place to live. Although marred somewhat by rather too many overpriced shops, it is still among the most evocative parts of the city, and one that particularly rewards detailed exploration.

Castlehill

The narrow uppermost stretch of the Royal Mile is known as **Castlehill**. On the side facing the Esplanade the pretty Art Nouveau Witches' Fountain commemorates the three hundred or more women burnt at the spot on charges of sorcery, the last of whom died in 1722. Rising up behind is the picturesque Ramsay Garden, centring on the octagonal Goose Pie House, home of the eighteenth-century poet Allan Ramsay, author of *The Gentle Shepherd* and father of the better-known portrait painter of the same name. The rest dates from the 1890s and was the brainchild of Patrick Geddes, a pioneer of the modern town-planning movement, who created these desirable apartments in an attempt to regenerate the Old Town.

At the top of the southern side of Castlehill, the so-called **Cannonball House** takes its name from the cannonball embedded in its masonry, which according to legend was the result of a poorly targeted shot fired by the Castle garrison at Bonnie Prince Charlie's encampment at Holyrood. The truth is far more prosaic: the ball marks the gravitation height of the city's first piped water supply. Alongside, the **Scotch Whisky Heritage Centre** (daily: June–Sept 9.30am–6pm; Oct–May 10am–5.30pm; £4.20) gives the lowdown on all aspects of Scotland's national beverage, featuring a gimmicky ride in a "barrel" through a series of uninspiring historical tableaux, plus a film on aspects of production and blending. It's worth popping into the shop, whose stock gives an idea of the sheer range and diversity of the drink, with dozens of different brands on sale.

Across the road, at the top of Castlehill, the former reservoir for the Old Town has been converted into the **Edinburgh Old Town Weaving Centre** (daily 9am–5.30pm; £3). Visitors can see the whole process of weaving before selecting their own tartan or creating a new one. Very much a commercial enterprise, the centre has a large shop and restuarant and also hosts Scottish evenings, encompassing a meal accompanied by bagpipes for a hefty £36.

A few doors further along, the **Outlook Tower** (April–Oct Mon–Fri 9.30am–6pm, Sat & Sun 10am–6pm; Nov–March 10am–5pm; £3.40) has been one of Edinburgh's top tourist attractions since 1853, when the original seventeenth-century tenement was equipped with a **camera obscura**. It makes a good introduction to the city: actual moving images are beamed onto a white table, accompanied by a running commentary. For the best views, visit at noon when there are fewer shadows. The viewing balcony is one of Edinburgh's best vantage points, and there are exhibitions on pinhole photography, holography, Victorian photographs of the city, and topographic paintings made between 1780 and 1860.

A few steps further on is the **Assembly Hall**, meeting place of the annual General Assembly of the Church of Scotland and, during the Festival, an extraordinarily effective venue for large-scale drama, normally staging the most ambitious event on the programme. It was built in 1859 for the breakaway Free Church; the established church previously met at the **Tolbooth Kirk** across the road. Stunningly sited at the foot of Castlehill, the Kirk is one of the most distinctive features of the Edinburgh skyline, thanks to its majestic spire, the highest in the city; vacated by its Gaelic-speaking congregation in 1981, it is due be converted into a centre for the Edinburgh Festival, incorporating ticket sales and press facilities. The church's superb neo-Gothic detailing is due to Augustus Pugin, co-architect of the Houses of Parliament in London.

Lawnmarket

Below the Tolbooth Kirk, the Royal Mile opens out into the much broader expanse of **Lawnmarket**, which, as its name suggests, was once a marketplace. At its northern end is the entry to **Milne's Court**, whose excellently restored tenements now serve as student residences, and immediately beyond, **James Court**, one of Edinburgh's most fashionable addresses prior to the advent of the New Town, with David Hume and James Boswell among those who lived there.

Back on Lawnmarket itself, **Gladstone's Land** (April–Oct Mon–Sat 10am–5pm, Sun 2–5pm; £2.80) takes its name from the merchant Thomas Gledstane (sic), who in 1617 acquired a modest dwelling on the site, transforming it into a magnificent six-storey mansion. The Gledstane family are thought to have occupied the third floor, renting out the rest to merchants, in the style of tenement occupation still widespread in the city today. The arcaded ground floor, the only authentic example left of what was once a common feature of Royal Mile houses, has been restored to illustrate its early function as a shopping booth. Several other rooms have been kitted out in authentic period style to give an impression of the lifestyle of a well-to-do household of the late seventeenth century; the Painted Chamber, with its decorated wooden ceiling and wall friezes, is particularly impressive. You can also stay here (see p62).

A few paces further on, steps lead down to Lady Stair's Close, in which stands **Lady Stair's House** (Mon–Sat: June–Sept 10am–6pm; Oct–May 10am–5pm; also Sun 2–5pm during the Festival; free), another fine seventeenth-century residence, albeit one subject to a considerable amount of Victorian refurbishment. It now serves as Edinburgh's literary museum, featuring a collection of personal mementoes (among them locks of hair and walking sticks) of the three lions of Scottish literature – Robert Burns, Sir Walter Scott and Robert Louis Stevenson.

On the south side of Lawnmarket is **Riddle's Court**, actually a double courtyard, each with its own pend. Further down the street, **Brodie's Close** is named after the father of one of Edinburgh's most morbid characters, Deacon William Brodie, burglar by night and apparent pillar of society by day. Following his eventual capture, he managed to escape to Holland, but was betrayed, brought back to Edinburgh and hanged in 1788 on gallows of his own design. His ruse of trying to cheat death by secretly wearing an iron collar under his shirt failed to save him.

The High Kirk of St Giles

Across George IV Bridge, the **High Kirk of St Giles** (Mon–Sat: April–Sept 9am–7pm; Oct–March 9am–5pm) closes off Parliament Square from High Street. The sole parish church of medieval Edinburgh and where John Knox (see box opposite) launched and directed the Scottish Reformation, the Kirk is almost invariably referred to as a cathedral, although it has only been the seat of a bishop on two brief and unhappy occasions in the seventeenth century. According to one of the city's best-known legends, the attempt in 1637 to introduce the English prayer book, and thus episcopal government, so incensed a humble stallholder named Jenny Geddes that she hurled her stool at the preacher, prompting the rest of the congregation to chase the offending clergy out of the building. A tablet in the north aisle marks the spot from where she let rip.

In the early nineteenth century, St Giles received a much-needed but over-drastic restoration, covering most of the Gothic exterior with a smooth stone coating that gives it a certain Georgian dignity while sacrificing its medieval character almost completely. The only part to survive this treatment is the late fifteenth-century tower, whose resplendent crown spire is formed by eight flying buttresses. The **interior** has survived in much better shape. Especially notable are the four massive piers supporting the tower, which date back, at least in part, to the church's Norman predecessor. In the nineteenth century, St Giles was adorned with a whole series of funerary monuments in order to give it the character of a national pantheon on the model of Westminster Abbey. It was also equipped with several Pre-Raphaelite stained-glass windows. The best of these, designed by Edward Burne-Jones and William Morris, showing Old Testament prophets and the Israelites crossing the River Jordan, can be seen on the facade wall of the **north aisle**. Alongside is the great **west window**, which was dedicated to Robbie Burns in 1985 causing enormous controversy – as a hardened drinker and womanizer, the national bard was far from being an upholder of accepted Presbyterian values. Look out, also, for an elegant bronze relief of Robert Louis Stevenson on the south side of the church.

At the southeastern corner of St Giles, the **Thistle Chapel** was built by Sir Robert Lorimer in 1911 as the private chapel of the sixteen knights of the Most Noble Order

JOHN KNOX

The Protestant reformer **John Knox** has been alternately credited with, or blamed for, the distinctive national culture that emerged from the Calvinist Reformation, which has cast its shadow over Scottish history and the Scottish character right up to the present.

Little is known about Knox's early years: he was born between 1505 and 1514 in East Lothian, and trained for the priesthood at St Andrews University under John Major (sic), author of a *History of Great Britain* that advocated the union of Scotland and England. Ordained in 1540, Knox then served as a private tutor, in league with Scotland's first significant Protestant leader, **George Wishart**. After Wishart was burnt at the stake for heresy in 1546, Knox became involved with the group who had carried out the revenge murder of the Scottish primate, Cardinal David Beaton, subsequently taking over his castle in St Andrews. The following year, this was captured by the French, and Knox was carted off to work as a galley slave.

He was freed in 1548, as a result of the intervention of the English, who invited him to play an evangelizing role in the spread of their own Reformation. Following successful ministries in Berwick-upon-Tweed and Newcastle-upon-Tyne, Knox turned down the bishopric of Rochester, less from an intrinsic opposition to episcopacy than from a wish to avoid becoming embroiled in the turmoil he guessed would ensue if the Catholic Mary Tudor acceded to the English throne. When this duly happened in 1553, Knox fled to the Continent, ending up as minister to the English-speaking community in Geneva, which was then in the grip of the theocratic government of the Frenchman **Jean Calvin**. Knox was quickly won over to his radical version of Protestantism, declaring Geneva to be "the most perfect school of Christ since the days of the Apostles".

In exile, Knox was much preoccupied with the question of the influence wielded by political rulers, believing that the future of the Reformation in Europe was at risk because of the opposition of a few powerful sovereigns. This prompted him to write his most infamous treatise, *The First Blast of the Trumpet Against the Monstruous Regiment of Women*, a specific attack on the three Catholic women then ruling Scotland, England and France, which has made his name synonymous with misogyny ever since.

When Knox was allowed to return to Scotland in 1555, he took over as spiritual leader of the Reformation, becoming minister of St Giles in Edinburgh, where he established a reputation as a charismatic preacher. However, the establishment of Protestantism as the official religion of Scotland in 1560 was dependent on the forging of an alliance with Elizabeth I, which Knox himself rigorously championed: the swift deployment of English troops against the French garrison in Edinburgh dealt a fatal blow to Franco-Spanish hopes of re-establishing Catholicism in both Scotland and England. Although the return of Mary, Queen of Scots the following year placed a Catholic monarch on the Scottish throne, reputedly Knox was always able to retain the upper hand in his famous disputes with her.

Before his death in 1572, Knox began mapping out the organization of the Scots Kirk, sweeping away all vestiges of episcopal control and giving lay people a role of unprecedented importance. He also proposed a nationwide education system, to be compulsory for the very young and free for the poor, though lack of funds meant this could not be implemented in full. His final legacy was the posthumously published *History of the Reformation of Religion in the Realm of Scotland*, a justification of his life's work.

For all his considerable influence, Knox was not responsible for many of the features which have created the popular image of Scottish presbyterianism – and of Knox himself – as austere and joyless. A man of refined cultural tastes, he did not encourage the iconoclasm that destroyed so many of Scotland's churches and works of art: indeed, much of this was carried out by English hands. Nor did he promote the unbending Sabbatarianism, the obsessive work ethic or even the inflexible view of the doctrine of predestination favoured by his far more fanatical successors. Ironically, though, by fostering an irrevocable rift in the "Auld Alliance" with France, he did do more than anyone else to ensure that Scotland's future was to be linked irrevocably with that of England.

of the Thistle. Self-consciously derivative of St George's Chapel in Windsor, it's an exquisite piece of craftsmanship, with an elaborate ribbed vault, huge drooping bosses, and extravagantly ornate stalls.

Parliament Square
The rest of **Parliament Square** is dominated by the continuous Neoclassical facades of the **Law Courts**, originally planned by Robert Adam (1728–92), one of four brothers in a family of architects (their father William Adam designed Hopetoun House; see p.94) whose work helped give the New Town much of its grace and elegance. Because of a shortage of funds, the present exteriors were built to designs by Robert Reid (1776–1856), the designer of the northern part of New Town, who faithfully quoted from Adam's architectural vocabulary without matching his flair. Mentor of William Playfair (see p.79), another architect, William Stark was flamboyant with design, and his **Signet Library**, which occupies the west side of the square, is one of the most beautiful interiors in Edinburgh – its sumptuous colonnaded hall a perfect embodiment of the ideals of the Age of Reason. Unfortunately it can only be seen by prior written application, except on very occasional open days.

Around the corner, facing the southern side of St Giles, is **Parliament House**, built in the 1630s for the Scottish Parliament, a role it maintained until the Union, when it passed into the hands of the legal fraternity. Today it is readily accessible during the week, used by lawyers and their clients for hushed conferrals in between court sittings. Inside, the most notable feature is the extravagant hammerbeam roof, and the delicately carved stone corbels from which it springs: in addition to some vicious grotesques, they include accurate depictions of several castles, including Edinburgh.

Outside on the square, an imposing equestrian **monument to King Charles II** depicts him in fetching Roman garb. Back on the High Street, beside a bloated memorial to the fifth Duke of Buccleuch, the brickwork pattern set in the pavement is known as the **Heart of Midlothian**. Immortalized in Scott's novel of the same name, it marks the site of a demolished tollbooth; you may see passers-by spitting on it for luck. Public proclamations have traditionally been read from the **Mercat Cross** at the back of St Giles. The present structure, adorned with coats of arms and topped by a sculpture of a unicorn, looks venerable enough, but most of it is little more than a hundred years old, a gift to the city from nineteenth-century prime minister, William Ewart Gladstone.

High Street: the western block
The third section of the Royal Mile proper is known as **High Street**, and occupies two blocks on either side of the intersection between North Bridge and South Bridge. Directly opposite the Mercat Cross, the U-shaped **City Chambers** were designed by John Adam, brother of Robert, as the Royal Exchange. Local traders never warmed to the exchange, however, so the town council established its headquarters there instead. Beneath the City Chambers lies **Mary King's Close**, one of Edinburgh's most unusual attractions. Built in the early sixteenth century, it was closed off for many years after the devastation of the 1645 plague, before being entirely covered up by the chambers in 1753. For many years tours of the close were occasional and sporadic, but are now taking place more frequently(contact Mercat Tours on☎661 4541 for details). A little further down the street is **Anchor Close**, site of the printing works of William Smellie, who published the first ever edition of the *Encyclopaedia Britannica* there in 1768.

Across the road is the **Tron Kirk**, best known as the favourite rendezvous for hardy Hogmanay revellers. The church was built in the 1630s to accommodate the Presbyterian congregation ejected from St Giles when the latter became the seat of a bishop; the spire is an 1820s replacement for one destroyed by fire. The Tron remained in use as a church until 1952. It was then closed for forty years, during which time excavations revealed sections of an old close, Marlin's Wynd, which ran from High Street down to the Cowgate.

High Street: the eastern block

Beyond the intersection of North Bridge and South Bridge back on the northern side of High Street, is **Paisley Close**, above whose entrance is a bust of a youth with the inscription "Heave awa' chaps, I'm no' dead yet", uttered in 1861 by a boy trapped by rubble following the collapse of a tenement in the close, and who was subsequently dug out by rescue workers.

In Chalmers Close, just to the west, **Trinity Apse** is a poignant reminder of the fifteenth-century Holy Trinity Collegiate Church, formerly one of Edinburgh's most outstanding buildings, but demolished in 1848 to make way for an extension to Waverley Station. The stones were carefully numbered and stored on Calton Hill so that it could be reassembled at a later date, but many were pilfered before sufficient funds became available, and only the apse could be reconstructed on this new site. A few years ago, it was transformed into a **Brass Rubbing Centre** (June–Sept Mon–Sat 10am–6pm; Oct–May Mon–Sat 10am–5pm; Sun 2–5pm during the Festival only; free), where you can rub your own impressions from Pictish crosses for around 40p.

On the other side of High Street, the noisy **Museum of Childhood** (Mon–Sat: June–Sept 10am–6pm; Oct–May 10am–5pm; also Sun 2–5pm during the Festival; free) was, oddly enough, founded by an eccentric local councillor who disliked children. Although he claimed that the museum was a serious social archive for adults, and dedicated it to King Herod, it has always attracted swarms of kids, who delight in the dolls' houses, teddy bears, train sets, marionettes and other paraphernalia.

Almost directly opposite is what's thought to be the city's oldest surviving dwelling, the early sixteenth-century **Moubray House** (closed to the public). The uses of the four-storeyed house have included tavern, bookshop and even, towards the end of the nineteenth century, temperance hotel. It also served as Daniel Defoe's office during his stay as an English government representative in 1707. Next door lies the picturesque **John Knox's House** (Mon–Sat 10am–4.30pm; £1.75), built some thirty years later. With its outside stairway, biblical motto, and sundial adorned with a statue of Moses, it gives a good impression of how the Royal Mile must have once looked. Whether or not it was ever really the home of Knox is debatable: he may have moved here for safety at the height of the religious troubles. The house did, however, once belong to goldsmith James Mosman, son of the designer of the Scottish crown, who was executed for his dogged loyalty to Knox's *bête noire*, Mary, Queen of Scots. The rather bare interiors, which give a good idea of the labyrinthine layout of Old Town houses, display explanatory material on Knox's life and career.

Canongate

For over seven hundred years, the district through which Canongate runs was a burgh in its own right, officially separate from the capital. In recent decades, it has been the subject of some of the most ambitious restoration programmes in the Old Town, two notable examples of which can be seen at the top of the street. On the south side is the residential **Chessel's Court**, a mid-eighteenth-century development with fanciful Rococo chimneys. It was formerly the site of the Excise Office, scene of the robbery that led to the arrest and execution of Deacon Brodie. Over the road the **Morocco Land** is a reasonably faithful reproduction of an old tenement, incorporating the original bust of a Moor from which its name derived.

Dominated by a turreted steeple, the late sixteenth-century **Canongate Tolbooth** (June–Sept Mon–Sat 10am–6pm; Oct–May 10am–5pm, Sun 2–5pm during the Festival only; free), a little further down the north side of the street, has served both as the headquarters of the burgh administration and as a prison, and now houses **The People's Story**, a lively museum devoted to the everyday life and work of Edinburgh people down the centuries, with sounds and tableaux on various aspects of city living – including a typical Edinburgh pub. Next door, **Canongate Kirk** was built in the 1680s to house the congregation expelled from Holyrood Abbey when the latter was commandeered by James VII (James II in England) to serve as the chapel for the Order of the Thistle. It's a curiously archaic design, still Renaissance in outline, and built to a cruciform plan wholly at odds with the ideals and requirements of Protestant worship. Its churchyard, one of the city's most exclusive cemeteries, commands a superb view across to Calton Hill. Among those buried here are Adam Smith, Mrs Agnes McLehose (better known as Robert Burns' "Clarinda") and Robert Fergusson, regarded by some as Edinburgh's greatest poet, despite his death at the age of 24; his headstone was donated by Burns, a fervent admirer, who also wrote the inscription.

Opposite the church, the local history museum in **Huntly House** (June–Sept Mon–Sat 10am–6pm; Oct–May Mon–Sat 10am–5pm; Sun 2–5pm during the Festival only; free) includes a quirky array of old shop signs, some dating back to the eighteenth century, as well as displays on indigenous industries such as glass, silver, pottery and clockmaking, and on the dubious military career of Earl Haig. Also on view is the original version of the National Covenant of 1638; modern science has failed to resolve whether or not some of the signatories signed with their own blood, as tradition has it.

Among the several fine seventeenth-century mansions on the easternmost stretch of Canongate, **Panmure House** was for a time the home of Adam Smith, father of the science of political economy and unwitting guru of latter-day Conservatism. At the very foot of the street, the entrance to the residential **Whitehorse Close** was once the site of the inn from where stagecoaches began the journey to London. Stridently quaint, it drips with all the most characteristic features of Scottish vernacular architecture, crow-stepped gables, dormer windows, overhanging upper storeys and curving outside stairways.

Holyrood

At the foot of Canongate lies **Holyrood**, Edinburgh's royal quarter, the **legend** of whose foundation in 1128 is described in a fifteenth-century manuscript which is still kept there. The story goes that King David I, son of Malcolm Canmore and St Margaret, went out hunting one day and was suddenly confronted by a stag who threw him from his horse and seemed ready to gore him. In desperation, the king tried to protect himself by grasping its antlers, but instead found himself holding a crucifix, whereupon the animal ran off. In a dream that night, he heard a voice commanding him to "make a house for Canons devoted to the Cross"; he duly obeyed, naming the abbey Holyrood (rood being an alternative name for a cross). More likely, however, is that David, the most pious of all Scotland's monarchs, simply acquired a relic of the True Cross and decided to build a suitable home for it.

ADMISSIONS TO HOLYROOD

Guided tours of Holyrood only take place from November to March; at other times of the year, visitors are free to move at their own pace. It is worth remembering that Holyrood is still a working palace, so the buildings are closed to the public for long periods during state functions; you won't be able to visit for a fortnight in the middle of May, and during the annual royal visit which usually takes place in the last two weeks of June and the first in July.

Holyrood soon became a favoured **royal residence**, its situation in a secluded valley making it far more agreeable than the draughty Castle. At first, monarchs lodged in the monastic guest house, to which a wing for the exclusive use of the court was added during the reign of James II. This was transformed into a full-blown palace for James IV, which in turn was replaced by a much larger building for Charles II, although he never actually lived there. Indeed, it was something of a white elephant until Queen Victoria started making regular trips to her northern kingdom, a custom that has been maintained by her successors.

The precincts

On the north side of **Abbey Strand**, which forms a sort of processional way linking Canongate with Holyrood, Abbey Lairds is a four-storey sixteenth-century mansion which once served as a home for aristocratic debtors and is now occupied by royal flunkies during the summer seat of the court.

Legend has it that Mary, Queen of Scots used to bathe in sweet white wine in the curious little turreted structure nearby known as **Queen Mary's Bath House**; it is more likely, however, that it was either a summer pavilion or a dovecote. Its architecture is mirrored in the **Croft an Righ**, a picturesque L-shaped house in a quiet, generally overlooked corner beside the eastern wall of the complex.

The Palace of Holyroodhouse

In its present form, the **Palace of Holyroodhouse** (April–Oct Mon–Sat 9.30am–5.15pm, Sun 10am–4.30pm; Nov–March daily 9.30am–3.45pm; £5.20) is largely a seventeenth-century creation, planned for Charles II. However, the tower house of the old palace was skilfully incorporated to form the northwestern block, with a virtual mirror image of it erected as a counterbalance at the other end. The three-storey **courtyard** is an early exercise in Palladian style, exhibiting a punctiliously accurate knowledge of the main Classical orders to create a sense of absolute harmony and unity.

Inside, the **State Apartments**, as Charles II's palace is known, are decked out with oak panelling, tapestries, portraits and decorative paintings, all overshadowed by the magnificent white stucco **ceilings**, especially in the Morning Drawing Room. The most eye-catching chamber, however, is the **Great Gallery**, which takes up the entire first floor of the northern wing. During the 1745 sojourn of the Young Pretender this was the setting for a banquet, described in detail in Scott's novel *Waverley*, and it is still used for big ceremonial occasions. Along the walls are 89 portraits commissioned from the seventeenth-century Dutch artist Jacob de Wet to illustrate the royal lineage of Scotland from its mythical origins in the fourth century BC; the result is unintentionally hilarious, as it is clear that the artist's imagination was taxed to bursting point by the need to paint so many different facial types without having an inkling as to what the subjects actually looked like. In the adjacent **King's Closet**, de Wet's *The Finding of Moses* provides a biblical link to the portraits, the Scottish royal family claiming descent from Scota, the Egyptian pharaoh's daughter who discovered Moses in the bulrushes.

The oldest parts of the palace, the **Historical Apartments**, are mainly of note for their associations with Mary, Queen of Scots and in particular for the brutal murder, organized by her husband, Lord Darnley, of her private secretary, David Rizzio, who was stabbed 56 times and dragged from the small closet, through the Queen's Bedchamber, and into the Outer Chamber. Until a few years ago, visitors were shown apparently indelible bloodstains on the floor of the latter, but these are now admitted to be fakes, and have been covered up. A display cabinet in the same room shows some pieces of **needlework** woven by the deposed queen while in English captivity; another case has an outstanding **miniature portrait** of her by the French court painter, François Clouet.

Holyrood Abbey

In the grounds of the Palace are the wonderfully evocative ruins of **Holyrood Abbey**. Of King David's original Norman church, the only surviving fragment is a doorway in the far southeastern corner. Most of the remainder dates from a late twelfth- and early thirteenth-century rebuilding in the Early Gothic style.

The surviving parts of the **west front**, including one of the twin towers and the elaborately carved entrance portal, show how resplendent the abbey must once have been. Unfortunately, its sacking by the English in 1547, followed by the demolition of the transept and chancel during the Reformation, all but destroyed the building. Charles I attempted to restore some semblance of unity by ordering the erection of the great east window and a new stone roof, but the latter collapsed in 1768, causing grievous damage to the rest of the structure. By this time, the Canongate congregation had another place of worship, and schemes to rebuild the abbey were abandoned.

Holyrood Park

Holyrood Park – or Queen's Park – a natural wilderness in the very heart of the modern city, is unquestionably one of Edinburgh's main assets, as locals (though relatively few tourists) readily appreciate. Packed into an area no more than five miles in diameter is an amazing variety of landscapes – mountains, crags, moorland, marshes, glens, lochs and fields – representing something of a microcosm of Scotland's scenery. The **Queen's Drive** circles the park, enabling many of its features to be seen by car, though you really need to stroll around to appreciate it fully.

Opposite the southern gates of the Palace a pathway, nicknamed the Radical Road, traverses the ridge immediately below the **Salisbury Crags**, one of the main features of the Edinburgh skyline. Even though there is no path, you can walk along the top of the basalt crags, from where there are excellent views of the Palace of Holyroodhouse and Holyrood Abbey. After the Salisbury Crags, Queen's Drive makes a sharp switchback, passing beneath **Samson's Ribs**, a group of basalt pillars strikingly reminiscent of the Hebridean island of Staffa (see p.298). It continues onto **Duddingston Loch**, the only natural stretch of water in the park, now a bird sanctuary. Perched above it, just outside the park boundary, **Duddingston Kirk** dates back in part to the twelfth century and serves as the focus of one of the most unspoilt old villages within modern Edinburgh.

Following Queen's Drive in the other direction from the Palace gates, you arrive at **St Margaret's Loch**, a nineteenth-century man-made pond, above which stand the scanty ruins of **St Anthony's Chapel**, another fine vantage point. From here, the road's loop is one-way only, ascending to **Dunsapie Loch**, again an artificial stretch of water, which makes an excellent foil to the eponymous crag behind.

This is the usual starting point for the ascent of **Arthur's Seat**, a majestic extinct volcano rising 823ft above sea level. The seat is Edinburgh's single most prominent landmark, resembling a huge crouched lion when seen from the west. The climb from Dunsapie, up a grassy slope, followed by a rocky path near the summit, is considerably less arduous than it looks, and is a fairly straightforward twenty-minute walk, though there are several other, somewhat longer and more taxing ways up from other points in the park. The views from the top are all you'd expect, covering the entire city and much of the Firth of Forth; on a clear day, you can even see the southernmost mountains of the Highlands. The composer, Felix Mendelssohn, climbed Arthur's Seat in July 1829, noting: "It is beautiful here! In the evening a cool breeze is wafted from the sea, and then all objects appear clearly and sharply defined against the gray sky; the lights from the windows glitter brilliantly." As there is little reason to associate it with the British king of the Holy Grail legends, there's no satisfactory story to explain the name.

The rest of the Old Town

Although most visitors to the Old Town understandably concentrate on the Royal Mile, the area has many other intriguing, and less commercial, corners.

Cowgate

Immediately south of the Royal Mile, and following a roughly parallel course from the Lawnmarket to St Mary's Street, is **Cowgate**. One of Edinburgh's oldest surviving streets, it was also formerly one of the city's most prestigious addresses. However, the construction of the great **viaducts** linking the Old and New Towns entombed it below street level, condemning it to decay and neglect and leading the nineteenth-century writer, Alexander Smith, to declare that "the condition of the inhabitants is as little known to respectable Edinburgh as are the habits of moles, earthworms, and the mining population". In the last decade or so Cowgate has experienced something of a revival, though few tourists venture here and the contrast with the neighbouring Royal Mile remains stark.

At the corner with Niddry Street, which runs down from the eastern block of High Street, the unprepossessing **St Cecilia's Hall** (Wed & Sat 2–5pm; £3) was built in the 1760s for the Musical Society of Edinburgh. Inside, Scotland's oldest and most beautiful concert room, oval in shape and set under a shallow dome, makes a perfect venue for concerts of Baroque and early music, held during the Festival and occasionally at other times of the year. The building is primarily worth visiting for the **Russell Collection** of antique keyboard instruments.

Towards the western end of Cowgate stands the **Magdalen Chapel** (Mon–Fri 9.30am–4.30pm; free), a sixteenth-century almshouse under the jurisdiction of the Incorporation of Hammermen, a guild to which most Edinburgh workers, other than goldsmiths, belonged. A few years later, as one of the focal points of the Reformation, it was probably the setting for the first ever General Assembly of the Church of Scotland. The Hammermen added a handsome tower and steeple in the 1620s, and later transformed the chapel into their guildhall, which was suitably adorned with fine ironwork. However, the main feature of the interior is the only significant pre-Reformation stained glass in Scotland still in its original location. That it escaped the iconoclasts is probably due to the fact that it is purely heraldic.

Grassmarket and George IV Bridge

At its western end, Cowgate opens out into **Grassmarket**, which has played an important role in the murkier aspects of Edinburgh's turbulent history. The public gallows were located here, and it was the scene of numerous riots and other disturbances down the centuries. It was here, in 1736, that Captain Porteous was lynched after he had ordered shots to be fired at the crowd watching a public execution. The notorious duo William Burke and William Hare had their lair in a now-vanished close just off the western end of Grassmarket, luring to it victims whom they murdered with the intention of selling their bodies to the eminent physician Robert Knox. Eventually, Hare betrayed his partner, who was duly executed in 1829, and Knox's career was finished off as a result. Today, Grassmarket can still be seamy, though the cluster of busy bars and restaurants along its northern side are evidence of a serious attempt to clean up its image.

At the northeastern corner of Grassmarket are five old tenements of the old **West Bow**, which formerly zigzagged up to the Royal Mile. The rest of this was replaced in the 1840s by the curving **Victoria Street**, an unusual two-tier thoroughfare, with arcaded shops below, and a pedestrian terrace above. This sweeps up to **George IV Bridge** and the **National Library of Scotland** which holds a rich collection of illuminated manuscripts, early printed books, historical documents, and the letters and papers of prominent Scottish literary figures, displayed in regularly changing thematic exhibitions (usually Mon–Sat 10am–5pm, Sun 2–5pm; free).

Greyfriars and around

The **statue of Greyfriars Bobby** at the southwestern corner of **George IV Bridge** must rank as Edinburgh's most sentimental tourist attraction. Bobby was a Skye terrier acquired as a working dog by a police constable named John Gray. When the latter died in 1858, Bobby began a vigil on his grave which he maintained until he died fourteen years later. In the process, he became an Edinburgh celebrity, fed and cared for by locals who gave him a special collar (now in the Huntly House Museum; see p.74) to prevent him being impounded as a stray. His statue, originally a fountain, was modelled from life, and erected soon after his death; his story has gained international renown, thanks to a spate of cloying books and tear-jerking movies.

The grave Bobby mourned over is in the **Greyfriars Kirkyard**, which among its clutter of grandiose seventeenth- and eighteenth-century funerary monuments boasts the striking mausoleum of the Adam family of architects. Greyfriars is particularly associated with the long struggle to establish presbyterianism in Scotland: in 1638, it was the setting for the signing of the National Covenant, while in 1679 some 1200 Covenanters were imprisoned in the enclosure at the southwestern end of the yard. Set against the northern wall is the Martyrs' Monument, a defiantly worded memorial commemorating all those who died in pursuit of the eventual victory.

The graveyard rather overshadows **Greyfriars Kirk** itself, completed in 1620 as the first new church in Edinburgh since the Reformation. It's a real oddball in both layout and design, having a nave and aisles but no chancel, and adopting the anachronistic architectural language of the friary that preceded it, complete with medieval-looking windows, arches and buttresses.

At the western end of Greyfriars Kirkyard is one of the most significant surviving portions of the **Flodden Wall**, the city fortifications erected in the wake of Scotland's disastrous military defeat of 1513. When open, the gateway beyond offers a short cut to **George Heriot's Hospital**, otherwise approached from Lauriston Place to the south. Founded as a home for poor boys by "Jinglin Geordie" Heriot, James VI's goldsmith, it is now one of Edinburgh's most prestigious fee-paying schools; although you can't go inside, you can wander round the quadrangle, whose array of towers, turrets, chimneys, carved doorways and traceried windows is one of the finest achievements of the Scottish Renaissance.

The Royal Museum of Scotland

On the south side of Chambers Street, which runs east from Greyfriars Bobby, stands the **Royal Museum of Scotland** (Mon–Sat 10am–5pm, Sun noon–5pm; free), a dignified Venetian-style palace with a cast-iron interior modelled on that of the Crystal Palace in London. Intended as Scotland's answer to the museum complex in London's South Kensington, it contains an extraordinarily eclectic range of exhibits; the scope will be broader still after the completion of a huge annexe in November 1998, when many items previously kept either in storage or at the Museum of Antiquities will be displayed. Among the most precious items to look out for in the new annexe are artefacts from the **prehistoric, Roman** and **Viking** eras and the famous **ivory chessmen** from the island of Lewis.

The **sculpture** in the lofty entrance hall begins with a superb Assyrian relief from the royal palace at Nimrud, and ranges via Classical Greece, Rome and Nubia to Buddhas from Japan and Burma and a totem pole from British Columbia. Also on the ground floor are collections of stuffed animals and birds, and a predominantly hands-on **technology** section featuring classic pieces of machinery of the Industrial Revolution. These include a double-action beam engine designed by James Watt in

1786; the *Wylam Dilly* of 1813, twin of the *Puffing Billy*; and the 1896 *Hawk Glider*, the earliest British flying machine. Upstairs there's a fine array of Egyptian mummies, ceramics from ancient Greece to the present day, costumes, jewellery, natural-history displays and a splendid selection of European decorative art ranging from early medieval liturgical objects via Limoges enamels and sixteenth-century German wood-carving to stunning **French silverware** made during the reign of Louis XIV. Finally, on the top floor, you'll come to a distinguished collection of historic scientific instruments, a small selection of arms and armour, plus sections on geology, fossils, ethnology, and the arts of Islam, Japan and China.

The University of Edinburgh
Immediately alongside the Royal Museum is the earliest surviving part of the **University of Edinburgh**, variously referred to as Old College or Old Quad, although nowadays it houses only a few University departments; the main campus colonizes the streets and squares to the south.

The Old College was designed by Robert Adam, but built after his death in a considerably modified form by William Playfair (1789–1857), one of Edinburgh's greatest architects. Playfair built just one of Adam's two quadrangles (the dome was not added until 1879) and his magnificent Upper Library is now mostly used for ceremonial occasions. The **Talbot Rice Art Gallery** (Tues–Sat noon–5pm; free), housed in the Old College, includes many splendid seventeenth-century works from the Low Countries, with Teniers, Steen and van de Velde well represented. There are also some outstanding bronzes, notably the *Anatomical Horse* by an unknown Italian sculptor of the High Renaissance, and *Cain Killing Abel* by the Dutch Mannerist Adrian de Vries.

The New Town

The **NEW TOWN**, itself well over two hundred years old, stands in total contrast to the Old Town: the layout is symmetrical, the streets broad and straight, and most of the buildings are Neoclassical. Originally intended to be residential, the entire area, right down to the names of its streets, is something of a celebration of the Union, which was then generally regarded as a proud development in Scotland's history. Today the New Town is the bustling hub of the city's professional, commercial and business life, dominated by shops, banks and offices.

The existence of the New Town is chiefly due to the vision of **George Drummond**, who made schemes for the expansion of the city soon after becoming Lord Provost in 1725. Work began on the draining of the Nor' Loch below the Castle in 1759, a job that was to last some sixty years. The North Bridge, linking the Old Town with the port of Leith, was built between 1763 and 1772 and, in 1766, following a public competition, a plan for the New Town by a 22-year-old architect, **James Craig**, was chosen. Its grid-iron pattern was perfectly matched to the site: the central George Street, flanked by showpiece squares, was laid out along the main ridge, with the parallel Princes Street and Queen Street on either side below, and two smaller streets, Thistle Street and Rose Street in between the three major thoroughfares to provide coach houses, artisans' dwellings and shops. Princes and Queen streets were built up on one side only, so as not to block the spectacular views of the Old Town and Fife. Architects were accordingly afforded a wonderful opportunity to play with vistas and spatial relationships, particularly well exploited by Robert Adam, who contributed extensively to the later phases of the work. The First New Town, as the area covered by Craig's plan came to be known, received a whole series of extensions in the first few decades of the nineteenth century, all carefully in harmony with the Neoclassical idiom.

In many ways, the layout of the New Town is its own most remarkable sight, an extraordinary grouping of squares, circuses, terraces, crescents and parks with a few set pieces such as **Register House**, the north frontage of **Charlotte Square** and the assemblage of curiosities on and around **Calton Hill**. However, it also contains an assortment of Victorian additions, notably the **Scott Monument**, as well as two of the city's most important public collections – the **National Gallery of Scotland**, and the **Scottish National Gallery of Modern Art**.

Princes Street

Although only allocated a subsidiary role in the original plan of the New Town, **Princes Street** had developed into Edinburgh's principal thoroughfare by the middle of the last century, a role it has retained ever since. Its unobstructed views across to the Castle and the Old Town are undeniably magnificent. Indeed, without the views, Princes Street would lose much of its appeal; its northern side, dominated by ugly department stores, is almost always crowded with shoppers, and few of the original eighteenth-century buildings remain.

It was the coming of the railway, which follows a parallel course to the south, that ensured Princes Street's rise to prominence. The tracks are well concealed at the far end of the sunken **gardens** that replaced the Nor' Loch, which provide ample space to relax or picnic during the summer. Thomas de Quincey (1785–1859), author of the classic account of drug addiction, *Confessions of an English Opium Eater* (published in 1821), spent the last thirty years of his life in Edinburgh and is buried in the graveyard of St Cuthbert's Church, beneath the castle at the western end of the gardens.

The East End

Register House (Mon–Fri 10am–4pm; free), Princes Street's most distinguished building, is at its extreme northeastern corner, framing the perspective down North Bridge, and providing a good visual link between the Old and New Towns. Unfortunately, the majesty of the setting is marred by the **St James Centre** to the rear, a covered shopping arcade now regarded as the city's worst ever planning blunder. Register House was designed in the 1770s by Robert Adam to hold Scotland's historic records, a function it has maintained ever since. Its exterior is a model of restrained Neoclassicism; the interior, centred on a glorious Roman rotunda, has a dome lavishly decorated with plasterwork and antique-style medallions.

Opposite is one of the few buildings on the south side of Princes Street, the **Balmoral Hotel**, formerly known as the *North British*. Among the most luxurious hotels in the city, it has always been associated with the railway, and the timepiece on its bulky clock tower is always kept two minutes fast in order to encourage passengers to hurry to catch their trains. Alongside the hotel, the **Waverley Market** is a sensitive modern redevelopment that carefully avoided repeating the mistakes of the St James Centre. Its roof makes an excellent open-air piazza, a favourite haunt of street theatre groups and other performing artists during the Festival.

The Scott Monument and the Royal Scottish Academy

Facing the Victorian shopping emporium Jenners, and set within East Princes Street Gardens, the 200ft-high **Scott Monument** (daily: Oct–March 9am–3pm; April–Sept 9am–6pm; £1.50) was erected by public subscription in memory of the writer within a few years of his death. The largest monument in the world to a man of letters, its magisterial, spire-like design is due to George Meikle Kemp, a carpenter and joiner whose only building this is; while it was still under construction, he stumbled into a canal one foggy evening and drowned. The architecture is closely modelled on Scott's beloved Melrose Abbey (see p.128), while the rich sculptural decoration shows 16 Scottish writers and 64 characters from the *Waverley* novels. Underneath the archway is a **statue** of Scott with his deerhound Maida, carved from a thirty-ton block of Carrara marble.

The monument's blackened condition is a pity, and it was recently hidden under shrouds for two years while studies were carried out as to the possibility of cleaning it by sandblasting, a technique successfully applied to many of Edinburgh's other historic buildings. This exercise divided professional opinion, some believing the monument to be too slender to stand up to the treatment. Eventually, it was decided that cleaning would not go ahead.

The Princes Street Gardens are bisected by the **Mound**, which provides a road link between the Old and New Towns. Its name is an accurate description: it was formed in the 1780s by dumping piles of earth brought from the New Town's building plots. At the foot of the Mound, Playfair's **Royal Scottish Academy** (Mon–Sat 10am–5pm, Sun 2–5pm; price varies) is a Grecian-style Doric temple used somewhat infrequently for temporary exhibitions during the year, notably for the RSA annual exhibition held from April to July.

The National Gallery of Scotland
To the rear of the Royal Scottish Academy the **National Gallery of Scotland** (Mon–Sat 10am–5pm, Sun 2–5pm; free) is another Playfair construction, built in the 1840s and now housing a choice display of Old Masters, many of which belong to the Duke of Sutherland. The knowledgeable staff wear tartan trousers, one of a series of innovations introduced by the flamboyant English director, Timothy Clifford. A few years ago, and more controversially, the original Playfair rooms on the ground floor were restored to their 1840s appearance, with the pictures hung closely together, often on two levels, and intermingled with sculptures and *objets d'art* to produce a deliberately cluttered effect (some lesser works, which would otherwise languish in the vaults, are a good 15ft up). Two small, late nineteenth-century works in Room 12 – one anonymous, the other by A E Moffat – show the gallery as it was, with paintings stacked up even higher than at present.

Though individual works are frequently rearranged, the layout is broadly chronological, starting in the upper rooms above the entrance, and continuing clockwise around the ground floor. The upper part of the rear extension is devoted to smaller panels of the eighteenth and nineteenth centuries, while the basement contains the majority of the Scottish collection.

EARLY NETHERLANDISH AND GERMAN WORKS
Among the gallery's most valuable treasures are the *Trinity Panels*, the remaining parts of the only surviving pre-Reformation altarpiece made for a Scottish church. Painted by **Hugo van der Goes** in the mid-fifteenth century, they were commissioned for the Holy Trinity Collegiate Church by its provost Edward Bonkil, who appears in the company of organ-playing angels in the finest and best preserved of the four panels. On the reverse sides are portraits of James III, his son (the future James IV) and Queen Margaret of Denmark. Their feebly characterized heads, which stand in jarring contrast to the superlative figures of the patron saints accompanying them, were modelled from life by an unknown local painter after the altar had been shipped to Edinburgh.

Of the later Netherlandish works, **Gerard David** is represented by the touchingly anecdotal *Three Legends of St Nicholas*, while the *Portrait of a Notary* by **Quentin Massys** is an excellent early example of northern European assimilation of the forms and techniques of the Italian Renaissance. Many of his German contemporaries developed their own variations on this style, among them **Cranach**, by whom there is a splendidly erotic *Venus and Cupid*, and **Holbein**, whose *Allegory of the Old and New Testaments* is a Protestant tract painted for an English patron.

ITALIAN RENAISSANCE WORKS

The Italian section includes a wonderful array of **Renaissance** masterpieces. Of these, *The Virgin Adoring the Child* is a beautiful composition set against a ruined architectural background shown in strict perspective: although known to have been painted in the workshop of the great Florentine sculptor **Andrea del Verrocchio**, its authorship remains a mystery. Equally graceful are the three works by **Raphael**, particularly *The Bridgewater Madonna* and the tondo of *The Holy Family with a Palm Tree*, whose striking luminosity has been revealed after recent restoration.

Of the four mythological scenes by **Titian**, the sensuous *Three Ages of Man*, an allegory of childhood, adulthood and old age, is one of the most accomplished compositions of his early period, while the later *Venus Anadyomene* ranks among the great nudes of Western art, notwithstanding its rough state of preservation. The companion pair of *Diana and Acteon* and *Diana and Calisto*, painted for Philip II of Spain, show the almost impressionistic freedom of his late style. **Bassano**'s truly regal *Adoration of the Kings*, a dramatic altarpiece of *The Descent from the Cross* by **Tintoretto**, and several other works by **Veronese**, complete a fine Venetian collection.

SEVENTEENTH-CENTURY SOUTHERN EUROPEAN WORKS

Among the seventeenth-century works is the gallery's most important sculpture, **Bernini**'s *Bust of Monsignor Carlo Antonio dal Pozzo*. **El Greco**'s *A Fable*, painted during his early years in Italy, is a mysterious subject whose exact meaning is unclear, while *The Saviour of the World* is a typically intense, visionary image from his mature years in Spain. Indigenous Spanish art is represented by **Velázquez**'s *An Old Woman Cooking Eggs*, an astonishingly assured work for a lad of 19, and by **Zurbaran**'s *The Immaculate Conception*, part of his ambitious decorative scheme of the Carthusian monastery in Jerez. There are two small copper panels by the short-lived but enormously influential Rome-based German painter **Adam Elsheimer**; of these, *Il Contento*, showing Jupiter's descent to earth to punish the ungodly, is a *tour de force* of technical precision.

The series of *The Seven Sacraments* by **Poussin** are displayed in their own room, whose floor and central octagaonal seat repeat, albeit loosely, some of the motifs in the paintings. Based on the artist's own extensive research into biblical times, the set marks the first attempt to portray scenes from the life of Jesus and the early Christians in an authentic manner, rather than one overlaid by artistic conventions. The result is profoundly touching, with a myriad of imaginative and subtle details. Poussin's younger contemporary **Claude**, who likewise left France to live in Rome, is represented by his largest canvas, *Landscape with Apollo, the Muses and a River God*, which radiates his characteristically idealized vision of Classical antiquity.

SEVENTEENTH-CENTURY FLEMISH AND DUTCH WORKS

Rubens' *The Feast of Herod* is an archetypal example of his grand manner, in which the gory subject matter is overshadowed by the lively depiction of the delights of the table; the painting's rich colours have been revived by recent restoration. Like all his large works, it was executed with extensive studio assistance, whereas the three small *modellos*, including the highly finished *Adoration of the Shepherds*, are all from his own hand. The trio of large upright canvases by **Van Dyck** date from his early Genoese period; of these, *The Lomellini Family* shows his mastery at creating a definitive dynastic image.

Among the four canvases by **Rembrandt** is a poignant *Self-Portrait Aged 51*, and the ripely suggestive *Woman in Bed*, which probably represents the biblical figure of Sarah on her wedding night, waiting for her husband Tobias to put the devil to flight. *Christ in the House of Martha and Mary* is the largest and probably the earliest of the thirty or so surviving paintings of **Vermeer**; as the only one with a religious subject, it inspired a notorious series of forgeries by Han van Meegeren. By **Hals** are a typical pair of portraits plus a brilliant caricature, *Verdonck*. There's also an excellent cross section of the specialist Dutch painters of the age, highlights being the mischievous *School for Boys* *and Girls* by **Jan Steen**, and the strangely haunting *Interior of the Church of St Bavo in Haarlem* by **Pieter Saenredam**, one of the gallery's most expensive purchases.

EUROPEAN WORKS OF THE EIGHTEENTH AND NINETEENTH CENTURIES

Of the large-scale eighteenth-century works, **Tiepolo**'s *The Finding of Moses*, a gloriously bravura fantasy (the Pharaoh's daughter and her attendants appear in sixteenth-century garb) stands out; despite its enormous size, it has lost a sizeable portion from the right-hand side. Other decorative compositions of the same period are **Goya**'s *The Doctor*, a cartoon for a tapestry design, and the three large upright pastoral scenes by **Boucher**. However, the gems of the French section are the smaller panels, in particular **Watteau**'s *Fêtes Vénitiennes*, an effervescent Rococo idyll, and **Chardin**'s *Vase of Flowers*, a copybook example of still-life painting. One of the gallery's most recent major purchases is **Canova**'s 1817 statue, *The Three Graces* – saved at the last minute from the hands of the J Paul Getty Museum in California.

There's also a superb group of Impressionist and Post-Impressionist masterpieces, including a particularly good cross section of the works of **Degas**, not least his seminal *Portrait of Diego Martelli*, depicting the Florentine critic who was one of the most fervent early champions of Impressionism. Also on display are three outstanding examples of **Gauguin**, set respectively in Brittany, Martinique and Tahiti, and **Cézanne**'s *The Tall Trees* – a clear forerunner of modern abstraction.

ENGLISH AND AMERICAN WORKS

Surprisingly, the gallery has relatively few English paintings, but those here are impressive. **Hogarth**'s *Sarah Malcolm*, painted in Newgate Prison the day the murderess was executed, once belonged to Horace Walpole, who also commissioned **Reynolds**' *The Ladies Waldegrave*, a group portrait of his three great-nieces. **Gainsborough**'s *The Honourable Mrs Graham* is one of his most memorable society portraits, while **Constable** himself described *Dedham Vale* as being "perhaps my best". There are two prime Roman views by **Turner**, by whom the gallery owns a wonderful array of watercolours, faithfully displayed each January, when the light is at its weakest.

Even more unexpected than the scarcity of English works is the presence of some exceptional American canvases: **Benjamin West**'s Romantic fantasy, *King Alexander III Rescued from a Stag*; **John Singer Sargent**'s virtuosic *Lady Agnew of Lochnaw*; and **Frederic Edwin Church**'s *View of Niagara Falls from the American Side*. The latter, having been kept in store for decades, was put back on display when the "rediscovery" of the artist in the late 1970s prompted astronomical bids from American museums keen to acquire the only work by the artist owned by a European gallery.

SCOTTISH WORKS

On the face of it, the gallery's Scottish collection, which shows the entire gamut of Scottish painting from seventeenth-century portraiture to the Arts and Crafts movement, is something of an anticlimax. There are, however, some important works displayed within a broad European context; **Gavin Hamilton**'s *Achilles Mourning the Death of Patroclus*, for example, painted in Rome, is an unquestionably arresting image. **Allan Ramsay**, who became court painter to George III, is represented by his intimate *The Artist's Second Wife* and *Jean-Jacques Rousseau*, in which the philosopher is shown in Armenian costume.

Of **Sir Henry Raeburn**'s large portraits, note the swaggering masculinity of *Sir John Sinclair* or *Colonel Alistair MacDonell of Glengarry*, both of whom are shown in full Highland dress. Raeburn's technical mastery was equally sure when working on a small scale, as shown in one of the gallery's most popular pictures, *The Rev Robert Walker Skating on Duddingston Loch*.

Other Scottish painters represented include the versatile **Sir David Wilkie**, whose huge history painting, *Sir David Baird Discovering the Body of Sultan Tippo Saib*, is in marked contrast to the early documentary and genre scenes displayed in the basement, and **Alexander Nasmyth**, whose tendency to gild the lily can be seen in his *View of Tantallon Castle and the Bass Rock*, where the dramatic scenery is further spiced up by the inclusion of a shipwreck.

George Street

Just north and parallel to Princes Street is **George Street**, the city's chief financial thoroughfare and the least prepossessing of the main streets of the First New Town, built up on both sides with a preponderance of unsympathetic development. At its eastern end lies **St Andrew Square**, in the middle of which is the Melville Monument, a statue of Lord Melville, Pitt the Younger's Navy Treasurer. On the eastern side of the square stands a handsome eighteenth-century town mansion, designed by Sir William Chambers. Headquarters of the Royal Bank of Scotland since 1825, the palatial mid-nineteenth-century banking hall is a symbol of the success of the New Town. On the south side of the street, the oval-shaped church of **St Andrew** (now known as St Andrew and St George) is chiefly famous as the scene of the 1843 Disruption led by Thomas Chalmers, which split the Church of Scotland in two. Famous visitors to George Street have included Percy Bysshe Shelley, who stayed at no. 60 with the 16-year-old Harriet Westbrook during the summer of 1811, and Charles Dickens who gave a number of readings of his works in the Assembly Rooms in the 1840s and 1950s.

At the western end of the street, **Charlotte Square** was designed by Robert Adam in 1791, a year before his death. For the most part, his plans were faithfully implemented, an exception being the domed and porticoed church of St George, which was simplified on grounds of expense. Its interior was gutted in the 1960s and refurbished as **West Register House**; like its counterpart at the opposite end of Princes Street, it features changing documentary exhibitions (Mon–Fri 10am–4pm; free).

The **north side** of the square has deservedly become the most exclusive address in the city. No. 6 is the official residence of the Secretary of State for Scotland, while the upper storeys of no. 7 are the home of the Moderator of the General Assembly, the annually elected leader of the Church of Scotland. Restored by the NTS, the lower floors are open to the public under the name of the **Georgian House** (April–Oct Mon–Sat 10am–5pm, Sun 2–5pm; £4), whose contents give a good idea of what the house must have looked like during the period of the first owner, the head of the clan Lamont. The rooms are decked out in period furniture, including a working barrel organ which plays a selection of Scottish airs, and hung with fine paintings, including portraits by Ramsay and Raeburn, seventeenth-century Dutch cabinet pictures, and a beautiful *Marriage of the Virgin* by El Greco's teacher, the Italian miniaturist Giulio Clovio. In the basement are the original wine cellar, lined with roughly made bins, and a kitchen, complete with an open fire for roasting, and a separate oven for baking; video reconstructions of life below and above stairs are shown in a nearby room.

Queen Street

Queen Street, the last of the three main streets of the First New Town, is bordered to the north by gardens, and commands sweeping views across to Fife. Much the best preserved of the area's three main streets, its principal attraction is its excellent gallery-cum-museum.

The Scottish National Portrait Gallery
At the far eastern end of Queen Street is the **Scottish National Portrait Gallery** (Mon–Sat 10am–5pm, Sun 2–5pm; free). The building is itself a fascinating period piece,

its red sandstone exterior, modelled on the Doge's Palace in Venice, encrusted with statues of famous Scots – a theme taken up in the entrance hall, which has a mosaic-like frieze procession by William Hole of great figures from Scotland's past, with heroic murals by the same artist of stirring episodes from the nation's history adorning the balcony above. The Museum of Antiquities used to be housed here too, but its exhibits have now moved to the new annexe at the Royal Museum of Scotland (see p.78).

On the ground floor of the western wing an exhibition on the **Stewart dynasty** traces the history of the family from its origins as stewards (hence the name) to medieval royalty, via its zenith under James VI, who engineered the union with England, to its final demise under Bonnie Prince Charlie.

From the early periods, look out for two superb artefacts from the reign of Robert the Bruce, the **Kames Brooch** and the **Bute Mazer** (a large wooden bowl). An excellent collection of Mary, Queen of Scots memorabilia includes her **Penicuik Jewels** and a portrait by Rowland Lockey. The reign of Charles I is represented by several outstanding paintings by Flemish artists including **Daniel Mytens** and **Alexander Keirinocx**, and there are fine official portraits of the later Stewart monarchs and members of their entourage. Mementoes of the Young Pretender include the ornate backsword and silver-mounted shield with which he fought at Culloden, and a Rococo **canteen** he left abandoned on the battlefield.

The floors above the Stewart exhibition are devoted to **portraits**, accompanied by potted biographies, of famous Scots – a definition stretched to include anyone with the slightest Scottish connection. From the seventeenth century, there's an excellent Van Dyck portrait of Charles Seton, second Earl of Dunfermline, and the tartan-clad Lord Mungo Murray, who died in the disastrous attempt to establish a Scottish colony in Panama. Eighteenth-century highlights include portraits of the philosopher-historian David Hume by Allan Ramsay, and the bard Robert Burns by his friend Alexander Nasmyth, and a varied group by Raeburn: subjects include Sir Walter Scott, the fiddler Niel Gow and the artist himself. The star portrait from the nineteenth century is that of physician Sir Alexander Morison by his patient, the mad painter **Richard Dadd** – Edinburgh's fishing port of Newhaven is in the background. Twentieth-century portraits include a very angular Alec Douglas-Home, briefly prime minister in the 1960s, the stern figure of union leader Mick McGahey, soccer star Danny McGrain (in a kilt) and film-maker Bill Forsyth.

Calton

Of the various extensions to the New Town, the most intriguing is **Calton**, which branches out from the eastern end of Princes Street and encircles a volcanic hill. For years the centre of a thriving **gay** scene (see p.108), it is an area of extraordinary showpiece architecture, dating from the time of the Napoleonic Wars or just after, and intended as an ostentatious celebration of the British victory. While the predominantly Grecian architecture led to Calton being regarded as a Georgian Acropolis, it is, in fact, more of a shrine to local heroes.

Waterloo Place forms a ceremonial way from Princes Street to Calton Hill. On its southern side is the sombre and overgrown **Old Calton Burial Ground**, in which you can see Robert Adam's plain, cylindrical memorial to David Hume and a monument, complete with a statue of Abraham Lincoln, to the Scots who died in the American Civil War. Hard up against the cemetery's eastern wall, perched above a sheer rockface, is a picturesque castellated building which many visitors arriving at Waverley Station below imagine to be Edinburgh Castle itself. In fact, it's the only surviving part of the **Calton Gaol**, once Edinburgh's main prison. Next door is the massive **St Andrew's House**, built in the 1930s to house civil servants.

Further on, set majestically in a confined site below Calton Hill, is one of Edinburgh's greatest buildings, the Grecian **Old Royal High School**, frontrunner in the contest to be Scotland's new parliament building. Previously in the Old Town, the new site for Edinburgh's oldest school – alma mater to, among others, Robert Adam, Walter Scott and Alexander Graham Bell – was built by Thomas Hamilton, himself an old boy. Across the road, Hamilton also built the **Burns Monument**, a circular Corinthian temple modelled on the Monument to Lysicrates in Athens, as a memorial to the national bard.

Robert Louis Stevenson reckoned that **Calton Hill** was the best place to view Edinburgh, "since you can see the Castle, which you lose from the Castle, and Arthur's Seat, which you cannot see from Arthur's Seat". Though the panoramas from ground level are spectacular enough, those from the top of the **Nelson Monument** (April–Sept Mon 1–6pm, Tues–Sat 10am–6pm; Oct–March Mon–Sat 10am–3pm; £1.50) are even better. Begun just two years after Nelson's death at Trafalgar, this is one of Edinburgh's oddest buildings, resembling a gigantic spyglass.

Alongside, the **National Monument** was begun in 1822 by Playfair to plans by the English architect Charles Cockerell. Had it been completed, it would have been a reasonably accurate replica of the Parthenon, but funds ran out with only twelve columns built. Various later schemes to finish it similarly foundered, earning it the nickname "Edinburgh's Disgrace". At the opposite side of the hill, the grandeur of Playfair's Classical **Monument to Dugald Stewart** seems totally disproportionate to the stature of the man it commemorates: a now-forgotten professor of philosophy at the University.

Playfair also built the **City Observatory** for his uncle, the mathematician and astronomer John Playfair, whom he honoured in the cenotaph outside. Because of pollution and the advent of street lighting, which impaired views of the stars, the observatory proper had to be relocated to Blackford Hill before the end of the century, though the equipment here continues to be used by students. The small domed pavilion at the northeastern corner, an addition of the 1890s, now houses the **Edinburgh Experience** (April–June, Sept & Oct Mon–Fri 2–5pm, Sat & Sun 10.30am–5pm; July & Aug daily 10.30am–5pm; £2), a twenty-minute 3-D show on the city's history viewed through special glasses. At the opposite end of the complex is the **Old Observatory**, one of the few surviving buildings by James Craig, designer of the New Town. New schemes for the development of Calton Hill, either grandiose or foolish (or both), are proposed every few months: with the possibility of funding from the Lottery Fund, one of these may even be carried out.

Elsewhere in the New Town

The **Northern New Town** was the earliest extension to the First New Town, begun in 1801, and today roughly covers the area north of Queen Street between India Street to the west and Broughton Street to the east, and as far as Fettes Row to the north. This has survived in far better shape than its predecessor: with the exception of one street, almost all of it is intact, and it has managed to preserve its predominantly residential character. One of the area's most intriguing buildings is the neo-Norman **Mansfield Place Church**, on the corner of Broughton and East London streets, designed in the late nineteenth century for the strange, now defunct Catholic Apostolic sect. Having lain redundant and neglected for three decades, it has suddenly acquired cult status, its preservation the current obsession of local conservation groups. The chief reason for this is its cycle of **murals** by the Dublin-born **Phoebe Traquair**, a leading light in the Scottish Arts and Crafts movement. She laboured for eight years on this decorative scheme, which has all the freshness and luminosity of a medieval manuscript, but desperately needs a thorough restoration to avert its already alarming decay. Interest in the murals was revived in 1993 when the church was opened to the public for the summer. The main body of the church, whose basement is now used regularly as a nightclub (*Café Graffiti*; see p.108 for review) will in the near future house a centre for Scottish voluntary groups.

Dean Village and Stockbridge

Work began on the western end of the New Town in 1822, in a small area of land north of Charlotte Square and west of George Street. Instead of the straight lines of the earlier sections, there were now the gracious curves of Randolph Crescent, Ainslie Place and the magnificent twelve-sided Moray Place, designed by the vainglorious James Gillespie Graham who described himself, with no authority to do so, as "architect in Scotland to the Prince Regent". Round the corner from Randolph Crescent, the four-arched **Dean Bridge**, a bravura feat of 1830s engineering by Thomas Telford, carries the main road high above Edinburgh's placid little river, the **Water of Leith**. Down to the left lies **Dean Village**, an old milling community that is one of central Edinburgh's most picturesque yet oddest corners, its atmosphere of terminal decay arrested by the conversion of some of the mills into designer flats. The riverside path into Stockbridge passes **St Bernard's Well**, a pump room covered by a mock Roman temple. Commissioned in 1788 by Lord Gardenstone to draw mineral waters from the Water of Leith, it has been recently restored, and is occasionally open to the public (contact Water of Leith Conservation Trust; ☎445 7367).

Stockbridge, which straddles both sides of the Water of Leith on the other side of Dean Bridge, is another old village which has retained its distinctive identity, in spite of its absorption into the Georgian face of the New Town, and is particularly renowned for its antique shops and "alternative" outlets. The residential upper streets on the far side of the river were developed by Sir Henry Raeburn, who named the finest of them **Ann Street**, which after Charlotte Square is the most prestigious address in Edinburgh (writers Thomas de Quincey and JM Ballantyne were residents); alone among New Town streets, its houses each have a front garden.

The West End

The western extension to the New Town was the last part to be built, deviating from the area's overriding Neoclassicism with a number of Victorian additions. Because of this, the huge **St Mary's Episcopal Cathedral**, an addition of the 1870s, is less intrusive than it would otherwise be, its three spires forming an eminently satisfying landmark for the far end of the city centre. The last major work of Sir George Gilbert Scott, the cathedral is built in imitation of the Early English Gothic style and was, at the time of its construction, the most ambitious church built in Britain since the Reformation.

The Scottish National Gallery of Modern Art

Set in spacious wooded grounds at the far northwestern fringe of the New Town, about ten minutes' walk from either the cathedral or Dean Village, the **Scottish National Gallery of Modern Art**, Belford Road (Mon–Sat 10am–5pm, Sun 2–5pm; free), was established as the first collection in Britain devoted solely to twentieth-century painting and sculpture. The grounds serve as a sculpture park, featuring works by Jacob Epstein, Henry Moore, Barbara Hepworth and the Constructivist creations of the Edinburgh-born Eduardo Paolozzi, soon to be honoured with his own museum in the massive Dean Centre on the opposite side of Belford Road. Inside, the display space is divided between temporary loan exhibitions and selections from the gallery's own holdings; the latter are arranged thematically, but are almost constantly moved around. What you get to see at any particular time is therefore a matter of chance, though the most important works are nearly always on view.

French painters are particularly well represented, beginning with **Bonnard**'s *Lane at Vernonnet* and **Vuillard**'s jewel-like *Two Seamstresses*, and by a few examples of the Fauves, notably **Matisse**'s *The Painting Lesson* and **Derain**'s dazzlingly brilliant *Collioure*; there's also a fine group of late canvases by **Leger**, notably *The Constructors*. Among some striking examples of German Expressionism are **Kirchner**'s *Japanese Theatre*, **Feininger**'s *Gelmeroda III*, and a wonderfully soulful wooden sculpture of a woman by **Barlach** entitled *The Terrible Year, 1937*. Highlights of the Surrealist section are **Magritte**'s haunting *Black Flag*, **Miró**'s seminal *Composition* and **Giacometti**'s contorted *Woman with her Throat Cut*, while Cubism is represented by **Picasso**'s *Soles* and **Braque**'s *Candlestick*.

Of works by Americans, **Roy Lichtenstein**'s *In the Car* is a fine example of his Pop Art style, while **Duane Hanson**'s fibreglass *Tourists* is typically cruel. English artists on show include Sickert, Nicholson, Spencer, Freud and Hockney, but, as you'd expect, considerably more space is allocated to Scottish artists. Of particular note are the so-called Colourists – **SJ Peploe**, **JD Fergusson**, **Francis Cadell** and **George Leslie Hunter** – whose works are attracting fancy prices on the art market, as well as ever-growing posthumous critical acclaim. Although they did not form a recognizable school, they all worked in France and displayed considerable French influence in their warm, bright palettes. The gallery also shows works by many contemporary Scots, among them **John Bellany**, a portraitist of striking originality, and the poet-artist-gardener **Ian Hamilton Finlay**.

The Suburbs

Edinburgh's principal sights are by no means confined to the city centre: indeed, at least three of its most popular tourist draws – the **Royal Botanic Garden**, the **Zoo** and the **Royal Observatory** – are out in the suburbs. Other major attractions in the outskirts include **Craigmillar Castle** and the southern hill ranges, the **Braids** and the **Pentlands**. Additionally, there are several districts with their own very distinct identity, among them the academic enclave of the **Southside**, the seaside resort of **Portobello** and the port of **Leith**.

The Royal Botanic Garden

Just beyond the northern boundaries of the New Town, with entrances on Inverleith Row and Arboretum Place, is the seventy-acre site of the **Royal Botanic Garden** (daily: March, April, Sept & Oct 10am–6pm; May–Aug 10am–8pm; Nov–Feb 10am–4pm; free), particularly renowned for the rhododendrons, which blaze out in a glorious patchwork of colours in April and May. In the heart of the grounds a group of hothouses designated the Glasshouse Experience (daily: March–Oct 10am–5pm; Nov–Feb 10am–3.30pm; free, but donation requested) displays orchids, giant Amazonian water lilies, and a 200-year-old West Indian palm tree, the latter being in the elegant 1850s glass-topped Palm House. Many of the most exotic plants were brought to Edinburgh by the aptly named George Forrest, who made seven expeditions to southwestern China between 1904 and 1932. There is also a major new Chinese-style garden, featuring a pavilion, waterfall and the world's biggest collection of Chinese wild plants outside China.

The southwest

The area **southwest of the Old Town** was formerly known as **Portsburgh**, a theoretically separate burgh outside the city walls that was nonetheless a virtual fiefdom of Edinburgh. Since the 1880s and the construction of the **Royal Lyceum Theatre** on Grindlay Street, the area has gradually developed into something of a theatre district. The **Museum of Fire** (by appointment only; ☎228 2401; free) situated on Lauriston Place next to the Art School, records the history of the oldest municipal fire brigade in Britain, formed in 1824. It contains a small collection of well-preserved manual, horse-drawn and motorized fire appliances. At its southern edge, the open parkland areas of the **Meadows** and **Bruntsfield Links** mark the transition to Edinburgh's genteel Victorian villa suburbs. South of the Meadows, a plaque on the wall of Sciennes Hill House in Sciennes House Place records the only known meeting, in 1787, of Robert Burns and Sir Walter Scott. On the opposite side of the street is a tiny Jewish graveyard. Prominent among the suburbs is **Morningside**, whose prim and proper outlook, accompanied by an appropriately plummy accent, was immortalized in Muriel Spark's *The Prime of Miss Jean Brodie*, and remains a favourite target for ridicule.

The Southside

The New Town was not the only mid-eighteenth-century expansion of Edinburgh: the city also spread in the opposite direction, creating a tenement suburb which became known as the **Southside**. Since the 1950s, this has developed into a lively academic quarter, having been progressively colonized by the overspill of University buildings.

On Nicolson Street, the southern extension of South Bridge, is **Surgeons' Hall**, a handsome Ionic temple built by Playfair as the headquarters of the Royal College of Surgeons. Most of it is accessible to the public only one day a year, an exception being the museum, entered from 9 Hill Square (Mon–Fri 2–4pm; free), which has intriguing, if somewhat specialist exhibits on the history of medicine. Across the street is the **Festival Theatre**, a refurbished music hall, which opened in 1994, giving the city a long-awaited venue capable of presenting the grandest opera.

Craigmillar Castle

Craigmillar Castle (April–Sept Mon–Sat 9.30am–6pm, Sun 2–6pm; Oct–March Mon–Wed & Sat 9.30am–4pm, Thurs 9.30am–noon, Sun 2–4pm; £1.50), where the murder of Lord Darnley, second husband of Mary, Queen of Scots was plotted, lies in a green belt five miles southeast of the centre. It's one of the best-preserved medieval fortresses in Scotland, marred only by the proximity of the ugly council housing scheme of Craigmillar, one of Edinburgh's most deprived districts.

The oldest part of the complex is the L-shaped **tower house**, which dates back to the early 1600s: it remains substantially intact, and the great hall, with its resplendent late Gothic chimneypiece, is in good enough shape to be rented out for functions. A few decades after Craigmillar's completion, the tower house was surrounded by a quadrangular wall with cylindrical corner towers pierced by some of the earliest surviving gunholes in Britain. The west range was remodelled as an aristocratic mansion in the mid-seventeenth century, but its owners abandoned the place a hundred years later, leaving it to decay into picturesque ruin. Take bus #14, #42 or #46 from the city centre to the junction of Duddingston Road West and Peffermill Road, from where the castle is a ten-minute walk along Craigmillar Castle Road.

The southern hills

The **hills** in Edinburgh's southern suburbs offer good, not overly demanding walking opportunities, with plenty of sweeping panoramic views. The **Royal Observatory** (daily: April–Sept noon–5.30pm; Oct–March 1–5pm; £2) stands at the top of Blackford Hill, just a short walk south of Morningside, or accessible by buses #40 and #41 direct from the centre. The visitor centre here seeks to explain the mysteries of the solar system by means of models, videos and space photographs, and you also get to see the observatory's two main telescopes.

At the foot of the hill, the bird sanctuary of Blackford Pond is the starting point for the **Hermitage of Braid** nature trail, a lovely shady path along the course of the Braid Burn. The castellated eighteenth-century mansion along the route, after which the trail is named, now serves as an information centre (Mon–Fri 10am–4pm, Sun 11am–6pm; café Sun only 11am–5pm). Immediately to the south are the **Braid Hills**, most of whose area is occupied by two golf courses, which are closed on alternate Sundays in order to allow access to walkers.

Further south are the **Pentland Hills**, a chain some eighteen miles long and five wide. The best entry point from within Edinburgh is **SWANSTON**, an unspoiled, highly exclusive hamlet of whitewashed thatched roof dwellings separated from the rest of the city by almost a mile of farmland. Robert Louis Stevenson (see below) spent his boyhood summers in Swanston Cottage, the largest of the houses, immortalizing it in the novel *St Ives*. To get a taste of the scenery of the Pentlands, follow the marked hik-

ROBERT LOUIS STEVENSON

Though **Robert Louis Stevenson** (1850–94) is often dismissed in highbrow academic circles for his deceptively simple manner, he was undoubtedly one of the best-loved writers of his generation, and one whose travelogues, novels, short stories and essays remain enormously popular a century after his death.

Born in Edinburgh into a distinguished family of engineers, Stevenson was a sickly child, with a solitary childhood dominated by his governess Alison "Cummie" Cunningham, who regaled him with tales drawn from Calvinist folklore. Sent to the University to study engineering, Stevenson rebelled against his upbringing by spending much of his time in the lowlife howffs and brothels of the city, and eventually switching to law. Although called to the bar in 1875, by then he had decided to channel his energies into literature: while still a student, he had already made his mark as an **essayist**, and published in his lifetime over a hundred essays, ranging from light-hearted whimsy to trenchant political analysis. A set of topographical pieces about his native city was later collected together as *Edinburgh: Picturesque Notes,* which conjure up nicely its atmosphere, character and appearance – warts and all.

Stevenson's other early successes were two **travelogues**, *An Inland Voyage* and *Travels with a Donkey in the Cevennes*, kaleidoscopic jottings based on his journeys in France, where he went to escape Scotland's bad weather. It was there that he met Fanny Osbourne, an American ten years his senior, who was estranged from her husband and had two children in tow. His voyage to join her in San Francisco formed the basis for his most important factual work, *The Amateur Emigrant*, a vivid first-hand account of the great nineteenth-century European migration to the United States.

Having married the now-divorced Fanny, Stevenson began an elusive search for an agreeable climate that led to Switzerland, the French Riviera and the Scottish Highlands. He belatedly turned to the **novel**, achieving immediate acclaim in 1881 for *Treasure Island*, a highly moralistic adventure yarn that began as an entertainment for his stepson and future collaborator, Lloyd Osbourne. In 1886, his most famous **short story**, *Dr Jekyll and Mr Hyde*, despite its nominal London setting, offered a vivid evocation of Edinburgh's Old Town; an allegory of its dual personality of prosperity and squalor, and an analysis of its Calvinistic preoccupations with guilt and damnation. The same year saw the publication of the historical romance *Kidnapped*, an adventure novel which exemplified his view that literature should seek above all to entertain.

In 1887 Stevenson left Britain for good, travelling first to the United States where he began one of his most ambitious novels, *The Master of Ballantrae*. A year later, he set sail for the South Seas, and eventually settled in Samoa; his last works include a number of stories with a local setting, such as the grimly realistic *The Ebb Tide* and *The Beach of Falesà*. However, Scotland continued to be his main inspiration: he wrote *Catriona* as a sequel to *Kidnapped*, and was at work on two more novels with Scottish settings, *St Ives* and *Weir of Hermiston*, a dark story of father–son confrontation, at the time of his sudden death from a brain hemorrhage in 1894. He was buried on the top of Mount Vaea overlooking the Pacific Ocean.

EDINBURGH'S PENTLAND HILLS

Ordnance Survey Landranger map no. 66.

Allow four hours for this walk. Exit the city on the A702 and look out for the *Flotterstone Inn* where there is a car park and small interpretive centre. A pleasant sideroad leads up to Glencorse Reservoir, a lochan, then swings round it to go through a tight pass and on to Loganlee Reservoir, a quite remote area that feels far away from city life. The more energetic can strike up onto Turnhouse Hill and cross Carnethy Hill (1900ft) to come down to the Howe, at the loch's west end.

A path leads on through a short pass to come out on the far side of the Pentland range, where the large expanse of Thriepmuir Reservoir stretches out in front of you. Cross a bridge over a "neck" in the reservoir; the path heads inland for a while, but take the first right to return to the reservoir and then follow it along Harlaw Reservoir beyond.

Here cross the dam to pass a trim cottage and then turn left on the woodside track. When the track bears left, take the righthand path, which leads up towards the hills again. After about 220yd, take the left fork which leads up to the pass between Bell's Hill and Harbour Hill. The path runs down the burn to rejoin Glencorse Reservoir.

There are quite a number of books and special maps about the Pentlands; *25 Walks, Edinburgh and Lothian* (HMSO, 1995) is excellent.

---

ing trail to the artificial ski slope of **Hillend** to the east; this traverses two summits and passes the remains of an Iron Age fort in addition to offering outstanding views over Edinburgh and Fife. The lazy way into the range is to take the **chair lift** from Hillend itself (Mon–Sat 9.30am–9pm, Sun 9.30am–7pm; £1.10), which is connected with the city centre by buses #4 and #15.

Portobello

Among Edinburgh's least expected assets is its **beach**, most of which falls within **PORTOBELLO**, once a lively **seaside resort** but now a forlorn kind of place, its funfairs and amusement arcades decidedly down-at-heel. Nonetheless, it retains a certain faded charm, and – on hot summer weekends at least – the beach can be a mass of swimmers, sunbathers, surfers and pleasure boats. A walk along the promenade is a pleasure at any time of the year. Portobello is about three miles east of the centre of town, and can be reached on buses #15, #26, #42 or #86.

Leith

For several hundred years **LEITH** was separate from Edinburgh. As Scotland's major east coast port, it played a key role in the nation's history, even serving as the seat of government for a time, and in 1833 finally became a burgh in its own right. In 1920, however, it was incorporated into the capital and, in the decades that followed, went into seemingly terminal decline: the population dropped dramatically, and much of its centre was ripped out, to be replaced by grim housing schemes.

The 1980s, however, saw an astonishing turnaround. Against all the odds, a couple of waterfront bistros proved enormously successful; competitors followed apace, and by the end of the decade the port had acquired arguably the best concentration of restaurants and pubs in Edinburgh (see p.103 & 107 for reviews). The surviving historic monuments were spruced up and a host of housing developments built or restored, a renaissance crowned by the completion of a vast new building housing civil servants from the Scottish Office.

To reach Leith from the city centre, take one of the many buses going down Leith Walk, near the top end of which is a statue of Sherlock Holmes, whose creator, Sir

Arthur Conan Doyle, was born nearby. Otherwise, it's a brisk walk of around twenty minutes plus, or you can travel on from Portobello by bus #2.

Around the port

While you're most likely to come to Leith for the bars and restaurants, the area itself warrants exploration; though the shipbuilding yards have gone, it remains an active port with a rough-edged character. Most of the showpiece Neoclassical buildings lie on or near **The Shore**, the tenement-lined road along the final stretch of the Water of Leith, just before it disgorges into the Firth of Forth. Note the former **Town Hall**, on the parallel Constitution Street, now the headquarters of the local constabulary, immortalized in the tongue twister, "The Leith police dismisseth us"; the Classical Trinity House on Kirkgate, built in 1816; and the massive Customs House on Commercial Street. To the west, set back from The Shore, is **Lamb's House**, a seventeenth-century mansion comparable to Gladstone's Land in the Old Town. Built as the home of the prosperous merchant Andro Lamb, it currently functions as an old people's day centre.

Leith Links is an area of predominantly flat parkland, just east of the police station. Documentary evidence suggests that The Links was a golf course in the fifteenth century, giving rise to Leith's claim to be regarded as the birthplace of the sport: in 1744 its first written rules were drawn up here, ten years before they were formalized in St Andrews.

To the west of Leith lies the village of **NEWHAVEN**, built by James IV, at the start of the sixteenth century, as an alternative shipbuilding centre to Leith: his massive warship, the *Michael*, capable of carrying 120 gunners, 300 mariners and 1000 troops, and said to have used up all the trees in Fife, was built here. It has also been a ferry station and an important fishing centre, landing at the height of its success (in the 1860s), some six million oysters a year. Today, although a few boats still operate from the harbour, the fish market is no more and the last of the colourfully dressed fishwives has long since retired. A variety of costumes and other memorabilia of the village's only industry can be found in the small **Newhaven Heritage Museum** (daily noon–5pm; free), a fascinating collection staffed by enthusiastic members of local fishing families.

The Zoo

Edinburgh's **Zoo** (April–Sept Mon–Sat 9am–6pm, Sun 9.30am–6pm; Oct & March Mon–Sat 9am–5pm, Sun 9.30am–5pm; Nov–Feb Mon–Sat 9am–4.30pm, Sun 9.30am–4.30pm; £6) lies three miles west of Princes Street on an eighty-acre site on the slopes of Corstorphine Hill (buses from town: #2, #26, #31, #36, #69, #85, #86). Here you can see 1500 animals, including a number of endangered species such as white rhinos, red pandas, pygmy hippos and Madagascar tree boas. However, its chief claim to fame is its crowd of penguins (the largest number in captivity anywhere in the world), a legacy of Leith's whaling trade in the South Atlantic. The penguin parade, which takes place daily at 2pm from April to September, and on sunny March and October days, has gained something of a cult status.

Lauriston Castle and Cramond

Lauriston Castle (40min guided tours April to mid-June & mid-Sept to Oct Sat–Thurs 11am–1pm & 2–5pm; mid-June to mid-Sept Sat–Thurs 11am–5pm; Nov–March Sat & Sun 2–4pm; £3) is a country mansion set in its own parkland overlooking the Firth of Forth, about five miles west of the centre. The original sixteenth-century tower house forms the centrepiece of what is otherwise a neo-Jacobean structure, which in 1902 became the retirement home of a prosperous local cabinet-maker. He decked out the interior with his private collection of furniture and antiques, which includes Flemish tapestries and ornaments made of Blue John from Derbyshire. The castle can be reached from the city centre by bus #41.

One mile further west, **CRAMOND** is one of the city's most atmospheric – and poshest – old villages. The enduring image of Cramond is of step-gabled whitewashed houses rising uphill from the waterfront, though it also boasts the foundations of a Roman fort, a medieval bridge and tower house, and a church, inn and mansion, all from the seventeenth century. In December 1996, a wonderful Roman sculpture of a lioness devouring a man was discovered in the River Almond: it is thought that it was simply thrown into the river after the departure of the Romans. The sculpture will eventually be seen by the public, though it has yet to be decided which of the city's museums will display it. There are a number of interesting **short walks** in the area: across the causeway at low tide to the uninhabited (except for seabirds) **Cramond Island**; eastwards along the seafront towards the gasometers of **Granton** with sweeping views out to sea; upstream along the River Almond past former mills and their adjoining cottages towards the sixteenth-century **Old Cramond Brig**; and, after a short ferry crossing, through the Dalmeny estate to **Dalmeny House** (see below). Apart from the last one, which is just a little longer, these walks should take around an hour each.

Dalmeny

In 1975, Edinburgh's boundaries were extended to include a number of towns and villages which were formerly part of West Lothian. Among them is **DALMENY**, two miles west of Cramond and accessible directly from the city centre by bus (#43 Scottish Eastern) or train. Another option is to take the coastal path from Cramond, which passes through the estate of **Dalmeny House** (July & Aug Mon & Tues noon–5.30pm; Sun 1–5.30pm; £3.60), the seat of the Earls of Rosebery. Built in 1815 by the English architect William Wilkins, it was the first stately home in Scotland in the neo-Gothic style, vividly evoking Tudor architecture in its picturesque turreted roofline, and in its fan vaults and hammerbeam ceilings. The family portraits include one of the fourth Earl (who commissioned the house) by Raeburn, and of the fifth Earl (the last British prime minister to govern from the House of Lords) by Millais; there are also likenesses of other famous society figures by Reynolds, Gainsborough and Lawrence. Among the furnishings are a set of tapestries made from cartoons by Goya, and the Rothschild Collection of eighteenth-century French furniture and *objets d'art*. There's also a fascinating collection of memorabilia of Napoleon Bonaparte – notably some items he used during his exile in St Helena – amassed by the fifth Earl, who wrote a biography of the French dictator.

Dalmeny **village** is a quiet community built around a spacious green. Its focal point is the mid-twelfth-century **St Cuthbert's Kirk**, a wonderful Norman church that has remained more or less intact. Although very weather-beaten, the south doorway is particularly notable for its illustrations of strange beasts. More vivaciously grotesque carvings can be seen inside on the chancel corbels and arch.

South Queensferry and around

Less than a mile of countryside separates Dalmeny from **SOUTH QUEENSFERRY**, a compact little town used by St Margaret as a crossing point for her frequent trips between her palaces in Edinburgh and Dunfermline. **High Street**, squeezed into the narrow gap between the seashore and the hillside above, is lined by a picturesque array of old buildings, among them an unusual two-tiered row of shops, the roofs of the lower level serving as the walkway for the upper storey. The small **museum**, 53 High St (Mon & Thurs–Sat 10am–1pm & 2.15–5pm, Sun 2–5pm; free), contains relics of the town's history and the building of the two bridges.

Everything in South Queensferry is overshadowed, quite literally, by the two great bridges, each about a mile and a half in length, which traverse the Firth of Forth at its narrowest point. The cantilevered **Forth Rail Bridge**, built from 1883 to 1890 by Sir John Fowler and Benjamin Baker, ranks among the supreme achievements of Victorian engineering. Some 50,000 tons of steel were used in the construction of a design that manages to exude grace as well as might. Derived from American models, the suspension format chosen for the **Forth Road Bridge** makes a perfect complement to the older structure. Erected between 1958 and 1964, it finally killed off the 900-year-old ferry, and now attracts a heavy volume of traffic. It's well worth walking across its footpath to Fife (see *Central Scotland*) for the tremendous views of the Rail Bridge.

Inchcolm

From South Queensferry's Hawes Pier, just west of the Rail Bridge, pleasure boats leave for a variety of cruises on the Forth (Easter, May & June Sat & Sun; July to mid-Sept daily; ☎331 4857; £6.50–8.95). Be sure to check in advance as sailings are always subject to cancellation in bad weather.

The most enticing destination is the island of **Inchcolm**, whose beautiful ruined **Abbey** was founded in 1123 by King Alexander I in gratitude for the hospitality he received from a hermit (whose cell survives at the northwestern corner of the island) when his ship was forced ashore in a storm. The best-preserved medieval monastic complex in Scotland, the abbey's surviving buildings date from the thirteenth to the fifteenth centuries, and include a splendid octagonal chapterhouse. Although the church is almost totally dilapidated, its tower can be ascended for a great aerial view of the island, which is populated by a variety of nesting birds and a colony of grey seals.

Hopetoun House

Immediately beyond the western edge of South Queensferry, just over the West Lothian border, **Hopetoun House** (April–Oct daily 10am–5.30pm; £4.50 house and grounds, £2.50 grounds only) is one of Scotland's grandest stately homes. The original house was built at the turn of the eighteenth century for the first Earl of Hopetoun by Sir William Bruce, the architect of Holyroodhouse. A couple of decades later, William Adam carried out an enormous extension, engulfing the house in a curvaceous main facade and two projecting wings – superb examples of Roman Baroque pomp and swagger. The scale and lavishness of the Adam interiors, most of whose decoration was carried out by his sons after the architect's death, make for a stark contrast with the intimacy of those designed by Bruce. Particularly impressive are the Red and Yellow Drawing Rooms, with their splendid ceilings by the young Robert Adam. Among the house's furnishings are seventeenth-century tapestries, Meissen porcelain, and a distinguished collection of paintings, including portraits by Gainsborough, Ramsay and Raeburn. The grounds of Hopetoun House are also open, with magnificent walks along the banks of the Forth and great opportunities for picnics.

Midlothian

Immediately south of Edinburgh lies the old county of **MIDLOTHIAN**, once called Edinburghshire. It's one of the hilliest parts of the Central Lowlands, with the Pentland chain running down its western side, and the Moorfoots defining its boundary with the Borders to the south. Though predominantly rural, it contains a belt of former mining communities, which are struggling to come to terms with the recent decline of the industry. Such charms as it has are mostly low-key, with the exception of the riotously ornate chapel at **Roslin**.

Dalkeith and around

Despite its Victorian demeanour, **DALKEITH**, eight miles southeast of central Edinburgh – to which it is linked by very regular buses (#3, #30, #82) – grew up in the Middle Ages as a baronial burgh under the successive control of the Douglases and Buccleuchs. Today it's a bustling shopping centre, with an unusually broad High Street at its heart.

At the far end of the street is the entrance to **Dalkeith Country Park** (April–Oct daily 10am–6pm; £2), the estate of the Dukes of Buccleuch, whose seat, the early eighteenth-century **Dalkeith Palace**, can only be seen from the outside. You can, however, visit its one-time chapel, now the episcopalian parish church of **St Mary**, adorned inside with extremely rich furnishings. Further north, Robert Adam's **Montagu Bridge** straddles the River North Esk in a graceful arch; beyond are some derelict but once wonderfully grandiose garden follies. There is also a large woodland playground, suitable for all but the youngest children.

A mile or so south of Dalkeith is **NEWTONGRANGE**, whose Lady Victoria Colliery is now open to the public as the **Scottish Mining Museum** (guided tours March–Oct daily 10am–4pm; £3), with a 1625ft-deep shaft, and a winding tower powered by Scotland's largest steam engine. A series of nostalgic tableaux depicts everyday life in the community.

Roslin

The tranquil village of **ROSLIN** lies seven miles south of the centre of Edinburgh, from where it can be reached by bus #87A or by regular Eastern Scottish services from St Andrew Square. An otherwise nondescript place, the village does boast the richly decorated late-Gothic **Rosslyn Chapel** (April–Oct Mon–Sat 10am–5pm, Sun noon–4.45pm; Nov–March Mon–Sat 10am–5pm, Sun noon–4pm; £2.25). Only the choir, Lady Chapel and part of the transepts were built of what was intended to be a huge collegiate church dedicated to St Matthew: construction halted soon after the founder's death in 1484, and the vestry built onto the facade nearly four hundred years later is the sole subsequent addition. After a long period of neglect, a massive restoration project has recently been undertaken: a canopy has been placed over the chapel which will remain in place for several years in order to dry out the saturated ceiling and walls, and other essential repairs are due to be carried out within the chapel.

The outside of the chapel bristles with pinnacles, gargoyles, flying buttresses and canopies, while inside the foliage carving is particularly outstanding, with botanically accurate depictions of over a dozen different leaves and plants. Among them are cacti and Indian corn, providing fairly convincing evidence that the founder's grandfather, the daring sea adventurer Prince Henry of Orkney, did indeed, as legend has it, set foot in the New World a century before Columbus. The rich and subtle figurative sculptures have given Rosslyn the nickname of "a Bible in stone", though they're more allegorical than literal, with portrayals of the Dance of Death, the Seven Acts of Mercy and the Seven Deadly Sins.

The greatest and most original carving of all is the extraordinary knotted **Prentice Pillar** at the southeastern corner of the Lady Chapel. According to local legend, the pillar was made by an apprentice during the absence of the master mason, who killed him in a fit of jealousy on seeing the finished work. A tiny head of a man with a slashed forehead, set at the apex of the ceiling at the far northwestern corner of the building, is popularly supposed to represent the apprentice, his murderer the corresponding head at the opposite side. The entwined dragons at the foot are symbols of Satan, and were probably inspired by Norse mythology.

A number of books have been published in recent years about Rosslyn Chapel, drawing on everything from Freemasons and the Turin Shroud to the True Gospels and the regular sightings of UFOs over Midlothian. Conspiracy theories notwithstanding, the chapel is well worth a visit.

THE FESTIVALS

The **Edinburgh Festival**, now the largest arts festival in the world, first took place in August 1947. Driven by a desire for reconciliation and escape from postwar austerity, the Austrian Rudolf Bing, who was administrator of the Glyndebourne opera, brought together a host of distinguished musicians from the war-ravaged countries of central Europe. The symbolic centrepiece of his vision was the emotional reunion of Bruno Walter, a Jewish refugee from Nazi tyranny, and the Vienna Philharmonic Orchestra. At the same time, eight theatrical groups, both Scottish and English, turned up in Edinburgh, uninvited, performing in an unlikely variety of local venues, thus establishing the Fringe. Today more than a million people come to the city over three weeks (the last three in August, or the last fortnight and first week in September) to see several separate festivals, each offering a wide variety of artists and events – everything is on show, from the highbrow to the controversial. However, the relationship between the official festival and the Fringe has become increasingly uneasy since the Fringe announced that, from 1998, it will begin and end a week earlier in order to coincide its final weekend with England's bank holiday.

The legacy of Rudolf Bing's Glyndebourne connections ensured that, for many years, the official **Edinburgh International Festival** was dominated by opera. Although, in the 1980s, efforts were made to involve locals and provide a broader cultural mix of international theatre, dance and classical music, the official Festival is still very much a highbrow event. The **programme** is published in April by the Edinburgh International Festival Society, 21 Market St, EH1 1BW (☎473 2000; Web site *www.go-edinburgh.co.uk*); bookings begin shortly afterwards.

For many years largely the domain of student revues – notable exceptions include Joan Littlewood's distinguished Theatre Workshop, with their early 1950s production of *The Other Animal*, about life in a concentration camp, and work by the great Spanish playwright, Lorca – the **Festival Fringe** began to really take off in the 1970s. Set up in 1951, the **Fringe Society** has grown from a small group to today's large-scale operation serving an annual influx of more than 500 acts – national theatre groups to student troupes – using around two hundred venues. In spite of this expansion, the Fringe has remained loyal to the original open policy and there is still no vetting of performers. This means that the shows range from the inspired to the truly diabolical and ensures a highly competitive atmosphere, in which one bad review in a prominent publication means box-office disaster. Many unknowns rely on self-publicity, taking to the streets to perform highlights from their show, or pressing leaflets into the hands of every passer-by. Performances go on round the clock: if so inclined, you could sit through twenty shows in a day. The full programme is usually available in June from the Festival Fringe Office, 180 High St, EH1 1QS (☎226 5257; Web site *www.edfringe.com*). Postal and telephone (☎226 5138) bookings can be made immediately afterwards.

Over the years in both the official Festival and the Fringe, there has been a remarkable choice of both performers and venues: both Jean-Louis Barrault (star of the 1945 movie *Les Enfants du Paradis*) and Richard Burton as Hamlet; Grace Kelly reading the works of early American poets; 65-year-old Marlene Dietrich in cabaret; *Macbeth* on Inchcolm Island in the Firth of Forth; and *2001: A Space Odyssey* performed to an audience sitting in a Hillman Avenger. The 1980s saw the anarchic circus performers Archaos, whose publicity involved sawing up cars outside the Fringe office. Although now disbanded, their spirit lives on in a number of ever more shocking shows, including a recent troupe of naked lesbian trapeze artists.

Edinburgh in August is also, of course, the place to witness the emergence of new **stars**; from actors Donald Pleasance and Penelope Keith in the 1950s, to the Beyond the

Cafés and restaurants

You can eat well in Edinburgh at almost any price, choosing from a wide range of cuisines. Plenty of places specialize in **traditional Scottish cooking**, using fresh local

Fringe comedy team of Alan Bennett, Jonathan Miller, Peter Cook and Dudley Moore in 1960; and, in the 1980s and 1990s, contemporary stars such as comedians Harry Enfield, Lee Evans and the late Bill Hicks, and actress Emma Thompson.

The **Film Festival** also began at the same time as the main Festival, making it the longest-running film festival in the world. After a period in the doldrums, it has grown to its current position as a respected fixture on the international circuit, incorporating both mainstream and independent new releases and presenting a series of valuable retrospectives from Sam Fuller to Shohei Immamura. It also hosts interviews and discussions with film directors; in recent years visitors have included Kenneth Anger, the Coen brothers, Clint Eastwood and Steve Martin. A particular feature has been the high profile support given to Scottish film: from Bill Douglas's austere and brilliant *Childhood* trilogy, through the lighter style of Bill Forsyth, to the recent small-budget hit, *Shallow Grave*. Tickets and information are available from the main venue, the Filmhouse, 88 Lothian Rd, EH3 9BZ (☎228 2688). The programme is usually ready by late June, when bookings start.

Meanwhile, other Festivals have emerged: the **Jazz Festival**, which has attracted the likes of Teddy Wilson and Benny Waters and stages a lively parade through the Grassmarket (programme available in July from the office at 116 Canongate, EH8 8DD; ☎557 1642); and the **Book Festival**, which evolved from existing meet-the-author sessions to become an annual jamboree held in the douce setting of a marquee-covered Charlotte Square. Hundreds of established authors from throughout the English-speaking world come to take part in readings, lectures, panel discussions and audience question-and-answer sessions. For further information, contact the Scottish Book Centre, 137 Dundee St, EH11 1BG (☎228 5444). The **Television Festival** is largely an in-house event, surfacing in the public consciousness only briefly as the keynote speaker indulges in the sport of deriding the latest changes at the BBC.

Although officially a separate event, the **Edinburgh Military Tattoo**, held in a splendid setting on the Castle Esplanade, is very much part of the Festival scene and an unashamed display of the kilt-and-bagpipes view of Scottish culture. Pipes and drums form the kernel of the programme, with a lone piper towards the end; performing animals, gymnastic and daredevil displays, plus at least one guest regiment from abroad, provide variety. Information and tickets are available from the Tattoo Office, 22 Market St, EH1 1QB (☎225 1188).

Although dubbed by many as elitist and irrelevant to locals, the Festival seems as much a part of the fabric of Edinburgh as its Castle (one-third of the tickets are sold to local people). Aside from providing a substantial boost to the city's economy, the Festival does stage two events which regularly bring in huge crowds of townspeople: Fringe Sunday, when Holyrood Park is taken over for a vast open-air party, and the massive firework display and free concert, held in Princes Street Gardens. And there are, of course, the annual Festival **rituals**: celebrity-spotting at the Assembly Rooms; newspaper gossip revolving around fears of imminent financial catastrophe for a major venue, if not the Festival itself; and the constant, raging debate about the strengths or otherwise of the Scottish element. Above all, though, there is a buzz to the city: the rumoured visit of a superstar, or even a soap star, the best and worst shows in towns, and the hot tips for the winners of the plethora of awards up for grabs, all become matters of supreme importance. By the Sunday following the end of the Festival, the performers have all departed: the winners to London for the various "Pick of the Fringe" seasons, and the losers back home to dream of next year. The church halls and Masonic lodges are locked up, the traders and hoteliers count their takings and the city streets are quiet once again.

For information on other festivals in the city, see p.109.

produce, while the city's ethnic communities, despite their small size, have drastically improved the **restaurant** scene, in particular with some great **Italian** trattorias and a host of excellent **Indian** restaurants serving regional dishes. In addition, the adaptation of home-grown ingredients to classic Gallic recipes is something the city does particularly well, resulting in some fabulous **French** restaurants. **Vegetarians** and vegans are well catered for, and there are plenty of **fish** specialists – seafood fans should head to **Leith**, whose waterside restaurants serve consistently good food. Most of Edinburgh's restaurants serve from noon to 2.30pm and 6pm to 11pm and close on Sundays, except where otherwise stated in our reviews. During the Festival, however, the majority of restaurants stay open all day until the early hours.

Although the city has nothing approaching the **café** society of other European capitals, if you fancy a snack a series of good establishments serves cakes and sandwiches. In choosing a place to eat, bear in mind that most **pubs** (which are covered in the following section) serve food, and that many have a restaurant attached. Edinburgh has a fairly high turnover of restaurants – some of impeccable repute have bitten the dust in the past few years – so don't be surprised if one or two of the listings have closed by the time you read this.

Old Town and Tollcross

Wonderful cafés and most of the upmarket Scottish and French restaurants are concentrated in the atmospheric streets of the **Old Town**, with a wide range of other cuisines also on offer, including vegetarian. **Tollcross**, handy for the city's theatres, also has a sprinkling of good restaurants, including some notable Chinese options.

Cafés and diners

Clarinda's, 69 Canongate (☎557 1888). Spruce olde-worlde café serving home-cooked breakfasts and light lunches. Inexpensive.

Deacon's Café, Brodies Close (☎226 1894). Quiet licensed café off the Royal Mile, claiming to have been the workshop of the infamous Deacon Brodie. It serves light snacks, home baking and even a nip of whisky. Daily 9am to around 6pm, later during the Festival. Inexpensive.

Edinburgh Fudge House, 197 Canongate (☎556 4172). Minimalist place serving snacks, sandwiches and cakes; notable for its huge range of delicious but pricey home-made fudges. Inexpensive.

Elephant House, 21 George IV Bridge (☎225 6267). Attractive new café with a large selection of coffees, teas, sandwiches and cakes and wonderful views of the castle. Open Mon–Sat 7.30am–10pm, Sun 10am–8pm. Inexpensive.

Elephant's Sufficiency, 170 High St (☎220 0666). This bright, lively café near the Fringe Office serves a great selection of sandwiches and baked potatoes. Inexpensive.

Lower Aisle, in the High Kirk of St Giles, High Street (☎225 5147). Popular with local lawyers, this café in the crypt serves good-value light lunches, with excellent home baking. Inexpensive.

Ndebele, 57 Home St (☎221 1141). New African café, named after a southern African tribe, offering tasty sandwiches, delicious fruit juices and a great selection of teas and coffees. Inexpensive.

Netherbow Café, Netherbow Arts Centre, 43 High St (☎556 9579). Excellent wholefood snacks using produce from the café's own allotment. Inexpensive.

Patisserie Florentin, 8–10 St Giles St (☎225 6267). French-style café off High Street whose extended opening hours and fabulous cakes and pastries make it a popular late-night rendezvous. Open 7am–11pm, closes 2am at weekends. It also has another, rather posher, branch at the Lyceum Theatre in Grindlay Street, which opens daily 7am–11pm. Inexpensive.

Chinese

Jasmine, 32 Grindlay St (☎229 5757). Good-value restaurant, with a strong line in fresh fish. Across the street from the Lyceum and the Usher Hall. Moderate.

Oriental Dining Centre, 8–14a Morrison St, Tollcross (☎221 1288). Three distinct restaurants, the most popular being the *Ho-Ho-Mei Noodle Shak*. Also contains the *Rainbow Arch Gourmet Restaurant* – try the three-course banquet for two for £20.95 – and *Henry's Dim Sum Cellar*, which also has a popular bar. All inexpensive–moderate.

French

L'Auberge, 58 St Mary's St (☎556 5888). French *nouvelle cuisine* in a luxurious setting. For a real treat, splurge on *Le Grand Menu Gourmand* at £38.50. Expensive.

La Bagatelle, 22a Brougham Place, Tollcross (☎229 0869). Fine French food in an authentic atmosphere, with a good-value three-course lunch for £8.50. Closed Sun lunch. Moderate.

Chez Jules, 1 Craigs Close (☎225 7007). French food in a fine, no-frills establishment. Also has a branch in the New Town branch at 61 Frederick St (☎225 7983). Moderate.

Grain Store, 30 Victoria St (☎225 7635). Another reasonably priced, solid Old Town French restaurant. Moderate.

Le Sept, Old Fishmarket Close (☎225 5428). Brasserie upstairs and à la carte restaurant downstairs. Walk in and (if necessary) wait for the brasserie, but book for the restaurant. Moderate–expensive.

Indian

Shamiana, 14 Brougham Place, Tollcross (☎229 5578). Established, first-class North Indian and Kashmiri cuisine in a tasteful environment located midway between the King's and Lyceum theatres. One of the more expensive restaurants in this category, but well worth it. Mon–Sat 6–10pm, Sun 6–9pm. Moderate.

Italian

Lazio's, 95 Lothian Rd (☎229 7788). Pick of the family-run trattorias on this block, handy for a late-night meal after a show in the nearby theatre district. Closes Fri 2am, Sat 3am. Moderate.

Mexican

Viva Mexico, 10 Anchor Close, off Cockburn Street (☎226 5145), and 50 E Fountainbridge, Tollcross (☎228 4005). Long-standing restaurant, with plenty of choice for vegetarians, and bargain options at lunchtimes; check out the tacos, burritos and refreshing margaritas. Moderate.

Scottish

The Atrium, 10 Cambridge St (☎228 8882). This award-winning restaurant is considered by many to be the city's best, though prices are high. Check out the tables which are made from railway sleepers. Very expensive.

Creelers, 3 Hunter Square (☎220 4447). Excellent seafood restaurant priding itself on fresh produce brought in from a sister restaurant/fish shop on Arran. Lunch £9.50, supper £15. Moderate.

Dubh Prais, 123b High St (☎557 5732). Basement restaurant offering innovative Scottish cuisine at affordable prices – the three-course dinner costs £25. Closed Sun & Mon. Expensive.

Jacksons, 209 High St (☎225 1793). Upmarket meat restaurant which turns the humble haggis into *haute cuisine*. The two-course set lunches are among Edinburgh's best bargains at around £5; dinners are nearer £20. Expensive.

Stac Polly, 8a Grindlay St (☎229 5405). Emphasis on game, fish and meat. Special pre- and post-theatre dinners for around £14. Expensive.

EDINBURGH CHAINS

One of Edinburgh's most popular French restaurants is the good value chain **Pierre Victoire**, which has branches in the Old Town at 10 Victoria St (☎225-1721) and 38 Grassmarket (☎226 2442), in the New Town at 8 Union St (☎557 8451) and 17 Queensferry St (☎226 1890) and in Leith at 5 Dock Place (☎555 6178). The service and food, which is unmistakably French and very affordable, can be erratic, but are normally good. All the branches close either on Sunday or Monday and are very popular so book ahead.

The city also boasts a series of **Oyster Bars**, at 10 Burgess St, Leith (☎554 6294), 6a Queen St, New Town (☎226 2530), 2 Calton Rd, Calton Hill (☎557 2925) and 28 W Maitland St, Haymarket (☎225 3861). These lively, wood-panelled bars serve a superb choice of cask beers and, as the name suggests, moderately priced fresh oysters.

Spanish

Igg's, 15 Jeffrey St (☎557 8184). A Spanish-owned hybrid, offering tapas snacks and Mediterranean dishes, plus traditional Scottish food. Good lunchtime tapas for around £5. Closed Sun. Expensive.

Vegetarian

Bann's Vegetarian Café, 5 Hunter Square (☎226 1122). Reliable café, halfway up the Royal Mile, with a frequently changing menu; two courses from around £4. Daily 10am–11pm. Moderate.

Black Bo's, 57 Blackfriars St (☎557 6136). Inventive non-meat diner with an earthy atmosphere and friendly service. Open after 11pm for drinks only. Closed Sun lunch. Moderate.

Henderson's at the Traverse, 10 Cambridge St (☎228 8003). Café in the basement of the Traverse Theatre with a small reliable menu and discreet music in the backgound. Open till 8pm daily, 10pm on performance nights. Inexpensive.

New Town and Stockbridge

With everything from Swiss and North African to organic Scottish food, the **New Town** and **Stockbridge** have a number of very good places to eat, with prices often cheaper than in the Old Town.

Cafés and diners

Bell's Diner, 7 St Stephen St (☎225 8116). Unpretentious little diner tucked away in Stockbridge. Good, inexpensive burgers, plus a wide choice of steaks and pancakes. Moderate.

Cyberia, 88 Hanover St (☎220 4403). Bright Internet café with fifteen computers (£2.50 per half-hour; email address: *edinburgh@easynet.co.uk*), and a wide range of snacks. Inexpensive.

Laigh Bake House, 117a Hanover St (☎225 1552). Long-established, homely New Town café with flagstone floor and cast-iron stoves. Good salads and soups, but best known for its wonderful home-baked scones and cakes. Inexpensive.

Scottish National Gallery of Modern Art Café, Belford Road (☎332 8600). Far more than a standard refreshment stop for gallery visitors, with many locals coming for lunch or a snack. It has a changing daily menu of salads, hot food and home baking, and there's a second branch in the National Portrait Gallery building. Moderate.

Seattle Coffee Company, Waterstone's, 128 Princes St (☎226 3610). A very welcome new arrival inside a bookshop, serving excellent coffee and with a fantastic view across Princes Street Gardens to the Castle. Inexpensive.

Terrace Café, Royal Botanic Garden (☎552 0616). Superior spot offering stunning views of the city, though the food is not that exciting. Changing menu includes hot dishes, sandwiches and cakes. Inexpensive.

Chinese

Bamboo Garden, 57a Frederick St (☎225 2382). Many of Edinburgh's Chinese community gather in this inexpensive place for great dim sum on Sunday lunchtime. Get the waiter to explain the choices rather than rely on the limited English-language menu. Moderate.

Loon Fung. 2 Warriston Place (☎556 1781). Something of a trailblazer for Cantonese cuisine in Scotland, near the eastern entrance to the Botanic Garden. Expensive.

French

Café St Honoré, 34 Thistle St Lane (☎226 2211). New Town brasserie serving good, inexpensive traditional French cooking, with fabulous pastries and coffee. Closed Sun. Moderate.

La Cuisine d'Odile, French Institute, 13 Randolph Crescent (☎225 5685). Popular French home cooking in a West End basement. Lunch only. Closed Sun, Mon & July. Inexpensive.

Indian

Indian Cavalry Club, 3 Atholl Place (☎228 3282). Upmarket, but moderately priced West End Indian restaurant with a pseudo-Raj decor and mildly spiced food. Five-course evening banquets for £15.95. Moderate–expensive.

Lancers, 5 Hamilton Place (☎332 3444). Aficionados rate the primarily Bengali and Punjabi curries at this moderately priced restaurant as the best in Scotland. Moderate.

Italian

Cosmo, 58a N Castle St (☎226 6743). Straightforward, delicious Italian cuisine at long-established trattoria. Main courses start at around £10. Closed Sun. Expensive.

Giuliano's, 18–19 Union Place (☎556 6590). Raucous trattoria across from the Playhouse, much favoured for family and office nights out. Does its best to conjure up the full Italian atmosphere. Closes 2am. Moderate.

Patio, 87 Hanover St (☎226 3653). The longest running of a clutch of reasonably priced, solid quality Italian restaurants on Hanover Street. Excellent fish and friendly service. Moderate.

Rafaelli, 10–11 Randolph Place (☎225 6060). Classy restaurant in a backstreet setting, specializing in northern Italian dishes, such as fish, veal and spinach pasta, and with a huge wine list. Closed Sun. Expensive.

San Marco, 10–11 Mary's Place (☎332 1569). Family-run Stockbridge pasta and pizza joint; good value and with a fun atmosphere. Moderate.

Vito's, 55a Frederick St (☎225 5052). Bustling, quality Italian cooking at mid-range prices with the emphasis on seafood. Closed Sun except during the Festival. Moderate.

Japanese

Tampopo, 25a Thistle St (☎220 5254). The closest thing to a budget Japanese restaurant, this noodle bar offers filling meals from around £5. Open daily noon–2.30pm & 6–9pm. Inexpensive.

Mexican

Tex Mex, 47 Hanover St (☎225 1796). Authentic, reasonably priced Mexican burritos and steaks, with a good value (£12.50) three-course pre-theatre menu available Mon–Fri 5–7pm. Moderate.

North African

Marrakech, 30 London St (☎556 7293). Scotland's only Moroccan restaurant, very reasonably priced, dishing up superb, authentic couscous, and *tajine,* plus a range of soups, fresh bread and pastries. Unlicensed, but you can take your own bottles and there's no corkage charge. Moderate.

Scottish

Duck's at Le Marché Noir, 2–4 Eyre Place, just off Dundas Street (☎558 1608). Adventurous Scottish menu, featuring such delicacies as haggis in filo pastry. The three-course dinner costs £26.50, and the three-course lunch is £15.50. Half the restaurant is non-smoking. Closed lunchtime Sat & Sun. Expensive.

Martin's, 70 Rose St (☎225 3106). The emphasis is on organic, unfarmed ingredients – salmon, venison, unpasteurized cheeses – in this long-standing restaurant hidden in an unlikely looking backstreet. It's at its priciest in the evenings, but well worth the money. Closed Sun & Mon. Expensive.

Stac Polly, 29–33 Dublin St (☎556 2231). Very much a carnivore's eating place, with good game, fish and meat dishes. Expensive.

Seafood

Café Royal Oyster Bar, 17a W Register St (☎556 4124). Splendidly ornate Victorian interior featured in *Chariots of Fire* – look out for the stained-glass windows showing sportsmen. Classic seafood dishes, including freshly caught oysters, served in a civilized, chatty atmosphere. Very expensive.

Spanish

The Tapas Tree, 1 Forth St (☎556 7118). Authentic, lively and extremely friendly tapas bar, featuring Spanish guitar music on Monday and Wednesday evenings. Moderate.

Swiss

Alp-Horn, 167 Rose St (☎225 4787). Fondues, air-dried meats and wonderful desserts in this handy little restaurant just off Charlotte Square. Good-value two-course lunches for £5.75. Closed Sun. Moderate.

Thai

Buntoms, 9–13 Nelson St (☎557 4344). Scotland's first Thai restaurant is still just as good as any of its competitors – don't miss its cracking *tom yum* soup. The three-course lunch for £6.50 is good value, and the menu includes several tasty vegetarian options. Moderate.

Siam Erewan, 48 Howe St (☎226 3675) Excellent Thai restaurant, serving a three-course lunch for £6.95 and evening banquets for around £19.95. Closed Sun lunch. Moderate.

Vegetarian

Henderson's, 94 Hanover St (☎225 2131). Self-service vegetarian basement restaurant, with adjacent bar. Freshly prepared hot dishes, plus a great choice of salads, soups, sweets and cheeses. An Edinburgh institution, so arrive early for lunch or be prepared to queue. Closed Sun. Inexpensive.

Southside

The **Southside** has a wide range of interesting restaurants, among them some of the best and most popular in Edinburgh.

Cafés and diners

Brattesani's, 85–87 Newington Rd (☎667 5808). Typical Italo-Scottish chippy, with choice of sit-down or carry-out meals. Daily 9.30am–midnight. Inexpensive.

Buffalo Grill, 14 Chapel St (☎667 7427). Charcoal-grilled steaks are the speciality in this popular and busy diner facing the main University campus. Moderate.

Café Q, 89 Clerk St (☎668 3456). In the Queen's Hall, a converted church, this café serves well-prepared salads, vegetarian dishes, soups and puddings as well as some decent wines and beers. Inexpensive.

Maxies, 32 W Nicolson St (☎667 0845). Large basement brasserie and wine bar with regular live music and some good vegetarian offerings. Popular with students and University staff. Closed Sun. Inexpensive.

Metropole, 33 Newington Rd (☎668 4999). Non-smoking Art Deco café with a good selection of coffees and excellent cakes. Moderate.

Nicolson's, 6a Nicolson St (☎557 4567). Spacious first-floor café opposite the Festival Theatre, with a varied daytime menu and three-course dinner for £14. Moderate.

Chinese

Chinese Home Cooking, 34 West Preston St (☎668 4946). Very reasonably priced: three-course lunch for £4, three-course dinner for £6. Inexpensive.

Good Year, 62 Ratcliffe Terrace (☎667 7532); 21 Argyle Place, south of the Meadows (☎229 4404). Both are very busy Chinese restaurants, particularly popular with students. Bring your own bottle (£1 corkage charge). Inexpensive.

French

La Bonne Vie, 49 Causewayside (☎667 1110). Very popular French restaurant serving a £15 set dinner. Moderate–expensive.

Indian

Annapurna, 45 St Patrick Square (☎662 1807). Excellent-value restaurant serving authentic Gujarati and southern Indian cuisine (so mainly vegetarian) – try the three-course lunch for £4.95. Moderate.

Kalpna, 2 St Patrick Square (☎667 9890). Outstanding vegetarian restaurant serving authentic Gujarati dishes. Offers a good-value eat-as-much-as-you-like lunchtime buffet for £4.50. Closed Sun. Moderate.

Khushi's, 16 Drummond St (☎556 8996). More a café than a restaurant, with only the basic comforts, but the food is reliable and cheap. Bring your own drink. Closed Sun. Inexpensive.

King's Balti, 79 Buccleuch St (☎662 9212). Edinburgh's best balti establishment is very popular with students and features an evening banquet for £25.95. You can bring your own bottle, but 50p corkage per person is charged. Moderate.

Suruchi, 14a Nicolson St (☎556 6583). Popular establishment serving genuine south Indian cooking. The emphasis is on rice and vegetables, with a few splendid poultry dishes. The set lunch is about £5, and there's a special pre-theatre menu around £9.95. Moderate.

North African

Phenecia, 55–57 W Nicolson St (☎662 4493). A basic food joint beside the main University campus, serving mostly Tunisian food but drawing on a variety of Mediterranean cuisines; the three-course lunch for £4.40 is very good value. Moderate.

Scottish

Howies, 75 St Leonard's St (☎668 2917). Smaller than its Haymarket partner, but serving similar brasserie-style Scottish cooking. No alcohol served, but you can bring your own bottle. Closed Mon lunch. Moderate.

Kelly's, 46b W Richmond St (☎668 3847). Enjoys virtual cult status among Edinburgh foodies, serving modern Scottish food and scrumptious desserts. Closed Mon lunch & Sun. Expensive.

Vegetarian

Engine Shed, 19 St Leonard's Lane (☎662 0040) Spacious, friendly vegetarian restaurant with a bakery on the premises. Lunchtime only. Inexpensive.

Pierre Lapin, 113 Buccleuch St (☎662 1849). Largely vegetarian offshoot of the *Pierre Victoire* chain, offering superb-value set menus. Closed Sun & Mon. Inexpensive.

Susie's Diner, 51 W Nicolson St (☎667 8729). The name has changed but this unlicensed café remains as popular as ever, serving inventive soups, savouries and puddings, and a range of vegan food, to crowds of students. Inexpensive.

Leith and Newhaven

Now a fashionable place to eat, **Leith** is packed with high-quality restaurants and waterfront brasseries, and is particularly good for seafood.

Brasseries

Malmaison Café Bar, 1 Tower Place (☎555 6969). Successful attempt to re-create the feel of a French café, serving excellent steak and chips and great fish dishes. The mashed potato is incredibly rich – not for those on a diet. Expensive.

Ship on the Shore, 24–26 The Shore (☎555 0409). The homeliest and least expensive of the waterfront brasseries serves good fresh fish, and has a changing range of cask ales. Moderate.

The Shore, 3 The Shore (☎553 5080). Non–smoking bar/restaurant with good fish dishes and decent wines. Great views at sunset, and live jazz and folk in the adjoining bar. Moderate.

Skippers, 1a Dock Place (☎554 1018). Across the Water of Leith from The Shore, with a vaguely nautical atmosphere and a superb – if expensive – fish-oriented menu that changes according to what's fresh. Closed Sun. Expensive.

Waterfront Wine Bar, 1c Dock Place (☎554 7427). Housed in the former lock-keeper's cottage with outdoor seating overlooking the waterfront, this popular wine bar/restaurant serves moderately priced fish dishes and good wines. Moderate.

Chinese

Yee Kiang, 42 Dalmeny St (☎554 5833). Homely little place, on a side street leading east off the middle of Leith Walk. The menu includes wonderful Pekinese specialities, notably the duck. Open 5.30–11.30pm; closed Mon. Moderate.

French

The Vintner's Rooms, 87 Giles St (☎554 6767). Splendid restaurant in a seventeenth-century warehouse, which is well worth the high prices. The bar in the cellar has a sombre, candlelit ambience and a coal fire; the ornate Rococo dining room serves expertly prepared food, using ingredients of the highest quality and is especially strong on fish and Gallic dishes. Very expensive.

Indian

Raj, 89–91a Henderson St (☎553 3980). An excellent ethnic alternative to the waterfront brasseries, serving Bangladeshi and north Indian dishes, but few vegetarian choices. Moderate.

Italian

Caprice Pizzerama, 327 Leith Walk (☎554 1279). Enormous place, almost exactly halfway between Princes Street and Leith. Specializes in giant pizzas baked in a wood-fired oven. Inexpensive.

Silvio's, 54 The Shore (☎553 3557). Non-smoking restaurant serving a variety of fresh pastas, excellent antipasto and fish dishes. The lunchtime menu offers two courses for £10.50, evenings are pricier. Moderate–expensive.

Tinelli, 139 Easter Rd (☎652 1932). Long-standing, very popular restaurant in an unlikely part of town, reputed to be Edinburgh's best Italian. Specializes in northern Italian food – try the spinach and pumpkin-stuffed pasta. Closed Sun. Moderate.

Umberto's, 2 Bonnington Road Lane (☎554 1314). The best place in Edinburgh for anyone with children. Play areas, sympathetic staff and the food's good as well. Moderate.

Scottish

(Fitz)henry, 19 Shore Place (☎555 6625). New brasserie which has already won a Michelin Red M. The three-course set dinner costs £22, and the two-course lunch will set you back a tenner. Closed Sun. Expensive.

Seafood

Harry Ramsden's, 5 Newhaven Place (☎551 5566). Just west of Leith in Newhaven, this branch of the Yorkshire chain offers substantial portions of fish and chips in an attractive harbourside setting. Inexpensive.

Swiss

Denzlers, 121 Constitution St (☎554 3268). Although it has moved premises a few times over the years, this has consistently ranked among Scotland's most highly praised restaurants. The ever-innovative menu is constantly changing, and prices are surprisingly reasonable, with most main courses under £10. Closed Sun & Mon. Moderate.

Pubs and bars

Many of Edinburgh's **pubs**, especially in the Old Town, have histories that stretch back centuries, while others, particularly in the New Town, are unaltered Victorian or Edwardian period pieces that rank among Edinburgh's most outstanding examples of interior design. Add in the plentiful supply of trendy modern bars, and there's a variety of styles and atmospheres to cater for all tastes. Many honest howffs stay open late and, during the Festival especially, it's no problem to find bars open till at least midnight.

Currently, Edinburgh has three **breweries**, including the giant Scottish and Newcastle (who produce McEwan's and Younger's). The small independent

Caledonian Brewery uses old techniques and equipment to produce some of the best beers in Britain, and there's also the tiny Rose Street Brewery, which has its own pub. In summer, the Caledonian Brewery, Slateford Road (☎337 1286) runs tours for groups of twenty or more: phone ahead to arrange a visit.

Edinburgh's main drinking strip is the near-legendary **Rose Street**, a pedestrianized lane of minimal visual appeal tucked between Princes and George streets. The ultimate Edinburgh pub crawl is to drink a half-pint in each of its dozen or so establishments – plus the two in West Register Street, its eastern continuation. Most of the **student pubs** are in and around Grassmarket, with a further batch on the Southside, an area overlooked by most tourists. **Leith** has a nicely varied crop of bars, ranging from the roughest type of spit-and-sawdust places to polished pseudo-Victoriana, while two of the city's best and most characterful pubs are further west along the seafront in **Newhaven**.

A fun way to expore Edinburgh's pubs is to take the **Original Edinburgh Literary Tour**, a lively trip round Old and New Town watering holes. Led by professional actors, the tour takes you through the major figures of Scottish literature from Burns and Scott to MacDiarmid and Welsh. The tour starts from the *Beehive Inn*, 18–20 Grassmarket (April–June, Sept & Oct Thurs–Sun 7.30pm; July & Aug daily 6pm & 8.30pm; Nov–March Fri 7.30pm; £6), and a minimum of six people is needed.

The Old Town and Tollcross

Bannermans, 212 Cowgate. The best pub in the street, formerly a vintner's cellar, with a labyrinthine interior and good beer on tap. On weekdays, tasty veggie lunches are on offer at rock-bottom prices; breakfasts available at weekends 11am–4pm. Open Mon–Sat till 1am.

Bar Kohl, 54 George IV Bridge. Trendy vodka bar with a choice of more than two hundred ways to give yourself a fearsome hangover.

Bennets Bar, 8 Leven St, Tollcross. Edwardian pub with mahogany-set mirrors and Art Nouveau stained glass; gets packed in the evening, particularly when there's a show at the King's Theatre next door. Mon–Sat serves lunch and opens till midnight.

Blue Blazer, 2 Spittal St. Traditional Edinburgh howff with oak-clad bar and church pews; serves a good selection of ales.

Bow Bar, 80 West Bow. Old wood-panelled bar that recently won an award as the best drinkers' pub in Britain. Choose from among nearly 150 whiskies, an almost equally wide range of other spirits, and a changing selection of first-rate Scottish and English cask beers.

Canon's Gait, 232 Canongate. Good food and ale is served in a tartan decor and there's folk and jazz music in the basement bar.

Cellar No.1, 2 Chambers St. Lively stone-clad vault that doubles as an imaginative restaurant. Excellent wines by the bottle or glass. Mon–Thurs & Sun open until 1am, Fri & Sat open till 3am.

Doric Tavern, 15 Market St. Favoured watering hole of journalists from the nearby *Scotsman* building. The downstairs *McGuffie's Tavern* is a traditional Edinburgh howff, while upstairs is a brasserie, with highly regarded food.

Fiddlers Arms, 9–11 Grassmarket. Traditional bar serving excellent McEwan's 80 Shilling. The walls are adorned with forlorn, stringless violins. Open Mon–Thurs till 11.30pm, Fri & Sat 1am.

Green Tree, 184 Cowgate. Popular student bar with occasional folk music and a walled beer garden.

Greyfriars Bobby, 34 Candlemaker Row. Long-established favourite with both students and tourists, named after the statue outside.

Hebrides Bar, 17 Market St. Home from home for Edinburgh's Highland community: ceilidh atmosphere with lots of jigs, strathspeys and reels, but no tartan kitsch.

International Bar, 15 Brougham Place. Good Tollcross pub offers toasted sandwiches to go with your pint and footie on the telly.

Jolly Judge, 7a James Court. Atmospheric bar in a close just down from the Castle. Popular with tourists.

Last Drop, 74–78 Grassmarket. "Drop" refers to the Edinburgh gallows, which were located in front, and whose former presence is symbolized in the red paintwork of the exterior. Cheapish pub food, and, like its competitors in the same block, patronized mainly by students.

Malt Shovel, 11–15 Cockburn St. Dimly lit, comfortable bar with an excellent range of cask beers and single malt whiskies, and serving big portions of chilli and haddock and chips at lunchtime. Open Sun–Thurs 11am–12.30am, Fri & Sat 11am–1am.

Oddfellows, 14 Forrest Rd. Hip hangout for students and hard-up fashion victims. An amazing clutter of paraphernalia reflects the building's previous incarnation as a flea market.

Sandy Bell's, 25 Forrest Rd. A folk music institution, hosting regular impromptu sessions. Small but busy with an impressive selection of beers and whiskies.

The New Town and Stockbridge

Abbotsford, 3 Rose St. Large-scale pub whose original Victorian decor, complete with wood panelling and "island bar", is among the finest in the city. Good range of ales, including Broughton Greenmantle. Restaurant upstairs serves hearty Scottish food. Closed Sun.

Baillie Bar, 2 St Stephen St. Basement bar at corner of Edinburgh's most self-consciously Bohemian street. English and Scottish ales are available, including some from the Caledonian Brewery.

The Basement, 10a Broughton St. Packed out, especially at the weekends, with a pre-club crowd, this trendy bar is run by young and enthusiastic staff and serves cheap Mexican food at the weekends.

Bert's Bar, 29 William St and 2–4 Raeburn Place. The former fills up with the office lunchtime crowd, the latter at night with Stockbridge yuppies. Both have excellent beer, good food and strive to be authentic, non-theme-oriented pubs.

Café Royal, 17 W Register St. The pub part of this stylish Victorian restaurant, the *Circle Bar*, is worth a visit for its decor alone, notably the huge elliptical "island" counter and the tiled portraits of renowned inventors. Thurs open until midnight, Fri & Sat till 1am.

Cumberland Bar, 1 Cumberland St. Highly popular bar with no jukebox and a wide variety of ales. There a garden in the summer and good, reasonably priced food is served from noon to 2pm.

The Dome Bar and Grill, 14 George St. Opulent conversion of a massive New Town bank, thronging with minor local celebrities. Sun–Thurs open till 11.30pm, Fri & Sat till 1am.

Guildford Arms, 1–5 W Register St. Excellent selection of ales, reasonable food and a mixed clientele in this splendidly Baroque bar.

Indigo Yard, 7 Charlotte Lane. Designer chic hits Edinburgh's West End: great for those who want Thai fish cakes with their draught beer. Daily till 1am.

Kay's Bar, 39 Jamaica St. Small, civilized one-time wine shop, warmed by a roaring log fire in winter, and serving fine cask ales. Closed Sun.

Kenilworth, 152–154 Rose St. Attractive high-ceilinged pub dating from 1899, with good beer and food. There's a family room at the back, with a special children's menu.

Mathers, 25 Broughton St. Relaxed, old-fashioned pub which attracts a mixed crowd. The best place in Edinburgh for stout, with Guinness and Murphy's on tap, as well as the local Gillespie's.

Milne's Bar, 35 Hanover St. Cellar bar once beloved of Edinburgh's literati, earning the nickname "The Poets' Pub" courtesy of Hugh MacDiarmid et al. Serves a good range of cask beers, including McEwan's 80 Shilling.

Oxford Bar, 8 Young St. Traditional city bar, unpretentious and somewhat of a shrine for rugby fans and off-duty policemen. Good Scottish pub food is available: try the Forfar bridies (similar to Cornish pasties) and mutton pie.

Po-Na-Na, 43b Frederick St. Trendy and very popular "souk" bar, offering simple snacks. Admission is charged after 11pm, Sun–Thurs £2, Fri & Sat £3. Open daily till 3am.

Rose Street Brewery, 55 Rose St. Edinburgh's only micro-brewery, whose equipment can be inspected in the upstairs restaurant; the two beers made there are also on tap in the ground-floor bar.

The Southside

Peartree House, 36 W Nicolson St. Fine bar in eighteenth-century house with courtyard, one of Edinburgh's very few beer gardens; serves decent bar lunches. Open daily until midnight.

Southsider, 3–5 W Richmond St. Genuine local pub with a superb range of draught and imported bottled beers.

Stewart's, 14 Drummond St. A Southside institution since the beginning of the century, and seemingly little changed since then; popular with lecturers and students.

Leith

Kings Wark, 36 The Shore, Leith. Real ale and good food in a restored eighteenth-century pub.

Malt and Hops, 45 The Shore. Real-ale pub offering basic bar snacks.

Merman, 42 Bernard St, Leith. Intimate pub that dates back to 1775, and is still preserved in its original state with a blazing log fire. Specializes in high-quality cask beers.

Starbank Inn, 64 Laverockbank Rd, Newhaven. Fine old stone-built pub overlooking the Forth with a high reputation for cask ales and bar food.

Tattler, 23 Commercial St, Leith. Bar-restaurant decked out in plush Victorian style and serving wonderful, award-winning bar meals of high-quality Scottish food including fish, meat and poultry.

Ye Olde Peacock Inn, Lindsay Road, Newhaven (☎552 8707). Serves cheap, homely food, including the best fish and chips in the city. Advance reservations are advisable for the main bar and restaurant; otherwise try for a table in the small lounge. Don't miss the gallery displaying prints of the pioneering Hill and Adamson calotypes of Newhaven fishwives.

Elsewhere in the city

Athletic Arms (The Diggers), 1 Angle Park Terrace. Out in the western suburbs, near Tynecastle football ground and Murrayfield rugby stadium, the pub's nickname comes from the cemetery nearby. For decades, it has had the reputation of being Edinburgh's best pub for serious ale drinkers.

Caley Sample Room, 58 Angle Park Terrace. Showpiece pub for the cask ales of the nearby Caledonian Brewery.

Canny Man's (Volunteer Arms), 237 Morningside Rd, Morningside. Atmospheric pub/museum adorned with anything that can be hung on the walls or from the ceiling. Mon–Sat open until midnight.

Hawes Inn, Newhalls Road, S Queensferry. Famous old whitewashed tavern virtually under the Forth Rail Bridge, immortalized by Stevenson in *Kidnapped*. The bar serves a wide range of food and drink and the rambling complex also includes a hotel and upmarket restaurant (☎319 1120).

Sheep Heid, 43 The Causeway, Duddingston. This eighteenth-century inn with a family atmosphere makes an ideal refreshment stop at the end of a tramp through Holyrood Park. Decent home-cooked meals are available at the bar, and more substantial fare in the upstairs restaurant.

Nightlife and entertainment

Inevitably, Edinburgh's **nightlife** is at its best during the Festival (see p.96), which can make the other 49 weeks of the year seem like an anticlimax. However, when not compared to the misleading yardstick of the Festival, the city has a lot to offer, especially in the realm of **performing arts** and **concerts**.

    Nightclubs don't offer anything startlingly original, but they serve their purpose, hosting a changing selection of one-nighters. In the bigger venues, you may find different clubs taking place on each floor. Most of the city-centre clubs stay open till around 3am. While you can normally hear **live jazz**, **folk** and **rock** every evening in one or other of the city's pubs, for the really big rock events, ad hoc venues – such as the Castle Esplanade, Meadowbank Stadium or the exhibition halls of the Royal Highland Show at Ingliston, which hosts occasional **raves** – are often pressed into service.

    With an estimated homosexual population of around 15,000–20,000, Edinburgh has a dynamic **gay** culture, for years centred round the top of Leith Walk and Broughton Street, where the first gay and lesbian centre appeared in the 1970s. Since the start of the 1990s, more and more gay enterprises, especially cafés and nightclubs, have moved into this area, now dubbed the "Broughton Triangle", and there is a constant stream of new places and old ones changing name.

The best way to find out **what's on** is to pick up a copy of *The List*, a fortnightly listings magazine covering both Edinburgh and Glasgow (£1.90). Alternatively, get hold of the *Edinburgh Evening News*, which appears daily except Sunday: its listings column gives details of performances in the city that day, hotels and bars included. **Tickets** and information on all events are available from the tourist office. Box offices of individual halls and theatres are likewise liberally supplied with promotional leaflets, and some are able to sell tickets for more than one venue.

Nightclubs

La Belle Angèle, 11 Hasties Close (☎225 2774). A rotating selection of Latin, soul, hip-hop and jazz. Edinburgh's best drum and bass club on Fridays, while House rules on Saturdays.

Café Graffiti, Mansfield Place Church, at the foot of Broughton Street (☎557 8003). Great venue in a church basement, with Latin and jazz playing at the weekend. Usually sells out very quickly, so arrive before 11.30pm.

The Cavendish, W Tollcross (☎228 3252). Packed out roots, ragga and reggae night on Friday; "The Mambo" on Saturday plays African and Latin rhythms.

The Citrus, 40–42 Grindlay St (☎229 6697). Eighties indie music along with some funk and disco.

Club Mercado 36–39 Market St (☎226 4224). Seventies night on Friday, while sharp clothes are required to get in to Saturday's busy thumping House nights.

Honeycomb, 36–38a Blair St (☎220 4381). A great sound system plays thumping house, hip-hop and garage music Thurs–Wed. Live jazz Mon–Wed.

Moray House Student Union, Holyrood Road (☎556 5184). Popular Saturday club nights ranging from 1970s funk to wistful indie.

Rocking Horse, Cowgate (☎225 7733). Rock nights including heavy metal, Goth-rock and grunge.

The Venue, 15 Calton Rd (☎557 3073). Each of the three levels hosts a variety of different one-nighters specializing in House, funk and garage. Friday nights see the long-running popular *Pure* with techno and live acts, and Saturdays alternate between 1970s disco and *Tribal Funktion* House and garage soul.

Wilkie House Cowgate (☎225 2935). *Lift*, held on alternate Fridays, is a busy techno and acid night, while *Joy,* a popular gay night, takes place monthly on Saturdays.

Gay clubs and bars

Blue Moon Café/Blue Moon Espresso, 1 Barony St and 36 Broughton St (☎557 0911). Eat in or take away at this stylish café/bar serving varied continental food and drink and attracting a mixed crowd. Open 7pm–1am.

Café Kudos, 22 Greenside Place (☎556 4349). Popular with smart young things, who throng to the outside tables in summer. Attracts both gays and lesbians at night, and a mixed crowd during the day.

CC Bloom's, 23 Greenside Place (☎556 9331). Big dance floor, stonking rhythms and a young, friendly crowd.

Newtown Club Bar, 26 Dublin St (☎538 7775). Men-only, with a high number of professionals. The raunchy *Intense Cellar Bar* downstairs is particularly good fun and opens Wed–Sun 9pm–late.

Route 66, 6 Baxter's Place (☎556 5991). Friendly and relaxed bar located in the heart of the "Broughton Triangle".

Stonewall Café, 60 Broughton St (☎478 7069). Light meals, snacks and drinks at the Edinburgh Gay, Lesbian and Bisexual Centre. Open April–Aug 11am–11pm; Sept–March noon–9.30pm.

Live music pubs and venues

La Belle Angèle, 11 Hasties Close (☎225 2774). A home to both indie bands and Latin divas.

Café Royal, 17 W Register St (☎556 4124). Regular folk nights upstairs in one of the city's most famous bars.

· EDINBURGH'S OTHER FESTIVALS

Quite apart from the Edinburgh Festival, the city is now promoting itself as a year-round festival city, beginning with a **Hogmanay Festival** (☎557 3990) which involves street parties, folk and rock concerts and drive-in cinema shows. The **Folk Festival** (☎556 3181) in April draws local and international performers, while the **Science Festival** (☎557 4296), also in April, incorporates hands-on children's events as well as numerous lectures on a vast array of subjects. There is a **Puppet and Animation Festival** (☎556 9579) in March, and a **Children's Festival** (☎554 6297) in May with readings, magicians, etc. In the summer, a series of concerts (usually free), ranging from tea dances to world music, is held in the **Ross Bandstand** in Princes Street Gardens. The Caledonian Brewery, 42 Slateford Rd, runs its own German-style **beer festival** in June, while the **Edinburgh Traditional Beer Festival**, with real ales from all over Britain, is held at Meadowbank Sports Stadium in October.

The **Open Doors Day**, around mid-September, provides an opportunity to visit a number of noteworthy buildings, otherwise closed to the public. In recent years, these have included private homes in the New Town, disused churches and company offices. Contact the **Cockburn Association** (☎557 8686) for details. The **Filmhouse** (☎228 2688) also has a number of annual seasons of international cinema, notably French (in November) and Italian (April), and a gay season (June).

Canon's Gait, 232 Canongate (☎556 4481). Local folk and jazz in a Royal Mile basement bar, which serves good beer.

Cas Rock Café, 104 W Port (☎229 4341). A mixture of sedate folk and raucous punky sounds.

The Liquid Room, 9c Victoria St (☎225 2564). Good-sized, recently renovated venue frequented by visiting indie and local R&B bands.

Negociants, 45–47 Lothian St (☎225 6313). Upstairs brasserie serves breakfast and lunch, and specializes in Belgian fruit beers. The downstairs bar hosts varied live bands and is popular with students. Open until 1am.

Nobles Bar, 44a Constitution St, Leith (☎553 3873). A standard of the local jazz scene, featuring regular live sessions in a lovely Victorian pub with leaded glass windows and horseshoe bar. Check out the all-day Sunday breakfasts.

The Queen's Hall, 37 Clerk St (☎668 3456). Housed in a former Southside church, with some pews still in place, hosting African, funk and rock bands, as well as smaller jazz, folk concerts and comedy nights with well-established comedians.

Royal Oak, 1 Infirmary St (☎557 2976). Cosy and friendly folk bar. Open till 2am.

Tron Ceilidh House, 9 Hunter Square (☎220 1500). Busy, huge complex of bars on different levels, with regular jazz and folk nights. Comedy on Friday nights.

The Venue, 15 Calton Rd (☎557 3073). Small, intimate sweaty club hosting up-and-coming indie bands.

Theatre and comedy

Assembly Rooms, 54 George St (☎220 4348). Varied complex of small and large halls. Used all year, but really comes into its own during the Fringe, featuring large-scale drama productions and mainstream comedy.

Bedlam Theatre, 2a Forrest Rd (☎225 9893). Housed in a converted Victorian church and used predominantly by student groups.

Festival Theatre, Nicolson Street (☎529 6000). Everything from the children's show *Singing Kettle*, to Engelbert Humperdinck and *La Traviata*.

Gilded Balloon Theatre, 233 Cowgate (☎226 6550). Fringe comedy venue, noted for the Late ' n' Live (1–4am) slot which gives you the chance to see top comedians whose main show elsewhere may be booked out. Also puts on regular comedy shows throughout the year.

King's Theatre, 2 Leven St (☎229 1201). Stately Edwardian civic theatre that offers the most eclectic programme in the city – includes opera, ballet, Shakespeare, pantomime and comedy.

Netherbow Arts Centre, 43 High St (☎556 9579). Although the centre is run by the Church of Scotland, the emphasis in their adventurous year-round drama productions is more Scottish than religious.

Playhouse Theatre, 18–22 Greenside Place (☎557 2590). The most capacious theatre in Britain, formerly a cinema. Recently refurbished, and used largely for extended runs of popular musicals and occasional rock concerts.

Pleasance Theatre, 60 The Pleasance (☎556 6550). Fringe Festival venue. Cobbled courtyard with stunning views across to Arthur's Seat and an array of auditoria used for a varied programme.

Royal Lyceum Theatre, 30 Grindlay St (☎229 9697). Fine Victorian civic theatre with compact auditorium. The city's leading year-round venue for mainstream drama.

St Bride's Centre, 10 Orwell Terrace (☎346 1405). Neo-Gothic church converted into an intimate stage that can be adapted for theatre in the round.

Theatre Workshop, 34 Hamilton Place (☎226 5425). Enticing programmes of international innovative theatre and performance art all year round.

Traverse Theatre, 10 Cambridge St (☎228 1404). A byword in experimental theatrical circles, and unquestionably one of Britain's premier venues for new plays. Going from strength to strength in its new custom-built home beside the Usher Hall.

Concert halls

Queen's Hall, 89 Clerk St (☎668 2019). Converted Georgian church with a capacity of around eight hundred, though many seats have little or no view of the platform. Home base of both the Scottish Chamber Orchestra and Scottish Ensemble, and much favoured by jazz, blues and folk groups. Also hosts established comedians.

Reid Concert Hall, Bristo Square (☎650 4367). Narrow, steeply pitched Victorian hall owned by the University, and hosting classical concerts.

St Cecilia's Hall, corner of Cowgate and Niddry Street (☎650 2805). A Georgian treasure that is again university-owned and not used as frequently as it deserves to be.

Usher Hall, corner of Lothian Road and Grindlay Street (☎228 1155). Edinburgh's main civic concert hall, seating over 2500. Excellent for choral and symphony concerts, but less suitable for solo vocalists. The upper circle seats are cheapest and have the best acoustics; avoid the back of the grand tier and the stalls, where the sound is muffled by the overhanging balconies.

Cinemas

ABC Filmcentre, Lothian Road (☎228 1638). Mainstream cinema.

Cameo, 38 Home St (☎228 4141). New arthouse releases and cult late-nighters.

Dominion, 18 Newbattle Terrace (☎447 4771). Latest releases.

Filmhouse, 88 Lothian Rd (☎228 2688). Eclectic programme of independent, arthouse and classic films.

Odeon, 7 Clerk St (☎667 7331). Five-screen cinema showing the latest releases.

UCI, Kinnaird Park (☎669 0777). Multiplex in the southeast of the city.

Shopping

Despite the relentless advance of the big chains, central Edinburgh remains an enticing place for **shopping**, with many of its streets having their own distinctive character. **Princes Street**, though dominated by standard chain outlets, retains a number of independent emporia. At the eastern end is the **Waverley Market**, a glossy mall of specialist shops, while the middle section of **Rose Street** has a good array of small jewellers and trendy clothes shops. Along the **Royal Mile** there are several distinctly offbeat places among the tacky-souvenir sellers, and in and around **Grassmarket** you'll find antique and arts and crafts shops plus some antiquarian booksellers. The main concentration of general, academic and remainder bookshops is in the area stretching from **South Bridge** to **George IV Bridge**. For antique shops the two best areas are **St Stephen Street** in Stockbridge and **Causewayside** in Southside.

Bagpipes Bagpipe Centre, 49 Blackfriars St (☎557 3090); Clan Bagpipes, 13a James Court, Lawnmarket (☎225 2415).

Books Bauermeisters, 19 George IV Bridge (☎226 5561), is a row of separate bookshops selling general and academic books, music, stationery and paperbacks. James Thin, 53–59 South Bridge (☎556 6743) and 57 George St (☎225 4495): the first a huge, rambling general and academic shop, the second smaller and more genteel, with a good café. Waterstone's is at 128 Princes St (☎226 2666), 13–14 Princes St (☎556 3034) and 83 George St (☎225 3436). There is a good selection of antiquarian bookshops in the city: Peter Bell, 68 West Port (☎229 0562); Castle Books, 204 Canongate (☎556 0624); Tolbooth Books, 175 Canongate (☎558 3411); West Port Books, 151 West Port (☎229 4431); also McNaughtan's Bookshop 3a–4a Haddington Place, Leith Walk (☎556 5897). The best of the secondhand bookshops are: Broughton Books, 2a Broughton Place (☎557 8010), and Second Edition, 9 Howard Place (☎556 9403).

Clothes (secondhand) Anna's, 2a Tarvit St (☎229 9126); Wm Armstrong, 313 Cowgate (☎556 6521); Herman Brown, 151 West Port (☎228 2589); Paddy Barass, 15 Grassmarket (☎226 3087); Elaine's, 55 St Stephen St; and Flip, 59–61 South Bridge (☎556 4966).

Haggis Charles MacSween & Son, 118 Bruntsfield Place (☎229 9141), has an international reputation, and also makes a tasty vegetarian version.

Maps Carson Clark, 173 Canongate (☎556 4710), sells antique maps, charts and globes.

Records Avalanche, 17 West Nicolson St (☎668 2374) and 28 Lady Lawson St (☎228 1939) for indie music; Fopp, 55 Cockburn St (☎220 0133); Ripping Records, 91 South Bridge (☎226 7010); and Vinyl Villains, 5 Elm Row (☎558 1170), stock secondhand records, tapes and ephemera.

Tartan Celtic Craft Centre, 101 High St (☎556 3228); Kinloch Anderson, on the corner of Commercial and Dock streets, Leith (☎555 1390); James Pringle Woollen Mill, 70 Bangor Rd, Leith (☎553 5161), who has an archive computer which tells you if you're entitled to wear a clan tartan, and gives full historic information; Geoffrey Tailor, 57–59 High St (☎557 0256).

Tweed Romanes and Paterson, 62 Princes St (☎225 4966).

Whisky Royal Mile Whiskies, 379–381 High St (☎225 3383); William Cadenhead, 172 Canongate (☎556 5864).

Woollen goods Bill Baber Knitwear, 66 Grassmarket (☎225 3249), designs and makes the garments on the premises; Ragamuffin, 276 Canongate (☎557 6007), for Skye knitwear; The Shetland Connection, 491 Lawnmarket (☎225 3525), and Simply Shetland, 9 West Port (☎228 4578), for Shetland knitting wool, lace and cobweb.

Listings

Airlines British Airways, 32 Frederick St (☎0345 222111). Other carriers handled by Servisair, Edinburgh Airport (☎344 3111).

American Express, 139 Princes St (Mon–Fri 9am–5.30pm, Sat 9am–4pm; July–Sept also Sun 10am–4pm; ☎225 9179).

Banks Bank of Scotland, The Mound (head office), 38 St Andrew Square, 141 Princes St; Barclays, 1 St Andrew Square; Clydesdale, 29 George St; Lloyds, 113–115 George St; Midland, 76 Hanover St; NatWest, 80 George St; Royal Bank of Scotland, 42 St Andrew Square; TSB, 120 George St.

Car rental Arnold Clark, Lochrin Place (☎228 4747); Avis, 100 Dalry Rd (☎337 6363); Budget, 111 Glasgow Rd (☎334 7739); Carnies, 46 Westfield Rd (☎346 4155); Europcar, 24 E London St (☎557 3456); Hertz, Waverley Station (☎557 5272); Mitchells, 32 Torphichen St (☎229 5384); Thrifty Car Rental, 24 Haymarket Terrace (☎313 1613).

Consulates Australia, 25 Bernard St (☎555 4500); Belgium, 21 The Square, Penicuik (☎01698/679969); Denmark, 4 Royal Terrace (☎556 4263); France, 11 Randolph Crescent (☎225 7954); Germany, 16 Eglinton Crescent (☎337 2323); Italy, 32 Melville St (☎226 3631); Netherlands, 53 George St (☎220 3226); Norway, 86 George St (☎226 5701); Poland, 2 Kinnear Rd (☎552 0301); Spain, 63 N Castle St (☎220 1843); Sweden, 6 St John's Place (☎554 6631); Switzerland, 66 Hanover Place (☎226 5660); USA, 3 Regent Terrace (☎556 8315).

Exchange Thomas Cook, 79a Princes St (Mon–Fri 9am–5.30pm, Sat 9am–5pm; ☎220 4039); currency exchange bureaus in the main tourist office (Mon–Sat 9am–8pm, Sun 10am–8pm) and in the accommodation office at Waverley Station (see p.60). To change money after hours, try one of the upmarket hotels – but expect to pay a hefty commission charge.

Football Edinburgh has two Scottish Premier Division teams, who are at home on alternate Saturdays. Heart of Midlothian (or Hearts) play at Tynecastle Stadium, Gorgie Road, a couple of miles west of the centre; Hibernian (or Hibs) play at Easter Road Stadium, a similar distance east of the centre. Between them, the two clubs dominated Scottish football in the 1950s, but neither has won more than the odd trophy since, though one or the other periodically threatens to make a major breakthrough. Tickets from £10.

Gay and lesbian contacts Gay Men's Health (☎558 9444); Gay Switchboard (☎556 4049); Lesbian Line (☎557 0751).

Genealogical research Scots Ancestry Research Society, 29a Albany St (☎556 4220); Scottish Genealogy Society, 15 Victoria Terrace (☎220 3677); Scottish Roots, 57–59 High St (☎557 6550).

Golf Edinburgh is awash with fine golf courses, but most of them are private. The best public courses are the two on the Braid Hills (☎447 6666); others are Carrick Knowe (☎337 1096), Craigentinny (☎554 7501) and Silverknowes (☎336 3843).

Hospital Royal Infirmary, 1 Lauriston Place (☎229 2477), has a 24hr casualty department.

Left luggage Lockers available at Waverley Station (Mon–Sat 7am–11pm, Sun 8am–11pm) and St Andrew Square bus station (Mon–Sat 6.35am–10pm, Sun 8am–10pm).

Libraries Central Library, George IV Bridge (Mon–Fri 9am–9pm, Sat 9am–1pm; ☎225 5584). In addition to the usual departments, there's a separate Scottish section, plus an Edinburgh Room which is a mine of information on the city. National Library of Scotland, George IV Bridge (Mon–Fri 9.30am–8.30pm, Sat 9.30am–1pm; ☎226 4531), a magnificent copyright library for research purposes only, is currently closed, but is due to reopen in autumn 1998. Reference facilities are available at the Map Room, 33 Salisbury Place (Mon–Fri 9.30am–5pm, Sat 9.30am–1pm).

Motoring organizations AA, 18–22 Melville St (☎225 3301); RAC, 35 Kinnaird Park (☎657 3444).

Pharmacy Boots, 48 Shandwick Place (Mon–Sat 8.45am–9pm, Sun 11am–4pm; ☎225 6757).

Post office 8–10 St James Centre (Mon 9am–5.30pm, Tues–Fri 8.30am–5.30pm, Sat 8.30am–6pm; ☎0345 223344).

Rape crisis centre ☎556 9437.

Rugby Scotland's international fixtures are played at Murrayfield Stadium, a couple of miles west of the city centre. Phone the stadium on ☎346 5000 for advice on ticket sales, but be warned that tickets can be very hard to come by.

Sports stadium Meadowbank Sports Centre and Stadium, 139 London Rd (☎661 5351), is Edinburgh's main venue for most spectator and participatory sports. Facilities include an athletics track, a velodrome and indoor halls.

Swimming pools The city has one Olympic-standard modern pool, the Royal Commonwealth Pool, 21 Dalkeith Rd (☎667 7211), and a number of considerably older pools at Caledonian Crescent (☎313 3964), Glenogle Road (☎343 6376), 15 Bellfield St, Portobello (☎669 4077), and 6 Thirlestane Rd (☎447 0052).

Travel agents Campus Travel (student and youth specialist), 53 Forrest Rd (☎225 6111) and 5 Nicolson Square (☎668 3303); Edinburgh Travel Centre (student and youth specialist), 196 Rose St (☎226 2019), 92 S Clerk St (☎667 9488) and 3 Bristo Square (☎668 2221). For three- and six-day coach trips to the Highlands, try Go Blue Banana, 16 High St (☎556 2000) or Haggis Backpackers, 11 Blackfriars St (☎558 1177).

travel details

Trains

Edinburgh to: Aberdeen (hourly; 2hr 40min); Aviemore (5 daily; 3hr); Birmingham (6 daily; 5hr 30min); Crewe (6 daily; 3hr 30min); Dundee (hourly; 1hr 45min); Fort William (change at Glasgow, 3 daily; 4hr 55min); Glasgow (38 daily; 50min); Inverness (4 daily; 3hr 50min); London (12 daily; 4hr 30min); Manchester (4 daily, direct; 4hr: 7 daily, change at Preston; 4hr); Newcastle upon Tyne (19 daily; 1hr 30min); Oban (3 daily, change at Glasgow; 4hr 10min); Perth (6 daily; 1hr 15min); Stirling (every 30min; 45min); York (20 daily; 2hr 30min).

Buses

Edinburgh St Andrew Square bus station to: Aberdeen (13 daily; express 3hr, standard 3hr 50min); Birmingham (2 daily; 6hr 50min); Campbeltown (3 daily; 6hr); Dundee (14 daily; express 1hr 25min–2hr); Fort William (3 daily; 5hr); Glasgow (44 daily; 1hr 10min); Inverness (11 daily; 3hr–4hr); London (2 daily; 7hr 50min); Newcastle upon Tyne (3 daily; 3hr 15min); Oban (3 daily; 5hr); Perth (14 daily; 1hr 20min); Pitlochry (11 daily; 2hr); York (1 daily; 5hr).

Flights

Edinburgh to: Birmingham (Mon–Fri 7 daily, Sat & Sun 4 daily; 1hr); Dundee (Mon–Fri 2 daily; 15min); London Gatwick (Mon–Fri 5 daily, Sat & Sun 3 daily; 1hr 15min); London Heathrow (Mon–Fri 20 daily, Sat & Sun 15 daily; 1hr); Manchester (Mon–Fri 3 daily; 50min); Stansted (Mon–Fri 5 daily, Sat & Sun 2 daily; 1hr 10min).

CHAPTER TWO

SOUTHERN SCOTLAND

Although **Southern Scotland** doesn't have the high tourist profile of other areas, in many ways the region is at the very heart of the country. Its inhabitants bore the brunt of long wars with the English, its farms have fed Scotland's cities since industrialization, and two of the country's literary icons, **Sir Walter Scott** and **Robbie Burns**, lived and died here. The main roads, the fast routes from northern England to Glasgow and Edinburgh, bypass the best of the region, but if you make an effort to get off the highways there's plenty to see, from the ruins of medieval castles and abbeys to well-preserved market towns and rural villages set within a wild, hilly countryside.

Geographically, southern Scotland is dominated by the **Southern Uplands** – a chain of bulging flat-peaked hills and weather-beaten moorland punctuated by narrow glens, fast-flowing rivers and blue-black lochs – extending south and west from an imaginary line drawn between Peebles and Jedburgh in central southern Scotland over to the Ayrshire coast. It's in the west, in the **Galloway Forest Park**, that they are at their most dramatic, with peaks soaring over 2000ft, and criss-crossed by many popular **walking** trails.

North of the inhospitable Cheviot Hills, which straddle the border with England, a clutch of tiny towns in the **Tweed River Valley** – including delightful **Melrose** – form the nucleus of the Borders, inspiration for countless folkloric ballads telling of bloody battles with the English and clashes between the notorious warring families, the Border Reivers. East of **Kelso**, one of four abbeys founded on the Borders by the medieval Canmore kings, the Tweed Valley widens to form the Merse basin, an area of flat farmland that boasts a series of grand stately homes, principally **Floors Castle**, **Manderston**, **Paxton** and **Mellerstain House**. These feature the work of the Adam family – William, and two of his four sons, John and Robert, whose fine skills are also displayed at Ayr's **Culzean Castle**.

North of the Tweed, a narrow band of foothills – the **Pentland**, **Moorfoot** and **Lammermuir** ranges – forms the southern edge of the Central Lowlands. These Lowlands spread west beyond Edinburgh, but here they constitute the slender coastal plain of **East Lothian**, which rolls down towards a string of fine sandy beaches. Further east, the coastline becomes more rugged, its cliffs and rocky outcrops harbouring a series of ruined castles, and inland, the flatness of the terrain is interrupted by the occasional extinct volcano, inspiration for all sorts of ancient myths.

The gritty town of **Dumfries** is gateway to **southwest Scotland**, where on the marshy Solway coast you can visit charming **Kirkcudbright** and see the magnificent remains of **Caerlaverock Castle**. The **Ayrshire coast** also rewards a visit for its strong associations with Robert Burns, especially at Ayr and **Alloway**, the poet's birthplace, as well as for its pastoral coastline and sandy beaches.

There's a **train** line along both coasts, and a good **bus** service linking all the major towns and many of the villages. The region is also excellent **walking** country and there are two marked treks for the ambitious hiker. The new **St Cuthbert's Way** follows a sixty-mile trail from Melrose, where St Cuthbert started his ministry, to Lindisfarne (the Holy Isle), where he died. The **Southern Upland Way**, a 212-mile path, stretches from Portpatrick on the west to Cockburnspath on the east coast. For the less dedi-

---

ACCOMMODATION PRICE CODES

Throughout this book, accommodation **prices** have been graded with the codes below, according to the cost of the least expensive double room in high season. Price codes are not given for campsites, most of which charge under £10 per person. Almost all hostels charge less than £10 a night for a bed – the few exceptions to this rule have the prices quoted in the text. For a full account of the accommodation price codes, see p.30.

① under £20	④ £40–50	⑦ £70–80
② £20–30	⑤ £50–60	⑧ £80–100
③ £30–40	⑥ £60–70	⑨ over £100

---

cated, both routes are parcelled up into easy-to-handle sections – and all the major tourist offices have leaflets on their nearest stretch. Ask also for details of the many **ranger-led walks** throughout the year and the annual **Festival of Walking** (late August to early Sept) which focuses on a different area each year. The combination of rolling landscape and quiet backroads also makes the region good for **cyclists**: many of the forested hills have mountain-biking tracks and hire centres, while the 88-mile Tweed Cycleway runs through attractive countryside from Biggar to Berwick-on-Tweed. Meanwhile, **golfers** can buy passes from tourist offices throughout the south, such as the Freedom of the Fairways pass (£46 for three days; £70 for five days), which allows access to ten of the Border region's nineteen courses.

EAST LOTHIAN AND THE EASTERN BORDERS

East Lothian consists of the coastal strip and hinterland immediately east of Edinburgh. Its western reaches, around Musselburgh, are an easy day-trip from the capital; the remainder takes a couple of overnight stays to explore. The prosperous market town of **Haddington** serves as a base for exploring the interior, whose bumpy farmland is bordered to the south by the Lammermuir Hills. But most people make a beeline for the shore, the fifty miles or so of coastline extending from **Aberlady** right round through the **Eastern Borders** to England's Berwick-upon-Tweed. There's something for most tastes here, from the sandy beaches and volcanic islets around the resort of **North Berwick** and neighbouring **Dirleton**, to the piercing cliffs of **St Abb's Head**, and a number of ruined medieval strongholds, the most dramatic at **Tantallon**. Inland, the **Lammermuir Hills** cross the boundary between East Lothian and the Borders to form the northern edge of the Merse, centring on modest **Duns**. Further south still, the busy Georgian town of **Kelso** is the key attraction of the **Lower Tweed Valley**.

Haddington and around

The East Lothian gentry keep a careful eye on **HADDINGTON**, their favourite country town. Its compact centre preserves an intriguing ensemble of seventeenth- to nineteenth-century architectural styles where everything of any interest has been labelled and plaqued. Yet the town's staid appearance belies an innovative past. During the early 1700s, Haddington became a byword for modernization as its merchants supplied the district's progressive landowners with all sorts of new-fangled equipment, stock and seed, and in only a few decades utterly transformed Lothian agriculture.

Haddington was also the birthplace of **John Knox**, the fiery sixteenth-century religious reformer who led the Protestant assault on Scotland's Catholic Church. He laid the foundations of the Presbyterian movement, but is mainly remembered for his treatise of 1558 entitled *The First Blast of the Trumpet Against the Monstrous Regiment of Women*: a specific attack on Mary of Guise, regent of Scotland; Mary, Queen of England; and Catherine de Medici. It didn't help him in his dealings with Queen Elizabeth I or Mary Stuart either (see p.71).

The Town

Haddington's centre is best approached from the west, where tree-trimmed **Court Street** ends suddenly with the soaring spire, stately stonework and dignified Venetian windows of the **Town House**, designed by William Adam in 1748. Close by, to the right and next door to a fine Italianate facade, the **Jane Welsh Carlyle House** (April–Sept Wed–Sat 2–5pm; £1) was the childhood home of the wife of essayist and historian Thomas Carlyle (see p.143). The dining room – the only part of the house open to the public – has been restored to its early nineteenth-century appearance and sports pictures of the influential personalities of the day, while the lovely garden is pretty much as Jane would have known it too. Carrying straight on, **High Street** is distinguished by its pastel-painted gables and quaint pends, a tad prettier than those in neighbouring **Market Street**. Keep an eye open for **Mitchell's Close** on Market Street, a recently restored seventeenth-century close with crow-stepped gables, rubble masonry and the narrowest of staircase towers.

Heading east from the town centre along High Street, it's a brief walk down Church Street – past the hooped arches of **Nungate Bridge** – to the hulking mass of **St Mary's Church** (daily 10am–4pm; free), Scotland's largest parish church. Built close to the reedy River Tyne, the church dates from the fourteenth century but it's a real hotchpotch of styles, the squat grey tower uneasy above clumsy buttressing and pinkishochre stone walls. Inside, on the **Lauderdale Aisle** a munificent tomb features the best of Elizabethan alabaster carving, moustached knights and their ruffed ladies lying beneath a finely ornamented canopy. In stark contrast, a plain slab in the choir is inscribed with Thomas Carlyle's beautiful tribute to his wife, who died on April 21, 1866, after forty years of marriage. Carlyle rounds the inscription off: "Suddenly snatched away from him, and the light of his life as if gone out." The church also offers brass rubbing, has a good tearoom and hosts internationally acclaimed concerts organized by the Lamp of Lothian Collegiate Trust (phone ☎01620/825111 for details). At nearby Haddington House, on Sidegate, the seventeenth-century medicinal gardens of **St Mary's Pleasance** (open during daylight hours; free) merit a brief stroll.

Practicalities

Fast and frequent **buses** connect Haddington with Edinburgh, fifteen miles to the west, and with North Berwick on the east coast, with all services stopping on High Street. There's no **tourist office**, but orientation is easy and *A Walk Around Haddington* (£1), detailing every building of any conceivable consequence, is available from local newsagents.

There are several central **B&Bs**, including Mrs Richards, whose well-kept Georgian town house is at 19 Church St (☎01620/825663; ④), and the *Plough Tavern*, 11 Court St (☎01620/823326; ⑤), a traditional inn in the town centre. Alternatively, try the more luxurious *Brown's Hotel*, 1 West Rd (☎01620/822254; ⑧), which occupies a fine Regency town house. *Monks' Muir Caravan Park* (☎01620/860340), on the eastern edge of town by the A1, also takes tents.

For **daytime snacks** and light lunches, *Simply Scrumptious*, next to the Town House, has an imaginative menu that outshines its main rival, the *Golden Grain* café, 13 High St, while *Peter Potter*, 10 The Sand, serves coffee and snacks and is attached to a craft shop where you can watch the artist in residence at work. The best place for an

evening meal is the *Waterside Bistro*, on the far side of Nungate Bridge, justifiably popular for its delicious seafood and varied vegetarian dishes. Alternatively try *Poldrate's Restaurant* at Poldrate Mill on Gifford Road, where the menu changes daily, or the restaurant at *Brown's Hotel*, though you'll need to book in advance. Decent bar meals are available at the *Victoria Inn* in Court Street, while real-ale fans should head to *The Pheasant* in Poldrate, rumoured to serve the best pint in East Lothian.

Around Haddington

A thorough exploration of Haddington will only take two or three hours, but there are several other attractions in its vicinity. If you're heading north to the coast on the A6137, stop off at **Byres Hill**, where you can climb up to the Hopetoun Monument for sweeping views over the Firth of Forth. Hidden away four miles or so northeast of Haddington, the **Museum of Flight** (April–June, Sept & Oct daily 10.30am–5pm; July & Aug daily 10.30am–6pm; Nov–March Mon–Fri 11am–3pm; £2) on the B1347 at East Fortune airfield, is one of Britain's largest museums. Its many exhibits include a Vulcan bomber, a Comet airliner, a Spitfire and a Tigermoth, all displayed in World War II hangars.

A mile south of Haddington, **Lennoxlove House** (Easter–Sept Wed, Sat & Sun 2–5pm; £3), a sprawling pile incorporating a medieval tower house, displays a splendid fine and applied art collection belonging to the Duke of Hamilton. An hour-long tour takes in portraits of the family, French furniture, porcelain and damask wall hangings, with the highlight being the death mask of Mary, Queen of Scots, and a silver casket in which she kept the letters that allegedly proved her involvement in Darnley's murder.

A further three miles south along the B6369 on the edge of the Lammermuir Hills, the pretty hamlet of **Gifford**, whose eighteenth-century estate cottages edge a trim whitewashed church, was the birthplace (in 1723) of the Reverend John Witherspoon, a signatory of the American Declaration of Independence. The hamlet makes a good base for walkers, with several footpaths setting out across the surrounding red-soiled farmland for the Lammermuir Hills, while longer trails connect with the Southern Upland Way. If you want **to stay**, try the traditional and well-reputed *Tweeddale Arms* (☎01620/810240; ⑤), or *Eaglescairne Mains* (☎01620/810491; ④), a huge country house with open fires and a tennis court. Gifford also boasts an exclusive **restaurant**, *Bonar's*, though you may prefer to make up a picnic of freshly baked breads, pizza and sandwiches from *The Little Bread Shop* opposite the green.

The east coast to the Lammermuir Hills

Skirting the southern shore of the Firth of Forth before curving down along the North Sea coast, the fifty-mile section of the **east coast** we've set apart from Edinburgh begins at **ABERLADY**, an elongated conservation village of Gothic-style cottages and mansions, just sixteen miles from the capital. The village served as Haddington's port until its river silted up in the sixteenth century, and the costly stained-glass windows of the honey-coloured stone medieval church act as a reminder of wealthier times. The salt marshes and sand dunes of the adjacent **Aberlady Bay Nature Reserve**, a birdwatchers' haven, mark the site of the old harbour.

From the nature reserve, it's a couple of miles to the modern villas and hotels of **GULLANE**, a disappointing location for the famous shoreline links of **Muirfield Golf Course**, established in the late 1800s. A half-mile detour off the Aberlady to Gullane road takes you to the **Myreton Motor Museum** (daily 10am–5pm; £3), a small stash of vintage cars, motorbikes, military vehicles and motoring memorabilia.

Two miles east of Gullane lies the genteel hamlet of **DIRLETON**, where a pair of triangular greens are bordered by tastefully refurbished cottages with thriving gardens.

Dirleton Castle (April–Sept Mon–Sat 9.30am–6.30pm, Sun 2–6.30pm; Oct–March Mon–Sat 9.30am–4.30pm, Sun 2–4.30pm; £2.30) has lovely gardens too, leading to a volcanic knoll crowned by Cromwell-shattered ruins. Scrambling round the castle is fun, and if the weather's good you can take the mile-long path from the village church to the sandy beach. Also near the beach, the *Yellowcraig Caravan Club Site* (☎01620/850217; April–Sept), with pleasant woodland walks to the shore, is the only budget place to **stay**; the splendid *Open Arms Hotel* opposite the castle (☎01620/850241; ⑨), on the other hand, has every luxury, including a fantastic restaurant serving moderate to expensive dinners from a varied and imaginative menu. Across the green, the *Castle Inn* (☎01620/850221; ④) falls somewhere in between and serves decent afternoon teas from 3pm to 5pm on Sundays.

North Berwick

NORTH BERWICK has a somewhat faded, old-fashioned air, its guest houses and hotels extending along the shore in all their Victorian and Edwardian sobriety. Set within sight of two volcanic heaps – the **Bass Rock** and **North Berwick Law** – the resort's pair of wide and sandy **beaches** are the main attraction. These fall either side of a narrow headland harbour that's an extension of Victoria Road, itself an extension of Quality Street. The only other attraction is the town's small **museum** on School Road (April–Oct daily 11am–5pm; free), housed in the old school house and displaying local curios, such as the old town stocks.

Little now remains of the original medieval town, but the fragmentary ruins of the **Auld Kirk**, next to the harbour, bear witness to one of the most extraordinary events of sixteenth-century Scotland. In 1590, while **King James VI** spent the summer in Denmark wooing his prospective wife, Francis Stuart, **Earl of Bothwell** was plotting against him. On hearing of the king's imminent return, Bothwell, a keen practitioner of the "black arts", summoned the witches of Lothian to meet the Devil in the Auld Kirk. Bothwell turned up disguised as the Devil and instructed his 200 acolytes to raise a storm that would shipwreck the king. To cast the spell, they opened a few graves and engaged in a little flagellation before kissing the bare buttocks of the "Devil" – reportedly "as cold as ice and as hard as iron" as it hung over the pulpit. Despite these shenanigans, the king returned safely – when rumours reached him of Bothwell's treachery he refused to believe them, and the earl went unpunished, possibly because James was reassured by his failure. After all, if the Devil himself was unable to harm him, he must surely be blessed by God, a belief the monarch was later to elaborate as the "Divine Right of Kings".

Bass Rock

Resembling a giant molar, the **Bass Rock** rises 350ft above the sea some three miles east of North Berwick. This massive chunk of basalt was bought by the government in 1671 and served as a prison, a fortress and a monastic retreat with a natural tunnel running east to west under the chapel building. Now it is home to millions of nesting seabirds, with Scotland's second-largest gannet colony after St Kilda in tight competition with razorbills, terns, puffins, guillemots and fulmars. Weather permitting, there are regular ninety-minute **boat trips** round the island from North Berwick harbour (Easter to early Oct daily; £3.50), but only Fred Marr (☎01620/892838) has landing rights. It's not to everyone's taste – as William Dunbar, a fifteenth-century poet, described it:

> *The air was dirkit with the fowlis*
> *That cam with jammeris and with youlis*
> *With shrykking, shrieking, skyrmming scowlis*
> *And meikle noyis and showtes.*

North Berwick Law

The other volcanic monolith, 613ft-high **North Berwick Law**, is about an hour's walk from the beach (take Law Road off High Street and follow the signs). On a clear day, the views out across the Firth of Forth, Fife and the Lammermuirs make the effort worthwhile, and at the top you can see the remains of a Napoleonic watchtower and an arch made from the jawbone of a whale.

Practicalities

It's a ten-minute walk east from North Berwick **train station**, with its frequent services from Edinburgh, to the town centre along Abbey Road, Westgate and High Street. **Buses** from Edinburgh (every 30min) run along the coast via Aberlady, Gullane and Dirleton and stop on High Street, while the hourly service from Haddington and Dunbar terminates outside the **tourist office**, on Quality Street (April & May Mon–Sat 9am–6pm; June & Sept Mon–Sat 9am–6pm, Sun 11am–4pm; July Mon–Sat 9am–7pm, Sun 11am–6pm; Aug Mon–Sat 9am–8pm, Sun 11am–6pm; Oct–March Mon–Fri 9am–5pm; ☎01620/892197).

Several excellent **B&Bs** are open from April to September, including Mrs Duns, at 20 Marmion Rd (☎01620/892066; ③), a Victorian house within easy walking distance of the sea, and Mrs McQueen's modern bungalow at 5 West Bay Rd (☎01620/894576; ③), next to the golf course. Out of season, first choice should be *The Glebe House*, Law Road (☎01620/892608; ③), a beautiful old manse in its own grounds overlooking the sea; alternatively, try Mrs Ralph, at 13 Westgate (☎01620/892782; ③), a spacious Victorian house. Of the **guest houses**, the seafront *Craigview*, 5 Beach Rd (☎01620/892257; ④), has four-poster beds and serves good vegetarian breakfasts, while *Point Garry*, 20 West Bay Rd (☎01620/892380; ⑦; April–Oct), is an upmarket **hotel** with a great cocktail bar. The nearest **campsite**, *Tantallon Rhodes Caravan Park* (☎01620/893348; April–Oct), occupies a prime clifftop location a couple of miles east of the centre – take the Dunbar bus (Mon–Sat six daily, Sun two daily).

Several little cafés, such as the *Buttercup*, High Street, sell cheap **food**; for an evening meal, there's the usual array of takeaways or decent bar meals at *The Grange*, *The County Hotel* (both on High Street) or the *Tantallon Inn* on Marine Parade.

East of North Berwick

The melodramatic ruins of **Tantallon Castle** (April–Sept Mon–Sat 9.30am–6.30pm, Sun 2–6.30pm; Oct–March Mon–Wed & Sat 9.30am–4.30pm, Thurs 9.30am–noon, Sun 2–4.30pm; £2), three miles east of North Berwick, on the A198, stand on the precipitous cliffs facing the Bass Rock. This pinkish sandstone edifice, with its imposing cylindrical towers, protected the powerful "Red" Douglases, Earls of Angus, from their enemies for over three hundred years. With a sheer drop down to the sea on three sides and a sequence of moats and ditches on the fourth, the castle's desolate invincibility is daunting, especially when the wind howls over the remaining battlements and the surf crashes on the rocks far below. In fact, the setting is more striking than the ruins: Cromwell's army savaged the castle in 1651 and only the impressive 50ft-high and 14ft-thick curtain wall has survived relatively intact. To reach Tantallon Castle from North Berwick, a fifteen-minute trip, take the Dunbar **bus** (Mon–Sat six daily, Sun two daily).

Birthplace of US conservationist John Muir, **DUNBAR** is in much the same vein as North Berwick, twelve miles away, with a wide High Street graced by several grand old stone buildings. One of the oldest is the **Town House** (daily April–Oct 12.30–4.30pm; free), formerly a prison and now home to a small archeology room and local-history centre. Of more significance, is the **John Muir House,** 126 High St (June–Sept Mon–Sat 11am–1pm & 2–5pm, Sun noon–5pm; free), birthplace of the explorer and naturalist who created the United States national park system. The house has been refurbished in period detail and contains a tiny museum dedicated the pioneer's life and work. A **country park** in Muir's honour, embracing Belhaven Bay and a rugged reach of coast, can be reached by a pleasant five-minute walk from the harbour in town. The delightfully intricate double **harbour** merits a stroll itself, with its narrow channels, cobbled quays and roughened rocks, set beside the shattered remains of the castle. The town's only other claim to fame is as the home of **Bellhaven beers**, which are still made on the original site of the monks' brewery, signposted off the Edinburgh road (guided tours can be arranged; phone ☎01368/864488 for details).

If you want to stay, the **tourist office**, 143 High St (May Mon–Sat 9am–6pm; June, July & Sept Mon–Sat 9am–7pm, Sun 11am–6pm; Aug Mon–Sat 9am–8pm, Sun 11am–6pm; ☎01368/863353) will help with **accommodation**. Alternatively, try the pleasant bay-windowed *Overcliffe Guest House*, 11 Bayswell Park (☎01368/864004; ③), a short walk west from the castle, or *Muirfield* B&B, Belhaven Road (☎01368/862289; ③; March–Oct;). The nearest **campsite** is *Belhaven Bay Caravan and Camping Park*, in the John Muir Park, just off the A1087 (☎01620/893348). For a light **lunch**, *The Food Hamper* and *William Smith's* on the High Street do good sandwiches, while the best evening meal options are *The Creel* on Victoria Street, which specializes in steaks and seafood, and *The Starfish*, a brightly painted quayside hostelry overlooking the old harbour with a great choice of hearty, freshly caught food.

St Abb's Head

Heading south from Dunbar, it's around seven miles to tiny Cockburnspath where the Southern Upland Way reaches its end about a mile from the coast – though there's now a five-mile extension which takes hikers from Cockburnspath square, underneath the A1 and down along the coast via Pease Bay, to **PENMANSHEIL**, back beside the A1. Nearby, the A1107 cuts off the main road for **ST ABBS**, a remote fishing village stuck onto the steepest of seashores. Flanked by jagged cliffs, St Abbs has a dramatic setting, with a jangle of old fishermen's cottages tumbling down to the surf-battered harbour. The village is named after Ebba, a seventh-century Northumbrian princess who struggled ashore here after being shipwrecked and promptly founded a nunnery. From the harbour, you can take sea angling, sub-aqua diving, birdwatching and regular sightseeing **boat trips** with local guide, Peter Gibson (☎018907/71681) or with St Abb's Marine Services (☎018907/71412). It's also an ideal base for visiting **St Abb's Head Nature Reserve**, reached from the tearoom and car park just half a mile back along the road. Owned by the NTS, this comprises 200 acres of wild and rugged coastline with sheer, seabird-encrusted cliffs rising 300ft above the water. An easy-to-follow walking trail ends at the lighthouse, a mile or so from the car park.

Twice daily the Edinburgh/Dunbar to Berwick-upon-Tweed **bus** passes through Coldingham on the A1107, where a **taxi-bus** service connects to St Abbs, a mile away down the B6438; connections are, however, only guaranteed for prebooked passengers (Mon–Fri 9am–4pm; ☎01289/308719). Buses south from St Abbs to Eyemouth run hourly. There are just two places to **stay** in St Abbs: the excellent *Castle Rock Guest House*, Murrayfield (☎018907/71715; ④; Easter–Oct), a Victorian manse whose spick-and-span bedrooms and gingerbread woodwork look out along the sea cliffs, and *Wilma Wilson's B&B*, a former fisherman's cottage at 7 Murrayfield (☎018907/71468; ③).

Coldingham itself is unremarkable, but a second minor road leaves here for the mile-long trip down to the coast at **COLDINGHAM SANDS**, where intrepid surfers gather. This pint-sized resort has a fine sandy beach and a **youth hostel** (☎018907/71298; March–Oct) in a large Victorian villa on a hill overlooking the seashore; the **B&B** *Cul-Na-Sithe* (☎018907/71565; ④; Feb–Nov) nearby also overlooks the sands. *Scoutscroft Holiday Centre*, one of two **campsites** (☎018907/71338), also has a **dive shop** for equipment rental and diving courses.

Eyemouth

Almost the entire 3500 population of **EYEMOUTH**, a few miles south of St Abbs – and accessible from there via a pleasant two-hour coastal walk – is dependent on the fishing industry, started by the thirteenth-century Benedictine monks of Coldingham Priory. Consequently, the town's slender harbour is very much the focus of activity, its waters packed with deep sea and inshore fleets and its quay strewn with tatters of old net, discarded fish and fish crates. It even boasts two annual fishy events, the week-long **Herring Queen Festival** in July and the weekend-long **Seafood Festival** each June.

Eyemouth's tiny centre, to the west of the harbour, is drearily modern, despite the town's medieval foundation. But the **Eyemouth Museum**, in the Auld Kirk on the Market Place (April–June & Sept Mon–Sat 10am–5pm, Sun 2–4pm; July & Aug Mon–Sat 10am–6pm, Sun 1–6pm; Oct Mon–Sat 10am–12.30pm & 1.30–4.30pm; £1.50) is just about worth a visit for the **Eyemouth Tapestry**, a recent composition commemorating the east coast fishing disaster of 1881 when a freak storm destroyed most of the inshore fleet: 129 local men were lost, a tragedy of extraordinary proportions for a place of this size. Nearby, along High Street, in the old **cemetery**, a stone memorial surmounted by a broken mast also pays tribute to the dead. Years before in 1849, the inhabitants had to raise the level of the cemetery by 6ft to cope with the victims of a cholera epidemic. However, the work was for nothing, as the site was soon abandoned (hence the lack of gravestones); but they did use the old tombstones to build the ghoulish **watch house** – a precaution against body snatchers – which you can still see today.

The elegant **Gunsgreen House**, standing alone on the far side of the harbour, was designed by James Adam (one of the famous family of architects) in the 1750s. Despite its respectable appearance – in keeping with its present use by the golf club – the house was once used by smugglers, with secret passages and underground tunnels leading back into town. This illicit trade in tobacco and booze peaked in the late eighteenth century, with local fishermen using their knowledge of the coast to regularly outwit the excise.

In the unlikely event that you'll want to **stay** overnight, the tourist office in the Auld Kirk (April–June & Sept Mon–Sat 10am–5pm, Sun 2–4pm; July & Aug Mon–Sat 10am–6pm, Sun 1–6pm; Oct Mon–Sat 10am–12.30pm & 1.30–4.30pm; ☎018907/50678) can recommend **B&Bs** in the area: the only two in town are Mrs MacKay (☎018907/50463; ③) and Mrs McGovern at Ebba House (☎018907/50350; ③). For **food**, a sprinkling of tawdry hotels along the harbour serve fish and standard bar fodder, but for snacks and great cakes try the licensed *Old Bakehouse* on Manse Road, across from the Auld Kirk. Underwater enthusiasts should head to the Eyemouth Diving Centre on Fort Road (☎018907/51202), which **rents out dive equipment**, charters boats and runs diving courses. Leaving town, regular **buses** from the stop opposite the old cemetery run north along the coast, west to Chirnside/Duns and south across the border to Berwick-upon-Tweed, eight miles away. If you're driving north, take the scenic A1107 for coastal views as far as Cockburnspath where you can rejoin the faster A1 to Dunbar and Edinburgh.

Duns

Heading inland from Eyemouth, the B6355 and then the A6105 cross the fertile farmland of the Merse to the little-visited market town of **DUNS**, birthplace of John Duns Scotus, a medieval scholar, from whose name the word "dunce" was derived. A more modern hero was also born here: Jim Clark, a farmer-turned-motor-racing ace whose brilliant career ended in death on the track at Hockenheim in Germany in 1968, is commemorated at the **Jim Clark Room**, 44 Newtown St (Easter–Oct Mon–Sat 10am–1pm & 2–5pm, Sun 2–5pm; £1). There's little else to do in Duns, but it's only a twenty-minute walk to the top of **Duns Law** (take North Castle Street and follow the signs). Most people make the trek up to the 714ft-high summit for the view, some to see the **Covenanters' Stone**, marking the spot where Alexander Leslie's army camped in 1639. Leslie assembled his troops on the Law to watch for Charles I's mercenaries, who had been sent north to crush the Covenanters. In the event, the royalist army faded away without even forcing a battle, and the king, by refusing to accept defeat, took one more step towards the Civil War. Other local **walks** are detailed in the leaflet *Walks Around Duns,* available from The Cherry Tree, a jeweller's shop on Market Square, with a good tearoom at the back.

Duns is well connected by **bus** to all the major settlements of the east Borders, so you don't have to stay the night. However, the town does have half a dozen **B&Bs**, such as the central *St Albans*, Clouds (☎01361/883285; ④), a former eighteenth-century manse. The wooden bar of the *Whip and Saddle* in Market Square is the best place for a **drink** and a traditional bar **meal**, but, if you fancy a splurge, the villages to the southeast of Duns boast two award-winning restaurants: the *Wheatsheaf Hotel* at Swinton (☎01890/860257; ⑦), and *Chirnside Hall Country House* (☎01890/818219; ⑧), both of which merit a detour.

Manderston House

Manderston House (May–Sept Thurs & Sun 2–5.30pm; £4), two miles east of Duns on the A6105, is the very embodiment of Edwardian Britain. Between 1871 and 1905, the Miller family spent most of their herring and hemp fortune on turning their home into a prestigious country house, with no expense spared as architect John Kinross added entire suites of rooms in the Classical Revival style. It's certainly a staggering sight, from the intricate plasterwork ceilings to the inlaid marble floor in the hall and the extravagant silver staircase, the whole lot sumptuously furnished with trappings worthy of a new member of the aristocracy: James Miller married Eveline Curzon, the daughter of Lord Scarsdale, in 1893. When you've finished inside the house, stroll round the fifty or so acres of garden, noted for their rhododendrons and azaleas.

The Lammermuir Hills and Lauder

Leaving Duns to the north, it's about three miles to the edge of the **Lammermuir Hills**, a slender, east–west chain whose flat-topped summits and quiet streams are a favourite haunt of ramblers. The hills are criss-crossed with footpaths, some of which follow ancient carting and droving trails as they slice from north to south. In the other direction, tracking along the body of the Lammermuirs between Lauder in the west and Cockburnspath on the coast, is the Southern Upland Way. If you're keen to sample a portion, leave Duns on the A6112, turn left along the B6355 and then follow the minor road to Abbey St Bathans, a hamlet beside the Whiteadder Water with a tiny **youth hostel** (☎01361/840245) and a pretty and undemanding ten-mile stretch of the trail which leads down to the sea. Alternatively, you could carry on up to East Lothian's Gifford (see p.118), some twenty miles from Duns on the other side of the Lammermuirs.

It is also easy to join the Southern Upland Way on the western edge of the Lammermuir Hills in **LAUDER**, a grey market town twenty miles west of Duns on the A68. Lauder's only attraction is **Thirlestane Castle** (May, June & Sept Mon, Wed, Thurs & Sun 2–5pm; July & Aug Mon–Fri & Sun 2–5pm; £4), an imposing pile on the eastern edge of town: the main entrance is half a mile south of Lauder, but pedestrians can take the signposted footpath from The Avenue, effectively the main square about halfway along High Street. Owned by the Maitland family since the sixteenth century, the castle has been refashioned and remodelled on several occasions, but its impressive reddish turrets and castellated towers appear as a cohesive whole nevertheless. The interior is disappointing, with little to see beyond the delicate plasterwork of the Restoration ceilings: most of the original furnishings were carted off to London in the 1840s to be replaced by inferior Victoriana.

The Lower Tweed Valley

Rising in the hills far to the west, the River Tweed snakes its way across the Borders until it reaches the North Sea at Berwick-upon-Tweed. The eastern reaches of the river, constituting the **Lower Tweed Valley**, run from Kelso to the coast and for the most part form the boundary between Scotland and England. This is a gentle, rural landscape of farmland and wooded river banks where the occasional military ruin, usually on the south side of the border, serves as a reminder of more violent days. For the English, the Eastern Borders were the quickest land route to the centre of Scotland and time and again they launched themselves north destroying everything in their way. Indeed, the English turned Berwick-upon-Tweed into one of the most heavily guarded frontier towns in northern Europe, and the massive fortifications survive today. The region also witnessed one of the most devastating of medieval battles when the Scots, under James IV, were decimated at **Flodden Field** in 1513. The heavily armoured Scottish noblemen got stuck in the mud at the bottom of a hill near Branxton, south of the border near Coldstream, and their overlong pikes and lances were simply no match for the shorter and sturdier English halberds.

Nowadays, the Lower Tweed Valley has one town of note, **Kelso**, a busy agricultural centre distinguished by the Georgian elegance of its main square and its proximity to Floors Castle (also Mellerstain House; see p.132). Perhaps surprisingly, Kelso is often visited for its abbey, even though the ruins of the colossal twelfth-century foundation, whose abbots claimed precedence over St Andrews, are scant indeed. Further downstream, close to Berwick-upon-Tweed, is the district's other main attraction, the Georgian **Paxton House**.

Paxton House

Built for Patrick Home in the middle of the eighteenth century, **Paxton House** (mid-April to Oct daily 11am–5pm; £3.50), some five miles west of Berwick-upon-Tweed along the B6461, was the last act of a would-be matrimonial fiasco. Resident in Germany, the young Scot had been a great success at the court of Frederick the Great, even seducing the king's only daughter, Charlotte de Brandt. The affair became public and Home was forced to leave Berlin, but not before the lovers "plighted their troth". Back in Scotland, Home built Paxton for his putative bride, but she never appeared – much to Frederick's dynastic satisfaction.

The building, designed by John and James Adam, is a grand neo-Palladian mansion, with a carefully contrived facade focused on the main house, whose imposing centrepiece comprises temple-like columns rising two storeys to an equally impressive pediment. This geometrical simplicity is continued inside, where a particular highlight of the guided tour is the contrast between John and James's Rococo and their more famous brother Robert's Neoclassical plasterwork. Also on display is a stunning collection of Chippendale and Regency rosewood furniture. Finally, the expansive **Picture Gallery**, completed in the 1810s, blends aspects of earlier Neoclassicism into a more austere design, with most of the plasterwork moulded to look like masonry. The National Gallery of Scotland uses this room as an outstation, displaying some of its lesser works here and changing the exhibits frequently.

The grounds (April–Oct 10am–sunset), eighty acres of mixed parkland and woodland abutting the Tweed, boast gentle footpaths, a salmon-fishing museum and a brand new hide from where you can spy on red squirrels.

Coldstream

The small town of **COLDSTREAM** sits tight against the Tweed, its long High Street part of the trunk road linking Newcastle across the border and Edinburgh. Entering

Coldstream from the south you cross Smeaton's handsome five-arched bridge on the site of the original ford across the **River Tweed** which marks the border with England. It was here that Edward I and his army invaded Scotland in 1296, Robert Burns first ventured "abroad" some five hundred years later and the Stone of Destiny re-entered Scotland in 1996. These events aside, the town's principal claim to fame is its association with the **Coldstream Guards**. General George Monck billeted his Cromwellian soldiers here in the winter of 1659–60, just before they were persuaded to discard their parliamentary allegiance and march on London to restore Charles II to the throne. Monck's regiment was thereafter recognized as the "Coldstream Guards" and the general became the first Duke of Albemarle – a handsome payoff for his timely change of heart. Oddly enough, in the sort of detail beloved of military historians, the Coldstreamers still sport the crownless tunic buttons they first wore as part of Cromwell's Model Army. The regiment's deeds are recorded in the **Coldstream Museum** (Easter–Oct Mon–Sat 10am–5pm, Sun 2–5pm; £1), on the attractively old-fashioned (and traffic-free) Market Square, just off High Street. Near the huge obelisk dedicated to an obscure nineteenth-century MP at the east end of town, is the bridge **Toll House**, an eighteenth-century building where "irregular marriages" were granted to runaway English couples as an alternative site to Gretna Green.

Coldstream's outdoor attractions include the pocket-size **Henderson Park**, opposite the tourist office, an aromatic garden for the blind with signs in braille and good views of the Tweed and the Cheviot Hills. Slightly further afield, on the western side of Coldstream, you can visit the 3000-acre estate **The Hirsel** (grounds open all year during daylight hours; parking charge £2). Hirsel House is not open to the public but you can walk around the attractive grounds, complete with lake, picnic area and rhododendron woods, which are particularly resplendent in early summer. A museum, housed in the old homestead outhouses, shows the workings of the estate, past and present (Mon–Fri 10am–5pm Sat & Sun noon–5pm; free).

Practicalities

Coldstream's **tourist office** is in the old town hall, about halfway down High Street (April–June & Sept Mon–Sat 10am–5pm, Sun 10am–1pm; July & Aug Mon–Sat 10am–6pm, Sun 10am–2pm; Oct Mon–Sat 10am–12.30pm & 1.30–4.30pm; ☎01890/882607). It has a comprehensive supply of brochures and booklets on the Borders as well as a list of local **B&Bs**. The best of these is the trimly kept *Attadale*, just off Market Square at 1 Leet St (☎01890/883047; ②); alternatively, try *Kengarth Guest House*, 7 Market St (☎01890/882477; ③). For daytime **snacks**, there's home baking in abundance at the little *Candy's Kitchen* on the High Street, while the *Castle Hotel*, 11 High St, offers substantial and reasonably priced **meals**. The best bet for a **drink** is the *Besom Inn*, next to the tourist office, a cosy pub decked out with all sorts of military mementoes.

Kelso and around

Compact **KELSO**, at the confluence of the Tweed and Teviot, grew up in the shadow of its abbey, once the richest and most powerful in southern Scotland. The abbey was founded in 1128 during the reign of King David (1124–53), whose policy of encouraging the monastic orders had little to do with spirituality. The bishops and monks David established here, as well as at Melrose, Jedburgh and Dryburgh, were the frontiersmen of his kingdom, helping to advance his authority in areas of doubtful allegiance. This began a long period of relative stability across the region which enabled its abbeys to flourish, until frequent raids by the English, who savaged Kelso three times in the early sixteenth century (in 1522, 1544 and 1545) brought ruin. The last assault – part of the "Rough Wooing" led by the Earl of Hertford when the Scots refused to ratify a marriage treaty between Henry VIII's son and the infant Mary Stuart – was the worst.

Such was the extent of the devastation – compounded by the Reformation – that the surviving ruins of **Kelso Abbey** (April–Sept Mon–Sat 9.30am–6pm, Sun 2–6pm; Oct–March Mon–Fri 9.30am–4pm, Sun 2pm–4pm; free) are disappointing: a heavy central tower and supporting buttresses represent a scant memorial to the massive Romanesque original that took over eighty years to build. Enough remains, however, to make out the two transepts and towers which give the abbey the shape of a double cross, unique in Scotland. Just behind the abbey, notice the Old Parish Church, constructed in 1773 to an octagonal design that excited universal execration. "It is", wrote one contemporary, "a misshapen pile, the ugliest Parish Church in Scotland, but it is an excellent model for a circus."

From the abbey, it's a couple of minutes' walk along Bridge Street to **The Square**, a cobbled expanse where the columns and pediments of the **Town Hall** are flanked by a splendid ensemble of three-storey eighteenth- and nineteenth-century pastel buildings. Beyond the general air of elegance, there's little to see, though if you're around the abbey, pop into the Kelso Pottery (Mon–Sat 10am–1pm & 2–5pm), beside the big car park at The Knowes, to see the ceramics which are fired in a large outdoor pit kiln.

Kelso has one other diversion. Leaving The Square along Roxburgh Street, take the alley down to the **Cobby Riverside Walk**, where a brief stroll leads to Floors Castle. En route, but hidden from view by the islet in the middle of the river, is the spot where the Teviot meets the Tweed. This junction has long been famous for its salmon fishing, with permits booked years in advance irrespective of the cost: currently around £5000 per rod per week. Permits for fishing other (less expensive) reaches of the Tweed and Teviot are available from Tweeside Fishing Tackle, 36 Bridge St (☎01573/225306). Details of last-minute fishing lets are available from the Tweedline on ☎01891/666412; for fishing catches and prospects, phone ☎01891/666410.

Six miles or so north of town lies the ruins of **Hume Castle**, one of the earliest types of Scottish castle, built on a rectangular plan. While the recently constructed folly on the ruined site gives you little idea of the life that existed within its walls, it's worth a visit for the panoramic views alone.

Floors Castle

There's nothing medieval about **Floors Castle** (late March to early Oct daily 10am–4.30pm; Oct Sun–Wed 10am–4.30pm; £4.50), a vast castellated mansion overlooking the Tweed about a mile northwest of Kelso. The bulk of the building was designed by William Adam in the 1720s, and, picking through the Victorian modifications, much of the interior demonstrates his uncluttered style. However, you won't see much of it, as just ten rooms and a basement are open to the public. Highlights include Hendrick Danckert's splendid panorama of Horse Guards Parade in the entrance hall; the Brussels tapestries in the ante and drawing rooms; paintings by Augustus John and Henri Matisse in the Needle Room; and all sorts of snuff boxes and cigarette cases in the gallery.

Floors remain privately owned, the property of the tenth Duke of Roxburgh, whose arrogant features can be seen in a variety of portraits. The duke is a close friend of royalty: it was here, apparently, that Prince Andrew proposed to Sarah Ferguson in 1986.

Practicalities

With good connections to Melrose and Jedburgh to the west and a less regular service to Coldstream and Duns, Kelso **bus station** on Roxburgh Street is a brief walk from The Square, where you'll find the **tourist office** in the elegant Town Hall building (April–June & Sept Mon–Sat 10am–5pm, Sun 10am–1pm; July & Aug Mon–Sat 9.30am–6.30pm, Sun 10am–6pm; Oct Mon–Sat 10am–4.30pm, Sun 10am–1pm; ☎01573/223464).

Other than during Kelso's main festivals – the Border Union Dog Show in late June, the Border Union Agricultural Show in late July, the Kelso Rugby Sevens in early

September and the Ram Sales a week or so later – **accommodation** is not a problem. The best B&Bs in town are the convenient *Wester House*, 155 Roxburgh St (☎01573/224428; ③); *Duncan House,* on Chalkheugh Terrace (☎01573/225682; ③), which is more basic but has river views; *Abbey Bank*, The Knowes (☎01573/226550; ④), a mansion house with large double beds; and, best of all, *Wooden* (☎01573/224204; ④ ; May–Sept), an ivy-clad country house set in its own grounds about half a mile east of Kelso on the B6350. There's also one rather special hotel, *Ednam House*, on Bridge Street, near The Square (☎01573/224168; ⑧), a splendid Georgian mansion, with antique furnishings and fittings, whose gardens abut the Tweed – make sure you're not put in the modern extension. There's a **campsite** at *Springwood Caravan Park* (☎01573/224596; March–Oct) overlooking the Tweed on the St Boswells road.

Most **eating** places are dotted around the The Square: for snacks, try the cheap *Hazel Lodge Tea Room*, on Horsemarket, with tables outside, or the quaint non-smoking *Cottage Garden*, opposite the abbey, which serves a wide range of home-made goodies. For something more substantial, *Cobbles* restaurant, tucked away in the alley off The Square, and *The Horse & Wagon,* in the street linking Horsemarket and Woodmarket, offer reasonable bar-type meals, while *The Queen's Head*, on Bridge Street, has an imaginative menu using fresh produce. The area boasts two upmarket restaurants: the traditional *Ednam House* hotel (see above) and, two miles or so south of Kelso on the A698 at Heiton, the outstanding *Sunlaws House*, owned by the Duke of Roxburgh, where top-quality food and service is matched by top prices.

Kirk Yetholm and Town Yetholm

Six miles southeast of Kelso along the B6352, Yetholm, perched on the edge of the Cheviot Hills, is actually two separate places, **KIRK YETHOLM** and **TOWN YETHOLM**, lying a quarter of a mile apart. The villages, accessible by bus from Kelso (4–8 daily; 20min), lie at the northern end of the **Pennine Way**, a long-distance footpath which travels the length of northern England finishing at the Kirk Yetholm **youth hostel** (☎01573/420631; late March to Sept). The hostel also marks the end of the second leg of **St Cuthbert's Way** (see p.130). Walkers who have completed the Pennine Way clutching a copy of Wainwright's guidebook are entitled to a celebratory free half-pint at the *Border Hotel* (☎01573/420637) in Kirk Yetholm, which serves good food, too. You'll find cheaper **accommodation** at *Spring Valley B&B* on the green in Kirk Yetholm (☎01573/420253; ③); or at the friendly *Plough Hotel* in Town Yetholm (☎01573/420215; ③).

CENTRAL SOUTHERN SCOTLAND

Central Southern Scotland encompasses a rough rectangle of land sandwiched between the Cheviot Hills on the English border and the chain of foothills – the Pentland and Moorfoot ranges – to the south of Edinburgh. The region incorporates some of the finest stretches of the **Southern Uplands**, with bare, rounded peaks and heathery hills punctuated by valleys.

Most of the roads stick assiduously to the valleys, and the main problem is finding a route that avoids endless to and froing. Whichever way you're travelling, be sure to take in the section of the **Tweed Valley** stretching from **Melrose** (the best base for your explorations) to **Peebles**, where you'll find a string of attractions, from the ruins of **Dryburgh** and **Melrose Abbey** to the eccentricities of Sir Walter Scott's mansion at **Abbotsford** and the intriguing Jacobite past of **Traquair House**. The extensive medieval remains of the abbey at **Jedburgh**, just south, also merit a visit.

Along with semi-industrialized Selkirk and Galashiels, these towns form the heart of the **Borders** region, whose turbulent history was, until the Act of Union, characterized by endless clan warfare and Reivers' raids. Consequently, the countryside is strewn with ruined castles and keeps, while each major town celebrates its agitated past in the **Common Ridings**, when locals – especially the "Callants", the young men – dress up in period costume and ride out to check the burgh boundaries. It's a boisterous business, performed with pride and matched only by the local love of **rugby union**, which reaches a crescendo with the **Melrose Sevens** tournament in April.

The Southern Uplands assume a wild aspect in **Liddesdale**, southwest of Jedburgh, and along the **Yarrow Water** and **Moffat Water** connecting Selkirk with Moffat. Choose either of these two routes for the scenery, using the old spa town of **Moffat** as a base.

Travelling around the region by **bus** takes some forethought: pick up timetables from any tourist office and plan your connections closely – it's often difficult to cross between valleys. Some relief is, however, provided by the Harrier Scenic Bus Service, which threads its way between the more noteworthy towns from early July to September: again, the tourist office has schedules (see "Travel details" at the end of the chapter).

Melrose

Tucked in between the Tweed and the Eildon Hills, minuscule **MELROSE** is the most beguiling of towns, its narrow streets trimmed by a harmonious ensemble of styles, from pretty little cottages and tweedy shops to high-standing Georgian and Victorian facades. Most of the year, it's a sleepy little place, but as the birthplace of the **Rugby Sevens** in 1883, it's swarming during Sevens Week (second week in April), and again in early September when it hosts the **Melrose Music Festival**, a popular weekend of traditional music attracting folkies from afar.

Behind the town square, the pink- and ochre-tinted stone ruins of **Melrose Abbey** (April–Sept Mon–Sat 9.30am–6.30pm, Sun 2–6.30pm; Oct–March Mon–Sat 9.30am–4.30pm, Sun 2–4.30pm; £2.80) soar above their riverside surroundings. The abbey, founded in 1136 by David I, grew rich selling wool and hides to Flanders, but its prosperity was fragile: the English repeatedly razed Melrose, most viciously under Richard II in 1385 and the Earl of Hertford in 1545. Most of the present remains date from the intervening period, when extensive rebuilding abandoned the original austerity for an elaborate, Gothic style inspired by the abbeys of northern England.

The site is dominated by the **Abbey Church**, where the elegant window arches of the nave approach the **monk's choir**, whose grand piers are disfigured by the masonry of a later parish church. The adjacent **presbytery** is better preserved, its dignified lines illuminated by a magnificent perpendicular window pointing piously high into the sky, with the capitals of the surrounding columns sporting the most intricate of curly kale carving. The legend that the heart of Robert the Bruce is buried here beneath the window was proven to be true when the cask containing it was publicly exhumed in 1996, although the burial location was not in accordance with Bruce's wishes. In 1329, the dying king told his friend, James Douglas, to carry his heart on a Crusade to the Holy Land in fulfilment of an old vow – "Seeing therefore, that my body cannot go to achieve what my heart desires, I will send my heart instead of my body, to accomplish my vow." Douglas tried his best, but was killed fighting the Moors in Spain – and Bruce's heart ended up in Melrose.

In the **south transept**, another fine fifteenth-century window sprouts yet more delicate, foliate tracery and the adjacent cornice is enlivened by angels playing musical instruments, though these figures are badly weathered. This kind of finely carved detail is repeated everywhere you look – and outside all sorts of **gargoyles** humour the majestic lines of the church, from peculiar crouching beasts and moaning men to, most unusual of the lot, a pig playing the bagpipes on the roof on the south side of the nave.

The fragmentary ruins of the old monastic buildings edge the church and lead across to the **Commendator's House** (same times as the abbey), which displays a modest collection of ecclesiastical bric-a-brac in the house of the abbey's sixteenth-century lay administrators. Next door to the abbey in the opposite direction is the delightful **Priorwood Garden** (April–Sept Mon–Sat 10am–5.30pm, Sun 1.30–5.30pm; Oct–Dec Mon–Sat 10am–4pm, Sun 1.30–4pm; free), whose walled precincts, owned by the NTS, are given over to an orchard and flowers that are suitable for drying – there's a dried flower shop, too.

Melrose's other museum, the **Trimontium Exhibition**, just off Market Square (March–Oct daily 10.30am–4.30pm; £1.25), is a quirky little centre that merits a browse. Its displays include Celtic bronze axe heads excavated from the Eildon hills, dioramas, models and the odd archeological find outlining the three Roman occupations of the region. For further Roman adventures, the four-mile circular **Trimontium Walk** (March–Oct Thurs 1.20–4.45pm; £2.50; phone ☎01896 822651 for details) visits various Roman sites in the area, including the Leaderfoot viaduct, and the most northerly amphitheatre in the Roman Empire. The walk includes a guide and tea in Newstead, the site of the Trimontium fort (Three Hills), whose remains are on display in Edinburgh's Royal Museum (see p.78).

Practicalities

Buses to Melrose stop in Market Square, a brief walk from both the abbey ruins and the adjacent **tourist office** (March–May Mon–Sat 10am–5pm, Sun 10am–1pm; June Mon–Sat 10am–6pm, Sun 10am–2pm; July & Aug Mon–Sat 9.30am–6.30pm, Sun 10.00am–6.00pm; Sept Mon–Sat 10am–6pm, Sun 10–2pm; Oct Mon–Sat 10am–5pm, Sun 10am–1pm; ☎01896/822555).

Melrose has a clutch of **hotels**, including the smart and tidy *Burts Hotel*, on Market Square (☎01896/822285; ⑦); the neat, ten-bedroom *Bon Accord* (☎01896/822645; ⑧) just across the street; and the far less expensive – but rather humdrum – *Station Hotel* (☎01896/822038; ③), up the hill from Market Square. It's among Melrose's **B&Bs**, however, that you'll get the real flavour of the place, most notably at the easy-going and comfortable *Braidwood*, on Buccleuch Street (☎01896/822488; ③), a stone's throw from the abbey, and the equally agreeable *Dunfermline House* (☎01896/822148; ④) opposite – advance booking is recommended at both during the summer. Other nearby options include *Little Fordel*, Abbey Street (☎01896/822206; ④), and the basic *Orchard House*, High Street (☎01896/822005; ③). The town also has a **youth hostel** (☎01896/822521) in a sprawling Victorian villa overlooking the abbey from beside the access road into the bypass. The *Gibson Caravan Park* (☎01896/822969) is at the foot of the High Street, opposite the Greenyards rugby grounds.

Melrose offers a reasonable variety of **eating** options: *Marmion's Brasserie*, on Buccleuch Street, serves well-prepared meals from an imaginative menu, while *Melrose Station*, in the old train station above the square, has a good range of daily specials featuring local produce. The busy *Burts Hotel* does excellent bar meals, although their attitude to backpackers can be a bit snooty. If you're feeling energetic, walk across the old suspension bridge to Gattonside, where the *Hoebridge Inn* (☎01896/823082), one of the Borders' best restaurants, serves home-made Italian and British food in relaxed, low-key surroundings. If you want a light lunch or snack, head to *Russel's* on Market Square; *Graham's*, just opposite Priorwood Gardens, for home-made ice cream and fudge; or *Haldane's Fish & Chip Shop* (closed Wed), just off the square. For **pubs**, try the friendly *King's Arms* on the High Street, or the *Ship Inn*, on East Port at the top of the square, the liveliest in town, especially during the Folk Festival and on Saturday afternoons when the Melrose rugby union team have played at home.

WALKING IN THE EILDONS AND ST CUTHBERT'S WAY

Ordnance Survey Landranger map No. 73

From the centre of Melrose, it's a vigorous three-mile walk to the top of the **Eildons Hills**, whose triple volcanic peaks are the Central Borders' most distinctive landmark. The tourist office sells a leaflet detailing the hike, which begins about 90yd south of – and up the hill from – Market Square, along the B6359 to Lilliesleaf. The path is signposted to the left and leads to the saddle between the North and Mid Hills. To the right of the saddle are **Mid Hill**, the highest summit at 1385ft, and further south **West Hill**; to the left **North Hill** is topped by the scant remains of an Iron Age fort and a Roman signal station. There are several routes back to town: one heading down from the northeast picks up a path to Newstead and you can return to Melrose by the river.

The hills have been associated with all sorts of legends, beginning with their creation by the wizard-cum-alchemist Michael Scott. It was here that the mystic Thomas the Rhymer received the gift of prophecy from the Faerie Queen, and Arthur and his knights are reckoned to lie asleep deep within the hills, victims of a powerful spell. The ancient Celts, who revered the number three, also considered the site a holy place and maintained their settlements on the slopes long after the Romans' departure.

Melrose is also the starting point for the popular **St Cuthbert's Way**, a sixty-mile walk which finishes at Lindisfarne (the Holy Isle) on the east coast. The tourist office can give details of the walk, though the trail is well marked by yellow arrows from the abbey up over the Eildons to the pretty village of **Bowden**, where you can make a detour to see a twelfth-century kirk, half a mile down the hill from the square.

Around Melrose

Melrose makes a great base for exploring the middle reaches of the **Tweed Valley**. The rich, forested scenery inspired Sir Walter Scott, and the area's most outstanding attractions – the elegiac ruins of **Dryburgh Abbey** and lonely **Smailholm Tower**, not to mention Scott's purpose-built creation, **Abbotsford House** – bear his mark. Perhaps fortunately, Scott died before the textile boom industrialized parts of the Tweed Valley, turning his beloved **Selkirk** and **Galashiels** into mill towns. Allow time, too, for a visit to **Mellerstain House**, an example of the work of William and Robert Adam.

A comprehensive network of **bus** services connects Melrose with its surroundings and footpaths line much of the river's length. However, if you have your own transport or **bikes** – Gala Cycles, 58 High St, Galashiels (☎01896/757587), and Herbert Cycles, 5 Bridge Place, Galashiels (☎01896/755340), both rent mountain bikes – you can explore the surrounding farmlands dotted with attractive villages which have remained almost unchanged for centuries.

Dryburgh Abbey

Hidden away on a bend in the Tweed a few miles east of Melrose, the remains of **Dryburgh Abbey** (April–Sept Mon–Sat 9.30am–6.30pm, Sun 2–6.30pm; Oct–March Mon–Sat 9.30am–4.30pm, Sun 2–4.30pm; £2.30) occupy a superb position against a hilly backdrop, with ancient trees and wide lawns flattering the reddish hues of the stonework. The Premonstratensians, or White Canons, founded the abbey in the twelfth century, but they were never as successful – or apparently as devout – as their Cistercian neighbours in Melrose. Their chronicles detail interminable disputes about land and money – in one incident, a fourteenth-century canon called Marcus flattened the abbot with his fist. Later, the abbey attained its own folklore: Scott's *Minstrelsy* records the tale of a woman who lived in the vaults with a sprite called Fatlips. She only

Edinburgh Castle

View over Princes Street from Calton Hill, Edinburgh

Street entertainers, Edinburgh

Scott's View, the Borders

Scotland's favourite drink

Barras Market, Glasgow

Victoria Street, Edinburgh

The Willow Tearooms, Glasgow

The Gallery of Modern Art, Glasgow

Salmon nets on the Solway Firth

Leith harbour

Statue of "Progress and posterity"
Kelvingrove Park, Glasgow

Kippford and Rockcliffe on the Solway coast

came out after dark to beg from her neighbours and was variously thought mad or demonic.

The abbey, demolished and rebuilt on several occasions, incorporates several architectural styles, beginning in the shattered **church** where the clumsy decoration of the main entrance contrasts with the spirited dog's-tooth motif around the east processional doorway. The latter leads through to the **monastic buildings**, a two-storey ensemble that provides an insight into the lives of the monks. Bits and pieces of several rooms have survived, but the real highlight is the barrel-vaulted **chapterhouse**, complete

SIR WALTER SCOTT

Walter Scott (1771–1832) was born in Edinburgh to a solidly bourgeois family whose roots were in Selkirkshire. As a child he was left lame by polio and his anxious parents sent him to recuperate at his grandfather's farm in Smailholm, where the boy's imagination was fired by his relatives' tales of derring-do, the violent history of the Borders retold amidst a rugged landscape that he spent long summer days exploring. Scott returned to Edinburgh to resume his education and take up a career in law, but his real interests remained elsewhere. Throughout the 1790s he transcribed hundreds of old Border ballads, publishing a three-volume collection entitled *Minstrelsy of the Scottish Borders* in 1802. An instant success, *Minstrelsy* was followed by Scott's own *Lay of the Last Minstrel*, a narrative poem whose strong story and rose-tinted regionalism proved very popular.

More poetry was to come, most successfully *Marmion* (1808) and *The Lady of the Lake* (1810), not to mention an eighteen-volume edition of the works of John Dryden and nineteen volumes of Jonathan Swift. However, despite having two paid jobs, one as the Sheriff-Depute of Selkirkshire, the other as clerk to the Court of Session in Edinburgh, his finances remained shaky. He had become a partner in a printing firm, which put him deeply into debt, not helped by the enormous sums he spent on his mansion, Abbotsford. From 1813, Scott was writing to pay the bills and thumped out a veritable flood of historical novels using his extensive knowledge of Scottish history and folklore. He produced his best work within the space of ten years: *Waverley* (1814), *The Antiquary* (1816), *Rob Roy* and the *The Heart of Midlothian* (both 1818) and, after he had exhausted his own country, two notable novels set in England, *Ivanhoe* (1819) and *Kenilworth* (1821). In 1824 he returned to Scottish tales with *Redgauntlet*, the last of his quality work.

A year later Scott's money problems reached crisis proportions after an economic crash bankrupted his printing business. Attempting to pay his creditors in full, he found the quality of his writing deteriorating with its increased speed and the effort broke his health. His last years were plagued by illness, and in 1832 he died at Abbotsford and was buried within the ruins of Dryburgh Abbey.

Although Scott's interests were diverse, his historical novels mostly focused on the Jacobites, whose loyalty to the Stuarts had riven Scotland since the "Glorious Revolution" of 1688. That the nation was prepared to be entertained by such tales was essentially a matter of timing: by the 1760s it was clear the Jacobite cause was lost for good and Scotland, emerging from its isolated medievalism, had been firmly welded into the United Kingdom. Thus its turbulent history and independent spirit was safely in the past, and ripe for romancing – as shown by the arrival of King George IV in Edinburgh during 1822 decked out in Highland dress. Yet, for Sir Walter the romance was tinged with a genuine sense of loss. Loyal to the Hanoverians, he still grieved for Bonnie Prince Charlie; he welcomed a commercial Scotland but lamented the passing of feudal ties; and so his heroes are transitional, fighting men of action superseded by bourgeois figures searching for a clear identity.

With the 1997 televised serial of *Ivanhoe*, British interest in Scott has been revived, and although many of his works are currently out of print, Edinburgh University Press has recently begun a long-term project to issue proper critical editions of the Waverley novels for the first time, correcting hitherto heavily corrupted texts and restoring passages and endings that had been altered – often drastically – by the original publishers. See "Books" in Contexts for details of books by Scott currently in print.

with low stone benches, grouped windows and carved arcade. The room was used by the monks for the daily reading of a chapter from either the Bible or their rule book, and was, as they prospered, draped with expensive hangings.

Finally, back in the church, the battered north transept contains the grave of **Sir Walter Scott**; close by lies Field Marshal Haig, the World War I commander whose ineptitude cost thousands of soldiers' lives.

Practicalities

If you're driving from Melrose to Dryburgh, you can either take the scenic route along the B6360 through Gattonside or go up the bypass to the A68 and turn right after the Leaderfoot viaduct following the back roads to the abbey. Either way, you'll pass the much-visited **Scott's View** overlooking the Tweed Valley, where writer and friends often picnicked and where Scott's horse stopped out of habit during the writer's own funeral procession. The scene inspired Joseph Turner's *Melrose 1831*, now on display in the National Gallery of Scotland (see p.81). Getting to Dryburgh by public transport, the only direct service is with the four-seater **postbus** (Mon–Fri 1 daily; 25min), but this doesn't make a return trip. Alternatively, you can take the Jedburgh **bus** (Mon–Sat hourly, Sun 8 daily; 10min) as far as St Boswells, then walk north from the village back along the main road and take the third right down the mile-long lane that leads to a footbridge and Dryburgh. Dryburgh has just one **place to stay**, the commodious **Dryburgh Abbey Hotel** (☎01835/822261; ⑧), a sprawling red-sandstone building right next to the ruins.

Smailholm Tower

Crossing the Tweed after St Boswells on the B6404, you'll pass **Mertoun Gardens** on the right-hand side of the road (April–Sept Sat, Sun, Mon & public holidays 2–6pm; £1), a 26-acre bird- and flower-filled garden that sprawls beside the Tweed like a tribute to Monet. In marked contrast is the craggy **Smailholm Tower** (April–Sept Mon–Sat 9.30am–6.30pm, Sun 2–6.30pm; £1.50), perched on a rocky outcrop a few miles further on. A remote and evocative fastness recalling Reivers' raids and border skirmishes, the fifteenth-century tower was designed to withstand sudden attack. The rough rubble walls average 6ft thick and both the entrance – once guarded by a heavy door plus an iron yett (gate) – and the windows are disproportionately small. These were necessary precautions. On both sides of the border, clans were engaged in endless feuds, a violent history that stirred the imagination of a "wee, sick laddie" who was brought here to live in 1773. The boy was Walter Scott and his epic poem *Marmion* resounds to the clamour of Smailholm's ancient quarrels:

> [The forayers], *home returning, fill'd the hall*
> *With revel, wassel-rout, and brawl.*
> *Methought that still with trump and clang,*
> *The gateway's broken arches rang;*
> *Methought grim features, seam'd with scars,*
> *Glared through the window's rusty bars.*

Inside, ignore the inept costumed models and press on up to the roof, where two narrow **wall-walks**, jammed against the barrel-vaulted roof and the crow-stepped gables, provide panoramic views. On the north side the watchman's seat has also survived, stuck against the chimney stack for warmth and with a recess for a lantern.

Mellerstain House

Mellerstain House (May–Sept daily except Sat 12.30–5pm; £4) is about four miles east of Smailholm via a series of signposted byroads, and six miles northwest of Kelso along the

A6089. The house represents the very best of the Adams' work: William designed the wings in 1725, and his son Robert the castellated centre fifty years later. Robert's love of columns, roundels and friezes culminates in a stunning sequence of plaster-moulded, pastel-shaded ceilings, from the looping symmetry of the library ceiling, adorned by medallion oil paintings of *Learning* and *Reading* on either side of *Minerva*, to the whimsical griffin and vase pattern in the drawing room. It takes an hour to tour the house; afterwards you can wander the formal Edwardian gardens, which slope down to the lake.

Abbotsford House

Abbotsford House (mid-March to May & Oct Mon–Sat 10am–5pm, Sun 2–5pm; June–Sept daily 10am–5pm; £3.40) was designed to satisfy the Romantic inclinations of Sir Walter Scott, who lived here from 1812 until his death twenty years later. Built on the site of a farmhouse Scott bought and subsequently demolished, Abbotsford took twelve years to evolve with the fanciful turrets and castellations of the Scots Baronial exterior incorporating copies of medieval originals: thus the entrance porch imitates that of Linlithgow Palace and the screen wall in the garden echoes Melrose Abbey's cloister. Scott was proud of his creation, writing to a friend, "It is a kind of conundrum castle to be sure [which] pleases a fantastic person in style and manner."

Inside, visitors start in the wood-panelled **study**, with its small writing desk made of salvage from the Spanish Armada. The **library** boasts Scott's collection of more than 9000 rare books and an extraordinary assortment of Scottish memorabilia, including Rob Roy's purse and *skene dhu* (knife), a lock of Bonnie Prince Charlie's hair and his *quaich* (drinking cup), Flora Macdonald's pocketbook, the inlaid pearl crucifix that accompanied Mary, Queen of Scots to the scaffold, and even a piece of oatcake found in the pocket of a dead Highlander at Culloden. You can also see Henry Raeburn's famous portrait of Scott hanging in the **drawing room** and all sorts of weapons, notably Rob Roy's sword, dagger and gun, in the **armoury**. In the barbaric-looking **entrance hall**, hung with elk and wild cattle skulls, is a cast of the head of Robert the Bruce.

Abbotsford is sandwiched between the Tweed and the B6360, about three miles west of Melrose. The fast and frequent Melrose–Galashiels bus provides easy access: ask for the Tweedbank island on the A6091 and walk up the road from there, for about ten minutes.

Selkirk and around

Whichever way you're heading, it's likely you'll pass through the royal burgh of **SELKIRK**, a textile town of high stone houses that spread along the hillside above Ettrick Water about four miles south of Abbotsford. The **tourist office**, at the west end of High Street, off Market Place (April–Oct Mon–Sat 10am–5pm, Sun 2–4pm; July & Aug Mon–Sat 10am–6pm, Sun 2–5pm; ☎01750/20054), shares a building with **Halliwell's House Museum** and **The Robson Gallery** (same hours as tourist office; both free). The museum features an old-style hardware shop and an informative exhibit on the industrialization of the Tweed Valley, while the gallery hosts a series of temporary exhibitions of paintings and ceramics. Also in Market Place, you can visit **Sir Walter Scott's Courtroom** (April–Oct Mon–Sat 10am–4pm, Sun 2–4pm; free), where he served as Sheriff for 33 years. At the other end of High Street, the statue of **Mungo Park**, the renowned explorer and anti-slavery advocate born in Selkirkshire in 1771, displays two finely cast bas-reliefs depicting his exploits along the River Niger, which came to an end with his accidental drowning in 1805. The bronze life-size figures of *Peace*, *War*, *Slavery* and *Home Life in the Niger* were added in 1913, after several petitions and newspaper editorials demanded that he be further commemorated.

The imposing greystone woollen mills by the riverside are mostly boarded up now, an eerie reminder of a once prosperous era, though a few now function as tweed and tartan outlets. In contrast, **Selkirk Glass**, on the A7 to Galashiels (Mon–Fri 9am–4.30pm, Sat 10am–4.30pm, Sun noon–4pm; free), is a thriving craft industry which draws visitors by the coachload to watch glass-blowers making intricate paperweights. It has a bright showroom and café, though glass-blowing displays only take place on weekdays.

Practicalities

There are frequent **buses** to Selkirk from most other border towns but out-of-season transport along the Yarrow Valley takes you only as far as the *Gordon Arms Hotel* and then turns north to Traquair and Peebles. Details of local **accommodation** are posted on the window of Halliwell's House Museum: among them is the upmarket eighteenth-century *Philipburn House Hotel* (☎01750/20747; ⑦), noted for its fine cuisine, and the white-turreted *Woodburn House Hotel*, with pleasant gardens (☎01750/20816; ④), a sharp left turn up from the road to Ettrick at Heatherlie Park. **Camping** facilities (☎01750/20897; April–Oct) are available beside the river, next to the swimming pool at *Victoria Park,* though the campsites in the Ettrick Valley are far more scenic (see p.135). **Eating** in Selkirk is confined to average bar meals and hotel restaurants: the *Woodburn House Hotel* serves a good range of food at reasonable prices. Other than that, you can snack on the traditional Selkirk Bannock fruit bread available from the *Courthouse Coffee Shop* in Market Place, or *Chatterbox* at West Port.

Bowhill House and the Yarrow Valley

Three miles west of Selkirk on the A708, nineteenth-century **Bowhill House** (July daily 1–4.30pm; £4) is the property of the Duke of Buccleuch and Queensberry, a seriously wealthy man. Beyond the mansion's grand and extensive facade is an outstanding collection of French antiques and European paintings: in the **dining room**, for example, there are portraits by Reynolds and Gainsborough and a Canaletto cityscape, while the **drawing room** boasts Boulle furniture, Meissen tableware, paintings by Ruysdael, Leandro Bassano and Claude Lorraine, as well as two more family portraits by Reynolds. Look out also for the **Scott Room**, which features another splendid portrait of Sir Walter by Henry Raeburn, and the **Monmouth Room**, commemorating James, Duke of Monmouth, the illegitimate son of Charles II, who married Anne of the Buccleuchs. After several years in exile, Monmouth returned to England when his father died in 1685, hoping to wrest the crown from James II. He was defeated at the battle of Sedgemoor in Somerset and subsequently sent to the scaffold: among other items, his execution shirt is on display.

The wooded hills of **Bowhill Country Park** adjoining the house (April–June & Aug daily except Fri noon–5pm; July daily noon–5pm; £1) are criss-crossed by scenic footpaths and cycle trails: **mountain bikes** can be rented from the visitor centre. Getting to Bowhill by **public transport** is difficult: the Peebles bus, leaving Selkirk daily at 2pm will drop you at General's Bridge (10min), from where it's a 1.5-mile walk through the grounds to the house. In addition, from July to late September, there's a weekly Harrier Scenic Bus Service from Selkirk and Melrose in the morning, returning in the afternoon.

A few miles beyond Bowhill on the A708, at the head of the **Yarrow Valley**, the roadside *Broadmeadows* **youth hostel** at Yarrowford (☎01750/76262; April–Sept) is a convenient starting point for some good hill walks. From here, you can reach the hilltop cairns of **The Three Brethren**, whose 1530-ft summit offers excellent views over the Borders. You can also link up with stretches of the Southern Upland Way by heading east down through Yair Forest, or by following an old drove road west to the Cheese Well at Minchmoor (so called because of offerings left by travellers for the faerie folk), and ending up at Trauqair House near Innerleithen.

Aikwood Tower

Aikwood Tower (April–Sept Tues, Thurs & Sun 2–5pm), four miles west of Selkirk on the B7009, is a sixteenth-century fortified tower house, whose stern rubble walls stand surrounded by forests of the Ettrick Water Valley. Inside, an exhibition explores the life and work of Sir Walter Scott's friend, **James Hogg**, otherwise the "Ettrick Shepherd". Born locally, in sheep-farming Ettrick Valley, self-taught Hogg was a poet of some contemporary renown who spent several years living among the Edinburgh literary elite. Today he's largely forgotten and – if you read any of his work – this is not entirely surprising. The old byres adjoining the tower are given over to temporary displays of local artists' work and during the summer months sculpture is exhibited in the gardens. Incidentally, Aikwood doubles as the home of retired Liberal politician David Steele.

Ettrick Water and Eskdalemuir

Running alongside **Ettrick Water** towards Langholm (see p.141), the B7009 passes through some of the Borders' loveliest scenery, from gentle, open hills, dotted with the occasional sheep farm to the progressively bleak moors of Eskdalemuir. After Aikwood Tower, the hamlet of Ettrickbridge, like every border town, boasts a *Cross Keys Inn* (☎01750/52224; ④), a seventeenth-century coaching inn with a cosy, oak-beamed bar. A few miles further on, just north of Ettrick, birthplace of Hogg in 1770, you'll find the picturesque *Angecoft Caravan Park* (☎01750/62251; March–Oct) and *Honey Cottage Caravan Park* (☎01750/62246; all year).

Nine miles further along the B709, the fluttering prayer flags, scarlet-robed Buddhists and golden temple domes of the only **Tibetan monastery** outside Tibet make a surreal sight against the bleak expanse of **ESKDALEMUIR**. Visitors are welcome to look round the impressive *Samye Ling* temple, and to attend courses on Buddhist meditation and Eastern philosophy (phone ☎013873/73232 for further details). Accommodation and a basic vegetarian canteen are available for people staying on retreats or attending courses, and there's a small shop and café for passing visitors.

The Tweed Valley: Galashiels to Peebles

There's a wide choice of routes on from Melrose; one of the more popular options is to travel 22 miles west along the **Tweed Valley** to the pleasant country town of **Peebles**. On the way, savour the wooded scenery and drop into **Traquair House**, just off the main road at **Innerleithen**. Public transport is no problem: frequent buses along the valley are supplemented by the seasonal Harrier Scenic Bus Service (see p.172). Just west of Peebles, the River Tweed curves south towards Tweedsmuir, from where it's just a few miles further to Moffat (see p.144).

Galashiels

Four miles west of Melrose, it's probably best to avoid **GALASHIELS**, a workaday textile town and home to the Scottish College of Textiles, spread along the valley of the Gala Water near its junction with the Tweed. You may, however, have to pass through the region's principal bus station, close to (and across the river from) the town centre. If you're delayed you could take a stroll along the main drag, High, then Bank, Street, whose eastern end is cheered by a melodramatic statue of a mounted Border Reiver. The long-demolished New Gala House, a mansion which stood at the top of the town, was taken over during World War II by an Edinburgh girls' school, St Trinnean's – Ronald Searle met two of the pupils in 1941, inspiration for the unruly school girls in his St Trinians novels. Galashiels **tourist office**, 3 St John's St, is across the square from the statue (April–June & Sept Mon–Sat 10am–5pm, Sun 2–4pm; July

& Aug Mon–Sat 10am–6pm, Sun 1–5pm; Oct Mon–Sat 10am–12.30pm & 1.30–4.30pm; ☎01896/755551).

Walkerburn and Innerleithen

Ten miles west of Galashiels on the A72, tiny **WALKERBURN** is home to the pint-sized **Museum of Woollen Textiles** (Mon–Sat 9am–5.30pm; April–Nov also Sun 11am–5pm; free). Some of the early wool and cloth patterns are of interest, but it won't be long before you're moving on the mile or so west to **INNERLEITHEN**, a rural village which gained prominence in the 1700s and 1800s as a mill town and spa centre. Aside from its main attraction, Traquair House (see below), the town boasts **Robert Smail's Printing Works** (Easter & May–Sept Mon–Sat 10am–1pm & 2–5pm, Sun 2–5pm; Oct Sat 10am–1pm & 2–5pm, Sun 2–5pm; NTS; £2.30), a working museum with original machinery from the nineteenth century where you can try your hand at typesetting, and the visitor centre at **St Ronan's Wells** (Easter–Oct daily 2–5pm; free), where Walter Scott used to imbibe the sulphur waters.

Most visitors make Peebles their base, but there are a few places **to stay** in Innerleithen, such as the central *Traquair Arms Hotel*, on Traquair Road (☎01896/830229; ④), and the *Caddon View Guest House*, Pirn Road (☎01896/830208; ③), though you have to book early during the Traquair Fair each August. Campers should head for the *Tweedside Caravan Park* on Montgomery Street (☎01896/831271), while **mountain bikes** can be rented from Bikesport on Peebles Road if you feel like checking out the many graded cycle routes through Glentress, Cardrona, or Elibank and Traquair forests.

Traquair House

Peeping out from the trees a mile or so south of Innerleithen on the B709, **Traquair House** (April, May & Sept daily 12.30–5.30pm; June–Aug daily 10.30am–5.30pm; Oct Fri, Sat & Sun 2–5pm; £4) is the oldest continuously inhabited house in Scotland, with the present owners – the Maxwell Stuarts – living here since 1491. The first of the line, **James**, first Laird of Traquair, inherited an elementary fortified tower, which his powerful descendants gradually converted into a mansion, visited, it is said, by 27 monarchs including Mary, Queen of Scots. Persistently Catholic, the family paid for its principles: the fifth earl got two years in the Tower of London for his support of Bonnie Prince Charlie, Protestant mill workers repeatedly attacked their property, and by 1800 little remained of the family's once enormous estates – certainly not enough to fund any major rebuilding.

Consequently, Traquair's main appeal is in its ancient shape and structure. The whitewashed facade is strikingly handsome, with narrow windows and trim turrets surrounding the tiniest of front doors – an organic, homogeneous edifice that's a welcome change from other grandiose stately homes. Inside, the house has kept many of its oldest features. You can see original vaulted cellars, where locals once hid their cattle from raiders; the twisting main staircase as well as the earlier medieval version, later a secret escape route for persecuted Catholics; a carefully camouflaged priest's hole; and even a **priest's room** where a string of resident chaplains lived in hiding until the Catholic Emancipation Act freed things up in 1829. Of the furniture and fittings, the carved oak door at the foot of the stairs is outstanding, as are the Dutch trompe l'oeils in the **still room** and the bright-yellow four-poster of the **king's room**, with a bedspread allegedly embroidered by Mary, Queen of Scots. That said, it's not any particular piece that impresses, but rather the accumulation of family bygones that give a real insight into the family's revolving-door fortunes and eccentricities. In the **museum room** there are several fine examples of Jacobite or **Amen glass**, inscribed with pictures of the Bonnie Prince or verses in his honour; a handful of personal items thought to have been owned by Mary, Queen of Scots; and the cloak worn by the fourth earl during his dramatic escape from the Tower of London. Under sentence of death for his part in the Jacobite Rising of 1715, the earl was saved by his wife, Lady Winifred Herbert, who got his jailers drunk and smuggled him out disguised as a maid.

It's worth sparing time for the surrounding **gardens** where you'll find a maze, several craft workshops and a **working brewery** dating back to 1566 which had lain unused for 150 years. The present owner restored it and opened it to the public in 1965, claiming it to be the only British brewery that still ferments totally in oak. You can taste the ales in the Malt Loft (Fri 3–4pm), and buy them from the laid-back tearoom and gift shop.

Peebles

Straddling the Tweed and circled by hills, the royal burgh of **PEEBLES** has a genteel, relaxing air, its wide High Street bordered by a complementary medley of architectural styles, mostly dating from Victorian times. A stroll around town should include a visit to the **The Tweedale Museum** (April–Oct Mon–Fri 10am–noon & 2–5pm, Sat 10am–noon, Sun 2–4pm; Nov–March Mon–Fri only; free), housed in the Chambers Institute on High Street. William Chambers, a local worthy, presented the building to the town in 1859, complete with an art gallery dedicated to the enlightenment of his neighbours. He stuffed the place with casts of the world's most famous sculptures and, although most were lost long ago, today's "Secret Room", once the Museum Room, boasts two handsome friezes: one a copy of the Elgin marbles taken from the Parthenon; the other of the Triumph of Alexander, originally cast in 1812 to honour Napoleon. **The Old Parish Church** (daily 10am–4pm) dominates the High Street and has some unusual features in its elegant oak, bronze and engraved-glass entrance screen and 22 modern oil paintings illustrating the scriptures. Suspended from the ceiling are tattered Napoleonic flags, emblems of 1816, the year the Peebleshire Militia disbanded.

WALKS AND CYCLING AROUND PEEBLES

A series of footpaths snake through the hills surrounding Peebles with their rough-edged burns, bare peaks and deep woods. The main local tracks are listed in the *Popular Walks Around Peebles* leaflet available from the tourist office. The five-mile-long **Sware Trail** is one of the easiest and most scenic, weaving west along the north bank of the river and looping back to the south. On the way, it passes **Neidpath Castle** (Easter–Sept Mon–Sat 11am–5pm, Sun 1–5pm; £2), a gaunt medieval tower house perched high above the river on a rocky buff. It's a superb setting, but think twice about the entrance fee – the interior, although it does possess a pit prison and an ancient well, is little more than an empty shell. The walk also slips by the splendid skew **rail bridge**, part of the Glasgow line which was finished in 1850. Other, longer footpaths follow the old drove tracks, like the thirteen-mile haul to St Mary's Loch or the fourteen-mile route to Selkirk via Traquair House (see opposite). For either of these, you'll need an Ordnance Survey map, a compass and proper hiking tackle (see "Outdoor pursuits" in Basics). A more gentle stroll is the 2.5-mile amble to the privately owned **Kailzie Gardens** (daily: April to mid-Oct 11am–5.30pm; £2; mid-Oct to March daylight hours; £1; ☎01721/720007), whose fifteen acres include a walled garden, trout pond (fishing costs £5 a day; fly-fishing tackle is available for rent), a lovely wood-panelled tearoom, a souvenir shop and small gallery.

From Peebles, you can link up to the clearly signposted ninety-mile **Tweed Cycleway**: mountain **bikes** can be rented from George Pennel Cycles, 3 High St (☎01721/720844), or Scottish Border Trails (☎01721/722934), at the entrance to Glentress Forest two miles east of town on the A72. If you need four or more, the latter deliver free within a ten-mile radius.

Practicalities

Buses to Peebles from Selkirk, Galashiels and Edinburgh stop outside the post office, a few doors down from the well-stocked **tourist office**, High Street (April & May Mon–Sat 10am–5pm, Sun 10am–2pm; June Mon–Sat 10am–5.30pm, Sun 10am–4pm; July & Aug Mon–Sat 9am–7pm, Sun 10am–6pm; Sept Mon–Sat 10am–5.30pm, Sun 1–4pm; Oct Mon–Sat 10am–4.30pm, Sun 10am–2pm; Nov & Dec Mon–Sat 10am–12.30pm & 1.30–4.30pm; ☎01721/720138), where you can buy the useful leaflet, *Peebles Town Walk* (25p). Peebles boasts more than twenty **B&Bs**; try the trim, pint-sized *Rowanbrae*, on Northgate, a turning off the east end of High Street (☎01721/721630; ③); the *Minniebank Guest House*, Greenside (☎01721/722093; ④), a Victorian villa set beside the river by the main bridge; or *Viewfield*, 1 Rosetta Rd (☎01721/721232; ③), an attractive Victorian house a ten-minute walk west of the bridge – take the Old Town road (the A72) and follow it round, turning right up Young Street. The best of the upmarket **hotels** is *The Park Hotel*, just east of the town centre on Innerleithen Road (☎01721/720451; ⑧), with cheaper alternatives including the mundane *Green Tree Hotel*, 41 Eastgate (☎01721/720582; ⑤), and the relaxing *Kingsmuir Hotel*, south of the river on Springhill Road (☎01721/720151; ⑦). For **camping**, the *Rosetta Caravan and Camping Park* (☎01721/720770; April–Oct) is a fifteen-minute walk north of the High Street (directions as for *Viewfield* B&B).

The best places for **food** are the *Crown Hotel*, High Street, featuring good daily specials, the *Kingsmuir Hotel*, Springhill Road, with more expensive but excellent bar meals, or the slightly dilapidated-looking *Tontine Hotel* on the High Street, which has a spacious lounge and restaurant serving good food. Other options on the High Street include the *Prince of India Tandoori Restaurant* and, during the day, the cheap-and-cheerful *Tatler Café* for good-value fish and chips, or the *Olive Tree* delicatessen for superb, imaginative sandwiches.

Jedburgh

Ten miles from the border with England, **JEDBURGH** nestles in the valley of the Jed Water near its confluence with the Teviot out on the edge of the wild Cheviot Hills. During the interminable Anglo-Scottish Wars, it was the quintessential frontier town, a heavily garrisoned royal burgh incorporating a mighty castle and abbey. Though the **Castle** was destroyed by the Scots in 1409 to keep it out of the hands of the English, its memory has been kept alive by local folklore: in 1285, for example, King Alexander III was celebrating his wedding feast in the Great Hall when a ghostly apparition predicted his untimely death and a bloody civil war; sure enough, he died in a hunting accident shortly afterwards and chaos ensued. Today the ruined **Abbey** is the main event though a stroll round Jedburgh's old town centre is a pleasant way to while away an hour or two.

The Town

The remains of **Jedburgh Abbey** (April–Sept Mon–Sat 9.30am–6.30pm, Sun 2–6.30pm; Oct–March Mon–Sat 9.30am–4.30pm, Sun 2–4.30pm; £2.80), right in the centre of town, date from the twelfth century. Benefiting from King David's patronage, the monks developed an extravagant complex on a sloping site next to the Jed Water, the monastic buildings standing beneath a huge sandstone church. All went well until the late thirteenth century, when the power of the Scots kings waned following the death of Alexander III and the prolonged war that ensued. The abbey was subsequently burnt and badly damaged on a number of occasions, the worst being inflicted by the English in 1544–45. The monastic way of life, however, had already fallen prey to corruption and only a few canons remained living in the ruins of the abbey, until the monastery closed in 1560 with the Reformation. However, the Abbey Church remained a parish kirk for another three centuries and has survived particularly well preserved.

Entry to the site is through the bright **visitor centre** at the bottom of the hill (arrangements can be made for wheelchair access), whose explanation of the abbey's history uses both contemporary quotations and "mood music" – chanting monks and the like. Next to the centre are the scant remains of the cloister buildings and chapter room, where day-to-day affairs were administered. The **Abbey Church**, lying on an east–west axis, is entered through the East Processional doorway, remarkably still in its original condition. Behind the doorway lies the splendidly proportioned three-storeyed nave, a fine example of the transition from Romanesque to Gothic design, with pointed window arches surmounted by the round-headed arches of the triforium, which, in turn, support the lancet windows of the clerestory. This delicacy of form is, however, not matched at the east end of the church, where the squat central tower is underpinned by the monumental circular pillars and truncated arches of the earlier, twelfth-century choir. On close inspection you can see the three places where the sculptor, Thomas Cranston, carved his initials and insignia.

It's a couple of minutes' walk from the abbey round to the tiny triangular **Market Place**. Up the hill from here, at the top of Castlegate, **Jedburgh Castle Jail and Museum** (March–Nov Mon–Sun 10am–4pm; £1.25) exhibits displays on prison life throughout the ages. The prison buildings themselves are, for the period, remarkably comfortable, reflecting the influence of reformer John Howard. Finally, **Mary, Queen of Scots' House** (March to mid-Nov Mon–Sat 10am–4.45pm, Sun 10am-4.30pm; £2), situated at the opposite end of the town centre, is something of a misnomer; the owner was actually her protector, Sir Thomas Kerr, ancestor of the present Lord Lothian of Ferniehurst Castle. It's true that Mary stayed here in this castle house during the assizes of 1566, but she didn't stay long and there's little on show connected with her visit. The attempt to unravel her complex life is cursory, the redeeming features being a copy of Mary's death mask and one of the few surviving portraits of the Earl of Bothwell. One curious feature of all Kerr houses is that the staircases spiral to the left for ease of sword-drawing, giving rise to the Scottish term for left-handedness, "kerry haunded" or "kerry fisted".

Practicalities

Jedburgh's **bus station**, a few yards from the abbey, is the starting point for a wide range of services around the Borders. Footsteps away on Murray's Green, the **tourist office** (April, May & Oct Mon–Sat 10am–5pm, Sun noon–4pm; June & Sept Mon–Sat 9.30am–6pm, Sun noon–4pm; July & Aug Mon–Fri 9am–8.30pm, Sat 9am–7pm, Sun 10am–7pm; Nov–March Mon–Fri 10am–4.30pm; ☎01835/863435) has a vast array of information, pamphlets detailing three circular walks and a town trail, and a comprehensive list of local **accommodation**. Try the *Kenmore Bank Guest House*, Oxnam Road (☎01835/862369; ⑥), a Victorian villa overlooking the Jed Water five minutes' walk south of the abbey, or *Glenfriars Hotel*, The Friars (☎01835/862000; ⑥), a big old house in its own grounds near the north end of High Street. Alternatively, there are several **B&Bs** among the pleasant and antique row houses of Castlegate, notably Mrs Bathgate, at no. 64 (☎01835/862466; ②; April–Oct) and Mrs Poloczek, at no. 48 (☎01835/862504; ④). A mile south of town on the A68, you'll find *Hundalee House* (☎01835/863011; ③; March–Oct), a historic mansion house in open grounds. The *Jedwater Caravan and Camping Park* (☎01835/840219; April–Oct) occupies a riverside site four miles south of town on the A68, while the *Elliot Park* caravan and **campsite** (☎01835/863393; March–Sept) is beside the Edinburgh road about a mile north of the centre. For **horse riders**, there are both stables and accommodation at *Ferniehurst*

JEDBURGH FESTIVALS

Jedburgh is at its busiest during the town's two main **festivals**. The Common Riding, or **Callants' Festival**, takes place in late June/early July, when the young people of the town – especially the lads – mount up and ride out to check the burgh boundaries, a reminder of more troubled days when Jedburgh was subject to English raids. In similar spirit, early February sees the day-long **Jedburgh Hand Ba'** game, an all-male affair between the "uppies" (those born above Market Place) and "downies" (those born below). In theory the aim of the game is to get hay-stuffed leather balls – originally the heads of English men – from one end of town to the other, but there's more at stake than that: macho reputations are made and lost during the two two-hour games.

Mill Lodge, two miles south of Jedburgh on the A68 (☎01835/863279; ④), from where experienced riders can venture out into the Cheviot hills.

During the day there are enough places **to eat** in Jedburgh, although evening meal choices are more limited. *Simply Scottish*, on the High Street, serves quality Scottish meals and snacks all day, while *Brown Sugar* coffee bar, by Market Place, offers sandwiches, salads and cakes. The *Castlegate Tea Room and Restaurant* around the corner has an evening menu, as well, and the friendly *Cookie Jar,* popular by day with locals and smokers, metamorphoses by night into an Italian restaurant. Other evening options are *The Wayfarer* down the High Street, whose German owners offer a variety of mainly meat dishes, and bar meals at *The Carter's Rest*, across from the abbey. Try the local speciality, Jethart Snails, which are sticky boiled sweets invented by a French POW in the 1700s and on sale everywhere.

Teviotdale, Ewes Water and Liddesdale

If you're heading southwest from Jedburgh, there are two clearly defined routes. The first, along the A698 and then A7, tracks up **Teviotdale** to **Hawick**, before slipping through the dramatic uplands which stretch as far as the English border. En route you change dales – joining **Ewes Water** at the Dumfries boundary.

The route down **Liddesdale**, along the B6357, is slower but even more picturesque, on a remote road flanked by dense forests, barren moors and secluded heaths. If you do come this way, stop off at solitary **Hermitage Castle**, a well-preserved fourteenth-century fortress.

The Galashiels to Carlisle **bus** travels the length of Teviotdale and Ewes Water (Mon–Sat 7 daily, Sun 3 daily), with buses from Jedburgh connecting with this service at Hawick. There are no buses along the length of Liddesdale – the best you'll do is the occasional, school-term-only service from Langholm to Canonbie and Newcastleton; ring Telfords Coaches (☎013873/75677) for details.

Hawick to Langholm and Liddesdale

Fourteen miles from Jedburgh, the unprepossessing mill town of **HAWICK** (pronounced "Hoyk") hit the headlines in 1996, when two local women attempted to join a traditional all-male ride-out which takes place each June. Having been refused permission to ride on grounds of their sex, the women took their case to the Equal Opportunities Commission. The Sheriff Court ruled that the ban was illegal under the Sex Discrimination Act, and the subsequent furore split the town. Controversy aside, Hawick is known for its many factory outlets which swarm with visitors, bearing witness to its history as centre of the region's knitwear and hosiery industry. Hawick's

tourist information office is in **Drumlanrig Tower** (Easter–May & Oct Mon–Sat 10am–5pm, June & Sept 10am–5.30pm, Sun noon–5.30pm, July & Aug Mon–Sat 10am–6pm, Sun noon–6pm; ☎01450/372547) and doubles as a **museum** (times as for tourist office; £2.25), telling the story of the tower from the sixteenth century.

Beyond Hawick, the road twists its way south between the bulging heathery hills that shadow the river to **TEVIOTHEAD**, home of the **Johnnie Armstrong Gallery** and workshops of the Moffat family who make gold and silver jewellery, specializing in Celtic, Viking and Scottish designs (daily 9am–7pm; ☎01450/850237). The museum is named after a local hero and defender of Scotland, who, in 1529, annoyed Henry VIII so much that he persuaded James V of Scotland to get rid of him – James then invited Johnnie Armstrong to a truce and had him murdered.

At Teviothead the road leaves the dale to cross over into Dumfries, where the **Ewes Water** strips down to **LANGHOLM**, a quiet, stone-built mill town, at the confluence of the Esk, Ewes and Wauchope waters, which flourished during the eighteenth-century textile boom, and is still dominated by the industry. In 1892 this was the birthplace of the poet **Hugh MacDiarmid**, a co-founder of the Scottish National Party and a key player in the literary renaissance that fired the nationalist movement between the two world wars. MacDiarmid, born Christopher Murray Grieve, looked to the Scotland of the eighteenth century, lionizing Walter Scott and Robbie Burns while heaping scorn on the anglicized gentry. This didn't go down well with some of the burghers of Langholm, who, when MacDiarmid died in 1978 at the age of 86, tried to prevent him being buried in the local churchyard. If you're passing through town, stop off at the **Armstrong Museum and Clan Centre**, at Castle Holm (Easter to end Sept Tues–Sun 1.30–4.30pm; £1), for further stories of the clan, or follow the MacDiarmid Trail round town.

The **tourist office** (April, May & Sept Mon–Sat 10.30am–4.30pm; June–Aug daily 10am–5pm; ☎013873/80976), on the main road leading into Langholm from the north, can provide details of **accommodation**, or try the convenient *Eskdale Hotel*, Market Place (☎013873/80357; ④), the *Reivers Rest*, High Street (☎013873/81343; ③), or one of the town's two **campsites**.

On from Langholm

Four roads lead out of Langholm, the most stunning being the narrow country lane that snakes its way east over the empty hills to **Newcastleton** in Liddesdale. Otherwise, choose between the rustic thirty-mile journey west to **Dumfries** (see p.149) via Lockerbie; the far slower trip northwest up **Eskdale** for Selkirk and the Tweed Valley (see p.135); or the shorter journey south past Canonbie to **Gretna Green**.

If you're travelling by **bus** from Langholm, it takes about three hours to get to Dumfries, changing at Lockerbie (4 buses weekly), whilst Gretna Green can be reached via the better-served Carlisle route. Buses to Selkirk (6–7 daily; 1hr) go along the A7 via Hawick – there aren't any services along Eskdale and only an occasional bus to Newcastleton (see p.141).

Liddesdale

Heading south out of Jedburgh on the A68, it's about a mile to the B6357, a narrow byroad that leads over the moors to the hamlet of Bonchester Bridge. From here, the road cuts south through Wauchope Forest and carries on into **Liddesdale**, whose wild beauty is at its most striking between Saughtree and Newcastleton. In between the two, take the turning to **Hermitage Castle** (April–Sept Mon–Sat 9.30am–6.30pm, Sun 2–6.30pm; Oct–March Sat 9.30am–4.30pm, Sun 2–4.30pm; £1.50), a bleak and forbidding fastness devilled by all sorts of horrifying legends: one owner, William Douglas, starved his prisoners to death; whilst Lord de Soulis, another occupant, engaged the help of demons to fortify the castle in defiance of the king, Robert the Bruce. Not entirely trusting his demonic assistants, Soulis also drilled holes into the shoulders of his vassals, the better to yoke them to sledges of building materials. Bruce became so tired of the complaints that he exclaimed, "Boil him if you please, but let me hear no more of him." Bruce's henchmen took him at his word and ambushed the rebellious baron. Convinced, however, that Soulis had a pact with his demonic familiar, Redcap, that made him difficult to kill ("ropes could not bind him, nor steel weapons touch"), they bound him with ropes of sifted sand, wrapped him in lead and boiled him slowly.

From the outside, the castle remains an imposing structure, its heavy walls topped by stepped gables and a tidy corbelled parapet. However, the apparent homogeneity is deceptive: certain features were invented during a Victorian restoration, a confusing supplement to the ad hoc alterations that had already transformed the fourteenth-century original. The ruinous interior is a bit of a letdown, but look out for the tight Gothic doorways and gruesome dungeon.

It's a short journey on to **NEWCASTLETON**, a classic estate village built for the hand-loom weavers of the third Duke of Buccleuch in 1793. The gridiron streets fall either side of a long main road that connects three geometrically arranged squares – nice enough to while away the odd hour. You can **stay** the night at the *Liddesdale Hotel* (☎013873/75255; ④) and sample some local trout or pheasant, or try the comfortable *Borders Honey Farm* B&B (☎013873/76737; ④), four miles north of Newcastleton on the B6357, but if you plan to stay during the hugely popular **Newcastleton Folk Festival** in July, book ahead. For **food**, try the *Copshaw Kitchen Restaurant* on Hermitage Street (closed Tues), provided you don't mind dining in an antique shop.

The road leaves Liddesdale ten miles southwest of Newcastleton at Canonbie. Around here, sandwiched between the **Esk** and the **Sark**, was what was known as the **"Debateable Land"**, a pocket-sized territory claimed – but not controlled – by both England and Scotland from the fourteenth to the early eighteenth century. In the prevailing chaos, the Border Reivers flourished and famed outlaws like Kinmont Willie, Jock o' the Side and Clym of the Cleugh established fabulous reputations for acts of cruelty and kindness in equal measure.

Annandale: Gretna Green to Moffat

Cutting through **Annandale**, the M/A74 connects Carlisle with Glasgow. This is the fastest way to cross Southern Scotland but it's an unpleasantly busy road, jam-packed with trucks and lorries. You could break your journey by stopping off at **Gretna Green**, whose name is synonymous with elopements and quick weddings, before travelling the thirty miles north to the charming market town of **Moffat**, bypassed by the main road, which makes an ideal base for exploring the surrounding uplands. Bus services along Annandale are quick and frequent.

Gretna to Lockerbie

There's not much to the twin villages of **GRETNA GREEN** and **GRETNA** except their curious history, the result of the quirks of the British legal system. Up until 1754 English couples could buy a quick and secret wedding at London's Fleet Prison, bribing imprisoned clerics with small amounts of money. The Hardwicke Marriage Act brought an end to this seedy wheeze, enforcing the requirement of a licence and a church ceremony. However, in Scotland, a marriage declaration made before two witnesses remained legal. The consequences of this difference in the law verged on farce: hundreds of runaway couples dashed north to Scotland, their weddings witnessed by just about anyone who came to hand – ferrymen, farmers, tollgate keepers and even self-styled "priests" who set up their own "marriage houses".

Gretna and Gretna Green, due to their position beside the border on the main turn-pike road to Edinburgh, became the most popular destination for the fugitives. In their rush, many people tied the knot at the first place to hand after dismounting from the stagecoach, which happened to be a blacksmith's shop situated at the crossroads, though the better off maintained class distinctions, heading for the staging post at Gretna Hall. The association with blacksmiths was strengthened by one of the first "priests", the redoubtable Joseph Paisley, a 25-stone Goliath who – in business from 1754 to 1812 – gave a certain style to the ceremony by straightening a horseshoe, a show of strength rather than a symbolic act. His melodramatic act led to stories of Gretna weddings being performed over the blacksmith's anvil, and later "priests" were more than happy to act out the rumour. Both villages boomed until the marriage laws were further amended in 1856, but some business continued right down to 1940, when marriage by declaration was made illegal. The **Old Blacksmith's Shop** now houses a museum, shops, workshops, restaurants, a pub and the **tourist office** (daily: April & Oct 10am–4.30pm; May, June & Sept 10am–5pm; July & Aug 10am–6pm; ☎01461/337834); year-round information is also available from the tourist office at the Gretna Services on the A74. Confusingly, the *Gretna Hall Hotel* (☎01461/338257; ⑤) also has a **Blacksmith's Shop and Museum** (April–Sept daily 9am–5pm; Oct–March Tues–Sat 10am–4pm; £1) containing a diverting collection of romantic bygones.

There are lots of places to **stay** in and around Gretna and Gretna Green and all the hotels serve **bar meals**. The tourist office has the full list, but the nicest options are in Gretna: try either of two modernized farmhouses, the *Surrone Guest House*, on Annan Road (☎01461/338341; ④), or *The Beeches*, Loanwath Road (☎01461/337448; ③; Feb–Nov), which has just two (non-smoking) rooms.

Ecclefechan and Lockerbie

It's about nine miles from Gretna to the tidy hamlet of **ECCLEFECHAN**, birthplace of the historian and essayist **Thomas Carlyle** (1795–1881). Born into a strongly Calvinist family, Carlyle's highly successful account of the *French Revolution* (1837) set out his theory of history as "Divine Scripture": the French aristocracy had reaped the rewards of their corruption and indulgence. However, with no clearly defined political ideology his radicalism soon began to wane – reinforced by the failure of contemporary activist movements to live up to his idealistic expectations. Disillusioned, Carlyle was eventually to become the strongest voice for the moral concerns of the Victorian bourgeoisie, and as such a litmus paper of his age. Supposedly an irritable and melancholic character, his marriage was turbulent, but when his wife died in 1866 he never recovered and was a semi-recluse for many years before his death. His old home, the whitewashed **Arched House** (May–Sept daily except Sat 1.30–5pm; £1.80), is now a tiny museum, featuring among the personal memorabilia a bronze cast of his hands, old smoking caps and his cradle. Perhaps surprisingly, there's little here to indicate either the man's stern demeanour or his Calvinist roots. There are several **hotels** and **B&Bs** in Ecclefechan, including *Carlyle House*, opposite the museum (☎01576/300322; ②), as well as the well-serviced *Hoddom Castle Campsite* nearby on the B725 (☎01576/300251).

The quiet country town of **LOCKERBIE**, eight miles from Ecclefechan, was catapulted into the headlines on Wednesday December 21, 1988, when a Pan-Am jumbo jet, flying from Frankfurt to New York via Heathrow, was blown up by a terrorist bomb concealed in a transistor radio. All the crew and passengers died and the plane's fragments crashed down on Lockerbie, killing a further eleven. Those who planted the bomb, apparently Arab terrorists now resident in Libya, have yet to be brought to book, and Anglo-American efforts to have them extradicted seem to be fizzling out. The local people have set up a Remembrance Garden on the outskirts of town, but this is no place for the casual visitor.

Moffat

Encircled by hills and dales, **MOFFAT** is a good-looking market town, its wide and elegant **High Street** flattered with Georgian mansions and flanked by streets of colourful brick cottages. The former hark back to the eighteenth century, when Moffat was briefly a modish spa, its sulphur springs attracting the rich and famous. One disappointed customer suggested they smelt of bilge water – but they were good enough for luminaries Robbie Burns and James Boswell, who came to "wash off the scurvy spots".

Moffat is no longer so fashionable, despite being winner of the "best kept small country town" in 1996, but boasts such low-key attractions as the John Adam-designed **Moffat House Hotel** and the neighbouring **Colvin Fountain**, whose sturdy bronze ram was accidentally cast without any ears. Not far away, the dark shadows of the **Black Bull** pub once quartered John Graham of Claverhouse as he planned his persecution of the Covenanters on behalf of Charles II. For details of the town's history, pop into the **museum**, at Church Gate (Easter–Sept daily except Wed 10.30am–1pm & 2.30–5pm; £1). The tourist office (see below) has a helpful compendium of local **walks**, one of the best being the short but brisk hike up to the top of Gallow Hill, from where there are great views out over Annandale; allow a couple of hours. For a more gentle stroll round the outskirts of the town by the River Annan, follow the "waterside walk" sign opposite Station Park. More strenuous walking is within reach in the Lowther Hills (see p.146), and nearby Beattock marks the midway point of the Southern Upland Way.

Practicalities

Buses to Moffat drop passengers on High Street near the **tourist office** (daily: April, May, Sept & Oct 10am–5pm; June–Aug 9.30am–6.30pm; ☎01683/220620). There is no shortage of accommodation in town: several **hotels** line the High Street, the best being the opulent *Moffat House Hotel*, High Street (☎01683/220039; ⑦). Some alternatives include the palatable *Buccleuch Arms* (☎01683/220003; ⑤) and the *Star Hotel* (☎01683/220156; ④), which claims to be Britain's narrowest free-standing hotel; both are on the High Street. For **B&Bs**, try along Beechgrove, a five-minute walk from the town centre: head north along High Street, continue down Academy Road, and turn beside Moffat Academy. Here you'll find an array of places to stay including *Queensberry* (☎01683/220538; ③; March–Sept), *Alba House* (☎01683/ 220418; ④; March–Oct), and *Gilbert House* (☎01683/220050; ③). The *Hammerland's Farm* **camping and caravan** site (☎01683/220436; March–Nov) sits beside the Selkirk road, about half a mile east of Moffat.

The *Buccleuch Arms* serves the best **bar meals** in town: alternatively, choose from two Italian restaurants, *Valle Verde Trattoria* (closed Wed) further up High Street for filling, cheap pizzas, and *Claudio's* in the old police station at Burnside for popular home cooking. You'll find a few cafés along High Street, including *Pacitti's* which serves great coffee, or go for the afternoon teas (May–Sept) at the *Moffat House Hotel*. If you've got a real sweet tooth, try the home-made fudge and local Moffat toffee from the sweet shop in the High Street.

Around Moffat

From Moffat, there are three beautiful routes you can take through the most dramatic parts of the Southern Uplands. Of the three, the finest is the A708 between Moffat and Selkirk (see p.133), via **Moffat Water** and **Yarrow Water**. On the way, the Grey Mare's Tail Waterfall provides the opportunity for an exhilarating ramble and St Mary's Loch gives easy access to an especially stimulating section of the Southern Upland Way. Further west, the second route uses the A701, which climbs over the hills at the head of Annandale, cuts down **Tweeddale**, and joins the Tweed Valley near Peebles (see p.137). The third option begins at Elvanfoot on the M/A74, where the B7040 leaves the main road to cross the **Lowther Hills**. Passing through the former lead-mining villages of **Leadhills** and **Wanlockhead**, this road reaches Nithsdale north of Drumlanrig Castle (see p.141).

Travelling these routes by **bus** remains difficult. The only service along the A708 is the Harrier Scenic Bus Service, which runs from Moffat to Melrose once weekly between July and late September. The Harrier also links Moffat and Peebles via the A701 once a week during the summer. The only way to reach Leadhills and Wanlockhead is on the once- or twice-daily service from Sanquhar in Nithsdale.

Moffat Water and Yarrow Water

Heading northeast from Moffat, the A708 snakes its way through the forests and hills along the lower stretches of **Moffat Water**. Before long the road climbs to wilder terrain, tracking along the bottom of a gloomy gully surrounded by desolate moorland. Beyond, ten miles from town, the 200ft **Grey Mare's Tail Waterfall** (NTS) tumbles down a rocky crevasse – one of Dumfries' best-known beauty spots. The base of the falls is approached by a precipitous footpath along the left side of the stream, a ten-minute clamber each way from the road. There's a longer hike, too, up the steep right-hand bank, past the head of the falls and on to the remote **Loch Skeen**, where you can fish without permits.

Back on the road, and crossing over into the Borders, it's a few miles further to the pair of icy lakes that mark the start of **Yarrow Water**. Tiny **Loch of the Lowes** to the south and the larger **St Mary's Loch** to the north are separated by a slender isthmus and magnificently set beneath the surrounding hills. This spot was popular with the nineteenth-century Scottish literati, especially Walter Scott and his friend James Hogg, the "Shepherd poet of Ettrick", who wrote:

> *Oft had he viewed, as morning rose*
> *the bosom of the lonely Lowes.*
> *Oft thrilled his heart at close of even*
> *to see the dappled vales of heaven*
> *with many a mountain, moor and tree*
> *asleep upon Saint Mary.*

The pair gathered to chew the fat at **Tibbie Shiels Inn** on the isthmus (☎01750/42231; ④), which takes its name from Isabella Shiel, a formidable and, by all accounts, amusing woman who ruled the place till her death in 1878 at the age of 96. Today, the inn is a famous watering hole on the Southern Upland Way and serves a limited range of bar meals. For a short and enjoyable walk, follow the footpath from the inn along the east side of St Mary's Loch into **Bowerhope forest**. Alternatively, the Southern Upland Way heads across the moors north to Traquair House and south to the valley of the Ettrick Water, both strenuous hikes that require an Ordnance Survey map, a compass and proper clothing (see "Outdoor pursuits" in Basics).

East of St Mary's Loch, the A708 is crossed by the B709 going north through the hills to Innerleithen or southeast to Hawick. The junction is marked by *The Gordon Arms Hotel* (☎01750/82232; ④), reputedly the last meeting place of Scott and Hogg, where framed fragments of letters from Scott are on display in an otherwise basic bar serving meals and real ale. From the hotel, which offers a transport service and a cheap bunkhouse dormitory for walkers, you can follow the course of the lovely Yarrow Water further east for about seventeen miles to Selkirk (see p.133).

Tweeddale

Just north of Moffat, the A701 ascends the west side of **Annandale** to skirt the impressive box canyon at its head. Best viewed from the road about six miles from town, the gorge – the **Devil's Beef Tub** – takes its name from the days when rustling Reivers hid their herds here. Walter Scott described the place aptly: "It looks as if four hills were laying their heads together to shut out daylight from the dark hollow place between them." The gorge was also a suitably secret hideaway for persecuted Covenanters during Charles II's "Killing Times".

Beyond the Tub, the road crosses over into **Tweeddale** and soon reaches tiny **Tweedsmuir**, where an alternative route turns right over the Tweedsmuir Hills to St Mary's Loch (see above). The eleven-mile single-track road, inaccessible in winter, climbs at a twenty percent gradient past Talla Reservoir, where many men lost their lives constructing a water supply for Edinburgh in 1905. Fishing permits for Talla and the neighbouring Megget Reservoir are available from *Tibbie Shiels Inn* at St Mary's Loch.

Back on the A701 a mile north of Tweedsmuir, you'll pass *The Crook Inn* (☎01899/880272; ⑤), one-time watering hole of Robbie Burns and a good base for climbing Broad Law, Southern Scotland's second highest hill. Behind the hotel, there's a small workshop and craft centre, where you can watch glass-blowing displays. Continuing north along the widening Tweeddale, you'll reach the village of **BROUGHTON**, where, inside the old Free Church, **The John Buchan Centre** (May to mid-Oct daily 2–5pm; £1) commemorates the novelist who spent his childhood holidays in the district.

The Lowther Hills

West of Moffat, sandwiched between the M74/A74 and Nithsdale, the **Lowther Hills** offer a wild landscape of tightly clustered peaks, bare until the heather blooms, hiding fast-flowing burns and narrow valleys – a dramatic terrain once known as "God's Treasure House" on account of its gold and silver ores. These mineral deposits were much sought after by the impoverished kings of Scotland, who banned their export and claimed a monopoly – draconian measures that only encouraged smuggling. There was lead here too, mined from Roman times right up to the 1950s, and used in the manufacture of pottery and glass.

Leadhills and Wanlockhead

Twenty-one miles north of Moffat, tiny **LEADHILLS** has a disconsolate air born of its wilderness surroundings. The terraced cottages of this classic "company town" were built by the mine owners for their employees, but the boom years ended in the 1830s, since when the village has been left pretty much to itself.

A couple of miles away, remote and windswept **WANLOCKHEAD**, at 1500ft the highest village in Scotland, is even smaller than its neighbour. It shares Leadhills' mining history, but Wanlockhead's attempts to lure the tourists have made the villages very different. The **Scottish Lead Mining Museum** (April–Oct daily 11am–4.30pm; £3.50) deserves a good hour or two, beginning with the spruce **visitor centre**, which traces the development of the industry and its workforce. Afterwards, highlights of the open-air site include a guided tour of the underground **Loch Nell Mine** and of a couple of restored miners' cottages. There's also a rare example of a wooden **beam engine** and all sorts of industrial bits and pieces, mostly dating from the late 1950s when government grants sponsored a brief revival in lead mining; the earlier workings were closed in the 1930s. Sometimes the eighteenth-century **library** is open too (early May to late Sept Wed, Sat & Sun 2–4pm), its books purchased from the voluntary subscriptions of its members: at its height, the library had a stock of 2000 volumes.

Wanlockhead straddles the Southern Upland Way, and is thus blessed with a **youth hostel** (☎01659/74252; April–Oct), sited in the old mine surgeon's house, while the museum's visitor centre can give details of a couple of cheap **B&Bs**.

Biggar and around

Five miles north of the Leadhills turning on the M/A74, Edinburgh traffic leaves the motorway to head northeast along the A702. Most people shoot straight through to the capital – it's only about forty miles – but, if you're looking to break your journey, the old market town of **BIGGAR** warrants an hour or two. Start your visit at the **Moat Park Heritage Centre** (April–Oct Mon–Sat 10am–5pm, Sun 2–5pm; £2.40), which occupies a grand neo-Romanesque church near the foot of Kirkstyle (off High Street). Inside, a well-presented exhibition traces the history of Upper Clydesdale, and on the upper floor you can see a display of extraordinary table covers made by local tailor Menzies Moffat (1828–1907). Don't miss the banquet-sized Royal Crimean Hero Tablecloth, which sets a cartoon strip of notable figures alongside scenes from Scottish country life. The heritage centre can also give details of **Hugh MacDiarmid's Cottage**, three miles from Biggar on the Edinburgh road, which can be visited by appointment only. Biggar has four other museums: the nearest, the **Gladstone Court Museum** (April–Oct Mon–Sat 10am–12.30pm & 2–5pm, Sun 2–5pm; £1.80), across Kirkstyle on North Back Road, boasts a shop-lined Victorian street illustrating different aspects of nineteenth-century life, from the telephone exchange and classroom to the bank and the cobblers. Returning to Kirkstyle, walk over the hill to the footpath beside Biggar burn. To the right is the **Greenhill Covenanters' Museum** (April to mid-Oct daily 2–5pm; £1.70), which attempts to explore the development of the Covenanting movement and the religious conflicts that ensued. To the left along the burn lies **Biggar Gasworks Museum** (June–Sept daily 2–5pm; £1). Before North Sea gas was piped across the UK, small coal-based gasworks like this one were common. Most were demolished in the 1970s, but Biggar's has survived and even manages to look quite spick-and-span. Lastly, on Broughton Road the unusual **Puppet Museum** (Easter–Sept Mon–Sat 10am–5pm, Sun 2–5pm; £1.50; phone ☎01899/220631 for details of shows), set up by the touring company Purves Puppets, features marionettes from around the world with regular workshops and shows held in the museum's Victorian theatre.

Back up High Street, the **sundial** outside the tourist office is the work of local poet-artist Ian Hamilton Finlay, a founder of the "concrete poetry" movement; you can see more of his work in Edinburgh's National Gallery of Modern Art (see p.87).

Practicalities

Regular **bus** services to Biggar arrive from a wide range of towns including Edinburgh, Peebles, Moffat and Dumfries. They stop on High Street, near the **tourist office** (Easter–Oct daily 10am–5pm; ☎01899/221066). There's a **B&B**, *Daleside,* 165 High St (☎01899/220097; ②), a stone's throw away, and **camping** is available at *Biggar Caravan Park* on Broughton Road (☎01899/220319). For **food**, both the *Elphinstone Hotel* and the *Crown*, on High Street, have good daily specials.

Around Biggar

Six miles west of Biggar along the A72/73, near the village of Thankerton, the solitary peak of **Tinto Hill** was the site of Druidic festivals in honour of the sun-god Baal, or Bel. It's relatively easy to walk the footpath up to the 2320ft-high summit, from where the views are splendid – you'll also see a Druidic Circle and a Bronze Age burial cairn. A regular **bus** links Biggar with Thankerton.

Just north of Biggar on the A702 lie the southern extremities of the **Pentland Hills**, the narrow belt of upland extending into the suburbs of Edinburgh. The hills are best visited from the capital, but the pretty medieval village of **WEST LINTON**, straddling the Lyne Water twelve miles from Biggar, gives ready access to several rambles across the neighbouring hills. If you want to **stay**, try the large Victorian country house of Mrs McCallum, on Carlops Road (☎01968/660795; ⑥; April–Oct), while the best **food** around is at *The Old Mill Inn* (☎01721/752220) in nearby Blyth Bridge. Its extensive menu specializes in local fare with excellent home-made puddings, and a free pick-up/drop-home service is available if you're based further afield (a minimum of six people; book in advance).

Nothing more than an unassuming row of whitewashed weavers' cottages, **CARLOPS**, three miles on from West Linton, gives access to some excellent walks along the farm tracks of rural hamlets hidden between the A702 and A701. The lesser-known poet, Alan Ramsey hailed from here and is honoured by the *Alan Ramsey Hotel* (☎01968/660258; ④), which serves standard bar fare and has an open fire.

SOUTHWEST SCOTLAND

Up until the eleventh century the whole of **Southwest Scotland** was known as Galloway, where independent chieftains maintained close contacts with the Vikings rather than the Scots. Gradually, this autonomy was whittled away and by the late thirteenth century the region, which comprises the rough triangle of land between the Solway Firth, the Firth of Clyde and the stretch from Dumfries to Kilmarnock, was integrated into Scotland. Indeed, it was here that both Robert the Bruce and William Wallace launched their wars against the English. Later on, from around the seventeenth century, the ports of the Solway coast prospered with the expansion of local shipping routes over to Ireland and, later still, the towns along the Firth of Clyde benefited from the industrialization of Glasgow. The region subsequently experienced economic decline as trade routes changed, turning busy ports into sleepy backwaters, and these days Southwest Scotland is agreeably laid-back, not crossed by motorway and – with most travellers skipping past on their way to the Highlands and islands – suffering little of the tourist crush familiar further north.

Robert Burns lived and died in this part of Scotland, a fact much exploited by the tourist offices. **The Burns Heritage Trail**, a motorist's route across much of the region, passes every conceivable place with which he had any connection, but frankly, unless you're particularly devoted, stick to the Burns sights in **Dumfries**, Ayr and Alloway. Extending southwest of Dumfries, the low-lying **Solway coast** boasts the delightfully tranquil township of **Kirkcudbright** and a handful of splendid medieval ruins, principally **Caerlaverock Castle** and **Sweetheart Abbey**. Criss-crossed by walking trails that cater for every level of athleticism and any amount of time, the **Galloway Hills** rise just to the north of the coast, their beautiful moors, mountains, lakes and rivers centred on the 150,000-acre **Galloway Forest Park**. After this come the rolling hills of the **Ayrshire Coast**, whose mostly agricultural landscapes are enlivened by a string of wide, flat sandy beaches and the occasional strip of coastal cliff. Here you'll also find the diverting town of **Ayr**, noteworthy for its Burns attractions and beach, and the district's other main resort, **Largs**, with its agreeable setting between hills and sea.

Travelling the region by **bus** presents few problems and there's a good **train** service from Glasgow along the Ayrshire coast to Stranraer. It's also easy to travel on from Southwest Scotland by **ferry**, from Stranraer to Belfast and Larne, in Northern Ireland, and from the port of Ardrossan, north of Ayr, to the Isle of Arran, where you can hop-scotch on up the Western Isles.

If you are keen to pursue a particular interest while visiting the area, Dumfries and Galloway Tourist Board has produced an excellent range of leaflets on local activities such as birdwatching, fishing and cycling, which are available from tourist offices.

Dumfries and around

With a population of 30,000, bustling **DUMFRIES** crowds the banks of the River Nith a few miles from the Solway Firth. Long known as the "Queen of the South", the town flourished as a medieval seaport and trading centre, its success attracting the attention of many English armies. The invaders managed to polish off most of the early settlement in 1448, 1536 and again in 1570, but Dumfries survived to prosper with its light industries supplying the agricultural hinterland. The town planners of the 1960s badly damaged the town, reducing it to an architectural hotchpotch, with – as the prime example – the graceful fifteenth-century lines of Devorgilla Bridge set against cereal-box apartment blocks. Nevertheless, the town makes a convenient base for exploring the Solway coast, and is at least worth a visit for its associations with Robert Burns, who spent the last five years of his life here.

The Town

Hemmed in by the river to the north and west, the snout-shaped centre of Dumfries radiates out from the pedestrianized **High Street**, which runs roughly parallel to the Nith. At its northern edge is the **Burns Statue**, a fanciful piece of Victorian frippery featuring the great man holding a poesy in one hand, whilst the other clutches at his heart. They haven't forgotten his faithful hound either, who lies curled around his feet.

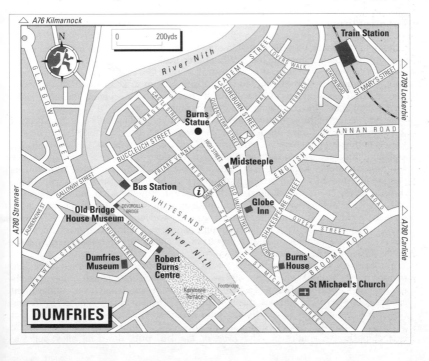

Heading south down High Street, it's a couple of minutes' walk to **Midsteeple**, the old prison-cum-courthouse, and the narrow alley that leads to the smoky, oak-panelled *Globe Inn*, one of Burns' favourite drinking spots, and still a tavern. Continuing down the street, follow the signs to the **Burns' House** (Easter–Sept Mon–Sat 10am–5pm, Sun 2–5pm; Oct–Easter Tues–Sat 10am–1pm & 2–5pm; free), a simple sandstone building where the poet died of rheumatic heart disease in 1796. Inside, there's an incidental collection of Burns memorabilia – manuscripts, letters and the like – and one of the bedroom windows bears his signature, scratched with his diamond ring.

Burns was buried in a simple grave beside **St Michael's Church**, a monstrous eighteenth-century heap just south of his house. Just twenty years later, though, he was dug up and moved across the graveyard to a purpose-built Neoclassical **Mausoleum**, whose bright white columns hide a statue of Burns being accosted by the Poetic Muse. The subject matter may be mawkish, but the execution is excellent – notice the hang of the bonnet and the twist of the trousers. All around, in contrasting brownstone, stand the tombstones of the town's bourgeoisie, including many of the poet's friends; a plan indicates exactly where each is interred.

From the mausoleum, saunter back along the Nith and cross Devorgilla Bridge to the tiny **Old Bridge House Museum** (April–Sept Mon–Sat 10am–1pm & 2–5pm, Sun 2–5pm; free) of local bric-a-brac – including a teeth-chattering range of Victorian dental gear – and the **Robert Burns Centre** (April–Sept Mon–Sat 10am–8pm, Sun 2–5pm; free), sited in an old water mill, which concentrates on the poet's years in Dumfries. On the hill above, occupying an eighteenth-century windmill, the **Dumfries Museum** (April–Sept Mon–Sat 10am–5pm, Sun 2–5pm; Oct–March Tues–Sat 10am–1pm & 2–5pm; free) traces the region's natural and human history and features a camera obscura on its top floor (April–Sept only; £1.20).

Practicalities

Dumfries train station, on the east side of town, is a five-minute walk from the centre. The **bus station** stands at the top of Whitesands beside the River Nith on the western edge of the centre. The **tourist office** (April, May & Oct daily 10am–5pm; June–Sept daily 9.30am–6pm; Nov–March Mon–Sat 10am–4.30pm & 2–5pm; ☎01387/253862), also on Whitesands on the corner with Bank Street, can book accommodation and give information about Burns attractions and town trails.

There are lots of **guest houses** and **B&Bs** in the handsome villas clustered round the train station, including *Morton Villa*, 28 Lovers Walk (☎01387/255825; ③), a large Victorian house with a pleasant garden, and *Lindean*, 50 Rae St (☎01387/251888; ③), a clean, comfortable red-sandstone house in a quiet street. For a more distinctive setting, try along Kenmure Terrace, a short block of attractive old houses overlooking the Nith from beside the footbridge below the Burns Centre. Of the three choices, *The Haven*, at no. 1 (☎01387/251281; ③), should be your first port of call. If you're looking for a **hotel**, head for Laurieknowe, a five- to ten-minute walk west from the bus station, where you'll find the welcoming, family-run *Edenbank Hotel* (☎01387/252759; ⑥), or splash out on *Comlongon Castle* at Clarencefield, seven miles south of Dumfries on the A75 (☎01387/870283; ⑨), an atmospheric manor house adjacent to the castle.

For **food**, try the child-friendly *Ben Veneto*, 42 Eastfield Rd, which serves Italian and seafood meals, or the *Station Hotel*, 49 Lovers Walk, specializing in fish and game dishes. The *Cairndale Hotel* offers a "Taste of Burns Country" menu and hosts Sunday night ceildhs (May–Oct). The cheapest meals in town are provided by the popular YMCA café *Grapevine*, behind the Burns Statue on Castle Street (Mon–Fri 10am–3pm, Sat 10am–2.30pm), while *Bruno*'s fish and chip shop on Balmoral Road claims to sell the best chips in the southwest. The *Hole in the Wa'* **pub**, down an alley opposite

Woolworth's on High Street, serves reasonable bar food, but for somewhere with more atmosphere, make your way to the earthy *Globe Inn*. Grierson and Graham, 10 Academy St (☎01387/259483), offer **bike rental**, useful for reaching the nearby Solway coast.

Around Dumfries: the east Solway coast and Nithsdale

The magnificent **Caerlaverock Castle** and the fine early Christian cross at **Ruthwell** are to be found on the shores of the Solway Firth southeast of Dumfries, from where a regular **bus** service runs to both. Alternatively, if you're heading north, the A76 travels the length of **Nithsdale** (there are also regular buses along this route), whose gentle slopes and old forests hide one major attraction: the massive, many-turreted seventeenth-century mansion of **Drumlanrig Castle**.

Caerlaverock Castle and Wildlife Centre

The remote and lichen-stained **Caerlaverock Castle**, eight miles from Dumfries (April–Sept Mon–Sat 9.30am–6.30pm, Sun 2–6.30pm; Oct–March Mon–Sat 9.30am–4.30pm, Sun 2–4.30pm; £2.30), is shaped like a dramatic triangle with a mighty gatehouse at the apex. Built around 1270, it clearly impressed medieval chroniclers. During the siege of 1300, Edward I's balladeer, Walter of Exeter, commented: "In shape it was like a shield, for it had but three sides round it, with a tower at each corner . . . and good ditches filled right up to the brim with water. And I think you will never see a more finely situated castle."

Nowadays, close inspection reveals several phases of construction, which reflect Caerlaverock's turbulent past: time and again, the castle was attacked and slighted, each subsequent rebuilding further modifying the late thirteenth-century original. For instance, the fifteenth-century machicolations of the gatehouse top earlier towers that are themselves studded with wide-mouthed gunports from around 1590. This confusion of styles continues inside, where the gracious Renaissance facade of the **Nithsdale Apartments** was added by the first earl in 1634. Nithsdale didn't get much value for money: just six years later he was forced to surrender his castle to the Covenanters, who proceeded to wreck the place. It was never inhabited again.

Three miles further on you'll find the **Caerlaverock Wildfowl and Wetlands Centre** (daily 10am–5pm; £3, with concessions for those arriving by public transport, bicycle or on foot), 1350 acres of protected salt marsh and mud flat edging the Solway Firth. A National Nature Reserve and a Wildfowl and Wetlands Trust Refuge, the centre is equipped with screened approaches that link the main observatory to a score of well-situated birdwatchers' hides. It's famous for the 12,000 or so barnacle geese which return here in winter. Between May and August, when the geese are away, walkers along a wetlands trail may glimpse the rare natterjack toad. Throughout the year at 2pm daily, the wild swans are fed and the wardens run free wildlife safaris. A varied **bird-watching and wildlife** programme is also on offer – ring ☎01387/770200 for up-to-date details. Both the castle and the centre are reached along the B725; this is the route the bus takes, mostly terminating at the castle but sometimes continuing to the start of the two-mile lane leading off the B725 to the centre.

The Ruthwell Cross

From the nature reserve it's about seven miles east along the B725 to both the village of **RUTHWELL** and the B724, the minor Dumfries–Annan road which trims its northern edge. Here you should turn down the short, signposted lane to the modest country church. The keys are kept at one of the houses at the foot of the lane; just look for the notice. Inside the church is the impressive **Ruthwell Cross**, an extraordinary early Christian monument dating from the late seventh century when Galloway was ruled by the Northumbrians. The 18ft-high cross reveals a striking diversity of influences, with Germanic and Roman Catholic decoration and, running round the edge, a poem written in both runic figures and Northumbrian dialect. But it's the biblical carvings on the main face that really catch the eye, notably Mary Magdalene washing the feet of Jesus.

If you want to **stay**, your best bet is the comfortable *Kirkland Country House Hotel* (☎01387/870284; ④) next to the church.

Nithsdale

North of Dumfries the A76 strips along the southern reaches of Nithsdale, a pastoral scene with the Forest of Ae and the Lowther Hills brooding in the distance. The road passes **Ellisland Farm** (April–Sept daily 10am–1pm & 2–5pm; Oct–March Tues–Sat 10am–1pm & 2–5pm; £1.50), built by Robert Burns and now housing a museum displaying many of his personal accoutrements. After fourteen miles you will reach the antiquated cottages of tiny **Thornhill**, where you can turn off onto the A702 to the conservation village of **MONAIVE**, which nestles between several glens and offers lovely walks and cycle rides. Stay at *Bainoon* B&B (☎01848/200440; ②) for huge cooked breakfasts, or the excellent *Craigdarroch Arms Hotel* (☎01848/200205; ④).

Back on the A76, three miles north of Thornhill lies **Drumlanrig Castle** (May–Aug daily except Thurs 11am–5pm; £4 or £2.50 for grounds only), not in fact a castle at all, but the grandiose stately home of the Duke of Buccleuch and Queensberry. The impressive driveway sweeps along an avenue of trees to confront the pink sandstone house with its cupolas, turrets and towers, surrounding an interior courtyard. The front is graced by a charming horseshoe-shaped stairway – a welcome touch of informality to the stateliness of the structure behind.

Inside, a string of luxurious rooms witness the immense wealth of the family. Among the priceless hoard of antique furnishings and fittings – which include a few mementoes dating from the overnight visit of Bonnie Prince Charlie in 1745 – are a trio of famous paintings exhibited in the **staircase hall**. These are Rembrandt's *Old Woman Reading*, a sensual composition dappling the shadow of the subject's hood against her white surplice, Holbein's formal portrait of *Sir Nicholas Carew*, and the *Madonna with the Yarnwinder* by Leonardo da Vinci. Other works are by Joost van Cleef, Breughel, Jan Grossaert (otherwise Mabuse) and Van Dyck, and there are endless family portraits by Allan Ramsay and Godfrey Kneller. Also look out for a striking 1950s portrait of the present duchess, all debutante coiffure and high-society shoulders, by John Merton and, in the serving room, John Ainslie's *Joseph Florence the Chef*, a sharply observed and dynamic portrait much liked by Walter Scott.

As well as the house, Drumlanrig offers a host of other attractions, including a forested **country park** criss-crossed by footpaths and cycle routes (**mountain bikes** are available for rent), an adventure playground, a cycle museum, craft workshops, a gift shop, a tearoom and a birds of prey collection with demonstrations at 1pm and 3pm daily (except Thursdays). If you're heading here by bus from Dumfries or Ayr, bear in mind it's a 1.5-mile walk from the road to the house.

Leaving Drumlanrig, the A76 slips through the wooded hills of Nithsdale, passing the turning to Wanlockhead (see p.146) en route to **SANQUHAR**, a trim market town which boasts the oldest working post office in Britain, dating from 1712 and now also home to the **tourist office** (Easter–May & Sept 10.30am–4.30pm; June–Aug 10am–5pm; ☎01659/50185). Pressing on, the mining village of **Kirkconnel** prefigures the industrial settlements further north, one of them being **Cumnock**, for many years the home of James Keir Hardie, whose bronze bust stands outside the Town Hall. At Cumnock, there's a choice of routes. The A76 ploughs on to Kilmarnock, whilst the A70 crosses the Ayrshire hills to reach the coast of Ayr.

The Solway coast to the Galloway Hills

The creeks, bays and peninsulas of the **Solway coast** string along the Solway Firth, a shallow estuary wedged between Scotland and England. Edged by tidal marsh and mud bank, much of the shoreline is flat and eerily remote, but there are also some fine rocky bays sheltering beneath wooded hills, most notably at **Rockcliffe**, about twenty miles west of Dumfries. **Kirkcudbright** and **Gatehouse of Fleet** were once bustling ports thronged with sailing ships, but they were bypassed by the Victorian train network and so slipped into economic decline which in effect preserved their handsome eighteenth- and early nineteenth-century town houses and workers' cottages. Both these towns are popular with – but not crowded by – tourists, as are **Sweetheart Abbey**, whose splendid Gothic remains are near Dumfries, and **Threave Castle**, a gaunt tower house perched on an islet just outside Castle Douglas.

Within comfortable striking distance of the coast are the **Galloway Hills**, whose forested knolls and grassy peaks flank lochs and tumbling burns – classic Southern Upland scenery, with scores of trails within **Galloway Forest Park**.

New Abbey

NEW ABBEY, a tidy hamlet eight miles south of Dumfries, is home to the red sandstone ruins of **Sweetheart Abbey** (April–Sept Mon–Sat 9.30am–6.30pm, Sun 2–6.30pm; Oct–March Mon–Sat 9.30am–4.30pm, Sun 2–4.30pm; £1). Founded by Cistercians in 1273, Sweetheart takes its name from the obsessive behaviour of its patron, Devorgilla de Balliol, who carried her husband's embalmed heart around with her for the last sixteen years of her life. The site is dominated by the remains of the Abbey Church, a massive structure that abandons the austere simplicity of earlier Cistercian foundations. The grand, high-pointed window arches of the nave, set beneath the elaborate clerestory, draw the eye to a mighty central tower with a battlemented parapet and flamboyant corbels. The opulent style reflects the monks' wealth, born of their skill in turning the wastes and swamps of Solway into productive farmland. Next door to the abbey, the **Abbey Cottage** tearooms serve great coffee and home-made cake, while the nearby *Criffel Inn* (☎01387/850305; ④) is a fine village pub with good beer. Alternatively, try the *Abbey Arms* (☎01387/850489; ④), opposite in the main square; both do food at lunch and dinner.

Just outside New Abbey on the Dumfries road, **Shambellie House** (April–Oct daily 11am–5pm; £2.50), set in beautiful gardens, houses a costume museum of dress and accessories from the late eighteenth century to the early twentieth century. One and a half miles south of New Abbey, Ardwell Mains Farm marks the start of the walk up **Criffel**, a 1871ft-high peak which offers great views of the Borders and the Lake District. A couple of miles further on at Kirkbean, a small turning on the left leads to **John Paul Jones Cottage** (April–June & Sept Tues–Sat 10am–1pm & 2–5pm, Sun 2–5pm; July & Aug Mon–Sat 10am–1pm & 2–5pm, Sun 2–5pm; £1.50), birthplace of the founder of the US navy, although interestingly he also fought for the Russians.

The Colvend coast: Rockcliffe and Kippford

South of New Abbey, the A710 cuts across a handsome landscape of rolling farmland following the **Colvend coast** past the aptly named **Sandyhills beach**, before heading inland to Dalbeattie. Along the road, you'll see turnings first to **ROCKCLIFFE**, a beguiling little place nestled around a beautiful cove, and then to **KIPPFORD**, a cosy yachting centre strung out along the Urr estuary. A pleasant thirty-minute coastal stroll, the Jubilee Path, links the two villages, passing the Celtic hill fort of the **Mote of Mark** en route. At low tide you can walk over the Rough Firth causeway from Kippford across the mud flats to **Rough Island**, a humpy twenty-acre bird sanctuary owned by the National Trust for Scotland, though it's out of bounds in May and June when the terns and oystercatchers are nesting.

Either of these villages would make a pleasant base for exploring the local countryside and beaches, or for tackling some of the excellent local walks: Rockcliffe has the bigger choice of accommodation, while Kippford is the more lively. In Rockcliffe, try the attractive *Albany* **B&B** (☎01556/630355; ③), right on the seafront, or the nearby *Millbrae House* (☎01556/630217; ③). The only **hotel** in the village is the grand *Barons Craig* (☎01556/630225; ⑨; April–Oct), a splendid Victorian mansion on the hill above the bay, but there are several cottages available for rent by the week – try *Westlin* (☎01556/630212; April–Oct; sleeps four; £120–215 per week), overlooking the bay, or the charming *Port Donnell* cottage rented out by the NTS (☎0131/243 9331; £240–390 per week). The best place to stay, and eat, in Kippford is the *Anchor Hotel* (☎01556 620205; ④), on the seafront, which serves excellent bar meals. There are a few lovely places to stay along the main A710 – both *Cairngill House* (☎01387/780681; ⑤) and *Craigbittern House* (☎01387/780247; ④) have stunning views of the coast at Sandyhills, and a couple of miles further on at Colvend is *Clonyard House* (☎01556/630372; ⑤), with wooded grounds and resident birds. There are various **campsites** in the area including the attractive *Kippford Caravan Park* (☎01556/620636), *Sandyhills Leisure Park* (☎01557/870267) on the beach at Sandyhills, and *Castle Point* (☎01556/630248) in Rockcliffe.

Beyond Kippford the A710 heads north to Dalbeattie, where you'll find the local **tourist office** (April, May & Sept Mon–Sat 10.30am–4.30pm; June–Aug daily 10am–5pm; ☎01556/610117) and a reasonable range of shops and supermarkets. From here, you can continue west along the attractive coastal road, the A711, to Kirkcudbright (see p.155), taking a brief signposted detour en route down a narrow country lane to see the evocative remains of **Orchardton Tower** (free), a mid-fifteenth-century fortified tower house, unusual in its circular design.

Around Castle Douglas

The eighteenth-century streets of **CASTLE DOUGLAS**, eleven miles north of Rockcliffe, were designed by the town's owner, William Douglas, a local lad who made a fortune trading in the West Indies. Douglas had ambitious plans to turn his town into a prosperous industrial and commercial centre, but, like his scheme to create an extensive Galloway canal system, it didn't quite work.

You'll only need to hang around town long enough to get your bearings as the district's two attractions are well outside the centre, but you might consider renting a **bike** here – at Ace Cycles, 11 Church St (Mon–Sat 9am–5pm; ☎01556/504542). The **tourist office** (April–June, Sept & Oct 10am–4.30pm; July & Aug 10am–6pm; ☎01556/502611) is at the end of the long main drag, King Street. Buses stop at the other end, on the lochside road to **Threave Garden** (daily 9.30am–sunset; £3.70), which can also be reached direct from the A75 – the signposted turning is at the roundabout on the west side of town. The garden features a magnificent spread of flowers and woodland, sixty acres subdivided into more than a dozen areas, from the bright, old-fashioned blooms of the Rose Garden to the brilliant banks of rhododendrons in the Woodland Garden and the ranks of primula, astilbe and gentian in the Peat Garden. In springtime thousands turn up for the flowering of more than two hundred types of daffodil and, from late May onwards, the herbaceous beds are the main attraction, with most of them arranged like islets in a sea of lawn (so that they can be viewed from all sides). The exception is the more formal beds of the Walled Garden (daily 9.30am–5pm), which adjoin the greenhouses and the nursery.

Threave Garden was developed by the National Trust for Scotland as a teaching arena for its School of Horticulture, whose students occupy Threave House, the hulking Victorian mansion that was the residence of the last laird. The **visitor centre** (April to late Oct daily 9.30am–5.30pm) has maps of and an exhibition about the garden and the surrounding estate (also NTS property), though the restaurant's (10am–5pm) fruit pies are more immediately satisfying.

To reach **Threave Castle** (April–Sept Mon–Sat 9am–6.30pm, Sun 2–6.30pm; £1.50), return to the A75 roundabout, where you will see signs to the Open Farm and Threave Wildfowl Refuge, and cut straight across, down the mile-long country lane which brings you to the start of the footpath to the River Dee. It's a lovely ten-minute walk down to the river, where you ring a brass bell for the boat over to the stern-looking stronghold, stuck on a flat and grassy islet. Built for a Black Douglas, Archibald the Grim, in around 1370, the fortress was among the first of its kind, a sturdy, rectangular structure completed shortly after the War of Independence when clan feuding spurred a frenzy of castle-building. The bleak lines of the original structure are, however, partly obscured by a rickety, fifteenth-century curtain wall, thrown up as a desperate – and unsuccessful – attempt to defend the castle against James II. Determined to crush the Black Douglases, the king personally murdered the eighth earl after dinner in Stirling and subsequently appropriated his estate. The Covenanters wrecked the place in the 1640s, but enough remains of the interior to make out its general plan, beginning with the storage areas and spitefully gloomy prison in the basement. Up above, the first – and entrance – floor was once reached from the outside by removable timber stairs, while inside a spiral staircase ascended to the upper floors – you can still make out its course. The roof was flat to accommodate stone-throwing machinery with projecting wooden galleries to enable the defenders to drop everything harmful onto the heads of the attackers – from the outside you can still discern the holes where the timber supports were lodged.

From Castle Douglas you can head north on the A713 which runs alongside **Loch Ken** to New Galloway (see p.159). The wooded banks of the loch are particularly stunning in autumn, and the area is a haven for the watersports fans, with waterskiing, powerboating, rowing, sailing, windsurfing, angling, birdwatching and more on offer. Contact Loch Ken Marina and Water Sports Club (☎01644/470220) for the action sports or Galloway Sailing Centre (☎01644/420626) for the non-powered variety; angling permits and boats are available from all the marinas and caravan parks. The village of Parton, halfway up the loch, is home to the **Scottish Alternative Games**, which takes place in early August and features the World Gird and Cleek Championships, amongst others.

There is a variety of **accommodation** available including the pleasant *Lochside* campsite on the Threave road (☎01556/502949), and several B&Bs in Castle Douglas itself: try the friendly and welcoming *Craignor House* (☎01556/1503315; ③), or *Balmaghie House* (☎01556/670234; ②), a huge mansion in its own grounds, with great home cooking. For considerably more luxury, head thirteen miles south of Castle Douglas to Auchencairn, where the award-winning *Balcary Bay Hotel* (☎01556/640217; ②) boasts a stunning location at the water's edge.

Kirkcudbright

KIRKCUDBRIGHT (pronounced "Kirkcoobrie"), hugging the muddy banks of the Dee ten miles southwest of Castle Douglas, has a quaint harbour and the most beguiling of town centres, a charming medley of simple brick cottages with medieval pends, Georgian villas and Victorian town houses, many attractively painted. This is the setting for **MacLellan's Castle** (April–Sept Mon–Sat 9.30am–6pm, Sun 2–6.30pm; Oct–March Sat 9.30am–4.30pm, Sun 2–4.30pm; £1), a sullen pink-flecked hulk towering above the harbourside. Part fortified tower house and part spacious mansion, the castle was built in the 1570s for Sir Thomas MacLellan of Bombie, when a degree of law and order permitted the aristocracy to relax its former defensive preoccupations and satisfy its increasing desire for comfort and domestic convenience. As a consequence, chimneys have replaced battle-ments at the wall-heads and windows begin at the ground floor. Nevertheless, the walls remain impressively thick, and there are a handful of wide-mouthed gun loops, though these are haphazard affairs designed to deter intruders rather than beat off an invading army. Inside, it's easy to pick out the vaulted basement – which accommodated the kitchen and storerooms – underpinning three upper storeys, home to a rabbit warren of well-appointed domestic apartments. Also, keep an eye out for a real curiosity, the laird's lug, or peephole, behind the fireplace of the Great Hall. Sir Thomas MacLellan is buried in the neighbouring **Greyfriars Church**, where his tomb is an eccentrically crude attempt at Neoclassicism – it even incorporates parts of someone else's gravestone.

Close by, on the L-shaped High Street, **Broughton House** (April to mid-Oct daily 1–5.45pm; £2.30) was once the home of Edward Hornel, an important member of the late nineteenth-century Scottish art establishment. Hornel and his buddies – The Glasgow Boys (see p.193) – established a self-regarding artists' colony in Kirkcudbright, and some of their work, impressionistic in style, is on display here. It's all pretty modest stuff, but Hornel's paintings of Japan, a country he often visited, are bright and cheery, and the house itself a delight. Hornel had the Georgian mansion he bought in 1901 modified to include a studio and a mahogany-panelled gallery decked out with a frieze of the Elgin marbles. He also designed the lovely **Japanese garden**.

A couple of minutes' walk away is the church-like **tollbooth**, which once served as court house, prison and town hall. Its clock faces are off-set so that they can be viewed down both parts of High Street. The building now houses the **Tolbooth Art Centre** (March, April & Oct–Feb Mon–Sat 11am–4pm; May & June Mon–Sat 11am–5pm & Sun 2–5pm; July & Aug Mon–Sat 10am–6pm, Sun 2–5pm; £1.50), featuring work by Hornel and his associates, whose history is detailed in an explanatory video. The studios on the upper floor are leased to artists and craftworkers, whom you can sometimes watch at work. The town's artistic connections are furthered by its several art galleries, including the picturesque **Harbour Cottage Gallery**, which hosts a variety of tempo-rary exhibitions (March–Nov 10.30am–12.30pm & 2–5pm; 50p).

Don't miss the **Stewartry Museum** on St Mary Street (same hours as the Tolbooth Arts Centre; £1.50), where, packed into a purpose-built Victorian building, hundreds of local exhibits illuminate the life and times of the Solway coast. It's an extraordinary col-lection, cabinets crammed with anything from glass bottles, weaving equipment, pipes, pictures and postcards to stuffed birds, pickled fish and the tricornered hats once worn by town officials. There are also examples of book jackets designed by Jessie King and EA Taylor, two of Hornel's coterie.

WALKS AROUND KIRKCUDBRIGHT

There are several easy and popular walks around Kirkcudbright including the seven-mile round-trip up the Dee to **Tongland Power Station** (May–Sept Mon–Sat guided tours 4 times daily; £1; bookings ☎01557/330114), whose turbines and generators are housed in a fine Art Deco building. Another option is the five-mile trek southeast along narrow country roads to **dundrennan**, an appealing little village hiding the greystone ruins of **Dundrennan Abbey** (April–Sept Mon–Sat 9.30am–6pm, Sun 2–6pm; £1). Enough remains of this twelfth-century foundation to be able to appreciate its architec-tural simplicity, in contrast to the more ornate style adopted by its daughter house, Sweetheart at New Abbey (see p.153). **Bus** service #501 connects Kirkcudbright and Dundrennan (Mon–Fri 4 daily, Sat 2 daily). Another eight-mile walk will take you along the coast through the **Stell** to **Nun Mill Bridge** looping back through the **Dhoon**. Further details of these and other local walks are available from the Kirkcudbright tourist office, and are contained in the leaflet, *Walks Around Kirkcudbright*.

Practicalities

Buses to Kirkcudbright stop by the harbour, next to the **tourist office** (April–June, Sept & Oct daily 10am–5pm; July & Aug daily 9.30am–6pm; ☎01557/330494), where you can get help finding accommodation, a service you will probably need in high season. The town has several quality **hotels** – the best among them being the *Gladstone House*, a renovated Georgian town house at 48 High St (☎01557/331734; ⑤), and the *Selkirk Arms*, an attractively refurbished eighteenth-century hotel just up the road (☎01557/330402; ⑦). For convenient **B&Bs**, try the bright, modern house run by Mrs Durok, 109a High St (☎01557/331279; ②); Mrs Callander at 110 High St (☎01557/330824; ④), who offers clean, basic accommodation; or Mrs Black at 1 Gordon Place, in a terrace of attactive whitewashed houses just off the High Street (☎01557/330472; ③). *Silvercraigs* caravan and **campsite** (☎01557/331079; Easter to late Oct) is on a bluff overlooking town at the end of St Mary's Place, five to ten minutes' walk from the centre. The town is also a popular spot for residential **painting courses**: contact Gracefield Arts Centre (☎01387/262084) or Kirkudbright Painting Holidays (☎01557/330274) for details.

Kirkcudbright is light on **restaurants**, but the cheap-and-cheerful *Belfry*, up along St Cuthbert Street from the tourist office, offers filling daytime snacks, while the *Selkirk Arms* serves excellent bar meals. The *Auld Alliance*, 5 Castle St (☎01557/330569), is a superior, if pricey, restaurant offering an imaginative mixture of French and Scottish cuisine. For a **drink**, the busy *Masonic Arms*, on Castle Street, pulls a reasonable pint.

Gatehouse of Fleet

The quiet streets of **GATEHOUSE OF FLEET**, easily reached by bus from Kirkcudbright ten miles to the east, give no clue that for James Murray, the eighteenth-century laird, this spot was to become the "Glasgow" of the Solway coast – a centre of the cotton industry whose profits had already made him immeasurably rich. Yorkshire mill owners provided the industrial expertise, imported engineers designed aqueducts to improve the water supply, and dispossessed crofters – and their children – yielded the labour. Between 1760 and 1790, Murray achieved much success, but his custom-built town failed to match its better-placed rivals. By 1850 the boom was over, the mills slipped into disrepair, and nowadays tiny Gatehouse is sustained by tourism and forestry.

It's the country setting that appeals rather than any particular sight, but there are some graceful Georgian houses along High Street, which also has an incongruous, granite clock tower and the **Mill on the Fleet Museum** (March–Nov daily 10am–5.30pm; £2.75), gallantly tracing the history of Gatehouse and Galloway from inside an old bobbin mill – check out its café with an attractive terrace overlooking the river. The nearby **tourist office** (daily: March, April & Oct 10am–4.30pm; May, June & Sept 10am–5pm; July & Aug 10am–6pm; ☎01557/814212) sells an excellent leaflet on local walks. One of them starts from the tourist office and heads along Old Military Road, passing through deciduous woodland before circling back to visit the stark remains of **Cardoness Castle** (April–Sept Mon–Sat 9.30am–6.30pm, Sun 2–6.30pm; Oct–March Sat 9.30am–4.30pm, Sun 2–4.30pm; £1.50), with its colourful and violent history. Perched on a hill, this late fifteenth-century stronghold is a classic example of the fortified tower house, with dense walls and tiny windows. It once edged the Water of Fleet river, but this was canalized long ago and today Cardoness overlooks the minor road linking Gatehouse with the A75, with stunning views of Fleet Bay in the distance. Another walk loops southeast from Gatehouse through the forests beside the Water of Fleet river on towards the Solway Firth. En route, you can't miss James Murray's country mansion, converted into the sumptuous *Cally Palace Hotel* (☎01557/814341; ⑧), though if you stay here make sure you are in the old house rather than the ugly modern extension. **Accommodation** in Gatehouse includes the *Murray Arms Hotel* (☎01557/814207; ⑧), a refurbished nineteenth-century mansion close to the clock tower; and some more affordable and convenient **B&Bs**, such as the *Bay Horse B&B*, 9 Ann St (☎01557/814073; ④). Farm accommodation is available in the surrounding countryside at *High Auchenlarie Farm* (☎01557/840231; ④), six miles west, off the A75, and *Holecroft Farm* (☎01557/840250; ③), half a mile or so further on. The *Murray Arms* serves delicious bar **meals** all day and has a very smart restaurant, as well as dispensing advice and permits for **fishing** locally.

Newton Stewart and Glen Trool

To the west of Gatehouse, the A75 skirts the mud flats of Wigtown Bay before cutting up to **NEWTON STEWART**, an unassuming market town beside the River Cree, famous for its **salmon and trout fishing**. The excellent **Creebridge House Hotel** (☎01671/402121; ⑤), in an old hunting lodge near the main bridge, arranges fishing permits for around £15 per day, can provide personal gillies (guides) for a further £25 daily, and at a pinch they'll even rent you all the tackle. The season runs from March to mid-October.

With its plentiful supply of accommodation (see below) and good bus connections along the A75, Newton Stewart has also become a popular base for **hikers** heading for the nearby **Galloway Hills**, most of which are enclosed within **Galloway Forest Park**. Many hikers aim for the park's **Glen Trool** by following the A714 north for about ten miles to Bargrennan, where a narrow lane twists the five miles over to the glen's **Loch Trool**. Halfway up the loch stands one of the area's two **Bruce's Stones**, this one marking the spot where Robert the Bruce ambushed an English force in 1307 after routing the main body of the army at Solway Moss. From here, there's a choice of magnificent hiking trails, including access to Merrick, at 2746ft the biggest hill in the southwest, as well as lesser tracks laid out by the Forestry Commission. Several longer routes curve round the grassy peaks and icy lochs of the Awful Hand and Dungeon ranges, whilst another includes part of the **Southern Upland Way**, which threads through the Minnigaff hills to Clatteringshaws Loch, beside the A712, the road that links Newton Stewart with New Galloway.

Practicalities

Newton Stewart is easily accessible by bus with services from Dumfries, Ayr and Stranraer, but reaching Loch Trool by **bus** is a bit of a pain: service #359 makes the twenty-minute trip from Newton Stewart to Glentrool village between three and six times daily, but you have to walk the final four miles. For the more adventurous **trails**, you'll need to be properly equipped; the Newton Stewart **tourist office** (April & Oct 10am–4.30pm; May, June & Sept 10am–5pm; July & Aug 10am–6pm; ☎01671/402431), just off the main street opposite the bus station, has bags of helpful literature. If you mean business, be sure to buy the relevant Ordnance Survey maps and *The Galloway Hills: A Walker's Paradise* by George Brittain (£2.50). In addition, the Forestry Commission produces leaflets on its various walks and other activities in the Forest Park: for further details, call ☎01671/402420.

The tourist office will provide a full list of local **accommodation** and book a bed on your behalf. In town, the cheapest choice is the convenient Minnigaff **youth hostel** (☎01671/402211; April–Sept) in an old schoolhouse 650yd from the main street, near the bridge. Alternatively – apart from the *Creebridge House Hotel* – you could try the **B&Bs** along Corvisel Road, a quiet residential street of Victorian brownstone houses near the tourist office – *Kilwarlin* at no. 4 (☎01671/403047; ③; April–Oct) is one of the best. On the southeast outskirts of town near the A75/A712 junction, there's the luxurious *Kirroughtree Hotel* (☎01671/402141; ⑨; mid–Feb to Dec), a splendid eighteenth-century mansion surrounded by beautiful gardens of azaleas and rhododendrons. Nearby are the well-appointed, two-bedroomed log chalets of the *Conifers Leisure Park* (☎01671/402107; £160–500 for four people depending on season; minimum stay three nights), with its own health centre. In Glen Trool village, the *House O'Hill Hotel* (☎01671/840243; ④) provides basic accommodation, beer, food and, occasionally, great music, while *Caldons Campsite* (☎01671/402420; April–Oct) is near the car park at the western tip of Loch Trool.

The best place **to eat** in Newton Stewart is the *Creebridge,* which has a wonderful but pricey restaurant as well as serving great pub food with its beers. A cheaper alternative is *Chatterbox* on the main street, which serves good snacks and cakes.

The Queen's Way: New Galloway and The Glenkens

The twenty-mile stretch from Newton Stewart to New Galloway, known as the **Queen's Way**, cuts through the southern periphery of **Galloway Forest Park**, a landscape of glassy lochs, wooded hills and bare, rounded peaks. You'll pass all sorts of **hiking trails**, some the gentlest of strolls, others long-distance treks. For a short walk, stop at the **Talnotry Campsite** (☎01671/402420; April–Oct), about seven miles from Newton Stewart, where the Forestry Commission has laid out three trails between two and four miles long: each delves into the pine forests beside the road, crossing gorges and burns. The campsite itself occupies an attractive spot among the wooded hills of the park; you can also buy fishing permits here. A few miles further on is **Clatteringshaws Loch**, a reservoir surrounded by pine forest, with a fourteen-mile footpath running right round. This runs past a second **Bruce's Stone**, a huge boulder where Robert the Bruce is supposed to have rested after victory over the English. The trail also connects with the Southern Upland Way as it meanders north towards the **Rhinns of Kells**, the bumpy hill range marking the park's eastern boundary.

From the loch, it's seven miles further to **NEW GALLOWAY**, nestling in the river valley at the northern tip of Loch Ken. Although little more than one long street lined by neat and attractive stone houses, it provides further easy access to the Southern Upland Way and the Rhinns of Kells, as does the neighbouring village of **DALRY** – which straddles the Southern Upland Way – a couple of miles upstream. New Galloway is in the valley of **The Glenkens**, which extends south to Castle Douglas via Loch Ken, and north along the river as far as Carsphairn, a desolate hamlet surrounded by wild moors. Midway between New Galloway and Carsphairn, you can visit the **Polmaddy Settlement**, a reconstructed Galloway village dating from before the Clearances. Continuing along the A713 through the attractive Doon Valley towards the coast at Ayr, you'll pass the old ironworks at **WATERSIDE,** which has been turned into a large, open-air **museum** portraying life for the workers of the iron industry a hundred years ago (April–Oct daily 10am–5pm; £2).

Practicalities

Connecting with services from Dumfries and Kirkcudbright, the fast and frequent Castle Douglas to Ayr **bus** stops in New Galloway. There's no official tourist office, but **The Smithy Teashop**, on High Street (daily: March, April & Sept 10am–8pm; May–Aug 10am–9pm; Oct 10am–6pm), provides all the essential information, rents out **bikes** and sells tasty oatcakes. The village has several **hotels** and **B&Bs** strung along the main drag: try the agreeable *Leamington Hotel* (☎01644/420327; ③; closed Nov), or *The Smithy* itself (☎01644/420269; ③; March–Oct). If you want to stay in Dalry, head for the attractive *Lochinvar Hotel* (☎01644/430210; ④). The nearest **youth hostel** is at Kendoon (☎01786/891400; mid-May to Sept), five miles north of Dalry along the B7000, near the

Southern Upland Way. It's about fifteen minutes' walk from the A713; if you're travelling there on the Castle Douglas–Ayr bus, ask the driver to tell you when to get off.

The Machars

The Machars, the name given to the peninsula of rolling farmland and open landscapes south of Newton Stewart, is a neglected part of the coastline, with a somewhat disconsolate air. Just six miles off the A75 is **WIGTOWN**, a modest country town whose spacious main street and square occupy a hill above Wigtown Bay. It's a five-minute walk from the square to the tidal flats below, where a simple stone obelisk commemorates two Covenanter martyrs, Margaret McLachlan and Margaret Wilson, who in 1685 were tied to stakes on the flats and drowned by the rising tide.

Whithorn

From Wigtown it's a further eleven miles south to **WHITHORN**, with a sloping, airy high street of pastel-painted cottages. This one-horse town occupies an important place in Scottish history, for it was here in 397 AD that **St Ninian** founded the first Christian church north of Hadrian's Wall. Ninian daubed his tiny building in white plaster and called it **Candida Casa**, translated as "Hwiterne" (White House), hence Whithorn, by his Pictish neighbours. Ninian's life is shrouded in mystery, but he does seem to have been raised in Galloway and was a key figure in the Christianization of his country. Indeed, his tomb became a popular place of pilgrimage and, in the twelfth century, a priory was built to service the shrine. For generations the rich and the royal made the trek here, but this ended with the Reformation – and the prohibition of pilgrimages in 1581.

Halfway down the main street, the **Whithorn Dig** (early April to Oct daily 10.30am–5pm; £2.70) exploits these ecclesiastical connections. A video gives background details and a handful of archeological finds serves as an introduction for a stroll round the dig. Be sure to take up the complimentary guide service – you won't make much sense of the complex sequence of ruins without one. Beyond the dig the meagre remains of the priory fail to inspire, unlike the adjacent **Whithorn Museum**, whose impressive assortment of early Christian memorials includes a series of standing crosses and headstones, the earliest being the Latinus Stone of 450 AD. For **lunch**, the *Diner*, near the Dig, offers basic meals.

The pilgrims who crossed the Solway to visit St Ninian's shrine landed at the **ISLE OF WHITHORN**, four miles south of Whithorn. Not an island at all, it's an antique and tiny seaport hiding the minuscule remains of the thirteenth-century **St Ninian's Chapel**. You can still follow in the pilgrims' footsteps by walking, cycling or riding the marked **Pilgrim Way** in a hundred-mile round-trip, starting from Glenluce and winding along paths and quiet roads to the Isle of Whithorn. For the less energetic, there's a pleasant twelve-mile round-walk between Whithorn and the Isle of Whithorn, which takes in St Ninian's Cave, the spot where the saint first put foot on Scottish soil. These and other shorter routes are detailed in a leaflet available from local tourist offices.

If you want to **stay** in the area, try the unassuming *Steam Packet Inn* (☎01988/500334; ④), right on the quay in Isle of Whithorn, or one of two farmhouses in Whithorn itself – *Baltier Farm* (☎01988/600241; ②) or *Clugston Farm* (☎01671/830338; ②). The owner of the *Queens Arms Hotel* (☎01988/500369; ④), in Isle of Whithorn, has a boat and takes people out on sea-angling trips.

Glenluce Abbey and Castle Kennedy Gardens

Heading west from Whithorn, the main road follows the wild and windy shore of Luce Bay on its way back to the A75 near the turning for **Glenluce Abbey** (April–Sept

Mon–Sat 9.30am–6.30pm, Sun 2–4.30pm; Oct–March Sat 9.30am–4.30pm, Sun 2–4.30pm; £1.50), whose ruins lie in a gentle valley a couple of miles north of the main road. There are no direct buses to the abbey, but the Glenluce to Newton Stewart bus will drop you off along the main road and you can walk from there. Founded in 1192, Glenluce prospered from the diligence of its Cistercian monks who drained the surrounding marshes, creating prime farmland. The brothers' fifteenth-century Chapter House has survived pretty much intact, and with its ribbed vault ceiling generates the clearest of acoustics – opera singers practise here. Notice, too, the green man motif carved into the corbels and bosses. Popularized in the twelfth century, these grotesques have human or cat-like faces, with large, glaring eyes, frowning foreheads and prominent teeth or fangs. All have greenery sprouting from their faces – a feature that originated with pagan leaf masks and the Celtic concept of fertility. The thirteenth-century wizard and alchemist **Michael Scot** lived here, supposedly luring the plague into a secret vault where he promptly imprisoned it. Scot, one-time magician to the court of the Emperor Frederick in Sicily, appears in Dante's *Inferno*.

Seven miles from Glenluce and three miles east of Stranraer, **Castle Kennedy Gardens** (April–Sept daily 10am–5pm; £2) flank the shattered, ivy-clad remains of a medieval fortress, situated on a narrow isthmus between two lochs. The gardens are noted for their monkey puzzle trees, magnolias and rhododendrons.

The Rhinns of Galloway

West of the Machars, the **Rhinns of Galloway** is a hilly, hammer-shaped peninsula at the end of the Solway coast, encompassing two contrasting towns, the grimy port of Stranraer, from where there are regular ferries over to Northern Ireland, and the beguiling resort of **Portpatrick**. Between the two, a string of tiny farming villages lead down to the **Mull of Galloway**, the windswept headland at the southwest tip of Scotland.

Stranraer

No one could say that **STRANRAER** was beautiful, though it has a nice feel to it and, if you're heading to (or coming from) Northern Ireland, you'll find everything's convenient. The **train station** is close to the Stena Sealink **ferry terminal** (☎0990/707070) on the Ross Pier, where boats depart for Larne; a couple of minutes' walk away, on Port Rodie, is the town's **bus station**; and nearby, further round the bay, Seacat **catamaran** services (☎0345/523523) leave from the West Pier to Belfast. Less handy, however, is the P&O ferry (☎0990/980777) to Larne, which leaves from the port of **CAIRNRYAN**, some five miles away.

Although a little dishevelled in parts, Stranraer has a pleasant walk from the recently renovated harbour area to a nearby beach. The main street, variously Charlotte, George and High streets, takes in the town's one specific attraction, a medieval tower which is all that remains of the **Castle of St John** (April–Sept Mon–Sat 10am–1pm & 2–5pm; £1). Inside, an exhibition traces the history of the castle down to its use as a police station and prison in the nineteenth century. Features of the castle include the old exercise yard on the roof and an interesting outdoor sculpture by Sibylle von Halem. If you've time to kill, pop into the **Stranraer Museum** in the Old Town Hall on George Street (Mon–Sat 10am–5pm; free) for a brief foray into the history of the area.

The **tourist office**, 28 Harbour St (April–June, Oct & Nov Mon–Sat 9.30am–5.30pm, Sun 10am–4pm; July–Sept daily 9.30am–6pm; Dec–March Mon–Sat 10am–4pm; ☎01776/702595) can arrange **accommodation**; alternatively, you could try the excellent family-run *Old Manse* on Lewis Street (☎01776/702135; ③), or *Fernlea*, on the same street (☎01776/703037; ③). For a real splurge, head to *Corsewall Lighthouse Hotel* at Kirkcolm on the peninsula eleven miles north of Stranraer (☎01776/853220; ⑦). You'll need your own transport to get to this converted lighthouse set in twenty acres of garden, though the owners will collect from the town, if you book in advance. For **camping**, *Aird Donald Camp & Caravan Park* (☎01776/702025) is ten minutes' walk east of the town centre along London Road.

Stranraer has plenty of basic **snack bars**, but it's well worth paying a little extra to enjoy a **meal** at the *Apéritif*, just up the hill from the bus station along Bellevilla Road. The *Ark House* on Church Street serves excellent (though fairly pricey) bar food, with the *Marine House Hotel* on the seafront being a cheaper alternative.

Portpatrick and south

Perched on the west shore of the Rhinns, the pastel houses of **PORTPATRICK** spread over the craggy coast above the slender harbour. Until the mid-nineteenth century, when sailing ships were replaced by steamboats, this was the main embarkation point for Northern Ireland, with coal, cotton and British troops heading in one direction, Ulster cattle and linen in the other. Nowadays, Portpatrick is a quiet, comely resort enjoyed for its rugged scenery and coastal hikes, including the twenty-minute stroll (take the steep steps near the garages beyond the lighthouse then follow the public footpath) along the sea cliffs to the shattered ruins of **Dunskey Castle**, an L-shaped tower house dating from the early sixteenth century. Portpatrick also has several intriguing and competitively priced craft-antique shops – check out the Old Lighthouse Pottery and the *Smugglers Cove*, around the harbour area – and offers excellent **sea fishing**; in summer daily trips cost £7 for three hours, £15 for seven. Walkers can tackle the first thirteen miles of the 212-mile coast-to-coast **Southern Upland Way**. It's a good day's walk past Castle Kennedy Gardens, and you can return by bus via Stranraer, but check times first.

Portpatrick has several good **hotels** and **guest houses**, the best of which is the *Portpatrick Hotel* (☎01776/810333; ⑧), a grand turreted Edwardian mansion on the hill above the harbour. Other options include the *Mount Stewart Hotel* (☎01776/810291; ③–④) with great food and good views of the harbour, the comfortable *Carlton Guest House*, beside the harbour on South Crescent (☎01776/810253; ③), and, close by, the bright, white *Knowe Guest House* (☎01776/810441; ④). There are three caravan and **campsites** in a row on the hill overlooking Portpatrick and Dunskey Castle. They are quite a distance from town, but it's a pleasant walk along the disused railway and clifftop trail – the *Galloway* (☎01776/810561) is the largest and has its own restaurant and shop, but all three have good facilities and nice views. The best place in Portpatrick for a **meal** and a **drink** is the *Crown* pub, on the seafront, or the *Auld Acquaintance* coffee shop nearby.

South to the Mull of Galloway

The remoter reaches of the Rhinns of Galloway, extending about twenty miles south from Portpatrick, consist of gorse-covered hills and pastureland crossed by narrow country lanes and dotted with farming hamlets. Of the two shorelines, the west has a sharper, rockier aspect and it's here, near the village of Port Logan, you'll find the uncrowded **Logan Botanic Garden** (mid-March to Oct daily 10am–6pm; £2), an outpost of Edinburgh's Royal Botanic Garden. There are three main areas: a peat garden, a woodland and a walled garden noted for its tree ferns and cabbage palms. The Gulf Stream keeps the Rhinns almost completely free of frost, allowing subtropical species to grow, including plants from South and Central America, southern Africa, Australasia and the Mediterranean.

It's a further twelve miles south to the **Mull of Galloway**, a bleak and precipitous headland where wheeling birds (guillemots, razorbills and kittiwakes) and whistling winds circle a bright whitewashed lighthouse. On clear days you can see over to Cumbria and Ireland.

The South Ayrshire coast

Fifty miles from top to bottom, the **South Ayrshire coast** between Stranraer and Ayr is easily seen from the windy A77 coastal road which leaves Stranraer to trim thirty miles of low, rocky shore before reaching **Girvan**, a low-key seaside resort where boats depart for **Ailsa Craig**, in the Firth of Clyde. Back on shore, the A77 presses on through the village of **Turnberry**, home to one of the world's most famous golf courses, where the A719 branches off for eighteenth-century **Culzean Castle** (pronounced "Cullane"). From the castle, it's twelve miles further to **Ayr**. Alternatively, if you keep to the main road, you'll pass by the medieval remains of **Crossraguel Abbey** on the way to the old market town of **Maybole**, just nine miles from Ayr. The whole area is steeped in links with its famous son, **Robert Burns**, and the association is exploited to the full. There's a reasonable **bus** service along the coast, a better one between Culzean and Ayr – plus a **train** line from Stranraer to Girvan, Maybole and Ayr.

Girvan and Ailsa Craig

Set beneath a ridge of grassy hills, **GIRVAN** is at its prettiest round the harbour, a narrow slit beside the mouth of the Girvan Water. Here, overlooked by old stone houses, the fishing fleet sets about its business, and, for a moment, it's possible to ignore the amusement arcades and seaside tat elsewhere in town. The long beaches around Girvan's otherwise rugged coastline are great for seaside strolls, though clambering down the cliff to the caves where the legendary Sawney Bean and his cannibal family lived is not recommended.

There are regular **bus** services from Stranraer and Ayr to Girvan, which is also on the Glasgow–Stranraer **train** line. The **tourist office**, on Bridge Street, just up from the harbour (Easter–May Mon–Fri 11am–1pm & 2–5pm, Sat & Sun 11am–5pm; June daily 11am–6pm; July & Aug daily 10am–7pm; Sept daily 11am–5pm; first two weeks of Oct daily noon–4pm; ☎01465/714950) has a full list of **accommodation**, or try one of the attractive Victorian villas along the seafront, such as the neat and tidy *Thistleneuk Guest House*, 19 Louisa Drive (☎01465/712137; ③), or *St Oswalds*, 5 Golf Course Rd (☎01465/713786; ③), with views out to Ailsa Craig. If you have money to burn and want to play the famous course which hosts the Open Golf Championship every few years, you can stay at the luxurious *Turnberry Hotel* (☎01655/331000; ⑨), five miles north of Girvan.

Ailsa Craig

From late May to September boats leave Girvan harbour for the ten-mile excursion west to the **Ailsa Craig**, "Fairy Rock" in Gaelic – though the island looks more like an enormous muffin than a place of enchantment. It would certainly have been less than enchanting for the persecuted Catholics who escaped to the island during the Reformation. With its jagged cliffs and 1114ft-high summit, Ailsa Craig is now a privately owned bird sanctuary that's home to thousands of gannets. The best time to make the trip is at the end of May and in June when the fledglings are trying to fly. Several companies cruise round the island, including the Rachel Clare (☎01294/833724), but only Mark McCrindle, who also organizes sea-angling trips, is licensed to land (once- or twice-daily sailings cost £10 per person for six hours, £9 for four; bookings required on ☎01465/713219). It takes about an hour to reach the island, so you've enough time to walk up to the summit of the rock and watch the birds – weather permitting.

Culzean Castle

The impressive **Culzean Castle** and its surrounding **country park** (both April–Oct daily 10.30am–5.30pm; Nov–March park open 9am–sunset; £6 for both, £3 for park only) is Ayrshire's premier tourist attraction. The best place to start is at the **visitor centre** in the modernized Home Farm buildings. Here, you can pick up free maps – as well as wildlife leaflets – that help you get your bearings, the layout of the place being rather confusing, or you can take a guided tour (castle daily 3.30pm; also July & Aug 11am: grounds April–June 2.30pm; July–Sept daily 11am & 2.30pm). From the visitor centre it's a few minutes' walk over to the **Castle**, whose towers and turrets rise high above the sea cliffs. Nothing remains of the original fifteenth-century structure, since, in 1777, David Kennedy, the tenth Earl of Cassillis, commissioned **Robert Adam**, the highly successful Scottish architect, to remodel the family home.

The work took fifteen years to complete, and, although the exterior, with its arrow slits and battlements, preserves a medieval aspect, the interior exemplifies the harmonious Classical designs Adam loved. On the ground floor, the subtle greens of the old eating room are enlivened by vine-leaf-and-grape plasterwork along the cornice, a motif continued in the adjacent dining room. Nearby, there's the brilliantly conceived oval staircase, where tiers of Corinthian and Ionic columns lead up to a huge cupola allowing light to stream down. All this is a fitting prologue to the impressive circular saloon, whose symmetrical flourishes deliberately contrast with the natural land and seascapes on view through the windows. Further on, a small exhibition celebrates President Eisenhower's military and civilian career as well as his association with Culzean; Ike stayed here on several occasions and the castle's top floor was given to him by the old owners, the Kennedys, for his lifetime. Nowadays, the top floor accommodates six double bedrooms done out in a comfortably genteel style. Guests eat together in the shared dining room and the chef comes in to do breakfast as well. Although hard to imagine a more distinctive setting, it's at a price: the smallest rooms cost £150 for bed and breakfast per night, the biggest £300 (reservations on ☎01655/760274).

Leave time for an exploration of the **country park**, whose 565 acres spread out along the seashore. A web of wooded trails lead you through the park, taking in cliffs, a beach, a walled garden, where the blooms are at their best in July and August, and the occasional reminder of earlier days – the laird's boat house and gun battery, the old ice and powder houses. Guided tours, craft shows, country dancing and a "fascinating fungi" walk are laid on throughout the year – details from the visitor centre and nearby tourist offices.

Crossraguel Abbey

Leaving Turnberry on the A77, it's a couple of miles to the hamlet of **KIRKOSWALD** and **Souter Johnnie's Cottage** (Easter–Sept daily 11.30am–5pm; Oct Sat & Sun 11.30am–5pm; £1.80), the simple thatched house that was once the home of John Davidson, the boon companion of Robert Burns and original Souter (cobbler) Johnnie of the poet's *Tam o' Shanter*. To the rear of the house, the restored alehouse has life-sized stone figures of Johnnie, Tam himself (called after his boat, Shanter being his farm) and other Burnsian characters, all of whom are buried in the nearby graveyard.

The substantial remains of **Crossraguel Abbey** (April–Sept Mon–Sat 9.30am–6.30pm; Sun 2–6.30pm; £1.50), a further three miles along the main road, are mostly overlooked – something of a surprise considering their singularity. Founded as a Cluniac monastery in the thirteenth century, Crossraguel benefited from royal patronage with its abbots holding land "for ever in free regality". The abbots took the temporal side of their work seriously and became powerful local lords. By the early sixteenth century, they had constructed an extensive private compound complete with a massive gatehouse and sturdy tower house. Both still stand – behind what remains of the abbey church – recalling the corruption of the monastic ideal that prodded the Reformation. Behind the gatehouse, you'll also spot the well-preserved dovecote, a funnel-shaped affair that was a crucial part of the abbey's economy; the monks not only ate the doves but also relied on them for eggs.

Ayr and around

With a population of around 50,000, **AYR**, the largest town on the Firth of Clyde coast, was an important seaport and trading centre for many centuries, and rivalled Glasgow in size and significance right up until the late seventeenth century. In recognition, Cromwell made it a centre of his administration and built an enormous fortress here, long since destroyed. With the relative decline of its seaborne trade, Ayr developed as a market town, praised by Robert Burns, who was born in the neighbouring village of **Alloway** (see p.168), for its "honest men and bonny lasses". In the nineteenth century, Ayr became a popular resort for middle-class Victorians, with a new town of wide streets and boulevards built behind the beach immediately southwest of the old town. Nowadays, Ayr is both Ayrshire's commercial centre and a holiday resort, its long sandy beach (and prestigious racecourse) attracting hundreds of Scotland's city dwellers.

The Town

The cramped, sometimes seedy streets and alleys of Ayr's **old town** occupy a wedge of land between Sandgate to Alloway Place in the west, and the south bank of the treacly

River Ayr to the east. Almost all the medieval buildings were knocked down by the Victorians, but the **Auld Brig**, with its cobbles and sturdy breakwaters, has survived from the thirteenth century. The bridge was saved by Robert Burns or, rather, by his poem *Twa Brigs*, which made it too famous to demolish; an international appeal raised the capital necessary for its refurbishment in 1907.

The bridge connects with High Street, where you should turn left and subsequently left again down Kirk Port, a narrow lane leading to the **Auld Kirk** (July & Aug Tues & Thurs only; phone ☎01292/262580 for further details), the church funded by Cromwell as recompense for the one he incorporated into his stronghold. At the lych gate, a plan of the graveyard shows where some of Burns' friends are buried. Notice also the mort-safe (heavy grating) on the wall of the lych gate. Placed over newly dug graves, these mort-safes were a sort of early nineteenth-century corpse security system meant to deter body snatchers at a time when dead bodies were swiftly bought up by medical schools with no questions asked. The church's dark and gloomy interior retains the original pulpit. Retracing your steps along High Street, take the first left down pedestrianized Newmarket Street, leading onto Sandgate, with the elegant spire of the **Town Buildings**, down towards the New Bridge.

Extending southwest of Sandgate to the Esplanade and the **beach**, the wide, gridiron streets of the Victorian **new town** contrast with the crowded lanes of old Ayr. It was the opening of the Glasgow to Ayr train line in 1840 that brought the first major influx of holiday-makers and Ayr remains a busy resort today, with many visitors heading for the plethora of trim guest houses concentrated around **Wellington Square**, whose terraces flank the impressive County Buildings dating from 1820. The new town extends north towards the river, with its comfortable villas spreading over what remains of the walls of Cromwell's fort. It's here, off Bruce Crescent, that you'll find St John's Tower, all that's left of the church Cromwell used as his armoury. The northern perimeter of the fortress once overlooked the harbour, which is now the place to go for either a summer **sea-angling trip** (details from the Sea Angling Centre, ☎01292/285297), or a **cruise** on the *Waverley*, the last seagoing paddle steamer in the world (July 8–Aug 27 Tues & Wed only 10am; ☎0141/221 8152). In addition, you can go on various excursions round the islands off the west coast, including those around Ailsa Craig (see p.163); the tourist office has details.

Practicalities

Ayr **bus station** is at the foot of Sandgate, a ten-minute walk west of both the **train station** and the **tourist office**, on Burns Statue Square (June & Sept to early Oct Mon–Sat 9.15am–6pm, Sun 10am–6pm; July & Aug Mon–Sat 9.15am–7pm, Sun 10am–7pm; Oct –May Mon–Sat 9.15am–5pm; ☎01292/288688). They can help with accommodation, a particularly useful service at the height of the season and during important race meetings.

At other times, head straight for the cluster of **hotels** and **guest houses** around Wellington Square, a couple of minutes' walk south of Sandgate along Alloway Place. In particular, try Queen's Terrace where, among others, there's the *Dargil Guest House*, no. 7 (☎01292/261955; ③), *Queens*, no. 10 (☎01292/265618; ④), and the *Daviot*, no. 12 (☎01292/269678; ④). There's another cluster of B&Bs among the attractive Victorian villas of Eglinton Terrace, a short walk north of Wellington Square. These include the *Grasmere Guest House*, no. 2 (☎01292/611033; ③; March–Oct) and the *Thornton*, no. 9 (☎01292/262948; ③). Cheaper accommodation is available at *Stamore*, 41 St Leonards Rd (☎01292/262597; ②), or at Ayr **youth hostel**, 5 Craigweil Rd (☎01292/262322; March–Oct), which occupies a grand neo-Gothic mansion behind the beach, a twenty-minute walk south of the town centre along Alloway Place (turn right down Blackburn Road – it's signposted). The *Heads of Ayr Leisure Park* (☎01292/442269; March–Nov), five miles south of town along the coastal A719, accepts **caravans** and **tents**, as does *Culzean Bay Holiday Park* (☎01292/500444; March–Oct), eight miles south of Ayr. If you prefer to stay out of town, try *Bona Lea Cottage* (☎01292/500233; ③), five miles south in the tiny village of **Dunure**, which consists of a couple of rows of cottages, a pub with decent food, an old harbour and the dramatic ruins of Dunure Castle.

The best **restaurant** in Ayr is *Fouters*, 2a Academy St, in a cellar off Sandgate (☎01292/261391); steaks and seafood are its specialities. Another good choice, which uses local produce, is the *Boathouse*, 4 South Harbour St, beside the river at the foot of Fort Street. For filling and more reasonably priced meals, try *Littlejohn's*,

ROBERT BURNS

The first of seven children, **Robert Burns**, the national poet of Scotland, was born in Alloway on January 25, 1759. His father, William, was employed as a gardener until 1766 when he became a tenant farmer at Mount Oliphant, near Alloway, moving to Lochlie farm, Tarbolton, eleven years later. A series of bad harvests and the demands of the landlord's estate manager bankrupted the family, and William died almost penniless in 1784. These events had a profound effect on Robert, leaving him with an antipathy towards political authority and a hatred of the landowning classes.

With the death of his father, Robert became head of the family and they moved again, this time to a farm at Mossgiel, near Mauchline. Burns had already begun writing poetry and prose at Lochlie, recording incidental thoughts in his *First Commonplace Book*, but it was here at Mossgiel that he began to write in earnest, and his first volume, *Poems Chiefly in the Scottish Dialect*, was published in Kilmarnock in 1786. The book proved immensely popular, celebrated by ordinary Scots and Edinburgh literati alike, with the satirical trilogy *Holy Willie's Prayer*, *The Holy Fair* and *Address to the Devil* attracting particular attention. The object of Burns' poetic scorn was the kirk, whose ministers had obliged him to appear in church to be publicly condemned for fornication – a commonplace punishment in those days.

Burns spent the winter of 1786–87 in the capital, lionized by the literary establishment. Despite his success, however, he felt trapped, unable to make enough money from writing to leave farming. He was also in a political snare, fraternizing with the elite, but with radical views and pseudo-Jacobite nationalism that constantly landed him in trouble. His frequent recourse was to play the part of the unlettered ploughman-poet, the noble savage who might be excused his impetuous outbursts and hectic womanizing.

Burns had, however, made useful contacts in Edinburgh and as a consequence was recruited to collect, write and rearrange two volumes of songs set to traditional Scottish tunes. These volumes, James Johnson's *Scots Musical Museum* and George Thomson's *Select Scottish Airs*, contain the bulk of his songwriting, and it's on them that Burns' international reputation rests with works like *Auld Lang Syne*, *Scots, Wha Hae*, *Coming Through the Rye* and *Green Grow the Rushes, O*. At this time, too, though poetry now took second place, he produced two excellent poems; *Tam o' Shanter* and a republican tract, *A Man's a Man for a' That*.

In 1788, Burns married Jean Armour and moved to Ellisland Farm, near Dumfries. The following year, he was appointed excise officer and could at last leave farming, moving to Dumfries in 1791. Burns' years of comfort were short-lived, however. His years of labour on the farm, allied to a rheumatic fever, damaged his heart, and he died in Dumfries on July 21, 1796, aged 37.

Burns' work, inspired by a romantic nationalism and tinged with a wry wit, has made him a potent symbol of "Scottishness". Ignoring the Anglophile preferences of the Edinburgh elite, he wrote in Scots vernacular about the country he loved, an exuberant celebration that filled a need in a nation culturally colonized by England. Today Burns Clubs all over the world mark every anniversary of the poet's birthday with the Burns' Supper, complete with Scottish totems – haggis, piper and whisky bottle.

231 High St, *Pierre Victoire*, 4 River Terrace, or the *Stables Restaurant*, at 41 Sandgate. If you fancy Italian food, head to *Bonfantis* at 64 Sandgate, or the *Royal Cafe* , 11 New Rd, for seriously good ice cream. The *Tudor Restaurant*, 8 Beresford Terrace, is famed for home baking and its Scottish "high teas" (5–6pm). The most enjoyable **pub** in town is the thatched *Tam o' Shanter*, on High Street, whose ancient walls sport quotes from Robert Burns. There are also several lively bars on and around Burns Statue Square, including *O'Briens*, which frequently showcases Irish folk bands.

Public transport to and from Ayr is easy, with plenty of buses and trains from Glasgow, Stranraer and Dumfries, as well as good local bus services. An open-topped bus "The Burns Country Tour" leaves Ayr bus station (mid-June to mid-Sept hourly 10am–5pm; £3) for the round-trip to Alloway and the coast, stopping at Burns attractions en route: you can get on and off as often as you like.

Alloway

There's little else but Burnsiana in **ALLOWAY**, formerly a small village but now part of Ayr's spreading suburbs, and a key stop on the **Burns Heritage Trail** (see p.147). The first port of call in Alloway is the whitewashed **Burns Cottage and Museum** (April–Oct daily 9am–6pm; Nov–March Mon–Sat 10am–4pm, Sun noon–4pm; £2.50) for a peep at the poet's birthplace, a dark and dank, long thatched cottage where animals and people lived under the same roof. The two-room museum boasts all sorts of memorabilia – the family Bible, letters and manuscripts – plus a potted history of his life, illuminated by contemporaneous quotes.

The modern, faceless building housing the **Tam o' Shanter Experience** (April–Oct daily 9am–6pm; Nov–March Mon–Sat 10am–4pm, Sun noon–4pm; £2.50 for each video), a few minutes further down the road, belies a marginally more interesting interior. Two videos recount the life of Burns, and you can watch a dramatic enactment of the poem *Tam o' Shanter* in a three-screen cinema. There is a large souvenir shop selling the works of Burns amid every other conceivable thing you could produce on the poet.

Across the road from here are the plain, roofless ruins of **Alloway Church**, where Robert's father William is buried. Burns set much of *Tam o' Shanter* here. Tam, having got drunk in Ayr, passes "By Alloway's auld haunted kirk" and stumbles across a witches' dance, from which he's forced to flee for his life over the **Brig o' Doon**, a humpbacked bridge. The dance was a riotous affair:

> *But hornpipes, jigs, strathspeys and reels,*
> *Put life and mettle in their heels.*
> *A winnock-bunker in the east* [*window recess*],
> *There sat auld Nick, in shape o' beast;*
> *A towzie tyke, black, grim and large* [*shaggy dog*],
> *To gie them music was his charge:*
> *He screw'd the pipes and gart them skirl* [*made; scream*],
> *Till roof and rafters a' did dirl* [*vibrate*].

Across the street from the church, the thirteenth-century bridge still stands, curving gracefully over the river below the **Burns Monument** (April–Oct only, same hours and ticket as Cottage), a striking Neoclassical temple in a small carefully manicured garden and housing yet another museum. True Burns junkies might want to stay here at the *Burns Monument Hotel* on the banks of the River Doon (☎01292/442466; ⑤), where you can eat in the poet's restaurant and sleep with his verse above your bed.

The North Ayrshire coast

The **North Ayrshire coast** extends some thirty miles or so from Ayr up to **Largs**, easily the area's most agreeable resort. The busy coastal road (the A78) cuts across this disparate shoreline, where rolling farmland is interrupted by the pockmarks of industrialization. Leaving Ayr, the road trims the outskirts of Prestwick, the site of an international airport, before bypassing **Troon**, an uninspiring resort with a seaside golf course.

IRVINE, the next settlement along, was once the principal port for Glasgow, its halcyon days recalled by the enjoyable **Scottish Maritime Museum** (April–Oct daily 10am–5pm; £2) down at the old harbour, a mile or so southwest of the town centre. The assortment of craft, which you can board, is moored to the museum docks and includes a dredger, a fishing skiff, a lifeboat, a tug and a "puffer" boat, the last used as an inshore supply vessel along the Clyde and between the islands. The history of the puffers forms part of the museum's well-presented display on Clydeside shipping. Close by, there's the Magnum Leisure Centre (daily 9am–10pm), with a swimming pool, cinemas and other leisure facilities and – at the mouth of the river – a sandy beach. Back on the west edge of the town centre, Irvine's **tourist office** (July & Aug Mon–Sat 9am–6pm, Sun noon–5pm; Sept–June Mon–Sat 9am–5pm, Sun noon–5pm; ☎01294/313886) adjoins the train and bus stations as well as the giant shopping centre which leads to High Street. Here a couple of narrow side alleys hint at the town's antiquity, amid the prevailing architectural gloom. One, **Seagate**, boasts ancient cottages and the sturdy remains of Irvine's castle; the other – **Glasgow Vennel** – features the house, no. 10, where Burns learnt to dress flax (he didn't enjoy it much), and his lodgings at no. 4. You're unlikely to want to stay in Irvine, but if you do, Kilwinning Road is the best place to head for – try *Conifers Guest House,* at no. 40 (☎01294/278070; ③), or *Laurelbank,* at no. 3 (☎01294/277153; ③).

Inland from Irvine on the A759, you can visit **Dundonald Castle** (April–Sept 1–4pm; £1.50), which dates from the 1370s although there's evidence that other structures existed on the site previously. Five miles further east, **KILMARNOCK,** a shabby manufacturing town, is known principally for being the home of **Johnnie Walker** whisky.

North from Irvine, it's just eight miles to **ARDROSSAN**, where Caledonian MacBrayne ferries (☎0990/650000) leave for Brodick on the Isle of Arran (see p.317), and another twelve miles to Largs, from where you can catch a ferry across to the nearby island of **Great Cumbrae**, a low-key but popular holiday spot.

Largs and Great Cumbrae

Tucked in between the hills and the sea, **LARGS** remains a traditional family resort, its guest houses and B&Bs spreading out behind an elongated seaside promenade. There's a tiny pier, too, set beside an unpretentious town centre that conceals one real surprise: **Skelmorlie Aisle** (June–Aug Mon–Fri 2–5pm; keys from the museum next door; free), a Renaissance gem hidden away beside the old graveyard off Main Street. Once the north transept of a larger church, the aisle was converted into a mausoleum for Sir Robert Montgomerie, a local bigwig, in 1636. Carved by Scottish masons following Italian patterns, the tomb is decorated with Montgomerie's coat of arms as well as symbols of mortality such as the skull, winged hourglass and inverted torch. Up above, the intricate paintwork of the barrel-vaulted ceiling includes the signs of the zodiac, biblical figures and texts, and – in tiny detail on the painted corbels – the legendary coats of arms of the tribes of Israel.

Back outside on the promenade, it's about a mile south along the shoreline footpath to the **Pencil Monument**, a modern obelisk commemorating the Battle of Largs of 1263. The battle was actually an accident, forced on King Hakon's Vikings when their longships were blown ashore by a gale. The invaders were attacked by the Scots as they struggled through the surf, and, although both sides claimed victory, the Norwegians retreated north, and abandoned their territorial claims to the Western Isles three years later. The Viking connection is exploited in the **Vikingar** exposition (daily: April–Sept 10.30am–6pm; Oct–March 10.30am–4pm; £3.50), a five-minute walk north of the pier, which traces the history of the Vikings in Scotland with dramatic mood music, dioramas and videos.

Alternatively you can venture out on the Firth of Clyde, with Clyde Marine **cruises** of Greenock (Mon–Fri; ☎01475/721281), or on the old paddle steamer, the *Waverley*, which visits Largs on its Tuesday trips during the summer (☎0141/221 8152). *Caledonian MacBrayne* (daily except Sat; ☎01475/674134) also operates from here to the islands just off the west coast – principally Bute and Cumbrae; Largs tourist office has all the details.

Largs practicalities

There are excellent connections to Ayr and Glasgow from Largs' **bus** and adjacent **train station**, on Main Street, a short stroll from the pier where **ferries** leave for Great Cumbrae. Beside the pier the **tourist office** (Easter–June Mon–Sat 9.15am–5pm, Sun 10am–5pm; July & Aug closes 6pm; Sept–Oct Mon–Sat 9.15am–5pm, Sun 11am–4pm; Oct to Easter Mon–Fri 9.15am–5pm, Sat 9.15am–1pm & 2–5pm; ☎01475/673765) has heaps of free literature and will help with accommodation. Being a holiday town, Largs has no shortage of **guest houses** and **B&Bs**. There is a cluster along Aubery Crescent, a short side street overlooking the coast a few minutes' walk north of the pier. Choose from the *Old Rectory B&B*, at no. 2 (☎01475/674405; ③), or the *Ardmore Guest House*, at no. 16 (☎01475/672516; ③; April–Oct;), both with excellent views over to Cumbrae and Arran. The cheapest joint in town is *Largs Tourist Hostel*, 110 Irvine Rd (☎01475/672851; ①), with doubles, family rooms and dorms available, whilst, at the other end of the scale, about three miles north of the centre on the A78, you can stay in the *Manor House Hotel* (☎01475/520832; ⑧), a grand Victorian pile set in its own grounds and looking out over the seashore. Churchill and Eisenhower met here to plan D-day landings – the decor is a little historic, too. *South Whittlieburn Farm Campsite* (☎01475/675881; March–Oct) lies about three miles northeast of town on a working farm, and *Skelmorlie Mains Campsite* is about four miles north on the A78 (☎01475/520794).

For **food**, the *Green Shutter Tearoom*, along the seafront just south of the pier, serves excellent meals, while the *Bagel Basket*, on Main Street, is cheap and simple. Largs' residents claim that no visit to the town is complete without trying one of the amazing ice creams from *Nardini's* on the Promenade, just north of the pier, which sports unadulterated 1950s decor and has a lively buzz.

Great Cumbrae Island

Immediately offshore from Largs lies **Great Cumbrae**, a plump, hilly island roughly four miles long and half as wide. The only settlement of any size is **MILLPORT**, which curves around an attractive hilly bay on the south coast. The town possesses Britain's smallest cathedral, the **Cathedral of The Isles** (daily 11am–4pm except during services), which was completed in 1851 to a design by William Butterfield, an enthusiastic member of the High Church Oxford Movement and one of the leading Gothic revival architects of the day. A mile or so away, along the south shore to the east, is the **Marine Life Museum** (Mon–Fri 9.30am–12.15pm & 2–4.45pm; June–Sept also Sat) of the universities of Glasgow and London. The aquarium is excellent, but you're more likely to remember the view of the nuclear power station and iron-ore terminal back on the mainland. Get away from this depressing sight by heading inland either on foot or by bike to enjoy the peaceful countryside, or head round the coast away from the mainland for some good beaches. **Bike rental** is available in Millport from Mapes on Guildford Street (☎01475/530444).

It takes fifteen minutes to cross by ferry from Largs to the island's northeast tip, where a connecting **bus** travels on to Millport. Caledonian MacBrayne **ferries** (☎0990/650000) run every fifteen minutes from June to August between 6.45am and 8.45pm, and every thirty minutes in the winter, so there's no need to overnight on the island, but if you decide **to stay** be sure to book a room beforehand at Largs' or Millport **tourist office** (Easter–May Sat & Sun 10am–5pm; June & Sept daily 11am–5pm; July & Aug daily 10am–6pm; first two weeks of Oct Sat & Sun 11am–4pm; ☎01475/530753). The *College of the Holy Spirit* (☎01475/530353; ③) in Millport is a retreat which offers accommodation and food in a very peaceful setting, while the *Millerstone Guest House* (☎01475/530480; ③) offers more conventional B&B. The return ferry fare is £2.75 per person, £11.70 per car (discounts on Day Saver returns Tues–Fri); bikes cost £2 return. Little Cumbrae, the islet opposite Millport, is privately owned.

travel details

Trains

Ayr to: Glasgow (approx every 30min; 50min); Stranraer (5–7 daily; 1hr 20min).

Dumfries to: Carlisle (5–15 daily; 35min); Glasgow (2–7 daily; 1hr 40min); Kilmarnock (2–7 daily; 1hr 5min).

Edinburgh to: Dunbar (Mon–Fri 7 daily, Sat 6 daily, Sun 4 daily; 20min); Musselburgh (Mon–Sat hourly, Sun 5 daily; 6 min); North Berwick (Mon–Sat hourly, Sun 5 daily; 30min).

Glasgow to: Ardrossan Harbour (5 daily; 50min); Ayr (every 30min; 50min); Carlisle (2–7 daily; 2hr 15min); Dumfries (2–7 daily; 1hr 40min); Kilmarnock (2–9 daily; 35min); Largs (hourly; 1hr); Stranraer (3–5 daily; 2hr).

Kilmarnock to: Carlisle (2–7 daily; 1hr 40min); Dumfries (2–9 daily; 1hr 5min); Glasgow (2–9 daily; 35min).

Largs to: Glasgow (hourly; 1hr).

Stranraer to: Ayr (5 daily; 1hr 20min); Glasgow (3–5 daily; 2 hr).

Buses

Ayr to: Castle Douglas (Mon–Sat 2 daily; 2hr); Culzean Castle (hourly; 30min); Girvan (every 30min; 1hr); Glasgow (hourly until 5.30pm; 55min); Largs (hourly; 1hr 10min); New Galloway (Mon–Sat 2 daily; 1hr 20min); Stranraer (10 daily; 2hr).

Dumfries to: Caerlaverock (Mon–Sat 5 daily; 35min); Carlisle (hourly; 50min); Castle Douglas (2–4 daily; 45min); Edinburgh (2 daily; 2hr 20min); Gatehouse of Fleet (2 daily; 55min); Glasgow (4 daily; 2hr); Gretna (6 daily; 1hr); Kirkcudbright (2 daily; 1hr 10min); Lockerbie (hourly; 35min); Newton Stewart (2 daily; 1hr 20min); Rockcliffe (2

daily; 1hr 10min); Sanquhar (4 daily; 50min); Stranraer (2 daily; 2hr); Thornhill (6 daily; 30min).

Edinburgh to: Aberlady (every 30min; 55min); Berwick-upon-Tweed (7–11 daily; 2hr); Carlisle (3 daily; 3hr 25min); Dirleton (every 30min; 1hr 5min); Dumfries (2 daily; 2hr 20min); Dunbar (hourly; 1hr 22min); Eyemouth (5–7 daily; 1hr 40min); Galashiels (hourly; 1hr 25min); Haddington (hourly; 55 min); Jedburgh (Mon–Sat 6 daily, Sun 4 daily; 2hr); Melrose (hourly; 2hr 15min); North Berwick (every 30min; 1hr 20min); Peebles (hourly; 1hr).

Galashiels to: Berwick-upon-Tweed (8–11 daily; 1hr 40min); Canonbie (Mon–Sat 6–7 daily, Sun 3 daily; 1hr 30min); Carlisle (6–7 daily; 2hr); Hawick (9–10 daily; 40min); Langholm (Mon–Sat 6–7 daily, Sun 3 daily; 1hr 15min); Selkirk (every 30min; 17min).

Haddington to: Gifford (hourly; 20min); North Berwick (Mon–Sat 10 daily, Sun 4 daily; 45min).

Jedburgh to: Hawick (hourly; 35 min); Kelso (3–6 daily; 30min).

Kelso to: Coldstream (3–8 daily; 20min); Kirk Yetholm (6 daily; 20min); Melrose (8 daily; 35min).

Largs to: Ayr (hourly; 1hr 10min).

Leadhills to: Wanlockhead (2 daily; 5min).

Lockerbie to: Dumfries (hourly; 35min); Langholm (4 weekly; 35min).

Melrose to: Duns (7 daily; 50min); Eyemouth (3 daily; 1hr 25min); Galashiels (hourly; 15min); Hawick (Wed & Fri 3 daily, Sat 2 daily; 40min); Jedburgh (hourly; 30min); Kelso (8 daily; 35min); Lauder (5–7 daily; 30min); Peebles (7 daily; 1hr 10min); Selkirk (Mon–Sat hourly, Sun 4 daily; 40min).

Moffat to: Dumfries (7–9 daily; 55min); Lockerbie (2 daily; 20min).

Newton Stewart to: Ayr (2–5 daily; 2hr 15min); Bargrennan (2–5 daily; 20min); Girvan (2–5 daily; 1hr 20min); Glentrool (2–5 daily; 25min); Stranraer (2–9 daily; 40min); Wigtown (Mon–Sat 10 daily, Sun 3 daily; 15min); Whithorn (3–8 daily; 50min); Isle of Whithorn (3–6 daily; 1hr).

Peebles to: Biggar (4–6 daily; 40min); Edinburgh (hourly; 1hr); Melrose (7 daily; 1hr 10min).

Selkirk to: Carlisle (Mon–Sat 6–7 daily, Sun 3 daily; 1hr 45 min); Hawick (Mon–Sat 6–7 daily, Sun 3 daily; 20min); Langholm (Mon–Sat 6–7 daily, Sun 3 daily; 1hr).

Stranraer to: Drummore (1–2 daily; 45min); Port Logan (1–2 daily; 35min); Portpatrick (5 daily; 25min).

Ferries

To Arran: Ardrossan–Brodick (up to 5 daily; 55min).

To Belfast: Stranraer–Belfast (hydrofoil 5 daily; July & Aug Sat & Sun 8 daily; 1hr 35min: Seacat 4 daily; 1hr 30min).

To Great Cumbrae Island: Largs–Millport (summer every 15min, winter every 30min; 15min).

To Larne: Cairnryan–Larne (Jetliner 6 daily; 1 hr: Ferry 3 daily; 2hr 15min).

SCENIC BUS ROUTES

Harrier Scenic Bus Services (with several bus companies involved in running this service it's best to contact tourist offices for details) run round-trip tours from July to September once a week along the following routes:

Melrose–Moffat via Galashiels, Selkirk, Bowhill House, Yarrow, St Mary's Loch (Thurs only; 2hr each way).

Selkirk–Eyemouth via Galashiels, Melrose, Kelso, Coldstream, Berwick-upon-Tweed (Tues only; 2hr 10min each way).

Hawick–Eyemouth via Denholm, Jedburgh, Town Yetholm, Berwick-upon-Tweed (Fri only; 2hr each way).

CHAPTER THREE

GLASGOW AND THE CLYDE

R ejuvenated, upbeat **Glasgow**, Scotland's largest city, has not traditionally enjoyed the best of reputations. Once an industrial giant set on the banks of the mighty River Clyde, it can still initially seem a grey and depressing place, with the M8 motorway screeching through the centre and crumbling slums on its outskirts. However, in recent years Glasgow has undergone a remarkable overhaul, set in motion in the 1980s by a self-promotion campaign featuring a fat yellow creature called Mr Happy, beaming beatifically that "Glasgow's Miles Better". The city proceeded to generate a brisk tourist trade, reaching a climax after beating Paris, Athens and Amsterdam to the title of European City of Culture in 1990.

The epithet is still apt: Glasgow has some of the best-financed and most imaginative museums and galleries in Britain – among them the showcase **Burrell Collection** of art and antiquities – and nearly all of them are free. There's also a robust social scene and nightlife that is remarkably diverse, though somewhat restricted by the Scottish licensing laws. Its **architecture** is some of the most striking in the nation, from the restored eighteenth-century warehouses of the **Merchant City** to the hulking Victorian prosperity of George Square. Most distinctive of all is the work of local luminary Charles Rennie Mackintosh, whose elegantly streamlined Art Nouveau designs appear all over the city, reaching their apotheosis in the **School of Art**. It is fitting that a Mackintosh creation, the Glasgow Herald building, will be used as the orientation point for the **City of Architecture and Design Festival** in 1999.

Despite all the upbeat hype, however, Glasgow's gentrification has passed by deprived inner-city areas such as the **East End**, home of the **Barras market** and some staunchly change-resistant pubs. This area, along with isolated housing schemes such as Castlemilk and Easterhouse, needs more than a facelift to resolve its complex social and economic problems, and has historically been the breeding ground for the city's much-lauded **socialism**.

Glasgow has also had a long-standing belief in the power of popular culture. Main attractions include the **People's Palace** – a celebrated social history museum – founded in 1898 to extol ordinary lives and achievements, and the **Citizens' Theatre**, formed in 1942 by playwright James Bridie to promote indigenous work for local people, and whose innovative productions still cost next to nothing to see. In addition, Glasgow's **Mayfest**, with its roots in the traditional working-class spring celebrations, could once claim to be Britain's second-largest arts bash after the Edinburgh Festival. Now somewhat reduced, it nevertheless continues to attract world-class acts to the city.

Quite apart from its own attractions, Glasgow makes an excellent base from which to explore the **Clyde Valley and coast**, made easy by the region's reliable rail service. Of the small communities in the Clyde Valley, **Lanark** is probably the best suited for overnight stays, as well as being the home of the remarkable eighteenth-century **New**

Lanark mills and workers' village. Beyond that, most of the inland towns (as well as the coastal resorts) are best approached as day-trips from Glasgow.

GLASGOW

GLASGOW's earliest **history**, like so much else in this surprisingly romantic city, is obscured in a swirl of myth. The city's name is said to derive from the Celtic *Glas-cu*, which loosely translates as "the dear, green place" – a tag that the tourist board are keen to exploit as an antidote to the sooty images of popular imagination. It is generally agreed that the first settlers arrived in the sixth century to join Christian missionary **Kentigern** – later to become St Mungo – in his newly founded monastery on the banks of the tiny Molendinar Burn.

William the Lionheart gave the town an official charter in 1175, after which it continued to grow in importance, peaking in the mid-fifteenth century when the **university** was founded on Kentigern's site – the second in Scotland after St Andrews. This led to the establishment of an archbishopric, and hence city status, in 1492, and, due to its situation on a large, navigable river, Glasgow soon expanded into a major **industrial port**. The first cargo of tobacco from Virginia offloaded in Glasgow in 1674, and the 1707 Act of Union between Scotland and England – despite demonstrations against it in Glasgow – led to a boom in trade with the colonies until American independence. Following the **Industrial Revolution** and James Watt's innovations in steam power, coal from the abundant seams of Lanarkshire fuelled the ironworks all around the Clyde, worked by the cheap hands of the Highlanders and, later, those fleeing the Irish potato famine of the 1840s.

The Victorian age transformed Glasgow beyond recognition. The population boomed from 77,000 in 1801 to nearly 800,000 at the end of the century, and new tenement blocks swept into the suburbs in an attempt to cope with the choking influxes of people. Two vast and stately **International Exhibitions** were held in 1888 and 1901 to showcase the city and its industries to the outside world, necessitating the construction of huge civic monoliths such as the Kelvingrove Art Gallery and the Council Chambers in George Square. At this time Glasgow became known as the "**Second City of the Empire**" – a curious epithet for a place that today rarely acknowledges second place in anything.

By the turn of the **twentieth century**, Glasgow's industries had been honed into one massive shipbuilding culture. Everything from tugboats to transatlantic liners were fashioned out of sheet metal in the yards that straddled the Clyde from Gourock to Rutherglen. In the harsh economic climate of the 1930s, however, unemployment spiralled, and Glasgow could do little to counter its popular image as a city dominated by inebriate violence and, having absorbed vast numbers of Irish emigrants, sectarian tensions. The **Gorbals** area in particular became notorious as one of the worst slums in Europe. The city's image has never been helped by the depth of animosity between its two great rival football teams: the Catholic **Celtic** and Protestant **Rangers**, whose warring armies of fans used to clash with monotonous regularity. Nowadays, post-match violence is rare, though the "Old Firm" clashes continue passionately on the field, with Rangers completely dominating the scene in recent years.

In the Eighties the promotion campaign began, snowballing towards the 1988 **Garden Festival** and year-long party as **European City of Culture** in 1990. Today, Glasgow is again preparing for another celebration after beating off Edinburgh and Liverpool to become **City of Architecture and Design** in 1999, expected to be the largest celebration of architecture and design ever held. The festival aims to rejuvenate Glasgow's blighted areas, involving schools and local communities in the process. Exhibitions and discussions will focus on the city's architectural heritage alongside visions of the future, including the importance of good design in modern everyday living. It proves that Glasgow, despite the many problems still remaining, has successfully broken off the industrial shackles of the past and evolved into a city of stature and confidence.

Orientation

Glasgow is a sprawling place, built upon some punishingly steep hills, and with no really obvious centre. However, as most transport services converge on the area around **Argyle Street** and, 200yd to the north, **George Square**, this pocket of the city is the most obvious candidate for city-centre status. However, with the renovated upmarket **Merchant City** immediately to the east and the main business and commercial areas to the west, the centre, when the term is used, actually refers to a large swathe from **Charing Cross** train station and the M8 in the west through to **Glasgow Green** in the **East End**. Although run-down, the latter boasts a wonderful social history museum, the People's Palace, and is close to Glasgow Cathedral at the city's medieval heart. Outside the city centre, the **West End** begins just over a mile west of Central station, and covers most of the area west of the M8. In the nineteenth century, as the East End tumbled into poverty, the West End ascended the social scales with great speed, a process crowned by the arrival of the **University**. Today, this is still very much the student quarter of Glasgow, exuding a decorous air, with graceful avenues, parks and cheap, interesting shops and cafés. It's also well connected with the city centre by Underground. The suburbs of Govan and the Gorbals, neither of which hold much for visitors, lie south of the Clyde, as does the area known as **South Side**, a relaxed version of the West End. Here the leafy enclaves of **Queen's Park** are home to the national football stadium, Hampden Park; the main attraction, though, has to be **Pollok Park** and the **Burrell Collection**. None of the sights here are within walking distance of the city centre, but can easily be reached by train or bus.

Arrival

Glasgow's **airport** (☎887 1111) is out at Abbotsinch, eight miles southwest of the city. To get into town, go to bus stop number two and take a Citylink or Glasgow Airport Express bus (both £2), which run to **Buchanan Street** bus station (☎332 7133), three roads north of George Square, every ten minutes during the day. From stop number three, regular buses run to **Paisley Gilmour Street** train station, from where you can catch a fast train into **Glasgow Central**, the terminus for trains from anywhere south of Glasgow.

Central station sits over Argyle Street, one of the city's main shopping thoroughfares. A **shuttle bus** (40p) from the front entrance on Gordon Street travels every ten minutes to **Queen Street station**, at the corner of George Square, for trains to Edinburgh and the north. The walk between the two takes about ten minutes.

All buses arrive at Buchanan Street station, except those run by Greater Glasgow and Kelvin Buses which terminate in various depots around the city.

Information

The city's excellent **tourist office**, at 11 George Square (May daily 9am–6pm; June & Sept daily 9am–7pm; July & Aug daily 9am–8pm; Oct–April Mon–Sat 9am–6pm; ☎204 4400) provides a wide array of maps and leaflets, and a free accommodation-booking service. You can also buy travel passes, theatre tickets and organize car rental. A couple of hundred yards southwest above the St Enoch Underground station sits the neo-Gothic hut of the **Strathclyde Travel Centre** (Mon–Sat 9.30am–5.30pm; ☎226 4826), where you can pick up sheaves of maps, leaflets and timetables. Their comprehensive and colour-coded *Visitors' Transport Guide* is the best free map of the city centre and West End, but if you're staying for longer, or want to explore the tiny streets and alleys that are invariably airbrushed off the tourist maps, it's probably worth investing in a *Bartholomew Glasgow Streetfinder* (£2.99).

City transport

Although it can be tough negotiating the steep hills, **walking** is the best way of exploring any one part of the city. However, as the main sights are scattered – the West End, for example, is a good thirty-minute walk from the centre – you'll need to use the comprehensive **public transport** system.

The best way to get between the city centre, southern suburbs and the West End is to use the city's **Underground**, whose stations are marked with a large U. Affectionately known as the "Clockwork Orange" (there's only one, circular route and the trains are a garish bright orange), the service is extremely easy to use. There's a flat fare of 65p, or you can buy a **day ticket** for £1.80; a **multi-journey ticket** gives ten journeys for £5.40 or twenty for £10. From Monday to Saturday, the whole system opens at 7am, and shuts down at 10.30pm. On Sundays, trains run from 11am to 5.30pm.

If you're travelling beyond the city centre or the West End, you may need to use the **bus** and **train** networks. After deregulation, the city was besieged with a horde of bus companies in hot competition. First Bus won the tender, operating under the names Greater Glasgow and Kelvin Buses – the *Visitors' Transport Guide* (see above) is a useful aid to sorting out the confusion.

The suburban train network is swift and convenient. Suburbs south of the Clyde are connected to Glasgow Central mainline station, while trains from Queen Street head into the northeast. The grim but functional **cross-city line**, which runs beneath Argyle Street (and includes a low-level stop below Central station), connects northwestern destinations with southeastern districts as far out as Lanark. Trains on both the Queen Street and Central station lines go through **Partick** station, west of the city centre; this is also an Underground stop.

If you are in the city for at least a week, it's worth investing in a **Zonecard**, which covers all public transport networks, and is valid for seven days or a month. Costs depend on the number of zones that you want to travel through – a two-zone card, for example, which gets you from Partick in the west to Rutherglen in the east, and as far as the Burrell Collection in the south, will set you back £10.20. This central two-zone core (divided by the Clyde) is ringed with a further six zones around its edge. The Strathclyde Travel Centre (see above) can give further details and help demystify the system. There is also a **Day-Tripper-Ticket**, which covers all the transport networks, going beyond the city zones, and costs £7 for one adult and up to two children, or £12.50 for two adults and up to four children, although you'd need to spend a very busy day sightseeing to make it worthwhile. Additionally, the **Roundabout Glasgow Ticket** (£3.40) gives unlimited travel for a day on the Underground and rail services from Milngavie in the north to Motherwell in the south. If you want to see the sights, the **Discover Glasgow** tour bus (April–Oct Mon–Sat 9.30am–5pm; £6) starts in George Square and runs a continuous route around all the major attractions in the city centre and West End, allowing you to get on and off as you please.

Should you want to avoid public transport altogether, you can hail a black **cab** from anywhere in the city centre. There are also taxi ranks at Central and Queen Street train stations and Buchanan Street bus station. Taxis run all day and night, and are very reasonable; the minimum fare is £1.50 and the journey from Central station to Pollok Park and the Burrell Collection (about three miles) costs £6.

As for **driving**, with the M8 motorway running right through the heart of Glasgow, it is one of the country's most car-friendly cities, with plenty of parking meters, and 24-hour multistorey car parks at Waterloo Street, Mitchell Street, Oswald Street and Cambridge Street. However, parking tariffs per day in the city centre are expensive, and significantly less in the outskirts.

Accommodation

There's a good range of **accommodation** in Glasgow, from an excellent youth hostel in the leafy West End through to some top international hotels in the city centre. Most of the rooms are in the city centre, the West End or down in the southern suburb of Queen's Park. Glasgow's speciality is its profusion of converted Victorian **town houses** in the middle of town, many of which are now privately run B&Bs that offer excellent value for money.

During Mayfest or in summer it's worth **booking ahead** to ensure a good room – at any time of year the **tourist office** can help secure you somewhere to stay. It also publishes a useful brochure of bargain weekend breaks.

Low-priced **self-catering** rooms and flats are available at the **University of Glasgow** (☎330 5385) from early July to mid-September. The **University of Strathclyde** has various sites, most of which are gathered around the cathedral. Bed-and-breakfast accommodation in single rooms is available near the main campus in Rottenrow for £22.50 per person, while self-catering flats cost £280 in high season for a four-person flat, and £300 for a six-person flat (☎553 4148). For better rooms, available all year (but pricier than many city hotels), call their **Graduate Business School**, Cathedral Street (☎553 6000; ⑧). The **YMCA** at 33 Petershill Drive, Balornock (☎558 6166), three miles northeast of the city centre (a 10min walk from Barnhill train station), offers clean, if rather lifeless self-catering flats (③) sleeping between four and six people which are available all year round; there are no dorms.

Glasgow Youth Hostel, 7–8 Park Terrace (☎332 3004), nuzzled deep in the splendour of the West End, is a ten-minute walk south from Kelvinbridge Underground station, or take #11, #44 or #59 Greater Glasgow bus from the city centre, after which it's a short stroll west up Woodlands Road. Bed and breakfast costs £11.95 per person in July and August and £10.95 from September to June; the hostel's very popular, so book in advance. In less magnificent surroundings, the **Berkeley Globetrotters Independent Hostel**, 63 Berkeley St (☎221 7880) provides a slightly cheaper alternative to the youth hostel, with dorm beds for £9.50 per person and twin-bedded rooms for £11 per person. The #57 Greater Glasgow bus from the city centre runs straight past the door; alternatively take a low-level train from Queen Street Station to Charing Cross; it is a five-minute walk west from there.

ACCOMMODATION PRICE CODES

Throughout this book, accommodation **prices** have been graded with the codes below, according to the cost of the least expensive double room in high season. Price codes are not given for campsites, most of which charge under £10 per person. Almost all hostels charge less than £10 a night for a bed – the few exceptions to this rule have the prices quoted in the text. For a full account of the accommodation price codes, see p.30.

① under £20	④ £40–50	⑦ £70–80
② £20–30	⑤ £50–60	⑧ £80–100
③ £30–40	⑥ £60–70	⑨ over £100

The only **campsite** within a decent distance of Glasgow is **Craigendmuir Park**, Campsie View, Stepps (☎779 4159), four miles northeast of the city centre, a fifteen-minute walk from Stepps train station. It has adequate facilities with showers, a laundry and a shop, but there are only ten pitches.

City centre

Adelaides, 209 Bath St (☎248 4970). Beautifully restored "Greek" Thomson building in a central location, with pleasant staff and large café. ④.

Babbity Bowster, 16–18 Blackfriars St (☎552 5055). A traditional and very lively hotel, bar and restaurant that makes much of its Scottishness, with haggis and neeps and tatties permanently on the menu. ⑥.

Baird Hall, 460 Sauchiehall St (☎553 4148). Lavish Art Deco building that belies the functional, ex-student rooms, near the School of Art and the upper end of Sauchiehall Street. ③.

Brunswick Hotel, 106 Brunswick St (☎552 0002). In the heart of the Merchant City, a good-value hotel decorated in designer colours with minimalist furniture, and a smart bar and restaurant. ④.

Central Hotel, Gordon Street (☎221 9680). Imposing, comfortable hotel, with its own leisure centre, in the heart of the action near the stations. ⑦.

Charing Cross Tower Hotel, Elmbank Gardens (☎221 1000). The top-floor rooms of this refurbished office block give excellent views of the city, and its location is good for trips to Sauchiehall Street. ④.

Copthorne Hotel, George Square (☎332 6711). Large and impressive eighteenth-century hotel occupying the entire northwestern corner of George Square; rooms are bright and flouncy, but prices rocket at the weekend. There's a popular bar in the ground-floor glass verandah. ⑦.

Hampton Court Hotel, 230 Renfrew St (☎332 6623 or 332 5885). Low-key, slightly downbeat and fairly small Victorian house conversion, close to the School of Art and Sauchiehall Street. ③.

Marriott, Argyle Street (☎226 5577). Large and luxurious chain hotel with a popular health centre. Ask for a room out of earshot of the M8. Considerable reductions available at weekends. ⑧.

Town House Hotel, Nelson Mandela Place, 54 W George St (☎332 3320). Sumptuously converted sandstone block with a "Scottish" feel. Good reductions are offered at weekends, and the restaurant serves expensive but original food. ⑨.

Victorian House, 212 Renfrew St (☎332 0129). Large and friendly terraced guest house, with some of the cheapest rooms in the city centre. ③.

Willow Hotel, 228 Renfrew St (☎332 2332 or 332 7075). Victorian town house on the north side of the city centre, which has been well converted into a clean and functional B&B, with spacious rooms. ③.

West End

Alamo Guest House, 46 Gray St (☎339 2395). Good-value, family-run boarding house next to Kelvingrove Park. Small but comfortable rooms. ③.

Ambassador Hotel, 7 Kelvin Drive (☎946 1018). Smallish but comfortable, family-run B&B in lovely surroundings next to the River Kelvin and Botanic Gardens. ⑤.

Argyll Hotel, 969 Sauchiehall St (☎337 3313). Well-placed, newly refurbished hotel with neat rooms and friendly staff. ⑤.

Hillhead Hotel, 32 Cecil St (☎339 7733). Quiet, welcoming hotel only a couple of minutes' stroll from Hillhead Underground and excellent local pubs and restaurants. ④.

Hillview Guest House, 18 Hillhead St (☎334 5585). Unassuming and peaceful small B&B near the University and the Byres Road. ③.

Kelvin Park Lorne Hotel, 923 Sauchiehall St (☎314 9955). Dependable, if slightly sterile, international hotel with food to match. Offers good weekend rates. ⑦.

Lomond Hotel, 6 Buckingham Terrace (☎339 2339). Discreet B&B in a beautifully restored Victorian terrace near the Botanic Gardens and Byres Road. ④.

One Devonshire Gardens, 1 Devonshire Gardens, Great Western Road (☎339 2001). A 10min walk up the Great Western Road from the Botanic Gardens, this hotel and its expensive gourmet restaurant are among the city's finest. ⑨.

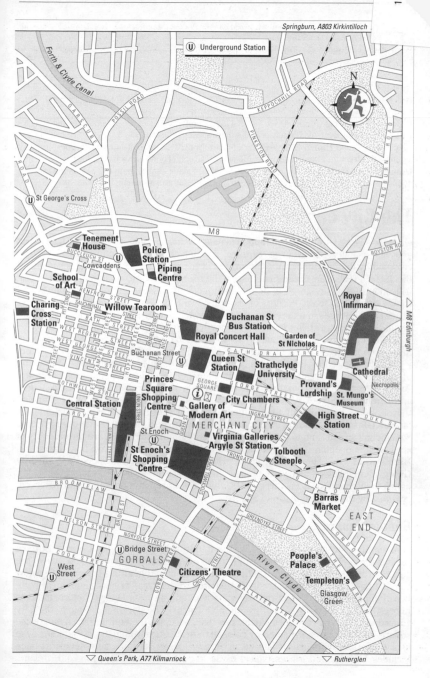

Springburn, A803 Kirkintilloch

U Underground Station

N

Forth & Clyde Canal

GARSCUBE ROAD

POSSIL ROAD

KEPPOCHHILL ROAD

PINKSTON ROAD

SPRINGBURN ROAD

U St George's Cross

P

M8

ROYSTON ROAD

△ M8 Edinburgh

Tenement House

BUCCLEUCH ST

Police Station

U Cowcaddens

Piping Centre

School of Art

RENFREW STREET

Charing Cross Station

SAUCHIEHALL STREET

Willow Tearoom

BATH STREET

WEST REGENT STREET

Buchanan Street

WEST GEORGE STREET

Buchanan St Bus Station

Royal Concert Hall

Garden of St Nicholas

Royal Infirmary

CASTLE STREET

Cathedral

Necropolis

CATHEDRAL STREET

Queen St Station

Strathclyde University

U

WEST NILE STREET

HOPE STREET

ST VINCENT STREET

PITT STREET

CAMPBELL STREET

BOTHWELL STREET

Princes Square Shopping Centre

GEORGE SQUARE

GEORGE STREET

Provand's Lordship

St. Mungo's Museum

Central Station

ARGYLE

i

City Chambers

Gallery of Modern Art

INGRAM STREET

DUKE ST

High Street Station

MERCHANT CITY

St Enoch

U

UNION STREET

QUEEN STREET

Virginia Galleries

Argyle St Station

HIGH STREET

St Enoch's Shopping Centre

TRONGATE

Tolbooth Steeple

GALLOWGATE

BROOMIELAW

BRIDGE ST

STOCKWELL STREET

ST MARKET ST

Barras Market

EAST END

LONDON RD

NELSON STREET

NORFOLK STREET

GREENDYKE STREET

River Clyde

COOK STREET

U Bridge Street

West Street

U

GORBALS

GORBALS STREET

CROWN STREET

Citizens' Theatre

People's Palace

Templeton's

BALLATER STREET

Glasgow Green

THE GREEN

▽ Queen's Park, A77 Kilmarnock

▽ Rutherglen

Sandyford Hotel, 904 Sauchiehall St (☎334 0000). A clean, comfortable hotel, well located for Kelvingrove Park and the SECC. ④.

Scott Guest House, 417 Woodside Rd (☎339 3750). Friendly B&B, well situated close to Kelvinbridge underground station. ③.

South Side

Boswell Hotel, 27 Mansionhouse Rd (☎632 9812). Informal, relaxing Queen's Park hotel with a superb real-ale bar, and regular folk and jazz nights. ⑤.

Ewington Hotel, 132 Queen's Drive (☎423 1152). Comfortable and peaceful hotel facing Queen's Park, with an excellent, moderately priced subterranean restaurant. ⑧.

Reidholme Guest House, 36 Regent Park Square (☎423 1855). Small and friendly guest house in a quiet side street that was designed by Alexander "Greek" Thomson (see p.185). ③.

Queen's Park Hotel, 10 Balvicar Drive (☎423 1123). Faintly shabby, but very welcoming and with good views over the hill of Queen's Park. Attracts a regular crowd of return visitors. ④.

The City centre

Glasgow's large **City centre** is ranged across the north bank of the River Clyde. At its geographical heart is **George Square**, a nineteenth-century municipal showpiece crowned by the enormous **City Chambers** at the eastern end. Behind this lies one of the 1980s' greatest marketing successes, the **Merchant City**, an area of massive gentrification partially restored to its nineteenth-century glory. The grand buildings and trendy cafés cling to the borders of the run-down **East End**, a strongly working-class district that chooses to ignore its rather showy neighbour. The oldest part of Glasgow, around the **Cathedral**, lies immediately north of the East End.

Called by John Betjeman "the greatest Victorian city in the world", Glasgow's commercial core spreads west of George Square, and is mostly built on a large grid system – possibly inspired by Edinburgh's New Town – with ruler-straight roads soon rising up severe hills to grand, sandblasted buildings. The main shopping areas here are **Argyle Street**, running parallel to the river east–west underneath Central train station, and **Buchanan Street**, which crosses it and leads up to the pedestrianized shopping thoroughfare, **Sauchiehall Street**. Just to the north of here is Rennie Mackintosh's famous **Glasgow School of Art**. Lying between the commercial bustle of Argyle and Sauchiehall streets, and to the immediate west of Buchanan Street, are the contours of an Ice age drumlin (one of three main drumlins in the area), now known as **Blythswood Hill**. The tightly packed grid of streets piled on its slopes are lined by Georgian buildings filled with offices. In comparison with the bustling shopping parades surrounding it on three sides, this area is remarkably quiet and reserved, crowned by the neat Blythswood Square.

George Square

Now hemmed in by speeding traffic, the imposing architecture of **George Square** reflects the confidence of Glasgow's Victorian age. Rising high above the centre of the square is an 80-ft column topped with Sir Walter Scott, although his links with Glasgow were, at best, sketchy. Haphazardly dotted around the great writer's plinth are a number of dignified statues of assorted luminaries, ranging from Queen Victoria to Scots heroes such as James Watt and wee Robbie Burns. The florid splendour of the **City Chambers**, opened by Queen Victoria in 1888, occupies the entire eastern end of the square. Built from wealth gained by colonial trade and heavy industry, it epitomizes the aspirations and optimism of late-Victorian city elders. Its intricately detailed facade includes high-minded friezes typical of the era: the four nations (England, Ireland,

Scotland, Wales) of the then United Kingdom at the feet of the throned queen, the British colonies and allegorical figures representing Religion, Virtue and Knowledge. It's worth taking a free guided tour (Mon–Fri 10.30am & 2.30pm; ☎227 4017) of the labyrinthine interior to get a look at the acres of intricate gold leaf and Italian marble.

Equally opulent is the **Merchant's House** opposite Queen Street station (entry by appointment only; ☎221 8272; free), where the grand Banqueting Hall and silk-lined Directors' Room are highlights.

The Gallery of Modern Art

Queen Street leads south from George Square to Royal Exchange Square, where the focal point is the graceful mansion built in 1780 for tobacco lord William Cunninghame. It was the most ostentatious of the Glasgow merchants' homes and, having served as the city's Royal Exchange and central library, now houses the excellent **Gallery of Modern Art** (Mon & Wed–Sat 10am–5pm, Sun 11am–5pm; free). Surrounded by controversy from the day it opened in 1996, the gallery has pleased the punters more than it has certain critics, who have damned the place for putting more emphasis on presentation than on content. The presentation is certainly unusual: the main part of the gallery is divided into four levels, named Fire, Earth, Water and Air, though these themes bear only a tenuous link with the work displayed. Once through the main portals, a mirrored reception area leads you straight into the **Earth Gallery**, a spacious zone that effortlessly absorbs large-scale socially committed works by the "Glasgow Pups" – Peter Howson, Adrian Wiszniewski, Ken Currie and Stephen Campbell. Felipe Linares' beautifully painted papier-mâché skeletons, exploring the seven deadly sins, shine defiantly from the end of the gallery, along with the evocative photos of Sebastião Salgado, whose most famous pictures record the plight of the world's economic underclasses.

Downstairs is the **Fire Gallery**, is a dark place packed with interactive creations, while upstairs you'll find the **Water Gallery**, a brightly lit room dealing with the flow of life and death through art that ranges from Andy Goldsworthy's sun-baked and cracked red clay floor to intricate Aboriginal paintings on canvas and bark. The blinding-white **Air Gallery** is a perfect setting for such displays of optical fireworks as *Punjabi*, an eye-shattering study in red, white, violet and green by Bridget Riley, or *Jubilee* by Patrick Hughes, a witty exercise in visual deception. A small set of stairs at the far end of the gallery leads down to an area filled with examples of well-designed everyday objects, from nappies to bookshelves. Don't miss the top-floor café, where a huge mural by Adrian Wiszniewski competes with the view of rooftops below (see p.200 for review of café).

Merchant City

The grid of streets that lies immediately east of the City Chambers is known as the **Merchant City**, an area of eighteenth-century warehouses and homes once bustling with cotton, tobacco and sugar traders, which in the last decade or so has been sandblasted and swabbed clean with greater enthusiasm and municipal money than any other part of Glasgow in an attempt to bring residents back into the city centre. The cost of living here is prohibitive for most people, however, and many of the warehouses remain smothered with "To let" signs. However, the expensive designer shops sitting neatly beside bijou bars and cafés bring some life back into this quiet area. Even though some of the buildings are literally no more than original facades, held in place with vast struts like a film set and nestled next to mock period reconstructions, the area has a simple elegance and upmarket charm. Towards dusk, when traffic has died down, floodlights bathe the scrubbed porticos in a range of colours. Look out for the delicate white spire of the National Trust for

Scotland's regional headquarters, **Hutcheson Hall**, at 158 Ingram St (Mon–Sat 10am–5pm). The NTS has a shop on the ground floor and visitors can see the ornately decorated hall upstairs. Almost opposite, on Glassford Street, the Robert Adam-designed **Trades House** (visits by appointment only; ☎552 2418; free) is easily distinguished by its neat, green copper dome. Purpose-built in 1794, it still functions as the headquarters of the Glasgow trade guilds. Its history can be traced back to 1605 when fourteen societies of well-to-do city merchants, who were the forerunners of the trade unions, first incorporated. These included a Bakers' Guild, and societies for Hammermen, Gardeners, Bonnet Makers, Wrights and Weavers, although they have since become little more than proto-Masonic lodges for men from all sections of Glasgow's business community. The former civic pride and status of the guilds is still evident, however, from the rich assortment of carvings and stained-glass windows, with a lively pictorial representation of the different trades in the silk frieze around the walls of the first-floor banqueting hall.

GLASGOW'S ARCHITECTURE

Glasgow, founded on religion, built on trade and now well established as a cultural centre, is rich in architectural styles: from its medieval cathedral to the modern glass-lined galleries of the Burrell Collection. Most dominant, however, is the legacy of the **Victorian age**, when booming trade and industry allowed merchants to commission the finest architects of the day. As World War II bombing was focused on the shipbuilding centre of Clydebank, most of the city's fine sandstone buildings have survived intact. The celebrated work of **Charles Rennie Mackintosh** (1868–1928) took Glasgow architecture to the forefront of early twentieth-century design, a final flowering of homespun genius before economic conditions effectively stopped the architectural trade in its tracks.

Glasgow's great expansion was initiated in the eighteenth century by wealthy tobacco merchants who, in an attempt to bask in the reflected glory of Classical times, built the grand edifices of public and municipal importance that still make up much of the **Merchant City**. One of the finest Merchant City views is down Garth Street, where the Venetian windows and Ionic columns of **Trades House**, designed by Robert Adam in 1791, close the vista with a flourish. **Hutcheson Hall**, closing off Hutcheson Street, is another fine monument of civic pride, with a five-bay facade and elegant tower that moves from a square through octagonals to a drum – an early nineteenth-century architectural nod to the Rennaissance by the architect David Hamilton.

Further west, **Royal Exchange Square** is one of the best examples of a typical Glasgow square: treeless, bare and centred around a building of importance, the 1829 **Royal Exchange** building, now housing the Gallery of Modern Art. The square itself is an excellent example of integrated municipal design, with closely matching Georgian buildings unifying the area into a harmonious whole. Further north, off Queen Street, the open space of **George Square** holds the emphatically Victorian **City Chambers**, its Venetian splendour a testimony to the confidence of the wealthy merchants, built only a couple of years after the crash of the Glasgow bank in 1878.

As workers piled into the centre of Glasgow in the early nineteenth century, filling up the already bursting tenements, wealthy residents began moving west. This expansion was completely uncontrolled and so the gridded streets that line **Blythswood Hill** (mostly developed after 1820) hold an eclectic range of buildings. However, a harmonious streetscape was created by the predominance of two- or three-storey terraces, their porches and heavy cornices providing textural relief to the endless sandstone monotony. The dignified proportions and design of **Blythswood Square** are a highlight of this area; at no. 5 the later Art Nouveau doorway designed by Charles Rennie Mackintosh sits incongruously amongst the Georgian solidity. Above all, the long streets provide a beautiful selection of open-ended views, one moment leading into the heart of the city, the next filled with distant hills and sky.

Now desiring to surround themselves with trees and fields, the well-to-do continued their migration west; in the early 1830s, beyond Charing Cross, the Woodlands Hill development

On Virginia Street, parallel to Glassford Street, the **Virginia Galleries** sit behind the intricate wrought-iron gate of no 33. Formerly the city's nineteenth-century tobacco and sugar trading house, the graceful market hall is now a sedate place, filled with a variety of shops selling anything from secondhand clothing to African artefacts.

From Trongate to the East End

Before 1846, **Glasgow Cross** – the junction of **Trongate**, Gallowgate and the High Street – was the city's principal intersection, until the construction of the new train station near George Square shifted the city's emphasis west. The turreted seventeenth-century **Tolbooth Steeple** still stands here, although the rest of the building has long since disappeared, and today the stern tower is little more than a traffic hazard at a busy junction. Further east, down Gallowgate, beyond the train lines, lies the **EAST END**,

was completed – a leafy parkland area in contrast to the treeless town squares of the city centre. Here **Woodside Crescent**, leading into Woodside Terrace, is a severe, fierce line of buildings, with splendid Doric porches and neatly organized gardens. **Park Circus**, on the other hand, is a parade of uninterrupted Georgian magnificence, with delicate detail – such as narrow window slots on either side of the doors – enhancing the dignified crescent. Now predominantly commercial, it is an excellent example of grand planning.

Long since overshadowed by Charles Rennie Mackintosh (see box p.188), the design of **Alexander "Greek" Thomson**, in the latter half of the nineteenth century, though well respected in its time, has been much maligned. As his nickname suggests, his work used the essence of Greek architecture and reprocessed it in a highly unique manner. Energetic and talented, he designed buildings from the lowly tenement to grand suburban villas. The St Vincent Street Church (1857), his best work, has a massive simplicity and serenity lightened by the use of exotic Egyptian and Hindu motifs, particularly in the tower with its decorated egg-shaped dome. This fusion of the classical and the Eastern stands out for its originality at a time when Gothic Revival or Renaissance work was all the rage. Thomson's buildings have not been given the treatment they deserve, and some were tragically torn down in the municipal clearances of the 1970s.

West from Park Circus lies **Glasgow University** (1866–86), its Gothic Revivalism – the work of Sir George Gilbert Scott – representing everything that Greek Thomson despised; he called it "sixteenth-century Scottish architecture clothed in fourteenth-century French details". Scottish features abound, such as crow-stepped gables, round turrets with conical caps and the top-heavy central tower. Inside, cloisters and quadrants sum up a suitably scholastic severity.

Originally conceived as a convenient way to house the influx of workers in the late 1800s, the Glasgow **tenement** design became more refined as the wealthy middle classes began to realize its potential. Tenements were built by private landlords, the majority constructed in a remarkably short space of time, from around 1860 to 1910. In general these buildings are three to five storeys with two or three apartments per floor. Important rooms are picked out with bay windows, middle storeys are emphasized by architraves or decorated panels below sill or above lintel, and street junctions are given importance by swelling bay windows, turrets and domes. West of the University, the streets off **Byres Road** are lined with such grand tenement buildings, in particular the Baronial red sandstone of Great George Street.

World War I put an end to the glorious century of Glasgow building, and the Depression years did little to enhance the city. More recently, glassy office buildings have sprung up, their mirrored walls basking in the reflected glory of the surrounding buildings to disguise their banality of design. More notable modern constructions include the **Burrell Collection** and St Mungo's Museum, both successfully designed to suit their surroundings, and the enormous extension to the **Scottish Exhibition and Conference Centre** (SECC), that now dominates the Clydeside vista.

the district that perhaps most closely corresponds to the old perception of Glasgow. Hemmed in by Glasgow Green to the south, and the old university to the west, this densely packed industrial area essentially created the city's wealth. The Depression caused the closure of many factories, leaving communities stranded in an industrial wasteland. Today isolated pubs, tatty shops and cafés sit amidst this dereliction, in sharp contrast to the gloss of the Merchant City only a few blocks to the west.

Three hundred yards down either London Road or Gallowgate, **The Barras** is Glasgow's largest and most popular weekend market. Red iron gates announce its official entrance, but boundaries are breached as the stalls – selling household goods, bric-a-brac, secondhand clothes and records – spill out into the surrounding cobbled streets. The fast-talking traders are sharp-witted and friendly, and there are plenty of bargains to be had, but you'll be in tenacious competition with locals vying for the goods.

Between London Road and the River Clyde are the wide and tree-lined spaces of **Glasgow Green**. Reputedly the oldest public park in Britain, the Green has been common land since at least 1178, when it was first mentioned in records. Glaswegians hold it very dear, considering it to be an immortal link between themselves and their ancestors, for whom a stroll on the Green was a favourite Sunday afternoon jaunt. It has also been the site of many of the city's major political demonstrations – the Chartists in the 1830s and Scottish republican campaigners in the 1920s – and was the traditional culmination of the May Day marches until the 1950s, when the celebrations were moved to Queen's Park. Various memorials (some in bad states of disrepair) are dotted around the lawns: the 146-ft **Nelson Monument**; the ornate but derelict terracotta **Doulton Fountain**, rising like a wedding cake to the pinnacle where the forlorn Queen Victoria oversees her crumbling Empire; and the stern monument extolling the evils of drink and the glory of God that was erected by the nineteenth-century Temperance movement – today, quite a meeting place for local drunks.

The People's Palace

On the northern end of Glasgow Green, the **People's Palace** (Mon & Wed–Sat 10am–5pm, Sun 11am–5pm; free) is a wonderfully haphazard evocation of the city's history. This squat, red-brick Victorian building, with a vast semicircular glasshouse tacked on the back, was purpose-built as a museum back in 1898 – almost a century before the rest of the country caught on to the fashion for social history collections. Although the building is currently undergoing refurbishment – it is due to be completed in spring 1998, in time for centenary celebrations – viewing is only slightly restricted.

On the top floor, glowing murals by local artist Ken Currie powerfully evoke the spirit of radical Glasgow, from the Carlton Weavers strike in 1787 to the Red Clydesiders of the 1920s (a radical Independent Labour Party formed during the post-World War I economic slump), and look down upon a potted history of Glasgow's social and economic development. Decorated by Suffragette flags and trade union banners, the room contains a host of memorabilia including the desk of John MacLean, who became consul to the Bolshevik Government in 1918. The west wing attempts to document Glasgow's eclectic history, with displays of everything from cast-iron railings and biscuit wrappers to a giant portrait of Billy Connolly. In the East Gallery, an interesting series of anecdotes and exhibits explore the daily life of Glasgow people through the years with music, songs and an interactive computer.

The glasshouse at the back of the palace contains the **Winter Gardens**, whose café, water garden, twittering birds and assorted tropical plants and shrubs make a pleasant place in which to pass an hour or so.

A hundred yards across the road from the People's Palace you can see the riotously intricate orange and blue facade of **Templeton's Carpet Factory**, built in 1889. William Leiper, Templeton's architect, is said to have modelled his industrial cathedral on the Doge's Palace in Venice; today it houses a centre for small businesses.

The Cathedral area

Rising north up the hill from the Tolbooth Steeple at Glasgow Cross is Glasgow's **High Street**. In British cities, the name is commonly associated with the busiest central thoroughfare, and it's a surprise to see how forlorn and dilapidated Glasgow's version is, long superseded by the grander thoroughfares further west. The High Street leads up to the **Cathedral**, on the site of Glasgow's original settlement.

Glasgow Cathedral

Built in 1136, destroyed in 1192 and rebuilt soon after, the stumpy-spired **Glasgow Cathedral** (April–Sept Mon–Sat 9.30am–1pm & 2–6pm, Sun 2–5pm; Oct–March Mon–Sat 9.30am–1pm & 2–4pm, Sun 2–4pm) was not completed until the late fifteenth century, with the final reconstruction of the chapterhouse and the aisle designed by Robert Blacader, the city's first archbishop. Thanks to the intervention of the city guilds, it is the only Scottish mainland cathedral to have escaped the hands of religious reformers in the sixteenth century. The cathedral is dedicated to the city's patron saint and reputed founder, St Mungo, about whom four popular stories are frequently told – they even make an appearance on the city's coat of arms. These involve a bird that he brought back to life, the bell with which he summoned the faithful to prayer, a tree that he managed to make spontaneously combust and a fish that he caught with a repentant adulterous queen's ring on its tongue.

Because of the sloping ground on which it is built, at its east end the cathedral is effectively on two levels, the crypt being part of the lower church. On entering, you arrive in the impressively lofty nave of the **upper church**, with the lower church entirely hidden from view. Most of this upper church was completed under the direction of Bishop William de Bondington (1233–58), although later design elements came from Blacader. Either side of the nave, the narrow **aisles** are illuminated by vivid stained-glass windows, most of which date from this century. Threadbare Union flags and military pennants hang listlessly beneath them, serving as a reminder that the cathedral is very much a part of the Unionist Protestant tradition. Beyond the nave, the **choir** is hidden from view by the curtained stone pulpit, making the interior feel a great deal smaller than might be expected from the outside. In the choir's northeastern corner, a small door leads into the cathedral's gloomy **sacristy**, in which Glasgow University was first founded over five hundred years ago. Wooden boards mounted on the walls detail the alternating Roman Catholic and Protestant clergy of the cathedral, testimony to the turbulence and fluctuations of the Church in Scotland.

Two sets of steps from the nave lead down into the **lower church**, where you'll see the dark and musty **chapel** surrounding the tomb of St Mungo. The saint's relics were removed in the late Middle Ages, although the tomb still forms the centrepiece. The chapel itself is one of the most glorious examples of medieval architecture in Scotland, best seen in the delicate fan vaulting rising up from the thicket of cool stone columns. Scots designer Robert Stewart was commissioned in 1979 to produce a tapestry detailing the four myths of St Mungo, which can be illuminated using the button at the bottom of the north-side stairs to reveal its swirl of browns and oranges. Also in the lower church, the spaciously light **Blacader Aisle** was originally built as a two-storey extension; today only this lower section survives, where the bright, and frequently gory, medieval ceiling bosses stand out superbly against the simple whitewashed vaulting.

Outside, the atmospheric **Necropolis** rises above the cathedral. Inspired by the Père Lachaise cemetery in Paris, developer John Strong created a garden of death in 1833, filled with Doric columns, gloomy catacombs and Neoclassical temples reflecting the vanity of the nineteenth-century industrialists buried here. From the summit, next to the column topped with an indignant John Knox, there are superb views over the cathedral and its surrounding area.

Cathedral Square

Back in Cathedral Square, the **St Mungo Museum of Religious Life and Art** (Mon & Wed–Sat 10am–5pm, Sun 11am–5pm; free) focuses on objects, beliefs and art from Christianity, Buddhism, Judaism, Islam, Hinduism and Sikhism. Portrayals of Hindu gods are juxtaposed with the stunning Salvador Dali painting *Christ Upon the Cross* – moved here from Kelvingrove Art Gallery – that draws the viewer into its morose depths. In addition to the main exhibition is a small collection of photographs, papers and archive material looking at religion in Glasgow, the power and zealotry of the nineteenth-century Temperance movement, Christian missionaries and local boy, David Livingstone, in particular. Outside is Britain's only permanent "dry stone" Zen Buddhist garden, with slabs of rock, white gravel and moss carefully arranged to suggest the forms of land and sea.

Across the square, the oldest house in the city, the **Provand's Lordship** (Mon & Wed–Sat 10am–5pm, Sun 11am–5pm; free) dates from 1471, and has been used, among other things, as an ecclesiastical residence and an inn. Many of the rooms have been kitted out with period furniture, including a re-creation of the fifteenth-century chamber of cathedral clerk Cuthbert Simon, who is seen as a contemplative bewigged wax dummy living in comparative luxury for the age. As a reminder of the manse's earthier history, the upper floor contains pictures of assorted lowlife characters, such as notorious drunkards and prostitutes of eighteenth- and nineteenth-century Glasgow.

CHARLES RENNIE MACKINTOSH

Dark-haired and confident, the figure of **Charles Rennie Mackintosh** (1868–1928) has come to be synonymous with the image of Glasgow. Whether his work was a forerunner of the Modernist movement or merely a sunset of Victorianism, he undoubtedly created buildings of great beauty, idiosyncratically fusing Scots Baronial with Gothic, Art Nouveau and modern design. Though the bulk of his work was conceived at the turn of the century, since the postwar years Mackintosh's ideas have become particularly fashionable, giving rise to a certain amount of ersatz "Mockintosh" in his home city, with his distinctive lettering and small design features used time and again by shops, pubs and businesses. Fortunately, there are also plenty of examples of the genuine article, making the city something of a pilgrimage centre for art and design students from all over the world.

Although his family did little to encourage his artistic ambitions, as a young child he began to cultivate his interest in drawing from nature during walks in the countryside, taken to improve his health. This talent was to flourish when he joined the **Glasgow School of Art**, in 1884, where the vibrant new director, Francis Newberry, encouraged his pupils to create original and individual work. Here he met Herbert MacNair and the sisters Margaret and Frances MacDonald, whose work seemed to be sympathetic with his, fusing the organic forms of nature with a linear, symbolic Art Nouveau style. Nicknamed "**The Spook School**", the four created a new artistic language, using extended vertical design, stylized abstract organic forms and muted colours, reflecting their interest in Japanese design and the work of Whistler and Beardsley. However, it was architecture that truly challenged Mackintosh, allowing him to use his creative artistic impulse in a three-dimensional and cohesive manner.

His big break came in 1896, when he won the competition to design a new **art school** (see p.190). This is his most famous work, but a number of smaller buildings created during his tenure with the architects Honeyman and Keppie, which began in 1889, document the development of his style. One of his earliest commissions was for a new building to house the **Glasgow Herald headquarters** on Mitchell Street, off Argyle Street. A massive tower rises up from the corner, giving a dynamism to the enclosed space, dispelling the regularity of the horizontal windows; this use of vertical lines was to play a significant part in his later work.

In the 1890s Glasgow went wild for tearooms, where the middle classes could play billiards and chess, read in the library or merely chat over some fine dining. The imposing

Behind this building lies the small **Garden of St Nicholas**; a herb garden contrasting medieval and Renaissance aesthetics and approaches to medicine; from the muddled clusters of herbs amid stone carvings of the heart and other organs, to the controlled arrangement of plants around a small ornate fountain. The garden, bordered by sandstone walkways where you can sit, is an aromatic and peaceful haven away from the High Street.

From Buchanan Street to Sauchiehall Street

The huge grid of streets that runs **from Buchanan Street** to the M8 a mile to the west, is home to Glasgow's main shopping district as well as its financial and business corporations, piling up the slopes of drumlins shaped by the receding glaciers of the last Icc age. The **St Enoch Shopping Centre**, south of George Square, sandwiched between Argyle and Howard streets, is a huge, lofty glass pyramid built around a redundant train station. Here, you can wander amongst the glossy shops and piped muzak, or sip a cappuccino whilst choosing from the array of stalls in the large food court area. A short walk north, on Buchanan Street, **Princes Square**, hollowed out of the innards of a soft sandstone building, is one of the most stylish and imaginative shopping centres in the country. The interior, all recherché Art Deco and ornate ironwork, has lots

Miss Cranston, who dominated the Glasgow teashop scene, running the most elegant establishments, gave Mackintosh great freedom of design, and in 1896 he started to plan the interiors for her growing business. Over the next twenty years he designed articles from teaspoons to furniture and, finally, as in the case of the **Willow Tea Rooms** (see p.190), the structure itself.

Mackintosh designed few **religious buildings**; the Queens Cross Church of 1896, still at the junction of Garscube and Maryhill roads in the northwest of the city, is the only completed one standing. Hallmarks include the sturdy box-shaped tower and asymmetrical exterior with complex heart-shaped floral motifs in the large chancel window. To give height to the small and peaceful interior, he used an open-arched timber ceiling, enhanced by carved detail and an oak pulpit decorated with tulip-form relief. It isn't the most unified of structures, but shows the flexibility of his distinctive style.

The spectre of limited budgets was to haunt Mackintosh throughout his career, and he never had the chance to design and construct with complete freedom. However, these constraints didn't manage to dull his creativity, as demonstrated by the **Scotland Street School** of 1904, near the Burrell Collection, (see p.199). Here, the two main stairways that frame the entrance are lit by glass-filled bays that protrude from the building. It is his most symmetrical work, with a whimiscal nod to history in the Scots Baronial conical tower roofs and sandstone building material.

Mackintosh's forceful personality and originality did not endear him to construction workers – he would frequently change his mind or add details at the last minute, often running a budget overboard. This lost him the support of local builders and architects, despite being admired on the continent, and prompted him to move to Suffolk in 1914, to escape the "philistines" of Glasgow and to re-evaluate his achievements. He now made use of his natural ability to draw flora and fauna, often in botanical detail and coloured with delicate watercolour washes. Whilst living in Port Vendres in 1923–27, on the Mediterranean side of the Franco-Spanish border, he produced a series of still lifes and landscape works which express something of his architectural style. Here, houses and rocks are painted in precise detail with a massive solidity and geometric form, and bold colours unite the patterned texture of the landscape, within an eerie stillness unbroken by human activity. These are a final flowering of his creative talent, a delicate contrast to the massive legacy of stonework left behind in the city that he loved.

of pricey, highly fashionable shops, the whole place set to a soothing background of classical music.

At the northern end of Buchanan Street, where it intersects with the eastern end of Sauchiehall Street, lies the £30-million **Royal Concert Hall**, given a prime city perspective but failing miserably to excite much attention. It looks like a hybrid of a car park and a power station, with three huge flagpoles protruding to proclaim that this is, in fact, a building of note. The showpiece hall plays host to world-class musical events, while the lobbies are used for temporary art exhibitions. These can be seen for free, or you can take a guided tour of the huge hall and its backstage areas (Tues & Thurs 2pm, Sat 11am; ☎332 6633; £1.50). It is a little-known fact that Glasgow runs second in the UK to London in terms of retail spending, so with this in mind developers are currently extending the East wing of the concert hall to provide a massive, swanky venue for upmarket outlets, due for completion in early 1998.

Sauchiehall Street runs in a straight line west past some unexciting shopping malls, leading to a few of the city's most interesting sights. Charles Rennie Mackintosh fans should head for the **Willow Tea Rooms**, at 217 Sauchiehall St (above a jewellery shop), a faithful reconstruction (opened in 1980 after over fifty years of closure) on the site of the 1904 original, which was created by the architect for Kate Cranston, one of his few contemporary supporters in the city. Everything from the fixtures and fittings right down to the teaspoons and menu cards were designed by Mackintosh. Taking inspiration from the word *Sauchiehall*, which means "avenue of willow", he chose the willow leaf as a theme to unify the whole structure from the tables to the mirrors and the ironwork. The motif is most apparent in the stylized linear panels of the bow window which continues into the intimate dining room as if to surround the sitter, like a willow grove, and is echoed in the distinctively high-backed silver-and-purple chairs. These elongated forms were used to enhance the small space and demonstrates Mackintosh's superb ability to fuse function with decoration. Tea is served here from 9.30am until 5pm (see p.201 for review).

A couple of footsteps west are the **McLellan Galleries**, 270 Sauchiehall St (Mon & Wed–Sat 10am–5pm, Sun noon–5pm; charges for some exhibitions), carefully restored after a severe fire in 1985. Despite its inauspicious frontage, inside the building is as soothing an example of classical architecture as anywhere in the city. A grand staircase sweeps you up into the main exhibition space, lit naturally by beautiful pedimented windows. There is no permanent display; the McLellan specializes in imaginative touring and temporary exhibitions, many of which have local themes – in recent years, anything from new Glaswegian art to an eccentric display of the city's rubbish, and in 1996 the biggest ever exhibition of Mackintosh's life and work. For relentlessly avant-garde art and culture, stroll down the same side of Sauchiehall Street to no. 350 and the **Centre for Contemporary Arts** (Mon–Sat 11am–6pm, Sun noon–5pm; free), with its eclectically internationalist exhibitions and performances, trendy café and bar that stays open till late (Mon–Wed till 11pm, Thurs–Sat till midnight, Sun till 7pm).

Glasgow School of Art

Rising above Sauchiehall Street to the north is one of the city centre's steepest hills, where Dalhousie and Scott streets veer up to Renfrew Street. Here, at no. 167, you'll find Charles Rennie Mackintosh's **Glasgow School of Art** (guided tours Mon–Fri 11am & 2pm, Sat 10.30am; extra tours May–Sept; booking advised; ☎353 4526; £3.50), one of the most prestigious in the country, with such notable alumni as artists Robert Colquhoun and Robert Macbryde and, more recently, Steven Campbell, Ken Currie and actor Robbie Coltrane. Widely considered to be the pinnacle of Mackintosh's work, the school is a characteristically angular building of warm sandstone which, due to financial constraints, had to be constructed in two sections (1897–99 and 1907–09). There's a clear change in the architect's style from the earlier severity of the mock-Baronial east wing to the softer lines of the western half.

The only way to see the school is by taking one of the student-led daily guided tours, the extent of which are dependent on curricular activities. You can, however, be sure of seeing at least some of the differences between the two halves and a handful of the most impressive rooms. All over the school, from the roof to the stairwells, Mackintosh's unique touches – light Oriental reliefs, tall-backed chairs and stylized Celtic illuminations – recur like leitmotivs. Even before entering the building up the gently curving stairway, you cannot fail to be struck by the soaring height of the north-facing windows, which light the art studios and were designed, in the architect's inimitable style, to combine aesthetics with practicality.

In the main entrance hall, the school shop sells tour tickets and a good selection of Mackintosh books, posters and cards. Hanging in the hall stairwell is the artist's highly personal wrought-iron version of the "bird, bell, tree, ring and fish" legend of St Mungo. You'll see excellent examples of his early furniture in the tranquil **Mackintosh Room**, flooded with soft, natural light, while the **Furniture Gallery**, tucked up in the eaves, shelters an Aladdin's cave of designs that weren't able to be housed elsewhere in the school – numerous tall-backed chairs, a semicircular settle designed for the Willow Tea Rooms, domino tables, a chest of drawers with highlighted silver panels and two bedroom suites. Around the room are mounted building designs including the House for an Art Lover, which Mackintosh submitted to a German competition in 1901. This building – which never saw the light of day during his lifetime – was recently constructed exactly to Mackintosh's specifications and now stands in the South Side's Bellahouston Park, providing offices and study areas for the Glasgow School of Art, with rooms open for public viewing.

You can peer down from the Furniture Gallery into the school's most spectacular room, the glorious two-storey **Library** below. Here, sombre oak panelling is set against angular lights adorned with primary colours, dangling down in seemingly random clusters. The dark bookcases sit precisely in their fitted alcoves, while of the furniture, the most unusual feature is the central periodical desk, whose oval central strut displays perfect and quite beautiful symmetry.

The Tenement House

Just a few hundred yards northwest of the School of Art – albeit on the other side of the sheer hill that rises and falls down to Buccleuch Street – is the **Tenement House** at no. 145 (March–Oct daily 2–5pm; Nov–Feb by appointment only; NTS; £2.80). This is the perfectly preserved home of the habitually hoarding Agnes Toward, who moved here with her mother in 1911, changing nothing and throwing very little out until she was hospitalized in 1965. On the ground floor, the NTS has constructed a fascinating display on the development of the humble tenement block as the bedrock of urban Scottish housing, with a display of relics – ration books, letters, bills, holiday snaps and so forth – from Miss Toward's life. Upstairs you have to ring the doorbell to enter the living quarters, which give every impression of still being inhabited, with a roaring hearth and range, kitchen utensils, recess beds, framed religious tracts and sewing machine all untouched. The only major change since Miss Toward left has been the reinstallation of the flickering gas lamps she would have used in the early days.

The Piping Centre

Behind the hulking Royal Scottish Academy for Music and Drama, the immaculate **Piping Centre**, at 30–34 McPhater St, prides itself on being a national centre for the promotion of the infamous bagpipe. Equipped with rehearsal rooms, performance halls, conference centre, accommodation, museum and an attractive café, it is a meeting place for fans and performers from all over the world. For the casual visitor, the **museum** (daily 10.30am–4.30pm; £1.50) is of most interest, with a collection of instruments and artefacts from the fourteenth century to the present day. Headsets provide a taped commentary with musical examples at relevant stages. The commentary is available in a number of languages (Gaelic included) and the museum shop contains a stack of related material from tapes and videos to manuscripts and piping accessories.

The West End

The urbane veneer of the **West End**, an area which contains many of the city's premier museums, seems a galaxy away from Glasgow's industrial image. In the 1800s, the city's focus moved west as wealthy merchants established huge estates away from the soot and grime of city life, and in 1870 the ancient university was moved from its cramped home near the cathedral to a spacious new site overlooking the River Kelvin. Elegant housing swiftly followed, the Kelvingrove Art Gallery was built to house the 1888 International Exhibition, and in 1896 the Glasgow District Subway – today's Underground – started its circuitous shuffle from here to the city centre.

The hub of life in this part of Glasgow is **Byres Road**, running down from the straight Great Western Road past Hillhead Underground station. Shops, restaurants, cafés, some enticing pubs and hordes of roving young people, including thousands of students, give the area a sense of style. Glowing red sandstone tenements and graceful terraces provide a suitably upmarket backdrop to this cosmopolitan district.

Straddling the banks of the cleaned-up River Kelvin, the slopes, trees and statues of **Kelvingrove Park** are framed by a backdrop of the Gothic towers and turrets of **Glasgow University** and the **Kelvingrove Museum and Art Gallery**, off Argyle Street in the park.

Kelvingrove Museum and Art Gallery

Founded on donations from the city's chief industrialists, the huge, red-brick fantasy castle of **Kelvingrove Museum and Art Gallery** (Mon–Sat 10am–5pm, Sun 11am–5pm; free) is a brash statement of Glasgow's nineteenth-century self-confidence. On the ground floor, a fairly dusty hall contains the **Scottish Natural History** display, where local and global events are marked in the rings of a slice of ancient Douglas fir. On the opposite side of the main hall sits an unremarkable exhibition of European and Scottish weapons.

However, it's the art collections, the majority of which are upstairs, that are of most interest. **Room 22** contains some superb Italian paintings, notably Botticelli's delicate *Annunciation*, Giorgione's rich and vibrant *The Adulteress Brought Before Christ*, and some fervent landscapes by Salvator Rosa. Further down the gallery, Rembrandt's symbolic portrayal of a crucified ox stands out darkly, along with his quiet portrait *The Man in Armour*. Continuing from the seventeenth century and leading up to the early nineteenth century, **Room 23** contains predominantly British work. The space is dominated by two paintings by Jacob More, a Scottish artist who worked in the elegiacally classical style of Claude; the spread of classicism in eighteenth-century Europe is also attested by pieces such as *Vestals Attending the Sacred Fire*, by David Allan, whose figures languish amongst ancient temples.

Room 24 is filled with quality work from Scottish and European artists from the eighteenth century to the early twentieth century. Among the biggest non-British names here are Courbet, Corot, Degas and Monet. As for the Scots, the angelic face of *Mrs William Urquhart* is testimony to Sir Henry Raeburn's skill as an informal portraitist, while the meticulous detail of *South and North Western View from Ben Lomond* – a dramatic pair of paintings by John Knox – makes a striking contrast with Turner's radiant *Modern Italy – The Pifferari*, a picture that glows amongst the dark glens and sombre portraits. Catching up on the twentieth century, **Room 26** contains such con-

THE GLASGOW BOYS

The traditional rivalry between Glasgow and Edinburgh was alive and kicking in the late nineteenth century when the Royal Scottish Academy resolutely refused to accept the work of any west coast artist. That was soon to change, however, when in the 1870s a group of painters formed a loose association, centred in Glasgow, that was to invest Scottish painting with a fresh approach inspired by contemporary European trends (in particular the *plein air* painting of the Impressionists). Derisively nicknamed "The Glasgow Boys", only in later years did their work come to be seen as quintessentially Glaswegian and reclaimed with considerable pride. The group was dominated by five men – Guthrie, Lavery, Hornel, Henry and Crawhall – who, despite coming from very different backgrounds, all violently rejected eighteenth-century conservatism that spawned little other than sentimental, anecdotal renditions of Scottish history peopled by "poor but happy" families, in a detailed, exacting manner. They called these paintings "**gluepots**" for their use of megilp, an oily substance that gave the work the brown patina of age, and instead began to experiment with colour, liberally splashing paint across the canvas. The content and concerns of the paintings, often showing peasant life and work, were as offensive as their style to the effete art establishment, as until then most of Glasgow's public art collections had been accrued by wealthy tobacco lords and merchants.

Sir James Guthrie spent his summers in the countryside, surrounded by like-minded artists, painting in the outdoors and observing everyday life. Instead of happy peasants, his work shows individuals staring out of the canvas, detached and unrepentant, painted with rich tones but without undue attention to detail or the play of light. Typical of his finest work during the 1880s, *A Highland Funeral* (on display in St Mungo's Museum; see p.188) was hugely influential on the rest of the group, who found inspiration in its restrained emotional content, colour and unaffected realism. Seeing it persuaded **Sir John Lavery**, then studying in France, to return to Glasgow. Lavery was eventually to become an internationally popular society portraitist, his subtle use of paint revealing his debt to Whistler, but his earlier work, of the middle class at play, is filled with fresh colour and figures in motion. In 1888 he documented the Glasgow International Exhibition and went on to paint a number of large-scale works, one of which – a massive depiction of Queen Victoria's visit to Glasgow – hangs in the Royal Concert Hall.

Rather than a realistic aesthetic, an interest in colour and decoration united the work of friends **George Henry** and **E.A. Hornel**. The predominance of colour, pattern and design in Henry's *Galloway Landscape*, for example, is remarkable, while their joint work *The Druids* (both on display in the Kelvingrove; see p.192), in thickly applied impasto, is full of Celtic symbolism. In 1893 both artists set off for Japan, funded by Alexander Reid and later William Burrell, where their work used vibrant tone and texture for expressive effect and took Scottish painting to the forefront of European trends.

Newcastle-born **Joseph Crawhall** was, by all accounts, a reserved and quiet individual. He combined superb draughtsmanship and simplicity of line with a photographic memory to create watercolours of an outstanding naturalism and freshness. Unlike the forceful Guthrie and Lavery, who craved wealth and success, Crawhall was a shy man who enjoyed hunting and riding in the countryside and was quite happy to paint delicate animal studies throughout his career. William Burrell was an important patron, and a good collection of his works resides at the Burrell Collection.

The school reached its height by 1900, and once its members had achieved the artistic respect – and for some the commercial success – they craved, it began to disintegrate and did not outlast World War I. However, the influence of their work cannot be under-estimated, shaking the foundations of the artistic elite and inspiring the next generation of Edinburgh painters now known as "Colourists".

tinental luminaries as Bonnard, Pissarro, Vuillard, Braque and Derain, and more excellent work by undervalued Scottish artists. *The Pink Parasol* by JD Fergusson, for example, reveals what he learned from Matisse and Cézanne, and the grittier *Two Children* by Joan Eardley makes use of collage and thick paint to convey the energy of Gorbals children in the 1960s.

In the east wing, **The Scottish Gallery** is entirely devoted to native artists. Here Raeburn's magnificent *Mr and Mrs Robert N. Campbell of Kailzie* almost overwhelms the room, the golden, life-size figures emerging from the loosely brushed background. A statue of Sir Walter Scott gazes upon a row of paintings depicting the romantic, Victorian view of Scotland, as exemplified by Horatio McCullochs' depiction of *Loch Maree*. On the far wall hangs the famous portrait of *Robert Burns* by Alexander Naysmyth, now found on biscuit tins the world over.

The **Glasgow 1900** room is dedicated to the era when Charles Rennie Mackintosh was in his prime: this marvellous collection of furniture is crowned by a pair of domino tables and chairs designed by Mackintosh for the tearooms of Miss Cranston (see p.190). The **Glasgow Boys** are well represented, with the decoratively patterned *In a Japanese Garden* by George Henry balanced by the bovine tranquillity of Crawhall's *Landscape with Cattle*. Works by Guthrie, Hornel and Lavery are also on display. Modern works by predominantly Scottish artists line the walls of **Room 16**. Brutish fishermen stare out from John Bellany's *The Fishers* to challenge traditional depictions of seamen happily mending nets on peaceful shores, whereas the austere beauty of *Edge of Storm, Turtle Lake* by James Morrison evokes the grandeur of a dramatic northern day. Bringing things right down to earth, a fibreglass replica of a chunk of Glasgow pavement, created by the Boyle family, encapsulates their dedication to revealing the landscapes that lie ignored beneath our feet.

The Transport Museum

The twin-towered **Kelvin Hall** is home to the excellent and enormous city **Transport Museum**, a collection of trains, cars, trams, circus caravans and prams, along with an array of old Glaswegian ephemera (Mon & Wed–Sat 10am–5pm, Sun 11am–5pm; free). Just inside the Bunhouse Road entrance, "Kelvin Street" is a re-created 1950s cobbled street featuring an old Italian coffee shop, a butcher (complete with plastic meat joints dangling in the window), a bakery (where labels claim that the buns were provided by the university's taxidermy department) and an old-time Underground station. A cinema shows fascinating films – mostly on themes based loosely around transport – of old Glasgow life, with crackly footage of Sauchiehall Street packed solid with trams and shoppers and hordes of pasty-faced Glaswegians setting off for their annual jaunts down the coast. The Clyde Room displays intricate models of ships forged in Glasgow's yards – everything from tiny schooners to ostentatious ocean liners such as the *QE2*.

Glasgow University and the Hunterian bequests

Dominating the West End skyline, the gloomy turreted tower of Glasgow's **University**, designed by Sir Gilbert Scott in the mid-nineteenth century, overlooks the glades of the River Kelvin (see "Glasgow architecture", p.184). Access to the main buildings and museums is from University Avenue, running east from Byres Road. In the dark neo-Gothic pile under the tower you'll find the **University Visitor Centre** (Mon–Sat 9.30am–5pm), which, as well as giving information for potential students, distributes leaflets about the various university buildings and the statues around the campus.

Next door to the University Visitor Centre, the collection of the **Hunterian Museum** (Mon–Sat 9.30am–5pm; free), Scotland's oldest public museum dating back to 1807, was donated to the university by ex-student William Hunter, a pathologist and anatomist whose eclectic tastes form the basis of a fairly dry, but frequently diverting zoological and archeological museum. Exhibitions include Scotland's only dinosaur, a look at the Romans in Scotland – the furthest outpost of their massive empire – and a vast coin collection .

The Hunterian Art Gallery

On the other side of University Avenue is Hunter's more frequently visited bequest: the **Hunterian Art Gallery** (Mon–Sat 9.30am–5pm; free), best known for its works by James Abbott McNeill Whistler – only Washington DC has a larger collection. Whistler's breathy landscapes are less compelling than his portraits of women, which give his subjects a resolute strength in addition to their fey and occasionally winsome qualities: look out especially for the trio of full-length portraits, *Harmony of Flesh Colour and Black*, *Pink and Gold – the Tulip* and *Red and Black – the Fan*.

The gallery's other major collection is of nineteenth- and twentieth-century Scottish art, including the quasi-Impressionist Scottish landscapes of William McTaggart, a forerunner of the Glasgow Boys movement, represented here by Guthrie and Hornel. Taking the aims of this group one step further, the monumental dancing figures of J.D. Fergusson's *Les Eus* preside over a small collection of work by the Scottish Colourists, such as Peploe, Hunter and Cadell, who left a vibrant legacy of thickly textured, colourful landscapes and portraits. A small selection of French Impressionism includes works by Boudin and Pissarro, with Corot's soothing *Distant View of Corbeil* being a highlight from the Barbizon school.

A side gallery leads to the **Mackintosh House**, a re-creation of the interior of the now-demolished Glasgow home of Margaret and Charles Rennie Mackintosh. An introductory display contains photographs of the original house sliding irrevocably into terminal decay, from where you are led into an exquisitely cool interior that contains over sixty pieces of Mackintosh furniture on three floors. Among the highlights are the Studio Drawing Room, whose cream and white furnishings are bathed in expansive pools of natural light, and the Japanese-influenced guest bedroom in dazzling, monochrome geometrics.

The Botanic Gardens

At the top of Byres Road, where it meets the Great Western Road, is the main entrance to the **Botanic Gardens** (daily 7am–dusk; free). The best-known glasshouse here, the hulking, domed **Kibble Palace** (daily summer 10am–4.45pm; winter 10am–4.15pm), originally known as the Crystal Palace, was built in 1863 for wealthy landowner John Kibble's estate on the shores of Loch Long, where it stood for ten years, before he decided to transport it into Glasgow, drawing it up the Clyde on a vast raft pulled by a steamer. It remained for over two decades on this spot, used not as a greenhouse but as a Victorian pleasure palace, before the gardens' owners put a stop to the drunken revels that wreaked havoc with the lawns and plant beds. Today the palace is far more sedate, housing a damp, musty collection of swaying palms from around the world. The smell is much sweeter on entering the **Main Range glasshouse** (summer Mon–Fri 10am–4.45pm, Sat 1–4.45pm Sun noon–4.45pm; winter closes 4.15pm), home to lurid and blooming flowers and plants – including stunning orchids, cacti, ferns and tropical fruit – luxuriating in the humidity. Quite apart from the main glasshouses, the Botanic Gardens have some beautifully remote paths that weave and dive along the closely wooded banks of the gorged River Kelvin.

Scottish Exhibition and Conference Centre

Down by the riverside, fifteen minutes' walk from Kelvingrove Park – and not strictly part of the West End – is the harshly re-landscaped **Scottish Exhibition and Conference Centre (SECC)**. It was built in 1985 to kick-start the revival of the

Riverbank: two vast adjoining red and grey sheds that make a dutifully utilitarian venue for travelling fairs, mega-concerts and anonymous bars and cafés. However, a sparkling new conference building now overshadows the area. Nicknamed "the Armadillo", it resembles a poor man's version of the Sydney Opera House but nevertheless stands as an architectural landmark, giving a bit of character to the riverside. The gleaming hotel alongside, and the expensive restaurants in the nearby rotunda – one of two access shafts to a long-closed tunnel under the Clyde – are reasonably successful, but the rotunda's twin on the opposite bank, the **Dome of Discovery**, once a hands-on science museum and showpiece of the 1988 Glasgow Garden Festival site, is an example of what happens when the money runs out: when the festival ended, the gardens rotted and the museum closed. However, plans are afoot to turn the area into an office park, housing the new Scottish headquarters of the BBC, which will hopefully regenerate this forlorn area.

South of the Clyde

The southern bank of the Clyde, facing the city centre, is home to the notoriously deprived districts of **Govan**, a community yet to find its niche after the shipbuilding slump, and the **Gorbals**, synonymous with the razor gangs of old. On the southern side of Govan the vast bowl of **Ibrox**, home to the overwhelmingly Protestant Rangers football team, proudly displays the Union flag. This Unionist fortress was totally overhauled following the disaster on January 2, 1971, when 66 fans died after a match against bitter arch-rivals Celtic – a stand collapsed as hundreds of early-leavers stampeded back into the stadium after an unlikely last-minute goal.

Inner-city decay fades into altogether gentler and more salubrious suburbs, commonly referred to as **South Side**. These include Queen's Park, a residential area which is home to Hampden Park football stadium, and the rural landscape of **Pollok Park**, three miles southwest of the city centre, which contains two of Glasgow's major museums: the **Burrell Collection** and **Pollok House**. Buses #34 and #34A from Govan Underground station set down outside the gate nearest to the Burrell. Slightly further to walk is the route from the Pollokshaws West station (don't confuse with Pollokshields West), served by regular trains from Glasgow Central and nearby bus stops on the Pollokshaws Road: take Greater Glasgow buses #45, #48 or #57 from Union Street. However, as Pollok Park is only three miles from the city centre, a taxi to the Burrell is an inexpensive option. A further reason to venture south is to see the newest attraction on the Charles Rennie Mackintosh trail, the **House for an Art Lover**, in Bellahouston Park.

The Burrell Collection

The lifetime collection of shipping magnate Sir William Burrell (1861–1958), the outstanding **Burrell Collection** (Mon & Wed–Sat 10am–5pm, Sun 11am–5pm; free) is, for some, the principal reason for visiting Glasgow. Unlike many other art collectors, Sir William's only real criterion for buying a piece was whether he liked it or not, enabling him to buy many "unfashionable" works, which cost comparatively little, and subsequently proved their worth. He wanted to leave his collection of art, sculpture and antiquities for public display, but stipulated in 1943 that they should be housed "in a rural setting far removed from the atmospheric pollution of urban conurbations, not less than 16 miles from the Royal Exchange". For decades, these conditions proved too difficult to meet, with few open spaces available and a pall of industrial smoke ruling out any city site. However, by the late 1960s, after the nationwide Clean Air Act had reduced pollution, and the vast land of Pollok Park, previously privately owned, had been donated to the city, plans began for a new, purpose-built gallery, which finally

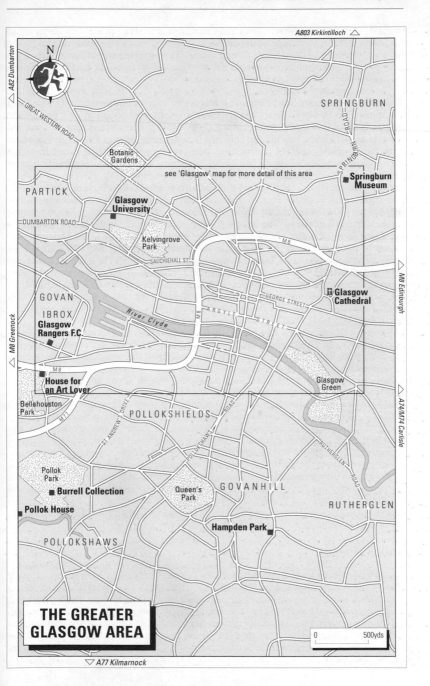

A803 Kirkintilloch

A82 Dumbarton

N

GREAT WESTERN ROAD

SPRINGBURN

Botanic
Gardens

see 'Glasgow' map for more detail of this area

PARTICK

**Springburn
Museum**

**Glasgow
University**

DUMBARTON ROAD

Kelvingrove
Park

SAUCHIEHALL ST.

M8

M8 Edinburgh

GOVAN

GEORGE STREET

**Glasgow
Cathedral**

IBROX
**Glasgow
Rangers F.C.**

M8 Greenock

River Clyde

ARGYLE

STREET

M8

M8

**House for
an Art Lover**

Glasgow
Green

Bellahouston
Park

M77

ST ANDREW'S DRIVE

POLLOKSHIELDS

POLLOKSHAWS ROAD

A74/M74 Carlisle

RUTHERGLEN ROAD

Pollok
Park

Burrell Collection

Queen's
Park

GOVANHILL

RUTHERGLEN

Pollok House

POLLOKSHAWS

Hampden Park

**THE GREATER
GLASGOW AREA**

0   500yds

A77 Kilmarnock

opened in 1983. Today the simplicity and clean lines of the Burrell building are its greatest assets, with large picture windows giving sweeping views over woodland and serving as a tranquil backdrop to the objects inside. The sculpture and antiques are on the ground level, arranged in six sections that overlap and occasionally backtrack, while a mezzanine above displays most of the paintings.

On entering the building, the most striking piece, by virtue of sheer size, is the Warwick Vase, a huge bowl containing fragments of a second-century AD vase from Hadrian's Villa in Tivoli. Next to it are the first of a series of sinewy and naturalistic bronze casts of Rodin sculptures, among them *The Age of Bronze*, *A Call to Arms* and the infamous *Thinker*. Beyond the entrance hall, on three sides of a courtyard, a trio of dark and sombre panelled rooms have been re-erected in faithful detail from the Burrells' Hutton Castle home, their heavy tapestries, antique furniture and fireplaces displaying the same eclectic taste as the rest of the museum.

From the courtyard, leading up to the picture windows, the **Ancient Civilizations** collection – a catch-all title for Greek, Roman and earlier artefacts – includes an exquisite mosaic Roman cockerel from the first century BC and a 4000-year-old Mesopotamian lion's head. The bulk of it is Egyptian, however, with rows of inscrutable gods and kings. Nearby, also illuminated by enormous windows, the **Oriental Art** forms nearly one-quarter of the complete collection, ranging from Neolithic jades through bronze vessels and Tang funerary horses to cloisonné. The earliest piece, from around the second century BC, is a lovable earthenware watchdog from the Han Dynasty, but most dominant is the serene fifteenth-century *Lohan* (disciple of Buddha), who sits cross-legged and contemplative up against the window and the trees of Pollok Park. Near Eastern art is also represented, in a dazzling array of turquoise- and cobalt-decorated jugs, and a swathe of intricate carpets.

Burrell considered his **Medieval and Post-Medieval European Art**, which encompasses silverware, glass, textiles and sculpture, to be the most valuable part of his collection. Ranged across a maze of small galleries, the most impressive sections are the sympathetically lit stained glass – note the homely image of a man warming his toes by the fire – and the numerous tapestries, among them the fifteenth-century riotous *Peasants Hunting Rabbits with Ferrets*. Among the church art and reliquary are simple thirteenth-century Spanish wooden images and cool fifteenth-century English alabaster, while a trio of period interiors span the period from the Gothic era to the eighteenth century. This is interrupted by a selection from Burrell's vast art collection, the highlight of which is one of Rembrandt's evocative early self-portraits.

Upstairs, the cramped and comparatively gloomy mezzanine is probably the least satisfactory section of the gallery, not the best setting for its sparkling array of paintings. The selection incongruously leaps from a small gathering of fifteenth-century religious works to Géricault's darkly dynamic *Prancing Grey Horse* and Degas's thoughtful and perceptive *Portrait of Émile Duranty*. Pissarro, Manet and Boudin are also represented, along with some exquisite watercolours by Glasgow Boy Joseph Crawhall, revealing his accurate and tender observations of the animal world.

Pollok House

A quarter of a mile away down rutted tracks lies the lovely eighteenth-century **Pollok House** (June–Sept Mon & Wed–Sat 10am–5pm, Sun 11am–5pm; free), the manor of the Pollok Park estate and once home of the Maxwell family, local lords and owners of most of southern Glasgow until well into this century. Designed by William Adam in the mid-1700s, the house is typical of its age: graciously light and sturdily built, looking out onto the pristine raked and parterre gardens, whose stylized daintiness contrasts with the heavy Spanish paintings inside, among them two El Greco portraits and works by Murillo and Goya.

The house itself is, however, like so many stately homes: a little sterile, a series of plush period rooms whose ornate furniture you view from behind red sash cordons. Only the servants' quarters downstairs capture the imagination – a virtually untouched labyrinth of tiled Victorian parlours and corridors that includes a good tearoom in the old kitchen.

Scotland Street School Museum of Education

A mile and a half northeast of the Burrell Collection is another great Mackintosh monument, the **Scotland Street School Museum of Education** (Mon & Wed–Sat 10am–5pm, Sun 2–5pm; free), slap opposite the Shields Road Underground station. Opened as a school in 1906 to Mackintosh's distinctively angular design, it closed in 1979, since when it has been refurbished as an entertaining education museum, housing a fascinating collection of memorabilia related to life in the classroom. There are reconstructed classrooms from the Victorian, Edwardian, World War II and 1960s eras, as well as changing rooms, a primitive domestic science room and re-creations of a headmaster's office, the school matron's sanitorium and a janitor's lair. If you visit on a weekday during term time, you may stumble on a period lesson going on with local schoolkids struggling to understand their ink blotters, gas masks and archly unsympathetic teachers. Even the faint smell of antiseptic will conjure up memories of scuffed knees and playground tantrums.

House for an Art Lover

Northwest of Pollok Park lies the smaller Bellahouston Park, home to Charles Rennie Mackintosh's **House for an Art Lover** (April–Sept daily 10am–5pm; Oct–March Sat & Sun 10am–5pm; £3.50), which was designed in 1901 for a German competition but not built until nearly a century later. In 1996, after years of detailed research and painstaking work, the building opened as a centre for Glasgow School of Art postgraduate students, with a limited number of rooms open for public viewing. Upon entering, you can watch a video giving a detailed account of the building's construction, then pass into the delicate **Oval room**, intended for women to retire to after dinner. From here, a small corridor leads into the main **hallway**, where massive windows cast a cool light upon an area designed for large parties. In direct contrast, the dazzling, white **Music Room** has bow windows opening out to a large balcony, though the garden view is marred by an artificial ski slope. The **Dining Room** is decorated with darkened

---

CYCLING IN AND AROUND GLASGOW

Thanks to the efforts of the *Sustrans* group, it is now possible to cycle from Glasgow to Edinburgh, Loch Lomond, Paisley, Irvine, Ardrossan and Greenock. Combining converted railway lines, minor roads and the Forth and Clyde Canal, tracks allow cyclists to safely explore the Glasgow area avoiding the heaving main roads. Some of the paths through the smaller towns can be a little confusing, so pick up a route planner from the local tourist board, detailing the well-kept paths which are peppered with interpretative sculpture and informative panels. Bikes are carried free on Strathclyde Transport trains, and you may wish to make use of them one way, as some of the routes are over twenty miles long. If you want to take your bike on the train to Edinburgh, however, you have to book in advance and pay a £3 fee. Despite the number of bike shops in Glasgow, only a few rent out bikes; Dales, 150 Dobbies Loan (☎332 2705), has reasonable weekend rates, and can be found a block north from the Buchanan Street bus station. Conveniently placed close to the start of the Glasgow to Loch Lomond route, West End Cycles, at 16 Chancellor St (☎357 1344), offers cheaper daily and weekly rental.

stained wood and enhanced by some beautiful gesso tiles. On the ground floor, the café is dotted with massive sofas, which are particularly popular with locals on Sunday mornings. To reach the house, take the Underground to Cessnock station and turn right at Paisley Road West which runs up to the park. By train, get off at Dumbreck, cross the road and continue straight on until you reach the park.

Cafés, restaurants and pubs

Glasgow's renaissance has seen an explosion of fine restaurants and European-style bars and cafés, which, in addition to the input of its diverse and ethnically mixed population, make eating possibilities pretty wide.

The city's **restaurants** cover an impressively international spectrum – incorporating cuisines such as Catalan and Irish along with more familiar dishes from France, Italy, India and China. Traditional **Scottish cuisine** has become very trendy in recent years, with an upsurge in the number of outlets that serve local specialities and cover most price ranges. There are few exclusively **vegetarian** restaurants, but most places – especially around the Merchant City – have good, imaginative vegetarian choices.

For **budget food**, cafés range from the cheapest, greasiest cholesterol-hole through to bars offering reasonable snacks all day, and frequently into the evening. Unlike in staid Edinburgh, where a lot of places close on Sunday, most of Glasgow's restaurants are open seven days a week.

City centre

The **city centre** boasts the widest range of cuisines in Glasgow, including most of its Oriental and vegetarian restaurants. The **Merchant City** contains the largest concentration of designer brasseries and some very pricey restaurants, while **Buchanan** and **Sauchiehall streets** feature the big restaurant and fast-food chains.

Cafés, diners and pubs

Café Alba, 61 Otago St (☎337 2282). Situated just off Gibson Street, this popular café sells a good selection of vegetarian food and the best home baking in the west. Mon–Sat 10am–5pm. Inexpensive.

Café Gandolfi, 64 Albion St (☎552 6813). Trendy Merchant City café-bar with distinctive wooden interior, that serves good-quality soup, salads and fish dishes. Mon–Sat 9am–11pm, Sun noon–11.30pm. Moderate.

CCA Café Bar, 350 Sauchiehall St (☎332 7864). Relaxed café and bar, perfect for a quick lunch or a full blowout; its varied menu caters well for vegetarians.

Fratelli Sarti, 133 Wellington St (☎248 2228) and 121 Bath St (☎204 0440). Authentic and popular, the frantic Wellington Street café also has a deli (open 9am–6pm) serving delicious takeaway pizza and pastas. The Bath Street restaurant (next door) is larger with the same quality menu; both café and restaurant open daily 8am–10pm. Moderate.

Gay and Lesbian Café, 11 Dixon St (☎204 5418). The only café of its kind in Glasgow, this colourful and relaxed establishment, tucked in a side street behind the St Enoch Centre, has a varied menu that includes soups, salads and bagels, and a three course special in the evening. Food served Mon–Sat 10am–midnight, Sun 11am–6pm. Inexpensive.

Gallery of Modern Art Café, Queen St (☎221 7484). Worth visiting for the mural alone and the view over the rooftops. Serves light lunches – the salads are good – and has a more extensive evening menu Thurs–Sat. Mon–Wed 10am–4.30pm, Thurs–Sat 10am–4.30pm & 6.30–10pm, Sun 11am–4.30pm. Moderate.

Granary, 82 Howard St. Well situated near the St Enoch Centre, an affordable café serving quiches, lasagne and other vegetarian favourites complemented by a good variety of salads. Open daily till 5pm. Inexpensive.

Junkanoo, 111 Hope St, near Central station (☎248 7102). Boisterous Latin American bar that successfully combines a pleasant drinking atmosphere with great food – tapas and chilli loom large. Mon–Thurs open till 11pm, Fri & Sat till midnight, Sun 6.30–10.30pm. Inexpensive.

Kings Café, 71 Elmbank St, off Sauchiehall Street. Good fish-and-chip shop with seating at the back, serving generous helpings of traditional greasy fare and quality pasta to boot. Mon–Fri 7am–midnight, Sat 7am–5am, Sun 10am–midnight. Inexpensive.

October Café, top floor, Princes Square Shopping Centre. A variety of different dishes, including some vegetarian options, served on the wraparound verandah peering down into the swish designer-shopping paradise. Mon–Sat 11am–midnight, Sun noon–5pm. Moderate.

Pipers' Tryst, 30–34 McPhater St (☎353 0220). Decorated with their very own tartan, this small, bright café in the Piping Centre uses fresh produce to create a variety of Scottish dishes including a hearty all-day breakfast. Daily 10.30am–9pm. Inexpensive.

Sloans, Argyll Arcade, off Argyle Street. Huge pub-cum-restaurant serving well-cooked food such as pasta and steaks in surroundings that become increasingly like a riotous Victorian gin palace the further up the building you rise. Mon–Sat restaurant noon–4.30pm, bar noon–8pm. Inexpensive.

13th Note, 80 Glassford St (☎553 1638). This Merchant City bar stands out for its all-vegan menu from vegeburgers to chilli with daily specials on an international theme. Food served daily noon–7pm. Inexpensive.

Tron Theatre, 63 Trongate (☎552 8587). Two atmospheres prevail here – the trendy wrought-iron café-bar caters for the quick-lunch and coffee crowd (daily 9.30am–10.30pm), while the old-fashioned Victorian bar is perfect for a laid-back lunch or dinner. Mon–Thurs noon–3pm & 5–10.30pm, Fri & Sat noon–10.30pm, Sun 10.30am–10.30pm. Inexpensive.

Vegville Diner, 93 St Georges Rd (☎333 1771). Good quality and value for money is the name of the game in this colourful diner. The menu consists of innovative and tasty dishes with several Japanese options. Mon 10am–7pm, Tues & Wed 10am–10pm, Thurs–Sat 10am–11pm. Inexpensive.

Wee Curry Shop, 7 Buccleuch St. Tiny Indian cafe, serving reasonably priced food, with an open kitchen so you can watch the cooking while you wait. Mon–Sat noon–2pm & 5.30–10.30pm. Inexpensive.

Willow Tea Rooms, 217 Sauchiehall St. Refined elevenses, lunches and afternoon tea in Mackintosh-designed splendour. Open till 5pm. Inexpensive.

Chinese

Amber Regent, 50 West Regent St (☎331 1655). Decisively Western decoration matched with authentic Chinese food characterizes this small, quality restaurant. The menu is extensive with half-price meals every Monday and Tuesday evening. Mon–Fri noon–2.15pm & 5.30–11pm, Sat noon–midnight. Moderate.

Blossom, 80 Miller St, Merchant City (☎221 1292). Chinese restaurant with a well-priced and wide-ranging menu including a good number of vegetarian options. Mon–Sat noon–2.30pm & 4.30–10.30pm. Moderate.

Canton Express, 407 Sauchiehall St, opposite the Garage nightclub. Open from noon until 4am every day, this formica palace is popular with shoppers and late-night clubbers alike, tempted by the Chinese and Sichuan fast food and cheap prices. Inexpensive.

Ho Wong, 82 York St, just off Argyle Street west of Central station (☎221 3550). Secluded restaurant offering a top-class range of Cantonese and Sichuan food; well worth the high prices. Mon–Sat noon–2pm & 6–11.30pm, Sun 6–11.30pm. Expensive.

Loon Fung, 417 Sauchiehall St (☎332 1477). Great dim sum but lacking in vegetarian options. Daily noon–11.30pm. Moderate.

Indian

Kama Sutra, 331 Sauchiehall St (☎332 0055). Thick velvet curtains, wrought ironwork and a designer interior give a new twist to the Glaswegians' love of curry. An unusual and wide-ranging menu including dishes from the northeast frontier plus low-fat, healthy options. Mon–Thurs noon–midnight, Fri & Sat noon–1am, Sun 5pm–midnight. Moderate.

Taj Mahal, 573–581 Sauchiehall St (☎226 5030). Pleasant restaurant serving huge portions of delicious Indian food – check out the enormous nan breads. Mon–Thurs noon–2.30pm & 5pm–midnight, Fri & Sat noon–midnight, Sun 2pm–midnight. Moderate.

Italian

Fire Station, 33 Ingram St (☎552 2929). Merchant City restaurant housed in a huge old fire station, dating from 1900 and walled with municipal cast-off marble tiling. The excellent menu, especially the pasta and the indulgent puddings, is good value, and the half-price pasta from 5pm to 7pm is a real bargain. Mon–Thurs noon–2.30pm & 5–9.30pm, Fri noon–2.30pm & 5–10.30pm, Sat noon–10.30pm, Sun 11am–9pm. Moderate.

O'Sole Mio, 32 Bath St. A superb, and easily affordable, city-centre restaurant for unusual pasta dishes, as well as pizzas from their log-fired oven. Go from 5pm to 6.30pm for extra-cheap food. Mon–Thurs noon–2.30pm & 5–11pm, Fri noon–2.30pm & 5pm–midnight, Sat noon–midnight. Moderate.

Paperino's, 283 Sauchiehall St (☎332 3800). Friendly and comfortable restaurant serving pizza and pasta dishes that are popular with students and shoppers alike. Mon–Thurs noon–3pm & 5–11pm, Fri noon–3pm, 5pm–midnight, Sat noon–midnight, Sun 5–11pm. Moderate.

Malaysian

Mata Hari, 17 W Princes St, Charing Cross (☎332 9789). Deservedly popular Malaysian restaurant with some unusual – and highly spicy – dishes on the moderately priced menu. Mon–Thurs & Sun 5.30–11pm, Fri & Sat 5.30–11.30pm. Moderate.

Mexican

Cantina Del Rey, 6 Kings Court (☎552 4044). Behind the St Enoch Centre in a converted railway vault, this spacious restaurant serves authentic Mexican cuisine including fajitas, burritos and frozen margaritas at reasonable prices. Open Sun–Thurs 5–10pm, Fri & Sat till 11pm. Moderate.

Scottish

Babbity Bowster, 16–18 Blackfriars St (☎552 5055). Atmospheric and popular Merchant City bar on the ground level serving excellent Scottish food – anything from hearty broths to haggis, salmon and kippers. The restaurant upstairs is pricier, and more sedate, serving venison, fresh fish and the like. Open Mon–Sat till 10.30pm. Expensive.

Buttery, 652 Argyle St (☎221 8188). A fine, if slightly snooty, restaurant serving lavish, imaginative and expensive food, with lots of tarted-up traditional Scottish dishes. Open Mon–Sat till 10.30pm. Very expensive.

City Merchant, 97 Candleriggs (☎553 1577). Popular restaurant in Merchant City that serves good food using Scottish produce from Dingwall haggis to fresh lobster. Open Mon–Sat till 10.30pm. Moderate.

Rab Ha's, 83 Hutcheson St (☎553 1545). Underneath this popular Merchant City bar lies a restaurant offering a version of the "Auld Alliance" with a combination of French and Scottish cuisine at reasonable prices. Daily 5.30–10.30pm. Expensive.

Rogano, 11 Exchange Place, near Buchanan Street (☎248 4055). Although the food here is not solely Scottish, the *Rogano* is a Glasgow institution, an absolutely superb but shockingly expensive fish restaurant decked out as an authentic replica of the 1930s Cunard liner, the *Queen Mary*. *Café Rogano*, in the basement, is cheaper but not so deliciously ostentatious. Café Mon–Thurs noon–11pm, Fri & Sat noon–11.30pm, Sun noon–10pm; moderate. Restaurant Mon–Sat noon–2.30pm & 6.30–10.30pm, Sun noon–2.30pm & 6–10pm. Very expensive.

VEGETARIAN EATING

Vegetarians will not have a hard time finding something to eat in Glasgow. Most restaurants and cafés have at least one vegetarian dish on their menus, whilst those listed below are either exclusively vegetarian, or offer a very good selection of meat-free dishes.

Bay Tree, see p.203
Café Alba, see p.200
Granary, see p.200
The 13th Note, see p.201
Vegville Diner, see p.201

West End

Predominantly due to the large local student population, the **West End** is the best area for cheap, stylish restaurants and cafés, and bars serving food, especially around Hillhead Underground station on Byres Road; nearby, the restaurants along **Ashton Lane** dish out unreservedly good meals. On the other side of Byres Road from the station, **Ruthven Lane** is home to some lively restaurants well known for their cheap happy hours.

Cafés, diners and pubs

Back Alley, 8 Ruthven Lane (☎334 7165). Great burgers smothered in assorted toppings, washed down with good beer and finished off with calorific puddings. Try the Mon–Thurs early-evening happy hour. Mon–Sat noon–midnight, Sun 11am–11pm. Inexpensive.

Bar Miro, 36 Kelvingrove St (☎353 0475). Friendly, relaxed bar with two levels: downstairs for drinks with outdoor seating, and upstairs for food. Sun–Thurs noon–11pm, Fri & Sat noon–midnight. Inexpensive.

Bay Tree, 403 Great Western Rd (☎334 5895). This small café offers a decent selection of vegeburgers, salads and soups with good daily specials. Try the sugar-free cakes for a guilt-free pudding. Mon–Sat 8.30am–9pm, Sun 10am–8pm. Inexpensive.

California Gourmet, 291 Byres Rd. Daytime American ice cream and sandwich bar, full of students enjoying the delicious submarines with up to thirteen different fillings. Mon–Fri 8.30am–9.30pm, Sat 9am–9.30pm, Sun 10am–9.30pm. Inexpensive.

Chimmy Chungas, 499 Great Western Rd (☎334 0884). Loud and popular Tex-Mex bar and café that is good for anything from a light snack to a full blowout. Looking down into a large bar, this restaurant is deservedly popular with students taking advantage of lunchtime bargains. Food Mon–Thurs & Sun until 9.30pm, Fri & Sat 10.30pm. Inexpensive.

Grosvenor Café, 31 Ashton Lane. Small, traditional Italo-Scots café tucked behind Hillhead Underground station with a die-hard clientele, addicted to the no nonsense food (pizzas, fried food, burgers) served at unbelievably low prices. Slightly more upmarket menu in the evening, but lacking in quality. Mon & Sun open till 7pm, Tues–Sat till 11pm. Inexpensive.

Java Café, 152 Park Rd. In the West End's only Internet café you can work up a hunger surfing the Net, then tuck into a huge burger, salad or the all-day vegetarian breakfast. With excellent coffee to match, this is a hip place to hang out. Open until midnight. Inexpensive.

Jinty McGinty's, 21–29 Ashton Lane. Wood-panelled and frosted-glassed Irish pub that, as well as serving excellent stout, maintains a small menu of Irish favourites such as bacon and cabbage, steak and Guinness pie or hearty soups. Inexpensive.

Insomnia, 38–42 Woodlands Rd. This 24hr café lies conveniently on the path from the city centre to the West End and gets very crowded once the pubs close. Choose from soups, sandwiches, pastries and coffee to beat those late-night blues.

French

Cul de Sac, 44 Ashton Lane (☎334 4749). Informal, relaxed restaurant, underneath a resolutely popular bar. A small but assorted menu with delicious half-price crêpes and burgers during the week 5–7pm. Mon–Thurs & Sun noon–11pm, Fri & Sat noon–midnight. Moderate.

Indian

Ashoka, 19 Ashton Lane (☎357 5904). Moderately priced West End *dhosa* house and Indian restaurant, popular with local students. Mon–Sat noon–midnight, Sun 5pm–midnight. Moderate.

Mother India, 28 Westminster Terrace (☎221 1663). Good-quality food at affordable prices in the refreshingly laid-back surroundings of this friendly Indian restaurant. It's unlicensed, so bring your own alcohol; small corkage fee. Mon–Thurs noon–2.30pm & 5.30–11pm, Fri & Sat till 11.30pm, Sun 5.30–11pm. Inexpensive.

Murphy's Pakora Bar, 1287 Argyle St (☎334 1550). Even picky eaters are spoilt for choice here, with over seventy varieties of pakora available as a light snack or mountainous meal. Close to the Kelvingrove Museum and open daily till midnight. Inexpensive.

Italian

The Big Blue, 445 Great Western Rd (☎357 1038). Whitewashed walls and colourful upholstery characterize this low-level bar and restaurant that serves simple but tasty pasta dishes. Food served till 10pm Mon–Thurs & Sun, till 8.30pm Fri & Sat. Moderate.

Di Maggio's, 61 Ruthven Lane (☎334 8560). Extremely popular West End pizzeria and pasta joint, usually packed solid with bargain-hungry students. Frantic atmosphere with occasional live music. Open daily until midnight. Inexpensive.

Joe's Garage, 52 Bank St, next to Glasgow University Union (☎339 5407). Fairly predictable range of pizza and pasta, but the food is good, inexpensive and the imaginative chef's specials are worth a try. Mon–Fri noon–3pm & 5pm–midnight, Sat & Sun noon–midnight. Inexpensive.

Mexican

Salsa, 184 Dumbarton Rd (☎337 1416). A smaller version of the *Cantina Del Rey* (see p.202), this West End branch serves the same good-quality food in a colourful and laid-back atmosphere. Open Sun–Thurs till 10pm, Fri & Sat till 11pm. Moderate.

Scottish

Ubiquitous Chip, 12 Ashton Lane (☎334 5007). Splendid West End restaurant with a covered patio that resembles an indoor forest. Glasgow's most delicious Scottish food – game, seafood and local cheeses, and occasionally oatmeal ice cream and venison haggis. Daily till 11pm. Very expensive.

South Side

Although the range isn't as great as elsewhere, **South Side**, a quieter less studenty alternative to the centre or the West End, does offer Glasgow's only Middle Eastern eating place and a couple of Greek restaurants.

Cafés, diners and pubs

Boswell Hotel, 27 Mansionhouse Rd, Queen's Park (☎632 9812). Unusually cheap and extensive bar-food menu with some offbeat house specialities – a good complement to the wide selection of real ales. Regular live music; food until 9pm. Inexpensive.

Stoat and Ferret, 1534 Pollokshaws Rd (☎632 0161). Wood-panelled real-ale pub close to Pollok Park. Bar meals including steak pie, pasta and haggis until 6pm, baked potatoes and lighter snacks until 9pm. Inexpensive.

Greek

Athena Taverna, 780 Pollokshaws Rd, near Queen's Park train station. Busy Greek restaurant serving authentic dishes, with a popular real-ale bar. Mon–Sat noon–2.30pm & 5–10.30pm. Moderate.

Café Serghei, 67 Bridge St (☎429 1579). One of the few Greek restaurants in Glasgow, serving traditional food in a lively atmosphere. Mon–Sat noon–2.30pm & 5–11pm, Sun 6–11pm. Moderate.

Italian

Enzo's Trattoria Da Maria, 221 St Andrew's Rd, E Pollokshields (☎429 4604). Cosy, traditional trattoria in an unlikely setting, with a few imaginative Italian dishes tucked among the standard pastas and pizzas. Open Mon–Sat till 11pm. Moderate.

Di Maggio, 1038 Pollokshaws Rd, Queen's Park (☎632 4194). Less studenty than the West End branch, offering the same selection of gargantuan pizzas and hefty pasta dishes. Mon–Fri noon–2.30pm & 5pm–midnight, Sat noon–midnight, Sun 12.30pm–midnight. Inexpensive.

Middle Eastern

Prince Armany's, 7 Clyde Place (☎420 6660). Tucked under the railway bridge near Bridge Street, this restaurant offers Middle Eastern food such as lamb kebabs and delicate vegetable stews served with couscous or deliciously light Arabian bread. The pre-theatre menu, 5–7pm, is a real bargain. Tues–Sun 5pm–midnight. Inexpensive.

Scottish

Ewington, at the *Ewington Hotel*, 132 Queen's Drive (☎423 1152). Facing Queen's Park, this sedate suburban hotel has a cellar restaurant whose very pink and flouncy decor is compensated for by the fine mix of traditional Scottish and continental cuisine. Food daily 6–8.45pm. Expensive.

Pubs and bars

Not so many years ago, Glasgow's rough image was inextricably associated with its **pubs**, widely thought of as no-go areas for any visitor. Although much of this reputation was exaggerated, there was an element of truth in it. Nowadays, however, you're just as likely to spend an evening in a succession of open and airy café-bars as in a dark, dangerous, nicotine-stained pub. The centre has an admirable range of reliable places to drink; if you tire of the glossy **Merchant City**, head for the **East End**, where a fair number of local spit-and-sawdust establishments make a welcome change. All in all, though, the liveliest area (once again) has to be the **West End**, its good cross section of pubs and bars matching its great restaurants.

> Inevitably there will be some overlap between bars, cafés and restaurants, with many pubs serving good food, restaurants having good bars, and cafés being lively places to drink. If a pub serves particularly good food, we have included it in our eating section; conversely, if we recommend it for its convivial drinking atmosphere, rather than its food, we have included it in the pubs and bars section.

City centre

Babbity Bowster, 16–18 Blackfriars St. Lively hangout at the heart of the Merchant City.

Bargo, Albion Street. Winner of the 1996 Pub Design Award with a spacious wood and stainless-steel interior, where the local Merchant City crowd and trendy set pose elegantly behind the massive glass frontage.

Bay Horse, 19 Bath St. Ordinary Glasgow pub, serving malt whisky, pies and peas.

Bar 91, 91 Candleriggs. Well-designed Merchant City bar, using wrought iron to evoke a stylish atmosphere.

Brahms and Liszt, 71 Renfield St. Candlelit cellar bar, popular with local students creating a loud, crowded atmosphere in the evenings.

Buzzy Wares, Princes Square Shopping Centre. Glossy bar popular at weekends as a pre-club stop.

Corn Exchange, 88 Gordon St. Slap opposite Central station, this bar has successfully re-created the feel of a traditional Victorian Glaswegian pub.

The Griffin, 226 Bath St. Friendly, if faintly tacky, three-bar pub with a firm crowd of regulars – mostly students.

Horseshoe Bar, 17 Drury St. Traditional old pub, reputedly Glasgow's busiest – loud, frantic and great fun, with a very mixed clientele. Karaoke upstairs, with a downstairs bar for quiet conversation.

McChuill's, 40 High St. Glasgows' skateboarders wheel into this brick-lined bar for the Wednesday hip-hop evenings; with live music most other nights, it attracts a faithful crowd.

Mitre Bar, 12–16 Brunswick St. Tucked away in a small side street between Wilson Street and Trongate, this unpretentious retreat sells decent beer to a mixed bag of locals.

Nico's, 375–379 Sauchiehall St. Trendy without being painfully so, the ambience in this popular bar strives towards a French flavour – prices, especially for the bottled beer, are steep.

RG's, 73 Queen St. Nostalgia-soaked bar that serves as a focus for Glasgow's rock music heritage – hence the large portraits of local musical luminaries that adorn the walls. A bit cramped, but a fun atmosphere.

Saracen Head, Gallowgate (opposite the Barras market). Unchanged East End pub that offers an enjoyably beery, sawdust-floored wallow. Look out for the tax demand from Robbie Burns displayed on the wall, from the days when he was the local tax officer.

Scotia Bar, 112 Stockwell St. Laid-back bar popular with writers and other tortured souls. Occasional live folk music – Billy Connolly began his career here, telling jokes in between singing folk songs.

Solid Rock Café, 19 Hope St. Glasgow's top rock pub, with heavy-rock DJs from Thurs–Sun.

Ten, Mitchell Lane. In a tiny street connecting Buchanan and Mitchell streets, *Ten* was designed by the same crew as Manchester's legendary *Hacienda* club. As you'd expect, it's suitably chic, though with a healthy dose of Glaswegian humour to take off the posey edge.

Variety Bar, 401 Sauchiehall St. Crowded bar with faded Art Nouveau appeal and frequented by local art school students.

Victoria Bar, 157–159 Bridgegate. Basic, folksy pub serving a wide selection of real ales.

West End

The Aragon, 131 Byres Rd. Old-fashioned bar with mixed crowd. The main attraction here is the vast beer selection, which includes European fruit beers and weekly guest ales.

Bonham's, 194 Byres Rd. Tall, spacious bar with splendid stained-glass windows. Popular, unpretentious, and serving reasonable daytime food.

Brewery Tap, 1055 Sauchiehall St. Well-known for its excellent selection of real ales and imported lager, this pub caters for students and locals alike with seating outside for those long summer evenings.

The Halt, 106 Woodlands Rd. Great beer and a vast selection of whiskies in this relaxed music pub. Regular live bands.

Living Room, 5–9 Byres Rd. Hotbed for the young and hip, at the southern end of Byres Road. Wrought iron and candles enhance the pre-club atmosphere.

Lismore, 206 Dumbarton Rd. Decorated with stained-glass panels depicting scenes from the Highland Clearances, this friendly pub is a meeting point for the local Gaels, who come here to chat, relax and listen to the impromptu music sessions.

Mitchell's, 157 North St. Next to the domed Mitchell's Library, a comfortable pub with a scholarly atmosphere. Good beer and an excellent refuge.

Tennent's, 191 Byres Rd. No-nonsense, beery den, a refreshing antidote to all the designer paradises nearby. Large and very popular, especially with real-ale aficionados.

Uisge Beatha, 232 Woodlands Rd. The plain frontage broken only by the bar's name in small green neon letters is far from indicative of the eclectic interior, where a lively mixed crowd relish the re-created Scottish atmosphere – all kilts, piped music and stripped wood. The name, by the way, is Gaelic for whisky, the "water of life".

The Western Bar, 80 Dumbarton Rd. A world apart from the student haunts nearby, this genuinely friendly working-class stronghold has walls that read like a city social-history treatise, with lots of old photographs and faded memorabilia.

Whistler's Mother, 116–122 Byres Rd. Combines a relaxed restaurant with the more basic bar, which is deservedly popular with students and legions of young people.

South Side

Boswell Hotel, 27 Mansionhouse Rd. Lively Queen's Park pub with great atmosphere and occasional live music. Good selection of real ales, including some unusually potent local brews. Fine bar food (see p.204).

Brazen Head, 1–3 Cathcart Rd. Close to the Citizens' Theatre and decorated by football strips, this Irish-Italian bar is a local haunt and well endowed with Guinness and Gillespies.

Church on the Hill, 16 Algie St. Perched on the hill behind Queen's Park, the wood panelling and brass fittings give an old time atmosphere to the bar and restaurant, which serves American-style food. Seating outside for sunny evenings.

Cul de Sac Southside, 1070 Pollokshaws Rd. Comfortable, trendy bar that serves food during the day. The pricier restaurant above serves meals with a Scottish-French influence, where main meals circle around £9.

The Granary, 10 Kilmarnock Rd, 10-min walk south from Queen's Park. Friendly bar, with a busy restaurant that serves a good selection of burgers, steak and Mexican food.

M J Heraghty, 708 Pollokshaws Rd. Tiny pub on the corner of Pollokshaws and Nithsdale roads. A rough working-men's hangout, particularly crowded when Celtic play, and so masculine that they don't even have a women's toilet – you have to go next door.

Samuel Dowes, 69–71 Northside Rd, close to Pollokshields West train station. This South Side favourite offers cheap bar meals and occasionally live music to a welcoming crowd. Ceilidh every Sun and poetry reading on the first Mon of every month.

Nightlife and entertainment

Glasgow's City of Culture tag resulted in a great liberalization of the city's licensing laws, which transformed the **clubbing** scene almost overnight. Since then, however, many of these laws have been repealed, and a curfew has been passed declaring that no one is to be allowed into a bar or club after 1am (the time has changed twice since being implemented, so check at the tourist office first). Considering that many clubs were licensed until 6am during 1990, encouraging club-hopping, the rules are, in the view of many, absurdly draconian. However, Glasgow still attracts some of the top DJs from around the world and can easily provide a good night out.

Most of Glasgow's nightclubs are in the heart of the main shopping areas off Argyle and Buchanan streets, many of them within walking distance of each other. Establishments are pretty mixed, and although there's still a stack of outdated mega-discos with rigorous dress codes, the last couple of years have seen the arrival of far more stylish haunts. Hours hover from around 9pm to 3am, and cover charges are variable – expect to pay around £3 during the week, and up to £10 at the weekend. Drinks are usually about thirty percent more expensive than in the pubs.

The city's traditional breadth of art, theatre, film and music is undeniably impressive, especially during **Mayfest**, Glasgow's most concentrated splurge of cultural activity, though this is suffering financial problems and has lost some of its momentum in recent years. The majority of the larger **theatres, cinemas** and showpiece **concert halls** are around the shopping streets of the city centre, while the West End is home to student-oriented venues such as the quirky Grosvenor cinema. The city's two trendiest theatres, the Citizens' and the Tramway, are both South Side. You can find **details** of the city's events in the *Glasgow Herald* or *Evening Times* newspapers, or the fortnightly listings magazine, *The List* (£1.80), which also covers Edinburgh. To book **tickets** for theatre productions or big concerts, call at the Ticket Centre, City Hall, Candleriggs, on the Trongate end of Argyle Street (Mon–Sat 9am–6pm, Sun noon–5pm; phone bookings Mon–Sat 9am–9pm, Sun noon–6pm; ☎227 5511).

Nightclubs

Archaos, 25 Queen St (☎204 3189). Massive nightclub with designer decor, and mixed, young crowd. Weekends are balanced between dance, hip-hop and garage.

The Arches, 30 Midland St (☎221 9736). Deservedly popular weekend club pounding out predominantly dance and rave-orientated music in converted railway arches, under Central station, off Jamaica Street. Slam on Fridays is legendary.

Fury Murray's, 96 Maxwell St, behind the St Enoch Centre (☎221 6511). Student-oriented and lively, with music spanning from the 1960s to rave and techno.

The Garage, 490 Sauchiehall St (☎332 1120). Medium-sized club at the heavier end of the rock spectrum; features some dance nights but lacks atmosphere.

Lime, 5 Scott St (☎332 0712). Busy, studenty club with mainstream music and Latin dance classes every Wednesday evening from 7.30–10.30pm.

Riverside Club, Fox Road, off Clyde Street (☎248 3144). Regular weekend ceilidh that gets packed out with good-natured, drunken Scottish dancers. Great fun, with a live band and callers involving everyone from seasoned ceilidh dancers to visiting novices. Get there early (8–9pm) to ensure a place.

Sub Club, 22 Jamaica St (☎248 4600). Nightclub aimed squarely at the dance and rave end of the market. Weekend nights are very trendy.

Tin Pan Alley, Mitchell Street (☎248 8832). Large dance club attracting a mixed crowd, with rave music dominating at the weekend. It has three floors, one of which hosts a world music night, "Virunga", on Fridays.

The Tunnel, 84 Mitchell St (☎204 1000). Stylish club with arty decor, though now a bit faded; the gents' toilet has cascading waterfall walls.

The Velvet Rooms, Sauchiehall Street (☎332 0755). Consists of a small bar with postage-stamp dance area for the posing set, and a larger bar above playing mainstream dance, garage and soul.

Gay clubs and bars

Austin's, 183 Hope St. Dingy but lively central cellar bar, with a mainly male – and fairly cruisey – crowd of all ages.

Bennett's, 90 Glassford St, Merchant City (☎552 5761). Glasgow's main gay club, predominantly male, fairly old-fashioned but enjoyable nonetheless. Straight nights on Tues.

The Court Bar, 69 Hutcheson St. Quiet back-street pub near George Square, mixed in daytimes and gay in the evenings. Friendlier, and less self-conscious, than most of Glasgow's gay pubs.

Del Monica's, 68 Virginia St. Glasgow's liveliest and most stylish gay bar, very near George Square, with a mixed and hedonistic crowd.

Polo Lounge, 84 Wilson St, off Glassford Street. The original decor in this converted insurance office – all marble tiles and open fires – and the dark pounding nightclub underneath attract a mixed crowd.

The Waterloo Bar, 306 Argyle St. Very central, garish but enjoyable bar, which gets packed at weekends. Mainly men.

Live music pubs and venues

Barrowlands, 244 Gallowgate (☎552 4601). Legendary East End dance hall, complete with spinning glitterball, that hosts some of the sweatiest, liveliest gigs you will ever encounter. Has a capacity of a couple of thousand, so tends to attract bands that are just breaking into the big time.

Curlers, 256 Byres Rd (☎334 1284). Studenty pub that hosts folk bands on Friday and Saturday nights.

The Garage, 490 Sauchiehall St (☎332 1120). Good-size venue for bands that are just about to make it big.

King Tut's Wah Wah Hut, 272a St Vincent St (☎221 5279). One of the city's best programmes of bands at this splendid city-centre live music pub. Good bar downstairs if you want to sit out the sweaty gig above.

Nice'n'Sleazy, 421 Sauchiehall St (☎333 9637). Alternative bands most nights in the somewhat cramped downstairs bar.

Scotia Bar, 112 Stockwell St, near the St Enoch Centre (☎552 8681). The folkies' favourite, a mellow musical pub that acts as a magnet for folk players and followers. Regular live gigs and frequent jam sessions.

The 13th Note, 80 Glassford St (☎553 1638). This double-level bar in the Merchant City is a good place to sample local music talent with live bands most nights.

Theatre and comedy

The Arches, 30 Midland St (☎221 9736). Trendy base for performances by touring theatre groups.

Blackfriars, 45 Albion Rd (☎552 5924). The city's premier comedy and cabaret venue, well sited in the Merchant City and renowned for its good-value Sunday-night line-ups. Also live music at the weekend, particularly jazz.

Centre for Contemporary Arts, 346 Sauchiehall St (☎332 7521). Radical theatre, dance and art.

Citizens' Theatre, 119 Gorbals St (☎429 0022). Glasgow's famous theatre grew from working-class roots to become one of the most respected and adventurous theatres in Britain. Three stages, with bargain prices for students and the unemployed, together with free preview nights.

King's Theatre, 297 Bath St (☎227 5511). Mainstream shows and comedy, south of Sauchiehall Street.

Mitchell Theatre, 6 Granville St, Charing Cross (☎227 5511). Enjoyable venue for touring groups.

Old Athenaeum, 179 Buchanan St (☎332 2333). A smallish base for the Scottish Youth Theatre, as well as for visiting companies and stand-up comedians.

Tramway Theatre, 25 Albert Drive, off Pollokshaws Road (☎227 5511). Good venue for experimental theatre, dance, music and regular art exhibitions.

Tron Theatre, 63 Trongate (☎552 4267). Varied repertoire of mainstream and experimental productions from visiting companies, together with one of the city's most laid-back bars.

Concert halls

Royal Concert Hall, 2 Sauchiehall St (☎227 5511). Big-name rock and soul stars, orchestras and opera companies.

Scottish Exhibition and Conference Centre, Finnieston Quay (☎248 3000). Soulless and overpriced huge shed with the acoustics and atmosphere of an aircraft hangar, but, unfortunately, the only venue in Glasgow (often the only venue in Scotland) visited by megastars on their world tours.

Theatre Royal, Hope Street (☎332 3321). Opulent home of the Scottish Opera and regular host to visiting classical orchestras, opera companies, theatre blockbusters and occasional comedy.

Cinemas

ABC Filmcentre, 326 Sauchiehall St (☎332 9513). Five-screen mainstream multiplex.

City Centre Odeon, 56 Renfield St (☎332 3413). Multiscreen cinema with similar programming to the ABC.

Glasgow Film Theatre, 12 Rose St (☎332 8128). The city's main arthouse and independent cinema.

Grosvenor, Ashton Lane (☎339 4298). Eclectic mix of mainstream and arthouse movies on two screens in this tiny West End alley. Occasional theme nights and frequent lates for local students.

Listings

Airlines Aer Lingus, 19 Dixon St (☎0645/737747); British Airways, 66 Gordon St (☎0345/222111); British Airways Express, Glasgow Airport (☎889 1311); Icelandair, Glasgow Airport (☎0345/581111); Lufthansa, 78 St Vincent St (☎0345/737747); Northwest, 177 W George St (☎226 4991); Qantas, 395 King St (☎0345/747767).

Airport enquiries ☎887 1111.

American Express 115 Hope St (Mon–Fri 8.30am–5.30pm, Sat 9am–noon; ☎221 4366).

Banks Bank of Scotland, 110 Queen St, 63 Waterloo St, 235 Sauchiehall St and 55 Bath St; Clydesdale Bank, 14 Bothwell St, 7 St Enoch Square, 30 St Vincent Place, 344 Argyle St and 120 Bath St; Royal Bank of Scotland, 98 Buchanan St, 22 St Enoch Square, 140 St Vincent St and 393 Sauchiehall St. English banks in Glasgow include Barclays, 90 St Vincent St; Lloyds, 12 Bothwell St and National Westminster, 14 Blythswood Square.

Bike rental see box on p.199.

Books John Smith's, 57 St Vincent St; Waterstone's, 132 Union St; and Dillons, 104–108 Argyle St, all have extensive local studies sections.

Bus enquiries Buchanan Street bus station. For local buses, call ☎332 7133; for national ones, ☎0990 505050.

Car rental Arnold Clark, 16 Vinnicomb St (☎334 9501); Avis, 161 North St (☎221 2827); Budget, 101 Waterloo St (☎226 4141); Hertz, 106 Waterloo St (☎248 7736). Car-rental firms at the **airport** include Avis (☎887 2261); Budget (☎887 0501); Eurodollar (☎887 7915); Europcar (☎887 0414); and Hertz (☎887 2451).

Consulates Germany, 158 W Regent St (☎221 0304); Italy, 24 St Enoch Square (☎226 3000); Norway, 80 Oswald St (☎204 1353); Spain, 389 Argyle St (☎221 6943); Sweden, 16 Robertson St (☎221 7845).

Exchange Outside banking hours you can change money at Thomas Cook in Central station (Mon–Wed & Sat 8am–7pm, Thurs & Fri 8am–8pm, Sun 10am–6pm; ☎204 4496).

Football Of the two big Glasgow teams, you can see Celtic at Celtic Park, 95 Kerrydale St, off the A749 London Road (☎554 8653), and bitter opponents Rangers at the mighty Ibrox stadium, Edminston Drive (☎427 8800). Glasgow's other, lesser teams include Partick Thistle in Firhill stadium, Firhill Road (☎945 4811), or, on the South Side, lowly Queen's Park at the national stadium Hampden Park, Mount Florida (☎632 1275). Tickets from £10 depending on the opposing team and match status.

Gay and lesbian contacts Lesbian and Gay Switchboard (daily 7–10pm; ☎332 8372); Lesbian Line (Wed 7–10pm; ☎552 3355).

Hospital 24hr casualty department at the Royal Infirmary, 84 Castle St (☎221 4000).

Left luggage Staffed office available at Buchanan Street bus station (daily 6.30am–10.30pm) and 24hr lockers at both Central and Queen Street train stations.

Pharmacies Munroes', 693 Gt Western Rd (daily 9am–9pm; ☎339 0012), and Superdrug, Central station (Mon–Wed 8am–8pm, Thurs–Sat 8am–9pm, Sun 10am–8pm; ☎221 8197).

Police Cranstonhill Police Station, 945 Argyle St (☎532 3200); and Stewart Street station, Cowcaddens (☎532 3000).

Post office 47 St Vincent St (Mon–Fri 8.30am–5.45pm, Sat 9am–7pm; ☎0345/'223344), with branch offices at 85–89 Bothwell St, 216 Hope St and 533 Sauchiehall St.

Taxis TOA Taxis (☎332 7070).

Train enquiries ☎0345/484 950.

Travel agents Campus Travel, The Hub, Hillhead St (☎357 0608), and 122 George St (☎553 1818); Glasgow Flight Centre, 143 W Regent St (☎221 8989).

THE CLYDE

The temptation to speed through the **Clyde Valley** is considerable, especially since the raw beauty of the Highlands, the islands and lakes of Argyll and the urbane sophistication of Edinburgh are all within easy reach of the city. Although many of the towns and villages surrounding Glasgow are decidedly missable, some receive far fewer visitors than they deserve, being tarnished with the frequently redundant reputation of dejected industrial towns clinging to the coat tails of Glasgow.

From the city regular trains dip down the southern bank of the Clyde to **Paisley**, where the distinctive cloth pattern gained its name, before heading up to the Firth of Clyde. Along the northern bank, the train rattles through some of Glasgow's oldest shipbuilding communities before arriving in the ancient Strathclyde capital of **Dumbarton**, whose twin-peaked **castle** dominates the flat estuary for miles around.

Heading southeast out of Glasgow, the river's industrial landscape gives way to a far more attractive scenery of gorges and towering castles. Here you can see the stoic town of **Lanark**, where eighteenth-century philanthropists built their model workers' community around the mills of **New Lanark**, and the spectacular **Falls of Clyde**, a mile upstream.

North of the city lies some wonderful upland countryside. Trains terminate at tiny **Milngavie**, which makes great play of its status as the start of the long-distance walk, the **West Highland Way**. Nearby, the rolling beauty of the **Campsie Fells** provides excellent walking and stunning views down onto Glasgow and the glinting river that runs through it (see "Central Scotland" for the full story).

The Firth of Clyde

The shipbuilding industry forged the **Firth of Clyde**. This is still evident today in the numerous yards that pepper the banks as you head west out of the city, especially in the north Clyde communities of **Clydebank**, **Yoker** and **Dalmuir**. The A82 and the rail line run along this northern bank, hemmed into the shore by the **Kilpatrick Hills** that rise menacingly above.

These days, the two river banks are connected by the concrete parabola of the **Erskine Bridge**, dominating the landscape in a way that even Dumbarton Castle has never managed. The bridge disgorges its traffic onto the M8, which runs straight down south to the textile centre of **Paisley** – billed rather meaninglessly as "Scotland's largest town". In the other direction, the M8/A8 and the main train line cling to the shipyard-lined estuary edge, passing the shipbuilding centre of **Greenock**, the old-fashioned seaside resort of **Gourock**, and **Wemyss Bay**, the ferry port for Argyll and Bute. Of the three, Greenock is by far the most interesting, with an excellent town museum that examines the life and achievements of local boy James Watt.

Paisley

Founded in the twelfth century as a monastic settlement around an abbey, **PAISLEY** expanded rapidly after the eighteenth century as a linen manufacturing town, specializing in the production of highly fashionable imitation Kashmiri shawls. Paisley quickly eclipsed other British centres producing the cloth, eventually lending its name to the swirling pine-cone design.

South of the train station, down Gilmour or Smithills streets, lies the bridge over the White Cart Water and the borough's ponderous **Town Hall**, seemingly built back to front as its municipal clock and mismatched double towers loom incongruously over the river instead of facing onto the town. Opposite the town hall, the **Abbey** was built on the site of the town's original settlement but was massively overhauled in the Victorian age. The unattractive, fat grey facade of the church does little justice to the renovated interior, which is tall, spacious and elaborately decorated. The elongated choir, rebuilt extensively throughout the last two centuries, is illuminated by jewel-coloured stained glass from a variety of ages and styles. The abbey's oldest monument is the tenth-century Celtic cross of St Barochan, which lurks like a gnarled old bone at the eastern end of the north aisle.

Paisley's tatty **High Street** leads from the town hall to the west and towards two churches that make far more of an impression on the town's skyline than the modest abbey. The steep cobbles of Church Hill rise away from the High Street up to the grand steps and five-stage spire of the **High Church**, while, beyond the civic museum at the bottom of the High Street, the **Thomas Coats Memorial Church** (May–Sept Mon, Wed & Fri 2–4pm; free) is a Victorian masterpiece of hugely overstated grandeur. Sitting squat like a giant red predator waiting to pounce, the church is one of the most opulent Baptist centres in Britain, with huge tower-top buttresses and an interior of seemingly endless marble and alabaster.

Between the two churches, Paisley's civic **Museum and Art Gallery** (Mon–Sat 10am–5pm; free) shelters behind pompous Ionic columns that face the grim buildings of Paisley University. The local-history section, nearest the entrance, contains an interesting collection of local artefacts from song sheets and spinning threads to the death warrant and executioner's contract for the last public hanging in Paisley in 1858. The most popular part of the museum, which deals with the growth and development of the Paisley pattern and shawls, shows the familiar pine cone (or teardrop) pattern from its simplistic beginnings to elaborate later incarnations. The Upper Gallery houses a small art collection including works by Glasgow Boys Hornel, Guthrie and Lavery (see p.193).

On Oakshaw Street, which runs along the crest of the hill above the Art Gallery, the **Coats Observatory** (Mon, Tues & Thurs 2–8pm, Wed, Fri & Sat 10am–5pm; free) has recorded astronomical and meteorological information since 1884. Today it houses a ten-inch telescope under its dome, and a couple of small exhibition areas display seismic recorders that documented the horrendous San Francisco earthquake of 1906. The telescopes are used for public viewing on Thursday evenings from the last Thursday in October until the last Thursday in March (7–9pm, weather permitting).

To bring you back down to earth, the harsh reality of eighteenth-century life is re-created in the **Sma' Shot Cottages** (April–Sept Wed & Sat 1–5pm; free) in George Place, off New Street. Each of these old houses has individual themes, and contains perfect re-creations of eighteenth- and nineteenth- century daily life complete with bone cutlery and ancient looms. The nineteenth-century artisan's home is filled with artefacts from ceramic hot-water bottles to period wallpaper and leads you into a cosy tearoom where you can enjoy some home baking.

Practicalities

Regular **trains** from Glasgow Central connect with Paisley's Gilmour Street station in the centre of town. Greater Glasgow **buses** #39, #53 and #54 stop at Paisley Abbey; however, the train is faster and more convenient. Buses leave Paisley's Gilmour Street forecourt every ten minutes for Glasgow Airport, two miles north of the town. The **tourist office** (April & May Mon–Fri 9am–1pm & 2–5pm; June–Sept Mon–Sat 9am–6pm; ☎889 0711) is a five-minute walk east from the Town Hall, tucked inside the unremarkable Lagoon Leisure Centre, on Mill Street.

Few people bother to stay in Paisley, except those catching an early flight, and **accommodation** in the town tends to be overpriced. If you do need to stay, the faded but comfortable *Brabloch Hotel*, at 62 Renfrew Rd (☎889 5577; ⑥), is the nicest option. **B&Bs** include *Ardgowan House*, 92 Renfrew Rd (☎889 4763; ④), and *Greenlaw*, 12 Greenlaw Drive, off the Glasgow road (☎889 5359; ③). Lunchtime and early-evening bar **meals**, together with a reasonably convivial atmosphere, can be found in *Gabriel's Bar* at 33 Gauze St, near the abbey, and *O'Neills'*, a large Irish theme pub on New Street. Close by, the Paisley Arts Centre has a small bar with seating outside, while the lively *Vodka Wodka* at 58 High St serves food until 8pm, with an impressive range of vodkas for those on a liquid diet.

From Port Glasgow to Wemyss Bay

PORT GLASGOW is the first of a string of unprepossessing towns that sprawl along the southern coast of the Firth of Clyde. A small fishing village until 1688, when the burghers of Glasgow bought it and developed it as their main harbour, it's a grim place, with nothing to detain you. The train line splits here, one branch heading west along the industrialized coast and the other heading inland before curving round to the ferry port at Wemyss Bay. You can get hourly City Link buses to Greenock and Gourock from Buchanan Street bus station.

Greenock and Gourock

GREENOCK was the site of the first dock on the Clyde, founded in 1711, and the community has grown on the back of shipping ever since. Despite its ranks of anonymous tower blocks and sterile shopping centres, the town still retains a few features of interest.

From the Central train station, it's a short walk down the hill to **Cathcart Square**, where an exuberant 245-ft Victorian tower looms high over the elegant Council House. Directly opposite, in rather shabbier surroundings, lies the **tourist office** (Mon–Fri 8.30am–4.45pm, Sat 9.30am–12.30pm; ☎01475/722007) for both Greenock and Gourock. On the dockside, reached by crossing the dual carriageway behind the square, the Neoclassical **Custom House** has an informative museum (Mon–Fri 10am–12.30pm & 1.30–4pm; free) featuring the work of the Customs and Excise departments, with a display on illicit whisky distilleries and a computer game in which you search a ship for contraband. From the dock in front, tens of thousands of nineteenth-century emigrants felt their last grain of Scottish soil before departing for the New World. On a happier note,

Clyde Marine Cruises (May–Sept; ☎01475/721281) operates from Princes Pier, past the Tesco superstore, with daily sailings to Dunoon, Largs, Rothesay, Millport and Tighna, allowing you to admire the stunning scenery and explore the local towns.

Greenock's town centre has been disfigured by astonishingly unsympathetic developments. More attractive, and indicative of the town's wealthy past, is the western side of town, with its mock-Baronial houses, graceful churches and quiet, tree-lined avenues. This area can be reached either via Greenock West station, or by taking a ten-minute walk up the High Street from the Council House. A hundred yards from the well-proportioned **George Square**, close to Greenock West station, the **Mclean Museum and Art Gallery** in Union Street (Mon–Sat 10am–5pm; free) contains pictures and contemporary records of the life and achievements of Greenock-born James Watt, prominent eighteenth-century industrialist and pioneer of steam power, as well as featuring exhibits on the shipbuilding industry and other local trades. The upper gallery houses a curious exhibition that purports to show the district's internationalism through its trading links, with a random selection of oddments from, among others, Japan, Papua New Guinea, India, China and Egypt. The small art gallery on the ground floor contains work by Glasgow Boys Hornel and Guthrie plus Colourists Fergusson, Cadell and Peploe.

Accommodation is particularly scarce in Greenock, so it's advisable to book ahead. *The Tontine Hotel* in Ardgowan Square, a few minutes' walk west of the Art Gallery, is expensive, but provides a pleasant atmosphere for afternoon tea or an evening meal (☎01475/723316; ⑦). Smaller and more intimate, though the rooms are large, the classical-style *Lindores Guest House* lies further west, at 61 Newark St (☎01475/783075; ③). The *James Watt Halls of Residence* (☎01475/731360; all-year) Customhouse Quay, offer clean and tidy single rooms with views across the water for £15 per person. *Bennicks' Brasserie* on West Blackhall Street, west of the shopping centre, serves a decent selection of soups, sandwiches and pasta dishes. Further west, *L'Arlecchino*, an Italian **restaurant**, is the best option for reasonably priced evening meals.

On the train line between Greenock and Gourock, **Fort Matilda** station perches below **Lyle Hill**, an invigorating 450-ft climb that is well worth the effort for the astounding views over the purple mountains of Argyll and the creeks and lochs spilling off the Firth of Clyde. West of here lies the dowdy old resort of **GOUROCK**, from where CalMac ferries (☎01475/650100) head across to Dunoon and Kilcreggan on the Cowal peninsula (see p.278). Generations of Glaswegians have holidayed here, but today the place is more or less a stopoff point for the ferry terminal. There's an enjoyable seafront swimming pool (Mon–Fri 10am–8pm, Sat & Sun 10am–5pm; £1.60) with a spectacular backdrop of the Argyll mountains, which can be seen in their full glory from Tower Hill, reached from John Street, past the Health Centre. It's a steep climb but the view makes the effort worthwhile.

Wemyss Bay

The southern branch of the train line from Port Glasgow heads inland, clipping the edge of Greenock before curling around the mountains and moors, playing a flirtatious game of peek-a-boo with the Clyde estuary. The terminus station, at **WEMYSS BAY**, is a startling wrought-iron and glass reminder of the great glory days, when thousands of Glaswegians would alight for their steamer trip "doon the watter". Today, Wemyss Bay station is far quieter, as the ferries chug their way from its exit over to Rothesay, capital of the Island of Bute (see p.281).

Dumbarton

Founded in about the fifth century, today the town of **DUMBARTON** is a brutal concrete sprawl, fulfilling every last cliché about postwar planning and architecture. Avoid the town itself – though Talking Heads fans might be interested to know that David

Byrne, of big suits fame, was born here – and head one mile southeast to the 2000-year-old **Dumbarton Castle** (April–Sept Mon–Sat 9.30am–6pm, Sun 2–6pm; Oct–March Mon–Wed & Sat 9.30–noon & 1.30–4pm, Thurs 9.30am–1pm, Sun 2–4pm; £1.50), sitting almost intact atop a twin plug of volcanic rock overlooking the Clyde. The castle is best reached from Dumbarton East train station, from where you turn right and take the second left, Victoria Street, continuing straight for just over half a mile. As a natural site, Dumbarton Rock could not be bettered – surrounded by water on three sides and with commanding views. First founded as a Roman fort, the structure was expanded in the fifth century by the Damnonii tribe, and remained Strathclyde's capital until its absorption into the greater kingdom of Scotland in 1034. The castle then became a royal seat, from which Mary, Queen of Scots sailed for France to marry Henri II's son in 1548, and to which she was attempting to escape when she and her troops were defeated twenty years later at the Battle of Langside. Since the 1600s, the castle has been used as a garrison and artillery fortress to guard the approaches to Glasgow – most of the current buildings date from this period.

The solid eighteenth-century Governor's House lies at the base of the rock, from where you enter the castle complex proper by climbing the steep steps up into the narrow cleft between the two rocks, crowned by the oldest remaining structure in the complex, a fourteenth-century portcullis arch. Vertiginous steps ascend to each peak – to see both you must climb more than five hundred steps. The eastern rock is the highest, with a windy summit that affords excellent views over to the lakes, rivers and mountains beyond Dumbarton town.

If you have an interest in shipbuilding, you may want to visit the **Denny Tank** (Mon, Tues, Fri & Sat 10am–4pm; £1), the world's oldest working ship model experiment tank; at around 110yd long, it's used to test scale models of ships prior to the expensive business of construction. Explanatory panels cover the whole process from wax modelling to the experiments themselves. It is on Castle Street, three streets west of Victoria Street.

Practicalities

Regular **trains** run from Glasgow's Queen Street station to Dumbarton East and Dumbarton Central stations. Take the first stop for access to the castle and accommodation. The **tourist office** (daily: June–Sept 9.30am–6pm; Oct–May 10am–5pm; ☎01389/742306) is situated out of town on the A82 and mainly caters for the vast number of car-bound tourists on their way to the Highlands. Likewise, most **accommodation** is clustered around this artery of traffic and the busy Glasgow Road, that leads into Dumbarton proper. The *Dumbuck Hotel*, Glasgow Road (☎01389/734336; ⑥), offers spacious and comfortable rooms, while *Kilmalid House*, 17 Glenpath, is a quiet **B&B** (☎01389/732030; ③), off Barnhill Road and opposite the conventional *Abbotsford Hotel*. To reach this area from Dumbarton East train station, turn left at the exit and continue until you reach Greenhead Road, which will take you straight up to the A82. Closer to Dumbarton Central, *Drummonds B&B* (☎01389/765984; ④), at 73 Bonhill Rd, offers a warm welcome. There is the usual selection of takeaways focused on the High Street in the centre of town or, for decent **pub food** during the day, try the *Burgh Bar*, on the High Street.

The Clyde valley

The landscape becomes more rural as the River Clyde heads east out of Glasgow, passing the last of a string of shipbuilding yards in Rutherglen, and criss-crossing the M74 as both river and road head southeast into Lanarkshire. Less than ten miles from central Glasgow, **Bothwell Castle** lies about a mile northeast from the **Blantyre** tenement, in which the explorer David Livingstone was born. Two miles further upstream, the valley's largest settlements, **Motherwell** and **Hamilton**, straddle either side of the river and motorway. Motherwell is a depressed town, hard-hit by the closure of its steel works in 1992 and, although Hamilton fancies itself as more upscale, there is little for the visitor in either place. Sandwiched between the two, the enormous **Strathclyde Country Park** features a glassy 200-acre man-made loch, the focus of many sports and outdoor pursuits.

From here the river winds through lush market gardens and orchards that bloom far below the austere lines of **Craignethan Castle**, before passing beneath the sturdy little town of **Lanark**, probably the best base from which to explore the valley. **New Lanark**, on the river bank, is a remarkable planned village dreamed up by eighteenth-century industrialists, David Dale and his son-in-law, Robert Owen. Travel around the area is relatively simple, with good train and bus services. Frequent low-level trains leave Central station for Lanark via Motherwell and Hamilton via Blantyre. At Buchanan Street bus station, Kelvin Central Buses operates a regular service to Hamilton, buses #55, #56, #63 or #67; for Blantyre take #63 and #67; and for Bothwell, #55 and #56. To Lanark, it's best to take the train, as there's only a very limited commuter bus service.

From Hamilton to Craignethan Castle

Although the town of **Hamilton** itself has little to offer the visitor, it lies under the watchful gaze of an old hunting lodge built in 1732 for the aristocratic Hamilton family. Designed by Scots architect William Adam, this building is the centrepiece of Chatelherault Park (daily: lodge 10.30am–4.45pm, park until 9pm; free), a pleasant area with walks that follow the Avon water and explore the surrounding countryside, past the ruins of Cadzow Castle and some 600-year-old oaks. To reach the park, take bus #53 or #54 from Hamilton Central train station, both of which stop at the entrance.

BLANTYRE, now a colourless suburb of Hamilton, was a remote Clydeside hamlet when explorer and missionary David Livingstone was born there in 1813. From Blantyre station, a right turn brings you to a quiet country lane. The entire tenement block at the bottom of the lane, now painted a brilliant white, has been taken over by the **David Livingstone Centre** (Mon–Sat 10am–6pm, Sun 12.30–6pm; £2.95), showing his life from early years as a mill worker up until his death in 1873 searching for the source of the River Nile. In 1813, the block consisted of 24 one-room tenements, each occupied by an entire family. Today the Livingstone family room shows the claustrophobic conditions under which he was brought up; all the others feature slightly defensive exhibitions on the missionary movement with tableaux of scenes from his life in Africa, including the infamous meeting with Stanley. Unfortunately, due to vandalism, the thatched huts donated by the government of Malawi which housed changing exhibitions on African themes have had to be removed. Smaller exhibitions on Blantyre and the Clyde valley area are now held inside the main "Africa Pavilion" building.

A mile or so from Blantyre, **Bothwell Castle** (April–Sept Mon–Wed & Sat 9.30am–6pm, Thurs 9.30am–1.30pm, Sun 2–6pm; Oct–March Sat–Wed 9.30am–4pm, Thurs 9.30am–12.30pm; £1.50) is one of Scotland's most dramatic citadels, a great red sandstone bulk looming high above a loop in the river. The oldest section is the solid donjon, or circular tower, at the western end, built by the Moray family in the late 1200s to protect themselves against the English king Edward I during the Scottish wars of independence. Such was the might of the castle, Edward only finally succeeded in capturing it in September 1301 after ordering the construction and deployment of a massive siege engine, wheeled from Glasgow to Bothwell in order to lob huge stones at the castle walls. Over the next two centuries, the castle changed hands numerous times and was added to by each successive owner, with the last section, the Great Hall, in the grassy inner courtyard. Despite its jigsaw construction, today the overwhelming impression is of the almost impenetrable strength of the castle, its solid red towers – whose walls reach almost 16ft thick in places – standing firm centuries after their construction. **Buses** #55 and #56 from Glasgow to Hamilton will drop you off on the Bothwell Road, near the castle entrance. By car, it is best approached from the B7071 Bothwell–Uddingston road.

Once known as the "Steelopolis" of Scotland, the small town of **MOTHERWELL**, a few miles east of Blantyre, has little to offer except the informative **Motherwell Heritage Centre** (Mon–Sat 10am–6pm, Sun noon–5pm; free), looming above the station on the High Road. The entrance foyer holds changing exhibitions on local themes, whilst the **multimedia exhibition** (£2) takes you through the history of the town. Reconstructed streets, cinemas and exhibits document the lives of the local community, and the future of Motherwell is explored with optimism despite widespread unemployment. On the first floor the **local-history lab** contains books, maps and photos of the area, as well as databases on Lanarkshire and Motherwell Football Club. From the top of the glass tower, there are spectacular views across Lanarkshire.

The section of the Clyde Valley southeast from Hamilton to Lanark has appropriately become known as "Greenhouse Glen", where the winding road, lined with small stone villages and inordinate numbers of garden centres, gives occasional glimpses of the river through the trees. Buses #17 and #217 from Hamilton and Lanark stop off at **CROSSFORD**, five miles short of Lanark, where the River Nethan forks off from the Clyde. From here you can either climb a difficult mile through the wooded Nethan valley up to the gaunt clifftop ruins of **Craignethan Castle** (March & Oct Mon–Wed, Sat & Sun 9.30am–4.30pm, Thurs 9.30am–12.30pm; April–Sept Mon–Sat 9.30am–6.30pm, Sun 2–6.30pm; £1.50), or, if driving, take the extremely tortuous three-mile signposted route. The last major castle to be built in Scotland, Craignethan was constructed by Sir James Hamilton of Finnart, Master of Works to James V, in 1530. Hamilton, inspired by new styles of artillery fortification in Italy, built a unique *caponier*, a dank vault wedged into the dry moat between the two sections of the castle. From here, defenders could spray the ditch with small-arms fire from behind the safety of walls 5ft thick. It was from Craignethan, owned by loyalist James Hamilton, that Mary, Queen of Scots left on May 13, 1568, ultimately for defeat at Langside, followed by exile and imprisonment in England. The castle, like so many others in Scotland, is said to be inhabited by her ghost, as Craignethan was probably the last time she was ever amongst true friends. Whatever the truth, Craignethan does have a spooky quality about it, its stillness only interrupted by the shriek of circling crows. The most intact parts of the castle are the gloomy *caponier* and the musty cellars underneath the vast main tower, from which gun holders still protrude.

Lanark and New Lanark

The neat little market town of **LANARK** is an old and distinguished burgh, sitting in the purple hills high above the River Clyde, its rooftops and spires visible for miles around. Beyond the world's oldest bell, cast in 1130 and visible in the Georgian Church of St Nicholas, there's little to see in town and most people make their way to **NEW LANARK** (daily 11am–5pm; £3.75), a mile below the main town on Braxfield Road.

Although New Lanark is served by an hourly bus from the train station, it's well worth the steep downhill walk to get there. The first sight of the village, hidden away down in the gorge, is unforgettable: large broken curving walls of honeyed warehouses and tenements, built in Palladian style, lined up along the turbulent river's edge. The community was founded by David Dale and Richard Arkwright in 1785 to harness the power of the Clyde waterfalls in their cotton-spinning industry, but it was Dale's son-in-law, Robert Owen, who revolutionized the social side of the experiment in 1798, creating a "village of unity". Believing the welfare of the workers to be crucial to industrial success, Owen built adult educational facilities, the world's first day nursery and playground, and schools in which dancing and music were obligatory and there was no punishment or reward.

The Neoclassical building at the very heart of the village was opened by Owen in 1816 under the utopian title of **The Institute for the Formation of Character**. With a library, chapel and dance hall, the Institute became the main focus of the community, and today you can see an introductory video about New Lanark and its founders in the spacious congregational hall. Of the three vast old mill buildings open to visitors, one houses the **Annie McLeod Experience**, where a chair lift whisks visitors through a social history of life here from the imaginary perspective of a young mill girl. With a plethora of special effects – low light diffused through aromatic fog, holograms and lasers – the ten-minute journey portrays honest and unsentimental pictures of village life. Other exhibits in the mills include huge spinning wheels and a massive steam engine.

The village itself is just as fascinating: everything, from the co-operative store to the workers' tenements and workshops, was built in an attempt to prove that industrialism need not be unaesthetic. You can wander through the 1920s shop, and find out how the workers lived from the 1820s to the 1920s in the **New Buildings**, then poke around the domestic kitchen, study and living areas of **Robert Owen's House**. Situated in the Old Dyeworks, **The Scottish Wildlife Trust Visitor Centre** (Feb, March & Oct–Dec Sat & Sun 1–5pm; April–Sept Mon–Fri 11am–5pm, Sat & Sun 1–5pm) provides information about the history and wildlife of the area. Friendly rangers give details of the walks around the tree-lined valley; the longest is an eight-mile round-trip. Further on, beyond the visitor centre, a path along the Clyde leads you past the small falls of green water on which the Lanark project was first founded, and the Bonnington hydroelectric station to the major **Falls of The Clyde**, where at the stunning tree-fringed **Cora Linn**, the river plunges 90ft in three tumultuous stages. It is a stunning marker point for the Clyde Walkway, a path that follows the river from Glasgow Green to this valley forest.

Practicalities

Lanark is the terminus on the **train** line from Glasgow Central station. The town's **tourist office** (May–Sept Mon–Sat 10am–6pm, Sun noon–5pm; Oct–April Mon–Sat 10am–5pm; ☎01555/661661) is housed in a circular building in the Horsemarket, next to Somerfields supermarket, 100yd west of the station. **Accommodation** varies from the spectacular wooded surroundings of the *Cartland Bridge Hotel* on the town's edge just off the A73 Glasgow Road (☎01555/664426; ⑧), to faintly seedy town-centre pubs such as the *Royal Oak*, opposite the train station at 39 Bannatyne St (☎01555/665895; ③). **B&Bs** include *Mrs Gray's*, 49 West Port, the continuation of High Street (☎01555/663663; ③), and *Parkview Guest House*, 27 Hynford Rd (☎0155/663313; ③), on the road to New Lanark. The **youth hostel** (☎01555/666710) is beautifully sited amongst the reconstructed buildings of New Lanark itself, and is an excellent spot for enjoying the surrounding countryside in peace. It has self-catering and drying facilities, and the occasional musical evening. There are plenty of cheap **cafés** and takeaways on High Street, and the *Courtyard Restaurant,* at 3 Castlegate, has a quiet patio to enjoy lunch away from the road. There are some more pricey Indian and Italian **restaurants** along Wellgate. The rather posh *Clydesdale Hotel*, at 15 Bloomgate, serves meals in the cellar bar until 9pm, while the far less pretentious *Crown Tavern*, a quiet drinking haunt in Hope Street, does reasonable food until 9.30pm. Other good local pubs include the *Horse and Jockey* in High Street and the *Wallace Cave* in Bloomgate. The current favourite amongst young people is the *Woodpecker Inn*, tucked behind High Street off the tiny Wide Close alley.

travel details

Trains

Glasgow Central to: Ardrossan (every 30min; 45min); Ayr (every 30min; 50min); Birmingham (5 daily; 3hr 50min); Blantyre (every 30min; 20min); Carlisle (hourly; 2hr 25min); Crewe (6 daily; 3hr 35min); Dumbarton (every 20min; 25min); East Kilbride (Mon–Sat every 30min; 30min); Gourock (every 30min; 47min); Greenock (every 30min; 40min); Hamilton (every 30min; 25min); Kilmarnock (hourly; 40min); Lanark (Mon–Sat hourly; 50min); Largs (hourly; 1hr); London (10 daily; 5hr 45min); Manchester (1 daily; 3hr 50min); Motherwell (every 20min; 30min); Newcastle-upon-Tyne (8 daily; 2hr 30min); Paisley (every 15min; 10min); Port Glasgow (every 15min; 30min); Queen's Park (every 15min; 6min); Rutherglen (every 20min; 10min); Stranraer (4 daily; 2hr 10min); Wemyss Bay (hourly; 55min); York (7 daily; 3hr 30min).

Glasgow Queen Street to: Aberdeen (hourly; 2hr 35min); Aviemore (3 daily; 2hr 40min); Balloch (Mon–Sat every 30min; 45min); Dundee (hourly; 1hr 20min); Edinburgh (every 30min; 50min); Fort William (3 daily; 3hr 40min); Helensburgh (every 30min; 45min); Inverness (3 daily; 3hr 25min); Mallaig (3 daily; 5hr 15min); Milngavie (Mon–Sat every 30min; 22min); Oban (3 daily; 3hr) (hourly; 1hr); Springburn (Mon–Sat every 30min; 13min); Stirling (hourly; 30min).

Buses

Glasgow to: Aberdeen (15 daily; 4hr); Aviemore (hourly; 3hr 30min); Campbeltown (3 daily; 4hr 20min); Dundee (hourly; 2hr 15min); Edinburgh (every 15min; 1hr 15min); Fort William (4 daily; 3hr); Glencoe (4 daily; 2hr 30min); Inverness (hourly; 4–5hr); Kyle of Lochalsh (3 daily; 5hr); Lochgilphead (3 daily; 2hr 40min); Loch Lomond (hourly; 45min); London (5 daily; 7hr 30min); Newcastle-upon-Tyne (2 daily; 4hr); Oban (4 daily; 3hr); Perth (hourly; 1hr 35min); Pitlochry (hourly; 2hr 20min); Portree (3 daily; 6hr); Stirling (hourly; 45min); York (1 daily; 6hr 30min).

Flights

Glasgow to: Birmingham (Mon–Fri 11 daily, Sat & Sun 6 daily; 1hr); London Heathrow (Mon–Fri 20 daily, Sat & Sun 12 daily; 1hr 30min); London Gatwick (Mon–Fri 4 daily, Sat & Sun 3 daily; 1hr 30min); London Stansted (Mon–Fri 4 daily, Sat 1 daily, Sun 4 daily; 1hr 30min); Manchester (Mon–Fri 8 daily, Sat 1 daily, Sun 2 daily; 1hr).

CHAPTER FOUR

CENTRAL SCOTLAND

Within easy reach of Edinburgh and Glasgow, **central Scotland** is a much-visited area; not least for its spectacular and varied countryside, ranging from the picture-postcard beauty of the Central Lowlands to the wilder more challenging terrain of the Highlands, which officially begin here. The **Highland Boundary Fault**, the dramatic physical divide running southwest to northeast across the region, has rendered central Scotland – from medieval to modern times – the main stage for some of the most important events in Scottish history. Today the landscape is not only littered with remnants of the past – well-preserved medieval towns and castles, royal residences and battle sites – but also coloured by the many romantic myths and legends that have grown up around it.

At the heart of the **Central Lowlands**, above the industrial belt around Falkirk and Grangemouth, is venerable **Stirling**, its imposing castle perched high above the town. Historically one of the most important bridging points across the River Forth, it was the site of two of the most famous battles fought under Robert the Bruce during the **Wars of Independence** (1296–1328). To the west and north of Stirling the magnificent scenery centres on the fabled mountains, glens, lochs and forests of the **Trossachs**, a unique and beautiful area of high peaks and steep-sided glens that stretches west from **Callander** to the eastern banks of Loch Lomond. The geography and history of the area caught the imagination of **Sir Walter Scott**, who took so much delight in the tales of local clansman **Rob Roy** MacGregor, the notorious seventeenth-century outlaw, that he set them down in his novel of the same name. Visitors flocked to the Trossachs and, according to one contemporaneous account, after Scott's *Lady of the Lake* was published in 1810, the number of carriages passing Loch Katrine rose from 50 the previous year to 270. Thanks to Scott and to William and Dorothy Wordsworth's effusive praise, Queen Victoria decided to visit, placing the area firmly on the tourist map. Today, however, the trappings of tourism – evident in twee shops and tearooms in every small town – don't impinge too much on the experience.

Lying to the east of the Central Lowlands is **Fife**, the only one of Scotland's seven original Pict kingdoms to survive relatively intact. Neither Norse nor Norman influence found its way to this independent corner, and nine and a half centuries later, when the government at Westminster redrew local boundaries in 1975 and again in 1995, the Fifers stuck to their guns and successfully opposed any changes. Here you'll find coastal fishing villages and sandy beaches and the self-assured town of **St Andrews**, inextricably linked in the public consciousness with **golf**.

North of St Andrews on the west bank of the River Tay is the ancient town of **Perth**, surrounded by beautiful rugged country. At nearby **Scone**, Kenneth Macalpine established the capital of the kingdom of the Scots and the Picts in 846. When this settlement was washed away by floods in 1210, William the Lion founded Perth as a royal burgh and it stood as Scotland's capital until 1452. The four great monasteries of Perth reflected the town's political and religious importance, but were all destroyed during the Reformation after a sermon by John Knox at St John's Church. North of Perth, the Highlands begin in earnest. From **Loch Tay** onwards, beyond the agreeable town of **Aberfeldy**, the countryside becomes more sparsely populated and more spectacular, with the **Grampian Mountains** to the east offering wonderful walks, especially around **Pitlochry**, and the wild expanses of **Rannoch Moor** to the west. This northerly part of the region also boasts Scotland's most popular tourist attraction, **Blair Castle**.

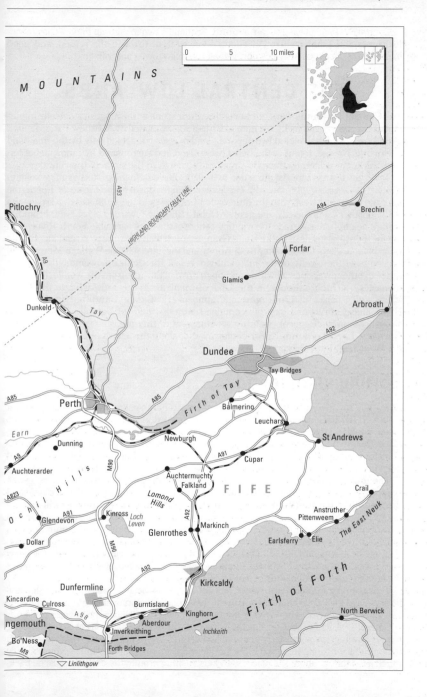

0   5   10 miles

M O U N T A I N S

HIGHLAND BOUNDARY FAULT LINE

A93

Pitlochry

A94

Brechin

A9

Forfar

Dunkeld

Tay

Glamis

Arbroath

A92

Dundee

Tay Bridges

A85

Perth

Balmerino

Firth of Tay

Leuchars

A85

Newburgh

St Andrews

Earn

Dunning

A91

Cupar

A9

Auchterarder

M90

Auchtermuchty

Falkland

F I F E

Crail

A823

O c h i l   H i l l s

*Lomond
Hills*

A91

Kinross

*Loch
Leven*

A92

Anstruther

Pittenweem

The East Neuk

Glendevon

Markinch

Dollar

Glenrothes

Earlsferry

Elie

M90

A92

Dunfermline

Kirkcaldy

Firth of Forth

Kincardine

Culross

Burntisland

A 9 8

North Berwick

ngemouth

Aberdour

Kinghorn

Bo'Ness

Inverkeithing

Inchkeith

M9

Forth Bridges

▽ Linlithgow

Central Scotland is easy to **get around**. Scotland's two main train lines – Glasgow to Inverness and Edinburgh to Aberdeen – cut straight through the region, and good intercity and local bus services connect all the main towns and villages.

THE CENTRAL LOWLANDS

The **Central Lowlands** were, for several centuries, one of the most strategically important areas in Scotland. In 1250 a map of Britain was compiled by Matthew Paris, a monk of St Albans, which depicted two separate land masses connected only by the thin band of **Stirling Bridge**. Lying at the heart of Scotland and surrounded by inhospitable terrain, Stirling was literally the gateway from the north to the south of the country.

Today the town is a tourist attraction in itself, its fine **castle** the perfect vantage point to look far out across the region. The castle rock plunges down to the **Carse of Forth**, the flat plain extending west, with the little-visited **Campsies** to the south and the **Trossachs** to the north. East of the city, the gentler **Ochil Hills** run towards Loch Leven. From the castle's heights you can trace the winding course of the once navigable **Forth River**, linking the industrial towns of **Falkirk** and **Grangemouth** with the rural west, and identify the great blunt tower of **Cambuskenneth Abbey** and the unmistakable **Wallace Monument**.

Alongside the beauty of the hills and villages of the Central Lowlands, there are a range of other diversions all within an hour's drive of Stirling: from the wonderful island monastery of **Inchmahome** in the Lake of Menteith in the Trossachs, to the Forth Valley's airy palace of **Linlithgow** and atmospheric **Castle Campbell** in the Ochil Hills. These attractions can be combined with a range of outdoor activities; the Trossachs provide great walking country, and the area is traversed by the **Glasgow–Loch Lomond–Killin cycleway** and, along the length of Loch Lomond, by the **West Highland Way**.

Stirling and around

Straddling the River Forth a few miles upstream from the estuary at Kincardine, at first glance **STIRLING** appears like a smaller version of Edinburgh. With its crag-top castle, steep, cobbled streets and mixed community of locals and students, it's an appealing place, though it lacks the cosmopolitan edge of Edinburgh or Glasgow. It's historic, due to its former importance as a much coveted river crossing, but – geographically trapped between Scotland's two main cities – Stirling remains at heart decidedly provincial.

The town was the scene of some of the most significant developments in the evolution of the Scottish nation. It was here that the Scots under William Wallace defeated the English at the **Battle of Stirling Bridge** in 1297, only to fight – and win again – under Robert the Bruce just a couple of miles away at the **Battle of Bannockburn** in 1314. Stirling enjoyed its golden age in the fifteenth to seventeenth centuries, most notably when its castle was the favoured residence of the Stuart monarchy and the setting for the coronation in 1543 of the young Mary, future Queen of Scots. By the early eighteenth century the town was again besieged, its location of strategic importance during the Jacobite rebellions of 1715 and 1745.

Today Stirling is known instead for its **Castle** – just as beautiful as its Edinburgh counterpart – and the lofty **Wallace Monument**, a mammoth Victorian monolith high on Abbey Craig to the northeast. The **University**, also, has helped to maintain the town's profile.

Stirling is at its liveliest during the summer, with buskers and street artists jostling for performing space in the pedestrianized centre. If you get decent weather – which isn't all that uncommon despite the proliferation of surrounding hills – there's very much a holiday air about the place, with kids rushing around the castle ramparts, back-

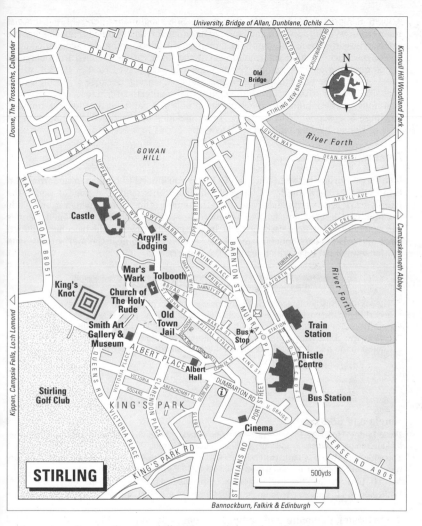

packers struggling up the steep hill to the youth hostel, and students, many of whom choose to stay here over the summer, spilling out of the cafés.

Arrival and information

The **train station** (☎0345/484950) is near the centre of town on Station Road; the **bus station** (☎01324/613777) nearby on Goosecroft Road. To reach the town centre from the train station, walk up Station Road and turn left at the mini-roundabout; from the bus station cut through the Thistle Shopping Centre opposite to reach the main drag, Port Street.

Stirling's **tourist office** is in the heart of the town centre at 41 Dumbarton Rd (June Mon–Sat 9am–6pm, Sun 10am–4pm; July & Aug Mon–Sat 9am–7.30pm, Sun

9.30am–6.30pm; Sept Mon–Sat 9am–6pm, Sun 10am–4pm; Oct–May Mon–Sat 10am–5pm; ☎01786/475019), and is the main office for Loch Lomond, Stirling and the Trossachs, with a wide range of books, maps and leaflets, and a free accommodation-booking service. Further information about the town can be gleaned from personal stereo guides, available from the Stags Audio Walk shop, 24 Broad St (£2.50), which cover all the major attractions, spiced up with ghost stories. Because of Stirling's compact size – barely five miles from the centre to the outermost fringes – sightseeing is best done on foot, though to avoid the steep hills you can take the "hop on, hop off" **Heritage bus** service whose circular route includes the castle, Wallace Monument, Stirling University, bus and train stations (June–Sept 10am–5pm; £5).

Accommodation

If you're in Stirling between May and October, you'll need to book your **accommodation** by lunchtime at the latest, or you're likely to be stranded. A good option is the **King's Park** area – immediately south of the tourist office – an opulent Victorian suburb built for Glasgow industrialists and merchants and composed of tree-lined avenues and splendid villas, some wonderfully Italianate with towers and balconies, though most of the **B&Bs** are concentrated in the residential area near the tourist office, and on Causewayhead Road which leads to the University.

ACCOMMODATION PRICE CODES

Throughout this book, accommodation **prices** have been graded with the codes below, according to the cost of the least expensive double room in high season. Price codes are not given for campsites, most of which charge under £10 per person. Almost all hostels charge less than £10 a night for a bed – the few exceptions to this rule have the prices quoted in the text. For a full account of the accommodation price codes, see p.30.

① under £20	④ £40–50	⑦ £70–80
② £20–30	⑤ £50–60	⑧ £80–100
③ £30–40	⑥ £60–70	⑨ over £100

Hotels and B&Bs
Park Lodge Hotel, 32 Park Terrace (☎01786/474862). Magnificently sited and luxurious, overlooking the park and castle and with a *haute cuisine* restaurant. ⑦.
The Heritage, 16 Allan Park (☎01786/473660). On the northern edge of King's Park, its pretty rooms look up at the castle, and it has a good Scottish/French restaurant too. ⑤.
No. 10, 10 Gladstone Place (☎01786/472681). Friendly and pleasant B&B. ④.
Whitegables, 112 Causewayhead Rd (☎01786/479838). A friendly B&B with TVs in all the rooms. ③.

Youth hostel, campsite and campus accommodation
At the top of the town (a strenuous trek with a backpack), the cheapest option is the **youth hostel** in a recently converted church on St John Street (☎01786/473442). All rooms have showers and toilets en suite, and continental breakfast is included; the high-season price is £11.95 per person.

   If you prefer to stay out of town, try the **campus accommodation** at Stirling University (☎01786/467141; ③; June–Aug), a couple of miles north of the town centre. Regular buses (#53 and #58) leave from Murray Place at the end of the main street (last services around 10.45pm). You can also rent Scandinavian-style **chalets** in the University's landscaped grounds (sleeps six for around £340 per week; June–Aug). Also on campus is the new Stirling Management Centre (☎01786/451666; ⑦), with luxurious en-suite rooms looking out at the Wallace Monument. There's a **campsite**, the

Witches Craig at Blairlogie, three miles east of the town off the A91 road to St Andrews (☎01786/474947; April–Oct).

The Town

Stirling evolved from the top down, starting with its castle and gradually spreading south and east onto the low-lying flood plain. At the centre of the original **Old Town**, Broad Street was the main thoroughfare, with St John Street running more or less parallel, and St Mary's Wynd forming part of the original route to Stirling Bridge below. In the eighteenth and nineteenth centuries, as the threat of attack decreased, the centre of commercial life crept down towards the River Forth, with the modern town – commonly called the **Lower Town** – growing on the edge of the plain over which the castle has traditionally stood guard.

Stirling Castle

Stirling Castle (daily: April–Sept 9.30am–6pm; Oct–March 9.30am–5pm; HS; £4.00 including entry to Argyll's Lodging) must have presented would-be invaders with a formidable challenge. Its impregnability is most daunting when you approach the town from the west, from where the sheer, 250ft drop down the side of the crag is most obvious. The rock was first fortified during the Iron Age, though what you see now dates largely from the fifteenth and sixteenth centuries. Presently undergoing a massive restoration scheme (due to be completed in 2001), small parts of the castle may be inaccessible.

The **visitor centre** (same times as castle) on the esplanade shows an introductory film giving a potted history of the castle, but the best place to get an impression of its gradual expansion is in the courtyard known as the **Upper Square**. Here you can see the magnificent **Great Hall** (1501–3), with its lofty dimensions and huge fireplaces perhaps the finest medieval secular building in Scotland. The exterior of the **Palace** (1540–42) is richly decorated with grotesque carved figures and Renaissance sculpture, including, in the left-hand corner, the glaring bearded figure of James V in the dress of a commoner. Inside in the royal apartments are the **Stirling Heads**, 56 elegantly carved oak medallions, which once comprised the ceiling of the Presence Chamber, where visitors were presented to royalty. Otherwise the royal apartments are bare, their emptiness emphasizing the fine dimensions and wonderful views. The **Chapel Royal** (1594) was built by James VI for the baptism of his son, and replaced an earlier chapel, not deemed sufficiently impressive. The interior is lovely, with a seventeenth-century fresco of elaborate scrolls and patterns.

The castle also houses the impressive Argyll and Sutherland Highlanders **museum**, with its collection of well-polished silver and memorabilia, including a seemingly endless display of Victoria Crosses won by the regiment. The setup in the restored castle **kitchens** re-creates the preparations for the spectacular Renaissance banquet given by Mary, Queen of Scots for the baptism of the future James VI. As well as an audiovisual display describing how delicacies for the feast were procured and an abundance of stuffed animals in various stages of preparation (who, we are assured, died natural deaths), the kitchens feature *faux* recipe books with such delights as sugar wineglasses, golden steamed custard and dressed peacock.

From the **Douglas Gardens** you can see the surprisingly small window from which the eighth Earl of Douglas, suspected of treachery, was thrown by James II in 1452. There is a bird's-eye view down to the **King's Knot**, a series of grassed octagonal mounds which in the seventeenth century were planted with box trees and ornamental hedges.

The Old Town

Leaving the castle, head downhill into the old centre of Stirling, fortified behind the massive, whinstone boulders of the **town walls**, built in the mid-sixteenth century and intended to ward off the advances of Henry VIII, who had set his sights on the young Mary as a wife for his son, Edward. The walls now constitute some of the best-preserved town defences in Scotland, and can be traced by following the path known as **Back Walk**. This circular walkway was built in the eighteenth century and in the upper reaches encircles the castle, taut along the edge of the crag, offering panoramic views of the surrounding countryside.

Five minutes' walk down the hill from the castle's visitor centre, you'll find **Argyll's Lodging** (daily: April–Sept 9.30am–6pm; Oct–March 9.30am–5pm; HS; £2.50), a romantic Renaissance mansion built by Sir William Alexander of Menstrie. Inside, an informative exhibition takes you through the history of the building in its various incarnations, from home to the first earl of Stirling, Sir William Alexander, and the ninth Earl of Argyll amongst others, to its later uses as military hospital and youth hostel. The oldest part of the building, marked by low ceilings and tiny windows, is the Great Kitchen, whose enormous fireplace comes complete with a special recess for salt, while the Drawing Room, hung with lavishly decorated purple tapestries, contains the ninth earl's imposing chair of state. An adjoining smaller room for his wife, Anna, still contains her personal chamber pot, an ornate affair in purple.

Further down Castle Wynd at the top of Broad Street, a richly decorated facade hides the dilapidated **Mar's Wark**, a would-be palace which the first Earl of Mar, Regent of Scotland and hereditary Keeper of Stirling Castle, started in 1570. His dream house was never to be realized, however, for he died two years later and what had been built was left to ruin, its degeneration speeded up by extensive damage during the 1745 Jacobite Rebellion. Behind here is the **Church of the Holy Rude** (May–Sept Mon–Fri 10am–5pm; Sunday service), a fine medieval structure, the oldest parts of which, including the impressive oak hammerbeam roof, date from the early fifteenth century. Go in during the day and imagine the ceremony that was held here in 1567 for the coronation of the infant James VI – later the first monarch of the United Kingdom – and come back in the evening to the atmospheric graveyard, from where you can watch the sun set. Just south of the church on the edge of the crag, the grand E-shaped **John Cowane's Hospital** was built as a 1649 almshouse for "decayed [unsuccessful] members of the Guild of Merchants". Above the entrance, John Cowane, the wealthy merchant who founded the hospital, is commemorated in a statue which, it is said, comes alive at Hogmanay.

A short walk down St John Street a sweeping driveway leads up to the impressive **Old Town Jail** (April–Sept 9.30am–5.30pm; Oct–March 9.30am–4pm; guided tours every 30min; £2.50), a formidable building rescued from dereliction in 1992 and superbly refurbished. Tours are brought to life by enthusiastic actors who change costumes and character a number of times, and there's a working example of the dreaded crank, a lever which prisoners had to turn 14,400 times per day for punishment. Take the glass lift up to the prison roof to admire spectacular views across Stirling and the Forth Valley.

Back on the ground, **Broad Street** was the site of the marketplace and centre of the medieval town. Many of its buildings have been restored in recent years, and preservation work continues. Down here, past the **Mercat Cross** (the unicorn on top is known, inexplicably, as "the puggy"), the **Tolbooth**, sandwiched between Broad and St John streets (with the entrance on Broad Street), was built in 1705 by Sir William Bruce, who designed the Palace of Holyroodhouse in Edinburgh. It was used as both a courthouse and, after 1809, a prison, from where the unfortunate were led to execution in the street outside. **Darnley's House**, at the bottom of Broad Street, was where Mary Queen of Scots' husband is believed to have lodged while she lorded it up in the castle; it now houses a coffee shop (see opposite).

The Lower Town
The further downhill you go in Stirling's Lower Town, the more recent the buildings become. Follow St John Street into Spittal Street, and then on down into King Street,

where austere Victorian facades block the sun from the cobbled road. Stirling's main **shopping** area is down here, along Port Street and Murray Place, while the **Smith Art Gallery and Museum** (Tues–Sat 10.30am–5pm, Sun 2–5pm) is a short walk west up Dumbarton Road. Founded in 1874 with a legacy from local painter and collector Thomas Stuart Smith, it houses a permanent exhibition relating the history of Stirling, and a range of changing displays of arts and crafts, contemporary art and photography.

The fifteenth-century **Old Bridge** over the Forth lies on the edge of the town centre (a 20min walk from Murray Place). Although once the most important river crossing in Scotland – the lowest bridging point on the Forth until the new bridge was built in 1831 – it now stands virtually forgotten, an almost incidental reminder of Stirling's former importance. An earlier, wooden **bridge** nearby was the focus of the Battle of Stirling Bridge in 1297, where William Wallace defeated the English.

Eating

At the top of town, *Stirling Merchants*, 39 Broad St, next to the Tolbooth Theatre, serves filling pub grub for under a fiver, including baked potatoes with vegetarian haggis. The elegant three-storey *Darnley Coffee House* on Bow Street (continuation of Broad Street), serves good, reasonably priced lunches and teas, amid an impressive plain barrel-vaulted interior. On Albert Place, the *Café Albert* in the Victorian grandeur of *Albert Hall*, is a good, well-priced place to lunch.

More upmarket is *Herman's* at 32 St John St (☎01786/450632), with its handsomely austere interior. The downstairs brasserie is open at lunchtime; the Austrian/Scottish evening main courses start at £8. The quality of the cooking at *Pierre Victoire*, 41 Friars St, just round the corner from the Murray Place bus stop (☎01786/448171), is unpredictable, but the set lunch is a great bargain at around £6 per person for three courses. *Italia Nostra*, close by at 25 Baker St (☎01786/473208), serves good well-priced Italian food and is very lively, especially at weekends. At the *East India Club*, 7 Viewfield Place, a five-minute walk from the centre (☎01786/471330), you can enjoy fabulous Indian food, postmodern "Raj" decor, and the friendliest service in town. Their buffet (Sun–Thurs) costs around £10 per person for three courses and as much as you can eat. Slightly more expensive is the delicious and elegantly served Cantonese food at *The Regent*, 30 Upper Craigs (☎01786/472513). Further afield, the *Sword Hotel* on Hillfoots Road (☎01786/473338), near the Wallace Monument, serves good lunches from a varied menu in a pleasant conservatory.

If you're planning a high-class **picnic**, head to *Clive Ramsay Delicatessen and Fine Foods* at 28 Henderson St, Bridge of Allan (buses #51 and #52 from Murray Place).

Nightlife and entertainment

Not known for its club scene, nightlife in Stirling revolves around **pubs** and **bars** and is dominated by the student population. The lively *Barnton Bar and Bistro*, on Barnton Street, serves a good selection of beers and food in a setting of wrought-iron and marble tables. Try to visit in the morning (from 10.30am) to sample one of their huge breakfasts. Also popular with students is the real ale at the *Settle Inn*, 91 St Mary's Wynd, Stirling's oldest alehouse; built in 1733 with a barrel-vaulted roof, its patina testifies to centuries of smoking and drinking. The *Hog's Head*, at the top of Friars Street, has a fairly convincing "old world" feel and a good range of real ales, while *The Meadowpark* pub, on Kenilworth Road near the university, is especially lively in term time.

If you want to carry on after the pubs close, you could try *Rainbow Rocks,* a mainstream music **nightclub** off Baker Street, or *Fubars* in Murray Place for a blast of cheesy house (see the *Stirling Observer* for weekly details). From June to September, **ceilidhs** take place in the wonderful venue of John Cowane's Hospital, near the castle (usually on Mon at 8pm, but check with the tourist office; £3.50). Although geared to tourists rather than locals, the ceilidhs can be fun and often singers and professional dancers are on hand too. The larger Albert Hall is a good venue for classical and pop/rock **concerts**, and recently summer rock concerts have been held on the castle esplanade.

The main venue for **theatre** and **film** is the excellent MacRobert Arts Centre (☎01786/461081) on the university campus (see below), which shows a good selection of drama and mainstream and arthouse films.

Around Stirling

North of Stirling, a ten-minute walk from the fine Victorian spa town of **BRIDGE OF ALLAN, Stirling University** was, until 1992 (when all British colleges and polytechnics acquired university status), the youngest university in Scotland, and once one of the most radical. The university exemplifies successful 1960s architecture, and the landscaped grounds are beautiful – resplendent with daffodils in spring, rhododendrons along the sides of the artificial Airthrey Loch in summer, and the rich colours of the Ochil Hills as a backdrop in autumn. Stranded on the northern edge, **Airthrey Castle** is a prepossessing late-eighteenth-century affair built by Robert Adam, now housing CELT (the Centre for English Language Teaching). The Pathfoot building displays in its main corridor a rich collection of portraits and landscapes by J.D. Fergusson (see p.263), given to the university by his widow. Frequent **buses** run to the university from Murray Place in Stirling, including the Heritage bus service (see p.224).

Overlooking the university from one mile to the southwest is the prominent 1860s **Wallace Monument** (daily: March–May & Oct 10am–5pm; June & Sept 10am–6pm; July & Aug 9.30am–6.30pm; Nov & Dec 10am–4pm; £2.50), a rocket-like tribute to Sir William Wallace ("the hammer and scourge of the English"), who was portrayed by Mel Gibson in the film *Braveheart*. It was from the nearby Wallace's Pass that the Scottish hero led his troops down to defeat the English at the Battle of Stirling Bridge in 1297. Exhibits inside the monument include Wallace's long steel sword and the Hall of (Scottish) Heroes, a row of stern white marble busts featuring John Knox and Adam Smith, among others. If you can manage the climb – 246 spiral steps up – there are superb views across to Fife and Ben Lomond from the top of the 220ft tower. A shuttle bus (70p) runs from the base of the hill to the tower every ten minutes, allowing you to avoid the initial steep climb; the Heritage bus service also calls here.

A woodland path weaves its way from the monument to the ruins of **Cambuskenneth Abbey**, about a mile east of Stirling (ruins April–Sept; grounds all year; HS; free). Founded in 1147 by David I on the site of an Augustinian settlement, the abbey is distinguished by its early fourteenth-century bell tower, though there's little else to see there now. Its history, however, makes it worth a brief look; the Scots parliament met here in 1326 to pledge allegiance to Robert the Bruce's son David, and James III (1451–88) and his wife, Queen Margaret of Denmark, are both buried in the grounds, their graves marked by a nineteenth-century monument erected at the insistence of Queen Victoria.

Above the university on the edge of the Ochil Hills (see p.241) are the wild moors of **Sheriffmuir**, where the Earl of Mar fought the crown forces in 1715. Access to the area is by car up steep single-track roads, but the splendid hills are worth the effort. In summer you can take "hacks" from the **Drumbrae Farm Riding Centre** (☎01786/832247), whose ponies are plump and reliable. The *Sheriffmuir Inn*, sitting in glorious isolation (follow the signs from Dunblane), serves food and is particularly popular in summer.

Frequent trains, bus #58 (and bus #358 in term time) make the journey four miles north of Stirling to **DUNBLANE**, indissolubly linked with the horrific massacre of

March 1996, when Thomas Hamilton entered a local primary school and shot dead fifteen children and their teacher, before turning the gun on himself. Prior to that atrocity, this small, attractive city was renowned for being an ecclesiastical centre since the seventh century, when the Celts founded the Church of St Blane here. **Dunblane Cathedral** (April–Sept Mon–Sat 9.30am–12.30pm & 1.30–6pm, Sun 2–6pm; Oct–March Mon–Sat 9.30am–12.30pm & 1.30–4pm, Sun 2–4pm; HS; free) dates mainly from the thirteenth century, and restoration work carried out a century ago has returned the cathedral to its Gothic splendour. Inside, note the delicate blue-purple stained glass, and the exquisitely carved pews, screen and choir stalls, all crafted in the early twentieth century. Also of interest is the little alcove with its thin stained-glass window, thought to be a hermit's cell, a tenth-century Celtic cross and a worn thirteenth-century double effigy of the fifth Earl of Strathearn and his countess. The cathedral, praised in the highest terms by John Ruskin ("I know not anything so perfect in its simplicity, and so beautiful, in all the Gothic with which I am acquainted"), stands serenely amid a clutch of old-world buildings, among them the seventeenth-century Dean's House, which houses the tiny cathedral **museum** (June–Sept Mon–Sat 10am–12.30pm & 2–4.30pm; free) with exhibits on local history. Close by, the oldest private library in Scotland, **Leighton Library** (May–Oct Mon–Fri 10am–12.30pm & 2–4.30pm), houses 4500 books printed between 1500 and 1840 in ninety languages; visitors can browse through some of the country's rarest books, including a first edition of Sir Walter Scott's *Lady of the Lake*. On a hill overlooking the city, the luxurious **Dunblane Hydro**, a great Victorian *palazzo* run by the Stakis Hotel group(☎01786/822551; ⑨), offers tennis and archery lessons and woodland walks.

Five miles northwest of Stirling (Mon–Sat buses #59 and #211), the **Blair Drummond Safari Park** (April–Oct daily 10am–4.30pm; £7), attempts to recreate the African bush and Limpopo. The only wildlife park in Scotland, it's good for a family day out, with everything from big cats to sea lions and Scotland's only elephants. There's also a pet farm, chimp island and waterfowl cruise, pedal boats and a small bus (50p) to visit the areas where lions, camel and bison roam free. The unlikely background to the park is **Blair Drummond Castle**, a Victorian Baronial extravaganza, now a Rudolf Steiner residential home. Just north past the safari park on the right hand side of the road to Doune is a secluded **graveyard**, the final resting place of the Home Drummond family, who owned Blair Drummond Castle, and their servants. One faithful retainer, as a stone records, served the family all his life, and to within an hour of his death.

DOUNE, eight miles northwest of Stirling, is a sleepy village with a violent past. The ruined, fourteenth-century **Castle** (April–Sept Mon–Sat 9.30am–6pm, Sun 2–6pm; Oct–March Mon–Wed & Sat 9am–4pm, Sun 2–4pm; HS; £2.30) is a marvellous pile standing on a small hill in a bend of the River Teith. Built by Robert, Duke of Albany, it eventually ended up in the hands of the Earls of Moray (whose descendants still own it), following the execution of the Albany family by James I. In the sixteenth century it belonged to the second earl, James Stewart – son of James V and half-brother of Mary, Queen of Scots – murdered in 1592 and immortalized in the ballad the *Bonnie Earl of Moray*. Today the most prominent features of the castle are its mighty 95ft gatehouse, with spacious vaulted rooms, and the kitchens, complete with medieval rubbish chute.

The present earl has a fabulous collection of flash vintage cars, which are on show one mile northwest of town in the **Doune Motor Museum** (April–Nov daily 10am–5pm; £3) off the A84. Among the examples of gleaming paintwork and tanned upholstery you can see legendary models of Bentley, Lagonda, Jaguar, Aston Martin and the second-oldest Rolls Royce in the world (built in 1905). To **get to Doune** from Stirling, take bus #59 which leaves hourly, or every two hours on Sunday.

A couple of miles south of Stirling, just north of the village of **BANNOCKBURN**, the **Bannockburn Heritage Centre** (April–Oct daily 10am–5.30pm; NTS; £2.30) stands close to where Robert the Bruce won his mighty victory over the English at the **Battle of Bannockburn** on June 24, 1314. It was this battle, the climax of the Wars of Independence, which united the Scots under Bruce and led to independence under the Declaration of Arbroath (1320) and the Treaty of Northampton (1328).

Outside, a concrete rotunda encloses a cairn near the spot where Bruce planted his standard after beating Edward II. Of the original bore stone, only a fragment remains, safely on display in the visitor centre. Over-eager visitors used to chip pieces off, and the final straw came when a particularly zealous enthusiast attempted to blast enough of it away to make two curling stones. Pondering the scene is an equestrian statue of Bruce, on the spot from where he is said to have commanded the battle, which was fought on the boggy carse down towards the burn. To reach Bannockburn, buses #51 and #52 leave from Stirling every half-hour.

The Campsies: hills and villages

Southwest of Stirling, the **Campsies**, an area of gently rolling hills and fertile farmland, include the Gargunnock and Fintry Hills and villages and, further south, the **Campsie Fells**. Although the area is often overlooked in the rush to reach the more spectacular Trossachs, it's worth taking a detour here for the fine walks and fishing on offer and the many quiet and pretty hamlets, most notably Fintry. To the north, the Campsies are bordered by the flat swath of the **Carse of Forth**, which separates it from the Trossachs. The carse, blocked in the east by the volcanic crag on which Stirling Castle is perched, partly accounts for Stirling's historical importance: for politicians, soldiers and merchants, the treacherous path north, edged by deep marshes and moss, was only accessible from the town. Finally drained in the eighteenth century by local landowners, the carse was transformed into lush and productive farmland, now traversed by the main road west from Stirling to the heart of theTrossachs, the A811. Heading this way, the first you'll see is the long stretch of the Gargunnock Hills to your left, which derive their distinctive stepped look from ancient lava flows. You can also approach and explore the area from the south from Falkirk, or Glasgow along the A803/A891, which winds along the northern edges of Glasgow's commuter belt, where almost every view is spoilt by industrial blight. Beyond **Lennoxtown**, however, the Campsie Fells are interrupted by nothing but sheep and waterfalls, the roads narrow and winding, and there are few signs of habitation. In winter it's an eerie sight, with the mists rolling in from the moors.

Hikers might want to follow the **Campsie Fells Trail** (for information, call ☎01786/475019 or ☎0141/204 4400), which links the Campsie villages (these include Fintry, Kippen, Gargannock, Balfron and Lennoxtown), or the **Forth and Clyde Canal** walk which gives access to the second-century **Antonine Wall** (see p.238). The area also encompasses part of the West Highland Way, which starts in Milngavie (see p.210), and there are various options for course and game fishing (you can get details from Stirling's tourist office; see p.223). Plenty of **buses** run through the region from Stirling (#10, #107, #210; three or four daily, fewer at weekends), and a **postbus** service (Mon–Sat 9.55am only) operates from **Denny**, roughly five miles south of Stirling (reached from Stirling bus station on buses #39, #81 or #81A). The postbus stops at **Fintry**, from where two buses (Mon–Sat) head further west to Balfron, the birthplace of architect Alexander "Greek" Thomson, who designed many of Glasgow's finest Victorian buildings (see p.571).

Gargunnock and Kippen

Six miles west of Stirling just off the A811, **GARGUNNOCK**, though mainly composed of eighteenth-century cottages, has a seventeenth-century grey crow-stepped church at the heart of the village. It is also home to the oldest **agricultural show** in Scotland which has been held here every summer since 1795. The views from the village over the great green of the carse and across to the mountains of the Trossachs are spectacular. To the east of the village in rolling parkland is handsome **Gargunnock House**, ancestral home of the Stirlings; Chopin is reputed to have spent two weeks here improving the family's keyboard skills. Recently restored and renovated, the house was begun in 1580, with pediments and a Classical facade added in 1794. It sleeps sixteen people, and can be rented from the Landmark Trust (☎01628/825925) for around £1500 a week, depending on the season. There is one **pub** in the centre of the village, the over-renovated *Gargunnock Inn*, which serves run-of-the-mill food.

More appetizing meals are available in **KIPPEN**, which can be reached by a lovely unmarked walk (1hr 30min). The track leads from the west of Gargunnock – the village is a dead-end – through a path of beech trees and into the Leckie Estate, at the heart of which is the privately owned **Leckie Castle**, a sixteenth-century Laird's House where the Lady of Leckie entertained Bonnie Prince Charlie in 1745. Following the farm road to the left as you look down at Leckie Castle, you will eventually come to the Burnton of Boqhuan, a row of eighteenth-century red-stone cottages; take the left-hand fork past the Burnton, until the track comes to a steep field. Cross the field to the far gate and continue up the track and you will soon begin the descent into Kippen. You can have a good **lunch** at *The Cross Keys*, an eighteenth-century hotel-pub on the main street (☎01786/870293; ③). There is little to do in Kippen other than wander along its pretty cobbled street of eighteenth-century houses, into the beautifully restored **smithy** (entry by arrangement only; NTS; ☎01738/631296), and round the adjoining ruined church and graveyard. Midland buses #10, #210 and #212 take you back to Stirling.

Fintry

The key settlement in the Campsies is **FINTRY**, a picture-postcard village at the head of Strathendrick valley and at the centre of the Campsie Fells Trail, that is a regular winner of the "Best Kept Small Village in Scotland" award. There are a couple of **places to stay**: if you're feeling flush, try the wonderful *Culcreuch Castle Hotel* (☎01360/860228; ⑧), a fourteenth-century thick-walled and parapeted pile on the northern side of the village. The castle is set in a country park which contains eight small wooden lodges, available for rent for £200–300 per week. The *Fintry Inn* (☎01360/860224; ③), a pretty white building on Main Street, offers pub food plus B&B accommodation.

Drymen

At the western end of the Campsie Fells, all roads meet at the small village of **DRYMEN**, which sits peacefully on the hills overlooking the winding Endrick water as it nears Loch Lomond. Although once you've seen the pretty eighteenth-century parish church, there's nothing more to do, Drymen's reputation as the "gateway to east Loch Lomondside" means it gets extremely busy during the summer. If you want **to stay**, the no-frills *Winnock Hotel* (☎01360/660245; ⑦) has a restaurant and is prettily sited on the village green, while those wanting to follow the Loch Lomond cycleway can **rent bikes** from Lomond Activities, 64 Main St (☎01360/660066; £10 per day). Ten miles southeast of the village in the Blane Valley, Lang Brothers' **Glengoyne Distillery** (April–Nov Mon–Sat 10am–4pm, Sun noon–4pm; £2.50) offers interesting guided tours of the whisky-making processes, though the staff are rather snooty.

Loch Lomond

Loch Lomond – the largest stretch of fresh water in Britain – is almost as famous as Loch Ness, thanks to the ballad about its "bonnie, bonnie banks", the Scottish folk song said to be written by a Jacobite prisoner. However, all is not bonnie at the loch nowadays, especially on its overdeveloped west side, fringed by the A82; on the water itself,

---

BEN LOMOND

Ordnance Survey Landranger map no.56

Ben Lomond (3192ft), the most southerly of the "Munros", is one of the most frequently climbed hills in Scotland, its commanding position above Loch Lomond affording amazing views of both the Highlands and Lowlands. You should allow five to six hours for the climb.

The tourist route, a beaten track, starts in Rowardennan at the car park at the rear end of the public road just beyond *Rowardennan Hotel*. The route rises through forest and crosses open moors to gain the southern ridge, which leads to the final pyramid. The path zigzags up, then rims the crags of the northeast corrie to reach the summit.

You can return the same way or start off westwards, then south, to traverse the subsidiary top of Ptarmigan down to the youth hostel in Rowardennan (see below) and then along the track to the start.

---

speedboats tear up and down on summer weekends, destroying the tranquillity which so impressed the likes of Queen Victoria, the Wordsworths and Sir Walter Scott.

Nevertheless, the west bank of the loch is an undeniably beautiful stretch of water, and despite the crowds gives better views than the heavily wooded east side. **LUSS**, the setting for the enormously popular Scottish TV soap *Take the High Road*, is the prettiest village, though its picturesque streets can become unbearably crowded in summer. **BALLOCH**, a brash holiday resort at the loch's southern tip, is the place to head for if you want to take a boat trip; various operators offer cruises around the 33 islands scattered near the shore.

The tranquil east bank is far better for walking than the west, and is traversed in its entirety by the West Highland Way footpath, from where you can head on through **Queen Elizabeth Forest Park** (see p.236), or take the stiff but hugely rewarding three-hour hike from **ROWARDENNAN** to the summit of Ben Lomond, the subject of the Scottish proverb "Leave Ben Lomond where it stands" – just let things be.

Practicalities

The West Highland **train** – the line from Glasgow to Mallaig, with a branch line to Oban – joins Loch Lomond seventeen miles north of Balloch at **TARBET**, and has one other station further on at **ARDLUI**, at the mountain-framed head of the loch. There are plenty of **buses** along the shore from Balloch.

Loch Lomond's **tourist office** (daily: April–June, Sept & Oct 10am–5pm; July & Aug 9.30am–7.30pm; ☎01389/753533) is above the marina in Balloch. They'll reserve a room for you without charge at one of the many local **hotels** and **B&Bs**, such as the comfortable *Balloch Hotel*, Balloch Road (☎01389/752579; ⑥), which also has a decent restaurant, or the friendly *Gowanlea Guest House*, Drymen Road (☎01389/752456; ③). A couple of miles up the west side of the loch at minuscule **ARDEN** is Scotland's most beautiful **youth hostel**, a turreted building complete with ghost (☎01389/850226). Caravan parks abound on the west side of the loch, and in Balloch itself there's the *Tullichewan Caravan Park* (☎01389/759475) which also rents out **bikes**; tents are best pitched at the secluded Forestry Commission **campsite** (☎01360/870234; April–Oct) two miles south of Rowardennan at Cashel on the east bank.

Passenger ferries cross between Inverbeg and Rowardennan, where there's an eponymous **hotel** (☎01360/870273; ⑥) and a wonderfully situated **youth hostel** (☎01360/870259; March–Oct), right on the West Highland Way. On the northeast shore of the loch is the *Inversnaid Lodge* (☎01877/386254; ⑤); once the hunting lodge of the Duke of Montrose, it now has a photography centre with instruction and workshops from guest tutors. There is no road from Rowardennan up the east of the loch to

Inversnaid; you have to take the B829 west from Aberfoyle. From Inversnaid you can take the mile-long loch-side walk to Rob Roy's cave, a hideout which is said to have given shelter to both Rob Roy and Robert the Bruce.

As for **eating**, on the west side of the loch, the *Inverbeg Inn* (signposted off the A82), is the most convenient place to stop, with bar snacks and outdoor seating from which to view the loch, as well as a few comfortable **rooms** (☎01436/860678; ⑤). On the east side, there's little option but to take a picnic.

The Trossachs

Often described as the Highlands in miniature, the **Trossachs** area boasts a magnificent diversity of scenery, with dramatic peaks and mysterious, forest-covered slopes that live up to all the images ever produced of Scotland's wild land. This is Rob Roy country, where every waterfall, hidden cave and barely discernible path was once frequented by the seventeenth-century Scottish outlaw who led the Clan MacGregor. Strictly speaking, the name "The Trossachs", normally translated as either "bristly country" or "crossing place", originally referred only to the wooded glen between **Loch Katrine** and Loch Achray, but today it is usually taken as being the whole area from **Callander** in the east to Queen Elizabeth Forest Park in the west, right up to the eastern banks of Loch Lomond.

This is fabulous walking territory. **Ben Venue** and **Ben A'an**, on the southern shores of Loch Katrine, and **Ben Ledi**, just northwest of Callander, especially, offer challenging climbs and, on clear days, stunning views. The weather, however, is unpredictable, and every year there are fatalities in the Trossachs Mountains, so be sure to follow the necessary safety precautions (see p.44). Less taxing walks can be made from the **Queen Elizabeth Park Visitor Centre**, on the A821 north of Aberfoyle. It's a good idea to consult the Bartholomew guide *Walk Loch Lomond and the Trossachs*, which grades walks according to difficulty. The **Trossachs Trundler** (June–Sept Mon–Fri & Sun; contact any tourist office for details) is a gleaming vintage bus which takes a circular route linking Callander, Loch Katrine and Aberfoyle, stopping at various points en route. The bus is timed to connect with sailings of the SS *Sir Walter Scott* on Loch Katrine, and costs £4.50 for a day-pass or £7.40 including the bus fare from Stirling to Callander.

The Trossachs' high tourist profile was largely attributable in the early days to Sir Walter Scott, whose *Lady of the Lake* and *Rob Roy* were set in and around the area. Since then, neither the popularity – nor beauty – of the region have waned, and in high season the place is jam-packed. Autumn is a better time to come, when the hills are blanketed in rich, rusty colours and the crowds are thinner. In terms of where to stay, **Aberfoyle** has a slightly dowdy air, even at the height of summer, so it is better to opt for the romantic seclusion of the **Lake of Menteith**, or the handsome country town of **Callander**.

Aberfoyle and Lake of Menteith

Like Brigadoon waking once a year from a mist-shrouded slumber, each summer the sleepy little town of **ABERFOYLE**, twenty miles west of Stirling, dusts itself down for the annual influx of tourists. Its position in the heart of the Trossachs is ideal, with **Loch Ard Forest** and **Queen Elizabeth Forest Park** stretching across to **Ben Lomond** and **Loch Lomond** to the west, the long curve of Loch Katrine and **Ben Venue** to the northwest, and **Ben Ledi** to the northeast.

Don't come here for lively nightlife or entertainment, but for a good, healthy blast of the outdoors. The town itself is well equipped to lodge and feed visitors (though booking is recommended), and is an excellent base for walking and pony trekking, or simply wandering the hills. You might like to wander to Doon Hill to the north of Aberfoyle;

cross the bridge over the Forth, continue past the cemetery and then follow signs to the **Fairy Knowe** (knoll). A toadstool marker points you through oak and holly trees to the summit of the Knowe where there is a pine tree, said to contain the unquiet spirit of the Reverend Robert Kirk, who studied local fairy lore and published his inquiries in *The Secret Commonwealth* (1691). Legend has it that, as punishment for disclosing supernatural secrets, Robert Kirk was forcibly removed to fairyland where he has languished ever since, although his mortal remains can be found in the nearby graveyard. This short walk should preferably be made at dusk, when it is at its most atmospheric.

About four miles east of Aberfoyle towards Doune, the **Lake of Menteith** is a superb fly-fishing centre and Scotland's only lake (as opposed to loch), so named due to a historic mix-up with the word *laigh*, the Scots for "low-lying ground", which applied to the whole area. To rent a **fishing boat**, contact the Lake of Menteith Fisheries (☎01877/385664). From the northern shore of the lake you can take a little ferry (April–Sept Mon–Sat 9.30am–5.15pm, Sun 10.30am–5.15pm, last boat returns 6pm; £3) to the **Island of Inchmahome**, and explore the lovely ruin of the Augustine abbey. Founded in 1238, **Inchmahome Priory** is perhaps the most beautiful island monastery in Scotland, with its remains rising tall and graceful above the trees. The masons employed to build the Priory are thought to be those who built Dunblane Cathedral (see p.229); certainly the western entrance there resembles that at Inchmahome. The nave of the church is roofless, but in the choir are preserved the graves of important families from the surrounding area. Most touching is a late thirteenth-century double effigy depicting Walter, the first Stewart Earl of Menteith, and his Countess Mary who, feet resting on lion-like animals, turn towards each other and embrace. Also buried at Inchmahome is Robert Bontine Cunninghame Graham (1852–1936), the adventurer, scholar, socialist and Scottish nationalist, who was Liberal MP for northwest Lanarkshire for 25 years and the first president of the National Party of Scotland. A pal of Buffalo Bill in Mexico as well as an intimate friend of the novelist Joseph Conrad, Cunninghame Graham had a ranch in Argentina, where he was affectionately known as "Don Roberto".

Five-year-old **Mary, Queen of Scots** was hidden at Inchmahome in 1547 before being taken to France; there's a knot garden in the west of the island known as Queen Mary's bower, where legend has it, the child Queen played. Traces remain of an

ROB ROY

"Rob Roy, hero or villain?" ponders the tourist literature, in the great spirit of inquiry. Given that Rob Roy's clan, the MacGregors, have the distinction of having invented the term "blackmail" (from the levying of black meal through protection rackets), and that Rob Roy himself achieved fame through cattle rustling and thieving, the evidence seems to point to the "villain" thesis. His life, though, dramatizes the clash between the doomed clan culture of the Gaelic-speaking Highlanders, and the organized feudal culture of lowland Scots, which effectively ended with the defeat of the Jacobites at Culloden in 1746.

Rob Roy (meaning "Red Robert" in Gaelic) was born in 1671 in Glengyle just north of Loch Katrine and started life as a cattle farmer, supported by the powerful Duke of Montrose. When the Duke withdrew his support, possibly having been robbed of £1000 by Rob Roy, the latter became a bankrupt and a brigand, plundering the rich carse land and avenging himself on the duke. He was present at the Battle of Sherrifmuir in 1715, ostensibly as a Jacobite but probably as an opportunist – the chaos would have made cattle raiding easier. Eventually captured and sentenced to transportation, Rob Roy was pardoned and returned to Balquhidder, where he remained until his death in 1734. Rob Roy's life has been much romanticized, from Sir Walter Scott's 1818 version of the story in his novel *Rob Roy*, to the 1995 film of the same name starring Liam Neeson.

orchard planted by the monks, but the island is thick now with oak, ash and Spanish chestnut. On an nearby but inaccessible island is the ruined castle of **Inchtalla**, the home of the Earls of Menteith in the sixteenth and seventeenth centuries.

Seven miles east of Aberfoyle on the A873 to Callander, the **Farm Life Centre** (April–Oct daily 10am–6pm; £3.50) makes an entertaining stop for children on a rainy day. Kids can pet a host of animals, make oatcakes, milk goats and ride tractors on this converted farm; there's also a picnic area, tearoom and small museum.

Practicalities

Regular **buses** from Stirling to Aberfoyle pull into the car park on Main Street. The **tourist office**, directly next door, has full details of local accommodation, sights and outdoor activities (daily: March–June, Sept & Oct 10am–5pm; July & Aug 9.30pm–7pm; ☎01877/382352). The nearby **Scottish Wool Centre**, in the car park (Easter–Oct Mon–Fri 9.30am–6pm, Sat & Sun 9.30am–6.30pm; Nov–Easter daily 10am–5.30pm) sells all the usual jumpers and woolly toys, and is a popular stopoff point with tour buses.

For **accommodation**, head to the *Inverard Hotel*, on Loch Ard Road (☎01877/382229; ⑤), a large country house with well-furnished rooms and good views over the River Forth and the hills beyond. Alternatively, you could try the warren-like, tartan-carpeted *Covenanter's Inn* (☎01877/382347; ④) at the northern end of town (turn left across the bridge and it's up behind the trees on the right). There are scores of **B&Bs** in Aberfoyle, including the comfortable Tudor-style *Craigend*, 1 Craiguchty Terrace (☎01877/382716; ③), and many dotted around the surrounding countryside, among them *Creag-ard House* (☎01877/382297; ④) in the pretty village of Milton, just two miles west of Aberfoyle. It looks out on Ben Lomond and Loch Ard, to which it has fishing and boating rights. More atmospheric than Aberfoyle, the **Lake of Menteith** is a beautiful place to stay – the *Lake Hotel and Restaurant* (☎01877/385258; ⑧) at Port of Menteith has a lovely lakeside setting next to the Victorian Gothic parish church, and a classy restaurant, or there's the handsome *Lochend Chalets* (☎01877/385268) on the lake, which sleep four to six people, and cost £240–645 per week in summer.

A couple of miles south of Aberfoyle on the edge of Queen Elizabeth Forest Park, *Cobleland Campsite* (☎01877/382392; March–Oct), run by the Forestry Commission, covers five acres of woodland by the River Forth (little more than a stream here). Further south the family-run *Trossachs Holiday Park* (☎01877/382614; April–Oct), is twice the size and has **bikes** for rent.

One of Scotland's best **restaurants**, the *Braeval Old Mill* (☎01877/382711; dinner Wed–Sat, lunch Thurs–Sun), lies just east of Aberfoyle on the road to Stirling. Plain on the outside and pleasingly austere inside, it serves delicious and exquisitely presented gourmet food for around £30 per head. For those on a smaller budget, there's a range of decent eating places in the town centre; try the *Country Kitchen* or *The Coach House*, both licensed restaurants on Main Street.

Duke's Pass

Even if you have to walk it, don't miss the trip from Aberfoyle to Callander, which for part of the way takes you along the **Duke's Pass** (so called because it once belonged to the Duke of Montrose), as it weaves through the **Queen Elizabeth Forest Park** to just south of Loch Katrine.

The A821 twists up out of Aberfoyle, following the contours of the hills and snaking back on itself in tortuous bends. About halfway up is the park's excellent **visitor centre** (April–Oct daily 10am–6pm; Nov–March Sat & Sun only 10am–4pm; ☎01877/382258), which details the local fauna and flora. From here various marked

---

QUEEN ELIZABETH FOREST PARK

Covering 75,000 acres on the edge of the Highlands, **Queen Elizabeth Forest Park** is a spectacular tract of wilderness bordering **Loch Lomond**, and incorporating **Loch Ard**, **Loch Achray** and **Loch Lubnaig**, as well as **Ben Venue**, **Ben A'an** and **Ben Ledi**. Managed by the Forestry Commission, it is used partly for leisure and recreation and is criss-crossed by waymarked paths and trails, including part of the **West Highland Way** and, on the western side, access to **Ben Lomond** (3192ft). Among its varied wildlife habitats are the forests north of Balmaha, which are home to red and roe deer, as well as wild goats. The park **visitor centre** is just outside **Aberfoyle** in the Trossachs (see above).

Accommodation in the park is available at two **campsites** – one on the banks of Loch Lomond at Cashel, near Rowardennan (see p.232), and the other beside the River Forth at Cobleland, south of Aberfoyle (☎01877/382383). There are also **log cabins** on the shores of Loch Lubnaig in Strathyre, south of Lochearnhead (cabins for five cost £350 per week; ☎0131/334 0303).

Full details about the park are available from the **Forest Enterprise**, Aberfoyle, Stirling FK8 3UX (☎01877/382383), and the **Countryside Ranger Service**, Enviromental Services, Viewforth, Stirling SK8 2ET (☎01786/432363).

---

paths wind through the forests giving splendid views over the lowlands and surrounding hills. About five miles further on, a track to the right marks the start of the **Achray Forest Drive**, a worthwhile excursion by car, foot or mountain bike which leads through the forest and along the western shore of **Loch Drunkie**, before rejoining the main road. After another couple of miles, a road branches off to the left, leading to the southern end of **Loch Katrine** at the foot of **Ben Venue** (2370ft, a strenuous walk), from where the historic steamer, the SS *Sir Walter Scott*, has been plying the waters since 1900, chugging up the loch to Stronachlachar and the wild country of Glengyle (April–Oct Sun–Fri 4 daily, Sat 2 daily; £3.70). To climb Ben A'an (1520ft), start from the *Trossachs Hotel* on the north bank of Loch Arhray. No longer a hotel, it retains the splendid exterior designed by the outlandishly named Lord Willoughby d'Eresby in 1852.

The final leg of the pass is along the tranquil shores of **Loch Venachar** at the southern foot of Ben Ledi. Look out for the small **Callander Kirk** in a lovely setting at the edge of the loch, where services are still held on the first Sunday of each month at 3pm – presumably because it takes all morning (or month) to get there.

Callander and around

CALLANDER, on the eastern edge of the Trossachs, sits quietly on the banks of the River Teith roughly ten miles north of Doune, at the southern end of the **Pass of Leny**, one of the key routes into the Highlands. Larger than Aberfoyle, it is an even more popular summer holiday base and a convenient springboard for exploring the surrounding area. Its wide main street recalls the influence of the military architects who designed the town after Bonnie Prince Charlie's Jacobite Rebellion of 1745.

Callander first came to fame during the "Scottish Enlightenment" of the eighteenth and nineteenth centuries, when the glowing reports given by Sir Walter Scott and William Wordsworth prompted the first tourists to venture into the wilds by horse-drawn carriage. Development was given a boost when Queen Victoria chose to visit, and then by the arrival of the train line – long since closed – in the 1860s.

The present community has not been slow to capitalize on its appeal, establishing a plethora of restaurants and tearooms, antique shops, secondhand bookstores, and shops selling local woollens and crafts. The chief formal attraction is the **Rob Roy and**

Trossachs Visitor Centre at Ancaster Square on the main street (Jan & Feb Sat & Sun only 10am–5pm; March–May & Oct–Dec daily 10am–5pm; June & Sept daily 9.30am–6pm; July & Aug daily 9am–7pm; £2.50), an entertaining and partisan account of the life of the diminutive redhead.

Practicalities

Callander's **tourist office** is in the Rob Roy and Trossachs Visitor Centre (same times; ☎01877/330342), and can book **accommodation**. The best options include *The Priory*, on Bracklinn Road (☎01877/330001; ④), a highly recommended Victorian house in its own gardens with good views; the handsome Victorian *Brook Linn Country House*, Leny Feus (☎01877/330103; ⑤), set above the town; and the *Ben A'an Guest House* (☎01877/330 317; ③) on the main street. A couple of miles out of town – cross the river at Bridge Street, follow the A81, turn right at the Invertrossachs Junction and continue for a mile – you'll find *Trossachs Backpackers*, a sparkling new hostel and activity centre with self-catering facilities and **bike rental** (☎01877/331100). For more luxury, try the *Roman Camp Hotel*, signposted off the main street (☎01877/330003; ⑨), a turreted and romantic seventeenth-century country house in twenty-acre gardens on the River Teith, or the *Invertrossachs Country House* (☎01877/331126; ⑧), west of Callander on the southern shores of Loch Venachar, a plush Edwardian mansion offering superior B&B. Despite its popularity, there are few **restaurants** worth recommending in Callander. The best place is in the *Roman Camp Hotel*, which serves splendid Scottish produce in refined surroundings. For good pub food, try the *Murtle Inn* on the eastern edge of Callander.

North to Lochearnhead

On each side of Callander, pleasant and less-than-arduous walks wind north through a wooded gorge to the **Falls of Leny** and **Bracklinn Falls** – both distances of only a mile or so. Longer **walks** of varying degrees of exertion thread their way through the surrounding countryside, the most challenging being that to the summit of **Ben Ledi** (2857ft), for which you should be well shod and well prepared (see p.44).

North of town, you can walk or ride the scenic six-mile **Callander to Strathyre Cycleway**, which forms part of the network of cycleways between the Highlands and Glasgow. The route is based on the old Caledonian train line to Oban, which closed in 1965, and runs along the western side of **Loch Lubnaig**. To the north, Rob Roy is buried in the small yard behind the ruined church at tiny **BALQUHIDDER**, where he died in 1734. Oddly enough, considering the Rob Roy fever that plagues the region, his grave – marked by a rough stone carved with a sword, cross and a man with a dog – is remarkably underplayed. If you want to **stay** in Balquhidder, go to the award-winning eighteenth-century farmhouse *Monachyle Mhor* hotel (☎01877/384622; ⑥), which has a terrific restaurant looking out to Loch Voil.

Watersports are the life force of the village of **Lochearnhead** (see p.268), at the western head of Loch Earn, a substantial body of water running east into Perthshire and fed by waters off the slopes of **Ben Vorlich** (3201ft) to the south. For a more impressive stretch of water, though, head to **Loch Tay**, about fifteen miles north of Callander, which points northeastwards like a fourteen-mile finger towards Aberfeldy (see p.269).

The Forth Valley

The **Forth Valley** stetches some forty miles southeast of Stirling along the Firth of Forth. The area has long been known for its industry, historically for the famous – but now redundant – Carron Ironworks near **Falkirk**, which was founded in 1759 and manufactured "carronades" (small cannons) for Nelson's fleet, and more recently for BP's petrochemical plant at **Grangemouth**. The lights and fires of the refineries are spectacular at night, and inspired Bertrand Tavernier to make the dour 1979 sci-fi film *Death Watch* in Scotland.

Given the lack of good accommodation in the Forth Valley, the area is best seen as a day-trip from either Stirling or Edinburgh. Unless you are particularly interested in steam trains – in which case definitely visit **Bo'ness** – the only unmissable outing is to **Linlithgow Palace**.

If you're coming from the east, across the Kincardine Bridge, you may want to pop into the signposted **tourist office** at Pine'N'Oak Layby, Kincardine Bridge (April, May & Sept Mon–Sat 10am–4pm, Sun noon–4pm; June–Aug daily 10am–5pm; ☎01324/831422). The regular train service between Stirling and Edinburgh makes Falkirk and Linlithgow easily accessible; for other destinations you'll have to rely on the comprehensive network of buses.

Falkirk and around

FALKIRK, the Forth Valley's main commercial centre, was the site of two major battles, one in 1298, when William Wallace fell victim to the English under Edward I, and the other in 1746, when Bonnie Prince Charlie, retreating northwards, sent the Hanoverians packing in one of his last victories over government troops. Traditionally a livestock centre, Falkirk was transformed in the eighteenth century by the construction of first the Forth and Clyde Canal, allowing easy access to Glasgow, and then the Edinburgh and Glasgow Union Canal, which continued the route through to Edinburgh. Just twenty years later, the trains arrived, and the canals became obsolete. However, a £78 million millennium project is currently under way to renovate the canal link to Glasgow –ultimately linking the North Sea to the Atlantic – with a massive canal interchange at Falkirk itself, using waterwheel technology to raise and lower boats between the locks. The wide network of old industrial canals in the area surrounding Falkirk offers good opportunities for **boating**, **canoeing** and **walks**.

The town itself is a busy local shopping centre, whose only formal attraction, set in Callendar Park, is **Callendar House** (April–Sept Mon–Sat 10am–5pm, Sun 2–5pm; Oct–March Mon–Sat 10am–5pm; £1.80), which was owned by the staunchly Jacobite Livingston family. Though more geared to conference guests than tourists, the house's fabulous Georgian kitchens are worth a look, with gleaming utensils, a huge mechanized spit and a costumed kitchen maid who dispenses information about life below stairs whilst chopping apples, while the **Historical Research Centre** (Mon–Fri 10am–12.30pm & 1.30–5pm; free) will gladly help you delve into local family history.

In **BONNYBRIDGE**, five miles west of Falkirk (take bus #37 from Falkirk), is **Rough Castle**. Built in 142 AD, this was one of the forts which were set up, at two-mile intervals, to defend the entire length of the Roman **Antonine Wall**. In the opposite direction, the industrial town of **GRANGEMOUTH** sits at the edge of the Forth, its huge chimneys spewing out smoke visible for miles around. If industrial heritage is your scene, head for the **museum** on Bo'ness Road in the Charing Cross area of town (Mon–Sat 10am–12.30pm & 1.30–5pm; free), which tells the history of Grangemouth as one of Scotland's first planned industrial towns.

The Pineapple, north of Falkirk (turn off the A905 onto the B9124, or take bus #75), qualifies as one of Scotland's most exotic and eccentric buildings, a 45ft-high stone pineapple built as a garden folly in the 1770s for the fourth Earl of Dunmore. The folly was an elaborate joke on Lord Dunmore's part; returning from a spell as Governor of Virginia, where sailors would put a pineapple on a gatepost to announce their return, he chose to signal his homecoming on a grand scale. The folly is now owned by the NTS, and the outhouse can be rented for holidays (see opposite).

Practicalities

Falkirk's centrally located **bus** station is at Callender Riggs. Regular **trains** run from Glasgow Queen Street, Edinburgh and Stirling to Falkirk Grahamston Station (as opposed to Falkirk High Station, which is further from the centre), from where it's a five-minute walk to the **tourist office**, 2–4 Glebe St (April & May daily 9.30am–5pm; June, July, Sept & Oct daily 9.30am–6pm; Aug daily 9.30am–7pm; Nov–March Mon–Sat 9.30am–12.30pm & 1.30–5pm; ☎01324/620244). If you want to **stay**, the best bet is the elegant *Darrioch House B&B,* on Camelon Road at the west end of town (☎01324/623041; ⑤), with large gardens, or try the modern *Stakis Falkirk Park Hotel*, directly opposite overlooking Dollar Park (☎01324/628331; ⑦), with comfortable rooms. The outhouse of The Pineapple folly can be rented through the Landmark Trust (☎01628/825925); it sleeps four, and costs around £550 per week.

You can **eat** Mexican food and hear **live music** at *Behind the Wall*, 14 Melville St, a brasserie-style café with a beer garden, while *Finn MacCools*, 1 Princess St, serves good bar meals. There's also an upmarket French **restaurant**, *Pierre's* (☎01324/635843), near the town centre at 140 Graham's Rd.

Linlithgow

Roughly equidistant (fifteen miles) from Falkirk and Edinburgh is the ancient royal burgh of **LINLITHGOW**. The town itself has largely kept its medieval layout, but development since the 1960s has sadly stripped it of some fine buildings, notably close to the **Town Hall** and **Cross** – the former marketplace – on the long High Street.

You should head straight for **Linlithgow Palace** (April–Sept Mon–Sat 9.30am–6pm, Sun 2–6pm; Oct–March Mon–Sat 9.30am–12.30pm & 1.30–4pm, Sun 2–4pm; £2.80), a splendid fifteenth-century ruin romantically set on the edge of Linlithgow Loch and associated with some of Scotland's best-known historical figures – including the ubiquitous Mary, Queen of Scots, who was born here in 1542. A royal manor house is believed to have existed on this site since the time of David I. Fire razed the manor in 1424, after which James I began construction of the present palace, a process that continued through two centuries and the reign of no fewer than eight monarchs. From the top of the northwest tower, Queen Margaret looked out in vain for the return of James IV from the field of Flodden in 1513. The ornate octagonal **fountain** in the inner courtyard, with its wonderfully intricate figures and medallion heads, flowed with wine for the wedding of James V and Mary of Guise. Bonnie Prince Charlie visited during the 1745 rebellion, and one year later the palace was burnt, probably accidentally, whilst occupied by General Hawley's troops.

This is a great place to take children: the rooflessness of the castle creates unexpected vistas and the elegant rooms with their intriguing spiral staircases seem labyrinthine. The galleried **Great Hall** is magnificent, as is the adjoining kitchen, which has a truly cavernous fireplace. Don't miss the dank downstairs **brewery**, which produced vast quantities of ale; 24 gallons was apparently a good nightly consumption in the sixteenth century.

St Michael's Church, adjacent to the palace, is one of Scotland's largest pre-Reformation churches, consecrated in the thirteenth century. The present building was completed three hundred years later, with the exception of the hugely incongruous aluminium spire, tacked on in 1946. Inside, decorative woodcarving around the pulpit depicts queens Margaret, Mary and Victoria.

A foil to the romantic historicism of the palace, the **Linlithgow Story** (March–Oct Mon & Wed–Sat 10am–5pm, Sun 1–4pm; £1), 143 High St, gives a realistic look at the transition from royal burgh via industrial centre to suburban backwater, with items such as a sword reputedly used at the Battle of Stirling Bridge and fifteenth-century coins on display. The second floor looks at local industries from paper mills to tanneries, where, it is said, the use of materials derived from animals was so efficient that "only the moo was left".

Running through Linlithgow is part of the **Union Canal**, the 31-mile artery opened in 1822, which linked Edinburgh with Glasgow via Falkirk. On summer weekends the Linlithgow Union Canal Society runs short trips on the *Victoria* (£2), a diesel-powered replica of a Victorian steam packet boat, and longer trips to the Avon Aquaduct on the *St Magdalene*, an electric canal boat (£6). The boats depart from the Manse Road canal basin, uphill from the train station at the southern end of town (☎01506/842575). An eighteen-mile walk along the canal towpath leads eventually to the centre of Edinburgh, but involves negotiating a path across a section of the Edinburgh ring road.

Practicalities

Frequent **buses** between Stirling and Edinburgh stop at the Cross, and the town is on the main train routes from Edinburgh to both Glasgow Queen Street and Stirling; the **train station** is at the southern end of town. From the station head downhill for High Street, where the **tourist office** is in the Burgh Halls building at the Cross (May & Sept daily except Sun 10am–5pm; June daily 10am–5pm; July & Aug daily 10am–6pm; Oct–April Tues–Sat 10am–4pm; ☎01506/844600).

For **accommodation** try *The Star and Garter*, 1 High St (☎01506/846362; ⑤), at the east end of town, a comfortable old coaching inn that also serves inexpensive bar meals. The Victorian *Pardovan House* is an excellent **B&B** (☎01506/834219; ③; May–Sept) at Philipstoun, a couple of miles west of Linlithgow, or you could try the friendly *Belsyde Farm*, Lanark Road (☎01506/842098; ③), a late-eighteenth-century house on a sheep and cattle farm beside the Union Canal. There are very few places to **eat** in Linlithgow, but for good pub food try *The Four Marys*, opposite the Cross on High Street, or, at the opposite end of the street, the smaller, more basic *West Port Hotel*, 18–20 West Port (☎01506/847456; ③), with a popular downstairs **bar** which also serves food. For more expensive Scottish cuisine, *Livingstone's* (☎01506/846505) on High Street serves meals in a small garden observatory.

The only official **campsite** in the area is at *Beecraigs Caravan Park* (☎01506/844516), about four miles south of town and part of the larger Beecraigs Country Park. There are only 39 pitches, however, so get there early or phone first.

Around Linlithgow

The small hillside town of **BO'NESS**, roughly four miles north of Linlithgow – which has traditionally looked down its nose at its pint-sized neighbour – sprawls in a less than genteel fashion down to the Forth, where a riverside path is separated from the road by a strip of scrub. On a clear day there are good views across the Forth to beautiful Culross (see p.245). The **Bo'ness and Kinneil train**, whose headquarters are in the old station at the eastern end of the waterfront road, is Scotland's largest vintage train centre, and in summer (July & Aug daily; April–Oct Sat & Sun; ☎01506/822298) runs lovingly kept steam trains to Birkhill, just over three miles away (£3.60 return). Here, you can wander along the wooded Avon Gorge, or take a guided tour through the **Birkhill Clay Mine** (four tours a day coincide with train times; £2.90), where 300 million-year-old fossils still line the walls. There's a small **tourist office** at Hamilton's Cottage (March & April Mon–Fri 9.30am–5.30pm; May & June Mon–Sat 9.30am–5.30pm, Sun 2–5pm; July–Sept Mon–Sat 9am–5.45pm, Sun 11am–5pm; Oct Mon–Fri 10am–5pm; ☎01506/826626), but if you can't find it – even some of the locals don't know it's there – ask at the post office on the waterfront road. If you want to **stay the night**, the best option is the *Richmond Park Hotel*, 26 Linlithgow Rd (☎01506/823213; ⑤), which has comfortable rooms and, set in its own grounds, offers good views across the Forth to the Fife hills. The moderately priced **restaurant** serves a fair choice of dishes, including some vegetarian, and the airy conservatory is a popular place to drink.

Further down the coast from Bo'ness and four miles northeast of Linlithgow, boldly positioned on a rocky promontory in the Forth, lies the village of **BLACKNESS**, once Linlithgow's seaport but now known for the fifteenth-century **Blackness Castle** (April–Sept Mon–Sat 9.30am–6pm, Sun 2–6pm; Oct–March Mon–Wed & Sat 9.30am–4pm, Thurs 9.30am–noon, Sun 2–4pm; £1.50), which, after the Treaty of Union in 1707, was one of only four castles in Scotland to be garrisoned. Said to be built in the shape of a galleon, the castle offers grand views of the Forth bridges from the narrow gun slits in its northern tower.

General Tam Dalyell, the seventeenth-century Scottish royalist, spent part of his youth at the **House of the Binns** (May–Sept daily except Fri 1.30–5pm; NTS; £3.50), occupying a hilltop site about two miles east of Linlithgow. Inside you can see ornate plaster ceilings, paintings, period furniture and family relics not much changed since Tam's day.

The Ochils

The rugged **Ochil Hills** stretch for roughly forty miles northeast of Stirling, along the northern side of the Firth of Forth, forming a steep-faced range which drops down to the flood plain of the Forth Valley and is sliced by a series of deep-cut, richly wooded glens. Although they provide a dramatic backdrop for the region's towns, villages and castles, this is gentler country than, say, the Trossachs, with the hills gradually giving way to the pastoral landscape of Fife.

The area has been at the centre of Scotland's wool production for centuries, rivalled only by the Borders. The cottage industry of **Clackmannanshire**, immediately east of Stirling, capitalized on the technological advances of the Industrial Revolution and by the mid-nineteenth century there were more than thirty mills in the space of half as many miles.

Recent times have seen a change in the industry, with the old family firms and handknitters unable to compete with modern technology. Nonetheless, you can still see traditional producers at work in shops and private houses, especially on the **Mill Trail** that starts in **Alva** (see below) and links the main towns, historic sites and modern mill shops. A glimpse of a different past is offered by various fortified tower houses – Clackmannanshire was a convenient base from which the country's powerful families could keep abreast of developments at the Royal Court at Stirling. None of them are open to the public at present, but substantial remains can still be seen at the Bruce house at Clackmannan and the Erskine's at **Alloa**, which has recently been restored. Above the picturesque town of **Dollar** (once Dolour) is a wooded glen which you ascend, with the Burn of Sorrow and the Burn of Care rushing by, to reach **Castle Campbell**, once called Castle Gloom. Despite the preponderance of mournful names, the town, the walk (see overleaf) and the castle make for a wonderful outing. Beyond Dollar the road runs south along the Devon Valley to Kinross, on the shores of Loch Leven.

There are no trains to destinations in the Ochils, but regular **buses** shuttle between Stirling and Yetts o' Muckhart (northeast of Dollar), and from Alloa to Tillicoultry.

The Ochil foothills

Three miles or so northeast of Stirling, the small and very appealing village of **BLAIRLOGIE** sits amidst orchards and gardens below a private castle. **Logie Old Kirk**, a ruined church and graveyard dating from the late seventeenth century, is beautifully sited by Logie Burn. Immediately to the rear looms **Dumyat** (pronounced "Dum-eye-at"), which offers spectacular views from its 1376ft summit.

MENSTRIE, a mile east, is noted for **Menstrie Castle** (May–Sept Sat & Sun 2–4pm; free), a much-restored, sixteenth-century stone-built mansion on Castle Road, which is totally at odds with the housing estate that now hems it in. The castle was the birthplace of Sir William Alexander, first Earl of Stirling, who in 1621 set off to found a Scots colony in Nova Scotia. There's little to see now, except an exhibition room displaying the coats of arms of the 109 subsequent baronets of Nova Scotia.

As well as a strong tradition of weaving, **ALVA**, five miles further on, was also known for its silver mining – an industry long since gone. From here you can follow **Alva Glen**, a hearty mile-and-a-half walk dipping down through the hills, which takes in a number of waterfalls. The **Mill Trail** starts from Glentana Mills, on Stirling Street, which doubles as a **tourist office** (daily: April–June & Oct–March 10am–5pm; July–Sept 9am–6pm; ☎01259/769696).

A few miles south of Alva on the A907, the nondescript town of **ALLOA** is home to the beautifully restored **Alloa Tower** (May–Sept daily 1.30–5.30pm; NTS; £2.30). Ancestral home of the Earls of Mar for four centuries, it's now incongrously surrounded by housing estates, though the parapet walk offers lovely views of the Forth. The only other reason to visit Alloa is to **stay** in the luxurious *Gean House* (☎01259/219275; ⑨), an elegant Edwardian mansion set in twenty acres of parkland, with a plush walnut-panelled restaurant, which serves simple, high-quality food.

Dollar

Nestling in a fold of the Ochils on the northern bank of the small River Devon where mountain waters rush off the hills, affluent **DOLLAR** is known for its Academy, founded in 1820 with a substantial bequest from local lad John MacNabb, and now one of Scotland's most respected private schools – its pupils and staff account for around a third of the town's population. Above the town, the dramatic chasm of **Dollar Glen** is commanded by **Castle Campbell** (April–Sept daily 9.30am–6pm; Oct–March Mon–Wed & Sat 9.30am–4pm, Thurs 9.30am–noon, Sun 2–4pm; NTS/HS; £2.30), formerly, and still unofficially, known as Castle Gloom – a fine and evocative tag but, prosaically, a derivation of an old Gaelic name. A one-and-a-half-mile road leads up from the main street, but becomes very narrow, very steep, and stops short of the castle, with only limited parking at the top. There is a marked walk through the glen to the castle, past mossy crags and rushing streams (see below).

WALKING ABOVE DOLLAR

Ordnance Survey Landranger map no. 58

The River Devon rises far in the Ochils but does a huge loop round Glendevon and the crook of Devon before turning to flow along the valley below the Ochil scarp. A walk combining the glen with Castle Campbell and Dollar Hill is highly recommended, and takes around three hours. A shorter (2hr) walk is possible, if you miss out the hill.

Walk up the Burnside from the town centre (clock tower) and then along a footpath from the top bridge beside the burn to pass an open area and reach the wooded glen (NTS). Keep an eye on small children, as in some places the path is steep and unfenced. Other bridges eventually lead you out near Castle Campbell, perched between the Burn of Care and the Burn of Sorrow.

You can return to Dollar by the small tarred road, which stops just short of the castle. But if you want to venture further Dollar Hill (Bank Hill on the OS map) is easily accessible by going up the burn to a bridge over the Sorrow. From here there's a direct descent to Dollar via the golf course. There is also an old drovers' road through to Glendevon, but you'll need to arrange transport back to Dollar from there. Leaving the castle the road dips, then climbs to a cottage (start of the track to Glendevon) and a car park (good view of the keep), before descending steeply to the town below.

The castle came into the hands of the Campbells in 1481, who changed its name from Castle Gloom in 1489. John Knox preached here in 1556, although probably from within the castle rather than from the curious archway in the garden as is traditionally claimed. In 1654 the castle was burnt by Cromwell's troops; the remains of a graceful seventeenth-century loggia and a roofless hall bear witness to the destruction. However, the oldest part of the castle, the fine fifteenth-century tower built by Sir Colin Campbell, survived the fire; look out for the claustrophobic pit-prison just off the Great Hall and the latrines with their vertiginous views. You can also walk round the roof of the tower, where there's a wonderful vista of the hills behind the castle, and down the glen to Dollar.

If you're tempted to **stay** at Dollar, try the modern *Tigh Ur*, 4 Hillfoots Rd (☎0374/182799; ③), or the comfortable *Castle Campbell Hotel* on Bridge Street (☎01259/742519; ⑥). The *Strathallen Hotel* on Chapel Road is a good spot for a pub **lunch** with real ale and outside seating, while three miles east of town, on the Tillicoultry road, the *Harvieston Inn* offers reasonably priced Scottish food.

The Devon Valley
Beyond Dollar, the A91 leads through the hills to Kinross and runs along the southern edge of the **Devon Valley**, passing through the hamlets of **Pool o' Muckhart** and **Yetts o' Muckhart**.

The scenic A823 cuts up from Yetts o' Muckhart through the valley itself, where there's a large **campsite** with good facilities (☎01259/781246) just beyond **GLENDEVON**. The village is also home to a simple **youth hostel** (☎01259/781206; April–Oct), which organizes pony trekking from mid-June to September, and can give advice on walks in the area. The road continues from here to **Gleneagles**, with its famous hotel and golf course (see p.266).

In the other direction, south of Yetts o' Muckhart, the same road crosses the River Devon at **Rumbling Bridge** – effectively two bridges; the newer one, built in the early nineteenth century, sweeping over the top of the old one, which dates from 1713. The observation point offers breathtaking views of the magnificent, 120ft-deep **gorge**, and you can follow a shady path along the river, through the lush vegetation flourishing in the damp, limestone walls of the chasm.

Kinross and Loch Leven
Although still by no means a large place, **KINROSS**, on the A977 a mile west of the loch, has been transformed in the last couple of decades by the construction of the nearby M90 Edinburgh–Perth motorway. The old village is still there, at the southern end of the main street, but apart from the views of Loch Leven its charm has been eroded by amorphous splodges of modern housing, which threaten to nudge it into the loch itself. The best time to visit is on Sunday, when the stalls of a large and lively **covered market** spring up on the southern edge of town, pulling in crowds who rifle through anything from kitsch ornaments to leather jackets.

During the summer a **ferry** departs regularly to ply the trout-filled waters of **Loch Leven**. In recent years the loch has become a National Nature Reserve and the location of international fishing competitions, and it also features **Castle Island**, where Mary, Queen of Scots was imprisoned for eleven months in 1567–68. On the island, the ruined fourteenth-century **Loch Leven Castle** (April–Sept Mon–Sat 9.30am–6pm, Sun 2–6pm; HS; £2.80) stands forlorn, little more than a tower. Nevertheless, it's easy to imagine the isolation of the incarcerated Mary, who is believed to have miscarried twins while here. She managed to charm the 18-year-old son of Lady Douglas into helping her escape: he stole the castle keys, secured a boat in which to row ashore, locked the castle gates behind them and threw the keys into the loch – from where they were retrieved three centuries later.

FIFE

The ancient Kingdom of **Fife**, designated as such by the Picts in the fourth century, is a small area (barely fifty miles at its widest point), but one which has a definite identity, inextricably bound with the waters which surround it on three sides – the Tay to the north, the Forth to the south, and the cold North Sea to the east. That the Fifers managed to retain their "Kingdom" when local government was reorganized in 1975 and 1995, is perhaps testimony to their will.

Despite its size, Fife encompasses several different areas, with a marked difference between the semi-industrial south and the rural north. In the **south**, the recent closure of the coal mines has left local communities floundering to regain a foothold, and the squeeze on the fishing industry may well lead to further decline. In the meantime many of the villages have capitalized on their unpretentious appeal and welcomed tourism in a way that has enhanced rather than degraded their natural assets; the perfectly preserved town of **Culross** is unmissable. East of Culross is **Dunfermline**, an overdeveloped town with stunning remains of the first Benedictine priory in Scotland.

Central Fife is dominated in the south by **Kirkcaldy**, the region's largest town, and in the north by **Cupar**, Fife's capital. Although only separated by twenty miles, they couldn't be more different: the former is something of an industrial blackspot in an otherwise green area, while the latter is a charming market town set in the rolling scenery for which central Fife is known.

Tourism and agriculture are the economic mainstays of the **northeast** corner of Fife, where the landscape varies from the gentle hills in the rural hinterland, to the windswept cliffs, rocky bays and sandy beaches on which scenes from the film *Chariots of Fire* were shot. The fishing industry is still prominent, as is evident in the beautiful and ancient villages lining the shore of the East Neuk from Crail on the eastern tip down to Earlsferry. **St Andrews**, Scotland's oldest university town, and the home of the world-famous Royal and Ancient Golf club, is on the northeast coast. Development here has been cautious, and the hills and hamlets of the surrounding area retain an appealing and old-fashioned feel.

The main **transport route** through the region is the M90 from Edinburgh to Perth, which edges Fife's western boundary. The coastal route is more attractive, however, and also affords relatively easy access into the centre of Fife. The train line follows the coast as far north as Kirkcaldy and then cuts inland, towards Dundee, stopping at Cupar and Leuchars (catch a bus from here to St Andrews) on the way. Exploration of the eastern and western fringes by public transport requires some thought as there is no train service, and buses are few and far between.

The south coast

Although the **south coast** of Fife is predominantly industrial – with everything from cottage industries to the refitting of nuclear submarines – thankfully only a small part has been blighted by insensitive development. Even in the old coal-mining areas, disused pits and left-over slag heaps have either been well camouflaged through landscaping or put to alternative use as recreation areas. If you're driving, it's tempting once you've crossed the river to beat a path directly north up the M90 motorway; however, if you do decide to stop off, you'll find the area has much to offer.

It was from **Dunfermline** that Queen Margaret ousted the Celtic Church from Scotland in the eleventh century; her son, David I, founded an abbey here in the twelfth century, which acquired vast stretches of land for miles around. Today, even though the lands no longer belong to the town, Dunfermline remains the chief town and focus of the coast. **Culross** was once a lively port, which enjoyed a thriving trade with Holland;

the Dutch influence obvious in the lovely gabled houses. After a period of about two hundred years of decline, the town but has been lovingly restored this century.

Fife is linked to Edinburgh by the two **Forth bridges**. You used to be able to take guided walks across the historic rail bridge, whose boldness of concept was all the more remarkable for coming so hard on the heels of the Tay Bridge disaster of 1879 (see p.260); today, however, you'll have to be satisfied with seeing it from a train or a boat (for more on the Forth bridges, see p.260). The towns and villages of the south coast are connected by **trains** from Edinburgh via the Forth Rail Bridge, and there is a good local **bus** service.

Culross

Crossing the bridge from the south, with unattractive views of the shipyard at Inverkeithing and the naval dock at Rosyth, the A985 heads west along the Forth before approaching **CULROSS** (pronounced "Cooros"). Buses from Glasgow via Stirling and Alloa stop here, and there are also services from Dunfermline and Falkirk. One of Scotland's most picturesque settlements, the town's development began in the fifth century with the arrival of St Serf on the northern side of the Forth at "Holly Point", or Culenros, and it is said to be the birthplace of St Mungo, who travelled west and founded Glasgow cathedral. The town today is in excellent condition, thanks to the work of the NTS, which has been renovating its whitewashed, red-tiled buildings since 1932.

Make your first stop the **National Trust Visitor Centre** (Easter–Sept daily 11am–5pm; combined ticket for Town House, Palace and Study £4), in the **Town House** on the main road in the centre of Culross, for an excellent introduction to the burgh's history. On the upper floor of the house, some of the 4000 witches executed in Scotland between 1560 and 1707 were tried and held while awaiting execution in Edinburgh. Behind the ticket office is a tiny prison with built-in mannacles, where people were locked up as punishment for minor offences. The focal point of the community is the ochre-coloured **Culross Palace** (Easter–Sept daily 11am–5pm), built by wealthy coal merchant George Bruce in the late sixteenth century. In fact, it's not a palace at all – its name comes from the Latin *palatium*, or "hall" – but a grand and impressive house, with lots of small rooms and connecting passageways. Inside, well-informed staff point out the wonderful painted ceilings, pine panelling, antique furniture and curios; outside, dormer windows and crow-stepped gables dominate the walled court in which the house stands. The garden is planted with grasses, herbs and vegetables of the period, carefully grown from seed. The café serves home-made food, and is open from 10.30am to 4.30pm.

A cobbled alleyway known as **Back Causeway**, complete with a raised central aisle formerly used by noblemen to separate them from the commoners, leads up behind the Town House to the **Study** (Easter–Sept daily 1.30–5pm), a restored house that takes its name from the small room at the top of the corbelled projecting tower, reached by a turnpike stair. Built in 1610, its oak panelling in Dutch Renaissance style dates from around twenty years later. Further up the hill lie the remains of **Culross Abbey**, founded by Cistercian monks on land given to the Church in 1217 by the Earl of Fife. The nave of the original building is a ruin, a lawn studded with great stumps of columns. Although it is difficult to get a sense of what the abbey would have looked like, the overall effect is of grace and grandeur. A ladder leads to a vaulted chamber, now exposed to the elements on one side, which feels as if it is suspended in mid-air. This adjoins the fine seventeenth-century **manse**, hung with clematis, and the choir of the abbey, which became the Parish Church in 1633. Inside, wooden panels detail the donations given by eighteenth-century worthies to the parish poor, and a tenth-century Celtic cross in the north transept is a reminder of the origins of the abbey as a religious site – there was a Celtic church here in 450. Alabaster figures of Sir George Bruce, his lady, three sons and five daughters decorate the splendid family tomb, the parents lying in state and the children lined up and kneeling in devotion. A brass plaque tells the story of Edward, Lord Bruce of Kinloss, who was defeated by Sir Edward Sackville in a duel fought in Bergen in Holland in 1613. The luckless lord had been buried in Holland, but a persistent rumour that his heart had been taken back to Scotland was proved true when it was found during building work in the church in 1808, embalmed in a "silver casket of foreign workmanship".

The graveyard of the church is fascinating. Many of the graves are eighteenth-century, with symbols depicting the occupation of the person who is buried; the gravestone of a gardener has a crossed spade and rake and an hourglass with the sand run out – the latter a symbol of mortality used on many of the graves. Note the Scottish custom, still continued, of marking women's graves with maiden names, even when they are buried with their husband.

Beyond Culross, the B9037 continues west to **Kincardine**, where the **Kincardine Bridge** provides a second crossing point over the Forth before the Old Bridge at Stirling.

Dunfermline

Scotland's capital until the Union of the Crowns in 1603, **DUNFERMLINE** lies seven miles inland east of Culross, north of the Forth bridges. This "auld, grey toun" is built on a hill, dominated by the abbey and ruined palace at the top. Up until the late nineteenth century, Dunfermline was one of Scotland's foremost linen producers, as well as a major coal-mining centre, and today the town is a busy place, its ever-increasing sprawl attesting to a booming economy. At the heart of the town is the imposing abbey, and the dramatic skeleton of the palace.

In the eleventh century, **Malcolm III** (Canmore) offered refuge here to Edgar Atheling, heir to the English throne, and his family, who while fleeing the Norman Conquest were fortuitously shipwrecked in the Forth. Malcolm married Edgar's sister, the Catholic Margaret, in 1067, and in so doing started a process of reformation that ultimately supplanted the Celtic Church. Margaret, an intensely pious woman who was canonized in 1250, began building a Benedictine priory in 1072, the remains of which can still be seen beneath the nave of the present church; her son, **David I**, raised the priory to the rank of abbey in the following century. In 1303, during the first of the **Wars of Independence** (1296–1328), the English king Edward I occupied the castle, conducting a military campaign which culminated in the siege of Stirling Castle the following year. He had the church roof stripped of lead to provide ammunition for his army's catapults, and also appears to have ordered the destruction of most of the monastery buildings, with the exception of the church and some of the monks' dwellings. **Robert the Bruce** helped rebuild the abbey, and when he died of leprosy was buried here 25 years later, although his body went undiscovered until building began on a new parish church in 1821. His heart, which was first taken on crusade to Spain by Sir James Douglas, now lies in Melrose Abbey in southern Scotland (see p.128).

The Town

Dunfermline's **centre**, at the top of the hill around the abbey and palace, holds an appeal of its own, with its narrow, cobbled streets, pedestrianized shopping areas and gargoyle-adorned buildings. One of the best of these, the **city chambers** on the corner of Bridge and Bruce streets, is a fine example of late nineteenth-century Gothic Revival style. Among the ornate porticoes and grotesques of dragons and winged serpents which adorn the exterior are the sculpted heads of Robert the Bruce, Malcolm Canmore, Queen Margaret and Elizabeth I.

Dunfermline Abbey (April–Sept Mon–Sat 9.30am–6.30pm, Sun 2–6.30pm; Oct–March Mon–Wed & Sat 9.30am–4.30pm, Thurs 9.30am–12.30pm, Sun 2–4.30pm; £1.50) is comprised of the twelfth-century nave of the medieval monastic church, with an early nineteenth-century parish church spliced on. A plaque beneath the pulpit marks the spot where Robert the Bruce's remains were laid to rest for the second time, while Malcolm and his queen, Margaret, who died of grief three days after her husband in 1093, have a shrine outside. The enormous stonework graffiti, "King Robert the Bruce", at the top of the tower is attributable to an overexcited architect thrilled by the discovery of Bruce's remains. The nearby pink harled **Abbot House** (daily 10am–5pm; £3), possibly fourteenth-century, is best seen from the outside. This building, variously used as an iron foundry, an art school and a doctor's surgery, has been recently restored, although nothing remains of the original interior, and there are no interesting artefacts on display. The upstairs rooms consist of "exhibitions": every square inch is painted with scenes of Dunfermline life, medieval and modern, with sinister life-size models of local figures dotted about. You can visit the witches'-coven-style café with a patio garden first to decide if you are willing to pay the entrance fee to see more.

The guest house of Margaret's Benedictine monastery, south of the abbey, became the **Palace** (same times as abbey; £1.50) in the sixteenth century under James VI, who gave both it and the abbey to his consort, Queen Anne of Denmark. Charles I, the last monarch to be born in Scotland, entered the world here in 1600. All that is left of it today is a long, sandstone facade, especially impressive when silhouetted against the evening sky. The four redundant walls next to the palace are those of the refectory, connected via the gatehouse to the kitchen, which was tacked on at the palace's eastern end.

Pittencrieff Park, known to locals as "the Glen", covers a huge area in the centre of town. Bordering the ruined palace, the 76-acre park used to be owned by the Lairds of Pittencrieff, whose 1610 estate house, built of stone pillaged from the palace, still stands within the grounds. In 1902, however, the entire plot was purchased by the local, rags-to-riches industrialist and philanthropist Andrew Carnegie, who donated it to his home town. This was just as much sweet revenge as beneficent public-spiritedness: the young Carnegie had been banned from the estate, according to a former laird's edict that no Morrison would pass through the gates. Since his mother had been a Morrison, Carnegie could do little but gaze through the bars on the one day a year that the estate was open to the rest of the public. Today **Pittencrieff House** (May–Oct daily except Tues 11am–5pm; free) displays exhibits on local history, the glasshouses are filled with exotic blooms, and the Pavilion coffee shop offers refreshment. In the centre of the park are the remains – little more than the foundations – of **Malcolm Canmore's Tower**, which may be the location of Malcolm's residence, known to have been somewhere to the west of the abbey. Dunfermline – meaning "fort by the crooked pool" – takes its name from the tower's location: *Dun* meaning "hill or fort"; *Fearum* "bent or crooked" and *Lin* (or *Lyne/Line*) "a pool or running water".

Just beyond the southeast corner of the park, the modest little cottage at the bottom of St Margaret Street is **Andrew Carnegie's Birthplace** (April–Oct Mon–Sat 11am–5pm, Sun 2–5pm; Nov–March daily 2–4pm; £1.50). The son of a weaver, the young Carnegie (1835–1919) lived upstairs with his family, while the room below housed his father's loom shop. Following the family's emigration to America in 1848, he worked on the railroads before becoming involved with the iron and then the steel industries. From 1873 he began his acquisition of steel-production firms, later to be consolidated into the Carnegie Steel Company; when he retired in 1901 to devote himself to philanthropy, Carnegie was a multi-millionaire. His house, an ordinary two up two down, has been preserved as it was at the end of the last century, and the adjacent Memorial Hall details his life and work.

Just north of the park, the holy shrine of **St Margaret's Cave** (Easter–Sept daily 11am–4pm; free) lies incongruously buried beneath the Glen Bridge car park. A dimly lit passageway descends deep into the ground, past displays and information panels that document the pious life of Margaret, who prayed here on a daily basis. At the bottom, the sparse stone praying area is small and damp, though in Margaret's day it would have been decorated with crosses and candles.

Practicalities

Trains from Edinburgh connect with Dunfermline, whose **train station** is southeast of the centre, halfway down the long hill of St Margaret's Drive. It's a fifteen-minute walk up the hill from here to the **tourist office**, on Maygate, next to Abbot House (April–Sept Mon–Sat 9.30am–5.30pm, Sun 11am–4pm; Oct–March Mon–Sat 9.30am–5.30pm; ☎01383/720999). An hourly bus from Edinburgh and two-hourly services from Glasgow, Perth and Dundee come in at the **bus station**, in the Kingsgate Centre, on the north side of town. If you want to **stay**, try the comfortable *Davaar House Hotel*, 126 Grieve St (☎01383/721886; ④), in a tastefully furnished Victorian town house, or the nearby B&B at 59 Buffies Brae (☎01383/733677; ③), which offers a warm welcome. There are some good, well-priced ethnic **restaurants** in Dunfermline, including *Blossom's*, 6–8 Chalmers St, for Chinese food, or *Khan's*, 33 Carnegie Drive, for Indian cuisine. Cheap-and-cheerful French cooking is on offer at *Café Rene*, also on Carnegie Drive, while, for great traditional Italian food, there's *Il Pescatore* (☎01383/872999; ⑤) on the coast at Limekilns (about five miles south of the town on the B9156), which also offers reasonable accommodation and boasts of patronage by Prince Andrew and his naval chums. If you want a drink in town, try the *Watering Hole*, New Row.

East of the bridges

Fife's **south coast** curves sharply north at the mouth of the River Forth, exposing the towns and villages to an icy east wind that somewhat undermines the sunshine image of their beaches. If you've got the time, though, or fancy an alternative route to St Andrews, after crossing the bridge, cut off to the east along the A921, following the train line as it clings to the northern shore of the mouth of the Forth. Here you'll find a straggle of Fife fishing communities which have depended on the crop of the sea for centuries, and now make popular, although not especially attractive, holiday spots. The **train** line from Inverkeithing and twice-hourly **buses** (#7 and #7A) from Dunfermline run along the coast, stopping at all the following towns.

North Queensferry

Cowering beneath the bridges is **NORTH QUEENSFERRY**, a small fishing village, which, until the opening of the road bridge, was the northern landing point of the ferry across the Forth, and a nineteenth-century bathing resort. Built on a rocky outcrop, the place is comparatively well preserved for somewhere which takes such a battering from the elements, and there are good views across the Forth and of the bridges. The massive spans of the rail bridge – inspiration for Iain Bank's postmodern novel, *The Bridge* – loom frighteningly large from such close range. Today, an ambitious programme to strip the old paint and replace it with a high-tech, long-lasting coating will render redundant the old saying for a seemingly endless task: "It's like painting the Forth Rail Bridge." Also here is the popular **Deep-Sea World** (daily 9.30am–6pm; £6), a huge aquarium that boasts the world's largest underwater viewing tunnel, through which you glide on a moving walkway while sharks, conger eels and all manner of creatures from the deep swim nonchalantly past.

Inverkeithing

The North Queensferry peninsula gives way to Inverkeithing Bay and **INVERKEITHING**, a medieval watering place established by David I in the twelfth century and granted a charter by William I around 1165, thanks to its strategic location and safe harbour. Modern Inverkeithing is unprepossessing, with housing estates sprawling around the more attractive old town centre. The **Parish Church of St Peter**, on Church Street near the train station, began as a wooden Celtic church before Queen Margaret set to work, and ended up as a Norman stone structure bequeathed to Dunfermline Abbey in 1139. The oldest part of it today is the fifteenth-century tower, the rest having been razed by fire in 1825.

Aberdour

Beyond Inverkeithing, **ABERDOUR** clings tight to the walls of its **Castle** (April–Sept Mon–Sat 9.30am–6.30pm, Sun noon–6.30pm; Oct–March Mon–Wed & Sat 9.30am–4.30pm, Sun 2–4.30pm; £1.50) at the southern end of the main street. Once a Douglas stronghold, the castle is on a comparatively modest scale, with gently sloping lawns, a large enclosed seventeenth-century garden and terraces. The fourteenth-century tower is the oldest part of the castle, the other buildings having been added in the sixteenth and seventeenth centuries, including the well-preserved dovecote. Worth more perusal is **St Fillan's Church**, also in the castle grounds, which dates from the twelfth century, with a few sixteenth-century additions, such as the porch restored from total dereliction earlier this century. There's little else to see here apart from the town's popular **silver sands** beach, which, along with its watersports, golf and sailing, has earned Aberdour the rather optimistic tourist board soubriquet the "Fife Riviera". From Aberdour you can take a ferry to Inchcolm Island to see its ruined medieval abbey (see p.94).

For **accommodation**, the real gem is *Hawkcraig House*, Hawkcraig Point (☎01383/860335; ④), a guest house with a good restaurant in an old ferryman's house overlooking the harbour. Alternatively, you could try the friendly *Aberdour Hotel* on High Street (☎01383/860325; ⑤), which also has an inexpensive **restaurant** downstairs.

Burntisland

From Aberdour it's three miles to the large holiday resort of **BURNTISLAND**, with its fine stretch of sandy beach. The busy High Street runs the length of the waterfront, hemmed in by buildings at the western end, where you'll find the unkempt **train station**. Offices now occupy **Rossend Castle** (beyond the west end of High Street), a fifteenth-century tower with sixteenth-century additions, sadly not open to the public. Mary, Queen of Scots stayed in 1563 and Pierre de Chastelard, an eager French poet, was discovered in her bedchamber. Chastelard, having been warned once already about hiding in the young queen's private rooms at Holyrood Palace, was whisked off to St Andrews where, proclaiming "Adieu, thou most beautiful and most cruel Princess in the world", he was executed.

Although almost every house along the Links, just beyond High Street, sports a **B&B** sign, the choice of **hotels** is limited to four. The *Inchview Hotel*, 69 Kinghorn Rd (☎01592/872239; ⑥), a listed Georgian building looking out across the sea, and *Kingswood Hotel*, Kinghorn Road (☎01592/872329; ⑥), are the most comfortable. The latter, in a leafy road just north of town, will also organize fishing and shooting trips for guests, and offers good bar meals, high teas and dinners. Other **eating** options include *The Smugglers Inn*, 14 Harbour Place, which does snacks and bar meals and has a good vegetarian selection. If you want to make up a picnic, *Delicate Essen*, 83 High St, is the place to go for bread, cheese, cakes and beer.

Kinghorn

Shortly before reaching **KINGHORN**, the coastal road from Burntisland passes a **Celtic cross** commemorating Alexander III, the last of the Celtic kings, who plunged over the cliff near here one night in 1286, when his horse stumbled. The ancient settlement of Kinghorn is today a popular but not too crowded holiday centre, with few formal attractions but a good beach. The ugly brown pebble-dashed **parish church**, looking over the beach and whipped by wintry winds at the land's edge, dates from 1894, though the site has been used as a church for centuries and the small graveyard – popular with local genealogists – is filled with lichen-covered, semi-legible tombstones from the eighteenth century. At the opposite (southern) end of town, a hill lined with Spanish-style villas leads down to the waterfront and the beach at **Pettycur Bay**, where fishing boats cluster round the small harbour and brightly coloured lobster nets dot the sands.

Regular trains from Edinburgh and Dundee arrive at Kinghorn's **train station**, just off High Street. The best place **to stay** is the *Longboat Inn*, 107 Pettycur Rd (✆01592/890625; ④), overlooking the River Forth, just above the beach at Pettycur Bay. Ask for a room with a balcony, from where you'll get good views across to Edinburgh and the Lothians. Cheaper B&Bs include *Craigo-er*, 45 Pettycur Rd (✆01592/890527; ③), and *The Anchorgate* further down the road at no. 55 (✆01592/890245; ③). Decent bar meals are available in the wine bar of the *Longboat Inn*, and full meals in its moderately priced **restaurant**.

Kirkcaldy and around

The ancient royal burgh of **KIRKCALDY** (pronounced "Kirkcawdy") is familiarly known as "The Lang Toun" for its four-mile-long esplanade which stretches the length of the waterfront. The esplanade was built in 1922–23 – not just to hold back the sea, but also to alleviate unemployment – and runs parallel for part of the way with the shorter High Street. If you're here in mid-April, you'll see the historic **Links Market**, a week-long funfair that dates back to 1305 and is possibly the largest street fair in Britain.

Incidentally, though there's little to show for it today, architect brothers Robert and James Adam were born in Kirkcaldy, as was the eighteenth-century scholar, philosopher and political economist Adam Smith, whose great work *The Wealth of Nations* (1776) established political economy as a separate science.

The Town

Kirkcaldy doesn't hold a great deal of interest for the visitor, its charms largely obliterated by overdevelopment. However, a stroll along the promenade is pleasant on a sunny day and there's a large range of the major chain stores in the town centre. The town's history is chronicled in its **Museum and Art Gallery** (Mon–Sat 10.30am–5pm, Sun 2–5pm; free) in the colourful War Memorial Gardens between the train and bus stations. The museum covers everything from archeological discoveries to the tradition of the local Wemyss Ware pottery and the evolution of the present town. Since its inception in 1925, the gallery has built up its collection to around three hundred works by some of Scotland's finest painters from the late eighteenth century onwards, including works by the fine portraitist Sir Henry Raeburn, the historical painter Sir David Wilkie, the Scottish "Colourists", the "Glasgow Boys" and William McTaggart. For a town which is known primarily for linoleum production and whose reputation is firmly rooted in the prosaic, the art gallery is an unexpected boon.

Just beyond the northern end of the waterfront, Ravenscraig Park is the site of the substantial ruin of **Ravenscraig Castle**, a thick-walled, fifteenth-century defence post, which occupies a lovely spot above a beach. The castle looks out over the Forth, and is flanked on either side by a flight of steps – the inspiration, apparently, for the title of John Buchan's novel, *The Thirty-nine Steps*. Sir Walter Scott also found this a place worthy of comment, using it as a setting for the story of "lovely Rosabella" in *The Lay of the Last Minstrel*.

Beyond Kirkcaldy lies the old suburb of **Dysart**, where tall ships once arrived bringing cargo from the Netherlands, setting off again with coal, beer, salt and fish. Well restored, and retaining historic street names such as Hot Pot Wynd (after the hot pans used for salt evaporation), it's an atmospheric place of narrow alleyways and picturesque old buildings. In Rectory Lane, the birthplace of John McDouall Stuart (who in 1862 became the first man to cross Australia from the south to the north) now holds the **McDouall Stuart Museum** (June–Aug daily 2–5pm; NTS; free), giving an account of his emigration to Australia in 1838 and his subsequent adventures.

Practicalities

Kirkcaldy's **train** and **bus stations** are in the upper part of town – keep heading downhill to get to the centre. For the **tourist office**, 19 Whytecauseway (Mon–Fri 10am–5pm, Sat 10am–1pm & 2–5pm; ☎01592/267775), follow the road for about ten minutes round to the right from the bus station. If you want to stay in Kirkcaldy, the office's accommodation booking service is a life-saver; there are few places to **stay** in the centre, and the layout of the rest of the town is not easy to follow because of the way it falls across the hillside. In Kirkcaldy town centre the *Parkway Hotel*, Abbotshall Road (☎01592/262143; ⑥), offers smart rooms and traditional breakfasts, while the smaller, more refined *Dunnikier House Hotel*, Dunnikier Park, Dunnikier Way (☎01592/268393; ⑥), serves fine local food and is set in pleasant grounds. The *Strathearn Hotel*, 2 Wishart Place, on Dysart Road (☎01592/652210; ⑤), is a welcoming place set in its own gardens, a couple of miles north of the centre of town. You can get cheaper rooms along the road in **Dysart**, at the *Royal Hotel*, Townhead (☎01592/654112; ③), which occupies one of the village's historic buildings.

The *Royal Hotel* is a good place for eating, as is the *Old Rectory Inn*, West Quality Street, also in Dysart. In Kirkcaldy itself, try *Giovanni's*, 66 Dunnikier Rd, for traditional Italian **food**, or *Maxin*, 5 High St, for Chinese.

There's a good **arts cinema** with a restaurant and bar, which is housed in the Adam Smith Theatre on Bennochy Road in the town centre (☎01592/260498).

Around Kirkcaldy

Inland from Kirkcaldy, the old **mining towns** of Cowdenbeath, Kelty, Lochgelly and Cardenden huddle together, their fires virtually extinguished by a blanket of economic depression. These are neglected places, and indeed are rarely even seen by visitors shooting up to St Andrews on the coastal route or zooming along the M90 to Perth. Take the train, however, and you'll weave through this forlorn stretch as the line leaves the coast and heads inland.

Ten miles inland from Kirkcaldy, **GLENROTHES** is a new town in much the same mould as any other. Stark, concrete and utilitarian, it is the European headquarters of the Californian company Hughes Microelectronics, who, along with similar operations, have given the town much-needed wealth and self-confidence. Only a short time ago, a sign at Markinch train station to the west (Glenrothes' nearest station) boldly announced, "Welcome to Glenrothes, the Capital of Fife". So outraged at this audacity were the residents of Cupar, Fife's real capital for centuries, that the sign had to be removed.

If you have even a passing interest in castles and their construction, try to visit **Balgonie Castle**, two miles east of Glenrothes on the B921 off the A911. Set above the River Leven, this splendid castle with its fourteenth-century keep and fine open courtyard has a somewhat unkempt appearance from the outside; only a small plaque stating that it is home to the Laird and Lady of Balgonie suggests it's inhabited. Don't be put off by the huge, but docile, Scottish deerhounds, or by the fact that you may have to wait some time at the door of the keep before anyone hears your knock. Once inside, you are guaranteed a uniquely personal tour from the laird or a member of his family; the castle has the distinction of being open every day of the year (roughly 10am–5pm) except when the fourteenth-century chapel is being used for candlelit weddings. The tour gives in-depth information on the architecture of the castle and its owners and occupiers, including Rob Roy who stayed here with 200 clansmen in 1716. Balgonie was partly restored in 1971 and the present laird, who hails from the West Midlands, but is always attired in a kilt, has continued the process.

The Howe of Fife

Completely different from the industrial landscape of Kirkcaldy and Glenrothes, the **Howe of Fife**, north of Glenrothes, is a low-lying stretch of ground ("howe") at the foot of the twin peaks of the heather-swathed **Lomond Hills** – West Lomond (1696ft) and East Lomond (1378ft). The area makes an ideal stopping point on the way to St Andrews, with **Falkland Palace** and the handsome market town of **Cupar**. Frequent **buses** run throughout the area, with regular services threading their way towards Dundee from Kirkcaldy. The **train** also comes this way, stopping at Cupar and Leuchars before crossing the Tay Bridge to Dundee.

Falkland

Nestling in the lower slopes of East Lomond, the narrow streets of **FALKLAND** are lined with fine and well-preserved seventeenth- and eighteenth-century buildings. The village grew up around **Falkland Palace** (April–Oct Mon–Sat 11am–5.30pm, Sun 1.30–5.30pm; NTS; £4.50, gardens only £2.30), which stands on the site of an earlier castle, home to the Macduffs, the Earls of Fife. James IV began the construction of the present palace in 1500; it was completed and embellished by James V, and became a favoured royal residence. Charles II stayed here in 1650, when he was in Scotland for his coronation, but after the Jacobite rising of 1715 and temporary occupation by Rob Roy the palace was left to ruin, remaining so until the late nineteenth century when the keepership was acquired by the third Marquess of Bute. He restored the palace entirely, and today it is a stunning example of Early Renaissance architecture, complete with corbelled parapet, mullioned windows, round towers and massive walls. A **guided tour** (40min) takes in a cross section of public and private rooms in the south and east wings. The former is better preserved and includes the stately drawing room, the Chapel Royal (still used for Mass) and the Tapestry Gallery, swathed with splendid seventeenth-century Flemish hangings. Outside, the **gardens** are also worth a look, their well-stocked herbaceous borders lining a pristine lawn, and with the oldest tennis court in Britain – built in 1539 for James V and still used.

Falkland is also a good base for **walks**, with several leading from the village; but for the more serious hikes to the summits of East and West Lomond, you have to start from Craigmead car park about two miles west of the village (always follow the usual safety precautions; see p.44).

If you want to **stay** in Falkland, try the **youth hostel**, Back Wynd (☎01337/857710; March–Sept; Nov–Feb Sat only), or, for B&B, the attractive *Oakbank Guest House*, The Pleasance (☎01337/857287; ③). Both the *Hunting Lodge Hotel*, on High Street, directly opposite the palace (☎01337/857226; ④), and the *Covenanter Hotel* (☎01337/857224; ④), just up the road, are comfortable.

Cupar and around

Straddling the small River Eden and surrounded by gentle hills, **CUPAR**, the capital of Fife, has retained much of its medieval character – and its self-confident air – from the days when it was a bustling market centre. A livestock auction still takes place here every week. In 1276 Alexander III held an assembly in the town, bringing together the Church, aristocracy and local burgesses in an early form of Scottish parliament. For his troubles he subsequently became the butt of Sir David Lindsay's biting play, *Ane Pleasant Satyre of the Thrie Estaitis* (1535), one of the first great Scottish dramas.

Situated at the centre of Fife's road network, Cupar's main street, part of the main road from Edinburgh to St Andrews, is plagued with thundering traffic. The **Mercat Cross**, stranded in the midst of the lorries and cars which speed through the centre, now consists of salvaged sections of the seventeenth-century original, following its destruction by an errant lorry some years ago.

One of the best reasons for stopping off at Cupar is to visit the **Hill of Tarvit** (Easter –Sept daily 1.30–5.30pm; NTS; £3.50; gardens open all year daily 9.30am–sunset; £1), an Edwardian mansion two miles south of town remodelled by Sir Robert Lorimer from a late seventeenth-century building. The estate, formerly the home of the geographer and cartographer Sir John Scott, includes the five-storey, late sixteenth-century **Scotstarvit Tower**, three-quarters of a mile west of the present house (keys available from the house during season only). Set on a little mound, the tower is a fine example of a Scots tower house, providing both fortification and comfort. The entire estate was bequeathed to the NTS in 1949 (part of which they rent out; see below), and the house contains an impressive collection of eighteenth-century Chippendale and French furniture, Dutch paintings, Chinese porcelain, and a restored Edwardian laundry.

Practicalities

Cupar's **train station** is immediately south of the centre; **bus** #23 from Stirling to St Andrews stops outside. If you want to **stay**, try the friendly *Eden House Hotel*, 2 Pitscottie Rd (☎01334/652510; ⑤), which also serves good inexpensive Scottish food, or *Rathcluan* B&B on Carslogie Road (☎01334/657857; ③). You can rent the small cottage at the foot of the Scotstarvit Tower from the NTS for around £250 per week (☎0131/243 9331). If money is no object, head for one of the luxury hotels out of the centre: *Balbirnie House Hotel*, Balbirnie Park (☎01592/610066; ⑨), is a magnificent Georgian mansion five miles southwest of town, complete with 416 acres of parkland; and five miles north of Cupar in **Letham**, the *Fernie Castle Hotel* (☎01337/810381; ⑧) occupies a real castle and offers bar meals as well as a more expensive à la carte menu. There is no shortage of good **restaurants** in the area; try the excellent *Ostler's Close*, 25 Bonnygate (☎01334/655574), or take the B940 east to the renowned *Peat Inn* (see p.258). For drinks and bar food, try *Watts* on Coal Road.

Around Cupar

To the west of Falkland are a couple of attractions particularly suitable for children. The **Scottish Deer Centre** (daily 10am–6pm; £2.50), three miles from Cupar on the A91, specializes in the rearing of red deer, and is also home to species of sika, fallow and reindeer. The tamer animals can be petted and there are falconry displays three times a day, as well as play and picnic areas and guided nature trails. A couple of miles further west along the A91, more unusual creatures are on show at the **Ostrich Kingdom** (daily 10am–5pm; £3.85), next to Birnie Loch Nature Reserve. Children will enjoy watching the giant birds cavort, and looking at chickens, goats and pot-bellied pigs in the children's farm.

A couple of miles southeast of Cupar, **CERES**, set around a village green, is home to the **Fife Folk Museum** (mid-May to Oct daily except Fri 2–5pm; £2). Occupying several well-preserved seventeenth- to-nineteenth-century buildings, it exhibits all manner of historical farming and agricultural paraphernalia. The pillory that used to restrain miscreants on market days still stands at the entrance of the old burgh tollbooth, and at the village crossroads is an unusual seventeenth-century stone carving of a man in a three-cornered hat with a toothy grin and a beer glass on his knee, said to be a depiction of a former provost.

Continuing east on the B939, you will soon come to **Magnus Muir**, halfway between Cupar and St Andrews, site of the murder of the controversial and oppressive Episcopalian Archbishop of St Andrews by a band of Covenanters in 1679; during the stuggle, Archbishop Sharp's daughter, Isabella, was wounded trying to protect him. One of the culprits, Hackston of Rathillet, was captured in Edinburgh and gruesomely executed. His hands were buried in Cupar's graveyard.

St Andrews and around

Confident, poised and well groomed, **ST ANDREWS**, Scotland's oldest university town and a pilgrimage centre for golfers from all over the world, is on a wide bay on the north-eastern coast of Fife. It's often referred to in tourist literature as "the Oxford or Cambridge of the North" and, like Cambridge, by and large St Andrews *is* its university.

According to legend, the town was founded, pretty much by accident, in the fourth century. St Rule – or Regulus – a custodian of the bones of St Andrew on the Greek island of Patras, had a vision in which an angel ordered him to carry five of the saint's bones to the western edge of the world, where he was to build a city in his honour. The conscientious courier set off, but was shipwrecked on the rocks close to the present harbour. Struggling ashore with his precious burden, he built a shrine to the saint on what subsequently became the site of the cathedral; St Andrew became Scotland's patron saint and the town its ecclesiastical capital.

Local residents are proud of their town, with its refined old-fashioned ambience. Thanks to a strong and well-informed local conservation lobby, many of the original buildings have survived. Almost the entire centre consists of listed buildings, while the ruined castle and cathedral have all but been rebuilt in the efforts to preserve their remains. If you're here in early August, don't miss the two-day **Lammas Fair**, Scotland's oldest surviving medieval market, complete with town crier. The other main event in the St Andrews calendar is the **Kate Kennedy Pageant**, usually held on the third Saturday in April, which involves an all-male procession of students taking to the streets dressed as characters associated with the university, from Kate Kennedy herself, niece of one of the university founders, to Mary, Queen of Scots.

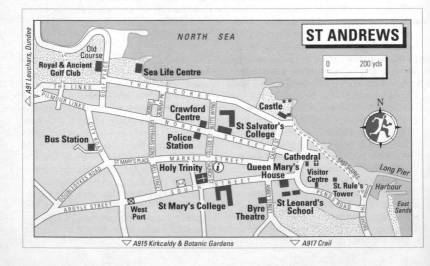

There are two main excursion areas from St Andrews. The most popular, with its beaches and little fishing villages is the **East Neuk**, stretching from Fife Ness to Largo Bay; the other is the **Tay coast**, which runs around Fife's northeast headland and along the Tay estuary almost to Perth. **Bus #95** runs from Leven up the coast to Dundee.

Arrival and information

St Andrews is not on the train line. The nearest **train station** is on the Edinburgh–Dundee–Aberdeen line at **Leuchars**, five miles northwest across the River Eden, from where regular (but not always connecting) buses make the fifteen-minute trip into town. The price of the rail ticket to Leuchars does not include the bus trip to St Andrews. Frequent **buses** from Edinburgh and Dundee terminate at the bus station on City Road at the west end of Market Street. The **tourist office**, 70 Market St (April & May Mon–Sat 9.30am–6pm, Sun 11am–4pm; June Mon–Sat 9.30–7pm, Sun 11am–6pm; July & Aug Mon–Sat 9.30am–8pm, Sun 11am–6pm; Sept to mid-Oct Mon–Sat 9.30am–7pm, Sun 11am–6pm; mid-Oct to March Mon–Sat 9.30am–5pm; ☎01334/472021), holds comprehensive information about St Andrews and northeast Fife.

If you're **driving**, the town's fiendish **parking** system requires vouchers (30p per hour) which you can get from the tourist office and some local shops. Scratch out the month, day, date and hour from the card, display it in your car, and cross your fingers that you've worked it out correctly.

Accommodation

Although rooms in St Andrews cost more than in the surrounding area, they often get booked up in the summer, when advance reservations are strongly recommended. Most of the **guest houses** are around Murray Place and Murray Park between The Scores and North Street. Good ones include *Aedel House*, 72 Murray Place (☎01334/472315; ③), and *Bell Craig Guest House* at 8 Murray Park (☎01334/472962; ③). On North Street, try *Aslar House*, at no. 120 (☎01334/473460; ④), or *Cadzow Guest House,* at no. 58 (☎01334/476933; ③). Between June and September, the **university** (☎01334/462000; ④) rents out about 200 rooms in various locations, all on a B&B basis with dinner optional. More upmarket are the various **hotels** lining The Scores, beyond the eastern end of the Old (golf) Course, overlooking the bay. The *St Andrews Golf Hotel*, at no. 40 (☎01334/472611; ⑨), occupies a three-storey town house, with chintzy, comfortable bedrooms – those at the front have great views – good food and an extensive wine list.

As you come into town from Leuchars, you'll see the entrance to the swanky *Rusacks Hotel*, 16 Pilmour Links (☎01334/474321; ⑨), on the left. From the airy lobby to its spacious rooms, this is a refined place whose old-fashioned style is in keeping with the town's air of respectability. A little further up the road is the *Tudor Inn*, 129 North St (☎01334/474906; ④) – its uncharacteristic black-and-white facade more English than Scottish. Although less luxurious than the above hotels, this is good value as long as you're not sleeping above the noisy downstairs bar. A couple of miles west of St Andrews on the B939 to Ceres is *Ruffets* (☎01334/472594; ⑧), an elegant 1920s country house, whose garden provides much of the produce for the hotel's restaurant. The *Peat Inn* hotel (☎01334/840206; ⑨), five miles south of town on the A915 and then one mile west on the B940, has plush suites in a modern building tucked behind the old coaching inn, and is renowned for its wonderful restaurant (see p.258).

The Town

The centre of St Andrews still follows the medieval layout. Wandering its three main thoroughfares, North Street, South Street and Market Street, which run west to east towards the ruined Gothic cathedral, are several of the original university buildings from the fifteenth century. Narrow alleys connect the cobbled streets, attic windows and gable ends shape the rooftops, and here and there you'll see old wooden doors with heavy knockers and black iron hinges.

The ruin of the great **St Andrews Cathedral** (visitor centre April–Sept Mon–Sat 9.30am–6pm, Sun noon–6pm; Oct–March Mon–Sat 9.30am–4pm, Sun 2–4pm; £1.50, joint ticket with St Andrew's Castle £3.30: grounds Sun only 9am–6.30pm; free), at the east end of town, gives only an idea of the former importance of what was the largest cathedral in Scotland. Though founded in 1160, it was not finished and consecrated until 1318, in the presence of Robert the Bruce. On June 5, 1559, the Reformation took its toll, and supporters of John Knox, fresh from a rousing meeting, plundered the cathedral and left it to ruin. Stone was still being taken from the cathedral for various local building projects as late as the 1820s.

Standing above the harbour where the land drops to the sea, the cathedral site can be a blustery place, with the wind whistling through the great east window and down the stretch of turf that was once the central aisle. In front of the window a slab is all that remains of the high altar, where the relics of St Andrew were once enshrined. Previously, it is believed that they were kept in **St Rule's Tower**, the austere Romanesque monolith next to the cathedral, which was built as part of an abbey in 1130. From the top of the tower (a climb of 157 steps), there's a good view of the town and surroundings, and of the remains of the monastic buildings which made up the priory. Around the entire complex is a sturdy wall dating from the sixteenth century, over half a mile long and with three gateways.

Southwest of the cathedral enclosure lies **the Pends**, a huge fourteenth-century vaulted gatehouse which marked the main entrance to the priory, and from where the road leads down to the harbour, passing prim **St Leonard's**, one of Scotland's leading private schools for girls. The sixteenth-century, rubble-stonework building on the right as you go through the Pends is **Queen Mary's House**, where she is believed to have stayed in 1563. The house was restored in 1927 and is now used as the school library.

Down at the **harbour**, gulls screech above the fishing boats, keeping an eye on the lobster nets strewn along the quay. If you come here on a Sunday morning, you'll see students parading down the long pier, red gowns billowing in the wind, in a time-honoured after-church walk. The beach, **East Sands**, is a popular stretch, although it's cool in summer and positively biting in winter. A path leads south from the far end of the beach, climbing up the hill past the caravan site and cutting through the gorse; this makes a pleasant walk on a sunny day, taking in hidden coves and caves.

North of the beach, the rocky coastline curves inland to the ruined **St Andrew's Castle** (April–Sept Mon–Sat 9.30am–6pm, Sun 9.30am–4pm; Oct–March Mon–Sat 9.30am–4pm, Sun 2–4pm; £2.30), with a drop to the sea on three sides and a moat on the fourth. Founded around 1200 and extended over the centuries, it was built as part of the Palace of the Bishops and Archbishops of St Andrews and was consequently the scene of some fairly grim incidents at the time of the Reformation. There's not a great deal left of the castle, since it fell into ruin in the seventeenth century, and most of what can be seen dates from the sixteenth century, apart from the fourteenth-century Fore Tower.

The Protestant reformer George Wishart was burnt at the stake in front of the castle in 1546, as an incumbent Cardinal Beaton looked on. Wishart had been a friend of John Knox's, and it wasn't long before fellow reformers sought vengeance for his death. Less than three months later, Cardinal Beaton was stabbed to death and his body displayed from the battlements before being dropped into the "bottle dungeon", a 24ft pit hewn out of solid rock which can still be seen in the Sea Tower. The perpetrators then held the castle for over a year, and during that time dug the secret passage which can be entered from the ditch in front. Outside the castle, the initials "GW" are carved in stone.

St Andrews University is the oldest in Scotland, founded in 1410 by Bishop Henry Wardlaw. The nominal founder is James I to whom the bishop was tutor, and the king was certainly a great benefactor of the university. The first building was on the site of the Old University Library and by the end of the Middle Ages three colleges had been built: St Salvator's (1450), on North Street, St Leonard's (1512), on The Pens, and St Mary's (1538), on South Street. At the time of the Reformation, St Mary's became a seminary of Protestant theology, and today it houses the university's Faculty of Divinity. The **quad** here has beautiful gardens and some magnificent old trees, perfect for flopping under on a warm day. A **guided tour** of the University buildings starts from the International Office, Butts Wynd, near St Salvator's Chapel (June–Aug Mon–Sat 11am & 2.30pm, 4.30pm on request; £3), or you can wander freely around the buildings at your own pace.

If you've got children in tow you may want to visit the huge **Sea Life Centre** (daily 10am–6pm; July & Aug closes 7pm; £4.25), on The Scores, at the west end of town close to the golf museum (see below). Here, you can see marine life of all shapes and sizes with displays, live exhibits, observation pools and underwater walkways. Also good for children is the fifty-acre **Craigtoun Country Park** (April–Sept daily 10.30am–6.30pm; £2), a couple of miles southwest of town on the B939. As well as several landscaped gardens there is a miniature train, trampolines, boating, crazy golf and picnic areas, and a country fair each May with craft stalls, wildlife exhibits and showjumping displays.

To escape the bustle of the town, head to the **Botanic Gardens** on Canongate (daily May–Sept 10am–7pm; Oct–April 10am–4pm; £1.50: glasshouses all year Mon–Fri 10am–4pm; £1.50), a peaceful retreat just ten minutes' walk south of South Street.

GOLF IN ST ANDREWS

St Andrew's **Royal and Ancient Golf Club** (or "R&A") is the governing body for golf the world over, dating back to a meeting of 22 of the local gentry in 1754, who founded the Society of St Andrews Golfers, being "admirers of the ancient and healthful exercise of golf". It acquired its current title after King William IV agreed to be the society's patron in 1834.

The game itself has been played here since the fifteenth century. Those early days were instrumental in establishing Scotland as the home of golf, for the rules were distinguished from those in the French game by the fact that participants had to manoeuvre the ball into a hole, rather than hit an above-ground target. (Early French versions were, in fact, more like croquet.) The game developed, acquiring popularity along the way – even Mary, Queen of Scots was known to have the occasional round. It was not without its opponents, however, particularly James II who, in 1457, banned his subjects from playing since it was distracting them from archery practice.

St Andrews' status as a world-renowned **golf** centre is obvious as you enter the town from the west, where the approach road runs adjacent to the famous **Old Course**. At the eastern end of the course lies the strictly private **clubhouse**, a stolid, square building dating from 1854. The first British Open Championship was held here in 1873, having been inaugurated in 1860 at Prestwick in Ayrshire, and since then the British Open has been held here regularly, pulling in enormous crowds. The eighteenth hole of the Old Course is immediately in front of the clubhouse, and has been officially christened the "Tom Morris", after one of the world's most famous golfers. Pictures of Nick Faldo, Jack Nicklaus and other golfing greats, along with clubs and a variety of memorabilia which they donated, are displayed in the admirable **British Golf Museum** on Bruce Embankment, along the waterfront below the clubhouse (April–Oct daily 9.30am–5.30pm; Nov–March Thurs–Mon 11am–3pm; £3.75). There are also plenty of hands-on exhibits, including computers, video screens and footage of British Open championships, tracing the development of golf through the centuries.

Eating and drinking

St Andrews has no shortage of **restaurants** and **cafés**. In town, *Littlejohns*, at the east end of Market Street, serves hearty burgers and steaks, while *The Vine Leaf Restaurant*, 131 South St (☎01334/477497), is known for its well-priced, good-quality dishes made from local produce and a good range of seafood.

Brambles, 5 College St, offers inexpensive homebaking, as does *The Merchant's House*, 49 South St, which also has good vegetarian options. The *Victoria Café*, 1 St Mary's Place, is a popular student haunt serving baked potatoes and toasted sandwiches, and a good place in which to have a few drinks in the evening. *Ma Belle's*, 40 The Scores, in the basement of the *St Andrews Golf Hotel*, is a lively pub serving cheap food and catering for locals as much as students. For the best views of the Old Course, *Rusacks Lounge Bar*, 16 Pilmour Links, has huge comfy chairs, where you can watch golfers through huge windows and sip pricey drinks.

For truly great food, head for the *Peat Inn* (see p.253), one of Britain's top restaurants, serving a varied menu of local specialities. The dining area is intimate without being cramped, and a three-course meal – perhaps featuring lobster broth, venison or roast monkfish – will set you back at least £40 per head.

With its big student population, St Andrews has lots of good **pubs**. Locals and tourists mix with the students at the *Tudor*, 129 North St, which has a late-night licence on Thursdays and Fridays and live bands from time to time. The *Central* on Market Street serves huge pies and a powerful beer brewed by Trappist monks. *Firkins*, St Mary's Place, at the bottom of Market Street, is a popular real-ale bar whose extensive beer selection attracts a young crowd.

The East Neuk

South of St Andrews, the **East Neuk** (*Neuk* is Scots for "corner") is a region of quaint fishing villages, all crow-stepped gables and tiled roofs. Perhaps the prettiest of these is **Crail**, with a picturesque pottery near the harbour, but the best beaches are at the resorts of **Elie** and **Earlsferry**, which lie next to each other about twelve miles south of St Andrews. The villages between St Andrews and Elie fall into two distinct types: either scattered higgledy-piggledy up the hillside like **St Monans**, between Pittenweem and Elie, or neatly lined along the harbour like **Anstruther**, between Crail and Pittenweem.

Anstruther

ANSTRUTHER is home to the wonderfully unpretentious **Scottish Fisheries Museum** (April–Oct Mon–Sat 10am–5.30pm, Sun 11am–5pm; Nov–March Mon–Sat 10am–4.30pm, Sun 2–4.30pm; £3.20), quite in keeping with the no-frills integrity of the area in general. Set in a complex of sixteenth- to nineteenth-century buildings on a total of eighteen different floors, it chronicles the history of the fishing and whaling industries in ingenious displays. Anstruther's helpful **tourist office** (Easter to mid-Sept Mon, Fri & Sat 10am–5pm, Tues–Thurs 10am–1pm & 2–5pm, Sun noon–5pm; ☎01333/311073) is next to the museum.

Several miles offshore from Anstruther on the rugged **Isle of May**, you can see a lighthouse, erected in 1816 by Robert Louis Stevenson's grandfather, as well as the remains of Scotland's first lighthouse, built in 1636, which burnt coals as a beacon. The island is now a nature reserve and bird sanctuary, and can be reached by boat from Anstruther (May–Sept; ☎01333/310103; one sailing daily; £12). Between April and July the dramatic sea cliffs are covered with breeding kittiwakes, razorbills, guillemots and shags, while inland there are thousands of puffins and eider duck. Grey seals also make the occasional appearance. Check up on departure times, as crossings vary according

---

SCOTLAND'S SECRET BUNKER

Inland between St Andrews and Anstruther on the B940 (bus #61 takes you to within two miles) is the idiosyncratic **Scotland's Secret Bunker** (April–Oct daily 10am—5pm; £5.95). Just off the official secrets list, the bunker was opened to the public in 1994, though part of the complex is still operational, and remains secret. Entrance is through an innocent-looking farmhouse, then you walk down a vast ramp to the bunker, which is 100ft below ground and encased in 15ft of reinforced concrete. In the event of a nuclear war the bunker was to have become Scotland's new administrative centre, from where government and military commanders would have coordinated firefighting and medical help for Scotland (the equivalent centres in England and Wales aren't open to the public). The bunker, which could house 300 people, was due to be equipped with air filters, a vast electricity generator, its own water supply, and a switchboard room with 2800 phone lines; the best of 1950s technology, today it has a rather kitsch James Bond feel about it. The only concession to entertainment was a couple of cinemas, which now show 1950s newsreel giving painfully inadequate instructions to civilians in the event of nuclear war. Appropriately, the bunker has not been spruced up for tourists, and remains uncompromisingly spartan.

---

to weather and tide, and allow between four and five hours for a round-trip: an hour each way, and a couple of hours there. Take plenty of warm, waterproof clothing.

At the end of a graceful avenue of trees, **Kellie Castle** (May–Oct daily 1.30–5.30pm; £3.50; garden and grounds all year daily 9.30am–sunset; £1), a couple of miles northeast of Anstruther on the B9171, has an unusual but harmonious mix of twin sixteenth-century towers linked by a seventeenth-century building. Abandoned in the early nineteenth century, the castle was discovered in 1878 by Professor James Lorimer, the distinguished political philosopher, who took on the castle as an "improving tenant". The professor, his artist wife and their children restored the building and made it their home; the family atmosphere evident in an upstairs nursery crammed with Victorian toys. The wonderful gardens, where space is broken up by arches, alcoves and paths which weave between profuse herbaceous borders, were designed by the Professor's son Robert aged just sixteen. Later Sir Robert Lorimer, he became a well-known architect specializing in restorations and war memorials; among his restoration works is the Hill of Tarvit in Cupar (see p.253).

Anstruther makes a pretty and peaceful base for exploring the surrounding area, and there are plenty of good **B&Bs**; try the lovely *Hermitage Guest House* (☎01333/310909; ④) on Ladywalk; the *Beaumont Lodge Guest House* (☎01333/310315; ③) and *The Spindrift* (☎01333/310573; ⑤), both on Pittenweem Road; or *The Sheiling* (☎01333/310697; ③) at 32 Glenogil Gardens. The *Sauchope Links* (☎01337/450460) is a very pleasant **campsite**, a few miles miles north at Crail. There is a fine **fish restaurant** in Anstruther, the *Cellar*, East Green (☎01333/310378), in one of the village's oldest buildings, once a cooperage and smokehouse. For tasty fish and chips, try the *Anstruther Fish Bar*, The Shore, reputed to be the best in Fife.

The Tay coast

Looking across to Dundee and Perthshire, the **Tay coast**, a peaceful wedge of rural hinterland on the edge of the River Tay, offers little in the way of specific attractions, but a lot of undiscovered hideaways. Gentle hills fringe the shore, sheltering the villages – several of which only acquired running water and streetlights in the past decade or two – that lie in the dips and hollows along the coast.

LEUCHARS, five miles north of St Andrews, is known for its RAF base, from where low-flying jets screech over the hills, appearing out of nowhere and sending sheep, cows and horses galloping for shelter. There is a beautiful twelfth-century church in the village, with fine Norman stonework. Romantic **Earlshall Castle** (private), just east of Leuchars, is the home of the Baron and Baroness of Earlshall, whose ancestor, Sir William Bruce, built the castle in 1546.

Northeast of Leuchars, **Tentsmuir Forest** occupies the northeasternmost point of the Fife headland, and is also a nature reserve with a good beach and peaceful woodland walks – so peaceful that you would never guess it's only five miles or so from the **Tay bridges** with Dundee just the other side (80p toll charge on the road bridge). The current Tay **rail bridge** is the second to span the river on this spot, the first having collapsed in a terrifying disaster during a storm on December 28, 1879, which claimed the lives of around a hundred people in a train crossing the bridge at the time. The event was recorded by the poet, William McGonagall, who has gone down in history as being responsible for some of the most banal verse ever written, including some memorably trite rhyme about the disaster:

> *So the train mov'd slowly along the Bridge of Tay,*
> *Until it was about midway,*
> *Then the central girders with a crash gave way,*
> *And down went the train and passengers into the Tay!*
> *The storm Fiend did loudly bray,*
> *Because ninety lives had been taken away,*
> *On the last Sabbath day of 1879,*
> *Which will be remember'd for a very long time.*

There's a **camping** and **caravan** site at **TAYPORT**, a popular resort a couple of miles east of the bridge, from where one of Scotland's oldest ferries once ran across the river. Here the "silvery Tay" more than justifies this traditional description, shimmering in the light whatever the season. There are good views across the river from the shingly cove at **BALMERINO**, a quaint hamlet five miles further on, just below the ruin of **Balmerino Abbey** (daily dawn–dusk; NTS; £1), surrounded by venerable old trees, including an enormous gnarled Spanish chestnut, which has stood here for four centuries. The Cistercian abbey was founded in 1229 by Alexander II and his mother Ermengarde, who is buried here, and built by monks from the abbey at Melrose in the Borders. Destroyed by the English in 1547, reconstruction work was halted for good by the Reformation. Unfortunately, the only substantial part remaining is unsafe and inaccessible.

Lindores Abbey, seven miles or so further west along the coast, dates from the century before and was a Benedictine settlement. The west tower still stands, silhouetted against the sky, and there are views down to nearby **NEWBURGH**, stunning on a summer evening, with the setting sun lighting up the mud flats below and skimming across the Tay. Newburgh itself is a fairly quiet, slightly rough-edged place. Originally a fishing village, it evolved due to its proximity to the abbey, and is now known for the admirable **Laing Museum** (April–Sept Mon–Fri 10am–5pm, Sat & Sun 2–5pm; Oct–March Wed & Fri noon–4pm, Sun 2–5pm; free). The collection, donated by the banker and historian Dr Alexander Laing in 1892, includes a fine array of antiques and geological specimens gathered in the area.

PERTH AND THE HIGHLANDS

Genteel **Perthshire**, although now officially part of Perthshire and Kinross, still retains its own identity: an area of scenic valleys and glens, rushing rivers and peaceful lochs, it's the long-established domain of Scotland's country-club set. First settled over

8000 years ago, it was taken by the Romans and then the Picts, before Celtic mission-aries established themselves here, enjoying the amenable climate, fertile soil and ideal defensive and trading location.

The hub of the region is the port of **Perth**, which for centuries has benefited from its inland position on the River Tay. Salmon, wool and, by the sixteenth century, whisky – Bell's, Dewar's (which has now moved to Glasgow) and the Famous Grouse whiskies all hail from this area – were exported from here, while a major import was Bordeaux claret. Today, perhaps Perth's greatest attraction is the wonderful **Fergusson Gallery**.

A place of magnificent beauty, where the snow-capped peaks of soaring mountains fall away down forested slopes to long, deep lochs on the valley floor, the area is domi-nated by the western **Grampian Mountains**, a mighty range that controls transport routes, influences the weather and tolerates little development. The **Breadalbane Mountains** run between **Loch Tay** and **Loch Earn**; as well as providing walking and watersports, the area is dotted with fine towns and villages, like **Aberfeldy** at the west-ern tip of Loch Tay and **Dunkeld** with its eighteenth-century whitewashed cottages and elegant ruined cathedral. Among the wealth of historical sites in Perthshire are the splendid Baronial **Blair Castle** north of Pitlochry, and the breathtaking Italianate gar-dens at **Drummond Castle** near Crieff.

Transport connections in the region are at their best if you head straight north from Perth, along the train line to Inverness, but buses – albeit often infrequent – also trail the more remote areas. Keep asking at bus stations for details of services, as the fur-ther you get from the main villages the less definitive timetables become.

Perth

Surrounded by fertile agricultural land and beautiful scenery, **PERTH** was for several centuries Scotland's capital. Viewed from the hills to the south, the town still justifies Sir Walter Scott's glowing description of it in the opening pages of his novel *The Fair Maid of Perth*. Scott writes of approaching Perth from the south:

. . . the town of Perth with its two large measures or inches, its steeples and towers; the hills of Moncreiff and Kinnoul faintly rising into picturesque rocks, partly clothed with woods; the rich margin of the river studded with elegant mansions; and the huge Grampian Mountains, the northern screen of this exquisite landscape.

During the reign of James I, Parliament met here on several occasions, but its glory was short-lived: the king was murdered in the town's Dominican priory in 1437 by the traitorous Sir Robert Graham, who was captured in the Highlands and tortured to death in Stirling. During the Reformation, on May 11, 1559, John Knox preached a rousing sermon in St John's Church, which led to the destruction of the town's four monasteries (by those Knox later condemned as "the rascal mulititude") and quickened the pace of reform in Scotland. Despite decline in the seventeenth century, the com-munity expanded in the eighteenth and has prospered ever since – today it is a finance centre, and still an important and bustling market town. Its long history in **livestock trading** is continued throughout the year, notably with the Aberdeen Angus shows and sales June to September, and the Perthshire Agricultural Show in August.

Arrival, information and accommodation

Perth is on the main train lines north from Edinburgh and Glasgow and is well con-nected by bus; the **bus** and **train stations** are on opposite sides of the road at the west end of town where Kings Place runs into Leonard Street. The **tourist office**, 45 High

St (April–June, Sept & Oct Mon–Sat 9am–6pm, Sun 11am–4pm; July & Aug Mon–Sat 9am–8pm, Sun 11am–6pm; Nov–March Mon–Sat 9am–5pm; ☎01738/638353), is a ten-minute walk away.

Of the numerous **hotels** in Perth's town centre, try the *Station Hotel*, on Leonard Street (☎01738/624141; ⑦), right by the station, or *Stakis Perth*, West Mill Street (☎01783/628281; ⑦). The spick-and-span *Salutation Hotel*, 34 South St (☎01738/630066; ⑥), claims to be one of Scotland's oldest hotels, having been established in 1699. There are **B&Bs** and guest houses all over town, notably on the approach roads from Crieff and Stirling. In the centre, Marshall Place, overlooking the South Inch, is the place to look. Of the many possibilities along here *Kinnaird House*, 5 Marshall Place (☎01738/628021; ④), offers a warm welcome in a lovely town house, with well-equipped en-suite rooms. In an elegant Georgian terrace facing the park is the *Park Lane Guest House*, 17 Marshall Place (☎01738/637218; ④). On the other side of the river, there's the friendly *Ballabeg*, 14 Keir St (☎01738/620434; ③), with spacious and comfortable rooms but shared facilities. The **youth hostel** is housed in an impressive old mansion with 64 rooms, at 107 Glasgow Rd (☎01738/623658; March–Oct) beyond the west end of York Place. Its a fair walk from the bus station – if you've got a heavy rucksack you might want to take bus #7.

The Town

Perth's compact **centre** occupies a small area, easily explored on foot, on the west bank of the Tay. Two large areas of green parkland, known as the North and South Inch, flank the centre. The **North Inch** was the site of the Battle of the Clans in 1396, in which thirty men from each of the clans Chattan and Quhele (pronounced "Kay") met in a battle, while the **South Inch** was the public meeting place for witch-burning in the seventeenth century. Both are now used for more civilized public recreation, with sports matches to the north, and boating and putting to the south.

A good variety of shops line **High Street** and **South Street**, as well as filling **St John's** shopping centre on King Edward Street. Opposite the entrance to the centre, the imposing **City Hall** is used by Scotland's politicians for party conferences. Behind here lies **St John's Kirk** (daily 10am–noon & 2–4pm; free), founded by David I in 1126, although the present building dates from the fifteenth century and was restored to house a war memorial chapel designed by Robert Lorimer in 1923–28. It was in St John's that John Knox preached his fiery sermon calling for the "purging of the churches from idolatry" in 1559.

A couple of minutes' walk north of here, the **Fair Maid's House**, on North Port, is arguably the town's best-known attraction, although you can only see it from the outside. Standing on the site of a thirteenth-century monastery, this cottage of weathered stone with small windows and an outside staircase was the setting chosen by Sir Walter Scott as the house of Simon Glover, father of the virginal Catherine Glover, in his novel *The Fair Maid of Perth*. Set in turbulent times at the close of the fourteenth century, the novel tells a traditional story of love, war and revenge, centring on the attempts by various worthies to win the hand of Catherine.

The nearby **Art Gallery and Museum** on George Street (Mon–Sat 10am–5pm; free), with exhibits on local history, art, natural history, archeology and whisky, gives a good overview of local life through the centuries. In similar vein, at **Lower City Mills**, West Mill Street (April–Oct Mon–Sat 10am–5pm; £1.50), a restored oatmeal mill driven by a massive waterwheel recalls Victorian Perth. The Round House, a domed circular structure on Marshall Place at the edge of the Tay, used to house the waterworks, and is the unlikely setting for the excellent **Fergusson Gallery** (Mon–Sat 10am–5pm; free). The gallery holds a collection of the paintings, drawings and sculpture of JD Fergusson, the foremost artist of the Scottish "Colourist" movement. Changing and imaginative exhibitions explore Fergusson's preoccupation with light and the sea, and his relationships with fellow modernists. His lifelong companion was the dancer and painter Margaret Morris; her summer schools, held annually for forty years, provided Fergusson with models and inspired his monumental paintings of bathers, in pure bright colours.

North of the town centre, and adjacent to the North Inch, the elegantly restored Georgian terraces beyond the Fair Maid's House give way to newer buildings, which have gradually encroached on the former territory of the fifteenth-century **Balhousie Castle**, off Hay Street (May–Sept Mon–Sat 10am–4.30pm; Oct–April Mon–Fri 10am–3.30pm; free). The castle sits incongruously in a peaceful residential area and has been restored in Scots Baronial style with turrets and crow-stepped gables. Originally the home of the Earls of Kinnoull, who have lent their name to Kinnoull Hill across the Tay to the east of Perth, it now houses the headquarters and **museum of the Black Watch**. This historic regiment – whose name refers to the dark colour of their tartan – was formed in 1739, having been built up earlier in the century by General Wade, who employed groups of Highlanders to keep the peace. The museum chronicles its history through a good display of paintings, uniforms, documents, weapons and photographs.

A number of attractions lie around Perth. A mile north of Perth on the A9, in the Inveralmond Industrial Estate, is the **Caithness Glass** factory (April–Oct Mon–Sat 9am–5pm, Sun 10am–5pm; Nov–March Mon–Sat 9am–5pm, Sun noon–5pm; free), with a viewing area where you can watch glass-blowing (take bus #4 from Mill Street in Perth).

For outdoor distractions, head for **Bell's Cherrybank Gardens** (April–Oct daily 9am–5pm; £2), a mile west of the centre, where you'll find eighteen acres of well-kept gardens, including the largest collection of heathers in Britain, interspersed with a waterfall, pools, aviary and children's play area. On the other side of the Tay, the **Branklyn Gardens**, Dundee Road (March–Oct daily 9.30am–sunset; NTS; £2.30), comprise an astonishing collection of Alpine plants and dwarf rhododendrons, spread across a compact two acres of hillside. Looking over the gardens from the north is **Kinnoull Hill**, which also offers splendid views of Perth, the Tay and the surrounding area from its 783ft summit (a 20min walk from the car park on Braes Road). Pick up a leaflet from Perth's tourist office for details of the hill's various woodland walks.

Eating and drinking

There's a fair selection of decent **eating places** in Perth: many ethnic restaurants and pubs offer cheap and satisfying food and there are several upmarket options. Within striking distance of the youth hostel is a good basic Indian restaurant, the *Café Kamran*, 13 York Place. The *Good Luck Food Palace*, 181 South St, serves well-priced Chinese cuisine, while *Pierre Victoire*, 38 South St (☎01738/444222), has cheap and cheerful French food. The best choice for a classier meal is *Number Thirty Three*, 33 George St (☎01738/633771), a stylish Art Deco fish restaurant, whose oyster bar serves delicious snacks, while the à la carte restaurant has more substantial fish dishes and good puds. *Strangeways*, 24 George St, is a popular bar and bistro, or, for delicious wholefood, home baking and coffee, try *The Lemon Tree*, 29–41 Skinnergate, just behind the tourist office (closes at 5pm). In addition, there are numerous little **coffee shops** in town like *Brambles*, 11 Princes St, and *Willows*, 12 St John's Place. An Irish **pub** in the town centre, *Mucky Mulligans*, 97 Canal St, claims to be the first "Dublin cottage-style" pub in Scotland and serves specialities like Irish stew all day, with live Irish folk music nightly. Nearby, *Twa Tams*, on Scott Street, and *Brennans*, on St John Street, have inexpensive meals and regular live music.

North of Perth

Just a couple of miles north of Perth on the A93 (bus #58 from South Street in Perth every 20min), on the eastern side of the Tay, **Scone Palace** (pronounced "Scoon") is worth every penny of the admission charge levied by its owners, the Earl and Countess of Mansfield, whose family has owned it for almost four centuries (mid-April to mid-Oct daily 9.30am–5pm; £5). The two-storey building is stately but not overpowering; it is far more a home than an untouchable monument, and the rooms, although full of priceless antiques and lavish furnishings, feel lived in and used.

Restored in the nineteenth century, the palace today consists of a sixteenth-century core surrounded by earlier buildings, most built of red sandstone, complete with battlements and the original gateway. The abbey that stood here in the sixteenth century, and where all Scottish kings until James I were crowned, was one of those destroyed following John Knox's sermon in Perth. In the extensive grounds which surround the palace lies the Moot Hill, which was once the site of the famous Coronation **Stone of Destiny** (see p.66).

Inside, a good selection of sumptuous rooms are open to visitors, including the library, which now houses an outstanding collection of porcelain, one of the foremost in the world, with items by Meissen, Sèvres, Chelsea, Derby and Worcester. Look out too for the beautiful papier-mâché dishes, Marie Antoinette's writing desk, and John Zoffany's exquisite eighteenth-century portrait of the *Lady Elizabeth Murray* [daughter of the second earl] *with Dido*. You could easily spend a morning here, enjoying strutting peacocks in the gardens, a fenced-off area with Highland cattle, picnic spot, donkey park, children's playground and a fragrant pine garden planted in 1848 with exotic conifers.

Huntingtower Castle

Not quite as grand as Scone, but nonetheless worth a visit, is **Huntingtower Castle** (April–Sept Mon–Sat 9.30am–6pm, Sun 2–6pm; Oct–March Mon–Wed & Sat 9.30am–4pm, Sun 2–4pm; HS; £1.50), three miles northwest of Perth on the A85 (bus #14, #15 or #55 from Scott Street in Perth). Two three-storey towers formed the original fifteenth- and sixteenth-century tower house, and these were linked in the seventeenth century by a range to provide more room. Formerly known as Ruthven Castle, it was here that the Raid of Ruthven took place in 1582, when the 16-year-old James VI, at the request of William, fourth Earl of Ruthven, came to the castle only to be held captive by a group of conspirators demanding the dismissal of favoured royal advisers. The plot failed and the young James was released ten months later. Today the castle's chief attractions are its splendid sixteenth-century painted walls and ceilings – you'll see them in the main hall in the east tower.

Dunkeld and Birnam

DUNKELD, twelve miles on from Perth up the A9 (trains from Perth to Inverness stop here; buses #23 and #27, Sun #22), was proclaimed Scotland's ecclesiastical capital by Kenneth MacAlpine in 850. Its position at the southern boundary of the Grampian Mountains made it a favoured meeting place for Highland and Lowland cultures, but in 1689 it was burnt to the ground by the Cameronians – fighting for William of Orange – in an effort to flush out troops of the Stuart monarch, James VII. Subsequent rebuilding, however, has created one of the area's most delightful communities, and it's well worth at least a brief stop to view its whitewashed houses and historic cathedral. The **tourist office** is at The Cross in the town centre (April–June, Sept & Oct Mon–Sat 9.30am–5.30pm, Sun 11am–4pm; July & Aug Mon–Sat 9am–7.30pm, Sun 11am–7pm; Nov & Dec Mon–Sat 9.30am–1.30pm; ☎01350/727688).

Dunkeld's partly ruined **cathedral** is on the northern side of town, in an idyllic setting amid lawns and trees on the east bank of the Tay. Construction began in the early twelfth century and continued throughout the next two hundred years, but the building was more or less ruined at the time of the Reformation. The present structure, in Gothic and Norman style, consists of the fourteenth-century choir and the fifteenth-century nave. The choir, restored in 1600 (and several times since), now serves as the parish church, while the nave remains roofless apart from the clock tower. Inside, note the leper's peep near the pulpit in the north wall, through which lepers could receive the sacrament without contact with the congregation. Also look out for the great effigy of "The Wolf of Badenoch", Robert II's son born in 1343. The wolf acquired his name and notoriety when, after being excommunicated from the Church for leaving his wife, he took his revenge by burning the towns of Forres and Elgin and sacking Elgin cathedral. He eventually repented, did public penance for his crimes and was absolved by his brother Robert III.

Dunkeld is linked to its sister community, **BIRNAM**, by Thomas Telford's seven-arched bridge of 1809. This little village has a place in history thanks to Shakespeare, for it was on "Dunsinane Hill" to the southeast of the village that Macbeth declared: "I will not be afraid of death and bane/Till Birnam Forest come to Dunsinane", only to be told by a messenger:

As I did stand my watch upon the Hill,
I look'd toward Birnam, and anon me thought
The Wood began to move ...

The **Perthshire Visitor Centre** just south of Birnam, down the A9 at Bankfoot (March–Oct daily 9am–8pm; Nov–Feb Mon–Fri 9am–7pm, Sat & Sun 9am–7.30pm; £2) offers "The Macbeth Experience", which documents – on film and through talking dummies – the true story of Macbeth, who in real life was quite the opposite of Shakespeare's scheming villain. Several centuries later another literary personality, Beatrix Potter, drew inspiration from the area, recalling her childhood holidays here when penning the *Peter Rabbit* stories. The **Beatrix Potter Garden** in Birnam celebrates the connection.

There are several large **hotels** in Dunkeld, including the *Atholl Arms Hotel*, Tay Terrace (☎01350/727219; ④), the *Royal Dunkeld*, Atholl Street (☎01350/727322; ⑤), and the Victorian Gothic *Birnam Hotel* on Perth Road (☎01350/727462; ⑥). Just to the north, the luxurious *Stakis Dunkeld* (☎01350/727771; ⑨) is set at the end of a long drive which winds through the hotel's lush estate, where you can fish, shoot, cycle and stroll. For **B&B**, try the non-smoking *Bheinne Mhor* (☎013502/727779; ④), Birnam Glen, Dunkeld, or the friendly *Heatherbank* (☎01350/727413; ③), on St Mary's Road in Birnam. There are a few mediocre **eating places** on Dunkeld's main street; the best food options are lunch at the *Atholl Arms* or a more expensive dinner at the *Stakis Dunkeld*.

Driving north on the A9 to Pitlochry, you can stop off and walk the mile and a half to **The Hermitage** (buses from Perth to Pitlochry stop near here), set in the wooded gorge of the River Braan. This pretty eighteenth-century folly, also known as Ossian's Hall, was once mirrored to reflect the water, but the mirrors were smashed by Victorian vandals and the folly more tamely restored. The hall, appealing yet incongruous in its splendid setting, neatly frames a dramatic waterfall.

Strathearn

Strathearn – the valley of the River Earn – stretches west of Perth, across to **Loch Earn** and the watersports centre at **Lochearnhead**. Agricola was here around two thousand years ago, trying to establish a foothold in the Highlands; later the area was frequented by Bonnie Prince Charlie and Rob Roy, both bound up in the north–south struggle between Highlands and Lowlands.

South of Strathearn, the small town of **AUCHTERARDER** sees its fair share of visitors, many of whom come to play golf at the swanky **Gleneagles Hotel** nearby (☎01764/662231; ⑨). There is a **tourist office** on High Street (April–June, Sept & Oct Mon–Sat 9.30am–5.30pm, Sun 11am–4pm; July & Aug Mon–Sat 9am–6pm, Sun 11am–5pm; Nov–March Mon–Fri 9.30am–1.30pm; ☎01764/663450). As well as the local bus service, a classic 1950s bus, the **Loch Earn Trundler**, links Callander, Lochearnhead, Comrie and Crieff, and the **Loch Tay Trundler** runs from Callander to Lochearnhead, Kenmore and Aberfeldy (for details call ☎01786/442707; July–Sept).

Dunning

Just southeast of the valley, it is worth taking a detour from the busy A9 to the quiet village of **DUNNING**, five miles east of Auchterarder on the B8062, which has an impressive history. The village was once the capital of the Picts and was the place where Kenneth I, King of the Picts and Scots, died in 860. Dunning was destroyed by the Jacobites and subsequently rebuilt, which accounts for its homogeneous appearance, the houses all being late eighteenth and early nineteenth century. Only **St Serf's** survived, a rugged church with a Norman tower and arch. Just west of the village is an extraordinary monument, a pile of stones surmounted by a cross, and scrawled with the words: "Maggie Wall, Burnt here, 1657". Maggie Wall was burnt as a witch, and rumour has it that local women replenish the white writing on the monument every year.

Crieff and around

At the heart of the valley is the old spa town of **CRIEFF**, in a lovely position on a south-facing slope of the Grampian foothills. Cattle traders used to come here in the eighteenth century, since this was a good location – between Highland and Lowland – for buying and selling livestock, but Crieff really came into its own with the arrival of the railway in 1856. Shortly after that, Morrison's Academy, now one of Scotland's most respected schools, took in its first pupils, and in 1868 the grand old *Crieff Hydro* (☎01764/655555; ⑨), then known as the *Strathearn Hydropathic*, opened its doors. It's still the nicest place to stay in town, despite being dry (of alcohol). Cheaper **B&B** options include *Eastview Guest House*, 98 East High St (☎01764/652132; ③), and the comely *Bank Guest House*, 32 Burrell St (☎01764/653409; ③). Crieff consists of a pleasing mixture of Edwardian and Victorian houses, with a busy little centre which still retains something of the atmosphere of the former spa town. The **Crieff Visitor Centre** (daily 9am–5pm) is a "craftsy" place, crammed with pottery and paperweights. The **tourist office** is in the town hall on High Street (April–June, Sept & Oct Mon–Sat 9.30am–5.30pm, Sun 11am–4pm; July & Aug Mon–Sat 9am–7pm, Sun 11am–6pm; Nov–March Mon–Fri 9.30am–5pm, Sat 9.30am–1.30pm; ☎01764/652578).

From Crieff, it's a short drive or a twenty-minute walk to the **Glenturret Distillery** (March–Dec Mon–Sat 9.30am–6pm, Sun noon–6pm, last tour 4.30pm; Jan & Feb Mon–Fri 11.30am–4pm, last tour 2.30pm; free), just off the A85 to Comrie. To get there on public transport, catch any bus going to Crieff, Comrie or St Fillans and ask the driver to drop you at the bottom of the Glenturret Distillery road, from where it's a five-minute walk. This is Scotland's oldest distillery, established in 1775, and a good one to visit, if only for its splendid isolation. Four miles southeast of Crieff on the B8062 (Crieff/Auchterarder bus) is the **Innerpeffray Library** (Feb–Nov Mon–Wed, Fri & Sat 10am–12.45pm & 2–4.45pm, Sun 2–4pm; £2). Founded in 1691, it is the oldest library in Scotland, and is a must for bibliophiles, with mainly theological and classical books.

If you enjoy ornate gardens, on no account miss the **Drummond Castle Gardens** (May–Oct daily 2–5pm; £3) near Muthill, two miles south of Crieff on the A822 (bus #47 from Crieff towards Muthill, then a mile and a half walk up the castle drive). The approach to the garden is extraordinary, up a dark avenue of trees. Crossing the courtyard of the castle to the grand terrace, you can view the garden in all its symmetrical glory. It was laid out by John Drummond, second Earl of Perth, in 1630, and shows clear French and Italian influence, although the central structural feature of the parterre is a St Andrews cross. Italian marble statues punctuate the long lines of the cross, and the overall effect is of exceptional harmony and grace. Behind this, everything from corn to figs and grapes grow in the Victorian greenhouse and kitchen garden. The castle itself (closed to the public) is a wonderful mixture of architectural styles. There is a blunt fifteenth-century keep on a rocky crag, adjoining a much modified Renaissance mansion house.

Comrie

COMRIE, a pretty conservation village another five miles along the River Earn, has the dubious distinction of being the location where more seismic tremors have been recorded than anywhere else in Britain, due to its position on the Highland Boundary Fault. Earthquake readings are still taken at **Earthquake House**, about 600yd off the A85, on the south side of the river. The building itself is not open to the public, but there are information panels outside, and if you're really keen you can look through the windows at a model of the world's first seismometer, set up here in 1874.

If you've got children, an excellent place to take them is the **Auchingarrich Wildlife Centre** (daily 10am–dusk; £4), a couple of miles south of Comrie on the B827 (bus #15 from Crieff to Comrie, then a two-mile walk). Recently established in a blustery hillside location, it covers 100 acres and provides lots of opportunities to pet the farm animals and admire the rare and ornamental birds.

Loch Earn

At the eastern edge of Strathearn is **Loch Earn**, a gently lapping Highland loch dramatically edged by mountains. The A85 runs north along the lochshore from the village of **ST FILLANS**, at the eastern tip, to the main settlement, **LOCHEARNHEAD**, at the western edge of the loch. This wide tranquil expanse of water is ideal for **watersports**, and particularly good for beginners. Lochearnhead Watersports (☎01567/830330) organizes and teaches a wide variety of activities, including water-skiing, windsurfing, Canadian canoeing and kayaking. Lochearnhead is also a good base for **walking**, and the watersports centre runs "heritage rambles". For **accommodation**, try the *Clachan Cottage Hotel* (☎01567/830247; ⑤), or the cheaper *Earnknowe* B&B (☎01567/830238; ③), both on Lochside, Lochearnhead. There are also some good **self-catering** options in the area: from *Earnknowe* you can rent attractive stone cottages close to Lochearnhead village (2–6 people; £120–355 per week). In addition, there are some Scandinavian-style wooden chalets, with good facilities (sleeps 6; £280–355 per week; ☎01567/830211), or a nice little whitewashed cottage in St Fillans (sleeps 2–4; £240 per week; ☎0131/313 0467 or 01764/670004). Perhaps the best choice for the area as a whole, though, is the chalet-like *Four Seasons Hotel* (☎01764/685333; ⑤) in St Fillans with a wonderful loch-side location. It's also the best choice for **eating**; there are few other options in the area.

Around Loch Tay

The mountains and valleys of **Glenalmond**, north of Strathearn, give way to the fourteen-mile-long, freshwater **Loch Tay**, just north of which is moody **Ben Lawers** (3984ft), Perthshire's highest mountain; from the top there are incredible views towards both the Atlantic and the North Sea. The ascent – which should not be tackled without all the right equipment (see p.44) – takes around three hours from the NTS **visitor centre** (mid-April to Sept daily 10am–5pm; ☎01567/820397), which is at 1300ft and reached by a track off the A827 along the northern side of the loch. The centre has an audio-visual show, slides of the mountain flowers – including the rare Alpine flora found here – and a nature trail with accompanying descriptive booklet.

The **mountains of Breadalbane** (pronounced "Bread-*al*bane"), named after the Earls of Breadalbane, loom over the southern end of Loch Tay. Glens Lochay and Dochart curve into the north and south respectively from the small town of **KILLIN**, where the River Dochart comes rushing out of the hills and down the frothy **Falls of Dochart**, before disgorging into Loch Tay. There's little to do in Killin itself, but it makes a convenient base for some of the area's best walks. The **tourist office** is located by the falls (March–May & Oct daily 10am–5pm; June & Sept daily 9.30am–6pm; July & Aug daily 9am–6pm; Nov, Dec & Feb Sat & Sun 10am–4pm), next to the **Breadalbane Folklore Centre** (same times as tourist office; £1). The centre explores the history and mythology of Breadalbane and holds the thirteen-hundred-year-old "healing stones" of St Fillan, an early Christian missionary who settled in Glen Dochart. Killin is littered with B&Bs, but one of the more unusual places **to stay** is the *Dall Lodge Hotel*, Main Street (☎01567/820217; ⑤), which is filled with all manner of exotic Far Eastern bits and pieces, and has a dining room serving fine local produce. There is also a **youth hostel** (☎01567/820546; April–Oct), in a fine old country house just beyond the northern end of the village, with views out over the loch.

North of the loch

Beyond Breadalbane, the mountains tumble down into **Glen Lyon** – at 34 miles long, the longest enclosed glen in Scotland – where, legend has it, the Celtic warrior Fingal built twelve castles. Access to the glen is usually impossible in winter, but the narrow roads are passable in summer. You can either take the road from Killin up past the **Ben Lawers Visitor Centre**, four miles up Loch Tay, and continue going, or take the road from Fortingall, which is a couple of miles north of the loch's northern end. The two roads join up, making a round-trip possible, but bear in mind there is no road through the mountains to Loch Rannoch further north. **FORTINGALL** itself is little more than a handful of thatched cottages, although locals make much of their 3000-year-old yew tree – believed (by them at least) to be the oldest living thing in Europe. The village also lays claim to being the birthplace of Pontius Pilate, reputedly the son of a Roman officer stationed here.

On a slight promontory at Loch Tay's northern end and overlooking the River Tay, **KENMORE**'s whitewashed houses and well-tended gardens cluster around the gate to **Taymouth Castle** – built by the Campbells of Glenorchy in the early nineteenth century and now a private golf club. Also in Kenmore, the **Scottish Crannog Centre** (April–Oct Mon–Fri 10am–5pm, Sat & Sun 10am–6pm; £2.80), perched above the loch on stilts, is an authentic reconstruction of a Bronze Age defensive house complete with sheepskin rugs and wooden bowls. There are various **boat rental** places around this end of the loch, as well as **Croft-na-Caber** (☎01887/830588), an impressive **outdoor pursuits** complex on the southern bank of the loch, where you can try water-skiing, fishing, hill walking, cross-country skiing, river sledging, rafting and jet biking. The complex also offers comfortable **accommodation** either in its own hotel (☎01887/830236; ⑤) or in well-equipped chalets overlooking the loch (sleeps 2–6; £250–550 per week). You don't have to stay here to use the facilities, however, and tuition or equipment rental is available by the hour, half-day, full day or longer. As an example of prices, a day's sailing or windsurfing instruction costs around £46. You can also stay at the overwhelmingly Scottish *Kenmore Hotel*, in the village square (☎01887/830205; ⑥), a descendant of Scotland's oldest inn, established here in 1572. Even if you don't stay, it's worth stopping for a meal or drink.

Aberfeldy

A largely Victorian town six miles or so further on, **ABERFELDY** makes a good base for exploring the area. The **tourist office** at The Square in the town centre (April–June, Sept & Oct Mon–Sat 9.30am–5.30pm, Sun noon–4pm; July & Aug Mon–Sat 9am–7pm, Sun 11am–6pm; Nov–March Mon–Fri 9.30am–5pm, Sat 9.30am–1.30pm; ☎01887/820276) gives details of the so-called Locus Project, a local initiative which has devised a series of looped trails that take in all the main sights.

Aberfeldy sits at the point where the Urlar Burn – lined by the silver birch trees celebrated by Robert Burns in his poem *The Birks of Aberfeldy* – flows into the River Tay. The Tay is spanned by **Wade's Bridge**, built by General Wade in 1733 during his efforts to control the trouble in the Highlands, and, with its humpback and four arches, is regarded as one of the general's finest remaining crossing points. Overlooking the bridge from the south end is the **Black Watch Monument**, a pensive, kilted soldier, erected in 1887 to commemorate the peacekeeping troop of Highlanders gathered together by Wade in 1739.

The small town centre is a busy mixture of craft and tourist shops, its main attraction the superbly restored early nineteenth-century **Aberfeldy Water Mill** (Easter–Oct Mon–Sat 10am–5pm, Sun noon–5pm; £1.80), a mill which harnesses the water of the Urlar to turn the wheel that stone-grinds the oatmeal in the traditional Scottish way.

One mile west of Aberfeldy, across Wade's Bridge, **Castle Menzies** (April to mid-Oct Mon–Fri 10.30am–5pm, Sun 2–5pm; £2.50) is an imposing, Z-shaped, sixteenth-century tower house, which until the middle of this century was the chief seat of the Clan

Menzies. With the demise of the Menzies line the castle was taken over by the Menzies Clan Society, who since 1971 has been involved in the lengthy process of restoring it. Now the interior, with its wide stone staircase, is refreshingly free of fixtures and fittings, with structural attributes such as the plasterwork ceilings on show.

If you want to **stay** in Aberfeldy, head for *Moness House Hotel and Country Club*, Crieff Road (☎01887/820446; ⑤), a whitewashed country house which also offers luxurious **self-catering** cottages (sleeps 2–6; £245–500 per week), as well as fishing, golf and watersports. Alternatively, there's *Guinach House*, by the Birks (☎01887/820251; ⑦), a tastefully decorated place in pleasant grounds near the famous silver birches, with a good dining room, or *Farleyer House* (☎01887/820332; ⑧), a mile out of Aberfeldy on the B846, which is highly recommended as a hotel and **restaurant**. For B&B, try *Novar*, 2 Home St (☎01887/820779; ③), or *Mavis Bank*, Taybridge Drive (☎01887/820223; ③), both attractive stone cottages.

Pitlochry

Surrounded by hills just north of the confluence of the Tummel and Tay rivers at Ballinluig, **PITLOCHRY** spreads gracefully along the eastern shore of the Tummel, on the lower slopes of Ben Vrackie (see box opposite). Even after General Wade built one of his first roads through here in the early eighteenth century, Pitlochry remained little more than a village. Queen Victoria's visit in 1842 helped put the area on the map, but it wasn't until the end of the century that Pitlochry established itself as a popular holiday centre.

Today the busy main street is a constant flurry of traffic, locals and tourists. Beyond the train bridge at the southern end of the main street (Atholl Road leading to Perth Road) is Bells' **Blair Atholl Distillery**, Perth Road (Oct–Easter Mon–Fri 9am–5pm; Easter–Sept also Sat 9am–5pm, Sun noon–5pm; tours every 10min; £3 including tastings), where the excellent visitor centre illustrates the process involved in making the Blair Atholl Malt. Whisky has been produced on this site since 1798, in which time production has been stepped up to around two million litres a year, making this a medium-sized distillery.

A perfect contrast to Blair Atholl is the **Edradour Distillery** (March–Oct Mon–Sat 9.30am–5pm, Sun noon–5pm; Nov–Feb group bookings only), Scotland's smallest, in an idyllic position tucked into the hills a couple of miles east of Pitlochry on the A924. A whistle-stop audiovisual presentation covering more than 250 years of production precedes the tour of the distillery itself.

On the western edge of Pitlochry, just across the river, lies Scotland's renowned "Theatre in the Hills", the **Pitlochry Festival Theatre** (☎01796/472680; Easter–early Oct). Set up in 1951, the theatre started in a tent on the site of what is now the town curling rink, before moving to the banks of the river in 1981. Backstage tours, covering all aspects of theatre production (generally Thurs & Fri 2pm; £3; booking essential), are on offer during the day, while a variety of productions – both mainstream and offbeat – are staged in the evening.

A short stroll upstream from the theatre is the **Pitlochry Power Station and Dam**, a massive concrete wall which harnesses the water of the man-made Loch Faskally, just north of the town, for hydroelectric power. Although the visitor centre (April–Oct daily 10am–5.30pm; £1.80) explains the ins and outs of it all, the main attraction here, apart from the views up the loch, is the **salmon ladder**, up which the salmon leap on their annual migration – a sight not to be missed.

Practicalities

Access to Pitlochry is easy by public transport, thanks to its position on the main train line to Inverness, and regular buses running from Perth. The **bus** stop and the

train station are on Station Road, at the north end of town, ten minutes' walk from the centre and the **tourist office**, 22 Atholl Rd (April to mid-May & Oct Mon–Sat 9am–6pm, Sun noon–6pm; mid-May to Sept daily 9am–8pm; Nov–April Mon–Fri 9am–5pm, Sat 9am–1.30pm; ☎01796/472215). The office gives out an informative free guide of walks in the surrounding area, and also offers an **accommodation** booking service.

Birchwood Hotel, East Moulin Road (☎01796/472477; ⑥), occupies a lovely Victorian country house at the top of town, set in four acres of grounds, and has a particularly good restaurant. South of the hotel, the magnificent and much pricier *Pitlochry Hydro*, Knockard Road (☎01796/472666; ⑧), looks out over the Tummel Valley. Five miles west of Pitlochry on the B8019, the *Queens View Hotel* (☎01796/473291; ⑥) has lovely views, good bar meals and a fine restaurant. In the town centre, there are a number of cheaper hotels along the main street, including the comfortable *McKays Hotel*, 138 Atholl Rd (☎01796/473888; ④), and many guest houses and **B&Bs**. Try *Craigroyston House*, 2 Lower Oakfield (☎01796/472053; ③), *Comar House*, Strathview Terrace (☎01796/473531; ③), or *Ferryman's Cottage* (☎01796/473681; ③), Port-na-Craig, in a beautiful position next to the River Tummel. The **youth hostel** (☎01796/472308) is a fine stone mansion on Knockard Road at the top of town.

WALKS AROUND PITLOCHRY

Ordnance Survey Landranger maps Nos. 43 & 52

Pitlochry is surrounded by good walking country. The biggest lure has to be **Ben Vrackie** (2733ft), which provides a stunning backdrop for the Festival Theatre and deserves better than a straight up-and-down walk; however, the climb should only be attempted in settled weather conditions, with the right equipment and following the necessary safety precautions (see p.44). A good round-walk goes via the quiet Loch Faskally to **Killiecrankie Visitor Centre** (refreshments available) and then heads up the hill by a seldom-used route before returning via Moulin. Allow a full day for the complete walk.

Head through Pitlochry northwards and branch off to pass the *Green Hotel* and reach attractive Loch Faskally. Another time you could walk right round it; for now follow the shore and take the signs up the River Garry to go through the **Pass of Killiecrankie**. This is looked after by the NTS, which has a visitor centre with interpretive displays, books and souvenirs for sale. To get this far takes a couple of hours.

From the NTS centre walk north up the old A9 and branch off on the small tarred road signposted **Old Faskally** which twists up under the new A9 and past a house and the gates of Old Faskally. Keep on the tarred road until you reach a diversion sign which leads up the embankment above the road onto a lesser track and through a kissing gate at the top of the field. Continue from here until you finally leave the cultivated land through the hill dyke.

The track zigzags up heathery pasture to an old wall and a gate in a fence just beyond: go through the gate then bear right across the open hillside, crossing the **Allt Eachainn**, the burn that drains this corrie, before heading up the hill opposite in another series of bends, clearly seen from below. Also visible from below is a footpath bearing off left as the slope gets steeper, which you should follow through the heather towards the pass. It goes over the saddle of a dark heathery prow and, 220yd beyond, brings you to the pass looking down on **Loch a' Choire**. The track from Pitlochry/Moulin crosses below the dam on the loch and heads directly up the peak. This steep track can be seen from the col; skirt north of the loch to join it. As Ben Vrackie is an isolated summit, the weather can change quickly and clouds render route-finding difficult, so Loch a' Choire may be a better place to picnic. The descent from Loch a' Choire is clearly pathed and runs across the moors to reach forest level. A stile crosses the fence into the birch and pine woods that lead down to a small car park. Follow the minor road from it down to the hamlet of **Moulin** and on to Pitlochry.

Pitlochry is the domain of the tearoom and pitifully short of **restaurants** and pubs; the best option is the *Killiecrankie Hotel* (☎01796/473220) at Killiecrankie three miles north on the A9, where the meals are hearty and well priced. In town, try the popular restaurant at the Festival Theatre, or the nearby *Porthacraig Inn & Restaurant*, both of which have beautiful riverside locations. For a pub lunch with spectacular views over the water, it's worth driving ten miles west to the *Loch Tummel Inn* (☎01882/634272; ④), halfway along Loch Tummel. Its restaurant is also highly recommended and booking ahead is essential for dinner.

Loch Tummel and Loch Rannoch

Between Pitlochry and Loch Ericht lies a sparsely populated, ever-changing panorama of mountains, moors, lochs and glens. Venturing into the hills is difficult without a car – unless you're walking – but infrequent local buses run from Pitlochry to the outlying communities, and the train to Inverness runs parallel to the A9.

West of Pitlochry, the B8019/B846 twists and turns along the Grampian mountainsides, overlooking **Loch Tummel** and then **Loch Rannoch**. These two lochs, celebrated by Harry Lauder in his famous song *The Road to the Isles*, are joined by Dunalastair Water, which narrows to become the River Tummel at the western end of the loch of the same name. This is a spectacular stretch of countryside and one which deserves leisurely exploration. **Queen's View** at the eastern end of Loch Tummel is a fabulous vantage point, looking down the loch across the hills to the misty peak of Schiehallion (3520ft), the "Fairy Mountain", whose mass was used in early experiments to judge the weight of the Earth. The Forestry Commission's **visitor centre** (April–Oct daily 10am–6pm; ☎01350/727284) interprets the fauna and flora of the area, and also has a café.

Beyond Loch Tummel, marking the eastern end of Loch Rannoch, the small community of **KINLOCH RANNOCH** is popular with backpackers, who stock up at the local store before taking to the hills. You can **stay** here in the converted eighteenth-century croft *Cuilimore Cottage* (☎01882/632218; ④), with a rustic atmosphere and delicious food. The road follows the loch to its end and then heads six miles further into the desolation of **Rannoch Moor**, where **Rannoch Station**, a lonely outpost on the Glasgow to Fort William West Highland train, marks the end of the line. The only way back is by the same road as far as Loch Rannoch, where it's possible – but not always advisable, depending on conditions – to return on a (very) minor road along the south side of the lochs. The round-trip is roughly seventy miles.

Blair Atholl to Loch Ericht

Four miles north of Pitlochry, the A9 cuts through the **Pass of Killiecrankie**, a breathtaking wooded gorge which falls away to the River Garry below. This dramatic setting was the site of the **Battle of Killiecrankie** in 1689, when the Jacobites quashed the forces of General Mackay. Legend has it that one soldier of the Crown, fleeing for his life, made a miraculous jump across the 18ft **Soldier's Leap**, an impossibly wide chasm halfway up the gorge. Queen Victoria, visiting here 160 years later, contented herself with recording the beauty of the area in her diary. Exhibits at the slick NTS **visitor centre** (April–Oct daily 10am–5.30pm; ☎01796/473233; £1) recall the battle and examine the gorge in detail.

Before leading the Jacobites into battle, Graham of Claverhouse, Viscount ("Bonnie") Dundee, had seized **Blair Castle** (April–Oct daily 10am–6pm; £5.50), three miles up the road at Blair Atholl. Seat of the Atholl dukedom, this whitewashed, turreted castle, surrounded by parkland and dating from 1269, presents an impressive sight as you approach up the drive. A piper may be playing in front of the castle: he is one of the Atholl Highlanders, a select group retained by the duke as his private army – a privilege afforded to him by Queen Victoria, who stayed here in 1844. Today the duke is the only British subject allowed to maintain his own force.

A total of 32 rooms are open for inspection, and display a selection of paintings, furniture and plasterwork that is sumptuous in the extreme, although the vast number of stuffed animals may not be to everyone's liking. The Tapestry Room, on the top floor of the original Cumming's Tower, is hung with Brussels tapestries and contains an outrageous four-poster bed, topped with vases of ostrich feathers which originally came from the first duke's suite at Holyrood Palace in Edinburgh. The Ballroom, also, with its timber roof, antlers and melange of portraits, is Baronial Scotland at its best.

Highland cows graze the ancient landscaped grounds and peacocks strut in front of the castle. There is a **riding stable** from where you can take treks, and formal woodland walks have been laid out – don't miss the neglected, walled Japanese water garden. There is also a **caravan park** (☎01796/481263) in the grounds.

Beyond Blair Atholl, the A9 follows the line of **Glen Garry** and the River Garry through the Grampian Mountains. The road climbs continuously, sweeping past the eastern end of **Glen Errochty**, on towards the barren **Pass of Drummochter** and to the bleak little village of Dalwhinnie at the northern end of **Loch Ericht**. The scenery is marvellous all the way, but there is literally nothing here apart from the mountains and moors.

travel details

Trains

Falkirk Grahamston to: Edinburgh (every 30min; 35min); Glasgow Queen Street (every 30min; 25min); Linlithgow (every 30min; 13min).

Kirkcaldy to: Aberdeen (hourly; 2hr); Dundee (hourly; 40min–1hr); Edinburgh (23 daily; 40min); Perth (7 daily; 40min); Pitlochry (4 direct daily; 1hr 15min; 4 indirect, change at Perth; 1hr 25min).

Linlithgow to: Edinburgh (hourly; 20min); Falkirk Grahamston (every 30min; 13min); Glasgow Queen Street (hourly; 30min).

Perth to: Aberdeen (hourly; 1hr 40min); Dundee (hourly; 25min); Edinburgh (9 daily; 1hr 25min); Glasgow Queen Street (hourly; 1hr 5min); Kirkcaldy (7 daily; 40min); Pitlochry (8 daily; 30min).

Pitlochry to: Edinburgh (5 daily; 2hr); Glasgow Queen Street (3 daily; 1hr 45min); Kirkcaldy (4 direct daily; 1hr 15min; 1 indirect, change at Perth; 1hr 45min); Perth (8 daily; 30min); Stirling (3–5 daily; 1hr 15min).

Stirling to: Aberdeen (hourly; 2hr 15min); Dundee (hourly; 1hr); Edinburgh (hourly; 1hr); Falkirk Grahamston (hourly; 28min); Glasgow Queen Street (hourly; 30min); Linlithgow (hourly; 35min); Perth (hourly; 30min); Pitlochry (3–5 daily; 1hr 15min).

Buses

Bo'ness to: Edinburgh (5 daily; 45min); Stirling (3 daily; 35min).

Dundee to: Glenrothes (every 30min; 1hr 10min); St Andrews (every 20min; 35min); Kirkcaldy (10 daily; 1hr 30min); Stirling (12 daily; 1hr 30min).

Dunfermline to: Edinburgh (2 daily; 40min); Glenrothes (15 daily; 1hr 5min); Kirkcaldy (hourly; 1hr); St Andrews (11–13 daily; 2hr).

Glenrothes to: Dundee (every 30min; 1hr 10min); Dunfermline (15 daily; 1hr 10min); Kirkcaldy (hourly; 20min); St Andrews (hourly; 45min).

Kirkcaldy to: Dundee (10 daily; 1hr 30min); Dunfermline (hourly; 1hr); Glenrothes (hourly; 20min); St Andrews (16 daily; 1hr).

Perth to: Dunblane (every 30min; 35min); Dunfermline (every 30min; 50min); Edinburgh (hourly; 1hr 20min); Glasgow (20 daily; 1hr 35min); Gleneagles (18 daily; 25min); Inverness (10 daily; 2hr 30min); London (4 daily; 9hr); Stirling (20 daily; 50min).

St Andrews to: Dundee (every 20min; 40min); Dunfermline (Mon–Sat 11–13 daily; 2hr); Edinburgh (12 daily; 2hr); Glasgow (6 daily; 2hr 50min); Glenrothes (hourly; 45min); Kirkcaldy (16 daily; 1hr); Stirling (6 daily; 2hr).

Stirling to: Aberfoyle (4 daily; 45min); Bo'ness (3 daily; 35 min); Callander (11 daily; 45min); Dollar (13 daily; 35min); Doune (14 daily; 30min); Dunblane (20 daily; 1hr 15min); Dundee (12 daily; 1hr 30min); Dunfermline (13 daily; 50min); Edinburgh (hourly; 1hr 35min); Falkirk (every 45min; 30min); Glasgow (34 daily; 1hr 10min); Gleneagles (16 daily; 30min); Inverness (12 daily; 3hr 30min); Killin (2 daily; 2hr); Linlithgow (hourly; 1hr); Lochearnhead (2 daily; 1hr 40min); Perth (20 daily; 50min); Pitlochry (2 daily; 1hr 30min); St Andrews (6 daily; 2hr).

CHAPTER FIVE

ARGYLL

C ut off for centuries from the rest of Scotland by the mountains and sea lochs that characterize the region, **Argyll** remains remote, its scatter of offshore islands forming part of the Inner Hebridean archipelago (the remaining Hebrides are dealt with in Skye and the Western Isles). Geographically, as well as culturally, this is a transitional area between Highland and Lowland, boasting a rich variety of scenery, from lush, subtropical gardens warmed by the Gulf Stream to flat and treeless islands far out in the Atlantic. It's in the folds and twists of the countryside and the views out to the islands that the strengths and beauties of mainland Argyll lie – the one area of man-made sights you shouldn't miss is the cluster of **Celtic and prehistoric sites** near Kilmartin. The overall population is tiny; even **Oban**, Argyll's chief ferry port, has just seven thousand inhabitants, while the prettiest, **Inveraray**, boasts a mere four hundred.

The eastern duo of **Bute** and **Arran** are the most popular of Scotland's more southerly islands, the latter – now strictly speaking part of North Ayrshire – justifiably so, with spectacular scenery ranging from the granite peaks of the north to the Lowland pasture of the south. Of the Hebridean islands covered in this chapter, mountainous **Mull** is the most visited, though it is large enough to absorb the crowds, many of whom are only passing through en route to the tiny isle of **Iona**, a centre of Christian culture since the sixth century. **Islay**, best known for its distinctive malt whiskies, is fairly quiet even in the height of summer, as is neighbouring **Jura**, which offers excellent walking opportunities. And for those seeking further solitude, there's the fertile island of **Colonsay**, and the more remote islands of **Tiree** and **Coll**, which, although swept with fierce winds, boast more sunny days than anywhere else in Scotland.

The region's name derives from *Aragàidheal*, which translates as "Boundary of the Gaels", the Irish Celts who settled here in the fifth century AD, and whose **kingdom of Dalriada** embraced much of what is now Argyll. Known to the Romans as *Scotti* – hence Scotland – it was the Irish Celts who promoted Celtic Christianity, and whose Gaelic language eventually became the national tongue. After a brief period of Norse invasion and settlement, the islands (and the peninsula of Kintyre) fell to the immensely powerful Somerled, who became King of the Hebrides and Lord of Argyll in the twelfth century. Somerled's successors, the MacDonalds, established Islay as their headquarters in the 1200s, but were in turn dislodged by Robert the Bruce. Of Bruce's allies, it was the **Campbells** who benefited most from the MacDonalds' demise, and eventually, as the dukes of Argyll, gained control of the entire area – even today they remain one of the largest landowners in the region.

In the aftermath of the Jacobite uprisings, the islands of Argyll, like the rest of the Highlands, were devastated by the **Clearances**, with thousands of crofters evicted from their homes in order to make room for profitable sheep farming – "the white plague" – and cattle rearing. Today the traditional industries remain under threat, leaving the region ever more dependent on tourism, EU grants and a steady influx of new settlers to keep things going, while Gaelic, once the language of the majority in Argyll, retains only a tenuous hold on the outlying islands of Islay, Coll and Tiree – all officially part of Scotland's Gaelic-speaking areas.

It's on Argyll's west coast that the unpredictability of the **weather** can really affect your holiday. If you can, avoid July and August, when the crowds on Mull, Iona and Arran are at their densest – there's no guarantee the weather will be any better than during the rest of the year, and you might have more chance of avoiding the persistent Scottish midge (for more on which see p.21). **Public transport** throughout Argyll is minimal, though buses do serve most major settlements, and the train line reaches all

---

ACCOMMODATION PRICE CODES

Throughout this book, accommodation **prices** have been graded with the codes below, according to the cost of the least expensive double room in high season. Price codes are not given for campsites, most of which charge under £10 per person. Almost all hostels charge less than £10 a night for a bed – the few exceptions to this rule have the prices quoted in the text. For a full account of the accommodation price codes, see p.30.

① under £20	④ £40–50	⑦ £70–80
② £20–30	⑤ £50–60	⑧ £80–100
③ £30–40	⑥ £60–70	⑨ over £100

the way to Oban. In the remoter parts of the region and on the islands, you'll have to rely on a combination of walking, shared taxis and the postbus. If you're planning to take a car across to one of the islands, it's essential that you book both your outward and return journeys as early as possible, as the ferries get very booked up. And lastly, a word on **accommodation**: a large proportion of visitors to this part of Scotland come here for a week or two and stay in self-catering cottages. On some islands and in more remote areas, this is often the most common form of accommodation available – in peak season, you should book several months in advance (for more on self-catering, see p.32).

Gare Loch and Loch Long

Most people approach Argyll from Glasgow, from where there's a choice of two routes: the most popular is along Loch Lomond (see p.231); a quieter route (and the one which the train takes for some of the way) is along the shores of **Gare Loch** and **Loch Long** to Arrochar, which marks the beginning of Argyll proper. Apart from **Helensburgh**, there's little to see along the shores of either loch, though the road is appealingly winding. Both shores are littered with decaying industrial remains, including the nuclear submarine base at Faslane on Gare Loch and the oil tanks at Finnart on Loch Long. Only occasionally is it possible to glimpse the unspeakably beautiful landscape described by eighteenth-century travellers.

Helensburgh

HELENSBURGH, twenty miles or so northwest of Glasgow, is a smart, Georgian grid-plan settlement laid out in an imitation of Edinburgh's New Town and overlooking the Clyde estuary. In the eighteenth century it was a well-to-do commuter town for Glasgow and a seaside resort, whose bathing-master, **Henry Bell**, invented one of the first steamboats, the *Comet*, to transport Glaswegians "doon the watter". Today Helensburgh is a stop on the route of the *Waverley,* the last sea-going paddle steamer in the world, which does a zigzag tour of the lochs of Argyll throughout the summer. In addition, there's a passenger-only ferry service across the Clyde from Helensburgh to Gourock (see p.213) and Kilcreggan (April to mid-Oct Mon–Sat) – pick up timetables for both from the tourist office.

The inventor of TV, John Logie Baird, was born here, as was Charles Rennie Mackintosh, who in 1902 was commissioned by the Glaswegian publisher Walter Blackie to design **Hill House** (Easter–Dec daily 1.30–5.30pm; NTS; £4.50), on Upper Colquhoun Street. Without doubt the best surviving example of Mackintosh's domestic architecture, the house – right down to light fittings – is stamped with his very personal interpretation of Art Nouveau, characterized by his sparing use of colour and stylized floral patterns. The effect is occasionally overwhelming – it's difficult to imagine actually living in such an environment – yet it is precisely Mackintosh's attention to detail that makes the place so special (for more on Mackintosh, see p.188). After exploring the house, head for the kitchen quarters, which have been sensitively transformed into a tearoom.

If you've got children to entertain (and your own transport), head for the **Cove Conservation Park** (daily: April–Oct 10am–5pm; Nov–March 10am–4pm; £3), fourteen miles' drive from Helensburgh on the nearby Kilcreggan peninsula. Not only can children watch and stroke a wide variety of farm animals, but there's a see-through bee-hive, a terrapinarium and lots of green technology for older kids and adults, too.

Practicalities

Hill House is a good twenty-minute walk from Helensburgh Central train station, up Sinclair Street, or just five minutes from Helensburgh Upper train station (where the Oban and Fort William trains stop). The **tourist office** is on the ground floor of the old

Italianate chuch tower by the loch (April to mid-May daily 10am–5pm; mid-May to June daily 9.30am–6pm; July–Sept daily 9.30am–7pm; early Oct Mon–Fri 10am–4.30pm, Sat & Sun 10am–5pm; ☎01436/672642). The best **accommodation** options are along West Clyde Street overlooking the loch – try the luxurious *Commodore* at no. 112–117 (☎01436/676924; ⑥), or the smaller *Imperial*, at no. 12–14 (☎01436/672320; ⑤). Of the **B&Bs**, the *Ardmore Guest House*, at no. 98 (☎01436/673461; ③), or *Ashfield*, 38 William St (☎01436/672259; ③), are both good bets.

Cowal and Bute

West of Helensburgh, the claw-shaped **Cowal peninsula**, formed by Loch Fyne and Loch Long, is the most visited part of Argyll, largely due to its proximity to Glasgow. The landscape here is extremely varied, ranging from the Highland peaks of the **Argyll Forest Park** in the north, to the gentle low-lying coastline of the southwest, but most visitors – and the majority of the population – confine themselves to the area around **Dunoon** (which has Cowal's chief tourist office) in the east, leaving the rest of the countryside relatively undisturbed. The island of **Bute** is in many ways simply an extension of the peninsula, from which it is separated by the merest slither of water, and is indeed now linked administratively with the rest of Argyll. Until 1975, however, it formed its own county, along with the Isle of Arran, to the south; its chief town, **Rothesay**, rivals Dunoon as the major seaside resort on the Clyde, and has the added attraction of two superb castles in its vicinity.

Argyll Forest Park and around

The **Argyll Forest Park** stretches from Loch Lomond south as far as Holy Loch, providing the most exhilarating scenery on the peninsula. The park includes the **Arrochar Alps**, north of Glen Croe and Glen Kinglas, whose Munros offer some of the best climbing in Argyll: Ben Ime (3318ft) is the tallest of the range, and Ben Arthur or "The Cobbler" (2891ft) easily the most distinctive. All are for experienced walkers only. Less threatening are the peaks south of Glen Croe, between Loch Long and Loch Goil (branching off Loch Long), known as **Argyll's Bowling Green** – no ironic nickname but an English corruption of the Gaelic *Baile na Greine* (Sunny Hamlet). At the other end of the scale, there are several gentle forest walks clearly laid out by the Forestry Commission.

Arrochar and Ardgartan

Approaching from Glasgow by road (A83), you enter the park from **ARROCHAR**, at the head of Loch Long. The village itself is ordinary enough, but the setting is dramatic, and it makes a convenient base for exploring the northern section of the park. There's a **train station**, a mile or so up the A83 to Tarbet, and numerous **hotels** and **B&Bs** – try the very friendly *Lochside Guest House* (☎01301/702467; ③), on the main road, which rents out bikes, or the *Mansefield Hotel* (☎01301/702282; ③), a little to the south on the quieter A814 to Garelochhead. If you want a bite **to eat**, try the *Village Inn*, near the *Mansefield*; the local nightlife revolves around *Callum's Bar*, two doors down from *Lochside Guest House*.

Two miles beyond Arrochar at **ARDGARTAN**, there's a loch-side Forestry Commission **campsite** (☎01301/702293; mid-March to Oct), a **youth hostel** (☎01301/702362; Feb–Dec), and a **visitor centre** (April–June, Sept & Oct daily 10am–5pm; July & Aug 10am–6pm; ☎01301/702432), run jointly by the tourist board and the Forestry Commission. It's a great source of advice on weather conditions and wildlife, and organizes various nature activities, ranging from hill climbing to deer spotting, though advance booking is essential.

Glen Kinglas to Loch Eck

Approaching Cowal from the east, you're forced to climb **Glen Croe**, a strategic hill pass whose saddle is called – for obvious reasons – Rest-and-be-Thankful. Here the road forks, with the single-track B828 heading down to **LOCHGOILHEAD**. The setting is difficult to beat, but the village has been upstaged by the *Drimsynie Holiday Resort*, whose triangular chalets pockmark the landscape for a mile to the west. A road tracks the west side of the loch, petering out after five miles at the ruins of **Carrick Castle**, a classic tower house castle built around 1400 and used as a hunting lodge by James IV.

If you'd rather skip Lochgoilhead, continue along the A83 from the Rest-and-be-Thankful down the grand Highland sweep of **Glen Kinglas** to **CAIRNDOW**, at the head of Loch Fyne. Just behind the village, off the main road, you'll find the **Ardkinglas Woodland Garden** (daily dawn–dusk; £2) which contains exotic rhododendrons, azaleas and a superb collection of conifers some of which rise to over 200ft. A mile or so further on the A83 around the head of the loch at **Clachan** is the famous *Loch Fyne Oyster Bar* (☎01499/600264), which sells more oysters than anywhere else in the country, plus lots of other fish and seafood treats. You can easily assemble a gourmet picnic here, and the restaurant is excellent.

If you're delving further into Cowal from Cairndow, take the A815 which follows the loch southwest to Strachur before heading inland to **Loch Eck**, an exceptionally narrow freshwater loch, squeezed between steeply banked woods, and a favourite for trout fishing. Superior bar food or an **overnight stay** can be had at the *Coylet Inn* (☎01369/840426; ③), halfway down the loch's eastern shores. At the southern tip of Loch Eck are the beautifully laid-out **Younger Botanic Gardens** (mid-March to mid-Oct daily 10am–6pm; £2), an offshoot of Edinburgh's Royal Botanic Gardens, especially striking for their avenue of Great Redwoods, planted in 1863 and now over 100ft high. You could combine a visit here with one of the most popular of the local **forest walks**, a leisurely stroll up the rocky ravine of **Puck's Glen**; the walk begins from the car park a mile south of the gardens (1hr 30min round-trip).

Dunoon

In the nineteenth century, Cowal's capital, **DUNOON**, grew from a mere village to a major Clyde seaside resort and favourite holiday spot for Glaswegians. Nowadays, tourists tend to arrive by ferry from Gourock and, though their numbers are smaller, Dunoon remains by far the largest town in all Argyll, with 13,000 inhabitants. The whole area is still suffering, however, from the closure of the US nuclear submarine base on nearby Holy Loch in 1992, which has severely depressed the local economy.

Apart from its practical uses, and its fine pier, there's little to tempt you to linger in Dunoon. The centre of town is dominated by a grassy lump of rock known as **Castle Hill**, crowned by Castle House, built in the 1820s by a wealthy Glaswegian, and subject of a bitter dispute with the local populace over closure of the common land around his house. The people eventually won, and the grounds remain open to the public to this day, as does the house, which is now home to the local museum (June–Oct Mon–Sat 10am–4.30pm; £1). Another more violent scene in local history is commemorated by a memorial on a nearby rock: at least 36 men of the Lamont clan were executed by their rivals, the Campbells, who hanged them from "a lively, fresh-growing ash tree" in 1646. The tree couldn't take the strain, and had to be cut down two years later – tradition has it that blood gushed from the roots when it was felled.

With an hour or so to spare, you could visit the **Cowal Bird Garden** (April–Oct daily 10.30am–6pm; £3), one mile northwest along the A885 to Sandbank, which harbours parrots, macaws, pheasants, peacocks and other fowl, plus a small rare-breeds farm. If the weather's fine, take the **Ardnadam Heritage Trail**, a mile further up the road, to the wonderful Dunan viewpoint looking out to the Firth of Clyde; if the weather's bad, you could head for Dunoon Ceramics, on Hamilton Street, which produces various styles of high-quality porcelain and bone china, and offers tours around the factory (Mon–Thurs 10am–4pm, Fri 10am–3pm).

Practicalities

It's a good idea to take advantage of Dunoon's **tourist office** (the main one in Cowal) on Alexandra Parade (April Mon–Fri 9am–5pm, Sat 11am–5.30pm, Sun 11am–3pm; May Mon–Fri 9am–5.30pm, Sat & Sun 10am–5pm; June & Sept Mon–Fri until 6pm; July & Aug Mon–Sat until 7pm; Oct Mon–Fri 9am–5.30pm only; ☎01369/703785). The shorter, more frequent of the two **ferry crossings** across the Clyde from Gourock to Dunoon is the half-hourly Western Ferries service to Hunter's Quay, a mile north of the town centre; CalMac has the prime position, however, on the main pier, and has better transport connections if you're on foot.

If you need to **stay** the night, there's an enormous choice of B&Bs: *Cedars* (☎01369/702425; ④) is better than average and central, as is *Claymore* (☎01369/702658; ③). The town's landmark *Argyll Hotel,* opposite the pier (☎01369/702059; ⑥), is not as plush as you might expect – for real class, at a price, head for the highly reputable *Ardfillayne,* West Bay (☎01369/702267; ⑨). The nearest **campsites** are the *Cot House* at Kilmun (☎01369/840351; April–Oct), on the north side of Holy Loch, or the *Stratheck* site by the Botanical Gardens at Loch Eck (☎01369/840472; March–Dec).

Chatters, 58 John St (March–Dec closed Sun), is Dunoon's best **restaurant**, offering delicious Loch Fyne seafood and Scottish beef – for something a bit less pricey, the *Argyll* does decent, filling bar snacks. Dunoon boasts a two-screen cinema (a rarity in Argyll) on John Street, but the town's most famous entertainment by far is the **Cowal Highland Gathering**, the largest of its kind in the world, held here on the last weekend in August, and culminating in the awesome spectacle of the massed pipes and drums of more than 150 bands marching through the streets. For **bike rental**, head for the Highland Stores, on Argyll Street.

Southwest Cowal

The mellow landscape of **southwest Cowal**, in complete contrast to the bustle of Dunoon or the Highland grandeur of the forest, becomes immediate as soon as you head west to Loch Striven, where, from either side, there are few more beautiful sights than the **Kyles of Bute**, the thin slithers of water that separate the bleak bulk of north Bute from Cowal, and constitute some of the best sailing territory in Scotland.

COLINTRAIVE, on the eastern Kyle, marks the narrowest point in the Kyles – barely more than a couple of hundred yards – and is the place from which the small CalMac car ferry to Bute departs. However, the most popular spot from which to appreciate the Kyles is the A8003 as it rises dramatically above the sea lochs before descending to the peaceful, loch-side village of **TIGHNABRUAICH** on the western Kyle. The **youth hostel** (☎01700/811622; April–Sept), situated above the village, is well used thanks to the excellent Tighnabruaich Sailing School (☎01700/811396), which offers week-long courses from beginners to advanced. The *Royal Hotel* (☎01700/811239; ④), by the waterside, has some cheaper rooms without en-suite facilities and does special deals for those enrolled at the sailing school; it also serves exceptionally good bar meals. In neighbouring **KAMES**, the *Kames Hotel* (☎01700/811489; ⑥) has wonderful views over the Kyles, as does *Piermount* (☎01700/811218; ③).

The Kyles can get busy in July and August, but you can escape the crowds by heading for Cowal's deserted west coast, overlooking Loch Fyne. The one brief glimpse of habitation en route is the luxurious, whitewashed *Kilfinan Hotel* (☎01700/821201; ⑦), set back from a sandy bay seven miles along the B8000 from Tighnabruaich. The road rejoins the coast at **OTTER FERRY**, which has a small sandy beach and a wonderful pub and oyster restaurant, *The Oystercatcher*, with tables outside if the weather's good. There was once a ferry link to Lochgilphead from here, though the "otter" part is not derived from the furry beast but from the Gaelic *an oitir* (sandbank), which juts out a mile or so into Loch Fyne. If you're heading for Kintyre, Islay or Jura, you can avoid the long haul around Loch Fyne – some seventy miles or so – by using the **ferry service to Tarbert** from Portavadie, three miles southwest of Kames.

Isle of Bute

Thanks to its consistently mild climate and Rothesay's ferry link with Wemyss Bay (see p.213), the island of **Bute** has been a popular holiday and convalescence spot for Clydesiders – particularly the elderly – for over a century. Even considering the island's small size (15 miles by 5 miles at its widest point), you can easily escape the crowds by heading for the sparsely populated west coast, since most of Bute's inhabitants are centred around the two wide bays on the east coast of the island which resembles one long seaside promenade.

Rothesay

Bute's one and only town, **ROTHESAY**, is a handsome Victorian resort, set in a wide sweeping bay, backed by green hills, with a classic palm-tree promenade and 1920s pagoda-style Winter Gardens. It creates a much better general impression than Dunoon, with its period architecture and the occasional flourishes of wrought-iron-work. Even if you're just passing through, you must pay a visit to the ornate **Victorian toilets** (daily: Easter–Oct 8am–9pm; Nov–Easter 9am–5pm; 10p) on the pier, which were built by Twyfords in 1899 and have since been declared a national treasure. Men have the best time as the porcelain urinals steal the show, but women can ask for a guided tour, if the coast is clear, and learn about the haunted cubicle.

Rothesay also boasts the militarily useless, but architecturally impressive, moated ruins of **Rothesay Castle** (April–Sept Mon–Sat 9.30am–6.30pm, Sun 2–6.30pm; Oct–March closes 4.30pm; £1.50), hidden amid the town's backstreets but signposted from the pier. Built around the twelfth century, it was twice captured by the Vikings in the 1200s; such vulnerability was the reasoning behind the unusual, almost circular curtain wall, with its four big drum towers, of which only one remains fully intact.

Rothesay's **tourist office**, opposite the pier at 15 Victoria St (April & Oct Mon–Fri 9am–5.30pm, Sat 10am–5.30pm, Sun 11am–3pm; May Mon–Fri 9am–5.30pm, Sat & Sun 10am–5pm; June & Sept Mon–Fri until 6pm; July & Aug Mon–Sat until 7pm; Nov–March Mon–Thurs 9am–5.30pm, Fri 9am–5pm; ☎01700/502151) can help with accommodation, though there's no shortage of B&Bs along the seafront from Rothesay to Port Bannatyne. The grandest **place to stay** is the giant, former spa sanatorium *Glenburn Hotel*, on Glenburn Road (☎01700/502500; ⑥) up East Princes Street, towards Mount Stuart. Others, like the *Commodore* at 12 Battery Place (☎01700/502178; ③) or the architecturally distinctive *Glendale*, 20 East Princes St (☎01700/502329; ②), are more modest. For **bike rental**, try the Mountain Bike Centre, 24 East Princes St, or *Calder Bros*, 7 Bridge St, both of which are open daily.

The best **restaurant** options are *Oliver's*, on Victoria Street, which serves decent pasta and steak (and occasionally local seafood), while the waterfront bistro in the Winter Gardens offers a good value pre-cinema three-course meal for £10, and a tea dance on Thursday afternoons. For Rothesay's finest fish and chips head for the *West End Café* on Gallowgate. Architecture enthusiasts might appreciate the council-run

Pavilion Café (closed Sat & Sun), housed in an Art Deco former cinema further up Victoria Street. Bute holds its own **Highland Games** on the last weekend in August – Prince Charles as Duke of Rothesay occasionally attends – plus a newly established international **folk festival** on the third weekend in July, and a (mainly trad) **jazz festival** during May Bank Holiday.

Mount Stuart

One very good reason for coming to Bute is to visit **Mount Stuart** (Easter & May to mid-Oct Mon, Wed & Fri–Sun 11am–5pm; £5.50 house and gardens), a fantasy Gothic house set amidst acres of lush woodland gardens, overlooking the Firth of Clyde just three miles south of Rothesay. Home of the obscenely wealthy seventh Marquess of Bute, the building was created by the marvellously eccentric third Marquess after a fire in 1877 had destroyed the family seat. With little regard for expense, the marquess shipped in tons of Italian marble, building a railway line to transport it down the coast and employing craftsmen who had worked with the great William Burges on the marquess's earlier medieval concoctions at Cardiff Castle. The building was by no means finished when the third Marquess died in 1900 and work continues even today, though subsequent family members haven't had quite the inspirational taste of their predecessor.

A bus runs from Rothesay approximately every 45 minutes to the gates of the Mount Stuart, while the house itself is a pleasant fifteen-minute walk through the gardens from the ticket office; if it's raining it might be worth taking the shuttle service provided. Inside the building, the showpiece is the columned **Marble Hall**, its vaulted ceiling and stained-glass windows decorated with the signs of the zodiac, reflecting the marquess's taste for mysticism. The marquess was equally fond of animal and plant imagery, hence you'll find birds feeding on berries in the dining-room frieze and monkeys reading (and tearing up) books and scrolls in the library. Look out also for the unusual heraldic plaster ceiling in the drawing room. After the heavy furnishings of the ground-floor rooms, you can seek aesthetic relief in the **Marble Chapel**, built entirely out of dazzling white Carrara marble, with a magnificent Cosmati floor pattern. Upstairs is less interesting, with the notable exception of the **Horoscope Room**, where you can see a fine astrological ceiling and adjacent observatory.

Although the sumptuous interior of Mount Stuart is not to everyone's taste, it's worth coming here to picnic and explore the wonderfully mature **gardens** (same hours as house, but open at 10am; £3 gardens only), established in the eighteenth century by the third Earl of Bute, who had a hand in London's Kew Gardens. Before you leave Mount Stuart, take a look at the planned village of **Kerrycroy**, just beyond the main exit, built by the second Marquess in the early nineteenth century for the estate workers. Semi-detached houses – alternately mock-Tudor and whitewashed stone – form an crescent overlooking a pristine village green and, beyond, the sea.

The rest of Bute

The Highland–Lowland dividing line passes through the middle of Bute around freshwater Loch Fad, which itself all but slices Bute in two. Consequently, the northern half of the island is hilly, uninhabited and little-visited, while the southern half is made up of Lowland-style farmland. The two highest peaks on the island are **Windy Hill** (913ft) and **Torran Turach** (745ft), both in the north; from the latter there are fine views of the Kyles, but for a gentler overview of the island you can simply walk up **Canada Hill** above Loch Fad, a few miles southwest of Rothesay.

Bute's early monastic history is recalled at **St Blane's Chapel**, a twelfth-century ruin beautifully situated in open countryside on the west coast, close to the island's southernmost tip. The medieval church stands amidst the foundations of an earlier Christian settlement established in the sixth century by St Catan, uncle to the local-born St Blane. Bute's finest sandy beach is **Scalpsie Bay**, four miles up the west coast, beyond which lies **St Ninian's Point**, where the ruins of a sixth-century chapel over-look another fine sandy strand and the uninhabited island of **Inchmarnock**, to which, according to tradition, alcoholics were banished in the last century.

Inveraray and around

A classic example of an eighteenth-century planned town, **INVERARAY** was built on the site of a ruined fishing village in 1745 by the third Duke of Argyll, head of the powerful Campbell clan, in order to distance his newly rebuilt castle from the hoi polloi in the town and to establish a commercial and legal centre for the region. Today Inveraray, an absolute set-piece of Scottish Georgian architecture, has a truly memorable setting, the brilliant white arches of Front Street reflected in the still waters of Loch Fyne, which separate it from the Cowal peninsula.

The town

With a population of just four hundred squeezed onto a headland some distance from the duke's new castle, there's not much more to Inveraray's "New Town" than its distinctive **Main Street** (running west from Front Street), flanked by whitewashed terraces, whose window casements are picked out in black. At the top of the street, the road divides to circumnavigate the town's Neoclassical church, originally built in two parts: the southern half served the Gaelic-speaking community, while the northern half – still in use and worth a peek for its period wood-panelled interior – served those who spoke English.

East of the church is **Inveraray Jail** (daily: April–Oct 9.30am–6pm; Nov–March 10am–5pm; £4.20), whose attractive Georgian courthouse and grim prison blocks ceased to function in the 1930s. The jail is now an imaginative and thoroughly enjoyable museum, which graphically recounts conditions from medieval times up until the nineteenth century. You can also sit in the beautiful semicircular courthouse and listen to the trial of a farmer accused of fraud.

Moored at the town pier is the **Arctic Penguin** (daily: April–Oct 9.30am–6pm; Nov–March 10am–5pm; £2.50), a handsome, triple-masted schooner built in Dublin in 1911 – it's full of nautical knick-knacks and displays on the maritime history of the Clyde, but only really worth a wander round in wet weather. During the replanning of the town, the **Inveraray Cross** was moved to its present position by the loch (another cross from Tiree was placed in the castle gardens); both date from the fifteenth century and feature intricate figural scenes.

For a panoramic view of the town, castle and loch, you can climb the **Bell Tower** (May–Sept daily 10am–1pm & 2–5pm; £1.50) of All Saints' Church, accessible through the screen arches on Front Street. Built after World War I as a memorial to the fallen Campbells by the tenth Duke of Argyll, the tower contains a ringing peal of ten bells, which are apparently the second heaviest in the world – it takes four hours to ring a complete peal.

Inveraray Castle

A ten-minute walk north of the New Town, the neo-Gothic **Inveraray Castle** (April–June, Sept & Oct Mon–Thurs & Sat 10am–1pm & 2–5.45pm, Sun 1–5.45pm; July & Aug Mon–Sat 10am–5.45pm, Sun 1–5.45pm; £4) remains the family home of the Duke of Argyll. Built in 1745 by the third duke, it was given a touch of the Loire with the addition of dormer windows and conical roofs in the nineteenth century. Inside, the most startling feature is the armoury hall, whose displays of weaponry – supplied to the Campbells by the British government to put down the Jacobites – rise through several storeys (look out for Rob Roy's rather sad-looking sporran and dirk handle, the traditional dagger worn in Highland dress). Gracing the castle's extensive grounds is one of three elegant bridges built during the relandscaping of Inveraray (the other two are on the road from Cairndow), while the **Combined Operations Museum** (April–Oct Mon–Thurs & Sat 11am–6pm, Sun 1–6pm; £1.25) in the old stables, recalls the wartime role of Inveraray as a training centre for the D-Day landings, during which over half a million troops practised secret amphibious manoeuvres around Loch Fyne.

Argyll Wildlife Park, Auchindrain and Crarae

If you've got children in tow, the **Argyll Wildlife Park** (daily 10am–5pm; £3.50), two miles south of Inveraray, along the A83 to Campbeltown, provides some light relief, allowing children to come face to face with Scotland's indigenous fauna, from sika deer to wildcats. Three miles further on, the **Auchindrain Folk Museum** (April–Sept daily 10am–5pm; £3) is in fact an old township of around twenty thatched buildings packed full of domestic memorabilia to give an idea of life here before the Clearances, and before the planning of towns like neighbouring Inveraray. Demonstrations illustrate the old "run rig" strip-farming methods used in the eighteenth and nineteenth centuries, and the informative **visitor centre** has a good bookshop and a tearoom. Another four miles down the road is **Crarae Garden** (daily: March–Oct 9am–6pm; Nov–Feb dawn–dusk; £2.50), laid out earlier this century as a "Himalayan ravine" in a deep glen that tumbles down into Loch Fyne. It is this dramatic setting that sets Crarae apart from the innumerable other gardens of Argyll, and provides the scenic backdrop for the garden's rhododendrons, azaleas and wide variety of eucalyptus and conifers.

Practicalities

Inveraray's **tourist office** is on Front Street (April Mon–Fri 10am–5pm, Sat & Sun noon–4pm; May & June Mon–Sat 9.30am–5pm, Sun 11am–5pm; July–Sept Mon–Sat 9am–6.30pm, Sun 9am–5pm; Oct Mon–Sat 9.30am–6pm, Sun noon–4pm; Nov–March Mon–Fri 11am–4pm, Sat & Sun noon–4pm; ☎01499/302063), as is the town's chief **hotel**, the historic and very comfortable *Great Inn* (☎01499/302466; ⑥), where Dr Johnson and Boswell stayed. A slightly cheaper, but equally well-appointed alternative is the Georgian *Fernpoint Hotel* (☎01499/302170; ④) round by the pier; otherwise there's a convenient **B&B** called *Lorona* (☎01499/302258; ②; April–Oct), on Main Street, or for a more secluded position try *Breagha Lodge* (☎01499/302061; ③) by the golf course. The **youth hostel** (☎01499/302454; mid-March to Oct) is just up the Oban road (A819). The old Royal Navy base, two miles down the A83, is now the *Argyll Caravan Park* (☎01499/302285; April–Oct). The **bar** of the *George Hotel* in the middle of town is the liveliest spot, while for tea and cakes head for *The Poacher*. The best place to sample Loch Fyne's delicious fresh fish is the restaurant of the *Loch Fyne Oyster Bar* (see p.279), six miles back up the A83 towards Glasgow.

Loch Awe

Legend has it that **Loch Awe** – at more than 25 miles in length, the longest stretch of fresh water in the country – was created by a witch and inhabited by a monster even more gruesome than the one at Loch Ness. The southern shores of the loch are the most peaceful, with gentle hills and, on the western side, the magnificent **Inverliever Forest**, where the Forestry Commission has laid out a series of none-too-strenuous **forest walks** around Dalavich. The most spectacular is the hour-long walk from Inverinan up to the Royal Engineers' wooden footbridge which takes you over a pretty waterfall.

Dotted around the north of the loch, where it's joined by the A819 from Inveraray, the A85 from Tyndrum and the railway from Glasgow, are several tiny islands sporting picturesque ruins; on **Inishail** you can see a crumbling thirteenth-century chapel which once served as a burial ground for the MacArthur clan; the ruined castle on **Fraoch Eilean** dates from the same period. Fifteenth-century **Kilchurn Castle**, strategically situated on a rocky spit – once an island – at the head of the loch and once a Campbell stronghold, has been abandoned to the elements since being struck by lightning in the 1760s, and is now one of Argyll's most photogenic loch-side ruins.

During the summer you can sail around Kilchurn Castle as part of an hour-long steamboat cruise that sets off from the pier at **LOCHAWE**, right by the village's train station. A mile further along the A85, it's worth pausing at **St Conan's Church**, an unusual architectural work fashioned in a sort of home-made Norman/Gothic style conceived in the early part of this century by Walter Campbell and completed by his sister Helen. The church contains a fair amount of historical bric-a-brac from a piece of Robert the Bruce to fragments from Iona Abbey and Eton College, but by far the finest sections are the ambulatory, with its tall, clear windows overlooking Loch Awe, and the dinky lead-roofed cloisters, to the north.

Further west, gorged into the giant granite bulk of Ben Cruachan (3695ft), is the underground **Cruachan Power Station** (daily 9am–5pm; £3), built in 1965. Half-hour guided tours set off every hour from the newly refurbished **visitor centre** by the loch, taking you to a viewing platform above the generating room deep inside the "hollow mountain". Using the water from an artificial loch high up on Ben Cruachan to drive the turbines, the power station can become fully operational in less than two minutes, supplying electricity during surges on the National Grid. Sadly it takes ten percent more electricity to pump the water back up into the artificial loch, so the station only manages to make a profit by buying cheap off-peak power and selling during daytime peak demand. If you're keen to go, make sure you get there before the queues start to form, particularly in summer.

In order to maintain the right level of water in Loch Awe itself, a dam was built at the mouth of the loch, which then had to be fitted with a special lift to transport the salmon – for which the loch is justly famous – upriver to spawn. From the dam, the River Awe squeezes through the mountains via the gloomy rock-walled **Pass of Brander** (which means "ambush" in Gaelic), where Robert the Bruce put to flight the MacDougall clan, cutting them down as they fought with one another to cross the river and escape.

Shortly before you reach **TAYNUILT**, a sign to the right invites you to visit the Inverawe Fisheries and Smokery, where you can buy traditionally smoked local fish and mussels, learn how to fly-fish, check out the exhibition on traditional smoking techniques, or go for a stroll down to nearby Loch Etive with your picnic. A few miles further on there's another signpost to **Bonawe Iron Furnace** (April–Sept Mon–Sat 9.30am–6.30pm, Sun 2–6.30pm; HS; £2.30), founded by Cumbrian ironworkers in 1753 and now restored as an industrial heritage site. It was clearly cheaper, in those days, to import iron ore from south of the border, rather than transport charcoal to the Lake District, since several iron furnaces were established in the area, of which Bonawe was the most successful. A whole series of buildings in various states of repair are scattered across the factory site, which employed 600 people at its height, and eventually closed down in 1876. From the pier beyond the iron furnace, daily or twice-daily **boat cruises** (Easter to mid-Oct) explore the otherwise inaccessible reaches of Loch Etive; phone Loch Etive Cruises (☎01866/822430) for more details.

Practicalities

Those who can afford it might like to stay at the grandiose Scots Baronial *Loch Awe Hotel* (☎01838/200261; ⑨) on the north shore of the loch in Lochawe, but in many ways the nicest **places to stay** are on the more peaceful western shores. At Dalavich, the *Forest*

Holidays campsite (☎01855/811397; April–Oct), near the loch, has chalets for rent, while at Kilchrenan, further north, there's the comfortable *Thistle-Doo* B&B (☎01866/833339; ③). For luxurious loch-side accommodation, head for the *Taychreggan Hotel* (☎01866/833211; ⑧) at Kilchrenan or the *Ardanaiseig Hotel* (☎01866/833333; ⑨), four miles to the northeast down a dead-end track with its own glorious gardens. An even wider choice of B&Bs and guest houses is on offer at Dalmally and Taynuilt, though neither enjoy a loch-side location. There are boats for hire, and fishing tackle (Loch Awe is stocked full of trout and salmon), from Loch Awe Boats (☎01866/833256) who are based southwest of Cladich on the east shore, though they will deliver boats to any other point on the loch for a fee.

Lorn

Oban lies at the centre of the coastal region known as **Lorn**, named after the Irish Celt Loarn, who, along with his brothers Fergus and Oengus, settled here around 500 AD. Given the number of tourists that pass through or stay in the area, it's hardly surprising that a few out-and-out tourist attractions have developed, which can be handy to know about if it's raining and/or you have children with you. The Lorn mainland is very picturesque, although its beauty is no secret – to escape the crowds, head off and explore the islands, like Lismore or Kerrera, just offshore.

Oban

The solidly Victorian resort of **OBAN** enjoys a superb setting – the island of Kerrera providing its bay with a natural shelter – distinguished by a bizarre granite amphitheatre, dramatically lit at night, on the hilltop above the town. Despite a population of just 8500, it's by far the largest port in northwest Scotland, the second-largest town in Argyll, and the main departure point for ferries to the Hebrides. If you arrive late, or are catching an early boat, you may have to spend the night here (there's no real need otherwise); if you're staying elsewhere, it's a useful base for wet-weather activities and shopping, although it does get uncomfortably crowded in the summer.

Arrival and accommodation

The CalMac **ferry terminal** (☎01631/566688) for the islands is on Railway Pier, a stone's throw from the **train station** (☎01631/563083), itself adjacent to the **bus terminus**. The **tourist office** (April Mon–Fri 9am–5pm, Sat & Sun 10am–5pm; May & June daily 9am–5.30pm; July & Aug Mon–Sat 9am–9pm & Sun 9am–7pm; early Sept Mon–Sat 9am–7pm, Sun 9am–5pm; late Sept–Oct Mon–Sat 9am–5.30pm, Sun 9am–5pm; Nov–March Mon–Fri 9am–5pm, Sat & Sun noon–5pm; ☎01631/563122) is currently tucked away on Argyll Square just east of the bus station (though a move is planned in the near future).

Oban is positively heaving with **hotels** and **B&Bs**, most of them very reasonably priced and many of them on or near the quayside. Although it's easy enough to search out a vacancy, in high season it might be wise to pay the small fee charged by the tourist office for finding you a room. If you're catching the 6am ferry to Coll or Tiree, you might want to consider staying overnight in one of the two- or four-bed berths on board the ferry, a cheaper option than a local B&B and one which allows you a longer lie-in – you can book your berth from any CalMac office, as long as you do so before 6pm on the evening before departure.

HOTELS AND B&BS

Ardview, Ardconnel Road (☎01631/565112). Above-average B&B in a street replete with them just below McCaig's Folly. ③.

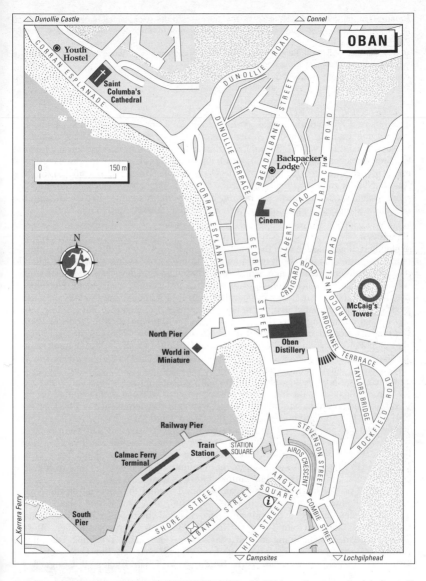

Briarbank, Glencruitten Road (☎01631/566549). B&B with glorious views over the bay from all three of its rooms. ④.

Caledonian, Station Square (☎01631/563133). Oban's large, comfortable landmark hotel right by the train station; all rooms are en suite. ⑥.

Glenbervie, Dalriach Road (☎01631/564770). Big Victorian guest house high above the town on a road heaving with accommodation; all rooms are en suite. ③.

Palace, George Street (☎01631/562294). If you can stand the strong smell of cats, and the floral decor, you can enjoy reasonably priced en-suite rooms, some of which come with great views across the harbour. ④.

Rahoy Lodge, Gallanach Road (☎01631/562301). Victorian guest house hidden away on the Gallanach Road, overlooking the Sound of Kerrera. ②.

Royal, Argyll Square (☎01631/563021). Pleasantly plush and recently refurbished hotel tucked behind the *Caledonian*; all rooms are en suite. ⑥.

HOSTELS AND CAMPSITES
The official *SYHA* **youth hostel** (☎01631/562025) is on the Corran Esplanade, just beyond the Catholic cathedral. More central is the relaxed *Backpackers' Lodge*, on Breadalbane Street (☎01631/562107), and the hostel run by the eccentric Jeremy Inglis at 21 Airds Crescent (☎01631/565065), which also offers cheap singles and doubles. There are two **campsites** to choose from: the *Oban Divers Caravan Park* (☎01631/562755; March–Nov), a mile and a half south of the ferry terminal on Glenshallach Road, or the more secluded *Oban Caravan & Camping Park* two miles southwest of Oban along the Gallanach Road beside the Sound of Kerrera (☎01631/566624; April to mid-Oct).

The Town

The only real sight in Oban is the town's landmark, **McCaig's Folly**, a stiff ten-minute climb from the quayside. Built in imitation of Rome's Colosseum, it was the brainchild of a local banker a century ago, who had the twin aims of alleviating off-season unemployment among the local stonemasons and creating a family mausoleum. Work never progressed further than the exterior walls before McCaig died, but the folly provides a wonderful seaward panorama, particularly at sunset. Equally beautiful evening views can be had by walking along the northern shore of the bay, past the modern, Roman Catholic **Cathedral of St Columba** – built by Sir Giles Gilbert Scott, architect of Battersea Power Station – to the rocky ruins of **Dunollie Castle**, a MacDougall stronghold on a very ancient site, successfully defended by the laird's Jacobite wife during the 1715 uprising but abandoned after 1745.

You can pass a few hours admiring the fishing boats in the harbour and looking out for scavenging seals in the bay; or, if the weather's bad, you can shelter in the McCaig's Centre by the new train station (the old Victorian one was demolished in 1988). You can also take a forty-minute guided tour of the **Oban Distillery** (Mon–Fri 9.30am–5pm; Easter–Oct also Sat; July–Sept until 8.30pm; £3), in the centre of town off George Street, which ends with a dram of whisky (and a refund of the admission fee if you buy a bottle). **The World in Miniature** (Easter–Oct Mon–Sat 10am–5pm, Sun 2–5pm; £1.60), on the North Pier, contains an assortment of minute "dolls' house" rooms, with even a couple of mini-Charles Rennie Mackintosh interiors to admire.

A host of private **boat operators** can be found around the harbour, on the North, South and Railway Pier: their excursions – to Mull, Iona, Staffa, Seal Island and the Treshnish Isles – are worth considering, particularly if you're pushed for time, or have no transport. Gordon Grant Tours (☎01631/700338), on Oban's South Pier, offers a whole range of trips, including an entire day's cruise around the Treshnish Isles. If you prefer, you can rent your own boat from Borroboats, on the Gallanach Road (☎01631/563292), or you can **rent bikes** from Oban Cycles, 9 Craigard Rd (☎01631/566996).

Eating, drinking and nightlife

Oban's best **restaurant** is *The Gathering* (☎01631/565421; evenings only) on Breadalbane Street, which excels in, among other things, moderately priced local fish and seafood; underneath is *O'Donnell's* Irish pub with live music at the weekend. The *Box Tree* on George Street offers an imaginative range of good-value meals, including a wide choice of veggie dishes and seafood, while the *Waterfront*, between the train station and the CalMac terminal, does cheaper bar food as well as à la carte meals. If you're looking for a quick bite to eat, try the excellent **take away** seafood counter by the side of the *Waterfront* restaurant, or any of the town's better-than-average **fish-and-chip** shops – in particular, *Onorio's*, at 86 George St.

Oban's only half-decent **pub** is the *Oban Inn* opposite the north pier, with a classic dark-wood-flagstone-and-brass bar downstairs and lounge bar with stained-glass upstairs. The town's nightlife doesn't bear thinking about (though you can read all about it in The Oban Times), however you might want to make use of the **cinema**, confusingly known as The Highland Theatre (☎01631/562444), at the north end of George Street.

Around Oban

A couple of miles east of Oban, along Glencruitten Road, the **Rare Breeds Farm Park** (daily: late March to Oct 10am–5.30pm; mid-June to Aug 10am–7.30pm; £4) displays rare but indigenous species of deer, cattle, sheep and so forth. Kids will love it, particularly the children's corner where they can meet the baby animals.

Dunstaffnage Castle (April–Sept daily 9.30am–6.30pm; HS; £1.50), three miles north of Oban, off the A85, is a thirteenth-century MacDougall fort, which was later handed over to the Campbells in 1470. Garrisoned by government forces during the 1745 rebellion, it served as a temporary prison for Flora MacDonald, but was destroyed by fire in 1810. The castle's substantial curtain wall battlements remain partially intact and are safe and fun to climb, giving great views across to Lismore and Morvern.

Isle of Kerrera

One of the best places to escape from the crowds that plague Oban is the low-lying island of **Kerrera**, which shelters Oban Bay from the worst of the westerly winds. The passenger and bicycle ferry departure point is about a mile and a half down the Gallanach road from Oban (daily 10.30am–12.30pm, 2–5pm & 6pm, Mon–Sat also 8.45am; 5–10min; £2.50 return). Measuring just five miles by two, the island is easily explored on foot, and gives panoramic views from its highest point – 600ft above the sea – over to Mull, the Slate Islands, Lismore, Jura and beyond. Kerrera has a total population of fewer than fifty – and no shop – so unless you're staying at *Ardantrive Farm* (☎01631/567180; ③), a mile or so up the coast from the jetty, you should bring your own food and drink.

The ferry lands by the lobster factory, roughly halfway down the east coast; it was on this spot that King Alexander II died in 1249. If the weather's fine and you feel like lazing by the sea, head for the island's finest sandy beach, **Slatrach Bay**, just one mile northwest of the ferry slip. Otherwise, the most rewarding trail is down to **Gylen Castle**, a clifftop ruin on the south coast, built in 1582 by the MacDougalls and burnt to the ground by the Covenanter General Leslie in 1647. You can head back to the ferry via the Drove Road, where cattle from Mull and other islands were once herded to be swum across the sound to the market in Oban. Those interested in pony trekking should ring ahead (☎01631/563668); mountain bikes are also available (☎01631/563665).

North of Oban

At **CONNEL**, five miles up the coast from Oban, you can't fail to admire the majestic steel cantilever bridge built in 1903 to take the old branch rail line across the sea cataract at the mouth of Loch Etive, north to Benderloch. The name "Connel" comes from the Gaelic *conghail* (tumultuous flood), which refers to the rapids, caused by the water at low ebb rushing over a ledge of rock between the two shores of the loch. The

A828 now crosses Connel Bridge to take you onto the hammerhead peninsula of **Benderloch** (from *beinn eadar dà loch*, "hill between two lochs").

Off the A828, on Benderloch's northern shores, you'll find **Barcaldine Castle** (May–Sept daily 11am–5.30pm; £2.95), an early seventeenth-century Campbell tower house. The house was abandoned by the Campbells in favour of Barcaldine House, three miles northeast, and eventually sold in 1842. Bought back by the family as a ruin in 1896 and restored, it is now occupied and run by the current heir, London-born and -bred Roderick, and his wife Caroline. There are no real treasures here, but the castle is fun to explore, with dungeons and hidden staircases, and has a pleasant, lived-in feel, with lots of family photos on display. To help balance the books, the Campbells also offer B&B at the castle (☎01631/720598; ④),but those with rather larger budgets might prefer to stay at Argyll's most exclusive hotel, the *Isle of Eriska*, a luxury turreted, Scottish Baronial pile situated on its own 300-acre island, off the northern point of Benderloch (☎01631/720371; ⑨; closed Feb).

Since the weather in this part of Scotland can be bad at almost any time of the year, it's as well to know about the **Sea Life Centre** (April–June daily 9am–6pm; July & Aug daily 9am–7pm; Sept, Nov, Feb & March daily 10am–5pm; Dec & Jan Sat & Sun 10am–5pm; £4.95), further east along the southern shores of Loch Creran on the A828 near Barcaldine House. Here you can see locally caught sea creatures at close quarters – look out for the octopus and stingray – before they are returned to the sea at the end of the season. The centre's self-service *Shoreline* restaurant features a small oyster bar.

Appin

Having circumnavigated the loch, you enter the district of **Appin**, setting for Robert Louis Stevenson's *Kidnapped*, a fictionalized account of the "Appin Murder" of 1752, when Colin Campbell was shot in the back, allegedly by one of the disenfranchised Stewart clan. The name "Appin" derives from the Gaelic *abthaine*, meaning "Lands belonging to the Abbey", in this case the one on Lismore (see opposite), which is linked to the peninsula by passenger ferry from **PORT APPIN**, a pretty little fishing village at the westernmost tip. The *Pierhouse Hotel* (☎01631/730302; ⑦), nicely situated right by the ferry, has en-suite rooms over looking the Lismore and Morvern, and a fairly pricey but excellent seafood restaurant. Alternatively, nearby there's a more modest guest house, *Fasgadh* (☎01631/730374; ③), with equally good views.

One of Argyll's most romantic ruined castles, the much-photographed **Castle Stalker**, occupies a tiny rock island to the north of Port Appin. Built by the Stewarts of Appin in the sixteenth century and gifted to King James IV as a hunting lodge, it inevitably fell into the hands of the Campbells after 1745. The current owners open the castle to the public for a short period only in July and August; ring ☎01631/730234 or ask at Oban tourist office for opening times. If you're looking for something to do in Appin, head for the Linnhe Marine Water Sports Centre (☎01631/730227), in Lettershuna (just beyond Port Appin), which rents out boats of all shapes and sizes, offers sailing and windsurfing lessons, not to mention water-skiing, shooting and even pony trekking.

Isle of Lismore

Legend has it that saints Columba and Moluag both fancied the skinny island of **Lismore** as a missionary base, but as they raced towards it Moluag cut off his finger and threw it ashore ahead of Columba, claiming the land for himself. Of Moluag's sixth-century foundation nothing remains, but from 1236 until 1507 the island served as the seat of the Bishop of Argyll. It was a judicious choice, as Lismore is undoubtedly one of the most fertile of the Inner Hebrides – its name, coined by Moluag himself, derives from the Gaelic *lios mór*, meaning "great garden" – and at one time it supported nearly 1400 inhabitants. The population today is around a tenth of that figure. Lying in Loch Linnhe to the north of Oban, and barely rising above a hillock, this narrow island offers wonderful gentle walking or cycling opportunities, with unrivalled views, in fine weather, across to the mountains of Morvern, Lochaber and Mull.

The ferry from Oban lands at **ACHNACROISH**, roughly halfway along the eastern coastline. To get to grips with the history of the island and its Gaelic culture (and have a cup of tea), head inland until you catch the signs for the **Comann Eachdraidh Lios Mòr**, or Lismore Historical Society (Mon–Sat 10am–5pm; £1). The island post office and shop are along the main road between Achnacroish and **CLACHAN**, a mile and a half northeast, where the diminutive, whitewashed former **Cathedral of St Moluag** stands. All that remains of the fourteenth-century cathedral is the choir, which was reduced in height and converted into the parish church in 1749; inside you can see a few of the original seats for the upper clergy, a stone basin in the south wall, and several medieval doorways. Due east of the church – head north up the road and take the turning signposted on the right – **Tirefour**, a circular stone broch over 2000 years old, occupies a commanding position and boasts walls almost 10ft thick in places. West of Clachan are the much more recent ruins of **Castle Coeffin**, a twelfth-century MacDougall fortress once believed to have been haunted by the ghost of Beothail, sister of the Norse prince Caiffen. Two other places worth exploring are **Sailean**, an abandoned quarry village on the west coast, with its disused kilns and cottages, and the ruins of **Achanduin Castle**, in the southwest, where the bishops are thought to have resided.

Two **ferries** serve Lismore: a small CalMac car ferry from Oban to Achnacroish (Mon–Sat 2–4 daily; 50min), and a shorter passenger-only crossing from Port Appin to the island's north point (daily every 2hr; 10min). There's a **postbus** round the island (Mon–Sat; pick up a timetable from Oban tourist office). **Accommodation** on the island is limited to a handful of B&Bs – try the excellent *Brynalen* (☎01631/760298; ③; Easter–Nov), or the *Schoolhouse* (☎01631/760262; ②), beyond Clachan.

South of Oban

Heading south along the A816 from Oban, you pass the **Salmon Centre** (Easter–Sept 10am–5.30pm; £3) after seven miles. There's an interesting exhibition on the life cycle of the salmon, and you can view the cages out in the loch where the fish are denied that life. The real reason for coming here, though, is to sample the wonderful seafood in the centre's excellent, reasonably priced restaurant.

If you're continuing south towards Lochgilphead, you couldn't want for a better place to stop and have a bite to eat than the *Loch Melfort Hotel* (☎01852/500284; ⑦), where you can enjoy great bar snacks from the hotel lawn overlooking Asknish Bay and the islands of Shuna, Luing, Scarba and Jura. Beside the hotel are the **Arduaine Gardens** (daily 9.30am–dusk; NTS; £2.30), which enjoy the same idyllic loch-side location. Gifted as recently as 1992, the gardens are stupendous, particularly in May and June, and have the feel of a intimate private garden, with pristine lawns, lily-strewn ponds, mature woods and spectacular rhododendrons and azaleas. The gardens' former owners, the Wright brothers, still live next door and have an equally lovely adjacent garden.

If the *Loch Melfort* is out of your price range, there are plenty of other options in the vicinity, like *Willow Cottage* (☎01852/200202; ③), or the lovely loch-side campsite (☎01852/200331; March–Oct), below the hotel. You can also stay in the slightly surreal surroundings of **Croabh Haven**, a planned marina village on the south side of Asknish Bay, either in the log-cabin-style *Buidhe Lodge* (☎01852/500291; ④), or in the old Baronial pile of *Lunga* (☎01852/500237; ③).

The Slate Islands and the Garvellachs

Eight miles south of Oban on the A816, a road heads off west to a small group of islands commonly called the **Slate Islands**, which at their peak in the mid-nineteenth century quarried over nine million slates annually. Today many of the old slate villages are sparsely populated, and an inevitable air of melancholy hangs over them, but their dramatic setting amid crashing waves make for a rewarding day-trip.

Isle of Seil

The most northerly of the Slate Islands is the **Seil**, separated from the mainland by the thinnest of sea channels and spanned by Thomas Telford's elegant hump-backed **Clachan Bridge**, built in 1793 and popularly known as the "Bridge over the Atlantic". The pub next door to the bridge is the *Tigh na Truish* (House of the Trousers), where kilt-wearing islanders would change into trousers to conform to the post-1745 ban on Highland dress.

The main village on Seil is **ELLANABEICH**, its neat white terrraces of workers' cottages crouching below the black cliffs of Dùn Mór on the westernmost tip of the island. This was once the tiny island of Eilean a'Beithich – hence Ellanabeich – separated from the mainland by a slim sea channel until the intensive slate quarrying succeeded in silting it up. Confusingly, the village is often referred to by the same name as the nearby island of Easdale, since they formed an interdependent community based exclusively around the slate industry.

Isle of Easdale

Easdale remains an island, though the few hundred yards that separate it from Ellanabeich have constantly to be dredged to keep the channel open. On the eve of a great storm on November 23, 1881, Easdale, less than a mile across at any one point, supported 452 inhabitants. That night, waves engulfed the island and flooded the quarries. The island never really recovered, slate quarrying stopped in 1914, and by the 1960s the population was reduced to single figures.

Recently many of the old cottages have been restored: some as holiday homes, others sold to new families (the present population stands at over thirty). One of the cottages now houses an interesting **museum** (April–Oct Mon–Sat 10.30am–5.30pm, Sun 10.30am–4.30pm; £1), near the main square, selling a useful historical map of the island, which you can walk round in about half an hour. The **ferry** from Ellanabeich runs partly to schedule, partly on demand (April–Sept Mon–Sat 7.50am–8.50pm, Sun 9.55am–5.50pm; Oct–March check at the Oban tourist office), and there's a nice **tearoom** near the quayside, plus a cosy, little whitewashed **B&B** at no. 22 (☎01852/300438; ③).

Isle of Luing

To the south of Seil, across the narrow, treacherous Cuan Sound lies **Luing** (pronounced "Ling"), a long, thin, fertile island which once supported more than 600 people. During the Clearances the population was drastically reduced to make way for cattle; Luing is still renowned for its beef and has cultivated a successful new crossbreed named after it. A car **ferry** (Mon–Sat 8am–4pm; June–Aug 8am–6pm; every 30min) crosses the Cuan Sound, while foot passengers enjoy a more frequent service (Mon–Thurs 7.30am–6pm, Fri & Sat 7.30am–11.30pm, Sun 11am–1pm & 3–6pm; every 30min).

CULLIPOOL, the pretty main village with its post office, general store and tearoom, lies a mile or so southwest; quarrying ceased here in 1965, and the place now relies on tourism and lobster fishing. Luing's only other village, **TOBERONOCHY**, lies on the more sheltered east coast, three miles southeast of Cullipool. Its distinctive white cottages, built by the slate company in 1805, nestle below a ruined church, which contains a memorial to the fifteen Latvian seamen who drowned off the nearby abandoned slate island of Belnahua during a hurricane in 1936. Other than self-catering cottages, the only **accommodation** available on the island is at *Bardrishaig Farm* (☎01852/314397; ③), on the road to Cullipool. For **bike rental**, ring ☎01852/314256 in the evening.

Isle of Scarba and the Garvellachs

Scarba is the largest of the islands around Luing, a brooding 1500ft hulk of slate, inhospitable and wild – most of the fifty or so inhabitants who once lived here had left by the mid-nineteenth century. To the south, the raging **Gulf of Corrievrechan** is the site of one of the world's most spectacular whirlpools, thought to be caused by a rocky pinnacle below the sea. It remains calm only for an hour or two at high and low tide; at flood tide, accompanied by a westerly wind, water shoots deafeningly some 20ft up in the air. Inevitably there are numerous legends about the place –known as *coire bhreacain* (speckled cauldron) in Gaelic – concerning *Cailleach* (Hag), the Celtic storm goddess.

If you're interested in taking a closer look at Corrievrechan or the string of uninhabited islands west of Luing, known collectively as the **Garvellachs**, contact Kingfisher Cruises (☎01852/500662), who operate out of Ardfern on the mainland, just south of Croabh Haven (see p.291), or Geminia Cruises (☎01546/830238), who operate from Crinan (see p.309). The Garvellachs take their name from the largest of the group, **Garbh Eileach** (Rough Rock), which was inhabited as recently as fifty years ago. The most northerly, **Dùn Chonnuill**, contains the remains of an old fort thought to have belonged to Conal of Dalriada, and **Eileach an Naoimh** (Holy Isle), the most southerly of the group, is where the Celtic missionary Brendan the Navigator founded a community in 542, some twenty years before Columba landed on Iona (see p.300). Nothing survives from Brendan's day, but there are a few ninth-century remains, among them a double-beehive cell and a grave enclosure. One school of thought has it that the island is Hinba, Columba's legendary secret retreat, where he buried his mother.

Isle of Mull

The second largest of the Inner Hebrides, **MULL** is by far the most accessible: just forty minutes from Oban by ferry. First impressions largely depend on the weather – it is the wettest of the Hebrides (and that's saying something) – for without the sun the large tracts of moorland, particularly around the island's highest peak, Ben More (3196ft), can appear bleak and unwelcoming. There are, however, areas of more gentle pastoral scenery around **Dervaig** in the north and **Salen** on the east coast, and the indented west coast varies from the sandy beaches around **Calgary** to the cliffs of Loch na Keal. The most common mistake is to try and "do" the island in a day or two: Mull is a place that will grow on you only if you have the time and patience to explore.

Historically, crofting, whisky distilling and fishing supported the islanders (*Muileachs*), but the population – which peaked at 10,000 – decreased dramatically in the nineteenth century due to the Clearances and the 1846 potato famine. On Mull, it is a trend that has been reversed, mostly due to the large influx of settlers from elsewhere in the country which has brought the current population up to over 2500. One of the main reasons for this resurgence is, of course, tourism – more than half a million visitors come here each year – although oddly enough, there are very few large hotels or campsites.

Craignure is the main entry point to Mull, with a frequent daily **car ferry** link to Oban; a much smaller car ferry crosses daily from Lochaline on the Morvern peninsula (see p.453) to the slipway at Fishnish, six miles northwest of Craignure; another even smaller car ferry connects Kilchoan on the Ardnamurchan peninsula (see p.454) with Tobermory, 24 miles northwest of Craignure. In addition, the Coll and Tiree ferry from Oban occasionally calls in at **Tobermory** to let foot passengers on and off – a good way to reach Mull for those without their own transport. **Public transport** on Mull is limited, and the roads are predominantly single-track, which can cause serious congestion on the main A849 in summer.

Craignure and around

CRAIGNURE is little more than a scattering of cottages, though there is a **tourist office**, right by the pier (April to mid-May Mon 6.45am–5.30pm, Tues–Fri 7.45am–7.15pm, Sat 6am–7.15pm, Sun 10am–5.15pm; mid-May to June Mon & Sun also until 7.15pm; July & Aug daily 9am–7pm; Sept daily 9.30am–6.30pm; Oct daily 10am–5pm; Nov–March Mon–Fri 10am–4pm; ☎01680/812377). The *Craignure Inn* (☎01680/812305; ③), just a minute's stroll up the road to Fionnphort, is a snug pub to hole up in. There are several other guest houses, too, and the well-equipped *Sheiling* **campsite** (☎01680/812496; May–Sept) by the sea, off the road to Fionnphort, which also offers hostel accommodation in "carpeted cottage tents". **Bus** connections with Fionnphort (2–3 daily) and Tobermory (2–4 daily) are infrequent, so check with Oban tourist office before you catch the ferry; **bike rental** (☎01680/812487) is available locally.

Two castles lie immediately southeast of Craignure. The first, a mile and a half away, **Torosay Castle** (mid-April to mid-Oct daily 10.30am–5pm; £4.50) is a full-blown Scottish Baronial creation. The fact that it is linked to Craignure by the narrow-gauge Mull & West Highland Railway (mid-April to mid-Oct; phone ☎01680/812494 for full details) ensures a steady flow of visitors. The house itself is stuffed with memorabilia relating to the present owners, the Guthries, all of it amusingly captioned but of no great import, with the possible exception of the belongings of the late David Guthrie-James, who was something of an adventurer and a POW in Colditz. Torosay's real highlight, however, are the magnificent **gardens** (daily 9am–7pm) with their avenue of eighteenth-century Venetian statues, Japanese section, and views over to neighbouring Duart. Also in the castle grounds is the workshop of the Isle of Mull Weavers (daily

9am–5pm; free), run by a couple who give demonstrations of traditional weaving using old dobby looms.

Lacking the gardens, but on a picturesque spit of rock a couple of miles east of Torosay, **Duart Castle** (May to mid-Oct daily 10.30am–6pm; £3.30) is clearly visible from the Oban–Craignure ferry. Headquarters of the once-powerful MacLean clan from the thirteenth century, it was burnt down by the Campbells and confiscated after the 1745 rebellion. Finally in 1911, the 26th clan chief, Fitzroy MacLean (1835–1936) – not to be confused with the Scottish writer of the same name – managed to buy it back and restore it. You can peek at the dungeons, climb up to the ramparts, study the family photos, and learn about the world scout movement – the 27th clan chief became Chief Scout in 1959. After your visit, you can enjoy home-made cakes and tea at the castle's excellent tearoom.

Both Torosay and Duart are inundated with visitors in the high season – not so **LOCHBUIE**, a peaceful, sandy bay ten miles or so southwest of Craignure. The shore is dominated by the fifteenth-century ivy-strewn ruins of **Moy Castle**, an old MacLean stronghold, and north of the castle is one of the few **stone circles** in the west of Scotland; with eight stones all about 6ft high and dating from the second century BC. A popular and fairly easy walk is the five-mile hike west along the coastal path to **CARSAIG**, where the Inniemore School of Painting enjoys an idyllic setting, at the end of a dead-end road, three miles south of Pennyghael.

Tobermory

Mull's chief town, **TOBERMORY**, is easily the most attractive fishing port on the west coast of Scotland, its clusters of brightly coloured houses and boats sheltering in a bay backed by a steep bluff. Founded in 1788 by the British Society for Encouraging Fisheries, it never really took off as a fishing port and only survived due to the steady influx of crofters evicted from other parts of the island during the Clearances. With a population of more than 700, it is, without doubt, the capital of Mull, and if you're staying any length of time on the island you're bound to end up here.

The harbour – known as **Main Street** – is one long parade of multicoloured hotels, guest houses, restaurants and shops, and you could happily spend an hour or so exploring: Mull Pottery and the Mull Silver Company are both worth a browse, as is The Gallery, a converted church more of interest for its architecture than the tartan and shortbread on sale. One of Tobermory's endearing features is the incessant chiming of its diminutive **Clock Tower**, erected by the author Isabella Bird in 1905 in memory of her sister who died of typhoid on the island in 1880. Close by is a polychrome watery cherub, donated by the local water-supply contractors in 1883.

THE TOBERMORY TREASURES

The most dramatic event in Tobermory's history was in 1588 when a ship from the Spanish Armada sank in mysterious circumstances while having repairs done to its sails and rigging. The story goes that one of the MacLeans of Duart was taken prisoner, but when the ship weighed anchor, he made his way to the powder magazine and blew it up. However, several versions of the story exist, and even the identity of the ship has been hotly disputed: for many years it was thought to be the treasure-laden Spanish galleon *Almirante di Florencia*, but it now seems more likely that it was the rather more prosaic troop carrier *San Juan de Sicilia*. Nevertheless, the possibility of precious sunken booty at the bottom of Tobermory harbour has fired the greed of numerous lairds and kings – in the 1950s Royal Navy divers were engaged by the Duke of Argyll in the seemingly futile activity of diving for treasure, and in 1982 another unsuccessful attempt was made.

A stiff climb up Back Brae will bring you to the island's new arts centre, **An Tobar** (Mon, Wed, Thurs & Sat 10am–6pm, Tues & Fri 10am–10pm, Sun 1–6pm; £1), housed in a converted Victorian schoolhouse. The centre hosts exhibitions, a variety of live events, and contains a small Internet café. The rest of the upper town is laid out on a classic grid-plan, and merits a stroll, if only for the great views over the bay. You could also pay a visit to the small **Mull Museum** (Mon–Fri 10.30am–4.30pm, Sat 10.30am–1.30pm; £1), on Main Street, a good wet weather retreat. Alternatively, there's the minuscule **Tobermory Distillery** (Easter–Sept Mon–Fri 10am–4pm; £2) at the south end of the bay, founded in 1795 but closed down three times since then. Today, it's back in business and offers a guided tour rounded off with a tasting.

Practicalities

The **tourist office** (April Mon–Fri 9am–5pm, Sat & Sun 10am–5pm; May & June Mon–Fri 9am–5.30pm, Sat & Sun 10am–5pm; July–Sept Mon–Sat 9am–6pm, Sun 10am–5pm; Oct Mon–Sat 9am–5pm, Sun 10am–4pm; ☎01688/302182) is in the same building as the CalMac ticket office at the far end of Main Street; while you're there, be sure to pick up Mull's free monthly listings broadsheet *Round & About*. If you want to rent a **bike**, head for the youth hostel (see below), or Tom-a'Mhuillin (☎01688/302164) on the Salen road. The island's only permanent bank, the Clydesdale is on Main Street (a mobile one tours the island; ask at the tourist office for details).

The tourist office can book you into a **B&B** for a small fee – not a bad idea since many of them are a stiff climb from the harbour. There are several places on Main Street – try the excellent *Fàilte* (☎01688/302495; ④), the *Harbour Guest House* (☎01688/302209; ③), or the lively *Mishnish Hotel* (☎01688/302009; ⑦). The island's friendly **youth hostel** is also on Main Street (☎01688/302481; mid-March to Oct). There are also several cheaper B&Bs such as *Ivybank* (☎01688/302250; ②), on Argyll Terrace overlooking the bay. The nearest **campsite** is *Newdale* (☎01688/302306; April–Nov), by a stream, one and a half miles outside Tobermory on the B8073 to Dervaig.

Main Street is heaving with **places to eat**, though there seems to be little between a five-course blowout at the *Tobermory Hotel* and the cheap, but unspectacular fare offered at the likes of *Gannets*. The *Lochinvar*, on Post Office Brae (closed Sun lunch), serves imaginative local seafood and meat dishes (it even does breakfasts from 9am on weekdays), though you might prefer to stuff yourself with the reasonably priced, huge portions of pub grub served in the bar at the *Mishnish*. There's an excellent bakery on Main Street, with topnotch picnic food available at the Tobermory Fish Farm shop, also on Main Street, and supplemented, perhaps, by goodies from the Chocolate Factory, up Back Brae. The lively bar of the *Mishnish Hotel*, is the local hangout, often featuring live music at the weekend, and the focus of Mull's annual **Traditional Music Festival**, a feast of Gaelic folk music held on the last weekend in April. Mull's other major musical event is the annual **Mendelssohn on Mull Festival**, held over ten days in early July, which commemorates the composer's visit here in 1829.

The west coast and the islets

The **west coast** provides some of the most beguiling scenery on the island. The B8073 to Dervaig is exceptionally dramatic, with fiendish switchbacks much appreciated during the annual Mull Rally, which takes place each October. Beyond **Dervaig**, the road is equally tortuous, following the heavily indented coastline.

Dervaig and Calgary

The only village of any size on the west coast is **DERVAIG**, nestling beside narrow Loch Chumhainn just eight miles southwest of Tobermory, and distinguished by its unusual pencil-shaped church spire and dinky whitewashed cottages set in twos along its main street. Dervaig is best known as the home of Mull Little Theatre, one of the smallest professional theatres in the world, which puts on an adventurous season of plays adapted for a handful of resident actors (May–Sept; booking recommended ☎01688/400245). The theatre lies within the grounds of the *Druimard Country House* (☎01688/400345; ⑦), which offers pricey but excellent pre-theatre dinners. A cheaper spot of refreshment is available from *Coffee and Books*, which offers just that (and a few provisions) from its premises opposite the *Bellacroy Hotel*, whose bar is a great place to shelter for the day in bad weather.

Dervaig has a wide choice of **places to stay**, aside from the aforementioned *Druimard*. Charles Dickens once stayed at the *Ardbeg House* (☎01688/400254; ④), still one of Dervaig's finest; other B&B options include the traditional *Antuim Farm* (☎01688/400230; ③; April–Oct) on the Salen road, the vegetarian-friendly *Glenbellart* (☎01688/400282; ③) on the main street, or *Adrioch Farm* (☎01688/400264; ③) on the Calgary road (the latter also run boat trips out to the islands off Mull). Head out on the rough road to Sea Life Surveys (daily 10am–1pm & 2–4pm; ☎01688/400223), which has an exhibition on whales and organizes boat trips to the Treshnish Isles, plus whale-watching and seal excursions, and you'll pass the excellent *Cuin House* (☎01688/400346; ③), overlooking the loch.

A little beyond Dervaig, the **Old Byre Heritage Centre** (Easter–Oct daily 10.30am–6.30pm; £2) is better than many of its kind, with a video on the island's history and a passable tearoom. The road continues cross-country to **CALGARY**, once a thriving crofting community, now an idyllic holiday spot boasting Mull's finest sandy bay, with wonderful views over to Coll and Tiree. There's just one **hotel**, the lovely *Calgary Farmhouse* (☎01688/400256; ⑥), whose excellent restaurant, *The Dovecote*, is (unsurprisingly) a converted dovecote. There's also an unofficial **campsite** by the beach and a splendid wild hillside **garden** at the House of Treshnish (April–Oct) overlooking the bay. For the record: the city of Calgary in Canada does indeed take its name from this little village, though it was not so named by Mull emigrants, but by one Colonel McLeod of the North West Mounted Police, who once holidayed here.

Salen and around

SALEN, though on the east coast halfway between Craignure and Tobermory, lies only three miles from the west coast at the narrowest point on the island. As such it makes a good central base for exploring the island, though it has none of Tobermory's charm. It does, however, have several **B&Bs** – try the solid Victorian *Glenmore* (☎01680/300442; ③; April–Oct) on Pier Road – plus hostel accommodation at *Arle Farm Lodge* (☎01680/300343; ②) in nearby Aros, north up the A848. Those with more substantial means should head three miles out of town to the west coast, where the award-winning *Killiechronan Hotel* (☎01680/300403; ⑦) awaits on the shores of Loch na Keal. On the main street, the *Coffee Pot* serves snacks, the *Puffer Aground* more substantial but inexpensive meals, and On Yer Bike **rents bikes**.

Four miles southwest, back on the west coast, you must pass through the pretty *Gruline Home Farm* (☎01680/300380; ③) in order to reach the **Macquarie Mausoleum**, a simple butressed tomb, set within a walled clearing surrounded by pine trees and rhododendrons, and lovingly maintained by the National Trust of Scotland, on behalf of the National Trust of Australia. Within lies the body of Lachlan Macquarie (1761–1824), the "Father of Australia", who, as the effusive epitaph explains, served as the enlightened governor of New South Wales for twelve years from 1809, when he was appointed by the British to replace the unpopular William Bligh, formerly of the *Bounty*.

Isle of Ulva

> A chieftain to the Highlands bound
> Cries "Boatman, do not tarry!
> And I'll give thee a silver pound
> To row us o'er the ferry!"

> "Now who be ye, would cross Lochgyle
> This dark and stormy water?
> "O I'm the chief of Ulva's isle,
> An this, Lord Ullin's daughter.

"Lord Ullin's Daughter", Thomas Campbell (1777–1844)

Around the time poet laureate Campbell penned this poem, **Ulva**'s population was a staggering 850, sustained by the huge quantities of kelp which were exported for glass and soap production. That was before the market for kelp collapsed and the 1846 potato famine hit, after which the remaining population was brutally evicted. Nowadays barely twenty people live here, and the island is littered with ruined crofts, not to mention a church which would once have seated three hundred parishioners. It's great walking country, with several clearly marked paths criss-crossing the island – and you're almost guaranteed to spot some of the abundant wildlife: at the very least deer, if not golden eagles and buzzards, with seals and divers offshore. Those who like to have a focus for their wanderings should head for the basalt columns, similar to those on Staffa, on the island's southwest coast.

To get to **Ulva** (from the Norse *ulv øy* or "wolf island") which, along with its tidal neighbour Gometra, lies just 100yd or so off the west coast of Mull, a small bicycle/passenger-only ferry (signposted "Ulva Ferry" from Salen) is available on demand (mid-April to mid-Sept Mon–Fri 8am–5pm; June–Aug also Sun; at other times by arrangement; £2.50 return).*The Boathouse*, near the ferry slip on Ulva, serves as a licensed tearoom selling cakes, snacks and Ulva oysters; you can learn more about the history of the island from the interpretive display upstairs. There's no accommodation, but with permission from the present owners (☎01688/500226) you can **camp** rough overnight.

Isle of Staffa and the Treshnish Isles

Five miles southwest of Ulva, **Staffa** is the most romantic and dramatic of Scotland's many uninhabited islands. On its south side, the perpendicular rockface features an imposing series of black basalt columns, known as the Colonnade, which have been cut by the sea into cathedralesque caverns, most notably **Fingal's Cave**. The Vikings knew about the island – the name derives from their word for "Island of Pillars" – but it wasn't until 1772 that it was "discovered" by the world. Turner painted it, Wordsworth explored it, but Mendelssohn's *Die Fingalshöhle*, inspired by the sounds of the sea-wracked caves he heard on a visit here in 1829, did most to popularize the place – after which Queen Victoria gave her blessing, too. The geological explanation for these polygonal basalt organ pipes is that they were created by a massive subterranean explosion some sixty million years ago. A huge mass of molten basalt ejaculated onto land and, as it cooled, solidified into what are, essentially, crystals. Of course, confronted with such artistry, most visitors have found it difficult to believe that their origin is entirely natural – indeed, the various Celtic folk tales, which link the phenomenon with the Giant's Causeway in Ireland, are certainly more appealing.

To **get to Staffa**, join one of the many boat trips from Oban, Dervaig, Ulva Ferry or Fionnphort, weather permitting (return trips for around £10–20 per person); Turus Mara (☎01688/400242), operating out of Ulva Ferry, is the nearest and cheapest, but Inter-Island Cruises (☎01688/400264), operating out of Dervaig, is worth the extra money. Several boat trips, including Turus Mara, combine a visit to Staffa with a tour of the archipelago of uninhabited volcanic islets that make up the **Treshnish Isles** northwest of Staffa. The most distinctive is **Bac Mór**, shaped like a Puritan's hat and popularly dubbed the Dutchman's Cap, while **Lunga**, the largest island, is a nesting place for hundreds of seabirds, in particular auks (mid-May to July) and puffins (late April to mid-Aug), as well as a breeding ground for common seals (June) and Atlantic greys (early Sept). The two most northerly islands, **Cairn na Burgh More** and **Cairn na Burgh Beg**, have the remains of ruined castles, the first of which served as a look-out post for the Lords of the Isles and was last garrisoned in the Civil War; Cairn na Burgh Beg hasn't been occupied since the 1715 Jacobite uprising.

Ben More and the Ardmanach peninsula

Round the coast from Ulva Ferry, the road (A8073) hugs the shores of Loch na Keal, which almost splits Mull in two. South of the loch rise the terraced slopes of **Ben More** (3169ft), a mighty extinct volcano, most easily climbed from Dishaig, halfway along the southern shores of Loch na Keal. Further west along the shore the road carves through spectacular overhanging cliffs before heading south past the Gribun rocks which face the tiny island of **Inch Kenneth**, where Unity Mitford died in 1948. There are great views out to Staffa and the Treshnish Isles as the road leaves the coast behind, cutting off the **Ardmanach** peninsula as it climbs over the pass to Loch Scribain, where it eventually joins the equally dramatic Glen More road (A848) from Craignure.

If you're properly equipped for walking, however, you can explore the Ardmanach peninsula by foot. On the north coast, a mile or so from the road, is **Mackinnon's Cave** – at 100ft high, one of the largest caves in the Hebrides, and accessible only at low tide. As so often, there's a legend attached to the cave, which tells of an entire party, led by a lone piper, who were once devoured here by evil spirits. Starting from the south coast, it's a longer, rougher six-mile hike from the road to **MacCulloch's Tree**, a huge 40ft-high fossil tree trunk embedded in the cliffs at Rubha na h-Uambha at the western tip of the peninsula. You'll need a good map and, again, you need to time your arrival with low tide; the area is NTS-owned and you should call in at Burg farm on the way to make your presence known (and get directions).

The Ross of Mull

Stretching for twenty miles west as far as Iona is Mull's rocky southernmost peninsula, the **Ross of Mull**, which, like much of Scotland, appears blissfully tranquil in good weather, and desolate and bleak in bad. Most visitors simply drive through the Ross en route to Iona, but, given that accommodation is severely limited on Iona, it's worth considering staying here. If you have children who need entertaining, be sure to check out the **Angora Rabbit Farm** (Easter–Oct daily except Sat 11am–5pm; £1.50), situated just east of Bunessan on the A849, where children can stroke the comical, long-haired bunnies, and watch their fur being clipped and then spun.

In **PENNYGHAEL** there are two very comfortable hotels overlooking Loch Scridain and Ben More: the luxury *Pennyghael Hotel* (☎01681/704288; ⑥; March–Dec), with its excellent restaurant, and the welcoming *Kinloch Hotel* (☎01681/704204; ⑤; April–Oct). **BUNESSAN**, roughly two-thirds of the way along the Ross and the only real village on the peninsula before you get to Fionnphort, has more choice with several inexpensive **B&Bs** such as *Ardtun House* (☎01681/700264; ②), and the excellent *Assapol House Hotel* (☎01681/700258; ⑥; Easter–Oct). Two miles away on the secluded south coast near **UISKEN**, there's a fine sandy beach, as there is at neighbouring **ARDALANISH**. Either of these can be enjoyed by staying at *Uisken Croft* (☎01681/700307; ②) or at *Ardalanish Farm* (☎01681/700265; ③), both of which are highly recommended.

The road ends at **FIONNPHORT**, facing Iona, a less attractive place to stay, though with a nice sandy bay backed by pink granite rocks to the north of the ferry slipway. Partly to ease congestion on Iona, and to give their neighbours a slice of the tourist pound, Fionnphort was chosen as the site for the **St Columba Centre** (Mon–Sat 10am–6pm, Sun 11am–6pm; £3.50), which opened in 1997 on the 1400th anniversary of the saint's death; inside, a small museum tells the story of Columba's life (for more on which, see below) using a combination of special effects and original artefacts.

If you're in need of a bed in Fionnphort, try the granite-built *Seaview* (☎01681/700235; ②) with views over Iona, or *Bruach Mhor* (☎01681/700276; ③), which stands on its own to the north of the village and caters for vegetarians and vegans. The basic *Fidden Farm* **campsite** (☎01681/700427), a mile south along the Knockvologan road by Fidden beach, is the nearest to Iona. Fidden beach looks out to the **Isle of Erraid**, accessible across the sands at low tide. Robert Louis Stevenson is believed to have written *Kidnapped* (its hero, David Balfour, gets shipwrecked here) in one of the island's cottages, overlooking the Torran Rocks, across the sea to the south, where his father and uncle built the Dubh Artach lighthouse in 1862. The island is now in Dutch ownership, and cared for by the Findhorn Community (see p.418).

Isle of Iona

Less than a mile off the southwest tip of Mull, **IONA** – just three miles long and not much more than a mile wide – has been a place of pilgrimage for several centuries now, and a place of Christian worship for more than 1400 years. For it was to this flat Hebridean island that St Columba fled from Ireland in 563 and established a monastery which was responsible for the conversion of more or less all of pagan Scotland as well as much of northern England. This history and the island's splendid isolation have lent it a peculiar religiosity; in the much-quoted words of Dr Johnson, who visited in 1773, "that man is little to be envied . . . whose piety would not grow warmer among the ruins of Iona". Today, however, the island can barely cope with the constant flood of day-trippers, so to appreciate the special atmosphere and to have time to see the whole island, including the often overlooked west coast, you should plan on staying at least one night.

Some history

Legend has it that **St Columba** (Colum Cille), born in Donegal in 521, was a direct descendant of the Irish king, Niall of the Nine Hostages. A scholar and soldier priest, who founded numerous monasteries in Ireland, he was not the peace-loving saint his name (meaning "dove") might suggest. It is thought that he became involved in a bloody dispute with the king when he refused to hand over a copy of the Gospels copied illegally from the original owned by St Finian, and was then excommunicated. At the Battle of Cul Drebene, Columba's forces won, though with great loss of life; repenting this bloodshed, he went into exile with twelve other monks, eventually settling on Iona in 563, allegedly because it was the first island he encountered from which he couldn't see his homeland. Columba became a legend in his own lifetime, and was credited with pacifying the Loch Ness monster and banishing snakes (and, some say, frogs) from the island; he also famously banned women and cows from Iona, banishing them to Eilean nam Ban (Woman's Island), just north of Fionnphort, for, as he believed, "where there is a cow there is a woman, and where there is a woman there is mischief".

During Columba's lifetime, Iona enjoyed a great deal of autonomy from Rome, establishing a specifically Celtic Christian tradition. Missionaries were sent out to the rest of Scotland and parts of England, and Iona quickly became a respected seat of learning and artistry; the monks compiled a vast library of intricately illuminated manuscripts – most famously the *Book of Kells* (now on display in Trinity College, Dublin) – while the masons excelled in carving peculiarly intricate crosses. Two factors were instrumental in the demise of the Celtic tradition: a series of Viking raids, the worst of which was the massacre of 68 monks on the sands of Martyrs' Bay in 806, and relentless pressure from the established church, which culminated in the suppression of the Celtic Church by King David I in 1144.

In 1203, Iona became part of the mainstream church with the establishment of an Augustinian nunnery and a Benedictine monastery by Reginald, son of Somerled, Lord of the Isles. During the Reformation, the entire complex was ransacked, the contents of the library burnt and all but three of the island's 360 crosses destroyed. Although plans were drawn up at various times to turn the abbey into a Cathedral of the Isles, nothing came of them until in 1899 its then owner, the eighth Duke of Argyll, donated the abbey buildings to the Church of Scotland, who restored the abbey church for worship over the course of the next decade. Iona's modern resurgence began in 1938, when George MacLeod, a minister from Glasgow, established a group of ministers, students and artisans to begin rebuilding the remainder of the monastic buildings. What began as a mostly male, Gaelic-speaking, strictly Presbyterian community is today a lay, mixed and ecumenical retreat. The entire abbey complex has been successfully restored and the island, apart from the church land and a few crofts, now belongs to the NTS.

Baile Mór

The passenger ferry from Fionnphort stops at the island's main village, **BAILE MÓR** (literally "large village"), which is in fact little more than a single terrace of cottages facing the sea. Just inland lie the extensive ruins of the **Augustinian nunnery**, disused since the Reformation. A beautifully maintained garden now occupies the cloisters, and if nothing else the complex gives you an idea of the state of the present-day abbey before it was restored. Across the road to the north, housed in a manse built, like the nearby parish church, by the ubiquitous Thomas Telford, is the **Iona Heritage Centre** (Mon–Sat 10.30am–4.30pm; £1.20), with displays on the social history of the island over the last 200 years, including the Clearances which nearly halved the island's population of 500 in the mid-nineteenth century. At a bend in the road, just south of the manse and church, stands the fifteenth-century **MacLean's Cross**, a fine late-medieval example of the distinctive, flowing, three-leaved foliage of the Iona school.

The abbey complex

At the entrance to the **abbey** complex, there's a small information hut, where you're asked to give a £2 donation and can pick up a plan of the abbey. No buildings remain from Columba's time: the present abbey dates from the arrival of the Benedictines in around 1200, was extensively rebuilt in the fifteenth and sixteenth centuries, and restored virtually wholesale this century. Iona's oldest building, the plain-looking **St Oran's Chapel**, lies south of the abbey, to your right, and boasts a Norman door dating from the eleventh century. Legend has it that the chapel could only be completed through human sacrifice. Oran, one of the older monks in Columba's entourage, apparently volunteered to be buried alive, and was found to have survived the ordeal when the grave was opened a few days later. Declaring that he had seen hell and it wasn't all bad, he was promptly reinterred for blasphemy.

Oran's Chapel stands at the centre of Iona's sacred burial ground, **Reilig Odhráin**, which is said to contain the graves of sixty kings of Norway, Ireland, France and Scotland, including Duncan and Macbeth. Archeological evidence has failed to back this up; it's about as likely as the story about Oran. The best of the early Christian gravestones and medieval effigies which once lay in the Reilig Odhráin have unfortunately been removed to the Infirmary Museum, behind the abbey (see overleaf). The grave that most visitors now head for, however, is that of the short-lived leader of the

---

In many ways the landscape of Iona – low-lying, treeless with white sandy coves backed by machair – is more reminiscent of the distant islands of Coll and Tiree than it is of neighbouring Mull. Few tourists bother to stray from Baile Mór, yet in high season there is no better way to appreciate Iona's solitary beauty.

Perhaps the easiest jaunt is up **Dùn I**, Iona's only real hill, which rises to the north of the abbey to a height of 300ft – a great place to wander at dawn or dusk. The west coast has some great sandy beaches; the **Camas Cuil an t-Saimh** (Bay at the Back of the Ocean) by the golf course is the longest. More sheltered is the tiny bay on the south coast, **Port na Curaich**, thought to be where Columba first landed in a coracle (*curaich*) made with tarred cowhides. The fifty-odd small cairns are said to have been piled up by the monks as a penance for their sins. More difficult to reach is the **disused marble quarry** at Rubha na Carraig-géire, on the southeasternmost point of Iona. Quarried intermittently for several centuries, it was finally closed down in 1914; much of the old equipment is still visible, rusting away by the shore.

Labour Party, **John Smith** (1938–94), who was buried here with permission from the local council, despite strong opposition from the islanders. Smith, a frequent visitor to Iona, but a mainlander born in the town of Ardrishaig, has drawn in so many political pilgrims that a new path has now been built to protect the rest of the gravestones.

Turning now to the abbey, you cross the medieval marble cobbles of the evocative **Road of the Dead**, which leads south to St Oran's Chapel. Beside the road stands the most impressive of Iona's Celtic high crosses, the eighth-century **St Martin's Cross**, smothered with figural scenes, including the Virgin and Child at the centre; the reverse side features Pictish serpent-and-boss decoration. Standing directly in front of the abbey are the base of St Matthew's Cross (now in the Infirmary Museum) and, to the left, a replica cast of the eighth-century **St John's Cross**, decorated with serpent-and-boss and Celtic spiral ornamental panels.

Before you enter the abbey, take a look inside **St Columba's Shrine**, a small steep-roofed chamber to the left of the main entrance. Columba is believed to have been buried either here or under the rocky mound to the west of the abbey, known as Tòrr an Aba. The **Abbey** itself has been simply and sensitively restored, to incorporate the original elements. You can spot many of the medieval capitals in the south transept and south aisle of the choir, where marble effigies of the eighth Duke of Argyll and his wife, Ina, lie in a side chapel. For reasons of sanitation, the **cloisters** were placed, contrary to the norm, on the north side of the church (where running water was available); entirely reconstructed in the late 1950s, they now shelter a useful historical account of the abbey's development. If you want to see some of the medieval grave slabs and the original fragments of St John's Cross, you should walk round the back of the abbey to the **Infirmary Museum**.

Baile Mór practicalities

There's no **tourist office** on Iona, and as demand far exceeds supply you should organize **accommodation** in advance. Of the island's two, fairly pricey, hotels, the *Argyll* (☎01681/700334; ⑦) is the nicer. B&Bs are cheaper but fill quickly: try *Cruachan* (☎01681/700523; ③; March–Oct), with sea views from all its rooms, *Finlay Ross* (☎01681/700357; ③), who run two B&Bs, or the vegetarian *Iona Cottage* (☎01681/700579; ③; Easter–Oct). If you want to stay with the Iona Community, contact the **MacLeod Centre** (☎01681/700404) – hostel accommodation is provided and you must be prepared to participate fully in the daily activities, prayers and religious services.

Camping is possible, but check with the crofter before setting up camp. Visitors are not allowed to bring cars onto the island, but **bikes** can be rented from *Finlay Ross* (see above). The Iona Community also organizes **guided walks** around the island (March–Oct Wed 10.15am). **Food** options are limited to the hotel restaurants (the *Argyll* is particularly good) or the self-service *Martyrs' Bay* restaurant by the pier. The coffee house (Mon–Thurs & Sat 11am–4.30pm, Fri & Sun noon–4.30pm) run by the Iona Community, just west of the abbey, serves home-made soup and delicious cakes.

Coll and Tiree

Coll and **Tiree** are among the most isolated of the Inner Hebrides, and if anything have more in common with the outlying Western Isles than with their closest neighbour, Mull. Each is roughly twelve miles long and three miles wide, both are low-lying, treeless and exceptionally windy, with white sandy beaches and the highest sunshine records in Scotland. Like most of the Hebrides, they were once ruled by Vikings, and didn't pass into Scottish hands until the thirteenth century. Coll's population peaked at 1440, Tiree's at a staggering 4450, but both were badly affected by the Clearances, which virtually halved their populations in a generation. Coll was fortunate to be in the hands of the enlightened MacLeans, but they were forced to sell in 1856 to the Stewart family, who sold two-thirds of the island to a Dutch millionaire in the 1960s. Tiree was ruthlessly cleared by its owner, the Duke of Argyll, who sent in the marines in 1885 to evict the crofters. After the passing of the Crofters' Act the following year, the island was divided into crofts, though it remains a part of the Duke of Argyll's estate. Both islands are Gaelic-speaking, but the percentage of English-speaking newcomers is rising steadily.

The CalMac ferry from Oban (sometimes allowing passengers off at Tobermory) calls at Coll and Tiree every day except Thursdays and Sundays throughout the year (June–Aug also Thurs), and there's a once-a-week sailing from Mallaig. Tiree also has an **airport** with daily flights (Mon–Sat) to and from Glasgow. The majority of visitors stay for at least a week in self-catering accommodation (see p.32), though there are B&Bs and hotels on the islands; wherever you choose to stay, it's as well to book as far in advance as possible (and that goes for the ferry crossing, too). The only **public transport** is a bus (Mon–Sat only) and a shared taxi service (☎01879/220311 or 220419), both on Tiree.

Isle of Coll

The fish-shaped rocky island of **Coll** (population 175) lies less than seven miles off the coast of Mull. The CalMac ferry drops off at Coll's only village, **ARINAGOUR**, whose whitewashed cottages dot the western shore of Loch Eatharna. Half the island's population lives in the village, and it's here you'll find the island's post office, churches, school and handful of shops; two miles northwest along the Arnabost road, there's even a golf course. However, there is currently no petrol station on the island, so fill up before you arrive.

On the southwest coast there are two edifices, both confusingly known as **Breachacha Castle**, and both built by the MacLeans. The oldest, at the head of Loch Breachacha, is a fifteenth-century tower house with an additional curtain wall, recently restored, and now a training centre for overseas aid volunteers. The "new castle", to the northwest, made up of a central block built around 1750 and two side pavilions added a century later, is currently boarded up. It was here that Dr Johnson and Boswell stayed in 1773 after a storm forced them to take refuge en route to Mull – they considered the place to be "a mere tradesman's box". The whole area around the castles, and to the west where a strip of **giant sand dunes** links Calgary Point (the westernmost tip of Coll) with the rest of the island, is now owned by the RSPB on account of its precious corncrake population.

For an overview of the whole island, you can follow in Boswell's footsteps and take a wander up **Ben Hogh** – at 339ft, Coll's highest point – two miles west of Arinagour, close to the shore. The island's northwest coast boasts the finest sandy beaches, though they take the full brunt of the Atlantic winds. In the nineteenth century, the rich machair meant that this was the most densely populated part of Coll, and a few of the old crofts in Bousd and Sorisdale, at Coll's northernmost tip, have recently been restored. From here, there's an impressive view over to the headland of Rubha Sgor-innis and the islands beyond, which in turn obscure the small crop of tidal rocks, known as the Cairns of Coll, a mile or so north of the headland.

In Arinagour, the *Isle of Coll* **hotel** (☎01879/230334; ⑤), *Taigh Solas* (☎01879/230333; ③) and *Tigh na Mara* (☎01879/230354; ④) all overlook the bay; two miles west of Arinagour, there's also *Achamore* **B&B** (☎01879/230430; ③), a nine-teenth-century farmhouse. The island's official **campsite** (☎01879/230374; April–Oct), which offers basic facilities, is on Breachacha Bay, in the old walled gardens of the castle; you can also stay in the adjacent *Garden House* B&B (phone as for campsite; ③). The *Isle of Coll* doubles as the island's social centre, but for a change from hotel **food** try the *Coll Malt and Wine Rack* (Easter–Oct) in Arinagour.

Isle of Tiree

Tiree, as its Gaelic name *tir-iodh* (land of corn) suggests, was once known as the bread-basket of the Inner Hebrides, thanks to its acres of rich machair. Nowadays crofting and tourism are the main sources of income for the resident population of around 800. One of most distinctive features of Tiree is its architecture, in particular the large numbers of "pudding" or "spotty" houses, where only the mortar is painted white. In addition, there are numerous "white houses" (*tigh geal*) and traditional "black houses" (*tigh dubh*); for more on these, see p.332. Wildlife lovers can also have a field day on Tiree, with lapwings, wheatcars, redshank, greylag geese and large laid-back brown hares in abundance. And with no shortage of wind, Tiree's sandy beaches attract large numbers of windsurfers for the International Windsurfers' Championships every October.

The CalMac ferry calls at Gott Bay Pier, close to the village of **SCARINISH**, home to a post office, a supermarket, a butcher's and a bank, with a petrol pump back at the pier; to the east is **Gott Bay**, backed by a two-mile stretch of sand. It's just one mile across the island from Gott to Vaul Bay, on the north coast, where the well-preserved remains of a drystone broch, **Dun Mor** – dating from the first century BC – lie hidden in the rocks to the west of the bay. From here it's another two miles west along the coast to the *Clach a'Choire* or **Ringing Stone**, a huge glacial boulder decorated with mysterious pre-historic markings, which when struck with a stone gives out a metallic sound. The story goes that, should the Ringing Stone ever be broken in two, Tiree will sink beneath the waves. A mile further west you come to the lovely **Balephetrish Bay**, where you can watch waders feeding in the breakers, and look out to sea to Skye and the Western Isles.

The most intriguing sights lie in the bulging western half of the island, where Tiree's two landmark hills rise up. The highest of the two, **Ben Hynish** (463ft), is unfortu-nately occupied by a "golf-ball" radar station which tracks incoming transatlantic flights; the views from the top, though, are great. Below Ben Hynish, to the east, is **HYNISH**, with its newly restored **harbour**, designed by Alan Stevenson in the 1830s to transport building materials for the 140ft **Skerryvore Lighthouse**, which lies on a sea-swept reef some twelve miles southwest of Tiree. The harbour features an inge-nious reservoir to prevent silting, and up on the hill behind, by the row of lightkeepers' houses, a stumpy granite signal tower. The tower, whose signals used to be the only contact the lighthouse keepers had with civilization, now houses a **museum** telling the history of the Herculean effort required to erect the lighthouse; weather permitting, you can see the lighthouse from the tower's viewing platform.

On the other side of Ben Hynish, a mile or so across the golden sands of Balephuil Bay, is the spectacular headland of **Ceann a'Mhara** (also known as Kenavara). The cliffs here are home to thousands of seabirds, including fulmars, kittiwakes, guillemots, razorbills, shags and cormorants, with gannets and terns feeding offshore; the islands of Barra and South Uist are also visible on the northern horizon. In the scattered west coast settlement of **SANDAIG**, to the north of Ceann a'Mhara, three thatched white houses in a row have been turned into the **Thatched House Museum** (June–Sept Mon–Fri 2–4pm), which gives an insight into how the majority of islanders lived in the last century.

Practicalities

From the **airport**, about three miles west of Scarinish, you can either catch the post-bus, phone for a shared taxi the night before (see p.303), or arrange for your hosts to collect (most will). Transport around the island is limited, though the postbus calls at all the main settlements; **bike rental** is available at the *Tiree Lodge* (see below). Of the island's two **hotels**, the *Tiree Lodge* (✆01879/220368; ④), a mile or so east of Scarinish along Gott Bay, is preferable to the *Scarinish* (✆01879/220308; ③), overlooking the old harbour. The *Kirkapol* (✆01879/220729; ④), just beyond the *Tiree Lodge*, is a great B&B in a converted kirk; overlooking Balephetrish Bay is *Sandy Cove* (✆01879/220334; ②; April–Oct); while *Matlock* (✆01879/220549; ④), in Crossapol, three miles west of Scarinish, has views over the south coast and is convenient for the airport. There are no official campsites, but **camping** is allowed with the local crofter's permission.

As for **eating**, apart from bar snacks or à la carte at the *Tiree Lodge*, the only other option is *The Glassary* (✆01879/220684; ③; Easter–Oct) over in Sandaig, an unpretentious, moderately priced restaurant that serves good food, much of it locally produced, and also offers accommodation. The island seriously lacks a tearoom of any description, and the only place you can be sure of getting a cuppa is at *Glebecraft*, off the main road to the north of Scarinish – it's an experience not to be missed, and they've got Jacob Sheep to look at out back. For a map of the island and the daily papers, you need to go to the supermarket at Crossapol.

Isle of Colonsay

Isolated between Mull and Islay, **Colonsay** – eight miles by three at its widest – is nothing like as bleak and windswept as Coll or Tiree. Its craggy, heather-backed hills even support the occasional patch of woodland, plus a bewildering array of plant and birdlife, wild goats and rabbits, and one of the finest quasi-tropical gardens in Scotland. That said, the population is precariously low at around 100, down from a pre-Clearance peak of just under 1000, and the ferry links with the mainland infrequent: three a week from Oban; one a week from Kennacraig via Islay. The number of self-catering cottages steadily increases year by year, but, with no camping or caravanning and just one hotel, there's no fear of mass tourism taking over.

The CalMac ferry terminal is at **SCALASAIG**, on the east coast, where there's a post office/shop, a petrol pump, a restaurant and the island's hotel. Right by the pier, in the old waiting room, the island's heritage trust puts on exhibitions about the island, and eventually hopes to mount a permanent display on its history – the building is usually open when the ferry docks. Two miles north of Scalasaig, inland, is **Colonsay House**, built in 1722 by Malcolm MacNeil. In 1904, the island and house were bought by Lord Strathcona, who made his fortune building the Canadian Pacific Railway (and whose descendants still own the island). He was also responsible for the house's lovely gardens and woods, which are slowly being restored to their former glory. The house and gardens are still off limits, but the outbuildings are now holiday cottages and you're free to wander round the woodland garden to the south, and inspect the strange eighth-century **Riasg Buidhe Cross** decorated with an unusually lifelike mug shot, east of the house.

To the north of Colonsay House where the road ends is the island's finest sandy beach, the breathtaking **Kiloran Bay**, where the breakers roll in from the Atlantic. There's another unspoilt sandy beach backed by dunes at Balnahard, two miles north-east along a rough track; en route, you might spot wild goats, choughs, and even a golden eagle. The island's west coast forms a sharp escarpment, quite at odds with the gentle undulating landscape that characterizes the rest of the island. Due west of Colonsay House around **Beinn Bhreac** (456ft), the cliffs are at their most spectacular and in their lower reaches provide a home to hundreds of seabirds, among them kittiwakes, cormorants and guillemots in spring and early summer.

The island's only **hotel**, the pricey *Isle of Colonsay* (☎01951/200316; ⑨; March–Oct), is within easy walking distance from the pier in Scalasaig; it serves very decent bar snacks and acts as the island's social centre. The best option for those with smaller budgets is to stay at the superb *Seaview B&B* (☎01951/200315; ④; April–Oct), in Kilchattan on the west coast. An alternative to eating out at the hotel bar is *The Pantry* (closed Sun) above the pier in Scalasaig, which offers simple home cooking as well as teas and cakes (ring ahead if you want to eat in the evening; ☎01951/200325). All accommodation (and ferry crossings) need to be booked well in advance for the summer; self-catering cottages tend to be booked from Friday to Friday, because of the ferries. Both the hotel and *Seaview* will rent out **bikes**, and there's a limited **bus** and **postbus** service (Mon–Sat) for those without their own transport. If you need a map or any books of the Highlands and islands, go to the very well-stocked **bookshop** (and tearoom) right by the hotel.

Isle of Oronsay

Whilst on Colonsay, most folk take a day out to visit the **Isle of Oronsay**, which lies half a mile to the south and contains the ruins of an Augustinian priory. The two islands are separated by "The Strand", a mile of tidal mud flats which act as a causeway for two hours either side of low tide (check locally for timings); you can drive over to the island at low tide, though most people park their cars and walk across. Although legends (and etymology) link saints Columba and Oran with both Colonsay and Oronsay, the ruins actually only date back as far as the fourteenth century. Abandoned since the Reformation and now roofless, you can, nevertheless, still make out the original church and tiny cloisters. The highlight, though, is the Oronsay Cross, a superb example of late medieval artistry from Iona which stands to the west of the chapel, and the beautifully carved grave slabs in the Prior's House. It takes about an hour to walk from the tip of Colonsay across the Strand to the priory (wellington boots are a good idea). If you don't have your own picnic, you can get tea, cakes and more substantial food from the *Barn Café* (daily except Sat; closed winter) on the Colonsay side of the Strand.

Mid-Argyll

Mid-Argyll is a vague term which loosely describes the central wedge of land south of Oban and north of Kintyre, extending west from Loch Fyne to the Atlantic. **Lochgilphead**, on the shores of Loch Fyne is the chief town in the area, though it has little to offer beyond its practical use – it has a tourist office, a good supermarket and is the regional transport hub, though public transport is thin on the ground. The highlights of this gently undulating scenery lie along the sharply indented west coast, in particular the rich Bronze Age and Neolithic remains in the Kilmartin valley, one of the most important prehistoric sites in Scotland.

Lochgilphead

The unlikely administrative centre of the entire Argyll and Bute region, **LOCHGILPHEAD**, as the name suggests, lies at the head of Loch Gilp, an arm of Loch Fyne. It's a planned town in the same vein as Inveraray, though nothing like as picturesque. If you're staying in the area, you're bound to find yourself here at some point, as Lochgilphead has the only bank and supermarket for miles. If you're desperate for something to do in wet weather, you could pay a visit to Highbank Pottery, a short distance up the Oban road (A816), where they make grotesque ceramic animals and offer guided tours of the premises (Mon–Fri 10.30am & 2pm; nominal fee). A better idea, in fine weather, is to head for Castle Riding Centre (☎01546/603274) at Brenfield Farm, three miles south, which runs highly enjoyable riding courses lasting from a day to a week, plus trekking and pub rides, and even **rents out bikes** and golf equipment.

The **tourist office**, 27 Lochnell St (April & Oct Mon–Fri 10am–5pm, Sat & Sun noon–5pm; May & June daily 10am–5pm; July–Sept Mon–Sat 9.30am–6.30pm, Sun 10am–5pm; ☎01546/602344) will help find you **accommodation**. If you are looking yourself, first choice is the lively *Argyll Hotel*, Lochnell Street (☎01546/602221; ③), or the loch-side, *Kilmory House*, on Paterson Street (☎01546/603658; ③); if you've money to spare, head three miles out of town to the excellent *Cairnbaan Hotel* (☎01546/603668; ⑦), overlooking the Crinan Canal and with a great restaurant and bar meals featuring locally caught seafood. *The Smiddy*, on Smithy Lane (closed Sun), does the best **home cooking** in town – for high-class picnic fare, call in at the *Alba Smokehouse* in Kilmory, a mile out of town on the Inveraray road.

Kilmartin Glen

The **Kilmartin Glen**, north of Lochgilphead up the A816 to Oban, is the most important prehistoric site on the Scottish mainland. The most significant relic is the **linear cemetery**, where several cairns are aligned for more than two miles, to the south of Kilmartin. These are thought to represent the successive burials of a ruling family or chieftains, but nobody can be sure. The best view of the cemetery's configuration is from the Bronze Age **Mid-Cairn**, but the Neolithic **South Cairn**, dating from around 3000 BC, is by far the oldest and the most impressive, with its large chambered tomb roofed by giant slabs.

Close to the Mid-Cairn, the two stone circles at **Temple Wood** appear to have been the architectural focus of burials in the area from Neolithic times to the Bronze Age. Visible to the south are the impressively cup-marked **Nether Largie standing stones** (no public access), the largest of which looms over 10ft high. **Cup- and ring-marked rocks** are a recurrent feature of prehistoric sites in the Kilmartin Glen and elsewhere in Argyll. There are many theories as to their origin: some see them as Pictish symbols, others as primitive solar calendars and so on. The most extensive markings are at **Achnabreck**, off the A816 towards Lochgilphead.

Kilmartin

Situated on high ground to the north of the cairns is the tiny village of **KILMARTIN**, where a new interpretive centre, **Kilmartin House** (March–Dec daily 10.30am–5.30pm; £3.90), is housed in the old manse adjacent to the village church. The fifteen-minute audiovisual is not half as interesting as the excellent museum, which is both enlightening and entertaining. Not only can you learn about the various theories concerning prehistoric crannogs, henges and cairns but you can practise polishing an axe, examine different types of wood and fur, and listen to a variety of weird and wonderful sounds (check out the Gaelic bird imitations). The café/restaurant is equally enticing, with local (often wild) produce on offer, which you can wash down with heather beer.

△ *Carnasserie Castle (1 mile)*

ᛤ	Standing Stones
⁘	Stone Circle
◎	Cup & Ring
	Marked Rocks
⌂	Cairns

Glebe Cairn
Kilmartin
North Cairn
Mid-Cairn
Temple Wood
Stockavullin
South Cairn
Nether Largie
Ri-Cruin
Duntrune Castle
Loch Crinan
Crinan
Crinan Canal
Mòine Mhòr
River Add
Dunadd
(ruined fort)
Kilmichael Glassary
Bridgend

N

KILMARTIN & DUNADD

Lochgilphead (2 miles) ▽

The nearby church is worth a brief reconnoitre, as it shelters the badly damaged and weathered **Kilmartin crosses**, while a separate enclosure in the graveyard houses a large collection of medieval grave slabs of the Malcolms of Poltalloch. Kilmartin's own castle is ruined beyond recognition; head instead for much less ruined **Carnasserie Castle**, on a high ridge a mile up the road towards Oban. The castle was built in the 1560s by John Carswell, an influential figure in the Scottish church, who published the first ever book in Gaelic, *Knox's Liturgy*, which contained the doctrines of the Presbyterian faith. Architecturally, the castle is interesting, too, as it represents the transition between fully fortified castles and later mansion houses, and has several original finely carved stone fireplaces, doorways, as well as numerous gun-loops and shot holes.

Dunadd

The raised peat bog of Mòine Mhór (Great Moss), opening up to the south of Kilmartin, is home to the Iron Age fort of **Dunadd**, which is also one of Scotland's most important Celtic sites, occupying a distinctive 176ft-high rocky knoll once surrounded by the sea but currently beside the winding River Add. It was here that Fergus, the first King of Dalriada, established his royal seat, having arrived from Ireland in around 500 AD. Its strategic position, the craggy defences and the view from the top are all impressive, but it's the **stone carvings** between the twin summits which make Dunadd so remarkable: several lines of inscription in ogam (an ancient alphabet of Irish origin), the faint outline of a boar, a hollowed-out footprint and a small basin. The boar and the inscriptions are probably Pictish, since the fort was clearly occupied long before Fergus got there, but the footprint and basin have been interpreted as being part of the royal coronation rituals of the kings of Dalriada. It is thought that the Stone of Destiny was used at Dunadd before being moved to Scone Palace (see p.264), then to Westminster Abbey in London, where it languished until its recent return to Edinburgh (see p.66).

Practicalities

If you don't fancy staying in Lochgilphead (see above), there are several **accommodation** options within a mile radius of Kilmartin. The *Kilmartin Hotel* (☎01546/510250; ④), with a lively bar, is in Kilmartin itself; *Ri-Cruin* (☎01546/510231; ③), near the cairn of the same name, and *Tibertich* (☎01546/810281; ②), north of Kilmartin off the A816, are local sheep farms offering **B&B**; and there are further possibilities in the nearby village of Kilmichael Glassary. The aforementioned café/restaurant at Kilmartin House is a great lunchtime **eating** option; alternatively *The Cairn* (☎01546/510254), opposite the church in Kilmartin, is also open in the evening, and features moderately priced Scottish and Mediterranean dishes.

Knapdale

Forested **Knapdale** – from the Gaelic *cnap* (hill) and *dall* (field) – forms a buffer zone between the Kintyre peninsula and the rest of Argyll, bounded to the north by the Crinan Canal and to the south by West Loch Tarbert.

Crinan Canal

In 1801 the nine-mile-long **Crinan Canal** opened, linking Loch Fyne, at Ardrishaig south of Lochgilphead, with the Sound of Jura, thus cutting out the long and treacherous journey around the Mull of Kintyre. John Rennie's original design, although an impressive engineering feat, had numerous faults and by 1816 Thomas Telford was called in to take charge of the renovations. The canal runs parallel to the sea for quite some way before cutting across the bottom of Mòine Mhór and hitting a flight of locks either side of Cairnbaan (there are fifteen in total); a walk along the towpath is both picturesque and pleasantly unstrenuous.

There are usually one or two yachts passing through the locks, but the best place to view the canal in action is at **CRINAN**, the pretty little fishing port at the western end of the canal. Crinan's tiny harbour is, for the moment at least, still home to a small fishing fleet; if you want to go on one of the boat trips organized by Gemini Cruises (☎01546/830238), however, you need to go to Crinan's other harbour, half a mile further along the coast. Every room in the *Crinan Hotel* (☎01546/830261; ⑨) looks across Loch Crinan to the Sound of Jura – one of the most beautiful views in Scotland, especially at sunset when the myriad islets and the distinctive Paps of Jura are reflected in the waters of the loch. If the *Crinan* is beyond your means, try one of the secluded **B&Bs**, such as *Tigh-na-Glaic* (☎01546/830261; ③), also with views out to sea. Lunch at the *Crinan* is pricey but recommended; the cheaper bar meals are also very good. Tea and delicious calorific cakes can be had from *Lock 16* right on the quayside.

Knapdale Forest and Loch Sween

South of the canal, **Knapdale Forest**, planted in the 1930s, stretches virtually uninterrupted from coast to coast, across hills sprinkled with tiny lochs. The Forestry Commission has set out several lovely **walks**, the easiest of which is the circular, mile-long path which takes you deep into the forest just past **Achanamara** (five miles south of Crinan). The three-mile route around **Loch Coille-Bharr**, which begins from a bend in the B8025, to Tayvallich, is fairly gentle; the other walk, although half a mile shorter, is more strenuous, starting from the B841 (halfway between Crinan and Lochgilphead), which runs along the canal, and ascending the peak of **Dunardry** (702ft).

Six miles south of Achanamara, on the shores of **Loch Sween** is the "Key of Knapdale", the eleventh-century **Castle Sween**, the earliest stone castle in Scotland, but in ruins since 1647. The tranquillity and beauty of the setting is spoilt by the nearby caravan park, an eyesore which makes a visit pretty depressing. You're better off continuing south to the thirteenth-century **Kilmory Chapel**, also ruined but with a new roof protecting the medieval grave slabs and the well-preserved MacMillan's Cross, an 8ft-high fifteenth-century Celtic cross showing the Crucifixion on one side and a hunting scene on the other. The best **accommodation** in the area is the *Kilberry Inn* (☎01880/770223; ⑥), twenty miles southwest of Lochgilphead on the B8024, which guarantees peace and quiet, plus excellent home cooking.

Kintyre

But for the mile-long isthmus between West and the much smaller East Loch Tarbert, **KINTYRE** (from the Gaelic *ceann tire*, "land's end") would be an island. Indeed, in the eleventh century, when the Scottish king, Malcolm Canmore, told Magnus Barefoot, King of Norway, he could lay claim to any island he could navigate his boat round, Magnus succeeded in dragging his boat across the Tarbert isthmus and added the peninsula to his Hebridean kingdom. After the Wars of the Covenant, when the vast majority of the population and property was wiped out by a combination of the 1646 potato blight coupled with the destructive attentions of the Earl of Argyll, Kintyre became a virtual desert until the earl began his policy of transplanting Gaelic-speaking Lowlanders to the region.

Getting around Kintyre without your own transport is a slow business, though services have improved. There are regular daily buses from Glasgow to Campbeltown, via Tarbert and the west coast, and even a skeleton service down the east coast. Bear in mind, though, if you're driving, that the new west coast road is extremely fast, whereas the single-track east coast road takes more than twice as long. Campbeltown has an airport, with regular flights from Glasgow, which is only forty miles away by air, compared to over 120 miles by road, and there's now a new ferry link from Campbeltown to Barrycastle in Northern Ireland.

Tarbert

A distinctive rocket-like church steeple heralds the fishing village of **TARBERT** (in Gaelic *an tairbeart*, meaning "isthmus"), sheltering an attractive little bay backed by rugged hills. Tarbert's herring industry was mentioned in the Annals of Ulster as far back as 836 AD – though right now the future of the local fishing industry is under threat from EU quotas. Tourism is an increasingly important source of income, as is the money that flows through the town during the last week in May, when the yacht races of the Rover Series take place, and in the following week when the village hosts the powerboat Grand Prix.

Of Robert the Bruce's fourteenth-century **castle** above the town to the south, only the ivy-strewn ruins of the keep remain, though the view from the overgrown rubble makes a stroll up here worthwhile. There are steps up to the castle from beside the excellent Ann Thomas bookshop and gallery on Pier Road, and, at the far end of the road, a lovely shell beach. Tarbert's main tourist attraction, though, is the **An Tairbeart Heritage Centre** (Easter–Oct daily 10am–7pm), five minutes' walk up the Campbeltown road. The shop sells local produce and runs an excellent restaurant serv-

---

FERRY CONNECTIONS IN AND AROUND TARBERT

One reason you might find yourself staying in Tarbert is its proximity to no fewer than four **ferry terminals**. The small CalMac ferry which connects Kintyre with **Portavadie** on the Cowal peninsula leaves from Pier Road; the busiest terminal, however, is at **Kennacraig**, five miles south along the A83, which runs daily sailings to Islay and a once-weekly service to Colonsay. From Kennacraig, the B8001 cuts across the peninsula to **Claonaig**, where a summer car ferry (April to mid-Oct) runs to Lochranza on Arran; and finally, south of Kennacraig on the A83 there is the Gigha ferry from **Tayinloan**.

---

ing the centre's own venison, Tayinloan snails and local seafood. Behind it is a child-centred nature park (£3) for viewing the local wildlife at close quarters; a whole range of activities such as wood turning and sheep shearing are on offer, too.

The **tourist office** (April Mon–Fri 10am–5pm, Sat & Sun 11am–5pm; May & June Mon–Sat 10am–5pm, Sun 11am–5pm; July–Sept Mon–Sat 9.30am–6.30pm, Sun 11am–5pm; Oct Mon–Sat 10am–5pm, Sun 11am–4pm; ☎01880/820429) is on the harbour. If you need to **stay**, try *Springside* B&B on Pier Road (☎01880/820413; ③), or the wonderful Victorian *Columba Hotel* further along the waterfront (☎01880/820808; ⑥). If you're just looking for a fill-up, the **bar snacks** at the *Islay Frigate Hotel* on the harbour suffice, but, for some excellent fish and seafood, head for the pricey *Anchorage* nearby (☎01880/820881), unforgettable not least for its eccentric proprietor. You can **rent bikes** from Mr Leitch (☎01880/820287), on the opposite side of the harbour from the tourist office.

Isle of Gigha

Gigha (pronounced "Geeya", with a hard "g") is a low-lying, fertile island, just three miles off the west coast of Kintyre. The island's Ayrshire cattle produce over a quarter of a million gallons of milk a year, despite the fact that Gigha's creamery closed down in the 1980s – some of it goes to produce the distinctive fruit-shaped cheese which is one of the island's main exports. Like many of the smaller Hebrides, the island was sold by its original lairds, the MacNeils, and has been put on the market three times in less than ten years, causing great uncertainty amongst the 140 or so inhabitants.

The ferry from Tayinloan, 23 miles south of Tarbert, deposits you at the island's only village, **ARDMINISH**, where you'll find the post office and shop. The only sights, as such, are the **Achamore Gardens** (April–Sept daily 9am–dusk; £2), a mile and a half south of Ardminish. Established by the first postwar owner, Sir James Horlick of hot drink fame, they are best seen in early summer, ablaze with rhododendrons and azaleas. The other attraction on Gigha, apart from the peace and quiet, is the white sandy beaches, including one at Ardminish, that dot the coastline.

Gigha is so small – six miles by one mile – that most visitors come here just for the day. However, it is possible to **stay**, either with the McSporrans at the *Post Office House* (☎01583/505251; ③), or at the *Gigha Hotel* (☎01583/505254; ⑥; March–Oct), which also runs self-catering flats dotted over the island. Caravans and camping are not allowed on Gigha. The *Gigha Hotel* is the place to go for tea and cakes, and for bar meals. **Bike rental** is available at the McSporrans'.

The west coast

Kintyre's bleak **west coast** ranks among the most exposed stretches of coastline in Argyll. Atlantic breakers pound the shoreline, while the persistent westerly wind forces the trees against the hillside. However, when the weather's fine, and the wind not too fierce, there are numerous deserted sandy beaches to enjoy with great views over to Gigha, Islay, Jura and even Ireland.

Two-thirds of the way down the coast you can visit **Glenbarr Abbey** (Easter–Oct daily except Tues 10am–5.30pm; £2.50), an eighteenth-century laird's house filled with tedious memorabilia about the once powerful MacAlister clan, now reduced to augmenting their income by giving personal guided tours of their house to the trickle of tourists that pass this way. Still, there are plenty of musty old sofas to lounge around in, a tearoom, and attractive grounds which provide a brief respite from the Atlantic winds.

The only major development along this coast is at **MACHRIHANISH**, at the southern end of Machrihanish Bay, the longest continuous stretch of sand in Argyll; you can approach the **beach** either from Machrihanish itself, or from Westport, at the north end of the bay, where the A83 swings east towards Campbeltown. Once a thriving salt-producing and coal-mining centre – you can still see the miners' cottages at neighbouring Drumlemble – Machrihanish now survives solely on tourism. The main draw, apart from the beach, is the tiny **seabird observatory** at Uisaed Point, ten minutes' walk west of the village, though it's best visited in the winter months when it provides a welcome shelter for ornithologists. There's also an exposed **golf links** between the beach and Campbeltown airport on the nearby flat and fertile swath of land known as the Laggan.

Practicalities

The best **accommodation** in Machrihanish is at the big Victorian *Ardell House* (☎01586/810235; ④; March–Nov), overlooking the golf links; for something simpler try *Kilgour* B&B (☎01586/810233; ④). **Campers** should head for the fully equipped site (☎01586/810366; March–Sept) close by, or one of the other blustery sites along the coast, such as the big *Point Sands Caravan Park* (☎01583/441263; April–Oct) in Rhunahaorine, two miles north of Tayinloan, near a long stretch of sandy beach, or the smaller, more informal *Muasdale Holiday Park,* three miles south of Tayinloan (☎01583/421207; April–Oct). Other places to stay along the coast include the luxury late-Victorian *Balinakill Country House* at Clachan (☎01880/740206; ⑤), north of Tayinloan. For **food** along the coast try the *Tayinloan Inn* (☎01583/441233; ③), a cosy pub offering better than average bar meals (and rooms), and the *North Beachmore Farm*, signposted off the A83, just south of Tayinloan, with superb views over the coast, and good, low-priced meals, tea and cakes. For **nightlife**,*The Beachcomber* bar, run by the owners of *Kilgour* B&B, is the liveliest place in Machrihanish.

Campbeltown

CAMPBELTOWN's best feature is its setting, in a deep bay sheltered by Davaar Island and the surrounding hills. With a population of 6500, it is also one of the largest towns in Argyll and, if you're staying in the southern half of Kintyre, here is by far the best place to stock up on supplies. Originally known as Kinlochkilkerran (*Ceann Loch Cill Chiaran*), the town was renamed in the seventeenth century by the Earl of Argyll – a Campbell – when it became one of the main points for immigration from the Lowlands. As is evident from the architecture, Campbeltown's heyday was the Victorian era, when shipbuilding was going strong, coal was shipped by canal from Drumlemble, the fishing fleet was vast and Campbeltown Loch was said to be made of whisky. With the decline of all its old industries, and its continuing geographical isolation, many folks' hopes are pinned on the positive impact of the new car-ferry link with Ballycastle in Northern Ireland.

The Town

Nineteenth-century visitors to Campbeltown frequently found the place engulfed in a thick fog of pungent peat smoke from the town's 34 **whisky distilleries**. Today, only

Glen Scotia and Springbank are left to maintain this regional subgroup of single malt whiskies which is distinct from Highland, Islay or Lowland varieties (see p.35 in Basics for more on whisky). The family-owned Springbank distillery offers tours by appointment (Mon–Thurs 2pm; ☎01586/552085; £2.50), and you can buy a guide to Campbeltown's former distilleries from the tourist office; aficionados should also peruse the huge range of whiskies for sale at Eaglesome on Longrow South.

The town's one major sight is the **Campbeltown Cross**, a fourteenth-century blue-green cross with figural scenes and spirals of Celtic knotting, which presides over the main roundabout on the quayside. Until the last war, it used to be rather more impressive in the middle of the main street outside the **Town House**, with its distinctive eighteenth-century octagonal clock tower. Back on the harbour is the "**Wee Picture House**", a dinky little Art Deco cinema on Hall Street, built in 1913 and now doubling as a bingo hall (Tues & Fri) and movie house. Next door is the equally delightful **Campbeltown Museum and Library** (Wed, Fri & Sat 10am–1pm & 2–5pm, Tues & Thurs 10am–1pm & 2–7.30pm; free), built in 1897 in the local sandstone, crowned by a distinctive lantern, and decorated on its harbourside wall with four relief panels depicting each of the town's main industries at the time. Inside, there's a timber-framed ceiling and etched glass partitions to admire, not to mention a rather unusual brass model of the Temple of Solomon (as it might have looked). The museum itself, which you enter through the library, is a less remarkable rundown of the local history; for a more enlightening version, head to the Heritage Centre (described below).

It used to be said that Campbeltown had almost as many churches as it did distilleries, and even today the townscape is dominated by its church spires; in particular, the top-heavy crown spire of **Longrow Church**, on the road to Machrihanish. The church known locally as the "Tartan Kirk", partly due to its Gaelic associations, but mainly for its stripy bell-cote and pinnacles, has now become the **Campbeltown Heritage Centre** (April–Oct Mon–Fri noon–5pm, Sat 10am–5pm, Sun 2–5pm; £2). A beautiful wooden skiff from 1906 stands where the main altar once was, and there's plenty on the local whisky industry and St Kieran, the sixth-century "Apostle of Kintyre", who lived in a cave – which you can get to at low tide – not far from Campbeltown. A dedicated ascetic, he would only eat bread mixed with a third sand and a few herbs; he wore chains, had a stone pillow and slept out in the snow – unsurprisingly, at the age of 33, he died of jaundice.

One of the most popular day-trips is to **Davaar Island**, linked to the peninsula at low tide by a mile-long shoal, or *dòirlinn* as it's known in Gaelic. Check the times of the tides from the tourist office before setting out; you have around six hours in which to make the return journey from Kildalloig Point, two miles or so east of town. Davaar is uninhabited and used for grazing (hence no dogs are allowed); its main attraction, besides the wealth of rock flora, is the cave painting of the Crucifixion executed in secret by local artist, Archibald MacKinnon, in 1887, and touched up by him after he'd owned up in 1934; a year later, aged 85, he died.

Practicalities

Campbeltown's **tourist office** is currently on the Old Quay (April Mon–Fri 9am–5.30pm; May–Sept Mon–Fri 9am–5.30pm, Sat & Sun 11am–5pm; Oct Mon–Fri 9.30am–5.30pm, Sat & Sun 10am–4pm; Nov–March Mon–Fri 10am–4pm; ☎01586/552056), though it's due to move in the future. The new pier for the CalMac ferry to Ballycastle lies just to the south. There's no shortage of **accommodation**: try the *Ardshiel Hotel*, on Kilkerran Road (☎01586/552133; ⑤), a very nice family-run hotel, or the landmark *White Hart Hotel* on Main Street (☎01586/552440; ⑤), another safe bet. The *Westbank Guest House* is a fine detached Victorian villa on Dell Road (☎01586/553660; ③), or there's the pretty, whitewashed *Feorlin* on Long Row (☎01586/552464; ③).

As for **places to eat**, it's best to stick to the value-for-money bar snacks at the afore-mentioned *White Hart Hotel* or *Ardshiel Hotel*; the *Locarno Café* on Longrow South is a period-piece greasy spoon, while the *Commercial Inn*, on Cross Street, is a good drinking hole. You can **rent bikes** at *The Bike Shop*, Longrow (☎01586/554443). If you're here in the middle of August, be sure to check out the **Mull of Kintyre Music Festival**, which features some great traditional Irish and Scottish bands.

Southend and the Mull of Kintyre

The bulbous, hilly end of Kintyre, to the south of Campbeltown, features some of the most spectacular scenery on the whole peninsula mixed with large swaths of Lowland-style farmland. **SOUTHEND** itself, a bleak, blustery spot, comes as something of a disappointment, though it does have a wide sandy beach. However, there are nicer beaches at **Carskey Bay** to the west, and **Macharioch Bay**, three miles east, looking out to distant Ailsa Craig in the Firth of Clyde. Jutting out into the sea at the east end of Southend's beach is **Dunaverty Rock**, where a force of 300 Royalists was massacred by the Covenanting army of the Earl of Argyll in 1647 despite having surrendered voluntarily. A couple of miles beyond lies **Sanda Island**, which contains the remains of St Ninian's chapel, plus two ancient crosses and a holy well; it's now a self-catering holiday retreat (☎01586/553134; April–Sept). Below the cliffs to the west of Southend, a ruined thirteenth-century chapel marks the alleged arrival point of St Columba prior to his trip to Iona, and on a rocky knoll nearby a pair of footprints carved into the rock are known as **Columba's footprints**, though only one is actually of ancient origin.

Most people venture south of Campbeltown to make a pilgrimage to the **Mull of Kintyre** – the nearest Britain gets to Ireland, whose coastline, just twelve miles away, is visible on clear days. Although the Mull was made famous by the mawkish number-one hit by one-time local resident Paul McCartney, with the help of the Campbeltown Pipe Band, there's nothing specifically to see in this godforsaken storm-racked spot but the view. The roads up to the "**Gap**" (1150ft) – where you must leave your car – and particularly down to the lighthouse, itself 300ft above the ocean waves, are terrifyingly tortuous. It's about a mile from the "Gap" to the lighthouse (and a long haul back up), though there's a strategic viewpoint just ten minutes' walk from the car park.

There are few places to **stay** in this remote region. Southend's only hotel has been closed for some time and cuts a forlorn figure, set back from the bay; try instead *Ormsary Farm* (☎01586/830665; ③), up Glen Breakerie, *Low Cattadale* (☎01586/830665; ③), near the golf links, or the **campsite** at *Machribeg Farm* (☎01586/830249; Easter–Sept) right by the beach. If you're interested in **horse riding**, call the Mull of Kintyre Equestrian Centre at Homeston Farm (☎01586/552437), signposted off the B842 to Southend.

The east coast

The **east coast** of Kintyre is gentler than the west, sheltered from the Atlantic winds and in parts strikingly beautiful, with stunning views across to Arran. However, be warned that bus services are very limited up the east coast and, if you're driving the thirty or so miles up to Skipness on the slow, winding, single-track B842, you'll need a fair amount of time.

The ruins of **Saddell Abbey**, a Cistercian foundation thought to have been founded by Somerled in 1160, lie ten miles up the coast from Campbeltown, set at the lush, wooded entrance to Saddell Glen. The abbey fell into disrepair in the sixteenth century, and though the remains are not exactly impressive, they do shelter a collection of medieval grave slabs decorated with full-scale relief figures of knights. Standing by the privately owned shoreline there's a splendid memorial to the last Campbell laird to live at Saddell Castle, which he built in 1774.

A little further north, the fishing village of **CARRADALE** is the only place of any size on the east coast and "popular with those who like unsophisticated resorts", as one 1930s guide put it. The village itself is drab, but the tiny, sandy, very pretty harbour with its small fishing fleet, and the sandy bay to the south, make up for it. There are a couple of **hotels** – the small *Ashbank* (☎01583/431650; ③) is the best value, while the bar of the *Carradale Hotel* (☎01583/431223; ④) is the hub of village social life – and several **B&Bs**, including the big Victorian *Dunvalanree Guest House* (☎01583/431226; ③), overlooking the sheltered little bay of Port Righ, towards Carradale Point, and *Seaview East* (☎01583/431316; ②), overlooking the old harbour, plus *Carradale Bay* **campsite** (☎01583/431665; Easter–Sept) right by the sandy beach.

There are several pleasant walks laid out in the woods around Carradale, not to mention a **vitrified fort** built more than two thousand years ago on a small tidal island off the headland of Carradale Point, to which you can walk at low tide. A little further up the road, a wet-weather possibility is a visit to **Grogport Tannery** (daily 9am–6pm), which produces naturally coloured, organically tanned, fully washable sheepskins (gloves and slippers too).

The B842 ends twelve miles north of Carradale at **CLAONAIG**, little more than a slipway for the summer car ferry to Arran. Beyond here, a dead-end road winds its way along the shore a few miles further north to the tiny village of **SKIPNESS**, where the considerable ruins of the enormous thirteenth-century **Skipness Castle** and a chapel look out across the Kilbrannan Sound to Arran. You can sit outside and admire both, whilst enjoying fresh oysters, delicious queenies, mussels and home-baked cakes from the excellent seafood cabin at *Skipness House*, which also offers **accommodation** in a family home (☎01880/760207; ⑦).

Isle of Arran

Shaped like a kidney bean, **Arran** is the most southerly (and therefore the most accessible) of all the Scottish islands. The Highland–Lowland dividing line passes right through its centre – hence the tourist board's aphorism about it being like "Scotland in miniature" – leaving the northern half underpopulated, mountainous and bleak, while the lush southern half enjoys a much milder climate. Despite its immense popularity, the tourists, like the population of around 4500, tend to stick to the southeastern quarter of the island, leaving the west and the north relatively undisturbed.

There are two big crowd pullers on Arran: **geology** and **golf**. The former has fascinated rock-obsessed students since James Hutton came here in the late eighteenth century to confirm his theories of igneous geology. A hundred years later, Sir Archibald Geikie's investigations were a landmark in the study of Arran's geology, and the island remains a popular destination for university and school field trips. As for golf, Arran boasts no fewer than seven courses, including three of the eighteen-hole variety at **Brodick**, **Lamlash** and **Whiting Bay**, and a twelve-hole course at **Blackwaterfoot**.

Although tourism is now by far its most important industry, Arran, at twenty miles in length, is large enough to have a life of its own. While the island's post-1745 history and the Clearances (set in motion by the local lairds, the dukes of Hamilton) are as depressing as elsewhere in the Highlands, in recent years Arran has not suffered from the depopulation which has plagued other, more remote islands. Once a county in its own right (along with Bute), Arran has been left out of the new Argyll and Bute district in the recent county boundary shake-up, and is coupled instead with mainland North Ayrshire, with which it enjoys year-round transport links, but little else.

Transport on Arran itself is good: daily **buses** circle the island (Brodick tourist office has timetables) and there are two **ferry services**: a year-round one from Ardrossan in Ayrshire to Brodick, and a smaller ferry from Claonaig on the Kintyre peninsula to **Lochranza** in the north (April to mid-Oct).

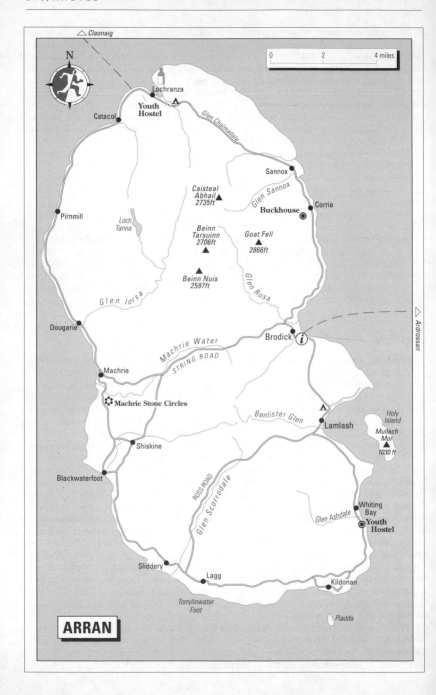

△ *Claonaig*

N

0   2   4 miles

Lochranza

**Youth
Hostel**

Catacol

Glen Chalmadale

Sannox

*Caisteal
Abhail*
2735ft ▲

Glen Sannox

Buckhouse ◎

Corrie

Pirnmill

*Loch
Tanna*

*Beinn
Tarsuinn*
2706ft ▲

Goat Fell
2866ft ▲

Beinn Nuis
2597ft ▲

Glen Rosa

G l e n   I o r s a

Dougarie

Machrie Water

Brodick ⓘ

△ *Ardrossan*

Machrie

STRING ROAD

:: **Machrie Stone Circles**

Benlister Glen

*Holy
Island*

⋀

Lamlash

*Mullach
Mor*
▲
1030 ft

Shiskine

Blackwaterfoot

ROSS ROAD

Glen Scorrodale

Glen Ashdale

**Whiting
Bay**
◎ **Youth
Hostel**

Sliddery

Lagg

Kildonan

*Torrylinwater
Foot*

⌒ *Pladda*

ARRAN

Brodick

Although the resort of **BRODICK** (from the Norse *breidr vik*, "broad bay") is a place of little charm, it does at least have a grand setting in a wide, sandy bay set against a backdrop of granite mountains. Its development as a tourist resort was held back for a long time by its elitist owners, the dukes of Hamilton, though nowadays, as the island's capital and main communication hub, Brodick is by far the busiest town on Arran.

The dukes lived at **Brodick Castle** (Easter–Oct daily 11.30am–5pm; NTS; £4.50), on a steep bank on the north side of the bay. The interior is for the dedicated period-furniture buff only; more accessible are the views over Brodick Bay, from the flower-filled walled grounds (daily 10am–dusk; £2.30) and the very good tearooms. The **Arran Heritage Museum** (Easter–Oct Mon–Sat 10am–5pm; £1.50), is a somewhat dry collection of old tools and furniture in a converted eighteenth-century crofter's farm halfway between the castle and the town centre – really only worth visiting to escape from bad weather.

Brodick's **tourist office** (May–Sept Mon–Sat 9am–7.30pm, Sun 10am–5pm; Oct–April Mon–Sat 9am–5pm; ☎01770/302401) is by the CalMac pier, and has reams of information on every activity from pony trekking to paragliding. Unless you've got to catch an early-morning ferry, however, there's little reason to stay in Brodick. Should you do so, there are plenty of **rooms** close to the ferry terminal, in the excellent *Dunvegan House Hotel* (☎01770/302811; ⑤), or the Victorian *Douglas Hotel* (☎01770/302155; ④), as well as in more secluded places like the *Glen Cloy Farm House* (☎01770/302351; ④; March–Nov). The best of the many **B&Bs** is the centrally located *Tigh-na-Mara*, on the seafront (☎01770/302538; ③; April–Oct). The nearest **campsite** is *Glenrosa* (☎01770/302380; April–Oct), a lovely farm site two miles from town on the B880 to Blackwaterfoot. For food, the only place which really stands out is the superb, but expensive, seafood restaurant *Creelers* (☎01770/302810; mid-March to Oct;), by the Arran Heritage Museum on the road to the castle; the bar snacks at the *Douglas Bar* in the *Kingsley Hotel* make a cheaper option. You can **rent bikes** from Brodick Cycles (☎01770/302460), opposite the village hall.

The south

The southern half of Arran is less spectacular, and less forbidding than the north; the land is more fertile, and for that reason the vast majority of the population lives here. The tourist industry has followed them, though with considerably less justification.

Lamlash and the south coast

With its distinctive Edwardian architecture and mild climate **LAMLASH** epitomizes the sedate charm of southeast Arran. Its major drawback is its bay, which is made not of sand but of boulder-strewn mud flats. You can take a boat out to the slug-shaped hump of **Holy Island** which shelters the bay, and is now owned by a group of Scottish Buddhists who have set up a meditation centre – providing you don't dawdle, it's possible to scramble up to the top of Mullach Mòr (1030ft), the island's highest point, and still catch the last ferry back. En route, you might well bump into the island's most numerous residents: feral goats, Highland cattle and rabbits.

If you want to **stay** in style in Lamlash, head for the *Glenisle Hotel* (☎01770/600 559; ⑦; closed Jan), or the much smaller *Lilybank Hotel* (☎01770/600230; ④), which does superb home-made food; cheaper B&Bs are easy enough to find – try *Blairmore Farmhouse* (☎01770/600004; ②) in the middle of the golf course. You can **camp** at *Middleton's Caravan Park* (☎01770/600255; mid-April to mid-Oct), just five minutes' walk south of the centre. Lamlash's best **restaurant** in is undoubtedly the *Carraig Mhor* near the pier (☎01770/604453; Mon–Sat eves only), which offers an exclusive and expensive menu featuring fresh local game, fish and seafood; for a cheaper alternative try the bar meals at the *Pier Head Tavern*.

Although it has been an established Clydeside resort for over a century now, **WHITING BAY**, four miles south of Lamlash, is actually pretty characterless. However, it's a good base for walking in the southern half of Arran and there are some excellent **places to stay**, including the *Royal Hotel* (☎01770/700286; ④; March–Oct), and the *Argentine House Hotel*, run (confusingly) by a Swiss couple (☎01770/700662; ④; closed Nov), both on Shore Road. Also worth a try are *View Bank House*, on Golf Course Road (☎01770/700326; ③; closed Dec), and *Rowallan*, on School Road (☎01770/700377; ③; March–Nov). Whiting Bay also boasts a **youth hostel** (☎01770/700339; March–Oct); for **bike rental** go to Whiting Bay Hires (☎01770/700382) on the jetty.

Access to the sea is tricky along the south coast, but worth the effort, as the sandy beaches here are among the island's finest. One place you can get down to the sea is at **KILDONAN**, a small village south of Lamlash, set slightly off the main road, with a nice sandy beach and, at its east end, a ruined castle looking out to the tiny island of Pladda. Those with kids might like to drop in at the nearby **South Bank Farm Park** (Easter–Sept daily 10am–5pm; £2), to see rare breeds and the occasional sheepdog demonstration (Tues & Thurs 2pm). If you want to stay in Kildonan, then book in at the architecturally splendid *Drimla Lodge* (☎01770/820296; ④; March–Oct) or at the local **campsite** (☎01770/820210).

Blackwaterfoot and Machrie

BLACKWATERFOOT, on the western end of String Road that bisects the island, is slightly less of a resort and more of a Hebridean fishing village and, like Lochranza, in the north, a good place to escape the worst of Arran's summer crowds. If you want to **stay**, the Victorian *Blackwaterfoot Hotel* (☎01770/860202; ⑤; March–Dec) is a good place to hole up, and there are plenty of cheaper B&Bs, too – try *Marvern House* (☎01770/860254; ③).

North of Blackwaterfoot, the wide expanse of **Machrie Moor** boasts a wealth of Bronze Age sites. No fewer than six **stone circles** sit east of the main road; although many of them barely break the peat's surface, the tallest surviving monolith is over 18ft high. The most striking configuration is at Fingal's Cauldron Seat, with two concentric circles of granite boulders; legend has it that Fingal tied his dog to one of them while cooking at his cauldron. Incidentally, **King's Cave**, two miles along the coast north from Blackwaterfoot, is one of several where Robert the Bruce is said to have encountered the famously patient arachnid, while hiding during his final bid to free Scotland in 1306.

The north

The desolate **north half of Arran** – effectively the Highland part – features bare granite peaks, the occasional golden eagle and miles of unspoilt scenery, within reach only to those prepared to do some serious hiking. Arran's most accessible peak is also the island's highest, **Goat Fell** (2866ft) – take your pick from the Gaelic, *goath*, meaning "windy", or the Norse, *geit-fjall*, "goat mountain" – which can be ascended in just three hours from Brodick (return journey 5hr), though it's a strenuous hike (for the usual safety precautions, see p.44). From Goat Fell, experienced walkers can follow the horseshoe of craggy summits and descend either from the saddle below Beinn Tarsuinn (2706ft) or from Beinn Nuis (2597ft).

Another good base for hiking is the pretty little seaside village of **CORRIE**, six miles north of Brodick, where a procession of pristine cottages lines the road to Lochranza. There are a couple of hotels and B&Bs – try the family-run *Corrie Hotel* (☎01770/810273; ④), or the traditional seafront *Blackrock House* (☎01770/810282; ④;

March–Oct) – and the *North High Corrie Croft* **bunkhouse** (☎01770/810253) above the village. **Bike rental** is available from The Spinning Wheel (☎01770/810640). At **SANNOX**, two miles north, the road leaves the shoreline and climbs steeply, giving breathtaking views over to the scree-strewn slopes around Caisteal Abhail (2735ft). If you make this journey around dusk, be sure to pause in **Glen Chalmadale**, on the other northern side of the pass, to catch a glimpse of the red deer that come down to pasture by the water.

The ruined castle which occupies the mud flats of the bay, and the gloomy north-facing slopes of the mountains which frame it, make for one of the most spectacular settings on the island – yet **LOCHRANZA**, despite being the only place of any size in this sparsely populated area, attracts far fewer visitors than Arran's southern resorts. Lochranza now boasts the island's first legal whisky **distillery** for more than 150 years, which offers guided tours (daily 10am–6pm; £2.50), but won't begin to offer its first single malt until 2001. Lochranza has a **youth hostel** (☎01770/830631; March–Oct) overlooking the castle, and a well-equipped **campsite** (☎01770/830273; Easter to mid-Oct) beautifully situated by the golf course on the Brodick Road. Plusher **accommodation** can be had at the superb *Apple Lodge Hotel* (☎01770/830229; ⑤), with excellent home cooking, the *Lochranza Hotel* (☎01770/830223; ③), whose bar is the centre of the local social scene, or the Edwardian B&B *Belvaren* (☎01770/830647; ③; Feb to mid-Dec).

An alternative is to continue a mile or so southwest along the coast to **CATACOL**, where the friendly *Catacol Bay Hotel* (☎01770/830231; ③) takes the prize as the island's best pub by far: good, basic pub food (with several veggie options and real chips), great beer on tap, a small adjoining **campsite**, and seals and shags to view on the nearby shingle. The pub also puts on live music most weeks, and hosts a week-long **folk festival** in early June.

Isle of Islay

Islay (pronounced "eye-la") is famous for one thing – single malt **whisky**. The smoky, peaty, pungent quality of Islay whisky is unique, recognizable even to the untutored palate, and all five of the island's distilleries will happily take visitors on a guided tour, ending with the customary complimentary tipple. Yet, despite the fame of its whiskies, Islay remains relatively undiscovered, much as Skye and Mull were some twenty years ago. Part of the reason, no doubt, is that it takes an expensive, two-hour ferry journey from Kennacraig on Kintyre to reach the island; and once there, you'll find no luxury hotels or fancy restaurants. Because the island is partially Gaelic-speaking, you'll see bilingual signs in Bowmore, Port Charlotte and elsewhere.

In medieval times, Islay was the political centre of the Hebrides, with **Finlaggan**, near **Port Askaig**, the seat of the MacDonalds, Lords of the Isles. The picturesque, whitewashed villages you see on Islay today, however, date from the planned settlements founded by the Campbells in the late eighteenth and early nineteenth centuries. Apart from whisky and solitude, the other great draw is the **birdlife**, in particular the scores of white-fronted and barnacle geese who winter here. For ten days in late May/early June, the Islay Festival *Feis Ile* takes place, with whisky tasting, pipe bands, folk dancing and other events celebrating the island's Gaelic culture.

Buses and postbuses will get you from one end of the island to the other, but it's as well to know that there is no **public transport** on a Sunday; pick up an area transport guide from the island's tourist office in **Bowmore**. The **airport**, which lies between Port Ellen and Bowmore, has regular flights to and from Glasgow, and the local bus or postbus will get you to either of the above villages. For a local point of view and news of up-and-coming events, pick up a copy of the fortnightly *Ileach*.

Port Ellen and the Oa

Notwithstanding the comings and goings of the ferry from Kennacraig, **PORT ELLEN**, the largest place on Islay, is a sleepy little place, laid out as a planned village in 1821 by Walter Frederick Campbell and named after his wife. The neat terraces along the harbour are pretty enough, but the bay is dominated by the now disused whisky distillery – the smell of malt which wafts across the harbour comes from the modern maltings just off the Bowmore road. For information about the southern half of Islay, check out the ad hoc **tourist office** (usually open Mon–Fri 9am–1pm) based in a caravan beside the *White Hart Hotel*, along the road to Bowmore. Mike Stuart, 91 Lennox St (☎01496/302391; ③), offers excellent **B&B**, while the *Trout Fly* on Charlotte Street (☎01496/302204; ③), also has rooms and a good restaurant. In nearby **KINTRA**, three miles northwest of Port Ellen, at the southern tip of Laggan Bay, there's an independent **hostel** and B&B at *Kintra Farm* (☎01496/302051; ①/③), whose adjacent

campsite has good facilities (April–Sept). Those with money to indulge themselves should head for the excellent *Glenmachrie Farmhouse* (☎01496/302560; ⑤), ten minutes' drive north of Port Ellen, on the A846 to Bowmore.

From Port Ellen, a dead-end road heads off east along the coastline, passing three distilleries in as many miles. First comes **Laphroaig distillery** (tours by appointment only; ☎01496/302418), which produces the most uncompromisingly smoky of the Islay whiskies. As every bottle of Laphroaig tells you, translated from the Gaelic the name means "the beautiful hollow by the broad bay", and, true enough, the whitewashed distillery is indeed in a gorgeous setting by the sea. It's also the first whisky ever to be officially supplied to a member of the royal family (Prince Charles, of course) and each bottle now bears the "By Appointment" stamp. The **Lagavulin distillery** (Mon–Fri tours by appointment; ☎01496/302400), a mile down the road, produces a superb sixteen-year-old single malt, while the **Ardbeg distillery**, another mile on, sports the traditional pagoda-style roofs of the malting houses – though sadly it's currently closed. Each tour offers a taster, but a bottle of the stuff is no cheaper at source, so expect to pay at least £20.

Armed with a bottle of your choice, you could do worse than head down to the shoreline just beyond Lagavulin and have a tot or two beside **Dunyvaig Castle** (*Dùn Naomhaig*), a romantic ruin on a promontory looking out to the tiny isle of Texa. There are a handful of **B&Bs** along the rapidly deteriorating road – *Tigh-na-Suil* (☎01496/302483; ③) has a lovely secluded position. A mile beyond this, the simple thirteenth-century **Kildalton Chapel** boasts a wonderful eighth-century Celtic cross made from the local "bluestone", which is, in fact, a rich bottle-green. The quality of the scenes matches any to be found on the crosses carved by the monks in Iona: Mary and child are on one side, with what look like elephants on the other.

The most dramatic landscape on Islay is to be found in the nub of land to the southwest of Port Ellen known as **The Oa** (pronounced "o"). This windswept and inhospitable landscape, much loved by illicit whisky distillers and smugglers over the centuries, culminates in some awesome cliffs around the Mull of Oa, inhabited by, among others, choughs, feral goats and, down below, basking seals. The road goes as far as **Upper Killeyan**, and you'll have to walk the last mile to the cliff's edge, for superb views and to see the monument erected by the American National Red Cross in memory of those who died when the *Tuscania* was torpedoed seven miles offshore in February 1918, and when the *Otranto* was shipwrecked in October of the same year. The memorial is inscribed with the unusual sustained metaphor: "On Fame's eternal camping ground, their silent tents are spread, while glory keeps with solemn round, the bivouac of the dead".

Bowmore

At the northern end of the seven-mile-long Laggan Bay lies **BOWMORE**, Islay's administrative capital, with a population of around 900. It was founded in 1768 to replace the village of Kilarrow, which was deemed by the local laird to be too close to his own residence. It's a striking place, laid out in a grid-plan rather like Inveraray, with Main Street climbing up the hill in a straight line from the pier on Loch Indaal to the town's crowning landmark, the **Round Church**. A little to the west of Main Street is **Bowmore distillery** (guided tours Mon–Fri 10.30am & 2pm; ☎01496/810441), the first of the legal Islay distilleries, founded in 1779 and still occupying its original buildings.

Islay's only official **tourist office** is in Bowmore (April–June Mon–Fri 9.30am–5.30pm; June also Sun 2–5pm; July–Sept Mon–Sat 9am–5.45pm, Sun 11am–5pm; Oct–March Mon–Fri 10am–4pm; ☎01496/810254), and can help you find accommodation anywhere on Islay or Jura. The nicest of Bowmore's several **hotels** is the *Lochside* on Shore Street (☎01496/810244; ④); *Lambeth House* on Jamieson Street (☎01496/810597; ③) is also worth a try. For **food**, head to the *Harbour Inn* (☎01496/810330; ⑤) on Main Street, to sample the local prawns and warm yourself by a peat fire, or try the homely food at *The Cottage*, further up on the same side of the street.

Gruinart Flats and Loch Gruinart

North of Bowmore, off the road to Port Charlotte, is the **RSPB nature reserve** of **Gruinart Flats**, in the fields to the south of **Loch Gruinart**. A working farm was purchased to encourage barnacle geese to winter here rather than on the Islay farmers' land. The geese come here for the first grass shoots of spring, which give them the energy to make the last leg of their journey to Greenland. The **RSPB visitor centre** (open at any reasonable time) at Aoradh (pronounced "oorig") houses an observation point with telescopes and a CCTV link with the flats; there's also a hide across the road looking north over the salt flats at the head of the loch. Barnacle and white-fronted geese begin to arrive in mid-September, and by late October more than 18,000 geese are living on the reserve. By the end of April, the geese have all left, but in summer you can see numerous lapwing, snipe and redshanks, and listen to the call of the corncrake.

From the nature reserve, a road heads north parallel to the west shore of Loch Gruinart looking down onto the sands. Halfway along, choughs nest in the ruins of **Kilnave Chapel**, whose graveyard contains an impressive Celtic cross. The road ends at Ardnave Loch, beyond which lie numerous sand dunes, where seals often sun themselves, while otters fish offshore. Nature lovers should hole themselves up in *Loch Gruinart House* (☎01496/850212; ③) by the reserve, or at the rudimentary *Craigens Farm* **campsite** by the head of the loch (☎01496/850256; April–Oct).

The Rhinns of Islay

PORT CHARLOTTE, founded in 1828 by Walter Frederick Campbell and named after his mother, is generally agreed to be Islay's prettiest village. Known as the "Queen of the Rhinns" ("rhinns" – more correctly "rinns" – is derived from the Gaelic word for promontory), its immaculate whitewashed cottages hug the sandy shores of Loch Indaal. East of the village, the imaginative **Museum of Islay Life** (Easter–Oct Mon–Sat 10am–4.30pm, Sun 2–4.30pm; £1.60), has a children's corner, a good library of books about the island, and tantalizing snippets about eighteenth-century illegal whisky distillers. The **Wildlife Information Centre** (Easter–Oct Tues & Thurs 10am–5pm, Fri & Sun 2–5pm; £1.50), housed in the former distillery warehouse, is also worth a visit for anyone interested in the island's fauna and flora. Tickets are valid for a week, allowing you to go back and identify things you've seen on your travels. As for **accommodation**, the best bet is the welcoming *Port Charlotte Hotel* (☎01496/850360; ⑦), down by the shore, which also has a decent (and not too expensive) restaurant. Other options include the inexpensive B&B run by *Mrs Brown* (☎01496/850495; ③) on the main street, or the youth hostel (☎01496/850385; mid-March to Oct), housed in an old bonded warehouse next door to the Wildlife Information Centre. The *Croft Kitchen* (mid-March to mid-Oct), near the museum, serves hot meals; including several vegetarian dishes.

The coastal road culminates seven miles south of Port Charlotte at **PORTNAHAVEN**, a fishing and crofting community since the early nineteenth century. The familiar Hebridean cottages wrap themselves prettily around the steep banks of a deep bay; in the distance, you can see Portnahaven's twin settlement, **PORT WEMYSS**, a mile south. The communities share a church, located between the two near the school, with separate doors for each village. A short way out to sea are two islands, the largest of which, Orsay, sports the **Rhinns of Islay Lighthouse**, built by Robert Louis Stevenson's father in 1825. There are few amenities in this isolated part of Islay, but you'll get **rooms** at the friendly, welcoming *Glenview House* (☎01496/860303; ③), or at the *Old School House* (☎01496/860242; ③) in Portnahaven.

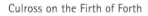

Culross on the Firth of Forth

Tobermory harbour, Mull

The Forth bridges

Celtic cross on the Isle of Oronsay

Iona Abbey

McCaig's Folly from Oban harbour

Autumn around Loch Tummel

Calanais Standing Stones, Lewis

Trotternish peninsula, Isle of Skye

EDMUND NÄGELE

Kilnave Chapel, Islay

JOHN NOBLE

Fingal's Cave, Isle of Staffa

EDMUND NÄGELE

Croft house in North Uist

Those in search of still more solitude should head for the isolated **west coast** of the Rhinns, inhabited mostly by sheep and peppered with sandy beaches. You can stay in great comfort in **KILCHOMAN** at *Kilchoman House* (☎01496/850382; ⑤), which boasts a fine restaurant. Kilchoman's church is in a sorry state of disrepair, but its churchyard contains a fine medieval cross with cups at its base and a wishing stone that should be turned sunwise when wishing; over towards the seashore is the burial ground of the sailors drowned when HMS *Otranto* sank in a storm in October 1918. Beyond lies the lovely golden beach of Machir Bay, which, like Saligo Bay to the north, has dangerous undercurrents.

Finlaggan and Port Askaig

About a mile to the north of Ballygrant, on the road from Bridgend to Port Askaig, lies **Loch Finlaggan**, site of a number of prehistoric crannogs (artificial islands) and, for four hundred years from the twelfth century, headquarters of the Lords of the Isles, who ruled over the Hebrides and Kintyre. You can learn a bit about the history of Finlaggan from the new **visitor centre** (Easter–Oct Tues, Thurs & Sun 2.30–5pm; £1.50), to the northeast of the loch, and view some of the finds from the site, including the head of a commemorative medieval cross. At any time of the day, it's also possible to walk out across the reed beds of the loch and explore **Eilean Mor**, where several carved grave slabs can be seen among the ruins, which seem to support the theory that the Lords of the Isles buried their wives and children, while having themselves interred on Iona. Further out into the loch is another smaller crannog, **Eilean na Comhairle**, originally connected to Eilean Mor by a causeway, where the Lords of the Isles are thought to have held meetings of the Council of the Isles.

Islay's other ferry connection with the mainland, and its sole link with Colonsay and Jura, is from **PORT ASKAIG**, a scattering of buildings which tumble down a little cove by the narrowest section of the Sound of Islay. The *Port Askaig Hotel* (☎01496/840245; ⑥) by the pier enjoys a wonderful position, with views over to the Paps of Jura; there are cheaper B&Bs to choose from, too, such as *Meadowbank* (☎01496/840679; ③). A short walk north along the shore from Port Askaig will bring you to the **Caol Ila distillery** (tours by appointment; ☎01496/840207), named after the Sound of Islay (*Caol Ila*) which it overlooks. The **Bunnahabhainn distillery** (tours by appointment; ☎01496/840646) is a couple of miles further up the coast.

Isle of Jura

The long whale-shaped island of **Jura** – or, to be more accurate, the distinctive Paps of Jura (so called because of their smooth breast-like shape, though there are three of them), the tallest of which, Beinn Oir, rises to 2571ft – seems to dominate every view off the coast of Argyll. Twenty-eight miles long and eight miles wide, Jura is one of the wildest and most mountainous of the Inner Hebrides, its entire west coast uninhabited and inaccessible except to the dedicated walker. The island's name derives from the Norse *dyr-oe* (deer island); appropriately enough, the current deer population outnumbers the two hundred humans 25:1.

Anything that happens on Jura happens in **CRAIGHOUSE**, which lies eight miles along the island's only road from Feolin Ferry, where the Western Ferries car ferry from Port Askaig on Islay arrives. There's an infrequent bus service on the island (Mon–Sat only), several of whose runs are request-only (phone ☎01496/820314 the day before). **Craighouse distillery** (tours by appointment; ☎01496/820240), which looks out across Small Isles Bay to the mainland of Knapdale, is the island's only industry besides crofting and tourism, and welcomes visitors. The one **hotel**, the family-run *Jura*

Hotel (☎01496/820243; ⑤), centre of the island's social scene, is supplemented by a smattering of local **B&Bs** – call Mr Gilmour (☎01496/820319; ②) or Mrs Boardman (☎01496/820379; ②) – and *Knockrome* (☎01496/820311; ②), a crofthouse overlooking the sea three miles north of the village. At Ardfin, three miles south of Craighouse, you can visit the organic walled garden of **Jura House** (daily dawn–dusk; £2) which specializes in Antipodean plants.

In April 1946, Eric Blair (better known by his pen name of **George Orwell**), suffering badly from TB and intending to give himself "six months' quiet" in which to write his novel, *1984*, moved to a remote farmhouse called Barnhill, on the northern tip of Jura. He lived out a spartan existence there for two years but was forced to return to London shortly before his death. The house, 23 miles north of Craighouse up an increasingly poor road, is as remote today as it was in Orwell's day, and sadly there is no access to the interior.

travel details

Trains
Glasgow (Queen St) to: Arrochar and Tarbert (Mon–Sat 3 daily, Sun 2 daily; 1hr 15min); Dalmally (Mon–Sat 3 daily, Sun 2 daily; 2hr 15min); Helensburgh Central (every 30min; 45min); Helensburgh Upper (Mon–Sat 4 daily, Sun 3 daily; 45min); Oban (Mon–Sat 3 daily, Sun 2 daily; 3hr).

Mainland buses
Campbeltown to: Airport (Mon–Fri 2 daily; 10min); Carradale (Mon–Sat 3–5 daily, Sun 2 daily; 45min); Machrihanish (Mon–Sat 11 daily, Sun 3 daily; 15min); Saddell (Mon–Sat 3–5 daily, Sun 2 daily; 25min); Southend (Mon–Sat 5–6 daily, Sun 4 daily; 23min).

Colintraive to: Dunoon (Mon–Sat 2–3 daily; 40min); Tighnabruaich (Mon–Thurs 1–2 daily; 35min).

Dunoon to: Colintraive (Mon–Sat 2–3 daily; 40min); Inveraray (Tues & Fri 2–4 daily, Sat 5 daily; 1hr 15min); Lochgoilhead (Mon & Fri 2 daily; 1hr 15min).

Glasgow to: Arrochar (Mon–Sat 6 daily, Sun 3 daily; 1hr 10min); Campbeltown (Mon–Sat 3 daily, Sun 2 daily; 4hr 25min); Dalmally (Mon–Sat 4 daily, Sun 2 daily; 2hr 20min); Inveraray (Mon–Sat 6 daily, Sun 3 daily; 1hr 45min); Kennacraig (Mon–Sat 2 daily, Sun 1 daily; 3hr 30min); Lochgilphead (Mon–Sat 3 daily, Sun 2 daily; 2hr 40min); Oban (Mon–Sat 4 daily, Sun 2 daily; 3hr); Tarbert (Mon–Sat 3 daily, Sun 2 daily; 3hr 15min); Taynuilt (Mon–Sat 4 daily, Sun 2 daily; 2hr 45min).

Kennacraig to: Claonaig (Mon–Sat 2–3 daily; 15min); Skipness (Mon–Sat 2–3 daily; 20min).

Inveraray to: Dalmally (Mon–Sat 4 daily, Sun 1 daily; 25min); Dunoon (Tues & Fri 2–4 daily, Sat 5 daily; 1hr 15min); Lochgilphead (Mon–Sat 5 daily, Sun 2 daily; 45min); Oban (Mon–Sat 3 daily, Sun 1 daily; 1hr 5min); Taynuilt (Mon–Sat 3 daily, Sun 1 daily; 45min).

Lochgilphead to: Campbeltown (2–4 daily; 1hr 25min); Crinan (Mon–Fri 1–3 daily, Sat 2 daily; 20min); Inveraray (Mon–Sat 5 daily, Sun 2 daily; 45min); Kilmartin (Mon–Sat 1–6 daily; 15–40min); Oban (Mon–Sat 1 daily; 1hr 25min); Tarbert (2–4 daily; 30min).

Oban to: Appin (2–4 daily; 45min); Benderloch (Mon–Sat 10–14 daily, Sun 6 daily; 20min); Ellenabeich (Mon–Sat 2–4 daily; 45min); Kilmartin (Mon–Sat 1 daily; 1hr 5min); Lochgilphead (Mon–Sat 1 daily; 1hr 25min).

Tarbert to: Campbeltown (4–6 daily; 1hr 10min); Claonaig (Mon–Sat 2–3 daily; 15min); Skipness (Mon–Sat 2–3 daily; 35min); Kennacraig (Mon–Sat 6–8 daily; 15min).

Tighnabruaich to: Portavadie (1–3 daily; 25min); Rothesay (Mon–Thurs 1–2 daily; 1hr).

Island buses
Arran
Brodick to: Blackwaterfoot (Mon–Sat 15–18 daily, Sun 3 daily; 25min–1hr 10min); Lamlash (Mon–Sat 15–16 daily, Sun 10 daily; 15min); Lochranza (Mon–Sat 5–8 daily, Sun 4 daily; 40min); Whiting Bay (Mon–Sat 15–16 daily, Sun 10 daily; 30min).

Bute
Rothesay to: Kilchattan Bay (Mon–Sat 4 daily, Sun 3 daily; 30min); Mount Stuart (1 daily except Tues & Thurs every 45min; 15min); Rhubodach (Mon–Sat 1–2 daily; 20min).

Colonsay
Scalasaig to: Kilchattan (Mon–Fri 2–4 daily; 30min); Kiloran Bay (Mon–Fri 2–3 daily; 12min); The Strand (Mon–Fri 1 daily).

Islay
Bowmore to: Port Askaig (Mon–Sat 7 daily, Sun 1 daily; 30–40min); Port Charlotte (Mon–Sat 5–7 daily; 30min); Portnahaven (Mon–Sat 5–7 daily; 50min).

Port Ellen to: Bowmore (Mon–Sat 4–8 daily, Sun 1 daily; 20–30min).

Jura
Craighouse to: Feolin (Mon–Sat 3–5 daily; 20min); Inverlussa (Mon–Sat 2 daily; 40min).

Mull
Craignure to: Fionnphort (Mon–Sat 3 daily, Sun 2 daily; 1hr 20min); Fishnish (Mon–Sat 3–4 daily; 15min); Salen (Mon–Sat 4 daily, Sun 2 daily; 30min); Tobermory (Mon–Sat 4 daily, Sun 2 daily; 1hr).

Salen to: Ulva Ferry (Mon–Sat 2 daily; 20min–1hr).

Tobermory to: Calgary (Mon–Fri 3 daily, Sat 2 daily; 45min); Dervaig (Mon–Fri 4 daily, Sat 2 daily; 30min); Fishnish (Mon–Sat 3–4 daily; 45min).

Car ferries (summer timetable)
To Arran: Ardrossan–Brodick (Mon–Sat 5–6 daily, Sun 4 daily; 55min); Claonaig–Lochranza (10 daily; 30min); Rothesay–Brodick (Mon, Wed & Fri 1 daily; 2–3hr).

To Bute: Brodick–Rothesay (Mon, Wed & Fri 1 daily; 2–3hr); Colintraive–Rhubodach (frequently; 5min); Wemyss Bay–Rothesay (every 45min; 30min).

To Campbeltown: Ballycastle (Northern Ireland)–Campbeltown (2 daily; 3hr).

To Coll: Oban–Coll (1 daily except Thurs & Sun; 3hr); Mallaig–Coll (June–Aug only Thurs 1 daily; 2hr 20min).

To Colonsay: Kennacraig–Colonsay (Wed 1 daily; 3hr 40min); Oban–Colonsay (Mon, Wed & Fri 1 daily; 2hr 10min); Port Askaig–Colonsay (Wed 1 daily; 1hr 20min).

To Dunoon: Gourock (hourly; 20min); McInroy's Point–Hunter's Quay (every 30min; 20min).

To Gigha: Tayinloan–Gigha (hourly; 20min).

To Islay: Colonsay–Port Askaig (Wed 1 daily; 1hr 20min); Kennacraig–Port Askaig (Mon–Sat 1–2 daily; 2hr); Kennacraig–Port Ellen (1 daily except Wed; 2hr 10min); Oban–Port Askaig (Wed 1 daily; 4hr).

To Kintyre: Portavadie–Tarbert (hourly; 20min).

To Lismore: Oban–Lismore (Mon–Sat 2–4 daily; 50min).

To Luing: Scil (Cuan Ferry) Luing (every 30min; 5min).

To Mull: Kilchoan–Tobermory (Mon–Sat 7–8 daily; July & Aug also Sun 5 daily; 35min); Lochaline–Fishnish (Mon–Sat every 40–45min, Sun hourly; 15min); Oban–Craignure (Mon–Sat 5–6 daily, Sun 4–5 daily; 40min).

To Tiree: Oban–Tiree (1 daily except Thurs & Sun; 4hr 15min); Mallaig–Tiree (June–Aug only Thurs 1 daily; 3hr 25min).

Passenger-only ferries (summer only)
To Coll: Tobermory–Coll (Mon, Wed & Sat 1 daily; 1hr 20min).

To Helensburgh: Kilcreggan–Helensburgh (Mon–Sat 2 daily; 30min); Gourock–Helensburgh (Mon–Sat 4 daily; 30–40min).

To Iona: Fionnphort–Iona (Mon–Sat frequently, Sun hourly; 5min).

To Lismore: Port Appin–Lismore (Mon–Sat 7–9 daily, Sun 5–6 daily; 10min).

To Mull: Oban–Tobermory (Mon, Wed & Sat 1 daily; 1hr 45min).

To Tiree: Tobermory–Tiree (Mon, Wed & Sat 1 daily; 2hr 30min).

Flights
Glasgow to: Campbeltown (Mon–Fri 2 daily; 35min–1hr 10min); Islay (Mon–Sat 1–2 daily; 40min); Tiree (Mon–Sat 1 daily; 45min).

CHAPTER SIX

SKYE AND THE WESTERN ISLES

A procession of Hebridean islands, islets and reefs off the northwest shore of Scotland, **Skye and the Western Isles** between them boast some of the country's most alluring scenery. It's here that the turbulent seas of the Atlantic smash up against an extravagant shoreline hundreds of miles long, a geologically complex terrain whose rough rocks and mighty sea cliffs are interrupted by a thousand sheltered bays and, in the far west, a long line of sweeping sandy beaches. The islands' interiors are equally dramatic, a series of formidable mountain ranges soaring high above great chunks of boggy peat moor, a barren wilderness enclosing a host of tiny lakes, or lochans.

Skye and the Western Isles were first settled by Neolithic farming peoples in around 4500 BC. They lived along the coast, where they are remembered by scores of remains, from passage graves through to stone circles – most famously at **Calanais** (Callanish) on Lewis. Viking colonization gathered pace from 700 AD onwards – on Lewis four out of every five place names is of Norse origin – and it was only in 1266 that the islands were returned to the Scottish crown. James VI (and I of England), a Stuart and a Scot, though no Gaelic-speaker, was the first to put forward the idea of clearing the Hebrides, though it wasn't until after the Jacobite uprisings, in which many Highland clans disastrously backed the wrong side, that the **Clearances** began in earnest.

The isolation of the Hebrides exposed them to the whims and fancies of the various merchants and aristocrats who caught "island fever" and bought them up. Time and again, from the mid-eighteenth century to the present day, both the land and its people were sold to the highest bidder. Some proprietors were relatively progressive – like **Lord Leverhulme**, who tried to turn Lewis into a centre of the fishing industry in the 1920s – while others were autocratic – such as **Colonel Gordon of Cluny**, who bought **Benbecula**, South Uist, **Eriskay** and Barra, and forced the inhabitants onto ships bound for North America at gunpoint – but always the islanders were powerless and almost everywhere they were driven from their ancestral homes, robbing them of their particular sense of place. However, their language survived, ensuring a degree of cultural continuity, especially in the Western Isles, where even today the mother tongue of the vast majority is **Gaelic**.

Aficionados of this part of Scotland swear that each island has its own distinct character, and that is to some extent true, although you can split the grouping quite neatly into two. **Skye** and the so-called **Small Isles** – the improbably named **Canna**, **Rum**, **Eigg** and **Muck** – are part of the Inner Hebrides, which also include the islands of Argyll (see the Argyll chapter). Beyond Skye, across the unpredictable waters of the Minch, lie the Outer Hebrides or Outer Isles, nowadays known as the **Western Isles**, a 130-mile-long archipelago stretching from **Lewis** and **Harris** in the north to **Barra** in the south.

Although this area is one of the most popular holiday spots in Scotland, the crowds only become oppressive on Skye, and even here most visitors stick to a well-trodden sequence of roadside sights that leaves the rest of the island unaffected. The main attraction, the spectacular scenery, is best explored on **foot**, following the scores of paths that range from the simplest of cross-country strolls to arduous treks. There are four obvious areas of outstanding natural beauty to aim for: on Skye, the harsh peaks of the **Cuillins** and the bizarre rock formations of the **Trotternish peninsula**, both of which attract hundreds of walkers and mountaineers; on the Western Isles, the mountains of **North Harris**, together with the splendid sandy beaches that string along the Atlantic seaboard of **South Harris** and the **Uists**.

ACCOMMODATION PRICE CODES

Throughout this book, accommodation **prices** have been graded with the codes below, according to the cost of the least expensive double room in high season. Price codes are not given for campsites, most of which charge under £10 per person. Almost all hostels charge less than £10 a night for a bed – the few exceptions to this rule have the prices quoted in the text. For a full account of the accommodation price codes, see p.30.

① under £20	④ £40–50	⑦ £70–80
② £20–30	⑤ £50–60	⑧ £80–100
③ £30–40	⑥ £60–70	⑨ over £100

The tourist world and that of the islanders tend to be mutually exclusive, especially in the Western Isles. There are, however, ways to meet people – not so much by sitting in the pubs (they are few and far between in these parts), than by staying in the B&Bs and getting to know the owners. You could, too, join the locals at church, where visitors are generally welcome. This is a highly **religious region,** dotted with numerous tiny churches, whose denominations differ from island to island. In general terms, the south is predominantly Roman Catholic, while the Calvinist north is a stronghold of the strict Free Church of Scotland – more familiarly known as the "Wee Frees" (see p.347). Another good way to get acquainted with local life is to read the weekly *West Highland Free Press*, a refreshingly vociferous campaigning paper published in **Broadford** on Skye.

Travelling around Skye and the Western Isles requires some degree of forethought. The CalMac **ferries** run to a complicated timetable, and the **bus** services are patchy to say the least. It's also worth reserving space on the ferries as far in advance as possible, as they get very booked up. Also, in accordance with Calvinist dogma, the entire public transport system of Lewis and Harris closes down on **Sunday**; elsewhere only a skeleton service remains. You should consider visiting the islands (particularly Skye) in the spring or early autumn, rather than the height of the summer, both to avoid the crowds and to elude the attentions of the pesky **midge** (see p.21).

SKYE AND THE SMALL ISLES

Justifiably **Skye** was named after the Norse word for cloud (*skuy*), earning itself the Gaelic moniker, *Eilean a Cheo* (Island of Mist). Yet despite the unpredictability of the weather, tourism has been an important part of the island's economy for almost a hundred years now, since the train line pushed through to Kyle of Lochalsh in the western Highlands in 1897. From here, it was the briefest of boat trips across to Skye, and the Edwardian bourgeoisie was soon swarming over to walk its mountains, whose beauty had been proclaimed by an earlier generation of Victorian climbers.

Most visitors still reach Skye from **Kyle of Lochalsh**, linked with Inverness by train, via the new Skye Bridge on one of the frequent buses over to **Kyleakin**, on the western tip of the island. However, this part of Skye is pretty dull, and the more scenic approach – and the main way to get to the **Small Isles** – is from the **ferry** port of **Mallaig**, further south (see p.456). Linked by **train** with Glasgow, the Mallaig boat (up to seven daily) takes thirty minutes to cross to **Armadale**, on the gentle southern slopes of the **Sleat peninsula**. A third option is the privately operated car **ferry** which leaves the mainland at Glenelg, about 25 miles south from Kyle of Lochalsh, to arrive at **Kylerhea**, from where the road heads inland towards **Portree**.

If you're carrying on to the Western Isles, it's 57 miles from Armadale to the opposite end of Skye, where **ferries** leave **Uig** for Tarbert on Harris and Lochmaddy on North Uist. From Mallaig, the round-trip passenger **ferry** crossing to the rocky and frugal Small Isles takes around seven hours depending on the route, and far longer in rough weather. The boat bypasses at least one of the islands each weekday, but it drops by each of the four – **Canna**, **Rum**, **Eigg**, and **Muck** twice on Saturdays, when the sailing times make a day-trip to one of them perfectly feasible.

Skye has several substantial **campsites**, four official **youth hostels** and numerous independent hostels or bunkhouses – all of which recommend advance bookings, par-

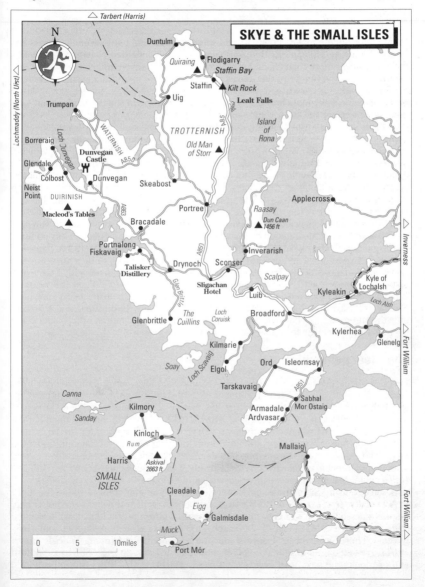

SKYE & THE SMALL ISLES

ticularly in July and August – and a string of very swanky **hotels**. Most visitors arrive by car, as the **bus** services, while adequate between the villages, peter out in the more remote areas, and virtually close down on Sundays. Accommodation on the Small Isles is more limited and requires forward planning at all times of the year; public transport is nonexistent and, for the most part, unnecessary.

Skye

Jutting out from the mainland like a giant wing, the bare and bony promontories of the **Isle of Skye** (An t-Eilean Sgiathanach) fringe a deeply indented coastline that makes the island never more than 25, and sometimes as little as seven, miles wide. This causes problems at the height of the tourist season when the main road system begins to bottleneck with coach tours and minibuses and caravans. Yet Skye is a deceptively large island, and you'll get most out of it – and escape the worst of the crowds – if you take the time to explore the more remote parts of the island.

Though some estimate that only half the island's population are *Sgiathanachs* (pronounced "Ski-anaks"), Skye remains the most important centre for **Gaelic culture** and language outside of the Western Isles. Despite the Clearances, which saw an estimated 30,000 emigrate in the mid-nineteenth century, around forty percent of the population is fluent in Gaelic, the Gaelic college on Sleat is the most important in Scotland, and the extreme Sabbatarian Free Church (see p.347) maintains a strong presence. As an English-speaking visitor, it's as well to be aware of the tensions that exist within this idyllic island. For a taste of the resurgence of Gaelic culture, try and get here in time for the Skye and Lochalsh Festival, *Feis an Eilean*, which takes place over two weeks in mid-July.

The most popular destination on Skye is the **Cuillins**, whose jagged peaks dominate the island during clear weather, though to explore them at close quarters you'll need to be a fairly experienced and determined walker. Equally dramatic in their own way are the rock formations of the **Trotternish** peninsula, in the north, from which there are inspirational views across to the Western Isles. If you want to escape the summer crush, shuffle off to **Glendale** and the cliffs of Neist Point or head for the island of **Raasay**, off Skye's east coast. Of the two main settlements, **Broadford** and **Portree**, only the latter has any charm attached to it, though both have tourist offices, and make useful bases, especially for those without their own transport.

The Sleat peninsula

Ferry services (Mon–Sat 6–7 daily; May to mid-Sept also Sun 6 daily; 30min) from Mallaig connect with the **Sleat** (pronounced "Slate") **peninsula**, Skye's southern tip, an uncharacteristically fertile area that has earned it the sobriquet "The Garden of Skye". The CalMac ferry terminal is at **ARMADALE** (Armadal), an elongated hamlet stretching along the wooded shoreline. If you've time to kill waiting for the ferry, take a look at the huge variety of Scottish and Irish knitwear on offer at Ragamuffin by the pier, or if you need a bite **to eat**, pop into the *Pasta Shed* next door, which does a great seafood pizza (eat-in or takeaway). Alternatively, a few hundred yards up the road, *The Gallery* café/restaurant serves inexpensive and delicious fish and seafood dishes.

If you're leaving Skye on the early-morning ferry, you may want to spend the night in Armadale – try *Skye Batiks* B&B (☎01471/844396; ③), near the pier – or, better still, head a mile southwest to neighbouring Ardvasar, where the traditional, whitewashed *Ardvasar Hotel* (☎01471/844223; ⑦; March–Oct) has an excellent restaurant and a lively bar. There are three **hostels** on the peninsula: *Armadale SYHA Hostel* (☎01471/844260; mid-March to Sept) is a ten-minute walk up the A851 to Broadford and overlooks the bay; *Sleat Independent Hostel* (☎01471/844440) is two miles up the same road, beyond Sabhal Mòr Ostaig; while *Hairy Coo Backpackers* (☎01471/833231) is another couple of miles further on, in Toravaig House by Knock Castle. The *SYHA* hostel **rents bikes**, as does the local petrol station (☎01471/844249), close to the pier.

Just past Armadale youth hostel, you'll find the **Clan Donald Visitor Centre** (March–Oct daily 9.30am–5.30pm; gardens open all year; £3.40), housed in the neo-Gothic Armadale Castle, which was built by the MacDonalds as their clan seat in 1815. Part of the castle has been turned into a touristy museum that traces the history of the Gaels, concentrating on medieval times when the MacDonalds were the Lords of the Isles. It's well done, and the sound effects – savage clanging swords and battle songs – just about compensate for the lack of original artefacts, but the handsome forty-acre gardens are the highlight.

A couple of miles up the road in an old MacDonald farm is the **Sabhal Mòr Ostaig** (☎01471/844373), a modern, independent Gaelic college of further education founded by Sir Iain Noble, an Edinburgh merchant banker, who owns a large chunk of the peninsula and is an untiring Gaelic enthusiast. The college runs a variety of extremely popular short courses in Gaelic language, music and culture, and longer full-time courses in Gaelic business, computing and media. If you're looking for a book and tape on beginners' Gaelic, the college bookshop has a good selection.

The loveliest part of the Sleat peninsula, by far, is the west coast: take the winding single-track road over to the scattered settlement of **Tarskavaig**, with its little sandy beach looking out over to Eigg. Further along the coast, through some ancient deciduous woods, you come to **Tokavaig**, where a stony, seaweedy beach overlooked by the ruined Dunscaith Castle boasts views over the entire Cuillin range – this, and neighbouring **Ord**, are the two best places on the whole of Skye from which to view the mountains in fine weather. If you're taken with the area, all three villages have a few small B&Bs dotted around.

Continuing northeast, it's another six miles to **ISLEORNSAY** (Eilean Iarmain), a secluded little village of ancient whitewashed cottages that was once Skye's main fishing port. With the mountains of the mainland on the horizon, the views out across the bay are wonderful, overlooking a necklace of seaweed-encrusted rocks and the tidal **Isle of Ornsay**, which sports a trim lighthouse built by Robert Louis Stevenson's father. You can **stay** at another of Sir Iain Noble's enterprises, the mid-nineteenth-century *Isleornsay Hotel* – also known by its Gaelic name *Hotel Eilean Iarmain* – a pricey place with excellent service, whose **restaurant** serves great seafood (☎01471/833332; ⑨). Also based in Isleornsay is Sir Iain's Gaelic whisky company, Prabann na Linne, which markets a number of unpronounceable Gaelic-named blended and single malt whiskies; the company offers tastings at its head office (phone ☎01471/833266 for opening hours).

Kyleakin and Kylerhea

The aforementioned Sir Iain Noble is also one of the leading advocates of (and investors in) the privately financed **Skye Bridge**, which now links the tidy hamlet of **KYLEAKIN** (Caol Acain) with the Kyle of Lochalsh (see p.460), just half a mile away on the mainland. The bridge, welcomed by the vast majority of islanders, was built entirely by private Anglo-German contractors for a cool £30 million, which they are currently trying to recoup by charging over £5 each way for cars and more than £30 for lorries and coaches, making it the most expensive toll bridge in Europe, and no cheaper than the ferry it replaced. With Labour now in power, the well-orchestrated campaign by SKAT (Skye & Kyle Against Tolls), 350 of whose members have refused to pay the tolls, may yet succeed in either reducing or abolishing the fee.

There's nothing much to see or do in Kyleakin, though you could have a quick look at the scant remains of **Castle Moil**, a fourteenth-century keep poking out into the straits on top of a diminutive rocky knoll. If you're marooned, the official **youth hostel** (☎01599/534585; open all year), an ugly, modern building, is a couple of hundred yards from the old pier; nearby*Skye Backpackers* (open all year; ☎01599/534510) is a more laid-back option. Alternatively, there are several cheap **B&Bs**. **Bike rental** is available from Skye Bikes (☎01599/534795) on the pier.

You can still avoid crossing the Skye Bridge by taking the ferry service (mid-March to mid-May & Sept to mid-Oct Mon–Sat 9am–6pm; mid-May to Aug Mon–Sat 9am–8.30pm, Sun 10am–6pm; 15min) from Glenelg to **KYLERHEA** (pronounced "Kile-ray"), a peaceful little place, some four miles down the coast from Kyleakin. **Seal trips**, organized by Castle Moil Seal Cruises, also set off from the ferry pier, taking you to view the seal colony on Eilean Mhal (4 daily; ☎01599/534641; £5.50). Alternatively, you can walk half an hour up the coast to the Forestry Commission **Otter Hide**, where, if you're lucky, you may be able to spot one of these elusive creatures.

Broadford

Heading west out of Kyleakin or Kylerhea brings you eventually to the island's second-largest village, charmless **BROADFORD** (An t-Ath Leathann), whose mile-long main street curves round a wide bay. Despite its rather unlovely appearance, Broadford makes a useful base for exploring the southern half of Skye, and something of a wet-weather retreat, with the unusual **Skye Serpentarium** (Easter–Oct Mon–Sat 10am–5pm; July & Aug daily 10am–5pm; £2), full of snakes, lizards and frogs to amuse bored children, and the **International Otter Survival Fund** visitor centre (March–Oct daily 9.30am–5pm; £1.50), where you can learn more about the otter and watch a video linkup with the centre's otter pen.

More pragmatically, Broadford has a **tourist office** (April, May & Sept Mon–Sat 9.30am–5.30pm; June Mon–Sat 9am–6pm; July & Aug Mon–Sat 9am–7pm, Sun 10am–5pm; Oct Mon–Sat 9.30am–5pm; ☎01471/822361), next to the Esso garage on the main road, and a bank and bakery at the west end of the village. The *SYHA* **hostel** is on the west shore of Broadford bay (☎01471/822442; March–Dec), or there's the much smaller, more beautiful and primitive *Fossil Bothy* hostel (☎01471/822297 or 822644; Easter–Oct), a mile or so east of the bay, in Lower Breakish, off the road to Kyleakin. Two **B&Bs** which stand out are the delightful old croft-house *Lime Stone Cottage*, 4 Lime Park (☎01471/822142; ③), and the modern, comfortable *Ptarmigan* (☎01471/822744; ④), on the main road. Close to the *Fossil Bothy*, the pleasant *Seagull* **restaurant** (Easter–Oct evenings & Sun lunch only) serves inexpensive local meat and seafood dishes, while you can **rent bikes** from the *SYHA* hostel or from *Fairwinds Guest House* (☎01471/822270; ③; March–Oct), just past the *Broadford Hotel*.

Scalpay, Luib and The Braes

The A850 from Broadford to Portree continues to hug the coast for the next ten miles, giving out views across Loch na Cairidh to the **Isle of Scalpay**, a huge heather-backed lump that looks something like a giant scone, rising to 1298ft at the peak of Mullach na Carn. The island is part red-deer farm, part forestry plantation, and is currently owned by a merchant banker.

As the road twists round into Loch Ainort, there's a turnoff to **Luib Folk Museum** (daily 9am–6pm; £1), a restored "black house", with a tearoom next door. Built low against the wind, the house's thick walls are made up of an inner and outer layer of loose stone on either side of a central core of earth, a traditional type of construction which attracted the soubriquet "black house" (*tigh dubh*) around 1850, when buildings with single-thickness walls known as "white houses" (*tigh geal*) were introduced from the mainland. The Luib museum is run by local museum magnate and restorer, Peter

MacAskill, who's also responsible for two other museums in restored "black houses" on the island.

From the head of Loch Ainort, the main road takes a steep short cut across a pass to Loch Sligachan, while a prettier, minor road meanders round the coast – either way, you'll reach **SCONSER**, departure point for the car ferry to Raasay (see below). On the opposite side of Loch Sligachan are the crofting communities of **The Braes**, who staged a successful rent strike in 1881 against their landlords, the MacDonalds. After eviction summonses were burnt by the crofters, a detachment of fifty Glasgow police were drafted in and took part in a "battle" which aroused a great deal of publicity for the crofters' cause (for more on which, see p.336).

Isle of Raasay

Though it takes only fifteen minutes for the CalMac car ferry to cross to the island from Sconser (Mon–Sat 9–10 daily), **Raasay**, a nature conservancy area with great walks across its bleak and barren hills, remains well off the tourist trail. For much of its history, the island was the property of a branch of the Jacobite MacLeods of Lewis, as a consequence of which it was practically destroyed by government troops in the aftermath of the 1745 uprising. Bonnie Prince Charlie spent a miserable night in a "mean low hut" on Raasay during his flight and swore to replace the burnt turf cottages with proper stone houses (he never did). Not long after the MacLeods were forced to sell up in 1843, the Clearances started in earnest, a period of the island's history immortalized in verse by Raasay poet, Sorley MacLean. In 1921, seven ex-servicemen and their families from the neighbouring isle of Rona illegally squatted crofts on Raasay, and were imprisoned, causing a public outcry. As a result both islands were bought by the government the following year. Rona is now uninhabited, and Raasay's ageing population stands at around 150, most of them members of the Free Presbyterian Church (see p.347). Strict observance of the Sabbath – no work or play on Sundays – is the most obvious manifestation for visitors, who should respect the islanders' feelings.

The ferry docks at the southern tip of the island, an easy fifteen-minute walk from **INVERARISH**, a tiny village set within thick woods on the island's southwest coast. A further half-mile along the coast is the Raasay Outdoor Centre, which occupies the grand Georgian mansion built by the MacLeods in the late 1740s – to be all but ruined by government troops a few years later. The place has since been restored, and now offers comfortable **accommodation** in tastefully Bohemian rooms (☎01478/660266; ③; March to mid-Oct). You can **camp** in the grounds and, for a daily cost of around £25, join in the centre's activity programme – anything from sailing, windsurfing and canoeing, to climbing and hill walking. Close by are two hotels that sit above the seashore looking out over Skye: the likeably old-fashioned *Isle of Raasay Hotel* (☎01478/660222; ⑤), which serves delicious traditional Scottish food, and the pleasant Victorian *Churchton House* (☎01478/660260; ③).

The grounds of the Outdoor Centre slope down to the tiny **harbour**, which is overlooked, from the top of a small hill, by two weathered stone mermaids. A mile or so north along the coast, lies the hamlet of **OSKAIG**, where Mrs MacKay's B&B, 6 Oskaig Park (☎01478/660207; ②), enjoys an idyllic setting with magnificent views; a rough track cuts up the steep hillside from the village to Raasay's isolated but beautifully placed *SYHA* **hostel** (☎01478/660240; mid-May to Sept).

Most of the rest of Raasay is starkly barren, a rugged and rocky terrain of sandstone in the south and gneiss in the north, with the most obvious feature being the curiously truncated basalt cap on top of **Dun Caan** (1456ft), where Boswell "danced a Highland dance" on his visit to the island with Dr Johnson in 1773 – you may feel like doing the same if you're rewarded with a clear view over to the Cuillins and the Outer Hebrides. The trail to the top of the peak is fairly easy to follow, a splendid five-mile trek up through the forest and along the burn behind Inverarish. The quickest return is made down the northwest slope of Dun Caan, but – by going a couple of miles further – you can get back to the ferry along the path by the southeast shore, passing the occasional abandoned crofters' village.

The Cuillins and around

For many people the **Cuillins**, whose sharp snowcapped peaks rise mirage-like from the flatness of the surrounding terrain, are Skye's *raison d'être*. When the clouds finally disperse, they are the dominating feature of the island, visible from every other peninsula on Skye. There are basically three approaches to the Cuillins: from the south, by foot or by boat from Elgol; from the *Sligachan Hotel* to the north; or from Glen Brittle to the west of the mountains. Glen Sligachan is one of the most popular routes, dividing as it does the granite of the round-topped **Red Cuillins** to the east from the dark, coarse-grained gabbro of the jagged-edged **Black Cuillins**, to the west. With some twenty Munros between them, these are mountains to be taken seriously, and many routes through the Cuillins are for experienced climbers only (for more on safety, see p.44).

Elgol and Glen Sligachan

The only reason to visit the desperate-looking village of **ELGOL**, fourteen miles west of Broadford at the tip of the Strathaird peninsula, is to take one of the boats that bob their way across Loch Scavaig (March–Sept 2–4 daily), past a seal colony, to the entrance of **Loch Coruisk** (*coire uish*, "cauldron of water"). A wild, glacial loch, this needle-like shaft of water, nearly two miles long but only a couple of hundred yards wide, lies in the shadow of the highest peaks of the Black Cuillins, a wonderfully dramatic landscape.

The return trip takes around two and a half hours and costs under £10 – for details of sailing times, ring the *Bella Jane* (☎01471/866244), or the *Nicola* (☎01471/866236). Walkers use the boat simply to get to Loch Coruisk, from where there are numerous possibilities for hiking amidst the **Red Cuillins**, the most popular of which is to head north over the pass into **Glen Sligachan**. Alternatively, you could walk round the coast to the sandy bay of **Camasunary**, to the east – a difficult walk that involves a tricky river crossing and negotiating "The Bad Step", an overhanging rock with a 30ft drop to the sea – and either head north to Glen Sligachan, continue south to Elgol, or continue east to the Am Mam shoulder, for a stunning view of mountains and the islands of Soay, Rum, Canna and Sanday. From Am Mam, the path leads down to the Elgol road, joining it at Kilmarie.

The only public transport is the **postbus** from Broadford (Mon–Sat 1–2 daily), which takes two hours to reach Elgol in the morning – so long, in fact, that you're almost bound to miss the afternoon service if you go on a boat trip (check with the tourist office in Broadford). Rather than stay in Elgol, head for *Rowan Cottage* (☎01471/866287; ③; March–Nov), a lovely **B&B** a mile or so east in Glasnakille, or the larger, more luxurious *Strathaird House* (☎01471/866269; ③; April–Sept) just beyond Kilmarie, three miles up the road to Broadford. By far the most popular place to stay, though, is the **campsite** by the *Sligachan Hotel* (☎01478/650204; ⑤) on the A850, at the northern end of Glen Sligachan. The hotel's huge *Seamus Bar* serves food for weary walkers until 10pm, and quenches their thirst with the full range of real ales produced by Skye's very own micro-brewery in Uig.

Glen Brittle and the Black Cuillins

Six miles along the A863 to Dunvegan from the *Sligachan Hotel*, a turning signed Carbost and Portnalong quickly leads to the entrance to stony **Glen Brittle**, edging the western peaks of the Black Cuillins – at the end of the glen, idyllically situated by the sea is the village of **GLEN BRITTLE**. Climbers and serious walkers tend to congregate at the *SYHA* **hostel** (☎01478/640278; mid-March to Sept) or the **campsite** (☎01478/640404;

April–Sept), a mile or so further south behind the wide sandy beach at the foot of the glen. During the summer, two buses a day (Mon–Fri; also Sat in July & Aug) from Portree will drop you at the top of the glen, but you'll have to walk the last seven miles; both the youth hostel and the campsite have grocery stores, the only ones for miles.

From the valley a score of difficult and strenuous trails lead into the **Black Cuillins**, a rough semicircle of peaks rising to about 3000ft, which surround Loch Coruisk. One of the easiest walks is the five-mile round trip from the campsite up **Coire Lagan**, to a crystal-cold lochan squeezed in among the sternest of rockfaces. Above the lochan is Skye's highest peak and the most difficult of the Munros, Sgurr Alasdair (3257ft), while Sgurr na Banachdich is the only other accessible Munro in the Cuillins (for the usual walking safety precautions, see p.44).

If the weather's bad, you could while away an afternoon at **Talisker whisky distillery** (April–Oct Mon–Fri 9am–4.30pm; July & Aug also Sat; Nov–March Mon–Fri 2–4.30pm; by appointment only; ☎01478/640314), which produces a very smoky, peaty single malt. Talisker is the island's only distillery, situated on the shores of Loch Harport at **CARBOST** (and not, confusingly, at the village of Talisker itself, which lies on the west coast). Hostellers might like to know that there are two year-round bunkhouses beyond Carbost near **PORTNALONG**: the *Croft Bunkhouse and Bothies* (☎01478/640254), where you can also camp, is signposted just before you get to Portnalong, while the *Skyewalker Independent Hostel* (☎01478/640250) is a converted school building beyond Portnalong, en route to Fiskavaig.

Dunvegan and the Duirinish peninsula

After the Portnalong and Glen Brittle turning, the A863 slips across bare rounded hills to skirt the bony sea cliffs and stacks of the west coast twenty miles or so north to **DUNVEGAN** (Dùn Bheagain), an unimpressive place strung out along the east shore of the sea loch of the same name. Just to the north of the village, **Dunvegan Castle** (mid-March to Oct daily 10am–5.30pm; £4.80) perches on top of a rocky outcrop, sandwiched between the sea and several acres of beautifully maintained gardens. It's been the seat of the Clan MacLeod since the thirteenth century, but the present greying, rectangular fortress with its uniform battlements and dummy pepper pots dates from the 1840s.

The half-dozen rooms open to the public sport all sorts of clannish trinkets, including a drinking horn, which each new chief was supposed to drain at one draught "without setting down or falling down", and an interesting display on the remote archipelago of St Kilda, long the fiefdom of the MacLeods. There's a lock of hair from the head of Bonnie Prince Charlie (whom the MacLeods, in fact, fought against), but most intriguing of all are the battered remnants of the **Fairy Flag** in the drawing room. This yellow silken flag from the Middle East may have been the battle standard of the Norwegian king, Harald Hardrada, who had been the commander of the imperial guard in Constantinople. Hardrada died trying to seize the English throne at the Battle of Stamford Bridge in 1066, after which his flag was allegedly carried back to Skye by his Gaelic boatmen. More fancifully, MacLeod family tradition asserts that the flag was the gift of the fairies, blessed with the power to protect the clan in times of danger – and as late as World War II MacLeod pilots carried pictures of it for luck.

From the jetty outside the castle there are regular seal-spotting **boat trips** out along Loch Dunvegan, as well as longer and less frequent sea cruises. Dunvegan's newest tourist attraction is the **Giant Angus MacAskill Museum** (daily 10am–6pm; £1), the weakest of Peter MacAskill's three museums on Skye, housed in a restored thatched smithy. The museum's eponymous hero was, in fact, born in the Outer Hebrides in 1825 and emigrated to Nova Scotia when he was just 6. Before his untimely death of a fever at the age of just 38, he toured with the midget, Tom Thumb, who it is said used to dance on his outstretched hand.

Duirinish and Glendale

The hammerhead **Duirinish peninsula** lies to the west of Dunvegan, much of it inaccessible to all except walkers prepared to scale or skirt the area's twin flat-topped peaks – Healabhal Bheag (1600ft) and Healabhal Mhor (1538ft) – known as **MacLeod's Tables**. The main areas of habitation lie to the north, along the western shores of Loch Dunvegan, and in the broad green sweep of **Glen Dale**, attractively dotted with white farmhouses and dubbed "Little England" by the locals, due to its high percentage of "white settlers", English incomers searching for a better life. Glen Dale's current predicament is doubly ironic given its history, for it was here in 1882 that local crofters, following the example of their brethran in The Braes (see p.333), staged a rent strike against their landlords, the MacLeods. Five locals – who became known as the "Glen Dale Martyrs" – were given two-month prison sentences, and eventually, in 1904, the crofters became the first owner-occupiers in the Highlands.

All this, and a great deal more about crofting, is told through contemporary news cuttings at **Colbost Folk Museum** (daily 10am–6pm; £1), the oldest of Peter MacAskill's three Skye museums, situated in a restored "black house", four miles up the road from Dunvegan. A guide is usually on hand to answer questions, the peat fire smokes all day, and there's a restored illegal whisky still round the back. A little further up the shores of the loch is the **Borreraig Park Exhibition Croft** (daily 9am–6pm or later; £1.50), run by the eccentric Spike Manwaring-Spencer, a Liverpudlian settler who has amassed a huge open-air museum of traditional horse-drawn farm machinery.

At **BORRERAIG**, where there was once a famous piping college, is the **MacCrimmon Piping Heritage Centre** (Easter to late May daily except Mon 11am–5.30pm; late May to early Oct daily 11am–5.30pm; £1.50), on the ancestral holdings of the MacCrimmons, hereditary pipers to the MacLeod chiefs for three centuries, until they were sent packing in the 1770s. The plaintive sounds of the *piobaireachd* of the MacCrimmons, the founding family of Scottish piping, fill this illuminating museum – to hear the real thing, go to the annual recital held in Dunvegan Castle early in August. In the village of **GLENDALE**, at Holmisdale House, an English settler has gathered together mountains of childhood toys and games from the last hundred years, and opened a **Toy Museum** (Mon–Sat 10am–6pm; £2), which manages to appeal to all ages.

The west coast of Duirinish is mostly uninhabited now, due to the Clearances of the 1830s, when the villagers were given the choice of emigration or prison. For walkers, though, it's a great area to explore, with blustery but easy footpaths leading to the dramatically sited lighthouse on **Neist Point**, Skye's most westerly spot, which features some fearsome sea cliffs, and wonderful views across the sea to the Western Isles – you can even stay at the lighthouse, too, in one of two self-catering cottages (☎01470/511200). Alternatively, you can head for the sheer 1000ft **Biod an Athair** at the western side of the mouth of Loch Dunvegan, though there's no path, and it's a bit of a slog.

Practicalities

It's unlikely you'll want to stay in Dunvegan, though it does boast several very good, reasonably priced **hotels** and **B&Bs** dotted along the main road, such as the converted traditional croft *Roskhill Guest House* (☎01470/521317; ⑤), *Atholl House Hotel* (☎01470/521219; ④), and the vegetarian B&B, *Kensalroag House* (☎01470/521306; ②; April–Nov). Other possibilities include the beautifully situated *Silverdale* (☎01470/521251; ③) just before you get to Colbost, or the luxurious *Harlosh House* (☎01470/521367; ⑦; April–Oct), four miles south of Dunvegan, plus a couple of B&Bs in Glendale itself. There's a basic lochside **campsite** (April–Sept) a short distance west along the head of Loch Dunvegan. The culinary mecca in the area is the expensive *Three Chimneys* restaurant (☎01470/511258; Mon–Sat), located beside Colbost Folk Museum, which serves sublime meals and is renowned for its marmalade pudding.

Portree

PORTREE, the only real town on Skye, is one of the most attractive fishing ports in northwest Scotland, its deep cliff-edged harbour filled with fishing boats and circled by multicoloured restaurants and guest houses. Originally known as *Kiltragleann* (the church at the foot of the glen), it takes its current name – some say – from *Portrigh* (port of the king), after the state visit James V made in 1540 to assert his authority over the chieftains of Skye. The harbour is overlooked by **The Lump**, a steep and stumpy peninsula with a flagpole on it, that was once the site of public hangings on the island, attracting crowds of up to 5000. Up above the harbour is the spick-and-span town centre, centred around **Somerled Square**, built in the late eighteenth century as the island's administrative and commercial centre, and now housing the bus station and car park.

The **Royal Hotel** occupies the site of the *McNab's Inn* where Bonnie Prince Charlie took leave of Flora MacDonald (see p.339). A mile or so out of town on the Sligachan road, the **Aros Heritage Centre** (daily 11am–5.30pm; £2.50) displays a collection of dioramas and videos that trace the troubled history of the island – an enjoyable way to pass a couple of hours if it's raining. For an alternative and more contemporary view of the island's heritage, head for **An Tuireann Arts Centre**, housed in a converted fever hospital on the Struan road (daily 10am–5pm; free), which puts on exhibitions, stages concerts, and has a fine café with a range of hot meals, including several veggie options.

Practicalities

The **tourist office**, just off Bridge Street (April to mid-May Mon–Sat 9am–5.30pm; mid-May to Aug Mon–Sat 9am–7/8pm, Sun 10am–5pm; Sept Mon–Sat 9am–6pm; Oct Mon–Sat 9am–5.30pm, Sun 11am–4pm; Nov–March Mon–Fri 9am–5.30pm, Sat 11am–4pm; ☎01478/612137), will, for a small fee, book **accommodation** for you – especially useful at the height of the season, when things can get very busy; they also have bus timetables and a good selection of maps and guides. Accommodation prices tend to be higher in Portree than elsewhere on the island, especially in the town itself, though B&Bs on the outskirts are usually cheaper. The *Bosville Hotel* (☎01478/612846; ⑤), on Bosville Terrace (☎01478/612641; ⑤), is the pick of the hotels, followed by the cosy *Tongadale* (☎01478/612115; ④) on Wentworth Street, and the *Rosedale Hotel*, converted from former fishermen's houses on the harbour front (☎01478/613131; ⑦), though the latter is pricey. Back on Bosville Terrace, the best option is *Coolin View Guest House* (☎01478/612300; ④), with *Harbour View* (☎01478/612069; ③) also worth a try. Of Portree's year-round **hostels**, the smartest is the *Portree Independent Hostel* (☎01478/613737) housed in the Old Post Office on the Green, though the *Portree Backpackers Hostel* (☎01478/613332), ten minutes' walk up the Dunvegan road, enjoys a more secluded location (and will pick you up from town if you ring ahead). Torvaig **campsite** (☎01478/612209; April–Oct) lies a mile and a half north of town off the A855 Staffin road.

The best **food** in town is at the *Bosville Hotel*'s *Chandlery* restaurant; it's pricey but serves excellent meals, with its sister *Bosville* restaurant being slightly cheaper. The *Lower Deck Seafood Restaurant* on the harbour has a wood-panelled warmth to it, and is reasonably priced at lunchtime (less so in the evenings); for a budget feast, pop next door to their excellent fish-and-chip shop. *The Café*, an ice-cream parlour on Wentworth Street, serves real cappuccino and espresso, plus a selection of cakes and snacks. The bar of the *Pier Hotel* on the quayside is the fishermen's drinking hole, while the bar of the *Royal Hotel* is also popular with locals.

For **bike rental**, go to Island Cycles (Mon–Sat; ☎01478/613121) on the Green; for **horse riding** head for Skye Riding Centre (April–Dec; ☎01470/532233), four miles along the Uig road (A856). Day or half-day **boat trips** leave the pier for daily excursions to Raasay and Rona (April–Oct; ☎01478/613718); **diving** can organized through Hebridean Diving Services in Lochbay, towards Dunvegan (☎01478/592219).

The Trotternish peninsula

Protruding twenty miles north from Portree, the **Trotternish peninsula** boasts some of the island's most bizarre scenery, particularly on the central mountain range, where volcanic basalt has pressed down on the softer sandstone and limestone underneath, causing massive landslides. These, in turn, have created sheer cliffs, peppered with outcrops of hard, wizened basalt, which run the full length of the peninsula. These pinnacles and pillars are at their most eccentric in the Quiraing, above Staffin Bay, on the east coast. The peninsula is best explored with your own transport, but an occasional bus service (Mon–Sat 4 daily) along the road encircling the peninsula gives access to almost all the coast.

The east coast

The first geological eccentricity on Trotternish, six miles north of Portree along the A855, is the **Old Man of Storr**, a distinctive column of rock, shaped like a willow leaf, which, along with its neighbours, is part of a massive landslip. Huge blocks of stone still occasionally break off the cliff face of the Storr (2358ft) above and slide downhill. At 165ft, the Old Man is a real challenge for climbers; less difficult is the half-hour trek up the new footpath to the foot of the column from the woods beside the car park.

Five miles further north, there's another turn-off to the **Lealt Falls**, at the head of a gorge which spends most of its day in shadow (and is home to a fiendish collection of midges). Walking all the way down to the falls is pointless, but the views across to Wester Ross from the first stage of the path are spectacular (weather permitting). Another car park four miles up the road gives access to **Kilt Rock**, whose tube-like, basaltic columns rise precipitously from the sea, set amongst sea cliffs dotted with nests for fulmars and kittiwakes. Close by, near the turn off to Elishader, is the slate-roofed **Staffin Museum** (sporadic opening hours; £1.25), which contains fossil finds from the area, and a dinosaur bone discovered here in 1994.

Over the brow of the next hill, Staffin Bay, where several fossilized dinosaur footprints were discovered in 1996, is spread out before you, dotted with whitewashed and "spotty" houses. A single-track road cuts across the peninsula from the north end of the bay, allowing access to the **Quiraing**, a spectacular forest of mighty pinnacles and savage rock formations. There are two car parks: from the first, beside a cemetery, it's a steep half-hour climb to the rocks; from the second on the saddle, it's a longer but more gentle traverse. Once you're in the midst of the rocks, you should be able to make out the Prison, to your right, and the 120ft Needle, to your left; the Table, a great sunken platform where locals used to play shinty, lies above and beyond the Needle, another fifteen-minute scramble up the rocks.

The **accommodation** on the east coast is among the best on Skye, with most places enjoying fantastic views out over the sea. Just before you get to the Lealt Falls, there's the modern *Lealt Falls Hostel* (☎01470/562363; ②; closed Feb), which also does B&B, and beyond it the charming *Glenview Inn* (☎01470/562248; ④), with a very good adjoining restaurant. One of the island's best B&Bs is *Quiraing Lodge* in Staffin (☎01470/562330; ③), set in an acre of well-tended garden a few minutes' walk from the main road, within sight of the Quiraing. It also has an excellent restaurant, this time serving delicious vegetarian food, and also offers **bike rental**. There's a **campsite** (☎01470/562213; April–Sept) south of Staffin Bay. For **food**, head to *The Oystercatcher* tearoom restaurant, in the local community hall, which serves excellent seafood platters. In fine weather, you can enjoy bar snacks on the castellated terrace of the *Flodigarry Country House Hotel* (☎01470/552203; ⑧), three miles up the coast from Staffin. Behind the hotel (and now part of it) is the cottage where local heroine Flora MacDonald and her family lived from 1751 to 1759. If the hotel's rooms are beyond your means, try the neat and tidy *Dun Flodigarry Backpackers' Hostel* (☎01470/552212; open all year), a couple of minutes' walk away.

BONNIE PRINCE CHARLIE

Prince Charles Edward Stewart – better known as **Bonnie Prince Charlie** or "The Young Pretender " – was born in Rome in 1720, where his father, "The Old Pretender", claimant to the British throne, was living in exile. At the age of 25, having little military experience, no knowledge of Gaelic, an imperfect grasp of English and a strong attachment to the Catholic faith, the prince set out for Scotland on a French ship, disguised as a seminarist from the Scots College in Paris. He arrived on the Hebridean island of Eriskay on July 23, 1745, and was immediately implored to return to France by the clan chiefs, who were singularly unimpressed by his lack of army. Charles was unmoved and went on to win the battle of Prestonpans, marching on London and reaching Derby before finally calling a retreat. Back in Scotland, he won one last victory at Falkirk, before the final disaster at Culloden in April 1746.

The prince spent the following five months in hiding, with a price of £30,000 on his head, and literally thousands of government troops searching for him. He certainly endured his fair share of cold and hunger whilst on the run, but the real price was paid by the Highlanders themselves, who risked their lives (and often paid for it with them) by aiding and abetting the prince. The most famous of these was, of course, 23-year-old **Flora MacDonald**, whom Charles met on South Uist in June 1746. Flora was persuaded – either by his beauty or her relatives, depending on which account you believe – to convey Charles "over the sea to Skye", disguised as an Irish servant girl by the name of Betty Burke. She was arrested just seven days after parting with the prince in Portree, and held in the Tower of London until July 1747. She went on to marry a local man, had seven children and lived to the age of 68.

Charles eventually boarded a ship back to France in September 1746, but, despite his promises – "for all that has happened, Madam, I hope we shall meet in St James's yet" – never returned to Scotland, nor did he ever see Flora again. After mistreating a string of mistresses, he eventually got married at the age of 52 to the 19-year-old Princess of Stolberg, in an effort to produce a Stewart heir. They had no children, and she eventually fled from his violent drunkenness; in 1788, a none-too-"bonnie" Prince Charles died in the arms of his illegitimate daughter in Rome. Bonnie Prince Charlie became a legend in his own lifetime, but it was the Victorians who really milked the myth for all its sentimentality, conveniently overlooking the fact that the real consequence of 1745 was the virtual annihilation of the Highland way of life.

The west coast

Beyond **Flodigarry**, the A855 veers off to the west coast, rounding the tip of the Trotternish ridge before reaching **DUNTULM** (Duntuilm), whose heyday as a major MacDonald power base is recalled by the shattered remains of a headland fortress abandoned by the clan in 1732 after a clumsy nurse dropped one of their babies from a window onto the rocks below. The swanky *Duntulm Castle Hotel* (☎01470/552213; ④; Easter–Oct) is close by, and provides wonderful views across the Minch to the Western Isles.

Heading down the west shore of the Trotternish, it's two miles to the **Skye Museum of Island Life** (Easter–Oct Mon–Sat 9.30am–5.30pm; £1.75), an impressive cluster of thatched "black houses" on an exposed hill overlooking Harris. The museum, run by locals, gives a fascinating insight into a way of life that was commonplace on Skye a hundred years ago. The "black house", now home to the ticket office, is much as it was when it was last inhabited in 1957, while the two houses to the east contain interesting snippets of local history. Behind the museum up the hill are the graves of **Flora MacDonald** and her husband. Thousands turned out for her funeral in 1790, creating a funeral procession a mile long – indeed, so widespread was her fame that the original family mausoleum fell victim to souvenir hunters and had to be replaced. The Celtic cross headstone is inscribed with a simple tribute by Dr Johnson, who visited her in

1773: "Her name will be mentioned in history, if courage and fidelity be virtues, mentioned with honour".

A further four miles south is the ferry port of **UIG** (Uige), which curves its way round a dramatic, horseshoe-shaped bay, and is the arrival point for ferries from Tarbet (Harris) and Lochmaddy (North Uist); the **tourist office** (April–Oct Mon–Sat 8.45am–6.30pm; mid-July to mid-Sept also Sun 8.45am–2pm; ☎01470/542404) is inside the CalMac office on the pier. Uig **campsite** (☎01470/542360; March–Oct) is by the shore near the dock, while the **youth hostel** (☎01470/542211; mid-March to Oct), high up on the south side of the village, has exhilarating views over the bay. At the other end of the accommodation spectrum is the *Uig Hotel* (☎01470/542205; ⑤; April–Oct), an attractive old coaching inn that serves good home-made **food**; cheaper B&Bs include *Braeholm* (☎01470/542396; ③) and the modern *Idrigill House* (☎01470/542398; ③). The *Pub at the Pier* offers filling meals, and serves the local Skye beers, which are brewed at the brewery close by (tours by appointment Mon–Fri; ☎01470/542477). **Bike rental** is available from North Skye Bicycle Hire, **pony trekking** from the *Uig Hotel*, and **windsurfing and canoeing** is organized by Whitewave (☎01470/542414) in Linicro, a couple of miles north of Uig.

The Small Isles

The history of the **Small Isles**, which lie to the south of Skye, is typical of the Hebrides: early Christianization, followed by a period of Norwegian rule that ended in 1266 when the islands fell into Scottish hands. Their support for the Jacobite cause resulted in hard times after the failed rebellion of 1745, but the biggest problems came with the introduction of the **potato** in the mid-eighteenth century. The consequences were as dramatic as they were unforeseen: the success of the crop and its nutritional value – when grown in conjunction with traditional cereals – eliminated famine at a stroke, prompting a population explosion. In 1750, there were just 1000 islanders, but by 1800 their numbers had almost doubled.

At first, the problem of overcrowding was camouflaged by the **kelp** boom, in which the islanders were employed, and the islands' owners made a fortune, gathering and burning local seaweed to sell for use in the manufacture of gunpowder, soap and glass. But the economic bubble burst with the end of the Napoleonic Wars and, to maintain their profit margins, the owners resorted to drastic action. The first to sell up was Alexander Maclean who sold Rum as grazing land for **sheep**, got quotations for shipping its people to Nova Scotia, and gave them a year's notice to quit. He also cleared Muck to graze cattle, as did the MacNeills on Canna. Only on Eigg was some compassion shown: the new owner, a certain Hugh MacPherson, who bought the island from the Clanranalds in 1827, actually gave some of his tenants extended leases.

Since the Clearances each of the islands has been bought and sold several times, though only **Muck** is now privately owned by the benevolent laird, Lawrence MacEwen. **Eigg** hit the headlines in 1997, when the islanders finally managed to buy the island themselves and put an end to more than 150 years of property speculation. The other islands were bequeathed to national agencies: **Rum**, the largest and most visited of the group, possessing a cluster of formidable volcanic peaks and the architecturally remarkable Kinloch Castle, passed to the Nature Conservancy Council (now Scottish Natural Heritage) in 1957; and **Canna**, by far the prettiest of the isles with its high basalt cliffs, has been under the auspices of the NTS since 1981.

Canna

Measuring a mere five miles by one, and with a Catholic and Gaelic-speaking population of just twenty, **Canna** is run as a single farm by the National Trust of Scotland. The island enjoys the best harbour in the Small Isles, a horn-shaped haven at its southeastern corner protected by the tidal island of Sanday, now linked to Canna by a footbridge. For visitors, the chief pastime is walking: from the dock it's about a mile across a grassy basalt plateau to the bony sea cliffs of the north shore, and about the same to the top of Compass Hill (458ft) – so called because its high metal content distorts compasses – in the northeastern corner of the island, from where you get great views across to Rum and Skye. The cliffs of the buffeted western half of the island are a breeding ground for both Manx shearwater and puffin; some seven miles offshore, you can see the **Heiskeir of Canna**, a curious mass of stone columns sticking up 30ft above the water.

With permission, you may **camp rough** on Canna, otherwise the only place is the NTS-owned *Tighard*, half a mile from the jetty, which sleeps a maximum of ten people and costs around £300 per week, rising to £500 in July and August. Booking forms are available from Holiday Cottages, NTS, 5 Charlotte Square, Edinburgh (☎0131/226 5922). Remember, however, that there are no shops on Canna (bar the post office), so you must bring your own supplies.

Rum

Like Skye, **Rum** is dominated by its Cuillins, which, though they only reach a height of 2663ft at the summit of Askival, rise up with comparable drama to the south of the island. The majority of the island's thirty or so inhabitants now live in **KINLOCH**, on the east coast, and most are employed by Scottish Natural Heritage. Loch Scresort, the pencil-thin harbour of Rum, is too shallow to take the passenger **ferry** from Mallaig, so incomers have to hop off onto the island tender, which lands them just a few minutes' walk along the shore from Kinloch. The island's best beach is at **KILMORY**, to the north, though it is periodically out of bounds to the public, since this part of the island is given over to the study of Rum's large red deer population. When the island's human head count peaked at 450 in 1791, the hamlet of **HARRIS** housed a large crofting community – all that remains now are several ruined "black houses" and the Bulloughs' extravagant Neoclassical **mausoleum**, built in the style of a Greek Doric temple, overlooking the sea.

Rum's chief attraction, though, is **Kinloch Castle** (whose caretakers are usually keen to show folk around), a reddish sandstone edifice completed in 1901, with elongated arcades and squat turrets that dominate the village of Kinloch. It's an odd-looking place, a hesitant attempt at the Gothic style, but the interior, past the main hall draped with animal skins and a forest of antlers, is extraordinary, packed with the knick-knacks collected by George Bullough, the eccentric son of self-made millionaire, Sir John Bullough, who had bought the place as a part-time hunting lodge in 1888. Bullough himself, keen to impress his guests, not only paid a piper to play at every sunset, but also had an orchestrion, an electrically driven barrel organ crammed in under the stairs to grind out an eccentric mixture of pre-dinner tunes – *The Ride of the Valkyries* and *Ma Blushin' Rosie*, among others, are still played. The *pièce de résistance*, though, has to be Bullough's **Edwardian shower**, whose six dials, on the hooded headpiece, fire high-pressure water from every angle. Outside, but long gone, great glasshouses once sheltered tropical trees, and heated pools were stocked with turtles and alligators, though these were eventually removed at the insistence of the terrified staff. The year before the house was completed, Bullough had, at his own expense, sent a hospital ship to the Boer War. He was rewarded with a knighthood, but, as the grandson of a Lancashire weaver, was still kept at arm's length by the aristocracy, who mocked both him and the unlettered taste of his castle. Hurt, Sir George began to keep strangers off the island and the house was barely used when he died in 1939.

Practicalities

Since **accommodation** is limited, many people simply come on a day -trip – if you plan to stay longer, book well in advance. Bear in mind, too, that Rum is the wettest of the

Small Isles, and a haven for midges (see p.21) – come prepared for both. *Kinloch Castle* (☎01687/462037; ⑤) still lets a few of its four-poster rooms, and has a small restaurant, but it's a shadow of its former self; there's also a thirty-bed independent **hostel** (number as for *Kinloch Castle*) in the old servants' quarters. Other accommodation options in Kinloch include two cheap and simple **bothies** (two nights maximum stay), and **camping** on the foreshore near the jetty – for both, contact the reserve manager at the *White House* (Mon–Fri 9am–12.30pm; ☎01687/462026). The resident reserve manager will also advise on local **walks**, the most dramatic being the trail along the southern shoreline beneath the mountain peaks, and you must ask his permission to climb any of the mountains.

Eigg

Having endured an unhappy history of private ownership – most notoriously with the Olympic bobsleigher and gelatine heir Keith Schellenburg – **Eigg** was finally bought for £1.5 million by the Eigg Heritage Trust, set up by the islanders in conjunction with the Scottish Wildlife Trust. The last owner, fire-worshipping German artist Professor Marlin Eckhard, aka Maruma, had to sell up after he got into problems with tax officials. The 63 islanders now plan to develop eco-friendly tourism and pursue their own small businesses without interference from an absentee landlord.

Eigg is without doubt the most easily distinguishable of the Small Isles from a distance, since it is almost entirely surrounded by 1000ft cliffs rising up to a plateau. The ferry drops anchor in the southeast at **GALMISDALE** (again passengers are transferred to the island on a smaller boat), overlooked by the island's great landmark, **An Sgurr** (1292ft), a basalt stump that rises out of the plateau another 290ft. The view from the latter out to Rum is spectacular, and around the summit is a large colony of Manx shearwater. The other special feature of the island – which measures just five miles by three – is the "Singing Sands", to the north of the island's main village **CLEADALE**. Here, the beach is comprised of quartz, which crunches underfoot when dry (hence the name).

Eigg's **B&Bs** charge around £28 per person for full board: try the croft house *Lageorna* (☎01687/482405) or *Laig Farm* (☎01687/482437). If you plan to **camp**, bring your own supplies, though there is a basic shop (and a post office) at Galmisdale.

Muck

Smallest and most southerly of the Small Isles, **Muck** is low-lying, mostly treeless and extremely fertile, and as such shares more characteristics with the likes of Coll and Tiree than its nearest neighbours. Its name derives from *muc*, the Gaelic for "pig" – or, as some would have it, *muc mara*, "sea pig" or porpoise, which abound in the surrounding water – and has long caused much embarassment to generations of lairds who preferred to call it the "Isle of Monk", because it had briefly belonged to the medieval church. **PORT MÓR**, on the southeast corner of the island, is where the ferry drops anchor and discharges its passengers onto a smaller vessel. The MacEwen family, which has owned the island since 1896, run the island's main farm, with two tenant farmers and around 25 inhabitants. You can **stay** at *Port Mór House* (☎01687/462365) for £32 per person full board, at the island's **bunkhouse** (☎01687/462042) or, with permission, **camp rough**.

THE WESTERN ISLES

The wild and windy **Western Isles** – also known as the Outer Hebrides – vaunt a strikingly hostile mix of landscapes from windswept golden sands to harsh, heather-backed mountains and peat bogs. An elemental beauty pervades each of the more than two hundred islands that make up the archipelago, only a handful of which are actually inhabited by a total of just over 30,000 people. The influence of the Atlantic Gulf Stream ensures a mild but moist climate, though you can expect the strong Atlantic winds to blow in rain on two out of every three days even in summer. Weather fronts, however, come and go at such dramatic speed in these parts, that there's little chance of mist or fog settling and few problems with midges.

The most significant difference between Skye and the Western Isles is that here tourism is much less important to the islands' fragile economy, still mainly concentrated around crofting, fishing and weaving, and the percentage of "white settlers" is a lot lower. The Outer Hebrides remain the heartland of **Gaelic** culture, with the language spoken by the vast majority of islanders, though its everyday usage remains under constant threat from the national dominance of English. Its survival is, in no small part, due to the all-pervading influence of the Free Church, whose strict Calvinism is the creed of the vast majority of the population, with only the sparsely populated South Uist, Barra and parts of Benbecula adhering to the more relaxed demands of Catholicism.

The interior of the northernmost island, **Lewis**, is mostly peat moor, a barren and marshy tract that gives way abruptly to the bare peaks of **North Harris**. Across a narrow isthmus lies **South Harris**, presenting some of the finest scenery in Scotland, with wide beaches of golden sand trimming the Atlantic in full view of the mountains and a rough boulder-strewn interior lying to the east. Further south still, a string of tiny, flatter islets, mainly **North Uist, Benbecula**, **South Uist** and **Barra**, offer breezy beaches, whose fine sands front a narrow band of boggy farmland, which, in turn, is mostly bordered by a lower range of hills to the east.

In direct contrast to their wonderful landscapes, the Western Isles claim the scrawniest of villages, unhappy-looking places that straggle out along the elementary road system. Only **Tarbert**, on Harris, and **Lochmaddy**, on North Uist, sustain a modicum of charm; **Stornoway**, Lewis's only town, is eminently unappealing. Many visitors, walkers and nature watchers forsake the settlements altogether and retreat to secluded cottages and B&Bs – though this is difficult without your own transport.

Visiting the Western Isles

British Airways Express operates fast and frequent **flights** (Mon–Sat only) from Glasgow and Inverness to Stornoway on Lewis, Barra and Benbecula on North Uist. But be warned, the weather conditions on the islands are notoriously changeable, making flights prone to both delay and stomach-churning bumpiness. On Barra, the other complication is that you land on the beach, so the timetable is adjusted with the tides. CalMac **car ferries** run from Ullapool in the Highlands to Stornoway (Mon–Sat only); from Uig, on Skye, to Tarbert and Lochmaddy (Mon–Sat only); and from Oban and Mallaig to South Uist and Barra (daily). There's also an **inter-island ferry** from Leverburgh, on Harris, to Otternish, on North Uist, and between South Uist and Barra (for more on ferry services, see "Travel details" on p.363).

Although travelling around the islands is time-consuming, for many people this is part of their charm. A series of inter-island causeways makes it possible to drive from one end of the Western Isles to the other with just two interruptions – the CalMac **ferry** trip from Harris to North Uist, and the one from South Uist to Barra. The islands boast a distinctly low-key **bus** service, with no buses on Sundays. Note, however, that several local companies offer very reasonable **car rental** – around £100 a week – though you're not permitted to take their vehicles off the Western Isles (see p.27 for details).

The islands' seven official **youth hostels** – there are also several independents – are geared up for the outdoor life, occupying remote locations on or near the coast. Several of them are run by the Gatliff Hebridean Hostels Trust, who have renovated some isolated crofters' cottages. None of these has phones, so you can't book in advance, and you really need to bring your own bedding; each has a simple kitchen, so take your own food. If you're after a little more comfort, then the islands have a generous sprinkling

---

GAELIC IN THE WESTERN ISLES

Except in Stornoway, and Balivanich on North Uist, **road signs** are now almost exclusively in **Gaelic**, a difficult language to the English-speaker's eye, with complex pronunciation (see p.588), though as a (very) general rule, the English names can often provide a rough pronunciation guide. Particularly if you're driving, it's essential to buy the bilingual Western Isles map, produced by the local tourist board, *Bord Turasachd nan Eilean*, and available at most tourist offices. To reflect the signposting we've put the Gaelic first in the text, with the English equivalent in brackets. Thereafter we've stuck to the Gaelic names, to try to familiarize readers with their (albeit variable) spellings – the only exceptions are in the names of islands and ferry terminals, where we've stuck to the English names after the first mention, partly to reflect CalMac's own policy.

---

of reasonably priced **B&Bs** and **guest houses** – many of which are a lot more inviting than the hotels and can be easily booked through the tourist offices for a small fee.

Leodhas (Lewis)

Shaped rather like the top of an ice-cream cone, **Lewis** is the largest and by far the most populous of the Western Isles and the northernmost island in the Hebridean archipelago. After Viking rule ended in 1266, the island was fought over by the MacLeods and MacKenzies, until it was eventually sold by the latter in 1844. The new owner, Sir James Matheson, invested heavily in new industries, though thousands were still forced to emigrate due to poverty. **Lord Leverhulme** ploughed money into the fishing industry when he aquired the island (along with Harris) in 1918. Though undoubtedly a benevolent despot, Leverhulme's unpopularity with many on Lewis, coupled with his financial difficulties, forced him to give up his grandiose plans in 1923. He gifted Stornoway to its inhabitants and offered free crofts to the islanders, but sadly only 41 took up the offer, and property speculation continues to cause problems. Leverhulme's departure also left a big gap in the economy, and between the wars thousands more emigrated.

Most of the island's 20,000 inhabitants – two-thirds of the Western Isles' total population – now live in the crofting and fishing villages strung out along the northwest coast, between **Calanais** and **Port Nis**, in one of the most densely populated rural areas in the country. On this coast you'll also find the islands' best-preserved **prehistoric remains** – Carloway broch and Calanais Standing Stones – as well as a smattering of ancient crofters' houses in various stages of abandonment. The landscape is mostly flat peat bog – hence the island's name, derived from the Gaelic *leogach* (marshy) – with a gentle shoreline that only fulfils its dramatic potential around Rubha Robhanais (Butt of Lewis), a group of rough rocks on the island's northernmost tip, near Port Nis. To the south, where it is physically joined with Harris, the land rises to just over 1800ft, providing a more exhilarating backdrop for the excellent beaches, peppered along the isolated coastline to the southwest of Calanais.

Most visitors use **Stornoway**, on the east coast, as a base for exploring the island, though this presents problems if you're travelling by **bus**. There's a regular service to Port Nis and Tarbert, and although the most obvious excursion – the 45-mile round trip from Stornoway to Calanais, Carlabhagh, **Arnol** and back – is difficult to complete by public transport, minibus tours make the trip on most days from April to October (see below).

Steornabhagh (Stornoway)

In these parts, **STORNOWAY** is a buzzing metropolis, with some 8000 inhabitants (including a small Gaelic-speaking Asian community), a one-way system, pedestrian precinct with CCTV and all the trappings of a large town. It's a centre for employment, a social hub for the island's youth and, perhaps most importantly of all, home to the **Comhairle nan Eilean Siar** (Western Isles Council), set up in 1974, which has done so much to promote Gaelic language and culture, and try to stem the tide of anglicization. Despite its valiant attempts in that quarter, it is perhaps better known for its

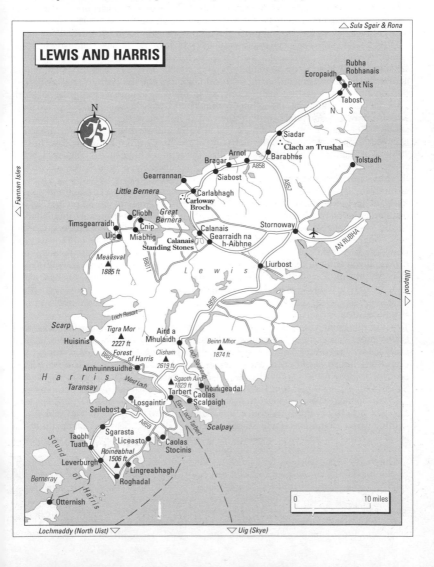

LEWIS AND HARRIS

supremely incompetent financial dealings, which lost the islands £23 million, following the collapse of the Bank of Credit and Commerce International (BCCI) in 1991. For the visitor, the town is unlikely to win any great praise – aesthetics are not its strong point, and the urban pleasures on offer are limited.

For centuries life in Stornoway has focused on its **harbour**, whose deep and shel-tered waters were thronged with coastal steamers and fishing boats in their nineteenth-century heyday, when more than 1000 boats were based at the port. Today, most of the catch is landed on the mainland, and, despite the daily comings and goings of the CalMac ferry from Ullapool, the harbour is a shadow of its former commercial self. The nicest section of the harbour is Cromwell Street Quay, by the tourist office, where the remaining fishing fleet ties up for the night, and the fish market takes place on Tuesday and Thursday evenings. On the other side of the water to the northwest stands **Lews Castle**, a nineteenth-century Gothic pomposity built by Sir James Matheson in 1863, and currently under renovation – the plan is to make it part of the new University of the Highlands and Islands, an ambitious project which aims to link various campuses across the north of Scotland using new technologies. For the visitor, the main attrac-tion, though, is the castle's mature wooded grounds, a unique sight on the Western Isles, for which Matheson had to import thousands of tons of soil from the mainland.

Stornoway's commercial centre, to the east, is little more than a string of unprepos-sessing shops and bars. The one exception is the old town hall, on South Beach, a splendid Scots Baronial building which currently houses the **An Lanntair Art Gallery** (Mon–Sat 10am–5.30pm; free), and features the work of local artists, plus a nice tea-room. Continuing up the pedestrian precinct into Francis Street, you'll eventually reach the **Museum nan Eilean** (April–Sept Mon–Sat 10am–5.30pm; Oct–March Tues–Fri 10am–5pm, Sat 10am–1pm; free). Apart from the chance to view a Gaelic/English CD-ROM on the Lewis Chessmen (see p.352), there is no permanent collection here as yet, but the temporary exhibitions are consistently good. Anyone remotely interested in Harris Tweed should sign up for a guided tour of the **Lewis Loom Centre** (Mon–Sat 10am–5pm; £2), located at the far end of Cromwell Street, in the Old Grainstore off Bayhead; here, you can watch the labour-intensive process of warping, spinning and dyeing. If you enter or exit Stornoway via Willowglen Road (A858), you'll see the town **War Memorial**, a castle tower set high above the town amidst gorse bushes, and a good place to take in the sprawl that is Stornoway.

Practicalities

The best thing about Stornoway is the convenience of its services. The island's **airport** is four miles east of the town centre, a £5 taxi ride away; the swanky new octagonal CalMac **ferry terminal** is on South Beach, close to the **bus station**. You can get bus timetables, a map of the town, and other useful information from the **tourist office**, near North Beach at 26 Cromwell St (April–May & Sept to mid-Oct Mon–Fri 9am–6pm, Sat 9am–5pm; June–Aug Mon, Tues & Thurs 9am–6pm & 8–9pm, Wed & Fri 9am–8pm, Sat 9am–5pm & 8–9pm; mid-Oct to March Mon–Fri 9am–5pm; ☎01851/703088); they also sell tickets for **minibus tours** to Calanais (Mon–Fri) and for Out and About **wildlife trips** round Lewis and Harris. There's a Bank of Scotland cashpoint and a small supermarket opposite the tourist office; the Western Isles' only superstore is ten minutes' walk up Cromwell Street, beyond the post office.

The tourist office will also, for a small booking fee, fix you up with **accommodation**. Of the hotels, the *Royal*, on Cromwell Street (☎01851/702109; ⑥), is the nicest; the solid Victorian *Park* (☎01851/702485; ④) and *Tower* (☎01851/702150; ③) guest hous-es, next door to each other on James Street, are the next best option. Of the **B&Bs** along leafy Matheson Road, try Mrs J Macleod, at no. 25 (☎01851/705419; ②), and Mrs A. Macleod, at no. 12 (☎01851/702673; ③). Stornoway's **independent hostel** is a basic affair about five minutes' walk from the ferry at 47 Keith St (☎01851/703628;

March–Nov). The nearest **campsite**, the *Laxdale Holiday Park* (☎01851/703234; April–Oct), lies a mile or so along the road to Barabhas, on Laxdale Lane.

As for **food**, you can get snacks from the *An Lanntair* tearoom, and good-value, filling meals from the *Fisherman Cafeteria* (Mon–Fri 8am–5pm) in the National Mission to Deep Sea Fishermen building on North Beach. Both the Crown Hotel, nearby on Castle Street, and the *Royal* have decent moderately priced restaurants, and serve bar snacks; for a more surreal experience, head for *Stornoway Balti House*, near the bus station on South Beach. As for **pubs**, try either *The Criterion* on Point Street, or the *Royal Hotel*, Cromwell Street – all pubs are closed on Sundays, while hotel bars are open for residents only. The most famous watering hole, though, is the bar of the *Crown*, where Prince Charles drank a cherry brandy whilst on a school sailing trip (and, more controversially, whilst still under 18). Last, but not least, Stornoway is home to the Western Isles' only **Internet café**, *Captions*, 27 Church St (Mon–Sat 10am–10pm; *bayble@captions.co.uk*), where you can go on line (at £5 an hour) whilst enjoying tea and home-made cakes.

RELIGION IN THE WESTERN ISLES

It is difficult to underestimate the importance of **religion** in the Western Isles, which are sharply divided – though with little enmity – between the Catholic southern isles of Barra and South Uist, and the Protestant islands of North Uist, Harris and Lewis. Most conflicts arise from the very considerable power the ministers of the Protestant Church, or Kirk, wield in secular life in the north, where the creed of **Sabbatarianism** is very strong. Here, Sunday is the Lord's Day, and virtually the whole community (irrespective of their degree of piety) stops work – all shops close, all pubs close, all garages close and there's no public transport; but, perhaps most famously of all, even the swings in the children's playgrounds are padlocked.

The other main area of division is, paradoxically, within the Protestant Church itself. Scotland is unusual in that the national church, the **Church of Scotland**, is presbyterian (ruled by the ministers and elders of the church) rather than episcopal (ruled by bishops). At the time of the main split in the Presbyterian Church – the so-called **1843 Disruption** – a third of its ministers left the Church of Scotland, protesting at the law which allowed landlords to impose ministers against parishioners' wishes, and formed the breakaway **Free Church**. Since those days there has been a partial reconciliation; although, in 1893, there was another break, when a minority of the Free Church became the Free Presbyterian Church; meanwhile others slowly made their way back to the Church of Scotland. The remaining rump of the Free Church – better known as the "**Wee Frees**" – has its spiritual heartland on Lewis. To confuse matters further, as recently as 1988, the Free Presbyterian Church split over a minister who attended a requiem mass during a Catholic funeral of a friend – he and his supporters have since formed the breakaway Associated Presbyterian Churches. Meanwhile, the Free Church itself is currently in crisis over the "heresies" of Professor Donald MacLeod, one its more liberal members, who writes a regular column in the West Highland Free Press. With a minority within the church determined to force the issue, another split looks inevitable, though as MacLeod himself says, "[Scotland] needs another denomination like it needs a hole in the head".

The various brands and subdivisions of the Presbyterian Church may appear trivial to outsiders, but to the churchgoers of Lewis, Harris and North Uist (as well as much of Skye and Raasay) they are still keenly felt. In part, this is due to social and cultural reasons: Free Church elders helped organize resistance to the Clearances, and the Wee Frees have done the most to help preserve the Gaelic language. A Free Church service is a memorable experience, and in some villages it takes place every evening (and twice on Sundays): there's no set service or prayer book and no hymns, only biblical readings, plainchant and a fiery sermon all in Gaelic; the pulpit is the architectural focus of the church, not the altar, and Communion is taken only on special occasions. If you want to attend one, the Free Church on Kenneth Street in Stornoway has reputedly the largest Sunday-evening congregation in the UK, of up to 1500 people.

For reasonably priced **car rental**, try Mackinnon Self-Drive, southeast of the town centre at 18 Inaclete Rd (☎01851/702984), or Arnol Motors (☎01851/710548), in Arnol (see p.350); you can **rent bikes** at Alex Dan, 67 Kenneth St (Mon–Sat 9am–6pm; ☎01851/704025 or 702934).

Barabhas (Barvas) to Nis (Ness)

Northwest of Stornoway, the A857 crosses the vast, barren **peat bog** of the interior, an empty undulating wilderness riddled with stretch marks formed by peat cuttings and pockmarked with freshwater lochans. The whole area was once covered by forests, but these disappeared long ago, leaving a smothering deposit of peat that is, on average, 6ft thick, and is still being formed in certain places. Tourists tend to cross this barren landscape at speed, while ecologists have identified these natural wetlands as important "carbon sinks", whose erosion should be protected. For the people of Lewis, the peat represents a valuable energy resource, with each crofter being assigned a slice of the bog. The islanders spend several very sociable weeks each spring cutting the peat, turning it over and leaving it neatly laid out in the open air to dry, returning in summer to collect the dried sods and stack them outside their houses. Though tempting to take home as souvenirs, these piles are the fruits of hard labour, and remain the island's main source of domestic fuel, its pungent smoke one of the most characteristic smells of the Western Isles.

Twelve miles across the peat bog the road divides, heading southwest towards Calanais (see p.351), or northeast through **BARABHAS** (Barvas), and a whole string of bleak and fervently Free Church crofting and weaving villages. These scattered settlements have none of the photogenic qualities of Skye's whitewashed villages; the churches are plain and unadorned, the crofters' houses fairly modern and smothered in grey, pebble-dash rendering, the stone cottages and enclosures of their forebears often lie half-abandoned in the front garden, while a rusting assortment of discarded cars and vans store peat bags and the like. Just beyond Barabhas, a signpost points to the pleasant **Morven Art Gallery**, with a handy café to hole up in during bad weather. Three miles further up the road, you pass the 20ft monolith of **Clach an Trushal**, the first of a series of prehistoric sights between the crofting and weaving settlements of **BAILE AN TRUISEIL** (Ballantrushal) and **SIADAR** (Shader).

Nis (Ness)

The main road continues through a string of straggling villages, until you reach the various densely populated settlements that make up **NIS** (Ness), at the northern tip of Lewis. The folk of Nis are perhaps best known for their annual culling of young gannets on Sula Sgeir (see below). For an insight into the social history of the area, take a look inside **Comunn Eachdriadh Nis** (Ness Historical Society; Mon–Sat noon–5.30pm; £2), on the left as you pass through **TABOST** (Habost). The museum, housed in an unlikely looking building, contains a huge collection of photographs, but its prize possession is a diminuitive sixth- or seventh-century cross from the Isle of Rona (see box opposite), decorated with a much eroded nude male figure, and thought by some to have been St Ronan's gravestone. The road terminates at the fishing village of **PORT NIS** (Port of Ness), with a tiny harbour and lovely golden beach.

Shortly before you reach Port Nis, a minor road heads two miles northwest to the hamlet of **EOROPAIDH** (Europie) – pronounced "Yor-erpee". Here, by the road junction that leads to Rubha Robhanais, the simple stone structure of **Teampull Mholuaidh** (St Moluag's Church) stands amidst the runrig fields. Thought to date from the twelfth century, when the islands were still under Norse rule, but restored in 1912 (and now used once a month by the Scottish Episcopal Church for sung Communion), the church features a strange south chapel with only a squint window connecting it to the nave. In the late seventeenth century, the traveller Martin Martin noted "they all went to church... and then standing silent for a little time, one of them gave a signal ... and immediately all of them went into the fields, where they fell a drinking their ale and spent the remainder of the night in dancing and singing, etc". Church services aren't what they used to be.

From Eoropaidh, a narrow road twists to the bleak and blustery northern tip of the island, **Rubha Robhanais** – well known to devotees of the BBC shipping forecast as the Butt of Lewis – where a lighthouse sticks up above a series of sheer cliffs and stacks, alive with kittiwakes, fulmars and cormorants, with skuas and gannets feeding offshore, and a great place for seal-, dolphin-, porpoise- and whale-spotting. The lighthouse is normally closed to the public and you're better off backtracking half a mile or so, where there's a path down to the tiny sandy bay of **Port Sto**, a more sheltered spot for a picnic than the Butt itself.

Practicalities

There are at least four buses a day from Stornoway to Port Nis, Sundays excepted, and several **accommodation** possibilities. One of the most comfortable is *Harbour View* (☎01851/810735; ③), located in an old-boat builder's house overlooking Port Nis harbour,

---

OFFSHORE ISLANDS

"Though three men dwell on Flannan Isle
To keep the lamp alight,
As we steer'd under the lee, we caught
No glimmer through the night."

"Flannan Isle", Wilfred Wilson Gibson

On December 15, 1900, a passing ship reported that the lighthouse on the **Flannan Isles**, built the previous year by the Stevensons some 21 miles west of the Butt of Lewis, was not working. Gibson's poem goes on to recount the arrival of the relief boat from Oban, on Boxing Day, whose crew found no trace of the three keepers. More mysteriously still, a full meal lay untouched on the table, one chair was knocked over, and only two oilskins were missing. Subsequent lightkeepers doubtless spent many lonely nights trying in vain to figure out what happened, until the lighhouse went automatic in 1971.

Equally famous, but for different reasons, is the tiny island of **Sula Sgeir**, 41 miles due north of the Butt of Lewis. Every August since anyone can remember, the young men of Nis have set sail from Port Nis to harvest the young gannet or guga that nest in their thousands high up on the islet's sea cliffs. It's a dangerous activity, and one that the RSPB has tried its best to stop, but for some unknown reason boiled gannet and potato continues to be a popular Lewis delicacy, and there's never any shortage of eager volunteers for the annual cull.

Somewhat incredibly, the island of **Rona**, less than a mile across and ten miles east of Sula Sgeir, was inhabited on and off until the mid-nineteenth century. The island's St Ronan's Chapel is one of the oldest Celtic Christian ruins in the country. St Ronan was, according to legend, the first inhabitant, moving here in the eighth century with his two sisters, Miriceal and Brianuil, until one day he turned to Brianuil and said, "My dear sister, it is yourself that is handsome, what beautiful legs you have". She apparently replied that it was time for her to leave the island, and made her way to neighbouring Sula Sgeir. Rona is now in the care of Scottish Natural Heritage (☎01870/705258), from whom you must get permission before landing.

The largest of all the offshore islands is the NTS-owned **St Kilda** archipelago, roughly a hundred miles west southwest of the Butt of Lewis and over forty miles from its nearest landfall, Griminish Point on North Uist. The last 36 Gaelic-speaking inhabitants of Hirta, St Kilda's main island, were evacuated at their own request in 1930, ending several hundred years of harsh existence – well recorded in Tom Steel's book *The Life and Death of St Kilda*. Today, the island is partly occupied by the army, who have a missile-tracking radar station here linked to South Uist. With a calm sea and permission from the NTS (☎01870/620238) – even tour operators have to negotiate long and hard – you may go ashore to visit the museum in the old village, recently restored by volunteers, and struggle up the massive cliffs, where the islanders once caught puffins, young fulmars and gannets.

with an adjoining **tearoom** (March–Nov Mon–Sat), serving toasted sandwiches and baked potatoes. Another option is the modern Gaelic croft of Catriona MacLeod (☎01851/810240; ③) in Coig Peighinnean (Five Penny Borve), four miles northeast of Barabhas; or else there's the luxury *Galson Farm* (☎01851/850492; ⑤), an eighteenth-century farmhouse in Gabhsann Bho Dheas (South Galson), halfway between Barabhas and Port Nis, with a **bunkhouse** close by (phone number as above). There are very few shops (other than mobile ones) in these parts, so it's as well to stock up in Stornoway before you set out.

Arnol to Calanais (Callanish)

Heading southwest from the crossroads near Barabhas brings you to the village of **ARNOL**, which meanders down towards the sea. At the far end of the village the **Black House Museum** (May–Sept Mon–Fri 10am–1pm & 2–5pm, Sat 11am–1pm & 2–5pm; HS; £1.50), dating from the 1870s and inhabited until 1964, is typical of its type, with a chimneyless roof overlaid with grassy sods and oat-straw thatch, lashed down with fish-nets and ropes. Beneath, a simple system of wooden tie beams supports the roof, which covers both the living quarters and the attached byre and barn. The postwar wallpaper inside has been removed to reveal sooty rafters above the living room, where, in the centre of the stone and clay floor, the peat fire was the focal point of the house.

Returning to the main road, it's about a mile or so to **BRAGAR**, where you'll spot a stark arch formed by the jawbone of a blue whale, washed up on the nearby coast in 1920. The spear sticking through the bone is the harpoon, which only went off when the local blacksmith was trying to remove it, badly injuring him. Another two miles on at **SIABOST** (Shawbost), local school children created the appealingly amateurish **Shawbost Crofting Museum** (Mon–Sat 9am–6pm; free) in 1970. The converted church contains a real hotchpotch of stuff – most of it donated by locals – including a rare Lewis brick from the short-lived factory set up by Lord Leverhulme, an old hand-driven loom and a reconstructed living room with a traditional box bed. Behind the church is a **campsite** (☎01851/710504; May–Oct). Just outside Siabost, to the west, there's a sign to the newly restored **Norse Mill and Kiln**. It's a ten-minute walk over a small hill to the two thatched bothies beside a little stream; the nearer one's the kiln, the further the mill. Mills and kilns of this kind were common in Lewis up until the 1930s, and despite the name are thought to have been introduced here from Ireland as early as the sixth century.

Five miles on, the landscape becomes less monotonous, with boulders and hillocks rising out of the peat moor, as you approach the sprawling trio of hamlets Mullach Charlabhaigh (Upper Carloway), then Carlabhagh (Carloway) and finally Dun Charlabhaigh (Doune Carloway). A mile-long road leads off north to the beautifully remote coastal settlement of **GEARRANNAN** (Garenin), where several thatched crofters' houses – the last of which was abandoned in 1973 – have been restored; one now serves as a primitive **youth hostel** (open all year; no phone), while another is ear-marked to be a museum. A night here is unforgettable, and there's a beautiful stony beach from which to view the sunset.

Carloway Broch and Calanais

Just before the turn off to Dun Charlabhaigh, about 400yd from the road, **Carloway Broch** perches on top of a conspicuous rocky outcrop overlooking the sea. Scotland's Atlantic coast is strewn with the remains of over 500 brochs, or fortified towers, but this is one of the best preserved, its drystone circular walls reaching a height of more than 30ft on the seaward side. The broch consists of two concentric walls, the inner one perpendicular, the outer one slanting inwards, the two originally fastened together by rough-ly hewn flagstones, which also served as lookout galleries reached via a narrow stairwell. The only entrance to the roofless inner yard is through a low doorway set beside a crude and cramped guard cell. As at Calanais (see below), there have been all sorts of theories about the purpose of the brochs, which date from between 100 BC and 100 AD; the most likely explanation is that they were built to provide protection from Roman slave-traders.

Five miles south of Dun Charlabhaigh lies the village of **CALANAIS** (Callanish), site of the islands' most dramatic prehistoric ruins, the **Calanais Standing Stones**, whose monoliths – nearly fifty of them – occupy a serene loch-side setting. There's been years of heated debate about the origin and function of the stones – slabs of gnarled and finely grained gneiss up to 15ft high – though almost everyone agrees that they were lugged here by Neolithic peoples between 3000 and 1500 BC. It's also obvious that the planning and construction of the site – as well as several other lesser circles nearby – was spread over many generations. Such an endeavour could, it's been argued, only be prompted by the desire to predict the seasonal cycle upon which these early farmers were entirely dependent, and indeed many of the stones are aligned with the position of the sun and the stars. This rational explanation, based on clear evidence that this part of Lewis was once a fertile farming area, dismisses as coincidence the ground plan of the site, which resembles a colossal Celtic cross, and explains away the central burial chamber as a later addition of no special significance. These two features have, however, fuelled all sorts of theories ranging from alien intervention to human sacrifice.

A "black house" adjacent to the main stone circle has been refurbished as a **tearoom** and shop, and it's to this you should head for refreshment rather than the superfluous **Calanais Visitor Centre** (April–Sept Mon–Sat 10am–7pm; Oct–March 10am–4pm; £1.50) on the other side of the stones (and thankfully out of view), to which all the signs direct you from the road. The centre runs a restaurant and a small museum on the site, but with so much information on the panels beside the stones there's little reason to visit it. You're politely asked not to walk between the stones, only along the path that surrounds them; so if you want to commune with standing stones in solitude head for the smaller circles in more natural surroundings a mile or two southeast of Calanais, around Gearraidh na h-Aibhne (Garynahine).

If you need a place to stay, there are several inexpensive **B&Bs** in Calanais itself: try Mrs Catherine Morrison, 27 Calanais (☎01851/621392; ③; March–Sept), or an excellent vegetarian B&B run by Debbie Nash (☎01851/621321; ③) in neighbouring Tolastadh a Chaolais (Tolsta Chaolais), three miles north. Back in Carlabhagh, beside a lochan, is the very reasonable *Doune Braes Hotel* (☎01851/643252; ③), whose bar serves up the same excellent seafood as its restaurant, only cheaper.

The Uig peninsula

From Gearraidh na h-Aibhne, the main road leads back to Stornoway, while the partially upgraded B8011 heads off west to the remote **Uig peninsula**, in the hillier, southwest coast of Lewis. After three miles there's another crossroads, with the B8059 heading eventually over a small sea channel to the island of **Bearnaraigh Mòr** (Great Bernera), the largest of the forty or so islands in Loch Roag, whose crofters successfully defied the attempts at eviction by the landlord and took part in the **Bernera Riot** of 1872, during which three locals were arrested and later acquitted – for more on the island's history, call in at the **Bernera Museum** (April–Sept Mon–Sat 11am–6pm), in the central settlement of **BREACLEIT** (Breaclete). Bernera is a rocky island, with a few small lobster-fishing settlements, but four miles from Breacleit on the north coast near the abandoned hamlet of **BOSTADH** (Bosta), there's a precious little bay of golden sand, which looks out to the nearby island of Bearnaraigh Beag (Little Bernera) and countless others. If you want to stay, there are a couple of **B&Bs** on the island, including Mrs A. A. MacDonald (☎01851/612347; ③; April–Oct) in Tobson, a mile south of Bostadh.

There are more superb golden sands on the western shores of West Loch Roag, though it's a long drive along the B8011 to reach them – sixteen miles from the crossroads to Miabhig (Miavaig), then a further mile off the main road northeast to **CLIOBH** (Cliff). The breakers on the beach below Cliobh make it unsafe for swimmers, who should continue another mile to **CNIP** (Kneep), to the east of which is **Traigh na Berie**, a glorious strand of shell sand, backed by dunes. Two miles southwest of Miabhig you'll find **Traigh Chapadail** (Uig Sands), the most prized of all the golden beaches on Lewis, overlooked by the lovely guest house, *Baile na Cille* (☎01851/672241; ④; March–Oct), in **TIMSGEARRAIDH** (Timsgarry). It was in the nearby village of **Eadar dha Fhadhail** (Ardroil) in 1831 that a local cow stumbled across the **Lewis Chessmen**, twelfth-century Viking chess pieces carved from walrus ivory that now reside in Edinburgh's Museum of Antiquities (see p.78) and the British Museum in London.

Na Hearadh (Harris)

The "division" between Lewis and **Harris** – they are, in fact, one island – is embedded in a historical split in the MacLeod clan, lost in the mists of time. The border between the two was also a county boundary until 1975, with Harris lying in Inverness-shire, and Lewis belonging to Ross and Cromarty. Nowadays, the dividing line is rarely marked even on maps; though, for the record, it comprises Loch Resort in the west, Loch Seaforth in the east, and the six miles in between. Harris itself is more clearly divided by a minuscule isthmus, into the wild, inhospitable mountains of North Harris and the gentler landscape and sandy shores of South Harris.

Along with Lewis, Harris was purchased in 1918 by **Lord Leverhulme**, and after 1923, when he pulled out of Lewis, all his efforts were concentrated here. In contrast to Lewis, though, Leverhulme and his ambitious projects were broadly welcomed by the people of Harris. His most grandiose plans were drawn up for Leverburgh (see p.355), but he also purchased an old Norwegian whaling station in Bun Abhain Eadara in 1922, built a spinning mill at Geocrab and began the construction of four roads. Financial difficulties, a slump in the tweed industry and the lack of market for whale products meant that none of the schemes was a wholehearted success, and when he died in 1925 the plug was pulled on all of them.

Since the Leverhulme era, unemployment has been a constant problem in Harris. Crofting continues on a small scale, supplemented by the Harris Tweed industry, though the main focus of this has shifted to Lewis. Fishing continues on Scalpay, while the rest of the population gets by on whatever employment is available: roadworks, crafts and, of course, tourism. There's a regular **bus** connection between Stornoway and Tarbert, and an occasional service which circumnavigates South Harris (see also "Travel details" on p.363).

Tairbeart (Tarbert)

The largest place on Harris is the ferry port of **TARBERT**, sheltered in a green valley on the narrow isthmus that marks the border between North and South Harris. The town's mountainous backdrop is impressive, though there's nothing much to the place – just a few terraces sloping up from the dock. However, it does boast the only **tourist office** (April–Oct Mon–Sat 9am–5pm; also open to greet the ferry; winter hours variable; ☎01859/502011) on Harris, close to the ferry terminal. The office can arrange modest, inexpensive B&B **accommodation** and has a full set of bus timetables, but its real value is as a source of information on local walks. If you wish to base yourself in Tarbert, you could do worse than stay at the easy-going, old-fashioned *Harris Hotel* (☎01859/502154; ⑤), five minutes' walk from the ferry towards Stornoway; the hotel bar acts as the local social centre and serves bar meals. You'll need to book ahead to stay in Tarbert's two most popular guest houses: *Allan Cottage* (☎01859/502146; ④; April–Sept), in the old telephone exchange, and *Leachin House* (☎01859/502157; ②), further up the road. It's also worth enquiring at the tourist office about Tarbert's new **bunkhouse** on the Main Street, which should be open from 1998 onwards.

Ceann a Tuath na Hearadh (North Harris)

The A859 north to Stornoway takes you over a boulder-strewn saddle between mighty **Sgaoth Aird** (1829ft) and **Clisham** (2619ft), the highest peak in the Western Isles. This bitter terrain offers but the barest of vegetation, with an occasional cluster of crofters' houses sitting in the shadow of a host of pointed peaks, anywhere between 1000ft and 2500ft high. These bulging, pyramidical mountains reach their climax around the dramatic shores of the fjord-like **Loch Seaforth**. If you're planning on walking in North Harris, and can afford it, consider using the spectacular *Ardvourlie Castle* (☎01859/502307; ⑧), ten miles north of Tarbert by the shores of Loch Seaforth, as a launch pad.

A cheaper, but equally idyllic spot is the Gatliff Trust's **youth hostel** (open all year; no phone) in the lonely coastal hamlet of **REINIGEADAL** (Rhenigdale), until recently only accessible by foot or boat. To reach the hostel without your own transport, walk east five miles from Tarbert along the road to **CAOLAS SCALPAIGH** (Kyles Scalpay). After another mile or so, watch for the sign marking the start of the path which threads its way through the peaks of the craggy promontory that lies trapped between Loch Seaforth and East Loch Tarbert. It's a magnificent hike, with superb views out along the coast and over the mountains, but you'll need to be properly equipped (see p.44) and should allow three hours for the one-way trip.

Caolas Scalpaigh looks out across East Loch Tarbert to the (former) island of **Scalpaigh** (Scalpay) – from the Norse *skalp-ray* (the island shaped like a boat) – now accessible via the brand-new single-track bridge. Scalpay's tightly knit fishing community is surprisingly bouyant, maintaining a relatively large population of 450. It's a pleasant and fairly easy three-mile hike across the island to the Stevensons' Eilean Glas lighthouse which looks out over the sea to Skye. The lighthouse buildings are now self-catering cottages, or you can stay on the island at *Suil-Na-Mara* **B&B** (☎01859/540278; ②); if you're interested in diving, contact Scalpay Diving Services (☎01859/540328).

The only other road on North Harris is the winding, single-track B887, which clings to the northern shores of West Loch Tarbert, and gives easy access to the awesome mountain range of the (treeless) Forest of Harris to the north. Immediately as you turn down the B887, you pass through **BUN ABHAINN EADARA** (Bunavoneadar), where some Norwegians established a short-lived whaling station – the slipways and distinctive red-brick chimney can still be seen. Seven miles further on, the road takes you through the gates of **Amhuinnsuidhe Castle** (pronounced "Avan-soo-ee"), built in Scottish Baronial style in 1868 by the Earl of Dunmore, and right past the front door, much to the annoyance of the castle's owners, who have tried in vain to have the road rerouted. As it is, you have time to admire the lovely salmon-leap waterfalls and pristine castle grounds. You can become a temporary neighbour by staying at the **B&B** in the *Post Office House* (☎01859/560207; ③; April–Oct), west of the castle.

It's another five miles to the end of the road at the small crofting community of **HUSINIS** (Hushinish), where you are rewarded with a south-facing beach of golden sand that looks across to South Harris. A slipway to the north of the bay serves the nearby island of **Scarp**, a hulking mass of rock rising to over 1000ft, once home to more than two hundred people and abandoned as recently as 1971 (it's now just a private holiday hideaway). It was owned until recently by Nazmu Virani, director of BCCI, who had big plans for the island until the bank crashed. The most bizarre moment in its history was undoubtedly in 1934, when the German scientist Gerhardt Zucher conducted an experiment with rocket mail, but the letter-laden missile exploded before it even got off the ground and the idea was shelved.

HARRIS TWEED

Far from being a picturesque cottage industry, as it's sometimes presented, the production of **Harris Tweed** is vital to the local economy with a well-organized and unionized workforce. Traditionally the tweed was made by women, from the wool of their own sheep, to provide clothing for their families. Each woman was responsible for the entire process: washing and scouring of the wool, dyeing it with lichen, heather flowers or ragwort, carding, spinning and warping. Finally the cloth was dipped in sheep urine and "waulked" by a group of women, who beat the cloth on a table to soften it whilst singing Gaelic waulking songs. Harris Tweed was originally made all over the islands, and was known simply as *clò mór* (big cloth).

In the mid-nineteenth century, the Countess of Dunmore, who owned a large part of Harris, started to sell surplus cloth to her aristocratic friends, thus forming the genesis of the modern industry, which now employs about 400 millworkers and a further 650 weavers – though demand, and employment, fluctuates wildly as fashions change. To earn the official Harris Tweed Association trademark of the Orb and the Maltese Cross – taken from the Countess of Dunmore's coat of arms – the fabric has to be hand-woven on the Outer Hebrides from 100 percent pure new Scottish wool, while the other parts of the manufacturing process must take place only in the local mills.

The main centre of production is now Lewis, where the wool is dyed, carded and spun; you can see all these processes by visiting the **Lewis Loom Centre** in Stornoway (see p.346). In recent years, there has been a revival of traditional tweed-making techniques, with several small producers, like Anne Campbell at **Clò Mór** in Liceasto (Mon–Fri 9am–5pm; ☎01859/530364), religiously following old methods. One of the more interesting aspects of the process is the use of indigenous plants and bushes to dye the cloth: yellow comes from rocket and broom, green from heather, grey and black from iris and oak, and, most popular of all, reddish brown from crotal, a flat grey lichen scraped off rocks.

Ceann a Deas na Hearadh (South Harris)

The mountains of **South Harris** are less dramatic than in the north, but the scenery is equally breathtaking. There's a choice of routes from Tarbert to the ferry port of **Leverburgh**, which connects with North Uist (passengers only): the east coast, known as **Na Baigh** (Bays), is rugged and seemingly inhospitable, while the west coast is endowed with some of the finest stretches of golden sand in the whole of the archipelago, buffeted by the Atlantic winds. A bus sets off from Tarbert, twice weekly, travelling out along the east coast, and returning via all points along the west coast a little under two hours later, so if you get off at any point you'll have to wait several days until the next bus – for more information see "Travel details" at the end of this chapter or contact Tarbert tourist office.

Na Baigh (Bays)

Paradoxically, most people on South Harris live along the harsh eastern coastline of **Bays** rather than the more fertile west side. But not by choice – they were evicted from their original crofts to make way for sheep-grazing. Despite the uncompromising terrain – mostly bare rock and heather – the crofters managed to establish "lazybeds" (small raised plots between the rocks fertilized by seaweed and peat), a few of which are still in use even today. The narrow sea lochs provide shelter for fishing boats, while the interior is speckled with freshwater lochans, and the whole coast now served by the meandering **Golden Road** (so called because of the expense of constructing it).

There are just a few places to stay along the coast, the most obvious being the two hostels south of Tarbert: the *SYHA* **youth hostel** (☎01859/530373; late March–Sept) is in a converted school in **CAOLAS STOCINIS** (Kyles Stockinish), six miles to the south; an **independent hostel** (☎01851/511255; open all year) lies only three miles to the south in **DRINISIADAR** (Drinishader), or there's *Hillhead* B&B (☎01859/511226; ③; April–Oct) in **SCADABHAGH** (Scadabay).

Six miles beyond Liceasto at **LINGREABHAGH** (Lingarabay), the road skirts the foot of **Roineabhal** (1508ft), the southernmost mountain of the island and known as *an aite boidheach* (the beautiful place). The vast majority of the locals are currently fighting to prevent Redland Aggregates building one of Europe's largest superquarries here, which would demolish virtually the entire mountain over the next seventy years. Environmentalists charge that local fishing grounds would be badly affected, the devout are up in arms over the possibility of Sunday working, and the initial promise of a hundred much-needed new jobs has been reduced on the evidence of a public enquiry to just 25. At the time of writing, the mountain's future is still undecided.

A mile or so from Rubha Reanais (Renish Point), the southern tip of Harris, is the old port of **ROGHADAL** (Rodel), where a smattering of ancient stone houses lies among the hillocks surrounding the dilapidated harbour where the ferry from Skye used to arrive. On top of one of these grassy humps, with sheep grazing in the graveyard, is **Tur Chliamainn** (St Clement's Church), burial place of the MacLeods of Harris and Dunvegan in Skye. Dating from the 1520s – in other words pre-Reformation, hence the big castellated tower – the church was saved from ruination in the eighteenth century, and fully restored in 1873 by the Countess of Dunmore. The bare interior is distinguished by its wall tombs, notably that of the founder, Alasdair Crotach (also known as Alexander MacLeod), whose heavily weathered effigy lies beneath an intriguing backdrop and canopy of sculpted reliefs depicting vernacular and religious scenes – elemental representations of, among others, a stag hunt, the Holy Trinity, St Michael, and the devil and an angel weighing the souls of the dead. Look out, too, for the *sheila-na-gig* halfway up the south side of the church tower; unusually, she has a brother displaying his genitalia, below a carving of St Clement on the west face.

The west coast

The main road from Tarbert into South Harris snakes its way west for ten miles across the lunaresque interior to reach the coast. Once there, you get a view of the most stunning **beach**, the vast golden strand of **LOSGAINTIR** (Luskentyre) – the village itself sits on the north side of the bay. The road continues to ride above a chain of sweeping sands, backed by rich machair, that stretches for nine miles along the Atlantic coast. In good weather, the scenery is particularly impressive, foaming breakers rolling along the golden sands set against the rounded peaks of the mountains to the north and the islet-studded turquoise sea to the west. A short distance out to sea is the island of **Tarasaigh** (Taransay), which once held a population of nearly a hundred, but was abandoned as recently as 1974.

Nobody bothers much if you **camp** or park beside the dune-edged beach, as long as you're careful not to churn up the machair; alternatively, try Losgaintir's good-value B&Bs, *Moravia* (☎01859/550262; ③; March–Oct), or *Seaview* (☎01859/550263; ③; April–Oct). The choicest accommodation, though, is five miles further south in **SGARASTA BHEAG** (Scaristabeg), where *Scarista House* (☎01859/550238; ⑨; May–Sept) overlooks the nearby golden sands; if you can't afford to stay, it's worth splashing out and booking for dinner, as the meat and seafood served here is among the freshest on the Western Isles. If you're intrigued by the local machair, you can go on guided walks (Mon & Fri 2.30pm; £2) across a stretch from the bayside village of **TAOBH TUATH** (Northton).

From Taobh Tuath the road veers to the southeast to trim the island's south shore, eventually reaching the sprawling settlement of **AN T-OB** (Leverburgh), where a series of brown clapperboard houses strikes an odd Scandinavian note. An t-Ob is better known as Leverburgh, after Lord Leverhulme, who planned to turn the place into the largest fishing port on the west coast of Scotland. There are several **B&Bs** strung out within a two-mile radius of Leverburgh: try *Caberfeigh House* (☎01859/520276; ③), a lovely stone-built Victorian building; Paula Williams (☎01859/520319; ③), who special- izes in vegetarian and vegan cooking; or the secluded *Shieldaig House* (☎01859/520378; ③), which is also vegetarian. On the north side of the bay, *An Clachan* general store (Mon–Sat: April–Sept 8.30am–8pm; Oct–Feb 9am–5.30pm) has a **café** upstairs, and an **exhibition** on the village's history. From the pier on the south side of the bay, a CalMac **car ferry** makes the seventy-minute journey across the skerry-strewn Sound of Harris for Otternish on North Uist on one of Scotland's most tortuous ferry routes, the ship tak- ing part in a virtual slalom race to avoid numerous hidden rocks.

Uibhist a Tuath (North Uist)

Compared to the mountainous scenery of Harris, **North Uist** – seventeen miles long and thirteen miles wide – is much flatter and for some comes as something of an anti- climax. Over half the surface area is covered by water, creating a distinctive peaty- brown lochan-studded landscape reminiscent of north Lewis. Most visitors come here for the trout and salmon fishing and the deerstalking, both of which (along with poach- ing) are critical to the survival of the island's economy. Others come for the solitude of North Uist's vast sandy beaches, which extend – almost without interruption – along the north and west coast, and the smattering of prehistoric sites.

There are two **car ferry** services to North Uist: the first is from Leverburgh on South Harris to Otternish (Mon–Sat 3–4 daily), from where there are two or three daily **buses**, plus the odd postbus and schoolday service, to Lochmaddy, the principal village on the east coast; the majority of people take either the Oban or the Tarbert ferry, which docks at Lochmaddy itself. Again, two or three daily buses leave for Lochboisdale in South Uist, but to travel the coastal road you'll have to rely on the school- or postbus.

Loch nam Madadh (Lochmaddy) and around

Despite being situated on the east coast, some distance away from any beach, the ferry port of **LOCHMADDY** makes the best base for exploring the island. The village itself, occupying a narrow, bumpy promontory, is nothing special, though incongruously it has sixteen brown weatherboarded houses, which arrived from Sweden in 1948. If the weather's bad or you've time to kill, take a look round **Taigh Chearsabhagh** (Mon–Sat 10am–5pm; £1.50), a converted eighteenth-century merchant's house, now home to an excellent local museum, arts centre and café.

The **tourist office** (mid-April to mid-Oct Mon–Sat 9am–5pm; also open to greet the evening ferry; ☎01876/500321), near the quayside, has local bus and ferry timetables, and can help with **accommodation**. Right by the tourist office is the island's bank, and the spick-and-span *Lochmaddy Hotel* (☎01876/500331; ⑤), with a restaurant specializ- ing in outstanding seafood; its bar is by far the liveliest place on North Uist and serves decent snacks. There are a couple of nice Victorian B&Bs: the *Old Courthouse* (☎01876/500358; ③) and the *Old Bank House* (☎01876/500275; ③). The *SYHA* **youth hostel** is in *Ostram House* (☎01876/500368; mid-May to Sept), half a mile from the ferry dock. Not far beyond, the independent hostel in the *Uist Outdoor Centre* (☎01876/500480; open all year) offers four-person bunk rooms.

The only **bike rental** on the island is from Morrison Cycle Hire (☎01876/580211), based nine miles away in Cairinis (Carinish), but they will deliver to Lochmaddy. The *Uist Outdoor Centre* also offers a wide range of outdoor activities from canoeing to rock climbing. The *Lochmaddy Hotel* is a favourite with the **fishing** fraternity – there's even

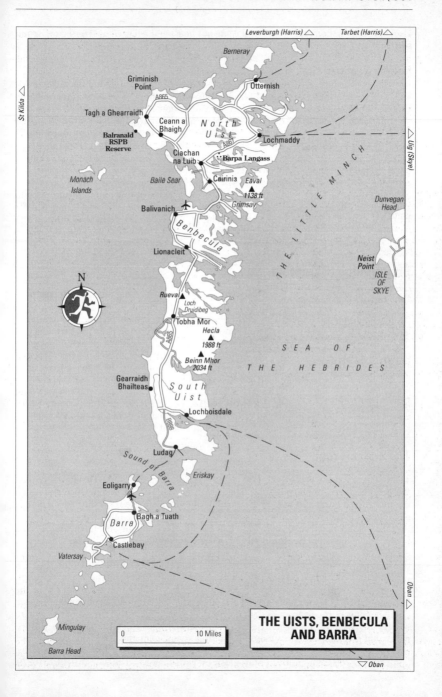

THE UISTS, BENBECULA AND BARRA

Leverburgh (Harris) △   Tarbet (Harris) △

St Kilda △

△ Uig (Skye)

Berneray

Griminish Point

Otternish

Tagh a Ghearraidh

Ceann a Bhaigh

North Uist

Lochmaddy

Balranald RSPB Reserve

Clachan na Luib

Barpa Langass

Monach Islands

Baile Sear

Cairinis

Eaval
1138 ft

Dunvegan Head

Balivanich

Grimsay

Benbecula

Lionacleit

THE LITTLE MINCH

Neist Point

ISLE OF SKYE

Rueval

Loch Druidibeg

Tobha Mor

Hecla
1988 ft

SEA OF

Beinn Mhor
2034 ft

THE HEBRIDES

Gearraidh Bhailteas

South Uist

Lochboisdale

Ludag

Sound of Barra

Eriskay

Eoligarry

Bagh a Tuath

Barra

Castlebay

Vatersay

△ Oban

N

Mingulay

0   10 Miles

Barra Head

▽ Oban

a set of scales in the hotel foyer – and rents out boats and sells permits for brown trout, sea trout and salmon.

Nearby Neolithic sites

Several prehistoric sites lie within easy cycling distance of Lochmaddy (or walking distance if you use the bus/postbus for the outward journey). The most remarkable is **Barpa Langass**, a huge chambered burial cairn a short walk from the A867, seven barren miles southwest. The stones are visible from the road and, unless the weather's good, it's not worth making a closer inspection as the chamber has collapsed and is now too dangerous to enter. A mile to the southeast, by *Langass Lodge* (☎01876/500358; ⑤), whose restaurant and bar snacks feature local seafood, a rough track leads to the small stone circle of **Pobull Fhinn**, which enjoys a much more picturesque location overlooking a narrow loch. The circle covers a large area and, although the stones are not that huge, they occupy an intriguing amphitheatre cut into the hillside. Three miles northwest of Lochmaddy along the A865 you'll find **Na Fir Bhreige** (The Three False Men), three standing stones which, depending on your legend, mark the graves of three spies buried alive or three men who deserted their wives and were turned to stone by a witch.

Bearnaraigh (Berneray)

For those in search of still more seclusion, there's the low-lying island of **Berneray** – eight miles in circumference with a population of just under 150 – accessible via a short car-ferry journey from Otternish, eight miles north of Lochmaddy, though a causeway is planned for the near future. The island's main claim to fame is as the birthplace of Giant MacAskill (see p.335) and as the favoured holiday hideaway of that other great eccentric, Prince Charles, lover of Gaelic culture and royal potato picker to local crofter, "Splash" MacKilliop. Apart from the sheer peace and isolation, the island's main draw for non-royals is a three-mile-long sandy beach on the west and north coast, backed by rabbit-free dunes. Should you wish to follow in the prince's footsteps, you can stay (and help out) at "Splash" MacKilliop's **B&B** (☎01876/540235; ④), or at the simple *SYHA* **youth hostel** (no phone; open all year), in a pair of thatched "black houses" a mile or so from the pier up the east coast, on the north side of Bays Loch.

The coastal road

The A865, which skirts the northern and western shoreline of North Uist for more than thirty miles, takes you through the most scenic sections of the island. Once you've left the boggy east coast and passed the turning to Otternish, the road slips past a couple of wide and sandy river estuaries before reaching the rolling hills that slope down to the sea in the northwest corner of the island. Here, about seventeen miles from Lochmaddy, you'll find **Scolpaig Tower**, a castellated folly on an islet in Loch Scolpaig, erected as a famine relief project in the nineteenth century. A footpath leads down from the road to the tower and beyond, to the rocky shoreline of **Griminish Point**, the closest landfall to St Kilda (see p.349) – which is sometimes visible on the horizon.

Roughly three miles south of Scolpaig Tower, through the sand dunes, is the **Baranald RSPB Reserve** (April–Sept), one of the last breeding grounds of the corncrake, among Europe's most endangered birds. Sightings are rare even here – you're slightly more likely to hear it. The two-hour marked walk along the headland, however, should give ample opportunity for spotting skuas, gannets and Manx shearwaters out to sea – guided walks take place throughout the summer (May–Aug Tues & Fri 2pm; ☎01878/602188). You can **stay** close by with Joan MacDonald (☎01876/510279;

②; April–Oct), overlooking the beautiful beach at **HOGHA GEARRAIDH** (Hougharry). A few miles down the road children might enjoy a visit to **Uist Animal Visitors Centre** (Mon–Sat 10am–10pm; £2) to see Eriskay ponies, Highland cattle and other rare Scottish breeds at close quarters; the centre also has **horse-drawn Romany caravans** for hire (☎01876/510223).

At **CLACHAN NA LUIB**, by the crossroads with the A867 from Lochmaddy, there's a post office and general store, where you can stock up on provisions, and a family-run hostel, *Taigh-mo-Sheannair* (☎01876/580246; open all year), a couple of miles east on the road to Loch Euphort (Locheport). Offshore, to the south, lie two tidal dune islands, the largest of which is **Baile Sear** (Baleshare), with its fantastic three-mile-long beach, connected by causeway to North Uist. In Gaelic the island's name means "east village", its twin "west village" having disappeared under the sea during a freak storm. This also isolated the **Monarch Islands** (sometimes known by their old Norse name of Heisker), once connected to North Uist at low tide, now eight miles out to sea. The islands, which are connected with each other at low tide, were inhabited until the 1930s when the last remaining families moved to North Uist.

On leaving North Uist the main road squeezes along a series of causeways, built by the military in 1960, that trim the west edge of **Griomasaigh** (Grimsay), a peaceful, little-visited lobster-fishing island, before heading across the tidal sands to Benbecula.

Beinn na Faoghla (Benbecula)

Blink and you could miss the pancake-flat island of **Benbecula** (put the stress on the second syllable), sandwiched between Protestant North Uist and Catholic South Uist. Most visitors simply trundle along the main road that cuts across the middle of the island in less than five miles – not such a bad idea, since nearly half the island's 1200 population are Royal Artillery personnel, working at the missile range on South Uist, and the noise on both islands can be deafening during practice sessions.

Economically, the area has, of course, benefited enormously, though the impact on the environment and Gaelic culture (with so many English-speakers around) has been less positive. There is talk of the military pulling out altogether – a devastating prospect for most islanders. Nearly all the military personnel live in the barracks-like housing developments of **BAILE A MHANAICH** (Balivanich), the grim, grey capital of Benbecula in the northwest. The only reason to come here at all is if you happen to be flying into or out of Balivanich airport (direct flights to Glasgow, Barra and Stornoway), need to take money out of the Bank of Scotland cashpoint, or stock up on provisions, best done at the only NAAFI "family store" in the UK that's open to the public, up the road to the west of the post office. If you're unfortunate enough to need **to stay** here, head for *Culla Bay View* (☎01870/602201; ③), a mile south of Balivanich overlooking a sandy beach, or the brand new **hostel** *Taigh-na-Cille* (☎01870/602522), within easy walking distance of the airport, on the road to North Uist. The best place to grab a bite to eat is *Stepping Stones* café and restaurant, situated in one of the barracks-type buildings opposite the post office. **Car rental** is available from Ask Car Hire (☎01870/602818) in neighbouring Uachdar.

The nearest **campsite**, *Shell Bay* (☎01870/602447; April–Oct) is in the south of the island at **LIONACLEIT** (Liniclate). Here, you'll also find the modern **Sgoil Lionacleit**, the only secondary school (and public swimming pool) on the Uists and Benbecula, and home to a small **museum** on local history (Mon, Tues & Thurs 9am–4pm, Wed 9am–12.30pm & 1.30–4pm, Fri 9am–8pm, Sat 11am–1pm & 2–4pm). Lionacleit also boasts the island's most comfortable hotel, *Dark Island Hotel* (☎01870/602414; ④) – no charmer from the outside, but with the best restaurant around, featuring local specialities such as peat-smoked salmon and lumpfish caviar.

Uibhist a Deas (South Uist)

To the south of Benbecula, the island of **South Uist** is arguably the most appealing of the southern chain of islands. The west coast boasts some of the region's finest beaches – a necklace of gold and grey sand strung twenty miles from one end to the other – while the east coast features a ridge of high mountains rising to 2034ft at the summit of Beinn Mhor. The only blot on the landscape is the Royal Artillery missile range, which occupies the northwest corner of the island, shattering the peace and quiet every so often.

The Reformation never reached South Uist (or Barra), and the island remains Roman Catholic, as is evident from the slender modern statue of *Our Lady of the Isles* that stands by the main road below the small hill of **Rueval**, known to the locals as "Space City" for its forest of aerials and golf balls, which help track the missiles heading out into the Atlantic. To the south of Rueval is the freshwater **Loch Druidibeg**, a breeding ground for greylag geese (there's a hide along the road to the north) and a favourite spot for mute swans.

A whole series of country lanes lead west from the main road to the old crofters' villages that straggle along the coast, but – although the paths are rarely more than three miles long – it's surprisingly easy to get lost, tramping round in circles before you stumble upon the shore. This is not the case, however, at **TOBHA MOR** (Howmore), with its easy mile-long walk from the main road to a gorgeous beach. The village is the prettiest place for miles, the shattered ruins of its medieval chapel and burial ground standing near a cluster of neat little "black houses", one of which the Gatliff Trust operates as a **youth hostel** (no phone;open all year); bring your own bedding.

Six miles south of Tobha Mor, the main road passes the cairn that sits amongst the foundations of **Flora MacDonald**'s childhood home (see p.339); she was born nearby, but the house no longer stands. It's another seven miles to the ferry terminal of **LOCH BAGHASDAIL** (Lochboisdale), which, like Lochmaddy in North Uist, occupies a narrow, bumpy promontory. Although the island's chief settlement, Lochboisdale has, if anything, even less to offer than Lochmaddy, with no youth hostel and just the *Lochboisdale Hotel* (☎01878/700332; ⑦), for somewhere to have a drink and a bite to eat. If you're arriving here late at night on the seven-hour boat trip from Oban (or Castlebay on Barra; 1hr 50min), you should try to book accommodation in advance; otherwise, head for the **tourist office** (Easter to mid-Oct Mon–Sat 9am–1pm & 2–5pm; also open to meet the night ferry; ☎01878/700286). There are several **B&Bs** within comfortable walking distance of the dock, including *Bayview* (☎01878/700329; ②; March–Oct) and *Lochside Cottage* (☎01878/700472; ②).

The best place to hole up in this part of South Uist, however, is the *Polochar Inn* (☎01878/700472; ⑤), eight miles from Lochboisdale, right on the south coast overlooking the Sound of Barra, with its own sandy beach close by. If you're heading for Barra without your own transport, you could take the passenger ferry from **Ludag jetty**, two miles east of the *Polochar Inn*, which lands at Eoligarry on Barra's north coast.

Eiriosgaigh (Eriskay)

Also from Ludag, a frequent passenger-only ferry (Mon–Sat only) slips across to Haun jetty on the hilly island of **Eriskay**, famous for its patterned jerseys (on sale at the post office), and a peculiar breed of pony, originally used for carrying peat and seaweed. For a small island, Eriskay has had more than its fair share of historical headlines. The island's main beach on the west coast was where Bonnie Prince Charlie landed on Scottish soil on July 23, 1745 – a big pink convolvulus grows there to this day, said to have sprung from the seeds Charles brought with him from France. The prince, as yet unaccustomed to hardship, spent his first night in a local "black house", and ate a cou-

---

ROCKALL

After years of anonymity – except to devotees of the BBC Shipping Forecast – **Rockall**, a tiny protuberance 80ft wide, 63ft high and 230 miles west of the Western Isles, hit the headlines in June 1997 when three Greenpeace protesters landed on the islet in a solar-powered survival capsule. The rock became part of Britain in 1955 as a security measure when the Royal Artillery established their rocket range on South Uist; a navigation beacon was added in 1972. By the 1980s, however, there was talk of oil, whereupon Ireland, Iceland and Denmark all laid claim to Rockall. In response, one hardy Brit lived there for forty days in 1985 so as to confirm British sovereignty. Greenpeace, naturally enough, wants to stop all gas and oil exploration in the area, since, they argue, the last thing the world needs is to tap into any more of its rapidly diminishing supply of fossil fuels. Understandably, the locals – that is, the people of Harris, to which parish Rockall nominally belongs – see things rather differently, as an offshore oil and gas industry would bring badly needed employment to a depressed area. However, before anyone can start drilling, ownership of the rock will have to be sorted out, with Ireland, for one, keen to take the issue to the European Court.

---

ple of flounders, though he apparently couldn't take the peat smoke and chose to sleep sitting up rather than endure the damp bed.

Eriskay's other claim to fame came in 1941 when the SS *Politician* sank on its way from Liverpool to Jamaica, along with its cargo of bicycle parts, £3 million in Jamaican currency and 264,000 bottles of whisky, inspiring Compton Mackenzie's book – and the Ealing comedy (filmed here in 1948) – *Whisky Galore!* (released as *Tight Little Island* in the US). The ship's stern can still be seen to the east of the Isle of Calvey at low tide, and one of the original bottles (and lots of other related memorabilia) is on show in the bar of *The Politician* in the main village of **BAILE** (Balla). Also worth a look is **St Michael's**, the island's Catholic church which stands on raised ground above the village, built in 1903 in a vaguely Spanish style. If you want to **stay**, try Mrs McInnes (☎01878/720232; ③); you can also **camp rough**, but there are few amenities – just a shop and a post office.

Barraigh (Barra)

Just four miles wide and eight miles long, **Barra** has a deserved reputation of being the Western Isles in miniature. It has sandy beaches, backed by machair, glacial mountains, prehistoric ruins, Gaelic culture, and a laid-back Catholic population of just over 1300. The only settlement of any size is the old herring port of **BAGH A CHAISTEIL** (Castlebay), which curves around the barren rocky hills of a wide bay on the south side of the island (ferries from Lochboisdale, on South Uist, and Oban stop here). Barra's religious allegiance is announced by the large Catholic church, Our Lady, Star of the Sea, which overlooks the castle bay; to underline the point, there's a Madonna and Child on the slopes of Heaval (1260ft), the largest peak on Barra, and a fairly easy hike from the bay.

As its name suggests, Castlebay has a castle in its bay, the medieval islet-fortress of **Kisimul Castle** (Mon, Wed & Sat tours at 2pm; £3), ancestral home of the MacNeil clan. The MacNeils owned Barra from 1427 to 1838, when they sold it to the infamous Colonel Gordon of Cluny, who offered to clear the island and turn it into a state penal colony. The government declined, so the colonel called in the police and proceeded with some of the most cruel forced clearances in the Hebrides. In 1937, the 45th chief of the MacNeil clan bought back the castle (and most of the island). It has since been restored to something of its original appearance, and you take a tour round it by catching the ferry from the slipway at the bottom of Main Street.

To learn more about the history of the island, and about the postal system of the Western Isles, it's worth paying a visit to **Dualchas** (Mon, Wed & Fri 11am–5pm; £1), Barra's cultural and heritage centre housed in an unprepossessing block on the road that leads west out of town. Following the west coast round will bring you to the island's finest sandy beaches, particularly those at Halaman Bay, and near the village of **ALLATHASDAL** (Allasdale). At **BAILE NA CREIGE** (Craigston), between the two, it's a fifteen-minute walk along a dead-end road inland to the **Thatched Cottage Museum** (Easter–Oct Mon–Fri 11am–5pm; £1), an isolated "black house", which remains much as it was when last inhabited in the 1970s.

One of Barra's most fascinating sights is its **airport**, on the north side of the island, where planes land and take off from the crunchy shell sands of **Tràigh Mhór** (Cockle Strand); the exact timing of the flights depends on the tides since at high tide the beach (and therefore the runway) is covered in water. Tràigh Mhór is also famous for its cockles and cockleshells, the latter being used to make harling (the rendering used on most Scottish houses). In 1994, mechanical cockle extraction using tractors was introduced, and quickly began to decimate the cockle stocks and threaten the beach's use as an airport – as a result it has now been banned, in favour of traditional hand-raking.

To the north of the airport, connected by a thin strip of land, is the coastal village of **EOLAIGEARRAIDH** (Eoligarry), with a passenger ferry link to Ludag on South Uist and several sheltered sandy bays close by. To the west of the village is **Cille-Bharra**, burial ground of the MacNeils (and Compton Mackenzie). The ground lies beside the ruins of a medieval church and two chapels, one of which has been reroofed to provide shelter for several carved grave slabs, some rather bizarre religious and secular objects and a replica of an eleventh-century rune-inscribed cross; the original is in the Royal Museum of Scotland in Edinburgh (see p.78).

To the south of Barra, the island of **Bhatarsaigh** (Vatersay), shaped rather like an apple core, is now linked to the main island by a causeway – a mile or so southwest of Castlebay – to try to stem the depopulation which has brought the current head count down to just over seventy. The main settlement (also known as Vatersay) is on the south coast, and to get to it you must cross a narrow isthmus, with the golden sands of Vatersay Bay to the east, and the stones and sands of Bàgh Siar a few hundred yards to the west. Above, on the dunes of the latter, is the **Annie Jane Monument**, a granite needle erected to commemorate the 350 emigrants who lost their lives when the *Annie Jane* ran aground off Vatersay in 1853 en route to Canada.

Barra practicalities

Situated on Main Street in Castlebay, just round from the pier, the **tourist office** (April to mid-Oct Mon–Sat 9am–5pm; also open to greet the ferry; ☎01871/810336) will advise on walking routes and has details of **accommodation**. The *Castlebay Hotel* (☎01871/810223; ⑥) is the most comfortable place to stay, and there are several decent B&Bs such as *Tigh-na-Mara* (☎01871/810304; ③; April–Oct), a couple of minutes' walk from the pier by the sea. Although architecturally something of a 1970s monstrosity, the *Isle of Barra Hotel* (☎01871/810383; ⑥; mid-March to mid-Oct) enjoys a classic location, overlooking Halaman Bay. There's no official campsite, though you can **camp rough** with permission and there's an *SYHA* **hostel** (no phone; open all year) in Breibhig (Brevig), a couple of miles east of Castlebay.

In contrast to the rest of the Western Isles, Castlebay is positively buzzing on a Sunday morning when all the shops open for the folk coming out of Mass. The *Kisimul Galley* serves breakfast all day every day, and specializes in cheap- and- cheerful Scottish fry-ups – try the stovies and the bridies. For more fancy fare, head to the *Castlebay Hotel*'s cosy bar which regularly has cockles, crabs and scallops on its menu, and good views out over the bay; the food at the *Isle of Barra Hotel* also features excellent local fish and seafood. There's a fairly decent **bus/postbus** service which does the rounds of the island (Mon–Sat), and you can rent **bikes** from Castlebay Cycle Hire (☎01871/810284), half a mile east of the town centre. Films are occasionally shown on Saturday evenings at the local school – look out for the posters. Those interested in a **boat trip** to the sea-cliffs of **Mingulay**, south of Barra, whose last two inhabitants were evacuated in 1934, should phone Mr Campbell (☎01871/810303) or enquire at the *Castlebay Hotel*.

travel details

Trains

Aberdeen to: Kyle of Lochalsh (Mon–Sat 1 daily; 5hr).

Glasgow (Queen St) to: Mallaig (Mon–Sat 3 daily, Sun 1 daily; 5hr 10min); Oban (Mon–Sat 3 daily, Sun 2 daily; 3hr).

Inverness to: Kyle of Lochalsh (Mon–Sat 3 daily; 2hr 30min).

Buses
Mainland

Edinburgh to: Broadford (1 daily; 7hr); Oban (1 daily; 3hr 45min); Portree (1 daily; 7hr 40min).

Glasgow to: Broadford (3 daily; 5hr 30min); Oban (Mon–Sat 4 daily, Sun 2 daily; 3hr); Portree (3 daily; 6hr 10min); Uig (Sun 1 daily; 7hr 40min).

Inverness to: Broadford (2 daily; 2hr 35min); Portree (2 daily; 3hr 15min).

Kyle of Lochalsh to: Broadford (5–6 daily; 30min); Portree (5–6 daily; 1hr 10min).

Skye

Armadale to: Broadford (Mon–Sat 6 daily; 1hr 5min); Kyleakin (Mon–Sat 6 daily; 45min); Portree (Mon–Sat 6 daily; 1hr 50min); Sligachan (Mon–Sat 6 daily; 1hr 35min).

Broadford to: Elgol (Mon–Fri 2 daily, Sat 1 daily; 35min–2hr 30min); Portree (14–15 daily; 40min).

Dunvegan to: Glendale (2–4 daily; 20min).

Kyleakin to: Broadford (13–16 daily; 15min); Portree (13–16 daily; 1hr 10min); Sligachan (13–16 daily; 55min); Uig (1–3 daily; 1hr 30min).

Portree to: Carbost (Mon–Fri 2 daily, July & Aug also Sun 1–2 daily; 35min); Duntulm (Mon–Sat 4 daily; 1hr); Dunvegan (Mon–Sat 2 daily; 50min); Fiskavaig (Mon–Fri 2 daily, July & Aug also Sun 1–2 daily; 50min); Staffin (Mon–Sat 2 daily; 40min); Uig (3 daily; 30min).

Lewis/Harris

Stornoway to: Barabhas (Mon–Sat 8–12 daily;

25min); Calanais (Mon–Sat 4–5 daily; 40min); Carlabhagh (Mon–Sat 4–5 daily; 1hr); Port Nis (Mon–Sat 4–8 daily; 1hr); Siabost (Mon–Sat 4–6 daily; 45min); Tarbert (Mon–Sat 4–5 daily; 1hr 15min); Timsgearraidh (Mon–Sat 1–2 daily; 1hr–1hr 30min).

Tarbert to: Caolas Scalpaigh (Tues, Fri & school-days 2–4 daily; 10min); Caolas Stocinis (Mon–Sat 2–4 daily; 30min); Husinis (Tues, Thurs & school-days 2–4 daily; 45min); Leverburgh (Mon–Sat 6–8 daily; 45min).

Uists/Benbecula

Lochboisdale to: Ludag (Mon–Sat 5 daily; 30–45min).

Lochmaddy to: Balivanich (Mon–Sat 4–7 daily; 45min–2hr); Lochboisdale (Mon–Sat 2–3 daily; 2hr).

Otternish to: Balivanich (Mon–Sat 2–4 daily; 1hr–2hr 20min); Lochmaddy (Mon–Sat 3–4 daily; 20–50min).

Barra

Castlebay to: Airport/Eoligarry (Mon–Fri 12 daily, Sat 5–6 daily; 35min/40min); Vatersay (Mon–Sat 3–4 daily; 20min).

Ferries (summer timetable)

To Barra: Mallaig–Castlebay (Tues & Sun; 5hr 30min); Oban–Castlebay (Mon, Wed, Thurs, Fri & Sat; 5–7hr); Lochboisdale–Castlebay (Tues, Thurs, Fri & Sun; 1hr 40min).

To Berneray: Otternish–Berneray (Mon–Sat 8–10 daily; 10min).

To Canna: Eigg–Canna (Mon & Sat; 2hr 45min–3hr); Mallaig–Canna (Mon, Wed, Fri & Sat; 2hr 30min–4hr 15min); Muck–Canna (Sat; 2hr 15min); Rum–Canna (Mon, Wed & Sat; 1hr–1hr 45min) .

To Eriskay: Ludag–Eriskay (at least 2 daily; 30min).

To Eigg: Canna–Eigg (Fri & Sat; 2hr 15min–3hr); Mallaig–Eigg (Mon, Tues, Thurs & Sat; 1hr 30–1hr

50min); Muck–Eigg (Tues, Thurs & Sat; 45–50min); Rum–Eigg (Fri & Sat; 1hr 15min–2hr).

To Harris: Lochmaddy–Tarbert (Mon–Sat 1–2 daily; 4hr); Otternish–Leverburgh (Mon–Sat 4 daily; 1hr 10min); Uig–Tarbert (Mon–Sat 1–2 daily; 1hr 45min).

To Lewis: Ullapool–Stornoway (Mon–Sat 2 daily; 2hr 40min).

To Muck: Eigg–Muck (Tues, Thurs & Sat; 1hr); Canna–Muck (Sat; 2hr 15min); Mallaig–Muck (Tues, Thurs & Sat; 2hr 40min–4hr 45min); Rum–Muck (Sat; 1hr 15min).

To North Uist: Leverburgh–Otternish (Mon–Sat 3 daily; 1hr 10min); Tarbert–Lochmaddy (Mon–Sat 1–2 daily;); Uig–Lochmaddy (1–2 daily; 1hr 50min).

To Raasay: Sconser–Raasay (Mon–Sat 9–10 daily; 15min).

To Rum: Canna–Rum (Wed, Fri & Sat; 1hr–1hr 15min); Eigg–Rum (Mon & Sat; 1hr 30min–2hr); Mallaig–Rum (Mon, Wed, Fri & Sat; 1hr 45min–3hr 30min); Muck–Rum (Sat; 1hr 15min).

To Skye: Glenelg–Kylerhea (frequently daily; 15min); Mallaig–Armadale (Mon–Sat 5–6 daily; May to mid-Sept also Sun; 30min).

To South Uist: Castlebay–Lochboisdale (Mon, Wed, Thurs & Sat; 1hr 40min); Mallaig–Lochboisdale (Tues & Sun; 3hr 35min); Oban–Lochboisdale (daily except Tues & Sun; 5hr–6hr 50min).

Flights

Glasgow to: Barra (Mon–Sat 1–2 daily; 1hr 20min); Benbecula (Mon–Sat 1 daily; 1hr); Stornoway (Mon–Sat 1–3 daily; 1hr–1hr 45min);

Inverness to: Stornoway (Mon–Sat 2 daily; 40–50min).

CHAPTER SEVEN

NORTHEAST SCOTLAND

A large triangle of land thrusting into the North Sea, the **northeast of Scotland** comprises the area east of a line drawn roughly from Perth up to Forres, on the fringe of the Moray Firth. The area takes in the county of Angus and the city of Dundee to the south and, beyond the **Grampian Mountains**, the counties of Aberdeenshire and Moray and the city of Aberdeen. Geographically diverse, the landscape in the south is made up predominantly of undulating farmland, but, north of the Firth of Tay this gives way to wooded glens, mountains and increasingly harsh land fringed by a dramatic coast of cliffs and long sandy beaches.

The northeast was the southern kingdom of the **Picts**, reminders of whom are scattered throughout the region in the form of numerous symbolic and beautifully carved stones found in fields, churchyards and museums – such as the one at **Meigle**. Remote, self-contained and cut off from the centres of major power in the south, the area never grew particularly prosperous, and a few feuding and intermarrying families, such as the Gordons, the Keiths and the Irvines, grew to wield disproportionate influence, building many of the region's **castles** and religious buildings and developing and planning its towns.

While the fishing industry is but a fondly held memory in many parts, a number of the northeast's ports have been transformed by the discovery of **oil** in the North Sea in the 1960s, particularly **Aberdeen**, Scotland's third-largest city. Aberdeen is the region's most stimulating urban centre; a fast, relatively sophisticated city that continues to ride on the crest of the oil boom. In contrast, **Dundee**, the next largest metropolis in the northeast, is low-key and only now beginning to emerge from a depressed post-industrial period. Having said that, it boasts a splendid site on the banks of the Tay and makes a useful base for visiting nearby **Glamis Castle**, famous as the setting for Shakespeare's *Macbeth*. A little way up the Angus coast lie the historically important towns of **Arbroath** and **Montrose**. Inland, the picturesque **Angus glens** cut into the hills, their villages, such as **Blairgowrie** and **Kirriemuir**, useful centres for hikers and skiers.

North of the glens, **Deeside** is a wild, unspoilt tract of land made famous by the royal family, who have favoured **Balmoral** as one of their prime residences since Queen Victoria fell in love with it back in the 1840s. Beyond, the **Don Valley** is less visited, while tranquil **Speyside**, a little way northwest, is best known as Scotland's premier

ACCOMMODATION PRICE CODES

Throughout this book, accommodation **prices** have been graded with the codes below, according to the cost of the least expensive double room in high season. Price codes are not given for campsites, most of which charge under £10 per person. Almost all hostels charge less than £10 a night for a bed – the few exceptions to this rule have the prices quoted in the text. For a full account of the accommodation price codes, see p.30.

① under £20	④ £40–50	⑦ £70–80
② £20–30	⑤ £50–60	⑧ £80–100
③ £30–40	⑥ £60–70	⑨ over £100

whisky-producing region. The route around the northeast coast offers the best of Aberdeenshire and Moray, with rugged cliffs, empty beaches and historic fishing villages tucked into coves and bays.

Northeast Scotland is well-served by an extensive **road** network, with fast links between Dundee and Aberdeen, while the area north and east of Aberdeen is dissected by a series of efficient routes. **Trains** from the south connect with Dundee, Aberdeen and other coastal towns, while an inland line from Aberdeen heads northwest to Elgin and on to Inverness. A reasonably comprehensive scheduled **bus service** is complemented by a network of **postbuses** in the Angus glens. Only in the most remote and mountainous parts does public transport disappear altogether.

DUNDEE AND ANGUS

The predominantly agricultural county of **Angus**, east of the A9 and north of the Firth of Tay, holds some of the northeast's greatest scenery and is relatively unspoilt by tourist crowds who tend to head further west for the Highlands proper. The coast from **Montrose** to **Arbroath** is especially inviting with scarlet cliffs and sweeping bays, then, further south towards Dundee, gentler dunes and long sandy beaches. **Dundee** itself, although not the most obvious tourist destination, has in recent years become a more dynamic and progressive city, and makes for a less snooty alternative to Aberdeen.

In the north of the county, the long fingers of the **Angus glens** – heather-covered hills tumbling down to rushing rivers – are overlooked by the southern peaks of the Grampian Mountains. Each has its own feel and devotees, **Glen Clova** being, deservedly, one of the most popular, along with **Glen Shee**, which attracts large numbers of people to its ski resort. Handsome market towns like **Brechin**, **Kirriemuir** and **Blairgowrie** are good bases for the area. Angus is also liberally dotted with **Pictish remains**.

Dundee

At first sight, **DUNDEE** can seem a grim place. In the nineteenth century it was Britain's main processor of jute – the world's most important vegetable fibre after cotton. Today, though economically depressed and somewhat overshadowed by its northerly neighbour, Aberdeen, it's still a refreshingly unpretentious and welcoming city, wonderfully placed on the banks of the Tay, with some good museums, a lively arts scene and useful transport connections throughout Angus.

Even prior to its Victorian heyday, Dundee was a town of considerable importance. It was here in 1309 that Robert the Bruce was proclaimed the lawful King of Scots, and during the Reformation it earned itself a reputation for tolerance, sheltering leading figures such as George Wishart and John Knox. During the Civil War, the town was destroyed by the Royalists and Cromwell's army. Later, prior to the Battle of Killiecrankie, the city was razed to the ground once more by Jacobite Viscount Dundee, who had been granted the place for his services to the Crown by James II. The city picked itself up in the 1800s, its train and harbour links making it a major centre for shipbuilding, whaling and the manufacture of jute. Today, however, there's little left of Dundee's former glory, and its self-image hasn't been helped by the imposition of a couple of garish central shopping malls and the seemingly endless spread of 1970s housing estates around the city edges.

Many of Dundee's populace still depend on DC Thomson, the local publishing giant that produces the timelessly popular *Beano* and *Dandy* comics, as well as the *Sunday Post*, for their dwindling employment prospects. Although they have now all closed down, the city's many jam factories used to be a further major source of employment,

DUNDEE

hence the saying that Dundee was built on three Js – jam, jute and journalism. In terms of tourist sights, the most impressive is Captain Scott's Antarctic explorer ship, **RRS Discovery**, while a recreated jute mill, **Verdant Works**, is the latest attempt to draw in a few more visitors to the city. However, museums like the **McManus Art Galleries** and the hilltop **Mills Observatory**, with breathtaking views over the road and rail bridges on the Tay, are less commercialized and just as interesting.

Arrival, information and city transport

Dundee's **airport** (☎643242; see p.420 for flight details) is five minutes' drive west from the city centre. There are no buses but a taxi will only set you back about £2. By **train**, you'll arrive at Taybridge Station on South Union Street (☎228046), about 300yd south of the city centre near the river. Long-distance **buses** arrive at the Seagate bus station (☎228345), a couple of hundred yards east of the centre.

Dundee's very helpful **tourist office** is right in the centre of things at 4 City Square (Jan–April & Oct–Dec Mon–Fri 9am–5pm, Sat 10am–5pm; May, June & Sept Mon–Sat 9am–6pm, Sun 10am–4pm; July & Aug Mon–Sat 9am–7pm, Sun 10am–4pm; ☎434664), and sells bus tickets as well as booking accommodation. You can also pick up the free monthly *What's On* and *Accent* listings magazines here, which detail local events and exhibitions. The city's two daily newspapers are the morning *Courier & Advertiser* and the *Evening Telegraph & Post*, available at any newsagent.

Dundee's centre is reasonably compact and you can walk to most sights; **local buses** leave from the High Street or from Albert Square, one block to the north (for bus information, call ☎201121). There are **taxi** ranks on Nethergate, or you could call City Cabs (☎566666), Handy Taxis (☎225825) or, in Broughty Ferry, Discovery Taxis (☎732111).

Accommodation

In a city that's only just getting used to tourists, **accommodation** isn't plentiful, but it is comparatively cheap and there are some excellent guest houses. You'll find plenty of rooms out by the suburb of Broughty Ferry if you don't mind a twenty-minute bus ride into the city; Travel Dundee buses #8, #10 and #12 and Strathtay buses #73 and #76 leave from outside Littlewoods in the centre of town – the journey costs 85p. The **tourist office** charges ten percent of the first night's tariff for booking accommodation, which is then reimbursed by the hotel.

Hotels

Discovery Quay Travel Inn, Riverside Drive (☎203240). Bland, new chain hotel which has cornered the only waterfront spot in the city centre, right beside Discovery Point and the railway station. ③.

Queens Hotel, 160 Nethergate (☎322515). Friendly, old hotel which has seen better days but still has a grand sweeping staircase and fine views of the Tay. Its location is good, too, right in the heart of the action between the city and the University. ⑤.

Shaftesbury Hotel, 1 Hyndford St (☎669216). A converted jute merchant's house in a residential area very near town. Has a good and pleasantly informal restaurant. ⑤.

Strathdon Hotel, 277 Perth Rd (☎665648). Family-run hotel in the west end of Dundee. The rooms are good, and the food is even better – breakfast is included and dinner is also available. ④.

Guest houses and B&Bs

Auld Steeple, 94 Nethergate (☎200302). Unglamorous but simple, neat guest house in an old tenement block right in the city centre. ③.

Beach House, Castle Terrace, Broughty Ferry (☎776614). Fairly upmarket guest house fronting the Tay. ④.

Errolbank, 9 Dalgleish Rd (☎462118). Victorian villa with good views of the Tay; some rooms have private bathrooms. ③.

Fisherman's Tavern, 12 Fort St, Broughty Ferry (☎775941). Rooms above a cosy pub with decent food and more than thirty malt whiskies. ③.

Hillside, 43 Constitution St (☎223443). Homely, central B&B with four comfortable rooms. ③.

Stonelee, 69 Monifieth Rd, Broughty Ferry (☎737812). The best option on a street filled with B&Bs. All rooms have en-suite bathrooms. ③.

Campus and hostel accommodation

University of Dundee (☎344039). Self-catering flats for weekly rental (from £220 a week for four-bedroom flat; July to mid-Sept), including use of the University swimming pool and sports centre. Short-term B&B is also available in student residences at 319 Perth Rd (☎647171; ③).

White House Backpackers, 208 Broughty Ferry Rd (☎455788). Large new independent hostel with dorms and communal facilities on the east side of city. Catch #75 bus from High Street.

The City

The best approach to Dundee is across the mile-and-a-half-long **Tay Road Bridge** from Fife. Offering a spectacular panorama of the city on the northern bank of the Tay, the bridge, opened in 1966, has a central walkway for pedestrians. An 80p toll is levied on cars leaving the city, but you can enter from the south for free. Running parallel is the **Tay Rail Bridge**, opened in 1887 to replace the spindly structure which collapsed in a storm only eighteen months after it was built in May 1878. The crew and 75 passengers on a train passing over the bridge at the time died. At over two miles long, the present construction is the longest rail bridge in Europe.

Dundee's city centre is focused on **City Square**, a couple of hundred yards north of the Tay. The square and its surrounding streets have been much spruced up in recent years, with fountains, benches and extensive pedestrianization making for a relaxing environment, though the grand old buildings and churches have been rather over-whelmed by large shopping malls filled with a mundane mass of chain stores.

The main street, which is pedestrianized as it passes City Square, starts as Nethergate in the west, becomes High Street in the centre, then divides into Murraygate (which is also pedestrianized) and Seagate. Opposite this junction is the mottled spire of **St Paul's Episcopal Cathedral** (not open to the public), a rather gaudy George Gilbert Scott Gothic Revival structure, notable for its vividly sentimental stained glass. Fifty yards further down Seagate, the **Seagate Gallery** (Tues–Sat 10am–5pm; free) houses temporary exhibitions of all kinds of contemporary art, as well as the work of local artists. Also in the building is the **Dundee Printmakers Workshop** (Mon–Fri 10am–5pm & 6–9pm, Sat 10am–5pm; free), where you can watch printmakers at work.

A hundred yards north of City Square, at the top of Reform Street, is the attractive **Albert Square**, home of the imposing DC Thomson building, Dundee High School and, on its eastern side, **McManus Art Galleries and Museum** (Mon 11am–5pm, Tues–Sat 10am–5pm; free). Designed by Gilbert Scott, the museum is Dundee's most impressive Victorian structure, with a delightful sweep of outside curved stone stair-cases and elaborate Gothic touches. Inside, the museum gives an excellent overview of the city's past, with displays ranging from Pictish stones to the Tay Bridge disaster. Upstairs, the magnificent **Albert Hall** – crowned by a roof of 480 pitch-pine panels in a Gothic arch – houses antique musical instruments, decorative glass, gold, silver, sculp-ture and some exquisite furniture. Don't miss the table at which the Duke of Cumberland signed the death warrants of captured Jacobites after the Battle of

Culloden. On the same floor, the barrel-roofed **Victoria Gallery**'s red walls are heaving with nineteenth- and twentieth-century paintings, including some notable Pre-Raphaelite and Scottish collections (William McTaggart's seascapes being a particular highlight).

Across Ward Road from the museum, the **Howff Burial Ground** on Meadowside (daily 9am–5pm or dusk) has some great carved tombstones dating from the sixteenth to nineteenth centuries. Originally gardens belonging to a monastery, the land was given to Dundee for burials in 1564 by Mary, Queen of Scots. Nearby is the run-of-the-mill **Barrack Street Natural History Museum** (Mon 11am–5pm, Tues–Sat 10am–5pm; free), with a motley collection of stuffed local wildlife. The most impressive exhibit is the skeleton of a whale, washed up on a nearby beach in 1883 and eulogized in a poem by William McGonagall, a strong contender for world's worst poet (for more on him, ask for a McGonagall Walking Trail leaflet from the tourist office).

Five minutes' walk west of here, on West Henderson Wynd in Blackness, an energetic new museum, **Verdant Works**, tells the story of jute from its harvesting in India to its arrival in Dundee on clipper ships (April–Oct Mon–Sat 10am–5pm, Sun 11am–5pm; Nov–March Mon–Sat 10am–4pm, Sun 11am–4pm; £3.25 or £6.50 joint ticket with Discovery Point). The museum has authentic-looking recreations of a turn-of-the-century jute-processing plant, and there are plans to extend the museum to cover Dundee's other two Js, jam and journalism, over the next few years.

Just south of the city centre, at the water's edge alongside the Tay Road Bridge, **Discovery Point** is an impressive development centring on the Royal Research Ship *Discovery* (same hours as Verdant Works; £4.50). A three-mast steam-assisted vessel built in Dundee in 1901 to take Captain Scott on his polar expeditions, it has been elegantly restored, with polished wood panels and brass trimmings giving scant indication of the privations suffered by the crew. Temperatures on board would plummet to -28° in the Antarctic, and turns at having a bath came round every 47 days. Enthusiastic guides spin some fascinating yarns about the boat's colourful history, and the audio-visual spectacular you experience before boarding is compelling enough, if mercilessly overhyped.

In total contrast is the endearingly simple wooden frigate **Unicorn** (mid-March to Sept daily 10am–5pm; £3), moored in Victoria Dock on the other side of the road bridge (there is a pathway between them). Built in 1824, it's the oldest British warship still afloat and was in active service up until 1968. During its service years, over 300 men would have lived and worked aboard. The fact that its 46 guns – eighteen-pounder cannons are still on display – were never fired in aggression probably accounts for its survival. Although the interior is sparse, the cannons, the splendid figureheads and the wonderful model of the ship in its fully rigged glory (23.5 miles of rope would have been used) are fascinating.

Out from the centre

A mile or so north of town, **Dundee Law** is the plug of an extinct volcano and, at 571ft, the city's highest point. Once the site of a seventh-century defensive hillfort, it is now an impressive lookout, with great views across the whole city and the Tay – although the climb is steep and often windy. It takes thirty minutes to walk to the foot of the law from the city centre, or you can take buses #3 or #4 from Albert Square.

The city's other volcanic plug of rock sits a mile to the west of Dundee Law. **Balgay Hill** is crowned by the wooded **Lochee Park**, at the summit of which sits the **Mills Observatory** (April–Sept Mon–Fri 11am–5pm, Sat 2–5pm; Oct–March Mon–Fri 4–10pm, Sat 2–5pm; free), Britain's only full-time public observatory with a resident astronomer. The best time to go is after dark on winter nights; in summer there's little to be seen through the telescope, but well-explained, quirky exhibits and displays chart the history of space exploration and astronomy, and on sunny days you can play at being a human sundial and take in the fantastic views over the city through little tele-scopes. The observatory also has special opening times to coincide with eclipses and other astronomic events (details on ☎435846). Buses #2, #36 and #37 drop you in Balgay Road, at the entrance to the park.

Four miles east of Dundee's city centre lies the seaside settlement of **BROUGHTY FERRY**, now engulfed by the city as a reluctant suburb. An eclectic mix of big villas built by jute barons up the hillside and small fishermen's cottages along the shoreline, "The Ferry" (as it's called by locals) has experienced a recent resurgence in popular-ity. Now a pleasant and relaxing spot with some good restaurants and pubs, it's far more unspoilt than Dundee, though the pollution level on the beach itself is pretty dire – all the city's sewage seems to end up here. The striking **Broughty Castle and Museum**, right by the seashore (Mon–Thurs & Sat 10am–1pm & 2–5pm; July–Sept also Sun 2–5pm; free), is worth a look. Built in the fifteenth century to protect the estu-ary, its four floors now house local-history exhibits, covering the story of Broughty Ferry as a fishing village and the history of whaling, as well as details of local geolo-gy and wildlife.

Just north of Broughty Ferry, at the junction of the A92 and B978, the chunky bricks of **Claypotts Castle** (April–Sept Mon, Sat & Sun 9.30am–6pm; £2.30) constitute one of Scotland's most complete Z-shaped tower houses. Built from 1569 to 1588, its two round towers have stepped projections to support extra rooms – a sixteenth-century archi-tectural practice that makes Claypotts look like it's about to topple.

Eating, drinking and nightlife

The West End of Dundee, around the principal University and Perth Road, is the best area for **eating and drinking**, while the city centre, though good for a few pubs, is a bit of a non-starter for decent food. Broughty Ferry is a pleasant spot with a good selec-tion of pubs and restaurants, which get particularly busy on summer evenings.

Restaurants

Agacan, 113 Perth Rd (☎644227). Tiny Turkish restaurant with colourful paintings on the rough walls, and equal artistry taking place over the charcoal grill; also does takeaways. Open Tues–Sun evenings.

Deep Sea, 81 Nethergate (☎224449). The best of Dundee's fish-and-chip restaurants, serving huge and tasty portions.

Nawab, 43a Gray St, Broughty Ferry (☎731800). An excellent and busy balti and tandoori restau-rant, popular with locals.

Pierre Victoire, 15 Shore Terrace (☎202077). Roomy, convivial French-style brasserie situated in the old Exchange Coffee House building just down from City Square.

Raffles, 18 Perth Rd (☎201139). Pricey but stylish wine bar/café with restaurant downstairs. Good for vegetarian meals and coffee at any hour.

Visocchi's, 40 Gray St, Broughty Ferry. Authentic and inexpensive Italian fare served in an infor-mal, popular ice-cream café.

Pubs

Drouthie Neebours, 142–146 Perth Rd. A cheerful bar with a Robbie Burns theme, lavish painted murals and a lively student clientele.

Laing's, 8 Roseangle, off Perth Road. Usually packed on warm summer nights, thanks to its beer garden and great views over the Tay.

Lucifer's Mill, Session Street. A converted jute mill, with a mainly student clientele. Good for up-and-coming indie/blues bands and a great chill-out room.

Mercantile, 100 Commercial St. Popular with the grey-suit brigade, but worth persevering for the excellent range of beers and quality pub snacks.

O' Neill's, North Lindsay Street. Beery Irish bar, with frequent live Celtic music.
Ship Inn, 121 Fisher St, Broughty Ferry. A narrow pub with a warm atmosphere right on the waterfront. The bistro upstairs has views over Tay and serves great food.

Nightlife

When it comes to post-pub nightlife, Dundee's offering is muted, to say the least. There are three **nightclubs** on top of each other along South Ward Road, midway between the centre and the University precincts – *Fat Sam's*, *De Stihl's* and the *Mardi Gras* – all of which have a regular student following. The current 'in' place is the centrally located *The Zone* on Commercial Street, which has regular theme nights.

On a cultural level, Dundee is showing signs of a lively renaissance: there are plans afoot to build a new arts centre around the Rep Theatre, and the Edinburgh Festival has even farmed out a few shows to Dundee over the last couple of years. Top of the bill is the prodigious Dundee Repertory Theatre (☎223530) on Tay Square, north of Nethergate, an excellent place for indigenously produced contemporary **theatre**. In St Mary Place (off Lochee Road) the Dundee Arts Centre (☎201035) is good for community-based theatre, dance and music. The best venue for **classical** music, including visits by the Royal Scottish Orchestra and other bigwigs, is Caird Hall (☎223141), whose bulky frontage dominates City Square. For **movies**, the ABC on Seagate (☎225247), or the Odeon multiplex, in the Stack Leisure Park off Harefield Road (☎400855), are predictably mainstream. For slightly more esoteric viewing, try the Steps Film Centre, an arts cinema at the back of the Wellgate Shopping Centre, off Victoria Road (☎434037).

Listings

Airport Riverside Drive, Dundee (☎643242).

Banks Bank of Scotland, 11 Reform St (☎229131); Clydesdale Bank, 96 High St (☎824404); Royal Bank of Scotland, 3 High St (☎228111); TSB, Meadowside (☎228801).

Bike rental Just Bikes, 57 Grey St, Broughty Ferry (☎732100); Nicholson's, 2 Forfar Rd (☎461212).

Bookshop James Thin, 7 High St; Waterstone's, 34 Commercial St.

Car rental Arnold Clark, 14–22 Trades Lane (☎225382); Eurodollar, 45–53 Gellatly St (☎224037); Hertz, 18 Marketgait (☎223711).

Bus enquiries National Express (☎0990 808080); Scottish Citylink (☎0990 505050); Strathtay Scottish for regional buses (☎228054); Travel Dundee (☎201121).

Currency exchange Thomas Cook, City Square (Mon–Fri 9am–5.30pm, Sat 9am–5pm; ☎200204), and at the tourist office.

Football Dundee has two leading football clubs, which face each other across Tannadice Street in the north of the city. Tickets for both the premier-league Dundee United (ticket sales and information on ☎833166) and first-division Dundee FC (ticket sales and information on ☎826104) cost around £12.

Gay, lesbian and bisexual Switchboard ☎202620.

Genealogical research Tay Valley History Society, 179 Princes St (☎461845).

Golf Public courses at Ashludie, Golf Avenue, Monifieth (☎532967); Caird Park (☎434706); and Camperdown Country Park (☎432688). Other courses along the Angus coast include Carnoustie (☎01241/853789), venue for the British Open in 1999.

Internet You can log onto the World Wide Web or send email from The Webgate Internet (☎434332) at the Central Library in the Wellgate Shopping Centre.

Hospital Dundee Royal Infirmary (with 24hr accident and emergency), Barrack Road (☎660111).

Pharmacy Boots, High St (Mon–Wed, Fri & Sat 8.30am–5.45pm, Thurs 8.30am–7pm); Sunday opening is done on a rota basis.

Police Tayside Police HQ, Bell St (☎223200).

Post office GPO, 4 Meadowside (Mon–Fri 9am–5.30pm, Sat 9am–7pm; ☎203532).

Rape crisis centre ☎201291.

Swimming pools Olympia leisure complex (Mon–Fri 9am–9pm, Sat & Sun 9am–5pm; ☎434888) beside Discovery Point.

Travel agents Campus Travel, Airlie Place (☎200412); Ramsay Travel, Crichton Street (☎200394).

The Angus coast

Two roads link Dundee to Aberdeen and the northeast coast of Scotland – by far the more pleasant option is the slightly longer A92 coast road which joins the inland A90 at Stonehaven, just south of Aberdeen. Intercity **buses** follow both main routes, while the coast-hugging train line from Dundee is one of the most picturesque in Scotland, passing attractive beaches and impressive cliffs, and stopping in the old seaports of **Arbroath** and **Montrose**.

Arbroath and around

Since it was settled in the twelfth century, local fishermen have been landing their catches at **ARBROATH**, situated on the Angus coast where it starts to curve in from the North Sea towards the Firth of Tay. The **Arbroath smokie** – line-caught haddock, smoke-cured over smouldering oak chips and then poached in milk – is one of Scotland's best-known dishes, and should be eaten the original way, with a knob of butter, rather than in the more fancy pâtés and mousses that are now becoming popular. Although it has a great location, with long sandy beaches and stunning sandstone cliffs on either side of town as well as a lively harbour area, Arbroath, like Dundee, has suffered from short-sighted development, its historical associations all but subsumed by pedestrian walkways, a mess of one-way systems and ugly shopping centres.

Chiefly due to its harbour, Arbroath had, by the late eighteenth century, become a trading and manufacturing centre, famed for boot-making and sail-making (the *Cutty Sark*'s sails were made here). Arbroath's real glory days, however, came much earlier in the thirteenth century with the completion of **Arbroath Abbey** in 1233 (April–Sept Mon–Sat 9.30am–6pm, Sun noon–6pm; Oct–March Mon–Sat 9.30am–4pm, Sun 2–4pm; £1.50), whose rose-pink sandstone ruins, described by Dr Johnson as "fragments of magnificence", stand on Abbey Street. Founded in 1178 but not granted abbey status until 1285, it was the scene of one of the most significant events in Scotland's history, when on April 6, 1320, a group of Scottish barons drew up the **Declaration of Arbroath**, asking the Pope to reverse his excommunication of Robert the Bruce and recognize him as king, asserting Scotland's independence from the English: "For, so long as one hundred remain alive, we will never in any degree be subject to the dominion of the English." It was duly dispatched to Pope John XXII in Avignon, who in 1324 agreed to Robert's claim.

The abbey was dissolved during the Reformation, and by the eighteenth century it was little more than a source of red sandstone for local houses. However, there is still enough left to get a good idea of how vast the place must have been: the semicircular west doorway is more or less intact, complete with medieval mouldings, and the south transept has a beautiful round window, once lit with a beacon to guide ships. In the early 1950s, the Stone of Destiny had a brief sojourn here when it was stolen from London by a group of Scottish nationalists and appeared, wrapped in a Scottish flag, at the High Altar. It was duly returned to Westminster Abbey, where it stayed until its recent move to Edinburgh Castle (see p.64).

Down by the harbour, the elegant Regency **Signal House Museum** (Mon–Sat 10am–5pm, July & Aug also Sun 2–5pm; free) stands sentinel as it has since 1813. The interior is now given over to some excellent local-history displays. A school room, fisherman's cottage and lighthouse kitchen have all been carefully re-created, with the addition of realistic smells.

WALKS AROUND ARBROATH

There's not much else to see in Arbroath besides the abbey, but there are some great **walks** in the vicinity. From the Signal House, you can wander through the huddled cottages of the **Fit o' the toon**, the harbour district where the smell of Arbroath smokies usually hangs heavy in the air. Beyond it, the seafront road heads into Victoria Park; at the far end of the road, a path climbs up over the red sandstone cliffs of **Whiting Ness**, stretching endlessly onto the horizon and eroded into a multitude of inlets, caves and arches that warrants hours of leisurely exploration. *The Arbroath Cliffs Nature Trail Guide*, available free from the tourist office, picks out twenty good viewing points along the first one and a half miles, and also gives details on the local fauna, flora and birds – you may even see puffins. After four miles the path comes to the foot of the neat little fishing village of **Auchmithie** (see below); a further four (very windy) miles north is the crest of **Lunan Bay**, a classic sweep of glorious sand crowned by the eerie ruins of Red Castle at the mouth of the Lunan Water.

St Vigeans and Auchmithie

Although now little more than a northwestern dormitory of Arbroath, the pristine and peaceful hamlet of **ST VIGEANS** is a fine example of a Pictish site colonized by Christians – the church is set defiantly on a pre-Christian mound at the centre of the village. Many Pictish and earlier remains are housed in the wonderful little **museum** (April–Sept Mon–Sat 9.30am–6.30pm, Sun 2–6.30pm; collect the key from cottage no. 7 if closed; free), including the Drosten Stone, presumed to be a memorial. One side depicts a hunt, laced with an abundance of Pictish symbolism, while the other side bears a cross, which dates it around 850 AD.

Four miles north of Arbroath by road or coastal footpath, the clifftop village of **AUCHMITHIE** is the true home of the Arbroath smokie. However, the village didn't have a proper harbour until last century – local fishermen, apparently, were carried to their boats by their wives to avoid getting wet feet – so Arbroath became the more important port and laid claim to the delicacy. Now an attractive little fishing village, Auchmithie's main attraction is the *But'n'Ben* restaurant (☎01241/877223; closed Tues), one of the best along this coast, which specializes in delicious Scottish dishes and seafood.

Practicalities

Arbroath's helpful **tourist office**, at Market Place right in the middle of town (April & May Mon–Fri 9am–5pm, Sat 10am–5pm; June–Aug Mon–Sat 9.30am–5.30pm, Sun 11am–4pm; Sept Mon–Sat 9.30am–5.30pm; Oct–March Mon–Fri 9am–5pm, Sat 10am–3pm; ☎01241/872609), can recommend local walks and book accommodation. **Buses** stop at the station on Catherine Street (☎01241/870646), about a five-minute walk south of the tourist office, while **trains** arrive at the station just across the road on Keptie Street (for enquiries, call ☎01382/228046).

The best place **to stay** is at the excellent *Five Gables Guest House* (☎01241/871632; ③), above the golf course a mile south of town on the A92: formerly the golf clubhouse, it has a great position overlooking the sea. Alternatively, try the *Harbour House Guest House*, 4 The Shore (☎01241/878047; ②), down by the harbour, which is also where you'll find the best **restaurants** and **pubs**. The best place to sample Arbroath smokies at *The Old Brewhouse* (☎01241/879945), a convivial and moderately priced restaurant-cum-pub by the harbour wall at the end of High Street, or check out some of the 180 varieties of rum on offer at the *Smugglers Tavern*, on The Shore.

Montrose and around

"Here's the Basin, there's Montrose, shut your een and haud your nose." As the old rhyme indicates, **MONTROSE**, a seaport and market town since the thirteenth century, can sometimes smell a little rich, mostly because of its position on the edge of a virtually landlocked two-mile-square lagoon of mud known as the Basin. But with the wind in the right direction Montrose is a great little town to visit, with a pleasant old centre and an interesting museum. The Basin too is of interest: flooded and emptied twice daily by the tides, it is a rich nature reserve for the host of geese, swans and waders who frequent the ooze to look for food. On the south side of the Basin, a mile out of Montrose along the A92, the **Montrose Basin Wildlife Centre** (daily: April–Oct 10.30am–5pm; Nov–March 10.30am–4pm; £2.50) has binoculars, high-powered telescopes, bird hides and remote-control video cameras to check out the diverse bird- and wildlife. In addition, the centre's resident ranger takes regular guided walks around the reserve.

Montrose locals are known as Gable Endies, because of the unusual way in which the town's eighteenth- and nineteenth-century merchants, influenced by architectural styles they had seen on the Continent, built their houses gable-end to the street. The few remaining original gabled houses line the wide **High Street**, off which are numerous tiny alleyways and quiet courtyards.

Two blocks behind the soaring kirk steeple at the lower end of High Street, the **Montrose Museum and Art Gallery** (Mon–Sat 10am–5pm; free) in Panmure Place on the western side of **Mid Links** park, is one of Scotland's oldest museums, dating from 1842. For a small town museum, it has some particularly unusual exhibits, among them the so-called Samson Stone, a Pictish relic dating from 900 AD, and bearing a carving of Samson slaying the Philistines. On the upper floor, the maritime history exhibits include a cast of Napoleon's death mask and a model of a British man-of-war, sculpted out of bone by Napoleonic prisoners at Portsmouth. Most intriguing, however, is the enigmatic message on a scrap of paper found in a bottle at nearby Ferryden beach in 1857, written by the chief mate of a brigantine eighty years earlier: "Blowing a hurricane lying to with close-reefed main topsails ship waterlogged. Cargo of wood from Quebec. No water on board, provisions all gone. Ate the dog yesterday, three men left alive. Lord have mercy on our souls. Amen."

Outside the entrance of the museum stands a winsome study of a boy by local sculptor William Lamb (1893–1951). More of his work can be seen in the moving **William Lamb Memorial Studio** on Market Street (July to mid-Sept daily except Mon 2–5pm; for entry at other times ask at the museum; ☎01674/673232; free), including bronze heads of the Queen, Princess Margaret and the Queen Mother. The earnings from these pieces enabled him to buy the studio in the 1930s, which he donated to the town of Montrose on his death. A superbly talented but largely unheralded artist, Lamb's work is made the more impressive by the fact that he taught himself to sculpt with his left hand, having suffered a war wound in his right.

After the impressive wildlife of Montrose Basin, it's easy to ignore the town's fabulous golden **seashore**. The beach road, Marine Avenue, across from the town museum, heads down through sand dunes and golf links to car parks fringing the fine, wide beach overlooked by a slender white lighthouse.

Around Montrose: the House of Dun

Across the Basin, four miles west of Montrose, is the Palladian **House of Dun** (Easter weekend & May–Sept daily 1.30–5pm; Oct Sat & Sun 1.30–5pm; NTS; £3.50, grounds free), accessible on the regular Montrose–Brechin bus (#30) – ask the driver to let you off outside. Built in 1730 for David Erskine, Laird of Dun, to designs by William Adam, the house was opened to the public in 1989 after extensive restoration, and is crammed full of period furniture and *objets d'art*. Inside, the ornate relief plasterwork is the most impressive feature, extravagantly emblazoned with Jacobite symbolism. You can also see some gorgeous pieces of intricate needlework, stitched by the illegitimate child of King William IV, Lady Augusta, who married into the Dun family in 1827.

The buildings in the courtyard – a hen house, gamekeeper's workshop and potting shed – have been renovated, and include a tearoom and a shop where local weavers give displays of their traditional skills.

Practicalities

The Montrose **tourist office** is squeezed into a former public toilet next to the library, at the point where Bridge Street merges into the lower end of High Street (April–June & Sept Mon–Sat 10am–5pm; July & Aug Mon–Sat 9.30am–5.30pm; ☎01674/672000). Most **buses** stop in High Street, while the **train** station lies a block back on Western Road (hourly trains from Dundee and Aberdeen). For B&B **accommodation**, try *Oaklands*, over the river bridge at 10 Rossie Island Rd (☎01674/672018; ③), or the friendly *Murray Lodge Hotel*, 2–8 Murray St, the northern continuation of High Street (☎01674/678880; ④). A nearby alternative is *Kirkside* (☎01674/830780; ③), an isolated converted fishing bothy situated on the edge of the sand dunes by St Cyrus Nature Reserve, just over two miles north of Montrose at the mouth of the North Esk River.

For **eating**, the liveliest place in Montrose is unquestionably *Roo's Leap*, a sports bar and restaurant by the golf club off the northern end of Traill Drive. The food is an unlikely, but excellent, mix of Scottish, American and Australian. If you want a **drink**, the vitality of *Roo's Leap* is matched in her sister café-bar, *Sharky's*, on George Street, which also serves coffee and light snacks, while on High Street the more traditional *Cornerhouse Hotel* hosts folk nights on Tuesdays. The *Salutation Inn*, 69–71 Bridge St, serves good, cheap food and has a beer garden.

Strathmore and the Angus glens

Immediately north of Dundee the low-lying Sidlaw Hills divide the city from the rich agricultural region of **Strathmore**, whose string of tidy market towns lie on a fertile strip along the southernmost edge of the heather-covered lower slopes of the Grampian Mountains. These towns act as gateways to the **Angus glens** – or "Braes o' Angus", a series of tranquil valleys penetrated by few roads and offering some of the most rugged and majestic landscapes of northeast Scotland. It's a rain-swept, wind-blown, sparsely populated area, whose roads become impassable with the first snows, sometimes as early as October, and in the summer there are ferocious midges to contend with. Nevertheless, most of the glens, particularly **Glen Clova**, are well and truly on the tourist circuit, with the rolling hills and dales attracting hikers, birdwatchers and botanists in the summer, grouse shooters and deerhunters in autumn and a growing number of skiers in winter. The most useful road through the glens is the A93, which

---

SKIING IN THE ANGUS GLENS

For **information on skiing** in the Angus glens, call Ski Glenshee (☎013397/41320), who also offer ski rental and lessons. In addition, lessons, skis and boards are available from Cairnwell Mountain Sports (☎01250/885255), at the Spittal of Glenshee. **Ski rental** starts at around £12 a day, while lessons are around £10 for two hours. **Lift passes** cost £16.50 per day or £66 for a five-day (Mon–Fri) ticket. For the latest snow and weather conditions, phone the Ski Hotline (☎0891/654656).

cuts through **Glen Shee** to Braemar on Deeside (see p.403). It's pretty dramatic stuff, threading its way over Britain's highest main road pass – the **Cairnwell Pass** at 2199ft. **Buses** ply along the A93 through most of Glen Shee en route to Deeside; for glens Clova and Prosen, you can use the **postbuses** from Kirriemuir.

Glen Shee

The most dramatic and best known of the Angus glens, **Glen Shee** is dominated by its ski fields, sprawled over four mountains above the Cairnwell mountain pass. During the winter season – December to March – skiers, predominantly from the cities of central Scotland, brave the ridiculously cold temperatures and bitter winds. Ski lifts and tows give access to gentle beginners' slopes, while more experienced skiers can try the more intimidating Tiger run. In summer it's all a bit sad, with lifeless chair lifts and bare, scree-covered slopes, although hang-gliders take advantage of the crosswinds between the mountains and there are some excellent hiking and mountain biking routes.

The well-heeled town of **BLAIRGOWRIE** (officially Blairgowrie and Rattray), little more than one main road set among raspberry fields on the glen's southernmost tip, is as good a place as any to base yourself – and is particularly useful in winter if you plan to ski. Right on the river, the town's only claim to fame is that St Ninian once camped at Wellmeadow, a pleasant grassy triangle in the town centre. If you've time to kill here, wander up the leafy river bank to **Keathbank Mill** (daily 10.30am–5pm; £2.95), a huge old jute mill with an 1862 steam turbine driven by the largest working water wheel in Scotland. Also housed within the complex are some fascinating workshops where the country's largest heraldic crests are carved.

Blairgowrie **tourist office** (Easter–June, Sept & Oct Mon–Sat 9.30am–5.30pm, Sun 11am–4pm; July & Aug Mon–Sat 9am–7pm, Sun 11am–6pm; Nov–Easter Mon–Fri 9.30am–5pm, Sat 9.30am–1.30pm; ☎01250/872960), on the high side of the Wellmeadow, can help with **accommodation**. Over the bridge spanning the fast-flowing River Ericht, Blairgowrie melts into its twin community of **Rattray**, where, on the main street (Boat Brae), you'll find the excellent *Ivy Lodge* B&B (☎01250/873056; ③), offering sweeping views of the river and surrounding hills, as well as use of a floodlit tennis court. Alternatively, there's the opulent, ivy-covered *Kinloch House* (☎01250/884237; ⑨), one of the area's most prestigious hotels, set in its own vast grounds three miles west of town on the A923, while, at the other end of the scale, **camping** is available at the year-round *Blairgowrie Holiday Park* on Rattray's Hatton Road (☎01250/872941). The town boasts plenty of places to **eat**: *Cargills* by the river on Lower Mill Street (☎01250/876735; closed Mon) is the best bet for a formal meal, while, for lighter meals and takeaways, there's the *Dome Restaurant*, just behind the tourist office, which has been run by two local Italian families since the 1920s. For good **pub** grub try the *Brig o'Blair* on the Wellmeadow, or head six miles out of town on the A93 to the delightfully situated *Bridge of Cally Hotel* (☎01250/886231; ⑤), which also has rooms. **Bikes** can be rented from the *Blairgowrie Holiday Park* (see above), and from Mountains and Glens (☎01250/874206), 300yd from the tourist office on Railway Road.

Nearly twenty miles north of Blairgowrie, the **SPITTAL OF GLENSHEE**, though ideally situated for skiing, is little more than a tacky service area, only worth stopping at for a quick drink or bite to eat. However, it does boast an excellent bunkhouse run by Cairnwell Mountain Sports, on the A93 (☎01250/885255), which rents out skis, bikes and even offers hang-gliding lessons. In addition, it's handily close to one of the nicest places to stay in the area, the *Dalmunzie House* (☎01250/885224; ⑧), a gorgeous, turreted, Highland sporting lodge, evoking the peace and tranquillity of the rugged scenery. From the Spittal the road climbs another five miles or so to the ski centre at the crest of the Cairnwell Pass.

Blairgowrie is well linked by **bus** to both Perth and Dundee by the hourly #57; to get up Glen Shee, however, you'll have to rely on the **postbus**, which leaves town (Mon–Sat) at 9.05am and returns from the Spittal of Glenshee at 2.15pm, or the thrice-weekly, summer-only Bluebird coach from Aberdeen and Braemar.

Glen Isla and Meigle

Running parallel to Glen Shee, and linked to it via the A926, is **Glen Isla**, dominated by Mount Blair (2441ft). A lot less dramatic than its sister glens, it suffers from an excess of angular conifers alongside great bald chunks of hillside waiting to be planted. At the mouth of the glen, on the B954, lies the tiny village of **MEIGLE**, fifteen miles north of Dundee and home to Scotland's most important collection of early Christian and Pictish inscribed stones. Housed in a modest former schoolhouse, the **Meigle Museum** (April–Sept Mon–Sat 9.30am–12.30pm & 1.30–6pm, Sun noon–6pm; £1.50) displays some thirty pieces dating from the seventh to the tenth centuries, all found in and around the nearby churchyard. The majority are either gravestones that would have lain flat, or cross slabs, inscribed with the sign of the cross and usually standing. Most impressive is the 7ft-tall great cross slab, said to be Guinevere's gravestone, carved on one side with a portrayal of Daniel surrounded by lions, a beautifully executed equestrian group, and mythological creatures including a dragon and a centaur. On the other side various beasts are surmounted by the "ring of glory" – a wheel containing a cross carved and decorated in high relief. The exact meaning and purpose of the stones and their enigmatic symbols is obscure, and why so many of the stones were found at Meigle is also a mystery. The most likely theory suggests that Meigle was once an important ecclesiastical centre which attracted secular burials of prominent Picts.

Heading north into Glen Isla along the B954, the River Isla narrows and then plunges some 60ft into a deep gorge to produce the classically pretty waterfall of **Reekie Linn**, or "smoking fall", so called because of the water mist produced when the fall hits a ledge and bounces a further 20ft into a deep pool known as the Black Dub. The glen cheers up enormously north of the tiny hamlet of **KIRKTON OF GLENISLA**, ten miles or so up the glen. Here, the cosy *Glenisla Hotel* (☎01575/582223; ③) is great for eating and drinking, as well as being a good base for walking. In the nearby Glenisla forest there are some trails for hiking, while, just before Kirkton, a turnoff on the right-hand side leads to the Glenmarkie Riding Centre (☎01575/582341), which offers pony trekking and wonderfully isolated B&B (③).

Transport connections into the glen are limited: the plain Strathmore town of Alyth, three miles north of Meigle, is on the main bus routes linking Blairgowrie with Dundee and Kirriemuir, while the hourly #57 bus from Dundee to Perth passes through Meigle. The only transport up to Kirkton is a postbus which leaves Alyth at 7.40am (Mon–Sat).

Forfar, Glamis and Aberlemno

Around fifteen miles north of Dundee, along the main A90, lies **FORFAR**, Angus's county town and the ancient capital of the Picts. Although hardly the most thrilling town in the district, exuding a solid conservatism, it warrants an afternoon's exploration. The old Picitsh connections are still evident in Forfar's strong support for the Scottish National Party (SNP), with a profusion of Scottish flags and stirring messages on civic buildings. The wide High Street is framed by some impressive Victorian architecture and small old-fashioned shops. Midway along, at no. 20, the **Meffen Institute Museum and Art Gallery** (Mon–Sat 10am–5pm; free) exhibits Neolithic, Pictish and Celtic remains and a thoroughly enjoyable collection of re-created historical street scenes. The most disturbing examines the town's seventeenth-century passion for witch-hunting, with a taped re-creation of locals baying for blood. There is also a comprehensive interactive computer catalogue of all the Pictish stones in Angus and an excellent art gallery.

A series of glacial lochs peter out in the west of the town at **Forfar Loch**, now surrounded by a pleasant country park with a visitors' centre and three-mile nature trail. Two miles east, high above the wooded Loch Fithie, are the impressive remains of **Restenneth Priory** (free access), approached along an easy-to-miss sideroad off the B9113. Built by King Nechtan of the Picts in about the eighth century, it was adapted as an Augustinian priory in the twelfth century. Still something of a Pictish shrine, it's common to find mementoes and flowers left by pilgrims. The splayed foot spire, first seen beckoning from the road, was added in the fifteenth century.

Forfar's small **tourist office** (April–June & Sept Mon–Sat 10am–5pm; July & Aug Mon–Sat 9.30am–5.30pm; ☎01307/467876) is at 45 East High St, opposite the soaring steeple of the parish church. Numerous shops and bakers stock the famous **Forfar Bridie**, a huge folded pastry case of mince, onion and seasonings, including Saddlers, a few door down from the tourist office, and McLarens (the locals' favourite), at 8 West High St. Otherwise, all-day **food** and **drink** can be found at the *Royal Hotel* on Castle Street, by the Town Hall.

Glamis Castle

Regular buses from Forfar (4 daily; 40min) to Dundee pass the pink-sandstone **Glamis Castle** (April–Oct daily 10.30am–4.45pm; castle and grounds £5.20, grounds only £2.40), a mile north of the picturesque village of **GLAMIS** (pronounced "Glahms"). A wondrously over-the-top, L-shaped five-storey pile set in an extensive landscaped park complete with deer and pheasants, this is one of the most famous Scottish castles. Shakespeare chose it as a central location in *Macbeth* and its royal connections (as the childhood home of the Queen Mother and birthplace of Princess Margaret) make it one of the essential stops on every bus tour of Scotland.

Approaching the castle down the long main drive, a melee of turrets, towers and conical roofs appear fantastically at the end of the sweeping avenue of trees, framed by the Grampian Mountains. The bulk of the current building dates from the fifteenth century, although many of the later additions (particularly from the seventeenth century) give it its startling Disneyesque appearance. Glamis began life as a comparatively humble hunting lodge, used in the eleventh century by the kings of Scotland. In 1372, King Robert II gave the property to his son-in-law, Sir John Lyon, who built the core of the present building. His descendants, the earls of Kinghorne and Strathmore – the fourteenth of which was the Queen Mother's father – have lived here ever since.

The guided tour starts upstairs in the Victorian **Dining Room**. The garish silver ship that forms the centrepiece of the table display was a golden wedding gift to the thirteenth earl from his estate workers in 1903. Another present – the grandfather clock in the corner – came from their 27 grandchildren, including a 3-year-old Elizabeth Bowes-Lyon, now the Queen Mother. The atmosphere changes dramatically in the fifteenth-century **Crypt**, more properly the Lower Hall of the original tower house. The crypt's 12ft-thick walls enclose a haunted "lost" room, reputed to be have been sealed with the red-bearded Lord of Glamis and Crawford (also known as Beardie Crawford) inside, after he dared to play cards with the Devil one Sabbath. From here, the tour passes up a seventeenth-century staircase, whose hollow central pillar was a primitive system of central heating.

Next is the arch-roofed **Drawing Room**, with delightful wedding-cake plasterwork (dated 1621). Classical portraits line the walls, the most notable being the vast Jacob de Wit family grouping of the third earl, who was responsible for many of the castle's seventeenth-century alterations. De Wit painted the earl in Classical armour that, unfortunately, looks like a flimsy negligee. The highlight of the tour is the family **Chapel**, completed in 1688. Jacob de Wit was commissioned to produce the frescoes from the family Bible, although his depictions of Christ wearing a hat and St Peter in a pair of glasses have raised eyebrows ever since. The chapel is said to be haunted by the spectre of a grey lady, the ghost of the sixth Lady Glamis who was burnt as a witch under orders of James V. The **Billiard Room**, complete with full-sized table and a beautiful polished walnut piano that cost £199 when it was commissioned in 1866, is lined with paintings and tapestries of which the vast and colourful *Fruit Market* by Flemish artist Frans Snyders draws the most attention. **King Malcolm's Room**, so called because it is believed he died nearby in 1034, is most notable for its carved wooden chimneypiece, on which many of its most decorative panels are, in fact, highly polished leather.

From here, the tour passes into the **Royal Apartments**, where you can see the Queen Mother's delicate gilt four-poster bed which was a wedding present from her mother, who embroidered the names and dates of birth of her ten children into its panels. **Duncan's Hall**, a fifteenth-century guardroom, is the traditional – but inaccurate – setting for Duncan's murder by Macbeth (it actually took place near Elgin). Finally, the tour concludes with a random set of family diplays that include the Queen Mother's old doll's house.

Glamis' grounds are worth a few hours in their own right. Highlights include the lead statues of James VI and Charles I at the top of the main drive, the seventeenth-century Baroque sundial, the formal gardens and the verdant walks out to Earl John's Bridge and through the woodland. In Glamis village the humble **Angus Folk Museum** (Easter weekend & May–Sept daily 11am–4.30pm, Oct Sat & Sun only; NTS; £2.30), housed in six low-slung cottages in Kirk Wynd, has a bewildering array of local ephemera, including bizarrely named agricultural implements, a nineteenth-century horse-drawn hearse and a section on local bothies.

Aberlemno

Five miles east of Forfar, straddling the ridge-topping B9134, the hamlet of **ABERLEMNO** is home to a superb collection of open-air Pictish stones (Oct–April boxed out of sight in weatherproofed wood). In the churchyard, just off the main road, an eighth-century cross slab combines a swirling Christian Celtic cross with Pictish beasts on one side and an elaborate Pictish battle scene on the other, thought to commemorate victory over the Northumbrians in 685 AD. Three other stones, bristling with Pictish and early Christian symbols, sit by the main road, overlooking huge sweeps of valley and mountain, though plans are afoot to move all the stones to a nearby indoor location to prevent further erosion. Bus #21A, from Forfar to Brechin, stops in Aberlemno.

Kirriemuir and glens Prosen, Clova and Doll

The sandstone town of **KIRRIEMUIR**, known locally as Kirrie, is set on a hill six miles northwest of Forfar on the cusp of glens Clova and Prosen. Despite the influx of hunters up for the "season", it's still a pretty special place, a haphazard confection of narrow closes, twisting wynds and steep braes. The main cluster of streets have all the appeal of an old film set, with their old-fashioned bars, tiled butcher's shop, tartan outlets and haberdasheries somehow managing to avoid being contrived and quaint – although the rapid recobbling of the town centre, around a twee statue of Peter Pan, undermines this somewhat.

In the nineteenth century, as a linen manufacturing centre, it was made famous by a local handloom-weaver's son, J.M. Barrie, with his series of novels about "Thrums", in particular *A Window in Thrums* and his third novel, *The Little Minister.* The author was to become more famous still as the creator of Peter Pan, the little boy who never grew up, a story which Barrie penned in 1904 – some say as a response to a strange upbringing dominated by the memory of his older brother, who died as a child. **Barrie's birthplace**, a plain little whitewashed cottage at 9 Brechin Rd (Easter weekend & May–Sept Mon–Sat 11am–5pm, Sun 1.30–5pm; Oct Sat 11am–5pm, Sun 1.30–5pm; NTS; £1.80), displays his writing desk, photos and newspaper clippings. The washhouse outside – romantically billed as Barrie's first "theatre" – was apparently the model for the house built by the Lost Boys in Never-Never Land for Wendy. Barrie chose to be buried at the nearby St Mary's Espiscopal Church in Kirrie, despite being offered a more prestigious plot at London's Westminster Abbey. Another local son who attracts a handful of rather different pilgrims is Bon Scott (1946–80) of the rock band AC/DC, who was born and lived here before emigrating to Australia.

High above the B957 to Brechin, Kirriemuir Hill is crowned by a **camera obscura** (contact the tourist office for opening hours) in an old cricket pavilion. This unexpected treasure was donated to the town in 1930 by Barrie and offers splendid views of Strathmore and the glens. On the other side of the town centre, a couple of hundred yards down the A928 to Glamis, is the **Aviation Museum** (April–Sept Mon–Sat 10am–5pm, Sun 11am–5pm; free), the lifetime collection of Richard Moss, who'll invariably be your guide through the jumble of military uniforms, photos, World War II memorabilia (including British and German propaganda leaflets) and Airfix models.

Kirrie's helpful **tourist office** is in Cumberland Close (April–June & Sept Mon–Sat 10am–5pm; July & Aug Mon–Sat 9.30am–5.30pm; ☎01575/574097), in the new development behind *Visocchi's* in the main square. **Accommodation** is available at *Crepto B&B*, Kinnordy Place (☎01575/572746; ②), or the respectable *Airlie Arms*, St Malcolm's Wynd (☎01575/572487; ④). *Visocchi's* is great for daytime **snacks** and ice cream, while the *Airlie*, and *Thrums Hotel*, on Bank Street, both serve good food in the evening. Of the **pubs**, the *Kilt and Clogs*, behind the tourist office, is the most lively. **Postbuses** into glens Clova and Prosen leave from the main post office, on Reform Street, at 8.30am (Mon–Sat). A second Glen Clova bus leaves around 3pm (Mon–Fri), but only goes as far as Clova village before returning to Kirriemuir. Hourly buses connect with Forfar for onward travel.

Glen Prosen

Five miles north of Kirrie, the low-key hamlet of **DYKEHEAD** marks the point where glens **Prosen** and Clova divide. **Accommodation** is available here at the *Royal Jubilee Arms Hotel* (☎01575/540381; ⑤), an old inn scarred by a grim modern conversion that, nonetheless, provides excellent all-day food, drink and Sunday-night **ceilidhs**. A mile or so up Glen Prosen, you'll find the house where Captain Scott and fellow explorer Doctor Wilson planned their ill-fated trip to Antarctica in 1910–11, with a roadside **stone cairn** commemorating the expedition. From here, Glen Prosen proper unfolds before you. Little has changed since Scott's time, and it remains essentially a quiet wooded backwater, with all the wild and rugged splendour of the other glens but without the crowds. To explore the area thoroughly you need to go on foot, but a good road circuit can be made by crossing the river at the tiny village of **GLENPROSEN** and returning to Kirriemuir along the western side of the glen via Pearsie.

The best walk in the area is the reasonably easy four-mile **Minister's Path** (so called because the local minister would walk this way twice every Sunday to conduct services in both glens). Take the footpath between the kirk and the bridge in Glenprosen village, then the right fork where the track splits and continue over the colourful burnt moorland down into Clova. As there is no afternoon return service by postbus from Prosen to Kirriemuir, you either have to stay the night or follow the path to its end, **Wester Eggie**, and pick up the Clova village postbus (Mon–Fri 3.30pm).

Glen Clova and Glen Doll

Of all the Angus glens, **Glen Clova** – which in the north becomes Glen Doll – with its stunning cliffs, heather slopes and valley meadows, is the firm favourite of many. Although it can get unpleasantly congested in peak season, the area is still remote enough to be able to leave the crowds with little effort. Wildlife is abundant, with deer on the mountains, wild hares and even grouse and the occasional buzzard. The meadow flowers on the valley floor and arctic plants (including great splashes of white and purple saxifrage) on the rocks also make it something of a botanist's paradise.

The B955 from Dykehead and Kirriemuir divides at the Gella bridge over the swift-coursing River South Esk (unofficially, road traffic is encouraged to use the western branch of the road for travel up the glen, and the eastern side going down). Six miles north of Gella, the two branches of the road join up once more at the hamlet of **CLOVA**, little more than the hearty *Clova Hotel* (☎01575/550222; ⑤), which also has an outside bunkhouse, and hosts regular barbecues, ceilidhs and even helicopter and balloon flights. An excellent, if fairly strenuous, four-hour walk from behind the old school at the back of the hotel leads up into the mountains and around the lip of **Loch Brandy**, which legend predicts will one day flood and drown the valley below.

North from Clova village, the road turns into a rabbit-strewn lane coursing along the riverside for four miles to the car park and informal **campsite** in **Glen Doll**, a useful starting point for numerous superb **walks** (see box). From the car park, it's only a few hundred yards further to the **youth hostel** (☎01575/550236; mid-March to Oct), a cheerful restored hunting lodge that boasts a squash court along with the usual facilities.

WALKS FROM GLEN DOLL

Ordnance Survey Landranger maps nos. 43 & 44.

These walks are some of the main routes across the Grampians from the Angus glens to Deeside, many of which follow well-established old drovers' roads. A number of them cross the royal estate of Balmoral, and Prince Charles's favourite mountain – Lochnagar – can be seen from all angles. The walks should always be approached with care; make sure to follow the usual safety precautions.

Capel Mounth to Ballater (fifteen miles/7hr). Head across the bridge from the car park, turning right after a mile when the track crosses the Cald Burn. Out of the wood, the path zigzags its way up fierce slopes before levelling out on the moorland plateau. Soon descending, the path crosses a scree near the eastern end of Loch Muick. With the loch to your left, walk down along the scree till you reach the River Muick, crossing the bridge to take the quiet track along the river's northern shore to Ballater.

Capel Mounth round trip (fifteen miles/8hr). Follow the above to Loch Muick, then follow the path down to loch level and double back on yourself along the loch's southern shore. When the track crosses the Black Burn, either take the steep left fork or continue along the shore for another mile, heading up the dramatic Streak of Lightning path that follows Corrie Chash. Both paths meet at the ruined stables below Sandy Hillock. Just beyond, take the path to the left, descending rapidly to the waterfall by the bridge at Bachnagairn, where a gentle burn-side track leads the three miles back to Glen Doll car park.

Jock's Road to Braemar (fourteen miles/7hr). Take the road north from the car park past the youth hostel. After almost a mile, follow the signposted Jock's Road to the right, keeping on the northern bank of the burn. Pass a barn, Davey's Shelter below Cairn Lunkhard and continue onto a wide ridge towards the path's summit at Crow Craigies (3018ft). From here, the path bumps down over scree slopes to the head of Loch Callater. Go either way round the loch, and follow the Callater Burn at the other end, eventually hitting the main A93 two miles short of Braemar.

Brechin

Twelve miles or so east of Kirriemuir, **BRECHIN** is a pretty if soporific town, whose chief attraction is the old **Cathedral** on Bishop's Close, off the High Street. There's been a religious building of sorts here since the arrival of evangelizing Irish missionaries in 900 AD, and the red sandstone structure has become something of a hotchpotch of architectural styles. What you see today chiefly dates from an extensive rebuilding in 1900, with the oldest surviving part of the cathedral being the 106ft round tower, one of only two in Scotland. The cathedral's doorway, built 6ft above the ground for protection against Viking raids, has some notable carvings, while inside you can see various Pictish stones, illuminated by the jewel-coloured stained-glass windows.

The library on St Ninian Square, to the north of the cathedral, houses Brechin's **museum** (Mon & Wed 9.30am–8pm, Tues & Thurs 9.30am–6pm, Fri & Sat 9.30am–5pm; free), a one-room jumble of history, civic memorabilia, geology and painting. Just off the square is the train station of the **Caledonian Railway** (talking timetable ☎01356/622992; inquiries ☎01674/810318), operating steam trains on summer Sundays and bank holidays along four miles of track from Brechin to the Bridge of Dun.

Opposite the library, the **tourist office** (April–June & Sept Mon–Sat 10am–5pm; July & Aug Mon–Sat 9.30am–5.30pm; ☎01356/623050) can organize accommodation and hand out information on hiking in Glen Esk. Brechin is on the main **transport** routes – bus #30 runs hourly to Montrose, nine miles east, and it's also served by regular Citylink coaches between Dundee and Aberdeen.

Edzell and Glen Esk

Travelling around Angus, you can hardly fail to notice the difference between organic settlements and planned towns built by paranoid landowners who forcibly rehoused local people in order to keep them under control, especially after the Jacobite uprisings. One of the better examples of this phenomenon, **EDZELL**, along the B966 five miles north of Brechin (and linked to it by buses #29 and #30), was cleared and rebuilt with Victorian rectitude a mile to the west of its original site in the 1840s. The long, wide and ruler-straight main street is lined with prim nineteenth-century buildings, now doing a roaring trade as genteel teashops and antique emporia.

The original village (identifiable from the cemetery and surrounding grassy mounds) lay immediately to the west of the impressive ruins of **Edzell Castle** (April–Sept Mon–Sat 9.30am–6pm, Sun 2–6pm; Oct–March Mon–Wed & Sat 9.30am–4pm, Thurs 9.30am–noon, Sun 2–4pm; HS; £2.30), itself a mile west of the planned village. It is a good example of a comfortable tower house, whose main priority became luxurious living rather than defence, with some intricate decorative corbelling on the roof, a vast fireplace in the first-floor hall and numerous telltale signs of building from different ages.

It is, however, the **pleasance garden** that makes a visit to Edzell essential, especially in late spring and early to mid-summer. The garden was built in 1604, at the height of the optimistic Renaissance by Sir David Lindsay, and its refinement and extravagance are evident. The walls contain sculpted images of erudition: the Planetary Deities on the east side, the Liberal Arts (including a decapitated figure of Music) on the south and, under floods of lobelia, the Cardinal Virtues on the west wall. In the centre of the garden, low-cut box hedges spell out the family mottoes and enclose voluminous beds of roses.

Four miles southwest of Edzell, lying either side of the lane to Bridgend, are the **Catherthuns**, twin Iron Age hillforts that were probably occupied at different times. The surviving ramparts on the White Caterthun (978ft) – easily reached from the small car park below – are the most impressive, and this is thought to be the later fort, occupied by the Picts in the first few centuries AD. Views from both, over the mountains to the north and the plains and foothills to the south, are stunning.

Just north of Edzell, a fifteen-mile road climbs alongside the River North Esk to form **Glen Esk**, the most easterly of the Angus glens and, like the others, scarcely populated. Nine miles along the Glen, the excellent **Glenesk Folk Museum** (Easter–May Mon, Sat & Sun noon–6pm; June to mid-Oct daily noon–6pm; £2), brings together records, costumes, photographs, maps and tools from the Angus glens, depicting the often harsh way of life for the inhabitants. The museum is housed in an old shooting lodge, which also has a noted tearoom. There are some excellent **hiking** routes further up the glen, including one to Queen Victoria's Well in Glen Mark and another up Mount Keen, Scotland's most easterly munro.

If you want to stay, there's **B&B** at Mrs De Costa's, 24 High St (☎01356/648201; ②), or you can **camp** one and a half miles north at the *Glenesk Caravan Park* (☎01356/648565; April–Oct).

ABERDEENSHIRE AND MORAY

Aberdeenshire and Moray cover some 3500 square miles of open and varied country dotted with historic and archeological sights, from neat NTS properties and eerie prehistoric rings of standing stones to quiet kirkyards, serene abbeys and a rash of dramatic castles. Geographically, the counties break down into two distinct areas: the **hinterland**, once barren and now a patchwork of farms, rising towards high mountains, sparkling rivers and gentle valleys; and the **coast**, a classic stretch of rocky cliff, remote fishing villages and long, sandy beaches.

For visitors, **Aberdeen** is of most obvious interest in the region, with its well-kept buildings (it's often voted Britain's cleanest city), museums and gorgeous parks. From here, it's a short hop west to **Deeside**, annually visited by the royal family and a popular holiday area. To the north lies the **Don Valley**, a usually quiet area which bursts into life in winter when skiers take to the slopes of the Lecht, and **Speyside**, the heart of Scotland's malt whisky industry. Further north, the **coast** offers some dramatic scenery, punctuated by picturesque villages left almost unchanged by the centuries.

Aberdeen has an **airport**, and **trains** run from here to Inverness and to major points further south. **Buses** can be few and far between, often running on schooldays only, but the main centres are well-served. By car, signposted **trails** set up by the tourist board make following the Speyside whisky trail and visiting the northeast coast and castles a painless experience.

Aberdeen

Some 120 miles from Edinburgh, on the banks of the rivers Dee and Don smack in the middle of the northeast coast, **ABERDEEN** is commonly known as the Granite City. The third-largest city in Scotland, it's a place that people either love or hate. As Lewis Grassic Gibbon, one of the northeast's most eminent novelists, summed it up: "One detests Aberdeen with the detestation of a thwarted lover. It is the one hauntingly and exasperatingly lovable city of Scotland." Certainly, while some extol the many hues and colours of Aberdeen's **granite** buildings, others see only uniform grey and find the city grim, cold and unwelcoming. The weather doesn't help: Aberdeen lies on a latitude north of Moscow and the cutting wind and driving rain (even if it does transform the buildings into sparkling silver) can be tiresome.

Since the 1970s, **oil** has made Aberdeen an almost obscenely wealthy and self-confident place – only four percent of Scotland's population live in the city, yet it has eight percent of

ABERDEEN

the country's spending power. Despite (or perhaps because of) this, it can seem a soulless city; there's a feeling of corporate sterility and sometimes, despite its long history, Aberdeen seems to exist only as a departure point and service station for the transient population of some ten to fifteen thousand who live on the 130 oil platforms out to sea.

That said, Aberdeen's **architecture** is undeniably striking: a granite cityscape created in the nineteenth century by three fine architects: Archibald Simpson and John Smith in the early years of the century and, subsequently, A. Marshall Mackenzie. Classical inspiration and Gothic Revival styles predominate, giving grace to a material once thought of as only good enough for tombs and paving stones. In addition, it sometimes seems like every spare inch of ground has been turned into **flower gardens**, the urban parks being some of the most beautiful in Britain. This positive floral explosion – Aberdeen has been debarred from "Britain in Bloom" competitions because it kept winning – has certainly cheered up the general greyness; nonetheless the new image, just like the first, is always at the mercy of the weather.

Staying in such a prosperous place has its advantages. There are plenty of good restaurants and hotels, local transport is efficient and nearly all the sights are free, including Aberdeen's splendid **Art Gallery** and the excellent new **Maritime Museum**. The city boasts a genuinely lively **harbour**, and stays alive at night with a thriving pub culture and a fair number of theatres, both mainstream and innovative.

Some history

In the twelfth century, Alexander I noted "Aberdon" as one of his principal towns, and by the thirteenth century it had become a centre for **trade and fishing**, a jumble of timber and wattle houses perched on three small hills, with the castle to the east and St Nicholas's kirk outside the gates to the west.

It was here that **Robert the Bruce** sought refuge during the Scottish Wars of Independence, leading to the garrison of the castle by Edward I and Balliol's supporters. In a night-time raid in 1306, the townspeople attacked the garrison and killed them all, an event commemorated by the city's motto "Bon Accord", the watchword for the night. The victory was not to last, however, and in 1337 Edward III stormed the city, forcing its rebuilding on a grander scale. A century later the Bishop Elphinstane founded the Catholic **University** in the area north of town known today as **Old Aberdeen**, while the rest of the city developed as a mercantile centre and important port.

Industrial and economic expansion led to the Aberdeen New Streets Act in 1800, setting off a hectic half-century of development that almost led to financial disaster. Luckily, the city was rescued by a boom in trade: in the **shipyards** the construction of **Aberdeen Clippers** revolutionized sea transport, giving Britain supremacy in the China tea trade, and in 1882 a group of local businessmen acquired a **steam** tugboat for trawl fishing: sail gave way to steam, and fisher families flooded in.

By the mid-twentieth century Aberdeen's traditional industries were in decline, but the discovery of **oil** in the North Sea transformed the place from a depressed port into a boom town. Today, Aberdeen remains an extremely prosperous city, though what will happen when the oil runs out is anybody's guess.

Arrival, information and city transport

Aberdeen's Dyce **airport**, seven miles northwest of town, is served by flights from most parts of the UK and a few European cities. The #27 airport bus (Mon–Fri every 35min until 5.15pm; £1.10) runs to Union Street and the bus station; after 6pm and at

The telephone code for Aberdeen is ☎01224.

weekends, you can take the #27A (every 60–90min). The **train station** is on Guild Street, in the centre of the city (☎594222), with the **bus** terminal for intercity and regional services right beside it (☎212266).

Aberdeen is also linked to Lerwick in Shetland and Stromness in Orkney by P&O **ferries** (☎594222), with regular crossings from Jamieson's Quay in the harbour.

Information

From the stations it's a two-minute walk up the hill to Union Street, Aberdeen's main thoroughfare, and only a little further to the **tourist office** at St Nicholas House, Broad Street, just off the north side of Union Street at its eastern (seaward) end (Oct–May Mon–Fri 9am–5pm, Sat 10am–2pm; June & Sept Mon–Sat 9am–5pm, Sun 10am–2pm; July & Aug Mon–Fri 9am–7pm, Sat 9am–5pm, Sun 10am–4pm; ☎632727). They'll book accommodation for you, charging ten percent of the first night's room rate, redeemable at your hotel. They also run tours of the city in open-topped buses, sell theatre tickets and maps, and have a good selection of pamphlets on the best **walks** in Aberdeen – well worth the small investment of 25p.

The tourist office also gives out two free monthly **listings** magazines, *Listings Aberdeen* and *What's On,* both of which have details of current events and scheduled art and entertainment. The local newspapers, the morning *Press and Journal* and the *Evening Express,* are good for more immediate events, and the tourist board also runs a 24-hour *What's On Line* (☎636363). The best place for more esoteric information – anything from t'ai chi workshops to festivals and ceilidhs – is the Lemon Tree Arts Centre, 5 West North St (☎642230), who produce a glossy bi-monthly programme.

OIL AND ABERDEEN

When **oil** was discovered in BP's Forties Field in 1970, Aberdonians rightly viewed it as a massive financial opportunity, and – despite fierce competition from other east coast British ports, Scandinavia and Germany – the city succeeded in persuading the oil companies to base their headquarters here. Land was made available for housing and industry, millions were invested in the harbour and offshore developments, new schools opened and the airport expanded to include a heliport, which has since become the busiest in the world.

The city's **population** swelled by 60,000, and earnings escalated from fifteen percent below the national average to a figure well above it. Wealthy oil companies built prestigious offices, swish new restaurants, upmarket bars and shops. At the peak of production in the **mid-1980s**, 2.6 million barrels a day were being turned out, and the price had reached $80 a barrel – from which it plummeted to $10 during the slump of 1986. The effect was devastating – jobs vanished at the rate of a thousand a month, house prices dropped and Aberdeen soon discovered just how dependent on oil it was. The moment oil prices began to rise again, crisis struck again with the loss of 167 lives in the **Piper Alpha disaster**, which precipitated an array of much-needed but very expensive safety measures.

In recent years production levels have steadily risen back up to those of the early 1980s, though with assurances that this time the dangers of boom-bust policies have been heeded. Oil remains the cornerstone of Aberdeen's economy, keeping unemployment down to one of the lowest levels in Britain and driving up house prices not just in the city itself but in an increasingly wide area of its rural hinterland. Predictions of the imminent decline in oil reserves and the end of Aberdeen's economic boom are heard regularly, as they have been since 1970, but reliable indicators suggest that the black gold will still be flowing well into the next millennium.

City transport

Aberdeen is best explored by foot, but you might need to use **local buses**, almost all of which pass along Union Street, to reach some of the sights. There is no all-inclusive day ticket, the minimum is a weekly bus pass (£11.30). If you plan to use the buses a lot, you should buy a **Farecard** (in £2, £5 or £10 denominations), which works rather like a phone card in that each time you travel the fare is deducted from the card. It can be bought from the main **transport office**, 395 King St, the City Council offices next to the tourist office, or the busy city-centre kiosk outside Marks & Spencer, on Union Street, which also sells decent transport **maps**. For information on local bus services, call Grampian Busline (4am–midnight; ☎650065).

Taxis, which operate from ranks throughout the city centre, are rarely necessary, except late at night. If you don't manage to hail one, call Mairs Taxis (☎724040).

Accommodation

As befits a high-flying business city, Aberdeen has a large choice of **accommodation**. Unfortunately, though, as most visitors *are* here on business, much of it is character-less and expensive, although some of the swankier places sometimes offer good-value weekend deals. Predictably, the best budget options are the **B&Bs** and **guest houses**, many of which are strung along Bon Accord and Crown streets (buses #6, #17 and #26 to and from Union Street), and the Great Western Road (buses #18, #19 and #24). Cheapest of all are the **youth hostel** and **student halls** left vacant for visitors in the summer months. There's also a **campsite** in the suburbs.

Hotels

Brentwood Hotel, 101 Crown St (☎595440). Spick-and-span refurbished old hotel south of Union Street. Popular with business people and often full during the week. ④.

Caledonian Thistle Hotel, 10–14 Union Terrace (☎640233). The best of the posh hotels – an impressive Victorian edifice just off Union Street. ⑧.

Cedars Private Hotel, 339 Great Western Rd (☎583225). Small hotel with friendly atmosphere. ⑤.

Ferryhill House Hotel, 169 Bon Accord St (☎590867). One of the most historic pubs in Aberdeen with colourful rooms and good food. ⑦.

Mannofield Hotel, 447 Great Western Rd (☎315888). Charming old granite building, once a posh private house, a mile west of town. Excellent-value three-course dinners. ④.

Palm Court Hotel, 81 Seafield Rd, (☎310351). Plush West End establishment with popular conservatory bistro-bar. ⑤.

Queen's Hotel, 51–53 Queen's Rd (☎209999). Cheerful city-centre hotel, recently refurbished, with a good culinary reputation. ④.

Speedbird Inn, Argyll Road, Dyce (☎772884). Large, modern chain hotel at the airport. ④.

Guest houses and B&Bs

Bracklinn Guest House, 348 Great Western Rd (☎317060). Welcoming Victorian house with elegant furnishings – one of the city's best B&Bs. ③.

Campbell's Guest House, 444 King St (☎625444). Highly recommended breakfasts. One mile from the city centre and handy for the beach. ③.

Crynoch Guest House, 164 Bon Accord St (☎582743). A welcoming guest house in a convenient location. ③.

Fourways Guest House, 435 Great Western Rd (☎310218). A converted manse in the West End of town. ④.

Klibreck, 410 Great Western Rd (☎316115). Non-smoking stately granite guest house. ②.

Salisbury Guest House, 12 Salisbury Terrace (☎590447). Family-run, comfortable and clean guest house. ③.

Hostel, campsite and campus accommodation

Crombie Johnstone Halls, College Bounds, Old Aberdeen (☎273301). Private rooms in the best of the student halls; located in one of the most interesting parts of the city.

Hazelhead Campsite, five miles west of centre on the A944 (☎321268). Grassy campsite with a swimming pool nearby. Follow signs from ring road or take buses #14 or #15. April–Sept.

King George VI Memorial Hostel, 8 Queen's Rd (☎646988). Rather soulless *SYHA* youth hostel with rooms for four to six, and a 2am curfew. Buses #14 and #15 from the train station.

The City

Aberdeen divides neatly into five main areas. The **city centre**, roughly bounded by Broad Street, Union Street, Schoolhill and Union Terrace, features the opulent **Marischal College**, the colonnaded **Art Gallery** with its fine collection, and homes that predate Aberdeen's nineteenth-century town planning and have been preserved as **museums**. Union Street continues west to the comparatively cosmopolitan **West End**, where much of the city's decent nightlife, plus a couple of sights, can be found amid the tall grey town houses. To the south, the **harbour** still heaves with boats serving the fish and oil industries, while north of the centre lies attractive **Old Aberdeen**, a village neighbourhood presided over by **King's College** and **St Machar's Cathedral** and influenced by the large student population. The magnificent **beach** marks the city's entire eastern border.

The city centre

Any exploration of the **city centre** should begin at the east end of the mile-long **Union Street**, whose impressive architecture, sometimes lost among the shoppers and chain stores, finishes up at **Castlegate**, where Aberdeen's long-gone castle once stood. An open cobbled area, it is dominated by the late seventeenth-century **Mercat Cross**, carved with a unique gallery of Stewart sovereigns alongside some fierce gargoyles. Castlegate was once the focus of city life but nowadays the best it can muster is a somewhat scruffy and uninteresting **market** (Thurs–Sat). However, the view up gently rising Union Street – a jumble of grey spires, turrets and jostling double-decker buses – is quintessential Aberdeen and well worth taking a moment or two to savour.

At the Union Street end of Castlegate, a discreet door on the side of the granite Town House leads into the **Tolbooth Museum** (April–Sept Tues–Sat 10am–5pm, Thurs 10am–8pm, Sun 2–5pm; free), quarried out of the seventeenth-century prison which lurks behind a steely-grey nineteenth-century exterior. The theme of the museum is law and imprisonment; climbing the claustrophobic staircases and squeezing into tiny, airless cells certainly gives plenty of opportunity to appreciate the harsh realities of incarceration. A suitably chilling audiovisual display featuring a talking model of a Jacobite prisoner complete with rattling chains can be seen, along with some fascinating maps and 3-D models charting Aberdeen's development from its old town beginnings.

Nearby, on King Street, the sandstone **St Andrew's Episcopal Cathedral** (mid-May to mid-Sept Mon–Sat 10am–4pm), where Samuel Seabury, America's first bishop, was consecrated in 1784, offers a welcome relief to the uniform granite. Inside, its spartan whiteness is broken by florid gold ceiling bosses representing the (then) 48 states of the USA and 48 local families who remained loyal to the Episcopal Church during the eighteenth-century Penal Laws. Even more resplendent is the gilded baldachino canopy over the High Altar and the brightly coloured Seabury Centenary window in the Suther Chapel.

West down Union Street brings you to Broad Street, where Aberdeen's oldest-surviving private house, **Provost Skene's House**, dating from 1545, cowers behind modern offices at 45 Guestrow (Mon–Sat 10am–5pm; free). In the sixteenth century all the well-to-do houses in the area looked like this, with mellow stone and rounded turrets –

yet it was only the intervention of the Queen Mother in 1938 which saved this house from the fate of its neighbours. Little has been altered since the Provost of Aberdeen lived here from 1676 to 1685, and the house is now a museum, giving an insight into the life of a rich Aberdonian merchant in the seventeenth century. Don't miss the Long Gallery, where a series of ornate tempera High Church paintings from 1622 shows a spirited defiance against the Protestant dogma of the time.

On Broad Street itself stands Aberdeen's most imposing edifice and the world's second-largest granite building after the Escorial in Madrid – the exuberant **Marischal College**, whose tall, steely-grey pinnacled neo-Gothic facade is in absolute contrast to the eyesore that houses the tourist office opposite. This spectacular architecture with all its soaring, surging lines has been painted and sketched more than any other in Aberdeen, and though not to everyone's taste – it was once described by a minor art historian as "a wedding cake covered in indigestible grey icing" – there's no escaping the fact that it is a most extraordinary feat of sculpture. The college itself was founded in 1593 by the fourth Earl Marischal, and coexisted as a separate Protestant university from Catholic King's, just up the road, for over two centuries. It was long Aberdeen's boast that their city had as many universities as the whole of England, and it wasn't until 1860 that the two were united as the University of Aberdeen. In 1893, the central tower was more than doubled in height by A. Marshall Mackenzie and the profusion of spirelets added, though the facade, which fronts an earlier quadrangle designed by Archibald Simpson in 1837–41, was not totally completed until 1906.

Behind the tower, through the college entrance, the Mitchell Hall's east window illustrates the history of the university in stained glass. The fan-vaulted lobby, once the college's old hall, now houses the wonderful **Anthropological Museum** (Mon–Fri 10am–5pm, Sun 2–5pm; free), made up of two large rooms that contain a wealth of weird exhibits, among them a series of Eskimo soapstone carvings, an outrigger canoe carved from a breadfruit tree from Papua New Guinea, a macabre Hawaiian head crafted from basketry and with real dogs' teeth, and a Tibetan prayer wheel. Most bizarre are the high-relief mummy case of an Egyptian 5-year-old girl, and a stomach-churning foot, unbound and preserved in brine. The "Encyclopaedia of the Northeast" exhibition – running alphabetically from Aberdeen through to Whisky – is well labelled and amazingly varied.

Between Upperkirkgate and Union Street stands the long **St Nicholas Kirk** (Mon–Fri noon–4pm, Sat 1–3pm; free), actually two churches in one with a solid, central bell tower rising from the middle, from where the 48-bell carillon, the largest in Britain, regularly chimes across the city. There's been a church here since at least 1157, but as the largest kirk in Scotland it was severely damaged during the Reformation and divided into the West and the East Church, separated today by the transepts and crossing; only the north transept, known as Collinson's aisle, survives from the twelfth century. The Renaissance-style **West Church**, formerly the nave of St Nicholas, was designed in the mid-eighteenth century by James Gibbs, architect of St-Martin-in-the-Fields in London's Trafalgar Square. The **East Church** was rebuilt over the groin-vaulted crypt of the restored fifteenth-century St Mary's Chapel (entered from Correction Wynd), which back in the 1600s was a place to imprison witches – you can still see the iron rings to which they were chained. Take time to explore the large peaceful churchyard, which with its green marble tombs and Baroque monuments seems a million miles from the bustling main street.

A little further west up Schoolhill, **James Dun's House** (Mon–Sat 10am–5pm; free) is a smallish, two-storey Georgian house built for the rector of Aberdeen's grammar school in 1769 and now housing contemporary art exhibitions and moderately interesting displays on the city's history. Opposite, Aberdeen's engrossing **Art Gallery** (Mon–Sat 10am–5pm, Sun 2–5pm; free) was purpose-built in 1884 to a Neoclassical design by Mackenzie. You enter into the airy **Sculpture Court**, whose walls are lined with contemporary British paintings, many by Scottish artists. Highlights of the room are a Barbara Hepworth sculpture – *Requiem* – in polished walnut, and a remarkable tubular alloy sculpture by Eduardo Paolozzi. Off to one side is the **Memorial Court**, a calming, white-walled circular room under a skylit dome that serves as the city's principal war memorial. It also houses the Lord Provost's *Book of Condolence* for the 167 people who died in the 1988 Piper Alpha oil rig disaster in the North Sea.

The **upstairs** rooms house the majority of the gallery's painting collection. The displays are changed fairly regularly, but you'll find some superb works by British Impressionists and modernists on the balcony overlooking the central Sculpture Court; look out for Stanley Spencer's joyful portrait of the British seaside in *Southwold*, and his dramatic *Crucifixion*, as well as Robert Brough's half-dazed *View of Elgin* and Duncan Grant's haunting *Self-Portrait*.

Heading back towards the top of the staircase, the two-room **MacDonald collection** of nineteenth-century British art leads off to the right. At first the sheer number of Victorian landscapes crowding the walls may be disconcerting, but closer inspection will prove rewarding. Highlights include John MacWhirter's vast, sun-drenched *Morning – Isle of Arran*, the sheer weariness of Robert McGregor's *Les Moulières* (The Mussel Gatherers), Pre-Raphaelite works by Rossetti and Burne-Jones, and various paintings by the Glasgow Boys (see p.193). The second MacDonald room houses 92 paintings of Victorian artists – mostly self-portraits. Local artists on display include John Phillip (1817–67), so heavily influenced by Velázquez and Murillo that he became known as "Spanish Phillip". Another Aberdonian, William Dyce (1806–64), features large, with several examples of his intensely photographic canvases.

The nineteenth-century foreign room leading off the balcony is, of course, popular for its Impressionist collection (including works by Boudin, Courbet, Sisley, Monet, Pissarro, and a deliciously bright Renoir, *La Roche Guyon*). A fabulous, sinewy cast of a Rodin male torso is the room's sculptural highlight. Off to the side, the dimly lit **Murray Room** contains prints, drawings and watercolours, features from a fifteenth-century Flemish illuminated manuscript and Edward Lear's comically annotated pen-ink and wash view of *Boche di Cattaro*.

West of the gallery, across the rail bridge, the sunken **Union Terrace Gardens**, bordered by the sparkling light-grey granite buildings of Union Terrace, are a welcome relief from the hubbub of heavy traffic on Union Street. In summer, free brass-band concerts and orchestral performances make it a great place to have a picnic. From here there are views across to the three domes of the Central Library, St Mark's Church and His Majesty's Theatre, traditionally referred to as "Education, Salvation and Damnation". Outside the theatre stands a hulking great statue of "Braveheart" William Wallace, erected in 1888.

The West End

Tatty gentility characterizes much of the **West End**, the area around the westernmost part of Union Street, which roughly begins at the great granite columns of the city's **Music Hall**. A block north is **Golden Square** – a misnomer, as the trim houses, pubs and restaurants surrounding the statue of the Duke of Gordon are uniformly grey. The city has invested much in gentrifying the area north of Union Street, resulting in neat cobbles, old-fashioned lamps and mushrooming designer boutiques. Huntly Street, west of Golden Square, heads off towards the curiously thin spire of **St Mary's Catholic Cathedral** (daily 8am–5pm), a typically foreboding example of Victorian Gothic church architecture.

On the southern side of Union Street, wedged between Bon Accord Street and Bon Accord Terrace, **Bon Accord Square**, is a typical, charming Aberdeen square. In the middle, a grassy centre surrounds a great hulk of granite, commemorating **Alexander Sampson**, architect of much of nineteenth-century Aberdeen. West of Bon Accord Terrace is Justice Mill Lane, home to many of the city's favourite bars and nightclubs, and also to the **Satrosphere** (school terms Mon & Wed–Fri 10am–4pm, Sat 10am–5pm, Sun 1.30–5pm; school holidays Mon–Sat 10am–5pm, Sun 1.30–5pm; £3.50), Aberdeen's thoroughly entertaining hands-on science exhibition. Unassuming from the outside, the Satrosphere – an ingenious illusion of a vast globe surrounded by numerous images of oneself – is created by walking into a open square of four mirrors with a patterned panel ahead of you. Other exhibits include a superb 3-D map of northeast Scotland, examples of interactive technology and a new biological section in which you can see inside beehives and an anthill.

The harbour

The old cobbled road of Shiprow winds down from Castlegate at the east end of Union Street to the north side of the harbour. Just off this steep road, peering out at the harbour through a striking modern glass facade, is the **Maritime Museum** (Mon–Sat 10am–5pm, Sun 11am–5pm; free), which combines a thoroughly modern, airy museum with Aberdeen's oldest-surviving building, **Old Provost Ross's House**, laced with small rooms, low doorways and labyrinthine corridors. The marriage has been successful, and the museum makes a thoroughly engrossing, imaginatively designed tribute to Aberdeen's maritime traditions.

As you walk in the front entrance, you'll see a series of blackboards, computer readouts and barometers showing everything from the time of high tide to the up-to-the-minute price of a barrel of crude oil. Suspended above the foyer and visible from five different levels is an 27ft high model of an oil rig, which, along with terrific views over the bustling harbour, serves as a constant reminder that Aberdeen's maritime links are very much alive today. The older industries of herring-fishing, whaling, shipbuilding and lighthouses also have their place with well-designed displays and audiovisual presentations, many of which draw heavily on personal reminiscences. Passages lead from various levels of the museum into Provost Ross's House, where intricate ship's models and a variety of nautical paintings and drawings are on display.

At the bottom of Shiprow, the cobbles meet Market Street, which runs the length of the **harbour**. Here, brightly painted oil-supply ships, sleek cruise ships and peeling fishing boats jostle for position to an ever-constant clatter and the screech of well-fed seagulls. Follow your nose down the road to the **fish market**, best visited early (7–8am) when the place is in full swing. The current market building dates from 1982, but fish has been traded here for centuries – the earliest record dating back to 1281 when an envoy of Edward I was charged for 1000 barrels of sturgeon and 5000 salt fish.

Back at the north end of Market Street, Trinity Quay runs to the shipbuilding yards and down York Street to the east corner of the harbour. Here you'll come to Aberdeen's **Footdee** or "fitee" (an easy walk or bus #14 from Union Street), a quaint nineteenth-century fishermen's village of higgledy-piggledy cottages which back onto the sea, their windows and doors facing inwards to protect from storms but also, so they say, to prevent the Devil from sneaking in the back door. On Thursday afternoons from June to August an excellent "Ships and Shorelines" **guided walk**, starting from the tourist office, takes in the sights, smells and stories of Footdee and the harbour area (2pm; £5).

From Market Street it's a twenty-minute walk or ten-minute bus ride (#6 from Market Street or #16 or #17 from Union Street) to **Duthie Park** (10am–dusk; free), situated on the banks of the Dee at the end of Polmuir Road. The rose garden here, known as Rose Mountain due to its profusion of blooms, can be stunning in summer, but the real treat is the Winter Gardens – a steamy jungle paradise of enormous cacti, exotic plants and tropical birds – jokingly held to be a favourite haunt with Aberdonians saving on their heating bills. From the northwestern corner of Duthie Park, a great cycle and walkway – the **Old Deeside Railway Line** – leads out of the city and past numerous old train stations.

Old Aberdeen

An independent burgh until 1891, the tranquil district of **Old Aberdeen**, a twenty-minute bus ride (#20) north of the city centre, has always maintained a separate village-like identity. Dominated by King's College and St Machar's Cathedral, its medieval cobbled streets, tiny wynds and little lanes are beautifully preserved.

The southern half of High Street is overlooked by **King's College Chapel** (Mon–Fri 9am–5pm), the first and finest of the college buildings, completed in 1495 with a chunky Renaissance spire. Named in honour of James IV, the chapel's west door is flanked by his coat of arms and those of his queen. The chapel stands on the quadrangle, whose gracious buildings retain a medieval plan but were built much later; those immediately north were designed by Mackenzie early this century, with the exception of Cromwell Tower at the northeast corner, which was completed in 1658. The first thing you notice inside the chapel is that there is no aisle. Within this unusual plan, the screen, the stalls (each unique) and the ribbed arched wooden ceiling are rare and beautiful examples of medieval Scottish woodcarving. The remains of Bishop Elphinstone's tomb and the carved pulpit from nearby St Machar's are also here. A **visitor centre** (Mon–Sat 10am–5pm, Sun noon–5pm) in the main college buildings tells the tempestuous tale of the establishment of the University of Aberdeen, which came about finally in 1860 when Protestant Marischal College and sceptical King's College were merged, well over 200 years after the first attempt. Rivalry between the two establishments (which led to well-charted brawls in the streets) has always been intense.

From the college, the cobbled High Street leads a short way north to **St Machar's Cathedral** on the leafy Chanonry (daily 9am–5pm; free), overlooking Seaton Park and the River Don. The site was reputedly founded in 580 by Machar, a follower of Columba, when he was sent by the latter to find a grassy platform near the sea, overlooking a river shaped like the crook on a bishop's crozier. This setting fitted the bill perfectly, and the cathedral, a huge fifteenth-century fortified building, became one of the city's first great granite edifices. Inside, the stained-glass windows are a dazzling blaze of colour, and above the nave the heraldic oak ceiling from 1520 is illustrated with nearly fifty different coats of arms from Europe's royal houses and Scotland's bishops and nobles. **Guided walks** round the cathedral and University take place throughout the summer, leaving from King's College (June–Aug Wed 7pm, Sun 2.30pm; £3).

Next door to the cathedral, the **Cruickshank Botanic Gardens** (May–Sept Mon–Fri 9am–4.30pm, Sat & Sun 2–5pm; Oct–April Mon–Fri 9am–4.30pm; free), laid out in 1898, offer lovely glimpses of the cathedral through the trees. In spring and summer it's worth checking out the flowerbeds, but don't bother with the dreary zoological museum.

A wander through Seaton Park will bring you to the thirteenth-century **Brig' o' Balgownie**, which gracefully spans the River Don, nearly a mile north of the cathedral. Still standing (despite Thomas the Rhymer's prediction that it would fall were it ever to be crossed by an only son riding a mare's only foal), the bridge is best visited at sunset – Byron, who spent much of his childhood in Aberdeen, remembered it as one of his favourite places.

The beach

Of Britain's large cities, Aberdeen can surely claim to have the best **beach**. Less than a mile to the east of Union Street is a great two-mile sweep of clean sand, broken by groynes and lined all along with an esplanade, where most of the city seems to gather on a sunny day. Towards the southern end of the beach is a burgeoning concrete expanse of cinemas and fast-food outlets, a couple of fairly tatty amusement parks and a vast leisure centre. As you head further north, most of the beach's hinterland is devoted to successive golf links. The #14 bus goes along the southern esplanade.

Eating, drinking and entertainment

Aberdeen is certainly not short of good places to **eat**, though you will find it more pricey than elsewhere in northeast Scotland. Union Street and the surrounding area has a glut of attractive **restaurants** and **cafés**. As for **nightlife**, like most ports Aberdeen caters for a transient population with a lot of disposable income and a desire to get drunk as quickly as possible. Although you'll find no shortage of loud, flashy bars catering to such needs, there are still a number of more traditional old **pubs** which, though usually packed, are well worth a visit.

Restaurants and cafés

Ashvale, 46 Great Western Rd. One of Scotland's finest, and biggest, fish-and-chip shops, with seating for 300. Open daily until late.

Café 52, The Green (☎590094). This pleasant place serves uncomplicated but original and inexpensive food down below the south side of Union Street. Closed Mon.

Courtyard on the Lane, 1 Alford Lane (☎213795). Highly regarded West End bistro with an excellent daily-changing menu of European/Scottish cuisine. There's a more formal restaurant upstairs. Closed Sun & Mon.

Drummonds, 1 Belmont St, just off Union Street (☎624642). A stylish café and wine bar during the day and a noisy music venue in the evening, with a wide-ranging menu.

Fortunes, 11 Dee St. Frugal-looking place serving good Chinese food.

Inversnecky, Beach Esplanade. Best of the beach cafés, great for big hangover breakfasts and ice-cream specials.

Lemon Tree, 5 W North St. Easy-going café inside an arts centre; serves good vegetarian and vegan snacks and meals.

La Lombarda, corner of Castlegate and King Street (☎640916). A smart upstairs trattoria with a lively, less formal basement bistro, both of which have pumped out pasta since 1922.

Owlies, Unit C, Littlejohn Street. Plain French brasserie food, with plenty of vegetarian options. Closed Sun.

Poldino's, 7 Little Belmont St (☎647777). Lively, expensive Italian restaurant.

Silver Darling Restaurant, Pocra Quay, North Pier (☎576229). Located at the mouth of the Dee in Footdee, this pricey restaurant serves the best seafood in town. Closed Sat lunch & Sun.

Wild Boar, 16 Belmont St. Upbeat brasserie with well-priced vegetarian food, soups, salads and pastas. A popular evening venue.

Pubs and bars

Bex Bar, Justice Mill Lane. A trendy spot which gets packed out at weekends; one of number of pubs and clubs along this West End street.

Café Continental, Esplanade. Large designer conservatory with windswept, rain-battered or sun-drenched views; serves more upmarket meals than the ice-cream cafés alongside.

Café Society, 9 Queen's Rd, opposite the youth hostel. Yuppie-ish bar, with a nice beer garden.

Carriages, *Brentwood Hotel*, 101 Crown St. Unusually lively hotel cellar bar with the city's largest range of real ales and ciders. Also serves excellent bar food.

Cocky Hunters, at the western end of Union Street. Small live music bar, popular with trendies and students.

Jock's, Netherkirkgate. Currently the "in" place with students, this Scottish-theme pub is full of tartan tat and excruciating Scottish music.

Ma Cameron's Inn, Little Belmont Street. Aberdeen's oldest pub, though only a section remains of the original. Serves food.

Nicky Tam's, 44 Market St. Olde-worlde-type pub, with unusual artefacts on its walls. One of the few bars in the harbourside area which feels safe to go into.

Prince of Wales, 7 St Nicholas Lane. Highly regarded Aberdeen pub with a long bar and flagstone floor. Very central and renowned for its real ales; often crowded.

St Machar Bar, 97 High St, Old Aberdeen. The medieval quarter's only pub, a pokey, old-fashioned bar inevitably full of King's College students.

Under the Hammer, 11 N Silver St. Basement wine bar located beneath some auction rooms, popular for after-work drinks.

Clubs and live music venues

De Niro's, 120 Union St. Techno-dance nightclub halfway along Union Street.

Franklyn's, Justice Mill Lane. Part of the same complex as the *Bex Bar* and catering for the same studenty crowd. Chart-oriented dance music is the staple.

Hogies, Bon Accord Crescent. Hip Latin American nightclub, specializing in steamy salsa.

Lemon Tree, 5 W North St. The fulcrum of the city's arts scene with a great buzz and regular live music, comedy and folk.

The Ministry, 16 Dee St. The hottest dance club for miles; Sunday nights are legendary. Occasionally has big-name guest DJs.

Oh Henrys, Adelphi Close. Flash studenty club just off Union Street with regular theme nights.

Theatres and concert halls

Tickets for most of the venues below can be bought from the **box office** beside the Music Hall on Union Street (Mon–Sat 10am–6pm; ☎641122).

Aberdeen Arts Centre, 33 King St (☎635208). Hosts a variety of theatrical productions alongside a programme of lectures and exhibitions.

Aberdeen Exhibition and Conference Centre, off Ellon Road at Bridge of Don. The biggest rock and pop acts play this huge hall.

Capitol Theatre, 431 Union St (☎583141). Venue for smaller visiting rock and pop acts.

Cowdray Hall, Schoolhill (☎646333). Classical music, often with visiting orchestras.

His Majesty's, Rosemount Viaduct (☎637788). Aberdeen's main theatre, in a beautifully restored Edwardian building, with a programme that ranges from highbrow drama and opera to pantomime.

Lemon Tree, 5 W North St (☎642230). Avant-garde events with off-the-wall comedians and plays, many coming hotfoot from the Edinburgh festivals.

Music Hall, Union Street (☎632080). Big-name comedy and music acts.

Cinemas

Arts Centre, King Street (☎635208). Small repertoire of lesser-known and arthouse movies.

Cannon, Union Street (☎591477). Mainstream general releases.

Odeon, Justice Mill Lane (☎916422 for programme details; ☎587160 for credit card booking). All the usual blockbusters in a similar line-up to the Cannon's.

Virgin, Beach Esplanade (☎572228) Huge, spanking-new multiscreen development by the beach.

Listings

Airport ☎722331.

Bike rental Aberdeen Cycle Centre, 188 King St (☎644542); Alpine Bikes, 66–70 Holburn St (☎211455).

Bookshops The two largest are Dillons, 269–271 Union St (☎210161); and Waterstone's, 236b Union St (☎571655), which boasts a particularly well-stocked Scottish section.

Car rental Budget, at the airport (☎771777); Thrifty, 76 Huntly St, in the West End (☎621033).

Exchange Thomas Cook, 335–337 Union St (Mon–Sat 9.30am–5.30pm; ☎212271); also available at the tourist office on Broad Street.

Ferries P&O ☎572615.

Football The local team, Aberdeen, is one of the top four in Scotland and plays at Pittodrie Stadium, between King's Road and the beach; phone ☎632328 for details of forthcoming fixtures and ticket sales.

Hospital The Royal Infirmary, on Foresterhill, northeast of the town centre, has a 24hr casualty department (☎681818).

Internet You can log onto the Internet and send email at RSC Internet, 15 Marischal St (☎585113).

Left luggage Small 24hr lockers at the train station cost £2.

Lesbian and Gay Switchboard (Wed & Fri 7–10pm; ☎633500).

Maps Aberdeen Map Shop, 74 Skene St (☎637999).

Pharmacy Boots, 161 Union St (Mon–Sat 8am–6pm; ☎211592).

Police The main police station is on Queen Street (☎639111).

Post office Aberdeen's central post office is in the St Nicholas Centre, between Union Street and Upperkirkgate (Mon–Sat 9am–5.30pm; ☎633065).

Public transport Grampian Transport Busline (☎650065).

Swimming Bon Accord Baths and Leisure Centre, Justice Mill Lane (☎587920), has an Olympic-sized pool; Beach Leisure Centre on the Esplanade has a fun pool with flumes and slides.

Travel agents STA Travel, 30 Kirkgate (☎658222); U Travel, 110 High St (Mon–Fri 9.30am–4.30pm; ☎273559).

Southern Grampians

South of Aberdeen, the A92 and the main train line follow the coast to **Stonehaven**, a pretty harbour town and base for the nearby **Dunnottar Castle**, a surreal ruin perched on the cliffs. The area to the south and west is known as the **Mearns**, an agricultural district of scattered population and gathering hills towards the Angus glens. **Fettercairn** is the most obvious base, for its proximity to **Fasque House**, family home of the former prime minister Gladstone.

Stonehaven is easily reached by **bus** or **train** from Aberdeen or Montrose, although public transport inland into the Mearns is virtually nonexistent.

Stonehaven and around

A busy pebble-dashed town, **STONEHAVEN** attracts hordes of holiday-makers in the summer due to its sheltered Kincardine coastline, and in mid-July in particular because of its respected **folk festival**. The town itself is split into two parts, the picturesque working harbour area being most likely to detain you. On one side of the harbour, Stonehaven's oldest building, the **Tolbooth** (June–Sept Mon & Thurs–Sat 10am–noon & 2–5pm; Wed & Sun 2–5pm; free), built as a storehouse during the construction of Dunnottar Castle (see opposite) is now a museum of local history and fishing. On calm summer evenings, you can also take **boat trips** from the harbour to the RSPB reserve at Fowlsheugh (June & July Tues & Fri 6.30pm).

The old High Street – lined with some fine town houses and civic buildings – connects the harbour and its surrounding old town with the late eighteenth-century planned centre on the other side of the River Carron. On New Year's Eve, High Street is the location for the ancient ceremony of **Fireballs**, when locals parade its length, swinging metal cages full of burning debris around their heads. This, it is said, wards off evil spirits for the year ahead. The **new town** focuses on the market square, overlooked by the dusky-pink granite market hall with its impressive steeple. From here, Evan Street heads inland before swinging right into Arduthie Road, which climbs up to the train station, a good fifteen-minute walk from the centre.

Practicalities

The **tourist office** is at 66 Allardice St, the main street past the square (April, May & Oct Mon–Sat 10am–1pm & 2–5pm; June & Sept Mon–Sat 10am–1pm & 2–6pm, Sun 1–6pm; July & Aug Mon–Sat 10am–7pm, Sun 1–7pm; ☎01569/762806). For **B&B** accommodation, *Arduthie House*, on Ann Street (☎01569/762381; ③), and the *Braemar*, on Evan Street (☎01569/764841; ③), are both good bets, while, a few miles south of town on the A92, *Dunnottar Mains Farm* (☎01569/762621; ③) is beautifully situated right beside Dunnottar Castle. For **food**, the *Tolbooth Seafood Restaurant* (☎01569/762287; closed Mon), above the museum on the harbour, is the place to go – it's pricey but worth it. For cheaper **pub** food or just a drink, try the entertaining *Marine Hotel* or the *Ship Inn*, both on the harbour. The most useful **buses** for Stonehaven are #107 and #117, which ply the coast road between Montrose and Aberdeen. For **bike hire** and advice about good local routes, head to Ruftrack Bikes, at 56 Barclay St, one block from the tourist office.

Dunnottar Castle, Kinneff and Arbuthnott

Two miles outside Stonehaven (the tourist office sells a walking guide for the scenic amble), **Dunnottar Castle** (late March–Oct Mon–Sat 9am–6pm, Sun 2–5pm; Nov to late March Mon–Fri 9am–dusk; £2.50) is one of the finest of Scotland's ruined castles, a huge ninth-century fortress set on a three-sided sheer cliff jutting into the sea – a setting striking enough to be chosen as the backdrop for Zeffirelli's movie version of *Hamlet*. Once the principal fortress of the northeast, the ruins are worth a good root around, and there are any number of dramatic views out to the crashing sea. Siege and bloodstained drama splatter the castle's past: in 1297 William Wallace burnt the whole English Plantaganet garrison alive here, while one of the more gruesome tales from the castle's history tells of the imprisonment and torture of 122 men and 45 women Covenanters in 1685 – an event, as it says on the Covenanters' Stone in the churchyard, "whose dark shadow is for evermore flung athwart the Castled Rock".

Four miles south of Dunnottar Castle, **CATTERLINE** is a clifftop hamlet typical of those along this stretch of coast – worth a visit for the views and the delicious, well-priced lobster at the *Creel Inn*, which also offers **B&B** (☎01569/750254; ③).

Four miles further down the coast, the tiny village of **KINNEFF** lies among fields tumbling down to the sea. Its church, for the most part eighteenth-century, is a successor to the one in which the Scottish crown jewels were hidden as Cromwell marched on Scotland in 1651. Popular tradition has it that the wives of the Dunnottar garrison commander and the Kinneff parish minister hid the crown under an apron and carried the state sceptre, disguised as a distaff, with bundles of flax. The state's most precious assets were successfully hidden here for nine years. Memorials and interpretive boards inside the beautifully light and simple old church tell the story.

Some five miles inland, the straggling village of **ARBUTHNOTT** was the home of prolific local author, **Lewis Grassic Gibbon** (1901–35), whose romanticized realism perfectly encapsulates the spirit of the agricultural Mearns area. His descriptions were often quite awesome – Glasgow, for example, he neatly penned as "the vomit of a cataleptic commercialism". *Sunset Song*, his most famous work, is an essential read for those travelling in this area. The community-run **Grassic Gibbon Centre** (April–Oct daily 10am–4.30pm; £2), on the B967 through the village, is a great introduction to this fascinating and self-assured man who died so young. He is buried (under his real name of James Leslie Mitchell) in the corner of the little village graveyard, overlooking the forested banks of the Bervie Water off the main road. The parish church itself, one of the few surviving intact in Scotland that predate the Reformation, is interesting for its Norman arch, unusual fifteenth-century circular bell tower and glorious thirteenth-century chancel.

Fettercairn and Fasque House

Eight miles southeast of Arbuthnott on the tiny B9120 (and served by buses from Montrose), the village of **FETTERCAIRN** is renowned for its handsome arch, which was erected in 1861 after Queen Victoria stayed at the local pub, the *Ramsay Arms* (☎01561/340334; ⑤), which is still a good place to stay or to stop for a drink. One mile west, and well signposted, the **Fettercairn distillery** (Mon–Sat 10am–4.30pm; free) is one of Scotland's oldest, with free tours and the customary free taster at the end.

A short drive north on the Edzel to Banchory road, the once beautiful, but now somewhat neglected **Fasque House** (May–Sept daily 11am–4.30pm; £3.50) – family home of four-times prime minister William Ewart Gladstone – is set in grounds filled with deer, pheasants and rabbits. Built between 1789 and 1809, the house passed into the Gladstone family in 1829 when Sir John Gladstone, William's father and a rich grain broker, bought the estate, on which members of the family still live. Sir John added various extensions to the house, developing the gardens and building roads and bridges. Today, in all its intriguing decrepitude, Fasque House offers a great insight into how the affluent landowner lived in the Victorian era. Downstairs, domestic implements litter the place in a refreshingly haphazard manner, while upstairs appears equally untouched, with a library crammed full of the Gladstones' books, a splendid Victorian bathroom complete with shower, and bedrooms looking much as the nineteenth-century maids would have left them.

Deeside

More commonly known as **Royal Deeside**, the land stretching west of the coast along the River Dee revels in its connections with the royal family, who have regularly holidayed here, at **Balmoral**, since Queen Victoria bought the estate. Eighty thousand Scots turned out to welcome her on her first visit in 1848, but some weren't so charmed – one local journalist remarked that the area was about to be "desolated by cockneys and other horrible reptiles". Today, however, the locals are fiercely protective of their connections, for ever retelling stories of their encounters with blue bloods.

Many of Victoria's guests weren't as enthusiastic about Deeside as she was: Count von Moltke, then aide-de-camp to Prince Frederick William of Prussia, observed, "It is very astonishing that the Royal Power of England should reside amid this lonesome, desolate, cold mountain scenery", while Tsar Nicholas II whined, "The weather is awful, rain and wind every day and on top of it no luck at all – I haven't killed a stag yet." However, the Queen adored the place, and the woods were said to remind Prince Albert of Thuringia, his homeland.

Deeside is undoubtedly handsome in a fierce, craggy Scottish way, and the royal presence has helped keep a lid on any unattractive mass development. The villages strung along the A93, the main route through the area, are well-heeled and the facilities for visitors first-class, with a number of bunkhouses and youth hostels, some outstanding hotels and plenty of castles and grounds to snoop around. It's also an excellent area for **outdoor activities**, with hiking routes into both the Grampian and Cairngorm mountains, and good mountain biking, canoeing and skiing.

Bluebird **bus** #201 from Aberdeen regularly chugs along the A93, serving most of the towns on the way to **Braemar**, past Balmoral to the west.

From Aberdeen to Banchory

West of Aberdeen is low-lying land of mixed farming, forestry and suburbs. Easily reached from the main road are the castles of **Drum** and **Crathes**, both interesting fortified houses with pleasant gardens, while the uneventful town of **Banchory** serves as gateway to the heart of Royal Deeside.

Drum and Crathes castles
Ten miles west of Aberdeen on the A93, **Drum Castle** (Easter–June & Sept daily 1.30–5.30pm; July & Aug daily 11am–5.30pm; Oct Sat & Sun 1.30–5.30pm; NTS; £4)

stands in a clearing in the ancient **woods of Drum**, made up of the splendid pines and oaks that once covered this whole area before the shipbuilding industry precipitated mass forest clearance. The castle itself combines a 1619 Jacobean mansion with Victorian extensions and the original, huge thirteenth-century keep. Given by Robert the Bruce to his armour-bearer, William de Irvine, in 1323 for services rendered at Bannockburn, the castle remained in Irvine hands for 24 generations until the NTS stepped in in 1976. To get a sense of the medieval atmosphere of the place, ascend the Turnpike Stair, above the Laigh Hall where a 700-year-old window seat gives views of the ancient forest.

Further along the A93, three and a half miles east of Banchory, **Crathes Castle** (mid-April to late Oct daily 11am–4.45pm; £4.50) is a splendid sixteenth-century granite tower house adorned with flourishes such as overhanging turrets, gargoyles and conical roofs. Its thick walls, narrow windows and tiny rooms loaded with heavy old furniture make Crathes rather claustrophobic, but it is saved by some wonderfully painted ceilings, either still in their original form or sensitively restored; the earliest dates from 1602. Don't miss the Room of the Nine Nobles, where great heroes of the past, among them Julius Caesar, King David and King Arthur, are skilfully painted on the beams. More intriguing still is the Green Lady's Room, where a mysterious child's skeleton was found beneath the floor and the ghost of a young girl, sometimes carrying a child, is said to have been spotted – most recently in the 1980s. The Muses Room, with portrayals of the nine muses and seven virtues, is also impressive. Beware the "trip stair", originally designed to foil seventeenth-century burglars.

By the entrance to Crathes, a cluster of restored stone cottages houses an interesting crafts shop, pottery and the *Milton Restaurant* (☎01330/844566), which serves high-class food, including a well-priced supper menu between 5pm and 7pm.

Banchory

BANCHORY, meaning "fair hollow", is really just a one-street town, and there's not much to see, though it can be a useful place to stay. The small local **museum** on Bridge Street, behind High Street (April, May & Oct Sat 11am–1pm & 2–5pm, Sun 2–4pm; June–Sept Mon–Sat 10am–1pm & 2–5.30pm, Sun 1–5pm; free), may warrant thirty minutes or so if you're a fan of local boy James Scott Skinner, renowned fiddler and composer of such tunes as *The Bonnie Lass o' Bon Accord*. Alternatively, you can watch salmon leap at the little footbridge where the Dee joins the Feugh River to the south of town.

Practicalities

The **tourist office**, in the museum (Easter–May & Oct Mon–Sat 10am–1pm & 2–5pm, Sun 1–5pm; June & Sept Mon–Sat 10am–1pm & 2–6pm, Sun 1–6pm; July & Aug Mon–Sat 10am–1pm & 2–7pm, Sun 1–7pm; ☎01330/822000), can provide information on walking and fishing in the area. There are several reasonable places **to stay** here and in the surrounding countryside. In town, the *Burnett Arms Hotel*, 25 High St (☎01330/824944; ⑥), a friendly former coaching inn, does Banchory's best pub grub, while *Primrose Hill*, on North Deeside Road on the eastern outskirts of town (☎01330/823007; ③), is a decent B&B. Outside Banchory on the Inchmarlo road, the smart *Tor-Na-Collie Hotel* (☎01330/822242; ⑧) was once a retreat for Charlie Chaplin and his family, and serves splendid Scottish salmon, venison and malt whisky in its upscale restaurant. More affordable escapism is available year-round at the *Wolf's Hearth* bunkhouse, ten miles northwest of Banchory, just outside Tornaveen on the B9119 (☎013398/83460). A converted farm building in a beautiful rural setting, it makes a great base for walking, cycling or skiing, and also offers a variety of creative activities such as painting and pottery.

Ballater and Balmoral

Heading west from Banchory on the A93, after twelve miles you'll come to the worka-day town of **ABOYNE**, notable only for the excellent *Black Faced Sheep* coffee shop just off the main road, and the *White Cottage* restaurant (☎013398/86265), a couple of miles before Aboyne on the Banchory side, which specializes in high-quality Scottish cooking made from fresh local produce. Another ten miles beyond Aboyne is the neat and ordered town of **BALLATER**, attractively hemmed in by the river and fir-covered mountains. The town was dragged from obscurity in the nineteenth century when it was discovered that the local waters were useful in curing scrofula. Although scrofula is no longer a problem, Ballater spring water is back in fashion and on sale around town.

It was in Ballater that Queen Victoria first arrived in Deeside by train from Aberdeen back in 1848 – she wouldn't allow a station to be built any closer to Balmoral, eight miles further west. Although the line has long been closed, you can still visit the ele-gant **train station** in the centre of town, which now houses a tearoom. The local shops, having provided the royals with household basics, also flaunt their connections, sport-ing oversized crests above their doorways.

Ballater is an excellent base for local **walks and outdoor activities**. There are numerous hikes from Loch Muik (pronounced "Mick"), nine miles southwest of town, including the Capel Mounth drovers' route over the mountains to Glen Doll (see p.384), and a well-worn but strenuous all-day trek up and around Lochnagar (3789ft), the mountain much painted and written about by the current Prince of Wales. The starting point for all these walks is the Balmoral Rangers' **visitors' centre**, on the shores of the loch (phone ☎013397/55059 for opening hours), which also offers a series of free guid-ed nature walks. **Bikes** can be rented from Making Treks (☎013397/55865), while for canoeing and ski **equipment** and **guides** for a range of outdoor activities contact Dave Latham (☎01330/850332). **Pony trekking** is available on the Balmoral Estate's ponies (☎013397/42334).

Ballater practicalities

The **tourist office** is opposite the station in Station Square (Easter–May & Oct Mon–Sat 10am–1pm & 2–5pm, Sun 1–5pm; June & Sept Mon–Sat 10am–1pm & 2–6pm, Sun 1–6pm; July & Aug Mon–Sat 10am–1pm & 2–7pm, Sun 1–7pm; ☎013397/55306). There are plenty of reasonable **B&Bs** in town, including the excellent no-smoking *Inverdeen House*, on Bridge Square (☎013397/55759; ③), which offers a choice of six breakfasts, many involving piles of Canadian pancakes. Other places to try include two options on Braemar Road – the welcoming *Deeside Hotel* (☎013397/55420; ④), or the nearby *Auld Kirk* (☎013397/55762; ③), set in a large old church. For **camping**, the *Anderson Road Caravan Park* (☎013397/55727; Easter–Oct) down towards the river, has around sixty tent pitches. There are numerous **places to eat**, from smart hotel restaurants to bakers and coffee shops: the award-winning *Green Inn*, 9 Victoria Rd (☎013397/55701), is pricey but excellent quality. For **drinking** with locals, try the back bar (entrance down Golf Street) of the *Prince of Wales*, which faces the main square.

Balmoral Castle and Crathie Church

Originally a sixteenth-century tower house built for the powerful Gordon family, **Balmoral Castle** (mid-April to May Mon–Sat 10am–5pm; June & July daily 10am–5pm; £3) has been a royal residence since 1852, when it was converted to the Scottish Baronial mansion that stands today. The royal family traditionally spend their summer holidays here, but despite its fame it can be something of a disappointment even for a dedicated royalist. For the three months when the doors are nudged open the general riffraff are permitted to view only the ballroom and the grounds; for the rest of the year it is not even visible to the paparazzi who converge en masse when the royals are in residence here in August.

Opposite the castle's gates on the main road, the otherwise dull granite church of **CRATHIE**, built in 1895 with the proceeds of a bazaar held at Balmoral, is the royals' local church. Princess Anne chose the place as the venue for her second marriage to her former equerry, Commander Tim Laurence, and princes William and Harry made their first public appearance here after the death of their mother, Princess Diana. A small **tourist office** operates in the car park by the church on the main road in Crathie (daily: April 10am–5pm; May–Aug 9.30am–6pm; Sept & Oct 10am–5.30pm; ☎013397/42414).

Braemar

Continuing for another few miles, the road rises to 1100ft above sea level to the upper part of Deeside and the village of **BRAEMAR**, situated where three passes meet and overlooked by an unimposing **castle** (Easter–Oct Mon–Thurs, Sat & Sun 10am–6pm; £2) of the same name. Signs as you enter Braemar boast that it's an "Award Winning Tourist Village", which just about sums it up, as everything seems to have been prettified to within an inch of its life or have a price tag on it. That said, it's an invigorating, outdoor kind of place, well patronized by committed hikers, although probably best known for its Highland Games, the annual **Braemar Gathering** (first Sat of Sept). Games were first held here in the eleventh century, when Malcolm Canmore set contests for the local clans in order to pick the bravest and strongest for his army. Since Queen Victoria's day, successive generations of royals have attended, and the world's most famous Highland Games have become rather an overcrowded, overblown event. You're unlikely to get in if you just turn up; tickets can be bought in advance from February 1, from the Bookings Secretary, BRHS, Coilacriech, Ballater AB35 5UH (☎013397/55377).

A pleasant diversion from Braemar is to head six miles west to the end of the road and the **Linn of Dee**, where the river plummets savagely through a narrow rock gorge. From here there are countless **walks** into the surrounding countryside or up into the heart of the Cairngorms (see p.448). There's a very basic **youth hostel** just before the falls at Inverey (June to early Sept; book through the Braemar hostel on ☎013397/41659).

MORRONE – BRAEMAR'S BEACON

Ordnance Survey Landranger map No. 43.

Late August and through autumn, when the mountain is plush with extravagant colours, is the best time to ascend Morrone. In winter, it can be a spectacular viewpoint but very exposed. Allow four hours for the walk.

Make your way up Chapel Brae at the west end of Braemar, passing a car park and pond, then Mountain Cottage, and swinging left up through fine birch woods (a nature reserve). Keep right of the fences and house. The track bears right (west), and at a fork take the left branch up to the Deeside Field Club view indicator. Skirt the crags above this to the left and the path is obvious thereafter. The summit provides a fantastic and huge view of the Cairngorms. You can descend by the upward route, but an easy continuation is to head down by the Mountain Rescue post's access path, which twists along and then down into Glen Clunie. Turn left along the minor road back to Braemar; the walk finishes by heading through the local golf course. In summer, you can take a Land Rover safari up Morrone; contact the tourist office in Braemar for details.

Practicalities

Braemar's **tourist office** is in the modern building known as the Mews in the middle of the village on Mar Road (daily: Jan–May & Sept–Dec 10am–5pm; June 9.30am–6pm; July–Aug 9.30am–7pm; ☎013397/41600). **Accommodation** is scarce in Braemar in the lead-up to the Games, but at other times there's a wide choice. *Clunie Lodge Guest House*, Clunie Bank Road (☎013397/41330; ③), on the edge of town, is a good **B&B** with lovely views up Clunie Glen, and there's a **youth hostel** at Corrie Feragie, 21 Glenshee Rd (☎013397/41659; Jan–Oct). Alternatively, the cheery *Rucksacks*, an easy-going bunkhouse well equipped for walkers and backpackers, is just behind the Mews complex (☎013397/41517); they also rent out **bikes**, and have a sauna inside. The *Invercauld Caravan Club Park* (☎013397/41373), just south of the village off the Glenshee Road, has fifteen **camping** pitches. Standard and fairly pricey hotel **food** is available from the bars of the various large hotels, or for some cheap stodge there's the *Braemar Takeaway* by the river bridge. For **drinking**, the *Invercauld Arms* in the middle of town is a youthful hangout with a pool table. For advice on outdoor activities, as well as ski, mountainbike and climbing **equipment rental**, head to Braemar Mountain Sports, opposite the *Takeaway*.

The Don Valley and the Lecht

The quiet countryside around the **Don Valley**, once renowned for its illegal whisky distilleries and smugglers, used also to be a prosperous agricultural area. As the region industrialized, however, the population drifted towards Dundee and Aberdeen, and nowadays little remains of the old farming communities but the odd deserted crofter's cottage. From Aberdeen, the River Don winds northwest through **Inverurie**, where it takes a sharp turn west to **Alford**, then continues past ruined castles through the **Upper Don Valley** and the heather moorlands of the eastern Highlands. This remote, and undervisited area, is positively littered with ruined castles, Pictish sites, stones and hillforts, all of which it is impossible to cover here. There are some excellent free leaflets in the Grampian Archeology series (available from all tourist offices), which give far more detail, and the well-signposted **Castle Trail** takes in the area's main castles. The Lecht Road, from Corgaff to the hilltop town of **Tomintoul**, rises steeply, making the area around it, simply known as the **Lecht**, an ideal skiing centre.

Inverurie is served by the regular Aberdeen to Inverness **train** and various **bus** services up the A96. Bluebird buses #215 and #210 link Alford with Aberdeen, but getting as far as Strathdon is much harder and public transport links with Tomintoul are all but nonexistent.

Inverurie and around

Some seventeen miles from Aberdeen, the prosperous granite farming town of **INVERURIE** makes a convenient base for visiting the numerous relics and castles in the area. The tiny **tourist office** is in the town hall on Market Place (July–Sept Mon–Sat 10am–1pm & 2–6pm; ☎01467/620600), not far from the station. Despite its size, it has a large stash of leaflets useful for finding the local sites, many of which are tucked away and confusingly signposted. While you're in Inverurie, don't miss the **Thainstone Mart**, just off the A96 south of town, one of Europe's largest and most impressive livestock sales (Mon & Wed–Fri around 10am).

Bennachie and Archaeolink

The granite hill **Bennachie**, five miles west of Inverurie, is possibly the site of Mons Graupius, Scotland's first ever recorded battle in 84 AD when the Romans defeated the Picts. At 1733ft, this is one of the most prominent tors in the region with tremendous views, and makes for a stiff two-hour walk. The best route starts from the Bennachie Information Centre (Tues–Sun 10.30am–5pm), a mile past **Chapel of Garioch** (pronounced "Geery"), itself a couple of miles off the A96. Immediately west of here is one of the most notable Pictish standing stones in the region, the **Maiden Stone**, a 10ft gravestone inscribed with such things as dragons and an elephant.

A further four miles from Chapel of Garioch, the **Archaeolink Prehistory Park**, on the B9002 at Oyne (daily 9.30am–5pm; £3.90), gives an insight into the area's Pictish heritage. The brand-new park includes a reconstructed Iron Age farm, a hillside archeological site, and a innovatively designed main building containing lively audio-visual displays designed to bring prehistory (anything from six thousand years ago to the battle of Mons Graupius) to life. Although it's a clear attempt to capture the imagination of young people, adults will be just as enthralled, partly because the experience is spread across a hillside with short walks, impressive views and interesting archeological projects.

Fyvie Castle

Some thirteen miles north of Inverurie stands the huge, ochre mansion of **Fyvie Castle** (April–June & Sept daily 1.30–4.45pm; July & Aug daily 11am–4.45pm; Oct Sat & Sun 1.30–4.45pm; NTS; £4). Scottish Baronial to the hilt, Fyvie's fascinating roofscape sprouts five curious steeples, one for each of the families who lived here from the thirteenth to the twentieth century. Beginning life as a typical courtyard castle, with a protective wall more than 6ft thick, over the ensuing centuries the place met with considerable architectural expansion. The Chancellor of Scotland bought Fyvie in 1596 and was probably responsible for the elaborate south front with its gables and turrets; his grandson sympathized with the Jacobites and, following his exile, the estate was confiscated and handed over to the Gordons. In 1889 the castle was sold to the Forbes-Leith, a local family who had made a fortune in America and were responsible for the grand Edwardian interior. The exquisite dining room is nowadays rented out for corporate entertaining by oil companies who hobnob among the Flemish tapestries, Delft tiles and the fine collection of paintings that includes feathery Gainsborough portraits and twelve works by Sir Henry Raeburn.

Alford and around

ALFORD, 25 miles west of Aberdeen, only exists at all because it was chosen, in 1859, as the terminus for the Great North Scotland Railway. The best of the sights is the **Grampian Transport Museum** on Main Street (April–Oct daily 10am–5pm; £2.75), a large display of transport through the ages. Unusual exhibits include the *Craigevar Express*, a strange, three-wheeled steam-driven vehicle developed by the local postman for his rounds before the invention of the engine; and, incongruously, a beautiful Art Deco Belgian dance organ with over 400 pipes and a full set of drums.

Practically next door is the terminus for the **Alford Valley Railway** (April, May & Sept Sat & Sun 1.30–4.30pm; June–Aug daily 1.30–4.30pm; ☎019755/62326), a two-foot narrow-gauge train that runs for about a mile from Alford Station through wooded vales to the wide open space of **Murray Park**; the return journey takes an hour. The station is also home to the neat **tourist office** (April–June, Sept & Oct Mon–Sat 10am–5pm, Sun 1–5pm; July & Aug Mon–Sat 10am–6pm, Sun 1–6pm; ☎019755/62052).

Craigievar Castle

Six miles south of Alford on the A980, **Craigievar Castle** (☎013398/83635; NTS) is a fantastic pink confection of turrets, gables, balustrades and cupolas bubbling over from the top three storeys. It was built by a Baltic trader known as Willy the Merchant in 1626, who evidently allowed his whimsy to run riot. The castle's massive popularity, however – it features on everything from shortbread tins to tea towels all over Scotland – has been its undoing, and the sheer number of visitors has caused interior damage. The NTS is currently limiting the number of people entering the house, but in any case the best part of the castle is its external appearance, which you can see free from the well-kept **grounds** (9.30am–sunset; free).

Lumsden and Rhynie

The A944 heads west from Alford, meeting the A97 just south of the tiny village of **LUMSDEN**, a surprising centre for Scottish sculpture. A contemporary **Sculpture Walk** – heralded by a fabulous skeletal black horse at its southern end – runs parallel to the main road, coming out near the premises of the **Scottish Sculpture Workshop** (Mon–Fri 9am–5pm or by arrangement; ☎01464/861372), very much an active workshop, rather than a gallery, at the northern end of town.

The village of **RHYNIE**, folded beautifully into the hills three miles further north up the A97, is for ever associated with one of the greatest Pictish memorials, the **Rhynie Man**, a remarkable 6ft boulder discovered in 1978, and depicting a rare whole figure, clad in a tunic and holding what is thought to be a ceremonial axe. The original can be seen in the foyer of the regional council's headquarters at Woodhill House in Aberdeen, but there is a cast on display at the school in Rhynie, across the road from the church; if you want to see it, contact Bill Inglis on ☎01464/861398. A further claim to fame for the village is that the bedrock lying deep beneath it, known as **Rhynie Chert,** contains plant and insect fossils up to 400 million years old, making them some of the earth's oldest fossils. A mile or so from the village, along the A941 to Dufftown, a car park gives access to the **Tap O'Noth**, Scotland's second-highest Pictish hillfort (1847ft), where substantial remnants of the wall around the lip of the summit show evidence of vitrification (fierce burning), probably to fuse the rocks together.

Rhynie is a reasonable – if very quiet – place **to stay**. The cheapest and the best choice is the *Gordon Arms Hotel*, on Main Street (☎01464/861615; ②).

The Upper Don Valley

Ten miles west of Alford stand the impressive thirteenth-century stone ruins of **Kildrummy Castle** (April–Sept Mon–Sat 9.30am–6pm, Sun 2–6pm; Oct–March Sat 9.30am–4pm, Sun 2–4pm; £1.50), site of some particularly hideous moments of conflict. During the Wars of Independence Robert the Bruce sent his wife and children here for their own protection, but the castle blacksmith, bribed with as much gold as he could carry, set fire to the place and it fell into English hands. Bruce's immediate family survived, but his brother was executed and the entire garrison hung, drawn and quartered. Meanwhile, the duplicitous blacksmith was rewarded for his help by having molten gold poured down his throat. Other sieges took place during the subsequent centuries: Balliol's forces attacked in 1335, Cromwell took over in 1654 and the sixth Earl of Mar used the castle as the headquarters of the ill-fated Jacobite risings in 1715. Following John Erskine's withdrawal Kildrummy became redundant and it was abandoned as a fortress and residence and fell into ruin. Beside the ruins is a Scottish Baronial-style castle built in 1901, now the *Kildrummy Castle Hotel* (☎019755/71288; ⑨), superbly endowed with wood-panelled rooms, Victorian furniture and a raised terrace on which you can enjoy afternoon tea overlooking the castle.

Ten miles further west, the A944 sweeps round into the dissipated parish of **STRATHDON**, little more than a succession of occasional buildings by the roadside. However, four miles from here, up a rough track leading into Glen Nochty, lies the unexpected **Lost Gallery** (Wed–Sun 11am–5pm; ☎019756/51287), which shows work by some of Scotland's leading modern artists in a wonderfully remote and tranquil setting. Heading west again on the A944, past the much-photographed signs to the village of Lost, you'll come to **Candacraig Gardens** (May–Sept Mon–Fri 10am–5pm; Sat & Sun 2–6pm; free), the walled grounds of Candacraig House, Highland retreat of Body Shop founder Anita Roddick. The house is private, but the gardens, an exuberant display of colour and energy, are open to the public. In the old laundry on the other side of the main house, *No. 3 Candacraig Square* (☎019756/51472; ③) is a stylish B&B with wooden floors, piles of books and a promise of fresh fish for breakfast.

A further eight miles on, just beyond the junction of the Ballater road, lies **Corgarff Castle** (Jan–March & Dec Sat 9.30am–4pm, Sun 2–4pm; April–Sept Mon–Sat 9.30am–6pm, Sun 2–6pm; Oct & Nov Mon–Wed & Sat 9.30am–4pm, Thurs 9.30am–2pm, Sun 2–4pm; HS; £2.30), an ugly white house with an unusual star-shaped wall and an eventful history. Built in 1537 – the wall was added in 1748 – it was first attacked in 1571, during a religious feud between the Forbes, family of the laird of the castle, and the Gordons, who torched the place killing the laird's wife, family and servants. In 1748, in the aftermath of Culloden, the Hanoverian government turned Corgarff into a barracks in order to track down local Jacobite rebels, and finally, in the mid-nineteenth century, the English Redcoats were stationed here with the unpopular task of trying to control whisky smuggling. Today there's little to see inside, but the place has been restored to resemble its days as a barracks, with stark rooms and rows of hard, uncomfortable beds.

Just before the castle by Rowan Tree Cottage, a track bumps south off the main road to *Jenny's Bothy* at Dellachuper (☎019756/51449), a beautifully remote and simple **hostel**, surrounded by empty scenery and wild animals.

Tomintoul

Just past Corgarff, at Cock Bridge, the road leaps up towards the ski slopes of the Lecht and, four miles further on, **TOMINTOUL** (pronounced "*Tom*-in-towel"), at 1150ft the highest village in the Scottish Highlands. Tomintoul owes its existence to the post-1745 landowners' panic when, as in other parts of the north, isolated inhabitants were forcibly moved to new, planted villages, where a firm eye could be kept on everybody. Its long, thin layout is reminiscent of a Wild West frontier town; Queen Victoria, passing through, wrote that it was "the most tumble-down, poor looking place I ever saw". That said, it makes a good base for **skiing** the Lecht area in winter, and there's some terrific **walking** hereabouts, with Tomintoul marking the end of the long-distance Speyside Way (see p.408).

SKIING THE LECHT

The Lecht offers dry ski-slope-skiing all year, and the recent introduction of snow-making equipment should help extend the snow season beyond January and February. While the gentle slopes are good for beginners, experienced skiers won't find much to tax them. Lift passes cost £12 a day for adults; ski and boot hire costs £11 a day from the ski school at the base station (☎019756/51440), which also provides tuition for £6 an hour.

For **information** on skiing and road conditions here, call the base station or the Ski Hotline (☎0891/654654).

Practicalities

In the central square, the **tourist office** (April, May & Oct Mon–Sat 10am–1pm & 2–5.30pm, Sun 2–5pm; June & Sept Mon–Sat 10am–1pm & 2–6pm, Sun 2–6pm; July & Aug Mon–Sat 10am–7pm, Sun 1–7pm; ☎01807/580285) also acts as the local **museum**, with mock-ups of an old farm kitchen and a smithie (same times; free). Information about the extensive Glenlivet Crown Estate, its wildlife (including reindeer) and numerous paths and bike trails is available from the **ranger's office** (phone ☎01807/580283 for opening hours) at the far end of the long main street.

If you need a place **to stay**, the *Tomintoul Bunkhouse,* immediately beside the tourist office (☎01343/548105), is plain but friendly and useful. Of the B&Bs, try *Conglass Hall*, on Main Street (☎01807/580291; ②), or *Milton* Farm, half a mile out of town on the B9008 to Dufftown (☎01807/580288; ③). Of the hotels gathered around the main square, the *Glenavon* (☎01807/580218; ③) is the most convivial for a drink, and serves ale made in the local Tomintoul Brewery. The best place to **eat** is at the *Clockhouse* bistro on Main Street.

Speyside

Strictly speaking, **Speyside** is the region surrounding the Spey River; however to most people the name is synonymous with the **whisky triangle**, stretching from just north of Craigellachie down towards Tomintoul in the south, and west to Huntly. Indeed there are more whisky distilleries and famous brands (including Glenfiddich and Glenlivet) concentrated in this small area than in any other part of the country. Running through the heart of the region is the River Spey, whose clean clear waters play such a vital part in the whisky industry and are home to thousands of salmon. At the centre of Speyside, the quiet market town of **Dufftown** makes a good base for a tour of the distilleries, while the only other settlement of any interest is **Huntly**, being well-served by road (A96) and rail links with Aberdeen and Elgin.

Dufftown and Craigellachie

The cheery community of **DUFFTOWN**, founded in 1817 by James Duff, the fourth Earl of Fife, proudly proclaims itself "Malt Whisky Capital of the World", and indeed it exports more of the stuff than anywhere else in Britain. Approaching the town from the south along the A941, you'll see the gaunt hilltop ruins of **Auchindoun Castle**. Although you can't go inside, it's enjoyable to wander along the track from the main road to this three-storey keep encircled by Pictish earthworks.

Following the A941 through the town brings you to the **Glenfiddich Distillery** (see opposite), past the old Dufftown train station, currently being restored for a steam line through to Keith. Behind the distillery, the ruin of the thirteenth-century **Balvenie**

THE SPEYSIDE WAY

The 45-mile-long **Speyside Way** follows the River Spey from its mouth at Spey Bay on the Moray Firth south to Tomintoul, on the edge of the Cairngorm mountains. It's a three- to five-day walk, or a day's cycle ride, but its proximity to main roads and small villages means that it is excellent for shorter walks, especially in the heart of distillery country between Craigellachie and Glenlivet. The path uses disused railway lines for much of its length, and there are simple campsites and good B&Bs at strategic points along the route.

Castle (April–Sept daily 9.30am–6pm; HS; £1) sits on a mound overlooking vast piles of whisky barrels. The castle was a Stewart stronghold, which was abandoned after the 1745 uprising, when it was last used as a government garrison.

Four miles north of Dufftown, the small settlement of **CRAIGELLACHIE** sits above the confluence of the sparkling waters of the Fiddich and the Spey. From the village, you can look down on a beautiful iron bridge over the Spey built by Thomas Telford in 1815. By the River Fiddich on the A95 Huntly road, there's a **visitor centre** for the Speyside Way (Easter–Oct daily 9am–5pm; ☎01340/881266), which sells maps of the route and gives advice on what to look for along the way.

Practicalities

Dufftown's four main streets converge on Main Square. For maps and information on the **whisky trail**, head straight to the **tourist office** inside the handsome clock tower at the centre of the square (April, May & Oct Mon–Sat 10am–1pm & 2–5pm; June & Sept Mon–Sat 10am–1pm & 2–6pm, Sun 1–6pm; July & Aug Mon–Sat 10am–7pm, Sun 1–7pm;

THE MALT WHISKY TRAIL

Speyside's **Malt Whisky Trail** is a clearly signposted seventy-mile meander around the region via eight distilleries, although there are others not on the official trail that you can visit by prior arrangement: The Macallan at Craigellachie (☎01340/871471), and Cragganmore at Ballindalloch (☎01807/500202) are both worth trying. Unless you're seriously interested in whisky, it's best to just pick out a couple that appeal, perhaps choosing one for the whisky and another for its setting. All the distilleries offer a guided **tour** (some are free, and some charge an entry fee, then give you a voucher which is redeemable against a bottle of whisky from the distillery shop) with a tasting to round it off – if you're driving you'll be offered a miniature to take away with you. Indeed, most people travel the route by car, though you could cycle it, or even walk using the Speyside Way (see opposite).

Cardhu, on the B9102 at Knockando (May–Sept Mon–Sat 9.30am–4.30pm; Oct–April Mon–Fri only; £2 with voucher). This distillery was established over a century ago when the founder's wife was nice enough to raise a red flag to warn local crofters when the authorities were on the lookout for their illegal stills. Sells good whisky, in an attractive bottle.

Dallas Dhu, Mannachie Road, Forres (April–Sept Mon–Sat 9.30am–6pm, Sun 2–6pm; Oct–March Mon–Wed & Sat 9.30am–4pm, Thurs 9.30am–noon, Sun 2–4pm; £2.30). Located apart from the others, this classic Victorian distillery no longer makes whisky, but all the equipment is in place and you can look around freely without a guided tour.

Glenfiddich, on the A941 just north of Dufftown (April to mid-Oct Mon–Sat 9.30am–4.30pm, Sun noon–4.30pm; mid-Oct to March Mon–Fri only; free). Probably the best known of the malt whiskies, and the biggest and slickest of all the distilleries. Uniquely, Glenfiddich is bottled on the premises – an interesting process to watch. Informative (and free) tours, though the place is thronged with tourists.

Glenlivet, on the B9008, ten miles north of Tomintoul (April–Oct Mon–Sat 10am–4pm, Sun 12.30–4pm; July & Aug last tour 5pm; £2.50 with voucher). With a famous name and a lonely hillside setting, this was the first licensed distillery in the Highlands, following the 1823 Act of Parliament which aimed to reduce illicit distilling and smuggling.

Speyside Cooperage, Craigellachie, four miles north of Dufftown (all year Mon–Fri 9.30am–4.30pm, plus Easter–Sept Sat 9.30am–4.30pm; £2). Gain an insight into the ancient and skilled art of cooperage, and watch the oak casks for whisky being made and repaired.

Strathisla, Keith (mid-May to mid-Sept Mon–Fri 9am–4.30pm; £4, with a £2 voucher). A small old-fashioned distillery claiming to be Scotland's oldest (1786) and situated in a highly evocative highland location on the strath of the Isla River. The malt itself is pretty rare, and used as the heart of the better-known Chivas Regal blend.

☎01340/820501). There's a good range of places to **stay** in Dufftown itself, as well as in the surrounding countryside. In town, *Morven,* on Main Square (☎01340/820507; ②), offers good, cheap B&B. A couple of miles out along the Maggieknockater road, the friendly *Tullich House* (☎01340/821008; ③) boasts a beautiful location, while the most comfortable option in Craigellachie is the B&B attached to the *Green Hall Gallery* on Victoria Street (☎01340/871010; ②). For unquestionable style and luxury, head to *Minmore House* (☎01807/590378; ⑨), the former home of Glenlivet owner George Smith, which sits right beside the distillery on a quiet hillside above the Livet Water.

The *Glenfiddich Café* just beyond the tourist office on Church Street does simple **meals** and takeaways, while the popular *Taste of Speyside* on Balverie Street, just off the square, serves a classier (and pricier) Scottish menu. Nine miles out of town along the B9009 towards Glenlivet, the *Croft Inn* is a cosy roadside **pub** with well-priced local dishes and beautiful views over Ben Rinnes, while the best selection of malts is at the *Grouse Inn* at Cabrach, ten miles out along the A941 to Rhynie. In Craigellachie, the tiny *Fiddichside Inn,* on the A95 Huntly road, is a wonderfully original and convivial pub with a garden by the river, while the busy *Highlander Inn* on Victoria Street serves good pub grub. The best place for takeaways of the liquid kind is The Whisky Shop, on Dufftown's main square, which stocks a superb range of whiskies and hosts occasional tastings. **Bikes** can be rented from Clarke's Cycle Hire (☎01340/881525), beside the *Fiddichside Inn* at Craigellachie.

Huntly

A small town set in attractive rolling farmland, the ancient burgh of **HUNTLY**, ten miles east of Dufftown and on the main train route from Aberdeen to Inverness, has little to offer the tourist other than its proximity to the Whisky Trail. It does boast, however, one of the smallest and prettiest castles in the area, albeit rather skeletal. **Huntly Castle**, power centre of the Gordon family (April–Sept Mon–Sat 9.30am–6pm, Sun 2–6pm; Oct–March Mon–Wed & Sat 9.30am–4pm, Thurs 9.30am–noon, Sun 2–4pm; HS; £2.30), sits in a peaceful clearing on the banks of the Deveron River, a ten-minute walk from the town centre down Castle Street and through an elegant arch. Built over a period of five centuries, it has sheltered the likes of Robert the Bruce and James IV (who attended a wedding here), and in 1562 became the headquarters of the Counter-Reformation in Scotland. After the Battle of Corrichie, brought about by the fourth earl's third son's wish to marry Mary, Queen of Scots, and which effectively ended the Gordons' 250-year rule, the castle was pillaged and its treasures sent to St Machar's Cathedral in Aberdeen. During the Civil War the Earl of Huntly, who had supported Charles I and declared, "you can take my head off my shoulders, but not my heart from my sovereign", was shot against his castle's walls with his escort, after which the place was left to fall into ruin.

Today you can still make out the twelfth-century motte, a grassy mound on the west side of the complex, while the main castle ruin, with its splendid doorway fronted by an elaborate coat of arms, dates from the mid-fifteenth century. In the basement, a narrow passage leads to the prisons, where medieval graffiti of tents, animals and people adorn the walls.

Seven miles south of Huntly and served by the occasional bus, the modest chateau-style **Leith Hall** (Easter weekend & May–Sept daily 1.30–4.45pm; Oct Sat & Sun 1.30–4.45pm; NTS; £4) is worth visiting, even when closed, for a wander around its 286-acre grounds (daily 9.30am–dusk). Home to the Leith and Leith-Hay family since 1650, the vast estate of varied farm and woodlands includes ponds, eighteenth-century stables, a bird-observation hide and signposted countryside walks. Inside, you can see personal memorabilia of the successive Leith lairds, a number of whom were in the armed services overseas, so anyone with military interests or a penchant for British imperial history will have a field day.

Three miles northwest of Huntly, between the A920 to Dufftown and the A96 to Keith (signposted from both), the **North East Falconry Centre** (daily: March–Sept 10am–5.30pm; Oct & Nov 10am–4pm; £3.50) is home to some fabulous falcons, owls and eagles, with flying demonstrations four times daily.

Practicalities

Huntly's **tourist office**, 7a The Square (daily: April to late Oct 10am–5pm; July & Aug till 7pm; ☎01466/792255), will book accommodation, but charges a ten percent deposit, redeemable on the first night's stay. One of the area's best **B&Bs** is *Faitch Hill Farmhouse* (☎01466/720240; ③), four miles outside town at Gartly; while, in Huntly itself, the *Dunedin Guest House*, 17 Bogie St (☎01466/794164; ③), near the train station, is a good bet. For serious luxury, head for the former home of the Duke of Gordon, *Huntly Castle Hotel* (☎01466/792696; ⑦), which stands at the end of a long driveway behind the castle ruins. The *Auld Pit* on Duke Street is a decent **pub** with regular folk music, and serves pub meals, while the home-brewed beers on offer at the *Borve Brew House* in Ruthven – four miles along the A96 to Keith and then a couple of miles along a narrow road – attract real-ale enthusiasts from across the country. **Bikes** can be rented from the Nordic Ski Centre near the castle (☎01466/704428), where you can also brush up your cross-country skiing skills.

The coast to Forres

The **coastal region** of northeast Scotland from Aberdeen to Inverness is a rugged, often bleak, landscape. Still, if the weather is good, it's well worth spending a couple of days meandering through the various little fishing villages and along the miles of deserted, unspoilt beaches. Keen walkers have the best run of the area: some of the cliffs are so steep that you have to hike considerable distances to get the best views of the coast.

Most visitors bypass **Peterhead** and **Fraserburgh**, the two largest communities, and head instead for quieter spots such as **Cruden Bay**, with its sandy beach and spooky castle, or the idyllic villages of **Pennan** and nearby **Cullen**. The other main attractions are **Duff House**, a branch of the National Gallery of Scotland, in **Banff**, the working abbey at **Pluscarden**, and the **Findhorn Foundation**, near **Forres**.

The main towns and larger villages are fairly well-served by **buses**, while **trains** from Aberdeen and Inverness stop at Elgin, Forres and Nairn. Even so, it's preferable to have your own transport for reaching some of the far-flung places.

Pitmedden Gardens to Peterhead

Fourteen miles north of Aberdeen, on the outskirts of Pitmedden village, **Pitmedden Gardens** (May–Sept daily 10am–5pm; NTS; £3.50) are the creation of Alexander Seton – formerly Lord Pitmedden, before James VII removed his title as punishment for opposing his Catholicism. Seton spent his enforced retirement on perfecting an elaborate garden project he had begun in 1675, and today the utterly orderly gardens, 471 feet square, have been restored to their seventeenth-century pattern, with neat box hedges, pavilions, fountains and sundials. In the lower garden (best viewed from the terrace), the layout of three of the flowerbeds mimics those of Holyrood Abbey in Edinburgh, while the fourth flowerbed – with its crest of arms, and a weather vane, surmounted by soldiers – are tributes to Seton's father who died fighting against the Covenanters in Aberdeen. Entrance to the gardens also takes in the **Museum of Farming Life**, where you'll see old tools and a chilly, dark bothy that was once home to the workers of the 100-acre Pitmedden estate.

Tolquhon Castle

One of the area's most secluded ruins, **Tolquhon Castle** (April–Sept Mon–Sat 9.30am–6pm, Sun 2–6pm; Oct–March Sat & Sun 9.30am–4pm, Sun 2–4pm; HS; £1.50), is tucked away off a dirt track a mile or so northwest of Pitmedden. Of the medieval remains, the gatehouse facade is the most impressive, with its handsome arched portal protected by drum towers and enriched with all manner of sculpted figures and coats of arms. You can still make out what each room was used for: the kitchen has two huge ovens gouged out of the wall, and one of the bedrooms has its own dungeon with an ominous trapdoor – at any one time there could have been eight or nine prisoners below.

Haddo House and Gardens

Four miles north of Pitmedden, the huge Palladian mansion of **Haddo House** (Easter weekend & May–Sept daily 1.30–4.45pm; Oct Sat & Sun 1.30–4.45pm; NTS; £4), completed to a design by William Adam in 1735, is set in 177 acres of woodland, lakes and ponds. Since 1731 Haddo has been the seat of the Gordons and several earls and marquesses of Aberdeen – the gardens, now home to otters, red squirrels, pheasants and deer, were created from a wasteland by the fourth earl in the early years of the last century. The house is now renowned for staging local music, drama and arts: check with the Haddo Arts Trust (☎01651/851770) for details of forthcoming productions.

Forvie Nature Reserve and Cruden Bay

Fifteen miles north of Aberdeen, a sideroad (signposted to Collieston) leads off the A90 past **Forvie National Nature Reserve**. This area incorporates the Sands of Forvie, one of Britain's largest and least disturbed dune systems, and boasts a rich array of birdlife. A network of trails winds along the coast and through the dunes, with one leading to a fifteenth-century village, buried by the shifting sands. Just south of here, at Newburgh, the *Udny Arms Hotel* on Mains Street (☎01358/789444; ⑦) has a superb restaurant, overlooking the mouth of the Ythan River, which is very popular with Aderdonians at the weekends.

Wonderful sandy beaches can also be found eight miles north of Forvie, at **CRUDEN BAY**, from where a pleasant fifteen-minute walk leads to the huge pink-granite ruin of **Slains Castle**. This eerie place, whose stark beauty overlooking the sea is said to have inspired Bram Stoker to write *Dracula*, was built in 1597 but remodelled in Gothic style in the nineteenth century. It is surprisingly badly signposted: from the car park at the end of Cruden Bay's Main Street, head for the sea then along the cliffs.

A precarious three-mile walk on from Slains Castle along the cliffs brings you to the **Bullers of Buchan**, a splendid 245ft-deep sea chasm, where the ocean gushes in through a natural archway eroded by the sea. This is some of the finest cliff scenery in the country and attracts a variety of (smelly) nesting seabirds. An alternative access point is the car park just off the A975, from where a short footpath leads past some old cottages to the very edge of the chasm.

Peterhead and around

Unless you have a particular penchant for baked-bean factories and power stations, **PETERHEAD**, the easternmost mainland town in Scotland, is best avoided. The busiest white-fish port in Europe, with annual catches valued at over $75 million, its harbour is a mass of large, aggressive-looking boats, with throbbing engines and an odour of stale fish. Fishing, along with a high-security jail, used to be Peterhead's sole source of income until the arrival of the oil industry in the 1970s. The town's population increased rapidly from 13,000 to 18,000, and now the community is one of the richest in Britain, though little of the wealth seems to have found its way into civic improvement.

The oldest building in Peterhead is the 400-year-old **Ugie Salmon Fish House** on Golf Road at the mouth of the River Ugie, at the north end of town (Mon–Fri 9am–noon & 2–5pm, Sat 9am–noon; free), where you can watch the traditional methods of oak-smoking salmon and trout in Scotland's oldest smoke-house – the finished product is for sale at reasonable prices. In contrast, one of the town's newest buildings houses the **Peterhead Maritime Heritage Museum** (April–Oct Mon–Sat 10am–5.30pm, Sun noon–5.30pm; Nov–March Sat 10am–4pm, Sun noon–4pm; £2.50), on South Road above a clean, spacious beach. The museum details the story of the town's fishing industry from the old herring fleet to the modern day, with a live relay of the harbourmaster's radio channel. Listen out too for the recordings of old fishermen and women, who still speak the distinctive Doric dialect.

Peterhead has no tourist office; if you need **to stay**, try *Alva House*, 128 Queen St (☎01779/477393; ③), a small centrally located B&B, or the modern *Waterside Inn,* on Fraserburgh Road (☎01779/471121; ⑦), on the banks of the River Ugie to the north of town. For **food**, head for the town's best fish-and-chip shop, the *Dolphin*, on Alexandra Parade on the northwest side of the harbour, beside the fish market.

Aden Country Park

From Peterhead, a direct bus travels the nine miles to the 230-acre **Aden Country Park** (daily 9am–dusk; free), just beyond the town of Mintlaw. In addition to woodlands, a lake and a huge variety of wildlife, the park is home to the **North East of Scotland Agricultural Heritage Centre** (April & Oct Sat & Sun noon–5pm; May–Sept 11am–5pm; free), whose highlight is a unique semicircular farmstead built around the beginning of the nineteenth century. Despite its uninspiring title, the centre is a well-thought-out and absorbing museum with atmospheric exhibits that recall a traditional farming life.

Fraserburgh and the north coast

Ten miles or so north of Aden Park, **FRASERBURGH** is a large and fairly severe-looking town in the same vein as Peterhead, although its economy still relies on fishing alone. At the northern tip of the town an eighteenth-century lighthouse protrudes from the top of sixteenth-century **Fraserburgh Castle**, where the highest wind speeds on mainland Britain (140mph) were recorded in 1989. The lighthouse was one of the first to be built in Scotland and now houses **Scotland's Lighthouse Museum** (April–Oct Mon–Sat 10am–6pm, Sun 12.30–6pm; Nov–April closes at 4pm; £2.50), where you can see a collection of huge lenses and prisms gathered from decommissioned lighthouses, and a display on various members of the Stevenson family (including the father and grandfather of Robert Louis Stevenson), who designed many of them. Highlight of the museum is the Kinnaird Head light itself, preserved as it was when the last keeper left in 1991, with its century-old equipment still in working order.

Fraserbugh's **tourist office**, in Saltoun Square (April–June & Sept Mon–Sat 10am–1pm & 2–5pm; July & Aug Mon–Sat 10am–1pm & 2–6pm, Sun 1–5pm; ☎01346/28315), gives out information about the surrounding area, while the friendly *Coffee Shoppe*, 30 Cross St, serves great sandwiches, soup and cakes.

Pennan, Crovie and Gardenstown

The coast road between Fraserburgh and **PENNAN**, twelve miles west, is particularly attractive; it's lined with pretty churches and cottages, and countless paths lead off it to ruined castles, clifftop walks and lonely beaches. Pennan itself, a tiny fishing hamlet, lies just off the road, down a steep and hazardous hill. Consisting of little more than a single row of whitewashed stone cottages, the village leapt into the limelight when the British movie *Local Hero* was filmed here in 1982. The only place to **stay** is the *Pennan*

Inn (☎01346/561201; ⑤), a convivial, lively spot with an excellent seafood **restaurant** and a cosy bar, whose customers spill out onto the sea wall on summer evenings. The tiny villages of **CROVIE** (pronounced "Crivie") and **GARDENSTOWN**, on the other side of Troup Head from Pennan, are just as appealing as their neighbour. Both are tucked in against the steep cliffs, with Crovie so narrow that its residents have to park at one end of the village and continue to their houses on foot.

Macduff and Duff House

Heading west along the coast from Pennan brings you, after ten miles, to **MACDUFF**, a famous spa town during the nineteenth century and now with a thriving and pleasant harbour. The **Macduff Marine Aquarium**, 11 High Shore (Mon–Fri 10am–8pm, Sat & Sun 10am–5pm; £2.50), displaying sea creatures from the Moray Firth in Britain's deepest aquarium tank, is a fun place for children, but the town's undoubted highlight is the extravagant **Duff House** (April–Sept daily 10am–5pm; Oct–March Thurs–Sun 10am–5pm; HS; £3), on the other side of the River Devoron over a beautiful seven-arched bridge. Built to William Adam's design in 1730, this elegant Georgian Baroque house was originally intended for one of the northeast's richest men, William Braco, who became Earl of Fife in 1759. It was clearly built to impress, and could have been even more splendid had Adam been allowed to build curving colonnades either side; Braco's refusal to pay for carved Corinthian columns to be shipped in from Queensferry caused such bitter argument that the laird never actually came to live here and even went so far as to pull down his coach curtains whenever he passed by.

The house has been painstakingly restored and reopened as an outpost of the **National Gallery of Scotland**'s extensive collection. The first room to the left off the rococo vestibule is the **Prince of Wales' Bedroom**, so called because it was used by the future Edward VII. His mother, Queen Victoria, can be seen, looking unusually fresh-faced, in the bust under the mirror. Beyond the back of the vestibule is the dining room, hung with ponderous eighteenth-century portraits, among which Allan Ramsay's *Elizabeth, Mrs Daniel Cunyngham* leaps out for its delightfully cool composition. To the left is the **Private Drawing Room**, containing a bust of William Adam and the sweeping canvases of Welsh landscapist Richard Wilson (1714–82). On the other side of the ground floor, Countess Agnes' Boudoir, formerly Lord Macduff's dressing room, contains a riotous gilded Rococo mirror and El Greco's heartfelt *St Jerome in Penitence*, which dominates a wall of mainly religious art. This leads into the **Hunting Room**, mainly filled with treasures from Dunimarle in Fife. Magdalene Erskine, who bought the house in 1835 and bequeathed its collection to be used to found an art gallery, can be seen as a little girl, added later to the painting of the family grouping by David Allen in 1788. Note how all the women are shown disproportionately tiny and doll-like next to the men and boys.

Ascending the **Great Staircase**, all eyes are drawn to the enormous copy of Raphael's *Transfiguration* by Inverness's Grigor Urquhart (1797–1846). Most of the accompanying portraits are also Scottish. Upstairs, the **North Drawing Room** contains the only piece of furniture original to the house, in the shape of a 1760s mirror, but more obvious is the bewilderingly bold gold and cherry-red ceiling, a not entirely successful Victorian pastiche of Adam's style. In the **Great Drawing Room**, William's son Robert Adam's symmetrical classicism meets French opulence head on, and somehow it works. The best example of this is the 1764 furniture suite of two gilded sofas and two chairs originally designed by the younger Adam and built by Chippendale, combining the Classical reference of lion's-paw feet and the Rococo influence of florid gold shells. Two chairs from the same collection recently sold at auction for £1.7 million – twice the amount ever paid for a piece of Chippendale furniture.

Beyond the house there are extensive grounds with some pleasant parkland walks, notably along the River Deveron to a local beauty spot, the **Bridge of Alvah**, a couple of miles south.

Banff

Macduff more or less merges with the town of **BANFF**, whose **tourist office** (April–Sept daily 10am–1pm & 2–5pm; July & Aug Mon–Sat until 6pm, Sun 1–6pm; ☎01261/812419) is housed in a Greek Doric lodge opposite the entrance to Duff House. Here, for £1 deposit, you can collect a thoroughly enjoyable **Walkman tour** of the town, which introduces both the grand Georgian upper town and, down by the harbour, the older, scruffier **Scotstown**. For sea swimming, head to Links Beach on the west side of town. The other beach, at the mouth of the Deveron, is susceptible to strong currents and is best avoided.

A mile southwest of town along the A97, the intiguing **Colleonard Sculpture Park** (daily 9.30am–5pm; free) is the world's only garden of archetypal abstractionism. Sculptor Frank Bruce, usually to be found around the site, began his outdoor collection in 1965. A man of immense talent, he carves figures and scenes of great vitality and intensity from tree trunks, which he then places around the wonderfully peaceful site.

If you want to stay, **B&Bs** include *Castlehill*, 58 Castle St, an extension of the High Street (☎01261/818372; ③), or, over the river in the heart of Macduff, Mrs Grieg's, 11 Gellymill St (☎01261/833314; ②). Four miles south of Macduff, off the A497 Turriff road, the elegant and welcoming Regency *Eden House* (☎01261/821282; ⑥) is set in extensive grounds overlooking the Deveron valley. **Camping** is best near the beach at the *Banff Links Caravan Park* (☎01261/812228; April–Sept). There are various pubs for **food and drink**: the *Aul' Fife*, at 12 Low St, just along from the tourist office, serves reasonable pub grub, or try the *Market Arms*, a sixteenth-century town house on High Shore.

Cullen

Twelve miles west of Banff, past the quaint village of **Portsoy**, renowned for its green marble once shipped to Versailles, is **CULLEN**, served by bus from Aberdeen. The town, strikingly situated beneath a superb series of arched rail viaducts, is made up of two sections – Seatown, by the harbour, and the new town on the hillside. There's a lovely stretch of sheltered sand by Seatown, where the colourful houses – confusingly numbered according to the order in which they were built – huddle end-on to the sea. Cullen's attractive old **kirk**, dating from the 1300s, lies a twenty-minute stroll south of the centre.

The town's enthusiastic **tourist office** (June–Aug daily 11am–5pm) is on the main square of the new town, and most of its **B&Bs** stand back from the seashore on Seafield Place. They're all much of a muchness, but no. 11 is friendly and comfortable (☎01542/840819; ②). If you want to try the local delicacy, Cullen skink – fish soup made from cream and smoked haddock – the friendly *Three Kings* **pub** on North Castle Street is your best bet, though most of the smarter hotels around town also serve it.

Elgin and around

Inland, about fifteen miles southwest of Cullen, the lively market town of **ELGIN** grew up in the thirteenth century around the River Lossie. It's an appealing place, still largely sticking to its medieval street plan, with a busy main street opening out onto an old cobbled marketplace and a tangle of wynds and pends.

On North College Street, just round the corner from the tourist office and clearly signposted, is the still lovely ruin of **Elgin Cathedral** (April–Sept Mon–Sat 9.30am–6pm, Sun 2–6pm; Oct–March Mon–Thurs & Sat 9.30am–4pm, Sun 2–4pm; £1.50, joint ticket with Spynie Palace £2.50). Once considered Scotland's most beautiful cathedral, rivalling St Andrews in importance, today it is little more than a shell, though it does retain its original facade. Founded in 1224, the three-towered cathedral was extensively rebuilt after a fire in 1270, and stood as the region's highest religious house until 1390 when the so-called Wolf of Badenoch (Alexander Stewart, Earl of Buchan and illegitimate son of Robert II) burnt the place down, along with the rest of the town, in retaliation for being excommunicated by the Bishop of Moray when he left his wife. The cathedral suffered further during the post-Reformation, when all its valuables were stripped and the building was reduced to common quarry for the locals. Unusual features include the Pictish cross slab in the middle of the ruins and the cracked gravestones with their memento mori of skulls and crossbones.

At the very top of High Street is one of the UK's oldest museums, the **Elgin Museum** (April–Sept Mon–Fri 10am–5pm, Sat 11am–4pm, Sun 2–5pm; £1), housed in this building since 1843. Along with the usual local exhibits, there's a weird anthropological collection including reptilian skulls, a shrunken head from Ecuador and a grinning mummy from Peru. In addition, you can see an excellent collection of fossils and well-explained Pictish relics.

The handsome, pedestrianized High Street, leading west, widens out onto the market place, the Plainstones, and the impressive Neoclassical parish **church of St Giles** (July & Aug Fri 2–5pm), built by Archibald Simpson in 1827–28.

Practicalities

Elgin is well-served by public transport, with the Aberdeen–Inverness train stopping here several times a day. The **bus station** is on Alexandra Road, a block from St Giles Church (☎01343/544222), while the **train station** is slightly less convenient, on the south side of town on Station Road (turn right out of the station, left at the island and up Moss Street to reach the centre).

The **tourist office**, 17 High St (April, May & Oct Mon–Sat 10am–1pm & 2–5pm, Sun 1–5pm; June & Sept daily till 6pm; July & Aug daily till 7pm; ☎01343/542666), will book **accommodation**. The *Saltire Bunkhouse*, on Pluscarden Road (☎01343/551467), offers hostel accommodation – it's a 25-minute walk from the centre of town. More central, *The Lodge*, 20 Duff Ave (☎01343/549981; ③), is a good-quality **B&B** in a house built for a former tea-plantation owner, while the castle-like *Mansion House Hotel*, The Haugh (☎01343/548811; ⑨), is one of the most exclusive in the region, and overlooks the river. For **food**, a popular place is *Flanagan's Irish Pub*, 48a High St, which serves good pub grub, and has regular live music; otherwise there's *Littlejohn's Brasserie*, 193 High St, a Tex-Mex and Cajun theme chain restaurant, or the *Ashvale* on Moss Street for fish and chips. The best **pubs** include *Thunderton House*, Thunderton Place, off High Street, which incorporates the seventeenth-century Great Lodge of Scottish kings, and *High Spirits*, in an old church on Moss Street. For great **picnic** foods, head to Gordon & McPhail, 58–60 South St, an Aladdin's cave of aromas, colours and delicacies, which sells one of the widest range of malt whiskies in the world.

Pluscarden Abbey

Set in attractive countryside seven miles southwest of Elgin, **Pluscarden Abbey** (daily 5am–10.30pm; free), looms impressively large in a peaceful clearing off an unmarked road. One of only a handful of abbeys in Scotland with a permanent community of monks, it was founded in 1230 for a French order and, in 1390, became another of the properties burnt by the Wolf of Badenoch (see above); recovering from this, it became a priory of the Benedictine Abbey of Dunfermline in 1454 and continued as such until monastic life was suppressed in Scotland in 1560. The abbey's revival began in 1897 when the Catholic antiquarian, John, third Marquis of Bute, started to repair the building. In 1948 his son donated it to the small group of Benedictine monks from Gloucester, who established the present community.

Lossiemouth, Spynie Palace and Duffus

Elgin's nearest seaside town, **LOSSIEMOUTH**, five miles north across the the flat land of the Laich of Moray, is generally known as Lossie, a cheery (if fairly golf-oriented) resort, blessed with two sandy beaches. The glorious duney spit of the East Beach is reached over a footbridge across the River Lossie from the town park. In the easternmost part of the older harbour's grid of stone streets, Pitgaveny Street has the tiny **Fisheries Museum** (Easter–Sept Mon–Sat 10am–5pm; 50p), which includes some interesting scale models of fishing boats and a re-creation of the study of James Ramsay Macdonald (1866–1937), Britain's first Labour prime minister. On Prospect Terrace, above the harbour district in the airier "new" town, laid out in the nineteenth century, there's an excellent viewpoint to his memory.

Lossiemouth's development as a port came when the nearby waterways of **SPYNIE**, three miles inland, silted up and became useless to the traders of Elgin. Little remains of the settlement, although the hulking shape of **Spynie Palace** (April–Sept Mon–Sat 9.30am–6pm, Sun 2–6pm; Oct–March Sat & Sun 2–4pm; HS; £1.50, joint ticket with Elgin Cathedral £2.50) indicates its former significance. Until 1224, Holy Trinity Church, which was part of the palace (there's no evidence of it today), was the cathedral of the Bishopric of Moray, before the honour passed to Elgin. The building remained, however, an integral part of the local ecclesiastical setup, primarily as the bishop's palace, right through until that office was abolished in the Scottish Church in 1689. The enormous rectangular David's Tower – seen looming for miles around – is the largest tower house in Scotland, and was built around a previously cylindrical corner tower during the time of Bishop David Stewart (1461–77). Views from the top over the Spynie Canal, the much-diminished sea loch and the Moray Firth, are stunning. Under the tower is a beautiful fourteenth-century beehive-roofed storage cellar. Next door, a slightly later cellar contains the wide-mouthed gun holes installed by Bishop Patrick Hepburn (1538–73), who, as a Catholic, survived the Reformation at Spynie for a full thirteen years.

Straight roads and water ditches criss-cross the flat land west of Spynie. Past the sinister shapes and frequent flights from RAF Lossiemouth is the spread-eagled settlement of **DUFFUS**, five miles west of Lossie. Old Duffus is no more than a farm or two and a motte and bailey **castle** (free access), part of which leans at a rakish angle. New Duffus, two miles northwest, is best known as the gateway to **Gordonstoun School**, the spartan (but hugely expensive) public school favoured by royalty, although Prince Charles reportedly despised its fresh-air-and-cold-showers puritanism. A quarter of a mile down the lane to Gordonstoun lie the remains of the Duffus old kirk, dating from at least 1226. A fine fourteenth-century parish cross, some beautifully inscribed graves and an 1830 watch house against grave-diggers are the highlights. Judging by the number of discarded cigarette packets, you're also likely to see a few Gordonstoun pupils at leisure.

Burghead

Windswept **BURGHEAD** was, before the imposition of the town in 1805–09 – a tightly packed grid of streets on the natural promontory – the site of an important Iron Age fort and the ancient Pictish capital of Moray. The **Burghead Bulls** were crafted here – a series of at least 25 unique Pictish stone carvings, all but six of which were destroyed when the town was built. One of these is on display in the window of the library on the main Grant Street; others can be seen in Elgin Museum, the Royal Museum in Edinburgh and the British Museum in London. A **well**, tucked away down King Street (key and interpretive boards are left in the porch at 69 King St), is the most remarkable surviving feature. Under a barrel roof, an impressive underground chamber fed by springs is believed to have been the water supply for the Iron Age and Pictish strongholds. The headland tip of the town is still pocked with the scant remains of early defences, including two earth ramparts, just off Bath Street, upon which an eerie burnt-out pillar sits. This is where the **Clavie** – a burning tar barrel still carried around the town on January 11, to mark the old calendar's new year – ends its annual journey. From the harbour, a wide sweep of sandy beach stretches five miles around Burghead Bay to Findhorn.

If you need to **stay** in Burghead, the *Red Craig* hotel, on the B9040 above the headland on the east side of town (☎01343/835663; ③), has B&B and camping, serves food and drink, and hosts regular music and dances. To get to Burghead, take bus #331 from Elgin.

The Findhorn Foundation

The **Findhorn Foundation** on the B9011, about ten miles east of Elgin (Mon–Sat 9am–noon & 2–5pm, Sun 2–5pm; free), is a spiritual community and magnet for soul-searchers from around the world. Set up in 1962 by Eileen and Peter Caddy, the foundation has blossomed from its early core of three adults and three children into a full-blown community, with classes and facilities for hundreds of people. Bizarrely enough, despite its enormous growth, the Foundation is still situated on the town's caravan and camping park (☎01309/690203; April–Oct), creating an intriguing combination of people on site. Many of the original caravans have metamorphosed into more permanent structures, including some fascinating houses and community spaces employing the latest in ecological methods. It's an amazing place and, however cynical you might be, well worth at least a flying visit. Guided **tours** (Mon, Wed & Sat 2pm), residential workshops and **B&B** accommodation are all available (for details contact the visitor centre on ☎01309/690310), and there's a smart **café** and richly stocked delicatessan/general shop on site.

A mile up the road, the tidy village of **FINDHORN** has a magnificent beach, a delightful harbour, a small **Heritage Centre** (May & Sept Sat & Sun 2–5pm, June–Aug daily except Tues 2–5pm; free) and a couple of good pubs. Bus #310 from Forres runs there via the Foundation.

THE FINDHORN FOUNDATION

In 1962, with little money and no employment, Peter and Eileen Caddy, their three children and friend Dorothy Maclean, settled on a caravan site at Findhorn. Dorothy believed she had a special relationship with what she called the "devas", in her own words "the archetypal formative forces of light or energy that underlie all forms in nature – plants, trees, rivers, etc", and from the uncompromising sandy soil they built a garden filled with remarkable plants and vegetables far larger than had ever been seen in the area.

The Original Caravan – as it is marked on the site's map – still stands, surrounded by a whole host of newer timber buildings and other caravans. The Foundation is now home to a couple of hundred people, with around 8000 visitors every year. The buildings, employing solar power, earth roofs and other green initiatives, such as an ecological sewage treatment centre, show the commitment of the Findhorners to a sustainable future.

As can be expected, the Foundation is not without its controversy, a local JP declaring that "behind the benign and apparently religious front lies a hard core of New Agers experimenting with hallucinatory techniques marketed as spirituality", a predictable enough charge from local conservative thought. Findhorn, now a public company, is also accused of being overly well-heeled: a glance into the shop or a tally of the large cars parked outside the houses does give some substance to such ideas. However, most people here, although honest about the downsides of community living, are extremely positive about its benefits.

Forres

FORRES, one of Scotland's oldest agricultural towns, is of little note except for its pretty flower-filled parks, and the 20ft **Sueno's Stone**, on the eastern outskirts of town, is one of the most remarkable Pictish stones in Scotland. Now housed in what looks like a huge glass telephone box as protection against further erosion, the stone was found buried in 1726 and mistakenly named after Swein Forkbeard, King of Denmark, though it more probably commemorates a battle between the people of Moray and the Norse settlers in Orkney. Carvings on the east face can be read as one of the earliest examples of war reportage, with the story told from the arrival of the leader at the top to the decapitated corpses of the vanquished at the bottom.

The #10 **bus** between Elgin and Inverness stops outside St Leonard's Church on High Street, further along from Forres' **tourist office** at no. 116 (Easter–June, Sept & Oct Mon–Sat 10am–1pm & 2–5pm; July & Aug Mon–Sat 10am–1pm & 2–6pm, Sun 1–6pm; ☎01309/672938); call Bluebird in Elgin (☎01343/544222) for details of other local services. If you want **to stay** in Forres, try the *Tormhor* **B&B**, 11 High St (☎01309/673837; ③), which has large, comfortable rooms in a Victorian house overlooking some colourful gardens.

Brodie Castle

Four miles west of Forres and eight miles east of Nairn (see p.436), just off the A96, **Brodie Castle** (April–Sept Mon–Sat 11am–4.30pm, Sun 1.30–4.30pm; Oct Sat & Sun only; NTS; £4), dating from 1567, is a classic Z-shaped Scottish tower house set in lovely grounds (open all year; free) with drifts of daffodils in spring. Although it's now the property of the NTS, the 25th Earl of Brodie still lives here, and his presence very much contributes to the country-house atmosphere. Inside, there are all the rooms you'd expect: a panelled dining room with fabulous plasterwork, several bedrooms complete with four-posters, and a massive Victorian kitchen and servants' quarters, all linked by winding passages. The collections of furniture, porcelain and especially paintings are outstanding, with works by Jacob Cuyp and Edwin Landseer, among others. To end your trip there's a **tearoom**, where the staff dishes out splendid home-baked cakes.

travel details

Trains

Aberdeen to: Arbroath (every 30min; 1hr); Dundee (every 30min; 1hr 15min); Edinburgh (1–2 hourly; 2hr 35min); Elgin (hourly; 1hr 30min); Forres (hourly; 1hr 45min); Glasgow (1–2 hourly; 2hr 35min); Huntly (hourly; 50min); Insch (hourly; 35min); Inverurie (hourly; 20min); Keith (hourly; 1hr 5min); Montrose (every 30min; 45min); Nairn (hourly; 2hr); Stonehaven (every 30min; 15min).

Dundee to: Aberdeen (every 30min; 1hr 15min); Arbroath (hourly; 20min); Montrose (hourly; 15min).

Elgin to: Forres (hourly; 15min); Nairn (hourly; 25min).

Buses

Aberdeen to: Arbroath (hourly; 1hr 20min); Ballater (hourly; 1hr 45min); Banchory (hourly; 55min); Banff (hourly; 1hr 55min); Braemar (4–6 daily; 2hr 10min); Crathie (for Balmoral) (4–6 daily; 1hr 55min); Cruden Bay (hourly; 50min); Cullen (hourly; 1hr 50min–2hr 30min); Dufftown (2 weekly; 2hr 10min); Dundee (hourly; 2hr); Elgin (hourly; 2hr 35min–3hr 40min); Forfar (2 daily; 1hr 20min); Forres (hourly; 2hr 35min); Fraserburgh (hourly; 1hr 20min); Fyvie (hourly; 1hr); Huntly (hourly; 1hr 35min); Inverurie (hourly; 45min); Macduff (hourly; 1hr 50min); Mintlaw (for Aden Park) (hourly; 50min); Montrose (hourly; 1hr); Nairn (hourly; 2hr

50min); Peterhead (every 30min; 1hr 15min); Pitmedden (hourly; 50min); Stonehaven (every 30min; 25–45min).

Ballater to: Crathie (June–Sept 1 daily; 15min).

Banchory to: Ballater (June–Sept 1 daily; 45min); Braemar (June–Sept 1 daily; 1hr 20min); Crathie (June–Sept 1 daily; 1hr); Spittal of Glenshee (June–Sept 1 daily; 2hr).

Dufftown to: Elgin (hourly; 1hr).

Dundee to: Aberdeen (hourly; 2hr); Arbroath (every 15min; 40min–1hr); Blairgowrie (every 30min; 50min–1hr); Forfar (every 30min; 30min); Glamis (2 daily; 40min); Kirriemuir (hourly; 1hr 10min); Meigle (hourly; 40min); Montrose (hourly; 1hr 15min).

Elgin to: Aberdeen (hourly; 2hr 35min–3hr 40min); Burghead (Mon–Sat hourly; 30min); Duffus (Mon–Sat hourly; 15min); Forres (hourly; 25min); Huntly (3 daily; 50min); Inverurie (3 daily; 1hr 45min); Lossiemouth (every 30min; 20min); Nairn (hourly; 40min); Pluscarden (1 daily; 20min).

Forres to: Elgin (hourly; 25min); Findhorn (Mon–Sat 8 daily; 20min).

Fraserburgh to: Banff (2 daily; 55min); Macduff (2 daily; 45min).

Montrose to: Brechin (hourly; 20min).

Peterhead to: Cruden Bay (every 30min; 20min).

Ferries
Aberdeen to: Lerwick, Shetland (6 weekly; 14hr); Stromness, Orkney (1 weekly; 10hr).

Flights
Aberdeen to: Birmingham (Mon–Fri 2 daily; 1hr 30min); Dundee (1 daily; 25min); Edinburgh (4 daily; 40min); Glasgow (3 daily; 45min); London (Heathrow 8 daily, Stansted 3 daily, Gatwick 4 daily; 1hr 30min); Manchester (Mon–Fri 6 daily, Sat 2 daily, Sun 1 daily; 1hr 20min).

Dundee to: Aberdeen (1 daily; 25min); Edinburgh (2 daily; 20min); Manchester (2 daily; 1hr 15min).

CHAPTER EIGHT

THE HIGHLANDS

Scotland's **Highlands** cover the northern two-thirds of the country and include some of its most spectacular scenery: mountains, glens, lochs and rivers contrast with moors and fertile farmland, and the whole sparsely populated area is surrounded by a magnificent coastline. This varied landscape and the tranquillity which it offers are without doubt the main attractions of the region. You may be surprised at just how remote much of it is: the vast peat bogs in the north, for example, are among the most extensive and unspoilt wilderness areas in Europe, while a handful of the west coast's isolated crofting villages can still only be reached by boat.

Exposed to slightly different weather conditions and, to some extent, different historical and cultural influences, each of the three coastlines has its own distinct character. Along the fertile east coast, green fields and woodland run down to the sweeping sandy beaches of the **Moray**, **Cromarty** and **Dornoch firths**, while further northeast, rolling moors give way to peaty wastes and sheep country. Stretching east–west from **John O' Groats** to the wind-lashed **Cape Wrath**, the **north coast** proper, backed by the vast and ecologically unique bog lands of the **Flow Country**, is wilder and more rugged, with sheer cliffs and sand-filled bays bearing the brunt of frequently fierce Atlantic storms. Visitors with limited time tend to stick to the more scenic **west coast**, whose jagged shoreline of sea lochs, rocky headlands and white-sand coves is set against some of Scotland's most dramatic mountains, looking across to Skye, Mull and the Hebrides on the horizon.

Cutting diagonally across the heart of the southern Highlands, the **Great Glen** provides an alternative focus for your travel, linking the long thin sliver of **Loch Ness**, in the centre of the region, with the key towns of Inverness on the east coast, and Fort William in the west. From here it's possible to branch out to some fine scenery, most conveniently the beautiful mass of **Glen Coe**, but also the remote and tranquil **Ardnamurchan peninsula** and the lochs and glens that lead up to **Kyle of Lochalsh** – the most direct route to Skye (see p.331). In the opposite direction, south of the Great Glen, the ski resort of **Aviemore** makes a convenient – if not the most appealing – base for exploring the spectacular **Cairngorm Mountains**.

Inverness, the only major urban centre in the Highlands, is an obvious springboard for more remote areas, with its good transport links and facilities, while on the

---

SAFETY IN SCOTTISH HIGHLANDS

The mountains of the Scottish Highlands, while not as high or as steep as the Alps, are so far north that weather conditions – including blizzards and icy winds of up to 100mph – can be fatal. In 1993, some 54 climbers died, many of them inexperienced walkers who did not realize the levels of danger involved. It's essential to take proper precautions. Always put safety first: never underestimate just how fast the weather can change (or how extreme the changes can be); don't venture off track if you're inexperienced; and be sure to set out properly equipped, with warm, waterproof clothing, decent footwear, a compass, all the maps you might need, and some food in case you get stuck. Make sure, too, that someone knows roughly where you have gone and when you expect to be back (remember to contact them again on your return).

---

western coast, **Fort William**, backed by Ben Nevis, and the planned eighteenth-century port of **Ullapool** are both well placed for exploring some of the spellbinding countryside. In the northeast, **Thurso** is a solid stone town with a regular ferry service to the Orkneys, and the old port of **Wick** was once the centre of Europe's herring industry – although it's fair to say that neither of these towns is particularly endearing in themselves. Further south lie **Dornoch**, with its sandstone fourteenth-century cathedral, and **Cromarty**, whose vernacular architecture ranks among Scotland's finest.

INVERNESS AND AROUND

Inverness, 105 miles northwest of Aberdeen on the A96, is the largest town in the Highlands – a good base for day-trips and a jumping-off point for many of the more remote parts of the region. You could do worse than spend a day here, looking around the shops, museums and the striking sandstone castle that presides imperiously over the town. The approach to the town over the barren Monadhliath Mountains from Perth and Aviemore provides a spectacular introduction to the district, with the **Great Glen** to the left, stretching southwestwards towards Fort William and, beyond, the massed peaks of Glen Affric. To the north is the huge, rounded form of Ben Wyvis, whilst to the east lies the **Moray Firth**, to some extent a commuter belt for Inverness, but also boasting a lovely coastline and some of the region's best castles and historic sites. The gentle, undulating green landscape is well tended and tranquil; a fertile contrast to the windswept moorland and mountains that virtually surround it.

A string of worthwhile sights punctuates the main coastal route from Aberdeen. The low-key holiday resort of **Nairn**, with its long white-sand beaches and championship golf course, stands within striking distance of several monuments, including the whimsical **Cawdor Castle**, featured in Shakespeare's *Macbeth*, and **Fort George**, one of several impressive Hanoverian bastions erected in the wake of the Jacobite rebellion. The infamous battle and ensuing massacre that ended Bonnie Prince Charlie's ill-fated uprising took place on the outskirts of Inverness at **Culloden**, where a small visitor centre and memorial stones recall the gruesome events of 1745.

Inverness

Straddling a nexus of major road and rail routes, **INVERNESS** is the busy and prosperous hub of the Highlands, and an inevitable port of call if you're exploring the region by public transport. **Buses** and **trains** leave for communities right across the far north of Scotland, and it isn't uncommon for people from as far afield as Thurso, Durness and Kyle of Lochalsh to travel down for a day's shopping here – Britain's most northerly chain-store centre. Though boasting few conventional sights, the town's setting on the leafy banks of the River Ness is appealing. Crowned by a pink crenellated castle and lavishly decorated with flowers – for which the town has won several awards – the compact centre has retained much of its medieval street layout (although unsightly concrete blocks overshadow the period buildings in places), while the salmon-packed River Ness, which flows through the centre, is lined with leafy parks and prosperous-looking stone houses.

Some history

Inverness's sheltered **harbour** and proximity to the open sea made it an important entrepôt and shipbuilding centre during medieval times. David I, who first imposed a feudal system on Scotland, erected a **castle** on the banks of the Ness to oversee maritime trade in the early twelfth century, promoting it to royal burgh status soon after. Bolstered by receipts from the lucrative export of leather, salmon and timber, the town grew to become the kingdom's most prosperous northern outpost, and an obvious target for the marauding Highlanders who plagued this remote border area.

A second wave of growth occurred during the eighteenth century as the Highland cattle trade flourished. The arrival of the **Caledonian Canal** and **rail** links with the east and south brought further prosperity, heralding a tourist boom that reached a fashionable zenith in the Victorian era, fostered by the British royal family's enthusiasm for all things Scottish. Over the last thirty years, the town has become one of the fastest-expanding in Britain, with its population virtually doubling due to the increasing tourist industry and improved communications.

Arrival and information

Inverness **airport** (☎232471) is at Dalcross, seven miles east of the town; the irregular **bus** #311 into town (Mon–Fri 3 daily, Sat 2 daily; check times on ☎01343/544222; 20min; £2.50) connects with only a few flights, and a **taxi** costs around £10. The **bus station** (☎233371) and **train station** (☎238924) both lie just off Academy Street to the east of the town centre. The **tourist office** (Mon–Fri 9am–5pm, Sat & Sun 10am–4pm; ☎234353) is in a 1960s block on Castle Wynd, just five minutes' walk from the station. It stocks a wide range of literature on the area, can book accommodation, and its friendly staff also hand out useful free maps of the town and environs.

The telephone code for Inverness is ☎01463.

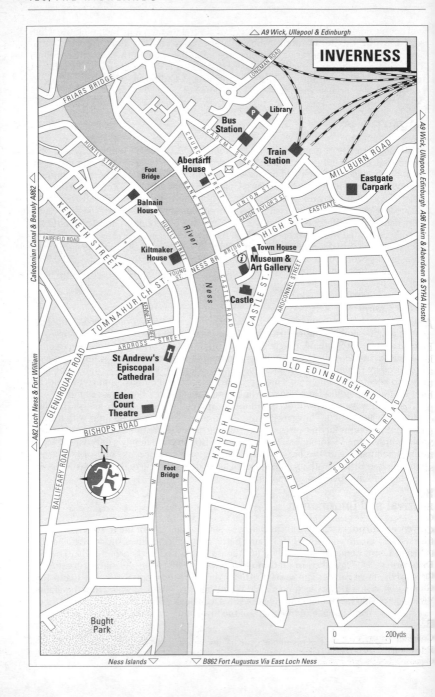

△ A9 Wick, Ullapool & Edinburgh

INVERNESS

Library

Bus Station

Train Station

Eastgate Carpark

Abertarff House

Foot Bridge

Balnain House

Kiltmaker House

Town House

Museum & Art Gallery

Castle

St Andrew's Episcopal Cathedral

Eden Court Theatre

Bught Park

FRIARS BRIDGE

HUNTLY STREET

KENNETH STREET

FAIRFIELD ROAD

TOMNAHURICH ST.

GLENURQUART ROAD

BALLIFEARY ROAD

BISHOPS ROAD

ARDROSS STREET

KENNETH STREET

YOUNG ST.

HUNTLY STREET

NESS BR.

River Ness

NESS WALK

LADIES WALK

Foot Bridge

ACADEMY STREET

CHURCH STREET

BANK STREET

UNION ST.

BARON TAYLOR'S S.

HIGH ST.

EASTGATE

BRIDGE ST.

CASTLE ST.

CASTLE ROAD

ARDCONNEL STREET

OLD EDINBURGH RD.

HAUGH ROAD

NESS BANK

CULDUTHEL RD.

SOUTHSIDE ROAD

LONGMAN ROAD

MILLBURN ROAD

N

0   200yds

△ Caledonian Canal & Beauly A862

△ A82 Loch Ness & Fort William

△ A9 Wick, Ullapool, Edinburgh A96 Nairn & Aberdeen & SYHA Hostel

▽ Ness Islands

▽ B862 Fort Augustus Via East Loch Ness

TOURS AND CRUISES

Inverness is the departure point for a range of day tours and cruises to nearby attractions, including Loch Ness and the Moray Firth. Among the most popular is Guide Friday's open-topped double-decker tour of **Inverness** (May–Sept every 45min; 30min; £4.50), which you can hop on and off all day; the bus also goes out to **Culloden** (1hr 20min; £6). Tickets can be bought on the buses, which leave from Bridge Street near the tourist office, or at Guide Friday's booth in the train station (May–Sept daily except Sat 9am–5.30pm, Sat 8.30am–5.45pm), which also acts as a booking agent for the tours below. In addition, tickets for all tours are available from the tourist office.

There are various **Loch Ness** tours leaving from the tourist office, such as a half-day-trip including a short cruise on the loch, and visits to the **monster exhibition at Drumnadrochit** and **Urquhart Castle** (£7.50 excluding admission fees), or a full day-trip right round the loch, including a boat ride (£10). Inverness Traction buses run a day-trip to **Ullapool**, **Lochinver**, **Durness** and **Smoo Cave**, which leaves from the tourist office and stops at several youth hostels en route (£12, or £15 if the trip is spread over four days). Finally, the Orkney Bus leaves Inverness bus station every day during the summer for a gruelling full-day whistle-stop tour of the **Orkney** islands (£39; advance bookings may be made at the tourist office or on ☎01955/611353).

Jacobite Cruises runs morning and afternoon **boat trips** to Loch Ness (April–Oct; ☎233999) from the Tomnahurich Canal Bridge on Glenurquhart Road, a mile and a half south of the town centre – to get here take Inverness Traction buses #3, #3A or #3C from Church Street. See p.433 for details of **dolphin**-spotting cruises on the Moray Firth.

Accommodation

Inverness is one of the few places in the Highlands where you're unlikely to have problems finding **somewhere to stay**, although in July and August you'll have to book ahead. You can reserve accommodation through the tourist office, or in the train station concourse at the Thomas Cook booth, but bear in mind that both places levy a booking fee, and charge the hotel or guest-house owner a hefty commission that is then passed onto you in your room tariff. Inverness boasts several good **hotels**, and nearly every street in the older residential areas of town has a sprinkling of **B&Bs**. Good places to look include both banks of the river south of the Ness Bridge, and Kenneth Street and its offshoots on the west side of the river. Several new budget travellers' **hostels** have opened recently, all reasonably central, and there are a couple of large **campsites**, one near the Ness Islands and the other farther out to the west.

Hotels

Brae Ness, Ness Bank (☎712266). A homely Georgian hotel overlooking the river and St Andrews Cathedral with a non-smoking licensed restaurant for residents. ⑥.

Columba, Ness Walk (☎231391). Huge, central hotel opposite the castle and just over the bridge from the town centre, whose tariffs, which include breakfast, drop at weekends. Popular with bus parties and businesspeople. ⑤.

Dunain Park (☎230512). Luxurious country house hotel off the A82 Fort William road, about three miles from the centre of town. Excellent food and beautiful rooms. ⑨.

Glenmoriston, 20 Ness Bank (☎223777). Very classy and comfortable hotel slap on the riverside with well-appointed rooms and a topnotch Italian restaurant. ⑦.

B&Bs

Craigside Lodge, 4 Gordon Terrace (☎231576). Spacious rooms, great views, and close to the centre. ③.

Edenview, 26 Ness Bank (☎234397). Very pleasant B&B in a riverside location as good as the more expensive hotels, 5min walk from the centre; non-smoking. ④.

ACCOMMODATION PRICE CODES

Throughout this book, accommodation **prices** have been graded with the codes below, according to the cost of the least expensive double room in high season. Price codes are not given for campsites, most of which charge under £10 per person. Almost all hostels charge less than £10 a night for a bed – the few exceptions to this rule have the prices quoted in the text. For a full account of the accommodation price codes, see p.30.

① under £20	④ £40–50	⑦ £70–80
② £20–30	⑤ £50–60	⑧ £80–100
③ £30–40	⑥ £60–70	⑨ over £100

Heathfield, 2 Kenneth St (☎230547). A very comfy and friendly B&B at the quiet end of a street packed with B&Bs. All rooms have central heating and some are en suite; non-smoking. ③

Old Drummond House, Oak Avenue (☎226301). Part of a nicely renovated 200-year-old mansion at the quiet end of a suburban avenue, a mile or so from the centre. Welcoming with delicious food, including vegetarian options. ③

Macrae House, 24 Ness Bank (☎243658). Right on the river, friendly, and with large, comfortable rooms. ③

Melrose Villa, 35 Kenneth St (☎233745). Very family-friendly, with excellent breakfasts. Three singles as well as doubles and twins, with most rooms en suite. ③

Hostels

Bazpackers, top of Castle Street (☎717663). Homely place with thirty beds including two double rooms and a twin; some dorms are mixed. Has good views and a garden, which is used for barbecues, as well as the usual cooking facilities; non-smoking.

Eastgate Hostel, Eastgate (☎718756). Well-maintained former hotel above *Le Déja Vu* restaurant. Sleeps 47 in dorms. Free tea and coffee is provided, and a continental breakfast costs £1.50.

Ho Ho Hostel, 23a High St (☎221225). Formerly the grand Highland Club, a town base for lairds; now has all the usual hostel facilities, plus a few echoes of its previous incarnation.

Inverness Student Hotel, 8 Culduthel Rd (☎236556). A laid-back fifty-bed hostel with laundry, self-catering facilities, breakfasts (£1.40), fine views and coffee and tea on tap.

SYHA Youth Hostel, Victoria Drive, off Millburn Road, about three-quarters of a mile from the centre (☎231771). Inverness's largest hostel with 166 beds, housed in a former school hall of residence.

Camping

Bught Caravan and Camping Site, Bught Park (☎236920). Inverness's main campsite, on the west bank of the river near the sports centre. Good facilities, but it can get very crowded at the height of the season.

Bunchrew Caravan and Camping Park, Bunchrew, three miles west of Inverness on the A862 (☎237802). Well-equipped site on the shores of the Beauly Firth, with hot water, showers, laundrette and a shop. It's very popular with families, so you'll have to contend with kids as well as midges.

The Town

The logical place to begin a tour of Inverness is the central **Town House** on High Street. Built in 1878, this Gothic-style pile hosted Prime Minister Lloyd George's emergency meeting to discuss the Irish crisis in September 1921, and now accommodates council offices. There's nothing of note inside, but the old **Mercat Cross** next to the main entrance is worth a look. The cross stands opposite a small square formerly used by merchants and traders and above the ancient *clach-na-cudainn,* or **"stone of tubs"** – socalled because washerwomen used to rest their buckets on it on their way back from the river. A local superstition holds that as long as the stone remains in place Inverness will continue to prosper.

Looming above the Town House and dominating the horizon is **Inverness Castle** (mid-May to Sept Mon–Sat 9am–5pm), a predominantly nineteenth-century red-sandstone edifice perched picturesquely above the river. The original castle formed the core of the ancient town, which had rapidly developed as a port trading with Europe after its conversion to Christianity by St Columba in the sixth century. Two famous Scots monarchs were associated with the building: **Robert the Bruce** wrested it back from the English during the Wars of Independence, destroying it in the process, and **Mary, Queen of Scots** had the governor of the second castle hanged from its ramparts after he had refused her entry in 1562. This structure was also destined for destruction, held by the Jacobites in both the 1715 and the 1745 rebellions, and blown up by them to prevent it falling into government hands. Today's edifice houses the Sheriff Court and, in summer, the **Castle Garrison Encounter** (£2.50) an entertaining and noisy interactive exhibition, in which the visitor plays the role of a new recruit in the eighteenth-century Hanoverian army. Around 7.30pm during the summer, a lone piper clad in full Highland garb performs for tourists on the castle esplanade. The statue of a woman staring south from the terrace is a memorial to **Flora MacDonald**, the clanswoman who helped Bonnie Prince Charlie escape to Skye in the wake of Culloden.

THE TRUTH ABOUT TARTAN

Tartan is big business and an essential part of the tourist industry. Every year, hundreds of visitors return home clutching tartan monsters, foreign-made souvenirs tied with foreign-made tartan ribbon, or lengths of cloth inspiringly named Loch This, Ben That or Glen Something-Else, fondly believing that they are bringing authentic history with them. The reality is that tartan is an ancient Highland art form that romantic fiction and commercial interest have enclosed within an almost insurmountable wall of myth.

Real tartan, the kind that long ago was called "Helande", was a fine, hard and almost showerproof cloth spun in Highland villages from the wool of the native sheep, dyed with preparations of local plants and with patterns woven by artist-weavers. It was worn as a huge single piece of cloth, which was belted around the waist and draped over the upper body, rather like a knee-length toga. The colours of old tartans were clear but soft, and the broken pattern gave superb camouflage; unlike modern versions, whose colours are either so strong that the pattern is swamped or so dull that it has no impact.

Tartan did not become popular in the Lowlands until the beginning of the eighteenth century, when it was adopted as the anti-Union badge of Jacobitism, and it was not until after 1745 that the Lowlands took it over completely. The 1747 ban on wearing tartan put an end to the making of tartan in Highland glens; instead, whole villages on the Lowland fringes devoted themselves to supplying the needs of the army and emigrant Highlanders in the colonies and, after the ban was lifted in 1782, those of the home market. The wars abated and the colonies became more self-sufficient, and what had become a major industry faced hard times. At first the remedy was sought in a proliferation of new patterns for, despite the existence of a handful with clan names, tartan was, in the main, a small-scale fashion fabric. Then Sir Walter Scott set to work, glamorizing the clans; George IV visited Edinburgh in 1822 and wore a kilt; and, finally, Queen Victoria set the royal seal of approval on both the Highlands and tartan.

At about this time, the idea that every clan had its own distinguishing tartan became highly fashionable. To have the right to wear tartan, one had to belong, albeit remotely, to a clan, and so the way was paved for the "what's-my-tartan?" lists that appear in the tartan picture books and the souvenir shops. Great feats of genealogical gymnastics were performed in the concoction of these lists, but they could not include every name, so "district", "national" and "political" tartans were developed.

Below the castle, the **Inverness Museum and Art Gallery** (Mon–Sat 9am–5pm; free) on Castle Wynd gives a good general overview of the development of the Highlands. Informative sections on geology, geography and history cover the ground floor, while upstairs you'll find a muddled selection of silver, taxidermy, weapons and bagpipes, alongside a mediocre art gallery.

Leading north from the Town House, medieval **Church Street** is home to the town's oldest-surviving buildings. On the corner with Bridge Street stands the **Steeple** (1791), whose spire had to be straightened after an earth tremor in 1816. Farther down Church Street is **Abertarff House,** reputedly the oldest complete building in Inverness and distinguished by its stepped gables and circular stair tower. It was erected in 1593 and is now owned by the NTS. The **Old High Church** (Fri noon–2pm & during services; tour at 12.30pm), founded by St Columba in 1171 and rebuilt on several occasions since, stands just along the street, hemmed in by a walled graveyard. Any Jacobites who survived the massacre of Culloden were brought here and incarcerated prior to their execution in the cemetery. If you take the guided tour, you'll be shown bullet holes left on gravestones by the firing squads.

Balnain House

One of Scotland's most novel museums stands over the footbridge that crosses the Ness just below the Old High Church. An immaculately restored, white-painted Georgian mansion, **Balnain House** (Tues–Sat 10am–5pm; £1.50) has a modest performance space and an interactive exhibition that will appeal as much to the casual visitor as folk-music aficionados. The exhibition traces the development of Highland **music** from its prehistoric roots (ringing rocks, cast-bronze battle horns and ancient Gaelic songs) to modern electric folk-rock. CD listening posts and a short video allow you to sample snatches of numerous other musical styles from the region, including clan-gathering and spell-casting songs, complex Shetland fiddle reels and the haunting singing of the Hebrides. There's also a congenial café downstairs where ceilidhs, music sessions and recitals take place throughout the summer, and a shop selling traditional Highland instruments, CDs and cassettes.

Elsewhere on the west bank

A five-minute walk upstream (south) from Balnain House brings you to the **Kiltmaker Centre** on the corner of Huntly Street (mid-May to Sept Mon–Sat 9am–9.30pm, Sun 10am–5pm; Oct to mid-May Mon–Sat 9am–5pm; £2). Entered through the factory shop, a small visitor centre sets out everything you ever wanted to know about tartan. The finished products are, of course, on sale in the showroom downstairs, along with all manner of Highland knitwear, woven woollies and Harris tweed.

Rising from the west bank directly opposite the castle, **St Andrews Episcopal Cathedral** was intended by its architects to be one of the grandest buildings in Scotland. However, funds ran out before the giant twin spires of the original design could be completed, hence Inverness isn't officially a city, but a town. The interior is pretty ordinary, too, though it does claim an unusual octagonal chapterhouse.

From the cathedral, you can wander a mile or so upriver to the peaceful **Ness Islands**, an attractive, informal public park reached and linked by footbridges. Laid out with mature trees and shrubs, the islands are the favourite haunt of local anglers. Further upstream still, the river runs close to the **Caledonian Canal**, designed by Thomas Telford in the early nineteenth century as a link between the east and west coasts, joining lochs Ness, Oich, Lochy and Linnhe. Today its main use is recreational, and there are cruises through part of it to Loch Ness, while its towpath provides relaxing walks with good views.

Three miles to the west of the town, on the top of **Craig Phadrig** hill, there's a vitrified **Iron Age fort**, reputed to be where the Pictish King Brude received St Columba in the sixth century. The walls of the fort were built of stone laced with timber and, when the timber was set alight, some of the stone fused to glass – hence the term "vitrified". Waymarked forest trails start from the car parks at the bottom of the hill and lead up to the fort, though only the outline of its perimeter defences are now visible. Buses #3 and #12 from the town centre (Mon–Sat every 15min) drop you to the bottom of the hill.

Eating and drinking

Inverness has lots of places **to eat**, including a few excellent-quality gourmet options, while for the budget-conscious there's no shortage of **pubs**, **cafés** and **restaurants** around the town centre. **Takeaways** cluster on Young Street, just across the river, and at the ends of Eastgate and Academy Street. Good places for **picnic food** include *Crumbs*, on Inglis Street, *Délifrance*, on Church Street, *The Gourmet's Lair*, on Union Street, and *Lettuce Eat*, on Drummond Street.

Restaurants

Bishop's Table Restaurant, Eden Court Theatre. Upmarket self-service restaurant with a nice bar and views. Imaginative food, with good salads, quiches, soups and a daily special. Inexpensive.

Café No. 1, 75 Castle St (☎226200). By far the most ambitious cooking in the town centre, with an impressive contemporary approach to recipes using good local ingredients. Moderate–expensive.

Castle Restaurant, 41 Castle St. Classic, long-established café that does a roaring trade in down-to-earth Scottish food – meat pies, chicken and fish, with piles of chips. Open at 8am for breakfast; closed Sun. Inexpensive.

Le Déja Vu, 38 Eastgate (☎231075). Unpretentious, relaxed place specializing in French country cooking using game, chicken, fish and shellfish. Great food, friendly service and the set lunch menu is astounding value at around £6. Moderate.

Dunain Park Hotel Restaurant, Dunain Park (☎224532). Award-winning Scots-French restaurant in a country-house hotel set in lovely gardens just southwest of town; a good choice for a leisurely dinner. Expensive.

Glen Mhor Hotel, 9 Ness Bank (☎234308). The bistro at the back of the hotel specializes in well-presented Scottish cuisine (mainly local salmon, beef and game) at moderate prices. The restaurant at the front is also good. Expensive.

Hayden's at The Islands, 11 Island Bank Rd (☎231833). Traditional Scottish dishes are served as well as specialities from around the world, including several pasta options. In a good position for after-dinner strolls beside the Ness. Inexpensive–moderate.

Littlejohn's, Church Street (☎713005). One of a chain, which serves a wide range of food, with many Mexican touches. Friendly and reasonable value. Moderate.

Il Palio Ristorante, 26 Queensgate (☎711950). Huge portions of Italian food including good pizza and pasta. Moderate.

Rajah, the Church Street end of Post Office Avenue (☎237190). An excellent Indian restaurant, tucked away in a backstreet basement. Moderate.

River Café and Restaurant, 10 Bank St, near the Grieg Street footbridge (☎714884). Healthy wholefood lunches and evening meals, with a great selection of freshly baked cakes and good coffee. Inexpensive–moderate.

Nightlife and entertainment

The liveliest **nightlife** in Inverness revolves around the pubs and the town's two main dance venues. The far end of Academy Street has a cluster of good **pubs**; the public bar of the *Phoenix* is the most original town-centre place, while the ersatz-Irish *Lafferty's* next door often has live music, as does the *Blackfriars* across the street. Over on Bridge Street, the *Gellions* is a legendary watering hole with several other congenial places in between.

The town's most trendy **music and dance** venue is the *Railway Club* on Strother's Lane behind the train station, which showcases local indie bands and DJs on Fridays and Saturdays. On the north side of the bus station, the larger *Blue* hosts local and nationally known DJs, plus occasional bands. The basement café at Balnain House museum, on the east bank of the Ness, opposite Grieg Street footbridge, has informal **folk sessions** that sometimes turn into ceilidhs. In addition, the museum stages regular recitals and workshops by Highland musicians and touring artists; details of all these are posted in the café, and the lobby upstairs. Balnain House also occasionally hosts "The Tickled Rib", billed as the north's best comedy club — it is, in fact, the north's only comedy club. Finally, if you crave a strong infusion of tartan and **bagpipes**, the nightly *Scottish Showtime* at the Cummings Hotel on Church Street is the place to be; the show has been running for years and is probably the most polished of its kind you'll find.

Listings

Bike rental Bikes of Inverness, 39/41 Grant Street (☎225965); go north down Academy Street, pass the roundabout and cross the grey metal Waterloo Bridge.

Bookshops Leakey's, Greyfriars' Hall, Church Street (☎239947), is good for secondhand books and is warmed in winter by a giant wood stove; James Thin, 29 Union St (☎233500), has an excellent range of Scottish books and maps; Waterstone's, 50–52 High St (☎717474).

Car rental Budget is on Railway Terrace, behind the train station (☎235337); Europcar has an office at the Highlander Service Station, Millburn Road, and a desk at the airport (☎235337); Hertz in the train station and at the airport (☎711479); and Thrifty is at 33 Harbour Rd (☎224466).

Cinemas The Eden Court Theatre and the attached Riverside Screen, on the banks of the Ness, host touring theatre productions, concerts and films; La Scala on Strother's Lane, just off Academy Street, has two screens; Warner Village, on the A96 Nairn road about two miles from the town centre, has seven screens.

Exchange American Express agents Alba Travel, 43 Church St (Mon–Sat 9am–5pm; ☎239188); the tourist office's bureau de change (Mon–Sat 9am–noon & 2–8.30pm, Sun 9am–noon & 2–6pm) changes cash and currency for £2.50 or 2.5 per cent; and Thomas Cook, 9–13 Inglis St (Mon–Fri 9am–5pm; ☎711921).

Hospital Accident and emergency care is provided by Raigmore Hospital (☎704000) on the southeastern outskirts of town close to the A9.

Left luggage Train station lockers cost from £2 to £4 for 24hr; the left luggage room in the bus station costs £1 per item (Mon–Sat 8.30am–6pm, Sun 10am–6pm).

Library Inverness library (☎236463), housed in the Neoclassical building on the northeast side of the bus station, has an excellent genealogical research unit (June–Sept 11am–1pm & 2–5pm; Oct–May Mon–Fri 2–5pm). Consultations with the resident genealogist cost £12 per hour, but are free if shorter than 10min. An appointment is advisable.

Post office 14–16 Queensgate (Mon–Thurs 9am–5.30pm, Fri 9.30am–5.30pm, Sat 9am–12.30pm; ☎234111).

Pharmacy Boots, Eastgate Shopping Centre (daily 9am–5.30pm, Thurs 9am–7pm; ☎225167).

Public toilets Usually immaculate ones in Mealmarket Close, north side of High Street.

Sports centre Inverness sports centre and Aquadome leisure pool (Mon–Fri 9am–10.30pm, Sat & Sun 9am–5.15pm; ☎713585), a mile or so south of the town centre off the A82, has a large pool, gym and other indoor sports facilities. Nearby is an ice rink (daily 2–4.30pm & 7–9.30pm).

The Moray Firth

East of Inverness lies the fertile, sheltered coastal strip of the **Moray Firth**, its many historic sites and castles accessible as day-trips from Inverness, or en route to Aberdeen. Both the countryside and the number of attractions around here make a good contrast to the purely scenic splendours you'll encounter once you head further north into the Highlands. The overloaded A96 traverses this stretch and the region is well served by public transport, details of which feature in the accounts below.

Culloden

The windswept moorland of **CULLODEN** (site open all year; visitor centre daily: Feb, March, Nov & Dec 10am–4pm; April–Oct 9am–6pm; NTS; £2.80), five miles east of Inverness, witnessed the last ever battle on British soil when, on April 16, 1746, the Jacobite cause was finally subdued – a turning point in the history of the Scottish nation.

THE DOLPHINS OF MORAY FIRTH

The **Moray Firth**, a great wedge-shaped bay forming the eastern coastline of the Highlands, is one of only three areas of UK waters that supports a resident population of **dolphins**. Just over a hundred of these beautiful, intelligent marine mammals live in the estuary, the most northerly breeding ground for this particular species – the bottle-nosed dolphin (*Tursiops truncatus*) – in Europe, and you stand a good chance of spotting a few, either from the shore or a boat.

Tursiops truncatus is the largest dolphin in the world, typically growing to a length of around 13ft and weighing between 396 and 660 pounds. The adults sport a tall, sickle-shaped dorsal fin and a distinctive beak-like "nose", and usually live for around 25 years, although a number of 50-year-old animals have been recorded. During the summer, herds of thirty to forty dolphins have been known to congregate in the Moray Firth; no one is exactly sure why, although experts believe the annual gatherings, which take place between late June and August, may be connected to the breeding cycle. Another peculiar trait of the Moray Firth school is its habit of killing porpoises. Several porpoise corpses with serrated tooth marks have been washed ashore in the area, the dolphins tossing dead or dying porpoises around in the waves as if for fun.

Both adults and calves frequently leap out of the water, "bow riding" in front of boats and performing elegant synchronized swimming routines together. This, of course, makes them spectacular animals to watch, and dolphin-spotting has become something of a craze in the Moray Firth area. One of the best places in Scotland, if not in Europe, to look for them is **Chanonry Point**, on the Black Isle (see p.482) – a spit of sand protruding into a narrow, deep channel, where converging currents bring fish close to the surface, and thus the dolphins close to shore; the hour or so before high tide is the most likely time to see them. **Kessock Bridge**, one mile north of Inverness, is another prime dolphin-spotting location. A team of zoologists from Aberdeen University studying the Moray Firth dolphins has set up a small listening post and visitor centre here (daily 10am–5pm; ☎01463/731866; £1 for the whole season), where hydrophones allow you to eavesdrop on the clicks and whistles of underwater conversations.

In addition, several companies run dolphin-spotting boat trips around the Moray Firth. However, researchers claim that the increased traffic is causing the dolphins unnecessary stress, particularly during the all-important breeding period, when passing vessels are thought to force calves underwater for uncomfortably long periods. They have therefore devised a code of conduct for boat operators, based on the experiences of other countries where dolphin-watching has become disruptive. So if you decide to go on a spotting cruise, make sure the operator is a member of the Dolphin Space Programme's Accreditation Scheme. Operators currently accredited include Peter MacDonald, 4 Craigview, Findochty (☎01542/833867); Karl Nielsen, 21 Great Eastern Road, Portessie, Buckie (☎01542/832289); Macaulay Charters, Harbour Offices, Longman Drive, Inverness (☎01463/717337); Moray Firth Cruises, Shore Street, Inverness (☎01463/717900); and Dolphin Écosse, Bank House, High Street, Cromarty (☎01381/600323).

The second Jacobite rebellion had begun on August 19, 1745, with the raising of the Stuarts' standard at **Glenfinnan** on the west coast (see p.455). Shortly after, Edinburgh fell into Jacobite hands, and Bonnie Prince Charlie began his march on London. The English, however, had appointed the ambitious young Duke of Cumberland to command their forces, and this, together with bad weather and lack of funds, eventually forced the Jacobites to retreat north. They ended up at Culloden, where, ill-fed and exhausted after a pointless night march, they were hopelessly outnumbered by the English. The open, flat ground of Culloden Moor was also totally unsuitable for the Highlanders' style of courageous but undisciplined fighting, which needed steep hills and lots of cover to provide the element of surprise, and they were routed. After the battle, in which 1500 Highlanders were slaughtered (many of them as they lay wounded on the battlefield), Bonnie Prince Charlie fled west to the hills and islands, where loyal Highlanders sheltered and protected him. He eventually escaped to France, leaving his erstwhile supporters to their fate – and, in effect, the end of the clan system. The clans were disarmed, the wearing of tartan and playing of bagpipes forbidden, and the chiefs became landlords greedy for higher and higher rents. Culloden also unleashed an orgy of violent reprisals on Scotland, as unruly English troops raped and pillaged their way across the region; within a century, the Highland way of life had changed out of all recognition.

Today you can walk freely around the battle site; flags show the position of the two armies, and **clan graves** are marked by simple headstones. The **Field of the English**, for many years unmarked, is a mass grave for the fifty or so English soldiers who died. Half a mile east of the battlefield, just beyond the crossroads on the main road, is the **Cumberland Stone**, thought for many years to have been the point from where the Duke watched the battle. It is more likely, however, that he was much further forward and simply used the stone for shelter. Thirty Jacobites were burnt alive outside the old **Leanach cottage** next to the visitor centre; inside, it has been restored to its eighteenth-century appearance. The **visitor centre** itself provides background information through detailed displays and a slide show. In April, on the Saturday closest to the date of the battle, there's a small commemorative service. The visitor centre has a reference library, and will check for you if you think you have an ancestor who died here. The site is served by Guide Friday **buses** from Bridge Street in Inverness (June–Sept; 10 daily from 10.30am; last bus back to town leaves Culloden at 5.45pm; 25min) and Highland Country bus #12 from Inverness post office (Mon–Sat 6 daily; last return service at 6.30pm).

The Clava Cairns

If you're visiting Culloden with your own transport, make a short detour to the **CLAVA CAIRNS**, an impressive collection of prehistoric burial chambers clustered around the south bank of the River Nairn, a mile southeast of the battlefield. Erected sometime before 2000 BC, the cairns, which are encircled by standing stones in a spinney of mature beech trees, are of two different kinds: one large and one very small **ring-cairn**, and two **passage graves**, which have a narrow passageway from edge to centre. Though cremated remains have been found in both types of structure, and unburnt remains in the passage graves, little is known about the nomadic herdsmen who are thought to have built them.

Kilravock Castle

Surrounded by lawns and pine trees, **Kilravock** (pronounced "Kilrawk") **Castle** (April–Sept Wed 2–5.30pm, or by prior arrangement; ☎01667/493258), five miles northeast of Culloden, is more like a stately home than a fortress. Dating from the fifteenth century, it is the seat of the Rose family, whose founding father, a Norman, settled here in 1190. The best-known Rose of Kilravock, however, is the one who entertained **Bonnie Prince Charlie** here on the eve of the battle of Culloden in 1745. Although not a Jacobite himself, the laird felt duty-bound by the traditional code of Highland hospitality to accommodate the rebel prince, even though he feared the consequences. According to one contemporary chronicler, the Duke of Cumberland rode out here himself on his 25th birthday to grill Rose over the affair, famously exclaiming, "I hear, sir, you've been entertaining my cousin!". He decided not to punish the Highlander, though, and for some reason left behind his knee-length **riding boots**, which are displayed in the castle, along with the bowl from which Bonnie Prince Charlie is alleged to have been served a glass of punch by his host.

Today, the Rose family maintain Kilravock as a wonderfully old-fashioned **guest house** (same number as above; ③), whose spacious, well-appointed rooms are superb value if you don't mind the ban on alcohol and cigarettes, or grace being said before meals (the establishment is run according to strict Christian principles). In addition, garden enthusiasts should not miss the opportunity to visit the castle grounds (Mon–Sat 10am–4pm; free), which harbour a tangle of woodland trails.

Cawdor Castle

The pretty, if slightly self-satisfied village of **CAWDOR**, eight miles east of Culloden, is the site of the **Cawdor Castle** (May to mid-Oct daily 10am–5.30pm; £4.50), apocryphally known as the setting for Shakespeare's *Macbeth* (the fulfilment of the witches' prediction that Macbeth was to become Thane of Cawdor sets off his tragic desire to be king). Though visitors descend here in their droves each summer because of the site's literary associations, the castle, which dates from the early fourteenth century, could not possibly have witnessed the grizzly historical events on which the Bard's drama was based. However, the immaculately restored monument – a fairy-tale affair of towers, turrets, hidden passageways, dungeons, gargoyles and crenellations whimsically shooting off from the original keep – is still well worth a visit.

The Cawdors have lived here for six centuries, and the castle still feels like a family home, albeit one with tapestries, pictures and opulent furniture. As you wander around, look out for the Thorn Tree Room, a vaulted chamber complete with the remains of an ancient tree – carbon-dated to 1372 and an ancient pagan fertility symbol believed to ward off fairies and evil spirits. According to Cawdor family legend, the fourteenth-century Thane of Cawdor dreamed he should build on the spot where his donkey lay down to sleep after a day's wandering – the animal chose this tree and building began right away.

The **grounds** of the castle are possibly the best part of the visit, with an attractive walled garden, a topiarian maze, a small golf course, a putting green and nature trails. Highland **bus** #12 (Mon–Sat 6 daily; 35min) runs to Cawdor from Inverness post office, with the last bus back leaving the castle just after 6pm.

Fort George

Eight miles of undulating coastal farmland separate Cawdor Castle from **Fort George** (April–Sept Mon–Sat 10am–6pm, Sun 2–6pm; Oct–March Mon–Fri 10am–4pm; £2.80), an old Hanoverian bastion considered by military architectural historians to be one of the finest fortifications in Europe. Crowning a sandy spit that juts into the middle of the Moray Firth, it was built (1747–69) as a base for George II's army, in case the Highlanders should attempt to rekindle the Jacobite flame. By the time of its completion, however, the uprising had been firmly quashed and the fort has been used ever since as a barracks; note the armed sentries at the main entrance and the periodic crack of live gunfire from the nearby firing ranges.

Apart from the sweeping panoramic **views** across the Firth from its ramparts, the main incentive to visit Fort George is the **Regimental Museum** of the Queen's Own Highlanders. Displayed in polished glass cases is a predictable array of regimental silver, coins, moth-eaten uniforms and medals, along with some macabre war trophies, ranging from blood-stained nineteenth-century Sudanese battle robes to Iraqi gas masks gleaned in the Gulf War. The heroic deeds performed by various recipients of Victoria Crosses make compelling reading. The **chapel** is also worth a look: squat and solid outside, and all light and grace within.

Walking on the northern, grass-covered casemates, which look out into the estuary, you may be lucky enough to see the school of bottle-nosed **dolphins** (see p.433) swimming in with the tide. This is also a good spot for birdwatching: a colony of kittiwakes occupies the fort's slate rooftops, while the white-sand beach and mud flats below teem with waders and seabirds.

The easiest way to get to Fort George by public transport is by Highland **bus** #11B from Queensgate in Inverness (Mon–Sat 7 daily; 25min), or Nairn (2 daily; 20min), eight miles east.

Nairn

One of the driest and sunniest places in the whole of Scotland, **NAIRN**, sixteen miles east of Inverness, began its days as a peaceful community of fishermen and farmers. The former spoke Gaelic, the latter English, allowing James VI to boast that a town in his kingdom was so large that people at one end of the main street could not understand those at the other end. Nairn became popular in Victorian times, when the train line offered a convenient link to its revitalizing sea air and mild climate, and today it still relies on tourism, with all the ingredients for a traditional seaside holiday – a sandy beach, ice-cream shops, and fish-and-chip stalls. Its windy, coastal **golf course**, the Links (venue for the 1999 Walker Cup), is one of the most popular in Scotland, and Thomas Telford's **harbour** is filled with leisure rather than fishing boats. Nearby, amid the huddled streets of old Fishertown – the town centre is known as new Fishertown – is the tiny **Fishertown Museum** (June–Aug Mon–Sat 10am–5pm; free), signposted from the town centre and the harbour. The more interesting exhibits focus on the parsimonious and puritanical life of the fishing families.

With a good map to help navigate the maze of minor roads, you can explore some pleasant countryside south of Nairn, particularly in the valley of the **River Findhorn**, with **Dulsie Bridge**, on the old military road linking Perth and Fort George, being a favourite local picnic spot. A few miles farther south, the waters of **Lochindorb** surround a ruined thirteenth-century castle.

Nairn's helpful **tourist office** is at 62 King St (Easter–May, Sept & Oct Mon–Sat 10am–5pm; June–Aug daily 9am–6pm; ☎01667/452753). For **accommodation**, try *Clifton House*, Viewfield Street (☎01667/453119; ⑦), which is stacked with antiques and paintings and hosts music and arts events, or *Greenlawns*, 13 Seafield St (☎01667/452738; ③), a spacious and friendly B&B, with most rooms en suite; most luxurious of all is the *Golf View Hotel* (☎01667/452301; ⑨), overlooking the golf course and sea. **Bike rental** is available from Nairn Watersports (☎01667/455416) down by the harbour.

West of Inverness: the Beauly Firth

West of Inverness, the Moray Firth becomes the **Beauly Firth**, a sheltered sea loch bounded by the Black Isle in the north and the wooded hills of the Aird to the south. Most northbound traffic uses Kessock Bridge to cross the Moray Firth from Inverness, so this whole area is quieter, and the A862, which skirts the shoreline and the mud flats, offers a more scenic alternative to the faster A9.

Beauly

The sleepy stone-built village of **BEAULY** lies ten miles west of Inverness, at the point where the Beauly River – one of Scotland's most renowned salmon-fishing streams — flows into the Firth. It's ranged around a single main street that widens into a spacious marketplace, at the north end of which stand the skeletal red sandstone remains of **Beauly Priory** (daily 10am–5pm; free). Founded in 1230 by the Bisset family for the Valliscaulian order, and later becoming Cistercian, it was destroyed during the Reformation and is now in ruins.

The locals will tell you that the name Beauly was bestowed on the village by Mary, Queen of Scots, who, when staying at the priory in the summer of 1564, allegedly cried, "Ah, quelle beau lieu!" (What a beautiful place!). In fact, it derives from the Lovat family, who came to the region from France with the Normans in the eleventh century. Among the more notorious members of this dynasty was Lord Simon Lovat, whose legendary mis-adventures included a kidnap attempt on a 9-year-old girl, followed by forced marriage to her mother. He was outlawed for this, but went on to play an active role in the Jacobite uprisings, expediently swapping sides whenever the one he was spying for looked likely to lose. Such chicanery earned him the nickname "The Old Fox of '45", but failed to save him from the chop: Lovat was eventually beheaded in London (ironi-cally enough for backing the wrong side at Culloden). The Victorian **monument** in the square, opposite the Priory, commemorates the more illustrious career of one of Simon Lovat's descendants, Simon Joseph, the sixteenth Lord Lovat, who founded a fighting unit during the South African Boer War.

As a change from distilleries, you can visit a **winery** at **Moniack Castle** (Mon–Sat 10am–5pm), four miles east of Beauly, just off the main Inverness road, where wine is produced from elderflower and birch (among other things), and sloe gin is also made.

Practicalities

Beauly has a surprising number of **places to stay**. The most comfortable is the modern *Priory Hotel* (☎01463/782309; ⑥) at the top of town, which also has a good restaurant. The *Lovat Arms Hotel* (☎01463/782313; ⑦), at the opposite end of the main street, is a more traditional option and hosts occasional ceilidhs. If you're looking for cheaper accommoda-tion, try the *Heathmount Guest House* (☎01463/782411; ③), one of several pleasant **B&Bs** in a row of large Victorian houses just south of the *Lovat* on the main road.

Finding somewhere to **eat** in Beauly isn't a problem, either. Both of the town's hotels sport pricey à la carte restaurants, while the *Archdale Hotel's* cosy café, at the bottom of the square, serves a range of inexpensive snacks and main meals, including several vegetarian specialities. Otherwise, head for the *Beauly Tandoori*, which dishes up mod-erately priced Indian food, or the *Friary* chippy; both are on the main square.

Muir of Ord

MUIR OF ORD, a sprawling village four miles north of Beauly, is visited in huge num-bers for the **Glen Ord Distillery** (July & Aug Mon–Sat 9am–4pm, Sun noon–5pm; Sept–June Mon–Fri 9.30am–5pm; free), on its northern outskirts. Its well-laid-out visi-tor centre explains the mysteries of whisky production with a tour that winds up in the cellars, where you get to sample a selection of the famously peaty Glen Ord malts, most of which find their way into well-known blends on sale in the distillery shop.

You can either visit Ord on a guided tour from Inverness (details from the tourist office), or take Inverness Traction **bus** #19 from Inverness bus station (Mon–Sat approximately hourly, Sun 4 daily; 25–40min); alternatively, the **train** from Inverness stops at Muir of Ord station (Mon–Sat 6–7 daily; June–Sept also Sun, 4 daily; 15min).

THE GREAT GLEN

The **Great Glen**, cutting diagonally across the Highlands from Fort William to Inverness, follows a major geological fault-line. This huge rift valley was formed when the northwestern and southeastern sides slid more than sixty miles towards each other along the fault, and were later smoothed by glaciers that only retreated around 8000 BC. The glen is impressive more for its sheer scale than its great beauty, but is an obvious and rewarding route between the east and west coast.

Of the Great Glen's four elongated lochs, the most famous is **Loch Ness**, home to the mythical beast and linked to the other three, **lochs Oich**, **Lochy** and **Linnhe** (a sea loch) by the **Caledonian Canal**. Surveyed by Thomas Watt in 1773, this famous waterway was completed in the early 1800s by Thomas Telford to enable ships to pass between the North Sea and the Atlantic without having to navigate Scotland's treacherous northern coast. However, only 22 miles of it are bona fide canal – the other 38 exploit the Glen's natural lochs and rivers flowing west to reach the Atlantic.

The traditional and most rewarding way to travel through the glen is by **boat**. A flotilla of kayaks, small yachts and pleasure vessels take advantage of the canal and its old wooden locks during the summer, among them Jacobite Cruises (see p.427 for details). The Forestry Commission has also established an excellent **cycle path** through the Glen, divided into twelve manageable stages that make a tranquil alternative to the hazardous A82. A leaflet outlining the route, through winding timber trails, towpaths and stretches of minor roads, is available at most tourist offices, or direct from Forestry Commission, Strathoich, Fort Augustus PH32 4BT (☎01320/366322). In addition, the Great Glen is reasonably well served by **buses**, with several daily services between Inverness and Fort William, and a couple of extra buses covering the section between Fort William and Invergarry during school terms.

Loch Ness

Loch Ness is long and undeniably scenic, with rugged heather-clad mountains rising steeply from a wooded shoreline and some attractive valleys opening up on either side, though the tree-lined A82 along its western side gives fewer views than you'd expect. Its fame, however, is based overwhelmingly on its legendary inhabitant, Nessie, the Loch Ness monster, whose notoriety ensures a steady flow of hopeful visitors to the settlements dotted along the loch, in particular **Drumnadrochit**. Nearby, the impressive ruins of **Castle Urquhart** — a favourite monster-spotting location — perch atop a rock on the loch-side and attract a deluge of bus parties during the summer. Almost as busy in high season is **Fort Augustus**, at the more scenic southwest tip of Loch Ness, where you can visit a working Benedictine monastery and watch queues of boats tackling one of the Caledonian Canal's longest flight of **locks**.

Although most visitors travel along the west shore of Loch Ness, on the A82, the opposite, eastern side, skirted by the sinuous single-track B862/852 (originally a military road built to link Fort Augustus and Fort George) is quieter and affords far more spectacular views. However, buses from Inverness only run as far south as **Foyers**, so – unless you take a bus tour from Inverness (see p.427) – you'll need your own transport to complete the whole loop around the Loch, taking in the most impressive stretch between Fort Augustus and the high, hidden Loch Mhor, where the imposing Monadhliath range looms to the south.

"NESSIE"

The world-famous Loch Ness monster, affectionately known as **"Nessie"** (and by serious aficionados as *Nessiteras rhombopteryx*), has been around a long time. The first mention of her crops up in St Adamnan's seventh-century biography of **St Columba**. While on his way to evangelize the pagan inhabitants of Inverness, the saint allegedly calmed the monster after she attacked one of his monks. Present-day interest, however, is probably greater outside Scotland than in, dating from the 1930s when the A82 was built along the loch's western shore. Recent encounters range from glimpses of ripples by anglers, to the famous occasion in 1961 when thirty hotel guests saw a pair of humps break the water's surface and cruise for about half a mile before submerging.

The most convincing sightings, however, have been those backed up by hard photographic evidence. Several seemingly conclusive images are showcased in the two "Monster Exhibitions" at Drumnadrochit, but the most impressive of these – including the renowned black-and-white movie footage of Nessie's humps moving across the water, and the photo of her neck and head – have been exposed as fakes. Hi-tech sonar surveys carried out over the past two decades have failed to come up with conclusive evidence, but it's hard to dismiss Nessie as pure myth. Too many locals have mysterious tales to tell, which they invariably keep to themselves for fear of ridicule by incredulous outsiders. Loch Ness also has an undeniably enigmatic air; even the most hardened cynics rarely resist the temptation to scan the waters for signs of life, just in case . . .

Drumnadrochit

Situated above a verdant, sheltered bay fifteen miles from Inverness, **DRUMNADROCHIT**, practically the first chance to draw breath as you head down the A82, is the epicentre of Nessie hype, sporting a rash of tacky souvenir shops and two rival monster exhibitions whose head-to-head scramble for punters occasionally erupts into acrimonious exchanges – detailed with relish by the local press. Of the pair, the **Original Loch Ness Monster Exhibition** (daily: April–June & Sept–Nov 10am–6pm; July & Aug 10am–9pm; £3.50) is the least worthwhile – basically a gift shop with a shoddy audiovisual show tacked on the side. If you're genuinely interested in "Nessie" lore, the **Official Loch Ness Monster Exhibition** (daily: April–June 9.30am–5.30pm July & Aug 9am–8.30pm; Sept & Oct 9.30am–6pm; £4.50), though more expensive (and no more "official" than the other), is a much better bet, offering an in-depth rundown of eyewitness accounts through the ages and mock-ups of the various research projects carried out in the loch. **Cruises** on the loch can also be booked here, and leave from Temple Pier (May–Sept hourly between 10am & 6pm; 1hr; £8).

Castle Urquhart

Most photographs allegedly showing the monster have been taken a couple of miles further south, around the fourteenth-century ruined loch-side **Castle Urquhart** (daily: April–Sept 9.30am–8.30pm; Oct–March 9.30am–4.30pm; last admission 45min before closing; £3.20). Built as a strategic base to guard the Great Glen, the castle played an important role in the Wars of Independence. It was taken by Edward I of England and later held by Robert the Bruce against Edward III, only to be blown up in 1692 to prevent it from falling to the Jacobites. It's pretty dilapidated today, but looks particularly splendid floodlit at night when all the crowds have gone. There are locally controversial plans to extend the hard-pressed car park and provide other facilities.

Practicalities

There's a good range of accommodation around Drumnadrochit, and in the adjoining village of Lewiston. Two very welcoming **B&Bs** are *Gilliflowers* (☎01456/450641; ③), a renovated farmhouse tucked away down a country lane in Lewiston, or the modern *Drumbuie* (☎01456/450634; ③), on the northern approach to Drumnadrochit, which has great views and a resident herd of Highland cattle. **Hotels** include the pleasant and secluded *Benleva Hotel* (☎01456/450288; ③) between Lewiston and the loch. Two miles from Drumnadrochit along the Cannich road is a particularly relaxed country-house hotel, *Polmaily House* (☎01456/450343; ⑨); it's very family-friendly and there's acres of space, a swimming pool, sauna, riding, and yacht on Loch Ness. For **hostel** beds, head to the immaculate and friendly *Loch Ness Backpackers Lodge* (☎01456/450807), at Coiltie Farmhouse in Lewiston; follow the sign to the left when coming from Drumnadrochit. As well as dorm beds, it has one double room (②), and excellent facilities, including boat trips and recommended walks.

All the hotels in the area serve good bar **food**; in Drumnadrochit the *Glen Restaurant* has a short and simple menu with basic grills, while the slightly more upmarket *Fiddlers' Bistro*, next door to the *Glen* on the village green, offers local steaks, salmon and appetizing home-baked pizza; it also rents out **mountain bikes** (☎01456/450554), and provides maps and rain capes on request.

Glen Urquhart and Glen Affric

You can head west from Drumnadrochit on the A831 through **Glen Urquhart**, a fairly open valley with farmland giving way to scrubby woodland and heather as you near **CANNICH**. The **youth hostel** here (☎01456/415244; mid-May to Sept) makes a good base for exploring **Glen Affric**, claimed by many to be Scotland's loveliest valley. It's real calendar stuff, with a rushing river and Caledonian pine and birch woods opening out onto an island-studded loch that was considerably enlarged after the building of the dam, one of many hydroelectric schemes around here. Hemmed in by a string of Munros, the glen is great for picnics and pottering, particularly on a calm and sunny day, when the still loch reflects the islands and surrounding hills.

The area also offers some tremendous **hiking**. Among the most popular routes is the one winding west through Kintail to Shiel Bridge, on the west coast near Kyle of Lochalsh (about 25 miles), which takes at least two full days; a remote but recently revamped **youth hostel** (no phone; April–Oct) makes a convenient stopover halfway into the walk on the banks of the burn above Loch Affric. The trail is easy to follow, but can get horrendously boggy if there's been a lot of rain, so allow plenty of time and take adequate wet-weather gear.

Invermoriston and Glen Moriston to Glen Shiel

Heading south, **INVERMORISTON** is a tiny, attractive village just above Loch Ness, from where you can follow well-marked woodland trails past a series of grand water-falls. Dr Johnson and Boswell spent a couple of nights here planning their journey to the Hebrides; you, too, could stay at the *Glenmoriston Arms Hotel* (☎01320/351206; ⑤), an old-fashioned inn with more than a hundred malt whiskies at the bar. Alternatively, the *SYHA* **Loch Ness Youth Hostel** (☎01320/351274), three and a half miles north of Invermoriston and overlooking the loch, is a more economical base.

If you're driving on from Invermoriston to the **west coast**, the roads (A887/A87) are good, as it's a main commercial and tourist route. Rugged and somewhat awesome, the stretch through **Glen Moriston**, beside **Loch Cluanie** has serious peaks on either side and little sign of human habitation as the road climbs. At the western end of the loch, you'll find the cosy *Cluanie Inn* (☎01320/340238; ⑦), which offers tasty bar meals. From here, the road drops gradually down **Glen Shiel** into the superb mountainscape of **Kintail** (see p.460).

Fort Augustus

FORT AUGUSTUS, the tiny village at the more scenic southwestern tip of Loch Ness, was named after George II's son, the chubby lad who later became the "Butcher" Duke of Cumberland of Culloden fame; it was built as a barracks after the 1715 Jacobite rebellion. Today, it's dominated by comings and goings along the Caledonian Canal, which leaves Loch Ness here, and by its large **Benedictine Abbey**, a campus of grey Victorian buildings founded on the site of the original fort in 1876. The abbey used to house a Catholic boys school, but this was forced to close in 1993 and has now been converted into a go-ahead **heritage centre** (daily: Easter–Oct 9am–5pm; Nov–Easter 10am–4pm; ☎01320/366233; £5), where a walkman tour-cum-sound-and-light-show canters through a large swath of Scottish history as well as covering the history of the abbey and the fort and explaining Benedictine life.

Traditional Highland culture is the subject of **The Clansmen Centre's** lively and informative exhibition (Easter to mid-Oct daily 10am–8.30pm; £2.50), on the banks of the canal. Guides sporting sporrans and rough woollen plaids talk you through the daily life of the region's seventeenth-century inhabitants inside a mock-up of a turf-roofed stone croft, followed by demonstrations of weaponry in the back garden, where you can be photographed in traditional Highland garb. Most of the young staff work here for fun, donning their kilts and dowdy women's period costumes on their free weekends to fight mock battles with enthusiasts from other parts of the Highlands, which must be why they are so unnervingly adept at wielding broadswords.

Practicalities

Fort Augustus's small **tourist office** (April–June Mon–Sat 10am–5pm; July & Aug 9am–8pm; Sept & Oct 9am–6pm; ☎01320/366367) hands out useful free maps detailing popular walks in the area. They'll also help sort out fishing permits if you fancy trying your luck in the loch or nearby river.

The best-value **accommodation** in Fort Augustus has to be the Benedictine Abbey's guest rooms (☎01320/366233; ③), which are clean, spacious and private. The entrepreneurial monks also run a small *Backpackers' Lodge* with self-catering and laundry facilities and, bizarrely, Internet pages at *www.monk.co.uk*. The *Bothy Bite Bunk House* (☎01320/366700), in the centre of the village by the canal, offers alternative hostel accommodation. The *Old Pier* (☎01320/366418; ⑤) is a particularly appealing B&B, right on the loch at the north side of the village; there are log fires in the evenings – often very welcome even in summer – and a riding centre is attached. Of the **hotels**, try the small, friendly *Caledonian* (☎01320/366256; ④), overlooking the Abbey, or the *Brae* (☎01320/366289; ⑤), just off the main road as you approach the village from the north, surrounded by woodland.

Places to **eat** include the *Gondolier*, on the southern side of the village, which serves ambitious food at reasonable prices, or the Benedictine Abbey for good, inexpensive fare that will appeal particularly to vegetarians and the health-conscious; in the evenings, you can take your own wine. Alternatively, try the *Bothy Bite* for Scottish specialities with a good range of moderately priced fish, steak and pies. The *Poachers* on the main road is the liveliest **pub**, drawing a mixed clientele of locals, yachties and backpackers.

North from Fort Augustus: East Loch Ness

The tranquil and scenic **east side of Loch Ness** is skirted by General Wade's old military highway, now the B862/852. From Fort Augustus, this narrow single-track

---

THE NEVIS RANGE SKI STATION

The **Nevis Range Ski Range** (☎01397/705825), seven miles northeast of Fort William on the A82, boasts Scotland's only cable-car system (daily: July & Aug 9.30am–8pm; otherwise 10am–5pm; closed mid-Nov to mid-Dec; £6 return), in the **AONACH MHOR** ski area – a popular attraction during both winter and the summer off-season period. Built in 1989 with a hefty grant from the regional council, the one-and-a-half mile gondola ride (15min) gives an easy approach to some high-level walking, but for most tourists it simply provides an effortless means to rise 2000ft and enjoy the spectacular views from the terrace of the self-service restaurant at the top. In July and August, you can also ski on the Nevis Range's 246ft **dry slope** (July & Aug Sun–Thurs 11.30am–1pm; £9 including ski rental and group instruction).

road swings inland through the near-deserted **Stratherrick** valley, dotted with tiny lochans and flocks of shaggy sheep, before dropping down to rejoin the loch at **FOYERS**, where there are numerous marked forest trails and an impressive waterfall.

Three miles further north at **INVERFARIGAIG** – where a road up the beautiful, steep-sided river valley leads over to Loch Mhor – stands **Boleskine House**, former residence of the infamous Satanist and occult guru, Alastair Crowley. The self-styled "Great Beast" of Black Magic lived here between 1900 and 1918, amid rumours of Devil worship and human sacrifice. In the 1970s, Led Zeppelin's Jimmy Page bought the place, but sold it after the tragic death of his daughter some years later. Set back in its own grounds, the house still has a gloomy air about it, and is not open to the public.

A much warmer welcome awaits visitors at the sleepy village of **DORES**, nestled at the top end of Loch Ness, where the *Dores Inn* makes a pleasant pit stop. Only nine miles from Inverness, the old pub, which serves an excellent pint of 80 shilling and inexpensive bar food, is popular with Invernessians, who trickle out here on summer evenings for a stroll along the grey-pebble beach, and some monster-spotting.

South from Fort Augustus to Fort William

The fast A82 runs south from Fort Augustus along the shores of **Loch Oich**, where, at Invergarry, the A87 strikes westwards towards Kyle of Lochalsh. Continuing south towards Spean Bridge and Fort William, there are fine views across Loch Lochy to the Glengarry mountains, including Ben Tee, on its northern side. The road comes into more open country near the **Commando Memorial**, a group of bronze soldiers, sculpted in 1952 by Scott Sutherland in memory of the men who trained in the area and lost their lives during World War II. The statue stands on a raised promontory that overlooks an awesome sweep of moor and mountain, taking in Lochaber and the Ben Nevis massif.

Nearby, the minor B8004 branches down to **GAIRLOCHY**, at Loch Lochy's southern tip, where you once more encounter the Caledonian Canal – you can easily walk anywhere along this stretch of the canal, although the best access point is where the B8004 crosses it. The canal debouches into the sea via a series of eleven locks, known as Neptune's Staircase, which cover a drop of 80ft and presented Telford with quite an engineering challenge. It's worth a detour round the northwest side of Loch Lochy to lonely Loch Arkaig, a twenty-minute drive that takes you through a pass, ablaze with rhododendrons in early summer, into country that feels a hundred miles from anywhere.

Fort William and around

The area **around Fort William** is a blend of rugged mountain terrain and tranquil sea loch. To the north, gentle and more rounded hills give way to altogether more dramatic scenes, while to the south **Ben Nevis** — at 4406ft Britain's highest peak – looms over **Loch Linnhe**, a long sea loch at the southern end of the Great Glen from whose western shore rise the peaks of **Ardgour**.

Fort William and the surrounding area has a turbulent and bloody **history**. Founded in 1655 and named in honour of William III, it was successfully held by government troops during both of the Jacobite risings; the country to the southwest is inextricably associated with Bonnie Prince Charlie's flight after Culloden. **Glen Coe**, half an hour's drive south of Fort William, is another historic site with a violent past, renowned as much for the infamous **massacre** of 1692 as for its magnificent scenery. Nowadays the whole area is unashamedly given over to tourism, and Fort William is swamped by bus tours throughout the summer, but, as ever in the Highlands, within a thirty-minute drive you can be totally alone.

Fort William

With its stunning position on Loch Linnhe and the snow-streaked bulk of Ben Nevis rising behind, **FORT WILLIAM**, known by the many walkers and climbers that come here as "Fort Bill", should be a gem. Sadly, ribbon bungalow development and an ill-advised dual carriageway complete with a grubby pedestrian underpass, have wrecked the waterfront. The main street and the little squares off it are more appealing, though occupied by some decidedly tacky tourist gift shops.

Arrival and information

Fort William is easily reached by **bus** from Inverness, and by **train** (the stations are next door to each other at the north end of High Street) direct from Glasgow via the famous, scenic **West Highland Railway** (see p.424). If you're driving, parking can be a nightmare: try the big car park down beside the loch, at the south end of town. The **tourist office**, Cameron Square, just off High Street (Mon–Sat 9am–8.30pm, Sun 9am–6pm; ☎01397/703781), hands out free town maps and can help arrange onward transport to many of the less-visited areas of the west coast. **Mountain bikes** are available for rent at Off Beat Bikes (☎01397/704008) on High Street; they also have a branch at the Nevis Range lower gondola station – good for exploring forest tracks in that area.

Accommodation

Fort William's plentiful **accommodation** ranges from large luxury hotels to budget hostels and bunkhouses. Numerous B&Bs are also scattered across the town, many of them in the suburb of Corpach, one and a half miles north along the Mallaig road. Note that a wide array of places to stay in this area may be reserved through the tourist office for a £1 booking fee, or you can ask for its free *Essential Guide* and telephone around yourself.

HOTELS AND B&BS
Alexandra Hotel, The Parade (☎01397/702241). Established hotel slap in the town centre, with well-appointed rooms and a restaurant. ⑤.
Beinn Ard, Argyll Road (☎01397/704760). A very central and comfortable B&B, offering some en-suite rooms and panoramic views of Loch Linnhe. ③.

Distillery House, North Road, just north of the town centre near the junction for Glen Nevis (☎01397/702980). Very comfortable and well-equipped upper-range B&B. ⑥.

Glenloy Lodge Hotel, about six miles from Fort William on the minor road running north from Banavie (☎01397/712700). Comfortable, friendly and secluded small hotel with views across to Ben Nevis. ⑨.

The Grange, Grange Road (☎01397/705516). B&B in an old stone house, with three en-suite doubles and a spacious garden. Vegetarian breakfasts on request; non-smoking. ⑤.

Inverlochy Castle, two miles north of Fort William on the A82 (☎01397/702177). A grand country house hotel set in wooded parkland, two miles north of Fort William; exceptional levels of service and outstanding food. ⑨.

Rhu Mhor, Alma Road (☎01397/702213). Congenial B&B 10min from the town centre, offering good breakfasts; vegetarians and vegans are catered for by arrangement. ③.

HOSTELS AND CAMPSITES

Ben Nevis Bunkhouse, Achintee Farm, Glen Nevis (☎01397/702240). A more civilized option than the neighbouring *SYHA*, with hot showers, self-catering kitchen and TV room. Reached by the road on the north side of the river Nevis, or from the south side by the Ben path.

Calluna, Heathcroft (☎01397/700451). Central, small family-run budget hostel with standard facilities, but tricky to find: head up Lundavra Road from the roundabout, then double back left along Connochie Road.

Fort William Backpackers, Alma Road (☎01397/700711). A friendly independent hostel 5min walk from the train station, whose all-in price includes bed linen, use of kitchen, and free tea and coffee.

Glen Nevis SYHA Hostel, two and a half miles up the Glen Nevis road (☎01397/702336). Large but best avoided in mid-summer when it's chock-full of teenagers. Closed Nov.

Glen Nevis Caravan and Camping Park, two miles up the Glen Nevis road (☎01397/702191). Good facilities include hot showers, a shop and restaurant.

The Smiddy Lodge, Station Road (☎01397/772467). A cosy twelve-bed hostel right next to Corpach train station, three miles or so out on the Mallaig road; regular buses run here from Fort William station.

The Town

Fort William's downfall started in the nineteenth century, when the original fort, which gave the town its name, was demolished to make way for the train line. Today, the town is a sprawl of dual carriageways, and there's little to detain you except the splendid and idiosyncratic **West Highland Museum**, on Cameron Square, just off High Street (Jan–March & Nov Mon–Sat 10am–4pm; April–Oct Mon–Sat 10am–5pm; July & Aug also Sun 2–5pm; £1.50). Its collections cover virtually every aspect of Highland life; the presentation is traditional, but very well done, making a refreshing change from state-of-the-art heritage centres. There's a good section on Highland clans and tartans and, among interesting Jacobite relics, a secret portrait of Bonnie Prince Charlie, seemingly just a blur of paint that resolves itself into a portrait when viewed against a cylindrical mirror. Look out, too, for the long Spanish rifle used in the assassination of a local factor (the landowner's tax-collector-cum-bailiff) – the murder that subsequently inspired Robert Louis Stevenson's novel, *Kidnapped*.

Excursions from town include the popular day-trip to Mallaig (see p.456) on the **Jacobite Steam Train** (mid-June to Sept Sun–Fri; depart Fort William 10.35am, depart Mallaig 2.10pm; day return £19.25). Heading along the north shore of Loch Eil to the west coast via historic Glenfinnan (see p.455), the journey takes in some of the region's most spectacular scenery. Several **cruises** also leave from the town pier every day, offering the chance to spot the marine life of Loch Linnhe, including seals, otters and seabirds.

Glen Nevis

A ten-minute drive out of town, **Glen Nevis** is indisputably among the Highlands' most impressive glens: a classic U-shaped glacial valley hemmed in by steep bracken-covered slopes and swaths of blue-grey scree. Herds of shaggy Highland cattle also graze the valley floor, where a sparkling river gushes through glades of trees. With the forbidding mass of Ben Nevis rising steeply to the north, it's not surprising this valley has been chosen as the location for scenes in several **movies** such as *Rob Roy* and *Braveheart*. Apart from its natural beauty, Glen Nevis is also the starting point for the ascent of Scotland's highest peak, and you can rent **mountain equipment** and **mountain bikes** at the trailhead. Highland Country **bus** #42 runs as far as the youth hostel from An Aird, Fort William (June–Sept approximately hourly; 10min).

Eating

Fort William has a reasonable range of places **to eat**. On the High Street, the *Grog and Gruel* serves an eclectic mix of pizzas, pasta and Mexican dishes with real ale, while the *Good Food Stop* at the *Alexandra Hotel* does inexpensive grills, fish and pasta dishes. *McTavish's Kitchen*, an American/Scottish restaurant on High Street, has a predictable menu of moderately priced steaks and seafood, with several vegetarian options; in summer, it also hosts nightly Scottish entertainment sessions (8.30–11.30pm). The pick of the bunch, though, is the *Crannog Seafood Restaurant*: an elegantly converted bait store on the pier, where oysters, langoustines, prawns and salmon are cooked with flair. The wine list is also excellent, although the prices make it best kept for a treat. Out of town, the *Old Pines* near Spean Bridge (☎01397/712324) is worth trying, or you can dine very

---

GLEN NEVIS: WALKS AND HIKES

Harvey's Ben Nevis Walkers Map and Guide
The above map is available in the Fort William tourist office and several shops around town. Anyone keen to do some serious planned walking should contact one of the guiding organizations, such as Lochaber Walks (☎01397/703828), or Donald Watt (☎01397/704340), leader of the Lochaber Mountain Rescue Team, who takes half- and whole-day walks.

Of all the walks in and around Glen Nevis, the ascent of **Ben Nevis**, Britain's highest summit, inevitably attracts the most attention. In high summer, the trail is teeming with hikers, whatever the weather. However, this doesn't mean the mountain should be treated casually. It can snow on top any day of the year and more people perish here annually than on Everest, so take the necessary precautions; in winter, of course, the mountain should be left to the experts.

The most obvious route to the summit, a Victorian pony path up the whaleback south side of the mountain, built to service the observatory that once stood on the top, starts from the Glen Nevis youth hostel, two miles southeast of Fort William. This climbs steadily from the trailhead, swinging onto a wide saddle with a small loch before veering right to cross the **Red Burn**. A series of seemingly endless zigzags rises from here over boulderfields onto a plateau, which you cross to reach the **summit**, marked by cairns, a shelter and a trig point. Return via the same route or, if the weather is settled and you're confident enough, make the sidetrip from the saddle mentioned earlier into the **Allt a'Mhuilinn** glen for spectacular views of the great cliffs on Ben Nevis's north face. The Allt a'Mhuilinn may be followed right down to valley level as an alternative route off the mountain, reaching the distillery on the A82 a mile north of Fort William. Allow a full day for the climb.

If you don't fancy a hike up the mountain, a great low-level walk runs from the end of the road at the top of the glen. The good but very rocky path leads through a dramatic **gorge** with impressive falls and rapids, then opens out into a secret hanging valley, carpeted with wild flowers, with a high waterfall at the far end. It's a pretty place for a picnic and if you're really energetic you can walk on over Rannoch Moor to Corrour Station, where you can pick up one of four daily trains (1–2 on Sundays) to take you back to Fort William.

well indeed in the more formal setting of *Inverlochy Castle* (☎01397/702177), though here the bill for two will probably run into three figures. A good place for **picnic food** as well as a snack is the *Café Chardon*, up a lane off High Street next to AT Mays; they do excellent baguettes, croissants and pastries to eat in or take away.

Glen Coe and Ballachulish

Breathtakingly beautiful, **Glen Coe** (literally "Valley of Weeping"), sixteen miles south of Fort William on the A82, is one of the best-known Highland glens: a spectacular mountain valley between velvety-green conical peaks, their tops often wreathed in cloud, and cascades of rock and scree. In 1692 it was the site of a notorious **massacre**, in which the MacDonalds were victims of a long-standing government desire to suppress the clans. Fed up with what they regarded as unacceptable lawlessness, and a grounds well of Jacobitism and Catholicism, the government offered a general pardon to all those who signed an oath of allegiance to William III by January 1, 1692. When clan chief **Alastair MacDonald** missed the deadline, a plot was hatched to make an example of "that damnable sept", and **Campbell of Glenlyon** was ordered to billet his soldiers in the homes of the MacDonalds, who for ten days entertained them with traditional Highland hospitality. In the early morning of February 13, the soldiers turned on their hosts, slaying between 38 and 45 and causing more than 300 to flee in a blizzard, some to die of exposure.

Today, the glen, a property of the NTS since the 1930s, is virtually uninhabited, and provides outstanding climbing and walking. A small **NTS visitor centre** (April–Oct 9.30am–5.30pm; 50p), in the middle of the glen just off the main road, shows a short video about the massacre, and has a gift shop selling the usual books, postcards and Highland kitsch; however, for information about the area, the tourist office at Ballachulish is more useful.

At the eastern end of Glen Coe beyond the demanding Buachaille Etive Mhor, the landscape opens out onto the vast Rannoch Moor, dotted with small lochs and crossed by the West Highland Way, the A82 and, farther east, the West Highland Railway. From the **Glen Coe Ski Centre**, a ski lift climbs 2400ft to Meall a Bhuiridh, giving spectacular views over Rannoch Moor and to Ben Nevis (all year; 15min; £3.75 return). At the base station, there's a tiny **Museum of Mountaineering** (daily 8.30am–5pm), where the rescue statistics make cautionary reading, and a simple but pleasant café. At the western end of the glen, **Glencoe village** lies on the shore of Loch Leven, an inlet of Loch Linnhe.

Two miles further west, **Ballachulish village** was a major centre for the production of roofing slates, from 1693 to 1955, while North and South Ballachulish were once the terminals for the ferry across the mouth of Loch Leven, now crossed by a bridge. On the seaward side of the main road, the pricey **Highland Mysteryworld** (daily 10am–6pm; £4.95), attempts to conjure up some of the myths and legends of the Highlands, with the help of a crew of enthusiastic actors, animatronics and lots of smoke; it has a reasonable café and relatively kitsch-free gift shop.

Practicalities

Ballachulish has a useful **tourist office**, on Albert Road (April & May Mon–Sat 9am–5pm Sun noon–4pm; June–Sept Mon–Sat 9am–6pm, Sun 10am–5pm; Sept & Oct Mon–Sat 10am–5pm, Sun 10am–4pm; ☎01855/811296), and there's a good selection of **accommodation** in Glen Coe and the surrounding area. Basic options include an *SYHA* **hostel** (☎01855/811219) in the lower part of Glen Coe, an NTS **campsite** (☎01855/811397) nearby, above the main road, and the *Inchree Bunkhouse* at Onich near North Ballachulish (☎01855/821287). Glencoe village has a few comfortable **B&Bs**, such as the secluded *Scorry Breac* (☎01855/811354; ③), and the *Glencoe Guest House* (☎01855/811244; ③). In Ballachulish village, *Fern Villa* (☎01855/811393; ③) is welcoming

WALKS AROUND GLEN COE

Ordnance Survey Landranger Map No. 41.

Flanked by sheer-sided Munros, Glen Coe offers some of the Highlands' most challenging **hiking** routes, with long steep ascents over rough trails and notoriously unpredictable weather conditions that claim lives every year. The walks outlined below number among the glen's less ambitious routes, but still require a map. It's essential that you take the proper precautions (see p.421), and stick to the paths, both for your own safety and the sake of the soil, which has become badly eroded in places.

A good introduction to the splendours of Glen Coe is the half-day hike over the **Devil's Staircase**, which follows part of the old military road that once ran between Fort William and Stirling. The trail, a good option for families and less experienced hikers, starts at the village of **Kinlochleven,** due north across the mountains from Glen Coe at the far eastern tip of Loch Leven (take the B863): head along the single-track road from the British Aluminium Heritage Centre to a wooden bridge, from where a gradual climb on a dirt jeep track winds up to Penstock Farm. The path, a section of the **West Highland Way**, is marked from here onwards by thistle signs, and is therefore easy to follow uphill to the 1804ft pass and down the other side into Glen Coe. The Devil's Staircase was named by 400 soldiers who endured severe hardship to build it in the seventeenth century, but in fine settled weather the trail is safe and affords stunning views of Loch Eilde and Buachaille Etive Mhor. A more detailed account of this hike features in *Great Walks: Kinlochleven* (No. 4) leaflet, on sale at most tourist offices in the area.

Another leaflet in the *Great Walks* series (No. 5: Glen Coe) gives a good description of the **Allt Coire Gabhail** hike, another old favourite. The trailhead for this half-day route is in Glen Coe itself, at the car park opposite the distinctive Three Sisters massif on the main A82 (look for the giant boulder). From the road, drop down to the floor of the glen and cross the River Coe via the wooden bridge, where you have a choice of two onward paths; the easier route, the less worn one, peels off to the right. Follow this straight up the Allt Coire Gabhail for a couple of miles until you rejoin the other (lower) path, which has ascended the valley beside the burn via a series of rock pools and lively scrambles. Cross the river here via the stepping stones and press on to the false summit directly ahead – actually the rim of the so-called "Lost Valley" which the Clan MacDonald used to flee to and hide their cattle in when attacked. Once in the valley, there are superb views of Bidean, Gearr Aonach and Beinn Fhada, which improve as you continue on to its head, another 20–30 minute walk. Unless you're well equipped and experienced, turn around at this point, as the trail climbs to some of the glen's high ridges and peaks.

Undoubtedly one of the finest walks in the Glen Coe area not entailing the ascent of a Munro is the **Buachaille Etive Beag** (BEB) circuit, for which we recommend you check out the *Ordnance Survey Pathfinder Guide*: Fort William and Glen Coe Walks. Following the textbook glacial valleys of Lairig Eilde and Lairig Gartain, the route entails a 1968ft climb in only nine miles of rough trail, and should only be attempted by relatively fit hikers. Park near the waterfall at **The Study** – the gorge part of the A82 through Glen Coe – and walk up the road until you see a sign pointing south to "Loch Etiveside". The path angles up from here, criss-crossing the Allt Lairig Eilde before the final pull to the top of the pass, a rise of 787ft from the road. The burn flowing through Glen Etive to Dalness is, confusingly, also called the Allt Lairig Eilde; follow its west bank path until you reach a fenced-off area, and then cross the stream, using the trail that then ascends Stob Dubh (the "black peat") directly from Glen Etive to gain some height. Next, pick a traverse line across the side of the valley to the col of the Lairig Gartain, and onwards to the top of the pass – a haul of around 984ft that is the last steep ascent of this circuit. The drop down the other side towards the estate lodge of Dalness is easy. When you reach the single-track road, follow the path signposted as the "Lairig Gartain", northeast to a second pass, from where an intermittent trail descends the west (left) side of the River Coupall valley, eventually rejoining the A82. Much the most enjoyable path back northeast down the glen from here is the roughly parallel route of the old military road, which offers a gentler and safer return with superb views of the Three Sisters – finer than those ever seen by any motorist.

and good, while *Cuildorag House* (☎01855/821529; ③) in Onich is a particularly pleasant vegetarian and vegan B&B, renowned for its great breakfasts. **Hotels** include the stark *Clachaig Inn* (☎01855/811252; ④), a great place to swap stories with fellow climbers, and the beer is good; it's up Glen Coe, on the minor road from the Glencoe village. In South Ballachulish, the *Ballachulish Hotel* (☎01855/811606; ⑤) is a grand but welcoming old place with good food, while the *Onich Hotel* (☎01855/821214; ⑤) is smart and friendly. **Mountain bikes** and **tandems** can be rented from the *Clachaig Inn*.

Glen Roy and Loch Laggan

From Fort William it's possible to reach Speyside along the relatively quiet A86 through **Roy Bridge**, northeast of Fort William, turnoff point for the minor road which runs up **Glen Roy**. A couple of miles along the glen, you'll see the so-called "parallel roads": not roads at all, but ancient beaches at various levels along the valley sides which mark the shorelines of a loch confined here by a glacial dam in the last Ice Age. Back on the A86, two miles beyond Roy Bridge, *Aite Cruinnichidh*, 1 Achluachrach (☎01397/712315), is a comfortable bunkhouse in a beautiful setting.

Further east, the A86 runs alongside the artificial **Loch Laggan**, raised in 1934 to provide water for the aluminium works at Fort William; the water travels in tunnels of up to 15ft in diameter carved through miles of solid rock. To the north of the loch is the **Creag Meagaidh National Nature Reserve**, where a hill track leads up through changing bands of mountain vegetation to **Lochan a Choire**. Right by the nature reserve car park, you can see several small herds of red deer, kept here for scientific study.

STRATHSPEY AND THE CAIRNGORMS

Rising high in the heather-clad hills above Loch Laggan, forty miles due south of Inverness, the **River Spey**, Scotland's second longest river, drains northeast towards the Moray Firth through one of the Highlands' most spellbinding valleys. Famous for its **ski slopes**, **salmon fishing** and **ospreys,** Strathspey forms a broad cleave between the mighty Monadhliath mountains in the north and the ice-sculpted Cairngorm range to the south. Outdoor enthusiasts flock here year-round to take advantage of the superb hiking, watersports and winter snows, but the valley is also a major transport artery connecting Inverness and the northern highlands with the south.

Of Strathspey's scattered settlements, **Aviemore** absorbs the largest number of visitors, particularly in midwinter when it metamorphoses into the UK's busiest ski resort. The village itself isn't up to much, but the 4000ft summit plateau of the Cairngorm is often snowcapped, providing stunning mountain scenery on a grand scale. Sedate **Kingussie**, further up the valley, is an older established holiday centre, popular more with anglers and grouse hunters than canoeists and climbers, while the Georgian town of **Grantown-on-Spey**, jumping-off point for **Loch Garten**, makes another good base for exploring the area. Most of upper Strathspey is privately owned by the Glen More Forest Park and Rothiemurchus Estate, who provide between them a plethora of year-round outdoor facilities, with masses of accommodation of all types. Both bodies actively encourage the recreational use of their land, which gives you the freedom to go virtually anywhere you want.

Aviemore

AVIEMORE was first developed as a resort in the mid-1960s, as the towering concrete **Aviemore Centre** bears witness: a shabby assortment of cavernous concrete buildings and incongruous high-rise hotels. The village proper, a sprawling jumble of traditional

---

WALKS AROUND AVIEMORE

Ordnance Survey Landranger Map No. 36.

Walking is an obvious attraction in the Aviemore area, but always follow the usual safety rules (see p.421).

If you want to walk the high tops, take the chair lift up from the Day Lodge (see below). However, as well as the high mountain trails, there are some lovely **low-level walks** around Aviemore. It takes an hour or so to complete the gentle circular walk around pretty **Loch an Eilean**, beginning at the end of the backroad that turns east off the B970 two miles south of Aviemore. The visitors' centre at the loch-side provides more information on the many woodland trails that criss-cross this area. A longer walk starts at the near end of **Loch Morlich**. Cross the river by the bridge and follow the dirt road, turning off after about twenty minutes to follow the signs to Aviemore. The path goes through beautiful pine woods and past tumbling burns, and you can branch off to Coylumbridge and Loch an Eilean. Unless you're properly prepared for a 25-mile hike, don't take the track to the **Lairig Ghru**, which eventually brings you out near Braemar. The routes are all well marked and easy to follow and, depending on what combination you put together, can take anything from two to five hours.

Another good shortish (half-day) walk leads along well-surfaced forestry track from Glenmore Lodge up towards the **Ryvoan Pass**, taking in An Lochan Uaine, known as the "Green Loch" and living up to its name, with amazing colours that range from turquoise to slate grey depending on the weather. The track narrows once past the loch and leads east towards Deeside, so retrace your steps if you don't want a major trek.

---

stone houses and tacky tourist shops set in a sea of car and coach parks, isn't much better. That said, Aviemore makes a convenient base for exploring more scenic parts of the valley, and has a wide range of facilities.

Winter sports

Scottish **skiing** on a commercial scale first really took off in Aviemore. By continental European and North American standards it's all on a tiny scale, but occasionally snow, sun and lack of crowds coincide and you can have a great day. February and March are usually the best times, but in some years the snow may still be good until April. Lots of places – not just in Aviemore itself – sell or hire equipment; for a rundown of ski schools and rental facilities in the area, check out the tourist office's *Ski Scotland* brochure.

The **Cairngorm Ski Area**, about eight miles southeast of Aviemore, above Loch Morlich in Glen More Forest Park, is well served by buses from Aviemore. You can rent skis and other equipment from the Day Lodge at the foot of the ski area (☎01479/861261), which also has a shop, a bar and restaurant, and sells tickets for the year-round chair lift.

If there's lots of snow, the area around **Loch Morlich** and into the **Rothiemurchus Estate** provides enjoyable cross-country skiing through lovely woods, beside rushing burns and even over frozen lochs. If you really want to know about survival in a Scottish winter, you could try a week at *Glenmore Lodge* (☎01479/861276) in the heart of the Glen More Forest Park at the east end of Loch Morlich. This superbly equipped and organized centre, run by the Scottish National Sports Council, offers winter courses in hill walking, mountaineering, alpine ski mountaineering, avalanche awareness and much besides. To add to the winter scene, there's a herd of **reindeer** at Loch Morlich, and the Siberian Husky Club holds its races in the area.

Summer sports

In summer, the main activities around Aviemore are **watersports**, and there are two centres that offer sailing, windsurfing and canoeing. The Loch Morlich Watersports

Centre (☎01479/861221), five miles or so east of Aviemore at the east end of the loch, rents equipment and offers tuition in a lovely setting with a sandy beach, while, up-valley, the Loch Insh Watersports Centre (see below) offers the same facilities in more open and less crowded surroundings. It also rents mountain bikes, boats for loch fishing, and gives ski instruction on a 164ft dry slope.

Riding and **pony trekking** are on offer up and down the valley; try Alvie Stables at Alvie near Kincraig (☎01540/651409), or the Carrbridge Trekking Centre, Station Road, Carrbridge, a few miles north of Aviemore (☎01479/84602).

Fishing is very much part of the local scene; you can fish for trout and salmon on the River Spey, and the Rothiemurchus Estate has a stocked trout-fishing loch at **Inverdruie**, where success is virtually guaranteed. Permits cost around £3.50 per day and are sold at Speyside Sports in Aviemore, one mile down the road toward the ski grounds from the tourist office, and at Loch Morlich Watersports Centre (see above), which also rents rods and tackle.

Practicalities

Aviemore's **tourist office** is just south of the train station on the main drag, Grampian Road (Mon–Sat 9am–5pm; ☎01479/810363). It offers an accommodation booking service, free maps and endless leaflets on local attractions. There's no shortage of **accommodation** in the area. The *Balavoulin Hotel* (☎01479/810672; ③) and *Ver Mont Guest House* (☎01479/810470; ③), both on Grampian Road, are good value, and there are also plenty of **B&Bs**: try Mrs Clark at *Sonas* (☎01479/810409; ③). However, the nicest place in the area is *Corrour House Hotel* at Inverdruie, two miles southeast of Aviemore (☎01479/810220; ⑤). As for **hostel** accommodation, Aviemore's large *SYHA* hostel (☎01479/810345; closed mid-Nov to Dec), is close to the tourist office, while at Glenmore, in the Glen More Forest Park a few miles east of Aviemore, the well-signposted *Badaguish Centre* (☎01479/861285), housed in three log cabins, has dorm beds for sixty people and good facilities for disabled visitors. There are also two more independent hostels near the village of Kincraig, six miles south of Aviemore: the *Loch Insh Watersports Centre* (☎01540/651272), beautifully sited beside the loch, and the *Glen Feshie Hostel* at Balachroick (☎01540/651323), where the all-in price includes bed linen and as much porridge as you like for breakfast. There's no shortage of **campsites** either: two of the best are the *Campgrounds of Scotland* site at Coylumbridge (☎01479/810120) and the Forestry Commission one at Glenmore (☎01479/861271).

All the hotels serve run-of-the-mill bar **food**, but for a more interesting option head to *The Old Bridge Inn*, on the east side of the railway, below the bridge, or *Littlejohn's*, on Grampian Road, which has more choice than most. Further afield, the Loch Insh Watersports Centre (see above) has a particularly pleasant restaurant overlooking the loch, with snacks available during the day and delicious meals in the evening.

Kingussie

KINGUSSIE (pronounced "Kingyoosee") lies twelve miles south of Aviemore and is far cosier, stacked around a single main street. Beyond its usefulness as a place to stay, the chief attraction here is the excellent **Highland Folk Museum** (April–Oct Mon–Sat 10am–6pm, Sun 2–6pm; Nov–March Mon–Fri 10am–3pm; £3). An absorbing collection of buildings, exhibitions and artefacts covering every aspect of Highland life, the complex includes a farming museum, an old smokehouse, a mill, a Hebridean "black house", and a traditional herb and flower garden; most days in summer there's a demonstration of various traditional crafts. East across the river on a hillock stand the ruins of **Ruthven Barracks**, the best preserved of the garrisons built to pacify the Highlands after the 1715 rebellion and stunningly floodlit at night. Taken by the Jacobites in 1744, it was blown up in the wake of Culloden to prevent it from falling into enemy hands. Ruthven was also the place from where clan leader Lord George Murray dispatched his acrimonious letter to Bonnie Prince Charlie, holding him personally responsible for the string of blunders that had precipitated their defeat.

Kingussie's **tourist office** is on King Street, off the High Street (May–Sept daily 9.30am–5.30pm, Sun 10am–12.30pm & 1.30pm–5pm; ☎01540/661297). If you want to base yourself here, try *The Auld Poor House*, Laggan Cottage (☎01540/661558; ③), a congenial **B&B**, ten minutes' walk northeast of the village on the B9152. As its name implies, this old stone building used to be a charitable home for local destitutes, and its present owner loves to quip that "soups is once again served and de-lousing rules still apply". Other good options are *St Helens* (☎01540/661430; ③), on Ardbroilach Road, noted for its great breakfasts, and the very central *Bhuna Monadh* (☎01540/661186; ③), 85 High St. Of the **hotels**, *Scot House* on Newtonmore Road (☎01540/661351; ⑥) is a comfortable place, where you can get imaginative meals at reasonable prices.

The most ambitious **food** in the area is served at *The Cross Restaurant*, in a converted tweed mill on Tweed Mill Brae (☎01540/661166; March–Nov & Christmas). Its pricey meals make interesting use of local ingredients and there's a vast wine list; they also have several rooms (⑨ including dinner). Cheaper food is available at several cafés and pubs on the High Street. The *Royal Hotel* serves standard bar meals, with some vegetarian options, a good choice of cask ales and some 250 malts, while the *Café Volante* does great cheap-and-cheerful fish and chips. *La Cafetière* has excellent coffee, with good home baking, soup, toasties and baked potatoes; it closes at 5pm.

Carrbridge

Worth considering as an alternative to Aviemore – particularly as a skiing base – **CARRBRIDGE** is a pleasant, quiet village about seven miles northeast. Its **Landmark Heritage Park** (daily: April to mid-July 9.30am–6pm; mid-July to Aug 9.30am–8pm; Sept & Oct 9.30am–5.30pm; Nov–March 10am–5pm; £4.65) combines multimedia presentations on history and natural history with forest walks, nature trails, a maze and fun rides; it's more tastefully done than some places of this kind and an excellent place for children to let off steam. There are some decent accommodation options, including the friendly *Cairn Hotel* (☎01479/841212; ③), the immaculate *Fairwinds Hotel* (☎01479/841240; ④) and, more basic, the tiny but cosy *Carrbridge Bunkhouse* (☎01479/841250), half a mile or so north of the village on the Inverness road.

Grantown-on-Spey

Buses run from Aviemore and Inverness to the tiny Georgian town of **GRANTOWN-ON-SPEY**, about 15 miles northeast of Aviemore, which, if you've got your own transport, makes another good base for exploring Strathspey and the Cairngorm area. Activity is concentrated around the attractive central square, and the nearby **tourist office** on High Street (May–Sept daily 9am–6pm; ☎01479/872773). The town has plenty of **accommodation**: *Cumbrae*, South Street (☎01479/873216; ②), Mrs Lawson, 2 Mossie Rd (☎01479/872076; ③), and *Fearna House*, Old Spey Bridge (☎01479/872016; ③), all do comfortable, good-value B&B. If you're after something more upmarket, head for the large seventeenth-century *Garth Hotel*, at the north end of the square (☎01479/872836; ⑦), or the less expensive *Tyree House Hotel* (☎01479/872615; ④) on its west side; both are open all year round and have good **restaurants** that serve Scottish specialities.

Loch Garten

The **Abernethy Forest RSPB Reserve** on the shore of **LOCH GARTEN**, eight miles south of Grantown-on-Spey (or seven miles north of Aviemore), is famous as the nesting site of one of Britain's rarest birds. A little over fifty years ago, the **osprey**, known in North America as the "fish hawk", had completely disappeared from the British Isles. Then, in 1954, a single pair of these exquisite white-and-grey eagles mysteriously reappeared and built a nest in a tree half a mile or so from the loch. Although efforts were made to keep the exact location secret, one year's eggs fell victim to a gang of thieves, and thereafter the area became the centre of an effective high-security operation. Now the birds are well established not only here but at an increasing number of other sites in the Highlands. The best time to visit is during the nesting season, between late April and August, when the RSPB opens an **observation hide** complete with powerful telescopes and television monitoring of the nest. The reserve is also home to several other species of rare birds and animals, including the Scottish crossbill, capercaillie, whooper swan and red squirrel.

Loch Garten can be difficult to reach without your own transport; check with one of the tourist offices in the area about inclusive tours combining a trip on the popular **Strathspey Steam Railway** from Aviemore to Boat of Garten, with a bus journey to the reserve.

THE WEST COAST

For many people, the Highlands' starkly beautiful **west coast** – stretching from the **Morvern** peninsula (opposite Mull) in the south, to wind-lashed Cape Wrath in the far north – is the epitome of "Bonnie Scotland". Serrated by long blue sea lochs, deep glens and rugged green mountains that sweep from the shoreline, its myriad islets, occasional white-sand beaches and turquoise bays can, on sunny days, look like a picture postcard of the Mediterranean. This also is the least populated part of Britain, with just two small towns, and yawning tracts of moorland and desolate peat bog between crofting settlements.

The **Vikings**, who ruled the region in the ninth century, called it the "South Land", from which the modern district of Sutherland takes its name. After Culloden, the Clearances emptied most of the inland glens of the far north, however, and left the population clinging to the coastline, where a herring-fishing industry developed. Today, tourism, crofting, fishing and salmon farming are the mainstay of the local economy, supplemented by EU construction grants and subsidies for the sheep you'll encounter everywhere.

For visitors, **cycling** and **walking** are the obvious ways to make the most of the superb scenery, and countless lochans and crystal-clear rivers offer superlative trout and salmon **fishing**. The shattered cliffs of the far northwest are an ornithologist's dream, harbouring some of Europe's largest and most diverse **seabird colonies**, and the area's craggy mountaintops are the haunt of the elusive golden eagle.

The most visited part of the west coast is the stretch between Kyle of Lochalsh and Ullapool. Lying within easy reach of Inverness, this area boasts the region's more obvious highlights: the awesome mountainscape of **Torridon**, **Gairloch**'s sandy beaches, the famous botanic gardens at **Inverewe**, and **Ullapool** itself, a picturesque and workaday fishing town from where ferries leave for the Outer Hebrides. However, press on further north, or south, and you'll get a truer sense of the isolation that makes the west coast so special. Traversed by few roads, the remote northwest corner of Scotland is wild and bleak, receiving the full force of the north Atlantic's frequently ferocious weather. The scattered settlements of the far southwest, meanwhile, tend to be more sheltered, but they are separated by some of the most extensive wilderness areas in Britain – lonely peninsulas with evocative Gaelic names like **Ardnamurchan**, **Knoydart** and **Glenelg**.

Tempered by the Gulf Stream, the west coast's weather ranges from stupendous to diabolical. Never count on a sunny morning meaning a fine day; it can rain here at any time, and go on raining for days. Beware, too, as always in this part of the world, of the dreaded **midge**, which drives even the hardiest of locals to distraction on warm summer evenings.

Without your own vehicle, **getting around** the west coast can be a problem. There's a reasonable **train** service from Inverness to Kyle of Lochalsh and from Fort William to Mallaig, and a useful **summer bus** service connects Inverness to Ullapool, Lochinver, Scourie and Durness. However, services peter out as you venture further afield, and you'll have to rely on **postbuses**, which go just about everywhere, albeit slowly and at odd times of day. **Driving** is a lot less problematic: the roads aren't busy, though they are frequently single-track and scattered with sheep. On such routes, re-fuel whenever you can, as pumps are few and far between, and make sure your vehicle is in good condition because, even if you manage to reach the nearest garage, spares may well have to be sent over from Inverness.

Morvern to Morar: the "Rough Bounds"

The remote and sparsely-populated southwest corner of the Highlands, from the **Morvern** peninsula to the busy fishing and ferry port of **Mallaig**, is a dramatic, lonely region of mountain, moorland and almost deserted glens fringed by a coast of stunning white beach-es, with wonderful views to Mull and Skye. Its Gaelic name translates as the **"Rough Bounds"**, implying a region geographically and spiritually outside current thought and behaviour. Even if you haven't got a car, you should spend a few days here exploring by foot – there are so few roads that some determined hiking is almost inevitable.

The southwest Highlands' main road is the A830, which winds in tandem with the rail line through the glens from **Fort William** to Mallaig. Along the way, the road passes **Glenfinnan**, the much photographed spot at the head of stunning Loch Shiel where Bonnie Prince Charlie gathered the clans to start the doomed Jacobite uprising of 1745. There are regular buses and trains along the main road; elsewhere in the region you'll usually have to rely on daily post- or school buses. If you have your own transport, the five-minute ferry crossing at **Corran Ferry** (every 15min), a nine-mile drive south of Fort William down Loch Linnhe, provides a more direct point of entry for Morvern and the rugged **Ardnamurchan** peninsula.

Morvern

Bounded on three sides by sea lochs and, in the north, by desolate Glen Tarbet, the remote southwest part of the Rough Bounds region, known as **Morvern**, is unremit-tingly bleak and empty. Most visitors only travel through here to get to **LOCHALINE** (pronounced "Loch*aa*lin"), a remote community on the **Sound of Mull**, from where a small ferry chugs to **Fishnish** – the shortest crossing from the mainland. The village, little more than a scattering of houses and a diving school (☎01967/421627) around a small pier, is a popular anchorage for yachts cruising the west coast, but holds little else to detain you. However, the easy stroll to the nearby fourteenth-century ruins of **Ardtornish Castle**, reached via a track that turns east off the main road one and a half miles north of Lochaline, makes an enjoyable detour. A further walk takes you to see the Loch Tearnait **crannog**, a defensive island dating back about 1500 years; this walk and others are detailed in the *Great Walks* series available from tourist offices in the area. If you're looking for somewhere to **stay**, try the tiny *Lochaline Hotel* (☎01967/421657; ③), which serves reasonable bar food and has a couple of small but comfortable **rooms**.

Sunart and Ardgour

The predominantly roadless regions of **Sunart** and **Ardgour** make up the country between Loch Shiel, Loch Sunart and Loch Linnhe, north of Morvern: the heart of Jacobite support in the mid-eighteenth century, and a Catholic stronghold to this day.

The area's only real village is sleepy **STRONTIAN**, grouped around a green on an inlet of Loch Sunart. In 1722, lead mines here yielded the first ever traces of the element **strontium**, subsequently named after the village. Worked by French POWs, the same mines also furnished shot for the Napoleonic wars. Strontian's other claim to fame is the "**Floating Church**", which was moored nearby in Loch Sunart in 1843. After being refused permission by the local laird to found their own "kirk", or chapel, on the estate, members of the Free Presbyterian Church (see p.347, bought an old boat on the River Clyde, converted it into a church and then had it towed up the west coast to Loch Sunart.

Travelling by **public transport**, you can get to Strontian (Mon–Sat) on the 8am bus from Kilchoan (see below), or on a bus that leaves Fort William at 11.50am and Ardgour at 12.20pm. Strontian's **tourist office** (Easter–Oct Mon–Fri 9am–5pm, Sat 10am–4pm, Sun 10am–2pm; ☎01967/402131) will book accommodation for a small fee. *Loch View* **B&B** (☎01967/402465; ②) is excellent value, with large rooms in a fine lochside Victorian house, while *Sea View* (☎01967/402060; ②), a small and very traditional cottage next door, is friendly but more basic; it welcomes dogs. The modern *Kinloch House* (☎01967/402138; ③) is very comfortable, with stunning views down the loch. Strontian also has a couple of good **hotels**, including the *Loch Sunart* (☎01967/402471; ⑥), in a splendid position right by the water, and the luxurious *Kilcamb Lodge* (☎01967/402257; ⑨ including dinner), a restored country house set in its own grounds on the loch-side, whose restaurant serves excellent food.

The Ardnamurchan peninsula

A tortuous single-track road (the B8007) winds west from **Salen** along the northern shore of Loch Sunart to the wild **Ardnamurchan peninsula**, the most westerly point on the British mainland. The unspoilt landscape is relatively gentle and wooded at the eastern end, but as you travel west the trees disappear and are replaced by a wild, salt-sprayed moorland. The peninsula, which lost most of its inhabitants during the infamous Clearances (see p.555), is today virtually deserted apart from the handful of tiny crofting settlements clinging to its jagged coastline. Ardnamurchan remains a naturalist's paradise, harbouring a huge variety of birds, animals and wildflowers like thrift and wild iris.

Glenborrodale and the Glenmore Natural History Centre

An inspiring introduction to the diverse flora, fauna and geology of Ardnamurchan is the superb **Glenmore Natural History Centre** (April–Oct 10.15am-5.30pm; £2.50), nestled near the shore just west of the hamlet of **GLENBORRODALE**. Brainchild of local photographer Michael MacGregor (whose stunning work enlivens postcard stands along the west coast), the centre is housed in a sensitively designed timber building, complete with turf roof and wildlife ponds. TV cameras relay live pictures of the comings and goings of the surrounding wildlife, from a pine marten's nest, a heronry and from underwater pools in the nearby river, while an excellent audiovisual show features MacGregor's photographs of the area accompanied by specially composed music. The small **café** serves sandwiches and good home-baked cakes and there's a useful bookshop. The nearby **RSPB reserve**, a mile to the east, is rich in wildlife too, being home to tree creepers, golden eagles, otters and seals, while for coastal wildlife-spotting – or trips to Tobermory on Mull or Fingal's Cave – contact Ardnamurchan Charters at Glenborrodale (☎01972/500208).

Kilchoan and Ardnamurchan Point

KILCHOAN, nine miles west of the Glenmore Centre, is Ardnamurchan's main village – a straggling but appealing crofting township overlooking the Sound of Mull. Between mid-April and mid-October, a **ferry** runs from here to Tobermory (6 daily; 35min), and the **tourist office** (Easter–Oct Mon–Sat 9am–6.45pm, Sun 10.30am–5.15pm; ☎01972/510222) will help with and book accommodation.

Hotels in Kilchoan include the *Meall mo Chridhe Hotel* (☎01972/510328; ③), with dinner ⑥), a converted eighteenth-century manse, or minister's house, set among trees above the road, and the very pleasant *Far View Cottage* (☎01972/510357; ⑤), on the road to the pier, which serves excellent food. In both cases, meal reservations are essential for non-residents. Further afield, a couple of miles before the Ardnamurchan Point lighthouse (see below), there's the *Sonachan Hotel* (☎01972/510211; ③), a cosy and friendly haven also offering good bar meals. For **B&B**, try *Doirlinn House* in Kilchoan (☎01972/510209; ③; March–Oct), or *Hillview* (☎01972/510322; ②), a traditional cottage about four miles north of the village at Achnaha (you'll need your own transport). The only direct bus to Kilchoan leaves from Corran Ferry at 12.05pm, arriving two and a half hours later.

Beyond Kilchoan the road continues to rocky, windy **Ardnamurchan Point**, with its unmanned **lighthouse** and spectacular views west to Coll, Tiree and across to the north of Mull. You can't normally get up the tower, but the lighthouse buildings house a café and an enthusiastically run **visitor centre** (April–Oct 9.30am–6pm; £2.50; ☎01972/510210), whose main theme is lighthouses, their construction and the people who lived in them. About three miles north of the point, the shell-strewn sandy beach of **Sanna Bay** offers truly unforgettable vistas of the Small Isles to the north, circled by gulls, terns and guillemots.

Acharacle

Back on the A861 towards the district of Moidart, the main settlement is **ACHARACLE**, an ancient crofting village lying at the seaward end of Loch Shiel. Surrounded by gentle hills, it's an attractive place whose scattered houses form a real community, with several shops, a post office, and plenty of places to stay. The informal *Loch Shiel Hotel* (☎01967/431224; ④) has nice rooms and simple but good food including local salmon and haddock. *Belmont* (☎01967/431266; ③) is a comfortable and central B&B, as is Mrs Crisp's (☎01967/431318; ③), just across the road. On the south side of the village, *Ardshealach Lodge* (☎01967/431301; ③) is secluded and welcoming. Acharacle's village hall is often used for ceilidhs: look out for notices in the shops.

Loch Moidart and Castle Tioram

A mile north of Acharacle, a sideroad running north off the A861 winds for three miles or so past a secluded estuary lined with rhododendron thickets and fishing platforms to **Loch Moidart**, a calm and sheltered sea loch. Perched atop a rocky promontory in the middle of the loch is **CASTLE TIORAM** (pronounced "cheerum"), one of Scotland's most atmospheric historic monuments. Reached via a sandy causeway, the thirteenth-century fortress, whose Gaelic name means "dry land", was the seat of the MacDonalds of Clanranald until destroyed by their chief in 1715 to prevent it from falling into Hanoverian hands while he was away fighting for the Jacobites. Today, the surviving walls and tower enclose an inner courtyard and a couple of empty chambers.

Glenfinnan

Approaching Moidart from the north by train, or via the fast Fort William–Mallaig road (the A830), you pass a historic site with great resonance for Scots. **GLENFINNAN**, nineteen miles west of Fort William at the head of Loch Shiel, was where Bonnie Prince Charlie raised his standard to signal the start of the Jacobite uprising of 1745. Surrounded by no more than 200 loyal clansmen, the young rebel prince waited to see if the Cameron of Loch Shiel would join his army. The drone of this powerful chief's pipers drifting up the glen was eagerly awaited, for without him and the Stuarts' attempt to claim the English throne would have been sheer folly. Despite strong misgivings, however, Cameron did decide to support the uprising, and arrived at Glenfinnan on a sunny August 19 with 800 men, thereby encouraging other less-convinced clan leaders to follow suit. Assured of adequate backing, the prince raised his red-and-white silk colour, proclaimed his father King James III of England, and set off on the long march to London from which only a handful of the soldiers gathered at Glenfinnan would return. The spot is marked by a column, crowned with a clansman in full battle dress, erected as a tribute by Alexander Macdonald of Glenaladale in 1815.

One doesn't need to be Scottish or to have Jacobite sympathies to appreciate the poignancy of this place, a beautiful stage for the opening scene in a brutal drama which was to change the Highlands for ever. The **visitor centre** and café (daily: April, May, Sept & Oct 10am–5pm; June–Aug 9.30am–6pm; £1), opposite the monument, gives an account of the "forty-five" uprising through to the rout at **Culloden** eight months later (see p.433).

Morar

Beyond Glenfinnan, the A830 runs alongside the captivating Loch Eilt in the district of Morar, through Lochailort – where it meets the road from Acharacle – and onto a coast marked by acres of white sands, turquoise seas and rocky islets draped with orange seaweed. **ARISAIG**, scattered round a sandy bay at the west end of the Morar peninsula, makes a good base for exploring this area. There's nothing in the way of specific attractions, but if the weather's fine you can spend hours wandering along the beaches and quiet backroads, and there's a small seal colony at nearby **RHUMACH**, reached via the single-track lane leading west out of the village along the headland. A daily boat also leaves from here during the summer for the Small Isles (see p.340); contact Arisaig Marine (☎01687/450224). **Accommodation** in the village is plentiful. *Kinloid Farm House* (☎01687/450669; ②, with dinner, ③) is one of several pleasant B&Bs with sea views, while the more upmarket *Old Library Lodge* (☎01687/450651; ⑥; April–Oct) has a handful of well-appointed rooms, some of them in a 200-year-old converted stable overlooking the waterfront. The restaurant downstairs, serving moderately priced lunches and excellent à la carte dinners (reservations recommended), is renowned for adding an exotic twist to fresh local ingredients – try Mallaig cod with Moroccan marinade.

Stretching for eight miles or so north of Arisaig is a string of stunning white-sand beaches backed by flowery machair, with barren granite hills rising straight up behind, though the views are somewhat marred by the abandoned cars, rusting metal and decrepit caravans which blight this part of the coast. The next settlement of any significance is **MORAR**, where the famous beach scenes from *Local Hero* were shot. Since the film crew left, however, a bypass has been built around the village, and the white sands, plagued by the rumble of frozen-cod lorries, are no longer the unspoilt idyll Burt Lancaster paddled ecstatically around in the early 1980s. **Loch Morar** – rumoured to be the home of **Morag**, a lesser-known rival to Nessie – runs east of Morar village into the heart of a huge wilderness area, linked to the sea by what must be one of the shortest rivers in Scotland. Hemmed in by heather-decked mountains, it featured in the movie *Rob Roy*: the cattle-rustling clansman's cottage was sited on its roadless northern shore.

Mallaig to Loch Duich

A cluttered, noisy port whose pebble-dashed houses struggle for space with great lumps of granite tumbling down to the sea, **MALLAIG**, 47 miles west of Fort William along the A830 (regular buses and trains run this route), is not a pretty village. Before the railway reached here in 1901, it consisted of only a few cottages, but now it's a busy, bustling place and, as the main ferry stop for Skye and the Small Isles (see p.328), is always full of visitors. The continuing source of the village's wealth is its thriving **fishing industry**: on the quayside piles of nets, tackle and ice crates lie scattered around a bustling modern market. When the fleet is in, trawlers encircled by flocks of raucous gulls choke the harbour, and the pubs, among the liveliest on the west coast, host bouts of serious drinking.

If you're waiting for a ferry or a train, you could fill in some time at **Mallaig Marine World**, north of the train station near the harbour (June–Sept Mon–Sat 9am–9pm, Sun 10am–6pm; Oct–May 9am–5pm, Sun 11am–5pm; £2.75), where tanks of sea creatures share space with informative exhibits about the port. Alongside the train station, the **Mallaig Heritage Centre** (May–Sept Mon–Sat 9.30am–5pm, Sun 1–5pm, £1.80), displaying old photographs of the town and its environs, is worth a browse. In addition, there are a couple of enjoyable **walks** around the town. The trail to **Mallaigmore**, a small cove with a white-sand beach and isolated croft, begins at the top of the harbour on East Bay; follow the road north past the tourist office and turn off right when you see the signpost between two houses. The round trip takes about an hour.

The stretch of coast **north of Mallaig** encompasses the lonely **Knoydart** and **Glenelg peninsulas**, two of Britain's last true wilderness areas, as it heads towards **Kyle of Lochalsh**, the main departure point for Skye. This whole region is also popular with Munro baggers, harbouring a string of summits over 3000ft. The famous Five Sisters massif and Kintail Ridge, flanking the A87 a short way south of Kyle, offer some of the Highlands' most challenging **hikes** and are easily accessible by road.

Practicalities

Mallaig is a compact place, concentrated around the harbour, where you'll find the **tourist office** (Mon–Sat 9am–8pm, Sun 10am–5pm; ☎01687/462170) – which will book accommodation for you – and the **bus** and **train stations**. The CalMac ticket office (☎01687/462403), serving passengers for Skye and the Small Isles, is also nearby, and you can arrange transport to Knoydart by telephoning Bruce Watt Cruises (☎01687/462320 or 462233), whose thrice-weekly boat to Inverie (Mon, Wed & Fri) continues east along Loch Nevis to Tarbet; the loch is sheltered, so crossings are rarely cancelled. Mr Watt also operates cruises (mid-May to mid-Sept) across to Rum and Canna on Tuesdays (10.30am) and to Loch Scavaig on Skye (see p.334) on Thursdays (11am).

There are plenty of places **to stay**; the *West Highland Hotel* (☎01687/462210; ⑤) is pleasantly old-fashioned, if a little shabby in places, and some rooms have excellent sea views, while the *Marine* (☎01687/462217; ⑥) is much smarter inside than first views suggest. For **B&B**, head around the harbour to East Bay, where you'll find the immaculate *Western Isles Guest House* (☎01687/462320; ③), with the nearby *Quarterdeck* (☎01687/462604; ③) a good alternative. Budget travellers should head for *Sheena's Backpackers' Lodge* (☎01687/462764), a refreshingly laid-back independent hostel overlooking the harbour, with mixed dorms, self-catering facilities and a sitting room. For **eating**, the *Marine Hotel* serves good-value bar meals featuring fresh seafood which are well above average, while the nearby *Seafood Restaurant* (also known as the *Cabin*) has a more ambitious menu but it's popular, so booking is wise.

The Knoydart peninsula

To get to the heart of the **Knoydart peninsula**, you have to catch a fishing boat from Mallaig or Glenelg, or else hike for a couple of days across rugged moorland and mountains and sleep rough in old stone bothies (most of which are marked on Ordnance Survey maps). Either way, you'll soon appreciate why many regard this as Britain's most dramatic and unspoilt wilderness area. Flanked by Loch Nevis ("Loch of

Heaven") in the south and the fjord-like inlet of Loch Hourn ("Loch of Hell") to the north, Knoydart's nobbly green peaks (three of them Munros) sweep straight out of the sea, shrouded for much of the time in a pall of grey mist. Unsurprisingly, the peninsula tends to attract walkers, lured by the network of well-maintained **trails** that wind east into the wild interior, where Bonnie Prince Charlie is rumoured to have hidden out after Culloden.

At the end of the eighteenth century, around a thousand people eked out a living from this inhospitable terrain through crofting and fishing. Evictions in 1853 began a dramatic decrease in the population and now Knoydart supports around seventy people, most of whom live in the tiny hamlet of **INVERIE**. Nestled beside a sheltered bay on the south side of the peninsula, it has a pint-sized post office, a shop and mainland Britain's most remote pub, *The Old Forge*.

Practicalities

Bruce Watt Cruises' boat chugs into Inverie from Mallaig (Mon, Wed & Fri 10.15am & 2.15pm; ☎01687/462320 or 462233). To arrange for a boat crossing from Arnisdale on Loch Hourn, contact Len Morrison (☎01599/522352) or Mr MacTavish (☎01599/522211); it costs between £8 and £25 depending on passenger numbers.

There are two main hiking routes into Knoydart: the trailhead for the first is Kinloch Hourn, a crofting hamlet at the far east end of Loch Hourn which you can get to by road (turn south off the A87 six miles west of Invergarry), from where a well-marked path winds around the coast to Barrisdale and on to Inverie; you can also pick up this trail by taking a boat from Arnisdale, on the north shore of Loch Hourn. The second path into Knoydart starts at the west side of Loch Arkaig, approaching the peninsula via Glen Dessary. These are both long hard slogs over rough, desolate country, so take wet-weather gear, plenty of food, warm clothes and a good sleeping bag, and leave your name and expected time of arrival with someone when you set off.

Most of Knoydart's **accommodation** is concentrated in and around Inverie. *Torrie Shieling* (☎01687/462669; £13 per person per night), an upmarket independent **hostel** located three-quarters of a mile east of the village on the side of the mountain, is popular with hikers and families, offering top-notch self-catering facilities, comfy wooden beds in four-person rooms, and superb views across the bay. They also have a landrover and boat for ferrying guests around the peninsula, and to neighbouring lochs and islands. The Knoydart Estate runs a cheaper, but rather grubby **bunkhouse** (☎01687/462331), in addition to the posh *Inverie House* (☎01687/462331; ⑦), where you can sleep in four-posters within staggering distance of the pub. In Inverie village itself, *Pier House* (☎01687/462347; ③, including dinner ⑥), a pleasant **B&B**, serves à la carte evening meals to non-residents (three courses for £15.20). If you want total isolation and all the creature comforts, though, book into the beautiful *Doune Stone Lodges* (☎01687/462667; ⑦ includes dinner), on the remote north side of the peninsula. Rebuilt from ruined crofts, this place has pine-fitted en-suite double rooms right on the shore, near the ruins of an ancient Pictish fort. They'll pick you up by boat from Mallaig if you book ahead. Most visitors eat at **Pier House** while in Knoydart; alternatively try the *Old Forge's* generous bar meals, served indoors beside an open fire.

The Glenelg peninsula

Further north, the **Glenelg peninsula**, jutting out into the Sound of Sleat, is the isolated and little-known crofting area featured in **Gavin Maxwell's** otter novel, *Ring of Bright Water*. Maxwell disguised the identity of this pristine stretch of coast by calling it "Camusfearnà", and it has remained a tranquil backwater in spite of the traffic that trickles through during the summer for the Kylerhea ferry to Skye. You can also approach the peninsula from the east by turning off the fast A87 at Shiel Bridge on Loch

Duich, from where a narrow single-track road climbs a tortuous series of switchbacks to the Mam Ratagan Pass (1115ft), affording spectacular views over the awesome Five Sisters massif. Following the route of an old military highway and drovers' trail, the road, covered each morning by the postbus from Kyle (departs 9.45am), drops down the other side through Glen More, with the magnificent Kintail Ridge visible to the southeast, towards the peninsula's main settlement, **GLENELG**, strewn along a pebbly bay on the Sound of Sleat. A row of little whitewashed houses surrounded by trees, the village is dominated by the rambling, weed-choked ruins of Fort Bernera, an eighteenth-century garrison for English government troops, but now little more than a shell. The *Glenelg Inn* (☎01599/522273; ④) has luxurious, cosy rooms overlooking the bay and an excellent à la carte restaurant, which also serves cream teas, cakes and quality coffee during the day.

The six-car **Glenelg–Kylerhea ferry** (April–Oct frequent; 5min; for more details call ☎01599/511305) shuttles across the Sound of Sleat from a jetty northwest of the village. In former times, this choppy channel used to be an important drovers' crossing: 8000 cattle each year were herded head to tail across from Skye to the mainland.

One and a half miles south of Glenelg village, a left turn up Glen Beag leads to the **Glenelg Brochs**, some of the best-preserved Iron Age monuments in the country. Standing in a sheltered stream valley, the circular towers – Dun Telve and Dun Troddan – are thought to have been erected around 2000 years ago to protect the surrounding settlements from raiders. About a third of each main structure remains with the curving drystone walls and internal passages still impressively intact.

A narrow backroad snakes its way southwest beyond Glenelg village through a scattering of old crofting hamlets and timber forests. The views across the Sound of Sleat to Knoydart grow more spectacular at each bend, reaching a high point at a windy pass that takes in a vast sweep of sea, loch and islands. Below the road at **Sandaig**, is where Gavin Maxwell and his otters lived in the 1950s: the site of his house is now marked by a cairn. Swinging east, the road winds down to the waterside again, following the north shore of Loch Hourn as far as **ARNISDALE**, departure point for the boat to Knoydart (see p.457). Arnisdale is made up of the two hamlets of **CAMUSBANE** and **CORRAN**, the former consisting of a single row of old cottages ranged behind a long pebble beach, with a massive scree slope behind, while the latter, a mile along the road, is a minuscule whitewashed fishing hamlet at the water's edge. Aside from the arrival of electricity and a red telephone box, the only major addition to this gorgeous hamlet in the last hundred years has been Mrs Nash's homely **B&B** (☎01599/522336; ②) and tea hut, where you can enjoy hot drinks and home-baked cake in a "shell garden", with breathtaking views on all sides. You can get to Arnisdale and Corran on the **postbus** from Kyle of Lochalsh (daily 9.45am; 3hr 40min; the return bus leaves Corran at 7am).

Loch Duich

Skirted on its northern shore by the A87, **Loch Duich**, the boot-shaped inlet that forms the northern shoreline of the Glenelg peninsula, features prominently on the tourist trail, with buses from all over Europe thundering down the 16 miles from **SHIEL BRIDGE** to Kyle of Lochalsh on their way to Skye. The most dramatic approach to the loch, however, is from the east through Glen Shiel, where the mountains known as the Five Sisters of Kintail surge up to heights of 3000ft – a familiar sight from countless tourist brochures, but an impressive one nonetheless. With steep-sided hills hemming in both sides of the loch, it's sometimes hard to remember that this is, in fact, the sea. There's a congenial *SYHA* **youth hostel** just outside Shiel Bridge at **RATAGAN** (☎01599/511243; March–Oct), popular with walkers newly arrived off the Glen Affric trek from Cannich (see p.440).

HIKING IN GLEN SHIEL

Ordnance Survey Map No. 33.

The mountains of **Glen Shiel**, sweeping southeast from Loch Duich, offer some of the best hiking routes in Scotland. Rising dramatically from sea level to over 3000ft in less than a couple of miles, they are also exposed to the worst of the west coast's notoriously fickle weather. Don't underestimate either of these two routes. Tracing the paths on a map, they can appear deceptively short and easy to follow; however, unwary walkers die here every year, often because they failed to allow enough time to get off the mountain by nightfall, or because of a sudden change in the weather. Neither of the routes outlined below should be attempted by inexperienced walkers, nor without a map, a compass and a detailed trekking guide – the SMC's *Hill Walks in Northwest Scotland* is recommended. Also make sure to follow the usual safety precautions outlined on p.421.

Taking in a bumper crop of Munros, the **Five Sisters traverse** is deservedly the most popular trek in the area. Allow a full day to complete the whole route, which begins at the first fire break on the left-hand side as you head southeast down the glen on the A87. Strike straight up from here and follow the ridge north along to Scurr na Moraich (2874ft), dropping down the other side to Morvich on the valley floor.

The distinctive chain of mountains across the glen from the Five Sisters is the **Kintail Ridge**, crossed by another famous hiking route that begins at the *Cluanie Inn* on the A87. From here, follow the well-worn path south around the base of the mountain until it meets up with a stalkers' trail, which winds steeply up Creag a' Mhaim (3108ft) and then west along the ridgeway, with breathtaking views south across Knoydart and the Hebridean Sea.

Eilean Donan Castle

After Edinburgh's hilltop fortress, **Eilean Donan Castle** (April–Oct daily 9am–5pm; £3), ten miles north of Shiel Bridge on the A87, has to be Scotland's most photographed monument. Presiding over the once strategically important confluence of lochs Alsh, Long and Duich, the forbidding crenellated tower rises from the water's edge, joined to the shore by a narrow stone bridge and with sheer mountains as a backdrop.

The original castle was established in 1230 by Alexander II to protect the area from the Vikings. Later, during a Jacobite uprising in 1719, it was occupied by troops dispatched by the King of Spain to help the **"Old Pretender"**, James Stuart. However, when King George heard of their whereabouts, he sent frigates to weed the Spaniards out, and the castle was blown up with their stocks of gunpowder. Thereafter, it lay in ruins until John Macrae-Gilstrap had it rebuilt between 1912 and 1932. Eilean Donan has also been the setting of several major **movies**, including *Highlander*, starring Christopher Lambert (large numbers of film stills are sold at the ticket office). Only the banqueting hall, the bedrooms and the troops' quarters are open to the public, with various Jacobite and clan relics also on display, though the large numbers of people passing through make it hard to appreciate them.

There are several **B&Bs** less than a mile away in the hamlet of **DORNIE**, including the delightful *Cuileann Cottage* (☎01599/555224; ③), a simple place surrounded by flowers and driftwood. The *Dornie Hotel*, Francis Street (☎01599/555205; ④), boasts comfortable rooms, while the *Loch Duich Hotel* (☎01599/555213; ⑤), has splendid doubles overlooking the loch and a small restaurant serving upmarket bar snacks and evening meals. Another good place for a bar meal is the popular *Clachan*, just along from the *Dornie Hotel*.

Kyle of Lochalsh to Scoraig peninsula

KYLE OF LOCHALSH, seven miles northeast of Eilean Donan Castle, is a busy town – a transit point on the route to Skye and an important train terminal. Straggling down the hill towards the pier and train station, it's not particularly attractive – concrete buildings, rail junk and myriad signs of the fishing industry abound – and is ideally somewhere to pass through rather than linger. Since the **Skye road bridge** was opened in 1995, the traffic rumbles freely over the channel a mile north of town, bypassing Kyle completely, leaving its shopkeepers bereft of the passing trade they used to enjoy. The new bridge, built with private sector money, has also sparked controversy over its high tolls (£5.40 for cars), with local protesters doing battle in Dingwall Sheriff Court and Edinburgh's Court of Session.

Practicalities

Buses run to the harbour in Kyle of Lochalsh from Glasgow via Fort William and Invergarry (3 daily; 5hr 30min–6hr 15min), and from Inverness via Invermoriston (4 daily; 2hr); there's also a summer service from Edinburgh (1 daily; 7hr 15min). These routes can become very crowded, so it's wise to book in advance (☎0990/505050). All these services continue at least as far as Portree, on Skye, and a shuttle service runs across the bridge to Kyleakin every thirty minutes or so. Three or four **trains** run daily, with one or two on summer Sundays, from Inverness (2hr 30min). Curving north through Achnasheen and Glen Carron, the train line is a rail enthusiast's dream, even if scenically it doesn't quite match the West Highland line to Mallaig.

The **tourist office** (April, May & mid-Sept to late Oct Mon–Sat 9.30am–5.30pm; June to mid-July & late Aug to mid-Sept Mon–Sat 9.30am–7pm; mid-July to late Aug Mon–Sat 9.30am–9pm, Sun 12.30–4.30pm; ☎01599/534276), on top of the small hill near the old ferry jetty, will book accommodation for you, which is useful as there are surprisingly few places to stay, particularly in high summer. If you're feeling flush, splash out at the *Lochalsh Hotel* (☎01599/534202; ⑨), a wonderfully located place looking out at Skye, with fabulous seafood and an air of dated luxury. For **B&B**, try Mrs Finlayson, on Main Street (☎01599/534265; ③), ten minutes' walk up the hill from the train station, or *Crowlin View* (☎01599/534286; ③), a traditional house with views to Skye, one and a half miles north of Kyle on the Plockton road. Between Kyle and Plockton, *The Old Schoolhouse* at Erbusaig (☎01599/534369; ⑤) is a good restaurant with comfortable rooms. The *Seagreen Restaurant*, also on the Plockton road on the edge of Kyle of Lochalsh, has good, moderately priced, fresh seafood and vegetarian meals, while the *Seafood Restaurant* at the train station is also recommended, if a little pricier.

Plockton

A fifteen-minute train ride north of Kyle at the seaward end of islet-studded Loch Carron lies the unbelievably picturesque **PLOCKTON**: a chocolate-box row of neatly painted cottages ranged around the curve of a tiny harbour and backed by a craggy landscape of heather and pine. Originally known as Am Ploc, the settlement was a crofting hamlet until the end of the eighteenth century, when a local laird transformed it into a prosperous fishery, renaming it "Plocktown". Its fifteen minutes of fame came in the mid-1990s, when the BBC chose the village as the setting for three series of the television drama *Hamish Macbeth*. Though the resulting spin-off has quietened down a little, in high season it's still packed full of tourists, yachtsmen and second-home owners. The unique brilliance of Plockton's light has also made it something of an artists' hangout, and during the summer the waterfront, with its row of shaggy palm trees, even shaggier Highland cattle, flower gardens and pleasure boats, is invariably punctuated by painters dabbing at their easels.

If you want **to stay**, the friendly, cosy *Haven Hotel,* on Innes Street (☎01599/544223; ⑦), is renowned for its excellent food, while the family-run *Creag-nan-Daroch Hotel*, also on Innes Street (☎01599/544222; ④), makes an informal and comfortable alternative. The *Plockton Hotel*, Harbour Street (☎01599/544274; ⑤), overlooking the harbour with some rooms in a nearby cottage, has a friendly bar and serves good seafood. Of the fifteen or so **B&Bs**, *The Shieling* (☎01599/544282; ③) has a great location on a tiny headland at the top of the harbour, while *The Manse* on Innes Street (☎01599/544442; ③) features beautifully furnished rooms and serves generous breakfasts. An interesting **self-catering** option is to stay at the *Craig Rare Breeds Farm*, midway between Plockton and Stromeferry, where you can rub shoulders with ancient breeds of Scottish farm animals, llamas and peacocks; ask for one of the cottages on the beach (one sleeps two, £235 per week; the other sleeps four to six; £360 per week, ☎01599/544205).

The top place **to eat** is the *Haven's* restaurant, whose gourmet food is in a league of its own, while *Off the Rails*, in the train station, serves good-value, imaginative snacks by day and dinner in the evening. *The Buttery*, part of Plockton Stores on the seafront, is also open all day for snacks and inexpensive meals. All the hotels, of course, are happy to feed non-residents. For **fishing** or **seal-spotting** boat trips from Plockton, try Leisure Marine (☎01599/544306) or Sea Trek Marine (☎01599/544356).

The Applecross peninsula

The most dramatic approach to the **Applecross peninsula** (the English-sounding name is actually a corruption of the Gaelic *Apor Crosan*, meaning "estuary") is from the south, along the infamous **Bealach na Ba** (literally "Pass of the Cattle"). Crossing the forbidding hills behind Kishorn and rising to 2053ft, with a gradient and switchback bends worthy of the Alps, this route, the highest road in Scotland and a popular cycling piste, is hair-raising in places, but the panoramic views across the Minch to Raasay and Skye more than compensate. The other way in is from the north: a beautiful coast road that meanders slowly from Shieldaig on Loch Torridon, with tantalizing glimpses of the Cuillins to the south.

The sheltered, fertile coast around **APPLECROSS** village, where the Irish missionary monk Maelrhuba founded a monastery in 673 AD, comes as a surprise after the bleakness of the moorland approach. It's an idyllic place: you can wander along lanes banked with wild iris and orchids, and explore beaches and rock pools on the shore. It's also quite an adventure to get here by **public transport**. The nearest railhead is seventeen miles northeast at Strathcarron Station, near Achnasheen, which you have to reach by 9.50am to catch the postbus to Shieldaig, on Loch Torridon. From here, a second postie leaves for Applecross at 11.30am (90min). No buses of any kind run over the Bealach na Ba. The old *Applecross Inn* (☎01520/744262; ④), right beside the sea, serves sandwiches and great seafood. Three friendly **B&Bs** lie south of here towards Toscaig, with its pier and inquisitive seals: try Mrs Thompson (☎01520/744260; ②) at Camusteel, Mrs Dickens (☎01520/744206; ③) at Camusterrach, or John Pearson (☎01520/744272; ③), whose cottage at Upper Toscaig is basic but traditional. There's also **camping** at the *Flowertunnel Restaurant*, off the road to the pass, which sells cakes and freshly baked bread.

Loch Torridon

Loch Torridon marks the northern boundary of the Applecross peninsula, its awe-inspiring setting backed by the appealingly rugged mountains of **Liathach** and **Beinn Eighe**, tipped by streaks of white quartzite. The greater part of this area is composed of the reddish 750-million-year-old Torridonian sandstone. The road which runs along the northern shore of the loch from **TORRIDON** village is scenic and dramatic, winding first along the shore then climbing and twisting past lochans, cliffs and gorges to the green wooded slopes of **DIABAIG**. There's a modern **youth hostel** at Torridon (☎01445/791284; Feb–Oct, Christmas & New Year), and one of the area's top hotels, the rambling Victorian *Loch Torridon Hotel* (☎01445/791242; ⑦), set amid well-tended

WALKING AROUND TORRIDON

Ordnance Survey Outdoor Leisure map No. 8.

There are difficult and unexpected conditions on virtually all hiking routes around Torridon, and the weather can change very rapidly. If you're relatively inexperienced but want to do the magnificent ridge walk along the **Liathach** (pronounced "*Lee*-a-gach", or "*Lee*-ach") massif, or the strenuous traverse of **Beinn Eighe** (pronounced "Ben *Ay*"), join a guided hike (details from the Ranger Service on ☎01445/791221).

For those confident to go it alone (using the above map), one of many possible routes takes you behind Liathach and down the pass, Coire Dubh, to the main road in Glen Torridon. This is a great, straightforward walk if you're properly equipped (see p.421), covering thirteen miles and taking in superb landscapes. Allow yourself the whole day. Start at the stone bridge on the Diabaig road along the north side of Loch Torridon. Follow the Abhainn Coire Mhic Nobuil burn up to the fork at the wooden bridge and take the track east to the pass (a rather indistinct watershed) between Liathach and Beinn Eighe. The path becomes a little lost in the boggy area studded with lochans at the top of the pass, but the route is clear and, once over the watershed, the path is easy to follow. At this point you can, weather permitting, make the rewarding diversion up to the Coire Mhic Fhearchair, widely regarded as the most spectacular corrie in Scotland; otherwise continue down the Coire Dubh stream, ford the burn and follow its west bank down to the Torridon road, from where it's about four miles back to Loch Torridon.

A rewarding walk even in rough weather is the seven-mile hike up the coast from **Lower Diabaig**, ten miles northwest of Torridon village, to **Redpoint**. On a clear day, the views across to Raasay and Applecross from this gentle undulating path are superlative, but you'll have to return along the same trail, or else make your way back via Loch Maree on the A832. If you're staying in Shieldaig, the track that winds up the peninsula running north from the village makes a pleasant ninety-minute round walk.

loch-side grounds. Also in Diabaig, Miss Ross (☎01445/790240; ②) has comfortable accommodation overlooking the rocky bay, and there's a good B&B, *Tigh Fada* (☎01520/755248; ②) at **DOIREANOR**, on the southwest side of Loch Shieldaig.

Loch Maree

About eight miles north of Loch Torridon, **Loch Maree**, dotted with Caledonian pine-covered islands, is one of the west's scenic highlights, best viewed from the road (A832) that drops down to its southeastern tip through Glen Docherty. It's also surrounded by some of Scotland's finest deerstalking country: the remote, privately owned Letterewe Lodge on the north shore, accessible only by helicopter or boat, lies at the heart of a famous deer forest. **Queen Victoria** stayed a few days here in 1877 at the *Loch Maree Hotel* (☎01445/791288; ⑥), which is comfortable and less formal than in her day.

The A832 skirts the southern shore of Loch Maree, passing the **Beinn Eighe Nature Reserve**, the UK's oldest wildlife sanctuary. Parts of the Beinn Eighe reserve are forested with Caledonian pinewood, which once covered the whole of the country, and it houses pine marten, wildcat, fox, badger, Scottish crossbill, buzzards and golden eagles. There's also a wide range of flora, with the higher rocky slopes producing spectacular natural alpine rock gardens. A mile north of Kinlochewe, the **Beinn Eighe Visitor Centre** (Easter & May–Sept daily 10am–5pm) on the A832, gives details of the area's rare species and sells pamphlets describing two excellent **walks** in the reserve: a woodland trail through loch-side forest, and a more strenuous half-day hike around the base of Beinn Eighe. Both start from the car park a mile north of the visitor centre.

Gairloch

Mostly scattered around the sheltered northeastern shore of the loch of the same name, the crofting township of **GAIRLOCH** thrives during the summer as a low-key holiday resort with several tempting sandy beaches and some excellent coastal walks within easy reach. The **Gairloch Heritage Museum** (April, May & Oct Mon–Sat 11am–4pm; June–Sept Mon–Sat 9.30am–5pm, Sun 1–5pm; for winter times phone ☎01687/462085) has eclectic, appealing displays covering geology, archeology, fishing and farming that range from a mock-up of a croft house to an early knitting machine. Probably the most interesting section is the archive – an array of photographs, maps, genealogies, lists of place names and taped recollections, mostly in Gaelic – made by elderly locals.

The area's real attraction, however, is its beautiful **coastline**. To get to one of the most impressive stretches, head around the north side of the bay and follow the single-track B8021 beyond Big Sand (a cleaner and quieter beach than the one in Gairloch) to the tiny crofting hamlet of **Melvaig** (reachable by the 9.05am Gairloch postbus), from where a narrow surfaced track winds out to **Rubha Reidh** (pronounced "Roo-a *Ree*") Point. The converted **lighthouse** here, which looks straight out to Harris in the Outer Hebrides, serves slap-up afternoon teas and home-baked cakes (Tues, Thurs & Sun noon–5pm). You can also stay in its comfortable and relaxed **bunkhouse**, or **double rooms** (book ahead in high season on ☎01445/771263; ②); if you phone ahead, you can be picked up from Gairloch for £4 return. Around the headland from Rubha Reidh lies the secluded and beautiful **Camas Mor** beach. For a great half-day walk, follow the marked footpath inland (southeast) from here along the base of a sheer scarp slope, and past a string of lochans, ruined crofts and a remote wood to Midtown on the east side of the peninsula, five miles north of Poolewe on the B8057. However, unless you leave a car at the end of the trail or arrange to be picked up, you'll have to walk or hitch back to Gairloch, as the only transport along this road is an early-morning post van.

A more leisurely way to explore the coast is on a wildlife-spotting cruise: Sail Gairloch departs (10am, 2pm & 5pm) from the Shieldaig mooring, five miles south of Gairloch, and heads off across the bay in search of dolphins, porpoises, seals and even the odd whale. You can also rent a boat for the day through Gairloch's chandlery shop (☎01445/712458) – popular with sea anglers.

Badachro and beyond

Three miles south of Gairloch, a narrow single-track lane (built with the Destitution Funds raised during the nineteenth-century potato famine) winds west from the main A832, past wooded coves and inlets on its way south of the loch to **BADACHRO**, a sleepy former fishing village in a very attractive setting.

Beyond Badachro, the road winds for five more miles along the shore to **Redpoint**, a minuscule hamlet with beautiful beaches of peach-coloured sand and great views to Raasay, Skye and the Western Isles. It also marks the trailhead for the wonderful coast walk to Lower Diabaig, described on p.463. Even if you don't fancy a full-blown hike, follow the path a mile or so to the exquisite beach hidden on the south side of the headland, which you'll probably have all to yourself. Redpoint is served by the Gairloch postbus (see below).

Gairloch practicalities

There's a late afternoon bus (Mon–Sat) from Inverness to **Gairloch**, though the route and arrival time varies. Without your own transport, you'll have to depend upon postbuses to get around once there. Two services (one for each side of the loch) leave from in front of the post office: one at 9.05am for Melvaig, and the other at 11.20am for Redpoint.

There's a good choice of **accommodation** in Gairloch, most of it mid-range; the central **tourist office** (Jan–March, Nov & Dec Mon–Thurs 9am–12.30pm & 1–5pm, Fri 9am–12.30pm & 1–4.30pm; April & May, Sept–Oct Mon–Sat 9am–5.30pm, Sun 1–6pm; June–Aug Mon–Fri 9am–6pm, Sat 10am–6pm, Sun 1–6pm; ☎01445/712130) will help if you have problems finding a vacancy. If you're looking for a **hotel**, try the family-run *Myrtle Bank Hotel* (☎01445/712214; ⑧), which has a good restaurant and is just above the loch. **B&Bs** are scattered throughout the area. In the village, options include the bright and pleasant *Newton Cottage* (☎01445/712007; ③), a little way up Mihol Road, and the friendly *Bains House* (☎01445/712472; ③), on the main street near the bus stop. A few hundred yards north on the Melvaig road, Gaelic-speaking Miss Mackenzie's *Duisary* (☎01445/712252; ③) is a good choice. Continuing towards Melvaig for about five miles, a little past the North Erradale junction, *Little Lodge* (☎01445/771237; ⑨ includes dinner) is outstanding, with immaculately furnished rooms, a log-burning stove, cashmere goats and dramatic sea views, as well as superb food. At Badachro, the recently built *Lochside* (☎01445/741295; ③) is spacious with a great view over the harbour and the Torridons. For **hostel** accommodation, there's a pleasant *SYHA* place at **Carn Dearg** two miles up the Melvaig road (☎01445/712219; mid-May to Sept), and **camping** is possible nearby at Big Sand or at Redpoint.

For **food**, *Myrtle Bank's* restaurant serves good meals at reasonable prices, while the child-friendly *Gairloch Sands Pizza Bar*, in the *Gairloch Sands Hotel* (a 5min walk round the bay from the tourist office), dishes up burgers and full-on American breakfasts with all the trimmings, as well as home-baked pizza. Inexpensive pasta and pricier seafood and meat are on offer at *Gino's* in the *Millcroft Hotel*, though service can be slow. For **snacks**, the *Conservatory Coffee Shop*, up the lane off the square, is a good bet, while *The Old Inn*, opposite the harbour, is a good real-ale **pub**.

Poolewe

It's a fifteen-minute hop by bus over the headland from Gairloch to the trim little village of **POOLEWE** on the sheltered south side of Loch Ewe, at the mouth of the River Ewe as it rushes down from Loch Maree. One of the area's best **walks** begins near here, signposted from the lay-by-cum-viewpoint on the main A832, a mile south of the village. It takes a couple of hours to follow the easy trail across open craggy moorland to the shores of Loch Maree, and thence to the car park at **Slatterdale**, seven miles southeast of Gairloch. If you reach Slatterdale just before 7pm on a Tuesday, Thursday or Friday, you should be able to pick up the Westerbus from Inverness back to Poolewe or Aultbea (confirm times on ☎01445/712255). Also worthwhile is the drive along the small sideroad running along the west shore of Loch Ewe to **COVE**. Here you'll find an atmospheric cave that was used by the "Wee Frees" as a church into this century; it's quite a perilous scramble up, however, and there's little to see once there. The route is also covered by a Poolewe **postbus** (1.55pm).

If you want **to stay** in the area, try the *Poolewe Hotel* (☎01445/781241; ⑤), on the Cove road; it's old-fashioned but very pleasant and serves straightforward but competent food. For **B&B** in Poolewe itself, *The Creagan* (☎01445/781424; ②), up the track on the village side of the campsite, is a welcoming modern house wreathed with honeysuckle. Up the Cove road, four miles north at **Inverasdale**, *Bruach Ard* (☎01445/781214; ③) has mostly en-suite rooms and great views to Assynt. At Cove, Mrs MacDonald (☎01445/781354; ④; April–Oct) offers upscale B&B with fine loch views. There's also an excellent NTS **campsite** between the village and Inverewe Gardens (☎01445/781229; April–Oct). The *Bridge Cottage Café*, just up the Cove road from the village crossroads, serves good coffee and home-baked cakes during the summer.

Inverewe Gardens

Half a mile across the bay from Poolewe on the A832, **Inverewe Gardens** (daily: Mid-March to Oct 9.30am–9pm; Nov to mid-March 9.30am–5pm; NTS; £4.50), a verdant oasis of foliage and riotously colourful flower collections, form a vivid contrast with the wild, heathery crags of the adjoining coast. They were the brainchild of the late **Osgood Mackenzie**, who inherited the surrounding 12,000-acre estate from his stepfather, the laird of Gairloch, in 1862. Taking advantage of the area's famously temperate climate (a consequence of the Gulf Stream, which draws a warm water current from Mexico to within a stone's throw of these shores), Mackenzie collected plants from all over the world for his walled garden, still the nucleus of the complex. Protected from Loch Ewe's corrosive salt breezes by a dense brake of Scots pine, rowan, oak, beech and birch trees, the fragile plants flourished on rich soil, brought here as ballast on Irish ships to overlay the previously infertile beach gravel and sea grass. By the time Mackenzie died in 1922, his garden sprawled over the whole peninsula, surrounded by 100 acres of woodland. Today the NTS strives to develop the place along the lines envisaged by its founder.

Around 180,000 visitors each year pour through here, but they are easily absorbed. Interconnected by a labyrinthine network of twisting paths and walkways, more than a dozen gardens feature exotic plant collections from as far afield as Chile, China, Tasmania and the Himalayas. Strolling around the lotus ponds, palm trees, and borders ablaze with exotic blooms, it's amazing to think you're at the same latitude as Hudson's Bay. Mid-May to mid-June is the best time to see the rhododendrons and azaleas, while the herbaceous garden reaches its peak in July and August, as does the wonderful Victorian vegetable and flower garden beside the sea. Look out, too, for the grand old eucalyptus in the Peace Plot, which is the largest in the northern hemisphere, and the nearby Ghost Tree (*Davidia involucrata*), representing the earliest evolutionary stages of flowering trees. You'll need at least a couple of hours to do the whole lot justice, and leave time for the **visitor centre** (mid-March to Oct daily 9.30am–5.30pm), which houses an informative display on the history of the garden. Guided walks (April–Oct Mon–Fri) leave from here every weekday at 1.30pm. The **restaurant** at the top of the car park does good snacks and lunches.

Gruinard Bay and the Scoraig peninsula

Three buses each week (Mon, Wed & Sat; eastwards in the morning, westwards in the evening) run the twenty-mile stretch along the A832 from Poolewe past **Aultbea**, a small NATO naval base, to the head of **Little Loch Broom**, surrounded by a salt marsh that is covered with flowers in early summer. From **Laide**, the road skirts the shores of **Gruinard Bay**, offering fabulous views and, at the inner end of the bay, some excellent sandy beaches. During World War II, **Gruinard Island**, in the bay, was used as a testing ground for biological warfare, and for years was ringed by huge signs warning the public not to land. The anthrax spores released during the testing can live in the soil for up to a thousand years, but in 1987, after much protest, the Ministry of Defence had the island decontaminated and it was finally declared "safe" in 1990.

The road heads inland before joining the A835 at **Braemore Junction** (three Inverness–Ullapool buses stop here daily) above the head of **Loch Broom**. Just nearby, and easily accessible from the A835, is the spectacular 164ft **Falls of Measach**, which plunge through the mile-long **Corrieshalloch Gorge**. You can overlook the cascades from a special observation platform, or from the impressive suspension bridge that spans the chasm, whose 197ft vertical sides are draped in a rich array of plant life, with thickets of wych elm, goat willow and bird cherry miraculously thriving on the cliffs. North from the head of Loch Broom to Ullapool is one of the so-called **Destitution Roads**, built to give employment to local people during the nineteenth-century potato famines.

DONALD M.T. REID

Three Sisters, Glencoe

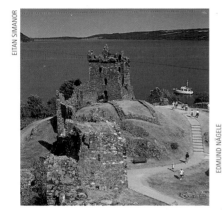

EITAN SIMANOR

Urquhart Castle, Loch Ness

EITAN SIMANOR

"Nessie"

EDMUND NÄGELE

EDMUND NÄGELE

Eilean Donan Castle, Loch Duich

Dunnottar Castle, Aberdeenshire

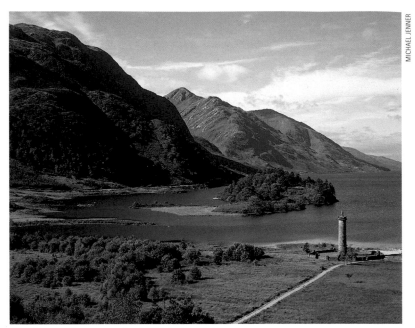

Glenfinnan Monument, Loch Shiel, the Highlands

Winter in the Cairngorms

Aberdeen Castlegate and Mercat Cross

Loch Duich

Puffins, Shetland

Traditional Highland dress

Eshaness, Shetland

Highland cow

Old Man of Hoy, Orkney

Hotels along here include the excellent *Old Smiddy* (☎01445/731425; ④, with dinner ⑧) on the main road in Laide, on the western shore of Guinard Bay and linked with Braemore and Achnasheen on the Kyle of Lochalsh railway by postbus. Crammed with travel trophies, family memorabilia, books and paintings by local artists (some on sale), the hotel has fine mountain views to the east, and serves outstanding food. Another option is *Cul-na-Mara* (☎01445/731295; ③), up the turning just past the *Ocean View Hotel*. At the head of Little Loch Broom, the *Dundonnell Hotel* (☎01854/612366; ⑨) is smart and comfortable and serves bar meals, while *Sail Mhor Croft* (☎01854/633224) is a small independent hostel in a lovely location on the loch-side at **Dundonnell**.

The Scoraig peninsula

The outer part of the rugged **Scoraig peninsula**, dividing Little Loch Broom and Loch Broom, is one of the remotest places on the British mainland, accessible only by boat or on foot. Formerly dotted with crofting townships, it is now deserted apart from tiny **SCORAIG** village, where a mostly self-sufficient community has established itself, complete with windmills, organic vegetable gardens and a thriving primary school. Understandably, Scoraig's inhabitants would rather not be regarded as tourist curiosities, so only venture out here if you're sympathetic to such a community. To reach **Scoraig**, you have three main options: you can drive to Badrallach and walk from there, catch the occasional ferry from Ullapool to the *Altnaharrie Hotel* (see p.468) then walk or phone the Scoraig **boat** operator (☎01854/633226), who serves the area two days a week. Accommodation on the Scoraig peninsula is limited to a small and particularly pleasant **campsite** at Badrallach, on the northeast shore of Little Loch Broom; there's also a good bothy available if you've an airbed or sleeping mat (☎01854/633281).

Ullapool

ULLAPOOL, the northwest's principal centre of population, was founded at the height of the herring boom in 1788 by the **British Fisheries Society**, on a sheltered arm of land jutting into Loch Broom. The grid-plan town is still an important fishing centre, though the ferry link to Stornoway on Lewis (see p.345) means that in high season its personality is practically swamped by visitors. Even so, it's still a hugely appealing place and a good base for exploring the northwest Highlands – especially if you are relying on public transport. Regular **buses** run from here to Inverness, Durness and (from May to early Oct) to the railhead at Lairg. Accommodation is plentiful and Ullapool is an obvious hideaway if the weather is bad, with cosy pubs, a new swimming pool and an arts centre, *The Ceilidh Place*.

Arrival and information

Forming the backbone of its grid plan, Ullapool's two main arteries are the loch-side **Shore Street** and, parallel to it, **Argyle Street**, further inland. **Buses** stop at the pier, in the town centre near the ferry dock, from where it's easy to get your bearings. The well-run **tourist office** (Easter–June & Sept–Nov Mon–Fri 9am–6pm, Sun 1–6pm; July & Aug Mon–Fri 9am–7pm, Sun 1–6pm; ☎01854/612135), on Argyle Street, offers an accommodation booking service. If you're heading onto the Outer Hebrides, there are two or three daily **ferries** (Mon–Sat; 2hr 30min); for precise timings, contact CalMac on ☎01584/612358.

Accommodation

Ullapool, a popular holiday centre in summer, has all kinds of **accommodation**, ranging from one of Scotland's most expensive hotels, the *Altnaharrie*, to innumerable

ULLAPOOL: WALKS, HIKES AND CYCLE RIDES

Ordnance Survey Maps nos. 15, 19 & 20.

Ullapool is at the start of several excellent **hiking trails**, ranging from sedate shoreside ambles to long and strenuous ascents of Munros. However, the weather here can change very quickly, so take the necessary precautions (see p.421). More detailed descriptions of the routes outlined below are available from the **youth hostel**, Shore Street (20p each), and are recommended; hostellers can also rent out the relevant up-to-date OS maps – essential for the hill walks.

An easy half-day ramble begins at the north end of Quay Street: cross the river here and follow its bank left towards the sea until you reach a second river and cross the bridge. A single-track road leads to a hilltop lighthouse from where you gain fine views across the sea to the Summer Isles. Return the same way or via the main road (A835).

For a harder half-day hike, head north along Mill Street on the east edge of town to Broom Court retirement home – trailhead for the Ullapool hill walk (look for the sign next to the electricity substation). A rocky path zigzags steeply up from the roadside to the summit of **Meall Mor**, where there are great views of the area's major peaks. This is also a prime spot for botanists, with a rich array of plants and flowers, including two insect-eating species: sundew and butterwort. The path then drops sharply down the heather-clad north side of Meall Mor into **Glen Achall**, where you turn left onto the surfaced road running past the limestone quarry; the main road back to Ullapool lies a further half-hour's walk west. A right turn where the path meets the road will take you up to Loch Achall and the start of an old drovers' trail across the middle of the Highlands to **Croick** (see p.486). A well-maintained bothy at **Knockdamph**, eleven miles further on, marks the midway point of this long-distance hike, which should not be undertaken alone or without proper gear.

If you're reasonably experienced and can use a map and compass, a day-walk well worth tackling is the rock path to **Achininver**, near Achiltiebuie. The route, which winds along one of the region's most beautiful and unspoilt stretches of coastline to a small **youth hostel** (book ahead on ☎01584/622254; May–Sept), is easy to follow in good weather, but gets very boggy and slippery when wet. Solid footwear, a light pack and a route guide are essential.

The warden and assistants at Ullapool hostel can also give advice on more serious mountain hikes in the area. Among the most popular is the walk to **Scoraig** (see p.467), following the old coast route over the pass to Badrallach, on the south side of the peninsula, and then northwest to Scoraig village itself. The only drawback with this rewarding route is that to get back to Ullapool you have to rely on the *Altnaharrie Hotel's* pricey and sporadic ferry boat (to check times, call ☎01854/633230); miss the boat and the only accommodation for miles is the ultra-expensive hotel or the bothy and campsite over at Badrallach (see p.467). If you have a **mountain bike**, the return trip to Scoraig via Badrallach can be completed in a single day.

Alternatively, try the **Rhidorroch** estate track, which turns right off the A835 just past the *Mercury Hotel* (two miles out of Ullapool), and then heads past the limestone quarry mentioned earlier to Loch Achall and beyond. At the East Rhidorroch Lodge, ignore the suspension bridge and strike up the steep hill ahead onto open moorland and secluded **Loch Damph**, where there's a small bothy. A much easier but no less scenic cycle route is the tour of Loch Broom, taking in the hamlets of **Letters** and **Loggie** on the tranquil western shore, which you can get to via a quiet single-track road (off the A832 once you've cycled south and round the loch from Ullapool). At the end of this, a jeep track heads for the vitrified Iron Age fort at **Dun Lagaidh**; you have to return by the same route.

guest houses and B&Bs, plus a well-situated **campsite** (up the hill from the pier and turn left) and an excellent **youth hostel** on Shore Street (☎01854/612254; mid-March to Oct).

Altnaharrie Hotel (☎01854/633230). A world-famous, select hotel with a very highly regarded restaurant across the loch from town – you're collected by launch. ⑨.

Brae Guest House, Shore Street (☎01854/612421). A great guest house in a beautifully maintained traditional building right on the loch-side. ③.

The Ceilidh Place, W Argyle Street (☎01854/612103). Tasteful and popular hotel, with the west coast's best bookshop, a relaxing first-floor lounge, a great bar-restaurant, sea views, and a laid-back atmosphere. ⑧. Also has a good-value bunkhouse (May–Oct), for £10 per person in dorms, otherwise ②.

Ferry Boat Inn, Shore Street (☎01854/612366). Traditional inn right on the waterfront with a friendly atmosphere and reasonable food. ⑤.

The Kist, Moss Road (☎01854/612269). Simple and cheap B&B, in the newer part of town. ③.

Point Cottage, 22 West Shore St (☎01854/612494). Very well-equipped rooms and good showers, at the quieter end of the seafront. Guests can borrow OS maps already marked up with walking routes. ⑤.

The Shieling, Garve Road (☎01854/612947). Outstandingly comfortable guest house overlooking the loch with immaculate, spacious rooms (rooms 4 and 5 have the best views), superb breakfasts (try their home-made venison and leek sausages) and a sauna. ④.

Tigh Na Mara, Ardinrean (☎01854/655282). Twelve miles from Ullapool on the opposite (west) shore of Loch Broom, but worth the trip. One of Scotland's most renowned vegetarian places, offering gourmet veggie/vegan breakfasts and simple rooms in a romantic setting. ⑥ including dinner.

Waterside House, 6 West Shore Street (☎01854/612140). Very appealing rooms in an outstandingly pleasant, friendly B&B on the seafront. ④.

The Town

Day or night, most of the action in Ullapool centres on the **harbour,** which has an authentic and salty air, especially when the boats are in. By day, attention focuses on the comings and goings of the ferry, fishing boats and smaller craft, while in the evening, yachts swing on the current, the shops stay open late, and customers from the *Ferry Boat Inn* line the sea wall. During summer, booths advertise trips to the **Summer Isles** – a cluster of uninhabited islets two to three miles offshore – to view seabird colonies, dolphins and porpoises, but if you're lucky you'll spot marine life from the waterfront. Otters occasionally nose around the rocks near the *Ferry Boat Inn*, and seals swim past begging scraps from the boats moored in the middle of the loch.

The only conventional "sight" in town is the **museum**, West Argyle Street (Jan–March, Nov & Dec Mon–Sat noon–4pm; April–Oct Mon–Sat 10am–6pm; also July–Aug some evenings; free), in the old parish church, with displays on crofting, fishing, local religion and emigration. During the Clearances, Ullapool was one of the ports through which evicted crofters left to start new lives in Canada, Australia and New Zealand.

Eating and drinking

Ullapool has a wide array of places to eat and drink, ranging from the cheap-and-cheerful chippies on the harbour front to one of Scotland's most expensive gourmet restaurants. The two best **pubs** are the *Arch Inn*, home of the Ullapool football team, and the *Ferry Boat Inn*, where you can enjoy a pint of real ale at the loch-side – midges permitting.

Altnaharrie Hotel (☎01854/633230). World-class cuisine by the renowned chef Gun Eriksen; superb, but steep at around £70 for dinner and hard to get a table if you're a non-resident.

The Ceilidh Place, W Argyle Street (☎01854/612286). Filling snacks are served at the excellent bar, while full meals, including imaginative seafood and vegetarian dishes, are on offer in the spacious restaurant, accompanied by occasional live music. The good coffee shop does great cakes and home-made ice cream.

Ferry Boat Inn, Shore Street. Ullapool's best pub, known locally as the "FBI", serves good food at moderate prices. Live folk sessions take place most Wed & Thurs.

John MacLean's, Shore Street. A wholefood shop/deli with a small café upstairs that serves blow-out breakfasts, pizzas, pies and grills, as well as a selection of freshly baked cakes.

Morefield, Morefield Lane (☎01854/612161). Huge portions of succulent seafood, easily Ullapool's best-value, are served in the restaurant, while the bar has good fish at lower prices. It's not so great for vegetarians, and is hard to find, being improbably hidden in a modern housing estate beyond the bridge on the north side of the town.

The Scottish Larder, Ladysmith Street (☎01854/612185). Creative and delicious food from local sources, specializing in interesting pies, at reasonable prices.

North of Ullapool

North of Ullapool, the landscape changes to consist not of mountain ranges but of extraordinary peaks rising individually from the moorland. As you head further north, the peaks become more widely spaced and settlements smaller and fewer, linked by twisting single-track roads and shore-side footpaths that make excellent hiking trails. You can easily sidestep what little tourist traffic there is by heading down the peaceful backroads, which, after twisting through idyllic crofts, invariably end up at a deserted beach or windswept headland with superb views west to the Outer Hebrides.

Ten miles north of Ullapool, a single-track road winds west off the A835 to squeeze between the northern shore of Loch Lurgainn and the lower slopes **of Cul Beag** (2523ft) and craggy Stac Pollaidh (2012ft) to reach the **Coigach** peninsula. To the southeast, the awesome bulk of **Ben More Coigach** (2439ft) presides over the district, which contains some spectacular coastal scenery including a string of sandy beaches and the Summer Isles scattered just offshore.

Coigach's main settlement is **ACHILTIBUIE**, an old crofting village stretched above a series of white-sand coves and rocks tapering into the Atlantic, from where a fleet of small fishing boats carries sheep, and tourists, to the island pastures during the summer. The village also attracts gardening enthusiasts, thanks to the space-station-like structure overlooking its main beach. Dubbed "The Garden of the Future", the **Hydroponicum** (Easter to early Oct 10am–5pm; £4; tours hourly on the hour) is a kind of glorified greenhouse that concentrates the sun's heat, while protecting the plants inside from winter cold and acidic soil. The results – exotic plants, fruit, fragrant flowers and herbs thriving in four separate "climate rooms" – speak for themselves; you can also taste its famous strawberries and other produce in the subtropical setting of the *Lily Pond Café*, which serves meals, desserts and snacks. Also worth a visit is the **Achiltibuie Smokehouse** (May–Sept Mon–Sat 9.30am–5pm; free), three miles north of the Hydroponicum at **Altandhu**, where you can see meat, fish and game being cured in the traditional way and can buy some afterwards.

The wonderful *Summer Isles Hotel* (☎01854/622282; ⑦; April–Oct), just up the road from the Achiltibuie school, enjoys a near-perfect setting above a sandy beach with views over the islands, and is virtually self-sufficient. The hotel buys in Hydroponicum fruit and vegetables, but has its own dairy, poultry, and even runs a small smokehouse, so the food in its excellent restaurant (open to non-residents) is about as fresh as it comes. A set dinner costs about £35, while superb bar snacks and lunches feature crab, langoustines and smoked mackerel starting from £5. Of Achiltibuie's several **B&Bs**, *Dornie House* (☎01854/622271; ③) in the north of the settlement is welcoming and has particularly fine views. There's also a beautifully situated, small twenty-bed *SYHA* **youth hostel** (☎01854/622254; mid-May to Sept), three miles down the coast at Achininver, which is handy for Coigach's many mountain hikes.

Lochinver

The narrow road north from Coigach through Inverkirkaig is unremittingly spectacular, threading its way through a tumultuous landscape of secret valleys, moorland and bare rock, past the startling shapes of **Cul Beag** (2523ft), **Cul Mor** (2785ft) and the distinctive sugar-loaf **Suilven** (2398ft). A scattering of pebble-dashed bungalows around a sheltered bay heralds your arrival at **LOCHINVER**, the last sizeable village before Thurso, also with the last cash machine. It's a workaday place, with a huge fish market, from where large trucks head off to the rest of Britain. There's a better-than-average **tourist office** (April–Oct Mon–Fri 10am–5pm, Sun 10am–4pm; ☎01571/844330), whose **visitor centre** gives an interesting rundown of the area's geology, wildlife and history; a countryside ranger is available to advise on walks. The village is popular with **fishing** enthusiasts, and equipment is available for rent from the Fish Selling Company, next to the pier, and the newsagents, on the main road.

Lochinver has a range of good **B&Bs**: on the north side of the harbour, *Ardglas* (☎01571/844257; ③) has superb views, though no en-suite rooms, while nearby *Davar* (☎01571/844501; ③) is better-equipped. More central, just above the tourist office, the comfortable *Polcraig* (☎01571/844429; ③) can arrange fishing. If you're looking for **hotel** accommodation, a pleasant and relaxing option is the *Albanach* (☎01571/844407; ⑨ includes dinner) at Baddaidarach, an attractive nineteenth-century building set in a walled garden, and renowned for its excellent seafood, caught locally and served in a lovely wood-panelled dining room. Lochinver's most imaginative **food** can be found in *Lochinver's Larder Riverside Bistro* on the main street: it has local seafood, venison and several vegetarian choices at reasonable prices. Steaks, chicken and some vegetarian dishes feature on the simpler menu at the nearby *Caberfeidh*, while the *Seamens' Mission*, down at the harbour, is a good option for filling meals (some vegetarian) if you're on a tight budget.

Inverkirkaig Falls

Approaching Lochinver from the south, the road bends sharply through a wooded valley where a signpost for **Inverkirkaig Falls** marks the start of a long but gentle **walk** to the base of **Suilven** – the most distinctive mountain in Scotland. Serious hikers use the path to approach the mighty peak, but you can follow it for an easy three-to-four-hour ramble, taking in a waterfall and a tour of a secluded loch. If you're travelling by vehicle, use the car park below the excellent Achins Bookshop near the trailhead, which is well stocked with titles on Scotland and the Highlands, and has a café serving cream teas, cakes and good coffee.

East of Lochinver

The area to the **east of Lochinver**, traversed by the A837 and bounded by the gnarled peaks of the Ben More Assynt massif, is a wilderness of mountains, moorland, mist and scree. Dotted with lochs and lochans, it's also an angler's paradise, home to the only non-migratory fish in northern Scotland, the brown trout, and numerous other sought-after species, including the Atlantic salmon, sea trout, Arctic char and a massive prize strain of cannibal ferox. **Fishing** permits for this area are like gold dust during the summer, snapped up months in advance by exclusive hunting-lodge hotels, but you can sometimes obtain last-minute cancellations (try the *Inver Lodge* on ☎01571/844496).

Although most of the land here is privately owned, nearly 27,000 acres are managed as the **Inverpolly National Nature Reserve**, whose visitor centre (mid-May to mid-Sept daily 10am–1pm & 2–5pm; ☎01854/666254) at Knockan Cliff, twelve miles north of Ullapool on the A835, gives a thorough overview of the diverse flora and wildlife in the surrounding habitats. The theory of thrust faults was developed here in 1859 by eminent geologist Nicol, and an interpretive **Geological Trail** shows you how to detect the movement of rock plates in the nearby cliffs.

Further north, on the rocky promontory that juts into eastern Loch Assynt, stand the jagged remnants of **Ardveck Castle** (free access), a MacLeod stronghold from 1597 that fell to the Seaforth Mackenzies after a siege in 1691. Previously, the Marquis of Montrose had been imprisoned here after his defeat at Carbisdale in 1650. The rebel duke, whom the local laird had betrayed to the government for £20,000 and 400 bowls of sour meal, was eventually led away to be executed in Edinburgh, lashed back to front on his horse.

The *Inchnadamph Hotel* (☎01571/822202; ⑦), on Loch Assynt, is a wonderfully traditional Highland retreat; inside the walls are covered with the stuffed catches of its past guests. The hotel offers fine old-fashioned cooking, usually with good vegetarian options, in its moderately priced restaurant and bar. It's popular with anglers, who get free fishing rights to Loch Assynt, as well as several hill lochs backing onto Ben More, haunts of the infamous ferox trout. Just along the road, the Assynt Field Centre at *Inchnadamph Lodge* (☎01571/822218) has basic but comfortable bunk rooms, as well as more spacious B&B accommodation (②), with breakfast included in the price.

North from Lochinver: the coast road

Heading **north from Lochinver**, there are two possible routes: the fast A837, which runs eastwards along the shore of Loch Assynt to join the northbound A894, or the narrow **coastal road** (the B869) that locals dub "The Breakdown Zone" because its ups and downs claim so many victims during summer. Hugging the indented shoreline, this route is the more scenic, offering superb views of the Summer Isles, as well as a number of rewarding side-trips to beaches and dramatic cliffs. **Postbuses** from Lochinver cover the route as far as Ardvar or Drumbeg (Mon–Sat). Unusually, most of the land and lochs around here are owned by local crofters rather than wealthy landlords. Helped by grants and private donations, the **Assynt Crofters' Trust** made history in 1993 when it pulled off the first ever community buyout of estate land in Scotland, and it's now pursuing a number of projects aimed at strengthening the local economy and conserving the environment. The Trust owns the lucrative fishing rights to the area, too, selling permits for £3 per day (£15 per week) through local post offices, and the newsagent and tourist office in Lochinver.

Heading north, the first village worthy of a detour is **ACHMELVICH**, a couple of miles along a sideroad, whose tiny bay cradles the whitest beach and most stunning turquoise water you'll encounter this side of the Seychelles. Unfortunately, there's a noisy **campsite** and a forty-bed **youth hostel** (☎01571/844480; April–Sept) just behind the largest beach. However, for total peace and quiet there are other equally seductive beaches beyond the headlands.

The sideroad that branches north off the B869 between **Stoer** and **Clashnessie**, both of which have sandy beaches, ends abruptly by the automatic **lighthouse** at **Raffin** – built in 1870 by the Stevenson brothers (one of whom was the author Robert Louis Stevenson's dad) – but you can continue for two miles along a well-worn track to Stoer Point, named after the colossal rock pillar that stands offshore known as "**The Old Man of Stoer**". Surrounded by sheer cliffs and splashed with guano from the seabird colonies that nest on its 200ft sides, it was climbed for the first time in 1961.

DRUMBEG, nine miles further on, is a major target for trout anglers, lying within reach of countless lochans. Permits to fish them are sold at the post office, but you'll need a detailed map and a compass to find your way in and out of this area without getting hopelessly lost. There's a lot of self-catering accommodation in the area, but few **B&Bs**. A good choice, however, is *Taigh Druimbeag* (☎01571/833209; ⑤), a comfortable old Edwardian house with period furniture and a large garden; to find it, turn off the main road at the primary school and follow the signs.

Kylesku to Kinlochbervie

KYLESKU, 33 miles north of Ullapool and around six miles west of Drumbeg, is the site of the award-winning road bridge spanning the mouth of lochs Glencoul and Glendhu. It's a pleasant place for a short stay, with plenty of good walks and a conge nial hotel by the water's edge above the old ferry slipway. The family-run *Kylesku Hotel* (☎01971/502231; ⑥; April–Nov) has en-suite rooms, a welcoming bar popular with locals, and an excellent restaurant serving outstanding fresh seafood, including lobster, crab, mussels and local salmon (you can watch the fish being landed on the pier). Alternatively, *Newton Lodge* (☎01971/502070; ⑤, including dinner ⑦) is a modern, friendly and comfortable small hotel a few hundred yards up the road towards Ullapool. Statesman Cruises runs boat trips (March–Oct daily 11am & 2pm; round trip 2hr; £7.50; ☎01571/844446) from the jetty below the hotel to the 650ft **Eas-Coul-Aulin**, Britain's highest waterfall, at the head of Loch Glencoul; seals, porpoises and minke whales can occasionally be spotted along the way.

It is also possible to reach Eas-Coul-Aulin on foot: a rough trail (3hr) leaves the A894 three miles south of Kylesku, skirting the south shore of **Loch na Gainmhich** (known locally as the "sandy loch") to approach the falls from above. Great care should be taken here as the path above the cliffs can get very slippery when wet; the rest of the route is also difficult to follow, particularly in bad weather, and should only be attempted by experienced, properly equipped and compass-literate hikers. However, there are several less demanding walks around Kylesku if you just fancy a gentle amble: one of the most popular is the half-day low-level route along the north side of Loch Glendhu, beginning at **Kylestrome**, on the opposite side of the bridge from the hotel. Follow the surfaced jeep track east from the trailhead and turn left onto a footpath that leads through the woods. This eventually emerges on to the open mountainside, dropping down to cross a burn from where it then winds to a boarded-up old house called Glendhu, where there's a picturesque pebble beach. Several interesting side-trips and variations to this walk may be undertaken with the help of the detailed Ordnance Survey Landranger Map No. 15, but you'll need a compass and wet-weather gear in case of bad weather.

Ten miles north of Kylesku, the widely scattered crofting community of **SCOURIE,** on a bluff above the main road, surrounds a beautiful sandy beach whose safe bathing has made it a popular holiday destination for families; there's plenty to do for walkers and trout anglers, too. Scourie itself has some good accommodation: try the charming *Scourie Lodge* (☎01971/502248; ③), an old shooting retreat with a lovely garden; the welcoming owners also do great evening meals. **UPPER BADCALL** village, three miles south of Scourie and even more remote, has a couple of B&Bs, including *Stoer View* (☎01971/502411; ③), whose clean and comfortable rooms look over Eddrachillis Bay to Stoer Point. For a little more luxury, try the nearby old-established *Eddrachillis Hotel* (☎01971/502080; ⑦, with dinner ⑧), which enjoys a spectacular situation on the bay, and serves reasonable bar food. There's also a good **campsite**, the *Scourie Caravan and Camping Park* (☎01971/502060) near the centre of the village.

Handa Island

Visible just offshore to the north of Scourie is **Handa Island**, a huge chunk of red Torridon sandstone surrounded by sheer cliffs and carpeted with machair and purple-tinged moorland. Teeming with seabirds, it's an internationally important wildlife reserve and a real feast for ornithologists, with vast colonies of razorbills and guillemots breeding on its guano-splashed cliffs during summer. From late May to mid-July, large numbers of puffins waddle comically over the turf-covered clifftops where they dig their burrows.

Apart from a solitary warden, Handa is deserted. Until midway through the last century, however, it supported a thriving, if somewhat eccentric, community of crofters. Surviving on a diet of fish, potatoes and seabirds, the islanders, whose ruined cottages still cling to the slopes by the jetty, devised their own system of government, with a "queen" (Handa's oldest widow) and "parliament" (a council of men who met each morning to discuss the day's business). Uprooted by the 1846 potato famine, most of the villagers eventually emigrated to Canada's Cape Breton; today, Handa is private property, administered as a nature sanctuary by the Scottish Wildlife Trust. If you're landing on the island, you're encouraged to make a donation of around £1.50 towards its upkeep.

You'll need about three hours to follow the footpath around the island – an easy and enjoyable walk taking in the north shore's Great Stack rock pillar and some fine views across the Minch: a detailed route guide is featured in the SWT's free leaflet available from the warden's office when you arrive. Weather permitting, boats (☎01971/502077; £6) leave for Handa throughout the day (until around 4pm) from the tiny cove of **TARBET**, three miles northwest of the main road and accessible by postbus from Scourie (Mon–Sat 1 daily; 1.50pm), where there's a small car park and jetty. However, if you're travelling south, you may prefer to pick up the Laxford Cruises (☎01971/502251) boat that sails from **FANAGMORE** (Easter–Oct Mon–Sat 10am, noon & 2pm; July & Aug also 4pm; £7.50), a mile further up the coast (reached by the same postbus as above). Camping is not allowed on the island, but the SWT maintains a **bothy** for birdwatchers (reservations must be made on ☎0131/312 7765, or with the warden on the island), while in Tarbet, Rex and Liz Norris (☎01971/502098; ③) run a comfortable little **B&B** overlooking the bay. For food, Tarbet's excellent *Seafood Restaurant* serves delicious, moderately priced fish and vegetarian dishes, and a good selection of home-made cakes and desserts in its airy conservatory just above the jetty.

Kinlochbervie and beyond

North of Scourie, the road sweeps inland through the starkest part of the Highlands; rocks piled on rocks, bog and water create an almost alien landscape, and the astonishingly bare, stony coastline looks increasingly inhospitable. After about eight miles, at **Rhiconich**, you can branch off the main road to **KINLOCHBERVIE**, a major fishing port set in a rugged, rocky inlet. Trucks from all over Europe pick up cod and shellfish from the trawlers here, crewed mainly by east coast fishermen. *The Old Schoolhouse Restaurant and Guest House* (☎01971/521383; ④) provides comfortable accommodation and home-cooked meals.

Beyond Kinlochbervie, a single-track road takes you through isolated **Oldshoremore**, a working crofters' village scattered above a stunning white-sand beach, to **BLAIRMORE**, where you can park for the four-mile walk across peaty moorland to deserted **Sandwood Bay**. Few visitors make this half-day detour north, but the beach at the end of the rough track is one of the most beautiful in Scotland. Flanked by rolling dunes and lashed by fierce gales for much of the year, the shell-white sands are said to be haunted by a bearded mariner – one of many sailors to have perished on this notoriously dangerous stretch of coast since the Vikings first navigated it over a millennium ago. Around the turn of the last century, the beach, whose treacherous undercurrents make it unsuitable for swimming, also witnessed Britain's most recent recorded sighting of a mermaid. Plans are afoot to bulldoze a motorable road up here, so enjoy the tranquillity while you can. Cape Wrath, the most northwesterly point in mainland Britain, lies a day's hike north. However, most people approach the headland from Durness on the north coast (see opposite). If you want **to camp** in the area, try the well-equipped site at Oldshoremore (☎01971/521281), or continue through Blairmore to **Sheigra**, where the road ends, for informal camping behind the beach.

THE NORTH COAST

Though a constant stream of sponsored walkers, caravans and tour groups makes it to **John O' Groats**, surprisingly few visitors travel the whole length of the Highlands' wild **north coast**. Those that do, however, rarely return disappointed. Pounded by one of the world's most ferocious seaways, Scotland's rugged northern shore is backed by barren mountains in the west, and in the east by lochs and open rolling grasslands. Between its far ends, mile apon mile of crumbling cliffs and sheer rocky headlands shelter bays whose perfect white beaches are nearly always deserted, even in the height of summer. This is a great area for **birdwatching**, too, with huge seabird colonies clustered in clefts and on remote stacks at regular intervals along the coast; **seals** also bob around in the surf offshore, and in winter **whales** put in the odd appearance in the more sheltered estuaries of the northwest.

Getting around this stretch of coast without your own transport can be a slow and frustrating business: **Thurso**, the area's main town and springboard for Orkney, is well connected by bus and train with Inverness, but further west, after the main A836 peters into a single-track road, you have to rely on a convoluted series of postbus connections or, in peak season, a single Highland Country bus.

Durness and around

Scattered around a string of sheltered sandy coves and grassy clifftops, **DURNESS**, the most northwesterly village on the British mainland, straddles the turning point on the main road as it swings east from the inland peat bogs of the interior to the north coast's fertile strip of limestone machair. First settled by the Picts around 400 BC, the area has been farmed ever since; its crofters being among the few not cleared off estate land during the nineteenth century. Today, Durness is the centre for several crofting communities and a good base for a couple of days, with some good walks. Even if only passing through, it's worth pausing here to see the **Smoo Cave**, a gaping hole in a sheer limestone cliff, and to visit beautiful **Balnakiel beach**, to the west. In addition, Durness is the jumping-off point for roadless and rugged **Cape Wrath**, the windswept promontory at the Scotland's northwest tip, which has retained an end-of-the-world mystique lost long ago by John O' Groats.

The Smoo Cave

A mile or so east of Durness village lies the 200ft-long **Smoo Cave**, a natural wonder, formed partly by the action of the sea, and partly by the small burn that flows through it. Tucked away at the end of a narrow sheer-sided sea cove, guides will show you the illuminated interior, although the much-hyped rock formations are less memorable than the short rubber-dinghy trip you have to make in the second of three caverns, where the whole experience is enlivened after wet weather by a **waterfall** that crashes through the middle of the cavern. A boat trip leaves from Smoo Cave on a wildlife tour of the coast around Durness, taking in stretches of the shoreline only accessible by sea. The trip (May–Sept daily, times depending on weather and tide; 90min; £6.50) takes a close look at **seabird colonies**, and sightings of seals, puffins and porpoises are common.

Balnakiel

A narrow road winds northwest of Durness to the tiny **BALNAKIEL**, whose name derives from the Gaelic *Baile ne Cille* (Village of the Church). The ruined **chapel** that today overlooks this remote hamlet was built in the seventeenth century, but a church has stood here for at least 1200 years. A skull-and-crossbones stone set in the south wall marks the grave of Donald MacMurchow, a seventeenth-century highwayman and contract killer who murdered eighteen people for his clan chief (allegedly by throwing them from the top of the Smoo Cave). The "half-in, half-out" position of his grave was apparently a compromise between his grateful employer and the local clergy, who initially refused to allow such an evil man to be buried on church ground. Balnakiel is also known for its **golf course**, whose ninth and final hole involves a 155-yard drive over the Atlantic; you can rent equipment from the clubhouse. The **Balnakiel Craft Village** (daily 10am–6pm; free), back towards Durness, is worth a visit. Housed in an imaginatively converted 1950s military base, the campus consists of a dozen or so workhops where you can watch painters, potters, leather workers, candle makers, woodworkers, stone carvers, knitters and weavers in action.

The white-sand beach on the east side of Balnakiel Bay is a stunning sight in any weather, but most spectacular on sunny days when the water turns to brilliant turquoise. For the best views, walk along the path that winds north through the dunes behind it; this eventually leads to **Faraid Head** – from the Gaelic *Fear Ard* (High Fellow) – where you stand a good chance of spotting puffins from late May until mid-July. The fine views over the mouth of Loch Eriboll and west to Cape Wrath make this round walk (3–4hr) the best in the Durness area.

Cape Wrath

An excellent day-trip from Durness begins three miles southwest of the village at **Keoldale**, where a foot-passenger ferry (May–Aug hourly 9.30am–4.30pm; Sept 4 daily; no motorcycles; ☎01971/511376) crosses the Kyle of Durness estuary to link up with a minibus (☎01971/511287; May–Sept) that runs the eleven miles out to **Cape Wrath**. The UK mainland's most northwesterly point, the headland takes its name not from the stormy seas that crash against it for most of the year, but from the Norse word *hvarf*, meaning "turning place" – a throwback to the days when Viking warships used it as a navigation point during raids on the Scottish coast. These days, a lighthouse (another of those built by Robert Louis Stevenson's father) warns ships away from the treacherous rocks. Looking east to Orkney and west to the Outer Hebrides, it stands above the famous **Clo Mor cliffs**, the highest sea cliffs in Britain and a prime breeding site for seabirds. You can walk from here to remote Sandwood Bay (see p.474), visible to the south, although the route, which cuts inland across lochan-dotted moorland, is hard to follow in places. Hikers generally continue south from Sandwood to the trail end at Blairmore; if you hitch or walk the six miles from here to Kinlochbervie you can, with careful planning, catch a bus back to Durness. Don't attempt this route from south to north, as, if the weather closes in, the Cape Wrath minibus stops running. Note also that much of the land bordering the headland is a military firing range, so check the firing times with Durness tourist office before you set off.

Durness practicalities

Public transport in the area is sparse; the key service on the north coast is the Highland Country link to Thurso (June–Aug Mon–Sat) leaving Thurso at 11.30am and Durness at 3pm. This connects at Durness with the daily Inverness Traction link (May to early Oct) from Inverness via Ullapool and Lochinver. Postbuses provide a more complicated year-round alternative; check at the post office, tourist office or youth hostel.

Durness has an enthusiastic **tourist office** (March–Oct Mon–Sat 9am–6pm; July & Aug also Sun 11am–7pm; ☎01971/511259), in the village centre, which can help with accommodation and arranges guided walks; its small visitor centre also houses some excellent interpretative panels detailing the area's history, geology, flora and fauna, with some good insights into the day-to-day life of the community. **Accommodation** is fairly limited in Durness itself, but there are further options along nearby Loch Eriboll (see opposite). Durness's best offering is the *Cape Wrath Hotel* (☎01971/511212; ⑥), which stands in a beautiful setting near the ferry jetty at Keoldale. Popular with walkers and fishermen, its rather austere character is offset by relaxed, friendly service and a stunning view from the dining room. Of the **B&Bs**, *Puffin Cottage* (☎01971/511208; ③) is small but pleasant, while the friendly **youth hostel** (☎01971/511244; mid-May to Sept), beside the Smoo Cave car park, a mile and a half east of the village, also rents out mountain bikes. There's **camping** at *Sango Sands Caravan and Camping Site*, Harbour Road (☎01971/511262), which has the added advantage of a good bar and restaurant. The other good **eating** option is the *Cape Wrath Hotel's* restaurant.

Loch Eriboll

Ringed by ghost-like limestone mountains, deep and sheltered **Loch Eriboll**, six miles east of Durness, is the north coast's most spectacular sea loch. Servicemen stationed here during World War II to protect passing Russian convoys nicknamed it "Loch 'Orrible", but if you're looking for somewhere wild and unspoilt, you'll find this a perfect spot. Porpoises and otters are a common sight along the rocky shore, and minke whales occasionally swim in from the open sea.

Overlooking its own landing stage at the water's edge, *Port-Na-Con* (☎01971/511367; ③; mid-March to Oct), seven miles from Durness on the west side of the loch, is a wonderful **B&B**, popular with anglers and divers (it'll refill air tanks for £2.50). Top-notch food is served in its small restaurant (open all year, including Christmas), with a choice of vegetarian haggis, local kippers, fruit compote and home-made croissants for breakfast, and adventurous three-course evening meals for around £12; the menu always includes a gourmet vegetarian dish. Non-residents are welcome, although you'll need to book. Another good option, half a mile further south, is *Rowan House* (☎01971/511347; ③), a child-friendly place overlooking the loch with a tiny eighteen-hole golf course; fresh local oysters often feature on its menu. A further half a mile south, *Choraidh Croft* (☎01971/511235; ③; Easter–Nov), also offers B&B and has a rare-breeds collection (£2), as well as a good café.

Tongue

It's a long slog around Loch Eriboll and east over the top of A Mhùine moor to the pretty crofting township of **TONGUE**. Dominated by the ruins of **Varick Castle**, the village, an eleventh-century Norse stronghold, is strewn over the east shore of the **Kyle of Tongue**, which you can either cross via a new causeway, or by following the longer and more scenic single-track road around its southern side. When the tide recedes, this shallow estuary becomes a mass of golden sand flats, superb on sunny days with the sharp profiles of **Ben Hope** (3040ft) and **Ben Loyal** (2509ft) looming to the south.

In 1746, the Kyle of Tongue was the scene of a naval engagement reputed to have sealed the fate of Bonnie Prince Charlie's **Jacobite rebellion**. In response to a plea for help from the prince, the king of France dispatched a sloop and £13,600 in gold coins to Scotland. However, the Jacobite ship *Hazard* was spotted by the English frigate, *Sheerness*, and fled into the Kyle, hoping that the larger enemy vessel would not be able to follow. It did, though, and soon forced the *Hazard* aground. Pounded by English cannon fire, its Jacobite crew slipped ashore under cover of darkness in an attempt to smuggle the treasure to Inverness, but they were followed by scouts of the local Mackay clan, who were not of the Jacobite persuasion. The next morning, a larger platoon of Mackays waylaid the rebels, who, hopelessly outnumbered and outgunned, began throwing the gold into **Lochan Hakel**, southwest of Tongue (most of it was recovered later). The Prince, meanwhile, had sent 1500 of his men north to rescue the treasure, but these too were defeated en route; historians have wondered ever since whether the missing men might have altered the outcome of the Battle of Culloden three weeks later.

If you want **to stay** in Tongue, try *Rhian Cottage* (☎01847/611257; ③, with dinner ⑥), a pretty whitewashed house with an attractive garden, about a mile down the road past the post office, or *Woodend* (☎01847/611332; ③), a mile north on the Bettyhill road, with panoramic views of the estuary. The *Ben Loyal Hotel* (☎01847/611216; ⑤) and

Tongue Hotel (☎01847/611206; ④) are more luxurious, and both do good food. There's also a beautifully situated and friendly *SYHA* **youth hostel** (☎01847/611301; mid-March to Sept), a mile north of the village centre on the east shore of the Kyle, and two **campsites**: *Kincraig Camping and Caravan Site* (☎01847/611218) just south of Tongue post office, and *Talmine Camping and Caravan Site* (☎01847/601225), just behind a sandy beach at Talmine, five miles north of Tongue on the western side of the Kyle.

Bettyhill to Dounreay

BETTYHILL, a major crofting village, straggles along the side of a narrow tidal estuary, and down the coast to two splendid beaches. Forming an unbroken arc of pure white sand between the Naver and Borgie rivers, **Torrisdale beach** is the more impressive of the pair, ending in a smooth white spit that forms part of the **Invernaver Nature Reserve**. During summer, arctic terns nest here on the river banks, dotted with clumps of rare Scottish primroses, and you stand a good chance of spotting an otter or two. The **Strathnaver Museum** (April–Oct Mon–Sat 10am–1pm & 2–5pm; £1.50), housed in the old church, is full of locally donated bits and pieces, and includes panels by local school children telling the story of the Strathnaver Clearances. You can also see some Pictish stones and a 3800-year-old early Bronze Age beaker found in Strathnaver, the river valley south of the village, whose numerous prehistoric sites are mapped on an excellent pamphlet sold at the entrance desk.

Bettyhill's small **tourist office** (Easter–May & Sept Mon–Sat 10am–5pm; June–Aug Mon–Sat 9.30am–5.30pm, Sun 3.30–5.30pm; ☎01641/521342) can book **accommodation** for you. The *Farr Bay Inn* (☎01641/521230; ③), just beyond the museum, has character, and does good bar food. There are also several good-value B&Bs, including *Shenley* (☎01641/521421; ②), a grand but homely detached house in an elevated spot in the middle of the village, and *Bruachmhor* (☎01641/521265; ②), a small but comfortable croft house, facing south over the village.

As you move east from Bettyhill, the north coast changes dramatically as the hills on the horizon recede to be replaced by fields fringed with flagstone walls. At the hamlet of **MELVICH**, twelve miles from Bettyhill, the A897 cuts south through Strath Halladale, the Flow Country (see below) and the Strath of Kildonan to Helmsdale on the east coast (see p.489). Melvich has some good accommodation, including the excellent *Sheiling Guesthouse* (☎01641/531256; ④) by the main road, whose impressive breakfast menu features locally smoked haddock and fresh herring.

Five miles further east, **DOUNREAY Nuclear Power Station**, a surreal collection of stark domes and chimney stacks marooned in the middle of nowhere, is still a fairly major local employer, though its three fast breeder reactors were decommissioned in April 1994 and it now reprocesses spent nuclear fuel rather than generating electricity. A permanent **exhibition** (Easter–Sept daily 10am–5pm; free) details the processes (and, unsurprisingly, the benefits) of nuclear power, but don't expect to hear much about the area's "leukemia cluster", nor the high levels of radiation reported over the years on the nearby beaches.

South from Melvich: the Flow Country

From Melvich, you can head forty miles or so south towards Helmsdale (see p.489) on the A897, through the **Flow Country**. This huge expanse of bog land came into the news a few years ago when ecology experts, responding to plans to transform the area into forest, drew attention to the threat to this fragile landscape, described by one contemporary commentator as of "unique and global importance, equivalent to the African Serengeti or Brazil's rainforest". Some forest was planted, but the environmentalists won the day, and the forestry syndicates have had to pull out. There's an excellent

RSPB Flow Country **visitor centre** (Easter–Oct daily 9am–6pm; ☎01641/571225), based in the train station at Forsinard, fifteen miles south of Melvich, which is easily accessible from Thurso, Wick and the south by train. Guided walks through the RSPB **nature reserve** leave from the visitor centre (May–Aug Tues & Thurs) and illuminate the importance of the area and its wildlife.

Thurso

Approached from the isolation of the west, **THURSO** feels like a metropolis. In reality, it's a relatively small service centre visited mostly by people passing through to the nearby port of **Scrabster** to catch the ferry to Stromness in Orkney. The town's name derives from the Norse word *Thorsa*, literally "River of the God Thor", and in Viking times this was a major gateway to the mainland. Later, ships set sail from here for the Baltic and Scandinavian ports loaded with meal, beef, hides and fish. Much of the town, however, dates from the 1790s, when Sir John Sinclair built a large new extension to the old fishing port, "according to the most regular plan that could be contrived and in a manner not only ornamental but also positively well adapted for preserving the health and promoting the convenience of the inhabitants". The nearby Dounreay Nuclear Power Station ensured continuing prosperity after World War II, when workers from the plant (dubbed "Atomics" by the locals) settled in Thurso in large numbers. Its gradual rundown over recent years has cast a shadow over the local economy, but investment in new industries such as telecommunications has improved matters.

Traill Street is the main drag, turning into the pedestrianized Rotterdam Street and High Street precinct at its northern end. However, the shops are uninspiring, and you're better off heading to the old part of town near the harbour, to see **Old St Peter's Church**, a substantial ruin with origins in the thirteenth century, but which has been much altered over the years. Alternatively, you could visit the **Thurso Heritage Museum**, High Street (Mon–Sat 10am–5pm; 50p) whose most intriguing exhibit is the Pictish **Skinnet Stone**, intricately carved with enigmatic symbols, and a runic cross.

Practicalities

It's a ten-minute walk from the **train station**, with services to Inverness and Wick, down Princes Street and Sir George Street, to the **tourist office**, on Riverside Road (April–Oct Mon–Sat 9am–6pm; July & Aug also Sun 10am–6pm; ☎01847/892371). The bus station, close by, runs regular **buses** to John O' Groats, Wick and Inverness and a summer service to Durness. **Ferries** operate daily from adjoining Scrabster to Orkney, which has less frequent links to Shetland and Aberdeen. You can book ahead through P&O Scottish Ferries, Aberdeen (☎01224/572615) or through any local tourist office. If you fancy a day-trip to Orkney, see "John O' Groats" (p.480).

Thurso is well-stocked with **accommodation**, with the recently refurbished *Royal Hotel* (☎01847/893191; ⑥) on Traill Street being a reasonable choice. Of the **B&Bs**, *Murray House*, 1 Campbell St (☎01847/895759; ③), is central and comfortable, or you could try the welcoming Mrs Oag, 9 Couper St (☎01847/894529; ②), east of High Street near the town hall, or Mrs Budge (☎01847/893205; ③), 6 Pentland Crescent, next to the beach front. The nearest **campsite** (☎01955/603761) is out towards Scrabster alongside the main road.

Food options include the *Fountain Restaurant*, Sinclair Street, which successfully juggles Chinese, Indian and European menus, and the *Upper Deck*, by the harbour at Scrabster, serving large, moderately priced steaks and seafood dishes. There are several **cafés** in the town centre which offer standard, filling snacks, including *Johnston's* on Traill Street, while the most enjoyably rowdy **pub** is the *Central*, on Traill Street. After the pub, head to *Evie's Nightclub* on Sir Georges Street, or for more traditional entertainment, the *Pentland Hotel*, on Princes Street, hosts a weekly Highland Night (£2.50).

Dunnet Head to Duncansby Head

Despite the plaudits that John O' Groats customarily receives, Britain's northernmost mainland point is in fact **Dunnet Head**. At the far side of Dunnet Bay, it's a vast sandy beach backed by huge dunes about six miles east of Thurso. The bay is popular with surfers, and even in the winter you can usually spot intrepid figures far out in the Pentland Firth's breakers. For Dunnet Head, turn off at **DUNNET**, at the east end of the bay, onto the B855, which runs for four miles over windy heather and bog to the tip of the headland, crowned with a Victorian lighthouse. The red cliffs below are startling, with weirdly eroded rock stacks and a huge variety of seabirds; on a clear day you can see the whole northern coastline from Cape Wrath to Duncansby Head, and across Pentland Firth to Orkney.

John O' Groats

Familiar from endless postcards, **JOHN O' GROATS** comes as something of an anti-climax. The views north to Orkney are fine enough, but the village itself turns out to be little more than a windswept grassy slope leading down to the sea, dominated by an enormous car park that is jammed throughout the summer with tour buses. The village gets its name from the Dutchman, Jan de Groot, who obtained the ferry contract for the crossing to Orkney in 1496. The eight-sided house he built for his eight quarrelling sons (so that each one could enter by his own door) is echoed in the octagonal tower of the much-photographed *John O' Groats Hotel*, good as a stopoff for a quick drink.

Aside from the frequent if irregular links with Land's End, maintained by a succession of walkers, cyclists, vintage-car drivers and pushers of baths, John O' Groats is connected by regular **buses** to Wick (4–5 daily; 50min) and Thurso (Mon–Fri 5 daily, Sat 2 daily; 1hr). John O' Groats Ferries (☎01955/611353) operates a daily passenger ferry across to Burwick in the Orkney Islands (May–Sept 4 daily, last one at 6pm; 45min; £22 return): officially this is a foot-passenger service, but it will take bicycles and motorbikes if it isn't too busy. The company also runs an afternoon wildlife cruise round the Stacks of Duncansby and the seabird colonies of Stroma (1hr 30min; £12). The **tourist office** (April–Oct Mon–Sat 9am–5pm; ☎01955/611373) by the car park can help sort out **accommodation**: alternatively, try *Swona View B&B* (☎01955/611297; ②) on the road to Duncansby Head, or *Haven Gore* (☎01955/611314; ②), a large, good-value B&B a mile west along the Thurso road. *Bencorragh House* (☎01955/611449; ③, with dinner ④) has very pleasant farmhouse accommodation at Upper Gills in Canisbay. If you're on a tight budget, head for the small **youth hostel** (☎01955/611424; April–Oct) at Canisbay, or the **campsite** (☎01955/611329) in John O' Groats.

Duncansby Head

If you're disappointed by John O' Groats, press on a couple of miles further east to **Duncansby Head**, which, with its lighthouse, dramatic cliffs and well-worn coastal path, has a lot more to offer. The birdlife here is prolific, and south of the headland lie some spectacular 200ft cliffs, cut by sheer-sided clefts known locally as *geos*. This is also a good place from which to view Orkney. Dividing the islands from the mainland is the infamous **Pentland Firth**, one of the world's most treacherous waterways. Only seven miles across, it forms a narrow channel between the Atlantic Ocean and North Sea, and for fourteen hours each day the tide rips through here from west to east at a rate of ten knots or more, flooding back in the opposite direction for the remaining ten hours. Combined with the rocky sea bed and a high wind, this can cause deep whirlpools and terrifying 30–40ft towers of water to form when the ebbing tide crashes across the reefs offshore. The latter, known as the "Bores of Duncansby", are the subject of many old mariners' myths from the time of the Vikings onwards.

THE EAST COAST

The **east coast** of the Highlands, between Inverness and Wick, is nowhere near as spectacular as the west, with gentle undulating moors, grassland and low cliffs where you might expect to find sea lochs and mountains. Washed by the cold waters of the North Sea, it's markedly cooler, too, although less prone to spells of permadrizzle, and midges. Although the Inverness–Thurso train line is twice forced by topography to head inland, the region's main transport artery, the A9 – slower here than in the south – follows the coast, which veers sharply northeast exactly parallel with the Great Glen, formed by the same geological fault.

From around the ninth century AD onwards, the **Norse** influence was more keenly felt here than in any other part of mainland Britain, and dozens of Scandinavian-sounding names recall the era when this was a Viking kingdom. Culturally and scenically, much of the east coast is more lowland than highland and Caithness in particular evolved more or less separately from the Highlands, avoiding the bloody tribal feuds that wrought such havoc further south and west. Later, however, the nineteenth-century **Clearances** hit the region hard, as countless ruined cottages and empty glens show. Hundreds of thousands of crofters were evicted, and forced to emigrate to New Zealand, Canada and Australia, or else take up fishing in one of the numerous herring ports established on the coast. The oil boom has brought a transient prosperity to one or two places over the past two decades, but the area remains one of the country's poorest, reliant on sheep farming, fishing and tourism.

The one stretch of the east coast that's always been relatively rich is the **Black Isle**, whose main village, **Cromarty**, is the region's undisputed highlight, with a crop of elegant mansions and appealing fishermen's cottages clustered near the entrance to the Cromarty Firth. In late medieval times, pilgrims including James IV of Scotland poured through here en route to the red-sandstone town of **Tain** to worship at the shrine of St Duthac, where the former sacred enclave has now been converted into one of the many "heritage centres" that punctuate the route north. Beyond **Dornoch**, a famous golfing resort renowned for its salubrious climate and sweeping beach, the ersatz-Loire chateau, **Dunrobin Castle**, is the main tourist attraction, a monument as much to the iniquities of the Clearances as to the eccentricity of Victorian taste. The award-winning **Timespan Heritage Centre** further north at Helmsdale recounts the human cost of the landlords' greed, while the area around the port of **Lybster** is littered with the remains of more ancient civilizations. **Wick**, the largest town on this section of coast, has an interesting industrial past, whose story is told in another good heritage centre, but is otherwise uninspiring. The relatively flat landscapes of this northeast corner – windswept peat bog and farmland dotted with lochans and grey and white crofts – are a surprising contrast to the more rugged country south and west of here.

The Black Isle and around

Sandwiched between the Cromarty Firth to the north and the Moray and Beauly firths to the south, the **Black Isle** is not an island at all, but a fertile peninsula whose rolling hills, prosperous farms and stands of deciduous woodland make it more reminiscent of Dorset or Sussex than the Highlands. It probably gained its name because of its mild climate: there's rarely frost, which leaves the fields "black" all winter; another explanation is that the name derives from the Gaelic word for black, *dubh* – a possible corruption of St Duthus (see p.485).

The Black Isle is littered with dozens of **prehistoric sites**, but the main incentive to make the detour east from the A9 is to visit the picturesque eighteenth-century town of

Cromarty, huddled at the northeast tip of the peninsula. A string of villages along the south coast is also worth stopping off in en route, and one of them, Rosemarkie, has an outstanding small museum devoted to **Pictish culture**. Chanonry Point is among the best **dolphin-spotting** sites in Europe.

Avoch, Fortrose and Rosemarkie

The most rewarding approach to Cromarty is along the south side of the Black Isle, along the A832, past the **Clootie Well**, just north of Munlochy, where coloured rags are hung on a fence to bring luck and health. Next comes the attractive harbourside fishing village of **AVOCH** (pronounced "Och"), where the *Station Hotel* serves good bar meals and real ale; there's a tiny heritage centre in the basement at the back. **FORTROSE**, a few miles further east, is another quiet village dominated by the ruins of an early thirteenth-century **cathedral**. Founded by King David I, it now languishes on a lovely yew-studded green bordered by red-sandstone and colourwashed houses, where a horde of gold coins dating from the time of Robert III was unearthed in 1880. There's also a memorial to the Seaforth family, whose demise the Brahan Seer famously predicted (see below).

There's a memorial plaque to the seer at nearby **Chanonry Point**, reached by a back-road from the north end of Fortrose; the thirteenth hole of the golf course here marks the spot where he met his death. Jutting into a narrow channel in the Moray Firth (deepened to allow warships into the estuary during the last war), the point, fringed on one side by a beach of golden sand and shingle, is an excellent place to look for **dolphins** (see p.433). Come here around high tide, and you stand a good chance of spotting a couple leaping through the surf in search of fish brought to the surface by converging currents.

ROSEMARKIE, a one-street village north of Fortrose at the opposite (northwest) end of the beach, is thought to have been evangelized by St Boniface in the early eighth century. **Groam House Museum** (Easter week & May–Sept Mon–Sat 10am–5pm, Sun 2–4.30pm; Oct–April Sat & Sun 2–4pm; £1.50), at the bottom of the village, displays a bumper crop of intricately carved standing stones (among them the famous Rosemarkie Cross Slab), and shows an informative video highlighting Pictish sites in the region. A lovely mile-and-a-half **woodland walk**, along the banks of a sparkling burn to Fairy Glen, begins at the car park just beyond the village on the road to Cromarty. Inexpensive bar food is also available at the wonderfully old-fashioned *Plough Inn*, just down the main street from the museum.

THE BRAHAN SEER

Legend has it that the seventeenth-century visionary Cùinneach Odhar (Kenneth Mackenzie, from Uig on Skye), who lived and worked on the Seaforths' estate, derived his powers from a small white divination stone passed on to him, through his mother, from a Viking princess. With the pebble pressed against his eye, Cùinneach foretold everything from outbreaks of measles in the village to the building of the Caledonian Canal, the Clearances and World War II. His visions brought him widespread fame, but also resulted in his untimely death. In 1660, Countess Seaforth, wife of the local laird, summoned the seer after her husband was late home from a French holiday. Reluctantly – when pressurized – he told the Countess that he had seen the earl "on his knees before a fair lady, his arm round her waist and her hand pressed to his lips". At this, she flew into a rage, accused him of sullying the family name and ordered him to be thrown head first into a barrel of boiling tar. However, just before the gruesome execution, which took place near Brahan Castle on Chanonry Point, Cùinneach made his last prediction: when a deaf and dumb earl inherited the estate, the Seaforth line would end. His prediction finally came true in 1815 when the last earl died.

Cromarty

An ancient legend recalls that the twin headlands flanking the entrance to the Cromarty Firth, known as The Sutors (from the Gaelic word for shoemaker), were once a pair of giant cobblers who used to protect the Black Isle from pirates. Nowadays, however, the only giants in the area are Nigg and Invergordon's colossal oil rigs, marooned in the estuary like metal monsters marching out to sea. Built and serviced here for the Forties North Sea oil field, they form a surreal counterpoint to the web of tiny streets and chocolate-box workers' cottages of **CROMARTY**, the Black Isle's main settlement. Sheltered by The Sutors at the northeast corner of the peninsula, the town, an ancient ferry crossing point on the pilgrimage trail to St Duthac's shrine in Tain, lost much of its trade during the nineteenth century to places served by the railway; a branch line to the town was begun but never completed. Although a royal burgh since the fourth century, Cromarty didn't became a prominent port until 1772 when the entrepreneurial local landlord, George Ross, founded a hemp mill here. Imported Baltic hemp was spun into cloth and rope in the mill, fuelling a period of prosperity during which Cromarty acquired some of Scotland's finest Georgian houses; these, together with the terraced fishers' cottages of the nineteenth-century herring boom, have earned the town a somewhat corny epithet, "the jewel in the crown of Scottish vernacular architecture".

To get a sense of Cromarty's past, head straight for the award-winning **museum** housed in the old **Courthouse**, Church Street (daily: Easter–Oct 10am–5pm; Nov–Easter noon–4pm; £3), which tells the history of the town using audiovisuals and animated figures (not as dreadful as they sound, and children love them). You are also issued with a personal stereo, a tape and a map for a walking tour around the town. **Hugh Miller** (1802–52) a stonemason turned author, geologist, folklorist and Free Church campaigner, was born in Cromarty, and his **birthplace** (May–Sept Mon–Sat 10am–1pm & 2–5pm, Sun 2–5pm; NTS; £2), a modest thatched cottage on Church Street, has been restored to give an idea of what Cromarty must have been like in his day. Aside from any formal sights, Cromarty is a pleasant place just to wander around, and there's an excellent **walk** out to the south Sutor stacks. You can pick up the path by leaving town on Miller Road, and turning right when the lane becomes "The Causeway"; follow this through the woods and past eighteenth-century Cromarty House until you reach the junction at Mains Farm; a left turn here takes you across open fields and through woods to the top of the headland, from where there are superb views across the Moray Firth.

Before you move on, bear in mind that Bill Fraser of Dolphin Écosse will take you out on half- or full-day **boat trips** to see seals, porpoises and bottle-nosed dolphins just off the coast, or killer whales (orcas) farther out; you can contact him on ☎01381/600323. The tiny two-car Nigg–Cromarty **ferry** (April–Oct 9am–6pm), Scotland's smallest, also doubles up as a cruiser on summer evenings; you can catch it from the jetty near the lighthouse.

Practicalities

Four **buses** each day run to Cromarty from Inverness (55min), returning from the stop near the playing fields on the western outskirts of town. During summer, **accommodation** is in short supply, so book ahead. Most upmarket is the traditional *Royal Hotel* (☎01381/600217; ⑤), down at the harbour, which has rather small but richly furnished rooms overlooking the Firth, and a good bar/restaurant. For **B&B**, try one of the attractive old houses on Church Street – Mrs Robertson at no. 7 (☎01381/600488; ②), or Mrs Brockman-More at Bellevue House (☎01381/600381; ③). Above the town, Mrs Ricketts (☎01381/600308; ③) offers well-equipped rooms and good views.

The most down-to-earth place to **eat** is the *Cromarty Arms*, which serves basic, inexpensive bar meals, and a good selection of ales and malts. It also hosts a lively karaoke night and occasional country and western bands on Fridays. If you're after something a little more sophisticated, you could try the *Thistle Restaurant,* on Church Street, or the *Royal Hotel's* restaurant, which features Scottish specialities. Cheaper meals are available in the cosy public bar or, on fine nights, on the terrace outside with great views over the firth.

Strathpeffer

STRATHPEFFER, a Victorian spa town surrounded by wooded hills, is a congenial place to stop over. During its heyday, this was a renowned European **health resort** complete with a Pump Room, where visitors could chat while they sipped the water. Today, sadly, some of its buildings are in a sorry state, including several huge faded hotels, though plans are afoot to restore the Pavilion Ballroom to its former glory. Activity is concentrated around the main square, where you can drink sulphur-laden water at the **Water Sampling Pavilion.**

Within striking distance of the bleak **Ben Wyvis,** Strathpeffer is also a popular base for walkers. One of the best hikes in the area begins from the *SYHA* **youth hostel,** at the west end of the village, from where a forestry track leads through dense woodland towards the hill of Cnoc Mor. Rather less than a mile farther on, you can turn up onto the ridge on the right and follow it to reach the vitrified Pictish hill fort of **Knock Farril,** that affords superb panoramic views to the Cromarty Firth and the surrounding mountains. From here, you can pick up a minor road and continue along the ridge to Dingwall, from where there are buses back to Strathpeffer. A shorter route drops back down from Knock Farril to the main road and then on to the village. Allow a full day for the longer route, a half-day for the shorter.

Practicalities

Buses run regularly between Dingwall and Strathpeffer (Mon–Sat), dropping passengers in the square, where you'll find a small **tourist office** (Easter–Nov Mon–Sat 10am–5pm; ☎01997/421415) with information on points west as well as local areas. The **hotels** in the village are very popular with bus tours, but often have room: the vast *Ben Wyvis* (☎01997/421323; ④) is adequate, in nice grounds east of the main square on the Dingwall road, while north of the main square a converted Victorian villa, complete with turrets, houses the *Holly Lodge Hotel* (☎01997/421254; ⑤). The *Inver Lodge,* west of the main square (☎01997/421392; ③), and *Francisville,* just past the church (☎01997/421345; ③), both offer good **B&B.** If you don't mind dorms, head for the rambling seventy-bed **youth hostel** (☎01997/421532; mid-March to Sept), a mile southwest of the main square up the hill towards Jameston.

Dingwall and the Cromarty Firth

Most traffic nowadays takes the upgraded A9 north from Inverness, bypassing the small provincial town of **DINGWALL** (from the Norse *thing,* "parliament", and *vollr,* "field"), a royal burgh since 1226 and former port that was left high and dry when the river receded during the last century. Today, it's a tidy but dull service and market town with one long main street that's bustling all day and moribund by dinner time. Dingwall's only real claim to fame is that it was the birthplace of Macbeth, whose family occupied the now ruined castle on Castle Street.

If you need **to stay,** Castle Street is a good place to look for B&Bs: try *The Croft* (☎01349/863319; ③) at no. 25, or *St Clements* (☎01349/862172; ③) at no. 17. The smartest hotel is the stylish *Tulloch Castle,* Castle Drive (☎01349/861325; ⑧), a former Highland clan headquarters, or there's the central *Royal Hotel,* High Street (☎01349/862130; ⑦).

Northeast of Dingwall, the **Cromarty Firth** has always been recognized as a perfect natural harbour. During World War I it was a major **naval base,** and today its sheltered waters are used as a centre for repairing North Sea oil rigs. The fifteen-mile stretch of the fast A9 from Alness to Tain passes several villages which have boomed with the expansion of the oil industry, notably **Invergordon**, on the coast just west of Nigg Bay. The extraordinary edifice on the hill behind **EVANTON,** ten minutes west along the A9 from Alness, is the **Fyrish Monument**, built by a certain Sir Hector Munro, partly to give employment to the area and partly to commemorate his own capture of the Indian town of Seringapatam in 1781 – hence the design, resembling an Indian gateway. If you want to get a close-up look, it's a tough two-hour walk through pine woods to the top.

Around the Tain peninsula

Bounded in the south by the Cromarty Firth, and in the north by the Dornoch Firth, the hammer-shaped **Tain peninsula** can still be approached by the ancient ferry crossing from Cromarty to Nigg. The peninsula's largest settlement is **TAIN**, a small town of grand whisky-coloured sandstone buildings, and the birthplace of **St Duthus**, a missionary who inspired great devotion in the Middle Ages. His miracle-working relics were enshrined in a sanctuary here in the eleventh century, and in 1360 St Duthus Collegiate Church was built, visited annually by James IV, who usually arrived here fresh from the arms of his mistress, Janet Kennedy, whom he had conveniently installed in nearby Moray. A good place to get to grips with the peninsula's past is the **Tain Through Time** exhibition (April–Oct daily 10am–6pm; Nov–March Mon & Thurs–Sun noon–4pm; £3), which uses sound-and-light shows and gregarious guides in period costumes to flesh out the historical facts. The ticket price also includes a tour of the church and neighbouring **museum** on Castle Brae (just off High Street), housing mediocre archeological finds and clan memorabilia. There's not a great deal more to see in Tain, but check out High Street's castellated sixteenth-century **Tolbooth**, with its stone turrets and old curfew bell. Tain's only other attraction, the **Glenmorangie whisky distillery** (Mon–Fri 10am–4pm; June–Oct also Sat 10am–4pm; book on ☎01862/892477), lies just off the A9 on the north side of town.

The *Mansfield House Hotel* (☎01862/892052; ⑦), a modernized mansion-hotel in the Scots-Baronial mould, is renowned for its cooking, while the more modest *Golf View House* (☎01862/892856; ③), three minutes' drive from the town centre on Knockbreck Road, offers comfortable **B&B**. For inexpensive typically Scottish-style hot meals, try *Strachan's Restaurant*, High Street (open all day).

Portmahomack

Although few people bother to explore the Tain area as far east as **Tarbat Ness** on the tip of the peninsula, if you're driving it's well worth setting aside a couple of hours to make the detour. The green, windswept village of **PORTMAHOMACK** sprawls downhill to a sandy beach and round a bay full of sailing boats. On top of the hill, a Pictish archeological site is being excavated next to the pretty whitewashed **Tarbat Old Church**, with its odd tower and balustraded entrance at the back. There's also a **lighthouse** (one of the highest in Britain) at the gorse-covered point, reached along narrow roads running through fertile farmland. A good seven-mile walk starts here (2–3hr round trip): head south from Tarbat Ness for three miles, following the narrow passage between the foot of the cliffs and the foreshore, until you get to the hamlet of Rockfield. A path leads past a row of fishermen's cottages from here to Portmahomack, then joins the tarmac road running northeast back to the lighthouse.

Back in Portmahomack, you could have lunch at the *Oystercatcher*, Main Street, which serves delicious seafood, home-made soups and salads; they also have a few very-good-value **rooms** (☎01862/871560; ③). Otherwise, if you want to stay, you could try the *Caledonian Hotel* (☎01862/871345; ⑤) further along Main Street, which looks over the beach to the Dornoch Firth.

Bonar Bridge and around

Before the causeway was built across the Dornoch Firth, traffic heading along the coast used to skirt around the estuary, crossing the Kyle of Sutherland at **BONAR BRIDGE**. In the fourteenth and fifteenth centuries, the village harboured a large **iron foundry**. Ore was brought across the peat moors of the central Highlands from the west coast on sledges, and fuel for smelting came from the oak forest draped over the northern shores of the nearby kyle. However, James IV, passing through here once on his way to Tain, was shocked to find the forest virtually clear-felled and ordered that oak saplings be planted in the gaps. Although now hemmed in by spruce plantations, the beautiful ancient woodland east of Bonar Bridge dates from this era.

Carbisdale Castle

Towering high above the River Shin, three miles northwest of Bonar Bridge, the daunting neo-Gothic profile of **Carbisdale Castle** (not open to the public) overlooks the **Kyle of Sutherland**, as well as the battlefield where the gallant Marquis of Montrose was defeated in 1650, finally forcing Charles II – if he wanted to be received as king (see p.553) – to accede to the Scots demand for presbyterianism. It was erected between 1906 and 1917 for the dowager **Duchess of Sutherland**, following a protracted family feud. After the death of her husband, the late Duke of Sutherland, the will leaving her the lion's share of the vast estate was contested by his stepchildren from his first marriage. In the course of the ensuing legal battle, the Duchess was found in contempt of court for destroying important documents pertinent to the case, and locked up in Holloway prison for six weeks. However, the Sutherlands eventually recanted (although there was no personal reconciliation) and, by way of compensation, built their stepmother a castle worthy of her rank. Designed in three distinct styles (to give the impression it was added to over a long period of time), Carbisdale was eventually acquired by a Norwegian shipping magnate in 1933, and finally gifted, along with its entire contents and estate, to the *SYHA*, which has turned it into what must be one of the most opulent **youth hostels** in the world, even if the finer furnishings have gone (☎01549/421232; March–Sept except May 6–16). The best way to get here by public transport is to take a train to nearby **Culrain** station, which lies within easy walking distance of the castle. **Buses** from Inverness (3 daily; 1hr 30min) and Tain (4 daily; 25min) only run as far as **Ardgay**, three miles south.

Croick Church

A mile or so southwest of Bonar Bridge, the scattered village of **ARDGAY** stands at the mouth of Strath Carron, a wooded river valley winding west into the heart of the Highlands. It's worth heading ten miles up the strath to **Croick Church**, which harbours one of Scotland's most poignant and emotive reminders of the **Clearances**. Huddled behind a brake of wind-bent trees, the graveyard surrounding the tiny grey chapel sheltered eighteen families (92 individuals) evicted from nearby Glen Calvie during the spring of 1845 to make way for flocks of Cheviot sheep, introduced by the Duke of Sutherland as a quick money earner (see p.489). A reporter from the *Times* described the "wretched spectacle" as the villagers filed out of the glen " . . . in a body, two or three carts filled with children, many of them infants". An even more evocative written record of the event is preserved on the diamond-shaped panes of the chapel windows, where the villagers scratched **graffiti memorials** still legible today: "Glen Calvie people was in the churchyard May 24th 1845", "Glen Calvie people the wicked generation", and "This place needs cleaning".

Lairg

North of Bonar Bridge, the A836 parallels the River Shin for eleven miles, to **LAIRG**, a bleak and scattered place at the eastern end of lonely **Loch Shin**. On fine days, the vast wastes of heather and deergrass surrounding the village can be beautiful, but in the rain it can be a deeply depressing landscape. This workaday village is predominantly a **transport hub** and the railhead for a huge area to the northwest, and there's nothing much to see in town. However, a mile southeast on the A839, there are signs of early settlement at nearby **Ord Hill**, where archeological digs have recently yielded traces of human habitation dating back to Neolithic times. The Countryside Centre and **tourist office**, on the west side of the river (Mon–Sat 9am–5pm, Sun 1–5pm; ☎01549/402160), hands out leaflets detailing the locations of hut circles and other sites and is the starting point for forest walks and an archeological trail to Ord Hill. Four miles south of Lairg, on the opposite side of the river – along the A836, then the B864 – the **Falls of Shin** is one of the best places in Scotland to see **salmon** leaping on their upstream migration; there's a viewing platform, and the café by the car park does good snacks and meals. Every August, Lairg hosts an annual lamb sale, the biggest one-day livestock market in Europe, when sheep from all over the north of Scotland are bought and sold.

Practicalities

Lairg, at the centre of the region's **road system**, is distinctly hard to avoid: the A838, traversing some of the loneliest country in the Highlands, is the quickest route for Cape Wrath; the A836 heads up to Tongue on the north coast; and the A839 links up to the A837 to push west through lovely Strath Oykel, to Lochinver on the west coast. For non-drivers, Lairg is on the **train line** connecting Inverness to Wick and Thurso and is the nexus of several **postbus routes** around the northwest Highlands. An Inverness Traction Heatherhopper service (May to early Oct Mon–Sat) runs from here to Ullapool, with a connection for Lochinver and Durness. Trains arrive north of the main road along the loch; buses stop right on the loch. Should you want **to stay**, *Carnbren* (☎01549/412259; ②), just south of the bridge on the Bonar Bridge road, is comfortable, as is the *Old Coach House* (☎01549/402378; ②; May–Oct), three miles south of Lairg on the B864 at Achany.

Dornoch

DORNOCH, eight miles north of Tain, lies on a flattish headland overlooking the **Dornoch Firth**. Surrounded by sand dunes and blessed with an exceptionally sunny climate by Scottish standards, it's something of a middle-class holiday resort, with solid Edwardian hotels, trees and flowers in profusion, and miles of sandy beaches giving good views across the estuary to the Tain peninsula. The town is also renowned for its championship **golf course**, ranked eleventh in the world and the most northerly first-class course in the world.

Dating from the twelfth century, Dornoch became a royal burgh in 1628. Among its oldest buildings, which are all grouped round the spacious Square, the tiny **Cathedral** was founded in 1224 and built of local sandstone. The original building was horribly damaged by marauding Mackays in 1570, and much of what you see today was restored by the Countess of Sutherland in 1835, though her worst Victorian excesses were removed this century, when the interior stonework was returned to its original state. A later addition were the stained-glass windows in the north wall, which were endowed by the expat American-based Andrew Carnegie (see p.247). You can climb the tower (July & Aug Mon–Fri 7.30am–8pm). Opposite, the fortified sixteenth-century Bishop's Palace, a fine example of vernacular architecture, with stepped gables and towers, has been refurbished as an upmarket hotel (see below). Next door, the **Old Town Jail** (Mon–Sat 10am–5pm; free) contains a mock-up of a nineteenth-century cell and a bookshop.

In 1722, Dornoch saw the last burning of a **witch** in Scotland. The unfortunate old woman, accused of turning her daughter into a pony and riding her around town, ruined her chances of acquittal by misquoting the Gaelic version of the Lord's Prayer during the trial, and was sentenced to burn alive in a barrel of boiling tar – an event commemorated by the **Witch's Stone**, just south of the Square on Carnaig Street.

Practicalities

Buses from Tain and Inverness stop in the Square, where you'll also find a **tourist office** (Mon–Sat 9am–1pm & 2–5pm; ☎01862/810400). There's no shortage of **accommodation**: the *Trentham Hotel* (☎01862/810391; ③), near the golf course on the northeast edge of town, is friendly and comfortable if a bit staid, while the characterful *Dornoch Castle Hotel* (☎01862/810216; ⑦), in the Bishop's Palace on the Square, has a cosy old-style bar and relaxing tea garden. Of the B&Bs, try *Trevose* (☎01862/810269; ③), on the Square, which is swathed in roses, or, a couple of miles out on the A949, *Evelix Farmhouse* (☎01862/810271; ③). Both the hotels do good bar and restaurant **meals** and the *Cathedral Café* serves delicious soup and snacks.

Golspie to Wick

Ten miles north of Dornoch on the A9 lies the straggling red-sandstone town of **GOLSPIE**, whose status as an administrative centre does little to relieve its dullness. It does, however, boast an eighteen-hole **golf course** and a sandy beach, while half a mile further up the coast the **Big Burn** has several rapids and waterfalls that can be seen from an attractive **woodland trail** (beginning at the *Sutherland Arms Hotel*).

Dunrobin Castle

The main reason to stop in Golspie, though, is to look around **Dunrobin Castle** (May–Oct Mon–Sat 10.30am–4.30pm, Sun 1–4.30pm; June–Sept Sun until 5.30pm; £4.80), overlooking the sea a mile north of town. Approached via a long tree-lined drive, this fairy-tale confection of turrets and pointed roofs – modelled by the architect Sir Charles Berry (designer of the Houses of Parliament) on a Loire chateau – is the seat of the infamous Sutherland family, at one time Europe's biggest landowners, with a staggering 1.3 million acres, and the principal driving force behind the **Clearances** in this area. The castle is on a correspondingly vast scale, boasting 189 furnished rooms, of which the tour only takes in seventeen. Staring up at the pile from the midst of its elaborate **formal gardens**, it's worth remembering that such extravagance was paid for by uprooting literally thousands of crofters from the surrounding glens. Much of the extra income generated by the evictions was lavished on the castle's opulent **interior**, which is crammed full of fine furniture, paintings (including works by Landseer, Allan Ramsay and Sir Joshua Reynolds), tapestries and *objets d'art*.

Set aside at least an hour for Dunrobin's amazing **museum**, housed in an eighteenth-century building at the edge of the garden. Inside, hundreds of disembodied animals' heads and horns peer down from the walls, alongside other more macabre appendages, from elephants' toes to rhinos' tails. Bagged mainly by the fifth Duke and Duchess of Sutherland, the trophies vie for space with other fascinating family memorabilia, including one of John O' Groat's bones, Chinese opium pipes, and such curiosities as a "picnic gong from the South Pacific". There's also an impressive collection of ethnographic artefacts acquired by the Sutherlands on their frequent hunting jaunts, ranging from an Egyptian sarcophagus to some more locally found, finely carved Pictish stones.

The Sutherland Monument

You can't miss the 100ft **Monument** to the first Duke of Sutherland, which peers proprietorially down from the summit of the 1293ft **Beinn a'Bhragaidh**, a mile northwest of Golspie. An inscription cut into its base recalls that the statue was erected in 1834 by ". . . a mourning and grateful tenantry [to] . . . a judicious, kind and liberal landlord . . . [who would] open his hands to the distress of the widow, the sick and the traveller". Unsurprisingly, there's no reference to the fact that the duke, widely regarded as Scotland's own Josef Stalin, forcibly evicted 15,000 crofters from his million-acre estate – a fact which, in the words of one local historian, makes the monument ". . . a grotesque representation of the many forces that destroyed the Highlands". Campaigners are lobbying, so far unsuccessfully, to have the monument broken into pieces and scattered over the hillside, so that visitors can walk over the remains to a new, more appropriate memorial. However, the Sutherland estate and local council have continually resisted moves to replace it.

It's worth the wet, rocky **climb** (round trip 90min) to the top of the hill for the wonderful views south along the coast past Dornoch to the Moray Firth and west towards Lairg and Loch Shin. It's a steep and strenuous walk, however, and there's no view until you're out of the trees, about ten minutes from the top. Take the road opposite Munro's TV Rentals in Golspie's main street, which leads up the hill, past a fountain, under the railway and through a farmyard – from here, follow the Beinn a'Bhragaidh footpath (BBFP) signs along the path into the woods.

Brora

BRORA, on the coast six miles north of Golspie, once boasted the only bridge in the region – whence its name, which means "River of the Bridge" in Norse. Until the 1960s, it was the only coal-mining village in the Highlands, having played host to the industry for four hundred years. These days, however, the small grey town harbours little of interest, although it's accessible by bus and train and does have *Capaldi's* on High Street, which sells brilliant homemade Italian ice cream. A mile or so north of town, the **Clynelish Distillery** (Mon–Fri 9.30am–4.30pm; free) will give you a guided tour and a free dram. The best **B&B** in the area is *Clynelish Farm* (☎01408/621265; ③) – turn left after the BP garage – a working Victorian stone farmhouse with en-suite rooms, built to provide employment for dispossessed crofters after the Clearances. The rooms here are spacious, with views over the fields to the Moray Firth, and evening meals are available by arrangement.

Helmsdale

Eleven miles up the A9 from Golspie, **HELMSDALE** is an old herring port, founded in the nineteenth century to house the evicted inhabitants of Strath Kildonan, which lies behind it. Today, the sleepy-looking grey village attracts thousands of tourists, most of them to see the **Timespan Heritage Centre**, beside the river (Easter–Oct Mon–Sat 9.30am–5pm, Sun 2–5pm; £2.75). It's a remarkable venture for a place of this size, telling the local story from prehistoric times to the present through hi-tech displays, sound effects and an audiovisual programme. For a spot of light relief after the exhibition, head across the road to the sugary pink and frilly *Mirage Restaurant*. The proprietor has become something of a Scottish celebrity, modelling herself on the romantic novelist Barbara Cartland, whose shooting lodge is nearby. Photographs proudly displayed on the walls show the peroxide-blonde restaurateuse posing with her heroine, while the fittings and furnishings reflect her predilection for all things pink and kitsch, with fish tanks, fake-straw parasols, and plastic seagulls set off to a T by the country and western soundtrack. She also dishes up great fish and chips, grills and puddings.

Helmsdale's **tourist office** (April–Sept Mon–Sat 10am–5pm; ☎01431/821640) will book accommodation for you. Most of the **B&Bs** are on the outskirts of town: *Broomhill House*, Navidale Road (☎01431/821259; ③), is the best of the bunch, with bedrooms in a turret added to the former croft by a miner who struck it lucky in the Kildonan gold rush (see below). Alternatively, try *Torbuie* (☎01431/821424; ③), in Navidale, on the A9 less than a mile from the village, or *Eastdale*, half a mile up the A897 (☎01431/821334; ③), both of which offer comfortable rooms. There's also a **youth hostel** (☎01431/821577; mid-May to Sept), about half a mile north of the harbour.

Baile an Or

From Helmsdale the single-track A897 runs up Strath Kildonan and across the Flow Country (see p.478) to the north coast, at first following the River Helmsdale river, a strictly controlled and exclusive salmon river frequented by the royals. Some eight miles up the Strath at **BAILE AN OR** (Gaelic for "goldfield"), gold was discovered in the bed of the Kildonan Burn in 1869; a gold rush ensued, hardly on the scale of the Yukon, but quite bizarre in the Scottish Highlands. A tiny amount of gold is still found every year: if you fancy **gold-panning** yourself, pick up a free licence and the relevant equipment from Helmsdale's gift and fishing-tackle shop, Strath Ullie, opposite the Timespan Heritage Centre.

From Helmsdale to Wick

Just north of Helmsdale, the A9 begins its long haul up the **Ord of Caithness**. This steep hill used to form a pretty impregnable obstacle, and the desolate road still gets blocked during winter snowstorms. Once over the pass, the landscape changes dramatically as heather-clad moors give way to miles of treeless green grazing lands, peppered with derelict crofts and latticed by long drystone walls. This whole area was devastated during the Clearances; the ruined village of **BADBEA**, reached via a footpath running east off the main road a short way after the pass, is a poignant monument to this cruel era. Built by tenants evicted from nearby Ousdale, the settlement now lies deserted, although its ruined hovels show what hardship the crofters had to endure: the cottages stood so near the windy cliff edge that children had to be tethered to prevent them from being blown into the sea.

DUNBEATH, hidden at the mouth of a small strath, twelve miles north of Ord of Caithness, was another village founded to provide work in the wake of the Clearances. The local landlord built a harbour here in 1800, at the start of the herring boom, and the settlement flourished briefly. Today it's a sleepy place, with lobster pots stacked at the quayside and views of windswept Dunbeath Castle (closed to the public) on the opposite side of the bay. The novelist Neill Gunn was also born here, in one of the terraced houses under the flyover that now swoops above the village; you can find out more about him at the **Dunbeath Heritage Centre** (Easter–Oct Mon–Sat 10am–5pm; £2.25), signposted from the road. The best of the handful of modest **B&Bs** here is *Tormore Farm* (☎01593/731240; ②), a large farmhouse with four comfortable rooms, half a mile north of the harbour on the A9.

The final stretch of road before Wick gives great views over the cliffs and out to sea to the oil rigs perched on the horizon. The planned village of **LYBSTER**, established at the height of the nineteenth-century herring boom, once had 200-odd boats working out of its harbour. Today, although still a busy fishing port, it's a grim collection of grey pebble-dashed bungalows centred on a broad main street. Most visitors head straight for the nearby **Grey Cairns of Camster**, seven miles due north and one of the most memorable sights on the northeast coast. Surrounded by bleak moorland, these two enormous prehistoric burial chambers, constructed 4000–5000 years ago, were immaculately designed, with corbelled drystone roofs in their hidden chambers, which you can crawl into through narrow passageways. More extraordinary ancient remains lie at **East Clyth**, two miles north of Lybster on the A9, where a path leads to the "**Hill o' Many Stanes**". Some 200 boulders stand in the ground here, forming 22 parallel rows that run north to south; no one has yet worked out what they were used for, although archeological studies have shown there were once 600 stones in place.

Wick

Originally a Viking settlement named *Vik* (meaning "bay"), **WICK** has been a royal burgh since 1589. It's actually two towns: Wick proper, and **Pultneytown**, immediately south across the river, a messy, rather run-down community planned by Thomas Telford, in 1806 for the British Fisheries Society, to encourage evicted crofters to take up fishing.

Wick's heyday was in the mid-nineteenth century, when it was the busiest herring port in Europe, exporting tons of fish to Russia, Scandinavia and the West Indian slave plantations. Robert Louis Stevenson described it as " . . . the meanest of man's towns, situated on the baldest of God's bays", and it's still a pretty grim place, in spite of a bustling shopping centre and some solid Victorian civic architecture. Pultneytown, lined with rows of fishermen's cottages, is the area most worth a wander, with the acres of largely derelict net-mending sheds, stores and cooperages around the harbour giving some idea of the former scale of the fishing trade. The town's story is told in the excellent **Wick Heritage Centre** in Bank Row, Pultneytown (June–Sept Mon–Sat 10am–5pm; £1), and illustrated by a huge photographic collection dating from the 1880s.

Rising steeply from a needle-thin promontory three miles north of Wick are the dramatic fifteenth- to seventeenth-century ruins of **Sinclair** and **Girnigoe castles**, which functioned as a single stronghold for the earls of Caithness. In 1570 the fourth earl, suspecting his son of trying to murder him, imprisoned him in the dungeon here until he died of starvation.

Practicalities

The **train** station and **bus** stops are next to each other behind the hospital. Frequent local buses run to Thurso and up the coast to John O' Groats. Wick also has an **airport** (☎01955/602294), a couple of miles north of the town, with direct flights from Edinburgh, Aberdeen and Orkney, and connections further south. From the train station head across the river down Bridge Street to the **tourist office**, just off High Street (Mon–Fri 9am–5pm, Sat 9am–1pm; ☎01955/602596), which gives out a full **accommodation** list. Just behind it, the *Wellington Guest House*, 41–43 High St (☎01955/603287; ④), is reasonable value, as are *The Clachan* B&B, South Road (☎01955/605384; ③), and *Greenvoe* on George Street (☎01955/609342; ②). The *Harbour Guest House*, on Rose Street, Pultneytown (☎01955/603276; ③) is friendly but more basic. The best of the hotels is *Mackay's*, by the river in the town centre (☎01955/602323; ⑧).

As for **eating**, the good-value *Lamplighter Restaurant*, High Street, serves enormous helpings of imaginative food; in the same building, *Houston's* cheerfully churns out good burgers. The *Lorne Restaurant*, on Bank Row near the Heritage Centre (open evenings only), is moderately priced and serves more than adequate portions. *Cabrelli's*, at the east end of the High Street, is a real find, trapped in a time warp, and serving piles of fish and chips, along with authentic pizza. A few doors further on, *Camps* is among the liveliest of the **pubs** in the evenings, with occasional live music.

travel details

Trains

Aviemore to: Edinburgh (Mon–Sat 8 daily, Sun 3 daily; 3hr); Inverness (Mon–Sat 8 daily, Sun 4 daily; 40min); Newtonmore (Mon–Sat 6 daily, Sun 4 daily; 20min).

Dingwall to: Helmsdale (Mon–Sat 3 daily, plus Sun 2 daily in summer; 2hr); Inverness (Mon–Sat 6–7 daily, plus Sun 4 daily in summer; 25min); Kyle of Lochalsh (Mon–Sat 3–4 daily, plus Sun 2 daily in summer; 2hr); Lairg (Mon–Sat 3 daily, plus Sun 2 daily in summer; 1hr 10min); Thurso (Mon–Sat 3 daily, plus Sun 2 daily in summer; 3hr 20min); Wick (Mon–Sat 3 daily, plus Sun 2 daily in summer; 3hr 20min).

Fort William to: Arisaig (Mon–Sat 4 daily, plus Sun 3 daily in summer; 1hr 10min); Crianlarich (Mon–Sat 3–4 daily, Sun 1–3 daily; 1hr 40min); Glasgow (Mon–Sat 3 daily, Sun 1–2 daily; 4hr); Glenfinnan (4 daily; 35min); London (1 nightly; 12hr); Mallaig (Mon–Sat 4 daily, Sun 1–3 daily; 1hr 25min).

Inverness to: Aviemore (Mon–Sat 8 daily, Sun 4 daily; 40min); Dingwall (Mon–Sat 6–7 daily, plus Sun 4 daily in summer; 25min); Edinburgh (Mon–Sat 8 daily, Sun 3 daily; 3hr 30min); Helmsdale (Mon–Sat 3 daily, plus Sun 2 daily in summer; 2hr 20min); Kyle of Lochalsh (Mon–Sat 3–4 daily, plus Sun 2 daily in summer; 2hr 40min); Lairg (Mon–Sat 3 daily, plus Sun 2 daily in summer; 1hr 40min); London (Mon–Fri & Sun 2 daily, Sat 1 daily; 8hr 35min); Plockton (Mon–Sat 3–4 daily, plus Sun 2 daily in summer; 2hr 15min); Thurso (Mon–Sat 3 daily, plus Sun 2 daily in summer; 3hr

45min); Wick (Mon–Sat 3 daily, plus Sun 2 daily in summer; 3hr 45min).

Kyle of Lochalsh to: Dingwall (Mon–Sat 3–4 daily, plus Sun 2 daily in summer; 2hr); Inverness (Mon–Sat 3–4 daily, plus Sun 2 daily in summer; 2hr 40min); Plockton (Mon–Sat 3–4 daily, plus Sun 2 daily in summer; 20min).

Lairg to: Dingwall (Mon–Sat 3 daily, plus Sun 2 daily in summer; 1hr 10min); Inverness (Mon–Sat 3 daily, plus Sun 2 daily in summer; 1hr 40min); Thurso (Mon–Sat 3 daily, plus Sun 2 daily in summer; 2hr 5min); Wick (Mon–Sat 3 daily, plus Sun 2 daily in summer; 2hr 5min).

Mallaig to: Arisaig (Mon–Sat 4 daily, plus Sun 3 daily in summer; 15min); Fort William (Mon–Sat 4 daily, plus Sun 3 daily in summer; 1hr 25min); Glasgow (Mon–Sat 3 daily, Sun 1–2 daily; 5hr 20min); Glenfinnan (Mon–Sat 4 daily, plus Sun 3 daily in summer; 35 min).

Newtonmore to: Aviemore (Mon–Sat 6 daily, Sun 4 daily; 20min); Inverness (Mon–Sat 6 daily, Sun 4 daily; 55min).

Thurso to: Dingwall (Mon–Sat 3 daily, plus Sun 2 daily in summer; 3hr 20min); Inverness (Mon–Sat 3 daily, plus Sun 2 daily in summer; 3hr 45min); Lairg (Mon–Sat 3 daily, plus Sun 2 daily in summer; 2hr 5min).

Wick to: Dingwall (Mon–Sat 3 daily, plus Sun 2 daily in summer; 3hr 20min); Inverness (Mon–Sat 3 daily, plus Sun 2 daily in summer; 3hr 45min); Lairg (Mon–Sat 3 daily, plus Sun 2 daily in summer; 2hr 5min).

Buses

Aviemore to: Grantown-on-Spey (6–9 daily; 35min); Inverness (15 daily; 40min); Newtonmore (8 daily; 20min).

Brora to: Thurso (4–5 daily; 1hr 50min); Wick (5–6 daily; 1hr 15min).

Dornoch to: Brora (5 daily; 35min); Inverness (10 daily; 1hr 10min).

Fort William to: Acharacle (Mon–Sat 2–4 daily; 1hr 30min); Drumnadrochit (6 daily; 1hr 30min); Fort Augustus (6 daily; 1hr); Inverness (6 daily; 2hr); Mallaig (1–2 daily; 2hr).

Gairloch to: Dingwall (3 weekly; 2hr); Inverness (3 weekly; 2hr 20min); Redpoint (1 daily; 1hr 35min).

Inverness to: Aberdeen (hourly; 3hr 40min); Aviemore (Mon–Sat 15 daily, Sun 12 daily; 40min); Cromarty (4 daily; 45min); Drumnadrochit (6 daily; 25min); Durness (May to early Oct 1 daily; 5hr); Fort Augustus (6 daily; 1hr); Fort William (6 daily; 2hr); Gairloch (1 daily; 2hr 20min); Glasgow (7 daily; 3hr 35min–4hr 25min); John O' Groats (1–2 daily; 3hr 40min); Kirkwall (April–Sept 2 daily; 5hr 20min); Kyle of Lochalsh (3–4 daily; 2hr); Lairg (Mon–Sat 2 daily; 2hr); Lochinver (May to early Oct 1 daily; 3hr 10min); Nairn (Mon–Sat hourly; 35min); Newtonmore (8 daily; 1hr 10min); Oban (Mon–Sat 2 daily; 4hr); Perth (10 daily; 2hr 35min); Portree (3–4 daily; 3hr 20min); Tain (hourly; 1hr 15min); Thurso (Mon–Sat 5 daily, Sun 4 daily; 3hr 30 min); Ullapool (2–4 daily; 1hr 25min); Wick (Mon–Sat 3 daily; 1hr 55min).

Kyle of Lochalsh to: Fort William (3 daily; 1hr 50min); Glasgow (3 daily; 5hr); Inverness (3–4 daily; 2hr).

Lochinver to: Inverness (May to early Oct 1 daily; 3hr 10min).

Mallaig to: Acharacle (1–3 daily; 1hr 45min); Fort William (1–2 daily; 2hr).

Thurso to: Bettyhill (2 daily; 1hr 20min); Inverness (Mon–Sat 5 daily, Sun 4 daily; 3hr 30min); Wick (Mon–Sat 2–4 daily, Sun 1 daily; 35min).

Wick to: Inverness (Mon–Sat 3 daily; 1hr 55min); Thurso (Mon–Sat 2–4 daily, Sun 1 daily; 35min).

Ferries

To Lewis: Ullapool–Stornoway, see p.364.

To Mull: Kilchoan–Tobermory, see p.325.

To Orkney: Scrabster–Stromness, see p.542.

To Skye: Mallaig–Armadale; Glenelg–Kylerhea, see p.364.

To the Small Isles: Mallaig–Eigg, Rum, Muck and Canna, see pp.363–4.

Flights

Inverness to: Amsterdam (1 daily; 1hr 35min); Edinburgh (Mon–Fri 1 daily; 50min); Glasgow (Mon–Fri 2 daily; 50min); Kirkwall (Mon–Fri 2 daily; 40min); London (7 daily; 1hr 25min); Shetland (Mon–Fri 1 daily; 1hr 50min); Stornoway (Mon–Sat 2 daily; 40min).

CHAPTER NINE

ORKNEY AND SHETLAND

R eaching up towards the Arctic Circle, and totally exposed to turbulent Atlantic weather systems, the Orkney and Shetland islands gather neatly into two distinct and very different clusters. Often referring to themselves first as Orcadians or Shetlanders, and with unofficial, but widely displayed, flags, their inhabitants regard Scotland as a separate entity. This feeling of detachment arises from their distinctive geography, history and culture, in which they differ not only from Scotland but also from each other.

To the south, just a short step from the Scottish mainland, are the seventy or so **Orkney Islands**. With the major exception of Hoy, which is high and rugged, these islands are mostly low-lying, gently sloping and fertile, and for centuries have provided a reasonably secure living for their inhabitants from farming and fishing. In spring and summer the days are long, the skies enormous and the meadows thick with wild flowers. There is a peaceful continuity to Orcadian life reflected not only in the well-preserved treasury of **Stone Age settlements**, such as Skara Brae, and standing stones, most notably the Stones of Stenness, but also in the rather conservative nature of society here today.

Another sixty miles north, the **Shetland Islands** are in nearly all respects a complete contrast. Dramatic cliffs, teeming with thousands of seabirds, rise straight out of the water to rugged, heather-coated hills, while ice-sculpted sea inlets cut deep into the

---

ISLAND WILDLIFE

Orkney and Shetland support huge numbers of **seabirds**, particularly during the breeding season from April to July, when cliffs and coastal banks are alive with thousands of guillemots, razorbills, puffins, fulmars and, particularly in Shetland, gannets. Terns are often to be found on small offshore islets or gravelly spits. On coastal heathland or moorland you should see arctic skuas, great skuas, curlews and occasionally whimbrel or golden plover, while in remoter meadows in Orkney, a corncrake may be heard. Many kinds of wild duck are present, especially in winter, but eiders are particularly common. In spring and autumn, large numbers of migrants drop in on their way north or south and very rare specimens may turn up at any time of year. Fair Isle, in particular, has a long list of rarities; and Shetland's isolation has produced its own distinctive subspecies of wren. Some of the best or most accessible bird sites have been noted in the text.

The separation of the islands from the mainland has also meant that some species of **land mammal** are absent and others have developed subspecies. For instance, Shetland has no voles but Orkney boasts its own distinctive type. However, both groups have considerable populations of seals and otters. Further offshore you may well see porpoises, dolphins and several species of whale including pilot, sperm and killer.

Neither of the island groups supports many **trees**, and very few are native. However, the clifftops and meadows of both Orkney and Shetland are rich with beautiful **wild flowers**, including pink thrift, the pale-pink heather-spotted orchid, red campion and, in wetter areas, golden marsh marigolds, yellow iris and insect-eating sundew. Notable **smaller plants** include the purple Scottish primrose, which grows only in Orkney and the far north of Scotland, and the Shetland (or Edmondston's) mouse-eared chickweed with its delicate white flower streaked with yellow, which grows only on the island of Unst.

land, offering memorable coastal walks in Shetland's endless summer evenings. With little fertile ground, Shetlanders have traditionally been crofters rather than farmers, often looking to the sea for an uncertain living in fishing or the naval and merchant services. Today islanders enthusiastically embrace new opportunities such as fish farming and computing. Nevertheless, the past is seldom forgotten; the Norse heritage is clear in every road sign and there are many well-preserved prehistoric sites, such as **Broch of Mousa** and **Jarlshof.**

Since people first began to explore the North Atlantic, Orkney and Shetland have been stepping stones on routes between Britain, Ireland and Scandinavia; and both groups have a long history of settlement, certainly from around 3500–4000 BC. The Norse settlers, who began to arrive from about 800 AD, with substantial migration from around 900 AD, left the islands with a unique cultural character. Orkney was a powerful Norse earldom, and Shetland (at first part of the same earldom) was ruled directly from

---

DIALECT AND PLACE NAMES

Between the tenth and seventeenth centuries the language of Orkney and Shetland was **Norn**, a Scandinavian tongue close to modern Faroese and Icelandic. After the end of Norse rule and with the transformation of the church, the law, commerce and education, Norn gradually lost out to Scots and English. Today, Orkney and Shetland have their own dialects and individual islands and communities within each group have local variations. The **dialects** have a Scots base, with some Old Norse words; however, they don't sound strongly Scottish, with the Orkney accent – which has been likened to the Welsh one – especially distinctive. Listed below are some of the words you're most likely to hear, including some birds' names and common elements in place names. In most cases, the Shetland form is given; the Orkney terms are very similar, if not identical.

alan	storm petrel	*noost*	hollow place where a boat is drawn up
ayre	beach		
böd	fisherman's store	*norie*	puffin
bonxie	great skua	(or *tammie-norie*)	
bruck	rubbish	*noup*	steep headland
burra	heath rush	*peerie* (in Orkney,	small
corbie	raven	often *peedie*)	
crö	sheepfold	*plantiecrub*	small drystone
du	familiar form of "you"	(or *plantiecrö*)	enclosure for
dunter	eider duck		growing cabbages
eela	rod-fishing from small boats	*quoy*	enclosed, cultivated common land
ferrylouper	incomer (Orkney)	*reestit*	cured (as in *reestit*
fourareen	four-oared boat		mutton)
foy	party or festival	*roost*	tide race
haa	laird's house	*scattald*	common grazing land
hap	hand-knitted shawl	*scootie alan*	arctic skua
kame	ridge of hills	*scord*	gap or pass in a
kishie	basket		ridge of hills
maa	seagull	*shaela*	dark grey
mallie (Shetland) or	fulmar petrel	*shalder*	oystercatcher
mallimak (Orkney)		*simmer dim*	summer twilight
mool	headland	*sixern*	six-oared boat
moorit	brown	*solan*	gannet
mootie	tiny	*soothmoother*	incomer (Shetland)
muckle	large	*tystie*	black guillemot
neesick	porpoise	*voe*	sea inlet

Norway for nearly 300 years after 1195. The Norse legacy is clearly evident today in place names and in dialect words; neither group was ever part of the Gaelic-speaking culture of Highland Scotland and the Scottish influence is essentially a Lowland one.

From October to April the weather can bring real drama; in late spring and summer, there are often long dry spells with lots of sunshine, but you need to come prepared for wind, rain and, most frustrating of all, the occasional sea fog.

ORKNEY

Just a short step from John O' Groats, the **Orkney Islands** are a unique and fiercely independent grouping. In spring and summer the meadows and clifftops are a brilliant green, shining with wild flowers, while long days pour light onto the land and sea. For an Orcadian, the "Mainland" invariably means the largest island in Orkney, rather than the rest of Scotland, and throughout their history they've been linked to lands much further afield, principally Scandinavia. In the words of the late Orcadian poet George Mackay Brown:

Orkney lay athwart a great sea-way
from Viking times onwards, and its lore
is crowded with sailors, merchants, adventurers,
pilgrims, smugglers, storms and sea-changes.
The shores are strewn with wrack, jetsam,
occasional treasure.

Small communities began to settle in the islands around 4000 BC, and the village at **Skara Brae** on the Mainland is one of the best-preserved Stone Age settlements in Europe. This and many of the other older archeological sites, including the **Stones of Stenness** and **Maes Howe**, are concentrated in the central and western parts of the Mainland. Elsewhere the islands are scattered with chambered tombs and stone circles, a tribute to the well-developed religious and ceremonial practices taking place here from around 2000 BC. More sophisticated **Iron Age** inhabitants built fortified villages incorporating stone towers known as brochs, protected by walls and ramparts, many of which are still in place. Later, Pictish culture spread to Orkney and the remains of several of their early Christian settlements can still be seen, the best at the **Brough of Birsay** in the West Mainland, where a group of small houses is clustered around the remains of an early church. Later, around the ninth century, **Norse** settlers from Scandinavia arrived and the islands became Norse earldoms, forming an outpost of a powerful, expansive culture which was gradually forcing its way south. The last of the Norse earls was killed in 1231, but they had a lasting impact on the islands, leaving behind not only their language but also the great **St Magnus Cathedral** in Kirkwall, one of Scotland's most outstanding pieces of medieval architecture.

After the end of Norse rule, the islands became the preserve of **Scottish earls**, who exploited and abused the islanders, although a steady increase in sea trade did offer some chance of escape. French and Spanish ships sheltered here in the sixteenth century, and the ships of the **Hudson Bay Company** recruited hundreds of Orcadians to work in the Canadian fur trade. The islands were also an important staging post in the **whaling industry** and the herring boom, which brought great numbers of small Dutch, French and Scottish boats. More recently, the naval importance of **Scapa Flow** brought plenty of money and activity during both world wars, but left the clifftops dotted with gun emplacements and the seabed scattered with wrecks, making for wonderful diving opportunities. Since the war, things have quietened down somewhat, although in the last two decades the large **oil terminal** on the island of Flotta, combined with EU funding, has brought surprise windfalls, stemming the exodus of young

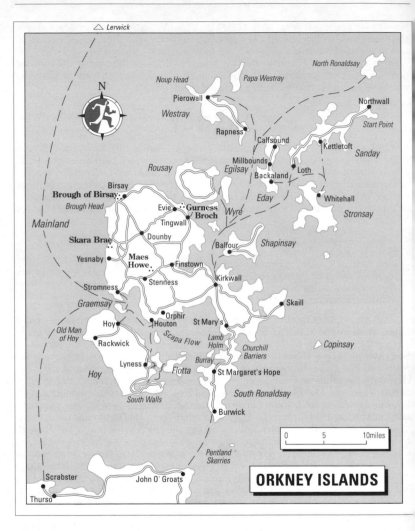

△ Lerwick

N

Noup Head
Pierowall
Westray
Rapness
Rousay
Egilsay
Birsay
Brough of Birsay
Brough Head
Evie **Gurness Broch**
Tingwall
Skara Brae
Dounby
Yesnaby **Maes Howe**
Stromness
Finstown
Stenness
Graemsay
Orphir
Houton
Old Man
of Hoy
Rackwick
Lyness
Hoy
South Walls
Scrabster
Thurso

Papa Westray
North Ronaldsay
Northwall
Start Point
Calfsound
Kettletoft Sanday
Millbounds
Backaland Loth
Eday
Whitehall
Wyre Stronsay
Shapinsay
Balfour
Kirkwall
Skaill
St Mary's
Lamb Holm
Scapa Flow
Churchill Barriers
Copinsay
Burray
Flotta St Margaret's Hope
South Ronaldsay
Burwick
John O' Groats
Pentland Skerries

Mainland

0   5   10miles

ORKNEY ISLANDS

people. Meanwhile, many disenchanted southerners have become "ferryloupers" (incomers) moving north in search of peace and the apparent simplicity of island life.

The Mainland is joined by causeways to the southern island of **South Ronaldsay**, and centres on the capital of **Kirkwall**; although you'll most likely arrive at the ferry port of **Stromness**, an attractive old fishing town on the far western shore. Dividing into distinct western and eastern sections, the Mainland is relatively heavily populated and farmed throughout. Further afield, the **smaller islands** (linked to the Mainland by regular ferries) are starker and quieter. The southern island of **Hoy**, the second largest in the archipelago, presents a superbly dramatic landscape, with some of the highest seacliffs in the country; most exposed of all are the ten **northern isles** – low, elemental outcrops of rock and sand scattered across the ocean.

GETTING TO ORKNEY

Orkney is connected to the Scottish mainland by three main **ferry** routes. P&O Scottish Ferries (☎01856/850655) runs weekly car ferries to **Stromness from Aberdeen** (June–Aug 2 weekly; 8hr), and daily services on the much shorter crossing (1hr 45min) to **Stromness from Scrabster**, about two miles northwest of Thurso on the north coast, which has train and bus connections from Inverness. A passenger ferry runs between **John O' Groats** and **Burwick** on South Ronaldsay (May to mid-Sept; 45min), with which the Orkney Bus service from Inverness connects. A day-trip is available from Inverness or John O' Groats, with a tour of some of the major sights on Orkney; details of both ferry and bus are available from John O' GroatsFerries (☎01955/611353). There's also a weekly (June–Aug twice-weekly) P&O service from Stromness to **Lerwick** in Shetland.

There are direct flights to Kirkwall airport from **Wick, Inverness, Aberdeen, Edinburgh** and **Glasgow**, with good connections from **Birmingham, London** and **Manchester**. There are also flights between Orkney and **Shetland**. All these services are operated by British Airways Express (☎0345/222111).

Rolling out of the sea "like the backs of sleeping whales" (Mackay Brown), the Orkney Isles offer excellent **walking** and beautiful sweeping white-sand beaches. There is also some good **fishing** to be had in both salt and fresh water, with the rivers and lochs providing some of the best trout and sea-trout fishing in Britain. A lively cultural life includes the **Orkney Folk Festival** in May, and a science festival in September, both of which have events throughout the islands, while June sees the celebration of St Magnus in Kirkwall.

Getting around

On the Orkney Mainland, **scheduled buses** connect Kirkwall to Stromness, Dounby, Houton, Tingwall, Evie, Rendall, Deerness, Burray and South Ronaldsay. However, services aren't frequent and many of the most interesting areas are some way from the bus routes. **Cycling** is cheap and effective as there are few steep hills, distances are not too long and, in summer at least, the weather is usually not prohibitive. Bikes can be rented in Kirkwall, Stromness and on some of the smaller islands. Bringing a **car** to Orkney is straightforward, if not exactly cheap; alternatively, you can rent one in Kirkwall, Stromness or on several of the islands. Especially if time is limited, it may be worth considering one of the informative bus or minibus **tours**, operated by Go-Orkney (☎01856/871871) or Wildabout (☎01856/851011) among others; details are available from the tourist offices.

Getting to the other islands from the Mainland isn't difficult; Orkney Ferries (☎01856/872044) operates several sailings daily to Hoy, Shapinsay and Rousay and between one and three, depending on route and season, to all the others except North Ronaldsay, which has a weekly boat on Fridays. British Airways Express flies to Eday, North Ronaldsay, Westray, Papa Westray, Sanday and Stronsay. Travel between individual islands by sea or air isn't so straightforward, but careful study of timetables can reduce the need to come all the way back to Kirkwall. Additional sailings on summer Sundays make useful inter-island connections.

Kirkwall

Relatively sheltered at the south end of its wide bay, Orkney's capital **KIRKWALL** huddles around St Magnus Cathedral. The town has two focal points: the busy **harbour**, where ferries come and go, and the main shopping street, whose name changes four

> The telephone code for Kirkwall is ☎01856.

times as it twists back past the **cathedral** through a tight knot of paved streets, old stone houses and narrow alleys.

By Orkney standards, Kirkwall is a bustling metropolis; a busy market town and home to the island's more exotic restaurants and better-stocked shops, as well as two distilleries. An interesting place to spend some time, with unusual, quietly impressive architecture and a gentle, unhurried atmosphere, Kirkwall also makes an ideal base from which to explore the Mainland or make day-trips to the northern isles.

Arrival, information and accommodation

Visitors coming to Orkney by sea from Scrabster, Aberdeen or Lerwick arrive at the ferry terminal in Stromness, in the southwest corner of the Mainland. **Ferries** are met by buses to Kirkwall (40min). There are also bus connections (45min) from the Burwick terminal on South Ronaldsay, served by ferry from John O' Groats. Kirkwall **airport** is about three miles southeast of Kirkwall on the A960. It's not served by buses, but a taxi into town should only set you back about £6.

Kirkwall itself is an easy place in which to orientate yourself, despite its **main street** taking four different names, Bridge Street, Albert Street, Broad Street and Victoria Street, as it winds through the town. Moreover, it's hard to get lost as the prominent spire of St Magnus Cathedral clearly marks the town centre. The helpful **tourist office**, on Broad Street, beside the cathedral graveyard (April daily 9am–6pm; May–Sept daily 8.30am–8pm; Oct–March Mon–Sat 9.30am–5pm; ☎872856), books accommodation, changes money and gives out an excellent free leaflet, the *Kirkwall Heritage Guide*, which takes you through all the buildings of interest. Most events are advertised in the *Orcadian* (Thurs) and there's a *What's on Diary* on BBC Radio Orkney (Mon–Fri 7.30–8am, 93.7MHz FM).

Kirkwall boats an excellent range of **accommodation**. For basic rooms, try the *SYHA* **youth hostel** (☎872243) on the road to Orphir, about half a mile southeast of the town centre – it isn't beautiful to look at, but is comfortable. A more central option is the small *Peedie Hostel* (☎874500), on the waterfront at the corner of Burgh Road. The tourist office has details of **B&Bs** and can book you in for a ten percent fee which is deducted from what you pay the owner. If you'd rather look yourself, try the comfortable *Whiteclett*, St Catherine's Place (☎874193; ②); *Craigwood* (☎872006; ②), one of several reasonable places on Cromwell Road; *Briar Lea*, 10 Dundas Crescent (☎872747; ③); or the B&Bs run by Mrs Bain, 6 Fraser's Close (☎872862; ②), and Mrs Forsyth, 21 Willowburn Rd (☎874020; ②). **Camping** is available at *Pickaquoy* (☎873535; mid-May to mid-Sept), on the west side of town; the site is well-equipped with clothes, washing and drying facilities.

ACCOMMODATION PRICE CODES

Throughout this book, accommodation **prices** have been graded with the codes below, according to the cost of the least expensive double room in high season. Price codes are not given for campsites, most of which charge under £10 per person. Almost all hostels charge less than £10 a night for a bed – the few exceptions to this rule have the prices quoted in the text. For a full account of the accommodation price codes, see p.30.

① under £20	④ £40–50	⑦ £70–80
② £20–30	⑤ £50–60	⑧ £80–100
③ £30–40	⑥ £60–70	⑨ over £100

Hotels and guest houses

Albert, Mounthoolie Lane (☎876000). Completely refurbished and in the heart of the town. ⑤.

Ayre, Ayre Road (☎873001) The best option in town: smart, friendly and on the waterfront. ⑧.

Foveran, two miles out on the A964 to Orphir (☎872389). A modern hotel set among fields, with comfortable rooms and a good restaurant. ⑦.

Queen's Hotel, Shore Street (☎872200). Comfortable and convenient for the centre. ④.

St Ola, Harbour Street (☎875090). Very central, overlooking the harbour, with comfortable accommodation and friendly bars. ④.

Sanderlay Guest House, 2 Viewfield Drive (☎872343). A welcoming place, with well-equipped rooms. ②.

West End Hotel, 14 Main St (☎872368). Comfortable and welcoming hotel in an old, characterful building; serves huge breakfasts. ⑤.

The Town

At the very heart of Kirkwall, **St Magnus Cathedral** (April–Sept Mon–Sat 9am–6pm, Sun 2–6pm; Oct–March Mon–Sat 9am–1pm & 2–5pm; also Sunday service at 11.15am) is the town's most intriguing conventional sight, a unique building that employs traditional architectural techniques but gives them a distinctively Orcadian twist. The building was begun in 1137 by the Orkney Earl Kol of Agdir, who decided to make full use of a growing cult surrounding the figure of his uncle Magnus Erlendson. Magnus had shared the earldom of Orkney with his cousin Hakon Paulson from 1103, but Hakon grew jealous of his cousin's popularity and had him killed in 1115. When Magnus's body was buried in Birsay a heavenly light was said to have shone overhead, and his grave soon became a place of pilgrimage attributed with miraculous powers and attracting pilgrims from as far afield as Shetland. When Kol of Agdir finally took over the earldom he built the cathedral in his uncle's honour, moving the centre of religious and secular power from Birsay to Kirkwall.

The first version of the cathedral, built using yellow stone from Eday and red stone from the Mainland, was somewhat smaller than today's structure, which has been added to over the centuries, with a new east window in the thirteenth century, the extension of the nave in the fifteenth century and a new west window to mark the building's 850th anniversary in 1987. Today the soft sandstone is badly eroded, particularly around the doorways, but it's still an immensely impressive building, its shape and style echoing the great cathedrals of Europe. Inside, the atmosphere is surprisingly intimate, the pink sandstone columns drawing you up to the exposed brickwork arches, while around the walls a series of gravestones and monuments include the bones of Magnus himself, a monument to the dead of HMS *Royal Oak* (which was torpedoed in Scapa Flow in 1939 with the loss of 833 men; see p.506) and the tomb of the Arctic explorer John Rae, who was born in Stromness. There's also a collection of gravestones from the sixteenth and seventeenth centuries, carved with chilling inscriptions calling on the reader to "remember death waits us all, the hour none knows".

Alongside the church are the ruined remains of the **Bishop's Palace** (April–Sept Mon–Sat 9.30am–6pm, Sun 2–6pm; £1.20). Built in the twelfth century for Bishop William of Old, the palace consisted of a main hall for ceremonial occasions and a tower which probably served as the bishop's private residence. The palace was rebuilt in the late fifteenth century and restored in the sixteenth, by Bishop Robert Reid, the founder of Edinburgh University. Today the walls and tower still stand, and a narrow spiral staircase takes you to the top for a good view of the cathedral and across Kirkwall's rooftops.

The neighbouring **Earl's Palace**, which dates from 1600, is rather better preserved; it's reckoned to be one of the finest examples of Renaissance architecture in Scotland. With its dank dungeons, massive fireplaces and magnificent central hall, it is a much grander building than the Bishop's Palace and has an confident solidity. Inside, a series of excellent displays analyses the uses of the various rooms, and it's easy enough to imagine the way in which the earl lived here and conducted his ruthless business. The roof is missing, but many domestic details remain, including a set of toilets and the stone shelves used by the clerk to do his filing.

The turreted towers of the Earl's Palace are echoed by those of the Victorian **Town Hall**, opposite the cathedral. Nearby **Tankerness House** (Mon–Sat 10.30am–12.30pm & 1.30–5pm; May–Sept also Sun 2–5pm; April–Sept £1, otherwise free), a former home for the clergy, has been renovated countless times over the years, first in 1574 and most recently in the 1960s. It is currently home to a simple but informative **museum** that takes you through Orkney history from the very beginning – well worth a look before you visit the main archeological sites. Among its more unusual artefacts are a collection of *ba* balls (used in a traditional Orkney street game played at Christmas and New Year), Pictish board games, an Iron Age bone shovel and early bowls made from whales' vertebrae. In addition, there are a couple of rooms which have been restored as they would have been in 1820, when the building was a private home. On a warm summer afternoon, the gardens (which can be entered either from the house itself or from a gate on Tankerness Lane) are thick with the buzz of bees and brilliant blooms.

At the harbour end of Junction Road, you can browse around the tiny **Orkney Wireless Museum** (April–Sept Mon–Sat 10am–4.30pm, Sun 2.30–4.30pm; £2), which is packed to the roof with every sort of radio equipment.

Further afield (a mile or so south of the town centre on the Holm road), is the Highland Park **distillery**, billed as "the most northerly legal distillery in Scotland". It's been in operation for more than 200 years, although it was closed during World War II, when the army used it as a food store and the huge vats served as communal baths. You can decide for yourself whether the taste still lingers by partaking of the regular guided tours of its beautiful old buildings and the customary dram afterwards (Easter–Oct Mon–Fri 10am–4pm; June–Aug also Sat 10am–4pm; Nov–March Mon–Fri tours at 2pm & 3.30pm only; £2).

Eating and drinking

Orkney is well-known for its beef and dairy produce, including excellent local cheeses, while the fish and shellfish are also of a high quality. Kirkwall offers a good selection of **cafés** and **restaurants**, where the range and quality of food continues to improve and local fresh ingredients take pride of place on most menus; vegetarian options are on the increase, too. Some **pubs** to try include the *Bothy Bar* in the *Albert Hotel*, which sometimes has live music and is attached to *Matchmakers* **disco** (open as a disco on Thurs, Fri & Sat nights, but selling bar meals at other times), and the cosy lounge bar in the *Queen's Hotel*. The liveliest option in town is the *Torvhaug Inn* at the harbour end of Bridge Street, while there's a good atmosphere and sometimes live music at the *Quoyburray Inn*, a couple of miles beyond the airport on the A960.

Albert Hotel, Mounthoolie Lane (☎876000). Good meals in the bar and restaurant with local produce widely used.

Buster's Diner, Mounthoolie Place. Inexpensive burgers, pizza, pancakes and ice cream, and friendly service.

Foveran Hotel, two miles out on the A964 to Orphir (☎872389). One of the best eating places in Orkney, with some good vegetarian choices. Strong on local produce.

Golden Dragon Chinese Restaurant, up the back steps at 25a Bridge St (☎872933). Probably the better of Kirkwall's two Chinese restaurants, but still a little bland.

International Takeaway, Bridge Street. Good fish and chips and other deep-fried delicacies, together with a wide range of baked potatoes.

Mumataz Indian Restaurant, 7 Bridge St (☎873537). Good food, friendly service and moderate prices. Also serves a small range of European dishes.

Pomona Café, Albert Street. Something of a local institution, with simple food: teas, coffees, cakes, pies, sandwiches and toasties.

Queen's Hotel, Shore Street (☎872200). Some ambitious bar meals are on offer, while the pricier *Buckingham Restaurant* is also good.

St Magnus Café, opposite the cathedral on Broad Street. Teas, sandwiches and soup in basic surroundings. Closes around 4pm; also Mon & Thurs 7–10pm.

Trenabies, 16 Albert St. Busy, easy-going restaurant serving a good breakfast, sandwiches, baked potatoes, pasta, pizza and other inexpensive meals.

West End Hotel, Main Street (☎872368). Good-value bar meals, including chicken, salmon, scampi and steak.

Listings

Airport ☎872421.

Banks There are branches of all the big Scottish banks on the main street.

Bike rental Paterson's, Tankerness Lane (☎873097).

Bookshops Leonard's or Stevenson at the corner of Bridge Street and Albert Street; Spence at 42 Broad St; secondhand books from M.E. McCarty at 54 Junction Rd.

Bus companies Causeway Coaches (Kirkwall to St Margaret's Hope; ☎831444); James D. Peace (Kirkwall to Houton, Stromness and Dounby; ☎872866); Rosie's Coaches (Kirkwall to Tingwall and Evie; ☎751227); Shalder Coaches (Kirkwall to Stromness to connect with Scrabster ferry, and Kirkwall to Burwick to connect with John O' Groats ferry; ☎850809); W.J. Stove (Kirkwall to Deerness; ☎741215).

Car rental James D. Peace, Junction Road (☎872866); Scarth, Great Western Road (☎872125); Shearer, Junction Road (☎872950); J. and W. Tait, Sparrowhawk Road (☎872490); W.R. Tullock, Castle Street (☎874458).

Consulates Denmark and Germany, J. Robertson, Shore Street (☎872961); Netherlands and Norway, J. Spence, 21 Bridge St (☎872268).

Exchange In addition to the banks, the tourist office in Broad Street runs an exchange service (summer daily 8.30am–8pm).

Fishing tackle and **diving equipment** Eric Kemp, 31–33 Bridge St (☎872137).

Golf The Orkney Golf Club, an exposed course west of the town with good views, is open to the public (☎872457).

Laundry Launderama, Albert Street (Mon–Fri 8.30am–5.30pm, Sat 9am–5.30pm).

Medical care Balfour Hospital, Kirkwall Health Centre and Dental Clinic, New Scapa Road (☎885400).

Post office Junction Road (Mon–Fri 9am–5pm, Sat 9.30am–12.30pm).

Travel agents Going Places, 15 Broad St (☎873734); Ridgway Travel, 67 Albert St(☎873359).

The West Mainland

The great bulk of the **West Mainland** is Orkney's most fertile, productive ground, fringed by some spectacular coastline and littered with impressive historical sites, ranging from the prehistoric village of **Skara Brae** to the battered concrete huts that mark the remains of Twatt military airfield, a large World War II air base. Today this part of the island is still heavily farmed, and there are few real villages. There are still some areas, however, which are too barren to cultivate, and the high ground and wild coastline are protected by several interesting **wildlife reserves**, while a handful of lochs offer superb **trout fishing**.

Evie and the Broch of Gurness

Overshadowed by the great wind turbines on Burgar Hill, the little village of **EVIE**, on the north coast, looks out across the turbulent waters of **Eynhallow Sound** towards the island of Rousay. At the western end of the white sands of Evie, the **Broch of Gurness** (April–Sept Mon–Sat 9.30am–6.30pm, Sun 2–6.30pm; £2.50) is the best preserved of more than 500 pre-Christian-era villages dotted across the islands – like the others, it's built to a simple pattern, with a compact group of homes clustered around a central tower. The walls and partitions of the houses have survived amazingly well, as has the main tower, which was probably retreated to in times of attack, with its thick, fortified walls and independent water supply.

To the south of Evie, a small road climbs high over the shoulder of **Burgar Hill**, skirting along the side of the huge **RSPB Birsay Moors Reserve**, which embraces most of Burgar Hill and reaches down to the marshland and the shores of Lowrie's Water. The high heather-coated ground provides good hunting for kestrels, merlins and hen harriers, while the loch is used as a nesting site by red-throated divers. The moor is also a source of traditional fuel, and you can make out the areas in which peat is cut, with small stacks often drying on the hillside. Just north of Evie, a road leads up to the **aerogenerators** established here in 1983 to harness Orkney's wind. Research done here has paved the way for wind-power developments elsewhere in Britain.

Birsay: the Earl's Palace, Brough of Birsay and Kirbuster

Northwest from Evie, the parish of **BIRSAY** was the centre of Norse power in Orkney for several centuries, until the earls moved to Kirkwall following the construction of the cathedral. Today a tiny cluster of homes is gathered around the ruins of the **Earl's Palace** at Birsay, which was built in 1574, behind a rocky, exposed bay. The crumbling walls and turrets retain plenty of their grandeur, although there is little remaining evidence of domestic detail. When it was occupied, the palace was surrounded by flower and herb gardens, a bowling green and archery butts. By comparison, the Earl's Palace in Kirkwall seems almost humble.

Just over half a mile northwest of the palace is the **Brough of Birsay**, a small Pictish settlement on a tidal island that is only accessible during the two hours each side of high tide. The focus of the village was the twelfth-century **St Peter's Church**, the shape of which is mapped out by the remains of its walls. Southwest, on the other side of Birsay Bay, is **Marwick Head**. On it stands the memorial to Lord Kitchener and the crew of the HMS *Hampshire* who died near here when the ship struck a mine in June 1916. Marwick Head is an **RSPB reserve**, as is the **Loons**, a mile or so to the east, from whose hide you can see a variety of duck and other wetland birds.

Two miles east of Birsay, at **KIRBUSTER** (between the Loch of Hundland and the Loch of Boardhouse), the **Kirbuster Farm Museum** (March–Oct Mon–Sat 10.30am–1pm & 2–5pm, Sun 2–5pm) offers an interesting insight into the hardships of life on an Orkney croft in the last century, when open peat fires filled the rooms with smoke and roofs were protected with heather thatch. Housed in a traditional structure, with cold stone floors, blackened cooking pots over the fire and fish fillets drying in the smoke, the display shows the dramatic improvements in croft life which took place last century; one room has bare stone walls and a fire in the centre of the room, while the other has wallpaper and a fireplace. Most remarkable of all is that the house was inhabited in much the same way until 1961.

Skara Brae

About five miles south of Birsay, the beautiful white curve of the **Bay of Skaill** is home to **Skara Brae** (April–Sept Mon–Sat 9.30am–6.30pm, Sun 2–6.30pm; Oct–March Mon–Sat 9.30am–4.30pm, Sun 2–4.30pm; £2.80), the remains of a small fishing and farming village that was inhabited between 3000 and 2500 BC and rediscovered in 1850 after a fierce storm. The village is very well preserved, its houses huddled together and connected by narrow passages which would have been covered over with turf. For centuries it was buried in the dunes, which protected a vast array of domestic detail, including dressers, fireplaces, beds and boxes, all carefully put together from slabs of stone. Archeologists have discovered two distinct types of house: an earlier, smaller structure, constructed around a central hearth, with beds built into the wall; and larger, later homes that have the beds in the main living area with cupboards behind them. Other evidence shows that the inhabitants were settled farmers eating sheep, cattle and grain, as well as fish and shellfish, and using lamps fuelled by the oil from whales, seals and seabirds.

Skara Brae was rediscovered by the laird of Skaill, whose massive **Skaill House**, 300yd inland, has been restored and is open to the public (April–Sept Mon–Sat 9.30am–6.30pm, Sun 11.30am–6.30pm; £3). The original house was built by Bishop George Graham in the 1620s, and has since been much extended. Its contents include Captain Cook's dinner service from the *Resolution*, as well as family and military memorabilia.

Maes Howe, the Stones of Stenness and the Ring of Brodgar

The main road leads back towards Kirkwall via **DOUNBY**, a quiet, former market village, then skirts the shores of Loch Harray (Orkney's most famous trout loch), to reach the great Neolithic burial chamber of **Maes Howe** (April–Sept Mon–Sat 9.30am–6pm, Sun 2–6pm; Oct–May Mon–Sat 9.30am–4pm, Sun 2–4pm; £2.30). The chamber occupies a central position on the Mainland and is proof positive of the ingenuity of prehistoric communities in Orkney. Dating from 2750 BC, its incredible state of preservation is partly due to the massive slabs of sandstone it was constructed from, the largest of which weighs over three tons. The central chamber, reached down a long stone passage, is aligned with the sun at the midwinter solstice and contains three cells built into the walls, each of which was plugged with an enormous stone. When the tomb was opened in 1861, it was found to be virtually empty, thanks to the work of generations of grave-robbers, who had only left behind a handful of human bones. The Vikings broke in here in the twelfth century, probably on their way to the Crusades, leaving large amounts of graffiti. These runic inscriptions, cut into the walls of the main chamber and still clearly visible today, include phrases such as: "Many a beautiful woman has stooped in here, however pompous she might be" and "These runes were carved by the man most skilled in runes in the entire western ocean".

The area surrounding Maes Howe was a Stone Age religious centre; of the many remains dating back to that era, the closest are the **Stones of Stenness**, just over a mile to the west – a circle of twelve rock slabs, the tallest of which is over 16ft high. Less than half a mile from these, the **Ring of Brodgar** is a nearly complete ring of 27 stones, dramatically sited on a narrow spit of land between two lochs.

West Mainland practicalities

You can easily base yourself in Kirkwall or Stromness, but there are many good **places to stay** scattered throughout the West Mainland, including welcoming **B&Bs** such as *Linnadale*, Heddle Road, in Finstown (☎01856/761300; ②), and *Duncraigon*, overlooking the loch at Sandwick (☎01856/841647; ②). *Netherstove*, northeast of the Bay of Skaill (☎01856/841625; ③), has a great view over the bay, comfortable rooms and self-catering cottages (two to four; £100 per week). Other places to try include *Dounby House* in Dounby (☎01856/771535; ③), *Primrose Cottage* at Marwick (☎01856/721384; ②), or *Woodwick House* at Evie (☎01856/751330; ④), a secluded, cultured and friendly place, with good food. **Hotels** include the *Smithfield Hotel* (☎01856/771215; ⑤), a pleasant village inn in the middle of Dounby, also serving good food. The *Barony Hotel*

(☎01856/721327; ④), on the north shore of the Loch of Boardhouse, specializes in fishing holidays, as does the *Merkister Hotel* (☎01856/771515; ⑤) at the north end of the Loch of Harray; it also boasts a bird hide. **Camping** is available at the *Eviedale Centre* (☎01856/751270; April–Oct).

All the hotels do lunches or bar **meals**; for a snack or something more filling try the *Dale Kitchen* at Evie, *Wylie's Tearoom* at Harray and the top-floor restaurant at *Tormiston Mill* opposite Maes Howe.

Stromness

> *The Orkney I was born into was a place*
> *Where there was no great distinction between*
> *the ordinary and the fabulous; the lives of*
> *living men turned into legend.*
>
> Edwin Muir

Vastly more appealing than most ferry ports, the great harbour town of **STROMNESS** has been one of the focal points of Orkney life since Viking times or before. It was here, in the sheltered Hamnavoe, on the edge of the great natural harbour of Scapa Flow, that ships from all around the world came and went, sweeping the town into a series of booms, unloading a cargo of sea tales and embarking hundreds of Orcadians on weird and wonderful expeditions.

French and Spanish ships sheltered in Hamnavoe in the sixteenth century, and for a long time European conflicts made it safer for ships heading across the Atlantic to travel around the top of Scotland rather than through the English Channel, many of whom called here to take on food, water and crew. Crews from Stromness were also hired for herring and whaling expeditions for which the town was an important centre. By 1842, the town boasted forty or so pubs and reports were made of "outrageous and turbulent proceedings of seamen and others who frequent the harbour". The herring boom brought large numbers of small boats to the town, along with thousands of young women who gutted and pickled the fish before they were packed in barrels. Today Stromness is still an important harbour town, serving as Orkney's main ferry terminal and as the headquarters of the Northern Lighthouse Board.

Information and accommodation

The **tourist office** (April–Oct Mon–Sat 8am–6pm, Sun 9am–4pm; Nov–March Mon–Fri 9am–5pm; ☎01856/850716) is in the ferry terminal building opposite the pier. The smartest **hotel** in the area is the *Standing Stones* (☎01856/850449; ⑤), four miles from Stromness on the southern shore of the Loch of Stenness. In Stromness itself, the *Stromness Hotel* (☎01856/850610; ⑥) was the town's first; it's showing its age a bit, but the welcome's warm. Stromness also boasts several good and friendly **B&Bs**, including the *Ferry Inn*, on John Street (☎01856/850280; ③), right by the ferry terminal, and Mrs Hourston (☎01856/850642; ③), just behind the *Ferry Inn* on the same street. At the southern end of town, on the Ness Road, *Stenigar* (☎01856/850438; ③) has lots of character. Further out, at Kirbister, *Brettobreck Farm* (☎01856/850373; ②) is a traditional and homely Orcadian farmhouse, while four miles out of town, on the road to Orphir, the carefully converted *Mill of Eyrland* (☎01856/850136; ③) has well-equipped rooms in a delightful setting by a mill stream, and serves enormous breakfasts.

Stromness has an official **youth hostel**, on Helly Hole Road (☎01856/850589; March–Oct), signposted from the car park outside the *Stromness Hotel*, but it's strictly run, with a curfew and single-sex dorms. More laid-back is the independent *Brown's Hostel*, 45–47 Victoria St (☎01856/850661), with bunk beds in shared rooms and kitchen facilities; it's open all day, and there's no curfew. There's also a well-equipped **camping** site (☎01856/873535) in a superb but exposed setting at Point of Ness, with views out to Hoy; to reach it, keep going southwards along the main street and follow the shore road (South End) for about half a mile.

The Town

Clustered along the shoreline, Stromness is a tight network of alleyways and slate roofs, crowded onto the lower slopes of **Brinkie's Brae**, which looms up from the harbour front. The main street, paved with great flagstones, takes six different names – John Street, Victoria Street, Graham Place, Dundas Street, Alfred Street and South End – as it threads its way southwards past the old houses on the harbour front. Originally all the waterfront houses had their own piers, from which merchants would trade with passing ships; the **cannon** at the southern end of town (on South End) was fired to announce the arrival of a ship from the Hudson's Bay Company. Today the trade in American rice and Canadian fur has gone, but the site of the cannon still gives magnificent views of the harbour, and there are a number of reminders of the town's trading heyday. **The Warehouse**, now home to the P&O and tourist offices, was originally built in the 1760s to store American rice. At the southern end of town, on the Ness road, **The Doubles** is a large pair of houses on a raised platform that were built as a home by Mrs Christian Robertson with the proceeds of her shipping agency, which sent as many as 800 men on whaling expeditions in one year.

The **Stromness Museum**, off the southern end of main street (May–Sept daily 10am–5pm; Oct–April Mon–Sat 10.30am–12.30pm & 1.30–5pm; £1.50), houses a collection of salty artefacts gathered from shipwrecks and Arctic expeditions, including crockery from the German fleet, beaver fur hats, Cree Indian cloth and part of the torpedo that sunk the HMS *Royal Oak*. The **Pier Arts Centre**, right on the waterfront (Tues–Sat 10.30am–12.30pm & 1.30–5pm; July & Aug also Sun 2–5pm), gives a more contemporary account of Orkney culture. The restored building has become an important focus of artistic life in the islands, with regular exhibitions, featuring painting and sculpture by local artists.

Eating and drinking

For its size, Stromness offers a good choice of **places to eat** scattered around the small town centre. The moderately priced *Hamnavoe Restaurant,* at 35 Graham Place (☎01856/850606), offers the town's most ambitious cooking, using local produce including shellfish, fish and beef and offering some delicious vegetarian dishes, in a very pleasant setting. For something less formal, the very popular *Ferry Inn* on John Street, beside the tourist office, serves good, inexpensive fish, steak and scampi dishes, while *The Café*, on the harbour front just across from the *Stromness Hotel*, serves straightforward meals of burgers, pizza and pasta. The *Valhalla Restaurant*, in the bar of the *Stromness Hotel*, offers a solid but uninspiring menu, including steak and haddock. For daytime food, head for the *Coffee Shop*, opposite the ferry terminal, a friendly little café offering enormous breakfasts, sandwiches, vegetarian dishes, afternoon tea, cakes and pies (closes at 5pm), or go southwards along Victoria Street to the *Peedie Coffee Shop*, the town's oldest establishment (closes at 4.30pm). Also on Victoria Street, *Argo's Bakery* has a wide range of **picnic** basics, while *Orkney Wholefoods*, a few doors down, sells cheeses and delicious made-to-order sandwiches featuring seafood.

Listings

Banks There are branches of the Bank of Scotland and Royal Bank of Scotland on the main street.
Bike rental *Brown's Hostel*, 45–47 Victoria St (☎01856/850661); Orkney Cycle Hire, 54 Dundas St (☎01856/850255).
Bookshops J. L. Broom, John Rae, or Scapa secondhand bookshop, are all on the main street.
Car rental Brass's Self Drive, Pierhead Office, John Street (☎01856/850750).
Fishing tackle W.S. Sinclair, just above the car park on John Street.
Laundry Next to the *Coffee Shop* on the north side of the car park (Mon–Sat 9am–5pm).

The East Mainland and South Ronaldsay

Southeast from Kirkwall, the narrow spur of the **East Mainland** juts out into the North Sea and is joined, thanks to the remarkable Churchill barriers, to the smaller islands of **Burray** and **South Ronaldsay**. The land here is densely populated and heavily farmed, but there are several interesting fishing villages and a scattering of unusual historical relics.

The East Mainland

The northern side of the East Mainland consists of a series of exposed peninsulas, the first of which, **Rerwick Head**, is marked by the remains of World War II gun emplacements. **Mull Head** – the furthest east – is an **RSPB reserve** with a large colony of seabirds, including arctic terns, that swoop and screech threateningly. The reserve is open to visitors at all times (although without your own transport it is hard to reach). There is a car park at the end of the road (a continuation of the B9050), which is about half a mile from the cliffs. A mile and a half south of the reserve, and a short walk from the car park, is **The Gloup**, an impressive collapsed sea cave; the tide still flows in and out through a natural arch, making strange gurgling noises. The name stems from the Old Norse *gluppa*, "a chasm". About two miles north of Deerness, the **Covenanters' Memorial** commemorates the death of around 200 people who were shipwrecked en route to a life of slavery in the West Indies – their offence had been to object to the new English Common Prayer Book.

On the south coast, just east of the village of **ST MARY'S**, is the **Norwood Museum** (May–Sept Tues–Thurs & Sun 2–5pm & 6–8pm; other times by arrangement ☎01856/781217; £2), a display of antiques collected by local stonemason Norrie Wood from the age of 13. Only about half of the collection is on display, but it's a fascinating and eccentric selection of bits and pieces from around the world, including pottery, painting, medals, furniture, cutlery, clocks, even a narwhal's tusk, all housed in a grand Orkney home. If you want to stay around here, St Mary's has Orkney's only motel, the *Commodore* (☎01856/781319; ③), which also serves good bar meals.

The Churchill barriers

The presence of the huge naval base in **Scapa Flow** during both world wars presented a tempting target to the Germans, and protecting the fleet was always a nagging problem for the Allies. During World War I, blockships were sunk to guard the eastern approaches, but in October 1939, just weeks after the outbreak of World War II, a German U-boat managed to manoeuvre past them and torpedo the battleship HMS *Royal Oak*, which sank with the loss of 833 lives. The U-boat captain claimed to have acquired local knowledge while fishing in the islands before the war.

Today the wreck of the *Royal Oak*, marked by an orange buoy off the Gaitnip Cliffs (on the west coast of the West Mainland, just off the A961 between Kirkwall and St Mary's), is an official war grave. Its sinking convinced the First Lord of the Admiralty, Winston Churchill, that Scapa Flow needed better protection, and in 1940 work began on a series of **barriers** to seal the waters between the Mainland and the string of islands to the south: the tiny uninhabited **Lamb Holm** and **Glimps Holm**, and the larger **Burray** and **South Ronaldsay**. Special camps were built to accommodate the 1700 men involved in the project; their numbers were boosted by the surrender of Italy in 1942, when Italian prisoners of war were sent to work here. Besides the barriers, which are an astonishing feat of engineering when you bear in mind the strength of Orkney tides, the Italians also left behind the extraordinary **Italian Chapel** on Lamb Holm. This, the so-called "miracle of Camp 60", must be one of the greatest adaptations ever, made from two Nissen huts, concrete, barbed wire and parts of a rusting blockship. The chapel deteriorated after the departure of the Italians, but its principal architect, Domenico Chiocchetti, returned in 1960 to restore the building. Today it is beautifully preserved and Mass is said regularly.

If you're travelling with children, you may like to stop off on Burray at the **Orkney Fossil and Vintage Centre** (daily: April–Sept 10am–6pm; Oct 10.30am–6pm; £2), on the main road. Attractions include a dinosaur's footprint, fossil fish, rocks that glow in ultraviolet light, and a café serving good teas, coffees and snacks.

South Ronaldsay

At the southern end of the series of four barriers is the low-lying **South Ronaldsay**. The island has a number of coastal hamlets and villages, of which the largest, **ST MARGARET'S HOPE,** takes its name either from Margaret, the maid of Norway, who died here in November 1290 while on her way to marry Edward II (then Prince Edward) or, less romantically, from an ancient chapel in the area. Margaret had already been proclaimed the queen of Scotland, and the marriage was intended to unify the two countries. Today, St Margaret's Hope is a pleasing little gathering of houses at the back of a sheltered bay, and it makes an excellent base from which to explore the area. The village **Smithy** has been turned into a museum (April–Aug most afternoons, times vary; Sept Mon 10am–noon; Oct Mon noon–2pm; free) with a few exhibits relating to this now-defunct business.

Despite the fact that it is heavily cultivated, South Ronaldsay also offers some excellent walking, particularly out on the **Howe of Hoxa**, where there is a small broch and a beach at the **Sands O'Right** – the scene of an annual ploughing match in August, in which local boys compete with miniature hand-held ploughs. Also at Hoxa, there's a **tapestry studio and gallery** (April–Sept daily 10am–6pm; free, gallery £2) where you can try tapestry-making and view a small but inspiring collection of the artists' work. Further south, seals and their pups can be seen in the autumn in **Wind Wick Bay**, and there is an ancient chambered burial cairn, known as the **Tomb of the Eagles**, at the southeastern corner of the island, where human remains were found alongside eagles' bones. The monument is privately operated and, as well as an engaging tour, there's hands-on contact with the exhibits (daily: April–Oct 10am–8pm; Nov–March 10am–noon; £2.50). Finally you reach **BURWICK**, where a passenger ferry connects South Ronaldsay with the Scottish mainland at John O' Groats.

South Ronaldsay practicalities

Getting to and from South Ronaldsay is relatively easy. There are four daily **buses** (40min) between Kirkwall and St Margaret's Hope, and all ferries arriving at Burwick are met by buses to Kirkwall. However, off the main road you'll have to rely on walking and hitching.

St Margaret's Hope is the best place to head for if you want **to stay**, and first choice should be the *Creel Restaurant and Rooms* (☎01856/831311; ⑦) on Front Road, one of the best restaurants in Scotland and winner of all sorts of awards for its superb food featuring local produce. It's friendly and relaxed, and the rooms are comfortable too. Other good accommodation in St Margaret's Hope includes the *Murray Arms Hotel* (☎01856/831205; ④), with its popular bar serving appetizing meals, and *The Anchorage* (☎01856/831456; ③), on the seafront; its *Galley Dining Room* offers teas, coffees, lunches, high teas and dinner all year round. Among the **B&Bs**, *West End House* (☎01856/831495; ④) is outstanding, with appealing rooms and a pleasant garden. Other comfortable places include *Windbreck*, on the main road southeast of St Margaret's Hope (☎01856/831370; ③), and *Bellevue Guest House* (☎01856/831294; ②), on a hill just east of the village. For basic but comfortable accommodation, head for *Wheems Bothy*, about a mile and a half from the War Memorial on the sideroad leading east (☎01856/831537). Mattresses and ingredients for a wholesome breakfast are provided, and organic produce from the croft is on sale. For good **snacks**, try the *Coach House Café* next to the Murray Arms in St Margaret's Hope.

Hoy

Hoy, Orkney's second-largest island, rises sharply out of the sea to the southwest of the Mainland. The least typical of the islands, but certainly the most dramatic, its north and west sides are made up of great glacial valleys and mountainous moorland rising to the 1500ft-high mass of Ward Hill and the enormous sea cliffs of St John's Head. This part of the island, though a huge expanse, is virtually uninhabited, with just the cluster of houses at **Rackwick** nestling dramatically in a bay between the cliffs, while most of Hoy's 400 or so residents live on the fertile land in the southeast in and around the villages of **Lyness** and **Longhope**.

Around the island

Much of Hoy's magnificent landscape is embraced by the **RSPB North Hoy Reserve** (which covers most of the northwest end of the island), in which the rough grasses and heather harbour a cluster of arctic plants and a healthy population of mountain hares, as well as merlins, kestrels and peregrine falcons, while the more sheltered valleys are nesting sites for snipe and arctic skua. The best access to the reserve is from the single-track road which follows the **White Glen** across the island to Rackwick. Along the way, the road passes the **Dwarfie Stane**, an unusual solid-stone tomb which dates from 3000 to 2000 BC. A couple of miles further on, the road passes the end of a large open valley which cuts away to the north and along which a footpath runs to the village of **HOY** at the island's northeast tip. On the western side of this valley is the narrow gulley of **Berriedale**, which supports Britain's most northerly native woodland, a huddle of birch, hazel and honeysuckle.

RACKWICK, on the west coast of the island, is a spread of crofts which boldly face the Atlantic weather, flanked by towering sandstone cliffs. Rackwick's crofting community went into a steady decline in the middle of this century: its school closed in 1954 and the last fishing boat put to sea in 1963. These days many of the houses have been renovated as holiday homes and the savage exposure of the place has provided inspiration to a number of artists and writers, including Orkney's George Mackay Brown, who wrote that "when Rackwick weeps, its grief is long and forlorn and utterly desolate". A small **museum** (open 24hrs), beside the outdoor centre, tells a little of Rackwick's rough history, and the croft of **Burnmouth Cottage**, just behind the beach (see opposite), gives a good idea of how things used to be.

The cliffs at Hoy's northwestern corner are some of the highest in the country and provide ideal rocky ledges for the nests of thousands of seabirds, including guillemots, kittiwakes, razorbills, puffins and shags. Standing just offshore is the **Old Man of Hoy**, a great sandstone column some 450ft high, perched on an old lava flow which protects it from the erosive power of the sea. The Old Man is a popular challenge for rock climbers, and a 1966 ascent was the first televised climb in Britain. For good views of the column, take the four-mile coastal footpath from Rackwick.

On the opposite side of Hoy, along the sheltered **eastern shore**, the high moorland gives way to a gentler environment, similar to that of the other islands. Hoy marks the western boundary of **Scapa Flow**, and during both world wars it played an important role in its defence, with several substantial gun emplacements along its eastern shore. At **LYNESS**, formerly the main naval base, the naval cemetery is surrounded by the scattered **remains** of hundreds of concrete structures which served as hangars and storehouses during the war, and are now used as barns and cowsheds. Among these are the remains of what was – incredibly – the largest cinema in Europe. Perhaps the most unusual of the remaining buildings is the black-and-white concrete facade of the old Garrison Theatre, on the main road to the south of Lyness. Formerly the grand front end of a huge Nissen hut, which disappeared long ago, it's now a private home. The old pump station, which now stands beside the new Lyness ferry terminal, has been turned into the **Scapa Flow Visitor Centre** (Mon–Fri 9am–4pm; May–Sept also Sat & Sun 10.30am–3.30pm; £1.50), a local museum displaying an interesting collection of pictures and photographs that show how busy the area was during the wars. Wartime exhibits include torpedoes, flags, guns, propellers and a paratrooper's folding bicycle.

Further south still, the secure waters of **North Bay** cut a deep inlet, a narrow spit of sand connecting north Hoy with **South Walls**, a fertile peninsula which is more densely populated. The bay itself is ringed with farms and homes and on its south side is the quiet little village of **LONGHOPE**. There is evidence of earlier conflict here, with two **Martello towers** that mark the island's southeastern outcrops of Hackness and Crockness, as well as the **Hackness battery**, built between 1813 and 1815 to guard against American and French privateers during the Napoleonic wars. If you want to see inside the restored Hackness tower, a sign indicates the nearby house where you can get the key. The eastern tip of the island looks out over treacherous waters and is marked by the **Cantick Head Lighthouse**, while the churchyard at **OSMUNDWALL** contains a monument to the crew of the Longhope lifeboat who died in 1969 when their boat overturned in strong gales on its way to the aid of a Liberian freighter. The entire eight-man crew was killed, leaving seven widows and ten fatherless children.

Practicalities

Two ferry services run to Hoy: a passenger ferry from **Stromness** to the village of Hoy, which also serves the small island of Graemsay (2–4 daily), and the roll-on/roll-off car ferry from **Houton** on the Mainland to **Lyness** and **Longhope**, also serving **Flotta** (6 daily).

If you have time, it's worth staying on Hoy; there are very good, friendly **B&Bs** at *Stonequoy Farm*, Lyness (☎01856/791234; ③), and at *Burnhouse Farm*, (☎01856/701263; ③) and the *Old Custom House* (☎01856/701358; ②), both in Longhope. There are also three **hostels** providing basic rooms, the first two of which can be booked through the Council's Education Department (☎01856/873535); they are the comfortable *Hoy Outdoor Centre*, just up from the pier in Hoy village, and the *SYHA*-affiliated *Rackwick Outdoor Centre*, where the accommodation is in bunk beds with blankets but no sheets (mid-March to early Aug). The third, the basic *Burnmouth Cottage* (☎01856/791316; no bedding), lies in a beautiful setting right at the top of the beach.

For **food**, there's little choice other than B&Bs, which will often provide an ample and delicious evening meal. Otherwise, the *Hoy Inn* in Hoy village, down beyond the post office, offers bar meals and snacks, and in Lyness the *Anchor Bar* serves typical pub food, with steaks and local fish available in the dining room. A good place for a snack or soup is the *Lyness Visitor Centre Café*.

The North Isles

Scattered loosely off the northwestern side of the Mainland, Orkney's **North Isles** are swept by strong tides and winter storms. Their spidery jigsaw-piece form is a product of this battering, and their stark beauty is based on a simple combination of mostly fertile soils, rock and sand. To get a feel for the Isles, it's best to stay at least a night or two, though all except North Ronaldsay can be easily visited on a day-trip from Kirkwall: occasional day-trips on summer Sundays take in North Ronaldsay, too. Each of the islands has its own character and the larger ones offer great walks and some outstanding archeological sites.

Shapinsay

Just a few miles northeast of Kirkwall, **Shapinsay** is the most accessible of the northern isles. The Balfour family, who had made a small fortune in India, constructed their castle in Baronial style here from 1847 by extending an eighteenth-century farmhouse. They also reformed the island's agricultural system and built **BALFOUR** village, a neat and disciplined cottage development, to house estate workers. **Balfour Castle** is a mile or so from the centre of the village and hidden from it by trees, though its towers and turrets are clearly visible from the ferry on the way in. Guided tours of the building are organized on Wednesday and Sunday afternoons and must be booked in advance through the Kirkwall tourist office (see p.498). It's also possible to stay in the castle; details are given below.

The Balfours' grandiose efforts in estate management have left some appealingly eccentric relics. Melodramatic fortifications around the harbour include the huge and ornate, if not exactly beautiful, **gatehouse**, which is now a pub. There's a stone **gasometer** which once supplied castle and village and, southwest of the pier, the castellated **Dishan Tower**, built as a dovecote but allegedly adapted as a cold-water shower. Elsewhere, the island is heavily cultivated, but within little more than a couple of miles from the ferry terminal there are nice walks by the shore to stretches of sand at the **Bay of Furrowend** in the west, with good birdwatching from the hide at **Vasa Loch**, and around the sweeping curve of **Veantro Bay** in the north.

Practicalities

Less than thirty minutes from Kirkwall by **ferry**, Shapinsay is an easy day-trip, but there's good accommodation on the island if you want to stay. **B&B** is available at comfortable *Girnigoe* (☎01856/711256; ②, full board ④), close to the north shore of Veantro Bay. It is also possible to stay in the distinguished and opulent *Balfour Castle* (☎01856/711282; full board ⑨), where the owners welcome house guests and offer visits by boat to nearby uninhabited islands as well as the use of their library and other beautiful rooms. The only lunch option is the *Smithy Café* (May–Sept), which serves teas and sandwiches and has a small heritage centre attached, too.

Rousay, Egilsay and Wyre

Just over half a mile away from the Mainland's northern shore, the island of **ROUSAY** is dominated by high, heather-covered moorland. It's one of the most interesting of the smaller isles, home to a number of intriguing archeological sites, as well as being one of the more accessible. The group of a dozen or so houses above the ferry terminal is the only settlement of any size, but a single road runs around the edge of the island, connecting a string of small farms. It's easy enough to reach the main points of interest on foot from the ferry terminal in the southeast corner of the island.

Only the coastal fringes of the island are cultivated, and the central section is dominated by rolling hills, the highest of which is the 750ft-high **Blotchnie Fiold**. This high ground offers good hill walking, with superb panoramic views of the islands, as well as excellent birdwatching: a sizeable section of moorland at the southern end of the island (a short walk from the ferry terminal) is a protected area in the **RSPB Trumland Reserve**. Here you may well catch a glimpse of merlins, hen harriers, peregrine falcons and red-throated divers, although the latter are more widespread just outside the reserve on one of the island's three lochs, which also offer good trout fishing. The north and western sides of Rousay are guarded by two sets of steep cliffs, separated by the rocky shores of **Saviskaill Bay**, and again provide spectacular walks and good birdwatching, with puffins, gulls, kittiwakes and arctic terns all nesting here in the summer.

The southwestern side of Rousay is home to the bulk of the island's archeological remains, strung out along the shores of the tide races of **Eynhallow Sound**, which run between the island and the Mainland. Most are on the **Westness Walk**, a mile-long heritage trail linking Westness Farm, about four miles northwest of the ferry terminal, with **Midhowe Cairn**, about a mile further on. Known as "the great ship of death", this well-preserved communal burial chamber dates from about 3500 BC and measures more than 98ft in length. The central chamber, a stone corridor, is partitioned with slabs of rock, with twelve compartments on each side. Archeologists discovered the remains of 25 people inside the tomb, generally in a crouched position with their backs to the wall. This form of burial in stalled tombs dates from the earliest period in the use of chambered burial cairns in Orkney.

A couple of hundred yards south of the Midhowe Cairn is the **Midhowe Broch**, the remains of a fortified Iron Age village which dates from the first century AD, and the best preserved of the six brochs that have been found along this shore. It's also thought to be one of the earliest brochs in Orkney, with a compact layout that suggests it was a fortified family house rather than a village.

There is evidence of more recent occupation at the **Knowe of Swandro** (on the shore about a mile south of Midhowe), where archeologists have unearthed the remains of a Norse farmstead of the eleventh or twelfth century. Although there isn't much to see today, a variety of artefacts have been found here, including bone remains from which scientists were able to determine the likely diet of the average person at the time – a mixture of seal, grouse, seabirds, whales, otters and deer. Nearby lie **The Wirk**, the remains of a grand ceremonial hall from the thirteenth or fourteenth century, and the abandoned **St Mary's Church**, on the coast a mile south of Midhowe, which dates from the sixteenth century but was abandoned in 1820, when the island was suffering rapid depopulation. Nearer the ferry terminal is **Blackhammar Cairn**, a stalled tomb of similar form and date to Midhowe. The smaller **Taversoe Tuick**, a near neighbour to the east, is a chambered tomb, unusual in that it exploits its sloping site by having two storeys, one entered from the upper side and one from the lower.

Despite its long history of settlement, Rousay is today home to little more than 200 people, as this was one of the few parts of Orkney to suffer Highland-style clearances, initially by George William Traill at **Quandale** in the northwest. His successor, General Traill Burroughs, built the unlovely **Trumland House** (in the trees, near the ferry terminal) in 1873. Continuing to substitute sheep for people, he built a wall to force crofters onto a narrow coastal strip and eventually provoked so much distress and anger that a gunboat had to be sent to restore order.

Egilsay and Wyre

Sheltering close to the eastern shore of Rousay, the two low-lying smaller islands of Egilsay and Wyre each contain some interesting historical remains. Both are served by the Rousay ferry, though on some sailings only by request (see below). The larger of the pair, **EGILSAY**, is dominated by the ruins of **St Magnus Church**, built around the twelfth century in a prominent position in the middle of the island, probably on the site of a much earlier version. The church, now missing its roof, is the only surviving example of the traditional round-towered churches of Orkney and Shetland and was built as a shrine to Earl Magnus who was murdered here in 1116 – a cenotaph marks the spot, about a quarter of a mile southwest of the church. Over on **WYRE** you can see the remains of "Cubbie Roo's" Castle, the twelfth-century Viking stronghold of Kolbein Hruga, and the neighbouring **St Mary's Chapel**, a ruined twelfth-century church, founded either by Kolbein or his son, a bishop of Orkney.

Rousay practicalities

Rousay makes a good day-trip from the Mainland, with regular **ferry** sailings from Tingwall and **bus** connections to and from Kirkwall. Most ferries call in at Egilsay and Wyre, but some need to be booked in advance at the Tingwall ferry terminal (☎01856/751360). Rousay Traveller (☎01856/821234) runs flexible and very informative minibus tours (late May to early Sept Tues–Fri; other months/days for groups by arrangement). Tours connect with ferries and last between two and six hours, the longer ones allowing extended walks. You can rent bikes from Helga's (☎01856/821293), behind the *Pier Restaurant* at the ferry terminal. Next to the pier, the **Trumland Orientation Centre** (Mon–Sat 7.30am–7pm; mid-May to mid-Sept also Sun) is packed with information on every aspect of Rousay past and present.

The only **hotel** on the island is the *Taversoe*, a couple of miles west of the terminal at Frotoft (☎01856/821325; ⑤), a modern building added onto an old croft. The hotel has a restaurant with excellent home cooking featuring local produce, especially seafood, and vegetarian options; a bar and beer garden overlook the sea. **B&B** is available at *Maybank*, three miles west of the ferry terminal (☎01856/821225; ③), while *Trumland Farm* (☎01856/821252), a mile or so west of the terminal, has a recently built **hostel** and a self-catering cottage sleeping four (£100 per week). The *Pier Restaurant* (☎01856/821359) right beside the terminal, serves bar-style meals; if you phone in advance, they will pack you a delicious picnic of crab, cheese, fruit and bannock bread. In the evenings, the restaurant functions as a pub.

Eday

Similar in many ways to Rousay and Hoy, the smaller island of **Eday** is dominated by a great block of heather-covered upland, with farmland confined to a narrow strip of coastal ground. Eday used to export peat cut on the high ground to the other northern isles for fuel, and yellow sandstone quarried from the island was used to build the St Magnus Cathedral in Kirkwall.

The island is very sparsely inhabited, and the nearest approximation to a village is the small gathering of houses at **CALFSOUND** in the north, which until its recent closure had the island's only pub. Unless you fly – into London Airport, in the middle of the island – you'll arrive at the ferry terminal in **BACKALAND**, at the island's southern tip. The southern end of the island offers some great walking, both on the high ground of **Ward Hill** and **Flaughton Hill** and along the jagged western shoreline to the sheltered curve of the **Sands of Mussetter**. However, the most dramatic cliffs are to be found in the far north (six miles from the ferry terminal) at **Red Head**, which also gives great views of the other islands and of the uninhabited **Calf of Eday** – itself home to some massive bird colonies.

The northern end of the island is also the focus of Eday's **archeological heritage**. The best way to explore this part of the island is to follow the signposted **Eday Heritage Walk**, which starts at the Eday Community Enterprise Shop on the main road in **MILLBOUNDS**, where there's also some information about the sites on the route. The walk covers around five miles and takes about three hours, initially following the road north past the bird hide at **Mill Loch** (an excellent place to watch red-throated divers) to the **Stone of Setter**. Centre stage in the landscape, visible from other prehistoric sites and around 15ft high, this eroded and cracked standing stone is Orkney's most spectacular. From here, passing the less spectacular Braeside and Huntersquoy chambered cairns en route, you can climb the hill to reach the Eday's finest, the **Vinquoy Chambered Cairn**, which has been partially restored and has a similar structure to that of the Maes Howe tomb on the Mainland, with large blocks of stone supporting the inside walls and four tomb chambers set into them. If you want to go inside, wear old clothes or waterproof trousers as the entrance is wet and muddy, and take a torch. From the cairn, you can either head back to the shop, or continue north past the viewpoint on the summit of Vinquoy Hill to the dramatic cliffs of Red Head, then walk around the coast to **Carrick House**, the grandest home on Eday (June to mid-Sept Sun pm, Wed groups by appointment; for times call ☎01857/622260). Built originally by the laird of Eday in 1633, it was extended in the original style by successive owners. It was once the prison of the pirate John Gow – on whom Sir Walter Scott's novel *The Pirate* is based – whose ship *The Revenge* ran aground here.

Practicalities

Eday's **ferry** terminal is at Backaland pier in the south, not ideal for visiting the more interesting northern section of the island, although if you haven't got your own transport you should find it fairly easy to get a lift with someone off the ferry, or you can rent a **taxi** from A. and R.M. Stewart by the pier (☎01857/622206). It's also possible to catch the British Airways Express plane from Kirkwall to Eday on Wednesdays; for times and fares, contact them on ☎01856/872494. You can **rent bikes** from Martin Burkett at Hamarr, in the valley below the post office (contact him through Eday Community Enterprises on ☎01857/622283).

Friendly **B&B** accommodation is available at *Skaill Farm*, a traditional farmhouse just south of the airport (☎01857/6222271; ⑤, including dinner; closed May); *Greentoft*, on the eastern side of Ward Hill in the south (☎01857/622269; ②); and *Blett* in the north of the island (☎01857/622248; ④, including dinner), which also has a pleasant **self-catering** cottage (sleeps two; £80 per week), and a small craft gallery. Another self-catering option is *Carrick Farmhouse*, sleeping eight (☎01857/622259; £200 per week). The *SYHA*-affiliated **hostel** just north of the airport is run by Eday Community Association (☎01857/622228 or 622206; April–Sept).

Stronsay

A three-pronged shape to the southeast of Eday, **Stronsay** consists of a beguiling combination of green pastures, white sands and clear turquoise bays. For a long time the islanders lived off the herring and kelp industries; indeed, at the end of the eighteenth century, the kelp business employed some 3000 people on the island, and during the 1880s Whitehall harbour was one of the main Scottish centres for the curing of herring caught by French, Dutch and Scottish boats, with four hundred boats working out of the port. By the 1930s, however, the herring stocks had been severely depleted and the industry began a long decline.

Today, Stronsay supports a sizeable population of farmers, and boasts some interesting bird and plant life and a scattering of vague archeological remains. The only village is **WHITEHALL**, made up of a couple of rows of small fishermen's cottages, and blessed with a hotel and pub. Wandering along the tranquil harbour front today, you'll find it hard to believe that the village supported 5000 people in the fishing industry during the summer season, as well as a small army of coopers, coal merchants, butchers, bakers, several Italian ice-cream parlours and a cinema. Unless you arrive by plane (at the airstrip at the northern end of the island), it's from Whitehall that you'll set out to explore the rest of the island. A good place to start is the interpretation centre housed in the old fish market by the pier (May–Sept daily 11am–5pm; Oct–March Wed & Sun 11am–5pm), where you can find out all about life on the island past and present.

Stronsay has few real sights, but like all of these northern isles it offers some fantastic walking. The low-lying central land is almost entirely given over to farming and it's on the coast that you'll see the island at its best, with cliffs home to several seabird colonies and seals basking on exposed rocks at low tide. On the island's western arm there are two broad, arching, dazzlingly white beaches, the **Bay of Holland** and **St Catherine's Bay**, while over in the east there's a small **bird reserve** and observatory on the shores of **Mill Bay**, just south of Whitehall. Birdwatching is at its best here in spring and autumn, when easterly winds bring migrants such as thrushes, warblers, flycatchers and wrynecks. The southeast of the island boasts Orkney's biggest and most dramatic natural arch at the **Vat of Kirbuster**.

Practicalities

Stronsay is served by a twice-daily **ferry** service to Whitehall. There are a few places to stay – try the welcoming **B&Bs** at *Airy* (☎01857/616231; ②) or *Clestrain* (☎01857/616340; ②). For more basic accommodation, the **hostel** in the old fish market by the pier (☎01857/616360 or 616346) has a well-equipped kitchen, comfortable double and four-bedded rooms, and a good café serving teas, coffees and snacks. Ornithologists might like to try the *Stronsay Bird Reserve* (☎01857/616363) which offers full board (④), bed and breakfast (③), or camping on the shores of Mill Bay. D.S. Peace. (☎01857/616335) operates taxis and **rents cars** and you can hire a boat from J. Stevenson (☎01857/616341). There's a **swimming pool** behind the school which is available for public use, but it's operated on a voluntary basis so check first at the interpretation centre.

Sanday

As its name suggests, **Sanday** is the most insubstantial of the North Isles, a great drifting dune strung out between several rocky points. The island's bays and clean white sands are the finest in Orkney, and in dry, clear weather it's a superb place to spend a day or two. The island has a long history as a shipping hazard, with many wrecks smashed against its shores, although the construction of the **Start Point Lighthouse** in 1802–06, on the island's exposed eastern tip, reduced the risk for seafarers. Today the islanders survive largely from farming and fishing, supplemented by a knitting business, based at Wool Hall southeast of Lady Village, and a rabbit farm at Breckan, which specializes in the production of Angora wool.

The shoreline supports a healthy seal and otter population, and behind the beaches are stretches of beautiful open grassland, thick with wild flowers during the spring and summer. The entire coastline presents the opportunity for superb walks, with splendid sandy bays protected by jaggy outcrops of rock. Sanday is particularly rich in archeology, with hundreds of mostly unexcavated sites including cairns, brochs and burnt mounds. The most impressive is the chambered cairn at **Quoyness** (on the peninsula opposite Kettletoft), which dates from the third millennium BC. The main chamber is 13ft long and holds six small cells, which contained bones and skulls.

Practicalities

Ferries to Sanday arrive at Loth, at the southern tip of the island, and are met by a minibus (book on ☎01857/600418), which will take you to most points on the island for £2.50 single. However, Sanday's main centre is **KETTLETOFT**, a little gathering of houses with a couple of hotels, a shop, a post office and a bank; the airfield is just north of here. *Kettletoft Hotel* (☎01857/600217; ③) has simple but comfortable rooms, good home cooking (including takeaways), and a bar that's popular with locals and visitors, while the *Belsair Hotel* (☎01857/600206; ③) is also comfortable and makes up delicious packed lunches as well as offering a varied restaurant menu. Cars, caravans and boats for trout fishing can be rented from from Mrs Muir (☎01857/600331), while bikes and cars are available from Kettletoft Garage (☎01857/600321).

Westray and Papa Westray

A pair of exposed islands on the western side of the group, Westray and Papa Westray – or **Papey** as Orcadians call it – bear the full brunt of the Atlantic weather. The southern end of **Westray**, where ferries put in, is relatively gentle, while at the northern end the island rises more sharply, forming dramatic cliffs. The cliffs of **Noup Head**, packed with nesting seabirds during the summer months, are very spectacular, particularly when a good westerly swell is up. The open ground above the cliffs, which is grazed by sheep, is superb maritime heath and grassland, carpeted with yellow, white and purple flowers. Further south, there's an interesting walk from Tuquoy to Langskaill taking in the Cross Kirk which, although ruined, is still one of the most complete medieval churches in Orkney. Along the shore nearby are the eroding remains of a Norse settlement; on the east side, the ruined walls on the sea stack known as the Castle of Burrian reveal the presence of an early Christian settlement. The stack is an excellent place to see puffins in the nesting season.

Westray has a fairly stable population of 700 or so, producing superb beef, scallops, shellfish and a large catch of white fish, with its own small fish-processing factory. The main village is **PIEROWALL** in the north, where a handful of impressive ruins includes the seventeenth-century **Notland Castle**, which stands just inland of the village, and the medieval parish church of **St Mary's** (on the northern side of the village), both of which can be visited at all times. The **Westray Heritage Centre** (mid-May to mid-Sept daily 2–5pm; £1) has permanent displays on the landscape and wildlife of the islands.

Across the short Papa Sound, the neighbouring island and former medieval pilgrimage centre of **Papa Westray** is connected to Westray by the world's shortest scheduled flight – two minutes in duration, less with a following wind. Try and stroll out to the **Knap of Howar**, on the western shore, a Neolithic farm building from around 3500 BC that makes a fair claim to being the oldest-standing house in Europe, and the remains of **St Boniface's Church**, dating from the twelfth century. On the northern tip of the island there's yet another **RSPB reserve**, which plays host to one of the largest arctic tern colonies in Europe, as well as arctic skuas, razorbills and guillemots.

Practicalities

Westray is served by roll-on/roll-off car **ferry** from Kirkwall operated by Orkney Ferries (mid-May to mid-Sept 2–3 daily, fewer at other times of the year; 1hr 25min; ☎01856/872044). On Tuesdays and Fridays, the ferries also go to Papa Westray; otherwise you can catch the passenger-only ferry from Westray to Papa Westray (3–6 daily), which connects with the Westray service from Kirkwall. You can fly on British Airways Express from Kirkwall to Papa Westray (Mon–Sat 1–2 daily) and to Westray (Mon–Sat 1–2 daily). Island Explorer (☎01857/677355) runs a guided tour of the island by minibus, which connects with ferries.

There are two **hotels** on Westray. The *Pierowall* (☎01857/677208; ③) is simple but welcoming with a popular bar and a reputation for excellent fish and chips. More luxurious is *Cleaton House* (☎01857/677508; ⑤), about three miles south of Pierowall, with excellent bar and restaurant meals at good prices. **B&B** accommodation is available at *Sand O' Gill* (☎01857/677374; ②), and you can also **camp** there. **Self-catering** options include *Taftend*, on the southwest shore of the island (sleeps six; ☎01857/677319; £220 per week). Cars can be rented from M. and J. Harcus (☎01857/677450), bikes from Taftend or Sand o' Gill. If you'd like to play the somewhat eccentric **golf course** on the links north of Notland Castle, clubs can be rented from Tulloch's (☎01857/677373) shop.

On Papa Westray, the island's Community Co-operative (☎01857/644267) runs a sixteen-bed **hostel** at *Beltane House* and has **self-catering** accommodation in a cottage sleeping up to seven (£190 per week plus fuel; June–Aug). **B&B** is available from Mrs Rendall (☎01857/644275; ③).

North Ronaldsay

Isolated by the treacherous waters of the North Ronaldsay Firth, **North Ronaldsay**, Orkney's most northerly island, has a unique outpost atmosphere, brought about by its extreme isolation. Measuring just three miles by one, and rising only 66ft above sea level, the island is almost overwhelmed by the enormity of the sky, the strength of wind and, of course, the ferocity of the sea – so much so that its very existence seems an act of tenacious defiance. Despite these adverse conditions, North Ronaldsay has been inhabited for centuries. Today the population is mostly aged over 60, but the island is still heavily farmed, the land dotted with old-style crofts, their roofs made from huge flagstones. With no natural harbours and precious little farmland, the islanders have been forced to make the most of what they have and seaweed has played an important role in the local economy. During the eighteenth century **kelp** was gathered here, burnt in pits and sent south for use in the chemicals industry. The island's sheep, which are a unique breed, tough and goat-like, feed mostly on seaweed, giving their flesh a dark tone and a rich, gamey taste. A **drystone dyke** running the thirteen miles around the edge of the island keeps them off the farmland. During the clipping and dipping season the islanders herd the sheep into stone "punds" in what is one of the last acts of communal farming practised in Orkney. The largest buildings on the island are **Holland House**, built by the Traill family who bought the island in 1727, and the **lighthouse**, which towers over 100ft in height, and is the only feature to interrupt the horizon.

Grey and common **seals** are prevalent on the island, and it serves as an important stopping-off point for migratory **birds** on their way to and from breeding grounds in Iceland, Greenland and Scandinavia. The peak times of year for migrants are from late March to early June, and from mid-August to early November, although there are also many breeding species which spend the spring and summer here, including gulls, terns, waders and cormorants.

Practicalities

There's a once-weekly ferry to North Ronaldsay, usually on Fridays, but sailings may be affected by bad weather so check with Orkney Ferries (☎01856/872044) a day before you hope to travel. Between late May and early September, look out for occasional Sunday excursions by ferry from Kirkwall which allow three or four hours on the island. A more flexible (if more costly) option is to catch a British Airways Express plane from Kirkwall (Mon–Sat 2 daily).

The North Ronaldsay Bird Observatory, at Twingness Croft on the southwest tip of the island (☎01857/633200), was established in 1987 by adapting a croft to wind and solar power; it offers full-board **accommodation** in its guest house (④) or in dorms (£16 per person). Full-board accommodation is available at *Garso*, in the northeast

(☎01857/633244; ④), or at the *Burrian Inn* (☎01857/633221; ④), both of which also have self-catering cottages. *Garso* also operates a **car rental** and **taxi** service and can provide guided tours. **Camping** is possible, but you must ask the permission of landowners. You can rent **bicycles** from Airfield Goods and Services (☎01857/633220), by the airfield in the west of the island.

SHETLAND

Many maps place the **Shetland Islands** in a box somewhere off Aberdeen, but in fact Bergen in Norway is a lot closer than Edinburgh and the Arctic Circle nearer than Manchester. The Shetland **landscape** is a product of the struggle between rock and the forces of water and ice that have, over millennia, tried to break it to pieces. Smoothed by the last glaciation, the surviving land has been exposed to the most violent **weather** experienced in the British Isles; it isn't for nothing that Shetlanders call the place "the Old Rock", and the coastline, a crust of cliffs with caves, blowholes and stacks, testifies to the continuing battle. Inland (a relative term, since you're never more than three miles from the sea), the terrain is a gentler mix of moorland, often studded with peaty lochs of a brilliant blue, and green farmland. In winter, gales are routine and Shetlanders take even the occasional hurricane in their stride, marking a calm fine day as "a day atween weathers". There are some good spells of dry, sunny weather from June to September, but it's the **"simmer dim"**, the twilight which replaces darkness at this latitude, which makes Shetland summers so memorable; in June especially, the northern sky is an unfinished sunset of blue and burnished copper. Insomniac sheep and seabirds barely settle, and golfers, similarly afflicted, play midnight tournaments..

People have lived in Shetland since **prehistoric times,** certainly from about 3500 BC, and the islands display spectacular remains, including the best-preserved broch anywhere. For six centuries the islands were part of the **Norse empire** which brought together Sweden, Denmark and Norway. In 1469, Shetland followed Orkney in being mortgaged to Scotland, King Christian of Norway being unable to raise the dowry for the marriage of his daughter, Margaret, to King James III. The Scottish king annexed Shetland in 1472 and the mortgage was never redeemed. Though Shetland retained links with other North Sea communities, religious and administrative practice gradually become Scottish; and **mainland lairds** set about grabbing what land and power they could. Later, especially in rural Shetland, the economy fell increasingly into the hands of **merchant lairds**; they controlled the fish trade and the tenants who supplied it through a system of truck, or forced barter. It wasn't until the 1886 Crofters' Acts and the simultaneous rise of herring fishing that ordinary Shetlanders gained some security; however, the boom and the prosperity it brought were short-lived – the economy soon slipped into depression.

During the two world wars, Shetland's role as gatekeeper between the North Sea and North Atlantic meant that the defence of the islands and control of the seas around them were critical: thousands of naval, army and air force personnel were drafted in and some notable relics, such as huge coastal guns, remain. **World War II** also cemented the old links with Norway, Shetland playing a remarkable role in supporting the Norwegian resistance. With a rebirth of the local economy in the 1960s, Shetland was able to claim, in the following decade, that the **oil industry** needed the islands more than they needed it. Careful negotiation, backed up by pioneering local legislation, produced a substantial income from oil which has been reinvested in the community. Now that income is gradually diminishing, local politicians are having to make difficult choices about how to spend what's left, and the islanders are thinking afresh how to carve out a living in a new century.

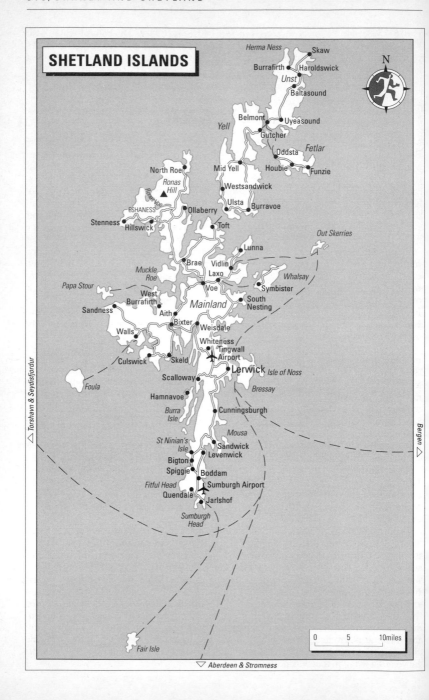

SHETLAND ISLANDS

N

Herma Ness • Skaw
Burrafirth • Haroldswick
Unst
Baltasound

Belmont • Uyeasound
Yell Gutcher
Oddsta
Fetlar
North Roe Mid Yell Houbie
Ronas Funzie
Hill Westsandwick
Ollaberry Ulsta Burravoe
ESHANESS Toft
Stenness
Hillswick *Out Skerries*
Lunna
Brae Vidlin
Muckle Laxo *Whalsay*
Roe Voe Symbister
Papa Stour West South
Burrafirth *Mainland* Nesting
Sandness Aith
Bixter
Walls Weisdale
Whiteness
Culswick Skeld Tingwall
Airport
Scalloway **Lerwick** *Isle of Noss*
Hamnavoe *Bressay*
Burra Cunningsburgh
Foula *Isle*
Mousa
St Ninian's Sandwick
Isle Levenwick
Bigton
Spiggie Boddam
Fitful Head Sumburgh Airport
Quendale Jarlshof
Sumburgh
Head

◁ *Torshavn & Seydisfjordur*

Bergen ▷

0   5   10miles

Fair Isle

▽ *Aberdeen & Stromness*

GETTING TO SHETLAND

There are two year-round **car ferry** routes to Shetland. From **Aberdeen**, P&O Scottish Ferries (☎01224/572615 or 01595/694848) operates a direct overnight service four times a week (5 times in winter) to Lerwick (14hr). There's also a twice-weekly afternoon/overnight indirect service (once weekly in winter) which calls at **Stromness** in Orkney (8hr to Stromness, 8hr on to Lerwick). For a very brief taste of Shetland, P&O offers short, ship-based mini-cruises to Shetland, some of which take in Orkney. From June to August, Shetland is also directly connected to **Bergen** in Norway (13hr), **Tórshavn** in Faroe (13hr) and, via Faroe, with **Seydisfjördur** in Iceland (33hr) and **Hanstholm** in Denmark (50hr) on Smyril Line (details from P&O Scottish Ferries).

By **air**, British Airways Express (☎01595/840246) flies from **Edinburgh, Glasgow, Aberdeen, Inverness, Kirkwall** and **Wick**, with connections from **Birmingham, Manchester** and **London**. The main airport is at **Sumburgh**, 25 miles south of Lerwick, with connecting bus services to the capital. Standard fares are high, but various cheaper tickets and special offers are available if you can meet the booking conditions.

Whatever else you do in Shetland you're sure to be based, at least for a day or two, in the lively port of **Lerwick**, the only town of any size and the hub of all transport and communications. Many parts of Shetland can be reached from here in a day-trip. South of Lerwick, a narrow finger of land runs some twenty miles to **Sumburgh Head**; this area is particularly rich in archeological remains, including the Iron Age **Broch of Mousa** and the ancient settlement of **Jarlshof**. Twenty-five miles south of Sumburgh Head is the remote but thriving **Fair Isle**, synonymous with knitwear and exceptional birdlife. To the **north** and **west**, the Mainland is bleaker and more sparsely inhabited, although the landscape, particularly to the north, opens out in scale and grandeur as it comes face to face with the Atlantic. Off the west coast, **Papa Stour** lies just a mile from Sandness and boasts some spectacular caves and stacks; much further out are the distinctive peaks and precipitous cliffs of the island of **Foula**. To the northeast, Shetland ends with the North Isles of **Yell**, **Unst** and **Fetlar**, reaching far up into the North Sea.

Supporting an impressive array of **birds and wildlife**, the islands offer excellent birdwatching and walking. The **fishing** is good, too, with lochs well stocked with brown trout, sea trout in the voes and the chance to go sea angling for ling, mackerel or even shark and halibut. If you are taking a tent with you, wild **camping** isn't usually discouraged in Shetland if done considerately and the landowner is asked first.

Getting around

On the **mainland**, there are **buses** from Lerwick to Sumburgh, Sandwick, Scalloway, Hamnavoe, Reawick, Skeld, Walls, Sandness, Brae, Hillswick, Laxo (for the Whalsay ferry) and Vidlin. A service involving two ferry crossings also runs from Lerwick to Yell and Unst. Various **tours** by bus, minibus or private car are available; operators include Leask's (☎01595/693162) or the more specialist Shetland Wildlife Tours (☎01950/460254). Shetland Field Studies Trust organizes nature walks (book through the tourist office), while the Shetland Tourist Guides Association (☎01595/696671) offers tailor-made tours for groups or individuals. If you want to **rent a car** once on the islands there are several firms to choose from (see "Listings" on p.524). **Hitching** is viable and pretty safe, and **cycling** is a reasonable choice in summer, though some long hills make it fairly energetic.

It's easy to **travel between the islands**: the larger ones have frequent **car ferry** services throughout the day, journey times are mostly less than 25 minutes and, although fares are steadily rising, they're still much cheaper than those in Orkney or the Western Isles. Adults are charged around £2.50 return on most routes (£5 or so to Foula, Fair Isle, Papa Stour and Skerries) and a car and driver cross for around £6 return. There are also British Airways Express services linking **Tingwall Airport** (☎01595/840226), five miles west of Lerwick, to Unst and Fair Isle and less frequently to Whalsay, Out Skerries, Papa Stour and Foula. Some Unst and Fair Isle flights leave from Sumburgh. It's also possible to take **boat trips** for pleasure, to explore the coastline and spot birds, seals, porpoises, dolphins and whales; operators include Bressaboats from Lerwick (☎01595/820205), and Tom Jamieson from Sandwick (for the Broch of Mousa) (☎01950/431367). Specialist services for **diving** or **sea angling** can be tracked down through the Lerwick tourist office (see below).

Lerwick and around

For Shetlanders, there's only one place to stop, meet and do business and that's "da toon", **LERWICK**. Very much the focus of Shetland's commercial life, Lerwick is home to about 7500 people, roughly a third of the islands' population. All year, its sheltered **harbour** at the heart of the town is busy with ferries, fishing boats, oil-rig supply vessels and a variety of more specialized craft including seismic survey and naval vessels from all round the North Sea. In summer, the quaysides come alive with local pleasure craft, visiting yachts, cruise liners, historic vessels such as the restored *Swan*, and the occasional tall sailing ship; in 1999 the port will play host to the Cutty Sark Tall Ships Race. Behind the old harbour is the compact town centre, solidly stone built with Commercial Street, the main shopping area, at its heart; from here, narrow **lanes** rise westwards to the late-Victorian "**new town**".

Lerwick began life as a **temporary settlement**, catering to the Dutch herring fleet in the seventeenth century, which brought in as many as 20,000 men. During the nineteenth century, with the presence of ever larger Scottish, English and Scandinavian boats, it became a major fishing centre, and whalers called to pick up crews on their way to the northern hunting grounds. In 1839, the visiting Danish governor of Faroe declared that "everything made me feel that I had come to the land of opulence". Business was conducted largely from buildings known as **lodberries**, each typically having a store, a house and small yard on a private jetty. **Smuggling** was part of the daily routine, and secret tunnels – some of which still exist – connected the lodberries to illicit stores. During the late nineteenth century, the construction of the Esplanade along the shore isolated several lodberries from the sea; but further south beyond the *Queen's Hotel* are some that still show their original form. Lerwick expanded considerably at this time and the large houses and grand public buildings established then still dominate, notably the impressive **Town Hall**. Another period of rapid growth began in the 1970s, with the farmland to the southwest disappearing under a suburban sprawl, the town's northern approaches becoming an industrial estate and some shopping and office development moving to new and more car-friendly sites.

Arrival, information and accommodation

Arriving in Lerwick is straightforward: the town is small and everything is within walking distance. Arriving by **ferry** you'll come ashore at the P&O terminal in the north harbour, about a mile from the town centre. If you arrive by **plane**, at **Sumburgh Airport**, you can take one of the regular buses to Lerwick; taxis (around £25) and car rental are also available. Buses stop on the Esplanade, very close to the old harbour and Market Cross, or at the bus station on Commercial Road about a quarter of a mile to the north.

The telephone code for Lerwick is ☎01595.

The **tourist office**, at the Market Cross on Commercial Street (May–Sept Mon–Fri 8am–6pm, Sat 8am–4pm, Sun 10am–1pm; Oct–April Mon–Fri 9am–5pm; ☎693434), is a good source of information and, for £1, will book accommodation. In July, August and over the Folk Festival weekend in April, accommodation is in short supply, so it's a good idea to book in advance.

As befits a town catering extensively to the oil business, Lerwick has a generous supply of **hotel** rooms, well equipped but often bland. You're likely to get closer to Shetland life in the older or smaller **B&Bs**, while the upper-range **guest houses** are usually good value for money. Most accommodation is either close to the old harbour or in the "new town". The Lerwick **youth hostel** (☎692114; mid-April to October) at Islesburgh House on King Harald Street, offers unusually comfortable surroundings, while **campers** should head for the *Clickimin Caravan and Camp Site*, Lochside (☎694555; late April to Sept), next to a leisure centre with plenty of facilities, including good hot showers.

Hotels, guest houses and B&Bs

Bona Vista Guest House, 26 Church Rd (☎692269) Central and friendly, this former laird's house stands just above Commercial Street and the old harbour. ③.

Carradale Guest House, 36 King Harald St (☎695411). Spacious, well-equipped guest house in a large, comfortable family home. ③.

Glen Orchy House, 20 Knab Rd (☎692031). A particularly comfortable guest house that's almost a hotel, licensed and with good home cooking. ⑤.

Kvelsdro House Hotel, Greenfield Place (☎692195). Lerwick's smartest and most luxurious place, with immaculate bedrooms and a good harbour view from the bar. It's hard to find, but locals will usually oblige (note: it's pronounced "Kelro"). ⑨.

Lerwick Hotel, 15 South Rd (☎692166). Modern hotel, with some good sea views, particularly favoured by business travellers. ⑧.

Mrs Gifford's B&B, 12 Burgh Rd (☎693554). Reasonably central but comfortable and secluded. ③.

Old Manse, 9 Commercial St (☎696301). Lerwick's oldest house dating mostly from 1685. ③.

Queen's Hotel, Commercial Street (☎692826). Right on the waterfront by the old harbour, with its feet in the sea; a beautiful old building with comfortable accommodation. ⑧.

Shetland Hotel, Holmsgarth Road (☎695515). Overlooking the ferry terminal, popular with business people and package-holiday operators. Its rooms and public areas are well equipped and fortunately more appealing than the ugly exterior. ⑧.

Woosung, 43 St Olaf St (☎693687). A friendly B&B in a quiet street, 5min walk from the old harbour. ③.

The Town

Commercial Street, universally known to locals as "da Street", is still very much the core of Lerwick. Its narrow, winding form provides shelter from the elements even on the worst days, and is where locals meet, shop, exchange news and gossip and bring in the New Year to the sound of a harbourful of ships' sirens. The Street's northern end is marked by the towering walls of **Fort Charlotte**: originally built, directly above the beach, for Charles II in 1665–67, during the war with the Dutch, it was attacked and burnt down by them in August 1673. In 1782 it was rebuilt and given its name in honour of George III's queen. Except on rare occasions when it's used by the Territorial Army, the fort affords good views from its solid battlements (daily: June–Sept 9am–10pm; Oct–May 9am–4pm; free). A walk along Commercial Street reveals an interesting mixture of **architectural styles** from the powerful Baroque of the Bank of Scotland at no. 117 to the plainer houses and lodberries at the south end, beyond the *Queen's Hotel*. Further along from the *Queen's* are the Anderson Homes and the Anderson High School, the latter's ornate, Franco-Scottish towers and dormers now unfortunately

UP HELLY-AA

On the last Tuesday in January, whatever the weather, the Victorian "new town" of Lerwick is the setting for the most spectacular part of the Lerwick **Up Helly-Aa**, a huge, fire festival, the largest of several held in Shetland in January and February. Around 900 torchbearing participants, all male and all in extraordinary costumes, march in procession behind a grand Viking longship. The annually appointed Guizer Jarl and his "squad" appear as Vikings and brandish shields and silver axes; each of the forty or so other squads is dressed for their part in the subsequent entertainment, perhaps as giant insects, space invaders or ballet dancers. Their circuitous route leads to the King George V Playing Field where, after due ceremony, all the torches are thrown into the longship, creating an enormous bonfire. A fireworks display follows, then the participants, known as "guizers", set off in their squads to do the rounds of more than a dozen "halls" (which usually include at least one hotel and the Town Hall) from around 8.30pm in the evening until 8am the next morning, performing some kind of act – usually a comedy routine – at each.

Up Helly-Aa itself is not that ancient, dating only from Victorian times; but it replaced an older Christmas tradition of burning tar barrels and other sorts of mischief. Around 1870, perhaps as a result of frustration at the controls increasingly imposed by the Town Council, the tar barrellers moved their activities into January, coined the name Up Helly-Aa and introduced both a torchlight procession and an element of disguise; it was some years, though, before the festival took on its Viking associations. Although this is essentially a community event with entry to halls by invitation only, visitors are welcome at the Town Hall, for which tickets are sold in early January; contact the tourist office well in advance. To catch some of the atmosphere of the event, check out the Up Helly-Aa exhibition (mid-May to Sept Tues & Sat 2–4pm, Thurs & Fri 7–9pm; £1) in the galley shed on St Sunniva Street, where you can see a full-size longship, costumes, shields and photographs.

rather lost among later additions. Both were the gift of **Arthur Anderson** (1792–1868), co-founder of the Peninsular and Oriental Steam Navigation Company (P&O).

Now a desirable place to live in, it's not so long ago that the narrow **lanes** that connect the Street to the Hillhead were regarded as slumlike dens of iniquity, from which the better off escaped to the Victorian gridiron "new town" laid out to the west. The stone-flagged lanes run uphill, lined by tall houses with trees, fuchsia, flowering currant and honeysuckle pouring over the garden walls. Hillhead is dominated by the splendid **Town Hall** (Mon–Fri 10am–noon & 2–3.30pm; free), a Gothic castle and a monument to civic pride. Built by public subscription, the many carved stone panels, coats of arms and stained-glass windows celebrate Shetland's history and, in particular, the islands' commercial and cultural links with other parts of Britain and Europe.

On Lower Hillhead, southwest of the Town Hall, the **Shetland Museum** (Mon, Thurs & Fri 10am–7pm, Tues, Wed & Sat 10am–5pm; free) is full to the brim with interesting Shetland artefacts relating to the islands' history and prehistory. More unusual exhibits include a stone carving by Adam Christie (1869–1950), a Shetlander who is perhaps best known for his application to patent a submarine invisible to enemies because it would be made of glass.

Eating

Shetland produces a huge harvest of fresh fish from the surrounding seas, including shellfish and salmon, and from the land there's superb lamb and even local tomatoes, cucumbers and peppers, grown under glass. The most celebrated local delicacy is *reestit* mutton; steeped in brine then air-dried, it's the base for a superb potato soup cooked by locals around New Year. Too often, the food on offer in hotels and pubs doesn't do these ingredients justice, but Lerwick has plenty of places which serve adequate bar food and no shortage of takeaway options either. The more interesting choices include a bistro and deli, a notable Indian restaurant and a pleasant Norwegian café.

Central Bakery, 124 Commercial St. Small café, in a baker's shop, serving soup, sandwiches, pies and cakes, and particularly good for lunch. Closes at 4pm.

The Golden Coach, 17 Hillhead (☎693848). Originally specializing in Cantonese and Pekinese food, the cuisine now takes in most of the far east. Erratic, but usually pretty good, and with comfortable surroundings. A cheaper lunch menu is served Mon–Fri.

Ian's Fish and Chips, the Esplanade. Decent fish and chips make for a pleasant alfresco fish supper by the harbour.

Havly Centre, 9 Charlotte St. A Norwegian Christian centre catering for the spiritual needs of visiting fishermen, but not at all evangelical and much frequented by locals and tourists. Friendly, with excellent snacks including delicious Norwegian open sandwiches.

Kvelsdro House Hotel, Greenfield Place (☎692195). Moderate to expensive dinner and bar menus feature local fresh produce including seafood cooked with care, though vegetarian options can be limited.

Lerwick Hotel, 15 South Rd. Wide choice of reasonable bar meals, with a restaurant overlooking the sea serving more elaborate food.

Monty's Bistro and Deli, 5 Mounthooly S (☎696555). Upstairs, an unpretentious bistro offers accomplished contemporary cooking – the best in Lerwick – with friendly service and moderate prices. The downstairs deli serves inexpensive and delicious snacks, soups, salads and baked potatoes (also does takeaways).

The New Harbour Café, behind the Thule Bar on the Esplanade. Basic, but bright place serving a range of simple snacks, soups and burgers. Gets very busy at lunchtime.

Queen's Hotel, Commercial Street (☎692826). Moderately priced local seafood, meat and vegetarian dishes are on offer, with a great view of the passing ships.

Raba Indian Restaurant, 26 Commercial Rd (☎695585). A consistently excellent curry house, with cheerful, efficient service and good prices.

Solotti's, Commercial Street by the Post Office. Something of an institution, this café serves generously filled rolls to eat in or take away, as well as cakes, teas, coffees and good ice cream; no smoking.

Drinking, nightlife and entertainment

At weekends or whenever the fishing fleet is confined to harbour, Lerwick's pubs are great social centres, packed full and brimming with atmosphere, though the range of beers is not huge. Uncompromisingly traditional places include the downstairs bar in the *Thule* on the Esplanade, an archetypal seaport pub, and the upstairs bar in the *Lounge*, up Mounthooly Street, where local musicians usually play Saturday lunchtime and some evenings. *Captain Flint's* is a very popular themed pub at the Market Cross, and afterwards the crowd heads on to the town's main dance venue, *Posers*, a small, lively and smartish nightclub at the back of the *Grand Hotel* on Commerical Street.

Music features very strongly in Shetland life and every style has an enthusiastic following. The emphasis in traditional music is firmly instrumental, not vocal; substantial numbers of young people learn the fiddle. In April, musicians from all over the world converge on Shetland for the excellent **Folk Festival**, which embraces a wider range of musical styles than the title might suggest; there are concerts and dances in every corner of the islands. For details, telephone the Folk Festival office (☎694757) or write to them at 5 Burns Lane, Lerwick. In October, there's an **Accordion and Fiddle Festival**: similar format, same mailing address, but a different musical focus. Throughout the year, there are traditional dances in local halls all over Shetland; the whole community turns up and you can watch, or join in with, dances like the Boston Two-Step, Quadrilles or the Foula Reel. There are also gigs featuring a surprising number of accomplished local groups; rock-tinged folk styles are particularly strong. Names to catch live or recorded include Rock, Salt and Nails, Bongshang, Hom Bru, Drop the Box and Fiddlers' Bid. Legendary local fiddler Aly Bain (see p.574) makes occasional appearances on the islands. For details of what's on listen in to *Good Evening Shetland* (BBC Radio Shetland, 92.7MHz FM, Mon–Fri 5.30pm), or buy the *Shetland Times* on Fridays. Some events are also advertised on Shetland's independent radio station, SIBC (96.2MHz FM, 24 hours).

Not surprisingly, another Shetland passion is **boating and yachting**, and regattas take place most summer weekends, in different venues throughout the islands. Lately, the sport of **yoal racing** has caught on in a big way and teams from different districts compete passionately in large six-oared boats which used to serve as the backbone of Shetland's fishing industry.

Listings

Airports Tingwall Airport (☎840306); Sumburgh Airport (☎01950/460654).

Banks Clydesdale, Bank of Scotland and Royal Bank of Scotland are all on Commercial Street; the Trustee Savings Bank is the gleaming and locally controversial structure on the Esplanade.

Bike rental Eric Brown, Grantfield Garage, Commercial Road (Mon, Tues & Thurs–Sat 9am–5pm; ☎01595 693733).

Bookshops Shetland Times Bookshop, 73–79 Commercial St (Mon–Sat 9am–5pm; June–Aug also Sun 11am–4pm; ☎695531).

Bus companies Leasks (Sumburgh Airport; Vidlin and Laxo for Whalsay; Yell, Unst and Fetlar; ☎01856/693162); Shalder Coaches, (Sandwick; Walls and Sandness; Brae and Hillswick; Scalloway; ☎880217); White's Coaches (Walls and Sandness; ☎809443).

Car rental Bolts Car Hire, 26 North Rd (☎693636); John Leask & Sons, Esplanade (☎693162); Star Rent-a-Car, 22 Commercial Rd (☎692075). All of these have offices at Sumburgh Airport.

Consulates Denmark, Iceland, Netherlands and Sweden at Hay and Company, 66 Commercial Rd (☎692533); Finland, France, Norway and Germany at Shearer Shipping Services, Garthspool (☎692556).

Dentists Alan Owen, 90 St Olaf St (☎695769); Reform Lane Dental Practice, 7 Reform Lane (☎694486).

Fishing tackle Rod and Line, 91 Harbour St.

Laundry Lerwick Laundry, 36 Market St (☎693043).

Medical care The Gilbert Bain Hospital (☎74300) and the Lerwick Health Centre (☎693201) are opposite each other on Scalloway Road. There's a Complementary Health Clinic at 47 North Rd (☎692924).

Post office Commercial Street (Mon–Fri 9am–5pm, Sat 9am–noon); there's a sub-post office in the Toll Clock Shopping Centre, 26 North Rd.

Sports There is a large, modern sports centre incorporating a superb leisure pool at the Clickimin Leisure Centre, Lochside, on the west side of town by Clickimin Loch (☎694555). There's also a café and bar.

Travel agents John Leask & Son, Esplanade (☎693162); Shetland Travelscope, Toll Clock Shopping Centre, 26 North Rd (☎696644).

Around Lerwick

A mile or so southwest from the town centre on the road leading to Sumburgh, **Clickimin Broch** stands on what was once a small island in Clickimin Loch. The settlement here began as a small farmstead around 700 BC and was later enclosed by a defensive wall. The main tower served as a castle and probably rose to around 40ft, though the remains are now not much more than 10ft high. There are two small entrances, one at ground level and the other on the first floor, which are carefully protected by outer defences and smaller walls. Despite the modern housing in the middle distance, it's not hard to imagine the original setting and sense the magical atmosphere of the place. Excavation of the site has unearthed an array of domestic goods that suggest international trade, including a Roman glass bowl thought to have been made in Alexandria around 100 AD.

In earlier times the seasonal nature of the Shetland fishing industry led to the establishment of small stores, often incorporating sleeping accommodation, beside the beaches where fish were landed and dried. These were known as **böds**, although the word was also applied to trading posts established by merchants of the Hanseatic League. About a mile and a half north of the town centre, right off the A970, stands the **Böd of Gremista** (June–Aug Wed–Sun 10am–1pm & 2–5pm; £1), the birthplace of **Arthur Anderson** (1792–1868). Though almost lost among the surrounding industry, the building has been beautifully restored and the displays explore Anderson's life as beach boy (helping to cure and dry fish), naval seaman, businessman, philanthropist, Shetland's first native MP and founder of Shetland's first newspaper. Built at the end of the eighteenth century for Anderson's father, the ground floor was originally used as an office and fish-curing station, while the trader and his family had permanent residence upstairs.

Bressay and Noss

Shielding Lerwick from the full force of the North Sea is the island of **Bressay**, dominated at its southern end by the conical Ward Hill and accessible on an hourly car and passenger ferry from Lerwick. At the end of the nineteenth century, Bressay had a population of more than 1000, due mostly to the prosperity brought by the Dutch herring fleet; now about 320 people live here. The island provides interesting cliff and coastal walks, notably to the lighthouse and huge World War I guns at the northern and southern ends of the island. In the past, Sir Walter Scott and royal visitors have stayed in the laird's Gardie House, one of the largest and, in its Classical detail, finest of Shetland laird houses. If you want to stay on Bressay, the *Maryfield House Hotel* (☎01595/820207; ⑤), by the ferry terminal, is friendly and serves good-value meals in the restaurant and cosy bar. There's also a tiny camping böd at the Lighthouse; book through the Lerwick tourist office.

Just off Bressay's eastern shore, the small but spectacular island of **Noss** – the name means "a point of rock" – was inhabited until World War II but is now given over to sheep farming. It is also a National Nature Reserve managed by Scottish Natural Heritage, who operate an inflatable as a ferry (late May to Aug; on demand except Mon, Thurs and when a red flag is flown on Noss; 2min; £2.50 return). You should wait at the landing stage below the car park at the east side of Bressay; if the weather is abnormally windy, check with the Lerwick tourist office whether the service is operating before setting off. On the island, the old farmhouse of Gungstie contains a small **visitor centre** (open whenever the ferry is operating), where you can find out about the island's amazing birdlife and its human history. The adjacent **Pony Pund**, a square stone enclosure, was built for the breeding of Shetland ponies. A stud was established here in the latter years of the nineteenth century, when the Marquis of Londonderry needed ponies to replace the women and children who had been displaced by new laws from his coal mines in County Durham. The animals were specially bred to produce "as much weight as possible and as near the ground as it can be got". The stud only lasted for about twenty years and was closed in 1899, studs in England having been established by then to supply demand at lower cost. There are no ponies on Noss today, but it's said that the influence of the breeding programme can still be seen in those roaming other parts of Shetland. The most memorable feature of Noss is its cliffed coastline rising to a peak at the massive 500ft **Noup**, from which can be seen vast colonies of cliff-nesting gannets, puffins, guillemots, shags, razorbills and fulmars; a truly wonderful sight and one of the highlights of Shetland. A route around the island is indicated on a map in the visitor centre and marked along the way. If you stray off it, the great skuas (locally called bonxies) and arctic skuas (alans) will do their best to intimidate you with dive-bombing raids that may hit hard. One of the features on the walk is the Holm of Noss; until 1864, it was connected to the main island by an extraordinary device called a cradle, a sort of basket suspended on ropes which was intended to allow access for the grazing of sheep. The Foula man who allegedly installed it in the seventeenth century is said to have died when, preferring to climb back down the cliffs, he fell.

The South Mainland

Shetland's **South Mainland** is a long, thin finger of land, only three or four miles wide, ending in the cliffs of **Sumburgh Head** and **Fitful Head**. The main road hugs the eastern side of the Clift Hills which form the peninsula's backbone; on the west side, there's no road between Scalloway and Maywick except for a short spur from Easter to Wester Quarff. It's a beautiful area with wild landscapes but also good farmland, and has yielded some of Shetland's most impressive archeological treasures.

Cunningsburgh and Catpund

The view opens up to the south soon after leaving Lerwick, at the shoulder of Shurton Hill above Gulberwick. To appreciate the coastal scenery here, it's best to leave the main road at **Fladdabister**, a favourite haunt of local artists who come to sketch and paint among the ruins of the old crofts and where, in summer, the meadows are a mass of wild flowers. In **CUNNINGSBURGH**, the first large settlement, the best views are again from the backroads to the east through the hamlets and hay meadows of Aith and Voxter. At the south end of Cunningsburgh is the Mail Kirkyard, where a remarkable stone carved with an image of a **dog-headed person** with an axe was found in 1992. The illustration is unusual in being secular rather than religious, which archeologists believe indicates a relatively early date.

Half a mile or so south of the Mail junction, the main road crosses the Catpund Burn. From the westward loop of the old road at this point, it's possible to scramble up the valley for about 300yd to a remarkable prehistoric industrial site, the **Catpund Quarries**. In Norse times, this area was the biggest soapstone (steatite) quarry in Britain, if not the world. Products would have included various types of bowl, weights for fishing nets or for looms, and possibly items of jewellery. It's not difficult to see where vessels were carved directly from the rock. Goods from here almost certainly found their way to Norse communities in Britain, Ireland, Iceland, Faroe or mainland Europe. The small area revealed by the 1988 excavation of the site is fenced off and a board gives more information, but there's similar evidence over much of the valley floor.

Sandwick to Boddam

Sandwick is a series of settlements about two miles south of Cunningsburgh. From one of these, **LEEBITTON**, in the northeast of the district, you can take a summer ferry to the small island of **Mousa** on which stands the best-preserved broch anywhere. Tom Jamieson (☎01950/431367) runs the ferry from the jetty near the impressive laird's house, **Sand Lodge**.

Mousa Broch features in both *Egil's Saga* and the *Orkneyinga Saga*, contemporary chronicles of Norse exploration and settlement. In the former, a couple eloping from Norway to Iceland take refuge after being shipwrecked in 900 AD, while in the latter the broch is besieged by an Earl Harald Maddadson when his mother is abducted and brought here from Orkney by Erlend the Young, who wanted to marry her. Rising to more than 40ft and with its curving stonework intact, it has a remarkable presence. The low entrance passage leads through two concentric walls to a central courtyard. Between the walls, there are cells and galleries in which storm petrels breed and a rough staircase leads to the top (a torch is useful). Elsewhere on Mousa, there are remains of several buildings, some of which housed the eleven families who lived here in the eighteenth century. **Seals** can often be seen at the bay on the east side.

To the southwest of Sandwick, is **HOSWICK**, where *Da Warp and Weft Visitor Centre* offers teas and snacks as well as an introduction to the history of Shetland **knitwear** (May–Sept Mon–Sat 10am–5pm, Sun noon–5pm; ☎01950/431533; free). At Channerwick on the main road south, it's possible to cross to the west side of the Mainland for St Ninian's Isle (see p.528). Staying on the east side, the next settlement is **LEVENWICK,** where there's a lovely beach of white sand and another broch site. The signposted sideroad through **BODDAM** winds around the shore to the **Shetland Crofthouse Museum** (May–Sept daily 10am–1pm & 2–5pm; £1.50), which portrays nineteenth-century crofting life with traditional furniture and fittings, including spinning wheels, high-backed Shetland chairs and baskets woven from heather fibres.

To Jarlshof and Sumburgh Head

From Boddam southwards, the landscape changes to a rolling agricultural one often compared with that of Orkney, but is still dominated from the west by the great brooding mass of Fitful Head. The main road leads to **Sumburgh Airport**, busy with helicopters and aircraft shuttling to and from the North Sea oilfields, and Shetland's main airport for external passenger services. The **Pool of Virkie**, just to the north, is a good place to see a variety of wading birds. Visible in the road cutting, to the south of the western end of the east–west runway, are the walls of a relatively complete **broch**, while the continuing excavation here is revealing other structures. Just above this site is **Betty Mouat's cottage**, recently reconstructed to provide basic accommodation (see p.528). In January 1886, Betty, then 60 years old, set off for Lerwick in the smack *Columbine* crewed by three local men. A storm swept the skipper overboard and the other two jumped in to try to rescue him; they failed, the skipper drowned and the two men, though they survived, lost contact with the smack. Betty and her boat were battered by the storm for nine days and nights, finally running ashore north of Aalesund in Norway. Astonishingly, she survived this experience, existing on some milk which she had with her. She returned to Shetland to become a celebrity, living into her nineties.

Of all the archeological sites in Shetland, **Jarlshof** (April–Sept Mon–Sat 9.30am–6.30pm, Sun 2–6.30pm; £2.30; Oct–March the grounds are always open; free) is the largest and most complex. There's evidence of more than 4000 years of continuous occupation, with buildings dating from the Stone Age to the early seventeenth century. The guidebook, available from the small visitor centre where you buy tickets, is almost essential in understanding the many layers of human activity. As well as Neolithic and medieval buildings, these include a **broch**, interconnected **wheelhouses** and Norse **longhouses**. Sir Walter Scott, rather than any Viking, was responsible for the name: while visiting Shetland in 1814 he decided to use part of the ruins, the Old House of Sumburgh, in his novel *The Pirate* (see p.513). The **Old House** (only the walls remain) dates from the late sixteenth century, when it was home first to Robert Stewart, Lord of the Northern Isles and later to William Bruce, first representative in Shetland of another immigrant Scottish family whose landholdings were to become substantial.

The Mainland comes to a dramatic end at Sumburgh Head, about two miles from Jarlshof. The **lighthouse**, designed by Robert Stevenson, was built in 1821; although not open to the public, its grounds offer great views to Noss in the north and Fair Isle to the south. This is also the easiest place in Shetland to get close to **puffins**. During the nesting season, you simply need to look over the western wall by the lighthouse gate to see them arriving at their burrows a few yards below with beakfuls of fish or giving flying lessons to their offspring; on no account should you try to climb over the wall.

North to St Ninian's Isle

Moving north again from Jarlshof, the road to **QUENDALE** leaves the main road at Boddam and leads to **Quendale Mill** (May–Sept daily except Mon 10am–1pm & 2–5pm; £1), a beautifully restored full-size watermill; although it's rarely operated, there are information panels and a video. Not far from here, near the head of a rocky inlet on the other side of Garths Ness, lies a rusting ship's bow, all that remains of the *Braer*, a Liberian-registered, American-owned oil tanker that ran onto the rocks here at 11.13am on January 5, 1993, a wild Tuesday morning etched in the memory of every Shetlander. The damage was less serious than it might have been, due to the thousands of tonnes of spilt oil being churned and ultimately cleansed by huge waves built by hurricane-force winds which, unusually even for Shetland, blew for most of January.

North of Quendale, the **Loch of Spiggie** is an RSPB reserve known particularly for large autumn flocks of almost 400 whooper swans, but several types of duck as well as greylag geese and waders can be seen, depending on the time of year. Otters also live here. There's information about the reserve at the hide on the northern shore. On the other side of the road, the district of Spiggie also boasts a long but reasonably sheltered sandy beach. North from here, the coast is spectacular: cliffs alternate with beaches and the vivid greens and yellows of the farmland contrast with black rocks and a sea which may be grey, deep blue or turquoise.

At **BIGTON** village, a signposted track leads down to the tombolo at **St Ninian's Isle**. The **tombolo** – a strip of sand with curving shorelines linking it to the Mainland – is the best example of its kind in Britain. It's usually exposed and you can walk over to the island, where there are the ruins of a church probably dating from the twelfth century but on the site of an earlier, Pictish, one. The site was excavated in 1958 and **treasure**, a hoard of 27 objects of Pictish silver, was found hidden in a larch box beneath a slab in the earlier building's floor; the larch probably came from the European mainland as it didn't grow in Britain at that time. The treasure included bowls, a spoon and brooches and probably dates from around 800 AD; it may have been hastily hidden during a Norse raid. Replicas are in the Shetland Museum in Lerwick and the originals can be seen in the Museum of Antiquities in Edinburgh.

South Mainland practicalities

Public transport to the South Mainland is relatively straightforward: there are between three and four buses a day between Lerwick and Sumburgh Airport (45min), and between four and six buses daily to Sandwick (35min). Bigton, Spiggie and Quendale are served by two buses on weekdays, one on Sundays.

Accommodation is in short supply; the *Sumburgh Hotel* (☎01950/460201; ⑤), next to Jarlshof, is convenient for the airport, serves generous bar meals, often including local fish or shellfish, and occasionally has live music. Of the **B&Bs**, try Mrs Harris in Cunningsburgh (☎01950/477408; ②), with comfortable accommodation, *Solbrekke* in Sandwick (☎01950/431410; ②) or, further south, *Columbine* (☎01950/460582; ②), on the sideroad to the Croft House Museum and identified by a railway signal. Simple accommodation is available at the *Cunningsburgh Community Club* (☎01950/477777 or 477241; June–Aug), which has dorm beds, good showers and a well-equipped kitchen. Those with **camping** gear minus a tent can try the reconstructed *Betty Mouat's Cottage* (no phone; book through the tourist office in Lerwick), immediately southwest of Sumburgh Airport. There's full-scale camping at *Levenwick Campsite* (☎01950/422207; May–Sept), which has basic facilities and a superb view over the east coast.

Fair Isle

Halfway between Shetland and Orkney and very different from both, **Fair Isle** supports a vibrant community of around seventy people. The north end of the island rises like a wall; the Sheep Rock, a sculpted stack of rock and grass on the east side, is one of the island's most dramatic features. The croft land and the settlement, consisting of scattered houses, are concentrated in the east and south.

At one time the population was not far short of 400, but clearances forced emigration from the middle of the nineteenth century. By the 1950s, the population had shrunk to just 44, a point at which evacuation and abandonment of the island was seriously considered. George Waterston, who'd bought the island and set up a bird observatory in 1948, passed it into the care of the NTS in 1954 and rejuvenation began. Since then, islanders, the Trust and the Shetland Islands Council have invested in many improvements to housing, the harbour and basic services, including an advanced **electricity system** integrating wind and diesel generation; and crafts including boat-building, the making of fiddles, felt and stained glass have been developed. The social and natural history of the island is compellingly told in the **George Waterston Memorial Centre** (opening times vary and are advertised locally; ☎01595/760244; free). Particularly memorable are stories of shipwrecks; *El Gran Grifon*, part of the retreating Spanish Armada, was lost here in 1588 and in 1868 the islanders undertook a heroic rescue of all 465 German emigrants aboard the *Lessing*.

The present **Bird Observatory**, just above the North Haven where the ferry from Grutness in Shetland arrives, dates from 1969. It's one of the major European centres for ornithology and its work in watching, trapping, recording and ringing birds goes on all year. Fair Isle is a landfall for a huge number and range of migrant birds during the spring and autumn passages. Migration routes converge here and more than 340 species, including many rarities, have been noted.

Fair Isle is even better known for its **knitting** patterns, still produced with as much skill as ever by the local knitwear co-operative, though not in the quantities which you might imagine from a walk around city department stores; there are demonstrations at the Hall from time to time, and the George Waterson Memorial Centre fills in the history. The idea that the islanders borrowed all their patterns from the 300 shipwrecked Spanish seamen is nowadays regarded as a patronizing myth.

Practicalities

The **ferry** connects Fair Isle with either Lerwick (on alternate Thurs; 4hr 30min) or Sumburgh (Tues, Sat & alternate Thurs; 3hr); for bookings contact J.W. Stout (☎01595/760222) in advance. You can also fly from the airport at Tingwall, six miles northwest of Lerwick (Mon, Wed, Fri & Sat; a day-trip is possible on Wed & Fri).

If you want **to stay**, the *Fair Isle Lodge and Bird Observatory* (☎01595/760258; ⑦, dorms with full board £25 per person; April–Oct) offers good home cooking and perhaps the opportunity to lend a hand with the observatory's research programme. For decent B&B accommodation, there's *Schoolton* (☎01595/760250; ③, full board ④), or *Barkland* (☎01595/760247; ⑤; full board), both in the south of the island.

Scalloway and around

The village of **SCALLOWAY** was once the capital of Shetland, but its importance waned through the eighteenth century as Lerwick, just six miles to the east, grew in trading success and status. Scalloway's prosperity, always closely linked to the

THE SHETLAND BUS

The story of the **Shetland Bus**, the link between Shetland and Norway which helped to sustain the Norwegian resistance through the years of Nazi occupation, is quite extraordinary. Constantly under threat of attack by enemy aircraft or naval action, small Norwegian fishing boats were used to run arms and resistance workers into lonely fjords. The trip took 24 hours and on the return journey brought back Norwegians in danger of arrest by the Gestapo, or those who wanted to join Norwegian forces fighting with the allies. For three years, through careful planning, the operation was remarkably successful; instructions to boats were passed in cryptic messages in BBC news broadcasts. Although local people knew what was going on, the secret was generally well kept. Eventually, 350 refugees were evacuated, and more than 400 tons of arms, large amounts of explosives and 60 radio transmitters were landed in Norway.

Originally established at **Lunna** in the northeast of the Mainland, the service moved to **Scalloway** in 1942, partly because the village could offer good marine engineering facilities at Moore's Shipyard at the west end of Main Street, where a plaque records the morale-boosting visit of the Norwegian Crown Prince Olav. Many buildings in Scalloway were pressed into use to support the work; explosives and weapons were stored in the Castle. **Kergord House** in Weisdale was used as a safe house and training centre for intelligence personnel and saboteurs. The hazards, tragedies and elations of the exercise are brilliantly described in David Howarth's book, *The Shetland Bus*; their legacy today is a closer, more heartfelt relationship between Shetland and Norway.

fluctuations of the fishing industry, has recently been given a boost with investment in new fish-processing factories, and in the impressive North Atlantic Fisheries College on the west side of the harbour.

The best way to approach Scalloway is on the main road from Lerwick; as it crosses the shoulder of the **Scord**, the view over the village and the islands to the south and west opens up dramatically. In spite of modern developments nearby, the scene is dominated by the imposing shell of **Scalloway Castle**, built in 1600 for **Earl Patrick Stewart** using forced labour and thus seen as a powerful symbol of oppression. Stewart, who'd succeeded his father Robert to the Earldom of Orkney and Lordship of Shetland in 1593, held court in the castle and gained a reputation for enhancing his own power and wealth through the calculated use of harsh justice, frequently including confiscation of assets. Eventually, he upset influential people and was arrested in 1609; his son attempted an insurrection and both were executed in Edinburgh in 1615. The castle was used for a time by **Cromwell's army**, but eventually fell into ruin and is nowadays carefully maintained in that state by HS. If the door is locked, the key can be borrowed from the knitwear shop immediately to the north.

On Main Street, a small **museum** (May–Sept Tues–Thurs 2–5pm, Sat 10am–1pm & 2–5pm; free) run by volunteers with local relics. It explains the importance of fishing and tells the story of the **Shetland Bus** (see above). West of Scalloway, there's a pleasant if energetic walk up **Gallows Hill** (allow 2–3hr), where alleged witches were put to death; and then on to the hamlet of Burwick, a former fishing settlement.

Scalloway practicalities

Transport in the area is provided by bus services from Lerwick (from the bus stop on the Esplanade) which run six times daily to Scalloway and three times most days to Hamnavoe. **Accommodation** in Scalloway includes the pleasant and welcoming *Hildasay Guest House* (☎01595/880822; ③), which specializes in angling holidays, and the *Broch Guest House* (☎01595/880767; ③). There aren't many places **to eat**, but the *Castle Café* has an excellent reputation for fish and chips, and the *Kiln Bar* and *Scalloway Hotel* both do restaurant and bar meals. The *North Atlantic Fisheries College* has a very pleasant restaurant with broad harbour views, and serves teas and snacks as well as meals.

Trondra and Burra

South of Scalloway – and connected to the Mainland by bridges – are the islands of **Trondra** and, further south and west, West and East Burra, which have some beautiful beaches with excellent coastal walks. Trondra is a small island whose main point of interest is at **Burland**, just west of the main road, where there's a **Croft Trail** (May–Sept Mon–Sat 10am–6pm; free) which provides an insight into life on a working croft; there are also some rare native breeds of livestock to be seen.

The next bridge leads west to **West Burra** and almost immediately to **HAMNAVOE**, a planned fishing settlement unlike any other in Shetland, established mainly in the early 1900s and still very much a working, seagoing community. The road south from Hamnavoe winds past the white sandy beach at **Meal**, deservedly popular on warm summer days, and to **Papil** at the south end of West Burra; a quarter of a mile beyond the end of the road, there's another fine beach at **Banna Minn**, with excellent walking nearby on the cliffs of Kettla Ness. The road south through **East Burra** ends at the hamlet of **Houss**, distinguished by the tall, ruined laird's house or haa. From the turning place outside the cattle-grid, continue walking southwards, following the track to the left, down the hill and across the beach, and after about a mile you'll reach the deserted settlement of **Symbister**, inhabited until the 1940s. You can now see ancient field boundaries and, just south of the ruins, a **burnt mound** (an overgrown pile of Neolithic cooking stones dumped when no longer usable). Half a mile further south, the island ends in cliffs, caves and wheeling fulmars. From there, the island of **South Havra**, topped by the ruins of Shetland's only **windmill**, is just to the southwest. Once supporting a small fishing community, the island was abandoned, except for the grazing of sheep, in 1923; it was such a perilous existence that children as well as animals had to be tethered to prevent them falling over the cliffs.

The Central Mainland

The districts of **Tingwall** and **Weisdale** in the **Central Mainland** are a captivating mix of farms, moors, lochs and Shetland's only significant woodland; the scale of the scenery ranges from the intimate to the vast, with particularly spectacular views from high points above **Whiteness** and Weisdale. The area also holds strong historical associations, with the Norse parliament at **Lawting Holm** and unhappy memories of nineteenth-century clearances at Weisdale.

Tingwall and the Lawting

The green farmland of the Tingwall Valley, containing the two lochs, **Tingwall** and **Asta**, both of which are good for fishing, stretches north from Scalloway. At the northern end of Tingwall Loch is the **Lawting Holm**, a small peninsula once an island and linked to the shore by a causeway. This was the site of the Lawting, *thing* being Old Norse for "**parliament**", where local people and officials gathered from time to time to make or amend laws and discuss evidence. From the late thirteenth century, Shetland's laws were based on those of Norwegian King Magnus the Lawmender. It seems that meetings to deal with these matters took place here up to the sixteenth century, after which judicial affairs were dealt with in Patrick Stewart's new castle at Scalloway. Although structures on the holm have long since vanished there's an information board which helps in visualizing the scene. A little further south, a 7ft **stone** by the roadside is said to mark the spot where, after a dispute at the Lawting in 1389, **Earl Henry Sinclair** killed his cousin and rival **Marise Sperra** together with seven of his followers.

Just north of the loch is **Tingwall Kirk** and in the burial ground a dank **vault** from a thirteenth-century church that was demolished in 1788. Inside the vault are several very old tombstones, including one to a local official called a *Foud* – a representative of the king – who died in 1603. It's an eerie place and a torch is useful; a grounding in Latin and Scots even more so.

This relatively fertile part of Shetland seems as appropriate a place as any for the **Agricultural Museum** (July–Sept daily 2–5pm; £1), about 200yd from the crossroads at Tingwall. The enthusiastic owner has amassed a remarkable treasure trove of equipment from Shetland's crofts and farms and has an intimate knowledge of all of it. West of Tingwall, the road crosses the ridge at Wormadale, giving excellent views, then curves northwards through **WHITENESS**, where the Hjaltasteyn workshop (April–Sept Mon 9.30am–noon, Wed 2–4.30pm, Thurs 9.30am–4.30pm; free) produces attractive jewellery, in polished stone, silver and gold. A little further north, by the shore of Weisdale Voe, another jewellery workshop, Shetland Silvercraft (Mon–Fri 9am–1pm & 2–5pm; free), also welcomes visitors.

Weisdale

Weisdale is an evocative name in Shetland; in this valley some of the cruellest clearances of people in favour of sheep took place in the middle of the nineteenth century. The perpetrator was **David Dakers Black**, a farmer from the county of Angus who began buying land in 1843. Hundreds of tenants were dispossessed and in 1850 the large house of **Kergord**, then called Flemington, was built towards the northern end of the valley from the stones of some of the older houses. The ruined shells of some of the rest still stand on the valley sides; local writers, particularly John J. Graham, have recounted the period in novels (notably his *Shadowed Valley*) and drama.

Around Kergord House and on the upper valley sides there are several **tree plantations** dating mainly from around 1920 but with a later experimental addition by the Forestry Commission. An amazing range of species is present, from the sycamores and willows which thrive in many Shetland gardens to examples of chestnut, copper beech, monkey puzzle and much else besides. Along with the trees comes a woodland ecosystem, with plants like **foxglove**, Britain's most northerly **rookery** and a reliable **cuckoo**. During the war, Kergord House played a role in the Shetland Bus operation; the saboteurs who trained here are said to have amused visitors by demonstrating booby traps and incendiary devices in the garden. Half a mile south of Kergord House is **Weisdale Mill**, built for grain milling and dating from 1855. It is now an arts centre, housing the small, beautifully designed **Bonhoga Gallery** (Wed–Sat 10.30am–4.30pm, Sun noon–4.30pm; free), in which touring and local exhibitions of painting, sculpture and other media are shown. There's also a very pleasant café, overlooking the stream.

South of the mill at the head of Weisdale Voe, it's also possible to turn southwards along the west shore where, among trees near the voe's narrowest point, is the ruined house once occupied by **John Cluness Ross** (1786–1853). He settled in the Cocos Islands in the Indian Ocean, went into coconut farming and appointed himself king, the first of three in a family dynasty which ruled (some would say oppressed) the islanders for decades.

Central Mainland practicalities

Transport to the Central Mainland from Lerwick is provided by **buses** heading for Walls or Skeld, all of which run through Tingwall, Whiteness and Weisdale. Buses heading to Brae, Mossbank and the North Isles also pass through Tingwall, as does one service a day from Scalloway via Lerwick to the Sullom Voe Terminal.

Accommodation in the Central Mainland is limited. Try Mrs Georgeson at Upper Hellister in Weisdale (☎01595/830440; ③) for pleasant B&B accommodation, or the *Westings Hotel* (☎01595/840242; ⑥) at Wormadale, which has a wonderful view over Whiteness Voe and the islands, and does good restaurant and bar meals. The appealing café at Weisdale Mill (see opposite) is the best place for a snack or light lunch.

The Westside and Papa Stour

The western Mainland of Shetland – known as the **Westside** – stretches west from Weisdale and Voe to Sandness and **Papa Stour**. Although there are some important archeological remains and wildlife in the area, the Westside's greatest appeal lies in its scenery and outstanding **walking**. At its heart, the Westside's rolling brown and purple moorland, dotted with patches of bright-green reseeded land, glistens with dozens of small, picturesque blue or silver lochs. On the west coast the rounded form of Sandness Hill (750ft) falls steeply away into the Atlantic. The **coastal scenery**, cut by several deep voes, is very varied; aside from dramatic cliffs, there are intimate coves and some fine beaches. The crossroads for the area is effectively Bixter, from where you can travel north towards Aith and Voe, south to **Skeld** and **Reawick** and west to Walls, **West Burrafirth** and Sandness.

A road winds northwest from **BIXTER** towards Aith and **Voe**; almost immediately there's a branch road to **Clousta** and **Noonsbrough**, hamlets by an intimate voe, and, like much of the rest of the Westside, dotted with archeological remains, including a ruined **broch** at Noonsbrough and a number of cairns, prehistoric houses and field systems. **AITH** is the main centre for the area, but there isn't a lot here except a shop and school, and the base for the west of Shetland lifeboat; you can buy sheepskins from an outlet on the south side of village. Just north, **Vementry** (also the name of a Mainland farm) is an island off the coast that boasts the best-preserved **heel-shaped cairn** in Shetland, right on top of the hill. To get there, make arrangements through the tourist office in Lerwick to rent a boat from Vementry Farm. Particularly towards Voe, the landscape is spectacular, with the road climbing high above the shores of the voes past tiny peaty lochs.

Southwest of Bixter, there's excellent walking along the coast between Silwick, Westerwick and **Culswick**, past cliffs, caves and stacks. About a mile west of Culswick is one of the better-preserved **brochs**. Five miles north, at **Staneydale**, stands a remarkable **Neolithic structure** measuring more than 40ft by 20ft internally with immensely thick walls, still around 4ft high, whose roof would have been supported by spruce posts. Called a temple by the archeologist who excavated it because it resembled one on Malta, this building, whatever its function, was twice as large as similarly shaped houses and was certainly of great importance, perhaps as some kind of community centre.

Once an important fishing port, **WALLS** (pronounced "Waas"), appealingly set round its harbour, is now a quiet village. There's a **swimming pool** and a small **museum**, mostly of knitwear (open by special arrangement and only for groups and tours; ☎01595/809366; free). To the south lies the island of **Vaila**, from where in 1837 Lerwick philanthropist Arthur Anderson operated a fishing station in an unsuccessful attempt to break down the system of **fishing tenures** under which tenants were forced to fish for the landlords under pain of eviction. Near Bridge of Walls, where the Walls and Sandness roads divide, there's a notable prehistoric site at **Scord of Brouster**. A helpful information board provides an explanation of the layout of various ruined houses and field boundaries, making it easier to imagine what life might have been like for the people who lived on this hil side between 3000 and 1500 BC.

The scattered crofting settlement of **SANDNESS** (pronounced "*Saa*ness"), which you can reach by road or by walking the coast from Walls past the dramatic **Deepdale** and across **Sandness Hill**, is an oasis of green meadows in the peat moorland, with a nice beach, too. The modern **spinning mill** (Mon–Fri 8am–5pm; free) produces pure Shetland wool and welcomes visitors; you can watch how they spin the exceptionally fine Shetland wool into yarn.

Papa Stour

A mile offshore from Sandness and reached by a foot passenger **ferry** from **West Burrafirth** is the quintessentially peaceful island of **Papa Stour** (big island of the priests); apart from early Christian connections, it was home, in the eighteenth century, to people who were mistakenly believed to have been lepers (also see opposite). The sea has eroded its volcanic rocks to produce some of the most impressive coastal scenery in Shetland, with **stacks, caves** and **natural arches**. The east side is the most fecund area, partly because much of the soil from the western side was painstakingly transported here. In the nineteenth century, Papa Stour supported around 300 inhabitants, but by the early 1970s there was a population crisis: the island's school had closed, the remaining sixteen inhabitants were all past child-bearing age and, worse still, it looked like the post office would close and the mailboat be withdrawn. The islanders made appeals for new blood to revive the fragile economy and managed to stage a dramatic recovery, releasing croft land to young settlers from Britain and overseas. Papa Stour was briefly dubbed "the hippie isle", but it wasn't long before some newcomers moved on, to other parts of Shetland or elsewhere, making a further appeal necessary. Today the island supports a community of thirty or so.

A trail leaflet (available from the tourist office in Lerwick) helps locate the island's prehistoric remains as well as the recently excavated remains of a thirteenth-century Norse house, which may have been a royal seat, at the **Biggins**, halfway along the island's only road.

Westside practicalities

Transport to the Westside from Lerwick is provided by **buses** to Walls (2–4 most days; 50min) and Skeld (1–2 most days; 65min). Minibus services connect with these routes to Aith (1–2 daily), Sandness (1–2 daily) and Dale of Walls (1 daily). In summer, the **ferry** runs from West Burrafirth to Papa Stour (Mon, Wed, Fri & Sat mornings, also on Fri, Sat & Sun evenings); always book in advance and reconfirm 24 hours before departure (☎01595/810460). British Airways Express also **flies** from Tingwall airport (near Lerwick) to Papa Stour daily and a day-trip is feasible (for details, phone ☎01595/840226).

The only **hotel** in the area is the beautifully situated *Burrastow House* (☎01595/809307; ⑨), about three miles west of Walls and dating from 1759, but recently extended. There are few **B&Bs**, most of which, in the remoter areas, will provide an evening meal. Try *Hogan*, Bridge of Walls (☎01595/809375; ②), a working croft with small rooms but a big welcome, or the friendly *Trouligarth*, west of Walls (☎01595/809373; ②). There's homely accommodation on Papa Stour at *North House* (☎01595/873238; ③, with dinner ④). For more **basic accommodation**, the beautifully restored *Voe House* at Walls is good if you have camping gear minus a tent; the modest price includes peat for the fires (book through the tourist office at Lerwick). *Aith Public Hall* is also usually available for indoor camping (☎01595/810327). The best place to **eat** in Shetland is at *Burrastow House*, which offers distinguished cooking in idyllic surroundings by the sea; meals, though expensive, are good value. Booking is advised for lunch, and essential for dinner.

Foula

Southwest of Walls, at "the edge of the world", the island of **Foula** is separated from the nearest point on Mainland Shetland by about fourteen miles of ocean. Seen from the Mainland, its distinctive form changes subtly, depending upon the vantage point, but the outline is unforgettable. Its western **cliffs**, the second highest in Britain after those of St Kilda, rise at the Kame to some 1241ft above sea level; from its highest point at the Sneug (1370ft), a clear day offers a magnificent panorama stretching from Unst to Fair Isle. On a bad day, the exposure is complete and the cliffs generate turbulent blasts of wind known in Shetland as "flans" which tear down the hills with tremendous force. The cliffs and moorland provide a home for a quarter of a million **birds** – the name of the island is based on the Old Norse for "bird island" – and host the largest colony of great skuas in Britain, with around 2500 pairs. Foula's human population peaked at around 200 at the end of the nineteenth century, but has fluctuated wildly over the years, dropping to three in 1720 following an epidemic of "muckle fever". Today, the gentler eastern slopes provide crofting land which, with sheep grazing, helps to support a community numbering about forty.

Inhabited since prehistoric times, the people here take pride in their separateness from Shetland, cherishing local traditions such as the observance of the Julian calendar, officially dropped in Britain in 1752 , where Old Yule is celebrated on January 6 and the New Year doesn't arrive until January 13. The island's isolation also meant that more of the Shetland dialect survived here than elsewhere; and in the late nineteenth century, Foula's people provided an enormous amount of information on the dialect and its roots in the Norn language for a study undertaken by the Faroese philologist Jakob Jakobsen. The island has a few visible prehistoric remains, but the peat probably covers many more.

Practicalities

A day-trip by **ferry** isn't possible. The summer passenger service to Foula runs from Walls on Tuesdays, Saturdays and alternate Thursdays (2hr 30min), with a sailing from Scalloway on remaining Thursdays (3hr). In winter the service runs to and from Walls on Tuesdays and Thursdays; it's essential to book and reconfirm (☎01595/753232). British Airways Express flies from Tingwall, near Lerwick, to Foula (Mon–Wed & Fri 1 daily; ☎01595/840226), with day-trips possible except on Tuesdays. If you want to stay on the island, **B&B** accommodation is available at Leraback (☎01595/753226; ④ including dinner). Even if you go to the island just for the day, bear in mind that there's no shop, so you'll need to take all your supplies with you.

The North Mainland, Whalsay and Out Skerries

Heading up the east side of the **North Mainland**, the districts of **Nesting** and **Lunnasting**, jutting out into the North Sea, offer appealing seascapes, gentle walks and numerous, if unspectacular, archeological remains. To the north, beyond the village of Vidlin, **Lunna House**, and the sheltered harbour below it, was the first base from which the Shetland Bus operation was conducted; the house dates in part from 1660. Down the hill lies the little, whitewashed Lunna Kirk, built in 1753, with a beautiful interior including a carved central pulpit. Among its features is a "lepers' squint" on the outside wall, through which those believed to have the disease could participate in the service without risk of infecting the congregation; there was, however, no leprosy here, the outcasts in fact suffering from a hereditary, non-infectious skin condition.

Whalsay and Out Skerries

The island of **Whalsay**, reached by ferry from Laxo (or in some weather conditions, Vidlin), is a thriving community devoted almost entirely to **fishing**. The islands' crews operate a fleet of large trawlers and have coped with the change and uncertainty that characterize the industry by investing huge sums in fishing further afield and catching a wider range of species, and have thus sustained a remarkable level of prosperity. The tiny **Pier House**, across **SYMBISTER** harbour from the ferry berth, is one of the two adjacent booths built for the **Hanseatic traders**, and contains a good display on how the Germans traded salt, tobacco, spirits and cloth for Whalsay's salted, dried fish.

At the hamlet of **Sodom**, about half a mile east, is the former home of celebrated Scots poet, writer and republican **Hugh MacDiarmid**, born Christopher Grieve in the Borders town of Langholm (1892–1978). He stayed here from 1933 until 1942, writing about half of his output, including much of his best work: lonely, contemplative poems honouring fishing and fishermen, with whom he sometimes went out to sea. Estranged from his first wife and family and with a drink problem, MacDiarmid, practically broken, had sought temporary relief in Shetland. At first, he seems to have fallen in love with the islands, but poor physical and mental health exacerbated (if not caused) by chronic poverty, dogged him. Eventually, unwillingly conscripted to work in a Glasgow munitions factory, he left with his new wife and young son, never to return. The cottage has recently been restored to provide basic accommodation for visitors (see p.538).

Of the several **prehistoric remains** on Whalsay, the most notable are **houses** at Yoxie and an **island fort** in the Loch of Huxter, both on the southeastern side of the island. The island also has an eighteen hole **golf course** in the northeast and a **leisure centre** with an excellent swimming pool close to the school in Symbister.

The **Out Skerries** (reached by ferry from Vidlin or Lerwick) consist of three tiny islands – Grunay, Bruray and Housay – the latter two linked by a bridge. That people live here at all is remarkable; that it is one of Shetland's most dynamic communities is astonishing, its affluence based on fishing from a superb, small natural harbour sheltered by all three islands, and on salmon farming in a nearby inlet. There are good, if short, walks, with a few prehistoric remains and an ingenious collection system for rainwater which involves a spiral channel around the island's main hill on Bruray.

Voe, Brae and Sullom Voe

The tight huddle of homes and workshops around the pier in the old, southern part of the village of **VOE** has a strongly Scandinavian appearance and is dominated by the **Sail Loft**. Painted in a rich, deep red, the building was originally used by fishermen and whalers, but later for the manufacture of knitwear. Woollen jumpers were knitted here for the 1953 expedition to Mount Everest, and Edmund Hillary wore one on his way to the summit. Today, the building provides simple visitor accommodation. From Voe the main road divides; the northern leg leads to Toft, the ferry terminal for the island of Yell (see p.539), while the other branch cuts northwest to Brae.

BRAE, a sprawling settlement that still has the feel of a frontier town, was one of four expanded in some haste in the 1970s to accommodate the workforce for the huge **Sullom Voe Oil Terminal**, just to the north. The longest in Shetland, Sullom Voe has always attracted the interest of outsiders in search of a deep-water harbour. During **World War II** it was home to the Norwegian Air Force and a base for RAF seaplanes. Although the terminal, built between 1975 and 1982, has passed its production peak, it is still the largest of its kind in Europe. Its size, however, isn't obvious from beyond the site boundary and few clues remain to the extraordinary scale of the construction effort, which for several years involved a workforce of 6000 accommodated in two large "construction villages" and two ships. It has, barring one early incident, a good environmental record. Its long-term future depends on whether it can attract sufficient business from the developing oilfields west of Shetland.

Past Brae, a branch off the main road to Mavis Grind and Hillswick leads over a bridge to the island of **Muckle Roe**. Its eastern side has relatively fei tile croft land; the western coastline is wilder and provides excellent walking country.

Northmaven

Mavis Grind, a narrow ithsmus at which it's said you can throw a stone from the Atlantic to the North Sea, or at least to Sullom Voe, marks the start of **Northmaven**, on the west of the North Mainland, unquestionably one of the most picturesque areas of Shetland with its often rugged scenery, magnificent coastline and wide open spaces. Three miles north of the isthmus, it's worth abandoning the main road to explore the remoter corners; the twisting sideroad west to **Gunnister** and **Nibon** travels through a wonderful tumbled landscape of pink and grey rock where abandoned fields and broken shells of croft houses provide abundant evidence of past human struggles to make a living. When the road ends, at Nibon, you can view a jigsaw of islands and rocky headlands which, even on a relatively calm day, smash the Atlantic into streams of white foam.

HILLSWICK, the main settlement in the area, was once served by the North of Scotland, Orkney and Shetland Shipping Company steamer, and in the early 1900s the firm also built a hotel, importing it in the form of a timber kit from Norway; it still stands, albeit somewhat altered. Nearer the shore is the much older Hillswick House and, attached to it, **Da Böd**, now a café but formerly the oldest pub in Shetland, said to have been founded by a German merchant in 1684.

Just outside Hillswick, a sideroad leads west to **Eshaness** (pronounced "*Ay*shaness"), celebrated for its splendid coastline views. Spectacular **cliffs** and **stacks** are spread out before you as the road climbs away from Hillswick, with stacks called the **Drongs** in the foreground and distant views to the Westside and Papa Stour. About three miles west of Hillswick, a turning northwards off the main road leads to the hamlet of **Hamnavoe**, birthplace of **Johnnie "Notions" Williamson** (1740–1803). A man of many talents, including blacksmithing and weaving, his fame rests on his work in protecting several thousand of the population against **smallpox** using a serum and a method of inoculation he'd invented himself, to the amazement of the medical profession. He used a scalpel to lift a flap of skin without drawing blood, then placed the serum he'd prepared underneath, dressing it with a cabbage leaf and a bandage.

Just before **Stenness** the road divides, the southern branch leading to a hamlet which was once one of the most important **deep-sea fishing stations** in Shetland. The remains of a few of the **böds** used by the fishermen are still visible along the sloping pebbly beach where they would dry their catch; nearby is an impressive natural arch, the **Dore Holm**. At the peak of operations in the early nineteenth century, as many as eighteen trips a year were made in up to seventy open six-oared boats, or "sixareens", to the fishing grounds thirty or forty miles to the west. A Shetland folk song, *Rowin' Foula Doon*, recalls how the crews rowed so far west that the island of Foula began to sink below the eastern horizon. A mile or so back along the main road) a south turning leads to **Tangwick Haa Museum** (May–Sept Mon–Fri 1–5pm, Sat & Sun 11am–7pm; free), which, through photographs, old documents and fishing gear, tells the often moving story of this remote corner of Shetland and its role in this dangerous trade. The northern branch of the road ends at the **Eshaness Lighthouse**, a great place to view the cliffs, stacks and, in rough weather, blowholes of this stretch of coast. A useful information board at the lighthouse details the dramatic features here, including a partially collapsed cave and a substantial br och, which can be reached in an easy three-hour walk.

North of **Ronas Voe**, by the shores of Colla Firth, an unmarked road leads up **Collafirth Hill**. At the top, there are the crumbling remains of a NATO radio station, but the natural landscape is much more impressive, with tremendous views on a clear day, and a foreground of large, scattered stones with hardly any vegetation. Though the walk isn't quite as straightforward as it looks, scale and distance being hard to judge in this setting, Collafirth Hill is the easiest place from which to approach the rounded contours of **Ronas Hill**, Shetland's highest point (1516ft). The climb, with no obvious path, is exhausting but rewarding (allow 2hr each way; also see the safety precautions on p.44): from the top you can look west to one of the most beautifully sculptured parts of the Shetland coast, as the steep slope of the hill drops down to the arching sand and shingle beach called the **Lang Ayre**, south and east over all of the Mainland, north along the coast of Yell, or out into the daunting expanse of the Atlantic. Also at the summit, among subarctic vegetation and stone patterns formed by freezing and thawing of the thin soil, is a Neolithic or Bronze Age **chambered tomb**, one of the best-preserved in Shetland and useful as a shelter from the wind.

North Mainland practicalities

From Lerwick, there are up to seven **buses** most days to Brae, and one or two in the late afternoon to Hillswick, which has minibus connections to Eshaness, Ollaberry and North Roe. Two buses daily travel from Lerwick to Vidlin, stopping at the nearby Laxo ferry terminal for Whalsay. **Ferries** between Laxo and Whalsay (30min) run about every 45 minutes from early morning until late evening; if you have a car, book ahead on ☎01806/566259. In bad weather, especially southeasterly gales, the service operates from Vidlin. Ferries to and from Skerries leave from Vidlin (Mon 1 daily, Fri–Sun 3 daily; 1hr), and Lerwick (Tues & Thurs 1 daily; 2hr 30min).

Just west of Brae is one of the best **hotels** in Shetland, *Busta House* (☎01806/522506; ⑦), which offers comfortable accommodation in historic surroundings. There's also the interesting, if less luxurious, timber-clad *St Magnus Bay Hotel* (☎01806/503371; ③) at Hillswick. For **guest houses,** try the friendly *Greystones* (☎01806/522322; ③), on the shore at Brae, or the modern *Valleyfield* (☎01806/522450; ④), just to the south, which also has a small **campsite**. Good **B&Bs** include Mrs Ford (☎01806/577302; ②) at Lunning, northeast of Vidlin. Near Brae, a good choice is *Westayre* (☎01806/522368; ③), at the end of the southern branch of the road on Muckle Roe. Nearer Eshaness, *Almara* (☎01806/503261; ③) in Urafirth offers good food, a family welcome and excellent views. On Out Skerries, Mrs Johnson (☎01806/515228; ②, with dinner ④) runs a friendly B&B at Rocklea. For **basic accommodation**, if you have an airbed or sleeping mat, try the camping böds at the *Sail Loft* in Voe, *The Grieve House* (Hugh MacDiarmid's) on Whalsay, or *Johnnie Notions* at Hamnavoe in Eshaness; book all these through the tourist office in Lerwick.

For a **meal** or a drink, good places to try include the *Mid Brae Inn*, in the centre of Brae, or *Busta House* (see above). In Hillswick, the *St Magnus Bay Hotel* serves bar and restaurant meals.

The North Isles: Yell, Fetlar and Unst

Shetland's three **North Isles** bring Britain to a dramatic, windswept end; north of Unst there's no land until eastern Siberia, beyond the North Pole. The landscapes and seascapes of the islands have been shaped by centuries of fierce storms and have an elemental beauty. Although the three islands differ markedly from one another, they all offer superb **walking**, some interesting **archeological sites,** and notable **bird reserves**. However, it's their wildlife which impresses most, with the coast of **Yell**, in particular, being home to abundant **otters**. The islands are easy to reach, and at less windy times of year they make good cycling country, with not too many steep hills. Accommodation, however, isn't abundant, so book ahead, especially in summer.

To get to the North Isles, a **bus** and ferry service leaves Lerwick for Yell, Unst and Fetlar every morning except Sunday, taking around two and a half hours to reach Belmont in Unst or Oddsta in Fetlar. There's also an afternoon service but the connection on Yell only runs on Tuesdays, Thursdays and Fridays, and Unst connections only on Thursdays and, between April and September, on Saturdays. There are also bus **tours** from Lerwick. Get details of all these services from Leasks (☎01595/693162). Taking a **car** is easy: using the inexpensive and frequent ferry services operated by Shetland Islands Council, it takes no more than two hours to Baltasound from Lerwick. The Mainland ferry terminal for Yell is at Toft; from there, **ferries** run to Ulsta about every thirty minutes from early morning to late evening (20min). Ferries leave from Gutcher in north Yell to Belmont on Unst (generally every 15–30min; 10min), and to Oddsta on Fetlar (4–7 daily; 25min). Booking in advance is wise; phone ☎01957/722259.

Yell

Historically, **Yell**, the largest of the North Isles, hasn't had good write-ups. The writer, Eric Linklater, described it as "dull and dark", while the Scottish historian Buchanan claimed it was "so uncouth a place that no creature can live therein, except such are born there". Certainly, if you keep to the fast main road via Westsandwick, which links the ferry terminal at **ULSTA** to the Fetlar and Unst one at **GUTCHER**, you'll pass a lot of uninspiring peat moorland, but the landscape is relieved by **Whale Firth, Mid Yell Voe** and **Basta Voe**, which cut deeply into it, providing superb natural harbours used as hiding places by German submarines during World War II. Yell's coastline is gentler and greener than the interior and provides an ideal habitat for a large population of **otters**; locals will point out the best places to watch for them.

A building dating from 1672 houses the **Old Haa Museum and Café**, at **BURRAVOE** (late April to Sept Tues–Thurs & Sat 10am–4pm, Sun 2–5pm; free), offering an ideal introduction to life on Yell past and present, with historical material, a small art gallery and the work of projects on local music and oral history. Just up the road is **St Colman's Church** (1900), an isolated but delightful example of Arts and Crafts architecture, built in three Gothic-windowed bays with a curved end, surmounted by a tiny ornate spire. Heading up the coast from Burravoe, you'll pass a ruined **broch** on the headland at Gossabrough and, north of Otterswick, a ship's figurehead known as the **White Wife,** from the wreck of the *Bohus* in 1924.

The island's largest village, **MID YELL**, has a couple of shops, a pub and a leisure centre with a good swimming pool. A mile or so to the west of the village, just beyond the main road, **Windhouse**, dating in part from the early eighteenth century, is said to be haunted by many ghosts – skeletons were found under the floor and in its walls. Its lodge now provides basic visitor accommodation; nearby are the remains of a **broch** and a **heel-shaped cairn**. North of Windhouse, at Lumbister, there's an **RSPB reserve** that's home to merlins and skuas and is scattered with wild flowers in summer. A pleasant walk is alongside the nearby narrow gorge known as **Daal of Lumbister**, where you can see a lush growth of honeysuckle, wild thyme and moss campion.

In the north of Yell, the area around **CULLIVOE** has relatively gentle, but attractive, coastal scenery, with a sandy beach at **Breckon**. To the west is **Gloup**, with its secretive, narrow voe. In the nineteenth century, this was one of the largest fishing stations in Shetland; a memorial commemorates the 58 men who were lost when a **great storm** overwhelmed six of their boats in July 1881. This area provides some excellent walking, as does the Atlantic coast further west, where there's an Iron Age fort and field system at **Burgi Geos**.

Practicalities

Yell's **B&Bs** include *Hillhead* (☎01957/722274; ②) in Burravoe, *Bayanne House* (☎01957/744219; ②) at Sellafirth, and Mrs Tulloch (☎01957/744201; ②) at Gutcher's post office. An alternative is the *Pinewood Guest House* (☎01957/702427; ③) at Aywick. All these places will provide an evening meal. For more **basic accommodation**, if you've an airbed or mat, you can stay in *Windhouse Lodge*, on the main road near Mid Yell; book through the tourist office in Lerwick. There isn't a great range of eating places on the island but the non-smoking café in the *Old Haa Museum* at Burravoe has soup, snacks and delicious home baking. The *Hilltop Bar* in Mid Yell offers lunches and suppers, while the *Seaview Café* at the Gutcher ferry terminal has filled rolls, snacks, soup, teas and coffees.

Fetlar

Known as "the garden of Shetland", **Fetlar** is the most fertile of the North Isles; much of it grassy moorland and lush green meadows with masses of summer flowers. Around 900 people once lived here; there might well be more than 100 now were it not for the activities of **Sir Arthur Nicolson**, who in the early nineteenth century cleared many of the people at forty days' notice to make room for sheep. Nicolson's architectural tastes were rather more eccentric than some other local tyrants; his rotting but still astonishing Brough Lodge, a rambling 1820s composition in stone and brick at the southwest corner of the island, owes something – perhaps an apology – to Gothic, Classical and maybe even Tudor styles.

Today Fetlar's population live on the southern and eastern sides of the island, where the main settlement, **HOUBIE,** has a rather less adventurously styled laird's house built by Fetlar's most famous son, **Sir William Watson Cheyne**, who with Lord Lister pioneered antiseptic surgery. Nearby is an excellent **interpretive centre** (May–Oct Wed–Sun noon–5pm; free) presenting the island's history and offering information on birdlife through an Internet site as well as by more conventional means. The island has several notable archeological remains, including the **Finnigert**, a Neolithic dyke which divides the island into two, a monastic site at Strandibrough, a ring of stones at Haltadans, brochs, soapstone workings, cairns and a Norse grave. The first three of these are within the **RSPB North Fetlar Reserve** (open all year, but from mid-May to mid-July visits are only possible with permission from the warden at Baelans on ☎01957/733246). The reserve boasts regular visits by one or more **snowy owls**, who bred here for the first time in Britain in 1967, on the southern limit of their range. Breeding continued for several years and around twenty chicks were raised, but recently only females have been present. Fetlar is also one of very few places you'll see graceful **red-necked phalarope** (late May and Aug); a hide has been provided at the east end of the island near **Funzie** (which incidentally is pronounced "Finnie").

Elsewhere on Fetlar, particularly on the remoter north coast and on Lambhoga, the higher moorland peninsula to the southwest, there is excellent walking. At Tresta, on the south coast, is a beautiful **sandy beach** and the loch behind it, Papil Water, is good for **fishing.**

Practicalities

The Oddsta ferry terminal is about three miles from Houbie; there are no buses on the island, so if you don't have a car you'll have to negotiate a lift on the ferry. Accommodation is in short supply and booking is advisable. There are two very welcoming **B&Bs**, *Gord* (☎01957/733227; ②), behind the island shop in Houbie, and *The Glebe* (☎01957/733242; ②), which is non-smoking, among the trees above Papil Water; both will provide an evening meal. *Garths Campsite* (☎01957/733269; May–Sept) is well-equipped with toilets, showers and drying facilities, and there's a café at the Fetlar Shop (Tues, Wed, Fri & Sat 10am–5pm, Thurs & Sun 10am–1pm).

Unst

Unst has a population of around 1000, of whom 300 or 400 are connected to the **RAF radar base** at Saxa Vord, listening out for uninvited intruders. Though much of the interior is rolling grassland, the coast is more dramatic: a fringe of cliffs relieved by some beautiful sandy beaches. Found widely on Unst is serpentine rock; most often it's greyish green, but it weathers to rusty orange, and in some stone walls there are pieces which are of an extraordinary deep turquoise hue. The serpentine soil also produces unusual vegetation; grass has a bluish-grey cast, and at the **Keen of Hamar National Nature Reserve**, north of Baltasound, numerous rare plants, including the unique mouse-eared chickweed, grow in an almost lunar landscape.

In the southeast of the island, not far from the ferry terminal, is **UYEASOUND** with nearby Muness Castle, built in 1598 by **Laurence Bruce**, half-brother of Robert Stewart and probably designed by Andrew Crawford who shortly afterwards built Scalloway Castle for Robert's son Patrick. A little to the north is a vast sandy beach, backed by the deserted crofting settlement of Sandwick. Northwest of Uyeasound, along the Westing road, is Shetland's largest **standing stone** near the Loch of Bordastubble; and further on, at Underhoull, are the ramparts of a ruined **broch** next to an Iron Age earth house.

The island's main settlement is at **BALTASOUND**, where the remains of old jetties around the bay testify to a bygone herring industry; there's a hotel with a pub, a shop, a post office and a leisure centre with a pool. Britain's most northerly post office is over the hill to the north, at **HAROLDSWICK**. Here, down near the shore, is the **Unst Boat Haven** (May–Sept daily 2–5pm; otherwise a key is available from the adjacent shop; free), displays a beautifully presented collection of historic boats with many tools of the trade and information on fishing; most of the boats are from Shetland, with one from Norway. A little to the north, off the main road, at the **Unst Heritage Centre** (May–Sept daily 2–5pm; free), you can find out about other aspects of Unst life. The road ends at **Skaw**, with a beautiful beach and the very last house in Britain.

West of Haroldswick is **Burrafirth**, a north-facing inlet surrounded by cliffs and guarded by the hills of **Saxa Vord** and **Hermaness**. Behind the beach and the links the **Loch of Cliff** is good for fishing. **Hermaness National Nature Reserve** is home to more than 100,000 seabirds, the best known of which is "Albert Ross", a disorientated black-browed albatross from the South Atlantic. Albert's return to the same ledge year after year, ever hopeful that a mate might turn up, soon became celebrated as a harbinger of spring but his presence has become more erratic of late. There's a **visitor centre** in the former lighthouse keepers' houses, and a marked route into the reserve allows you to look down over the jagged rocks of **Muckle Flugga** and the most northerly bit of Britain, **Out Stack**. There are few more dramatic settings for a lighthouse, and few sites could ever have presented as great a challenge to the builders. The views from here are inevitably marvellous and the walk down the west side of Unst towards Westing is one of the finest in Shetland.

Practicalities

The island's guest houses and hotel are all in Baltasound: there's historic *Buness House* (☎01957/711315; ④), *Clingera Guest House* (☎01957/711579; ③), and Britain's most northerly hotel, the *Baltasound Hotel* (☎01957/711334; ⑤), which serves lunches and dinners to non-residents. **B&Bs** include *Barns* (☎01957/755249; ③) at Westing, Mrs Ritch (☎01957/711323; ②) at Haroldswick, and Mrs Firmin (☎01957/775234; ③) at Uyeasound. For more **basic accommodation**, the independent youth hostel at Uyeasound is well-equipped (☎01957/755298 or 755311). Snacks and teas can be had at the *Nornova Tearoom* just north of Muness Castle or, often on a help-yourself basis, at the *Haroldswick Shop*.

ONWARDS TO NORWAY, THE FAROE ISLANDS AND ICELAND

Thanks to the historical ties and the attraction of a short hop to continental Europe, **Norway** is a popular destination for Shetlanders and Orcadians. Norwegians often think of Shetland and Orkney as their western isles and, particularly in west Norway, old wartime bonds with Shetland are still strong. Norwegian yachts and sail training vessels are frequent visitors to Lerwick and Kirkwall. Shetlanders can also go by ferry to the **Faroe Islands** – steep, angular shapes rising out of the North Atlantic – and from Faroe, on to **Iceland**.

There are weekly **flights** between June and September from Kirkwall, Orkney (1hr 45min) and twice-weekly from Sumburgh, Shetland (1hr) to Bergen in Norway. Short inclusive breaks are available by air from Shetland (book through Hay & Co; ☎01950/460661). From June to August the large, comfortable and fast Faroese car **ferry** *Nörrona* makes weekly return trips from her home port in Faroe to Shetland, Norway, Iceland and Denmark. From Shetland, Bergen in Norway and Torshavn in Faroe are thirteen hours away; to Iceland the journey takes 33 hours including a brief stop in Faroe; on the way back there's a two-day stopover in Faroe while the ship makes a return trip to Denmark.

travel details

ORKNEY
Buses

Kirkwall to: Houton (5–6 daily; 30min); St Margaret's Hope (4 daily; 40min); Stromness (hourly; 40min); Tingwall (3 daily; 25min).

Ferries

Burwick to: John O' Groats (passengers only; 2–4 daily; 45min).

Houton to: Hoy (Lyness) and Flotta (6 daily; 45min).

Kirkwall to: Eday (1–3 daily; 1hr 15min); North Ronaldsay (1 weekly; 2hr 40min); Papa Westray (2–3 daily; 2hr 15min); Sanday (1–3 daily; 1hr 25min); Shapinsay (4–6 daily; 45min); Stronsay (1–3 daily;1hr 35min); Westray (2–3 daily; 1hr 25min).

Stromness to: Aberdeen (1 weekly in winter, 2 weekly in summer; 8–10hr); Hoy (passengers only; 2–3 daily in summer; 30min); Lerwick (1 weekly in winter, 2 weekly in summer; 8hr); Scrabster/ Thurso (1–3 daily except Sun in winter; 1hr 45min).

Tingwall to: Egilsay (7 daily; 50min); Rousay (7 daily; 30min); Wyre (7 daily; 45min).

Flights

Kirkwall to: Aberdeen (2–4 daily; 45min); Eday (Wed 2 daily; 12min); Edinburgh (1 daily; 2hr); Glasgow (1 daily; 2hr 10min); Inverness (2 daily; 50min); North Ronaldsay (Mon–Sat 2 daily; 15min); Papa Westray (Mon–Sat 1–2 daily; 12min); Sanday (Mon–Sat 1–3 daily; 20min); Stronsay (Mon–Fri 1–2 daily; 25min); Westray (Mon–Sat 1–2 daily; 12min).

SHETLAND
Buses

Cullivoe to: Ulsta (1–3 daily; 50min).

Lerwick to: Brae (3–7 daily; 40min); Culswick (daily; 1hr 20min); Fetlar (1–2 daily; 3hr 10min); Hamnavoe (Mon–Sat 3 daily; 30min); Hillswick (1–2 daily; 1hr 15min); Laxo (2–3 daily; 30min); Sandwick (Mon–Sat 4–6 daily, Sun 3 daily; 35min); Scalloway (Mon–Sat 6 daily; 15min); Sumburgh (3–4 daily; 45min); Unst (Mon–Sat 1–2 daily; 2hr 45min); Vidlin (Mon–Sat 2 daily; 40min); Walls and Sandness (2–4 daily, 50min); Yell (Mon–Sat 3 daily, Sun 1 daily; 1hr 20min).

Ferries
Mainland

Grutness to: Fair Isle (May–Sept Tues, Sat & alternate Thurs; 2hr 30min).

Laxo to: Whalsay (16–18 daily; 30min).

Lerwick to: Aberdeen (4–5 weekly overnight; direct sailings 14hr, via Orkney 20hr); Bressay

(20–22 daily; 5min); Fair Isle (alternate Thurs; 4hr 30min); Out Skerries (Tues & Thurs 1 daily; 2hr 30min).

Scalloway to: Foula (May–Sept alternate Thurs; 3hr).

Toft to: Yell (25–28 daily; 20min).

Vidlin to: Out Skerries (Mon 1 daily; Fri, Sat & Sun 3 daily; 1hr 30min).

Walls to: Foula (May–Sept Tues, alternate Thurs & Sat 1 daily; 2hr 30min).

West Burrafirth to: Papa Stour (Mon & Wed 1 daily; Fri–Sun 2 daily; 35min).

Other islands

Unst (Belmont) to: Fetlar (3 daily; 25min).

Yell (Gutcher) to: Fetlar (4–7 daily; 25min); Unst (29 daily; 10min).

Flights

Sumburgh to: Aberdeen (Mon–Fri 5 daily, Sat & Sun 2 daily; 1hr); Fair Isle (1 weekly; 15min); Glasgow (1 daily; 2hr 5min); Kirkwall (1–2 daily; 40min); Unst (Mon–Fri 1 daily; 35min); Wick (Mon–Sat 1 daily; 50min).

Tingwall to: Fair Isle (Mon, Wed, Fri & Sat 1–2 daily; 25min); Foula (Mon–Wed, Fri 1–2 daily; 15min); Out Skerries, calling at Whalsay on request (Mon & Wed–Fri 1 daily; 30min); Papa Stour (Tues 1 daily; 10min); Unst (Mon–Fri 1 daily; 25min).

PART THREE

THE
CONTEXTS

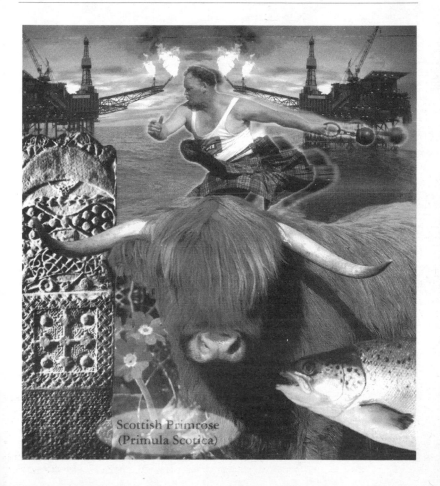

Scottish Primrose
(Primula Scotica)

THE HISTORICAL FRAMEWORK

PREHISTORIC SCOTLAND

Scotland, like the rest of prehistoric Britain, was settled by successive waves of peoples arriving from the east. These first inhabitants were **hunter-gatherers**, whose heaps of animal bones and shells have been excavated, amongst other places, in the caves along the coast near East Wemyss, in Fife. Around 4500 BC, **Neolithic farming peoples** from the European mainland began moving into Scotland. To provide themselves with land for their cereal crops and grazing for their livestock, they cleared large areas of upland forest, usually by fire, and in the process created the characteristic moorland landscapes of much of modern Scotland. These early farmers established permanent settlements, some of which, like the well-preserved village of **Skara Brae** on Orkney, were near the sea, enabling them to supplement their diet by fishing and to develop their skills as boatbuilders. The Neolithic settlements were not as isolated as was once imagined: geological evidence has, for instance, revealed that the stone used to make axe-heads found in the Hebrides was quarried in Northern Ireland.

Settlement spurred the development of more complex forms of religious belief. The Neolithic peoples built large chambered burial mounds or **cairns**, such as Maes Howe in Orkney. This reverence for human remains suggests a belief in some form of afterlife, a concept that the next wave of settlers, the **Beaker people**, certainly believed in. They placed pottery beakers filled with drink in the tombs of their dead to assist the passage of the deceased on their journey to, or their stay in, the next world. The Beaker people also built the mysterious **stone circles**, thirty of which have been discovered in Scotland. Such monuments were a massive commitment in terms of time and energy, with many of the stones carried from many miles away, just as they were at Stonehenge in England, the most famous stone circle of all. One of the best known Scottish circles is that of **Callanish** on the Isle of Lewis, where a dramatic series of monoliths (single standing stones) form avenues leading towards a circle made up of thirteen standing stones. The exact function of the circles is still unknown, but many of the stones are aligned with the position of the sun at certain points in its annual cycle, suggesting that the monuments are related to the changing of the seasons.

The Beaker people also brought the **Bronze Age** to Scotland. Bronze, an alloy of copper and tin, was stronger and more flexible than its predecessor flint, which had long been used for axe-heads and knives. New materials led directly to the development of more effective weapons, and the sword and the shield made their first appearance around 1000 BC. Agricultural needs plus new weaponry added up to a state of endemic warfare as villagers raided their neighbours to steal livestock and grain. The Bronze Age peoples responded to the danger by developing a range of defences, among them the spectacular **hillforts**, great earthwork defences, many of which are thought to have been occupied from around 1000 BC and remained in use throughout the Iron Age, sometimes far longer. Less spectacular but equally practical were the **crannogs**, smaller settlements built on artificial islands constructed of logs, earth, stones and brush, such as Cherry Island in Loch Ness.

Conflict in Scotland intensified in the first millennium BC as successive waves of **Celtic** settlers, arriving from the south, increased competition for land. Around 400 BC the Celts brought the technology of **iron** with them and, as Winston Churchill put it, "Men armed with iron entered Britain and killed the men of bronze". These fractious times witnessed the construction of hundreds of **brochs** or fortified towers. Concentrated along the Atlantic coast and in the northern and western isles, the brochs were drystone fortifications (built without mortar or cement) often over 40ft in height. Some historians claim they provided protection for small coastal settlements from the attentions of Roman slave traders. Much the best-preserved broch is on the Shetland island of **Mousa**; its double walls rise to about 40ft, only a little short of their original height. The Celts continued to migrate north almost up until Julius Caesar's first incursion into Britain in 55 BC.

At the end of the prehistoric period, immediately prior to the arrival of the Romans, Scotland was divided among a number of warring Iron Age tribes, who, apart from the raiding, were preoccupied with wresting a living from the land, growing barley and oats, rearing sheep, hunting deer and fishing for salmon. The Romans were to write these people into history under the collective name Picti, or **Picts**, meaning painted people, after their body tattoos.

THE ROMANS

The **Roman conquest** of Britain began in 43 AD, almost a century after Caesar's first invasion. By 80 AD the Roman governor, Agricola, felt secure enough in the south of Britain to begin an invasion of the north, building a string of forts across the Clyde–Forth line and defeating a large force of Scottish tribes at Mons Graupius. The long-term effect of his campaign, however, was slight. Work on a major fort – to be the base for 5000 – at Inchtuthill, on the Tay, was abandoned before it was finished, and the legions withdrew south. In 123 AD the **Emperor Hadrian** decided to seal the frontier

against the northern tribes and built **Hadrian's Wall**, which stretched from the Solway Firth to the Tyne and was the first formal division of the island of Britain. Twenty years later, the Romans again ventured north and built the **Antonine Wall** between the Clyde and the Forth. This was occupied for about forty years, but thereafter the Romans, frustrated by the inhospitable terrain of the Highlands, largely gave up their attempt to subjugate the north, and instead adopted a policy of containment.

It was the Romans who produced the first written accounts of the peoples of Scotland. In the second century AD, the Greco-Egyptian geographer Ptolemy drew up the first known map of Scotland, which identified seventeen tribal territories. Other descriptions were less scientific, compounding the mixture of fear and contempt with which the Romans regarded their Pictish neighbours. Dio Cassius, a Roman commentator writing in 197 AD, informed his readers that:

They live in huts, go naked and unshod. They mostly have a democratic government, and are much addicted to robbery. They can bear hunger and cold and all manner of hardship; they will retire into their marshes and hold out for days with only their heads above water, and in the forest they will subsist on barks and roots.

THE DARK AGES

In the years following the departure of the Romans, traditionally put at 450 AD, the population of Scotland changed considerably. By 500

THE NORTHERN ISLES

With their sophisticated ships and navigational skills, the **Vikings**, who began their expansion in the eighth century, soon gained supremacy over the Pictish peoples in Shetland, Orkney, the extreme northeast corner of the mainland and the Western Isles. In 872, the King of Norway set up an earldom in **Orkney** from which **Shetland** was also governed: for the next six centuries the northern isles took a path distinct from the rest of what is now called Scotland, becoming a base for raiding and colonization in much of the rest of Britain and Ireland, and a link in the chain that connected Faroe, Iceland, Greenland and, more tenuously, North America. Norse culture flourished, and buildings such as St Magnus Cathedral in Kirkwall, Orkney, begun in 1137, give some idea of its energy (see

p.499). However, there were bouts of unrest, and finally Shetland was brought under direct rule from Norway at the end of the twelfth century.

When Norway united with Sweden under the Danish crown in the fourteenth century, Norse power began to wane and Scottish influence to increase. In 1469, a marriage was arranged between Margaret, daughter of the Danish King Christian I, and the future King James III of Scotland. Short of cash for her dowry, Christian mortgaged Orkney to Scotland in 1468, followed by Shetland in 1469; neither pledge was ever successfully redeemed. The laws, religion and administration of the northern isles became Scottish, though their Norse heritage is still very evident in place names, dialect and culture.

AD the **Picts** occupied the northern isles, and the north and the east as far south as Fife. Today their settlements can be generally identified by place names with a "Pit" prefix, such as Pitlochry, and by the existence of carved symbol stones, like those found at Aberlemno in Angus. To the west, between Dumbarton and Carlisle, was a population of **Britons**. Many of the Briton leaders had Roman names, which suggests that they were a Romanized Celtic people, possibly a combination of tribes maintained by the Romans as a buffer between the Wall and the northern tribes, and peoples pushed west by the Anglo-Saxon invaders landing on the east coast. Both the Britons and the Picts spoke variations of P-Celtic, from which Welsh, Cornish and Breton developed.

On the west coast, to the north and west of the Britons, lived the **Scotti**, Irish-Celtic invaders who would eventually give their name to the whole country. The first Scotti arrived in the Western Isles from Ireland in the fourth century AD, and about a century later their great king, Fergus Mor, moved his base from Antrim to Dunadd, near Lochgilphead, where he founded the kingdom of Dalriada. The Scotti spoke Q-Celtic, the precursor of modern Gaelic. On the east coast, the Germanic Angles had sailed north along the coast to carve out an enclave around Dunbar in East Lothian. The final addition to the ethnic mix was also non-Celtic; from around 800 AD, **Norse** invaders began to arrive, settling mainly in the northern isles (see box) and the northeast of the mainland.

The next few centuries saw almost constant warfare among the different groups. The main issue was land, but this was frequently complicated by the need of the warrior castes, who dominated all of these cultures, to exhibit martial prowess. Military conquests did play their part in bringing the peoples of Scotland together, but the most persuasive force was **Christianity**. Many of the Britons had been Christians since Roman times and it had been a Briton, St Ninian, who conducted the first missionary work among the Picts at the end of the fourth century. Attempts to convert the Picts were resumed in the sixth century by St Columba, who, as a Gaelic-speaking Scotti, demonstrated that Christianity could provide a bridge between the different tribes.

Christianity proved attractive to pagan kings because it seemed to offer them extra super-natural powers. As St Columba declared, when he inaugurated his cousin Aidan as king of Dalriada in 574, "Believe firmly, O Aidan, that none of your enemies will be able to resist you unless you first deal falsely against me and my successors." This combination of spiritual and political power, when taken with Columba's establishment of the island of **Iona** as a centre of Christian culture, opened the way for many peaceable contacts between the Picts and Scotti. Intermarriage became commonplace, and the Scotti king Kenneth MacAlpine, who united Dalriada and Pictland in 843, was the son of a Pictish princess – the Picts traced succession through the female line. Similarly, MacAlpine's creation of the united kingdom of **Alba**, later known as **Scotia**, was part of a process of integration rather than outright conquest. Kenneth and his successors gradually extended the frontiers of their kingdom by marriage and force of arms until, by 1034, almost all of what we now call Scotland was under their rule.

THE MIDDLE AGES

By the time of his death in 1034, **Malcolm II** was recognized as the king of Scotia. He was not, though, a national king in the sense that we understand the term, as under the Gaelic system kings were elected from the *derbfine*, a group made up of those whose great-grandfathers had been kings. The chosen successor, supposedly the fittest to rule, was known as the *tanist*. By the eleventh century, however, Scottish kings had become familiar with the principle of heredity, and were often tempted to bend the rules of *tanistry*. Thus, the childless Malcolm secured the succession of his grandson **Duncan** by murdering a potential rival tanist. Duncan, in turn, was killed by **Macbeth** in 1040. Macbeth was not, therefore, the villain of Shakespeare's imagination, but simply an ambitious Scot of royal blood acting in a relatively conventional way.

The victory of **Malcolm III**, known as Canmore (bighead), over Macbeth in 1057 marked the beginning of a period of fundamental change in Scottish society. Having avenged his father Duncan, Malcolm III, who had spent the previous seventeen years at the English court, sought to apply to Scotland a range of ideas he had brought back with him. He and his heirs established a secure dynasty based on succession through the male line and introduced **feudalism** into Scotland, a system that was diametrically opposed to the Gaelic system, which rested on blood ties: the followers of a Gaelic king were his kindred, whereas the followers of a feudal king were vassals bought with land. The Canmores successfully feudalized much of southern and eastern Scotland by making grants to their Norman, Breton and Flemish followers, but beyond that, traditional clan-based forms of social relations persisted.

The Canmores, independent of the local nobility, who remained a military threat, also began to reform the **Church**. This development started with the efforts of Margaret, Malcolm III's English wife, who brought Scottish religious practices into line with those of the rest of Europe and was eventually canonized. **David I** (1124–53) continued the process by importing monks to found a series of monasteries, principally along the border at Kelso, Melrose, Jedburgh and Dryburgh. By 1200 the entire country was covered by a network of eleven bishoprics, although church organization remained weak within the Highlands. Similarly, the dynasty founded a series of **royal burghs**, towns such as Edinburgh, Stirling and Berwick, and bestowed upon them charters recognizing them as centres of trade. The charters usually granted a measure of self-government, vested in the town corporation or guild, and the monarchy hoped this liberality would both encourage loyalty and increase the prosperity of the kingdom. Scotland's Gaelic-speaking clans had little influence within the burghs, and by 1550 Scots – a northern version of Anglo-Saxon – had become the main language throughout the Lowlands.

The policies of the Canmores laid the basis for a cultural rift in Scotland between the Highland and Lowland communities. Before that became an issue, however, the Scots had to face a major threat from the south. In 1286 **Alexander III** died, and a hotly disputed succession gave Edward I, the king of England, an opportunity to subjugate Scotland. In 1291 Edward presided over a conference where the rival claimants to the Scottish throne presented their cases. Edward chose John Balliol, in preference to Robert the Bruce, his main rival, and obliged John to pay him homage, thus turning Scotland into a vassal kingdom. Bruce refused to accept the decision, thereby continuing the conflict, and in 1295 Balliol renounced his allegiance to Edward and formed an alliance with France – the beginning of what is known as the "Auld Alliance". In the conflict that followed, the Bruce family sided with the English, Balliol was defeated and imprisoned, and Edward seized control of almost all of Scotland.

Edward had shown little mercy during his conquest of Scotland – he had, for example, had most of the population of Berwick massacred – and his cruelty seems to have provoked a truly national resistance. This focused on **William Wallace**, a man of relatively lowly origins who forged an army of peasants, lesser knights and townsmen that was fundamentally different to the armies raised by the nobility. Figures like Balliol, holding lands in England, France and Scotland, were part of an international aristocracy for whom warfare was merely the means by which they struggled for power. Wallace, by contrast, led proto-nationalist forces determined to expel the English from their country. Probably for that very reason Wallace never received the support of the nobility and, after a bitter ten-year campaign, he was betrayed and executed in London in 1305.

With Wallace out of the way, feudal intrigue resumed. In 1306 **Robert the Bruce**, the erstwhile ally of the English, defied Edward and had himself crowned king of Scotland. Edward died the following year, but the unrest dragged on until 1314, when Bruce decisively defeated a huge English army under Edward II at the Battle of **Bannockburn**. At last Bruce was firmly in control of his kingdom, and in 1320 the Scots asserted their right to independence in a successful petition to the pope, now known as the **Arbroath Declaration**.

In the years following Bruce's death in 1329, the Scottish monarchy gradually declined in influence. The last of the Bruce dynasty died in 1371, to be succeeded by the "Stewards", hence **Stewarts**, but thereafter a succession of Scottish rulers, culminating with James VI in 1567, came to the throne when still children. The power vacuum was filled by the nobility, whose key members exercised control as Scotland's regents while carving out territories where they ruled with the power, if not the title, of kings. At the close of the fifteenth century, the Douglas family alone controlled Galloway, Lothian, Stirlingshire, Clydesdale and Annandale. The more vigorous monarchs of the period, notably **James I** (1406–37), did their best to curb the power of such dynasties, but their efforts were usually nullified at the next regency. **James IV** (1488–1513), the most talented of the early Stewarts, might have restored the authority of the crown, but his invasion of England ended in a terrible defeat for the Scots – and his own death – at the battle of Flodden Field.

The reign of **Mary, Queen of Scots** (1542–67) typified the problems of the Scottish monarchy. Mary came to the throne when just one week old, and immediately caught the attention of the English king, Henry VIII, who sought, first by persuasion and then by military might, to secure her hand in marriage for his 5-year-old son, Edward. Beginning in 1544, the English launched a series of devastating attacks on Scotland, an episode Sir Walter Scott later called the "Rough Wooing", until, in the face of another English invasion in 1548, the Scots – or at least those not supporting Henry – turned to the "Auld Alliance". The French king proposed marriage between Mary and the Dauphin Francis, promising in return military assistance against the English. The 6-year-old queen sailed for France in 1548, leaving her loyal nobles and their French allies in control, and her husband succeeded to the French throne in 1559. When she returned thirteen years later, following the death of Francis, she had to pick her way through the rival ambitions of her nobility and deal with something entirely new – the religious Reformation.

THE REFORMATION

The **Reformation** in Scotland was a complex social process, whose threads are often hard to unravel. Nevertheless, it is quite clear that, by the end of the sixteenth century, the established Church was held in general contempt. Many members of the higher clergy regarded their relationship with the Church purely in economic terms, and forty percent of known illegitimate births (ie those subsequently legitimized) were the product of the "celibate" clergy's liaisons.

Another spur to the Scottish Reformation was the identification of Protestantism with anti-French feeling. In 1554, Mary of Guise, the French mother of the absent Queen Mary, had become regent, and her habit of appointing Frenchmen to high office was seen as part of an attempt to subordinate Scotland's interests to those of France. There was considerable resentment, and in 1557 a group of nobles banded together to form the **Lords of the Congregation**, whose dual purpose was to oppose French influence and promote the reformed religion. With English military backing, the Protestant lords succeeded in deposing the French regent in 1560, and, when the Scottish Parliament assembled shortly afterwards, it asserted the primacy of Protestantism by forbidding the Mass and abolishing the authority of the pope. The nobility proceeded to confiscate two-thirds of Church lands, a huge prize that did much to bolster their new beliefs.

Even without the economic incentives, Protestantism was a highly charged political doctrine. Luther had argued that each individual's conscience was capable of discerning God's will. This meant that a hierarchical priesthood, existing to interpret God's will, was unnecessary and that the people themselves might conclude their rulers were breaking God's laws, in which case the monarch should be opposed or even deposed. This point was made very clearly to Queen Mary by the Protestant reformer **John Knox** at their first meeting in 1561. Subjects, he told her, were not bound to obey an ungodly monarch.

Knox, a Protestant exile who had returned to Scotland in 1559, was a follower of the Genevan reformer Calvin, who combined Luther's views on individual conscience with a belief in predestination. He argued that an omnipotent God must know everything, including the destinies of every human being. Consequently, it was determined before birth who was to be part of the Elect, bound for heavenly glory, and who was not, a doctrine that placed enormous pressure on its adherents to demonstrate by their godly behaviour that they were of the Elect. This was the doctrine that Knox brought back to Scotland and laid out in his Articles of Confession of Faith, better known as the **Scot's Confession**, which was to form the basis of the reformed faith for over seventy years.

Mary ducked and weaved, trying to avoid an open breach with her Protestant subjects. The fires of popular displeasure were kept well-stoked by Knox, however, who declared "one Mass was more fearful than if ten thousand enemies were landed in any part of the realm, of purpose to suppress the whole religion". At the same time, Mary was engaged in a balancing act between the factions of the Scottish nobility. Her difficulties were exacerbated by her disastrous second marriage to **Lord Darnley**, a cruel and politically inept character, whose jealousy led to his involvement in the murder of Mary's favourite, David Rizzio, who was dragged from the queen's supper room at Holyrood and stabbed 56 times. The incident caused the Scottish Protestants more than a little unease, but they were entirely scandalized in 1567, when Darnley himself was murdered and Mary promptly married the **Earl of Bothwell**, widely believed to be the murderer. This was too much to bear, and the Scots rose in rebellion, driving Mary into exile in England at the age of just 25. The queen's illegitimate half-brother, the Earl of Moray, became regent, and her son, the infant James, was left behind to be raised a Protestant prince. Mary, meanwhile, became perceived as such a threat to the English throne that Queen Elizabeth I had her executed in 1587.

Knox could now concentrate on the organization of the reformed Church, or **Kirk**, which he envisaged as a body empowered to intervene in the daily lives of the people. **Andrew Melville**, another leading reformer, wished to push this theocratic vision further. He proposed the abolition of all traces of Episcopacy – the rule of the bishops in the Church – and that the Kirk should adopt a **presbyterian** structure, administered by a hierarchy of assemblies, part-elected and part-appointed. At the bottom of the chain, beneath the General Assembly, Synod and Presbytery, would be the Kirk session, responsible for church affairs, the performance of the minister and the morals of the parish. In 1592, the Melvillian party achieved a measure of success when presbyteries and synods were accepted as legal church courts and the office of bishop was suspended.

James VI (1567–1625) disliked presbyterianism because its quasi-democratic structure – particularly the lack of royally appointed bishops – appeared to threaten his authority. He was, however, unable to resist the reformers until 1610, when, strengthened by his installation as James I of England after Elizabeth's death in 1603, he restored the Scottish bishops. The argument about the nature of Kirk organization would lead to bloody conflict in the years after James's death.

THE RELIGIOUS WARS

Raised in Episcopalian England, **Charles I** (1625–49) had little understanding of Scottish reformism. He believed in the Divine Right of Kings, an authoritarian creed that claimed the monarch was God's representative on earth and, therefore, his authority had divine sanction, a concept entirely counter to Protestant thought. In 1637, Charles attempted to impose a new prayer book on the Kirk, laying down forms of worship in line with those favoured by the High Anglican Church. The reformers denounced these changes as "Popery" and organized the **National Covenant**, a religious pledge that committed the signatories to "Labour by all means lawful to recover the purity and liberty of the Gospel as it was established and professed".

Charles declared all the "**Covenanters**" to be rebels, a proclamation endorsed by his Scottish bishops. Consequently, when the king backed down from military action and called a General Assembly of the Kirk, the assembly promptly abolished the Episcopacy. Charles pronounced the proceedings illegal, but lack of finance stopped him from mounting an effective military campaign – whereas the Covenanters, well-financed by the Kirk, assembled a proficient army under Alexander Leslie. In desperation, Charles summoned the English Parliament, the first for eleven years, hoping it would pay for an army. But, like the calling of the General Assembly, the decision was a disaster and Parliament was much keener to criticize his policies than to raise taxes. In response Charles declared war on Parliament in 1642.

Until 1650 Scotland was ruled by the Covenanters and the power of the Presbyterian Kirk grew considerably. Laws were passed establishing schools in every parish and, less usefully, banning trade with Catholic countries. The only effective opposition to the theocratic state came from the **Marquis of Montrose**, who had initially supported the Covenant but lined up with the king when war broke out. His army was drawn from the Highlands and islands, where the Kirk's influence was weakest. Montrose was a gifted campaigner who won several notable victories against the Covenanters, but the reluctance of his troops to stay south of the Highland Line made it impossible for him to capitalize on his successes, and he was eventually captured and executed in 1650.

Largely confined to the peripheries of Scotland, Montrose's campaigns were a sideshow to the **Civil War** being waged further south. Here, the Covenanters and the English Parliamentarians faced the same royal enemy and in 1643 formed an alliance. Indeed, it was the Scots army that captured Charles at Newark in Nottinghamshire, in 1646. There was, however, friction between the allies. Many of the Parliamentarians, including Cromwell, were **Independents**, who favoured a looser form of doctrinal control within the state Church than did the Presbyterians, and were inclined towards religious toleration for the law-abiding sects outside the state Church. In addition, the Scots believed the English were tainted with **Erastianism** – a belief in placing the secular authority of Parliament over the spiritual authority of the Church.

The Parliamentarians in turn suspected the Scots of hankering for the return of the monarchy, a suspicion confirmed when, at the invitation of the Earl of Argyll, the future Charles II came back to Scotland in 1650. To regain his Scottish kingdom, Charles was obliged to renounce his father and sign the Covenant, two bitter pills taken to impress the population. In the event, the "presbyterian restoration" was short-lived. Cromwell invaded, defeated the Scots at Dunbar and forced Charles into exile. Until the Restoration of 1660, Scotland was united with England and governed by seven commissioners.

Although the restoration of **Charles II** (1660–85) brought bishops back to the Kirk, they were integrated into an essentially presbyterian structure of Kirk sessions and presbyteries, and the General Assembly, which had been abolished by Cromwell, was not re-established. Over 300 clergymen, a third of the Scottish ministry, refused to accept the reinstatement of the bishops and were edged out of the Church, forced to hold open-air services, called **Conventicles**, which Charles did his best to suppress. Religious opposition inspired military resistance and the Lowlands witnessed scenes of brutal repression as the king's forces struggled to keep control in what was known as "The Killing Time". In the southwest, a particular stronghold of the Covenanters, the government imported Highlanders, the so-called "Highland Host", to root out the opposition, which they did with great barbarity.

Charles II was succeeded by his brother **James VII** (James II of England), whose ardent Catholicism caused a Protestant backlash in England. In 1689, he was forced into exile in France and the throne passed to **Mary**, his Protestant daughter, and her Dutch husband, **William of Orange**. In Scotland, William and Mary restored the full presbyterian structure and abolished bishops, though they chose not to restore the political and legal functions of the Kirk, which remained subject to parliamentary control. This settlement ended Scotland's religious wars and completed its reformation.

THE UNION

Although the question of Kirk organization was settled in 1690, the political issue of the relationship between the Crown and the Scottish Parliament was not. From 1689 to 1697, William was at war with France, partly financed by Scottish taxes and partly fought by Scottish soldiers. Yet many Scots, mindful of the Auld Alliance, disapproved of the war and others suffered financially from the disruption to trade with France. There were other economic irritants too, principally the legally sanctioned monopoly that English merchants had over trade with the English colonies. This monopoly inspired the **Darien Scheme**, a plan to establish a Scottish colony in Panama. The colonists set off in 1698, but, thwarted by the opposition of both William and the English merchants, the scheme proved a miserable failure. The colony collapsed with the loss of £200,000 – an amount equal to half the value of the entire coinage in Scotland – and an angry Scottish Parliament threatened to refuse the king taxes as rioting broke out in the cities.

Meanwhile, in the north, the Highlanders blamed William for the massacre of the **MacDonalds of Glencoe**. In 1691, William had offered pardons to those Highland chiefs who had opposed his accession, on condition that they took an oath of allegiance by New Year's Day 1692. Alasdair MacDonald of Glencoe had turned up at the last minute, but his efforts to take the oath were frustrated by the king's officials, who were determined to see his clan, well-known for their support of the Stewarts, destroyed. In February 1692, Captain Robert Campbell quartered his men in Glencoe and, two weeks later, in the middle of the night, his troops acted on their secret orders and slaughtered as many MacDonalds as they could. Thirty-eight died, and the massacre caused a national scandal, especially among the clans, where "Murder under Trust" – killing those offering you shelter – was considered a particularly heinous crime.

The situation in Scotland was further complicated by the question of the succession. Mary died without leaving an heir and, on William's death in 1702, the crown passed to her sister **Anne**, who was also childless. In response, the English Parliament secured the Protestant succession by passing the Act of Settlement, which named the Electress Sophia of Hanover as the next in line to the throne. The Act did not, however, apply in Scotland, and the English feared that the Scots would invite James Edward Stewart back from France to be their king. Consequently, Parliament appointed commissioners charged with the consideration of "proper methods towards attaining a union with

Scotland". The project seemed doomed to failure when the Scottish Parliament passed the **Act of Security**, in 1703, stating that Scotland would not accept a Hanoverian monarch unless they had first received guarantees protecting their religion and their trade.

Nevertheless, despite the strength of anti-English feeling, the Scottish Parliament passed the **Act of Union** by 110 votes to 69 in January 1707. Some historians have explained the vote in terms of bribery and corruption. This certainly played a part (the Duke of Hamilton, for example, switched sides at a key moment and was subsequently rewarded with an English dukedom), but there were other factors. Scottish politicians were divided between the Cavaliers – Jacobites (supporters of the Stewarts) and Episcopalians – and the Country party, whose

THE HIGHLANDS

The country that was united with England in 1707 contained three distinct cultures: in south and east Scotland, they spoke Scots; in Shetland, Orkney and much of the northeast the local dialect, though Scots-based, contained elements of Norn (Old Norse); in the rest of north and west Scotland, including the Western Isles, Gaelic was spoken. These linguistic differences were paralleled by different forms of social organization and customs. The people of north and west Scotland were mostly pastoralists, moving their sheep and cattle to highland pastures in the summer, and returning to the glens in the winter. They lived in single-room dwellings, heated by a central peat fire and sometimes shared with livestock, and in hard times they would subsist on cakes made from the blood of their live cattle mixed with oatmeal. Highlanders supplemented their meagre income by raiding their clan neighbours and the prosperous Lowlands, whose inhabitants regarded their northern compatriots with a mixture of fear and contempt. In the early seventeenth century, Montgomerie, a Lowland poet, suggested that God had created the first Highlander out of horseshit. When God asked his creation what he would do, the reply was "I will doun to the Lowland, Lord, and thair steill a kow".

It would be a mistake, however, to infer from the primitive nature of Highland life that the institutions of this society had existed from time immemorial. This is especially true of the "**clan**", a term that only appears in its modern usage in the sixteenth century. In theory, the clan bound together blood relatives who shared a common

ancestor, a concept clearly derived from the ancient Gaelic notion of kinship. But in practice many of the clans were of non-Gaelic origin – such as the Frasers, Sinclairs and Stewarts, all of Anglo-Norman descent – and it was the mythology of a common ancestor, rather than the actuality, that cemented the clans together. Furthermore, clans were often made up of people with a variety of surnames, and there are documented cases of individuals changing their names when they swapped allegiances.

At the upper end of Highland society was the **clan chief** (who might have been a minor figure, like MacDonald of Glencoe, or a great lord, like the Duke of Argyll, head of the Campbells), who provided protection for his followers: they would, in turn, fight for him when called upon to do so. Below the clan chief were the **chieftains of the septs**, or subunits of the clan, and then came the **tacksmen**, major tenants of the chief to whom they were frequently related. The tacksmen sublet their land to **tenants**, who were at the bottom of the social scale. The Highlanders wore a simple belted plaid wrapped around the body – rather than the kilt – and not until the late seventeenth century were certain **tartans** roughly associated with particular clans. The detailed codification of the tartan was produced by the Victorians, whose romantic vision of Highland life originated with George IV's visit to Scotland in 1822, when he appeared in an elaborate version of Highland dress, complete with flesh-coloured tights (for more on tartan, see p.4290).

presbyterian members dreaded the return of the Stewarts more than they disliked the Hanoverians. There were commercial considerations too. In 1705, the English Parliament had passed the Alien Act, which threatened to impose severe penalties on cross-border trade, whereas the Union gave merchants of both countries free access to each other's markets. The Act of Union also guaranteed the Scottish legal system and the Presbyterian Kirk, and offered compensation to those who had lost money in the Darien Scheme.

Under the terms of the Act, both parliaments were to be replaced by a new British Parliament based in London, with the Scots apportioned 45 MPs and 16 peers. There were riots when the terms became known, but no sustained opposition.

THE JACOBITE RISINGS

When James VII/II was deposed he had fled to France, where he planned the reconquest of his kingdom with the support of the French king. In 1702, James's successor, William, died and the hopes of the Stewarts passed to his cousin James, the "Old Pretender" (Pretender in the sense of having pretensions to the throne; Old to distinguish him from his son Charles, the "Young Pretender"). The crown passed to Anne, however, and after her death and the accession of the Hanoverian George I, the first major **Jacobite uprising** occurred in 1715. Its timing appeared perfect. Scottish opinion was moving against the Union, which had failed to bring Scotland any tangible economic benefits. The English had also been accused of bad faith when, contrary to their pledges, they attempted to impose their legal practices on the Scots. Neither were Jacobite sentiments confined to Scotland. There were many in England who toasted the "King across the water" and showed no enthusiasm for the new German ruler. In September 1715, the fiercely Jacobite John Erskine, Earl of Mar, raised the Stewart standard at Braemar Castle. Just eight days later, he captured Perth, where he gathered an army of over 10,000 men, drawn mostly from the Episcopalians of northeast Scotland and from the Highlands. Mar's rebellion took the government by surprise. They had only 4000 soldiers in Scotland, under the command of the Duke of Argyll, but Mar dithered until he lost the military advantage. There was an indecisive

battle at Sheriffmuir in November, but by the time the Old Pretender arrived the following month 6000 veteran Dutch troops had reinforced Argyll. The rebellion disintegrated rapidly and James slunk back to exile in France in February 1716.

The **Jacobite uprising of 1745**, led by James's dashing son, Charles Edward Stewart (Bonnie Prince Charlie), had little chance of success. The Hanoverians had consolidated their hold on the English throne, Lowland society was uniformly loyalist, and even among the Highlanders Charles only attracted just over a half of the 20,000 clansmen who could have marched with him. Nevertheless, after a decisive victory over government forces at Prestonpans, Charles made a spectacular advance into England, getting as far as Derby. London was in a state of panic: its shops were closed and the Bank of England, fearing a run on sterling, slowed withdrawals by paying out in sixpences. But Derby was as far south as Charles got. On December 6, threatened by superior forces, the Jacobites decided to retreat to Scotland. The Duke of Cumberland was sent in pursuit and the two armies met on **Culloden Moor**, near Inverness, in April 1746. Outnumbered and outgunned, the Jacobites were swept from the field, losing over 1200 men compared to Cumberland's 300 plus. After the battle, many of the wounded Jacobites were slaughtered, an atrocity that earned Cumberland the nickname "Butcher". Jacobite hopes died at Culloden and the prince lived out the rest of his life in drunken exile.

In the aftermath of the uprising, the wearing of tartan, the bearing of arms and the playing of bagpipes were all banned. Rebel chiefs lost their land and the Highlands were placed under military occupation. Most significantly, the government prohibited the private armies of the chiefs, thereby effectively destroying the clan system.

THE HIGHLAND CLEARANCES

Once the clan chief was forbidden his own army, he had no need of the large tenantry that had previously been a vital military asset. Conversely, the second half of the eighteenth century saw the Highland population increase dramatically after the introduction of the easy-to-grow and nutritious potato. Between 1745 and 1811, the population of the Outer Hebrides, for example, rose from 13,000 to 24,500. The clan chiefs adopted different policies to deal with the new situation. Some encouraged emigration, and as many as 6000 Highlanders left for the Americas between 1800 and 1803 alone. Other landowners developed alternative forms of employment for their tenantry: mainly fishing and kelping. **Kelp** (brown seaweed) was gathered and burnt to produce soda ash, which was used in the manufacture of soap, glass and explosives. There was a rising market for soda ash until the 1810s, with the price increasing from £2 a ton in 1760 to £20 in 1808, making a fortune for some landowners and providing thousands of Highlanders with temporary employment. Other landowners developed **sheep runs** on the Highland pastures, introducing hardy breeds like the black-faced Linton and the Cheviot. But extensive sheep farming proved incompatible with a high peasant population, and many landowners decided to clear their estates of tenants, some of whom were forcibly moved to tiny plots of marginal land, where they were to farm as **crofters**.

The pace of the **Highland Clearances** accelerated after the end of the Napoleonic Wars in 1815, when the market price for kelp, fish and cattle declined, leaving sheep as the only profitable Highland product. The most notorious Clearances took place on the estates of the Countess of Sutherland, who owned a million acres in northern Scotland. Between 1807 and 1821, around 15,000 people were thrown off her land, evictions carried out by Patrick Sellar, the estate factor, with considerable brutality. Those who failed to leave by the appointed time had their homes burnt in front of them, and one elderly woman, who failed to get out of her home after it was torched, subsequently died from burns. The local sheriff charged Sellar with her death, but a jury of landowners acquitted him – and the sheriff was sacked. As the dispossessed Highlanders scratched a living from the acid soils of some tiny croft, they learnt through bitter experience the limitations of the clan. Famine followed, forcing large-scale emigration to America and Canada and leaving the huge uninhabited areas found in the region today.

The crofters eked out a precarious existence, but they hung on throughout the nineteenth century, often by taking seasonal employment away from home. In the 1880s, however, a sharp downturn in agricultural prices made it

difficult for many crofters to pay their rent. This time, inspired by the example of the Irish Land League, they resisted eviction, forming the **Highland Land Reform Association** and the **Crofters' Party**. In 1886, in response to the social unrest, Gladstone's Liberal government passed the **Crofters' Holdings Act**, which conceded three of the crofters' demands: security of tenure, fair rents to be decided independently, and the right to pass on crofts by inheritance. But Gladstone did not attempt to increase the amount of land available for crofting, and shortage of land remained a major problem until the **Land Settlement Act** of 1919 made provision for the creation of new crofts. Nevertheless, the population of the Highlands has continued to decline during the twentieth century, with many of the region's young people finding city life more appealing.

INDUSTRIALIZATION

Glasgow was the powerhouse of Scotland's **Industrial Revolution**. The passage from Glasgow to the Americas was much shorter than that from rival English ports and a lucrative transatlantic trade in tobacco had developed as early as the seventeenth century. This in turn stimulated Scottish manufacturing since, under the terms of the Navigation Acts, the Americans were not allowed to trade manufactured goods. Scottish-produced linen, paper and wrought iron were exchanged for Virginia tobacco, and when the American Revolution disrupted the trade in the 1770s and 1780s, the Scots successfully turned to trade with the West Indies and, most important of all, to the production of cotton textiles.

Glasgow's west coast location gave it ready access to the sources of raw cotton in the Americas, while the rapid growth of the British Empire provided an expanding market for its finished cloth. Initially, the city's **cotton industry**, like the earlier linen industry, was organized domestically, with spinners and weavers working in their homes, but increased demand required mass production and a need for factories. In 1787, Scotland had only nineteen mills; by 1840 there were nearly 200.

The growth of the textile industry spurred the development of other industries. In the mid-eighteenth century, the **Carron Ironworks** was founded near Falkirk, specializing in the production of military munitions. Here, the capital and expertise were English, but the location was determined by Scottish coal reserves, and by 1800 it was the largest ironworks in Europe. The basis of Scotland's **shipbuilding** industry was laid as early as 1802, when the steam vessel *Charlotte Dundas* was launched on the Forth–Clyde canal. Within thirty years, 95 steam vessels had been built in Scotland, most of them on Clydeside. The growth of the iron and shipbuilding industries, plus the extensive use of steam power, created a massive demand for coal, and pit shafts were sunk across the coalfields of southern Scotland.

Industrialization led to a concentration of Scotland's **population** in the central Lowlands. In 1840, one-third of the country's industrial workers lived in Lanarkshire alone, and Glasgow's population grew from 17,000 in the 1740s to over 200,000 a century later. Such sudden growth created urban overcrowding on a massive scale and, as late as 1861, 64 percent of the entire Scottish population lived in one- or two-room houses. For most Clydesiders, "house" meant a couple of small rooms in a grim tenement building, where many of the poorest families were displaced Highlanders and Irish immigrants, with the Irish arriving in Glasgow at the rate of one thousand a week during the potato famine of the 1840s.

By the late nineteenth century a measure of prosperity had emerged from industrialization, and the well-paid Clydeside engineers went to their forges wearing bowler hats and starched collars. They were confident of the future, but their optimism was misplaced. Scotland's industries were very much geared to the export market, and after **World War I** they found conditions much changed. During the war years, when exports had been curtailed by a combination of U-boat activity and war production, new industries had developed in India and Japan, and the eastern market for Scottish goods never recovered. The postwar world also witnessed a contraction of world trade, which hit the shipbuilding industry very hard and, in turn, damaged the steel and coal industries. By 1931, for instance, pig-iron production was at less than 25 percent of its 1920 output.

These difficulties were compounded by the financial collapse of the early 1930s, and by 1932 28 percent of the Scottish workforce was unemployed. Four hundred thousand Scots emigrated between 1921 and 1931, and those who stayed endured some of the worst social conditions in the British Isles. By the late 1930s, Scotland had the highest infant mortality rate in Europe, while some thirty percent of homes had no toilet or bath. There was a partial economic recovery in the mid-1930s, but high unemployment remained until the start of **World War II**.

THE LABOUR MOVEMENT

In the late eighteenth century, conditions for the labouring population varied enormously. At one extreme, the handloom weavers, working from home, were well-paid and much in demand, whereas the coal miners remained serfs, bought and sold with the pits they worked in, until 1799. During this period, the working class gave some support to the **radical movement**, those loosely connected groups of reformers, led by the lower middle class, who took their inspiration from the French Revolution. One of these groups, "The Friends of the People", campaigned for the extension of the right to vote, and such apparently innocuous activities earned one member, Thomas Muir, a sentence of fourteen years' transportation to Australia.

In 1820, the radicals called for a national strike and an insurrection to "show the world that we are . . . determined to be free". At least 60,000 workers downed tools for a week, and one group set off for the Carron Ironworks to seize arms. The government was, however, well prepared. It slammed radical leaders into prison and a heavy military presence kept control of the streets. The strike fizzled out and three leading radicals, all weavers, were later executed.

The 1832 Scottish Reform Act extended the franchise to include a large proportion of the middle class and thereafter political radicalism assumed a more distinctive working-class character, though its ideals still harked back to the American and French revolutions. In the 1840s, the **Chartists** led the campaign for working-class political rights by sending massive petitions to Parliament and organizing huge demonstrations. When Parliament rejected the petitions, the more determined Chartists – the "physical-force men" – urged insurrection. This call to arms was not taken up by the Scottish working class, however, and support for the Chartists fell away. The insurrectionary phase of Scottish labour was over.

During the next thirty years, as Scotland's economy prospered, skilled workers organized themselves into **craft unions**, such as the

Amalgamated Society of Engineers, dedicated to negotiating improvements for their members within the status quo. Politically, the trade unions gave their allegiance to the Liberal Party, but the first major crack in the Liberal-Union alliance came in 1888, when **Keir Hardie** left the Liberals to form the Scottish Socialist Party, which was later merged with the Independent Labour Party, founded in Bradford in 1893. Scottish socialism as represented by the ILP was ethical rather than Marxist in orientation, owing a great deal to the Kirk background of many of its members. But electoral progress was slow, partly because the Roman Catholic priesthood consistently preached against socialism.

In the early years of the twentieth century, two small Marxist groups established themselves on Clydeside: the **Socialist Labour Party**, which concentrated on workplace militancy, and the party-political **British Socialist Party**, whose most famous member was the Marxist lecturer John MacLean. During World War I, the local organizers of the SLP gained considerable influence by playing on the fears of the skilled workers, who felt their status was being undermined by the employment of unskilled workers. After the war, the influence of the shop stewards culminated in a massive campaign for the forty-hour working week. The strikes and demonstrations of the campaign, including one of 100,000 people in St George's Square in Glasgow, panicked the government into sending in the troops. But this was no Bolshevik Revolution – as Emmanuel Shinwell, the seamen's leader and future Labour Party politician, observed, "[the troops] had nothing much to do but chat to the local people and drink their cups of tea". The rank-and-file may have had little interest in revolution, but many of the activists did go on to become leaders within the newly formed Communist Party of Great Britain.

The ILP, now an affiliated part of the socialist **Labour Party**, made its electoral breakthrough in 1922, when it sent 29 Scottish MPs to Westminster. They set out with high hopes of social progress and reform, aspirations that were dashed, like trade union militancy, by the 1930s Depression. At the 1945 general election, Labour won forty seats in Scotland and, in more recent times, the party has dominated Scottish politics with its gradual eclipse of the Scottish

Conservatives. In 1955 the Conservatives held 36 Scottish seats, by 1995 they had just ten, and the 1997 general election left them with none at all.

The ILP MPs of the 1920s combined their socialism with a brand of Scottish nationalism. In 1924, for instance, the MP James Maxton had declared his intentions to "make English-ridden, capitalist-ridden Scotland into the Scottish socialist Commonwealth". The Labour Party maintained an official policy of self-government for Scotland, endorsing home rule in 1945 and 1947, but these endorsements were made with less and less enthusiasm. In 1958, Labour abandoned the commitment altogether and adopted a unionist vision of Scotland, much to the chagrin of many Scottish activists.

In 1971, **Upper Clyde Shipbuilders** stood on the brink of closure, its demise symbolizing the failure of traditional Labour politicians to revive Scotland's industrial base, which had resumed its decline after the end of World War II. In the event, UCS was partly saved by the work-in organized by two Communist shop stewards, Jimmy Reid and Jimmy Airlie. After fourteen months, the work-in finally succeeded in winning government support to keep part of the shipyard open, and Scots saw the broadly based campaign waged on its behalf as a national issue – Scottish industries set against an indifferent London government. Many socialist Scots, like James Jack, General Secretary of the Scottish TUC, moved towards some form of nationalism. Twenty-one years later, the closure of the steelworks at **Ravenscraig**, Motherwell, revived many of the same emotions.

TOWARDS DEVOLUTION

The **National Party of Scotland** was formed in 1928, its membership averaging about 7000 people, mostly drawn from the non-industrial parts of the country. Very much a mixture of practical politicians and left-leaning eccentrics, such as the poet Hugh MacDiarmid, in 1934 it merged with the right-wing Scottish Party to create the **Scottish National Party**. The SNP, after years in the political wilderness, achieved its electoral breakthrough in 1967 when Winnie Ewing won Hamilton from Labour in a by-election. The following year the SNP won 34 percent of the vote in local government elections and gained control of Cumbernauld, successes that had repercussions within both the Labour and Conservative parties. Both parties, wishing to head off the Nationalists, began to work on schemes to give Scotland a measure of self-government, and the term **"Devolution"** was coined. However, when the Conservatives came to power in 1970, Edward Heath, the prime minister, shelved plans for devolution because the SNP had only secured a twelve percent share of the Scottish vote.

The situation changed dramatically in 1974, when Labour were returned to power with a wafer-thin majority. The SNP held seven seats, which gave them considerable political leverage, and devolution was back on the agenda. The SNP had also run an excellent election campaign, concentrating on North Sea oil, which was now being piped ashore in significant quantities. Their two most popular slogans, "England expects.... Scotland's oil" and "Rich Scots or Poor Britons?", seemed to have caught the mood of Scotland.

In 1979, the Labour government, struggling to hold onto office after a "winter of discontent", put its devolution proposals before the Scottish people in a **referendum**. The "yes" vote gained 33 percent, the "no" vote 31 percent; although a majority was in favour, it was not by the required 40 percent. Not for the first time, Scottish opinion had shifted away from home rule; the reluctance to embrace it was based on uncertainty about what might follow, a concern about too many layers of government and, in some areas, a fear that the resulting assembly might be dominated by the Clydeside conurbation. The incoming Conservative government of Margaret Thatcher set its face against any form of devolution. It argued that the majority of Scots had voted for parties committed to the Union – namely Labour, the Liberal Democrats and themselves – and that only a minority supported the separation advocated by the SNP. At the same time, the government asserted that any form of devolution must lead inevitably to the break-up of the United Kingdom and, therefore, that the devolution solutions put forward by other parties could not be what the Scottish people wanted, because the inescapable result would be separation.

As the Thatcher years rolled on, growing evidence from opinion polls and central and local government elections suggested that few Scottish voters accepted either this reasoning or the implication that Scots did not know what was good for them. The Conservatives' support

in Scotland was further eroded by their introduction of the deeply unpopular Community Charge – universally nicknamed the **Poll Tax** – a form of local taxation that was charged essentially on a per capita basis and took little account of income. The fact that it had been imposed in Scotland a year earlier than in England and Wales was the source of further resentment.

In 1992, having largely rejected Conservative ideology and all but a few of the party's candidates, Scots found themselves still under a Tory government, this time with John Major at the helm. Though some Scottish Conservatives quietly supported devolution, their limited influence in the party as a whole was evident in the appointment of Michael Forsyth, one of the most articulate advocates of Thatcherite policy, as Secretary of State for Scotland in the 1995 Cabinet reshuffle.

Throughout the 1980s and early 1990s, the case for devolution had been made consistently by both Labour and the Liberal Democrats. In 1989, they, together with a cross section of Scottish organizations, including local government, churches and trade unions, co-operated in the establishment of the **Scottish Constitutional Convention**, a standing conference which developed detailed proposals for the introduction of a devolved Scottish legislature. Initially, the SNP saw the Convention as a diversion from their aim of an independent Scotland firmly attached to the European Union and did not join. Later, however, nationalists began to argue that devolution might after all offer a stepping stone to independence.

In the May 1997 general election, the Labour party won an enormous landslide victory and the Tories lost every single one of their Scottish seats. The new Labour government, headed by Tony Blair, moved swiftly to publish its proposals for devolution and a **referendum** was organized for that September. Voters were asked whether or not they agreed with two propositions: first, that a Scottish parliament should be established; and second, that it should have the power to vary income tax by up to three pence in the pound. Labour, the Liberal Democrats and the Scottish National Party united in calling for a "Yes, Yes" vote.

The referendum result was a clear "Yes, Yes" – 74.3 percent voted for a Scottish Parliament and 63.5 percent supported tax-varying powers.

Every part of the country supported the principle of a parliament and all but two regions were in favour of the tax proposals. In the autumn of 1997, the government introduced legislation to give Scotland's parliament control over education, health, law and order, social work, local government, planning and the environment, economic development, agriculture and fisheries, sport and the arts. Westminster was to retain control over defence, foreign affairs and major economic and tax issues, along with a number of legal provisions, including abortion, race relations and some aspects of road safety. The first elections for the new parliament are planned for May 1999, with powers due to take effect in 2000.

However, many questions have yet to be resolved, not least the issue of the consequences for the British parliament and **constitution**. For years, outspoken Labour MP for West Lothian, Tam Dalyell has criticized his own party for its alleged failure to answer what has become known as the West Lothian Question. Simply put, should Scottish MPs continue to have the same amount of influence over the affairs of the rest of Britain once a Scottish parliament has been established? This is a tricky issue for the government, since, although it currently enjoys a huge majority, any reduction in Scottish MPs at Westminster could, in the future, threaten its ability to form a British government.

Meanwhile, the Scottish National Party, who hope to form the principal opposition in the new parliament, have said that, while they are committed to making devolution work, they are adamant that it should be a stepping stone towards full independence.

THE FUTURE

With the nation set on a new and exciting political course, Scots hope that the **economy** can keep pace and sustain its recent prosperity. There have been hard times, particularly in central Scotland, where the decline of the heavy industries, including deep coal-mining, steelmaking, shipbuilding and engineering, has been all but complete, and unemployment has produced profound social problems in parts of Glasgow, Edinburgh and smaller towns. However, there has been a notable growth in service industries; for example, financial services and insurance have had a substantial impact in Edinburgh, Glasgow and some smaller centres such as Perth and Dunfermline. In northeast Scotland, particularly around Aberdeen, the oil industry – although past its boom – continues to underpin an economy which might otherwise have struggled to cope with the uncertainties of agriculture and, especially, fishing.

Though there have been encouraging signs of recent progress, the Highlands and islands remain an economically fragile area that needs special measures – distance from markets being an obvious and fundamental problem. Prosperity of a temporary sort has been provided in some areas by oil, but the best options for the future are likely to lie in selective, high-quality development in fishing, fish farming and other food-based industries, activities based on the advanced telecommunications network, primary industries such as forestry and quarrying and, last but certainly not least, tourism. Increasingly, the local environment is seen as a major asset for the attraction and success of most kinds of employment. One of the keys to Highland development, some would say the most important of all, is the ownership and control of land. Some of the largest Highland estates continue to be owned and managed from afar, with little regard to local needs or priorities; the success of a group of crofters in buying an estate in Assynt and the purchase of the island of Eigg by its inhabitants may point the way ahead for other communities.

Unquestionably the most striking change in Scotland in the last decade has been a **cultural renaissance**. Especially notable has been the revival of Gaelic, supported by large investments in broadcasting and publishing, and demonstrated by the huge popularity among young audiences – few of them Gaels – of bands like Runrig and Capercaillie. But the transformation goes beyond that: old inhibitions about writing in Scots or in Shetland dialect have been laid to rest too, and much of Glasgow's recent success is attributed to the city's focus on the arts. It remains to be seen whether Scotland's new cultural confidence and political life will act as the catalysts for the country's potential in a new century.

THE WILDLIFE OF SCOTLAND

A comprehensive account of Scotland's wildlife would take a whole book to cover; what follows is a general overview of the effects of climate and human activity on the country's flora and fauna.

CLIMATE

Scotland's mountains are high enough to impose harsh conditions, especially in the Highlands, and the **Cairngorm plateau** (the largest area of high ground in the whole of Britain) is almost arctic even in summer. Despite this, however, since the easing of the Ice Age about 10,000 years ago, Scotland has developed a rather complex climate, and some areas of the country are quite mild.

The warmish water of the Gulf Stream tempers conditions on the west coast, so that at **Inverewe**, for example, you'll find incongruously lush gardens blooming with subtropical plants. Inland, the weather becomes more extreme, but what restricts plant life on many Scottish hills is not the cold so much as the stress of wind and gloomy cloud cover. **Ben Nevis**, for example, is clouded and whipped by 50mph gales for more than two-thirds of the year, and as a result, the tree line – the height to which trees grow up the slopes – may be only 150ft above sea level near the west coast, but up to over 2000ft on some of the sheltered hillsides inland.

A BRIEF HISTORY

After the Ice Age, "arctic" and "alpine" plants abounded, eventually giving way to woody shrubs and trees, notably the **Scots pine**. Oak and other hardwood trees followed in some places, but the Scots pine remained the distinctive tree, spreading expansively to form the great **Caledonian Forest**. Parts of this ancient forest still remain, miraculously surviving centuries of attack, but it is only comparatively recently that attempts at positive conservation have been made.

Early **settlement**, from the Picts to the Norsemen, led to clearance of large areas of forest, and huge areas were burnt during the clan wars. When centuries of unrest ended with the Jacobite defeat at Culloden in 1745, the glens were ransacked for timber, which was floated downriver to fuel iron smelting and other industries. The clansmen had had a freebooting cattle economy, but during the infamous **Clearances** both the cattle and the defeated Highlanders were replaced by the more profitable sheep of the new landlords. As also happened on the English downland and moorland, intensive sheep grazing kept the land open, eventually destroying much woodland by preventing natural regeneration.

In Victorian times **red deer** herds, which also graze heavily, provided stalking, and when rapid firing breech-loading guns came into general use around the 1850s, **grouse shooting** became a passion. It's strange to think of birds changing the scenery, but grouse graze heather and thus large areas are burnt to encourage fresh green growth. No tree saplings survive and the open moorland is maintained.

The flatter **lowlands** are now dominated by mechanized farming; barley, beef, turnips and potatoes conspire against wildlife, and pollution and development are as damaging here as elsewhere. Even the so-called "**wilderness**" is under threat. Its own popularity obviously holds dangers, and the unique flora of the Cairngorm peaks, for example, is in danger of being stamped out under the feet of the summer visitors using the ski lifts. But even more damaging than tourism is **conifer planting**. In recent decades, boosted (if not caused) by generous grant aid and tax dodges, large areas of open moorland have been planted with tightly packed monocultural ranks of foreign conifers, forbidding to much wildlife.

Coniferization is particularly threatening to large areas of bogland in the "Flow Country" of Caithness and elsewhere, areas that are as unique a natural environment as the tropical rainforests. For these and other similar habitats, registration as an **SSSI** – a Site of Special Scientific Interest – has proved barely adequate, and the only real safeguard is for such areas to be owned or managed by organizations such as Scottish Natural Heritage (the national agency) or the Scottish Wildlife Trust, the Royal Society for the Protection of Birds and similar voluntary groups.

WILD FLOWERS

Relic patches of the Scots pine Caledonian Forest, such as the Black Wood of Rannoch and Rothiemurchus Forest below the Cairngorms, are often more open than an oak wood, the pines, interspersed with birch and juniper, spaced out in hilly heather. These woods feature some wonderful wild flowers, such as the **wintergreens** which justify their name, unobtrusive **orchids** in the shape of creeping lady's tresses and lesser twayblade and, in parts of the northeast especially, the rare beauty of the **twinflower**, holding its paired heads over the summer needle litter.

You'll also find old oak woods in some places, especially in the lower coastward lengths of the southern glens. Here the Atlantic influence encourages masses of spring flowers including **wood anemone** and **wild hyacinth**, the Scottish term for what in England is called a bluebell. (In Scotland the name "bluebell" describes the summer-flowering English harebell that grows on more open ground.) Scotland, or at least lowland Scotland, has many flowers found further south in Britain – **maiden pink**, orchids, **cowslip** and others in grassy areas. Roadside flowers, such as **meadowsweet** and **meadow buttercup**, **dog rose**, **primrose** and **red campion**, extend widely up through Scotland, but others, such as the **white field rose** and **mistletoe**, **red valerian**, **small scabious**, **cuckoo pint** and **traveller's joy** (and the elm tree), reach the end of their range in the Scottish central lowlands.

Scotland's mountains, especially where the rock is limey or basic in character, as on Ben Lawers, for example, are dotted with arctic-alpine plants, such as mountain **avens**, with their white flowers and glossy oak-like leaves, and handsome **purple saxifrage**, both of which favour a soil rich in calcium. Here as elsewhere, the flowers are to be found on ledges and rock-faces out of reach of the sheep and deer. Other classic mountain plants are **alpine lady's mantle** and **moss campion**, which grows in a tight cushion, set with single pink flowers.

Higher up on the bleak wind-battered mountain tops, there may be nothing much more than a low "heath" of mosses and maybe some tough low grasses or rushes between the scatterings of rubble. Because this environment encourages few insects, such plants are generally self-fertilizing and some even produce small plants or "bulbils" in their flower heads instead of seed.

A variety of ferns shelter in the slopes amid the tumbled rock screes or in cracks in the rock alongside streams. In Scotland's damp climate, you'll also see many ferns on lower ground, but some, the **holly fern** for one, are true mountain species. **Lichens**, too, are common on exposed rocks, and in the woods bushy and bearded lichens can coat the branches and trunks.

Bogs are a natural feature of much of the flatter ground in the Highlands, often extending for miles. Scottish bogland comprises an intricate mosaic of domes of living bog moss (sometimes bright green or a striking orange or yellow), domes of drier, heathery peat, and pools dotted in between. The wettest areas give rise to specialized plants such as **cranberry, bearberry** and also the **sundews**, which gain nutrients in these poor surroundings by trapping and absorbing midges with the sticky hairs on their flat leaves.

At sea level, the rivers spawn estuaries; these and some sea lochs are edged with **salt marshes**, which in time dry out into "meadows" colourful with **sea aster** and other flowers. The west coast, especially the cliffs of Galloway, shimmers blue with **spring squill** as soon as the winter eases, while the Galloway shore marks the southernmost limit of **Scots lovage**, a celery-scented member of the cow parsley family. A relic of arctic times, the **oysterplant**, with blue-grey leaves and pink bell flowers, also grows here, as it does on the shores of Iceland and Scandinavia.

Scotland has some wonderful **sand dune** systems, which on the back shores harden into grassy patches often grazed by rabbits to create a fine turf.

BIRDLIFE

It might seem unexpected to find birds nesting at over 3000ft, but in Scotland the wind is strong enough to blow patches of icy ground clear of snow, enabling birds to make their homes on the mountains. The **dotterel**, a small wader with a chestnut stomach, is a rare summer visitor to the Cairngorms and other heights – in the Arctic it nests down to sea level. Even rarer is the **snow bunting**, the male black and white, the female brownish – perhaps only ten pairs nest on Scotland's mountains, although they are seen much more widely around the coasts in winter, when the male also becomes brown. The **snowy owl**, at the southern limit of its range, is a regular visitor to Shetland.

More common on the heights is the **ptarmigan**, shy and almost invisible in its summer coat, as it plays hide and seek amongst the lichen-patched boulders – you're most likely to see it on the Cairngorms, as it ventures out for the sandwich crusts left by the summer visitors using the ski lifts. It is resident up here, and moults from mottled in summer to pure white in winter.

The ptarmigan's camouflage helps protect it from the **golden eagle**. This magnificent bird ranges across many Highland areas – there are perhaps three hundred nesting pairs on Skye, the Outer Hebrides, above Aviemore and Deeside, and in the northwest Highlands, each needing a territory of thousands of acres over which to hunt hares, grouse and ptarmigan. The **raven** also has strong links with the mountains, tumbling in crazy acrobatics past the rockfaces.

Where the slopes lessen to moorland, the domain of the **red grouse** begins. This game bird not only affects the landscape but also, via the persecution of gamekeepers, threatens eagles and other birds of prey, although they are all theoretically protected. The **cuckoo** might be heard as far north as Shetland – one of its favourite dupes, the **meadow pipit**, is fairly widespread on any rough ground up to 3000ft. Dunlin and other waders nest on the wet moorlands and boglands, where the soft land allows them to use their delicate bills to probe for insects and other food.

You'll come across many notable birds where pine woods encroach onto open moor. One such is the **black grouse**, with its bizarre courtship rituals, when both sexes come together for aggressive, ritualistic display in a small gathering area known as a "lek". The **capercaillie**, found deeper in the forest and perhaps floundering amongst the branches, is an unexpectedly large, turkey-like bird, about 3ft from bill to

end of tail, which also has a flamboyant courting display. A game bird, it was shot to extinction but reintroduced into Scotland from Europe in 1837. Other birds that favour the pine woods are the **long-eared owl**, many of the tit family (including the **crested tit** in the Spey Valley), the **siskin** and the **goldcrest**. The Speyside woods, especially, are a stronghold of the **crossbill**, which uses its overlapping bill to prise open the pine cones.

Scottish **lochs** are as rich in birdlife as the moorlands that embrace them. After fifty years of absence, the **osprey** returned and more than a hundred pairs now breed; the best site to see them is near Loch Garten on Speyside. In addition to common species such as **mallard** and **tufted duck**, you might also see **goosander**, **red-breasted merganser** and other wildfowl. The superbly streamlined fish-eating **red-** and **black-throated divers** nest in the northwest, while the **great northern diver**, with its shivery wailing call, is largely a winter visitor on the coasts, although one or two pairs may occasionally nest.

Scotland is also strong on **coastal birds**. **Eider duck** gather in their thousands at the mouth of the Tay, and the estuaries are also a magnet for **waders** and **wild geese** in winter: the total population of barnacle geese from the Arctic island of Spitsbergen winters in the Solway estuary and on the farmland alongside. Other areas to head for if you're interested in seabirds are remote cliffs such as St Abb's Head in the Borders, and the many offshore "**bird islands**", which, although often little more than bare rock, attract vast colonies that fish the sea around them. Some have their own speciality – **Manx shearwaters** have vast colonies on Rhum, for example, while the Shetland isle of Foula has about a third (three thousand pairs) of all the **great skuas** breeding in the northern hemisphere. Remote St Kilda is also stunning, with snowstorms of **gannets, puffins, guillemots, petrels** and **shearwaters**.

In addition to Scotland's resident bird population, and the winter and spring migrants, the western coasts and islands often see transatlantic "accidentals" blown far off course, which give rise to inbred **subspecies**. St Kilda is of particular interest to specialists, not only for its sheer numbers of resident birds but also for the St Kilda wren, a distinct subspecies. Fair Isle also sees large numbers of migrant and vagrant birds from both sides of the Atlantic. In northern and parts of eastern Scotland, the English all-black carrion crow is replaced by the "hoodie" or **hooded crow**, also found around the Mediterranean, with its distinctive grey back and underparts. Where the ranges of carrion crow and hoodie overlap, they interbreed, producing offspring with some grey patches of plumage.

MAMMALS

By the mid-eighteenth century, much of Scotland's wild animal life – including the Scottish **wolf, beaver, wild boar** and **elk** – had already disappeared. Although the indigenous **reindeer** was wiped out in the twelfth century, more recently a semi-wild herd of Swedish stock was reintroduced to the slopes of the Cairngorms above Aviemore. Of two other semi-wild species – **Highland cattle** and **Shetland ponies** – the former is a classic case of breeding fitting conditions (they can survive in snowy conditions for fifty days a year), while the latter, the smallest British native pony, probably arrived in the later stages of the Ice Age when the ice was retreating but still gave a bridge across the salt water. There are feral goats in some places, but probably the most interesting of such animals is the Soay sheep of St Kilda. This, Britain's only truly wild sheep, notable for its soft brown fleece, can be seen as a farm pet and in wildlife parks – and is even used to graze some nature reserves in the south of Britain.

Although there are **sika** and **fallow deer** in places, and **roe deer** are widespread, Scotland is the stronghold of wild **red deer** herds, which, despite culling, stalking for sport and harsh winters, still number more than quarter of a million head. By origin a woodland animal, they might graze open ground – of necessity when the forest has been cleared – but they also move up to high ground in summer to avoid the biting flies and the tourists, and to graze on heather and lichens. They're most obvious in the snowy depths of winter, when, forced downhill in search of food, large numbers may be seen by road or rail travellers on Rannoch Moor or between Blair Atholl and Drumochter Pass.

The **fox** is widespread, as are the **mole** and **hedgehog**, but the **badger** is rather more rare. The **wild cat** and **pine marten** live in remote areas, hiding away in the moors and forests.

The former, despite its initial resemblance to the family pet, is actually quite different – larger, with longer, striped fur, and a blunt-ended bushy tail that is also striped. The agile cat-sized pine marten, although hunted by gamekeepers, is maintaining reduced numbers, preying on squirrels and other small animals.

Native red **squirrels** are predominantly found in the Highlands, where they are still largely free from competition from the greys, which began to establish themselves about a century ago and now have a strong presence in many lowland areas. **Rabbit** and **brown hare** are widespread, as are the **blue** or **mountain hare** in the Highlands, usually adopting a white or patchy white coat in winter. The north Scottish **stoat** also dons a white winter coat, its tail tipped with black, when it is known as ermine. Although Scotland is too far north for the dormouse and the harvest mouse, **shrews, voles** and **field mice** abound and, though there are few bats, the related **pipistrelle** is quite widely seen.

You may also be lucky enough to encounter the **otter**, endangered in the rest of Britain. In Scotland, the otter is found not only in the rushing streams but more often along the west coast and in the northern and western isles, where it hunts the seashore for crabs and inshore fish. The otter is not to be confused with the feral **mink**, escaped from fur farms to take up life in the wild; these mink are a scourge in some areas, destroying birds.

Whales and their kin are frequent visitors to coastal waters and **seals**, including the shy grey seal, are quite common. However, in the hitherto virgin sea lochs of the west coast, both the seals and the coastal otters are under threat from the spread of **fish farms** (for salmon and sea trout). Not only are they poisoned by the chemicals used to keep the trapped fish vermin-free, but they also face the threat of being shot by the fish-farm owners when they raid what is to them simply a natural larder.

FISH, REPTILES AND INSECTS

Quite apart from the Loch Ness monster, Scotland has a rich water life. The Dee and other rivers are fished when the **salmon** swim upstream to breed in their ancestral gravel headwaters. The fish leap waterfalls on the way, and many rivers which have been dammed for hydroelectric power generation have "salmon ladders" to help them – these make great tourist attractions. The **sea trout** is also strongly migratory, the **brown** or **mountain trout** less so, although river or stream dwellers do move upstream and loch dwellers up the incoming rivers to spawn. Related to these game fish is the **powan** or **freshwater herring**, found only in the poorer northern basins of Loch Lomond, and possibly a relic from Ice Age arctic conditions. The richer southern waters of Loch Lomond and similar lakes contain **roach**, **perch** and other "coarse" fish.

Although the **adder** is common, the grass snake is not found in Scotland. Both **lizards** and the snake-like **slowworm** (in fact a legless lizard) are widespread, as are the **frog** and **toad**; the natterjack toad, however, is rarely seen this far north.

Scottish boglands are notable for their **dragon flies**, which prefer acid water, and **hawkers, darters** and **damselflies** feature in the south. One Scottish particular is the **blue hawker**, common in parts of the western Highlands. As for **butterflies**, some of the familiar types from further south – common blue, hairstreaks and others – are scattered in areas where conditions are not too harsh. One species with a liking for the heights is the **mountain ringlet**, only seen elsewhere in the English Lake District and in the Alps, which flies above 1500ft in the Grampians. Adapted to quite harsh conditions, it is clearly a relic of early post-glacial times. Another mountain butterfly, the **Scotch argus**, no longer found in England or Wales, is widespread in Scotland, and the **elephant hawk moth** can be seen in the Insh marshes below the Cairngorms.

THE ARCHITECTURE OF SCOTLAND

From crofts to castles, the Victorian grand residence to the "new towns", Scotland has a rich legacy of strong, unique buildings. Stonework predominates, from the long houses of the Western Isles to the soft red sandstone that fills the streets of Glasgow. Surrounding countries have also had a substantial influence: some settlements in Orkney and Shetland evoke links with the Norse kingdoms, while the ruined church architecture of the central belt is testimony to a long history of battles with the marauding English.

PREHISTORIC TIMES TO THE THIRTEENTH CENTURY

One morning in 1850, after a ferocious storm, the villagers of Orkney woke to find **Skara Brae** (see p.502 – one of the earliest prehistoric sites in Scotland – revealed beneath the beautiful white sands. Situated nineteen miles northwest of Kirkwall, this **Neolithic** stone village is so well preserved that you can still see domestic details, typical of the age, such as flagstone box beds, built due to the lack of timber on the islands. Small passages unite what must have been quite a large and intricate settlement of stock farmers, who originally came to Scotland from mainland Europe; a turf roof provided insulation from wind and cold. The chambered tombs

at **Maes Howe** (Orkney; see p.503) are another great architectural achievement, dating from 2750 BC and complete with Viking graffiti from later raids on the islands. These tombs are remarkably well constructed, incorporating monoliths into the fine masonry that supports the narrow passages and small tomb cells. A fairly large community also existed at the **Jarlshof** prehistoric and Norse settlement on Shetland (see p.527), where small stone cells grouped around a central hearth provided the main accommodation, with now ruined outhouses used for bronze work and sheltering cattle. The survival of a number of ritual sites, including many **stone circles**, suggests some form of religious activity in Scotland at this time. One of the most beautiful and well-preserved stands at **Callanish** (Lewis; see p.350), where a circle of megaliths rise majestically from the ground with radiating lines of stone in a mysteriously symbolic form. The central stone is nearly 16ft high and sits next to a small chambered cairn, which may have once contained human remains.

During the **Bronze Age**, from around 1000 BC, the two predominant types of defensive settlements, made from earth and timber, were spectacular **hillforts**, and artificial islands built in the middle of lochs, called **crannogs**; little now remains of either of these. It wasn't until the **Iron Age** (from around 400 BC) that the next significant architectural development was to occur. For residents of the northwest mainland and the northern islands the need for protection from attack or invasion and from the harshness of the weather was particularly extreme, and so it's here that most of Scotland's 400 or so **brochs**, the majority in ruins, can be found. Circular, windowless and tall – some over 40ft high – these drystone buildings were sturdily built to protect the inhabitants who lived inside, sheltered underneath wooden constructions. Broad at the bottom and narrow at the top, the unusual shape was due to the necessity for a thick base to support the high walls and provide storage and guard rooms. Brochs also had two walls and a spiral staircase leading up to a timber roof – a very useful vantage point. Some were inhabited for several centuries; the finest example is the **Broch of Mousa** from c.100 BC in Shetland (see p.526), which is remarkably well preserved due to its isolated position on a small island, free from the stone stealing that plagued subsequent settlements.

In 83 AD, the Scottish border came under threat from the **Romans**. Their success was limited, however, and the civilizing influence of Rome was to have barely any effect on the life and tribes of Scotland, who continued to live in brochs and crannogs, or erect primitive buildings of timber, wattle and clay, regardless. Of the Roman structures that have survived, the most impressive are the remnants of the **Antonine Wall**, a 36-mile-long construction that stretched from Kilpatrick to Bo'ness. Less substantial than the great Hadrian's Wall, it was originally built as a temporary measure to aid the overthrow of the fierce Pictish tribes, but was soon abandoned.

The subsequent introduction of **Christianity** left a much greater architectural legacy in Scotland. The primitive church of 397 AD at **Whithorn** of (see p.160) marks one of the earliest Christian sites in Scotland and, with the arrival of St Columba at Iona in 563, the Celtic Christian community really came to dominate the country's religious matters. Evidence of this can be seen in the characteristic **round towers** at **Brechin** (Angus; see p.385) and **Egilsay** (Orkney; see p.512). Places of refuge for the monastic fellowship during times of attack, these were well defended, with a raised entrance and few windows. The simple and basic structures of the Irish Celtic church conveyed their ascetic religious beliefs, while artistic and creative energies were poured into the making of sculpted crosses and illuminated manuscripts. Fine carving survives at the monastic foundation on **Iona** (see p.301), a religious community that still thrives today. Few other such buildings remain, indicating that they were constructed from materials like timber, clay and turf.

The marriage of Malcolm III to the Saxon princess Margaret, in 1070, signified a dramatic upsurge in Scottish architecture. Malcolm created a feudal society based on agriculture and, more importantly, his wife orchestrated the reintroduction of Latin Christianity to the central areas of Scotland, founding many ecclesiastical buildings and finally bringing a European influence to this region – while the Highlands and Islands continued to build in the vernacular tradition. The **Romanesque** (or Norman) style can be seen at its best in **Dalmeny Church** (see .93). This simple, thick-walled three-cell church has narrow window openings and a round arched doorway crowned by typically Romanesque wall arcading. The Anglo-Norman influence also created larger buildings, cruciform in plan with aisled naves and three-storey elevations; these were not actual physical levels but would consist of arches, a middle storey, usually formed by blind arches or decorative wall hangings but sometimes an actual gallery for the local notables and, at the top, stained-glass windows. The thick piers and semicircular arches of **Dunfermline Abbey** (Fife; see p.247) are typically Norman. However, it was the Cistercians who brought the significant pointed arch and lancet window to Scotland and introduced the **Gothic** style to the country's craftsmen. As buildings were either reconstructed or modified in future centuries, the church at **Dunstaffnage** (Argyll; see p.289), with its simple rectangular plan and lancet windows, is a rare example of Early Gothic design. The twelfth-century abbey at **Jedburgh** in the Borders (see p.138) was just one of the abbeys that housed the religious communities being imported from England and France to southern and central parts of the country. Now in ruins, this church is very much in the transitional style between Romanesque and Gothic, as the west front contains a Romanesque round-arched doorway with a thirteenth-century rose window in the main gable. One of the most complete of the ruined Border Abbeys, **Dryburgh Abbey** (see p.130), in beautiful red sandstone, has an unusual vertical emphasis in the main arcade. **Melrose Abbey** (see p.128) contains examples of High Gothic detail, such as delicate tracery and flying buttresses, while **Kelso Abbey** (see p.126) stands out for its simplicity and massive proportions. These great Scottish Abbeys, with the exception of the austere Cistercian communities, would have been richly decorated with tapestries, murals and carved furnishings. Unfortunately, their position in the southeast of Scotland left them vulnerable to attack from the English and they suffered badly as a result.

In the thirteenth century, the Norman kings brought a more settled period, establishing their authority through a network of loyal nobles who controlled parts of the country but recognized the king as overall ruler. This allowed for the building of great cathedrals, notably those of Glasgow and Elgin. **Glasgow Cathedral** (see p.187) is Scotland's only complete medieval cathedral to survive the Reformation, the verticality of the interior and elegance of the clustered piers monuments to the power of the Gothic tradition. The building itself is an amalgam of influences, from the Early Pointed style of the east end of the choir to the magnificent Late Gothic vaulting of the lower church, and is a poignant reminder of the wealth of architecture that has been lost to the nation over the years. **Elgin Cathedral** (see p.415), once "the ornament of the realm", with its unusual double aisles and rich furnishings, was an extravagant Anglo-Saxon statement of refinement and power, built to impress the Highland clans. It is now in ruins after it was destroyed in 1390 by an earl angry at being excommunicated for leaving his wife.

The popular image of the great Scottish **castle**, the stuff of myth and legend, perched on a rocky crag and often surrounded by woodlands, heather and deer, is remarkably different from the cold reality of daily castle living. Rising in stone above the small peasant dwellings of turf and timber, the castle was a centre of administrative and judicial control, as well as a secure place in times of conflict. **Castle Sween** on Loch Sween (see p.310) is the earliest stone castle in Scotland, built in the eleventh century with a Norman-style round-arched doorway leading into the centre of the quadrangular building, once roofed with timber. With its origins in the twelfth century, **Edinburgh Castle** (see p.64) stands out as the archetypal royal Scottish castle. Built on an extinct volcano, it commanded a strong strategic position and served throughout much of its history as a resonant symbol of power and protection. The epitome of the romantic Highland castle, on the other hand, is the beautifully picturesque **Eilean Donan** on Loch Duich (see p.460), ten miles south of the Kyle of Lochalsh. Originally a small thirteenth-century castle of enclosure, it was used to garrison Spanish troops as part of the Jacobite Rising, and was destroyed by English warships in 1719. The present building is predominantly a reconstruction, initiated at the beginning of the twentieth century, an immaculate three-storey keep perched on a rocky outcrop with a dramatic arched bridge.

Developments in warfare and architecture marched hand in hand, and thirteenth-century castles employed a number of defensive techniques: the use of catapults and assault towers, the strengthening of outer walls, and construction of round towers to allow for a better view

of the base. Two miles north of Oban, the tall thick walls of **Dunstaffnage** (see p.289) are topped with a crenellated wall walk and contain few windows but many well-placed firing slits; an outer defence like the moat at **Rothesay** (Isle of Bute; see p.281), which was established c.1204, was also common. Natural defences such as rocky outcrops were particularly impenetrable; **Dirleton Castle** (near North Berwick; see p.119) uses one to great advantage, its weaker side protected by three towers forcing outwards in an aggressive manner, and **Stirling Castle** is similarly well defended (see p.225). Situated on a grassy hilltop, the reinforced tower at **Bothwell Castle** (near Blantyre; see p.215) provided an effective last refuge in an attack.

THE FOURTEENTH AND FIFTEENTH CENTURIES

With the power of the monarch declining and the nobility fighting for territory and power, the **fourteenth century** was a time of great strife and warfare in Scotland; consequently, law and order were overthrown and few buildings constructed. The destruction predominantly affected the Lowlands, the Highlanders being a law unto themselves within their own social system, strategically using the mountains to defend their proud autonomy. Castles continued to be strengthened, often growing in size to accommodate larger buildings. The impressive four teenth-century castles of **Tantallon** (near North Berwick; see p.120) and **Doune** (Perthshire; see p.229) both contain a massive gatehouse employed to protect the entrance, and provide the lord with accommodation. This gave him full control of the castle's defences, necessary at a time when hired mercenaries were commonly used in private armies. For lesser nobles, the **tower house** was the perfect solution to the conflicting problems of comfort and defence. The tower house became a popular high-security residence, being smaller and cheaper than a great castle. Tall and narrow with smooth walls and few windows, these buildings featured a raised entrance and crenellated parapet as the main elements of passive defence – relying on thick walls and great height for effect. Being of a simple yet flexible design, the majority were expanded and decorated in later centuries, and none exist in their original form (see "Sixteenth and Seventeenth Centuries" for examples).

The **fifteenth century**, fluctuating between periods of war and peace, allowed tower houses to retain their popularity among the lesser nobles, being secure, yet comfortable enough for everyday living. High Gothic principles became established in ecclesiastical buildings, and the construction of the great royal residences introduced the spirit of the **Early Renaissance** to Scotland. In the 1420s, James I began to rebuild **Linlithgow Palace** (see p.239) and by 1500 it had become a large and symmetrical structure, in contrast to the random organization of medieval castles. Designed as a quadrangle with an open central court, it was primarily a domestic royal residence with a system of corridors and stair-wells and large, regularly placed windows. This hint of Renaissance order and elegance was markedly different from the usual defensive principles of high walls and small window openings. Once considered the finest in the realm, the central chambers would have been luxuriously decorated with painted plaster and wall hangings.

The Gothic style was still favoured in ecclesiastical architecture, most apparent in **Melrose Abbey** (see p.128). Twice destroyed in the fourteenth century, the rebuilding left excellent examples of High Gothic, the east window being the work of the York school of masons, and the richly carved south transept by a French master mason, which accounts for the lavish use of decoration. The flying buttresses are of particular note, being structural not merely decorative. Due to an increase in trade with other countries, wealthy landowners could afford to construct small churches, staffed by secular clergy to pray for the soul of the benefactor. Many small collegiate buildings were built at this time, predominantly with a Late Gothic flavour: the most unusual and extreme is the mid-century **Rosslyn Chapel** (Edinburgh; see p.95), with its elaborate carving and decorative flying buttresses. Also around this time, the castellated features of castles and towers began to creep into church architecture, seen in the use of crow-stepped gables at **St Michael's Church** (Linlithgow; see p.239), or the crenellated parapet at **King's College Chapel** (Aberdeen; see p.395).

THE SIXTEENTH AND SEVENTEENTH CENTURIES

The massacre of the Scots at Flodden in 1513 set the tone for unrest in the early part of the **sixteenth century**, leaving little opportunity for new buildings or styles. However, the Stewart dynasty continued to breathe the Renaissance spirit into their opulent palaces. A royal holiday home for the Stewart monarchs, **Falkland Palace** (Fife; see p.252), with its reconstructed south range, is an excellent example of **French Renaissance** design, the solid buttresses transformed into Classical columns. This courtly look is also apparent at **Stirling Castle** (see p.225), a true amalgam of styles, perched high up on a rocky outcrop. Here, the Renaissance facade of the Royal Palace, completed in 1540, is merely tacked onto the Gothic structure, with a line of restless statues perched on elegant wall shafts. Ultimately, this fashion did not catch on, as nobles preferred security and comfort over superficial elegance.

The Reformation of 1560 released a tragic wave of wholesale destruction of sculptural and other decorative items in church buildings. The tower house, however, resumed popularity, as a considerable amount of church land had been sold off to nobles, who then wanted to create a mini-castle as an emblem of power and prestige. These buildings developed right through to the seventeenth century, often changing dramatically in plan; for example at **Drum Castle** (Aberdeen; see p.400). Originally built in the late thirteenth century, the dignified tower was extended to its full Jacobean glory in the seventeenth century, when the desire for greater comfort and space called for a larger building. The **Scottish Baronial** style, characterized by crow-stepped gables and conical roofs, lightened the austerity of the original tower form and took these buildings to their peak. Excellent examples include **Claypotts Castle** (near Dundee; see p.373), where defensive features have been subsumed to the need for extra accommodation, which is corbelled out at the top of the Z-plan towers. Other castles of note are **Crathes** (Deeside; see p.401), **Fyvie** (near Inverurie; see p.405) and **Glamis Castle** (north of Dundee; see p.381), which was constructed in the early seventeenth century. A later, even more decorative approach can be found at the absurdly pink-hued **Craigievar Castle**, 26 miles west of Aberdeen (see p.406). Built in 1626 and hailed as the finest tower house in Scotland, the crenellation serves to enhance the top-heavy accommodation area, but the beautifully preserved interior contains excellent stucco work. In all of these examples, useful defensive elements have been manipulated for effective decorative purposes.

The religious Wars of the Covenant (1639–44) and invasion of Cromwell (1650) initially discouraged contemporary building in the **seventeenth century**. However, it did see the final development of the **Early Scottish Renaissance**, marked by regular, symmetrical plans, the use of pediments and other decorative details of Classical origin, and an ordered dignified facade. Initiated in 1628, the elaborate **George Heriot's Hospital** in Edinburgh, which is now a school, is an excellent example. Here, Renaissance ideas are not merely decorative items tacked onto the front but incorporated by the architect, **William Wallace**, into the overall design. The quadrangular plan with a tower at each corner is a feast of turrets, chimneys and cupolas that top the symmetrical facade. As the century progressed, the landed classes, having travelled and become more aware of the cultural conditions in England and Europe, began to take a serious interest in the design of their mansions, led by the influential figure of Sir William Bruce, who essentially founded the **Classical** school in Scotland. He undertook the major reconstruction of the **Palace of Holyrood** (Edinburgh; see p.75) in 1671–79, creating a delicate and restrained courtyard frontage of fine proportion and exacting detail. **Drumlanrig Castle** (Dumfries; see p.152), built between 1679 and 1690, is an extravagant mansion, more obviously Classical with a balanced plan and a sweeping double staircase at the entrance.

THE EIGHTEENTH CENTURY

In the early years after the Act of Union (1707), the Scottish economy was at a low ebb. Gradually conditions began to improve as trade, encouraged by the union, began to take off, further enhanced by the agricultural revolution. By mid-century, the industrial age had ignited an architectural explosion. The towns of Edinburgh and Glasgow were to receive the best in **Neoclassical** architecture, as steadily increasing industrial production called for more housing, warehouses and municipal buildings. In line with the rationality and order of the Enlightenment, symmetry and proportion in design came into stride with the English Classicism of Sir Christopher Wren and Inigo Jones. Edinburgh's **New Town**, designed by

James Craig in 1767, is characterized by symmetrical wide streets and large tree-filled squares, with service lanes that follow the main axis of the roads. Amongst this sandstone glory lies **Charlotte Square** (see p.84), the north side of which was designed by the renowned Classicist **Robert Adam** in 1791. The Venetian windows and restrained use of decoration create a unified facade, the main rooms clearly defined by angular stonework in comparison to the smooth sandstone of the other storeys. Compared with the medieval High Street that descends from the Castle, and the narrow lanes that run from it, these formal squares reflect a new approach to civilized urban living, allowing the upper classes to dwell in their own spacious areas away from the huddle of the Old Town. Adam was the shining light in a talented family of architects, who modified the elegant **Hopetoun House** (Edinburgh; see p.94) in c.1721–60. Set in an excellent position overlooking the Forth, this delicate and symmetrically designed building makes full use of triangular pediments and round-headed windows to recall the noble spirit of Classical times.

Concurrently, an interest in medieval architecture, encouraged by romantic fiction and the cult of the picturesque, led to **Gothic Revivalism**. Here, the pointed arch took over from the geometric rigours of Classicism. **Inveraray Castle** (Argyll; see p.283), built between 1745 and 1761, is one of the first Georgian castles to recreate itself in this neo-Gothic style. Although the interior is inspired by Classicism, the exterior makes use of pointed arches and crenellated parapets, the conical roofs being a later addition. Another neo-Gothic building is **Culzean Castle** (1771–92), attractively situated on a clifftop south of Ayr (see p.163) and extensively remodelled by Robert Adam in the latter part of the century. He designed every detail, from the fine interior plasterwork, complete with swags and urns, to the castellated exterior with mock arrow slits, to give a romantically medieval touch to the dramatic setting.

THE NINETEENTH CENTURY

By the turn of the century, Scotland had changed dramatically, climbing from a poor backwater to become one of the Empire's leading industrial centres. Furthermore, after Queen Victoria "discovered" Scotland in 1842, it became highly fashionable, fuelled by the image of wild clans and rugged, lonely landscapes – a far cry from the bitter reality of life within the rapidly industrializing central belt, populated increasingly by families left homeless by the Highland Clearances. The major cities of Glasgow, Edinburgh and Dundee were expanding at great speed, filling up with warehouses, municipal buildings and workers' accommodation. This ushered in the **Victorian Age** of architecture. Marked by a continuation of the Romantic and Classical idioms established in the eighteenth century, grand buildings celebrated the pride and self-confidence of the industrial giants. A fusion of historical styles became common, and architects increasingly looked for novel ways to decorate their buildings. For instance, the Tudor-Gothic **Donaldson's Hospital** in Edinburgh, designed by **William Playfair** in 1851, fuses a symmetrical plan with elaborate turrets and a central decorated tower. Playfair was also responsible for creating the rich facade at **Floors Castle** (near Kelso; see p.126), in 1838, cloaking the building in a new fashionable guise without changing the basic structural design.

Inspired by simple proportion and logical harmony, the followers of the **Greek Revival** created buildings of massive serenity, using little decoration. In Glasgow, **Alexander "Greek" Thomson** brought a unique interpretation to this style. He created buildings from warehouses to tenements and churches, such as Glasgow's impressive **St Vincent Street Church** (see p.185), an imposing construction that mixes the massive solidity of Greek design with exotic motifs and decoration. In Edinburgh, it was **William Playfair** who created the city's icons of Greek Revivalism: the **Royal Scottish Academy** of 1836 (see p.81), and the **National Gallery of Scotland** of 1857 (see p.81), are both well proportioned with precise detail, the former making more use of scrolls and wreaths, the latter slightly less ponderous and more elegant. With the Gothic style no longer restricted to ecclesiastical architecture, the majestic **Glasgow University** building of 1870, designed by George Gilbert Scott, dominates the skyline of the West End in pseudo-medieval splendour. Similarly in Edinburgh, The **Scottish National Portrait Gallery** of 1885–90, designed by Sir R. Rowand Anderson, is richly detailed with pointed arches and turrets.

New materials of the industrial age, such as cast iron, were being used to great effect, in such as buildings as **Kibble Palace** in the Botanic Gardens (Glasgow; see p.195) and the interior of the **Royal Museum of Scotland** (Edinburgh; see p.78), which was based on London's Crystal Palace. The industrial age also gave birth to such great figures of **engineering** as **William Telford**, **Sir Benjamin Baker** and **Sir John Fowler**, who constructed roads and bridges throughout Scotland. Baker and Fowler were responsible for the pinnacle of Scottish engineering that straddles the Firth of Forth in cantilevered steel glory – the **Forth Railway Bridge** spans more than a mile, took seven years to build and employed more than 5000 men at a time, rivalling the Eiffel Tower in its complexity.

THE TWENTIETH CENTURY

At the turn of the century, Scotland was riding on the crest of a wave, with a healthy economy and solid industrial base; soon, however, a long period of postwar depression was to destroy this security. In any case, while the Victorian well-to-do had been luxuriating in their fine buildings, the workers had lived in slums, a situation that was to result in mass demolition later in the century.

Despite many financial difficulties, Glasgow's **Charles Rennie Mackintosh** began to design exciting new buildings, motivated by the desire for complete organic unity of structure and decoration. Associated with the Art Nouveau school and their push for change after the conservatism of the previous century, he produced some buildings of excellent quality and form. The **Glasgow School of Art** (see p.190) is the archetypal Mackintosh work, fusing the curvilinear shapes of Art Nouveau with the crow-stepped gables and conical roofs of the Scots Baronial tradition. The interior effectively combines practicality with decorative beauty; and the library, in particular, promotes his forward-thinking style as it makes use of a strong vertical motif for its columns, lighting and furnishing (for more on Mackintosh, see p.188). Outside the bustling city at **Hill House** in Helensburgh (see p.277), Mackintosh created a domestic building in 1902 that unites the turrets and chimney stack of the Baronial tradition with a modern interior. In the drawing room he creates two "zones", the wide bay window overlooking the Firth, for summer, and a cosy fireplace with a bookcase as a backdrop for winter evenings.

World War I brought a dramatic shift in scientific and artistic sensibilities; with the old ways undermined, people looked more and more to the future. This new atmosphere was represented in the **Art Deco** style, celebrating speed and technology. Typical features include modern, flat roofs, soaring geometric motifs and the use of reinforced concrete, which allowed semicircular glazed bays to project out from the building. However, due to financial constraints, few buildings were actually being erected; some gems that were include Glasgow's **Baird Hall of Residence** in Sauchiehall Street, built in 1938. The architect W. Beresford Inglis used two soaring projecting towers with bay windows to give a dynamic prominence to the general bulk of the building. In contrast, the large, brick-covered planes of the **Glasgow Film Theatre** (see p.209), constructed one year later and designed by James McKissack, enhance the squat flat-roofed building. **The Maybury**, on the outskirts of Edinburgh, is a typical "roadhouse" built to cater for the new car-bound tourist, who could gaze up into the regularly spaced windows of the tower, designed to emulate the radiator of a huge limousine.

Despite the innovative ideas for town planning after World War I and the great rehousing plans set in motion after World War II, few public or private buildings of note were produced. Instead, vast **suburban sprawls** were constructed in the most economical manner, resulting in their bland architectural character. More recently, the development of housing associations has allowed residents to have some influence over their living space, and tower blocks have been replaced with small, brick buildings laid out in crescents and tree-lined streets. In the public realm, the possibilities of modern technology continued to be explored, for example at the **Exhibition Plant Houses** at Edinburgh's Royal Botanic Garden (see p.88). Built in 1967, the glass skin is held in place by an outside structure of steel and iron to provide the maximum use of space inside. The manipulation of glass to enhance space is also apparent at the **Burrell Collection** (Pollok Park, Glasgow; see p.196), built in 1983 to house the great collection of Sir William Burrell. The architect Barry Gasson effectively fused nature and art, employing large panes of glass to take advantage of the surrounding woodland light, while the geometric use of red sandstone contrasts well with the roughness of the park land.

The current trend for conservation and renovation has produced some fine work: the glass-fronted **Festival Theatre** in Edinburgh is a successful and dynamic conversion of an older building, while the massive bulk that is the **Royal Concert Hall** in Glasgow (see p.209) is still waiting for its union with a proposed shopping centre. However, this bias has restricted the possibility for any really distinguished modern buildings or radical flights of fancy to be constructed in Scotland. With few patrons willing or able to push the boundaries towards the 21st century, despite the enthusiasm of young Scottish architects, the nation's architecture is in danger of becoming frozen in time and trapped by historicism, a sad irony after the far-sighted construction of the Victorian era.

THE MUSIC OF SCOTLAND

Scottish music heads towards the 21st century in remarkably buoyant mood, with a wide range of groups – Silly Wizard, The Tannahill Weavers, Runrig, Wolfstone, Boys Of The Lough, Ossian (who re-formed in 1997) and the still vibrant Capercaillie, to name but a few – having rewritten the music scene over the last two decades. All these performers have embellished traditional music with a degree of passion, vision, technical excellence and enthusiasm scarcely imaginable in the days when most people felt that Scots music involved little more than Andy Stewart and the Bay City Rollers.

There used to be a British television show – still fondly remembered by people who buy Max Bygraves and Val Doonican records – called *The White Heather Show*. This, the British public were gleefully informed each week, was the sound of Scotland, all men in kilts, led by the likes of Andy Stewart and Jimmy Shand, with their accordions and sentimental songs of the Highlands. The show ran for many years, and – let's not be mean – probably gave an awful lot of people an awful lot of pleasure. It also damned Scottish music with an image of banal glibness from which it looked like never recovering.

While Jimmy Shand's gung ho accordion playing became an institution and the nation hooted along with Andy Stewart's *Scottish Soldier* and *Donald Where's Your Troosers* (a

British number one in the 1960s and the 1990s), Scots musicians were donated a legacy that was to dog them for the next two decades. To make any credible headway beyond the shackles of an image decimated by kilts and Highland flings, they were forced to deny the very thing that provided their one claim to be unique in the first place – their Scottishness.

For two decades even the best exponents of a purely Scots music had teetered on the edge of ridicule. The admirable Ian Campbell Folk Group (who included future Fairport Daves, Swarbrick and Pegg, while Ian's sons, Aly and Robin, went on to form UB40) had flirted with commercialism and pop sensibilities – as virtually every folk group of the era was compelled to do – and was too often unfairly bracketed with England's derided Spinners as a result. A similar cross was borne by others of the period, particularly Robin Hall and Jimmie MacGregor (remembered in Britain for the awful *Football Crazy* novelty hit) and The Corries, both of whom were too closely associated with the curse of the White Heather Club. Yet The Corries, especially, laced their blandness with bold enterprise, inventing their own instrumentation and writing the new unofficial national anthem, *Flower of Scotland*.

Pop and rock, of course, always had a thriving tradition of Scots bands but mostly their origins were incidental, or laid on as thick as the tartan on the Bay City Rollers' trousers. It was to be the late 1970s before Scots musicians investigated their own musical history with any real sense of purpose. The Boys of the Lough led the way, initially driven on by the instinctive brilliance of their Shetland fiddler Aly Bain (see box on p.574), and they were followed by Battlefield Band, who consciously attempted to hack away the old Scots clichés, and the Dick Gaughan-fronted electric band Five Hand Reel.

Then Alba did the unthinkable and introduced bagpipes to a contemporary rock line-up, paving the way for a rush of groups like Silly Wizard, Battlefield Band and Tannahill Weavers to sweep Scots music into the 1980s with pride. Scots bands could at last draw on their evocative national fund of music, free of self-consciousness, and the results were encouraging. In the 1990s, the Scots variant of Celtic music has found contemporary-sounding champions in bands like Runrig, Capercaillie, Seelyhoo and Shooglenifty, who have blended mass rock appeal and techniques with ancient inspirations, while essentially rock bands like Deacon Blue and Simple Minds have drawn liberally on traditional Scottish modes of melody and instrumentation. In an era of revived nationalism, Scots artists of varying genres – from Eddi Reader to Texas – wear invisible Celtic Pride badges: Rod Stewart, even, has recorded a cover version of *Wild Mountain Thyme*, a folk-club favourite popularized by the McPeake Family and usually associated with the Scottish Highlands.

The White Heather Club is now well and truly buried, and at last some of the traditions are also being aired in their older forms. The dance music of Bob Smith's Ideal Band has had a couple of albums devoted to it, and the extraordinary strathspey rhythms of legendary fiddle player Scott Skinner have had belated exposure, too. Also getting a fresh listening – especially with the CD releases of the Scottish Tradition Series – are traditional Gaelic songs, like those of the wonderful Cathie-Ann McPhee, and the old travelling singers, such as the Stewarts of Blairgowrie, Isla Cameron, Lizzie Higgins and, the greatest of them all, Lizzie's mother, Jeannie Robertson. Belle Stewart died in the autumn of 1997, but not before her songs – and equally

SHETLAND MUSIC: ALY BAIN

Aly Bain has been one of Scotland's most-respected Scottish musicians for over three decades. A fiddle player of exquisite technique and individuality, he has been the driving force of one of Scotland's all-time great bands, **Boys of the Lough**, throughout that time, while latterly diversifying into the roles of TV presenter and author. In these guises, he has been instrumental in spreading the wings of Scottish music to an even greater extent. First and foremost, though, Bain is a Shetlander and his greatest legacy is the inspiration he has provided for a thriving revival of fortunes for Shetland's own characteristic tradition.

Aly was brought up in the capital of Shetland, Lerwick, and was enthused to play the fiddle by **Bob Duncan** – who endlessly played him records by the strathspey king Scott Skinner – and later the old maestro **Tom Anderson**. Duncan and Anderson were the last of an apparently dying breed, and the youthful Aly was an odd sight dragging his fiddle along to join in with the old guys at the Shetland Fiddlers Society. Players like Willie Hunter Jnr and Snr, Willie Pottinger and Alex Hughson were legends locally, but they belonged to another age and the magic of Shetland fiddle playing – one inflected with the eccentricity of the isolated environment and the influence of nearby Scandinavia.

By the time the teenage Aly was persuaded to leave for the mainland, Shetland was changing by the minute, and the discovery of North Sea oil altered it beyond redemption, as the new industrial riches trampled its unique community spirit and sense of tradition. The old fiddlers gradually faded and died, and Shetland music seemed destined to disappear too.

That it didn't was largely down to Aly. After a spell with Billy Connolly (then a folk artist, before finding comedy success as a professional Glaswegian) on the Scottish folk circuit, Aly found himself working with blues iconoclast Mike Whellans, before they both tumbled into a linkup with two Irishmen, Robin Morton and Cathal McConnell, in a group they called Boys of the Lough. The last thing Aly Bain imagined was that he'd spend the next quarter of a century answering to this name. But he did, and his joyful artistry, unwavering integrity and unquenchable appetite and commitment to the music of his upbringing kept Shetland music alive in a manner he could never have imagined. Even more importantly, it stung the imagination of the generation that followed.

A series of collaborations with fellow artists has sustained the pace. Closest to Aly's roots is his long-standing partnership with Shetland musicians **Violet Tulloch** on piano and guitarist **"Peerie" Willie Johnson**, but he has also ventured into new areas, linking up with the brilliant accordionist **Phil Cunningham** for a foray into the Cajun tradition, as well as playing more classically orientated work with the BT Scottish Ensemble.

These days, Shetland music is buzzing again, with its own annual festival a treat of music making and drinking that belies the impersonal industrialization of Shetland. There are young musicians pouring out of the place: **Catriona MacDonald** – who was also taught by Tom Anderson, in his last days – blends traditional and classical skills, while half a dozen young bands – the best known of which is **Rock Salt and Nails** – have successfully mixed Shetland traditions with all sorts of contemporary influences.

importantly her style – became deeply embedded in a national consciousness.

THE PIPES OF WRATH

Bagpipes are synonymous with Scotland, yet they are not, oddly enough, a specifically Scottish instrument. The pipes were once to be found right across Europe, and pockets remain, across the English border in Northumbria, all over Ireland, in Spain and Italy, and notably in eastern European countries like Romania and the Czech and Slovak republics, where bagpipe festivals are still held in rural areas. In Scotland, bagpipes seem to have made their appearance around the fifteenth century, and over the next hundred years or so they took on several forms, including quieter varieties, both bellows and mouth-blown, which allowed a diversity of playing styles.

The Highland bagpipe form known as **pibroch** (*piobaireachd* in Gaelic) evolved around this time, created by clan pipers for military, gathering, lamenting and marching purposes. Legend among the clan pipers of this era were the MacCrimmons (they of the famous "MacCrimmon's Lament", composed during the Jacobite rebellion), although they were but one of several important piping clans, among which were the MacArthurs, Mackays, MacDonalds and others. In the seventeenth and eighteenth centuries, through the influence of the British army, reels and strathspeys joined the repertoire, and in the early nineteenth century a tradition of military pipe bands had emerged, and with it a network of piping competitions.

The bagpipe tradition has continued uninterrupted to the present, although for much of this century under the domination of the military and the folklorist Piobaireachd Society. Recently, however, a number of Scottish musicians have revived the pipes in new and innovative forms. **Alan McLeod** succeeded in knitting the pipes into a framework of instruments, playing as a teenager with the band **Alba**, and his lead has been consolidated by **Battlefield Band**, whose arrangements involve the beautifully measured piping of **Duncan McGillivray**, and Iain MacDonald, who had previously piped along with rock instruments in **Ossian**. Rab Wallace of **The Whistlebinkies** and Jimmy Anderson in **The Clutha** have also been crucial figures while, although he hates playing them, the brilliant young **Martyn Bennett** has been instru-

mental in making the pipes sexy, merging them into trip-hop arrangements and introducing them into the club scene.

Alongside all this came a revived interest in traditional piping, and in particular the strathspeys, slow airs and reels, which had tended to get submerged beneath the familiar military territory of marches and laments. The century's great modern-day bagpipe players, notably **John Burgess**, **John MacLean** and **Terry Tully** have received a belated wider exposure. Burgess's legacy includes a masterful album and a renowned teaching career to ensure that the old piping tradition marches proudly on. With Robert Matheson's 1997 album *The Big Birl* being a huge seller, a constant stream of CDs being released (the Lismor label has its own Greatest Pipers series), pipe band concerts regularly attracting healthy business and four bagpipe magazines on the market, bagpiping is set to ride into the next century on a new wave of popularity.

FOLK AND CELTIC FESTIVALS

The Scots' first forays into a new "traditional music" grew out of the folk and acoustic scene in mid-1960s Glasgow and Edinburgh. It was at Clive's Incredible Folk Club, in Glasgow, that **The Incredible String Band** made their debut, led by Mike Heron and Robin Williamson. The Incredibles took an unfashionable glance back into their own past on the one hand, while plunging headlong into psychedelia and other uncharted areas on the other. Their success broke down significant barriers for them and others, both in and out of Scotland, and a quarter of a century on Robin Williamson is still tinkering around with his Celtic roots, with perhaps less gusto but just as much guile. In 1997 the Incredibles delighted fans by reuniting for a tour.

In the wake of the Incredibles' success came a succession of Scottish folk-rock crossover musicians. Glasgow-born **Bert Jansch** launched "folk supergroup" **Pentangle** with Jacqui McShee, John Renbourn and Danny Thompson, and the flute-playing Ian Anderson found rock success with **Jethro Tull**. Meanwhile, the folk clubs in Glasgow and Edinburgh gave rise to an interesting mix of traditional and pop artists. Among the latter, Barbara Dickson, Gallagher & Lyle, Rab Noakes and Gerry Rafferty went on to mainstream success, while a more traditional Scottish sound was promoted by the likes of **Archie**, **Ray** and

Cilla Fisher, who sang new and traditional ballads, individually and together, **The McCalmans**, who employed bodhráns, mandolins and traditional material, and, perhaps most crucially, **Dick Gaughan**.

Gaughan's passionate artistry towers like a colossus above three decades. He started out in the Edinburgh folk-club scene with an impenetrable accent, a deep belief in the socialist commitment of traditional song, and a guitar technique that had old masters of the art hanging on to the edge of their seats. For a couple of years in the early 1970s, he played along with Aly Bain (see p.574) in **The Boys of the Lough**, an Irish-Scottish band that was knocking out fiery versions of trad Celtic material. Gaughan became frustrated, however, by the limitations of a primarily instrumental (and fiddle-dominated) group and subsequently formed **Five Hand Reel**. Again playing Scots-Irish traditional material, they might have been the greatest folk-rock band of them all if they hadn't marginally missed the Fairport/Steeleye Span boat.

Leaving to pursue an independent career, Gaughan became a fixture on the folk circuit and made a series of albums exploring Scots and Irish traditional music and reinterpreting the material for guitar. *His Handful of Earth* (1981) was perhaps the single best solo folk album of the decade, a record of stunning intensity with enough contemporary relevance and historical belief to grip all generations of music fans. And, though sparing in his output and modest about his value in the genre, he's also become one of the best songwriters of his generation. An amazing man.

While local record labels issue collections of Rabbie Burns' material, the best songs of recent years specifically about Scotland are by **Dougie MacLean**, who maintains the currently unfashionable traditions of the singer-songwriter. If The Corries' *Flower of Scotland* is now the unofficial national anthem, MacLean's beautiful and moving *Caledonia* is unequivocal first reserve.

GAELIC ROCKING

Scottish music took an unexpected twist in 1978 with the low-key release of an album called *Play Gaelic*. It was made by a little-known group called **Runrig**, who took their name from the old Scottish oilfield system of

EWAN MACCOLL: THE MAN FROM AUCHTERARDER

The single most gifted, influential and inspirational figure in modern British folk song was a man from Auchterarder, Perthshire, called **Ewan MacColl**. He was enthused with the unique spirit and dignity of Scottish music by his parents, both lowlanders, and became a superb ballad singer, devoting himself to the music with such zeal and political sense of purpose that it still colours people's thinking years later.

He is perhaps best remembered now as a gloriously evocative songwriter – with the ability to switch from tender love songs to crushing political venom without apparent change in demeanour. But it was his revolutionary championing of indigenous folk song that caused such a furore, and played such a fierce role in the preservation of folk song, wherever it came from. Singers and musicians, decreed MacColl, should only play music of their own country: a rule which gained him much notoriety when imposed at his own folk clubs. It seems a ludicrous notion in hindsight, but with American music sweeping the world in the late 1950s and early 1960s, it may well have saved large swaths of traditional British folk music.

Initially MacColl made his mark in the theatre, and later moved to the BBC, where he allied his theatrical leanings with his love of folk music in a series of documentary dramas in which the lives of people in different industries were illustrated by the shrewd interspersal of his own songs, written in a folk idiom, for the series. These eight "radio ballads" were major breakthroughs for folk music, and from that point on MacColl was a central figure in the evolution of British roots music. He continued to perform with his American wife Peggy Seeger almost to his death in 1989, his hatred of the Thatcher government inspiring him to ever greater heights of savagery in his songwriting.

Elvis Costello made his public debut down the bill at a Ewan MacColl gig. Shane MacGowan of The Pogues says the only time he ever set foot in a folk club was when MacColl was appearing. And Elvis Presley recorded one of his songs – the Grammy award-winning *First Time Ever I Saw Your Face*. They should be thinking about building some kind of statue up there in Auchterarder.

agriculture, and worked primarily in the backwaters of the Highlands and islands. The thing, though, that stopped people in their tracks was the fact that they were writing original material in Gaelic. This was the first time any serious Scottish working band had achieved any sort of attention with Gaelic material, although Ossian were touching on it around a similar time, as were Nah-Oganaich.

Runrig subsequently marched to unprecedented heights. They chipped away at prejudices, conducting their own musical experiments, adopting accordions and bagpipes, sharper arrangements, electric instruments, full-blown rock styles, and surviving the inevitable personnel changes and the continuous carping of critics who accused them of selling out with every new market conquered. They even made one epic concept album, *Recovery*, which effectively related the history of the Gael in one collection, provoking unprecedented interest in the Gaelic language after years of it being regarded in Scotland as moribund and defunct.

Although few made the connection, because of their geographical remoteness and isolation from the rest of the scene, Runrig were basically making a logical step on from the work of those classic Edinburgh/Glasgow bands whose names roll off with such ease you imagine there's an umbilical link binding them together: **The Corries** and **The McCalmans**; **The Whistlebinkies** and the **JSD Band**; Silly Wizard and **The Tannahill Weavers**; **Alba** and the **Battlefield Band**; **Ossian** and **The Boys of the Lough**; Mouth Music and Capercaillie. Not all of these, by any means, sung in Gaelic, but in each the Gaelic element was strong within the music, in the use either of traditional material or instruments.

Among the ranks of these bands, each with their own agenda and style, are some of Scotland's most important and influential contemporary musicians. **Silly Wizard**, especially, featured a singer of cutting quality in Andy M. Stewart (and did he need that M.), while **Phil and Johnny Cunningham** have subsequently gone on to display a pioneering zeal in their efforts to use their skills on accordion and fiddle to knit Scottish traditional music with other cultures. Johnny Cunningham, fiddle maestro and celebrated party animal, has been especially influential in broadening the boundaries of

Scottish music, working with various bands — notably Relativity and Celtic Fiddle Festival — and conceiving the music for the American touring production of Peter and Wendy. **Mouth Music**, too, were innovative: a Scots-origin duo of Martin Swan and Talitha MacKenzie, who mixed Gaelic vocals (including the traditional "mouth music" techniques of sung rhythms) with African percussion and dance sounds. **Talitha MacKenzie** has subsequently worked solo, radically transforming traditional Scottish songs with wonderful multitracked vocals and Mouth Music's characteristic African rhythms. On a more roots front, The Whistlebinkies were notable for employing only traditional instruments, including fine *clarsach* (Celtic harp) played by Judith Peacock.

These bands' collective success has paved the way for more tolerance and encouragement for the "purer" Scots musicians and singers: *clarsach* player **Alison Kinnaird**; singers **Gordeanna McCulloch**, **Savourna Stevenson**, **Christine Primrose**, **Arthur Cormack** and **Heather Heywood**; and the amazing **Wrigley sisters** from Orkney — now at the forefront of an exciting upsurge of young musicians combining traditional Scottish music with unlimited technical accomplishment, and attitude with a capital A.

Above all, though, the Runrig baton has been grabbed by the excellent **Capercaillie**, who themselves have risen from Argyll pub sessions to flirt with mass commercial appeal, reworking Gaelic and traditional songs from the West Highlands. As yet, they don't appear to have compromised their ideals one iota on the way, and don't look as if they intend to, either. After a two-year break in which singer Karen Matheson recorded a solo album and performed for France in the Eurovision Song Contest, Capercaillie returned in startling style in 1997 with the *Beautiful Wasteland* album, featuring African singers Paloma Loribo and Piruchi Apo of the group Sibeba from Equatorial Guinea.

Towards the end of the 1990s, young Scottish bands such as Wolfstone, Shooglenifty, Seelyhoo, Ceolbeg and Tartan Amoebas have seen an upsurge in popularity, while Cape Breton's Scottish heritage has achieved international credence, largely as a result of the exploits of brilliant Gaelic singer **Mary Jane Lamond** and the wild, flamboyant fiddler **Ashley McIsaac**. More significant still is **Martyn Bennett**, a trained classical musician, master fiddler and bagpipe player who has immersed himself in club culture to blend Gaelic traditions with hip-hop, dub and house styles. Dreadlocked, occasionally bare-chested and wonderfully uninhibited, he inevitably upset a few purists with his astonishing 1997 album

Bothy Culture, which drew a direct line from the great traditional musicians of old. A reluctant visionary, Martyn Bennett is surely the guy to take Scots music into the 21st century.

Colin Irwin
(taken from the *Rough Guide to World Music.*)

SCOTTISH ROCK AND POP

In the early 1980s, a small independent record label, **Postcard**, was set up in Glasgow, which was to have a crucial and long-lasting effect on the Scottish music industry. It started out by signing up virtually unknown bands such as **Aztec Camera** and **Orange Juice** – whose lead singer **Edwyn Collins** went solo in the 1990s to great acclaim. The nationwide popularity of these bands proved that commercial success was not necessarily dependent upon the London marketing scene, and gave other independent Scottish labels and bands the confidence to challenge international markets.

By the late 1980s, a small clique of Glasgow-based musicians began to gain a small but dedicated cult following in Britain, Japan and the US. **The Pastels**, led by Stephen Pastel, and the sugar-sweet pop of **The BMX Bandits** started the ripples that were to culminate with Grunge rockers Nirvana covering **The Vaselines** track *Jesus Don't Want Me for a Sunbeam.* By this point it was clear that Scotland had become an influencial force in the music industry. Today, country rockers **Teenage Fanclub**, retaining their Glasgow indie roots, enjoy substantial acclaim, while guitar group **Del Amitri** have created a huge US following by sheer persistence and constant Stateside touring. Country and western fans, **The Proclaimers**, renowned for their political approach to lyrics and style, achieved US recognition principally through their single *Five Hundred Miles*, which featured in the film *Benny and Joon.* In contrast, the esoteric **Blue Nile** whose simple, sparse, electronic music and mournful lyrics have led to their selling out venues

such as the Royal Albert Hall, with virtually no promotion at all.

On a more commercial level, stadium rockers **Deacon Blue** dominated the British charts in the mid-1980s, while **Simple Minds** effortlessly moved onto the international scene, where they continue to enjoy success. Of course, the contribution of Aberdonian **Annie Lennox**, who notched up several chart hits in the 1980s with The Eurythmics, cannot be underestimated, and she continues to be Scotland's most successful female artist. Clydebank boys **Wet Wet Wet** regularly sell out the massive SECC in Glasgow, having enjoyed one of the decade's biggest selling hits on both sides of the Atlantic with *Love is all around.* In a similar vein, **Texas**, disregarded as an 1980s one-hit wonder, have recently shot back onto the scene, losing their characteristic slide guitar sound, gaining some electronic dance beats and turning lead singer Sharleen Spiteri into something of a pop icon.

More recently in Scotland, the **dance scene** has flowered to become one of the liveliest in Europe. Independent labels such as Soma – who signed French dance-groovers **Daft Punk** – Bellboy Records and Hook Records all continue to release top-quality dance tracks. DJs **Stuart MacMillan** and **Orde Meikle**, creators of Slam – recently voted the 22nd best club in the world – continue to perform globally, returning with world-class DJs to pack out Glasgow clubs. More recently DJ **Howie B** has been breaking the boundaries of live performance by mixing **U2** live on their 1997 tour, while the camera-shy **Blue Boy** is a club favourite with his fantastic fusion of dance and funky soul.

BOOKS

Wherever a book is in print, the UK publisher is given first in each listing, separated, where applicable, from the US publisher by an oblique slash. Where books are published in only one of these countries we have specified which one; when the same company publishes the book in both, its name appears just once. Out of print titles are indicated as o/p – these should be easy to track down in secondhand bookshops.

ART, ARCHITECTURE AND HISTORIC SITES

Lesley Astaire, Roddy Martine and Fritz von Schulenburg *Living in Scotland* (Thames & Hudson/Abbeville). A fascinating, if rather intense, photographic tour of the interiors of the main country homes, inhabited castles and grand town houses of Scotland.

Roger Billcliffe *The Scottish Colourists* (UK John Murray). An impressive, perhaps the definitive, study of a group of artists reckoned by many to be Scotland's finest.

Kitty Cruft and Andrew Fraser, eds *James Craig 1744–95* (UK Mercat Press). Distinguished authors offer reassessments of Craig's achievement in designing Edinburgh's New Town.

Exploring Scotland's Heritage (UK The Stationery Office). Detailed, beautifully illustrated series with the emphasis on historic buildings and archeological sites. Recently updated titles include Orkney, Shetland, the Highlands, Aberdeen and Northeast Scotland, Fife, Perthshire and Angus, and Argyll and the Western Isles.

Bill Hare *Contemporary Painting in Scotland* (UK Craftsman House). Features the work of 48

contemporary artists – including John Bellany, Bruce McLean and Elizabeth Blackadder – and gives special attention to the "New Painting" that emerged in the 1980s and developed into a distinctive Scottish style. Expensive and serious.

David King *Complete Works of Robert and James Adam* (Butterworth-Heinemann o/p). Comprehensive and scholarly look at the work of the Adam brothers.

Charles McKean, David Walker and Frank Walker *Central Glasgow* (Rutland Press). An architectural romp through the city centre and West End, with plenty of photographs and informed comment, *Central Glasgow* is part of the Rutland Press series of illustrated guides to Scottish architecture. Whilst authoritative, they are not at all stuffy and are conveniently pocket-sized. In addition, the Press has produced studies of such notable figures as James Miller, Basil Spence and Peter Womersley.

Duncan MacMillan *Scottish Art 1460–1990* (Mainstream). Lavish overview of Scottish painting with good sections on landscape, portraiture and the Glasgow Boys.

Colin McWilliam, ed. *The Buildings of Scotland* (UK Penguin). There are volumes on various regions of Scotland, including Fife, Edinburgh and Lothian, all of which provide comprehensive and scholarly coverage of every building of importance. Though easy to understand, they would best suit visitors intending to spend more than a couple of weeks in Scotland.

Alistair Moffat and Colin Baxter *Remembering Charles Rennie Mackintosh* (Colin Baxter Photography/Voyageur Press). Illustrated biography of Scotland's most celebrated early twentieth-century architect, artist and designer.

Andrew Gibbon Williams and Andrew Brown *The Bigger Picture: A History of Scottish Art* (UK BBC Books). Originally published to accompany a TV series, this is a richly illustrated survey of Scottish art from 1603 to the present day. Suitable for the lay reader.

HISTORY, POLITICS AND CULTURE

Adamnan (trans. by John Marsden) *The Illustrated Life of Columba* (UK Floris Books). The original story of the life of St Columba, annotated and accompanied by beautiful photos of the places associated with him, in particular the Hebridean island of Iona.

Ian Adams and Meredith Somerville *Cargoes of Despair and Hope* (UK John Donald Publishing). Riveting mixture of contemporary documents and letters telling the story of Scottish emigration to North America from 1603 to 1803.

Ian Bell *Dreams of Exile* (Headline/Holt). Admirable biography of Robert Louis Stevenson that seeks to explain his work in terms of Scottish emigration, exile and escape. Does a good job of balancing the real man against his over-romanticized image.

Andrew Campbell and Roddy Martine *The Swinging Sporran* (UK Penguin o/p). An entertaining guide to bluffing your way in Scottish country dancing.

David Daiches, ed. *The New Companion to Scottish Culture* (Polygon/Subterranean). A dense if wide-ranging tome with more than 300 articles on Scottish culture in its widest sense, from eating to marriage customs to the Scottish Enlightenment.

George MacDonald Fraser *The Steel Bonnets* (HarperCollins). Immensely enjoyable and erudite account of cattle rustling, feud, blackmail, murder and mayhem on the Anglo-Scottish border of the sixteenth century.

Rosemary Goring *Chambers Scottish Biographical Dictionary* (UK Chambers). More than 2000 mini-biographies of important Scots, both well-known and utterly obscure, in fields such as law, medicine, education, the Church, music and the stage.

Historic Scotland (Stationery Office/Seven Mills). A series of books covering many aspects of Scotland's history and prehistory, including the Picts, Vikings, Romans and Celts. All are colourful, accessible and well-presented. Available at many Historic Scotland sites as well as bookshops.

William Laughton Lorimer *The New Testament* (UK Penguin). Magnificent translation into the Scots tongue. Interestingly, only the Devil's words are rendered in English.

Michael Lynch *Scotland: A New History* (UK Pimlico). Probably the best available overview of Scottish history, taking the story up to 1992 and the arguments for and against a national parliament.

James MacKay *Burns: A Biography of Robert Burns* (UK Mainstream). An attempt to clear the myths surrounding Scotland's most famous poet, including those created by the man himself.

James MacKay *William Wallace* (UK Mainstream). An authoritative biography, and the best of a rash of books capitalizing on the success of the movie *Braveheart* – the book is more of a stickler for historical fact than the film.

R.F. Mackenzie *A Search for Scotland* (UK Fontana o/p). Combining travelogue, autobiography and polemic, Mackenzie presents a highly personal account of the contradictions of Scottish culture and character. Inquisitive and incisive, the book is full of fierce but not uncritical affection for his homeland.

Fitzroy Maclean *Bonnie Prince Charlie* (UK Canongate). Very readable and more or less definitive biography written by the "real" James Bond.

John McLeod *No Great Mischief If You Fall* (Mainstream/Trafalgar). Gloom and doom on the rape of the Highlands; an enraging, bleak but stimulating book debunking some of the myths upheld by the Highland industry.

Ann McSween and Mick Sharp *Prehistoric Scotland* (Batsford o/p/New Amsterdam Books). Thematic introductory guide to many of Scotland's prehistoric sites, with atmospheric black-and-white photographs and imaginative illustrations.

Andrew Marr *The Battle for Scotland* (UK Penguin o/p). An intelligent and readable account of Scottish political history from the nineteenth century to 1992, written by the editor of the *Independent*.

W.H. Murray *Rob Roy MacGregor* (UK Canongate). Yet another tie-in to a recent Scottish movie, with fact and legend being inextricably interwoven.

John Prebble *Glen Coe* (Penguin/Secker & Warburg o/p), *Culloden* (Penguin/Athenium o/p) and *The Highland Clearances* (Penguin/Secker & Warburg o/p). Emotive and subjective accounts of key events in Highland history. Essential reading for Jacobite sympathizers.

John Purser *Scotland's Music* (Mainstream). Comprehensive overview of traditional and classical music in Scotland – thorough and scholarly but readable.

James D. Scarlett *Tartan: The Highland Textile* (Shepheard-Welwyn/Paul & Co Publishing). Detailed and authoritative, Scarlett's up-to-date and near definitive work debunks the myths surrounding tartan and analyses 500 patterns.

T. C. Smout *A History of the Scottish People 1560–1830* (Fontana/Scribner o/p) and *A Century of the Scottish People 1830–1950* (Fontana/Yale University Press o/p). Widely acclaimed volumes, brimful of interest for those keen on social history. Smout combines enormous learning with a clear and entertaining style.

Tom Steel *Scotland's Story* (UK Fontana). Good people-based introduction written to accompany a popular British television series.

Andy Wightman *Who Owns Scotland* (UK Canongate). A detailed and revealing breakdown of the patterns of land ownership and use in Scotland, but rather dry for general reading.

GUIDES AND PICTURE BOOKS

Colin Baxter *Scotland from the Air* (UK Lomond), **Baxter and Jim Crumley** *Portrait of Edinburgh* (UK Colin Baxter Photography) and **Baxter and Jack McLean** *The City of Glasgow* (UK Colin Baxter Photography). Best known for his ubiquitous postcards, Baxter's photographs succeed in capturing the grandeur of Scotland's moody landscapes and characterful cityscapes.

Moira Burgess *Reading Glasgow* (UK Book Trust Scotland). A lively literary guide to Glasgow, with pictures, sketch maps, extracts and narrative to guide you around different sections of the city.

Collins Gem Scots Dictionary (UK HarperCollins). Handy, pocket-sized guide to the mysteries of Scottish vocabulary and idiom.

Joe Fisher *The Glasgow Encyclopedia* (Mainstream). The essential Glasgow reference book, covering nearly every facet of this complex urban society.

Hamish Haswell-Smith *The Scottish Islands* (UK Canongate). An exhaustive and impressive gazetteer with maps and absorbing information on all the Scottish islands. Filled with attractive

sketches and paintings, the book is breathtaking in its thoroughness and lovingly gathered detail.

Magnus Magnusson and Graham White, eds *The Nature of Scotland – Landscape, Wildlife and People* (UK Canongate). Glossy picture-based book on Scotland's natural heritage, from geology to farming and conservation. Good section on crofting.

Oscar Marzaroli *Glasgow's People: 1956–1988* (Mainstream) and *Shades of Grey* (Mainstream). Two wonderful collections by Glasgow's most sympathetic photographer: both contain the pictures of local people missing from so many other coffee-table books.

Richard Muir *The Coastlines of Britain* (UK Macmillan o/p). An exploration of all aspects of Scotland's varied coast with chapters on cliffs, beach, dunes, flora and fauna.

Anne Shade *Scotland for K'ds* (Mainstream). Indispensable advice on where to go and what to do with children in Scotland, written by a mother of two.

Cecil Sinclair *Tracing your Scottish Ancestors* (UK The Stationery Office). Probably the best guide to ancestry research in the Scottish Record Office; definitely worth reading before visiting General Register House.

Michael and Elspeth Wills *Walks in Edinburgh's Old Town* (UK Mercat Press). A small guide which takes you into the nooks and crannies of Britain's most historically intensive city centre.

FOLKLORE AND LEGEND

Margaret Bennett *Scottish Customs from the Cradle to the Grave* (Polygon). Fascinating and sympathetic extensive oral history.

Michael Brander *Tales of the Borders* (UK Mainstream). Part social history and part guidebook, a collection of romantic nineteenth-century Border tales retold and put into historical context.

Alan J. Bruford and Donald Archie McDonald, eds *Scottish Traditional Tales* (Polygon). A huge collection of folk stories from all over Scotland, taken from tape archives.

Anne Ross *Folklore of the Scottish Highlands* (Barnes and Noble). A comprehensive collection, with sections on clan lore, witchcraft, spells and taboos, festivals and scores of obscure customs.

Jennifer Westwood *Albion: A Guide to Legendary Britain* (Grafton o/p/Salem House). Highly readable volume on the development of myth in literature, with a section on Scottish legends.

MEMOIRS AND TRAVELOGUES

David Craig *On the Crofter's Trail* (UK Pimlico). Using anecdotes and interviews with descendants, Craig conveys the hardship and tragedy of the Highland Clearances without being mawkish.

Jim Crumley *Gulfs of Blue Air – A Highland Journey* (Mainstream). Recent travelogue mixed with nature notes and references to Scottish poets such as MacCaig and Mackay Brown.

David Duff ed *Queen Victoria's Highland Journals* (UK Hamlyn). The daily diary of the Scottish adventures of "Mrs Brown" – Victoria's writing is detailed and interesting without being twee, and she lovingly conveys her affection for Deeside and the Highlands.

James Hunter *Scottish Highlanders* (Mainstream). Attempts to explain the strong sense of blood ties held by people of Scottish descent all over the world; lots of history and good photographs.

Samuel Johnson and James Boswell *A Journey to the Western Isles of Scotland* and *The Journal of a Tour to the Hebrides* (UK Penguin). Lively accounts of a famous journey around the islands taken by Johnson and his biographer and friend.

Tom Morton *Spirit of Adventure: A Journey Beyond the Whisky Trails* (Mainstream). Offbeat and funny view of Scotland's whisky industry as seen from the back of a motorcycle in appalling weather.

Edwin Muir *Highland Journey* (Mainstream). A classic travelogue written in 1935 by the troubled Orcadian writer on his return to Scotland from London.

Kenneth Roy *Travels in a Small Country* (UK Carrick Publishing o/p). An attempt to discover the "real" Scotland by an engaging and talented commentator. Village halls, fish auctions and second-division football grounds take the starring role.

Robert Louis Stevenson *Edinburgh: Picturesque Notes* (Barnes and Noble). Charming evocation of Stevenson's birthplace –

its moods, curiosities and influences on his work.

Mike Tomkies *A Last Wild Place* (UK Jonathan Cape). Written by a journalist who lived in a derelict croft in Northwest Scotland for twenty years, this is a great perceptive and loving account of the natural world around him.

FOOD AND DRINK

Annette Hope *A Caledonian Feast* (UK Mainstream). Authoritative and entertaining history of Scottish food and social life from the ninth to the twentieth century. Lots of recipes.

Michael Jackson *Malt Whisky Companion* (UK Dorling Kindersley). An attractively put together tome, considered by many to be the "bible" on malt whisky tasting.

G.W. Lockhart *The Scots and Their Fish* (UK Birlinn). Tells the history of fish and fishing in Scotland, and ends with a selection of traditional recipes.

Charles McLean *Pocket Guides: Scotch Whisky* and **Charles McLean and Jason Lowe** *Malt Whisky* (UK Mitchell Beazley o/p). The first is a small, thorough, fact-filled book covering malt, grain and blended whiskies, plus whisky-based liqueurs. The second is an attractive coffee-table book with inspiring photographs of the places whisky comes from, as well as detailed background information.

F. Marian McNeill *The Scots Kitchen* (UK Mercat Press) and *The Scots Cellar* (UK Lochar o/p). The first is a definitive, learned and entertaining guide to the history of Scots cooking; the second a history on the consumption and appreciation of whisky, ale and wine, with some good, alcoholic recipes.

Nick Nairn *Wild Harvest/Wild Harvest 2* (UK BBC Books). Glossy TV tie-ins by a fashionable young Scottish chef, who takes up the challenge of gathering and eating from the wild. Both books have fascinating, if difficult to recreate, recipes.

FICTION

Iain Banks *The Crow Road* (UK Abacus), *The Wasp Factory* and *Song of Stone* (both Abacus/Simon and Schuster). Banks's work can be funny, pacy, thought-provoking, imaginative and downright disgusting. It is never dull.

D. K. Broster *The Jacobite Trilogy* (UK Mandarin). Tear-jerking trilogy centred round the tribulations of the Jacobite supporters.

George Mackay Brown *Beside the Ocean of Time* (UK Flamingo). A child's journey through the history of an Orkney island, and an adult's effort to make sense of the place's secrets in the late twentieth century.

John Buchan *The Complete Richard Hannay* (UK Penguin/Godine). This one volume includes *The 39 Steps, Greenmantle, Mr Standfast, The Three Hostages* and *The Island of Sheep*. Good gung ho stories with a great feel for Scottish landscape. In the US, both Oxford University Press and Godine publish various editions of the Hannay stories. Less well-known but better are Buchan's historical romances: for example, *The Free Fishers* (UK B&W Publishing), *John Burnet of Barnes* (UK B&W Publishing) and *Witchwood* (UK Canongate).

Isla Dewar *Women Talking Dirty* (UK Headline Review). Set in Edinburgh suburbia, the outrageous, funny and poignant soul-bearing of two women who become fast friends over a bottle of vodka and detailed post-match analysis. *Keeping up with Magda* and *Giving up on Ordinary* (both UK Headline Review) are in a similar style.

George MacDonald Fraser *The General Danced at Dawn* (Fontana HarperCollins), *McAuslain in the Rough* and *The Sheikh and the Dustbin* (Fontana HarperCollins). Touching and very funny collections of short stories detailing life in a Highland regiment after World War II.

Janice Galloway *The Trick is to Keep Breathing* (Minerva Dalkey Archive). The story of a woman's mind as she slowly spirals into madness. Almost unwittingly the reader is drawn into the vortex and suddenly finds themself empathizing with the heroine's confusion. A brilliantly written, intense book.

Lewis Grassic Gibbon *A Scots Quair* (Penguin/Schocken o/p). A landmark trilogy, set in northeast Scotland during and after World War I, the events are seen through the eyes of Chris Guthrie, "torn between her love for the land and her desire to escape a peasant culture". Strong, seminal work.

Alasdair Gray *Lanark* (Picador/Harcourt Brace). A postmodern blend of social realism and labyrinthine fantasy: Gray's extraordinary debut as a novelist, with his own allegorical illustrations, takes invention and comprehension to their limits.

Neil M. Gunn *The Silver Darlings* (UK Faber & Faber). Probably Gunn's most representative and best-known book, evocatively set on the northeast coast and telling the story of the herring fishermen during the great years of the industry. Other examples of his romantic, symbolic works include *The Lost Glen, The Silver Bough* and *Wild Geese Overhead* (UK Chambers).

James Hogg *The Private Memoirs and Confessions of a Justified Sinner* (Penguin). Complex, powerful mid-nineteenth-century novel dealing with possession, myth and folklore, as it looks at the confession of an Edinburgh murderer from three different points of view.

James Kelman *The Busconductor Hines* (UK Phoenix). The wildly funny story of a young Glasgow bus conductor with an intensely boring job and a limitless imagination. *How Late it Was, How Late* (Minerva/Dell) is Kelman's award-winning and disturbing look at life as seen through the eyes of a foul-mouthed, blind Glaswegian drunk.

A. L. Kennedy *Looking for the Possible Dance* (UK Vintage). Young Scottish writer dissects the difficulties of human relationships on a personal and wider social level. More recent novels *So I Am Glad* and *Original Bliss* (both UK Minerva) have the same deft touch.

Alexander MacArthur and Kingsley Long *No Mean City* (UK Corgi). Classic story of razor gangs in 1935 Glasgow.

William McIlvanney *Docherty* (UK Sceptre). Tale of a hard, poverty-wracked Scottish coal-mining community by one of the country's most-respected contemporary authors.

Compton Mackenzie *Whisky Galore* (UK Penguin). Comic novel based on a true story of the wartime wreck of a cargo of whisky on a Hebridean island. Full of predictable stereotypes but still funny.

Naomi Mitchison *The Bull Calves* (UK Virago). Moving story of a family facing personal and political realities after the failed Jacobite Rebellion of 1745. A generous, humane and thoroughly engrossing read.

Neil Munro *The Complete Edition of the Para Handy Tales* (UK Pan). Engaging and witty stories relating the adventures of a Clyde puffer captain as he more or less legally steers his grubby ship up and down the west coast. Despite a fond – if slightly patronizing – view of the Gaelic mind, they are enormous fun.

Sir Walter Scott *The Waverley Novels* (Penguin). The books that did much to create the romanticized version of Scottish life and history. A series of critical hardback editions have been published by Edinburgh University Press: *Kennilworth*, *Tale of Old Mortality*, *Black Dwarf*, *St Ronan's Well* and *The Antiquary*. For more on Scott, see p.131.

Iain Crichton Smith *Consider the Lillies* (UK Canongate). Poetic lament about the Highland Clearances by Scotland's finest bilingual (English and Gaelic) writer.

Muriel Spark *The Prime of Miss Jean Brodie* (Penguin/NAL Dutton). Wonderful evocation of middle-class Edinburgh life and aspirations, still apparent in that city today.

Alan Spence *The Stone Garden* (UK Phoenix). Perceptive, gently humorous and well-crafted short stories based on childhood experiences in Glasgow.

R. L. Stevenson *Dr Jekyll and Mr Hyde* (Penguin/Vintage), *Kidnapped* (Penguin/Signet), *The Master of Ballantrae* (Penguin/Oxford University Press) and *Weir of Hermiston* (UK Penguin). Nineteenth-century tales of intrigue and adventure. For more on Stevenson, see p.90.

Nigel Tranter *The Bruce Trilogy* (Hodder & Stoughton). Massive tome by prolific and hugely popular author on Scottish themes.

Alan Warner *Morven Caller* (UK Jonathan Cape). The tantalizing story of a supermarket shelf-packer from Oban who follows her vision to the rave clubs of Ibiza and the quiet beauty of the West Highlands. Sequel is called *These Demented Lands* (UK Jonathan Cape).

Irvine Welsh *Irvine Welsh Omnibus* (Vintage/Norton). A compendium including *Trainspotting*, *The Acid House* and *Marabou Stork Nightmares*, all of which can also be found as separate titles. Welsh trawls through the horrors of drug addiction, sexual fantasy, urban decay and hopeless youth, making you either rejoice at an authentic and unapologetic new voice for the dispossessed, or throw up.

Thankfully, his unflinching attention is not without humour.

Kevin Williamson, ed. *Children of Albion Rovers* (Canongate/Overlook Press). A fast-track introduction to some of the best Scottish writers of the drug-culture generation, with novellas by the likes of Irvine Welsh, Alan Warner, Gordon Legge and Laura J. Hird.

POETRY

J. K. Annaud *Dod and Davie* (UK Canongate o/p). Translation into Scots of Wilhelm Busch's tongue-in-cheek morality tale. Robust and wickedly funny, the book appeals to badly behaved children of all ages.

George Mackay Brown *Selected Poems 1954–1983* (John Murray). Brown's work is as haunting, beautiful and gritty as the Orkney islands which inspire it.

Robert Burns *The Complete Illustrated Poems, and Songs and Ballads* (UK Lomond). Facsimile edition of the works of Scotland's most famous bard. Oxford University Press publish much of Burns' work in the US.

Douglas Dunn, ed. *The Faber Book of Twentieth-Century Scottish Poetry* (Faber & Faber). All the big names and some lesser-known works.

Douglas Dunn, ed. *Scotland: An Anthology* (UK Fontana o/p). Wide-ranging anthology featuring both Scottish writers and outsiders that attempts to provide a background to past and present notions of Scottish nationality.

Liz Lochhead *Bagpipe Muzak* (UK Penguin). A great collection of monologues and poems examining contemporary everyday life from a deceptively simple angle.

Norman MacCaig *Selected Poems* (Chatto & Windus). Justly celebrated for its keen observation of the natural world, MacCaig's work remains intellectually challenging without being arid. His poetry, rooted in the Highlands, uses detail to explore a universal landscape.

Hugh MacDiarmid *Selected Poetry* (edited by Alan Riach; Penguin/New Directions). Nationalistic, challenging works by Scotland's finest modern poet.

William McGonagall *McGonagall: A Selection* (edited by Colin Walker; UK Birlinn).

Compulsive selection of works by Scotland's much-loved worst poet.

MacCaig, Morgan, Lochhead *Three Scottish Poets* (UK Canongate). A representative selection from the work of three well-known poets. Contrasting perspectives – natural, metaphysical, urban, political and feminist – reflect the complexity of the modern Scottish experience.

John McQueen and Tom Scott, eds *The Oxford Book of Scottish Verse* (UK Oxford University Press). Claims to be the most comprehensive anthology of Scottish poetry ever published.

Alastair Reid *Oases* (Canongate). A rich selection of poetry and prose by Scottish exile, Alastair Reid, who also translates the work of Borges and Neruda.

Tom Scott, ed. *The Penguin Book of Scottish Verse* (UK Penguin). Good general selection.

Roderick Watson, ed. *The Poetry of Scotland* (UK Edinburgh University Press). An accessible anthology of poems in English, Scots and Gaelic (with notes and translations) from the fourteenth century to the present day.

OUTDOOR PURSUITS

Bartholomew Walks Series (UK Bartholomew). The series covers different areas of Scotland, including Perthshire, Loch Lomond and the Trossachs, Oban, Mull and Lochaber, and Skye and Wester Ross. Each booklet has a range of walks of varying lengths with clear maps and descriptions.

Donald Bennet *The Munros*, and **Scott Johnstone et al.** *The Corbetts* (UK Scottish Mountaineering Trust). Authoritative and attractively illustrated hillwalkers' guides to the Scottish peaks. SMT also publishes guides to districts and specific climbs.

Hamish Brown *Hamish's Mountain Walk and Climbing the Corbetts* (Bâton Wicks). The best of the travel narratives about walking in the Scottish Highlands.

Andrew Dempster *Classic Mountain Scrambles in Scotland* (UK Mainstream). Guide to hill walks in Scotland that combine straightforward walking with some rock-climbing.

Richard Fitter, Alastair Fitter and Marhorie Blanney *Collins Pocket Guide to the Wild Flowers of Britain and Northern Europe* (UK HarperCollins). An excellent, easy-to-use field guide.

Muriel Gray *The First Fifty* (UK Corgi). Described as "munro bagging without a beard" Scottish TV presenter Gray takes an enthusiastic and irreverent tour of her favourite Scottish peaks.

David Hamilton *The Scottish Golf Guide* (Canongate). An inexpensive paperback with descriptions of and useful information about 84 of Scotland's best courses.

John Hancox *Collins Pocket Reference – Cycling in Scotland* (UK HarperCollins). Spiral-bound edition with over fifty road routes of all grades up and down the country, each with a useful route map. For more off-road mountain bike routes, try **Derek Purdy** *Scotland: The Central Valley* (UK Haynes Publishers) in the *Ride Your Bike* series, or **Harry Henniker** *101 Bike Routes in Scotland* (UK Mainstream).

Michael Madders and Julia Welstead *Where to Watch Birds in Scotland* (UK Christopher Helm). Region-by-region guide with maps, details on access and habitat, and notes on what to see when.

Ian Mitchell *Mountain Days and Bothy Nights* (Luath Press). A slim but highly entertaining volume describing the characters and experiences of modern-day hill climbing.

Ordnance Survey Pathfinder Series (Jarrold Publishing/Seven Hills Book Distribution). Top-quality maps, colour pictures and clear text. Titles include: *Loch Lomond and the Trossachs, Fort William and Glen Coe* and *Perthshire*.

Robert Price *Scotland's Golf Courses* (UK Mercat Press o/p). A thorough lowdown on Scottish courses for serious golfers, with good photographs.

Pastime Publications *Scotland for Game, Sea and Coarse Fishing* (UK Pastime Publications). General guide on what to fish, where and for how much, along with notes on records, regulations and convenient accommodation. Published in association with the Scottish Tourist Board.

Roger Smith *The West Highland Way, The Southern Upland Way* (both The Stationery

Office o/p). Comprehensive guides to long-distance paths, containing information on sights, history, nature and help on planning your trek, as well as specially orientated maps. The Stationery Office also publishes a series called *Twenty-Five Walks*, each volume covering a particular city or region of Scotland with colour pictures and excellent maps.

Ralph Storer *100 Best Routes on Scottish Mountains* (UK David and Charles). A compilation of the best day-walks in Scotland, including some of the classics overlooked by the Munroing guides.

LANGUAGE

Gaelic remains a living language in many regions of Scotland, particularly in the *Gàidhealtachd* or Gaelic-speaking areas of the Western Isles, parts of Skye and a few scattered islands of Argyll. The recent revival of interest in the language, encouraged by schools and the media, has meant that, in addition, you may well pick up snatches of the language in some mainland parts of the northwest and in Inverness or Glasgow. However, even in these areas you are far more likely to have a conversation with locals in Scots, a dialect of English whose peculiar accent, vocabulary and grammar have led many to declare it, too, to be a separate language. In Orkney and Shetland, the language has a Scots base too, but some words are carried over from Old Norse (or Norn), the language of the Viking settlers; for more on this and a list of place-name terms and other words you are most likely to hear, see p.494.

Scottish **Gaelic** (*Gàidhlig*, pronounced "Gallic") is one of only four Celtic languages to survive into the modern age (Welsh, Breton and Irish Gaelic are the other three). Manx, the old language of the Isle of Man, died out earlier this century, while Cornish was finished as a community language way back in the eighteenth century. Scottish Gaelic is most closely related to Irish Gaelic and Manx – hardly surprising, given that it was introduced to Scotland from Ireland around the third century BC. From the fifth to the twelfth centuries, Gaelic enjoyed an expansionist phase, gradually becoming the national language, thanks partly to the backing of the Celtic church in Iona. At the end of this period, Gaelic was spoken throughout virtually all of what is now Scotland – the main exceptions being Orkney and Shetland – but from that point onwards it began a steady decline.

Over the next few centuries, even before union with England, power, religious ideology and wealth gradually passed into non-Gaelic hands. The royal court was transferred to Edinburgh and an Anglo-Norman legal system was put in place. The Celtic church was Romanized by the introduction of foreign clergy, and, most importantly of all, English and Flemish merchants colonized the new trading towns of the east coast. In addition, the pro-English attitudes held by the Covenanters led to strong anti-Gaelic feeling within the Church of Scotland from its inception.

The two abortive Jacobite rebellions of 1715 and 1745 furthered the language's decline, as did the Clearances that took place in the Gaelic-speaking Highlands from the 1770s to the 1820s, which forced thousands to migrate to central Scotland's new industrial belt or emigrate to North America. Although efforts were made to halt the decline in the first half of the nineteenth century, the 1872 Education Act gave no official recognition to Gaelic, and children were severely punished if they were caught speaking the language in school.

Current estimates put the number of Gaelic speakers at 86,000 (about two percent of the population), the majority of whom live in the *Gàidhealtachd*, with an extended Gaelic community of perhaps 250,000 who have some understanding of the language. In the last decade or so the language has stabilized and even recovered, thanks to the introduction of bilingual primary and nursery schools, and a huge increase in the amount of broadcasting time given to Gaelic-language programmes. The success of rock bands such as Runrig has shown that it is possible to combine traditional Gaelic culture with popular entertainment and reach a mass audience.

While Gaelic has undergone something of a renaissance, **Scots**, or "Lallans", as spoken by the "English-speaking" majority of Scottish people, is still struggling for recognition. In form, at least, it is closely related to the English spoken south of the border, since it began life as a northern branch of Anglo-Saxon. In the early fifteenth century, it replaced Latin as the country's main literary and documentary language, but has since been drawn closer to southern varieties of English. Some people claim it to be a separate language, which has suffered the same systematic repression as Gaelic, while others reject this view, considering it to be, at best, an artificial amalgamation of local dialects. Robbie Burns is the most obvious literary exponent of the Scots language, but there has been a revival this century led by poets such as Hugh MacDiarmid. (For examples of the works of both writers, see "Books".)

GAELIC GRAMMAR AND PRONUNCIATION

Gaelic is a highly complex tongue, with a fiendish, antiquated grammar and, with only eighteen letters, an intimidating system of spelling. Pronunciation is actually easier than it appears at first glance – one general rule to remember is that the **stress** always falls on the first syllable of a word. The general rule of syntax is that the verb starts the sentence whether it's a question or not, followed by the subject and then the object; adjectives generally follow the word they are describing.

SHORT AND LONG VOWELS

Gaelic has both short and long vowels, the latter being denoted by an acute or grave accent.

a as in c**a**t; before nn and ll, like the _ow_ in b**ow** (of a boat)
à as in b**a**r
e as in p**e**t
é like the _ai_ in r**ai**n
i like the _ee_ in str**ee**t, but shorter
í like the _ee_ in fr**ee**
o as in p**o**t
ò like the _a_ in the enthr**a**l
ó like the _ow_ in b**ow** (of a boat)
u like the _oo_ in sc**oo**t
ù like the _oo_ in l**oo**

VOWEL COMBINATIONS

Gaelic is littered with diphthongs, which, rather like in English, can be pronounced in several different ways depending on the individual word.

ai like the _a_ in c**a**t, or the _e_ in p**e**t; before dh or gh, like the _ee_ in str**ee**t
ao like the _ur_ in s**ur**ly
ei like the _a_ in m**a**te
ea like the _e_ in p**e**t, or the _a_ in c**a**t, and some-

times like the _a_ in m**a**te; before ll or nn like the _ow_ in b**ow** (of a boat)
èa as in h**ea**r
eu like the _ai_ in tr**ai**n, or the _ea_ in f**ea**r
ia like the _ea_ in f**ea**r
io like the _ea_ in f**ea**r, or the _ee_ in str**ee**t, but shorter
ua like the _ooe_ in w**ooe**r

CONSONANTS

The consonants listed below are those that differ substantially from the English.

b at the beginning of a word as in **b**ig; in the middle or at the end of a word like the _p_ in **p**air
bh at the beginning of a word like the _v_ in **v**an; elsewhere it is silent
c as in **c**at; after a vowel it has aspiration _before_ it
ch always as in lo**ch**, never as in **ch**urch
cn like the _cr_ in **cr**owd
d like the _d_ in **d**og, but with the tongue pressed against the back of the upper teeth; at the beginning of a word before e or i, like the _j_ in **j**am; in the middle or at the end of a word like the _t_ in ca**t**; after i like the _ch_ in **ch**urch
dh before and after a, o or u an aspirated _g_, rather like someone gargling; before e or i like the _y_ in **y**es; elsewhere silent
fh usually silent; somtimes like the _h_ in **h**ouse
g at the beginning of a word as in **g**et; before i like the _y_ in **y**es; in the middle or end of a word like the _ck_ in so**ck**; after i like the _ch_ in lo**ch**
gh at the beginning of a word as in **g**et; before or after a, o or u rather like someone gargling; after i sometimes like the _y_ in ga**y**, but often silent
l after i and sometimes before e like the _l_ in **l**ot; elsewhere a peculiarly Gaelic sound produced by flattening the front of the tongue against the palate
mh like the _v_ in **v**an
p at the beginning of a word as in **p**et; elsewhere it has aspiration _before_ it
rt pronounced as **sht**
s before e or i like the _sh_ in **sh**ip; otherwise as in English
sh before a, o or u like the _h_ in **h**ouse; before e like the _ch_ in lo**ch**
t before e or i like the _ch_ in **ch**urch; in the middle or at the end of a word it has aspiration _before_ it; otherwise as in Englis'ı
th at the beginning of a word, like the _h_ in **h**ouse; elsewhere, and in the word _thu_, silent

GAELIC PHRASES AND VOCABULARY

The choice is limited when it comes **teach-yourself Gaelic** courses, but the BBC *Can Seo* cassette and book is perfect for starting you off. Drier and more academic is *Teach Yourself Gaelic* (Hodder & Stoughton), which is aimed at bringing beginners to Scottish "O" grade standard. *Everyday Gaelic* by Morag MacNeill (Gairm) is the best phrasebook around.

BASIC WORDS AND GREETINGS

yes	*tha*	night	*oidhche*	music	*ceòl*
no	*chan eil*	here	*an seo*	book	*leabhar*
hello	*hallo*	there	*an sin*	tired	*sgìth*
how are you?	*ciamar a tha thu?*	this way	*mar seo*	food	*lòn*
OK	*tha gu math*	that way	*mar sin*	bread	*aran*
thank you	*tapadh leat*	pound/s	*not/aichean*	water	*uisge*
welcome	*fàilte*	tomorrow	*a-màireach*	milk	*bainne*
come in	*thig a-staigh*	tonight	*a-nochd*	beer	*leann*
goodbye	*mar sin leat*	cheers	*slàinte*	wine	*fion*
goodnight	*oidhche mhath*	yesterday	*an-dé*	whisky	*uisge beatha*
who?	*cò?*	today	*an-diugh*	post office	*post oifis*
where is...?	*càit a bheil...?*	tomorrow	*maireach*	Edinburgh	*Dun Eideann*
when?	*cuine?*	now	*a-nise*	Glasgow	*Glaschu*
what is it?	*dé tha ann?*	hotel	*taigh-òsda*	America	*Ameireaga*
morning	*madainn*	house	*taigh*	Ireland	*Eire*
evening	*feasgar*	story	*sgeul*	England	*Sasainn*
day	*là*	song	*òran*	London	*Lunnain*

SOME USEFUL PHRASES

It's a nice day	*tha latha math ann*	Do you speak Gaelic?	*a bheil Gàidhlig agad?*
How much is that?	*dè tha e 'cosg?*	What is the Gaelic for?	*Dé a' Ghàidhlig a tha*
What's your name?	*dè 'n t-ainm a th'ort?*		*. air?*
Excuse me	*gabh mo leisgeul*	I don't understand	*chan eil mi 'tuigsinn*
What time is it?	*dé am uair a tha e?*	I don't know	*chan eil fhios agam*
I'm thirsty	*tha am pathadh orm*	That's good	*'s math sin*
I'd like a double room	*'se rùm dùbailte tha mi 'g*	It doesn't matter	*'s coma*
	. iarraigh	I'm sorry	*Tha mi duilich*

NUMBERS AND DAYS

1	*aon*	10	*deich*	1000	*mìle*
2	*dà/dhà*	11	*aon deug*	Monday	*Diluain*
3	*trì*	20	*fichead*	Tuesday	*Dimàirt*
4	*ceithir*	21	*aon ar fhichead*	Wednesday	*Diciadain*
5	*còig*	30	*deug ar fhichead*	Thursday	*Diardaoin*
6	*sia*	40	*dà fhichead*	Friday	*Dihaoine*
7	*seachd*	50	*lethcheud*	Saturday	*Disathurna*
8	*ochd*	60	*trì fichead*	Sunday	*Didòmhnaich/*
9	*naoi*	100	*ceud*		*. La na Sàbaid*

SURNAMES

The prefix **Mac** or **Mc** in Scottish surnames derives from the Gaelic, meaning "son of". In Scots, Mac is used for both sexes; but in Gaelic, women are referred to as Nic. For example:

Donnchadh Mac Aodh   Duncan MacKay   *Iseabail Nic Aodh*   Isabel MacKay

GEOGRAPHICAL AND PLACE-NAME TERMS

The purpose of the list below is to help with place-name derivations and with more detailed map reading.

ach or **auch**, from **achadh**	field	**ess**, from **eas**	waterfall
ail, **aileach**	rock	**fin**, from **fionn**	white
Alba	Scotland	**gair** or **gare**, from **geàrr**	short
ardan or **arden**, from **àird**	a point of land or height	**garv**, from **garbh**	rough
		glen, from **gleann**	valley
ault, from **allt**	stream	**gower** or **gour**, from **gabhar**	goat
bal or **bally**, from **baile**	town, village	**inch**, from **innis**	meadow or island
balloch, from **bealach**	mountain pass	**inver**, from **inbhir**	rivermouth
bad	clump of trees	**ken** or **kin**, from **ceann**	head
bagh	bay	**knock**, from **cnoc**	hill
bàrr	summit	**kyle**, from **caolas**	narrow strait
beg, from **beag**	small	**lag**	hollow
ben, from **beinn**	mountain	**loch**	lake
blair, from **blàr**	field or battlefield	**meall**	round hill
cairn, from **càrn**	pile of stones	**mon**, from **monadh**	hill
craig, from **creag**	rock	**more**, from **mór**	large, great
cnoc	hill	**rannoch**, from **raineach**	bracken
coll or **colly**, from **coille**	wood	**ross**, from **ros**	promontory
corrie, from **coire**	round hollow in mountainside, whirlpool	**rubha**	promontory
		sgeir	sea rock
		strath, from **srath**	broad valley
cruach	bold hill	**tarbet**, from **tairbeart**	isthmus
drum, from **druim**	ridge	**tir** or **tyre**, from **tìr**	land
dubh	black	**torr**	hill, castle
dun or **dum**, from **dùn**	fort	**traigh**	shore
eilean	island		

A SCOTTISH GLOSSARY

AULD Old.

AYE Yes.

BAIRN Baby.

BEN Mountain peak.

BLACK HOUSE Thick-walled traditional dwelling.

BONNIE Pretty.

BOTHY Primitive cottage or hut; farmworker's or shepherd's mountain shelter.

BRAE Slope; hill.

BRIG Bridge.

BROCH Circular prehistoric stone fort.

BURN Small stream or brook.

BYRE Shelter for cattle; cottage.

CAIRN Mound of stones.

CARSE Riverside area of flat alluvium.

CEILIDH Social gathering involving dancing, drinking, singing and storytelling.

CLAN Extended family.

COVENANTERS Supporter of the Presbyterian Church in the seventeenth century.

CORBETT Mountain between 2500ft and 3000ft high.

CORBIE-STEPPED Architectural term; any set of steps on a gable.

CORRIE Circular hollow on a hillside.

CRAIG Steep peak or crag.

CRANNOG Celtic lake or bog dwelling.

CROFT Small plot of farmland with house, common in the Highlands.

CROW-STEPPED Same as *corbie-stepped*.

DOLMEN Grave chamber.

DRAM Literally, one-sixteenth of an ounce. Usually refers to a small measure of whisky.

DRUM Narrow ridge.

DUN Fortified mound.

FIRST-FOOT The first person to enter a household on *Hogmanay* (see below).

FIRTH Narrow inlet.

GILLIE Personal guide used on hunting or fishing trips.

GLEN Deep, narrow mountain valley.

HARLING Limestone and gravel mix used to cover buildings.

HOGMANAY New Year's Eve.

HOWE Valley.

HOWFF Meeting place; pub.

INCH Small island.

KEN Knowledge; understanding.

KILT Knee-length tartan skirt worn by Highland men.

KIRK Church.

KYLE Narrow strait or channel.

LAIRD Landowner; aristocrat.

LAW Rounded hill.

LINKS Grassy coastal land; coastal golf course.

LOCHAN Little loch or lake.

MACHAIR Sandy, grassy, lime-rich coastal land, generally used for grazing.

MANSE Official home of a Presbyterian minister.

MUNRO Mountain over 3000ft high.

MUNRO-BAGGING Sport of trying to climb as many Munros as possible.

PEEL Fortified tower, built to withstand Border raids.

PEND Archway or vaulted passage.

PRESBYTERIAN The official (Protestant) Church of Scotland, established by John Knox during the Reformation.

SASSENACH English.

SHINTY Simple form of hockey.

SNP Scottish National Party.

SPORRAN Leather purse worn in front of a kilt.

STRATH Broad, flat river valley.

TARTAN Check-patterned woollen cloth, particular patterns being associated with particular clans.

THANE A landowner of high rank; the chief of a clan.

TREWS Tartan trousers.

WEE Small.

WYND Narrow lane.

YETT Gate or door.

INDEX